Ι

if

v

INTERNATIONAL ECONOMIC POLICIES AND THEIR THEORETICAL FOUNDATIONS

A Sourcebook

SECOND EDITION

This is a volume in
ECONOMIC THEORY, ECONOMETRICS,
AND MATHEMATICAL ECONOMICS

A Series of Monographs and Textbooks

Consulting Editor: Karl Shell, *Cornell University*

A list of recent volumes in this series appears at the end of this volume.

INTERNATIONAL ECONOMIC POLICIES AND THEIR THEORETICAL FOUNDATIONS

A Sourcebook

SECOND EDITION

Edited by

JOHN M. LETICHE

Department of Economics
University of California, Berkeley
Berkeley, California

ACADEMIC PRESS, INC.

Harcourt Brace Jovanovich, Publishers

San Diego   New York   Boston   London   Sydney   Tokyo   Toronto

Academic Press Rapid Manuscript Reproduction

Contents

Preface

The momentous events that occurred as the world economy entered the 1990s made the comprehensive revision of this book a formidable challenge. In the early 1980s, there was increasing differentiation among the developed and developing market economies, and the centrally planned economies, in world trade and payments policies. By the early 1990s, international economic policies were converging toward freer market-oriented economies among an ever-larger number of developed and developing nations throughout the world. I have tried to draw on works that recognize these changes without sacrificing the analysis of fundamental principles of international economics. The objective has been to serve the interests of teachers, students, and government officials over the long run. Cogency, relevance, and basic principles were, therefore, given high degrees of priority.

The book aims to complement textbooks in international economics. During the past decade, a substantial advance occurred in international trade theory and related policy formation. Sixteen new articles have been selected for this edition, some never before published. They range from authoritative contributions on the emerging prospects of trade, growth, and development for the major regions of the world to the modern analysis of imperfect competition, increasing returns to scale, and differentiated products in international trade. Literature on restructuring in Western Europe, the shift from centrally planned to market economies, the new protectionism, contemporary exchange rate economics, monetary and portfolio-balance models of exchange rate determination, the new IMF and GATT procedures all receive expert consideration. I owe the authors sincere appreciation and acknowledge them and the publishers for generous permission to use materials held in copyright.

Gratitude is due to a long line of able students who have shared their judgment with me in the selection of articles: Menzie Chinn, Charles Engel, Charles Marston, Ronald L. Solberg, Richard Stern, Steven Phillips, Henri Vandendriessche, and Shangjin Wei gave me not only highly valued advice but also assistance in checking references and using libraries. To my colleagues at Berkeley in the field of international economics, professors Pranab Bardhan, Barry Eichengreen, Albert Fishlow, Jeffrey Frankel, Bent Hansen, Maurice Obstfeld, Kenneth Rogoff, and Laura D. Tyson, I am indebted for ever available intellectual counsel and stimulus. To my wife Emily Kuyper Letiche, to my friend Robin Gaster, and to my assistant Louise Sullivan, I am thankful for literary criticism and for the inspiration that renders every form of scholarly activity a satisfying experience.

Introduction

JOHN M. LETICHE

This book is composed of ten parts. Part I deals with the world economy entering the 1990s. First, for historical perspective, a classic text traces the evolution of the international order. It is followed by an article that appraises the opportunities and risks for the world economy in an era of extraordinary challenge and increasing complexity. Then, with perceptive brevity, a United Nations document discusses the state of the world economy at the end of 1989 and short-term prospects, providing data on trade and growth for the world, by region, and by selected country groupings for the period 1981–1990. Since this document was published 8 January 1990, estimates for 1989 have been updated, and the projections for the medium term revised following the Iraqi invasion of Kuwait, German reunification, and the occurrence of deeper structural changes than had been anticipated in Eastern Europe and the Soviet Union. These events, inter alia, significantly slowed the rate of expansion of world economic activity (compare Tables 1 and 2 here with Table 1 of Chapter 3). The projected real GNP growth rate of the world for 1990 declined from 3.0 percent to 1.2 percent, and the downward trend is expected to affect both the developed and the developing market economies. The economic outlook for Eastern Europe and the Soviet Union is particularly bleak; there appears little chance of avoiding a substantial decline in real living standards in these countries during a period of critical transition.

The effects of the Persian Gulf crisis were felt all over the world, nowhere more dramatically than in the oil-importing developing countries. The average dollar price of oil increased by about 28 percent in 1990, and the trade deficit of the net energy importing-developing countries widened from $17.3 billion in 1989 to $40.0 billion in 1990. Although the early end of the war kept oil prices from rising to extremely high levels, many oil-importing countries suffered considerable losses in merchandise and service trade during the crisis. Debt service burdens continue to be heavy for many countries, and the slower growth in the industrial world will further damage many heavily indebted and least developed nations. In a number of cases the loss of workers' remittances from the Persian Gulf intensified the international debt problem. A significant short-term deceleration therefore occurred for all oil-importing countries in Africa, Latin America, and Asia; growth fell 2 to 3 percentage points compared to earlier expectations. Even in the economically robust newly industrialized economies (NIEs) of Southeast Asia

TABLE 1

World Gross National Product (1970 U.S. $): 1990–1995 and Mean

	1990	1991	1992	1993	1994	1995	Mean
World total	1.2	0.9	2.9	2.9	3.4	3.4	2.4
Developed market economies	2.4	1.7	3.0	2.7	2.8	3.0	2.6
North America	1.0	0.9	3.1	2.7	3.0	3.0	2.3
United States	1.0	0.9	3.1	2.7	2.9	3.0	2.3
Developed East	4.8	3.4	4.3	3.9	4.0	3.6	4.0
Japan	5.7	3.4	4.6	4.0	4.0	3.7	4.3
European Community	3.5	2.1	2.6	2.3	2.2	2.6	2.6
Germany (Federal Republic)	4.5	2.7	2.2	1.7	1.6	2.3	2.5
France	2.7	2.1	3.1	3.3	3.0	3.2	2.9
United Kingdom	0.9	−0.8	2.5	1.9	2.2	2.8	1.6
Rest of industrialized world	1.2	0.4	1.8	3.0	3.1	3.9	2.2
Developing countries	2.7	3.7	5.1	5.1	5.3	5.4	4.6
Latin America and Caribbean	−1.1	1.5	3.8	4.4	4.6	4.6	3.0
Argentina	−2.1	1.6	1.5	1.4	1.7	2.0	1.0
Brazil	−4.9	−0.9	4.2	5.5	5.7	5.5	2.4
Mexico	2.6	3.4	4.6	5.2	6.0	5.8	4.6
Venezuela	4.4	5.3	5.2	3.9	1.3	3.4	3.9
Africa	2.9	2.8	2.6	2.3	3.2	3.3	2.9
North Africa	2.8	2.9	2.3	2.1	3.3	3.2	2.8
Algeria	4.6	4.6	2.9	3.4	4.1	4.2	4.0
Egypt	1.3	1.7	1.2	1.1	2.5	2.2	1.7
Sub-Saharan Africa	3.0	2.8	2.9	2.5	3.2	3.4	3.0
Nigeria	4.9	4.1	2.7	2.0	3.8	4.0	3.6
Southeast Asia	5.8	5.5	6.0	6.1	6.2	6.2	6.0
Hong Kong	2.6	4.0	5.5	5.6	5.1	4.7	4.6
India	4.4	3.9	4.8	5.2	5.4	5.4	4.8
Indonesia	6.5	7.1	7.7	7.3	7.6	7.7	7.3
Korea (Republic)	9.0	7.8	7.8	7.8	7.8	7.3	7.8
Taiwan Province	5.1	6.9	6.5	6.0	6.1	6.1	6.1
Thailand	10.0	7.3	6.8	7.3	7.6	7.9	7.8
China	5.0	5.7	6.3	6.3	6.4	6.4	6.0
West Asia	−6.5	−7.9	8.8	6.1	6.3	6.6	2.0
Oil-exporting countries	−8.2	−11.1	10.6	7.1	7.4	7.7	1.9
Oil-importing countries	1.2	4.7	2.6	2.4	2.4	2.4	2.6
Mediterranean	−1.4	1.8	4.1	2.7	2.4	3.3	2.1
Eastern Europe and the USSR	−5.6	−6.6	−1.1	0.2	3.1	2.7	−1.3
USSR	−4.8	−5.1	−1.0	−0.1	2.3	1.9	−1.2
Memo							
FRG + GDR	3.4	0.3	1.8	1.7	2.0	2.6	2.0
Eastern Europe	−6.8	−3.1	−0.5	1.0	4.6	4.1	−0.2
Developing countries (excluding China)	1.9	3.0	4.6	4.7	4.9	5.0	4.0
Least developed countries	1.9	1.7	2.7	2.4	2.5	2.8	2.3
Net energy exporting countries	3.8	4.5	5.6	5.5	5.8	5.9	5.2
Net energy importing countries	1.6	3.0	4.6	4.7	4.9	5.0	4.0

Source: World Economic Situation and Prospects 1991–1995: "Report on the Meeting of the Expert Group on Short- and Medium-term Projections of the World Economy (Project LINK)," New York, 6–8 March 1991, United Nations, New York, forthcoming. The cutoff date for the preparation of this forecast was 18 April 1991.

TABLE 2

Per Capita World Gross National Product (1970 U.S. $):
1990–1995 and Mean

	1990	1991	1992	1993	1994	1995	Mean
World total	−0.5	−0.8	1.1	1.1	1.6	1.7	0.7
Developed market economies	0.9	0.2	1.5	1.2	1.3	1.4	1.0
North America	0.1	0.1	2.3	1.9	2.2	2.2	1.4
United States	0.1	0.1	2.3	1.8	2.1	2.2	1.4
Developed East	4.2	2.8	3.7	3.3	3.4	3.1	3.4
Japan	5.0	3.2	4.1	3.5	3.5	3.3	3.8
European Community	3.3	1.9	2.4	2.1	2.0	2.4	2.3
Germany (Federal Republic)	4.6	2.8	2.3	1.8	1.8	2.4	2.6
France	2.4	1.8	2.8	2.9	2.7	2.8	2.6
United Kingdom	0.9	−0.8	2.4	1.9	2.1	2.7	1.5
Rest of industrialized world	−0.2	−0.9	0.4	1.5	1.7	2.4	0.8
Developing countries	0.8	1.9	3.2	3.2	3.4	3.5	2.6
Latin America and Caribbean	−3.2	−0.5	1.8	2.3	2.5	2.5	2.5
Argentina	−3.5	0.3	0.2	0.1	1.4	2.7	−0.3
Brazil	−6.8	−2.7	2.3	3.6	3.7	3.6	0.5
Mexico	0.3	1.2	2.4	3.0	3.7	3.6	2.4
Venezuela	1.8	2.9	2.7	1.5	−1.0	1.0	1.5
Africa	−0.3	−0.3	−0.6	−0.8	0.1	0.1	−0.3
North Africa	0.5	0.7	0.2	0.0	1.1	1.0	0.6
Algeria	3.2	3.0	3.0	3.0	3.0	3.0	3.0
Egypt	1.3	1.7	1.2	1.1	2.5	2.2	1.7
Sub-Saharan Africa	−0.2	−0.5	−0.4	−0.7	−0.1	0.2	−0.3
Nigeria	1.3	0.5	−0.9	−1.6	0.2	0.4	0.0
Southeast Asia	3.9	3.6	4.1	4.2	4.3	4.3	4.1
Hong Kong	1.0	2.6	4.1	4.2	3.7	3.3	3.1
India	2.7	2.2	3.1	3.5	3.7	3.7	3.2
Indonesia	4.7	5.4	5.9	5.6	5.9	6.0	5.6
Korea (Republic)	6.3	6.3	6.3	6.3	6.3	5.9	6.2
Taiwan Province	3.6	5.5	5.2	4.7	4.8	4.8	4.8
Thailand	8.2	5.6	5.1	5.5	5.8	6.2	6.1
China	3.8	4.5	5.1	5.1	5.2	5.2	4.8
West Asia	−9.3	−10.6	5.6	3.0	3.2	3.5	−1.0
Oil-exporting countries	−10.9	−13.6	7.5	4.1	4.3	4.7	−1.0
Oil-importing countries	−2.1	1.3	−0.8	−1.0	−1.0	−1.0	−0.8
Mediterranean	−3.0	0.3	2.6	1.2	0.9	1.7	0.6
Eastern Europe and the USSR	−6.3	−7.3	−1.8	−0.4	2.4	2.0	−2.0
USSR	−5.7	−5.9	−1.8	−0.9	1.5	1.1	−2.0
Memo							
FRG + GDR	2.9	−0.1	1.4	1.3	1.6	2.1	1.5
Eastern Europe	−7.3	−3.6	−1.0	0.5	4.1	3.6	−0.7
Developing countries							
(excluding China)	−0.3	0.8	2.4	2.5	2.7	2.8	1.8
Least developed countries	−1.0	−1.3	−0.3	−0.5	−0.5	−0.1	−0.6
Net energy exporting countries	2.2	2.9	4.0	3.9	4.2	4.2	3.5
Net energy importing countries	−0.5	0.9	2.4	2.6	2.7	2.8	1.8

Source: World Economic Situation and Prospects 1991–1995: "Report on the Meeting of the Expert Group on Short- and Medium-term Projections of the World Economy (Project LINK)," New York, 6–8 March 1991, United Nations, New York, forthcoming. The cutoff date for the preparation of this forecast was 18 April 1991.

(South Korea, Taiwan, Hong Kong, and Singapore), economic growth slowed to an average rate of about 5 percent in 1990, from 5.5 percent in 1989. Except for South Korea, export growth in the NIEs is projected to decelerate in the short term. Nonetheless, these robust economies are expected to maintain high growth rates in the medium and long terms. In South Asia, however, growth performance is projected to be mixed, with current accounts deteriorating markedly in commodity-exporting and oil-importing countries. As the growth of the world economy is expected to decline in 1991, growth even in Asia will probably decrease. Modest improvement in the Chinese economy, however, should stabilize the region's growth at about the 1990 rate.

According to the revised United Nations data, the short-term outlook hence appears distinctly unpromising. Growth in West Asia, particularly, is expected to fall due to large output declines in Iraq, Jordan, and Kuwait. However, the rise that occurred in oil prices had a one-time effect. Therefore, as the world economy entered the 1990s in much better economic shape than it did the 1980s, and the Gulf War did not substantially damage Saudi Arabian oil production facilities — oil prices have sharply fallen to pre-war levels — the medium- and long-term prospects of the world economy are not expected to be seriously affected by the Gulf crisis or its aftermath. Thus, the world economy is likely to return to long-term average growth rates by 1993 or 1994 (see Tables 1 and 2). The projections suggest that the recovery will be broad-based and spread across all regions of the world. Highly indebted oil-importing developing countries may, however, require 2 or 3 additional years to resume significantly higher growth rates. Consequently, with additional stimuli expected from a strengthening of economic activity in the European Community after 1992, a resumed expansion of the economies in Eastern Europe, continued robust growth in Japan and Southeast Asia, and the rebound of the North American economy, the revised United Nations projections shown in Tables 1 and 2 are quite optimistic with regard to the resurgence of growth rates in world GNP and in the volume of world trade.

Nonetheless, the articles in Part I rightly emphasize the opportunities and risks facing the emerging "new world order." Practically every major country is in the process of attempting to restore domestic and international equilibrium. Indeed, since the end of 1987, the United States, Japan, and Germany have made important progress in reducing their current account imbalances as a percentage of GNP — and the process is likely to continue. But there remain, of course, very significant complexities, risks, and uncertainties. Among them are growth dispersions among regions and nations that are a notable and disturbing fact of the recent growth data. Since about 1982, an asymmetry has arisen between the quite satisfactory growth record of North America, the European Community, and Southeast Asia on the one side, and that of Latin America, the Caribbean, Africa, and West Asia on the other. High budget deficits in the United States and Germany are likely to continue for the foreseeable future, with an accompanying uncertain impact of high real interest rates. Understandably, there has recently been a severe tightening in financial markets, especially in the United States and Japan, where banks have been under severe pressure from regulatory agencies to purge impaired assets from their balance sheets. And this has occurred while global excess demand for both financial and physical capital has greatly increased as a result of restructuring of the eastern part of Germany, the transformation of Eastern Europe and the U.S.S.R., and the rebuilding of infrastructure in the Gulf region. Further, the narrowing of saving minus investment balances as a percentage of GNP in the United States, Japan, and Germany, combined with the global contraction of credit, will probably continue to constrain the flow of capital to most developing countries.

Experience in the 1980s has shown, however, that a number of Latin American and African countries have depended not only on internal and external stabilization and debt-reduction measures for their structural reforms, but also crucially on access to external financial resources. But, unfortunately, in Latin America the investment rate during the last decade has been about half as high as in earlier decades, a phenomenon resulting from, inter alia, low domestic savings and net capital transfers abroad. The latter was related to the foreign debt overhang despite improvements in reducing sovereign debt and debt-service ratios. Though there has been an increase in development aid, particularly to sub-Saharan Africa, most developing countries continue to face increasing financial difficulties.

The likelihood that, in the short and medium term, new and enlarged trading blocs may adversely affect a substantial number of countries is yet another source of uncertainty. The recent dissolution of the Council for Mutual Economic Assistance (CMEA) as an institutional organization and the decision of the former members to conduct their foreign trade on the basis of convertible currencies holds out promise, but not without risk. Given the variations in growth rates, inflation, and unemployment in the Eastern European countries, as well as the speed of implementing reforms, and the fact that "perestroika" in the U.S.S.R. has entered its critical phase, it is not surprising that a recent United Nations report on The World Economic Situation and Prospects concludes:

> If current trends of low national saving rates and unfavorable prospects for external finance [continue], they will reduce the effectiveness of adjustment efforts considerably and the early 1990s will become a period of increased saving-investment imbalances with a sustainable danger of these countries experiencing into another decade of unstable and low growth.

Though this may be an unduly pessimistic outlook, it is fitting that articles in Part I consider these issues and include Cooper's contribution on "Opportunities and Risks for the World Economy: The Challenge of Increasing Complexity."

Part II presents the foundations of terms-of-trade and gains-from-trade theory underlying key policy issues of economic growth and development. Fundamental contributions to this literature were made in the 1980s, and these have been incorporated in a thorough update.

Part III consists of studies in world food production, international trade, and agriculture. In Chapters 6 and 7, Schultz shows economic productivity and human well-being to be vitally interrelated in both poor and rich countries. Powerful arguments emerge for rejecting the view that limitations of space, energy, crop land, and other physical properties are the decisive constraints to human betterment. Instead, Schultz argues that the acquired characteristics of the peoples of the earth — their education, experience, skills, and health — are the vital factors in economic progress. Attention is devoted to the attributes of traditional agriculture and to allocated efficiency, including its implications for commercial policy throughout the world. A general argument, with supporting evidence, is presented in terms of the increasing value of human time, a formulation that is applicable to both theory and policy pertaining to various terms-of-trade concepts. In an update, Schultz appraises his contributions in terms of his most recent thought.

Because Chapter 7 is taken from a book, and limitations of space have necessitated severe condensation, the broader framework of its context must be examined.[1] Schultz explains why even the giants of economics such as Adam Smith, David Ricardo, and Thomas Malthus could not have foreseen that the economic development of western industrial nations would depend primarily on "population quality." A predominant part of national income (⅘ in the United States) is now derived from earnings and only a small part from property. Drawing on his expertise in agriculture, trade, and development, the author provides fresh insights into the following fundamentals: (1) the process whereby advances in knowledge enhance both physical and human capital; (2) the underlying reasons why economists in rich countries find it exceedingly difficult to comprehend the implications of the severe resource constraints in low-income countries; (3) the nature of the performances of poor people that determine their economic choices; and (4) the implications of the ample evidence that poor people in developing countries are no less motivated to work hard, to adapt efficiently to domestic and international market forces (if proper incentives are adopted), and to improve their lot and that of their children, than are those with incomparably greater advantages. Schultz pays particular attention to the effects of government actions on national economies and on trade. The theory developed is robust and applicable to the following issues bearing on this book: (1) to the impact of international economic policies on basic research in agriculture, (2) to investment in developing and improving domestic and international market structures, (3) to investment in entrepreneurial ability in developed and developing countries, (4) to economic distortions caused by the international donor community, and (5) to trade discrimination by higher-income countries. A major economic implication of this discrimination is that free internal market

---

[1]Theodore W. Schultz, *Investing in People: The Economics of Population Quality* (Berkeley: University of California Press, 1981), especially Chapters 2, 3, 6, and 7; and for related discussions consistent with these views, see *Restoring Economic Equilibrium: Human Capital and the Modernizing Economy* (New York: Basil Blackwell, 1990), Chapters 8 and 16.

prices would be a boon for consumers in high-income countries, and would also contribute substantially to the export opportunities for many low-income countries. "Gains from such trade," Schultz observes, "would probably contribute more to the agricultural development of low-income countries than foreign aid."[2] Systematic research on this issue, particularly as it pertains to existing uneconomic and obsolete forms of overt and covert "tied aid," should yield high returns to both donor and recipient countries.

The world food situation is the topic of Chapter 8. Johnson reveals gross error, exaggeration, and oversimplification in numerous current policy approaches and government pronouncements. The author calls attention to unsettled issues and to promising policy research. The update demonstrates the power of Johnson's analysis for explaining the underlying economic trends, the cogency of which appears to have long-term relevance. Thus, a recent study of the Organization for Economic Cooperation and Development (OECD), entitled *Agricultural Policy for the 1990s*, showed that overall grain production has — globally speaking — been adequate and world food prices relatively stable in the last 15 years, although arrangements to maintain food reserves and to meet unexpected emergencies need to be improved. On a national level, however, the growth of food production per head in the 1980s was negative in 46 out of 95 developing countries. Consistent with Johnson's analysis, the OECD study notes that between 1965 and 1980 the volume of agricultural trade grew threefold. This momentum, however, was not maintained in the 1980s; between 1980 and 1985, such trade stagnated, before recovering slightly in 1986 and 1987. Developing countries' share in world agricultural exports fell from about 45 percent in 1970 to less than 30 percent in 1987, partly because their total demand for agricultural goods grew faster than their production, and partly because of the heavy subsidies provided by the governments of the OECD countries.

The OECD study suggests that successful policy reforms in agriculture in the 1990s will depend on whether (1) many more developing countries begin to achieve positive growth rates in agricultural production per head; (2) the world's poor have better food security in the year 2000 than in 1990; (3) agricultural OECD countries are more market-oriented and less dependent on government support and, consequently, the share of developing countries in world trade in farm products increases; and (4) net returns for farmers improve because of both higher international prices and productivity gains.[3]

---

[2]*Ibid., Investing in People*, p. 143, and *Restoring Economic Equilibrium*, Chapters 12 and 15. Attention has also been directed to the effect of differential growth rates of productivity in food and manufacturing on trade between tropical and industrial countries. This trade has failed as an engine of economic growth. See W. Arthur Lewis, "Aspects of Tropical Trade: 1883–1965," Wicksell Lectures, Stockholm, 1969.

[3]Sartaj Aziz, *Agricultural Policies for the 1990s* (Paris: OECD, 1990); see also *Agricultural Trade Liberalization: Implications for Developing Countries*, edited by Ian Goldin and Odin Knudsen (Paris: OECD and The World Bank, 1990).

Part IV considers the economics of common markets. A key passage from the modern, classic formulation is given, and subsequent chapters survey the more recent literature with reference to developed and developing nations. The new texts deal to a greater extent with the economics of integration, and with particular emphasis on the macroeconomic impacts of "Europe 1992" and beyond. Under the usual assumptions, it appears that less developed countries (the LDCs) are unlikely to derive economic gains from the formation of common markets. However, earlier econometric projections for the 1980s and 1990s suggested that the growth rates of world output and trade were more likely to approximate those of the dismal 1970s rather than those of the heady 1960s. In fact, these growth rates for the period 1982–1990 were between the two extremes; but many developing countries did not share in that greater world prosperity.

In fact, the performance of most economies in Latin America and the Caribbean, in sub-Saharan Africa, in the low-income developing countries of South Asia, and, of course, in Eastern Europe and the Soviet Union, was abysmal — especially in per capita terms. Consequently, and because no realistic, gradual, and step-by-step process has emerged to expand specified categories of West–East and North–South foreign trade, these factors have led to a resurgence of interest in new forms of economic integration among countries of Latin America and the Caribbean, sub-Saharan Africa, the Pacific Basin region, and of Eastern Europe with an expanded European Community. These issues need to be discussed in more concrete terms, especially in relation to trade among the more — and the less — rapidly industrializing nations. At present, the industrial countries of Europe are preoccupied with their own restructuring; and the restructuring of reunified Germany will clearly take longer and cost more than was expected. Economic blocs in the Americas, in Europe, and in Asia are likely to expand, and the means of reducing their protectionist effects on the world economy will require much new theoretical and policy analysis. Recent Uruguay Round negotiations strongly suggest that the responsibility will fall primarily on the U.S. government.[4]

Chapter 14 by Prebisch deals with the global system of capitalism in Latin

[4]As Richard G. Lipsey observes in the update to his article on "The Theory of Customs Unions: A General Survey," (Chapter 10), probably the biggest change since he wrote his essay is in empirical measures of the gains from trade. Experience of the European Community taught economists that most of the specialization following on tariff reductions was intraindustry. In Chapter 11 (b), entitled "Empirical Studies: Measuring the Extent and Effects of Integration," Robson presents this data. Some projections are also appraised by Dornbusch in Chapter 12 on "Europe 1992: Macroeconomic Implications." As for the formation of economic blocs, see the essays in *Free Trade Areas and U.S. Trade Policy*, J. J. Schott, ed. *The Free Trade Areas and U.S. Trade Policy* (Washington: Institute for International Economics, 1989); *The European Internal Market — Trade and Competition*, edited by Alexis Jacqemin and André Sapir (Oxford: Oxford University Press, 1989); *The Political Economy of Trade Policy*, edited by R. Jones and Anne Krueger (Oxford: Basil Blackwell, 1989); and Richard G. Lipsey, "Growth, Erosion and Restructuring of the Multilateral Trading System," paper presented at the American Economic Association meetings, Atlanta, December 28, 1989 (forthcoming).

America.[5] Because this chapter is a resumé of a critically important book published in Spanish, the book itself needs to be placed in perspective.

After World War II, Prebisch raised the key economic issues facing Latin America and proferred solutions for dealing with them. He also perceptively and provocatively altered some of his fundamental approaches and recommendations in the light of new evidence and superior analysis. Prebisch had more influence on Latin American international development policy than any other economist, and his influence on government officials and academic economists in other less developed countries (LDCs) has also been marked. This is understandable, for the fundamental issue facing Latin America — the struggle for orderly development in an epoch of revolutionary change, characterized by massive migrations from rural to urban areas, often aggravating the spread of urban decay and mounting unemployment in the major cities — has also plagued other industrializing nations. As projected growth rates for GNP and international trade declined for the 1980s, the "interior concept" of economic development underwent a resurgence (though a moderate one) and the author once again drew attention to fundamental, emerging issues. Four developments in Prebisch's writings can be distinguished:

1. The emphasis in the late 1950s on strengthening the Latin American industrialization process through differential tariff protection, import substitution, and the creation of a common market for trade and investment integration;[6]

2. The recognition by the mid-1960s that the "first" or "easy" stage of substitution of domestic manufacturing production for imports had passed, and that Latin American exports should be promoted through the removal by industrial countries of their trade barriers to imports of manufactures from Latin America;[7]

3. The call in the late 1960s for tariff preferences with respect to Latin American exports of manufactures to the United States and other industrial nations, as well as for more effective economic integration among the major Latin American nations through the use of Special Drawing Rights (SDRs) and the elimination of their overvalued exchange rates;[8] and

---

[5]Raúl Prebisch, Chapter 14 in this publication; also Raúl Prebisch, "Dependence, Development and Interdependence," in *The State of Development Economics: Progress and Perspectives*, T. Paul Schultz and Gustav Ranis, eds. (New York: Basil Blackwell, 1988).

[6]Raúl Prebisch, "Commercial Policy in the Underdeveloped Countries," *American Economic Review* **49** (May 1959), pp. 251–273.

[7]Raúl Prebisch, *Towards a Dynamic Development Policy for Latin America* (New York: United Nations, 1963); *Towards a New Trade Policy for Development* (New York: United Nations, 1964), pp. 20–25.

[8]Cf. United Nations Economic Commission for Latin America, *Economic Bulletin for Latin America* (New York: United Nations, 1967), vol. 12, no. 1, pp. 35–55; also vol. 12, no. 2, pp. 146–147. Prebisch also expressed similar views at a conference on the 25th anniversary of Bretton Woods held at Queen's University, Kingston, Ontario, Canada, June 2–3, 1967.

4. The synthesis of his views in the early 1980s, the essence of which is an enhanced rate of capital accumulation; this is to be achieved via a reduced proportion of GNP devoted to profligate government expenditures and class-conscious conspicuous consumption, and an enlarged proportion (directed by government) devoted to more productive investment through the greater use of private entrepreneurial capacity and improved market structures, supported by preferences on exports of manufactures and selective import substitution.[9]

Prebisch had much practical experience in guiding and evaluating the process of Latin American economic development. With reference to his earlier views, he believed that after World War II an import-substitution strategy was essential for Latin America because imports were "undercutting" the development of "nascent" industries. To overcome this handicap, trade barriers had to be erected but they were to be temporary — not permanent. Prebisch also recommended policies for Latin American economic integration, which were to help achieve essential internal and external economies of scale. In the early 1980s, he wrote that trade barriers against the outside world should be moderate, whereas most Latin American countries pushed them to the extreme. Furthermore, he advocated North–South economic cooperation, which, in his judgment, the industrial countries failed to implement: "The centres," Prebisch contends in Chapter 14 of this volume, "have by no means encouraged this process through changes in their production structure; and by failing to open their doors to manufacturing imports from the periphery, they force the latter to continue with import substitution."[10]

Prebisch appears to agree, however, with the general consensus concerning the effects of tariffs and of quantitative restrictions imposed by most Latin American governments in the 1950s and 1960s: they inordinately reduced foreign competition. Domestic firms became relatively more inefficient as they expanded the production of substandard commodities for highly priced, and comparatively small, internal markets. These factors contributed to his focus on the markets of the "centre countries" — the United States, Western Europe, and Japan. But Latin American manufacturers could not compete in these markets without preferential tariff treatment. Consequently, the United Nations Conference on Trade and Development (UNCTAD) was formed in 1963 to help Latin American countries compete. As its first secretary general, a post he held for 6 years, Prebisch made this organization the focal point of the North–South dialog. The concepts developed by UNCTAD induced the United Nations General Assembly in 1974 to pass the unattainable, even if desirable, comprehensive resolutions calling for a "new international economic order."

Prebisch's most promising paradigm, advocated in his final work, confronted the serious errors made both by the industrializing and the industrial countries in

---

[9]Raúl Prebisch, Chapter 14 in this publication.
[10]*Ibid.*

recent decades. The extreme trade restrictions of the LDCs hindered competition from imports, and also discriminated against their own exports — explicitly through high taxes on exportables, implicitly through overvalued exchange rates stemming from the cost-increasing tendencies of immoderate trade restrictions. It was the *combination* of ill-advised economic policies and the movement from the first stage of import substitution to the second stage that resulted in vast and costly economic distortions. The first stage usually entailed the replacement by domestic production of imported nondurable consumer goods (e.g., clothing, shoes, and household wares) and of their inputs (e.g., textiles, leather, and wood products). Characteristically, the LDCs had a dynamic comparative advantage in these industries. They are usually labor intensive, and do not require highly skilled workers, sophisticated technologies, and a network of suppliers of parts and components in order to attain and maintain international competitiveness. Their efficient scale of output is relatively low and their expansion tends to generate an increasing supply of entrepreneurial ability, improved labor training, and technology.[11]

The second stage of import substitution involved the replacement of imported consumer and producer durables (as well as intermediate inputs) by domestic production. The intermediate inputs were goods such as steel products and petrochemicals. The required conditions for efficient production, understandably, were the opposite of those prevailing in first stage industries. Propelled by exorbitantly high rates of effective tariff protection, these products generated exceedingly high domestic resource costs relative to foreign exchange earnings, because the need to import key materials and machinery was virtually always enlarged. Further, neglected intraindustry relationships led to enormous economic waste, as overpricing industrialization was matched only by the underpricing of agriculture. The result was an uneconomic relative contraction of output in food and agriculture, which aggravated inflationary pressures and external deficits. Since nominal interest rates usually lagged behind the increase in domestic prices, much wasteful private and public investment was undertaken, and credit rationing was imposed by the banks and/or government.

Not surprisingly, in his final writings, Prebisch regarded the immense economic waste in the policies of overextended LDC governments and in the new consumption patterns of the elite and middle classes — especially in his native Latin America — as basic factors in their distorted economic structures. Nevertheless, he contends that market forces are not and cannot be "the supreme regulator of the development of the periphery and its relations with the centre."[12] Notwithstanding

---

[11]For an extensive analysis, see Bela Belassa, *The Process of Industrial Development*, pp. 4–9; and the sources cited therein. This essay retains the format of the Frank D. Graham Memorial Lecture delivered by the author at Princeton University. It eschews footnote references, but a list of the author's publications from which the empirical evidence cited in the essay (and in Chapter 22 of this publication) is derived, is contained in an appendix. *Ibid.*, pp. 29–30.

[12]Raúl Prebisch, Chapter 14 in this publication.

their satisfactory growth rates in the 1960s and 1970s, he points out, income distribution in Latin America remained appallingly skewed: the bottom 40 percent of the population earned only 8 percent of the national income.

"Dynamic redistribution," according to Prebisch's concluding position, is a primary requisite of successful economic development, not through aid from industrial nations, but through harnessing the LDCs' own resources that are now misallocated in waste. Prebisch did not abandon his criticism of what he regarded as the "major flaws in centre–periphery relations."[13] Nor did he believe that the economic transformation of Latin America is feasible without the state playing a critical role in enforcing essential austerity. The free market and authoritarian governments, he argued, have not solved the major problems of Latin American economic development. Recognizing the immensity of the task, Prebisch did not take a dogmatic theoretical stand. At the core of his concluding analysis remained the division of the world into the "centre" and "the periphery," with the center controlling the world economy and the LDCs reduced to a dependency relationship of providing raw materials and markets. If the LDCs are to prosper and to attain equality, he wrote, this form of economic dependency must be broken: "Individual decisions in the market place must be combined with collective decisions outside it which override the interests of the dominant groups. All this, however, calls for a great vision, a vision of change, both in peripheral development and in relations with the centres. . . ."[14]

Prebisch formulated his final analysis in different terms from those of his previous writings. Accumulation — in its human and physical forms — is the key to economic development. Much of the capital stock required for accelerated growth, he said, already exists in Latin America. But it is wasted in huge government establishments, in ornamental military outlays, and in purchases of apartments abroad and fancy automobiles by the elites, and of smaller luxuries such as color television sets by the middle class. They are indulging in the frenetic imitation of consumption in the center, which is a form of waste they cannot afford. Prebisch therefore suggested that if a larger proportion of GNP were allocated to more productive investment, the growth rate of Latin American LDCs would be enhanced and the distribution of income improved.

As an antidote to "frenetic consumption," Prebisch challenged the Latin American governments to "build an interior concept of development" along the lines of

[13]See the discussion of Prebisch's views on this issue by Edward Schumacher, "North-South by South: A New Axis of Waste," *New York Times*, May 31, 1981, p. 19 EY. For a more critical view of the North–South dilemma, see W. M. Corden, *The NIEO Proposals: A Cool Look*, Thames Essay No. 21 (London: Trade Policy Research Centre, 1979); and the introduction in *The New International Economic Order: The North–South Debate*, J. N. Bhagwati, ed. (Cambridge, Mass.: The MIT Press, 1977), pp. 1–24.

[14]Raúl Prebisch, Chapter 14 in this publication, "Dependence, Development and Interdependence," *ibid.*; and *La Crisis*.

Japan, with high savings and austerity dedicated to economic growth. Short of that, he recommended progressive taxation on consumption expenditures — not on income — and an enlarged use of government outlays on productive industrial and agricultural development. The aided industries, he emphasized, should be *private*, not government owned. Although the governments of Latin American LDCs have to play an active role in the accumulation of capital, Prebisch no longer concentrated his attack on the international and domestic market system as such. The major flaws of the system, he wrote, do not lie in private property itself but in the harmful consequences of the concentration of the means of production. Prebisch acknowledged that the market is an extremely useful mechanism, economically and politically. "If you abolish it," he observed, "the decisions are all made by a few at the top and that is not favorable for democracy."[15] If the state takes into its own hands the ownership and management of the means of production, this option "is incompatible with the paramount concept of democracy and the human rights inherent in it."[16] Compared with his earlier views, Prebisch here manifestly accords a more balanced role to government and to import substitution. Exportables, entrepreneurial capacity, freer markets, and private capital formation received more emphasis in his new and improved paradigms.

When his more comprehensive formulation becomes available in English, it will doubtless require analytical examination and testing. But even cursory examination of comparative evidence suggests that the misallocation of resources in Latin America has been massive. In the 1960s and 1970s, the proportion of gross national saving to GNP, and gross investment to GNP, was not significantly different in Latin America and the Caribbean from the proportion in East Asia and the Pacific.[17] But the rate of growth in gross investment and in total GNP — and particularly in GNP per capita — was substantially lower in Latin America and the Caribbean. However, the new emphasis should mark even more than an improved direction in paradigms. It calls for a recognition that the international economic policies of individual governments are more important to the success of their economic growth and development than the arbitrarily assumed structural economic forces ascribed to various "centers" or "peripheries."

Following the oil and other crises of the early and late 1970s, this recognition has been growing among leaders of the LDCs. They increasingly appreciate that the economic problems of their countries are no less the result of domestic economic distortions than of those emanating from either the capitalist or former

[15]See Schumacher's article listed in footnote 13. Limitations of space have proscribed the inclusion of a paper in this publication dealing specifically with the issue of "unequal exchange." The reader interested in the exploration of literature on this problem may wish to consult the survey article by Alain de Janvry and Frank Kramer, "The Limits of Unequal Exchange," *The Review of Radical Political Economies* (Winter 1979), pp. 3–15, and the sources cited therein.

[16]*Ibid.* and Chapter 23 in this publication.

[17]*Annual Report*, World Bank, Washington, D.C., 1978, pp. 118–19 and 1980, pp. 130–31.

communist centers. Action based on this recognition is an indispensable element for even a modest improvement in international economic policies. A caveat, however, is in order: Prebisch insisted that the route to democracy is through better income distribution. If, by this, he meant that a larger proportion of GNP devoted to more productive human and physical capital is likely to enhance real per capita growth rates, reduce unemployment, and improve income distribution, the argument appears tenable under the conditions that he finally postulated. It may, furthermore, apply to new Latin American arrangements for more effective private entrepreneurship in the management of enterprises now publicly owned and managed — a problem that deserves serious attention. If, however, Prebisch meant that the route to democracy is by way of direct income distribution in the shape of wealth redistribution and/or enlarged transfer payments, the growing literature on macroeconomic populism in Latin America provides ample evidence that the argument is untenable on economic grounds.[18]

Part V includes selections on international cartels, commodity agreements, and the oil problem. The emphasis centers on the economic analysis and historical experience of relevant price fluctuations and price trends. The economics of exhaustible resources and of the world oil outlook is examined in the light of modern trade theory, and is realistically applied to the exigencies of contemporary world reality. This appraisal lends itself to comparison with the Link System simulations for 1981–1990, presented in the concluding chapter of this volume, which offers a long-term projection of world trade, output, and prices when the real price of oil remains steady, rises gradually, or rises by way of discontinuous shocks. It is high praise, indeed, to observe that the effects of the third oil shock, brought about by the Persian Gulf crisis, called for no significant alterations in these texts.[19]

Part VI considers multinationals and international investment. The chapters examine the roles of direct foreign investment and foreign trade under competitive and monopolistic conditions. Original contributions appear on the "product cycle" and on "uneven development." These presentations offer objective formulations

[18]See the papers in Michael Bruno, Guido di Tella, Rudiger Dornbusch, and Stanley Fischer, eds., *Inflation Stabilization* (Cambridge: The MIT Press, 1989); and the "Symposia: The State and Economic Development," in *The Journal of Economic Perspectives*, vol. 4, no. 3 (Summer 1990), pp. 3–61.

[19]For excellent background discussions, see R. M. Solow, "The Economics of Resources or the Resources of Economics," *American Economic Review* **64**, no. 2 (May 1974), pp. 1–14; D. M. G. Newbery, "Oil Prices, Cartels, and the Problem of Dynamic Inconsistency," *Economic Journal* **91** (September 1981), pp. 617–646; L. R. Klein, S. Fardoust, V. Filatov, and V. Su, "Simulations of the World Impact of Oil Price Increases: An Exercise in Supply Side Economics," in Lawrence R. Klein, *The Economics of Supply and Demand* (Baltimore: The Johns Hopkins University Press, 1983), pp. 51–88. An analysis by the IMF, *Economic Outlook*, appendix (Washington, D.C., 1990), emphasizes that the oil price increase in 1990 was small relative to the previous oil shocks of 1973–74 and 1979–80. Moreover, the industrial economies are now less vulnerable to oil-price increases because oil consumption and imports declined significantly in relation to GNP during the 1970s and 1980s. The IMF and the U.S. Department of Energy expect a surplus of world oil supplies following a resolution of the Gulf crisis. See *The New York Times*, June 1990, p. C-16

for strikingly different points of view. The updates by Caves and Vernon incorporate new work by the authors and, with stimulating brevity, review the most recent research in these fields.

Part VII concentrates on commercial policies: first, for developing market economies; second, for centrally planned economies, with considerable emphasis on the role of foreign trade in their economic reform, and an update on shifting from socialist economies to market-oriented economies; and third, of developed market economies, with chapters on the new GATT and foreign aid.

Salient elements of the industry and trade of seven developing countries have been published by the OECD.[20] Basic information is further provided in nine volumes of a special conference series published by the National Bureau of Economic Research.[21] In addition, two volumes summarize the experience of these foreign trade regimes and their impact on development. One explains the successes and failures of economic liberalization attempts, the other outlines the overall results.[22] Even the summaries of these volumes, however, are either too lengthy or too closely linked to their context for feasible inclusion in this book. Nonetheless, an appraisal of current commercial policies in developing market economies requires a brief review of this research.

The evidence is generally consistent with the following economic conclusions. The more closed the regime, the lower the growth rate in exports and in GNP. Furthermore, for the middle-income LDCs, the more closed regimes were usually associated with the following characteristics: (1) more comprehensive import-substitution programs; (2) greater "bias" against exports, denoted by the greater extent to which relative incentives for domestic production of items not traded and import substitution were distorted away from international relative prices; (3) higher variance in price differentials among commodity categories; (4) more distorted relative factor prices and less efficient relative factor use, and less efficient finished product markets; (5) larger investment in capital-intensive sectors; (6) lower domestic value added to capital employed; (7) lower real profits; (8) smaller inflow of governmental and private capital, signifying lower gross

[20]See especially I. M. D. Little, T. Scitovsky, and M. Scott, *Industry and Trade in Some Developing Countries: A Comparative Analysis* (Paris: OECD, 1970).

[21]See "A Special Conference Series on Foreign Trade Regimes and Economic Development," resulting from a National Bureau of Economic Research Project. The series includes 9 country studies: Turkey, Ghana, Israel, Egypt, the Philippines, India, South Korea, Chile, and Colombia, and synthesis volumes noted in footnote 22. For a series of 7 volumes, covering 19 developing countries, published on behalf of the World Bank, see *Liberalizing Foreign Trade*. Demetris Papageorgian, Michael Michaely, and Armeane M. Choksi, eds. (Cambridge, Mass.: Basil Blackwell, 1990).

[22]Anne O. Krueger, *Liberalization Attempts and Consequences* (Cambridge, Mass.: Ballinger Publishing Co., 1978); Jagdish N. Bhagwati, *Anatomy and Consequences of Exchange Control Regimes* (Cambridge, Mass.: Ballinger Publishing Co., 1978); also Anne O. Krueger, "The Relationship Between Trade, Employment and Development," in *The State of Development Economics: Progress and Perspectives*, T. Paul Schultz and Gustav Ranis, eds. (New York: Basil Blackwell, 1988).

investment relative to gross national saving as a percent of GNP; (9) less optimal, and more erratic, composition of imported inventories; (10) greater instability of agricultural and food supplies; (11) larger excess capacity of plant utilization in manufacturing production; and (12) higher unemployment rates.

The first selection in Part VII succinctly outlines the lessons and prospects for development strategies.[23] Belassa first analyzes the results of inward- and outward-oriented development strategies. The lessons of experience — such as the exceedingly high costs that many developing nations incurred after their governments implemented erroneous economic policies — stand out clearly. Chapter 23, by Myint, an important article in the history of economic thought, examines the relevance of classical international trade theory as a guide to commercial policy and to the economic growth of underdeveloped countries.

In Part VII, Chapter 24, Wolf considers the theoretical and institutional determinants of foreign trade in centrally planned economies and their policy implications for internal and external balance. It is an exemplary analysis of the microeconomic and macroeconomic effects and policy responses of trade and financial flows among the countries of the CMEA and with the developed and developing market economies. The members of the CMEA included Bulgaria, Cuba, Czechoslovakia, the German Democratic Republic, Hungary, Mongolia, Poland, Rumania, the Soviet Union, and Viet Nam. The analysis demonstrates how the exchange rate system in conjunction with a distorted domestic price structure created significant problems for the crumbling communist economies. Indeed, procedures for intra-CMEA foreign trade distorted even the possible measurement, on a basis comparable to that for market economies, of national income, the structure and level of foreign trade, and the degree of openness of the planned economies. An update deals with the shift of the centrally planned economies to market-oriented economies, leading to the collapse of CMEA.[24] The controversial and unsettled issues of the Uruguay Round negotiations, leading to the new GATT, are then presented in Chapter 25, and the section concludes with a brief essay on the international assistance policies of the United States.

[23]Bela Belassa, *The Process of Industrial Development and Alternative Development Strategies*, Essays in International Finance (Princeton: Princeton University Press, 1980).

[24]For a brief discussion on the evolution of East–West Trade Relations, with an analysis of the concentration and competition in east-west trade in Europe; data on trade in the former CMEA countries; and a bibliography on these issues, with emphasis on government documents, respectively, see the following: Centre for Economic Policy Research, *Monitoring European Integration: The Impact of Eastern Europe* (London: 1990), pp. 19–25, 43–50; IMF, *The Economy of the U.S.S.R., 1990*, (IMF, IBRD, OECD, and EBRD: Washington, D.C., 1990); and John M. Letiche, "Toward a Market-Oriented Economy in China: The Long View," *Shanghai Academy of Sciences, United States–China Economic Relations* (Shanghai, 1991). For background information, see also the excellent discussion by Ed. A. Hewett, *Reforming the Soviet Economy: Equality Versus Efficiency* (Washington: Brookings Institution, 1988), Chapters 2 and 8.

Part VIII consists of fundamental readings on the new international economics. Chapter 27, by Krugman, reviews the relationships between imperfect competition, increasing returns, and differentiated products in international trade. Recent research on the causal relations between industrial organization and international trade receives particular attention. Five strands in the literature are discussed: first, the role of external and internal economies of scale as causes of intraindustry trade, modeled with the use of monopolistic competition; second, the effect of tariffs and quantitative trade restrictions on domestic market power; third, the analysis of dumping as a form of international price discrimination; fourth, the potential strategy role of government policy, pro and con, as an aid to domestic firms in ologopolistic competition; and fifth, an appraisal of recent work providing a new argument for protectionism. A concluding section discusses three efforts at quantifying modern trade theory: (1) econometric studies testing aggregate predictions of the intraindustry trade model; (2) attempts to "calibrate" theoretical models to fit the facts of particular industries; and (3) efforts to introduce aspects of industrial organization into a general equilibrium model of a specified economy. Krugman points out that international economics, like industrial organization, is becoming a field in which many models are used and research is an eclectic mix of approaches. This transformation of the subject, he writes, has been extremely valuable and is based on a fundamental insight, long requiring analytical application — markets are seldom perfectly competitive, and returns to scale are often not constant. The new approaches have brought creativity to an area that had begun to lose vitality. Now the central problem of international trade, Krugman suggests, is how to go beyond the proliferation of models to some kind of new synthesis. He concludes: "Probably trade theory will never be as unified as it was a decade ago, but it would be desirable to see empirical work again to narrow the range of things that we regard as plausible outcomes."[25] As other facets of the new international economics, in Chapter 28, Baldwin examines the new protectionism as a response to shifts in national economic power. In Chapter 29, Fishlow presents alternative approaches and solutions to the debt problem of developing countries.

Part IX contains outstanding readings on international payments, classic and modern. Chapter 30, by Meade, incisively formulates the meaning of internal and external balance. It is followed by Johnson's authoritative statement on the monetary approach to the balance of payments, and then by Cooper's seminal article on currency devaluation in developing countries. Chapter 33, by Dornbusch, provides a guide to contemporary exchange rate economics, carefully formulating relations between theory and policy. There then follow chapters by Frankel, appraising the monetary and portfolio-balance models of exchange rate determination, by Giovannini on the operating principles and procedures of the European Monetary System, and by Rogoff on conditions under which international monetary coop-

---

[25]Krugman, Chapter 27 in this publication.

eration can be counterproductive. Recent monetary policy under exchange rate flexibility is analyzed by Artus and Crockett, as is the need for surveillance by the International Monetary Fund. The final selection, Chapter 38, presents in rigorous and tabular form the kinds of exchange rate regimes now in practice, and describes how members use the Fund's resources to meet balance of payment needs.[26]

Part X, which provides perspectives on the present state of the international economy — and its relation to the troubled environment in which international economic-policy targets will operate — consists of Klein's Nobel lecture and an update on likely economic scenarios.

---

[26]For related works on the present international monetary system in historical perspective and on exchange rate instability, see Robert Solomon, *The International Monetary System*, 1945–1981 (New York: Harper and Row, 1982), especially Chapters 1–14; Barry Eichengreen, ed., *The Gold Standard in Theory and History* (London: Methuen, 1985), especially Chapter 11 on "Hegemonic Stability Theories of the International Monetary System," pp. 271–311; Committee for the Study of Economic and Monetary Union, (1) *Report on Economic and Monetary Union in the European Community*, and (2) *Collection of Papers Submitted to the Committee for the Study of Economic and Monetary Union* (Luxembourg: Official Publications of the European Communities, 1989); and Paul R. Krugman, *Exchange-Rate Instability* (Cambridge: The MIT Press, 1989).

Part I

Evolution and Prospects of the International Economy

Lewis
Cooper
Secretary-General

THE EVOLUTION OF THE
INTERNATIONAL ECONOMIC ORDER

W. Arthur Lewis

INTRODUCTION

In international circles the topic of the day is the demand of the Third World for a new international economic order. My topic is the evolution of the existing economic order: how it came into existence not much more than a century ago, and how it has been changing.

The phrase "international economic order" is vague, but nothing would be gained by trying to define it precisely. I will discuss certain elements of the relationship between the developing and the developed countries that the developing countries find particularly irksome. These are:

First, the division of the world into exporters of primary products and exporters of manufactures.

Second, the adverse factoral terms of trade for the products of the developing countries.

Third, the dependence of the developing countries on the developed for finance.

Fourth, the dependence of the developing countries on the developed for their engine of growth.

My purpose in treating these topics is not to make recommendations, but to try to understand how we come to be where we are.

Reprinted from "The Evolution of the Economic Order." pp. 3–25,
with permission of Princeton University Press. Princeton. Copyright
1978.

THE DIVISION
OF THE WORLD

How did the world come to be divided into industrial countries and agricultural countries? Did this result from geographical resources, economic forces, military forces, some international conspiracy, or what?

In talking about industrialization, we are talking about very recent times. England has seen many industrial revolutions since the thirteenth century, but the one that changed the world began at the end of the eighteenth century. It crossed rapidly to North America and to Western Europe, but even as late as 1850 it had not matured all that much. In 1850 Britain was the only country in the world where the agricultural population had fallen below 50 percent of the labor force. Today some 30 Third World countries already have agricultural populations equal to less than 50 percent of the labor force—17 in Latin America, 8 in Asia not including Japan, and 5 in Africa not counting South Africa. Thus, except for Britain, even the oldest of the industrial countries were in only the early stages of structural transformation in 1850.

At the end of the eighteenth century, trade between what are now the industrial countries and what is now the Third World was based on geography rather than on structure; indeed India was the leading exporter of fine cotton fabrics. The trade was also trivially small in volume. It consisted of sugar, a few spices, precious metals, and luxury goods. It was then cloaked in much romance, and had caused much bloodshed, but it simply did not amount to much.

In the course of the first half of the nineteenth century industrialization changed the composition of the trade, since Britain captured world trade in iron and in cotton fabrics; but the volume of trade with the Third World continued to be small. Even as late as 1883, the first year for which we have a calculation, total imports into the United States and Western Europe from Asia, Africa, and tropical Latin America came only to about a dollar per head of the population of the exporting countries.*

There are two reasons for this low volume of trade. One is that the leading industrial countries—Britain, the United States, France, and Germany—were, taken together, virtually self-sufficient. The raw materials of the industrial revolution were coal, iron ore, cotton, and wool, and the foodstuff was wheat. Between them, these core countries had all they needed except for wool. Although many writers have stated that the industrial revolution depended on the raw materials of the Third World, this is quite untrue. Not until what is

* For the sources of this and other statistics used here, and generally for more detailed historical analysis, the reader may consult my book, *Growth and Fluctuations 1870-1913*, Allen and Unwin, London 1978.

sometimes called the second industrial revolution, at the end of the nineteenth century (Schumpeter's Third Kondratiev upswing based on electricity, the motor car and so on), did a big demand for rubber, copper, oil, bauxite, and such materials occur. The Third World's contribution to the industrial revolution of the first half of the nineteenth century was negligible.

The second reason why trade was so small is that the expansion of world trade, which created the international economic order that we are considering, is necessarily an offshoot of the transport revolutions. In this case, the railway was the major element. Before the railway the external trade of Africa or Asia or Latin America was virtually though not completely confined to the seacoasts and rivers; the railway altered this. Although the industrial countries were building railways from 1830 on, the railway did not reach the Third World until the 1860s. The principal reason for this was that, in most countries, railways were financed by borrowing in London—even the North American railways were financed in London—and the Third World did not begin to borrow substantially in London until after 1860. The other revolution in transport was the decline in ocean freights, which followed the substitution of iron for wooden hulls and of steam for sails. Freights began to fall after the middle of the century, but their spectacular downturn came after 1870, when they fell by two-thirds over thirty years.

For all these reasons, the phenomenon we are

exploring—the entry of the tropical countries significantly into world trade—really belongs only to the last quarter of the nineteenth century. It is then that tropical trade began to grow significantly—at about four percent a year in volume. And it is then that the international order that we know today established itself.

Now it is not obvious why the tropics reacted to the industrial revolution by becoming exporters of agricultural products.

As the industrial revolution developed in the leading countries in the first half of the nineteenth century it challenged the rest of the world in two ways. One challenge was to imitate it. The other challenge was to trade. As we have just seen, the trade opportunity was small and was delayed until late in the nineteenth century. But the challenge to imitate and have one's own industrial revolution was immediate. In North America and in Western Europe, a number of countries reacted immediately. Most countries, however, did not, even in Central Europe. This was the point at which the world began to divide into industrial and non-industrial countries.

Why did it happen this way? The example of industrialization would have been easy to follow. The industrial revolution started with the introduction of new technologies in making textiles, mining coal, smelting pig iron, and using steam. The new ideas were ingenious but simple and easy to apply. The capital requirement was remarkably small, except for the cost of building railways, which could be had on loan. There were no great economies of scale, so the skills required for managing a factory or workshop were well within the competence and experience of what we now call the Third World. The technology was available to any country that wanted it, despite feeble British efforts to restrict the export of machinery (which ceased after 1850), and Englishmen and Frenchmen were willing to travel to the ends of the earth to set up and operate the new mills.

Example was reinforced by what we now call "backwash." A number of Third World countries were exporting manufactures in 1800, notably India. Cheap British exports of textiles and of iron destroyed such trade, and provided these countries an incentive to adopt the new British techniques. India built its first modern textile mill in 1853, and by the end of the century was not only self-sufficient in the cheaper cottons, but had also driven British yarn out of many Far Eastern markets. Why then did not the whole world immediately adopt the techniques of the industrial revolution?

The favorite answer to this question is political, but it will not wash. It is true that imperial powers were hostile to industrialization in their colonies. The British tried to stop the cotton industry in India by taxing it. They failed because the Indian cotton industry had the protection of lower wages and of lower transportation costs. But they did succeed in holding off iron and steel production in India till as late as 1912. The hostility of imperial powers to industrialization in their colonies and in the "open door" countries is beyond dispute. But the world was not all colonial in the middle of the nineteenth century. When the coffee industry began to expand rapidly in Brazil around 1850, there was no external political force from Europe or North America that made Brazil develop as a coffee exporter instead of as an industrial nation. Brazil, Argentina, and all the rest of Latin America were free to industrialize, but did not. India, Ceylon, Java, and the Philippines were colonies, but in 1850 there were still no signs of industrialization in Thailand or Japan or China, Indo-China or the rest of the Indonesian archipelago. The partition of Africa did not come until 1880, when the industrial revolution was already a hundred years old. We cannot escape the fact that Eastern and Southern Europe were just as backward in industrializing as South Asia or Latin America. Political independence alone is an insufficient basis for industrialization.

We must therefore turn to economic explanations. The most important of these, and the most neglected, is the dependence of an industrial revolution on a prior or simultaneous agricultural revolution. This argument was already familiar to eighteenth-century economists, including Sir James Steuart and Adam Smith.

In a closed economy, the size of the industrial sector is a function of agricultural productivity. Agriculture has to be capable of producing the surplus food and raw materials consumed in the industrial sector, and it is the affluent state of the farmers that enables them to be a market for industrial products. If the domestic market is too small, it is still possible to support an industrial sector by exporting manufactures and importing food and raw materials. But it is hard to begin industrialization by exporting manufactures. Usually one begins by selling in a familiar and protected home market and moves on to exporting only after one has learnt to make one's costs competitive.

The distinguishing feature of the industrial revolution at the end of the eighteenth century is that it began in the country with the highest agricultural productivity—Great Britain—which therefore already had a large industrial sector. The industrial revolution did not create an industrial sector where none had been before. It transformed an industrial sector that already existed by introducing new ways of making the same old things. The revolution spread rapidly in other countries that were also revolutionizing their agriculture, especially in Western Europe and North America. But countries of low agricultural productivity, such as Central and Southern Europe, or Latin America, or China had rather small industrial sectors, and there it made rather slow progress.

If the smallness of the market was one constraint on industrialization, because of low agricultural productivity, the absence of an investment climate was another. Western Europe had been creating a capitalist environment for at least a century; thus a whole new set of people, ideas and institutions was established that did not exist in Asia or Africa, or even for the most part in Latin America, despite the closer cultural heritage. Power in these countries—as also in Central and Southern Europe—was still concentrated in the hands of landed classes, who benefited from cheap imports and saw no reason to support the emergence of a new industrial class. There was no industrial entrepreneurship. Of course the agricultural countries were just as capable of sprouting an industrial complex of skills, institutions, and ideas, but this would take time. In the meantime it was relatively easy for them to respond to the other opportunity the industrial revolution now opened up, namely to export agricultural products, especially as transport costs came down. There was no lack of traders to travel through the countryside collecting small parcels of produce from thousands of small farmers, or of landowners, domestic or foreign, ready to man plantations with imported Indian or Chinese labor.

And so the world divided: countries that industrialized and exported manufactures, and the other countries that exported agricultural products. The speed of this adjustment, especially in the second half of the nineteenth century, created an illusion. It came to be an article of faith in Western Europe that the tropical countries had a comparative advantage in agriculture. In fact, as Indian textile production soon began to show, between the tropical and temperate countries, the differences in food production per head were much greater than in modern industrial production per head.

Now we come to another problem. I stated earlier that the industrial revolution presented two alternative challenges—an opportunity to industrialize by example and an opportunity to trade. But an opportunity to trade is also an opportunity to industrialize. For trade increases the national income, and therefore increases the domestic market for manufactures. Import substitution becomes possible, and industrialization can start off from there. This for example is what happened to Australia, whose development did not begin until the gold rush of the 1850s, and was then based on exporting primary products. Nevertheless by 1913 the proportion of Australia's labor force in agriculture had fallen to 25 percent, and Australia was producing more manufactures per head than France or Germany. Why did this not happen to all the other agricultural countries?

The absence of industrialization in these countries was not due to any failure of international trade to expand. The volume of trade of the tropical countries increased at a rate of about 4 percent per annum over the thirty years before the first world war. So if trade was the engine of growth of the tropics, and industry the engine of growth of the industrial countries, we can say that the tropical engine was beating as fast as the industrial engine. The relative failure of India tends to overshadow developments elsewhere, but countries such as Ceylon, Thailand, Burma, Brazil, Colombia, Ghana, or Uganda were transformed during these thirty years before the First World War. They built themselves roads, schools, water supplies, and other essential infrastructure. But they did not become industrial nations.

There are several reasons for this, of which the most important is their terms of trade. Thus, we must spend a little time analyzing what determined the terms of trade.

THE FACTORAL TERMS
OF TRADE

The development of the agricultural countries in
the second half of the nineteenth century was promoted by two vast streams of international migration. About fifty million people left Europe for the
temperate settlements, of whom about thirteen
million went to what we now call the new countries of temperate settlement: Canada, Argentina,
Chile, Australia, New Zealand, and South Africa.
About the same number—fifty million people—
left India and China to work mainly as indentured
laborers in the tropics on plantations, in mines, or
in construction projects. The availability of these
two streams set the terms of trade for tropical and
temperate agricultural commodities, respectively.
For temperate commodities the market forces set
prices that could attract European migrants, while
for tropical commodities they set prices that would
sustain indentured Indians. These were very different levels.

A central cause of this difference was the difference in agricultural productivity between Europe
and the tropics. In Britain, which was the biggest
single source of European migration, the yield of
wheat by 1900 was 1,600 lbs. per acre, as against
the tropical yield of 700 lbs. of grain per acre. The

European also had better equipment and cultivated more acres per man, so the yield per man must have been six or seven times larger than in tropical regions. Also, in the country to which most of the European migrants went (the United States), the yield differential was even higher, not because of productivity per acre, which was lower than in Europe, but because of greater mechanization. The new temperate settlements could attract and hold European immigrants, in competition with the United States, only by offering income levels higher than prevailed in Northwest Europe. Since Northwest Europe needed first their wool, and then after 1890 their frozen meat, and ultimately after 1900 their wheat, it had to pay for those commodities prices that would yield a higher-than-European standard of living.

In the tropical situation, on the other hand, any prices for tea or rubber or peanuts that would offer a standard of living in excess of the 700 lb. of grain per acre level were an improvement. Farmers would consider devoting idle land or time to producing such crops; as their experience grew, they would even, at somewhat higher prices, reduce their own subsistence production of food in order to specialize in commercial crops. But regardless of how the small farmer reacted, there was an unlimited supply of Indians and Chinese willing to travel anywhere to work on plantations for a shilling a day. This stream of migrants from Asia was as large as the stream from Europe and set the level of tropical prices. In the 1880s the wage of a plantation laborer was one shilling a day, but the wage of an unskilled construction worker in Australia was nine shillings a day. If tea had been a temperate instead of a tropical crop, its price would have been perhaps four times as high as it was. And if wool had been a tropical instead of a temperate crop, it could have been had for perhaps one-fourth of the ruling price.

This analysis clearly turns on the long-run infinite elasticity of the supply of labor to any one activity at prices determined by farm productivity in Europe and Asia, respectively. This is applied to a Ricardian-type comparative cost model with two countries and three goods. The fact that one of these goods, food, is produced by both countries determines the factoral terms of trade, in terms of food. As usual one can elaborate by increasing the number of goods or countries, but the essence remains if food production is common to all.

One important conclusion is that the tropical countries cannot escape from these unfavorable terms of trade by increasing productivity in the commodities they export, since this will simply reduce the prices of such commodities. Indeed we have seen this quite clearly in the two commodities in which productivity has risen most, sugar and rubber. The factoral terms of trade can be improved only by raising tropical productivity in the common commodity, domestic foodstuffs.

There are interesting borderline cases where the two groups of countries compete. Cotton is an example. In the nineteenth century, the United

States was the principal supplier of cotton, but the crop could also grow all over the tropics. The United States maintained its hold on the market despite eager British efforts to promote cotton growing in the British colonies. The U.S. yields per acre were about three times as high as the Indian or African yields, but this alone would not have been enough to discourage tropical production. The United States could not have competed with tropical cotton had southern blacks been free to migrate to the North and to work there at white Northern incomes. It was racial discrimination in the United States that kept the price of cotton so low; or, to turn this around, given the racial discrimination, American blacks earned so little because of the large amount of cotton that would have flowed out of Asia and Africa and Latin America at a higher cotton price.

Cotton was one of a set of commodities where low agricultural productivity excluded tropical competition. The tropics could compete in any commodity where the difference in wages exceeded the difference in productivity. This ruled out not only cotton and tobacco, which fell to the ex-slaves in North America, but also maize, beef, and timber, for which there were buoyant markets, and ground was lost steadily in sugar as beet productivity increased. This left a rather narrow range of agricultural exports and contributed to the over-specialization of each tropical country in one or sometimes two export crops. Low productivity in food set the factoral terms of trade, while relative productivity in other agriculture determined which crops were in and which were out.

Minerals fall into this competing set. Labor could be had very cheaply in the tropical countries, so high productivity yielded high rents. These rents accrued to investors to whom governments had given mining concessions for next to nothing, and the proceeds flowed overseas as dividends. Mineral-bearing lands were not infinitely elastic, but the labor force was. With the arrival of colonial independence over the last two decades, the struggle of the newly independent nations to recapture for the domestic revenues the true value of the minerals in the ground, whether by differential taxation, by differential wages for miners, or by expropriation, has been one of the more bitter aspects of the international confrontation.

Given this difference in the factoral terms of trade, the opportunity that international trade presented to the new temperate settlements was very different from the opportunity presented to the tropics. Trade offered the temperate settlements high income per head, from which would immediately ensue a large demand for manufactures, opportunities for import substitution, and rapid urbanization. Domestic saving per head would be large. Money would be available to spend on schools, at all levels, and soon these countries would have a substantial managerial and administrative elite. These new temperate countries would thus create their own power centers, with money, education, and managerial capacity, independent of and somewhat hostile to the imperial power. Thus, Australia, New Zealand, and Canada ceased to be colonies in any political sense long before they acquired formal rights of sovereignty, and had already set up barriers to imports from Britain. The factoral terms available to them offered them the opportunity for full development in every sense of the word.

The factoral terms available to the tropics, on the other hand, offered the opportunity to stay poor—at any rate until such time as the labor reservoirs of India and China might be exhausted. A farmer in Nigeria might tend his peanuts with as much diligence and skill as a farmer in Australia tended his sheep, but the return would be very different. The just price, to use the medieval term, would have rewarded equal competence with equal earnings. But the market price gave the Nigerian for his peanuts a 700-lbs.-of-grain-per-acre level of living, and the Australian for his wool a 1600-lbs.-per-acre level of living, not because of differences in competence, nor because of marginal utilities or productivities in peanuts or wool, but because these were the respective amounts of food that their cousins could produce on the family farms. This is the fundamental sense in which the leaders of the less developed world denounce the current international economic order as unjust, namely that the factoral terms of trade are based on the market forces of opportunity cost and not on the just principle of equal pay for equal work. And of course nobody understood this mechanism bet-

ter than the working classes in the temperate settlements themselves, and in the United States. The
working classes were always adamant against Indian or Chinese immigration into their countries
because they realized that, if unchecked, it would
drive wages down close to Indian and Chinese
levels.*

* I have borrowed passages from my paper "The Diffusion
of Development" in Thomas Wilson, Editor, *The Market and
the State*, Oxford University Press, Oxford 1976.

CUMULATIVE FORCES

Now let me come to more recent developments. I must first make the point that, in spite of the poor factoral terms of trade, the opportunity to trade did substantially raise the national incomes of those tropical countries that participated in trade. This was partly because prices had to be set at levels that would bring the produce out. So, although prices were based on the low productivity in food, they had to be set somewhat higher. Just as wages were higher in Australia and Argentina than in Paris or London, so also wages were higher in Ceylon or Burma than in India or China.

The other reason national incomes of some tropical countries increased was that these countries developed by bringing unused resources into use—both unused land and unused labor—so that to a large extent what they produced for export was additional to what they would otherwise have produced. In particular the tropical countries continued to be self-sufficient in food. The agricultural exports were extra output.

This steady increase in income over some sixty or seventy years, right down to the great depression of 1929, very considerably expanded the demand for manufactures. Imports of textiles and of iron goods mounted, putting domestic handicrafts

out of business. Why did not these countries set up
their own modern factories to cope with this rising
demand?

Some did—especially India, Ceylon, Brazil, and
Mexico—but progress was slow. Apart from co-
lonialism, which restricted some but not others,
three other factors worked against industrialization.

The first reason is that to a large extent the import and export trades of these countries were controlled by foreign hands. This was where the profits were, in a complex of wholesaling, banking,
shipping, and insurance. Railway, plantation, and
mining profits were much more volatile. Profits
provide a major source of funds for reinvestment.
Had trading profits accumulated in domestic
hands, there would have been more domestic reinvestment, and almost certainly more interest in
domestic manufacturing.

Foreigners participated heavily in the external
trade of these countries for a variety of economic,
cultural, and political reasons. On the economic
side there was advantage in large scale operations
because they minimized the usual riskiness of trading and avoided the possibility facing small traders, who could be wiped out by a bad season. On
the cultural side Europeans had been running big
shipping and trading enterprises since the
seventeenth century; in this as also in banking and
insurance, they had a considerable lead over Latin
Americans and Africans, though not over Indians
or Chinese. The political factor was a further com-

plication in that some imperial governments deliberately favored their nationals at the expense both of indigenous and of other foreign competitors. Whatever the reason, the points where profits were greatest (wholesaling, banking, shipping, insurance) tended to be foreign-controlled, and this certainly diminished the availability of funds and enterprise for investment in domestic manufacturing.

A second factor to which some nationalist historians attach much importance is the fact that participation in trade itself whets the appetite for foreign goods, in the process destroying local industry. The consumer learns to prefer wheat to yams and cement to local building materials. This is all right if the country has the raw materials and can acquire the new skills for processing them. Otherwise it reduces the export multiplier—the extent to which the proceeds of exports circulate within the country, stimulating domestic industry, before flowing out again. It is difficult to give this quantitative significance for the nineteenth century, since the products destroyed by imports from Britain were mostly cotton and iron manufactures not essentially different from the imports which replaced them. Some of the difference lay in consumer preference, but most of the difference lay in cost. The situation evolved differently in the twentieth century when brand names established their footing in many consumer markets and proved difficult to dislodge even with domestic products of equal cost and quality.

As long ago as 1841, Friederich List emphasized

that the market forces in an agricultural economy work to keep it agricultural unless special measures are taken to arrest their momentum and change their direction. List's remedy was for the government to protect an infant manufacturing industry with tariffs and quotas. But this presupposes that the industrial forces have already conquered the government and can use it to their advantage. The fact that they had not is the third explanation why the agricultural countries, though becoming more prosperous and consuming more and more manufactures, did not industrialize. Imperial power was of course an obstacle in the colonial countries, but is not a necessary explanation since the same happened in the independent countries. The fact is that the very success of the country in exporting created a vested interest of those who lived by primary production—small farmers no less than big capitalists—and who opposed measures for industrialization, whether because such measures might deflect resources from agriculture and raise factor prices, or because they might result in raising the prices of manufactured goods. The outcome therefore depended on the relative political strengths of the industrial and the agricultural interests.

It is not to be supposed that in this confrontation the entrenched agricultural forces always won. On the contrary, they lost in most European countries and in most of the countries of new settlement. In Latin America at the end of the century the liveliness of Brazilian and Mexican entrepreneurs is notable. Egypt contrasts with India in not producing a single industrialist from its prosperous landowning and merchant classes. To unravel the different responses of countries experiencing apparently similar forces is a source of historical excitement. The contrast between Argentina and Australia is particularly instructive. These two countries began to grow rapidly at the same time, the 1850s, and sold the same commodities—cereals, wool, and meat. In 1913 their incomes per head were among the world's top ten. But Australia industrialized rapidly, and Argentina did not, a failure which cost her dearly after the war when the terms of trade moved against agriculture. Some Argentinian nationalists blame this failure on British interests in Argentina, but the British had even more influence in Australia or Canada, which were industrializing rapidly. The crucial difference between the two countries was that Argentinian politics were dominated by an old, landed aristocracy. Australia had no landed aristocracy. Its politics were dominated by its urban communities, who used their power to protect industrial profits and wages. The slowness with which industrial classes emerged in Latin America, or Central Europe, North Africa or much of Asia is explained as much by internal social and political structure as by the impact of external forces.

OPPORTUNITIES AND RISKS FOR THE WORLD ECONOMY:
THE CHALLENGE OF INCREASING COMPLEXITY

by Richard Cooper

Introduction

The subject of international economic cooperation has been under much discussion in recent years. People usually have in mind such events as the Plaza Agreement of September 1985 for coordinated intervention in exchange markets, or the coordinated lowering of central bank discount rates by the United States, Japan, and Germany that took place in March 1986. They also have in mind the apparent unwillingness of major countries to cooperate in framing their fiscal policies, and notably the reluctance of Japan and the Federal Republic of Germany to be "locomotives" for their trading partners as US fiscal policy moves into a contractionary stance.

But economic cooperation is much broader in scope than just the coordination of monetary or fiscal policy, and it is worthwhile to put cooperation into this broader context. Already 100 years ago nations agreed on a global framework for reckoning time and location; on common standards and a clearing mechanism for expenses of international postal service and, later, international telegraphic service (the latter also required agreed signals); on important navigational aids, and, early in the 20th century, on procedures for prompt reporting on contagious diseases and agreement on what should and (equally important) should not be done to limit their spread. Subsequent agreement was reached on the allocation of radio frequencies for the new wireless, and also on emergency signals for ships in distress; on air traffic control (as well as quarantine measures) for international aviation; on common nomenclature, measures, and standards for pharmaceuticals and other biological products; and more recently on common standards labelling and methods of shipping for toxic chemicals; on safety and control standards for nuclear energy; and on a host of other matters.

Most of these international cooperative measures are known only to the industries directly affected and to a few government and outside specialists. But all contribute toward the smooth flow of international commerce, and indeed have become taken for granted[1]. It is noteworthy that these measures were motivated in large measure by the realization that the reduction or removal of artificial or even natural obstacles to commerce can benefit all trading nations. Even those measures with apparent humanitarian aim, such as control of the spread of contagious disease, had their origin in the desire to reduce arbitrary national actions that had been taken out of fear but that were duplicative or ineffectual and at the same time impeded commerce.

Of course, one of the major barriers to commerce historically has been tariffs. Negotiations for mutual tariff reduction started seriously in the 19th century as well, if we exclude the customs union among thirteen former British colonies in the late eighteenth century. The German Zollverein, partly with political motivation, was formed in the nineteenth century, and the Cobden-Chevalier Treaty of 1860 began a series of bilateral negotiated reductions in tariff barriers to trade within Europe. This process suffered a major reversal in the 1930s, but then proceeded with unprecedented success after 1945. These recent negotiations involved not only tariff reduction, but also rules to prevent erosion of the trade liberalisation through other channels, for example by prohibiting quantitative restrictions on imports or direct subsidies to exports.

Published by the Organisation for Economic Cooperation and Development, Paris, 1986

All this is to suggest that the current preoccupation with the not very successful cooperation in the macroeconomic arena is only part of the story, and a relatively recent and one may even say, minor part of the broader picture of international economic cooperation among nations.

A Brief History

International cooperation in the macroeconomic arena is not, however, entirely a post-1945 endeavour. Various international conferences were held in the nineteenth century to preserve a bi-metallic system in the face of strong market pressure on silver. And there is the justly celebrated Genoa Conference of 1922, which addressed the question of how to preserve an international gold standard in view of the large price increases that had taken place during the First World War. The agreed solution was that central banks should concentrate monetary gold in their own hands, rather than allowing gold to circulate as coinage with the public, and furthermore that some countries would hold as their international reserves currencies (mainly the pound sterling) that were in turn convertible into gold. In these two ways the limited monetary gold stock could be stretched under the very different post-war conditions that prevailed in the 1920s. Finally, there was the abortive London Economic Conference of 1933, in which countries placed their hopes to raise the world economy out of the Great Depression, hopes which were dashed when the new Roosevelt Administration declined to agree to fix the dollar exchange rate. Then came the Tripartite Agreement of 1936 among Britain, France, and the United States, which in effect ended the exchange rate floating of 1931-36.

The unhappy experience of the 1920s and 1930s led wartime planners to attempt to build a better, more durable international economic system from the bottom up. This was an extraordinary endeavour. The results of these efforts provide the framework which, broadly speaking, we still use. It resulted in the Bretton Woods Agreement in the area of international money and finance, and the General Agreement of Tariffs and Trade in the area of trade, the latter being a residuum of a more ambitious proposal for an International Trade Organisation designed to cover investment as well as trade. The new system had several components: it involved rules, both proscriptions and prescriptions for national behaviour; it involved putting up capital; it involved the creation of new institutions; and it involved a commitment to a course of action beyond obedience to the formal rules, for example the liberalisation of trade.

For various reasons, this system stalled on the European payments problems of the late 1940s. An alternative route toward cooperation was therefore established, which involved the Marshall Plan, the creation of the Organisation of European Economic Cooperation (OEEC) to coordinate the distribution of Marshall aid within Europe and to provide a forum for assuring rough compatibility of policies, and the creation of the European Payments Union to clear payments as they became multilateralised among European countries. This regional system allowed the discrimination against North America that the Bretton Woods system and GATT had prohibited.

The period of transition from the disruptions of the Second World War were completed by 1960, and the OEEC was transformed into the Organisation for Economic Cooperation and Development (OECD), with Canada and the United States becoming full members, later to be joined by Japan, Australia and New Zealand. The European Community was also formed around this time to carry trade liberalisation to its extreme among a limited number of countries. The OECD was charged with fostering economic cooperation among all of its Member countries. Committees were created along functional lines. Among them was the Economic Policy Committee to provide a forum for discussion of macroeconomic policies, and its limited membership Working Party III to provide for reasonably confidential discussion of sensitive balance of payments issues. An annual ministerial meeting permitted high level pronouncements on the state of the world economy and decisions on the work program for the OECD.

The oil shock of 1974 gave rise to new calls for international economic cooperation, and spawned a host of new fora; a special session of the UN General Assembly, the Washington Energy Conference which led to creation of the International Energy Agency, the North South Conference on International Economic Cooperation (CIEC), and, starting in 1975, the economic summit meetings among the heads of government of at first five, then seven, leading democratic nations. The economic summit became an annual event for focusing high level political attention on a variety of issues of international economic cooperation, including but not limited to macroeconomic cooperation. Some of the preparatory work was done within the OECD. In the meantime, the European Community had eliminated tariffs and created a common agricultural policy. It faltered at first on monetary cooperation, but by 1979 was able to establish among some of its members the European Monetary System (EMS).

Forms of Economic Cooperation and Rationale

As should be clear from reflection on the history of international economic cooperation, there are diverse forms of cooperation. Too often "coordinated policy action" comes to mind when international cooperation is mentioned. But it is useful to distinguish at least six distinct forms of cooperation, in a rough hierarchy from less to more intensive engagement.

1. Exchange of information on the current situation and on current national policies. This form of cooperation is designed to assure the same information base, so to speak, and to avoid misunderstandings about what any country's policy actually is.

2. Agreement on common definitions of concepts and measurements, so all parties are reasonably confident that they are talking about the same thing.

3. Agreement on norms or objectives so all parties are assured that some of their actions are aimed in the same direction, at shared if not completely common objectives.

4. Exchange of information on prospective policy actions, so that each party is not caught unaware by the actions of others and can prepare its own actions to offset unwelcome side effects or to pursue the same objective in parallel action.

5. Coordination of national actions, so that the various parties work in prearranged concert in the pursuit of common objectives.

6. Joint action, in which the actions are decided together, taken together in the name of all participating parties, and often involve joint expenditure with shared contributions.

Examples of all these forms of economic cooperation can be found among the industrialised democracies, but the list of examples shortens as we proceed down the hierarchy, because the demands for strongly shared objectives and mutual trust typically become greater, as does the intrusion into national decision making procedures, as we proceed from (1) toward (6). Calls for international cooperation or coordination of policy are vague on exactly what is meant, although cooperation at level (5) is often implicit. On occasion it has actually occurred, as at the Bonn Economic Summit of 1978 and again in early 1986 with the coordinated reduction of central bank discount rates.

There is a school of thought, however, that contends that this kind of cooperation is unnecessary, undesirable, and possibly even dangerous. The argument takes three distinct forms. The first, drawing its inspiration from Adam Smith and by analogy to the competitive economic system, argues that decentralised decision making, with each agent pursuing its own interest, will lead to a social optimum. Any attempt to centralise, or "coordinate" decisions is likely to move away from this optimum. As with collusion among business firms within a national economy, so the argument runs, so also among governments within the international community, collusion is at the expense of the general public. It is better to let national governments pursue their national objectives in an internationally competitive environment (see Vaubel, 1983). This argument by analogy has double appeal, because coordination of actions among democratic governments is in fact extremely difficult to achieve. If it is unnecessary and even undesirable, that will make matters that much easier for national decision makers.

Unhappily, but perhaps not surprisingly, certain strong conditions must be met for decentralised decision making to lead to optimal results, and these conditions are manifestly not met in all economic relations aong nations. One condition is that the actions of one economic agent must not impinge significantly on the economic circumstances of others. Another condition is that no economic agent can have any monopoly power over the prices it pays or receives. A third condition is that economic agents can respond quickly to new economic circumstances. A fourth is that there be no "public goods", that is goods that can benefit many parties without additional cost (a lighthouse is the classic example). A fifth condition is that there be adequate insurance markets covering diverse future contingencies.

All of these conditions are violated in contemporary economic intercourse among nations. The most obvious violation is that nations are of unequal size, and some of them are able to influence the prices they pay or receive, including notably their real exchange rate, but also including particular goods for which they are especially large suppliers or markets. Changes in general business conditions in medium to large countries of course also affect their trading partners; and there are even some genuine international public goods – navigational aids have been mentioned, as well as elimination of contagious diseases such as smallpox, but providing a macroeconomically stable environment might also be included here. The upshot is that it is at least necessary to examine whether in practice the condition of nations can be improved by cooperation, since they clearly can be in principle.

A second objection to international economic cooperation arises from the possibility that such cooperation, aimed at improving conditions for all participating nations, may actually make them worse off because of the anticipatory response of private parties. The standard example is that labour unions leaders may hold out for higher wages if they anticipate that a cluster of closely related nations will frame their economic policy so as to maintain a high level of employment, whereas in the absence of international collaboration the leaders will recognise more clearly that striking for higher wages will reduce employment by weakening the international competitiveness of each nation's labour (Rogoff, 1985). In short, collaboration might weaken the "disciplinary role" of an open economy, which role, however, it should be noted, presupposes that certain rules are obeyed, e.g. with respect to import barriers. To the extent that this loss of internal discipline is a serious risk, it should of course be taken into account in framing any collaborative action.

A third objection to international cooperation arises from the possibility that cooperation may make the participating nations worse off in this case if it is based on deep ignorance of how economies actually function. If national authorities set out to cooperate, for example, to expand aggregate demand, or to stimulate investment for future production, on the basis of a badly inaccurate "model" of how their economies work, there is the possibility – not the certainty – that they will be made worse off (Frankel, 1986). This objective is of course in principle remediable; I return to it below.

At bottom, the case for international economic cooperation, including joint action, is that independent national actions will leave nations worse off than they need be, and that improvements can be made through cooperation. But this basic assumption should be examined critically in each proposal for international cooperation.

Current Problems

What then are the main areas where uncoordinated national action now and in the future runs the risk of impinging unfavourably on one's economic neighbours? Four different areas are worth mentioning, but the list is not exhaustive.

1. Mercantilistic tendencies still exist in most nations. Exports are thought to be more important than imports, and in many subtle or not so subtle ways governments try to improve their nation's trade balance. Tariffs are under reasonably tight international control among developed countries – developing countries have unfortunately but successfully pressed for exemption from this international discipline – so the pressure pushes action into other channels, such as official export credits, production subsidies, tax systems tilted to favour exports, and subsidies for new product development. These often favour so-called high-tech industries, where high-tech is defined in terms of the stage of development of the country in question. To protect traditional industries from new foreign sources of supply, import quotas and so-called voluntary restraint agreements have proliferated. As a result, while tariffs in developed countries are unprecedentedly low, trade is probably more encumbered by policy restrictions today than was true twenty-five years ago when the OECD was established. And the proliferation of such measures continues. Each country perceives its interest to lie in the extension of these incentives/restrictions. Yet we know from general principles that it cannot be in all countries' interests to have these incentives/restrictions become universal. Taken to its logical extreme, each village would become autarkic. The introduction of heavy steel subsidies in several European countries forced other members of the common market reluctantly to introduce their own subsidies in self defence and similarly led the United States to introduce the trigger price mechanism to ward off many private subsidy cases, and later to negotiate quota restrictions on European imports into the United States. That in turn led both Europe and the United States to introduce restrictions on steel coming from such new suppliers as Brazil, South Korea, Romania, and so on. The end result is to deny the benefits of competitive steel prices to many steel users in the advanced industrial countries.

2. The competitive spread of financial deregulation offers another example. Much of this deregulation is no doubt healthy, clearing out restrictions that had become outmoded. Many safeguards were put in at the time of the last major financial crisis in the early 1930s. Conditions today are very different from what they were then. But memories of what a financial crisis can be like have also faded. Are we really sure that the present system retains adequate safeguards against a new financial crisis? The rush to deregulation is driven in part by obsolescence of past restrictions, but in greater part by the new international mobility of capital and of financial institutions, and it represents a defensive reaction by governments to keep or attract newly mobile financial services on home shores. Those who believe that the system was over regulated will welcome this development, and I will join them in part. But the fundamental potential instability of a system of paper credit remains, and safeguards – at a minimum, the obligation of financial institutions to provide accurate, comprehensible, and up-to-date information – are needed. The rush to deregulate under competitive pressure of mobility may go too far, and internationally cooperative action would be required to establish a common framework of regulation.

An analogous problem arises in the area of antitrust policy, or as Europeans prefer to call it competition policy. For *each* country world sources of supply are increasingly relevant, not merely national sources, so concern with national concentration ratios and other traditional indicators of lack of competition are less and less relevant. But who is looking with a critical eye at the *world* structure of industry?

3. The industrialised nations are still extraordinarily dependent on imported oil to fuel their economies. This dependence, plus collusion among major oil exporting countries, has twice resulted in serious worldwide macroeconomic disruptions, in the form of bursts of inflation combined with economic contraction, high unemployment, and low investment, with highly undesirable consequences both for present and for future generations. The world at present seems to be in a period of remission – indeed, the sharp drop in oil prices is also a source of macroeconomic disruption, although less malign than sharp oil price increases have been. Each country has some incentive to protect itself against another price increase, which is likely to occur some time in the 1990s. But here is a classic case of a public good: insufficient protection will be purchased by each nation, because some of the benefits from each country's actions accrue to other countries, via downward pressure on world oil prices. So each country will underestimate the full benefits of its actions, and will engage in too little. This tendency is reinforced by the fact that action now is typically costly, both in economic and in political terms, and the future is uncertain. One can always hope that the feared contingency will not arise and, if it does, that it will be beyond my country's control. Yet a collective countermove could be highly beneficial to all.

4. Under a system of floating exchange rates, the short run "trade off" between inflation and unemployment that individual countries face results in more extensive price level changes for any given change in unemployment than would be true under fixed exchange rates or (which comes to about the same thing) than is true for the community of trading nations taken as a whole. The reason is that a given monetary action will immediately affect the exchange rate, and hence the level of consumer prices. This is true for each country acting alone. As a result, countries acting exclusively on their own will tend to maintain tighter monetary conditions than would be appropriate, given their objectives, with a consequential deflationary bias in the short run and a bias against investment in the long run. By acting in concert, nations would overcome this bias. (It should be noted that this macroeconomic deflationary bias may be offset in part or in full by the mercantilistic leanings noted in the first point above, which would press national authorities toward a weaker rather than a stronger currency.)

In addition, problems may arise because of the mis-timing of national actions. This problem is especially present in the area of fiscal action, where execution lags are long and action can only with difficulty take place more often than once a year. Mis-timing of actions could be corrected by the provision of adequate information on *prospective* actions by other nations, combined with confidence that they will actually be executed. Otherwise, we will be subject to episodes like 1972, when most major countries expanded at the same time, making inadequate allowance for the fact that other countries were also expanding; or 1974-75 when the reverse occurred, and major countries contracted without making adequate allowance for the fact that other major countries were also contracting.

Impediments to Cooperation

In all of these areas, and others, cooperation in the future might be mutually beneficial. Can we therefore be confident that it will occur? Not at all. There are a number of reasons that cooperation might not occur despite mutual benefit, and despite the presence of objectives that are broadly consonant (but need not be identical). First, disagreement among potentially cooperative parties may occur over the *distribution* of the benefits and the costs associated with cooperative action. All parties may want the action, but each wants it at a cost as low as possible to itself. In the limit, this gives rise to the so-called free-rider problem, where each party assumes that it will reap the benefits but can do so without incurring any costs or responsibility for maintenance of a mutually beneficial set of arrangements. That is left to someone else.

Second, there may be disagreement over prognostication. Everyone may agree that certain outcomes or events are undesirable, but they may disagree strongly over the likelihood of their occurrence. Since preventive actions are typically costly, they may therefore fail to agree on taking the preventive action.

Third, there may be disagreement on the method to achieve common objectives, partly because of different impacts of costs or unwanted side effects (the first point above), but mainly because of different assessments of efficacy of the proposed course of action toward attainment of the desired objectives – what I have elsewhere called differences of view on means-ends relationships, or more generally, disagreements on how the world actually works.

Fourth, countries may fail to cooperate because each party does not trust the others sufficiently to carry out their parts of a complex bargain. Sometimes cooperation involves one-time actions; but more often it involves a sequence of reinforcing actions (or proscriptions), and often countries will be reluctant to commit to a given course of action because they fear other countries will not carry out their roles, leaving the leaders of the country in question appearing naive to their home constituencies for having trusted "foreigners".

All of these factors are present to some extent in inhibiting economic cooperation, but the mix varies greatly from one issue to another. For instance, the main obstacle to trade liberalisation is distributional concerns. Adjustment to more open trading conditions is difficult, but it is eased if there are new export opportunities associated with the liberalisation. In addition countries are concerned about their terms of trade and/or emergent trade imbalances. Politically speaking, there have to be clear gainers within each country to compensate for the losers. Without this distributional problem, countries could generally gain by unilateral trade liberalisation[2].

In the cases of regulation and energy, the main disagreement is over prognostication: will the foreseen problems actually come to pass in the absence of action? Beyond this, there are means-ends disagreements with respect to whether proposed regulations are really necessary and sufficient for their assigned tasks. Distributional considerations also play a major role. Since oil is a major and pervasive input into modern industry, it is costly to cut back on it or even to store it. Who should bear these costs? Agreement was difficult and half-hearted at the 1979 Tokyo economic summit even in the midst of a world oil crisis, when disagreements over prognostication were minimal since the problem was real and the crisis palpable. Furthermore, cooperation was impeded by scepticism about whether others would carry out their part of the proposed agreement on targeted cutbacks in demand for imported oil.

In the macroeconomic arena, disagreements over objectives and in particular over nationally acceptable levels of inflation and unemployment have typically been emphasised. No doubt that is part of the story. But I believe a much more significant obstacle is ignorance about means-ends relationships, about how economies actually work. There are also differences over prognostication, which make anticipatory actions difficult by any government, much less agreement on them by several governments. But I suspect that such differences, while occasionally important, are secondary to disagreements over how the macroeconomic world works. One has only to recall the surprising propositions of supply-siders that dominated the first Reagan Administration. Or the continuing debate between monetarists and non-monetarists over the ability of central banks to influence the economy through their actions, and in particular over their alleged (by monetarists) inability to influence real interest rates or real economic activity beyond a relatively short and unpredictable period. Or the views expressed by various senior German economic officials to the author over the past ten years. They have alleged on occasion that increased government spending is inflationary, even when unemployment exceeded 8 per cent, but at the same time that increased exports are not inflationary, even when unemployment was below 4 per cent. They have alleged that reduced government spending is not contractionary, but on the contrary would stimulate investment through its confidence building effects, and that reduced personal taxation would not be expansionary, since all of the tax reduction would be saved or would be spent abroad. It is implausible that all of these propositions are valid. But policy judgments hinged on them or, more correctly, these propositions were used to rationalise not taking certain actions. Each of these is a testable proposition, and we should not remain in ignorance about their validity or invalidity. Perhaps some of them will prove to be valid under certain circumstances but not under others, that is, our current analytical categories are not drawn sufficiently finely. If that is the case, we should be able to discover that as well.

An illuminating exercise, the first of its kind, was undertaken by the Brookings Institution in early 1986. Twelve global macroeconomic models were aligned approximately to the same baseline over the period 1984-90 and were put through the same set of policy simulations. There were certain similarities in the results. For example, an increase in US government spending increased US GNP, and expansionary US monetary policy depreciated the dollar. Such similarities are not surprising, since all the models were drawn from a similar *corpus* of economic theory. But there were startling quantitative differences among them. For instance, the impact in the first year on US real GNP (in billions of 1972 dollars) arising from a one per cent cut in government expenditure (about $36 billion in 1985) ranged from a decline of $1 billion to a decline of $35 billion, and the impact on the government deficit ranged from a drop of $9 billion (in 1985 dollars) to a drop of $38 billion. Thus there were enormous differences among these models in the required cut in government spending to achieve a given reduction in the budget deficit. These quantitative differences reflect great divergences about how the US economy, in its interaction with the rest of the world, actually performs under stipulated circumstances.

It is difficult to imagine macroeconomic cooperation on a regular basis so long as there are large divergences of views on means-ends relationships. That was the experience with respect to international cooperation in containment of the spread of contagious diseases. The problem was early recognised as one calling for international cooperation, but cooperation proved impossible so long as there was serious contention over the etiology of diseases. Once a workable consensus was reached on the mechanism of disease propagation, serious cooperation began to take place (see Cooper: 1986a).

A similar phenomenon can be observed with respect to fisheries. International cooperation in limiting access to ocean fisheries is clearly required for optimal management of this common property resource, since free entry will deplete the source of fish unduly, such that yields will fall way below their optimum. Limited success at international cooperation has been achieved with respect to fur seals, some whales, and Pacific salmon, where there was a workable consensus on the rate of growth of the stock and the harvest that could be taken while maintaining its health. Where such consensus has been lacking, distributional disputes become embedded in apparently scientific disputes over what is required to maintain the stocks in order to achieve anything near the optimum harvest over time. The move within the last decade to the 200 mile national fishery zone does not solve this problem, it simply reduces the number of potential parties required to solve it. In some cases it pushes the issue back to the national level, where the history of fisheries' management has also been abysmal, again because of distributional squabbles mixed with scientific ignorance.

This is not to say that international cooperation is impossible until knowledge is extensive. First, as noted above, there are many levels of cooperation, some of which involve the exchange of information and the pursuit of knowledge. Second, as Putnam and Maynes have pointed out, there may be occasions in which a coalition of common interests across national boundaries may form to collaborate on a particular coordinated program of action. This seems to have been the case at the 1978 Bonn summit, where a grand bargain was struck whereby West Germany and Japan agreed to introduce expansionary fiscal actions, the United States agreed to pull in its fiscal reins and to decontrol domestic oil prices, and France and the United Kingdom agreed to remove their hold on trade liberalisation under the Tokyo round. Successive rounds of trade liberalisation have also involved an international coalition of forces interested in enlarging the world market, aligned against often strong domestic interests in each country intent on preventing greater competition from imports.

A Glimpse into the Future

The need for international economic cooperation is likely to become more rather than less important in the future, for the reasons outlined by Vernon. Economies are becoming more interdependent in both trade and finance. Factors of production are becoming more mobile. These developments will tend to weaken traditional instruments of policy applied at the national level. Their efficacy can be restored by applying them at the international level, that is, through international collaboration. Technological advances and higher incomes will create pressures against common property resources and will generate new public goods or public bads, as they have in the past with respect to whaling, the electromagnetic spectrum, the atmospheric disposal of radioactive waste, geostationary satellite locations, global deforestation, and possibly ozone depletion.

What are the problems for the future calling for economic cooperation? Some important ones are implicit in the four headings that have been discussed above:

1. maintaining foreign trade free from undue interference and the inevitable restrictive reactions to it;
2. assuring adequate soundness and resiliency to the world financial system;
3. avoiding another oil crisis or responding to it at relatively low cost; and
4. maintaining the world economy on a reasonably even path of non-inflationary growth through adequate macroeconomic management.

We currently have institutional arrangements for dealing with the first and third of these problems in the GATT, the OECD, and the IEA although these arrangements have serious weaknesses and need attentive cultivation. The second of these issues has been addressed in a preliminary way by central bankers under BIS auspices, resulting in two concordats concerning cooperation among central banks in crisis (see Lomax), but much deeper analysis is needed and there are gaps and uncertainties in the cooperative arrangements. The fourth issue has been sporadically and unsystematically considered by the OECD and in the economic summit meetings, and for Europe within the European Community. Global economic forecasting is now done by the OECD and by the International Monetary Fund.

As noted above, systematic progress on the fourth issue is unlikely until there is greater consensus on how economies actually work. That places a high premium on gaining that information, which itself is in part a task calling for international cooperation. Among others, it should be pursued by the OECD. In the meantime, close coordination of macroeconomic policy should be approached gingerly, since proceeding on the basis of a seriously incorrect view of how the world works could leave everyone worse off, as Frankel has illustrated.

Coordination of national policy actions is ambitious. Less ambitious forms of cooperation are equally valuable, indeed sometimes essential preconditions to collaborative action. The OECD has played a key role in the exchange of information, in the standardization of concepts, and in the development of norms of behaviour over its 25 year life. This is useful work, and should continue.

Institutions for international cooperation abound. We do not need new institutions until we have found tasks that are necessary or desirable and cannot be performed well under existing arrangements. The argument above suggests that the absence of suitable institutions is not at present the critical obstacle to effective international economic cooperation in the macroeconomic arena.

What needs to be done from a substantive point of view? I have four suggestions. First, the GATT staff needs to be given more direct initiative and resources for identifying and analysing trade distorting practices, to provide systematic information and analysis of them, and thereby to draw more attention to them. At present the initiative is exclusively with Member states.

Second, we will need to continue to negotiate codes of behaviour with respect to trade-affecting domestic economic policies, including codes on services, of the type now being pursued in the new round of trade negotiations. "Subsidies" need to be defined, along with permissible reactions to them. The detailed discussion of these issues themselves would bring some benefit, and if norms can be agreed so much the better.

Third, the IMF needs to be given greater capacity to help stabilise the world economy. A straightforward step, but one that requires amendment of its Articles, would be to authorise it to augment its ordinary lending resources by issuance of SDRs to itself, and in parallel to authorise it to alter the borrowing rights of Member states according to world economic conditions. Peter Kenen (1986) has recently emphasized the importance of shifting the IMF from a supplier of reserve credit at country initiative to a global responsibility with respect to reserve creation.

Fourth, real exchange rate uncertainty is likely to prove increasingly distasteful and distortionary of both trade and international investment. I have boldly suggested elsewhere that the key OECD countries should move to a single currency with a single monetary policy and a system of international governance to determine that monetary policy (Cooper: 1984). This would represent the ultimate form of international cooperation, joint monetary action on a continuing basis. It is too radical for early implementation, but not too radical to begin thinking seriously about. Perhaps by the 50th anniversary of the OECD such an arrangement will be in place.

NOTES

1. It is possible for example to order a given drug in most major cities of the world, and the druggist will know what you are talking about and the measurements will be comprehensible to the user. It is also possible for a plane or ship to arrive from an area endemic with cholera or other contagious diseases, and the passengers will be landed with a minimum of fuss and with a minimum of risk. Both contrast sharply to the condition one hundred years ago, when for example a passenger ship left Genoa and because of a case of cholera on board was refused landing rights at Montevideo and at Rio de Janeiro and had to re-cross the Atlantic and ended up at Livorno less than one hundred miles from where it started, without disembarking any of its passengers.

2. It must be said also that differences in means-ends relationships still play a role in that some observers continue to press the "infant industry" argument with apparent conviction, that is, with more than just a cover-up for self-serving distributional gains. There should in principle be consensus on which industries are true infant industries in that they can expect to grow out of their infant status and be successful. If that could be achieved, means-ends disagreements would have disappeared or would have been transformed into distributional disagreements revolving around the question whether country A's established industry should bear the costs of nurturing by country B of that same industry as an infant.

REFERENCES

Camps, Miriam, with Catherine Gwin, *Global Management*, McGraw Hill, 1981.

Cooper, Richard N., 1984, "A Monetary System for the Future", *Foreign Affairs*, Fall, 1984.

Cooper, Richard N., 1986a, "International Cooperation in Public Health as a Prologue to Macroeconomic Cooperation", Brookings Discussion Paper No. 44.

Cooper, Richard N., 1986b, "US Macroeconomic Policy, 1986-88: Are the Models Useful?", mimeo.

Frankel, Jeffrey A., "The International Macroeconomic Policy Coordination when Policymakers Disagree on the Model", mimeo, June 1986.

Kenen, Peter B., *Financing, Adjustment, and the International Monetary Fund*, The Brookings Institution, Washington, 1986.

Lomax, David F., *The Developing Country Debt Crisis*, McMillan, London, 1986.

Putnam, Robert, and Nicholas Bayne, *Hanging Together – The Seven-Power Summits*, Heinemann Educational Books Ltd, London, 1984.

Rogoff, Kenneth, "Can International Monetary Policy Cooperation Be Counterproductive?", *Journal of International Economics*, No. 18, May, 1985, pp. 199-217.

Vaubel, Roland, "Coordination or Competition among National Macroeconomic Policies?" in F. Machlup et al, eds., *Reflections on a Troubled World Economy*, Macmillan, London, 1983.

Vernon, Raymond, "Global Interdependence: A Long View", mimeo, 1986.

THE WORLD ECONOMY ENTERING THE 1990s

by The Secretary-General, United Nations

The world scene in 1989 was dominated by spectacular political developments. Superpower relationships and the political structure in Eastern Europe changed dramatically. In themselves, these changes are epoch-making; their implications for the world economy are far reaching. At the end of the year they tended to overshadow developments in the international economy.

As predicted in the World Economic Survey, 1989, 1/ the world economy slowed down in 1989 after strong growth in 1988. Growth decelerated in all major groups of economies, but unevenly (see table 1). The deceleration was relatively modest in the developed market economies and the developing countries and sharp in Eastern Europe. Differences in growth rates among countries remained large, particularly among developing countries. Per capita output increased fairly significantly in the industrial countries, but in Africa and Latin America the average level of income continued to fall, as it has throughout the decade. In Asia, per capita output rose rapidly, although mass poverty remained pervasive.

The developed market economies, which have had the longest economic expansion in post-war history, slowed down in 1989 but no recession is forecast in the near future. Growth remains strong in the major economies. Business confidence remains high and has been buoyed by the prospects of European integration. In a number of developing countries which had been growing fast in the 1980s, growth has been slowing down but still remains high. The growing economic relations with Eastern Europe and the Soviet Union, while fraught with great problems, should on balance be expected to stimulate trade and investment.

Yet there are threats to the world economy. The most likely development is a continuation of present trends, but those imply growing tensions and great challenges to policy makers. The problems of the dollar, interest rates, external debts and commodity prices continue to weigh heavily over the world economy.

1/   United Nations publication, Sales No. E.89.II.C.1.

Published by the Economic and Social Council, United Nations, 16 January 1990.

37

Table 1. Growth of output by region and selected country
groupings and world exports, 1981-1990

	Annual percentage rate of change						Population 1988 (million)
	1981- 1985	1986	1987	1988	1989 a/	1990 b/	
World	2.7	3.3	3.5	4.4	3.2	3.0	5 112
Developed market economies	2.2	2.7	3.3	4.2	3.2	2.7	809
North America	2.4	2.9	3.4	4.6	2.7	2.2	272
Western Europe	1.5	2.6	2.6	3.3	3.3	2.6	356
Developed Asia	3.6	2.5	4.0	5.4	4.7	4.3	142
Eastern Europe and the Soviet Union c/	3.3	4.3	2.6	4.1	2.5	..	396
Developing countries	2.5	3.9	4.1	4.5	3.3	4.0	3 907
Western hemisphere	1.0	3.6	2.5	0.2	0.7	3.0	430
West Asia	-0.9	0.1	-1.3	1.0	2.0	3.5	66
South and East Asia	4.8	5.5	5.5	7.4	6.4	6.0	1 653
China	10.2	8.3	10.6	11.2	5.0	4.0	1 104
Africa	-0.9	-2.1	0.9	2.3	2.6	3.0	576
Mediterranean	2.9	5.6	3.7	3.2	3.7	4.5	78
Memorandum items:							
Heavily indebted countries d/	-3.0	3.3	2.5	0.9	1.3	3.2	588
Sub-Saharan Africa e/	-0.7	-0.2	0.0	2.3	2.5	2.8	359
Volume of world exports	2.0	3.8	5.7	8.5	6.5	6.0	-

Source: Department of International Economic and Social Affairs of the United
Nations Secretariat, based on data provided by the regional commissions, Project LINK
and other sources.

a/ Preliminary estimates.

b/ Forecast. For the groups of developing countries, estimates are rounded to the
nearest half percentage point.

c/ Net material product; data for 1981-1988 are government estimates.

d/ The countries in this group are Argentina, Bolivia, Chile, Colombia, Côte
d'Ivoire, Ecuador, Mexico, Morocco, Nigeria, Peru, the Philippines, Uruguay, Venezuela
and Yugoslavia.

e/ Excluding Nigeria.

The following appraisal of the world economy and its prospects for 1990 was prepared for the information of United Nations delegates and the international community by the Department of International Economic and Social Affairs of the United Nations Secretariat. It draws on the analyses of the regional commissions of the United Nations in Europe, Latin America and the Caribbean, Africa, Asia and the Pacific, and Western Asia.

I. DEVELOPMENTS IN 1989

A. Growth of output

World production and trade continued to expand in 1989, but more slowly than in 1988. According to preliminary estimates, world output increased by around 3 per cent compared with 4.4 per cent in the preceding year. After an extraordinary growth of 8.5 per cent in 1988, international trade is estimated to have grown by around 6.5 per cent in 1989, which is high by historical standards.

1. Developed market economies

The developed market economies continued to grow in 1989, the seventh year of uninterrupted expansion. But, as widely expected, the rate of growth slowed down; it declined from 4.2 per cent in 1988 to just over 3 per cent in 1989. This was still above the average for the decade.

The deceleration varied considerably between countries. Among the large economies, the sharpest slow-down was in Canada and the United States of America. Growth in the United States is estimated at around 2.7 per cent for 1989, or less than two thirds of the 4.4 per cent growth in 1988. The deceleration in Canada was of similar magnitude. Most other major economies grew almost as fast in 1989 as in 1988 or even faster. Japan's economic growth dropped from about 5.7 per cent to around 5 per cent, and the Federal Republic of Germany grew by around 4 per cent, which was faster than in 1988 and its fastest rate in the 1980s. The British, French and Italian economies grew only slightly more slowly in 1989 than in 1988, and some of the smaller economies, notably Spain, grew faster.

The continued strength of the developed market economies in Western Europe and Japan was fueled largely by an investment boom which had begun earlier and remained strong in 1989. In Europe, the growth of investment was due to buoyant business confidence and industrial restructuring in the run-up to the introduction of the single market in the European Economic Community (EEC) in 1992. In Japan, the strong growth in capital spending was geared to the shift towards expansion of the domestic market.

The growth of these economies in recent years was reflected in a significant decline in unemployment, though it remains high in a number of countries. The relatively large slow-down in the United States in 1989 was accompanied by a slight edging up of the unemployment rate which at around 5.5 per cent, remains among the lowest in the major economies. In Europe, the rate of unemployment, though still high, was projected to decline further in 1989.

Expansion in the developed market economies over the last three years was accompanied by accelerated inflation. Consumer prices rose faster in almost all the major economies during 1987-1988 and well into the second quarter of 1989, but the rate of increase slowed somewhat in the third quarter. The rate of inflation remains relatively low, however. For the developed market economies as a whole, consumer prices rose by an annual rate of 4.7 per cent in the first nine months of 1989, compared with 3.0 per cent in 1987 and 3.3 per cent in 1988. Price increase rose from 4.1 per cent in 1988 to 4.9 per cent in the first nine months of 1989 in the United States, from 0.9 per cent to 2.2 per cent in Japan, and from 1.2 per cent to 2.9 per cent in the Federal Republic of Germany. Among the major economies, the rate of inflation was the highest in the United Kingdom of Great Britain and Northern Ireland, where it increased from 5.1 per cent to 7.8 per cent.

The macro-economic response to the inflationary pressure has been a tightening of monetary policy. The Federal Republic of Germany raised official interest rates by 1 percentage point and Japan by almost 2 percentage points. Interest rates were high and rising in the United Kingdom. Credit policy remained tight in the United States in the midst of continuing concern over inflation, but was eased slightly by mid-year as the economy began to slow down.

2. Developing countries

In the developing countries, growth slowed in 1989. The slow-down was pronounced in some of the rapidly growing economies, while the declining ones showed only marginal improvement.

South and East Asia

South and East Asia continued to be the most rapidly expanding region in the world in 1989, but even that region did not maintain the rapid pace of the previous year. Several of the export-oriented economies have been adversely affected by the deceleration in some of the developed market economies and China and, in some cases, by the earlier revaluations of their currencies and increasing unit labour costs. In some of these countries, the deterioration in export prospects is being offset by a boom in private domestic consumption brought about by several years of steady growth.

Although weather conditions in South Asia were generally favourable in 1989, agricultural output is unlikely to have surpassed the previous year's level. As a result, the rate of growth of GDP in India is likely to be about 2 per cent lower than in 1988 but will still be around 6 per cent. Growth in Sri Lanka has suffered as a result of civil unrest.

Latin America and the Caribbean

In Latin America, output increased modestly in 1989 after a decrease in 1988. The improvement was due almost entirely to a turn-around in Brazil, although Mexico also improved on its 1988 growth performance. The rate of growth of the other countries in the region was less than in 1988, and growth in the region as a whole was insufficient to avoid a fall in per capita output for the second consecutive year.

In most countries in the Latin American region, economic stagnation in 1989 was largely the result of stabilization measures. The main economic concern in many of these countries was inflation and hyper-inflation. In Argentina, Nicaragua and Peru, economic stabilization measures resulted in negative growth for the second consecutive year; policy actions also resulted in a sizeable fall in output in Venezuela in 1989. At the other end of the spectrum, Chile experienced another year of robust growth, while Colombia, the only country in the region to have made sustained progress during the previous years of the decade, slowed down in 1989. For many countries in the region, a large net outflow of resources resulting from the debt crisis remains a serious constraint to growth.

Africa

Economic conditions in Africa remain disconcerting. The formulation in 1989 by the Economic Commission for Africa (ECA) of an African Alternative Framework for Structural Adjustment Programmes and the publication of a comprehensive report by the World Bank, entitled <u>Sub-Saharan Africa: From Crisis to Sustainable Growth</u>, reflected the widespread concern about Africa's continuing development crisis. In 1989, growth is estimated to have been only slightly higher than in the previous year. This means a further decline in per capita output. Regional wars and civil unrest continue to be a major impediment to economic and social progress in several countries. In particular, conflicts in Ethiopia and the Sudan, coupled with a drought in the affected regions, are putting hundreds of thousands of people at risk of starvation in the immediate future.

West Asia

The dependence of the economies of West Asia on the international oil market remains undiminished. Oil prices on average have been some 20 per cent higher in 1989 than in 1988. The energy-exporting countries of the region have benefited accordingly. Output in this sub-group of countries is estimated to have grown by some 2-3 per cent in 1989 after negligible growth in 1988. Despite this, these economies are still in the process of adjusting to the lower oil prices that have prevailed since 1986. This adjustment has also had a major influence on neighbouring countries through three main channels: a decrease in energy-exporting countries' imports from them; a collapse in workers' remittances; and a reduction of development assistance flows. Some of the energy-importing countries in the region have also accumulated large external debts, which they are finding difficult to service in the less favourable economic environment.

China

Economic growth in China slowed in 1989 to about 5 per cent, one of its lowest levels in the 1980s. Industrial output increased by about 7 per cent, compared with almost 18 per cent in 1988. Agricultural output probably increased by around 4 per cent. The economy, which had been growing very fast in the 1980s, grew by 11 per cent in 1988. Such growth was becoming unsustainable. Serious imbalances developed in the economy, and the rate of inflation rose to an unprecedented 25 per cent in the first half of 1989. The economic slow-down in China in 1989 was mainly due to contractionary measures taken. The growth of money supply was severely curtailed and interest rates raised. Central government investment expenditure was substantially cut and real wages in state enterprises reduced.

These policies have started to produce the intended result of checking inflation, which declined to an annual rate of around 9 per cent in October.

With the moderation of domestic demand and imposition of import restrictions, the growth of imports slowed, while exports increased faster than before. Yet, a drastic fall in tourism and increased interest payments on foreign loans led to a worsening of the current account deficit in 1989. The currency was devalued by 21 per cent in December as part of efforts to reduce the payments imbalance.

3. Eastern Europe and the Union of Soviet Socialist Republics

Political upheavals and continuing striving for political and economic reforms acquired far greater significance for the economies of Eastern Europe and the Soviet Union than any measure of their growth in 1989. Output grew only modestly, even in comparison with the average rate of the 1980s. After growing by around 4 per cent in 1988, net material product in these economies probably increased by about 2.5 per cent in 1989. The growth of industrial production slowed considerably, especially in Bulgaria, the German Democratic Republic, Poland and the Soviet Union. Agricultural production in most of these economies also fell far short of the rather ambitious targets and probably increased by about 2 per cent.

The Soviet Union and virtually all countries in Eastern Europe are in the throes of reforms aiming to reshape their political and economic systems fundamentally in the direction of greater reliance on market mechanisms and democratic governance, though the shape of both of these is still under debate. They are encountering severe transition problems ranging from high inflation to acute scarcities and labour unrest. A great number of changes have to be made simultaneously, and harsh adjustment policies are necessary. External assistance will also be needed for industrial restructuring, debt relief and stabilization of government finances.

B.   International trade

International trade remained buoyant in 1989 after a remarkable growth in 1988. There were signs, however, that the growth of trade was slowing in the latter part of the year. Preliminary data suggest that for the year as a whole, trade may have grown by around 6.5 per cent.

Significant progress was made in negotiations under the Uruguay Round to liberalize trade and strengthen the trading system. Activities in all the negotiating groups picked up and participating countries reaffirmed their commitment to complete the negotiations by the end of 1990, as agreed at Punta del Este. An early result of the negotiations was an agreement to strengthen the General Agreement on Tariffs and Trade (GATT) dispute settlement machinery. Indeed, greater use is now being made of the GATT dispute settlement mechanism. The trade policy review mechanism initiated early in the year is in operation, and the trade policies of Australia, Morocco and the United States have already come under review. GATT membership is increasing and a number of countries have applied for membership. The Soviet Union is close to receiving observer status in GATT, and China's re-entry application is under examination.

However, there was little actual trade liberalization, and quantitative trade restrictions continued to proliferate. The trend towards bilateralism in trade relationships continued. The United States has emphasized bilateralism in action taken under the Omnibus Trade and Competitiveness Act of 1988. The Canada-United States trade agreement further strengthened bilateral trade relations among two major participants in international trade.

There were further moves towards the formation of trading blocs in 1989. At the December 1989 summit, EEC made significant progress towards the creation of a single market in 1992, which will free trade and capital flows between member States. The decision to move towards monetary union was a major step in that direction. An agreement between EEC and the European Free Trade Association (EFTA) for further liberalization of movement of goods, services, capital and people between the two country groups was nearly complete by the end of the year. In November, ministers from a group of 12 countries of the Pacific rim met in Canberra to discuss increased regional co-operation, trade liberalization and a common position in multilateral trade negotiations. Although the Conference on Asia-Pacific Economic Co-operation is intended to be an association that is looser than a trading bloc discriminating against outsiders, it may turn out to be the first step towards the formation of a new trade alignment.

The implications of such developments for the multilateral trading system are as yet unclear. The dynamic effects of regional integration will often benefit outsiders as well, but new discriminatory treatment will create new tensions. Above all, if world commercial policy issues are to be settled in negotiations between a few major blocs rather than among the States that are now members of GATT, the trading system will take on a new character.

C. Debt and the net transfer of financial resources

A major international concern in the 1980s was that many developing countries had to severely cut back essential domestic expenditures, especially investment, in order to make a net transfer abroad of financial resources. The countries most affected are heavily indebted and largely middle-income. Since 1983, their net capital inflows have been less than the net payment of interest and profits (figure I illustrates the effects for an indicative sample of 15 developing countries). 2/ Others, generally low-income countries, including many that also have heavy debt burdens, have continued to enjoy a positive net transfer from abroad, albeit at a lower rate than in the early 1980s (see figure II for the case of sub-Saharan Africa). 3/

2/   The 15 countries are Argentina, Bolivia, Brazil, Chile, Colombia, Côte d'Ivoire, Ecuador, Mexico, Morocco, Nigeria, Peru, the Philippines, Uruguay, Venezuela and Yugoslavia.

3/   Nigeria is excluded from the sub-Saharan Africa group since its large economy would otherwise mask the results of the many smaller African countries. It is included in the group of 15 heavily indebted countries.

The total outstanding external debt of the capital-importing developing
countries reached $1.1 trillion in 1987, a level at which it remained in 1988 and
in 1989 as well, according to preliminary data. The group of 15 heavily indebted
countries probably spent over 40 per cent of their export earnings in 1989 on
servicing their debt, only slightly less than in 1988, while the corresponding
ratio for the countries of sub-Saharan Africa was about 27 per cent, somewhat more
than in 1988. Interest payments alone were estimated at 23 per cent of the export
earnings of the former group in 1989 and 13 per cent of that of the latter.

In 1989, higher interest rates in international capital markets raised the
interest payments required on debt owed to international commercial banks, while
there was little new lending to these countries except from official institutions.
Capital flight has been arrested or reversed in countries that were able to offer
sufficiently attractive conditions to retain the capital of their citizens, but the
present communication facilities ensure that capital flight will continue if the
only impediment is administrative controls on capital flows. It is a symptom of
the difficulties that many debtor countries were accumulating new arrears of
interest and principal to their foreign creditors, including the International
Monetary Fund (IMF) and the World Bank.

All in all, preliminary and partial data suggest that the net financial
transfer out of the 15 country sample, rose from $33 billion in 1988 to about
$37 billion in 1989, almost 4 per cent of their GDP. The net transfer into the
sub-Saharan group is estimated at about $5 billion (almost 4 per cent of GDP),
essentially the same in nominal dollar terms as in 1988.

It is now widely recognized that in the case of heavily indebted middle-income
countries, the solution of the debt problem cannot be to add more loans to a debt
that already cannot be serviced. Debt reduction has an important role in
straightening out such situations. That is why creditor Governments adopted the
March 1989 proposal of the United States Secretary of the Treasury (the "Brady
Plan"), under which loans from IMF and the World Bank, as well as from the
Government of Japan, would help underwrite a negotiated reduction of commercial
bank debt and debt servicing.

The experience of the first Brady Plan case, that of Mexico, was that the
negotiations with the banks proved very difficult and protracted. In the end
intensive creditor Government involvement was required to bring them to a close. A
long period was then needed to arrange details and "sell" the package to Mexico's
500 creditor banks. The programme was expected to reduce the burden of commercial
bank debt by roughly 35 per cent through a combination of debt reduction, interest
reduction and "new money" loans, although the net benefit would be less since the
official credits that were used to enhance the debt reduction scheme also had to be
serviced. No overall framework was set by the Mexican case, as subsequent Brady
Plan negotiations settled on very different packages for the Philippines and Costa
Rica. In any event, by late December 1989, none of the agreements had been
completed and implemented.

Meanwhile, informal and formal debt/equity swap programmes and related
arrangements have captured some of the secondary market discounts and continue to

chip away at the stock of outstanding debt in some countries, notably Brazil, Chile, Mexico and the Philippines. In addition, the Governments of Belgium, Canada, France, the Federal Republic of Germany and the United States have begun over the last year to cancel outright certain debts of low-income countries undertaking major economic adjustment programmes. Operations of the Paris Club under the 1988 Toronto Summit agreement have also added a measure of concessionality to rescheduling of mainly official export credits owed by low-income countries. But there too, the experience has been that negotiations were long and difficult, especially when the debtor had to reach agreement with each creditor Government separately after the framework agreement in the Paris Club itself.

In sum, although there is now a patchwork of policies for partial reduction of debt or debt service, the international design of a comprehensive policy to resolve the debt crisis is far from complete.

D. Commodity prices

Prices of non-fuel commodity exports of the developing countries rose significantly in 1988 after years of decline, but levelled off by mid-1989 and have since been declining again (see figure III). For the period January-October, average dollar prices were practically at the same level as in the corresponding period a year earlier. The overall weakness largely reflects a sharp fall in prices of tropical beverages, in particular coffee and cocoa, which account for a high proportion of the foreign exchange earnings of a large number of countries. Coffee prices declined as quota arrangements under the International Coffee Agreement were suspended. A continuing excess supply depressed cocoa prices in 1989 below the record low levels of 1988. Sugar prices, on the other hand, rose from the very low levels of the mid-1980s as output continued to fall short of consumption. The decline in prices was not, however, confined to tropical beverages. Metal and mineral prices also weakened, largely as a result of a slack in demand, after substantial increases in 1988 and early 1989. Supply disruptions due to labour strikes caused a large increase in copper prices in September, but they resumed their fall later in the year.

Measured in terms of prices of manufactured imports from developed countries, commodity prices rose in 1988. But in such real terms, they were lower in the third quarter of 1989 than in the same period of 1988 and were about 30 per cent below their peak in 1979-1981.

While non-fuel prices stagnated or declined, fuel prices rose, though with considerable fluctuations (see figure IV). With world oil consumption increasing by around 2 per cent a year and with cutbacks of exports from the Soviet Union and decline in output in the United States and the North Sea, the demand for oil exports of developing countries has been increasing. Average world prices of oil were about 20 per cent higher in 1989 than in 1988. As prices of manufactured imports were stable, oil prices in real terms rose by a similar magnitude.

E. United States international payments deficit and the dollar

An orderly reduction of the large United States payments deficit on current
account remains an issue of international concern. The deficit narrowed in 1988
and a further modest improvement was achieved in the first nine months of 1989.
Nevertheless, it stood at an estimated $125 billion for 1989, or only slightly
lower than in 1988, and amounted to 2.4 per cent of GNP, which was a slight
improvement over the previous year. The reduction was achieved through a very
large expansion of exports, helped by a depreciating dollar. The narrowing of the
trade deficit did not, however, compensate for the deterioration of the balance in
services, which reflected the growing net debtor position of the United States and
the increasing flow of net interest and investment income payments abroad.

The large United States deficit corresponded to the surpluses generated
elsewhere, especially by Japan and, to a lesser extent, the Federal Republic of
Germany. The estimated combined surplus of these two countries stood at
$125 billion in 1989. This surplus shows little sign of decline.

Foreign capital is still attracted to the United States and thus sustains the
deficit, since confidence in the economy remains high. If expectations about a
fall in the dollar arise, they might become self-fulfilling and discourage the
foreign capital inflow. But such concerns have so far proved misplaced.

As the fall in the value of the dollar since 1985 was a major factor that
helped to reduce the trade deficit, the consensus among policy makers appears to
have been that the dollar had again risen too high by mid-1989. Central bank
intervention to bring it to a more stable level was very large. Yet the dollar
continued to rise for most of 1989. Although the appreciation of the dollar helped
to reduce the trade deficit in 1989 through an improvement in the dollar prices of
foreign goods, it will have an adverse effect on the deficit in the longer run
since it is eroding the competitiveness of United States exports.

II. PROSPECTS FOR 1990 AND INTERNATIONAL POLICY CHALLENGES

The world economy is expected to slow down further in 1990 (see table) but
retain a considerable diversity of growth experience among countries. The latest
forecasts suggest that the rate of growth in the developed market economies may
decline somewhat below 3 per cent, compared with slightly above 3 per cent in
1989. The year 1989 has been one of slow growth in a large number of developing
countries, mostly in Latin America and Africa. Modest growth is expected in these
economies in 1990. A further moderate deceleration is expected for South and East
Asia, but the average rate of growth in the economies of the region will still
remain high by most standards. In China, growth in 1990 is expected to be close to
the sharply reduced rate of 1989, and a quick return to the rapid growth of the
1980s is not expected.

Although the rate of growth of the developed market economies is expected only
to slow down, a sharper deceleration or a recession remains a possibility. The
persistence of a large United States payments deficit continues to be a danger to

the stability of the world economy. The risk of instability could be reduced by a speedier narrowing of the United States fiscal deficit, which mirrors the payments gap. Foreign savers have been financing the United States fiscal deficit for a number of years, and their continuing willingness to do so at the present scale is not guaranteed. The relaxation of tension between East and West and the mutual desire to cut military expenditure provide an opportunity to reduce the deficit by more than was foreseen even a few months ago.

For a large number of developing countries, their ability to stay on the course of policy reform that they have undertaken will be essential. That ability will, however, depend in part on developments in the world economy and progress in resolving the debt crisis. The predicted slow-down in the world economy may depress commodity prices further and compound their difficulties.

The need for a quick resolution of the debt crisis is no longer in question; neither is the need for debt reduction as an essential part of the solution. The current negotiations for debt reduction have proved cumbersome and drawn-out. They have demonstrated the need for greater and more persuasive involvement of the Governments of creditor countries in the negotiating process. Creation of a new international facility for debt restructuring should remain on the international agenda.

An open world trading system is a pre-condition of a continuing expansion of the world economy. The current round of trade negotiations to strengthen the multilateral trading system will enter a critical phase in 1990. Though progress has been made, difficult areas of negotiation lie ahead. A determined effort will be required to bring them to a successful conclusion. Meanwhile, national trade policies must not undo what international efforts are seeking to achieve.

The revolutionary changes in Eastern Europe and the Soviet Union will have profound implications not only for them, but for the rest of the world as well. The possibility of an end to the debilitating arms race of the super-Powers changes both the political and economic prospects of the world as a whole. The next few years will presumably be one of consolidation of the transition to new economic systems with closer ties to the rest of the world. Substantial additional demands on international resources will be made by countries of Eastern Europe.

Governments in many developing countries fear that these changes in the international situation will deflect resources and attention from their development problems. However, this is to ignore the repercussions of future disarmament, the waning of the threat of nuclear war and the stimulus to the world economy that is likely to flow from the reduction of the trade barriers between the rest of the world and Eastern Europe and the Soviet Union. Nevertheless, developing countries must be fully assured, in particular, that the additional demands for resources in Eastern Europe will not involve any diversion of resources from their development needs.

The present economic prospects hold a wide spectrum of opportunities and risks, but they are above all marked by the same diversity that characterized developments in 1989. There is the risk of a slow-down in the major industrial countries that have a decisive influence on the buoyancy of international trade, but this is overshadowed by the concerns about the debt crisis of Latin America, the development crisis of Africa and the problems of transition in Eastern Europe and the Soviet Union.

On balance, 1989 has, in most parts of the world, been a year of considerable policy change, of greater realism and much convergence in approaches to stability and growth. The short-term outlook is clouded, and 1990 may not see much progress, but the medium-term outlook for the world economy has greatly improved.

Figure I. Investment and net financial transfer of 15 middle-income, highly indebted developing countries, 1980-1989

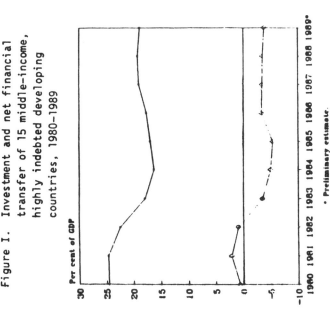

Per cent of GDP

• Preliminary estimate.

—•— Investment   —▲— Net transfer

Source: UN/DIESA, based on data of IMF and the World Bank.

Figure II. Investment and net financial transfer of sub-Saharan Africa excluding Nigeria, 1980-1989

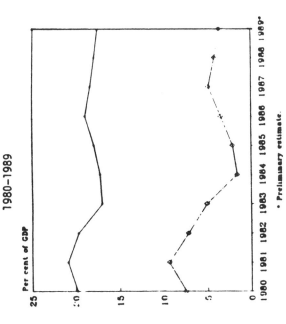

Per cent of GDP

• Preliminary estimate.

—•— Investment   —◆— Net transfer

Source: UN/DIESA, based on data of IMF and the World Bank.

Figure III. Prices of non-fuel commodity
exports of the developing
countries, 1980-1989

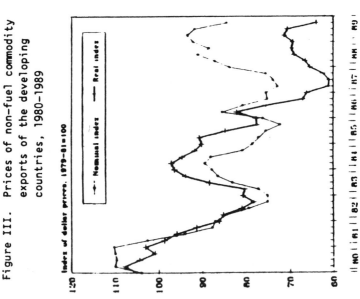

Source: Data of UNCTAD and UN/DIESA.

Figure IV. Prices of crude petroleum,
1986-1989

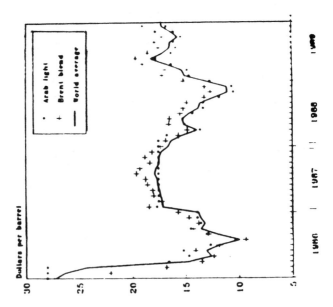

Source: UN/DIESA, based on U.S.
Department of Energy data.

Part II

Terms of Trade and Gains from Trade in Goods and Services, Capital, and Assets

Meier
Letiche, Chambers, and Schmitz

Terms of Trade

Gerald M. Meier

1. Despite all the ambiguities obscuring their use, the terms of trade still receive considerable attention in discussions of economic development. This is so not only because the terms of trade have sizeable quantitative significance for most poor countries, but also because they are a convenient indication of the net result of many diverse forces, and may have important welfare implications. We shall therefore analyze in this chapter the determinants of secular changes in the terms of trade and attempt to assess the influence of these changes on the development of a poor country.[1]

2. Several different concepts of the terms of trade may be distinguished: the gross barter, net barter or commodity, income,

[1] The short-run problem of cyclical fluctuations in the terms of trade and export earnings is analyzed in Chapter 9.

Reprinted from "The International Development of Economics: Theory and Policy," pp. 41–65, with permission of Harper and Row, Copyright 1968.

single-factoral, double-factoral, real cost, and utility terms of trade.[2] These several concepts fall into three groups: (1) those that relate to the ratio of exchange between commodities—the gross barter, net barter, and income terms of trade; (2) those that relate to the interchange between productive resources—the single-factoral and double-factoral terms of trade; and (3) those that interpret the gains from trade in terms of utility analysis—the real cost and utility terms of trade.

In considering the barter terms of trade, Taussig introduced the distinction between "net" and "gross" barter terms.[3] The commodity or net barter terms of trade (N) are expressed as $N = P_x/P_m$, where P_x and P_m are price index numbers of exports and imports, respectively. A rise in N indicates that a larger volume of imports could be received, on the basis of price relations only, in exchange for a given volume of exports. According to Taussig, however, the net barter terms are relevant only when nothing enters into the trade between countries except sales and purchases of merchandise.

If the balance of payments includes unilateral payments, so that there is an excess in money value of either exports or imports, then the relevant concept is the gross barter terms (G). This measures the rate of exchange between the whole of a country's physical imports as compared with the whole of its exports, and is expressed as $G = Q_m/Q_x$, where Q_m and Q_x are vol-

---

[2] Jacob Viner, *Studies in the Theory of International Trade*, Harper & Row, 1937, pp. 558–564; W. W. Rostow, "The Terms of Trade in Theory and Practice," *Economic History Review*, Second Series, Vol. III, No. 1, 1950, pp. 1–20; R. G. D. Allen and J. E. Ely, eds., *International Trade Statistics*, John Wiley, 1953, pp. 207–209; Gottfried Haberler, *A Survey of International Trade Theory*, International Finance Section, Princeton University, rev. ed., 1961, pp. 24–29.

[3] F. W. Taussig, *International Trade*, Macmillan Co., 1927, pp. 113, 117, 248–249.

ume index numbers for imports and exports, respectively. A rise in G represents a "favorable" change in the sense that more imports are received for a given volume of exports than in the base year. Since $G = N$ only if the value of imports and value of exports are equal,[4] G and N diverge when there are unilateral transactions. But one must distinguish among the different types of unilateral transactions that cause changes in G. It is then more meaningful to consider the significance of various unilateral transactions directly, instead of incorporating them in the terms of trade index.[5]

Since it is especially important for a poor country to take changes in its volume of exports into account, we may want to correct the movements in N for changes in export volume. The income terms of trade (I) do this, and are expressed as $I = N \cdot Q_r$, where Q_r is the export volume index.[6] A rise in I indicates that the country can obtain a larger volume of imports from the sale of its exports; its "capacity to import"—based on exports—has increased. The export-based capacity to import should be distinguished, of course, from the total capacity to import, which depends not only on exports but also capital inflow and other invisible exchange receipts. Nor should a change in

[4] If V_m and V_x are index numbers of values of imports and exports, respectively, $\dfrac{G}{N} = \dfrac{Q_m}{Q_x} \cdot \dfrac{P_m}{P_x} = \dfrac{V_m}{V_x}$.

[5] Cf. Gottfried Haberler, *The Theory of International Trade*, William Hodge & Co., 1936, pp. 164–165; Viner, *op. cit.*, p. 563; Erick Schiff, "Direct Investments, Terms of Trade, and Balance of Payments," *Quarterly Journal of Economics*, February, 1942, pp. 310–316.

[6] G. S. Dorrance, "The Income Terms of Trade," *Review of Economic Studies*, 1948–49, pp. 50–56. The income terms of trade have also been referred to as "the export gain from trade"; A. H. Imlah, "The Terms of Trade of the United Kingdom, 1798–1913," *Journal of Economic History*, November, 1950, p. 176.

the income terms of trade be interpreted as a measure of the gain from trade or an indicator of welfare; it should be used simply as a measure of the quantity of imports bought by exports.

It is significant that, according to the direction and magnitude of the changes in P_x and Q_x, the changes in I and N may be in opposite directions. If, for example, with unchanged import prices, export prices have fallen, but export quantities (Q_x) have increased by a greater percentage than the decrease in P_x, the income terms of trade will have improved despite a deterioration in the commodity terms of trade.

Changes in productivity are obviously also of prime significance in considering development, and one may therefore want to refer to the factoral terms of trade. The single-factoral terms (S) correct the commodity terms for changes in productivity in producing exports, and may be expressed as $S = N \cdot Z_x$, where Z_x is an export productivity index. A rise in S is a favorable movement in the sense that a greater quantity of imports can be obtained per unit of factor-input used in the production of exportables.

If N is corrected for changes in productivity in producing imports as well as exports, the result is the double-factoral terms of trade (D), expressed as $D = N \cdot Z_x/Z_m$, where Z_m is an import productivity index. A rise in D shows that one unit of home factors embodied in exports now exchanges for more units of the foreign factors embodied in imports. D will diverge from S when there is a change in the factor cost of producing imports, but this has no welfare significance for the importing country, even though it indicates a change in productivity in the other country from which commodities are imported. What matters to the importing country is whether it receives more goods per unit of its "exported factor-input" (an improvement in S)—not whether these imports contain more or less foreign inputs than before.

It may also be noted that N will equal D when constant returns to scale prevail, and there are no historical changes in costs and no transport costs. But if costs are variable with respect to output or time, or there are transport costs, N and D will diverge. Although this divergence is analytically significant, it is difficult to measure as long as a productivity index remains an elusive concept. In the offer curve analysis of the preceding chapter, the terms of trade as determined at the positions of equilibrium in Fig. 3 are the commodity terms. If, however, we had followed Marshall, and considered on each axis "representative bundles" or "bales" of commodities that contained a constant quantity of "productive resources," the terms of trade would have been the double-factoral terms.

Proceeding more directly to the level of welfare analysis, we may define in utility terms the total amount of gain from trade as the excess of the total utility accruing from imports over the total sacrifice of utility involved in the surrender of exports.[7] To consider the amount of disutility involved in the production of exports, we may correct the single-factoral terms of trade index by multiplying S by the reciprocal of an index of the amount of disutility per unit of productive resources used in producing exports.[8] The resultant index would be a real cost terms of trade index (R). If R rises as a result of a change in the methods of producing exports, or a change in the factor proportions used in exports, this would indicate that the amount of imports obtained per unit of real cost was greater.

On the side of demand, we may want to allow for changes in the relative desirability of the imports and the domestic commodities whose home consumption is foregone because of the use of resources in export production. It is then necessary to in-

[7] Viner, *op. cit.*, p. 557.
[8] *Ibid.*, p. 559.

corporate into R an index of the relative average utility per unit of imports and of foregone domestic commodities. The resultant index is the utility terms of trade (U), equal to R multiplied by an index of the relative utility of imports and foregone commodities.[9]

The difficulty with the use of R and U is, of course, that of calculating the disutility involved in export production, or the relative average utility of various commodities. The welfare significance of changes in the terms of trade must therefore be considered only indirectly, along the lines suggested below in section 5, and not directly through any measurement of R or U.

Having minimized the significance of changes in G, D, R, and U, we are thus left with N, S, and I as the most relevant concepts of the terms of trade for poor countries. Movements in N, S, and I may diverge, however, and these divergences are not merely technical but are due to fundamentally different circumstances. Accordingly, they have different consequences for the country's development. To assess the significance for a poor country of an alteration in its commodity terms of trade—the most frequently cited change—we must therefore analyze the determinants of this change and also the attendant movements in the income and single-factoral terms of trade.

3. Over the short period, the terms of trade may vary as a consequence of changes in commercial policy, exchange rate variations, unilateral transfer payments, or cyclical fluctuations. Over the long period, however, the determinants of changes in the terms of trade are associated with more fundamental structural variations in production and consumption that may be examined in the light of the offer curve analysis of the preceding chapter.

[9] *Ibid.*, pp. 560–561.

As already noted, the shifts in the offer curves will cause movements in the terms of trade, and the various possible shifts in the offer curves can be attributed, in turn, to different types of development.[10]

Assuming that development occurs only in country E, so that G's offer curve remains fixed while E's offer curve shifts, we can summarize the various changes in E's commodity terms of trade, according to the different total biases in development, as follows:

Type of Total Bias in Development	Direction of Change in Commodity Terms of Trade
N	$(-)$
X	$(-)$
M	$(-)$
UM	$(+)$
UX	$(-)$

N = neutral UX = ultra-export-bias
X = export-bias $(-)$ = deterioration
M = import-bias $(+)$ = improvement
UM = ultra-import-bias

When development occurs only in E, and G's offer curve is not infinitely elastic, the terms of trade for E deteriorate for each

[10] For other analyses of the effects on international trade of shifts in reciprocal demand schedules of different elasticities, see Murray C. Kemp, "The Relation between Changes in International Demand and the Terms of Trade," *Econometrica*, January, 1956, pp. 41–46; W. R. Allen, "The Effects on Trade of Shifting Reciprocal Demand Schedules," *American Economic Review*, March, 1952, pp. 135–140; J. Bhagwati and H. G. Johnson, "Notes on Some Controversies in the Theory of International Trade," *Economic Journal*, March, 1960, pp. 84–93; Frederic L. Pryor, "Economic Growth and the Terms of Trade," *Oxford Economic Papers*, March, 1966, pp. 45–57.

type of total bias except an ultra-import-bias. As indicated previously (Fig. 3), the deterioration for a given increase in total output is least, however, when there is an import-bias, and the demand for imports increases less than proportionately to the expansion in total output. The deterioration is greatest when there is an ultra-export-bias, and the absolute demand for imports increases more than total output. In general, the rate of deterioration in E's commodity terms of trade will be greater under the following conditions: the larger is the degree of export-bias on balance in E; the higher is the rate of increase in E's total output; the lower is E's elasticity of demand for G's goods; and the lower is G's elasticity of demand for imports from E.

4. When development occurs in both E and G, the movement of the terms of trade depends on the rate of increase in each country's demand for imports from the other country—in other words, on the relative shifts of the offer curves as determined by the type of total bias and the rate of development in each country.

If the total bias in the development of each country is neutral, each country's offer curve shifts outwards, with the extent of the shift depending on the rate of development. The terms of trade will therefore deteriorate for the country that has the higher rate of development.

If in each country development is ultra-export-biased, or export-biased, or import-biased, each country's offer curve again shifts outwards. The terms of trade would then remain constant only if the types and degrees of bias and rates of development had the same total effect on the growth of demand for imports in each country. In the general case, the terms of trade deteriorate for that country which has the greater rate of growth of demand for imports as determined by its degree of bias, as well as rate of development.

If the over-all effects are export-biased in E, but import-biased in G, then, assuming the rate of development is the same in each country, the terms of trade will deteriorate for E. If, however, the rate of development in E is sufficiently lower than in G, the terms of trade will improve for E, even though its development is export-biased.

The relative rates of development in the two countries may, in many cases, be significant in offsetting the different degrees or types of bias. If, however, the development is ultra-import-biased in only one of the countries, the terms of trade will improve for that country regardless of the type of bias in the other country and the relative rates of development.

From these diverse cases it is apparent that there is no invariant relationship between a country's development and movements in its commodity terms of trade. Depending on the type and degree of bias and the rate of development in each country, the terms of trade may either improve or deteriorate.

5. The connection between changes in the terms of trade and economic welfare is an especially difficult problem: In what sense may a movement in a country's terms of trade be accepted as an index of the trend in economic welfare? Considerable care must be exercised to avoid the fallacy of equating a change in any of the various terms of trade with a variation in the amount or even direction of change in the gains from trade. Such an equation cannot be adduced until we determine the underlying forces associated with the change in the terms of trade, and until we connect the terms of trade, relating to a unit of trade, with the volume of trade.

The welfare implications of a change in the commodity

terms of trade are most directly seen in the effect on real national income. When a country's commodity terms of trade improve, its real income rises faster than output, since the purchasing power of a unit of its exports rises. This increase in real
income will supplement the benefit that the country derives from
its own development.[11] If, however, a country experiences a deterioration in its terms of trade as it develops, part of the benefit
from an expansion in its own output is thereby cancelled.

Insofar as a slower rate of development might allow a country's commodity terms of trade to improve, whereas a higher
rate would cause a deterioration, it is possible that the gain from
the improvement in the terms of trade might be more than sufficient to compensate for the output foregone by the slower expansion in home output. In the case of an ultra-import-bias,
however, a lower rate of development would not tend to augment the improvement in the commodity terms of trade. On the
contrary, unlike the other cases, a higher rate of development in
this situation will not only increase domestic output further, but
will also cause a greater improvement in the commodity terms of
trade.

As an extreme case, it is possible that the type and rate of
development may cause so severe a deterioration in the terms of
trade that the gain from the growth in output is more than offset
by the loss from adverse terms of trade, so that the country ends
up with a lower real income after growth. This theoretical possibility has been demonstrated by Professor Bhagwati, who de-

---

[11] An improvement in the commodity terms of trade might facilitate
an expansion in domestic output by permitting the release of resources
from export production to domestic production. If the improvement is
due to a rise in export prices, this may contribute to an increase in public
saving through export taxes, income taxes, or a rise in the profits of governmental marketing boards.

scribes it as a case of "immiserizing growth."[12] For example, an increase in factor supply or technical progress would raise real income by the amount of the change in output at constant prices, but if the factor accumulation or "factor-saving" is so export-biased that the terms of trade worsen, the negative income effect of the actual deterioration in the terms of trade may then be greater than the positive effect of the expansion in output.

Although analytically interesting, the practical bearing of this possibility is very limited. The conditions necessary for immiserization to result are highly restrictive. In the case of incomplete specialization, the possibility can arise only if the increased quantity of the factor is allocated to export industries, and either the foreign demand for the growing country's exports is inelastic or the country's expansion actually reduces the domestic production of importables.[13] But if external demand is so unfavorable, then additional resources will not flow into the export sector when the situation is such that the very growth of factor supplies may actually have to be induced by the existence of profitable

[12] Jagdish Bhagwati, "Immiserizing Growth: A Geometrical Note," *Review of Economic Studies*, June, 1958, pp. 201–205; "International Trade and Economic Expansion," *American Economic Review*, December, 1958, pp. 941–953; "Growth, Terms of Trade and Comparative Advantage," *Economia Internazionale*, August, 1959, pp. 395–398.

Some classical and neoclassical economists also recognized this possibility when they considered the impact of technological change upon the terms of trade. See J. S. Mill, *Principles of Political Economy*, Longmans, Green, 1848, Book III, chap. XVIII, sec. 5; C. F. Bastable, *The Theory of International Trade*, Macmillan Co., 1903, appendix C, pp. 185–187; F. Y. Edgeworth, "The Theory of International Values, I," *Economic Journal*, March, 1894, pp. 40–42.

[13] Bhagwati, "International Trade and Economic Expansion," *op. cit.*, pp. 949–952. In the case of complete specialization, it is necessary that both the foreign demand for exports and the domestic demand for imports be inelastic. This proposition is demonstrated by Bhagwati and Johnson, *op. cit.*, pp. 80–81.

openings for the employment of these additional factors. Moreover, even if there is an autonomous increase in factors, there is
still no basis for "immiserizing growth," inasmuch as increments
in factor supplies are as a rule mobile and the economy has some
capacity for transforming its structure of output. Factor increments, therefore, need not flow into the export sector in accordance with a predetermined pattern of production.[14] To be valid,
the "immiserizing growth" argument depends on highly restrictive conditions with respect to elasticities of demand and supply
—conditions which are unlikely to apply when an economy has
some flexibility in its structure of output and some capacity for
adapting to changed circumstances. It should also be realized
that, even if the necessary conditions do exist, the country can
still institute offsetting policies and impose taxes on its trade sufficient to gain some of the benefits of the expanded production.[15]

If we examine the welfare implications of a change in the
terms of trade more broadly, we can readily identify circumstances under which a country need not be worse off, even
though its commodity terms deteriorate. When the deterioration
results from a shift only in the foreign offer curve, with the
country's own offer curve unchanged, the resultant deterioration
in the country's terms of trade is clearly unfavorable. If, however, the domestic offer curve also shifts, then it is necessary to
consider the causes of this shift and also the possible changes in
the factoral and income terms of trade.

[14] Ragnar Nurkse, *Patterns of Trade and Development*, Wicksell Lectures, Almqvist & Wiksell, 1959, pp. 56, 58–59 (reprinted in *Equilibrium
and Growth in the World Economy. Economic Essays by Ragnar Nurkse*,
Harvard Univ. Press, 1961, pp. 332–334).
[15] R. A. Mundell, "The Pure Theory of International Trade," *American Economic Review*, March, 1960, p. 85; Bo Södersten, *A Study of Economic Growth and International Trade*, Almqvist & Wiksell, 1964, pp.
53–54.

For instance, development may occur in both countries E and G, but the rate of growth of demand for imports may be greater in E than in G, so that E's commodity terms of trade deteriorate. Nonetheless, E may still be better off than before if the deterioration in its commodity terms is due to export-biased increases in productivity. In this case the single-factoral terms of trade improve, and the deterioration in the commodity terms is only a reflection of the increased productivity in E's export industries. As long as productivity in E's export sector is rising faster than the prices of its exports are falling, its real income rises despite the deterioration in its commodity terms of trade. If the prices of exports in terms of imports fall by a smaller percentage than the percentage increase in productivity, the country clearly benefits from its ability to obtain a greater quantity of imports per unit of factors embodied in its exports.

Classical and neoclassical economists recognized this possibility and attempted to go behind the quantities of exports and imports to consider what, as Pigou remarked, "underlie the exports, namely a given quantity of labor and service of capital." It may then be that although the commodity terms of trade deteriorate when the production costs of exports fall, the country may receive more imports than previously for what "underlies its exports." A divergence between the commodity terms and the factoral terms was meant to be avoided by J. S. Mill's conception of "cost," Bastable's "unit of productive power," and Marshall's "representative bales of commodities," each of which contains a constant quantity of "productive resources." But as already noted, if we allow for more than two commodities, transportation costs, or variable costs of production, the commodity terms and the factoral terms of trade may diverge.

It is also relevant that even if productivity is not rising in the export sector, and the commodity terms of trade are deteriorating, it is still possible for the real income of the factors to rise. This may occur under conditions of a "dual economy" in which factors are initially employed in the backward domestic sector with lower productivity than exists in the advanced export sector. If export production should then expand and attract these factors into the export sector, the factors will gain to the extent that their marginal productivity in the export sector remains above their marginal productivity in the sector from which they withdraw. At the same time, the real prices of export products may be falling, and the commodity terms of trade may be worsening.[16]

A high degree of export-bias on the side of consumption may also cause a deterioration in E's commodity terms of trade. But if this export-bias is due to a change in tastes or a redistribution of income, it is difficult to reach any welfare conclusion. For the intervening change in the preference system makes it impossible to conclude that the later result is inferior to the previous situation merely because the commodity terms have deteriorated. If the terms worsen because demand increases for imports, it may not be true that from the criterion of "utility" a loss is incurred. What must be considered is not the utility of the import alone, but also its utility relative to that of the domestic commodities whose domestic consumption is precluded by allocation of resources to production for export. Were it measurable, the utility terms of trade index would be appropriate for this type of change.

We should also realize that it is possible for the country's income terms of trade to improve despite, or sometimes even because of, a deterioration in the country's commodity terms of

[16] Theodore Morgan, "The Long-Run Terms of Trade Between Agriculture and Manufacturing," *Economic Development and Cultural Change*, October, 1959, pp. 17–18.

trade. If the foreign offer curve is elastic,[17] or if the foreign offer curve shifts out sufficiently, the volume of exports may increase enough to improve the income terms of trade despite the deterioration in the commodity terms. The country's capacity to import is then greater, and this can be of decided significance for a developing country. Such an improvement in the capacity to import is especially important for a poor country which has a high average propensity to import. It would, of course, be even better for the country if its greater volume of exports could be traded at unchanged prices. But this involves a comparison with a hypothetical situation, whereas the relevant consideration is the effect of the actual change between the previous and present situations.

In contrast, a country's development program may be handicapped, despite an improvement in its commodity terms, if its capacity to import is reduced because of a fall in the volume of exports that is not offset sufficiently by the improved commodity terms. If, for example, a country's development is ultra-import-biased so that its commodity terms improve, but the foreign offer curve is not inelastic, or it shifts inwards relatively more than does the domestic offer curve, the country's income terms will deteriorate. Regardless of its more favorable commodity terms, the country's capacity to import is then reduced, and this may hamper the country's developmental efforts if the growth in output has not been sufficiently import-saving.

These examples illustrate that the mere knowledge of a change in the commodity terms of trade does not in itself allow a firm conclusion as to the effect on the country's economic welfare. It is essential to proceed beyond this superficial level and consider whether the change has been caused by a shift only in

---

[17] When the offer curve is of the normal "elastic" sort, more imports are demanded and more exports are supplied as the price of imports falls.

the foreign offer curve or by a shift in the domestic offer curve. If
by the latter, then the cause of the shift becomes relevant and
may deserve more emphasis than the fact of the change itself.
Attention to the underlying cause is especially needed for recognizing movements in the single-factoral terms as well as commodity terms of trade, and for determining possible changes in
the pattern of demand. Finally, changes in the volume of trade
must always be considered along with price variations.

6. With the foregoing general considerations in mind, we may
now examine the validity of the often-repeated contention that
the poor countries have suffered a secular deterioration in their
commodity terms of trade.[18] On the basis of inferences from the
United Kingdom's commodity terms of trade, proponents of this
view claim that "from the latter part of the nineteenth century
to the eve of the second world war . . . there was a secular
downward trend in the prices of primary goods relative to the
prices of manufactured goods. On an average, a given quantity
of primary exports would pay, at the end of this period, for only
60 percent of the quantity of manufactured goods which it could
buy at the beginning of the period."[19]

[18] This allegation appears in several reports of the United Nations and
in various writings by Raúl Prebisch, Hans Singer, W. A. Lewis, and
Gunnar Myrdal, among others. It is noteworthy that this view is completely at variance with that commonly held by classical economists who
believed that the operation of diminishing returns in primary production
would cause the prices of primary products to rise relatively to prices of
manufactures. Keynes restated the classical view in his "Reply to Sir William Beveridge," *Economic Journal*, December, 1923, pp. 476–488; also,
D. H. Robertson, *A Study of Industrial Fluctuation*, P. S. King & Son,
1915, p. 169.

[19] United Nations, Department of Economic Affairs, *Relative Prices
of Exports and Imports of Underdeveloped Countries*, 1949, p. 72. The

The causes of this deterioration are supposedly associated with differences in the distribution of the gains from increased productivity, diverse cyclical movements of primary product and industrial prices, and disparities in the rates of increase in demand for imports between the industrial and primary producing countries. Since technical progress has been greater in industry than in the primary production of poor countries, it is suggested that if prices had been reduced in proportion to increasing productivity, the reduction should then have been less for primary products than for manufactures, so that as the disparity between productivities increased, the price relationship between the two should have improved in favor of the poor countries. It is alleged, however, that the opposite occurred: In respect to manufactured commodities produced in more developed countries, it is contended that the gains from increased productivity have been distributed in the form of higher wages and profits rather than lower prices, whereas in the case of food and raw material production in the underdeveloped countries the gains in productivity, although smaller, have been distributed in the form of price reductions.[20]

---

indices used are based on Werner Schlote, *Entwicklung und Struktur-wandlungen des englischen Aussenhandels von 1700 bis zur Gegenwart* Probleme der Weltwirtschaft, No. 62, Jena, 1938. Other indices constructed by Professors Imlah and Kindleberger do not show as marked an improvement for Britain as do Schlote's; A. H. Imlah, *Economic Elements in the Pax Britannica*, Harvard Univ. Press, 1958, chap. IV, Table 8; C. P. Kindleberger, *The Terms of Trade, A European Case Study*, John Wiley, 1956, pp. 53 ff.

W. A. Lewis' consideration of the prices of primary products and manufactures also relies heavily on Schlote's data; Lewis, "World Production, Prices and Trade, 1870–1960," *Manchester School of Economic and Social Studies*, May, 1952, Table II.

[20] United Nations, Department of Economic Affairs, *The Economic Development of Latin America and Its Principal Problems*, 1950, pp. 8–14;

This contrasting behavior of prices in industrial and primary producing countries is also attributed to the different movements of primary product prices and industrial prices over successive business cycles and to the greater number of monopoly elements in industrial markets.[21] According to this reasoning, the prices of primary products have risen sharply in prosperous periods, but have subsequently lost their gain in the downswing of the trade cycle. In contrast, it is asserted that although manufacturing prices have risen less in the upswing, they have not fallen as far in depression as they have risen in prosperity, because of the rigidity of industrial wages and price inflexibility in the more monopolistic industrial markets. It is therefore concluded that over successive cycles the gap between the prices of the two groups of commodities has widened, and the primary producing areas have suffered an unfavorable movement in their terms of trade.

Proponents of the secular deterioration hypothesis also argue that the differential price movements between poor and rich countries have been accentuated by a relative decrease in the demand for primary products and a relative increase in the demand for industrial products. This is attributed to the operation of Engel's law, and also, in the case of raw materials, to technical progress in manufacturing, which reduces the amount of raw ma-

Relative Prices of Exports and Imports of Underdeveloped Countries, op. cit., pp. 13–24, 126; H. W. Singer, "The Distribution of Gains Between Investing and Borrowing Countries," American Economic Review, Papers and Proceedings, May, 1950, pp. 477–479; W. A. Lewis, "Economic Development with Unlimited Supplies of Labour," Manchester School of Economic and Social Studies, May, 1954, pp. 183–184; F. Mehta, "The Effects of Adverse Income Terms of Trade on the Secular Growth of Underdeveloped Countries," Indian Economic Journal, July, 1956, pp. 9–21.

[21] The Economic Development of Latin America and Its Principal Problems, op. cit., pp. 12–14.

terials used per unit of output.[22] The low income elasticity of demand and the structural changes result in a secular decline in the demand for primary products. In other words, the consumption effect of development in the poor country is export-biased (pro-trade-biased), whereas in the rich country it is import-biased (anti-trade-biased).

If the alleged secular deterioration in the terms of trade of poor countries were true it would mean that there has been an international transfer of income away from the poor countries, and this decrease in purchasing power would be significant in reducing their capacity for development. The thesis is, however, highly impressionistic and conjectural. When its content is examined more rigorously, the argument appears weak—both statistically and analytically.[23]

Although the relevant long-run data for individual poor countries are not readily available, the substitution of the "inverse" of the United Kingdom's terms of trade is merely an expedient and does not provide a sufficiently strong statistical foundation for any adequate generalization about the terms of

[22] Singer, op. cit., p. 479; Raúl Prebisch, "Commercial Policy in Underdeveloped Countries," American Economic Review, Papers and Proceedings, May, 1959, pp. 261–264. For a quantitative approach to some of the factors considered by Singer and Prebisch, see M. K. Atallah, The Terms of Trade Between Agricultural and Industrial Products, Netherlands Economic Institute, 1958.

[23] The most systematic and thorough-going critiques of the argument have been presented by Gottfried Haberler, "Terms of Trade and Economic Development," Howard S. Ellis, ed., Economic Development for Latin America, St. Martin's Press, 1961, pp. 275–297; M. June Flanders, "Prebisch on Protectionism: An Evaluation," Economic Journal, June, 1964, pp. 309–316. On the basis of several objections, largely similar to those we discuss below, both of these papers conclude that the reasons which have been advanced for the alleged trend are either fallacious or are entirely inadequate in their explanation.

trade of poor countries.[24] The import-price index is a mixed bag, concealing the heterogeneous price movements within and among the broad categories of foodstuffs, raw materials, and minerals. An aggregation of primary products cannot be representative of the wide variety of primary products exported by poor countries. Nor, of course, is it legitimate to identify all exporters of primary products as poor countries. Some primary producing countries are also importers of primary products. Moreover, the composition of exports from other industrial countries differs markedly from the United Kingdom's, making it unlikely that the United Kingdom's terms of trade can be truly representative for other industrial countries. It has been shown that the terms of trade for other industrial countries have behaved quite differently from those of the United Kingdom.[25]

Even if we were willing to use the British terms of trade as indirect evidence for the terms of trade between industrial and nonindustrial countries, we should still have to be extremely skeptical about the reliability of the British data. Apart from all

[24] Morgan, op. cit., pp. 6–20. From a consideration of six countries other than the United Kingdom, Professor Morgan concludes that the highly diverse demand and supply experience for particular commodities of the different countries emphasizes the importance of refraining from generalizing about the experience of other countries by using the experience of the United Kingdom. Particular supply influences, and particular demand changes, for different commodities, countries, and times, have dominated the historical picture (p. 20).

Also see Morgan, "Trends in Terms of Trade and Their Repercussions on Primary Producers," R. F. Harrod and D. C. Hague, eds., *International Trade Theory in a Developing World*, Macmillan Co., 1963, pp. 57–59; Robert E. Lipsey, *Price and Quantity Trends in the Foreign Trade of the United States*, Princeton Univ. Press, 1963, pp. 8–24, 76; Harry G. Johnson, *Economic Policies toward Less Developed Countries*, Brookings Institution, 1967, appendix A.

[25] Kindleberger, op. cit., pp. 53 ff., 233.

the statistical pitfalls connected with the construction of import and export price indices, there are strong biases in the United Kingdom series that make the terms of trade appear less favorable to poor countries than they actually were.[26] No allowance is made for changes in the quality of exports and imports; nor is there adequate coverage for the introduction of new commodities. Insofar as the improvements in quality and the introduction of new commodities have undoubtedly been more pronounced for industrial products than for primary products, a simple inversion of the United Kingdom's terms of trade would thus overstate any unfavorable movement for countries exporting primary products to the United Kingdom and importing industrial products from it.

Furthermore, there is no allowance for the fact that transportation costs were falling, making it invalid to infer from the British data what the terms of trade were for the primary producing countries trading with Britain. If the recorded terms of trade were corrected for the decline in transportation costs that occurred, the improvement in the United Kingdom's terms would appear substantially less. This is because British exports are valued at the port of exit, while the value of imports includes shipping costs. A large part of the decline in British import prices, however, was caused by the fall in ocean freights, and if Britain's export price index were corrected for transportation costs it would show a greater decline than does the recorded British export price index.[27] A proper consideration of transportation costs

[26] Morgan, "The Long-Run Terms of Trade Between Agriculture and Manufacturing," *op. cit.*, pp. 4–6; R. E. Baldwin, "Secular Movements in the Terms of Trade," *American Economic Review, Papers and Proceedings*, May, 1955, pp. 267–268.

[27] Statistical confirmation is given by L. Isserlis, "Tramp Shipping Cargoes and Freights," *Journal of Royal Statistical Society*, 1938, p. 122;

makes the terms of trade of primary producers appear less unfavorable.

These statistical imperfections do not allow much support
for the hypothesis of a secular deterioration in the terms of trade
for poor countries. It might even be maintained that their terms
of trade improved because of quality improvements in their imports, access to a wider range of imports, and the great relative
decline in transportation costs as compared with the prices of the
commodities transported.

If the empirical evidence does not bear close scrutiny, still
less does the analytical explanation. The validity of the appeal to
monopolistic elements in the industrial countries depends on the
existence of monopoly in not only factor markets but also product markets,[28] so that the increasing productivity could be distributed in the form of rising money wages and profits, with
stable or rising prices. It is an open question whether trade unions
and firms actually possessed and exercised sufficient monopoly
powers. But even if they did, the existence of such monopoly elements would at most explain movements in the absolute domestic
price level and not changes in relative world prices of manufactures and primary products. World price levels depend on
world conditions of supply and demand, and a country with a
relatively high domestic price level may simply find itself priced
out of international markets unless it makes some adjustment in
its domestic prices or exchange rate.

Further, allowing for the neglected influence of transport

Kindleberger, *op. cit.*, pp. 20–21, 336–339; C. M. Wright, "Convertibility
and Triangular Trade as Safeguards against Economic Depression," *Economic Journal*, September, 1955, pp. 424–426; P. T. Ellsworth, "The
Terms of Trade Between Primary Producing and Industrial Countries,"
Inter-American Economic Affairs, Summer, 1956, pp. 47–65.

[28] Kindleberger, *op. cit.*, pp. 246–247, 304.

costs over the cycle, we may also note many instances in which during a recession the prices of primary products declined in the United Kingdom, while actually rising at the ports of shipment in the primary producing countries.[29] Nor is the pre-1914 evidence on the purchasing power of primary products consistent with the cyclical explanation: Britain's terms of trade actually deteriorated during most depressions before 1914; Britain's food import prices fluctuated less in most trade cycles before 1914 than did British export prices; and a substantial number of primary products—especially foodstuffs—actually gained in purchasing power during many pre-1914 depressions.[30]

As for the appeal to disparities in the rates of increase in the demand for imports, it is true that, *ceteris paribus*, different Engel curves could cause a deterioration in the terms of trade. It is, however, essential to consider also the rates of development and changes in supply conditions, as has been stressed in the analysis of shifts in the offer curves. For even though the percentage of expenditure on a given import might be a decreasing function of income, the absolute demand for the import may still be greater as development proceeds. In addition, shifts of the long-term supply elasticities within industrial countries may be such as to prevent the domestic output of importables from keeping up with demand, so that the import requirements may rise relatively to income growth in the industrial countries. It should also be remembered that Engel's law applies only to foodstuffs—not to industrial raw materials or minerals. And even if an income

---

[29] Wright, *op. cit.*, pp. 425–426.

[30] K. Martin and F. G. Thackeray, "The Terms of Trade of Selected Countries, 1870–1938," *Bulletin of the Oxford University Institute of Statistics*, November, 1948, pp. 380–382; W. W. Rostow, "The Historical Analysis of the Terms of Trade," *Economic History Review*, Second Series, Vol. IV, No. 1, 1951, pp. 69–71.

elasticity of demand of less than unity is accepted as reasonable for primary products, what is significant for a specific primary producing country is not this over-all elasticity but the expansion in demand for its own exports.

Finally, aside from its statistical and analytical weaknesses, the entire argument has been unduly restricted to only the commodity terms of trade. Also significant are changes in the income terms of trade and especially the single-factoral terms. It is clearly possible, as already noted, that a country's income terms and single-factoral terms might improve at the same time as its commodity terms deteriorate. Since the exports from poor countries have grown so considerably, and productivity in export production has increased, the income terms and single-factoral terms have undoubtedly improved for poor countries. This is actually implicit in the secular deterioration argument, insofar as it relies on productivity increasing in both primary producing and industrial countries, but at a higher rate in the latter. Although their double-factoral terms of trade may have deteriorated, this did not affect the welfare of poor countries; they were better off when their own single-factoral terms improved and they received more imports per unit of their "exported factors," regardless of whether the single-factoral terms also improved for other countries exporting to them. Their capacity to import and their imports per unit of productive resources exported have increased—regardless of any changes in the relative prices for their products.

The most favorable situation, of course, would be an improvement in the commodity terms of trade as well as in the single-factoral and income terms. But the ruling conditions may frequently be incompatible with such a simultaneous improvement. Nonetheless, to look only at changes in the commodity terms is to neglect the favorable effects of the greater capacity to import through improvement in the income terms and the benefits from the improvement in the single-factoral terms. When it is assessed within this wider analysis, a change in the commodity terms of trade may prove to be of small moment for a developing economy in comparison with the more fundamental changes that have occurred at the same time.

Terms of Trade

Gerald M. Meier

In the period since the foregoing was written, the terms of trade controversy (discussed in Section 6) has still continued. Although many economists have criticized the Prebisch-Singer thesis of deteriorating terms of trade for primary producing developing countries, Singer has recently again argued on behalf of the thesis [H. W. Singer, "The Terms of Trade Controversy and the Evolution of Soft Financing: Early Years in the U.N.," in Gerald M. Meier and Dudley Seers, eds., *Pioneers in Development*, Oxford University Press, 1984, pp. 280-93].

There have also been more recent empirical studies that claim to support the thesis of deteriorating terms of trade of developing countries. Prominent is the study by John Spraos, *Inequalizing Trade*, Clarendon Press, 1983. Spraos incorporates two later arguments advanced by Raul Prebisch—namely, that primary commodities suffer from a downward demand bias, the measure of which is their lower income elasticity compared with manufactures, and second, they suffer from a upward supply bias because they draw on the pool of excess labor in the less progressive sectors of the developing countries' economies. Spraos also evaluates the factorial terms of trade as a measure of inequalization.

David Sapsford also claims to have presented "some quite strong evidence in support of the Prebisch-Singer hypothesis " [Sapsford, "The Statistical Debate on the Net Barter Terms of Trade Between Primary Commodities and Manufacture: A Comment and Some Additional Evidence." *Economic Journal* September 1985, pp. 781-788.] Sapsford extends Spraos' earlier (1980) work, considers some econometric issues, and introduces more recent evidence.

Against Singer's conclusion, however, Bela Balassa has argued that the data that both Singer and Spraos rely upon are not statistically significant. [Bela Balassa, "Comment" in Gerald M. Meier and Dudley Seers, eds. *Pioneers in Development*, Oxford University Press, 1984, pp. 304-311.] In contrast, on the basis of studies by Irving B. Kravis and Robert E. Lipsey [*Price Competitiveness in World Trade*, New York: National Bureau of Economic Research, 1971] and Michael Michaely, [*Trade, Income Levels and Depenence*, Amsterdam: North-Holland], together with his own revisions of some price indices, Balassa concludes that his "cited estimates effectively refute the Prebisch-Singer thesis on the alleged tendency of the secular deterioration of the terms of trade of the developing countries" (p. 308).

With the marked decline in primary commodity prices during the 1980s, however, and with the continual interest in issues of distributive justice between the more developed and less developed countries, it is likely that the Prebisch-Singer thesis will remain controversial. And some may well claim with Singer that the early Prebisch-Singer forecasts have stood the tests of time rather better than many other economic forecasts.

THE DEVELOPMENT OF GAINS FROM TRADE
THEORY: CLASSICAL TO MODERN
LITERATURE

John M. Letiche
Professor of Economics, University of California, Berkeley

Robert G. Chambers
Assistant Professor of Agricultural Economics, Ohio State University

Andrew Schmitz
Professor of Agricultural and Resource Economics, University of California, Berkeley

CONTENTS

Even though classical, neoclassical, and every school of post-classical economists have long emphasized that nations can gain from an expanding volume of world trade, in the last years of the 1970s, many sectors of national economies were once again becoming more protectionist. In view of that fact, this paper will examine the arguments supporting the free trade doctrine in the context of major theoretical developments in the gains from trade literature. The classical writings on the issue are voluminous. They have been excellently apparised, however, making it possible to present the essential foundations with comprehensive brevity.[1] Most of the focus will be on the normative aspects of neoclassical trade theory, and only the standard results will be considered.[2]

Reprinted from "Economic Perspectives: An Annual Survey of Economics" (M.B. Ballabon, ed.), Vol. 1, pp. 119–149, with permission of Harwood, Copyright 1979.

THE EARLY WRITINGS

The classical theory of international trade was formulated primarily to provide guidance on important questions of national policy. It originated in Britain, where a major issue revolved around the potential gains to England from free trade, as well as the distribution of gains from trade between England and the rest of the world. The classical economists utilized three methods in dealing with the question of the gains from trade: (1) the doctrine of comparative costs; (2) the increase in income as a criterion of gain; and (3) the terms of trade as an index of the gains from trade and its distribution.

The free trade doctrine, as presented by Adam Smith was based on the apparent advantage to a country of importing, in exchange for domestic products, those goods which either could not be produced at home or could be produced only at costs absolutely greater than those at which they could be produced abroad. Accordingly, the producer of exportables had to have an absolute advantage; and this advantage was generally measured in terms of the labor costs of production. Under free trade all products entering international commerce would be produced in those countries where the real costs were lowest, and from this doctrine Adam Smith drew laissez-faire conclusions. As he wrote over 200 years ago:

> If a foreign country can supply us with a commodity cheaper than we ourselves can make it, better buy it from them with some part of the produce of our own industry, employed in a way in which we have some advantage. The general industry of the country . . . will not thereby be diminished . . . but only left to find out the way in which it can be employed with the greatest advantage.[3]

David Ricardo and Robert Torrens corrected Smith's theorizing to show that a country can gain from trade even if it has no absolute real cost advantage in the production of any commodity. The early theory of comparative cost was formulated in terms of a single factor of production (labor) and assumed that, in the absence of trade, goods were exchanged internally at their relative unit labor cost. In the case of free trade, gains from trade resulted when countries specialized in the production of those commodities in which they had a comparative advantage, denoted by the respective ratio of productivity of the resources between the countries concerned.[4]

The case for a large volume of profitable trade, it was held, depends on the width of these gaps in comparative advantage of different countries for the production of different goods. If a country has an absolute advantage in agriculture, this does not stop it from specializing in something in which it has a greater advantage still. The comparative-cost approach, in effect, emphasized that trade minimizes the aggregate real cost at which a given level of real income can be obtained or maximizes the aggregate level of real income obtainable from a given (full employment) utilization of resources. Theoretical contributions made by J. S. Mill, Alfred Marshall, F. Y. Edgeworth, and F. W. Taussig demonstrated that comparative costs are an essential element in the gains from trade, but that reciprocal demand functions have to be incorporated into the analysis insofar as they are welfare functions representing net income.[5]

In this connection Mill contributed a brilliant discussion on the relationship between reciprocal demand and the commodity terms of trade. Marshall in turn generalized the analysis by an ingenious fusion of "reciprocal demand-and-supply"—a simultaneous incorporation of macroeconomic and microeconomic theory which, for its time, achieved not only a remarkable degree of theoretical "generality" but also a constructive link with reality. In this theoretical framework, production is carried on under diminishing marginal value productivity, resulting from the combined operation of the law of diminishing returns and the law of diminishing utility. Hence it is assumed that output per unit of input of labor and/or capital diminishes after a point. Further, as output of some commodities increases, the exchange value per unit of this commodity declines; i.e., its terms of trade for other commodities diminishes. Therefore, if all commodities are produced under increasing costs, each country produces some of each good and, with minor exceptions, imports or exports the difference between its domestic demand and supply, respectively. By implication at least, for developed countries partial specialization is the rule, its extent depending upon how rapidly relative costs rise.

The classical school believed that in the medium term manufactures were produced at constant or decreasing costs per unit of output, with the check to specialization occurring via a decline in the relative value of the commodity as its supply increases. Agricultural production, however, was assumed to occur under increasing costs. But even to classical economists this formulation leads logically to free trade conclusions, in some cases, only under these assumptions:

1. Free competition exists in each country entering into international trade.

2. Labor and capital migrate within the same country more easily and freely than among different countries.

3. Costs and prices are appreciably more variable than employment; hence full employment conditions are taken for granted in the assumed long-term analysis.

4. Costs incurred during the process of occupational mobility and during production adjustment are abstracted from, and transportation costs usually are assumed to be zero, internally and internationally.

5. Entrepeneurs expect current prices to continue for that part of the future that is relevant to their decisions.

6. Maximization of national real income or aggregate world real income is considered to be the most important economic objective, with some recognition (but not of practical importance) of the possible conflict between countries as to the relative level of real income or its distribution.

7. Multilateral convertibility prevails in the modern sense of the term plus approximately stable exchange rates; monetary and credit systems work either automatically or under central bank management in such a way as to bring the monetary and real factors easily and readily toward domestic and international equilibrium.

Since free trade makes imports cheaper and exports dearer, the wages of labor employed in import fields would tend to fall and in export fields to rise. Distribution of income would therefore be affected. With this important exception, on the basis of their assumptions, there appear to be no qualifications of consequence to the free trade position. Even changes in the distribution of income resulting from free trade could be compensated for by changes in taxation.

There was, however, a logical error in this early free trade doctrine. The argument was expressed in terms of free trade versus no trade, whereas the real choice usually was between free trade and tariff protection. Implicitly, some of the writers might have assumed that the movement from protection to free trade would not alter a country's terms of trade. But in time this issue was explicitly faced and it brought about a rift in the ranks of free traders. Torrens, Mill, Marshall, Edgeworth, and Taussig conceded the theoretical error. They realized that by imposing a tariff a country would tend to reduce the volume of its imports; the price of its exportables would tend to be raised and that of importables lowered, improving its terms of trade. Such gains were likely to be offset by losses from resource misallocation. The gains from protection were only to be derived up to a point, Edgeworth noted, and they were not accurately ascertainable. Even if a country gave careful consideration to the national interest, rather than to pressure groups, all these writers believed that it would still probably err in the direction of excess protection. Torrens qualified his argument by advocating reciprocal rather than unilateral tariff reductions. The gains from trade to be derived by tariff protection, however, were regarded as national—not cosmopolitan—gains, for a gain in terms of trade to one country is a loss to another, while the misallocation of resources is a general loss.

Even to a single country, if the terms of trade argument were to hold, the reciprocal demand of the outside world should have a low elasticity and its own reciprocal demand a high elasticity. Not only should the tariffs be administered with skill and integrity, but there should be no retaliation—an important issue reconsidered in the later literature on the "second-best." Understandably, therefore, the classical writers before World War I believed that in the long run the scope for nationally profitable protection was in practice narrowly limited. From a cosmopolitan point of view, they believed the free trade doctrine to have remained intact. Long-term protection, they held, may injure all who practice it, and can benefit none except at the cost of greater injury to others. The only exception would entail the effective use of tariff protection by a poor country that would benefit at the expense of its rich trading partners. The resulting reduction in aggregate world income would hence justify the use of income-offsets from the rich countries to the poor in order to maximize world welfare.

Although the classical economists considered the long-term arguments for free trade as substantive arguments against protection, they conceded the theoretical validity of the short-term "young country" or "infant industry" arguments for protection. In its crude form the argument was often stated in the seventeenth century. The classical economists, however, formulated the argument in specific terms.[6] Gains from trade could therefore be derived through the use of temporary protection by speeding the establishment and development of potentially profitable industries. The argument was sometimes rejected, however, on these practical grounds: (1) the selection of industries was likely to be arbitrary or irrational; (2) it would open the door to promiscuous protection and "ad hoccery"; (3) it would stifle or delay genuine progress through the spread of industrial inertia, inefficiency, and restrictive monopoly; (4) temporary protection would tend to become permanent when market forces revealed the incapacity to operate without artificial support; (5) the ex-

tensive use of infant industry protection for the economic development
of a young country would tend to increase costs as a whole and thereby
hinder its specialization in domestic industries and export fields by way
of comparative advantage; (6) the widespread use of temporary protection tends to make commodities too expensive for the budget of many
consumers and thereby hinders the development of mass production and
distribution; (7) when justified, infant industries could be more efficiently
protected through the use of subsidies rather than tariffs.[7] For these reasons plus noneconomic arguments for free trade, the classical writers for
the most part did not regard tariff protection as an intelligent form of
economic planning, but a perversion to laissez-faire.

Many of the conclusions concerning the gains from trade derived from
later theoretical developments are similar to those obtained from the
models presented by these early writers. To investigate one of these
models more fully, consider Figure 1. Let S^X, D^X represent the supply
and demand situation in the exporting country and S^M, D^M represent
the supply and demand situation in the importing country. Without
trade, price in the importing country is P^M, in the exporting country, P^X.
With trade, in the absence of transportation costs and other impediments,
price P^W obtains in both countries. The movement to free trade results in
a net welfare gain of the two crosshatched areas. For example, in the exporting country the introduction of trade results in a loss of consumers'
surplus of $BP^W P^X C$ while producers' surplus is increased by the area of
$AP^W P^X C$.[8]

The early writers also used this framework to examine the welfare impacts of restrictive trade policies, especially tariffs. In Figure 1, consider
the introduction of a tariff, T. The effect on the importing country, for
example, is a loss in consumer surplus equal to the area $GIEP^W$, a gain
in producer surplus equal to the area $GHFP^W$, and the tariff revenue obtained is $HIKJ$. Interestingly, modern facets of the optimal tariff were
developed within this framework.[9] Thus, for the importing country to
gain from the imposition of a tariff, the sum of the tariff revenue and
the gain in producers' surplus must exceed the loss in consumers' surplus.
This will always be the case for the optimal tariff when the foreign excess supply curve is upward sloping.

POST-WORLD WAR I LITERATURE

The main theme of the normative aspects of modern trade theory supports the claim of the classical economists that, with "appropriate compensation," trade results in an improvement in economic welfare. In pur-

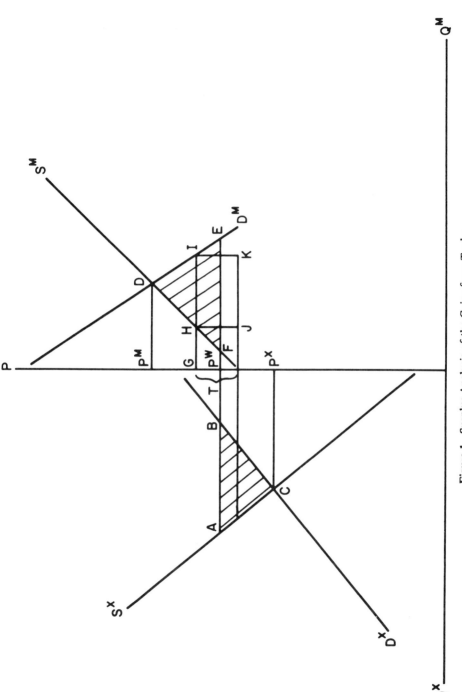

Figure 1. Surplus Analysis of the Gains from Trade.

suing the normative aspects of trade theory, Leontief, in a classic paper, demonstrated how standard consumer theory can be extended to the analysis of international trade.[10] Let TT in Figure 2 represent the transformation curve of the home country derived under conditions of increasing costs, and let U_i represent community indifference curves. Autarkic equilibrium occurs where community curve U_0 is tangent to TT at α. The home country produces and consumes OF of A and OD of B. Let p^0p^0 represent the free trade terms of trade.[11] In equilibrium, the home country now produces OE of A but consumes OC of A and exports EC of A for XY of B. Clearly, there are gains from trade since utility level U_0 is below utility level U_1.[12]

A more rigorous proof of the existence of either actual or potential gains from trade was provided by Samuelson.[13] Assuming perfect competition, the existence of monotonic ordinal preferences for each individual [i.e., $x^* \geqslant x$ implies $u(x^*) \geqslant u(x)$] —profit maximization and utility maximization—denote commodities consumed by the vector $x = (x_1 \ldots x_n)$, commodities produced by the vector $\bar{x} = (\bar{x}_1 \ldots \bar{x}_n)$, productive services by the vector $a = (a_1 \ldots a_n)$, and prices of commodities and productive services by the respective vectors $p = (p_1 \ldots p_n)$ and $w = (w_1 \ldots w_n)$. Let superscript o denote autarkic quantities and prices. In autarkic equilibrium it is clear that $\bar{x}^o = x^o$.

Consider the opening of trade. Denote free trade commodity prices and factor prices, respectively, by p' and w'. Under these assumptions the optimal bundles of commodities produced and productive services utilized will maximize the difference betwen total commodity value and total productive service value for any feasible production set. That is,

$$p'\bar{x}' - w'a' \geqslant p'\bar{x} - w'a \qquad Vx \neq x', w \neq w' \qquad (1)$$

and specifically

$$p'\bar{x}' - w'a' \geqslant p'\bar{x}^o - w'a^o$$

where $p'\bar{x}'$ is understood to be the inner product. Then assuming balanced trade, i.e., $p'(\bar{x}' - x') = 0$, (1) can be rewritten as

$$p'x' - w'a' \geqslant p'x^o - w'a^o \qquad (1')$$

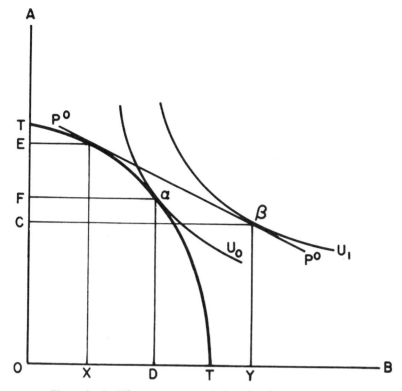

Figure 2. Indifference curves and the gains from trade.

Based on expression (1'), Samuelson derived the following theorem on the assumption that all members of the economy are identical in every respect.[14]

The introduction of outside (relative) prices differing from those which would be established in our economy in isolation will result in some trade, and as a result every individual will be better off than he would be at the prices which prevailed in the isolated state.[15]

When individuals are not alike (given that the introduction of outside relative prices generates trade), trade may make some people actually worse off. However, there are *potential* gains to be had from trade since the trade consumption bundle can be redistributed by means of lump-sum income transfers such that everyone could be made better off.

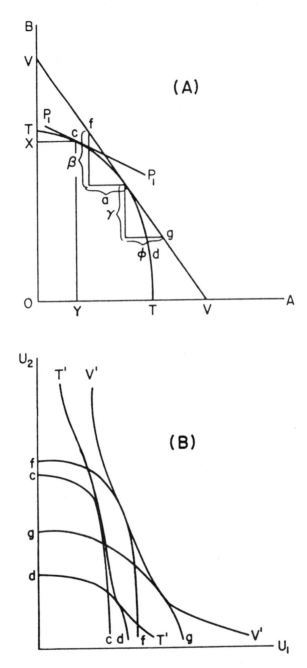

Figure 3. The new welfare economics and the gains from trade.

In other words, if a unanimous decision were required in order for trade to be permitted, it would always be possible for those who desired trade to buy off those opposed to trade, with the result that all could be made better off.[16]

The New Welfare Economics and the Gains from Trade

In a later article, Samuelson showed in a broader framework that nations can potentially gain from international trade.[17] Let TT in Figure 3A represent the transformation curve in the home country. VV represents the free trade consumption possibility frontier.[18] Assume c represents the no trade equilibrium with relative prices P_1P_1. At c, OX of B and OY of A are produced and consumed. The utility possibility frontier corresponding to this bundle is represented by cc in Figure 3B. Consider any other point, d, on the transformation curve. The corresponding utility possibility frontier for d is dd in Figure 3B. The envelope of all such frontiers is known as the grand utility possibility frontier under no trade $(T'T')$.[19] Now, consider point f which is a bundle obtainable through international trade, i.e., α of A is exported for β of B. The utility possibility frontier for f is ff in Figure 3B. Likewise, consider point g where γ of B is traded for ϕ of A. The utility possibility frontier for g is gg in Figure 3B. The envelope of all such frontiers is $V'V'$. It follows that, for all positive trade, everyone can be made better off, with proper income redistribution, than in the no trade case because $V'V'$ lies everywhere outside of $T'T'$ (at the limit $V'V'$ may touch $T'T'$).

This argument can be seen in another way. Let TT in Figure 4 represent the home country's transformation curve. Suppose c represents autarkic equilibrium and free trade prices are given by the slope of VV. Evaluating c at the free trade prices $(V'V')$, it is clear that national income is greater in the trading case than in the no trade case.

An alternative geometric proof for the proposition that free trade is always potentially superior to autarky has been provided by Peter B. Kenen, who developed the commodity space analogue to the utility possibility frontier known as the Paretian contract curve.[20]

The classical economists conjectured that, typically, the more the terms of trade for a country improved, the larger the gains from trade. Samuelson has posed the question, "Is it possible to state that the more prices 'deviate' from those of the isolated state the better off all individuals will be?"[21] In this regard it has been demonstrated that if the terms of trade improve it is possible for society to consume at least as much of each commodity without employing more of any factor.[22] Furthermore,

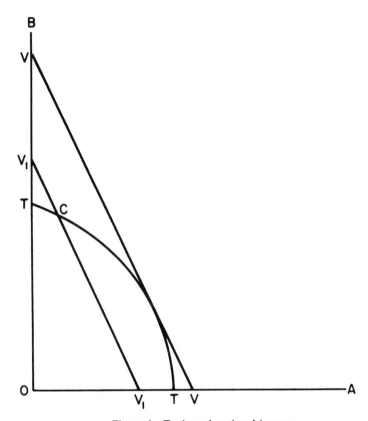

Figure 4. Trade and national income.

for two commodities produced with fixed factor supplies, it has been
shown that the more the terms of trade improve the greater the gains from
trade.[23] This result, however, does not apply to a country engaged in
tariff-ridden trade.[24] In such a case, as illustrated in Figure 5, if the export good is inferior in consumption it is possible that an improvement
in terms of trade will leave everyone worse off. Suppose the home
country always produces a fixed amount of A, say a, which it exports
for B. The original free trade terms of trade are given by the slope of ab.
Free trade quilibrium is at c where a community indifference curve (not
drawn) is tangent to ab. Now suppose that a duty is levied at B at a constant ad valorem rate. Equilibrium will then obtain at c' where ab intersects a community indifference curve U_1 at the point where the indifference curve has the same slope as the internal price ratio (represented by

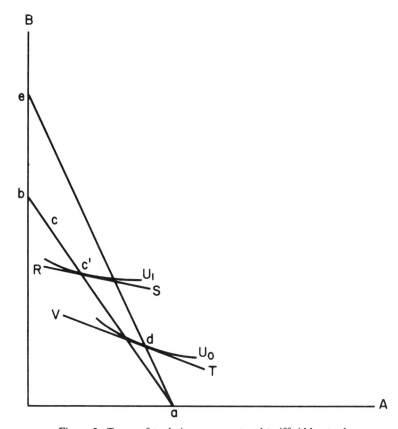

Figure 5. Terms of trade improvement and tariff ridden trade.

the slope of *RS*). If the terms of trade improve to, say, the slope of *ae*, the new equilibrium can be found anywhere along *ae*. Figure 5 illustrates the possibility of a deterioration of the home country's welfare—a deterioration possible only when the export good is inferior: A rise in the domestic price of exportables (the new internal price ratio, given by the slope of *VT*, is greater than that of *RS*) is associated with an increase of their domestic consumption.

Tariffs and the Gains from Trade

As already noted, a considerable amount of attention was given in the early writings to the welfare effects of tariffs. In the neoclassical literature many authors have rigorously demonstrated, in a general equilibrium framework,

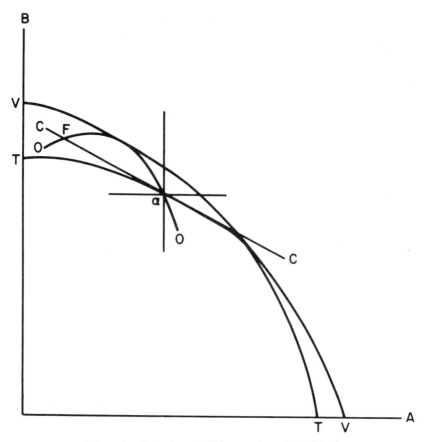

Figure 6. Gains from tariff or quota restricted trade.

the conditions under which tariffs can bring about a higher level of national welfare than free trade.

In a well known article Robert E. Baldwin used the "envelope curve" to show how a country potentially can gain from restricting trade by imposing a tariff or a quota.[25] Assuming nonintersecting community indifference curves, let TT in Figure 6 represent the home country's transformation curve and OO the foreign country's offer curve. The envelope, VV, can be derived by sliding the foreign country's offer curve around TT, always keeping its axis parallel to the axis of the transformation curve. Suppose that the free trade terms of trade, determined by the intersection of the home country's offer curve and OO, is given by the slope of cc. The free trade point, F, will always lie within the envelope VV. Hence the grand utility possibility frontier of the bundles represented by the envelope will lie everywhere to the northeast of the grand utility possibility frontier derived from the free trade bundles.[26] Therefore, by imposing tariffs or quotas—in the absence of retaliation—there is a potential gain from restricting trade, since points on the envelope denoting higher levels of community welfare can be reached by these means. This result follows from the fact that the imposition of tariffs or quotas by countries having monopoly power on imports (and, symmetrically, of taxes and quotas on exports) can in the postulated conditions improve their terms of trade.[27]

In one of his early articles on optimum tariffs and retaliation, Harry G. Johnson refuted the conclusion of earlier writers that tariff retaliation would necessarily leave both (all) countries worse off than under free trade. Using a myopic Cournot-type of retaliation mechanism such that each country in turn imposed on optimal tariff, Johnson demonstrated that the country initially imposing an optimum tariff could be made better off than under free trade. But in his later writings he reversed the policy implications of this *curiosum*, reducing the case for tariffs to a *second-best* category in the presence of all distortions *other* than that of the traditional case implied by the presence of monopoly power in foreign trade. In a related note, he provided yet another argument against protection: if a small country grew subject to a distortionary tariff, the country could experience immiserization with no change in either domestic or international terms of trade. Furthermore, if technical change in the protected industry was the source of growth, the likelihood of immiserating growth was even greater, since the primary gain from growth (measured as optimal policy) could now be more outweighed by the accentuation of the loss from the distortion imposed by the tariff following growth. This argument reinforced the importance of measuring growth at world rather than domestic prices in trade-distorted economies, and furnished an important explanation of why import-substituting LDCs have as a rule done worse than the export-promoting LDCs.

Not only have these contributions stimulated scholars to examine whether tariff-induced capital flows would necessarily be welfare-improving, but they led Johnson and others to theoretic-empirical work on the cost of protection, on the gains or losses to a country of joining a customs union, on the so-called "scientific tariff," and on a more generalized theory of distortions and welfare.[28]

As the objectives of tariff policy became more extensive, new concepts were developed to analyze and appraise them. Listing a large number of commonly recognized arguments of modern tariff protection, Johnson applied the "scientific tariff" for an examination of the following objectives: (1) to promote national self-sufficiency, independence, diversification, agriculturalization, or industrialization; (2) to increase military preparedness; and (3) to strengthen a country's international bargaining position. With regard to gains from trade, he formulated alternative maximization policies for a developing country's exports of primary products, in terms of both export and import tariffs designed to maximize government tariff revenue.

In comparing the results of tariff protection with other commercial policies, the problem has been further analyzed as to whether a higher tariff is necessarily preferable to a lower one. In Figure 7, let TT be the transformation curve, A the exportable good and ab the international terms of trade. Manifestly, an appropriate tariff on B could lead to production at a and consumption at b. A higher tariff would lead to production at c and consumption at d, where d is on a higher indifference curve than b. In this illustration given by Bhagwati, a higher tariff provides superior results to a lower one, refuting the assertion that a higher tariff is necessarily inferior to a lower one. It will be noted, however, that in this illustration the export good is inferior in consumption: evaluated at the original tariff-level price, d represents an increase in real income, but consumption of A has declined. In a controversy on this issue, Kemp criticized some of the welfare comparisons which were made on the basis of this particular example. He showed that the maximum feasible utility one individual can attain—given all other utility levels as fixed—is greater in a comparatively low-tariff situation.[29]

Having unified a considerable body of literature on the theory of distortions and welfare, Bhagwati derived "duality" relationships between the analysis of policy rankings under various market imperfections and policy rankings to achieve noneconomic objectives. The seven areas treated, and key conclusions reached, point to the strength and weakness of this form of analysis. Postulating the existence of four important market imperfections—for example, in factor markets a wage differential between sectors, in product markets a production externality, in consumption a consumption externality, and in trade monopoly power—the suboptimality of laissez-faire is demonstrated. In other words, under such conditions laissez-faire would not be the optimal policy. Providing examples of immiserization—economic growth bringing about a deterioration in the country's terms of trade; an optimum tariff (before growth)

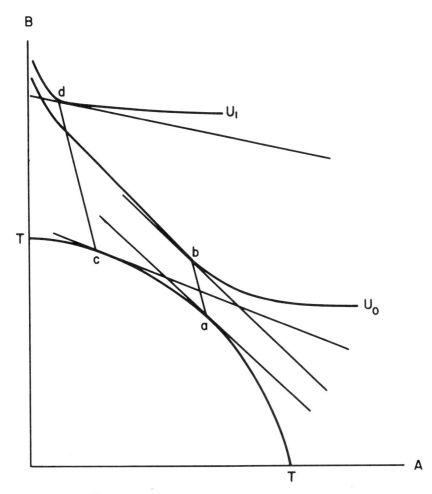

Figure 7. The gains from high vs. low tariff protection.

becoming suboptimal after growth; a distortionary tariff used for the purpose of import-substitution; and cases where a wage differential exists in the factor market—it is shown that all these distortions may result in the country becoming worse off after growth. Ranking alternative policies under these market imperfections, Bhagwati demonstrates the optimal policy intervention in regard to them. Under the heading of "ranking of tariffs," policies constituting impediments to the attainment of optimality are evaluated. This is the category in which Kemp's theorem can be

illustrated—that a country without monopoly power in trade (and no
other imperfection), but with no inferior goods, would be worse off with
a higher tariff than a lower one. Similarly, tariffs around the optimal
tariff for a country with monopoly power in trade may be evaluated. Introducing various kinds of market imperfections (e.g., Hagen's case of
wage differentials or Haberler's case of production externalities), or the
existence of commodity taxes, it is feasible to rank conditions of free
trade and autarky demonstrating that free trade is not necessarily superior
to self-sufficiency. Finally, noneconomic objectives are considered with
the attendant ranking of policies. This analysis comprises optimal policy
intervention when the values of certain variables are constrained so that
full optimality is unattainable.

After considering the theory of distortions in terms of four "pathol-
ogies," representing cases where the economic system would not satisfy
conditions for an economic maximum, viz., where the equalities for the
marginal rate of transformation in domestic production, the marginal
foreign rate of transformation, and the marginal rate of substitution in
domestic consumption are not met, Bhagwati analyzes the distortions
arising potentially from endogenous (existing market imperfections),
policy-imposed (concrete government acts), and autonomous (accidental)
distortions. With regard to gains or losses from trade, these are the noteworthy conclusions. Where market imperfections exist and noneconomic
objectives are postulated, the required policy directly attacks the source
of the distortion. Hence, when distortions are introduced into the economy, because the values of certain variables (e.g., production or employment of a factor in an activity) have to be constrained, the least-cost
method of achieving this objective is to choose the policy intervention
affecting directly the constrained variable. Specifically, a trade-level noneconomic objective is achieved at least cost by introducing a policy-imposed distortion via a trade tariff or subsidy; a production noneconomic
objective by introducing a policy-imposed distortion via a production
tax-cum-subsidy; a consumption noneconomic objective by introducing a
policy-imposed distortion via a consumption tax-cum-subsidy; and a
factor-employment (in a sector) noneconomic objective by introducing a
policy-imposed distortion via a factor tax-cum-subsidy.[30]

Bhagwati has shown that although each distortion, whether endogenous, policy-imposed, or autonomous in origin, may be welfare-ranked
and symmetrical with a "corresponding" class of imposed distortions
(e.g., the ranking of policies for a production externality is identical with
the ranking of policies when production is constrained as a noneconomic

objective), the policies can be ranked as optimal or second-best, etc.—as well as when they may be superior to free trade—but they cannot be ranked uniquely vis-a-vis one another. When several distortions exist, successive reductions in a tariff will not necessarily improve welfare steadily, if at all, and the gains from trade may turn into losses. The theorems on the possible inferiority of free trade (i.e., zero tariff) to no trade (i.e., prohibitive tariff) when there is a production externality or a wage differential are thus only special cases of the general theorem that reductions in the "degree" of a distortion will not necessarily be welfare-increasing if there is another distoriton in the system. Similarly, if distortions exist under free trade and under autarky, the free trade situation may be immiserizing (therefore, free trade inferior to autarky) if the loss from the distortion is accentuated and outweighs the primary gain from the shift to (free) trade itself. The conclusion that deserves particular attention for policy formation is that distortions cannot be ranked vis-à-vis one another, which applies to all classes of distortions.

This literature on distortions and welfare, with its related emphasis on potential gains or losses from trade, grew primarily out of the conditions and ferment of ideas in Delhi, India, during 1963-68. In many ways, with differences being no smaller than similarities, the problems of growth, development, and trade under extreme uncertainty of the industrial countries of North America, Western Europe, Australasia, and Japan have brought about an illuminating literature with references to the "gains from trade." Inter alia, these writings have dealt with customs union theory, optimum-currency areas, various exchange rate regimes, as well as with import-substitution, effective tariffs, and the relation of these phenomena to geographical and national income distribution.

A considerable emphasis has been placed on the notion of "effective tariffs." The concept of the effective rate of protection was developed within the traditional framework of tariff theory. It is a tariff measure that takes into account tariffs on both intermediate and final products. In the simplest case of one imported input, the effective rate of protection is:

$$ERP = \frac{t_c - A_{yc}\, t_y}{V_c}$$

where t_c is the nominal tariff on the output, t_y is the nominal rate on the imported input, A_{yc} is the share of the input in the total value of the output, and V_c is the value added.[31] The literature on effective tariffs has endeavored to show the impact of various restricted trade policies upon growth and development. Understandably, much attention has been given to the implications for the LDCs of reduced gains from trade resulting from high effective tariffs of developed countries on imports of processed goods and semifinished manufactures. To date the results of this literature have been highly controversial, and the theoretical concepts are still being integrated into the corpus of modern trade and development theory.[32]

GAINS FROM TRADE: SOME RECENT MATHEMATICAL CONTRIBUTIONS

With the emergence of a new economic era in the 1970s—deceleration in the rates of economic growth and volume of foreign trade among the major capitalist countries—not surprisingly there appeared a series of articles providing a reexamination of the gains from trade under nonautarkic versus autarkic conditions. These works were written in mathematical terms and their authors either confirmed or derived the following results. Free trade is *potentially noninferior* to autarky. Trade restriction via tariffs, or quotas, is *potentially noninferior* to autarky. If a small country is in trade equilibrium and experiences an autonomous change in prices that is potentially beneficial, a further change in prices in the same direction is potentially unharmful. Similarly, if a large country experiences this phenomenon, an expansion of foreign trade is potentially unharmful.[33]

Proofs have been provided for the existence of a world "Pareto-optimal" competitive equilibrium, as well as for "equilibrium" under conditions of autarky. A general theorem demonstrates the existence of a competitive world equilibrium which is potentially noninferior for the consumers of each nation as compared with "equilibrium" under autarky.[34] The relationships between welfare criteria in utility space and in commodity space have been rigorously formalized.[35] The concept of a social utility frontier has been used to prove a variant of the proposition that free trade is potentially noninferior to autarky.[36]

Furthermore, the gains from trade have been investigated for situations where the trading economy is faced with nonmarket externalities and the conditions formulated under which trade would still be superior to autarky.[37] A unified analysis of many of these problems shows that conditions can be postulated under which economic growth with free trade, or growth with tariffs, is potentially noninferior to trade under autarky; trade with subsidies—solely financed by tariff revenues—is not

worse than no trade; and a generalization has been provided for the relationship between price divergence and terms-of-trade improvement.[38] It
has also been shown that, if there exists an economy, say A, such that
every agent in A benefits from the movement from autarky to trade, an
economy A' comprised of agents sufficiently similar to those of A will
benefit from the opening of trade.[39]

This mathematical literature has had the beneficial effect not only of
defining the precise conditions under which restricted trade can better
all members of society as compared with autarky, but indirectly of providing the foundation for empirical investigations of the feasibility of
achieving greater gains from trade by reducing serious fluctuations in the
terms of trade.

TRADE, DEVELOPMENT AND UNCERTAINTY

In the last two decades, full-length analytical studies have appeared on
trade, development and uncertainty. Basically this work was founded on
a two-sector growth model with trade. It has also been utilized to analyze such problems as the impact of slow-export-demand growth upon
the growth of per capita income in developing countries. Bardhan has
shown that, if a less-developed country faces an externally determined
rate of growth of demand for its exports and if its domestic production
requires the use of an imported intermediate product, the long-run rate
of growth for this country will be influenced by export demand factors.
The long-run rate of growth will be a weighted average of the rate of
growth of the primary factors (as in standard neoclassical models) *and*
the rate of growth of export demand. If exports grow at a sluggish rate
so that the latter rate is lower than the former, long-run capital accumulation for such a country will be slower than the "natural" growth rate.[40]
More generally, several articles have reconsidered the problems of factor
proportions and comparative advantage within the framework of long-run
growth and development. Important results have been obtained: the basic
conclusion of the static Heckscher-Ohlin theory, which maintains that a
labor- (capital-) abundant country will have a comparative advantage in
producing labor- (capital-) intensive goods, also applies to the long run
when an economy experiencing population growth and capital accumulation has reached a steady growth path.[41] Moreover, it has been demonstrated that in the long run a higher savings ratio will inevitably lead to
relatively higher output of capital-intensive goods. This analysis was
carried out for a small country which, by means of labor and capital,

produces three goods, one of which is a nontraded capital good. As is the case with most such analyses, the results may not be generalizable but the basic conclusions appear to be of prime importance to the theory and practice of the gains from trade. In the long run, the *form* of comparative advantage will differ from the initial situation; per se, however, dynamic considerations do not contravene the results of standard comparative advantage theory—arguments to the contrary of many critics notwithstanding.

The gains from trade via import-substitution have also been reconsidered. It has been shown convincingly that a heavy-industry emphasis does not necessarily lead to the most rapid growth process. Clearly this conclusion has an important bearing on the trade and development policies of LDCs.

Attempts have also been made to relate monetary and exchange rate arrangements to the gains from trade. Specifically, in analyzing the controversy between monetarists and structuralists on the issue of inflation in Latin American countries, Findlay has designated market imperfections and lack of factor mobility for special consideration. This has opened the way for the incorporation of these conditions into standard international trade theory via well-developed economic techniques. Similarly, it has been shown that certain exchange-rate regimes have important distribution effects on production and consumption.[42] An overvalued exchange rate regime benefits importers and consumers of internationally traded goods and penalizes producers; it restricts the inflow of foreign captial. *Per contra*, devaluation shifts income from consumers to producers of these goods. Although many country-studies have appeared indicating the distorting effects of inflexible—usually overvalued—exchange rate regimes on the gains from trade and its distribution, further theoretical-quantitative research on this issue is long overdue.

An important and growing literature has devoted attention to the more general incorporation of uncertainty into gains from trade theorizing. One author has investigated the case of a small trading country experiencing large fluctuations in terms of trade as a result of uncertain transaction costs and/or of erratic movements in spot exchange rates. Under otherwise customary assumptions, the following nonautarky theorem was derived: Given trade uncertainty (and excluding "pathological" distortions), autarky will not be optimal regardless of variations in the terms of trade. Similarly, by introducing forward markets into the analysis, it was shown that in the long run autarky cannot be optimal regardless of the variations in terms of trade and whatever the level of forward prices.[43] In a jointly authored paper, Batra and Russell examined the effects of increasing uncertainty of world prices on the social welfare of a trading nation and demonstrated that it would bring about a decline of expected utility. Under conditions of uncertainty, therefore, free trade may not be an optimal policy. To reduce the effects of uncertainty, and to increase the potential gains from trade, the authors considered various governmental policies designed to minimize the cost to consumers resulting from variations in actual as compared with expected terms of trade.[44]

Batra further examined these issues by adopting the well known approach of introducing a random variable in the production function and proceeding with the assumption that the expected utility of the producers is to be maximized. With this change in assumptions the theory of international trade was reconsidered along standard lines.[45] The analysis was confined to the narrow world of two commodities, two factors, and two countries. It also utilized a special form of the production function, for uncertainty appears as a multiplicative factor grafted on to a standard production function with full certainty. The conclusions therefore depend not only on the producers being risk averters but upon the precise nature of their risk-aversion. Although the theorems derived are narrow in scope, they provide insights for the development of gains from trade theory and practice, especially in regard to the "commodity problem" and the stabilization of terms of trade.

In effect, the introduction of uncertainty is shown to have important consequences for standard trade theory. Uncertainty cannot be assumed away as a minor modification. Contrary to the standard Heckscher-Ohlin conclusion, given constant commodity prices and the customary assumptions regarding homogeneity—with uncertainty, changes in factor endowments do affect relative factor prices. Still, the following related theorems remain robust: (1) the Stopler-Samuelson theorem, which demonstrates that a tariff increases the return to factors used intensively in the import-competing industry—although Kemp has pointed out that the Stolper-Samuelson theorem may not hold in the many-commodity, many-factor case;[46] (2) the Samuelson theorem on the one-to-one correspondence between international commodity-price ratios and factor-price ratios;[47] and (3) the celebrated Rybczynski theorem: At constant commodity prices, accumulation of a factor increases the output of the commodity that uses that factor intensively and reduces the output of the other commodity.[48] Even the Heckscher-Ohlin theorem, it is shown, can be rescued for conditions of uncertainty if we define factor abundance in physical terms. However, under certain specifications of risk aversion, complete factor-price equalization is ruled out. But the weak factor-equalization theorem, i.e., the existence of a *tendency* toward factor-price equalization, remains. The volume of trade and the gains from trade, it is conclusively demonstrated, are smaller under uncertainty than under certainty.

The Ricardian model of international trade also has been reworked and this conclusion reached: Expected gains from trade for a risk-averse country which, under certainty, would wish to trade may, under postulated assumptions with price uncertainty, become negative, causing it to cease trading.[49] Several authors have formulated a trading model in which both price uncertainty and storage activities were included. They showed that with nonincreasing risk aversion but increased price uncertainty, both importers and exporters of the stored commodity tend to reduce the volume of their trade and, at the limit, would be better off not trading.[50] A framework has been developed for the analysis of trade under conditions of substantial fluctuations in prices, given alternative specifications of risk by the governments of respective trading partners.[51]

Although models based on the analysis of "economic surplus" cannot provide general conclusions on the potential gains or losses from trade, a number of papers have extended such models by comparing various restricted trade situations rather than confining the analysis to the comparison of autarkic and free trade equilibria.[52] The sources of instability, it has been noted, have different effects under different trading regimes.[53] Marketing boards engaged in foreign trade are likely to stabilize producers' prices (although in developing countries they have been notorious for destabilizing producers' incomes) whereas private firms engaged in "marketing" are more likely to destabilize producers' prices. By relaxing the linearity assumption made in previous studies, the conclusion has been reached that producers of an export good generally would be better off with price instability, while consumers and importers would be better off with price stability. In a cosmopolitan framework, however, they would jointly be better off with price stability.[54]

Theoretically, the presence of uncertainty in the foreign trade of goods and assets can, to a degree, be treated as an additional or joint "commodity," denoted as "risk." In the absence of satisfactory, or feasible, risk-sharing arrangements—reflected by the fact that this "commodity" is not internationally traded—the prices of these risk elements in production and distribution are manifestly different in different countries. As a consequence, some of the basic properties of international trade theory may not hold. Without such minimal risk-sharing arrangements, analysis of the effects of substantial uncertainty on the basic properties of trade theory (e.g., comparative advantage) has little predictive value for international specialization and the pattern of trade. Nevertheless, studies which have considered a planning model in which a social welfare function (expected utility) is maximized subject to the country's technological constraint, can be interpreted as models which include *domestic* stock markets and/or *domestic* Arrow-Debreu contingent commodity markets.[55] For effective gains-from-trade analysis under uncertainty, the incorporation into these models of international trade in firms' equities and/or other national and international risk-sharing arrangements appears to be a primary requisite.

CONCLUDING REMARKS

The classical literature first compared the effects of free trade versus no trade; then, those of free trade versus protection. The neoclassical literature, in turn, increasingly compared the general effects of protection versus quantitative trade restrictions; then, those of various forms of trade restrictions versus autarky. By examining the precise conditions under which restricted trade can improve the welfare of society as compared to autarky, the recent literature on trade and welfare also provided the foundation for empirical research on optimizing the gains-from-trade by reducing extreme fluctuations in the terms of trade. These theoretical developments reflected both the growing interdependence of the world economy and the increasing pressures for protection—particularly in times of deep and prolonged recession—resulting from this interdependence. Unless the standard theory accords these factors their due importance, a pendular reaction to free-trade doctrine may have the effect of institutionalizing new and excessive forms of protection unwarranted by either modern gains-from-trade theory or by relevant statistical evidence.

NOTES

1. The *locus classicus* of international trade theory before Adam Smith is Jacob Viner, *Studies in the Theory of International Trade* (New York: Harper & Bros., 1937), Ch. 1 and 2. For evidence on increasing protectionism in the latter 1970s, see International Monetary Fund, *Annual Report on Exchange Restrictions*, e.g., 1977; Jan Tinbergen, ed., *R. I. O. Reshaping the International Order* (New York: Dutton, 1976), Ch. 3; and Harold B. Malmgren, "Trade Policies of the Developed Countries for the Next Decade," in Jagdish Bhagwati, *The New International Economic Order: The North-South Debates* (Cambridge: M.I.T. Press, 1977), Ch. 8.

2. The many paradoxes in modern trade theory are discussed by Stephen P. Magee, "Twenty Paradoxes in International Trade Theory," Chapter 5, ed. Jimmye S. Hillman and Andrew Schmitz, *International Trade and Agriculture: Theory and Policy* (Boulder: Westview Press, 1979). Some of the material presented in this

paper is based on an earlier work by Chambers, Letiche, and Schmitz, *ibid.*, Chapter 4.

3. Adam Smith, *The Wealth of Nations*, eds. R. H. Campbell and A. S. Skinner (Oxford: Clarendon Press, 1976), vol. 1, p. 457.

4. David Ricardo is deservedly given credit for the first clear and reasonably comprehensive exposition of the comparative cost doctrine. See *The Works and Correspondence of David Ricardo*, ed. Piero Sraffa with M. H. Dobb (New York: Cambridge University Press, 1951), vol. 1, *On the Principles of Political Economy and Taxation* (first published in 1817), especially pp. 133-49; and Robert Torrens, *An Essay on the External Corn Trade* (London: J. Hatchard, 1815), especially pp. 264-66.

5. The most precise exposition of their views is to be found in the following original sources. John Stuart Mill, *Essays on Some Unsettled Questions of Political Economy* (London: Parker West Strand, 1844), pp. 47-74; Alfred Marshall, "The Pure Theory of Foreign Trade," in *Pure Theory (Foreign Trade-Domestic Values)* (London: London School of Economics, 1949), pp. 1-28; Francis Y. Edgeworth, "The Theory of International Values," *Economic Journal* 4 (March 1894):34-50; and F. W. Taussig, whose earlier writings are incorporated in *International Trade* (New York, 1927).

6. See Francis Y. Edgeworth, *Papers Relating to Political Economy* (London: Macmillan and Co., 1925); and Philip E. Sorensen, "Edgeworth on Monopoly, Taxation and International Trade" (Ph.D. dissertation, University of California, Berkeley, 1966), pp. 127-63.

7. The detailed evolution of these views is discussed by Viner in his *Studies in the Theory of International Trade* (Chs. 8 and 9) and *International Trade and Economic Development* (Glencoe: Free Press, 1952), Ch. 3.

8. Enrico Barone used this form of back-to-back diagram to reach conclusions with respect to gains from trade. He borrowed the diagram from H. Cunynghame, *A Geometric Political Economy* (Oxford, 1904), Figure 51, p. 98. Cf. Enrico Barone, *Grundzüge der theoretischen Nationalökonomie* (German trans. by Hans Staehle of the original Italian ed. of 1908; Bonn, 1927), Figure 30, p. 102, and Figure 32, p. 105. Barone, however, makes no reference to Cunynghame. On the formidable errors of using such Marshallian domestic-trade demand and supply curves in terms of monetary forces for gains-of-trade theory, see Viner, *Studies in the Theory of International Trade*, pp. 589-93; and John M. Letiche, *Balance of Payments and Economic Growth* (New York: Harper & Bros., 1958), pp. 71-73. See also the survey paper by John M. Currie, John A. Murphy, and Andrew Schmitz, "The Concept of Economic Surplus and its Use in Economic Analysis," *Economic Journal* 81 (December 1971):741-99.

9. See, e.g., Steven Enke, "The Monopsony Case for Tariffs," *Quarterly Journal of Economics* 58 (February 1944):229-44.

10. Wassily W. Leontief, "The Use of Indifference Curves in the Analysis of Foreign Trade," *Quarterly Journal of Economics* 48 (May 1933):493-503.

11. The terms of trade $p^o p^o$ can be obtained under the small-country assumption or derived from the standard offer curve analysis for large-country models. For an excellent exposition of offer curves, with illustrative diagrams, see James E. Meade, *A Geometry of International Trade* (London: George Allen, 1952).

12. An important assumption made by Leontief is that community indifference curves do not intersect.

13. Paul A. Samuelson, "The Gains from International Trade," *Canadian Journal of Economics and Political Science* 5 (May 1939):195-205, reprinted in *Readings in the Theory of International Trade*, eds. Howard S. Ellis and Lloyd A. Metzler (Philadelphia: Blakiston Co., 1949), pp. 239-52.

14. This means that the same ordinal preference schedule relating commodities and productive services is assumed for every individual as well as the same ownership in the means of production. It does not mean, however, that the utilities of different individuals are comparable. For as Samuelson notes, since all individuals are identical, if one is bettered (in an ordinal sense) by the introduction of trade, all will be bettered, and this makes it unnecessary to make any welfare comparisons between individuals.

15. Samuelson, pp. 245-46 (italics in original). Although Samuelson's original, rigorous proof on the gains from trade used the small-country assumption, Murray C. Kemp demonstrated that the proof holds for countries of any size in "The Gains from International Trade," *Economic Journal* 72 (December 1962):803-19.

16. Samuelson, p. 251. Samuelson suggests that the reader see "Professor Viner's interesting remarks in his *Studies in the Theory of International Trade*, pp. 532-4." An arithmetic illustration, which Viner used in his international trade course at Chicago, may be of interest to some readers: *Before trade,* with customary free competitive assumptions, France's output was: 20 units of labor produced 200 cotton; the remaining 20 units of labor produced 50 wine. Therefore 4 cotton exchanged for 1 wine. *After trade,* assuming France had a comparative advantage in wine, France could produce with its 40 units of labor 100 wine. The rate of interchange would be 1 wine = 4(+) cotton. Therefore, for 50 wine France could obtain 200(+) cotton. Hence France could always have at least 50 wine and more than the original amount of 200 cotton; or, 50(+) wine and 200 cotton.

17. Paul A. Samuelson, "The Gains from International Trade Once Again," *Economic Journal* 72 (December 1962):820-29.

18. Slope of *VV* represents the free trade price line (i.e., the terms of trade). Profit maximization insures production at a point like *U*. Free trade allows consumption along the *VV* frontier; the volume of trade depends upon consumer preferences.

19. This terminology was used by Francis M. Bator, "The Simple Analytics of Welfare Maximization," *American Economic Review* 47 (1957):22-59.

20. See Peter B. Kenen, "On the Geometry of Welfare Economics," *Quarterly Journal of Economics* 71 (August 1957):426-47.

21. Samuelson, "The Gains from International Trade," p. 250.

22. Kemp, "The Gains from International Trade," passim.

23. A. O. Krueger and H. Sonneschein, "The Terms of Trade, the Gains from Trade and Price Divergence," *International Economic Review* 8 (February 1967):pp. 121-27.

24. Murray C. Kemp, "Some Issues in the Analysis of the Gains from Trade," *Oxford Economic Papers* 20 (July 1968): 149-61.

25. Robert E. Baldwin, "The New Welfare Economics and Gains in International Trade," *Quarterly Journal of Economics* 66 (February 1952):91-101. A key assumption in the analysis on the gains from trade is that factors of production are internationally immobile. For example, see the work by Robert Mundell, "International Trade and Factor Mobility," *American Economic Review* 47 (June 1957): 321-35; and A. Schmitz and P. Helmberger, "Factor Mobility and International Trade: The Case of Complementarity," *American Economic Review* LX (September 1970):761-67, where this assumption is relaxed.

26. The envelope *VV* and the free trade possibility frontier will coincide at the no-trade point. Correspondingly, the grand utility possibility frontier for the *VV* envelope may be tangent to the trade grand utility possibility frontier.

27. On the basis of this proposition, an expression can be obtained for the optimal tariff. It is simply: $1/(\epsilon - 1)$, where ϵ is the elasticity of the foreign offer curve. For a graphic and algebraic proof, see Richard E. Caves and Ronald W. Jones, *World Trade and Payments* (Boston: Little Brown, 1973), pp. 239-40. Among

outstanding contributions on the subject of tariffs and quotas are: Wolfgang F. Stolper and Paul A. Samuelson, "Protection and Real Wages," *Review of Economic Studies* 9 (November 1941):58-73; Tibor Scitovsky, "A Reconsideration of the Theory of Tariffs," *Review of Economic Studies* 9 (Summer 1942):89-100; Lloyd A. Metzler, "Tariffs, the Terms of Trade and the Distribution of National Income," *Journal of Political Economy* 62 (February 1949):2-29, reprinted in *Readings in International Economics,* eds. Richard E. Caves and Harry G. Johnson (Homewood, Ill.: Richard D. Irwin, 1968), pp. 24-57; and A. P. Lerner, "The Symmetry between Import and Export Taxes," *Economica* 3 (August 1936):306-13, reprinted in *Readings in International Economics,* rev., pp. 197-203.

28. Harry G. Johnson, "Optimum Tariffs and Retaliation," *Review of Economic Studies* 21 (1953-54):142-53; idem, "Optimal Trade Intervention in the Presence of Domestic Distortions," in R. E. Baldwin et al., *Trade, Growth and the Balance of Payments,* Essays in Honor of Gottfried Haberler (Chicago: Rand McNally, 1965), pp. 3-34; and idem, "The Possibility of Income Losses from Increased Efficiency or Factor Accumulation in the Presence of Tariffs," *Economic Journal* 77 (March 1967):151-54. This brief paper also induced Richard Brecher and Carlos Diaz-Alejandro to show that distortionary tariff-induced capital inflows will necessarily be immiserizing if the protected industry is capital intensive; see R. Brecher and Carlos Diaz-Alejandro, "Tariffs, Foreign Capital and Immiserizing Growth," *Journal of International Economics* 7 (November 1977), 317-22. For further work on the theory of tariffs, see Harry G. Johnson, "The Cost of Protection and the Scientific Tariff," *Journal of Political Economy* 68 (August 1960):327-45; and "The Alternative Maximization Policies for Developing Country Exports of Primary Products," *Journal of Political Economy* 43 (May/June 1968): 489-93.

29. Kemp, "Gains from International Trade," pp. 803-19, and "Some Issues in the Analysis of the Gains from Trade," pp. 149-61; Jagdish Bhagwati, "The Gains from Trade Once Again," *Oxford Economic Papers* 28 (July 1960):137-48. One of the issues dealt with here is the question of ranking policies that themselves constitute impediments to the attainment of optimality: e.g., for a country *without* monopoly power in trade (but no other imperfections), the question is whether a higher tariff is worse than a lower tariff. In addition to the results given, *supra,* Bhagwati and Kemp have analyzed the problem for tariffs around the optimal tariff for a country *with* monopoly power in trade. See J. Bhagwati and M. C. Kemp, "Ranking of Tariffs under Monopoly Power in Trade," *Quarterly Journal of Economics* 83 (May 1969): The Kemp and Bhagwati-Kemp theorems dealing with these issues have deduced the proposition that reductions in the degree of *an only* distortion are successively welfare-increasing until the distortion is fully eliminated. But cases relating to this proposition require the exclusion of inferior goods and attendant multiple equilibria if the possibility of the competitive system "choosing" an inferior-welfare equilibrium under the lower degree of distortion is to be ruled out. See, J. N. Bhagwati, "The Generalized Theory of Distortions and Welfare," in *Trade, Balance of Payments and Growth,* Papers in International Economics in Honor of Charles P. Kindleberger, ed. Jagdish Bhagwati, Ronald W. Jones, Robert A. Mundell, and Jaroslav Vanek (New York: North-Holland Publishing Co., 1971), p. 84. Bhagwati demonstrates, moreover, that Kemp's theorem of the superiority of tariff-restricted trade over no trade does not extend to cases in which trade is restricted instead by policies such as consumption and production tax-cum-subsidies. In this instance two distortions are being compared: (1) a consumption tax-cum-subsidy with a situation of autarky and (2) a production tax-cum-subsidy with a situation of autarky. Unique

ranking is also impossible between autarky and restricted trade where trade restriction occurs via use of a factor tax-cum-subsidy. In these cases, a more general proposition applied: "Distortions cannot be ranked (uniquely) vis-à-vis one another" (p. 88).

30. Bhagwati, "Generalized Theory of Distortions and Welfare," p. 78. See also Gottfried Haberler, "Some Problems in the Pure Theory of International Trade," *Economic Journal* 60 (June 1950):223-40; W. M. Corden, "Tariffs, Subsidies and the Terms of Trade," *Economica* 24 (August 1957), and E. Hagen, "An Economic Justification of Protectionism," *Quarterly Journal of Economics* 72 (November 1958).

31. Although aspects of this problem were referred to in the pre-World War II literature on commercial treaties and tariff protection, the modern literature gained much impetus from the writings by C. L. Barber, W. M. Corden, G. Bascvi, B. Belassa, and J. H. Young. An extensive bibliography is to be found in Herbert G. Grubel and Harry G. Johnson, eds., *Effective Tariff Protection* (Geneva, 1971), pp. 299-305. (However, the reference on p. 305 to J. H. Young, *Canadian Commercial Policy*, is misdated; it should read 1957 rather than 1967.) See especially Clarence L. Barber, "Canadian Tariff Policy," *Canadian Journal of Economics and Political Science* 21 (November 1955):513-30; W. M. Corden, "Effective Protective Rates in a General Equilibrium Model: A Geometric Note," *Oxford Economic Papers* 21 (July 1969), *The Theory of Protectionism* (New Jersey: Oxford University Press, 1971), and *Trade Policy and Economic Welfare* (Oxford: Cloverdon Press, 1974).

32. Cf. Herbert G. Grubel "Effective Tariff Protection: A Non-specialist Introduction to the Theory, Policy Implications and Controversies," *Effective Tariff Protection*, pp. 1-15; Wilfred K. Ethier, "General Equilibrium Theory and the Concept of the Effective Rate of Protection," *Effective Tariff Protection*, pp. 17-43; and the critical analysis by V. K. Ramaswami and T. N. Srinivasan, "Tariff Structure and Resource Allocation in the Presence of Factor Subsiitution," in *Trade, Balance of Payments and Growth*, ed. Bhagwati, et al., in which the authors "conclude that substitution effects will often be significant and that, therefore, effective protective rates are likely to be a poor guide to the resource movements resulting from the levy of a tariff. . . . Domestic distortions, externalities, and noneconomic objectives are appropriately handled through taxes and subsidies on domestic economic variables. Thus in many situations the optimal policy with regard to foreign trade is nonintervention. When the levy of trade taxes is justified, the optimal tariff must be determined with reference to a specified objective: and the effective protective rates entailed by this tariff are of no relevance" (p. 298). Regarding American agriculture, empirical estimates of effects of these tariffs were made by Rachel Dardis and J. Dennisson, "The Welfare Costs of Alternative Methods of Protecting Raw Wool in the United States," *American Journal of Agricultural Economics* 51 (May 1969):303; and by Larry J. Wipf, "Tariffs, Nontariff Distortions and Effective Protection in U.S. Agriculture," *American Journal of Agricultural Economics* 53 (August 1971):423-30.

33. Murray Kemp and Henry Y. Wan, "The Gains from Free Trade," *International Economic Review* 13 (October 1972):509-22.

34. J. M. Grandmont and Daniel McFadden, "A Technical Note on Classical Gains from Trade," *Journal of International Economics* 2 (May 1972):109-28.

35. Yoshihiko Otani, "Gains from Trade Revisited," *Journal of International Economics* 2 (May 1972):127-56.

36. John S. Chipman and James C. Moore, "Social Utility and the Gains from Trade," *Journal of International Economics* 2 (May 1972):157-72.

37. Henry Y. Wan, "A Note on Trading Gains and Externalities," *Journal of Interna-*

tional Economics 2 (May 1972):173-80. For an early, classical contribution to this problem, see Gottfried Haberler, "Some Problems in the Pure Theory of International Trade," *Economic Journal* 60 (June 1950):223-40.
38. See the report by Akira Takayama on Ohyama's work in *International Trade: An Approach to the Theory* (New York: Holt, Rinehart & Winston, 1972), Ch. 17.
39. Donald J. Roberts, "Continuity in the Gains from Trade with Similar Consumers," *Journal of International Economics* 4 (February 1974):25-36.
40. Pranab K. Bardhan, *Economic Growth, Development and Foreign Trade: A Study in Pure Theory* (New York: John Wiley & Sons, 1970), Ch. 4; also, H. Oniki and H. Uzawa, "Patterns of Trade and Investment in a Dynamic Model of International Trade," *Review of Economic Studies* XXXII (January 1965):15-38.
41. Ronald E. Findlay, "Factor Proportions and Comparative Advantage in the Long-Run," *Journal of Political Economy* (February 1970), republished in *International Trade and Development Theory* (1973), Ch. 7 (rev.), and Ch. 2 and 11, to which the immediate discussion refers.
42. Cf. Carlos Diaz-Alejandro, *Exchange Rate Devaluation in a Semi-Industrialized Country* (Cambridge, Mass.: M.I.T. Press, 1965) and *Essays on the Economic History of the Argentine Republic* (New Haven: Yale University Press, 1970), pp. 362-90 and Ian Little, Tibor Scitovsky, and Maurice Scott, *Industry and Trade in Some Developing Countries* (New York: Oxford University Press, 1970), especially pp. 67-69; see, also, I. A. McDougall and R. H. Snape, eds., *Studies in International Economics* (Amsterdam: North-Holland Publishing Co., 1970); Jagdish Bhagwati, *Anatomy and Consequences of Exchange Control Regimes*, Vol. 11 of the National Bureau of Economic Research, Inc., *Foreign Trade Regimes and Economic Development* (Cambridge, Massachusetts: Ballinger Publishing Company, 1978), Chs. 2-7; Ann O. Krueger, *Liberalization Attempts and Consequences*, Vol. 10, *ibid.*, Chs. 10-12; and Bent Hansen and Jagdish Bhagwati, "Should Growth Rates be Evaluated at International Prices?" eds. J. H. Baghwati and R. Eckaus, *Development and Planning*, essays in honor of P. Rosenstein-Rodan (London: George Allen & Unwin, 1973), pp. 53-68.
43. R. J. Ruffin, "International Trade under Uncertainty," *Journal of International Economics* 4 (August 1974):243-59.
44. Raveendra N. Batra and William R. Russell, "Gains from Trade under Uncertainty," *American Economic Review* 64 (December 1974):1040-48.
45. Raveendra N. Batra, *The Pure Theory of International Trade under Uncertainty* (New York: John Wiley & Sons, 1975), especially Chs. 3-7.
46. Murray C. Kemp, *Three Topics in the Theory of International Trade: Distribution, Welfare, and Uncertainty* (Amsterdam: North Holland Publishing Co., 1976). Chs. 4 and 5 analyze an "n x m" model, which includes intermediate goods. Elaborating on the essence of the Stolper-Samuelson theorem, viz., that an increase in any commodity price must lead to a decrease in the price of *at least one* other factor, Kemp shows that this result holds for the more realistic conditions examined. However, Chs. 1, 2, and 3 examine whether a small increase in any product price, all other product prices remaining the same, is associated with an *unambiguous* increase in the real reward of the factor used relatively intensively in this sector and with an unambiguous decline in the real reward of any other factor or in the real reward of the factor used relatively unintensively in this sector. Kemp shows that this requires setting extreme restrictions on the technology in the "n x n" model which makes it very much like the "2 x 2" model. Cf. Assaf Razin's careful review in *Journal of Political Economy* 86 (February 1978):162-65.
47. Paul A. Samuelson, "International Trade and the Equalization of Factor Prices," *Economic Journal* 58 (June 1948):163-84. "I learn from Professor Lionel Robbins," Samuelson has written, "that A. P. Lerner, while a student at L.S.E.,

dealt with this problem. I have had a chance to look over Lerner's mimeographed report, dated December 1933, and it is a masterly, definitive treatment of the question, difficulties and all." Paul A. Samuelson, "International Factor-Price Equalization Once Again," *Economic Journal* 59 (June 1949):181.

48. T. M. Rybczynski, "Factor Endowments and Relative Commodity Prices, *Economica* (November 1955):336-41, republished in *Readings in International Economics* (1968), pp. 72-77. The figure I has been redrawn to meet a criticism of E. J. Mishan, "Factor Endowment and Relative Commodity Prices: A Comment," *Economica* 23 (November 1956):352-59.

49. Stephen J. Turnovsky, "Technological and Price Uncertainty in a Ricardian Model of International Trade." *Review of Economic Studies* 61 (April 1974): 201-17. This conclusion, it will be noted, is different from that derived by Ruffin, under somewhat different assumptions.

50. Gershon Feder, Richard E. Just, and Andrew Schmitz, "Storage with Price Uncertainty in International Trade," *International Economic Review* 18 (October 1977):553-68.

51. James Anderson and J. Riley, "The International Trade with Fluctuating Prices," *International Economic Review* 17 (February 1976):76-97.

52. See especially Kemp, *Three Topics in the Theory of International Trade*, Part 2; and Jagdish Bhagwati, *The Theory and Practice of Commercial Policy: Departures From Unified Exchange Rates* (International Finance Section, Princeton University, 1968), pp. 11-66, and "The Generalized Theory of Distortions and Welfare," pp. 78ff.

53. C. F. Darrell Hueth and Andrew Schmitz, "International Trade in Intermediate and Final Goods: Some Welfare Implications," *Quarterly Journal of Economics* 86 (August 1972):351-65; Jurg Bieri and Andrew Schmitz, "Market Intermediaries and Price Instability," *American Journal of Agricultural Economics* 56 (May 1974):280-85. The work on the welfare aspects of market intermediaries in trade has recently been extended by R. Just, A. Schmitz, and D. Zilberman, "Price Controls and Optimal Export Policies Under Alternative Market Structures," *American Economic Review* (forthcoming).

54. Richard E. Just, Ernst Lutz, Andrew Schmitz, and Stephen J. Turnovsky, "The Distribution of Welfare Gains from International Price Stabilization under Distortions," *American Journal of Agricultural Economics* 59 (November 1977): 652-61.

55. See K. J. Arrow, "Le rôle des valeurs boursières pour la répartition la meilleure des risques," *Econométric* (Centre National de la Recherche Scientifique, Paris, 1953), pp. 41-48; idem, *Aspects of a Theory of Risk-Bearing* (Helsinki: Yrjo Jahnsson Lectures, 1965); Gérard Debreu, "Une économie de l'incertain," (Electricité de France, 1953); idem, *Theory of Value* (New Haven: Yale University Press, 1959), Ch. 7; E. Helpman and A. Razin, "Uncertainty and International Trade in the Presence of Stock Markets," *Review of Economic Studies* (forthcoming); and *idem,* "Welfare Aspects of International Trade in Goods and Securities," *Quarterly Journal of Economics* XCII (August 1978):489-508.

UPDATE

By John M. Letiche

Since the preceding article was written, in all categories of gains-from-trade analysis the literature has become more technical, providing further impetus to the trend away from simple models based on overly restrictive assumptions. Techniques of intertemporal optimization and general equilibrium theory increasingly have been used with considerable mathematical sophistication. The analysis has concentrated on three different types of gains from trade: (1) those resulting from a country's contemporary trade of goods and services for foreign goods and services; (2) from intertemporal trade that entails the exchange of goods and services for foreign assets, i.e., for claims to future goods and services; and (3) from trade of assets of one country for foreign assets possessing different properties of risk and function.

As for the first category, new significant contributions have been made to gains-from-trade theory by distinguishing between interindustry and intraindustry trade. Under competitive conditions, interindustry trade is assumed to be determined by comparative advantage; under imperfectly competitive conditions, intraindustry trade is assumed to be determined by economies of scale and differentiated products. To deal with conditions of long-run equilibrium, the literature has developed two models of intra-industry trade based on assumptions including increasing returns to scale in manufacturing sectors. [1]

The first case applies to external economies of scale in manufacturing at the industry level but not at the firm level. Average unit cost is thus assumed to be decreasing with the size of the industry; large firms, however,

have no advantage over small firms. For simplicity, productivity in the second
industry, say agriculture, is assumed to be the same in both countries before
and after the opening of trade. In consequence, if for whatever reason one
country begins with a larger volume of production in a manufacturing sector
than another, its cost advantage would continue until at least one of the two
countries would become specialized. Even if the two countries had the same
capital-labor ratio and technology, external economies of scale would give rise
to international trade. Moreover, expansion of trade would continue to raise
productivity in manufacturing and lower the price of these exports, thereby
raising the level of income in both countries and increasing the gains from trade
even for the country that loses increasing-returns sectors. Though the initial
cost advantage can accumulate over time, it has been shown that under the
postulated assumptions, a stable pattern of production must have at least one
of the two countries specializing in the production of one good.[2] Different
possible outcomes have been analyzed, but the fundamental conclusion remains
robust: although comparative advantage is ruled out, long-run equilibrium is
established with countries specializing in the production of different goods.
Recognizing that many things can influence the initial conditions leading to
lower unit cost in a manufacturing sector characterized by external economies
of scale, the originators of this model have suggested that the unpredictability
of the resulting pattern of specialization and trade does not reflect in -
determinancy but rather a greater impact of historical accident or institutional
conditions than that of national economic structures.

The criterion for gains from trade, therefore, in a world characterized
by external economies of scale in manufacturing sectors is that all countries
would gain provided that the world's scale of increasing-returns industries
is larger as a result of trade than the national scale of those industries would

have been in the absence of trade. Because the world market is larger than that
of any one country, the presumption is extremely strong that the scale of
production would be larger in a trading world economy than any one country
would achieve. In effect, according to this model, industrial countries with
similar levels of economic development, per capita income, technology, and
capital-labor ratios would likely have a pattern of trade dominated not by
comparative advantage but by external economies of scale in manufacturing.
Such countries would specialize <u>within</u> industries, giving rise to international
trade in addition to that brought about by comparative advantage.

As noted in our article, under conditions of comparative advantage the
gains from trade operate through a change in relative prices, often with
strong effects on the distribution of income. Potentially, as has been shown, everyone
can benefit from trade; but without compensatory payments, not everyone would
necessarily do so. Under conditions of intraindustry trade, however, it has
been plausibly argued--though definitive evidence not yet produced--that
industrial countries producing prime manufacturers and services are most likely
to benefit from high growth rates in foreign trade, with minor income-
distribution defects.

Since some economies of scale are internal to firms, the external
economies-of-scale model is incomplete as an explanation of intraindustry trade.
Accordingly, the core of the second model consists of an application of
"Chamberlain analysis" of monopolistic competition with differentiated products
to international trade. In this analysis, it will be recalled, entry of many
firms into an industry eliminates monopoly profits. Applied to a two-country,
two-factor, two-commodity model, the further assumption is introduced
that one country has a higher overall capital-labor ratio than the other. The two

industries, manufacturing and agriculture, are assumed to be located in each
country before and after the opening of trade. The manufacuting industry is the
more capital-intensive. Firms in agriculture produce a homogeneous product, while
firms in manufacturing produce differentiated products. Because of internal
economies of scale in manufacturing, it is postulated that neither country is
able to produce efficiently the full range of differentiated products by itself.
Through trade, however, firms in each country can produce a smaller variety of
manufactures at a larger scale, with higher productivity and lower costs.
Hence consumers in both countries would benefit from an increasing range of
choice at lower prices. Some consumers in the country with a higher capital-labor
ratio would probably prefer certain varieties produced in the second country.
Imports and exports of differentiated manufactures would therefore appear in
the same industry. The country with the higher capital-labor ratio would,
understandably, have an export surplus in manufactures. This category of trade,
represented by an exchange of manufactures for manufactures, is part of the
aggregate intraindustry trade. Another category of trade, represented by an
exchange of manufactures for agricultural goods, is part of the aggregate
interindustry trade, reflecting comparative advantage. Clearly, the capital-
abundant country would be a net exporter of capital-intensive manufactures and
a net importer of labor-intensive agricultural goods. Thus it has been shown
via this model that under conditions of monopolistic competition long run
equilibrium in international trade can be established:[2] internal economies of
scale in manufacturing with differentiated products can serve as an independent
motivation for foreign trade, furnishing extra gains from trade over those
brought about by comparative advantage. However, while the new literature has

demonstrated how external and internal economies of scale can induce intraindustry trade in manufactures and, by implication, in many forms of assets and services, whether or not the specific explanatory features of these models are a satisfactory first approximation of reality in regard to the trade in manufactures that has actually occurred in recent decades must await systematic and comprehensive empirical investigation.

As regards intertemporal gains from trade through the exchange of goods for assets, the new literature on international finance has become increasingly concerned with the determinants of real income, and the intertemporal allocation of consumption in open economies significantly linked to world trade and payments. As compared with earlier models the fundamental parameters of which were extremely time-specific both with respect to economic structures and government policies--often providing conclusions that were soon shown to be erroneous out-of-sample--the more recent research has been based on much improved macroeconomics. This research has concentrated on open-economy models of demand and supply functions derived from seemingly relevant optimal rules of maximizing firms and households. Specifically, it has been shown that to achieve an intertemporal optimal current-account deficit, the analysis must specify the economy's real opportunities for shifting consumption and investment over time. The technological, market, and government policies for the relevant range of time must be specified. Fundamentally, the analysis entails the intertemporal public and private budget constraints that specify the terms on which an economy can borrow and lend abroad. In this way the analysis illuminates the links between these budget constraints and the current account. As authors have shown, an important implication of this analysis is that external balance may be defined, roughly, as a current account which enables a country to maintain the highest possible, steady consumption level consistent with an economy's expected intertemporal budget constraints.[3] Other goals, of course, may be set. Temporary shocks may approximately be offset by temporary current-account deficits, while temporary surpluses may be an approximate response to temporary favorable shocks. Permanent shocks, however, would require adjustments in "economic fundamentals" to current-account balances. Accordingly, the analysis points the way for dealing with path-dependent equilibria or disequilibria in current accounts.

An important exceptional conclusion also is derived from this analysis: if a country is large enough economically to affect the relative real interest rates and terms of trade, the normative guidelines offered by the maximizing-intertemporal utility approach would not be directly applicable to policy formation. And the government in question would, instead, have to condition its actions on the conjectural responses of other governments. As cogently put:

"A Nash-Cournot equilibrium, in which each government maximizes over policy settings taking as given the policies of other governments, will in general be Pareto-inefficient from a global viewpoint. When governments recognize their policy interdependence, welfare in each country can be improved through policy cooperation. The practical difficulty lies in the negotiation process through which all parties agree to choose a particular point on the world contract curve." [4]

This intertemporal analysis of external balance, however, has given insufficient emphasis to the asymmetries of countries; it assumes a world in

which governments can borrow unlimited sums in the world capital markets subject
only to their intertemporal budget constraints. In reality, only a few
countries come close to approximating these conditions, setting serious limits
to the optimizing-intertemporal-utility models.

Nonetheless, changing conceptions about the prudent proportion of current-
account balances to GNP did take place during the 1980s. Many governments
adopted policies to prevent their current-account balances from becoming so
negative that their economies might become destablized by policies of creditors,
or so positive that their trading partners would become unable to repay their
foreign debts. A confluence of historical conditions and advances in
economic theory brought about, as will soon be noted, significant contributions
on the relationships between the gains-from-trade and different forms of
financial risk, industrial policy, and exchange-rate systems for different
economies.

World trade in asssets for assets has grown at a phenomenal rate in the
last few decades, and the following normative rule of economics has generally
been applied to it: For the variance of a portfolio's net returns to be
minimized subject to achieving a given average rate of return, the best
investment policy is to diversify holdings, or the maximization of average
returns subject to a given variance, will tend to lead to the same result.
Applied globally, authors have emphasized that portfolio diversification is a
basic motive for international asset trade since, theoretically, all
participants in it could gain through the exchange of different degrees of
risky assets. The gains of such trade would take the form of reducing the
riskiness of each country's income and wealth. An original simple model has
been developed illustrating that for a world of two exchange economies with

equal international risk-sharing, consumption levels can be perfectly correlated internationally without current-account imbalances ever taking place.[5] The problem of external balance never arises in this idealized setting because the contingency of risk regarding the consumption levels is exactly met by the financial returns from the portfolio diversification. As would be expected from historic, legal, and information criteria, the extent of international portfolio diversification of the major world economies is, in fact, very much smaller than plausible financial models of contemporary risk conditions would indicate. As a result, the recent literature has devoted attention to the means of dealing with unpredictable financial contingencies that require a longer period of adjustment than had been customarily anticipated.

In the 1980s, larger current-account imbalances of the major industrial countries and debt crises of the heavy indebted LDCs called attention to the dichotomy between the new theorizing on external balance and the state of international portfolio diversification. For countries with well-developed international financial markets, authors have suggested that the traditional way of holding precautionary foreign reserves to finance unexpected current-account deficits--including IMF facilities--should be supplemented by governments holding a larger volume of diversified foreign assets that could be enlarged or reduced, respectively, in accordance with the state of their current accounts.[6] With a few important exceptions, a typical loan contract between banks and developed, or creditworthy developing, countries has been indexed only to the London Inter-Bank Offered Rate (LIBOR), but not to other factors that might alter the borrower's ability to repay. Many developing countries, furthermore, have faced binding credit restraints affected by the probability of sovereign

debt default. Authors have therefore explicitly analyzed the issue of sovereign
debt repudiation. Initially, it was hypothesized that a sovereign debtor would
default whenever the present discounted benefit of doing so would exceed the
present discounted cost.[7] Accordingly, sovereign borrowers would find themselves
credit-rationed; they would be unable to borrow in international markets as much
as would normally be optimal at the going rate of interest. The changing meaning
of external balance, therefore, required analysis incorporating, inter alia, more
complex prospects of default. By the end of the 1980s, with insignificant
exceptions, a professional consensus appears to have emerged on the basis of
both theoretical foundations and political realities that, for the improved
performance of the major industrial countries and the heavily indebted LDCs,
various forms of debt relief were indispensable. In effect, the policy
proposals called for the ex-post indexation of debt contracts to adverse
contingencies that had not been entirely under the debtor's control.

New conclusions have appeared on the connections between different exchange
rate systems, sterilized intervention in international financial markets, and
the gains from trade. In the 1980s, considerable volatility of floating
exchange rates among key industrial countries does not appear to have had a
significant effect on the trend growth rate of their total foreign trade.[8]
Floating rates, furthermore, helped to prevent international financial crises
from transmitting injurious economic effects on domestic output and employment.
Hence most industrial countries eschewed the worst elements of any exchange
rate system: rigid rates that become seriously overvalued. No exchange rate
system can work well, however, under conditions of macroeconomic instability
and breakdown of multinational cooperation such as had occurred during most of
the 1980s. Understandably, floating rates did not prevent major industrial

countries from having large imbalances in their current accounts. Nor did
floating rates play a major role in restoring such equilibrium in the medium
term. For many governments the removal of responsibility to maintain reasonably
stable exchange rates, in effect, also removed the last bulwark for controlling
inflation. [9] Studies have shown that the hybrid exchange rate mechanism which
has been adopted by most members of the European Monetary System--fairly stable
rates among the members and floating rates with the rest of the world--has worked
more successfully than had been generally anticipated. To date, these countries
have pursued more disinflationary policies than heretofore. This has been at
the cost of greater flexibility in their short term rates of interest, but
fluctuations in their long term rates of interest do not appear to have been
affected. Their competitiveness vis a vis the rest of the world has substantially
improved, with attendant improvement in their gains from trade. [10]

Critical work also has appeared on the relationships between exchange
rate fluctuations and sterilized intervention in the domestic money market.
The aim has been to determine econometric causality and to examine whether
central banks have been able to influence exchange rates by altering the supply
of domestic and foreign assets while sterilizing the impact on domestic monetary
aggregates. Generally, the results have been negative; but recent research
has shown that the Deutsche Bundesbank has had considerable success in dampening
exchange rate volatility in the short term. [11]

The empirical evidence is mixed about the foreign-exchange market's
record in communicating appropriate price signals to international traders and
investors. Econometric tests on the interest parity condition appear to
suggest that the market ignores readily available information in setting exchange

rates, a questionable presumption. Since the interest parity theory ignores
risk aversion and the resulting risk premiums, it appears more likely that the
theory is an oversimplification of reality. Attempts to model risk factors have
not been very successful. Tests of excessive exchange rate volatility also have
reached a mixed verdict on the foreign exchange market performance.[12] Nonetheless,
the literature cited marks important advances in theory and measurement. The
relationships between monetary and real variables have attained greater
attention, empirical exchange rate modelling has been substantially improved, a
broader and more relevant framework has been developed on the problem of
international lending in the presence of default risk, as well as on
international macroeconomic coordination.[13] A professional consensus appears to
have emerged that severe limits on exchange rate flexibility for most countries
are unlikely to be reinstated in the foreseeable future. It would appear most
likely that the world will continue to experience different groups of countries
with different degrees of exchange rate flexibility. Notwithstanding the
possibility of exceptional cases, the most convincing conclusion appears to be
that increased economic coordination among policy makers   in the industrial
countries would improve the performance of floating exchange rates. As for the
European Monetary System, in the longer term greater credibility and commitment
to the goals of monetary and fiscal coordination are likely to improve the
performance of their reasonably stable exchange rate mechanism. The theoretical
and empirical studies seem to suggest that, for open economies, such long term
developments would have a positive impact on the relations between exchange-rate
systems and the gains from trade.

Unusually high levels of unemployment in most countries of Western Europe
during the 1980s induced new analysis of macroeconomic adjustment in open

economies, with implications to gains from commodity trade, direct foreign investment, and international financial assets. Provisional research was conducted on wage and price rigidities as they applied to the fix-price disequilibrium approach to macroeconomics.[14] New models were developed to analyze the effects of devaluation, quantitative trade restrictions, and the transfer problem: the incorporation of an explicit treatment of effective demand could radically transform conventional conclusions on the effects of policy intervention, say such as the response of the trade balance to an exchange rate variation. The results, it was shown, are contingent on whether the labor market is characterized by excess supply and the commodity market by excess demand, or conversely.[15] The model has been extended to include the existence of uncertainty, engendered by exchange rate volatility, when investment decisions are made on entering into or exit from foreign markets.[16] An improved framework has thus been constructed for research on international trade and industrial organization within which the welfare effects of competition in the presence of product differentiation could be examined. This has led, in turn, to the analysis of strategic competition between two countries when more than one strategic variable is taken into account.[17]

An interrelated literature on strategic industrial policy related to gains from trade has clarified several theoretical issues but, to date, has brought about adversarial debate rather than a solid foundation for policy formulation. Subsidizing the export of a commodity produced under increasing returns to scale, it has been shown, could enhance a country's welfare: for excluding retaliation, a strategic industrial policy of this kind could result in shifting oligopolistic profits from foreign to domestic firms.[18] In the case examined by the authors, the social return by expanding output of the subsidized industry would exceed the private return, raising the gains from trade. However, this argument locates the "market failure" that justifies government intervention primarily in the existence of imperfect competition, few firms and excess profits. The success of the policy rests on such key conditions as the subsidy having the effect of raising profits of domestic firms by more than the subsidy payment itself because of its deterrent effect on foreign competition. In a general equilibrium framework, it has been pointed out, rather than in a partial-equilibrium one with much unemployment, subsidies would divert resources from the non-subsidized industries, raising costs and lowering profits in those industries, with indeterminate effects on the nation's total profits.[19]

Another branch of research has continued to generalize the literature on the relations between variations in terms of trade, distortions, and welfare optimization. Contrary to previous conclusions, it has been shown that, under more general assumptions than usually postulated, a price shock raising the cost of an intermediate input (such as oil) may lead to an appreciation of the exchange rate (of an oil importing country) rather than a depreciation--both in the short run and in the long.[20] Moreover, the oil importing country is likely to occasion a current account surplus rather than a deficit. The article concludes: "The terms of trade between foreign and domestic finished goods always improve in the long run."[21] Since the author of this article has had a significant influence on the advance of modelling away from the partial approach that characterized models of the late 1970s toward more general equilibrium analysis, it warrants particular attention. The analysis is carried out in the framework of general equilibrium markets for goods and assets in an open economy with a floating exchange rate. An important objective is to consider the determinants of the stationary-state stock of foreign assets, based on the endogenous time-preference notion as applied to gains-from-trade problems. It is assumed that the nominal wage and the domestic-currency price of national output are perfectly flexible; they adjust instantaneously to ensure both full employment and goods-market equilibrium. The economy's sustainable utility level, it is postulated, is the constant level of utility it could enjoy forever by spending all its income but nothing more. It is assumed that economic agents possess perfect foresight concerning the time path of the exchange rate, so that expected and actual variations in the exchange rate coincide. After analyzing the effects of the price rise on the economy's real equilibrium, a dynamic model is employed to examine the following issues: the impact of the price disturbance, the dynamics of the exchange rate under perfect foresight, and the transition to stationary-state equilibrium.

Since it is assumed that the economy must return eventually to its assumed utility level, it follows that, at the initial terms of trade, demand for home goods would be unchanged. In the short term, however, home output following the price shock would be lower: hence the initial terms of trade would be inconsistent with long-run equilibrium. Therefore, when the assumed sustainable utility at first falls, in order for the economy to return to its stationary utility level, under the postulated conditions, the result would be achieved by accumulating claims on foreigners. "This process," it is explained, "augments both the stationary-state inflow of interest payments and stationary-state spending, increasing sustainable utility through a direct service-account effect and an induced [heightened] terms of trade effect." [22] Theoretically, the possibility

of such a long-term equilibrium effect is incontrovertible. The article well
demonstrates the partial, particular results of previous analysis and formulates
a more general set of alternative solutions. This represents an important
analytical advance, but the predictive power of more general equilibrium analysis,
based on very special assumptions, is not necessarily more credible for a given
long-range period of time than the less satisfactory, more partial analysis. The
cogency of the different possible solutions, it would appear, depends on the
relevance of the assumptions over time and on the results of empirical
investigation. [23]

Another article reexamined the view that a deterioration in the terms of
trade which lowers real income would, along Keynesian lines, necessarily lower
saving, raise the domestic-goods value of aggregate spending, and bring about
a current account deficit.[24] The analysis describes an economy in which households
consume "a nonproduced exportable good and an imported foreign good, face
given terms of trade, and maximize an integral of discounted instantaneous utilities
over an infinite horizon by optimally allocating income each moment between
current consumption and the accumulation of real claims on foreigners."[25] It is
shown that an unanticipated permanent worsening of the terms of trade occasions
a surplus rather than a deficit in the current account, implying that when net
claims on future units of the foreign goods are zero--so that the Laursen-Metzler
assumption of complete specialization in production is valid--aggregate spending
measured in units of the domestic good would fall rather than rise. That is,
the economy would choose a transition path that allows it in the long run to

obtain its original utility level, and this implies that the long-run utility
level must rise. Since the current account must eventually be in balance, and
domestic spending measured in home goods cannot be higher in the new stationary-
state unless income is higher as well, a rise in income can be accomplished
only through the accumulation of interest-earning claims on foreigners. Hence,
the terms-of-trade shift leaves the domestic-goods value of output unchanged,
and so the required surplus must be accommodated, in the case of perfect capital
markets, by a fall in the domestic-goods value of expenditure.[26] An unanticipated
change in real income, the author argues, conveys new information and so
dictates a revision of the previous lifetime consumption plan. While it is
possible that, as Keynes and Laursen-Metzler assumed, the subsequent expenditure
path may be smoothed, a sharp initial reduction in spending cannot be ruled out.
It is precisely such a discontinuous expenditure shift that would give rise to
a current account surplus. Furthermore, in examining another case, the author
shows that a positive expenditure response could result from a sufficiently
large endowment of claims on the foreign good.[27] Therefore, although the
Laursen-Metzler prediction concerning spending is in this instance verified,
"the emergence of a deficit remains impossible." [28]

This conclusion, the author claims, has relevance to concrete policy
issues such as the impact of oil shocks on the current-account adjustment
problems of industrial countries. He believes that the conclusions of his
analysis are more important to "permanent" terms of trade shocks whereas the
Laursen-Metzler conclusions would be more pertinent to discussions of cyclical
phenomenon.[29] Significant as this analysis may be, it concentrates on the effects
of a permanent terms of trade deterioration on an economy "peopled by infinitely

lived, utility maximizing families."[30] It is in the context of explicit,
intertemporal optimization that he finds the well-known Laursen-Metzler
relationship, which predicts a decline in saving and thus a current account
deficit to be invalid. Contrariwise, in his paper, the deterioration in the
terms of trade leads to a current account surplus as households acquire
interest-bearing claims on foreigners in order to restore their stationary-
state utility to its original level, entailing a fall in the home-good value
of spending when the initial net bond holdings are zero. As the author himself
states, his conclusions are based on "a particular set of assumptions concerning
preferences and the opportunities for transforming present utility into future
utility.[31] Indeed, the intertemporal transformation possibilities assumed by
him differ from those assumed by Laursen-Metzler. Considering the specifications
of both sets of analyses, the relevance of economic projections based on them
would depend, of course, on their correspondence to reality, the conditions
of which may, or may not, approximate more closely to those of long-run
equilibrium or cyclical theorizing. In both these respects, again, the state
of our knowledge calls for systematic, empirical work.

Similarly, authors have reexamined the role of subsidies in the gains
from trade and have derived new conclusions.[32] According to the standard
two-good trade model, export subsidies always lower a country's welfare, since
they lead to a deterioration in its terms of trade. But the new research has
demonstrated that, in a trade model with more than two goods, a certain type
of export-subsidy policy may improve a country's terms of trade and its
economic welfare. Moreover, part of the analysis has been conducted under the
assumptions of perfect competition and complete price flexibility. Subsidizing

exports, in the standard two-good model, it is pointed out, is equivalent to
a uniform export subsidy in a many-good trade model, because a uniform subsidy
on all exported goods lowers or, at best, does not alter the country's terms
of trade. If export subsidies are not uniform, however, this conclusion
does not necessarily hold. In simplest terms, the argument is as follows.

The authors define "marginal goods" as those which would be exported by
the country in question in very small amounts, or not at all, under free trade.
These exports can be promoted, however, through the use of export subsidies:
for, thereby, it is assumed that the country will expand the exportation of
these goods and cause a contraction of their supply by competitors in world
markets. In a continuum-of-goods model, it is shown, that export subsidies
of this kind can have the effect of improving the country's terms of trade
and its economic welfare. Assuming no retaliation, consider a country
exporting three goods, I, II, and III, and the government subsidizes the
exports of only one of these goods ("marginal good" II). Therefore, the
external relative price of good II in terms of the other goods falls. But
this does not necessarily imply that the country's overall terms of trade
deteriorate. "Quite possibly," the authors write, "the relative price of the
other export goods in terms of the import good will rise."[33] Because, the
external price of good II falls relative to the price of good I, but it may
remain relatively stable to the price of good III. For the relative price of
good I, a nonmarginal good of the home country, and assumed to be a
complement of good II, rises in price in terms of good III. This follows,
primarily, from the shift in foreign factors of production from the marginal
good II industry to the good III industry, bringing about a rise in the
output of good III and a fall in its relative price. Therein centers the

mechanism through which export subsidies on marginal goods may improve the country's terms of trade.[34]

The authors of this article note that it "is not easy,"[35] in practice to select the types of export subsidy that would actually improve the country's terms of trade and gains from trade. Even in theory, small differences in the assumptions upon which these arguments are based may result in strikingly different conclusions. In practice, governments would require more foresight and information than they usually possess for the arguments to be widely applicable.

Nonetheless, the aforementioned literature has had a strong influence on policy discussions, providing support for so-called "managed trade." It has been shown, precisely, that it could be to a country's economic advantage to impose countervailing duties on imports from foreign countries subsidizing their exports, or to relax certain domestic anti-trust activities as a means of counteracting foreign subsidization.[36] Most international trade theorists, however, including those who have developed these models, do not adhere to the more general restrictions of managed trade. Indeed, differentiating between partial and general analysis, authors have applied their theorizing to conditions under which freer trade is Pareto improving when the standard assumptions of feasible lump-sum transfers are eliminated; whereas previous formulations of the proposition have been shown to be less satisfactory.[37] The techniques used have also been applied to reexamine the relationship between factor endowments and commodity trade, leading to robust conclusions on the extent to which the H-O-S model carried over to a multi-product, multi-factor setting. An important objective of this work has been to generalize the range

of assumptions concerning patterns of demand and supply under which gains from
international trade can be precisely analyzed. The literature has had the
effect of broadening the analysis of foreign trade under increasingly relevant
assumptions about the structure of production, thereby endogenizing the stage
at which a good-in-process is traded internationally. As resource endowments may
effect the determinants of international trade, an expanding volume of trade and
investment, in turn, may significantly change a country's resource endowment;
the newly emerging pattern of trade and related commercial policies in both
countries can quickly shift the margin of comparative advantage and competitiveness
in a vertical production framework.

Thus the relation between international trade theory and industrial
organization theory has been among the most important advances of recent
theoretical literature. Applications have been made to general equilibrium
analysis as well as to applied fields, such as the relation between strategic
industrial policy and commercial policy; commitment analysis as related to
credibility of government macroeconomic policies; monetary and fiscal coordination
policies conducted in an environment of oligopolistic competition. These theoretical
advances all have indirect implications for gains-from-trade theory, since policies
based on them may seriously affect the structure, volume, direction, and terms of
trade. Moreover, gains from trade also may be seriously affected by entry and
exit deterrents, a problem of firms being able to maintain a credible commitment
to a price low enough to deter potential foreign rivals from entering the industry.
Contrariwise, firms may face conditions under which commitments may not be
feasible, and, if made, are not credible. Important contributions have recently
been made examining such alternative conditions. Provocative, though as yet
indefinite, contributions also have been made on the possible effects of
international economic coordination of fiscal and monetary policies under various

conditions. The analysis has been applied to varying exchange rate mechanisms and their effects on the gains from trade, demonstrating the importance in this field of feasible commitment and distinguishing between feasible and infeasible stratgegies. [38]

Though the analogy between domestic taxes and tariff barriers has long been recognized, it has recently been extended to derive optimal configurations under different assumptions regarding mobility of factors and products. For example, the literature has generalized the previous treatment of the welfare consequences of trade policy when lump-sum taxes are precluded and redistribution can be accomplished only through distorting factor and commodity taxes. The international trade literature on the welfare effects of monopolistic commercial policies, including the effects of commercial relations in non-cooperative equilibrium, apply also to tax policies when countries engage in international economic transactions. The applications are cogent to problems of economic growth and variations in terms of trade. When the analysis has been modeled for developed countries, or newly developing countries, producing primarily manufactured goods under increasing returns and monopolistic competition, while less developed countries suffer from extremely low rates of growth and productivity of all their industries, previously held conclusions on secularly declining terms of trade and gains from trade of LDCs have been shown to be seriously misleading. In the modern framework, no single standard concept in terms of trade--commodity terms of trade, single factoral terms of trade, or investment terms of trade--is adequate to explain or to project the impact of international trade on the gains from trade, on economic growth, or on the welfare of developing countries.

As noted in our article, a general principle regarding international trade and industrial policy is that policy should be targeted specifically on the activity in which the market distortion, or market failure, has occurred. Understandably, such a policy would seek to subsidize the generation of knowledge that firms cannot appropriate. However, it would be a blunt instrument to provide a general subsidy for a set of industries in which this kind of knowledge is believed to prevail. Technological spillovers are probably the best case one can make intellectually for an active industrial policy. Spillovers of investment in human capital, it has recently been argued, are of a different character than those of investment in physical capital.[39] Though the two forms of investment may in practice be interrelated, the case for or against targeting knowledge-intensive industries, and their potential effects on gains from trade, still awaits incisive analysis.

General equilibrium analysis also has cast serious doubt on the argument according to which the "home country" loses while the "foreign country" gains when responsibility for "voluntary" trade restrictions devolves on the foreign country.[40] As firms compete for a share of the trade-restricting and premium-fetching licenses, lobbying occurs not only among firms participating in the arrangement within each country, but also between firms of the participating countries. The analysis calls for more systematic quantitative research under postulated conditions. Since the H-O-S model is too highly aggregated to explain long-term changes in overall tariff structures, it has been shown how a minority of factor owners can succeed in gaining tariff protection of its industry under majority voting, provided that voting costs are significant.[41] The many-commodity model, with specific factors, seems to be more appropriate in explaining day-to-day attempts by individual

industries or interest groups in gaining tariff protection and thereby
influencing gains from trade and their distribution. While significant
contributions along these lines have been made, it has been suggested that future
research should explore factors such as nonhomothetic tastes, multi-issue
voting, and log-rolling policy formation with the objective of examining the
operational impacts of multi-party systems in the formation of tariff structures.

Time inconsistency, authors have shown, may be an important cause of
trade restrictions and foregone gains from trade.[42] Government's inability to
make credible commitments on freer trade logically leads to a time-consistent
policy for tariff protection. Given a preference for time-consistent policy
formation, it is analytically shown that government would choose a time-
consistent tariff policy over a time-consistent production subsidy. Many
market imperfections, it is also shown, can generate time-inconsistencies
in the implimentation of optimal activist policies. "Whenever this happens,"
the authors conclude, "a government pursuing a discriminatory trade policy
finds itself trapped in a sub-optimal equilibrium. Thus, a commitment to a
simple set of trading rules may often be superior to an activist but
discretionary trade policy." [43]

With emphasis on the widespread phenomenon of rent-seeking contemporary
societies, it has been demonstrated that the welfare cost of quantitative
restrictions equals that of a tariff equivalent plus the value of rents
obtained.[44] Even if the political process were ideal, the creation of these
possibilities for rents establishes the conditions for rent-seeking activities.
If the market mechanism is suspect in the sense that people do not associate
pecuniary rewards with social product, governments usually resort to greater

and greater intervention, thereby increasing the amount of activity to rent-seeking. Accordingly, a political-economic "vicious circle" may develop: people perceive much monopoly gains from the quantitative restrictions, and the market function does not operate in a way compatible with social approval. Hence, further and further government intervention follows, more and more rent-seeking activity, more and more corruption, and skewed income distribution. The author cogently argues that neither the extreme of a "perfect market" with no intervention nor a system of "perfect restrictions" with optimal qualitative and/or quantitative restrictions could ever exist in practice.[45] As restrictions expand, however, "there might be some point along the continuum beyond which the market fails to perform its allocated function to any satisfactory degree."[46] Clearly, under such conditions, rent-seeking activities greatly reduce the potential gains from trade. A model has been constructed to explain rent-seeking activities between producers in both exporting and importing countries. The analysis extends the effects of export cartels to the case of export-import cartels, applying the model to bilateral marketing arrangements between countries in agricultural products.[47]

As for risk bearing and gains from trade, a new article has shown that between two competitive but risky economies with no insurance markets, free trade may be Pareto inferior to no trade.[48] The model is simple enough to illustrate intuitively the role prices play in transferring and sharing risk when there is an incomplete set of markets; it exhibits the resulting inefficiencies in a powerful manner. Fundamentally, the case considered is one in which exporters are assured a stable income before the opening of trade, whereas under free trade and uncertainty, a decline in the price of the exportable and an increase in its output (a demand elasticity, say, of unity) may bring about a reduction of output in the second industry, preventing consumers from gaining as much from the opening of free trade as compared with the loss incurred by producers. While the author recognizes that the assumptions are extremely restrictive, the conclusions may nonetheless be significant; especially for the least developed countries and for the command economies moving toward market-oriented economies. The analysis points to the importance of developing improved futures markets for many primary exports. In a similar vein, another article directs attention to the widespread contemporary phenonemenon whereby via government promotion the volume of trade may be substantially increased but the gains from trade actually lowered, if not entirely eliminated. It is shown by way of rent-seeking arguments and illustrative data that, at times, leading industrial nations have used high price supports and export subsidies to expand the volume of some of their key agricultural exports at the cost not only of careening budgetary outlays and losses from trade, but also of retaliatory action by third parties injuriously affected by a reduction of their agricultural exports in traditionally competitive markets. In seeking economic rents via government protection, it is further averred, the expenditure of corporate time and scarce resources often have the effect of reducing incentives of management to pursue more aggressive marketing of their products abroad and of supporting policies for freer international markets more generally. [49]

As for commodity price stabilization, new work has been done on nonstorable commodities that constitute a large volume of world trade. Models have been developed to demonstrate the effects of buffer-fund schemes based on taxing producers during high-price periods and subsidizing them during low-price periods. Measures designed to replace, or supplement, less appropriate physical storage activities. The research has called attention to the need for combining appropriate buffer-fund schemes and physical-storage facilities that would be partiularly applicable to many agricultural products exported by small and medium sized economies.[50]

Statistical work on gains from trade has primarily analyzed the long-run evidence on the relationship between primary commodity prices, manufactured goods prices, and the terms of trade of developing countries. Authors have reexamined the validity of the original Prebisch-Singer hypothesis in the context of alternative and updated data, and greater levels of disaggregation.[51] It will be recalled that both Prebisch and Singer suggested that the net barter terms of trade (N) for the LDCs would suffer a secular decline due mainly to the asymmetrical effects of productivity growth in the developed versus the less developed regions of the world. Cet. par., a decline in N would be synonymous with a decrease in welfare, a conclusion in accord with classical views of the gains from trade. The recent research has used more satisfactory alternative measures of commodity prices as proxies for LDCs' export prices.[52] The basic version is base-weighted to 1977-79 nonfuel export values (GYCPI). Alternative wieghts to account specifically for LDCs' shares (GYCPI 1) and time-varying weights (GYCPI II) do not yield appreciably different price indexes. Including fuel in the commodity basket (as is done in GYCPI III) does alter the index's time profile substantially, since this index includes petroleum-product prices.

For LDCs' imports, the authors use two proxies: the U.N. manufacturing unit value index (MUV) and the price of U.S. manufactured goods (USMPI). The proxy for the LDCs' net barter terms of trade is hence either of the commodity price indexes divided by MUV or by USMPI. The results do not vary significantly from one to the other, with the exception of GYCPI III divided by USMPI.

Using these data, the authors have found a rate of decline for all primary product prices of 0.5 percent per annum over the period 1900-86, somewhat lower than Prebisch's implicit 0.61 percent. Only when excluding fuels, the weight was 0.6 percent. Hence the authors' assertion that Prebisch's results are confirmed in sign, although not in magnitude.

The authors then conduct two exercises: the first is aggravated by commodity and the second by region. In the first exercise, a wide diversity of experience is revealed. Metals and non-food agricultural products suffered the worst price decline, about 0.8 percent per year. Food products fell 0.3 percent, but within the aggregate food index, tropical beverages (a typical LDC export) experienced a marked improvement, between +0.63 to +0.68 percent, while cereals (an important export during the period examined)of the United States, Canada, and Australia suffered a serious decline of 0.68 percent. This result illustrates the hazards of inferring specific conclusions from highly aggregated data. In the second comparison, across regions, the authors compute partial correlations between regional non-oil terms of trade, and aggregate proxies, such as GYCPI over MUV, and find the correlations substantially less than one, the figures range from 0.28 to 0.57. This is true even for the aggregate non-oil LDCs and for GYCPI over MUV. Moreover, the correlation has lessened over time, in accord with accepted priors: For LDCs' exports have moved substantially into manufactured products, as exemplified by the NIEs. Hence, commonly used commodity terms of trade indexes may not measure well LDCs' terms of trade.

The authors have presented an exhaustive analysis of the LDCs' net barter terms of trade for the period 1900-86. They still have found a long-term secular decline. However, here one theoretical question, with important policy implications, appears relevant: How to accord to the net barter terms of trade an appropriate degree of significance as a measure of the long-term gains from trade? Under classical assumptions of full employment of resources (i.e., being on the economy's production possibility frontier), this measure is appropriate. But in cases, normally common in most LDCs, of improving total factor productivity, the single factoral terms of trade and/or the income terms of trade may be more relevant concepts. Generally, these measures have been unambiguously increasing, even when fuel prices are excluded from the index. Not surprisingly, the authors have found that the net barter terms of trade (as measured by commodity prices versus manufacturing prices) has fallen, but not as rapidly as predicted by Prebisch and Singer. Moreover, the significance of that decline is mitigated by the fact that LDCS' trade patterns do not correspond closely to the "stylized facts" that Prebisch and Singer presented. Modernizing LDCs have been increasing their productivity in both agriculture and manufacturing with an ever larger proportion of their exports comprising higher quality manufactures.

Theoretical advances in the recent literature on contempory and intertemporal gains from trade in goods and services, in human and physical capital, and in international financial assets has not been matched by empirical work.[53] Considering the emphasis that the economics profession has devoted to means of improving the allocation of economic activity on a global scale, to increasing returns to scale and scope, to the growth and extension of freer markets, as well as to other higher-income yielding activities, the need for systematic, comprehensive and continuous measures of the gains from trade, demonstrating their interdependence with commodity, single factoral, and income terms of trade appears to be long overdue.

1. The locus classicus   of these new models of international trade is
    Elhanan Helpman and Paul Krugman, <u>Market Structure and Foreign Trade</u>:
    <u>Increasing Returns, Imperfect Competition, and the International Economy</u>
    (Cambridge: MIT Press, 1985). Since the late 1970s, an extensive
    literature has appeared on the monopolistic-competion model of foreign
    trade and other formal treatments of increasing returns to scale.
    Professor Staffan Burenstan Linder published an early version of the
    view that trade in manufactures among advanced countries reflects forces
    other than comparative advantage. Cf. <u>An Essay on Trade and Transformation</u>
    (New York: John Wiley and Sons, 1961). For excellent formal contributions
    on issues ranging from gains-from-trade theories with increasing returns
    to scale to economic growth and terms of trade under imperfect competition, as
    well as welfare analysis of factor movements and of protection under such
    conditions, see the papers in <u>Monopolistic Competition and International</u>
    <u>Trade</u>, edited by Henryk Kierzkowski (Oxford: Clarendon Press, 1984).

2. For a presentation in excellent textbook form, see Paul R. Krugman and
    Maurice Obstfeld, <u>International Economics: Theory and Policy</u> (Glenview,
    Ill.: Scott, Foresman & Co., 1988), chapter 6, and especially the section
    on "The Gains from Trade," pp. 131-32.

3. For an incisive review of this literature, see Maurice Obstfeld and Alan
    C. Stockman, "Exchange-Rate Dynamics," in <u>Handbook of International</u>
    <u>Economics</u>, vol. 2, edited by Ronald W. Jones and Peter B. Kennan (New
    York: North-Holland Press, 1985), especially pp. 957-973, and references
    cited on pp. 973-977. For a less mathematical presentation,

see Maurice Obstfeld, "International Finance," in <u>The New Palgrave:</u>
<u>A Dictionary of Economics</u>, edited by John Eatwell, Murray Milgate, and
Peter Newman, vol. 2 (London: Macmillan, 1987), pp. 898-906.

4. Maurice Obstfeld, "International Finance," listed in footnote 3, p. 905.

5. For examples, see Paul R. Krugman and Maurice Obstfeld, <u>International</u>
<u>Economics: Theory and Policy</u> (Glenview, Ill.: Scott, Foresman & Co.,
1988), pp. 625-26.

6. See Albert F ishlow, "Alternative Approaches and Solutions to the Debt of
Developing Countries," chapter 29 in this publication and sources
cited therein.

7. J. Eaton and M. Gersovitz, "Debt With Potential Repudiation: Theoretical
and Empirical Aspects," <u>Review of Economic Studies</u> 48 (April 1981),
pp. 289-309

8. See Giovanni, chapter 35 in this publication and, for the earlier period,
Richard N. Cooper, "Flexible Exchange Rates, 1973-1980: How Bad Have
They Really Been?" in <u>The International Monetary System</u> (Cambridge:
The MIT Press, 1987), pp. 103-117.

9. See Dornbusch, chapter 33 in this publication.

10. See Giovanni, "The European Monetary System," chapter 35 in this publication.
For estimates on projected continuing improvements in the gains from
further European integration, see Dornbusch, "Europe 1992: Macroeconomic
Implications," chapter 33 in this publication and sources cited therein.

11. See Kathryn Dominguez and Jeffrey Frankel, "Does Foreign Exchange
Intervention Matter? Disentangling the Portfolio and Expectations
Effects for the Mark," (March 1990, forthcoming).

12. See Jeffrey Frankel, "Monetary and Portfolio-Balance Models of Exchange Rate Determination," chapter 34 in this publication; R. A. Meese and K. Rogoff, "Empirical Exchange Rate Models of the Seventies: Do They Fit Out of Sample? Journal of International Economics, vol. 14, pp. 3–24; and Richard Meese, "Currency Fluctuations in the Post Bretton Woods Era," (forthcoming).

13. For empirical evidence on international market efficiency and international capital markets, see Richard M. Levich, "Empirical Studies of Exchange Rates: Price Behavior, Rate Determination and Market Efficiency," in Handbook of International Economics, vol. 2, edited by Ronald W. Jones and Peter B. Kennan (New York: North-Holland Press, 1985), chapter 19; and Maxwell Watson, Donald Mathieson, Russell Kincaid, David Folkerts-Landau, Klaus Regling, and Caroline Atkinson, International Capital Markets: Developments and Prospects (Washington, D.C.: IMF, January 1988), especially pp. 46–49.

14. For a brief, excellent discussion, see Edmond Malinvaud, Mass Unemployment (Oxford: Basil Blackwell, 1984), pp. 51–66; and for an important original contribution, Robert M. Solow, The Labor Market as a Social Institution (Cambridge: Basil Blackwell, 1990), pp. 28–56, 82–87, and sources cited therein.

15. Avinash Dixit, "Hysteresis, Import Penetration, and Exchange Rate Pass-through," working paper, Princeton, NJ: Princeton University, November 1987.

16. Avinash Dixit, "Entry and Exit Decisions Under Uncertainty," Quarterly Journal of Economics (forthcoming).

17. See Avinash Dixit and Gene Grossman, "Targeted Export Promotion With Several Oligopolistic Industries," Journal of International Economics, vol. See also Avinash Dixit and Joseph E. Stiglitz, "Monopolistic Competition and Optimum Product Diversity,"

18. Itoh and Kiyono, "Welfare-Enhancing Export Subsidies," Journal of Political Economy, vol. 95, no. 1 (February 1987), pp. 115-137.

19. For the first exposition of the case for "strategic" industrial policy, see James A. Brander and Barbara J. Spencer, "International R & D Rivalry and Industrial Strategy," Review of Economic Studies, vol. 50 (1983), pp. 707-722; these authors have also written a seminal article on the potential role of subsidies as a tool of strategic trade policy, see "Export Subsidies and International Market-Share Rivalry," Journal of International Economics, vol. 16 (1985), pp. 83-100; and for an extension of the Brander-Spencer analysis in a more general equilibrium framework, see Avinash Dixit and A. S. Kyle, "The Use of Protection and Subsidies for Entry Promotion and Deterrence," American Economic Review, vol. 75 (1985), pp. 139-152.

20. Maurice Obstfeld, "Intermediate Imports, The Terms of Trade, and The Dynamics of the Exchange Rate and Current Account," Journal of International Economics, vol. 10 (1980), pp. 461–480.

21. Ibid., p. 461, italics added.

22. Ibid., p. 468.

23. In an article on "The Mathematization of Economic Theory," Gerard Debreu cautioned that in the past two decades "economic theory was carried away" by forces which can be explained only partly by the intellectual success of the mathematization; these forces include, "the values imprinted on an economist by his study of mathematics," American Economic Review (March 1991, forthcoming). This fact, I believe, has played a decisive role even in some of the best recent contributions to the theory of international trade.

24. Maurice Obstfeld, "Aggregate Spending and the Terms of Trade: Is There a Laursen-Metzler Effect?" Quarterly Journal of Economics (May 1982), pp. 253–270.

25. Ibid., p. 252.

26. Ibid., p. 262.

27. Ibid., p. 268.

28. Ibid., p. 263.

29. Ibid., p. 269.

30. Ibid., p. 268.

31. Ibid., p. 268.

32. Itoh and Kiyono, "Welfare-Enhancing Export Subsidies," Journal of Political Economy, vol. 95, no. 1 (February 1987), pp. 115–137.

33. Ibid., p. 122.

34. Ibid.

35. Ibid.

36. Cf the papers in Strategic Trade Policy and The New International Economics, ed. Paul R. Krugman (Cambridge: The MIT Press, 1986).

37. Cf. Avinash Dixit, "International Trade Policy for Oligopolistic Industries," Economic Journal, ibid.; "Anti-Dumping and Countervailing Duties Under Oligopoly," European Economic Review, ibid.; Gene Grossman and Avinash Dixit, "Targeted Export Promotion With Several Oligopolistic Industries," Journal of International Economics, ibid.; Avinash Dixit and Victor Norman, "Gains From Trade Without Lump-Sum Compensation," Journal of International Economics, ibid.

38. See Kenneth Rogoff, "The Optimal Degree of Commitment to an Intermediate Target," ibid.

39. See Robert E. Lucas Jr., "On the Mechanics of Economic Development," his Marshall Lecture (Cambridge University, May 1985), Journal of Monetary Economics, vol. 22 (1988), pp. 3-42.

40. Cf. Richard A. Brecher and Jagdish N. Bhagwati, "Voluntary Export Restrictions Versus Import Restrictions: Welfare-Theoretic Comparison," Journal of International Economics (1985), pp. 41-53; Richard Harris, "Why Voluntary Export Restraints are 'Voluntary,'" Canadian Journal of Economics, vol. 18, no. 4 (November 1985), pp. 99-109; and Aryeln Hillman and Henrich W. Ursprung, American Economic Review (September 1988), pp. 729-745.

41. See Wolfgang Mayer, "Endogenous Tariff Formation," American Economic
    Review, vol. 74, no. 5 (December 1984), pp. 970–985.

42. Robert W. Staiger and Guido Tabellini, "Discretionary Trade Policy and
    Excessive Protection," American Economic Review, vol. 77, no. 5
    (December 1987), pp. 823–837.

43. Ibid., p. 836. See Anne O. Krueger, "The Political Economy of the
    Rent-Seeking Society," American Economic Review, vol. 64, no. 3,
    (June 1974), pp. 291–303; and M. Bredahl, A. Schmitz, and J. Hillman,
    "Rent Seeking in International Trade," American Journal of Agricultural
    Economics (1987), pp. 1–16.

45. Ibid., p. 302.

46. Ibid., p. 303.

47. See Andrew Schmitz, Dale Sigurdson, and Otto Doering, "Domestic Foreign
    Policy and the Gains From Trade," American Journal of Agricultural
    Economics, vol. 68, no. 4 (November 1986), pp. 820–827.

48. David M. G. Newbery, "Pareto Inferior Trade," Review of Economic Studies,
    vol. 51, no. 12 (1984), pp. 1–11.

49. Cf. Schmitz, Sigurdson, and Doering, ibid.

50. See G. C. Van Koten and Andrew W. Schmitz, "Commodity Price Stabilization:
    The Price-Uncertainty Case," Canadian Journal of Economics, vol. 17
    (1985), pp. 426–34; and G. C. Van Koten, A. Schmitz, and W. H.
    Furtan, "The Economics of Storing a Non-storable Commodity,"
    Canadian Journal of Economics, vol. 21 (1988), pp. 579–586.

51. See Enzo Grilli and Maw Cheng Yang, Primary Commodity Prices, Manufactured
     Goods Prices, and the Terms of Trade of Developing Countries: What
     the Long Run Shows," The World Bank Economic Review, vol. 2 (1)
     (January 1988) pp. 1–48.

52. Ibid.

53. For references to recent efforts at quantifying modern trade theory,
     in general, see Krugman, chapter 27 in this publication, pp.

Part III

World Food, International Trade, and Agriculture

Schultz
Johnson

THE ALLOCATIVE EFFICIENCY
OF TRADITIONAL AGRICULTURE

Theodore W. Schultz

The economic acumen of people in poor agricultural communities is generally maligned. It is widely held that they save and invest too little of their income in view of what capital earns, that they pay no heed to changes in prices, and that they disregard normal economic incentives at every turn. For these and other reasons, it is frequently said they do badly in using the factors they have. But is this true? The aim of this chapter is to examine the efficiency with which farmers within traditional agriculture allocate the factors at their disposal.

THE ECONOMIC EFFICIENCY HYPOTHESIS

There is, as has already been noted, a large class of poor agricultural communities in which people have been doing the same things for generations. Changes in products and factors have not crowded in on them. For them neither consumption nor production is studded with new gadgets.

Reprinted from "Transforming Traditional Agriculture," pp. 36–52, with permission of Yale University Press, New Haven, Copyright 1964.

The factors of production on which they depend are known through long experience and are in this sense "traditional." While the communities in this class differ appreciably one from another in the quantity of factors they possess, in what they grow, in the arts of cultivation, and culturally, they have one fundamental attribute in common: they have for years not experienced any significant alterations in the state of the arts. This means simply that farmers of this class continue year after year to cultivate the same type of land, sow the same crops, use the same techniques of production, and bring the same skills to bear in agricultural production. To examine the allocative behavior of these farmers, the following hypothesis is proposed:

> *There are comparatively few significant inefficiencies in the allocation of the factors of production in traditional agriculture.*

The factors of production under these circumstances consist of traditional factors, and the hypothesis is restricted to those factors at the disposal of the people of a particular community. It should be made clear that not all poor agricultural communities have the economic attributes of traditional agriculture. Some are excluded on the ground that they have been subject to change. Any community that has experienced a significant alteration to which it has not had time to adjust fully is excluded. When a new road or railroad is built, as a rule it takes some years for the communities affected to adapt to it. The economic routine of the affected communities is also disturbed by a new large dam, irrigation canals, structures to control floods and to reduce soil erosion. A serious adversity of nature—a flood or a drought followed by famine—can be a source of disequilibrium. Some poor agricultural communities must be excluded because they have been subject to large political changes, for example by partition, by recruitment of many men into the armed services, or by the destruction of both human and nonhuman resources by war. Large changes in relative prices of products because of outside developments affecting the terms of trade can also upset the quiet economic life of particular communities. In modern times, the most pervasive force disturbing the equilibrium of agricultural communities is the advance in knowledge useful in agricultural production. Any poor agricultural community that is adjusting its production to one or more of these circumstances is excluded from traditional agriculture to which the *efficient but poor hypothesis* applies. The fact that particular communities are excluded because they are making major adjustments in production does not imply that they are inherently inefficient in making the adjustments. The test in that case, however, is different.

Whether one wishes to test or to examine the implications of the proposed hypothesis, it will be necessary to distinguish between an efficient allocation of the stock of factors devoted to current production and an optimum rate of investment to increase the stock of such factors. It will be convenient at this stage, in working with this hypothesis, to assume that the rate of return to investment is given and, whether the rate is low or high, that the total stock of factors can be increased only a little per year. Accordingly, the rate of return can be either low or high, or, if one prefers, the price of additional income streams can be either dear or cheap. The hypothesis at this point pertains only to the allocation of the existing factors in current agricultural production, with the prevailing rate of return to investment given. The question of investment will be considered later.

It may be helpful to mention a few of the implications of

the hypothesis. The principal implication is of course that no appreciable increase in agricultural production is to be had by reallocating the factors at the disposal of farmers who are bound by traditional agriculture. It follows, therefore, that the combination of crops grown, the number of times and depth of cultivation, the time of planting, watering, and harvesting, the combination of hand tools, ditches to carry water to the fields, draft animals and simple equipment—are all made with a fine regard for marginal costs and returns. Implied also is that significant indivisibilities will not show their ugly heads. Product and factor prices will reveal themselves as flexible. Another implication is that an outside expert, however skilled he may be in farm management, will not discover any major inefficiency in the allocation of factors. To the extent that any of these implications are contrary to the observable and relevant facts, the hypothesis here proposed would be under a cloud of doubt.

Mindful of what an outside expert can usefully do that goes beyond a reallocation of existing factors, it must be underscored that in testing this hypothesis it is not permissible to alter the technical properties of the factors of production at the disposal of the community. Nor is it permissible to provide new useful knowledge about superior factors that exist in other communities, that is, provide such knowledge at a cost that would be less than it was formerly. Doing so would alter the costs and the return to the search for information pertaining to alternative economic opportunities. Obviously, the introduction of better varieties of seeds and other technically superior inputs by the expert is precluded in making this test. If the outside expert were successful in these respects, he would alter the established equilibrium that may otherwise have characterized the economic activities of the community being investigated.

Still another implication of this hypothesis is that no productive factor remains unemployed. Each parcel of land is used that can make a net contribution to production, given the existing state of the arts and other available factors. So are irrigation ditches, draft animals, and other reproducible forms of capital. Also, each laborer who wishes and who is capable of doing some useful work is employed. It is of course possible to conceive of exotic technical conditions in agriculture that preclude "full" employment. Workers conceivably could become so numerous as to be in each other's way. There could be indivisibilities in factors of production. But these seem to be paper tigers, for they are not found in this class of agricultural communities. The recent doctrine that agricultural production activities are often such that capable workers contribute nothing to production at the margin—that is, that a part of the agricultural labor force has a marginal productivity of zero value—will be examined in the following chapter. The efficient but poor hypothesis does not imply that the real earnings (production) of labor are not meager. Earnings less than subsistence are not inconsistent with this hypothesis provided there are other sources of income, whether from other factors belonging to workers or from transfers within the family or among families in the community.

In turning to the real world to test the hypothesis here advanced, the main difficulty is the paucity of usable data. The propensity to take any estimates, however weak they may be, and force them into a Cobb-Douglas type of production function, is as a rule a sheer waste of time. Fortunately, some social anthropologists studying particular communities of this type for extended periods have diligently recorded product and factor prices, costs and returns of the major economic activities, and the institutional framework in which

production, consumption, savings, and investment occur.
Two of these studies—one pertaining to a Guatemalan Indian community and another to an agricultural community
in India—are especially useful and relevant. These two
studies will now be examined in relation to the proposed
hypothesis.

PANAJACHEL, GUATEMALA:
VERY POOR BUT EFFICIENT

A classic study by Sol Tax, *Penny Capitalism*,[1]
opens with these words: it is "a society which is 'capitalist'
on a microscopic scale. There are no machines, no factories,
no co-ops or corporations. Every man is his own firm and
works ruggedly for himself. Money there is, in small denomi-
nations; trade there is, with what men carry on their backs;
free entrepreneurs, the impersonal market place, competition—these are in the rural economy." Tax leaves no doubt
that this community is very poor, that it is under strong
competitive behavior, and that its 800 people are making
the most of the factors and techniques of production at their
command.[2]

No one ought to be surprised that the people are very
poor. Tax puts their poverty this way: they "live without
medical aid or drugs, in dirt-floored huts with hardly any
furniture, the light only of the fire that smokes up the room,
or of a pitch-pine torch or a little tin kerosene lamp; the

1. Originally published by the Smithsonian Institution, Institute of
Social Anthropology, Publication No. 16 (Washington, U.S. Government
Printing Office, 1953). Reprinted by the University of Chicago Press,
1963.
2. This study is keyed to data covering the period from 1936 to 1941.
Professor Tax lived in the community on and off from the autumn of
1935 to the spring of 1941 (see his preface).

mortality rate is high; the diet is meager and most people cannot afford more than a half-pound of meat a week. . . . Schools are almost nonexistent; the children cannot be spared from work in the field. . . . Life is mostly hard work."[3] Tax presents many data measuring the consumer goods and the level and cost of living to support this poignant testimony on the poverty of the community.

Competition is present everywhere in the way products and factors are priced. "All household utensils—pottery, grinding stones, baskets, gourds, china, and so on—and practically all household furnishings such as tables and chairs and mats, must be brought in from other towns. So must many articles of wearing apparel, such as material for skirts and cloaks, hats, sandals, blankets, and carrying bags, as well as cotton and thread for weaving the other things. So must most of the essential foodstuffs: the greater part of the corn, all lime, salt and spices, most of the chile, and most of the meat. . . . To get the money they depend upon the sale of agricultural produce . . . . Onions and garlic, a number of fruits, and coffee are the chief commodities produced for sale."[4] Prices are in every respect highly flexible.

Tax goes on to document the fact that the Indian is "above all else an entrepreneur, a business man," always looking for new means of turning a penny. He buys the goods he can afford with a close regard for price in various markets, he calculates with care the value of his labor in producing crops for sale or for home consumption against his working for hire, and he acts accordingly. He rents and pawns parcels of land with a shrewd eye to the return, and he does likewise in acquiring the few producer goods that he buys from others. All of this business, "may be characterized as *a money econ-*

3. Tax, p. 28.
4. Ibid., pp. 11–12.

*omy organized in single households as both consumption
and production units, with a strongly developed market
which tends to be perfectly competitive.*"[5]

The economy has been geared to a stable, virtually stationary, routine pattern. Not that the Indian is not always
looking for new ways to improve his lot. Tax notes that "he
is on the lookout for new and better seeds, fertilizer, ways
of planting." But such improvements come along infrequently, and their effects upon production are exceedingly small.
There was a growing demand by "foreigners" for some shore
land along Lake Atitlan but this development was having
very little effect upon the land Indians used for producing
crops and on which they built their huts. Some buses and
trucks had become available for transport to more distant
towns and they were being used to go to and from markets
in these towns because it was "cheaper" than walking and
carrying the goods. There were more tourists in and about
the lake but these too were having little or no discernible
influence on the community.[6]

All the evidence revealed in the careful documentation
of the behavior of the people in *Penny Capitalism* and in
the many tables showing prices, costs, and returns strongly
supports the inference that the people are remarkably efficient in allocating the factors at their disposal in current
production. There are no significant indivisibilities in
methods of production, none in factors, and none in products.
There is no disguised unemployment, no underemployment
of either men, women, or children old enough to work, and

5. Ibid., p. 13. Italics are from Tax.
6. Professor Tax had occasion to revisit this Indian community in
Guatemala after a lapse of 20 years. The overwhelming impression of
the brief visit was that life and the economy had remained virtually
unchanged.

for the least of them there is no such thing as a zero marginal product. Because even very young children can contribute something of value by working in the field, they cannot be spared the time to go to school. Product and factor prices are flexible. People respond to profit. For them every penny counts.

SENAPUR, INDIA: POOR BUT EFFICIENT

A study by W. David Hopper, "The Economic Organization of a Village in North Central India,"[7] portrays an economy in another part of the world performing as if it too were highly efficient in using the factors at hand. Hopper, like Tax, entered upon his study of this village as an anthropologist. Like Tax, after having lived in the community for a period and having observed its cultural, social, and other characteristics, he decided to concentrate heavily on the economy of the village.

For students of anthropology, there are undoubtedly important cultural and social differences between Senapur, India, and Panajachel, Guatemala.[8] There are also some

7. An unpublished Ph.D. thesis presented at Cornell University, June 1957. The village of Senapur is located on the Ganges Plain. At the time of the study, it comprised 1,046 acres and had a population of about 2,100. Hopper resided in Senapur from October 1953 to February 1955.

8. Senapur, for instance, has a long-established caste system, whereas the Guatemalan community has singular flexibility in the movement of families up and down its social status scale. In Senapur the families of the privileged castes, mainly the Thakur, have perpetuated their wealth, privileges, and social status for many generations. In the Guatemalan community, Tax found marriages cutting across wealth lines and much mobility on the economic and social scale; moreover, the social and economic gap separating the top and the other families has not been substantial. Thus even the varying winds of fortune make for much mobility from one generation to the next as one sees these families in *Penny Capitalism*.

differences in the level of production and consumption. Senapur is not as poor as Panajachel, but by Western standards it is nevertheless poor. Senapur has a school with grades 1 to 5 which until very recently served mainly the more privileged castes. The number of "productive" animals is unbelievably large: 270 milch cows and buffaloes; 480 bullocks to work in the fields. The stock of capital includes irrigation wells, ditches, storage ponds, digging tools, plows, chaff-cutters, and some small equipment. There is more specialization in Senapur than in the Guatemalan community: well-diggers, potters, carpenters, brick-makers, a blacksmith, and others. But for all that Senapur is poor.

Hopper examines with care the factors of production over which the people of Senapur have command. There is a fine set of natural resources characteristic of that part of India, and there is a substantial set of reproducible resources both within this community and outside that also serves its production and consumption activities. He then traces the behavior of the competitive forces as these are revealed through the established product and factor markets.

Hopper summarizes an important part of this study thusly: "An observer in Senapur cannot help but be impressed with the way the village uses its physical resources. The age-old techniques have been refined and sharpened by countless years of experience, and each generation seems to have had its experimenters who added a bit here and changed a practice there, and thus improved the community lore. Rotations, tillage and cultivation practices, seed rates, irrigation techniques, and the ability of the blacksmith and potter to work under handicaps of little power and inferior materials, all attest to a cultural heritage that is richly endowed with empirical wisdom." Hopper then puts this question to himself: "Are the people of Senapur realizing the full economic potential of their physical resources? . . . From the point of view of the villagers the answer must be 'Yes' for in general each man comes close to doing the best that he can with his knowledge and cultural background."[9]

Fortunately, the data that Hopper collected have permitted him to make a rigorous test of the allocative hypothesis under consideration.[10] He made such a test by determining the set of relative prices of products and factors implicit in the allocation decisions revealed in the data. In determining the allocative efficiency of the farmers from the prices implicit in their production activities, Hopper used the price of barley as the numeraire. The implicit prices in terms of barley for each product estimated from factor allocations, with barley at 1.00, are wheat, 1.325; pea, .943; and gram, .828. The implicit price estimates for each factor based on its production use at the average product prices and their standard errors are as follows.[11]

	Barley	Wheat	Pea	Gram	Average
Average Price	1.00	1.325	.943	.828	
Price of:	Used in Production of:				
Land (acres)	4.416	4.029	4.405	4.845	4.424
	(1.056)	(.855)	(1.185)	(.857)	
Bullock time	.0696	.0716	.0820	.0834	.0774
(hours)	(.0116)	(.0098)	(.0180)	(.0156)	
Labour (hours)	.0086	.0097	.0087	.0076	.0086
	(.0026)	(.0037)	(.0021)	(.0030)	
Irrigation Water	.0355	.0326	.0305	.0315	.0325
(750 gals.)	(.0122)	(.0078)	(.0111)	(.0234)	

9. Hopper, p. 161.

10. W. David Hopper, "Resource Allocation on a Sample of Indian Farms," University of Chicago, Office of Agricultural Economics Research, Paper No. 6104 (April 21, 1961, mimeo.).

11. W. David Hopper, "Allocation Efficiency in Traditional Indian Agriculture," *Journal of Farm Economics* (forthcoming).

From these data and his test, Hopper infers that "there is a remarkably close correspondence between the various price estimates. It would appear that the average allocations made by the sample of farms were efficient within the context of the prevailing technical relationships. There is no evidence that an improvement in economic output could be obtained by altering the present allocations as long as the village relies on traditional resources and technology."

The implicit prices also match closely the market prices of products and factors for which there were market prices. These prices follow:

Product or factor	Relative barley price	Adjusted to the barley price (in rupees)	Actual market price (in rupees)
Barley (md.)	1.00	9.85	9.85
Wheat (md.)	1.325	13.05	14.20
Pea (md.)	.943	9.29	10.40
Gram (md.)	.828	8.16	10.85
Land (acres)	4.424	43.57	8.00 to 30.00 (cash rent only)
Bullock time (hrs.)	.0774	.762	not available
Labor (hrs.)	.0086	.085	.068 (cash and kind only)
Irrigation water (750 gals.)	.0325	.321	not available

The implicit prices of these products, except for gram, match closely the actual market prices. Hopper observes that in the case of gram there is a lagged response under way to a strengthening market for gram; the relative price of gram had been rising for three years prior to the date of Hopper's study. The findings in this important study show that there is a "close approximation between market and implicit prices." The factors of production available to the people of Senapur were allocated efficiently, and the test therefore strongly supports the hypothesis here proposed.

INFERENCES AND IMPLICATIONS

The data pertaining to the allocation of factors for current production in Panajachel and Senapur are consistent with the hypothesis proposed at the outset of this chapter. It is important to note, however, in drawing the inference that there are no significant inefficiencies in the allocation of factors in these two communities, that the concept of factors includes more than land, labor, and capital as these are commonly defined. It also includes the state of the arts, or the techniques of production, that are an integral part of the material capital, skills, and technical knowledge of a people. In other words, factors are not treated by abstracting from the state of the arts. By this all-inclusive concept of factors, the community is poor because the factors on which the economy is dependent are not capable of producing more under existing circumstances. Conversely, under these simplified conditions, the observed poverty is not a consequence of any significant inefficiencies in factor allocation.

Although it is not feasible to show that these two communities are typical of a large class of poor agricultural communities, the assumption that they are seems highly plausible. Moreover, this plausibility is supported by the fact that the hypothesis under consideration appears to be consistent with a wide array of other empirical studies of such communities. The well-known studies of the farm economy of China by

Buck[12] lend support as do the many examples cited by Bauer and Yamey.[13] A comprehensive examination of all such data is, however, beyond the scope of this study.

The economic premises on which the hypothesis rests, and the support it receives empirically, warrant treating it as a proposition likely to be widely useful. As such, it has a number of implications, some already mentioned.

What does illiteracy imply? The fact that people are illiterate does not mean that they are therefore insensitive to the standards set by marginal costs and returns in allocating the factors they have at their disposal. What it does indicate is that the human agent has fewer capabilities than he would have if he had acquired the skills and useful knowledge associated with schooling. Although schooling may increase greatly the productivity of the human agent, it is not a prerequisite to an efficient allocation of the existing stock of factors. The notion that these poor agricultural communities do not have enough competent entrepreneurs to do a satisfactory job in using the factors at hand is in all probability mistaken. In some cases these entrepreneurs may be subject to political or social restraints that give rise to allocative inefficiencies, but the adverse production effects of such restraints are quite another matter.

There is another inference that is contrary to a widely held view, namely that farmers in these communities do not respond to developments that alter the stock of factors at their disposal. This view holds that the farmers do not adjust to changes in relative prices of products and factors.

12. John Lossing Buck, *Chinese Farm Economy* (Chicago, University of Chicago Press, 1930).

13. Peter T. Bauer and Basil S. Yamey, *The Economics of Under-Developed Countries,* a Cambridge Economic Handbook (Chicago, University of Chicago Press, 1957), Ch. VI.

If this is true, it is inconceivable that the community could ever become essentially efficient in factor allocation, except by sheer accident. Both Hopper and Tax, however, are explicit in noting that these farmers do respond. The question may be formulated thusly: if an irrigation canal is constructed or a new and better variety of a particular crop becomes available, do they respond? A pioneering study by Raj Krishna[14] of the supply responses of farmers in the Punjab during the twenties and thirties indicates that the lag in adjustment in producing cotton was about the same as it has been for cotton farmers in the United States. Quite aside from the rate at which they adjust to alterations in economic conditions, however, the important fact at this juncture of the analysis is that they do respond. It therefore follows that whenever such a community has for decades been living a quiet, routine economic life it has long since achieved an essentially efficient allocation of factors at its disposal.

There is one set of estimates based on cross-sectional Cobb-Douglas type production functions which includes six classes of farms in India that appear to show extraordinary inefficiencies in factor allocations. Heady includes these six Indian sets in a list of 32 that covers locations in various parts of the world.[15] The six sets covering farms in India are based presumably on data for the middle 1950s. In these the marginal returns to labor range from .03 to 1.78 for each

14. Raj Krishna, "Farm Supply Response in the Punjab (India-Pakistan): A Case Study of Cotton," (unpublished Ph.D. dissertation, University of Chicago, 1961).

15. Earl O. Heady, "Techniques of Production, Size of Productive Units, and Factor Supply Conditions," Paper presented at the Social Science Research Council Conference on Relations between Agriculture and Economic Growth, Stanford University, Stanford, California, November 11–12, 1960.

1.00 (unit) of labor costs.[16] For land, the range of the marginal returns to costs is even wider, with the lowest at .05 and the highest at 3.60 for 1.00 (unit) of land rental. The most extreme results, however, are those reported for reproducible material capital. For these the marginal returns range from –.85 to 6.97 per 1.00 (unit) of capital costs.

Although Heady mentions the possible limitations that qualify the usefulness of these estimates,[17] they are nevertheless treated as if they could be taken seriously. Hopper's careful examination of the data problem in Senapur, India, makes it abundantly clear that such "monthly wage rates" and "rental returns" to land are most inaccurate. In the case of capital, Heady reveals that the "selection of interest rate for capital is itself a problem,"[18] because it ranges "from 6 to 200 percent." It is no wonder that the results of working with such data are so meaningless. If these agricultural communities in India had been experiencing rapid economic development and were therefore confronted by large changes in factor and product prices to which they had not as yet had time enough to adjust, there would be a logical basis for some inequalities in marginal returns relative to the costs of factors. But no such major developments had taken place in India at that time. It is noteworthy that no logical explanation of the extreme ranges in the estimates cited for

16. In the case of labor, no estimate is shown for wheat farming in Uttar Pradesh, India, undoubtedly the most absurd of the lot, for it is this set that shows a marginal return to land of 2.22 and to capital of 6.97 for each unit (1.00) of input costs.

17. Among these possible limitations, Heady lists "(a) specification bias, (b) aggregation, (c) algebraic form, (d) sampling, and (e) other facets of statistical inference. However, we believe that the data do, even though they represent a small stratum of national agriculture, provide some qualitative types comparisons." P. 35.

18. Heady, "Techniques of Production," p. 35.

the six sets of farming in India is offered. Had one been attempted, the untenable nature of the results would have become apparent.

Still another implication stemming from the proposition that a large class of poor agricultural communities shows comparatively few significant inefficiencies in factor allocation is that competent farm managers, whether national or foreign, cannot show the farmers how to allocate better the existing factors of production. Once again it must be stressed that this implication holds provided these competent experts are restricted in advising farmers to the existing factors, which means that they do not alter the opportunity to increase production by introducing other factors, including knowledge about the availability of such other factors.

Lastly, then, there is the implication that no part of the labor force working in agriculture in these communities has a marginal productivity of zero. But since this particular implication runs counter to a well-established doctrine, the next chapter is devoted to an examination of the basis of this doctrine and the reasons why it is a misleading conception of the economics of labor productivity in poor agricultural communities.

THE ECONOMICS OF THE VALUE OF HUMAN TIME[1]

THEODORE W. SCHULTZ

The difference in the economic value of human time between low- and high-income countries is very large At the time when the foundations of classical economics were established, however, the value of human time throughout Western Europe was exceedingly low. In view of economic changes since then, are corresponding improvements possible for low-income countries? While it is all too convenient to believe that it can be accomplished by law supported by rhetoric, it is clearly not possible to achieve this objective on command by government. Increases in the earnings of labor depend basically on achieving increases in the value productivity of labor. Investment in population quality is one of the important means of doing so. The economic dynamics are, however, exceedingly complex, as is evident in accounting for the increases in the value of human time that have occurred over time in high-income countries.

In the United States, for instance, real earnings per hour of work have risen fivefold since 1900. The upward trends in real wages in industry in France, Germany, Sweden, and the United Kingdom are much like that in the United States, with some notable differences. France and the United Kingdom show no increase between 1900 and 1910, and, as of 1925, the increases show Sweden and the United States substantially ahead of the other three countries (was this a consequence mainly of differences in the effects of the war and its aftermath). Sweden and the United States maintain their advantage over the others up to 1960, with the United Kingdom losing ground in relative terms. Finally, at the end of the 1960s, France and Germany join Sweden and the United States in showing a fourfold and more relative increase in real annual wages in industry over the period from 1900 to 1970, whereas the relative increase for the United Kingdom is slightly less than threefold.

The trend of the deflated natural resource commodity prices over this period was slightly downward, compared to the more than fivefold rise in real hourly wages. In agriculture, the deflated prices of crops declined about one-third, despite various government price supports during parts of this period; the index for livestock closed at the level at which it began. In general, the costs of producing livestock products have been affected more by the increase in the price of human time than have the costs of producing crops. The deflated prices of mineral fuels indicate that whereas the deflated price index for all mineral fuels was about one-fourth less at the end of this period compared to 1900, the price of bituminous coal rose and that of petroleum fell. It is undoubtedly true that the rise in real wages accounts for a good deal of the increase in coal prices.

[1]This is a condensation entirely in the words of the original; all changes were made with author approval.

Reprinted (with author approved deletions) from "Investing in People: The Economics of Population Quality," pp. 59–84, with permission of California University Press, Berkeley, Copyright 1981.

Without a useful theory, there can be no satisfactory analysis of the determinants that account for the changes in relative prices. Since "growth" implies changes over time, the theory that is required could be referred to as a theory of economic growth. But it is fair to say that, as yet, there is no growth theory that is sufficiently comprehensive in specifying the factors and events that determine the changes in relative prices and stocks of resources that occur as a consequence of observable economic behavior, and that are in turn consistent with that behavior.

A simple supply-and-demand approach helps to clarify matters. It is the intercept of the supply of and the demand for human time that reveals the price we observe. Shifts in the supply and demand schedules then account for the recorded increases in this price over time. The key to this pricing problem is in the factors that determine such shifts. We know a good deal about the factors that increase the *supply*, both in terms of the size of the labor force and of the quality attributes of the workers. But this is, at best, a partial picture of the price changes that occur. The nub of the unresolved problem is that we know very little about the factors that shift the demand upward over time so strongly.

In devising an approach to get at the factors that explain the shifts in these two schedules, an all-inclusive concept of capital formation is necessary. In using this concept, it is essential to see the heterogeneity of the various old and new forms of capital and to specify them in sufficient detail to determine not only the substitutions but also the interacting complementarity between these forms of capital. Inasmuch as captial formation entails investment, it is important not to conceal the changes over time in incentives—that is, the anticipated rates of return to be had from alternative investment.

Changes in investment opportunities, events, and human behavior alter the scale of value and the composition of the stock of capital. Alterations that enhance the scope of choices are favorable developments. The various forms of capital differ significantly in their attributes. Natural resources are not reproducible, but structures, equipment, and inventories of commodities and goods are. Human beings are productive agents with the attributes of human capital, and they are also the optimizing agents. In a fundamental sense, human preferences determine what use is made of the various forms of capital. It is noteworthy that in high-income countries the rate at which human capital increases exceeds that of nonhuman capital.

To specify the heterogeneity of capital, it is not sufficient to classify the capital forms as natural resources, reproducible material forms, and human capital, because of the important role that new forms of capital within each of these classes play in altering relative prices (returns) and in shifting supply-and-demand schedules. It will be necessary to make room in this approach to growth and changes in relative prices for the following propositions:

1. The Ricardian principle that an increasing share of national income accrues to land rent (natural resources) needs to be replaced by the proposition that this share tends to decline as a consequence of man-made substitutes for land. A notable example is the creation of hybrid corn, which may be viewed either as a substitute or

as a new input augmenting the yield from land. Plastics and aluminum become substitutes for various metals and wood, and nuclear energy becomes a substitute for fossil fuels. The economics of producing such substitutes (research and development) is still in its infancy, and the prospective output of this sector is subject to the same uncertainty as are other advances in useful knowledge.

2. Some new forms of capital complement other forms of capital in production. A consequence of such complementarity is that particular new forms of material capital increase the demand for particular human skills (a subclass of human capital). These complementary forms of capital need to be identified and included in the analytical model.

3. Making room in economic growth models for changes in relative prices over time is a return to the approach of early classical economics. Since modern macrogrowth models tend to take prices as given (usually fixed), the inclusion of relative prices and their function is a radical analytical proposition. Be that as it may, relative prices, which include the alternative rates of return on investment, are the mainspring that drives the economic system. If this mainspring did not exist, we would have to invent it by appealing to shadow prices.

The shifts in demand in favor of productive services of labor that contribute to increases in the price of human time are, in large part, a consequence of the complementarity proposed in the second of these propositions. But the state of the art of economics does not as yet permit us to identify and determine the effects of this complementarity on the demand for labor.

The price and income effects of increases in the value of human time include enlargement of institutional protection of the rights of workers, favoring human capital relative to property rights; increases in the value added by labor, relative to that added by materials in production; a decline in hours worked; increases in labor's share of national income; a decline in fertility; and the high rate at which human capital increases. The human agent becomes ever more a capitalist by virtue of his personal human capital, and he seeks political support to protect the value of that capital. The rise in the value of human time makes new demands on institutions. Some political and legal institutions are especially subject to these demands. What we observe is that these institutions respond in many ways. The legal rights of labor are enlarged and in the process some of of the rights of property are curtailed. The legal rights of tenants are also enhanced. Seniority and safety at work receive increasing protection. The history of national income by type indicates clearly that large changes have occurred over time that parallel, and are associated with, a rise in the real earnings of workers.

By 1970, about ¾ of the official United States national income by type consisted of employee compensation. The remaining one-fourth is classified as proprietors' income, rental income, net interest, and corporate profits. These four classes of "property" income include considerable earnings that accrue to human agents for the productive time they devote to self-employed work and to the management of their property assets. A conservative estimate of the aggregate contribution of human agents in 1970, measured by employee compensation, plus self-employment earnings and management of assets within the domain of the market sector, was fully $\frac{4}{5}$ of the value of the production accounted for in national income.

The price and income effects of hourly earnings explain a wide array of changes in the allocation of time. When expected future earnings from more education rise, the response of youth is to postpone work-for-pay in order to devote more years to education. The advantage of youth in acquiring additional education is twofold: the wages foregone are lower than they would be later, and there are more years ahead to cash in on the anticipated higher earnings and satisfactions. As wages increase, people who earn their income by working can afford to retire at an earlier age because of the larger retirement income that they are able to accumulate. This is counterbalanced by the improvement in health that is purchased, which extends the years that individuals may opt to work. The rise in the value of the time of women is an incentive to substitute various forms of physical capital in household production, and, inasmuch as children are labor-intensive for women, the demand for children is reduced, and an increasing part of women's time is allocated to the labor market.

Economic theory has in recent years been extended to explain the accumulation of human capital, and the price and income effects of this form of capital. The theory has led to important new approaches in bringing economics to bear on human behavior in both developed and developing countries. Throughout most of the world, labor still earns a pittance. In a few countries, however, the value of the time of working people is exceedingly high. The high price of human time that characterizes these exceptional countries is, from the viewpoint of economic history, a recent development. In these countries, the increases in real wages and salaries represent gains in economic welfare that are the most significant achievement of their economic growth. Much less time is allocated to work-for-pay. Most of the work is no longer hard physically. Ever more skills are demanded, and the supply response of skills is strong and clear. But the increases in demand are still concealed in the complementarity between the various new forms of capital.

The historical fact is that, despite the vast accumulation of capital, the real rate of return on investment has not diminished over time. There has been much aimless wandering in analyzing growth that could have been avoided had the perceptions of Alfred Marshall been heeded.

> Capital consists in a great part of knowledge and organization: knowledge is the most powerful engine of production. . . . The distinction between public and private property in knowledge and organization is of great and growing importance: in some respects of more importance than that between public and private property in material things.[1]

Public and private investment in human capital and in useful knowledge are a large part of the story in accounting for the increases in the value of human time.

[1]Alfred Marshall, *Principles of Economics,* 8th ed. (New York: Macmillan, 1920), bk. 4, pp. 138–39.

The economics of my Traditional Agriculture and of my approach to The Value of Human Time have fared well in a wide array of empirical studies. A quarter of a century has elapsed since Traditional Agriculture was written. A number of additional insights are now evident.

Contrary to classical expectations, agricultural land rent declines as a fraction of national income, as modern economic growth occurs even though population increases. The influence of landlords in national politics also declines.

The fraction of the labor force engaged in agriculture becomes ever smaller indeed, so small that it seems unbelievable. In the U.S., it is down to less than 3 percent and declining. The value of the time that farm people devote to agricultural activities in an open and well integrated national labor market is determined predominantly by the value of time of workers throughout the economy.

Costs of producing food and feed grains per ton decline. Since 1910-14, the real price of these commodities have declined by one-third to one-half. We now know that declines in food grain prices contribute to reducing the inequality in the distribution of personal income.

In countries where the economic functions of markets and of farm entrepreneurs are performed by governments, the gains in agricultural productivity to be had from modernization are in large measure lost as a consequence of allocative inefficiencies. In retrospect, gains in agricultural productivity contribute importantly to economic growth and to the decline in the economic importance of agricultural land.

Continuing with the <u>long view</u> of agriculture and human capital, the modernization of agriculture has become a strong dynamic process. The sources of the remarkable productivity gains on the part of agriculture are no longer a mystery. As yet, however, the economic value of the specialized human capital of agricultural scientists has not received its due. Nor has the value of the education of farmers which enhances their entrepreneurial ability.

The importance of the search for markets is told repeatedly by economic historians. Nation-states, however, here and now pursue policies that distort world trade and impair the gains to be had from international trade. Thus, nation-states reduce specialization, reduce productivity, and reduce economic growth. Much evidence is now at hand which shows that nations pursuing in-ward oriented economic policies, even though they are large nations, are doing poorly. Whereas, an array of small nations pursuing outward oriented policies are doing well in achieving economic growth.

Specialized human capital is an important source of increasing returns. Growth theory that excludes the formation of such human capital is far from adequate. So is growth theory that excludes the contributions of entrepreneurs to growth. These two factors are crucial both for the advance of economic growth and for the explanation of growth experience. On various important issues pertaining to economic progress early economists had comprehensive insights that economists now omit. Smith's division of labor made possible by specialization constrained by the extent of the market, is a fundamental insight. So are Marshall's tendencies to increasing returns.   What is hard to explain is the long silence on the part of economists following Young's classic paper.

Taking the <u>long view</u> human capital is a crucial component in economic modernization and growth. It consists of the abilities and knowledge embodied in people. It calls for investments in population quality.   Incentive to undertake such investments privately and publicly entails specialization, markets and trade.

Anxieties about food, space, energy and other physical properties of the earth are not new. They were expressed cogently at the beginning of the nineteenth century by David Ricardo and T.R. Malthus.   I reject present forebodings that are based predominantly on assessments of the declining physical capacity of the earth because a valid assessment must reckon the abilities of man to deal with changes in the physical properties of the earth. These abilities are ignored in these earthview assessments. Increases in the acquired abilities of people throughout the world and advances in useful knowledge hold the key to future economic productivity and to its contributions to human well-being.

The elaboration of the short view by economists with increasing subtlety, refinement and elegances is nevertheless a structure built on shifting sand. Viner's stand made him a special custodian for society of the <u>long view</u> in economic matters.

THE WORLD FOOD SITUATION: DEVELOPMENTS DURING THE 1970s AND PROSPECTS FOR THE 1980s AND 1990s[1]

D. GALE JOHNSON

INTRODUCTION

The lead sentence in an Associated Press story of November 11, 1979, was "the Third World is moving toward a massive food shortage that could result in 'economic disaster' within 20 years, a United Nations report says."[2] This gloomy projection was a reporter's interpretation of a conference report by the director-general of the Food and Agriculture Organization (FAO) of the United Nations. The report expressed the fear that developing countries would require ever-increasing grain imports and that the cost of these imports would become a burden that many low-income countries could not bear.

Has the world food situation deteriorated during the 1970s? Have the prices of basic foods increased over time? Are the majority of the world's poor eating less and less as time goes by? If the dire predictions concerning the world's food situation, which were so common in 1973 through 1975, had proven to be valid, the answer to each of these questions would be in the affirmative.

But such is not the case. The world food situation did not deteriorate during the 1970s. The prices of basic foodstuffs are low by historical standards. There is no evidence that the world's poor people are eating less well now than they did a decade ago. In fact, on each point the evidence is to the contrary. The 1970s, as did each of the two prior decades, saw an improvement in per capita food supply for the world and in the low-income countries.

In *World Food Problems and Prospects,* published in early 1975, I concluded, "I am cautiously optimistic that the food supply situation of the developing countries will continue to improve over the coming decades. If I had as much confidence in

[1] This is a condensation entirely in the words of the original; all deletions were made with the author's approval.

[2] *Sunday Sun-Times* (Chicago), November 11, 1979. My reading of this United Nations report entitled *Agriculture: Toward 2000* leaves me with a quite different impression than the newspaper article gives. First, the report makes no projections of future events; instead it presents what is likely to occur if recent trends persist and what could be achieved if substantial increases were made in investments in agricultural inputs and research and if appropriate incentives were provided for farmers. To quote from the introduction: "in the study no attempt has been made to forecast or to predict what is likely to happen by the end of the century." Second, there is very little emphasis given to energy. Of course, it is possible that discussion of the report at the conference did emphasize the bleakest possible picture of the future. *Agriculture: Toward 2000* was prepared by the Food and Agriculture Organization (FAO) of the United Nations and presented at the twentieth FAO Conference held in Rome, November 10–29, 1979.

Reprinted from "Contemporary Economic Problems 1980," pp. 301–339, with permission of American Enterprise Institute for Public Policy Research 1980, Washington, D.C., Copyright 1980.

the political process in both the industrial and developing countries as I do in the farmers of the world, I would drop the qualification *cautiously.*"[3] For the 1970s the cautious optimism was justified. Per capita food supplies in the developing countries improved. The improvement, however, was modest, and it was far from uniform. In fact, in Africa, per capita food production declined during the decade, but there were substantial differences in growth of food production within Africa that cannot be attributed primarily to natural conditions.

FOOD SUPPLY AND DEMAND DURING THE 1970s

In the mid-1970s the predominant view was that demand was likely to grow more rapidly than supply and that the real prices of food would quite probably increase rather than decrease from the high levels of 1973 and 1974. A number of reasons were given for the expectation that the food supply situation would deteriorate after the early 1970s. These included the assumption that higher energy prices would greatly increase the price of farm inputs, especially fertilizer; that expanding the cultivated area was no longer a possibility as a significant means of increasing food production; and that the growing use of grain as feed would reduce the food supplies of low-income countries.

It is appropriate to look at what actually happened to per capita food supplies during the 1970s and, especially, after 1972. For all low-income countries (except centrally planned) per capita food production in 1972 was at the 1961–1965 level, a decline from the 1970 index of 106 (1961–1965 = 100). The recovery from the low 1972 level was rapid, and by 1975 the index of per capita food production stood at 107. Further progress occurred through 1978, by which time the index had increased to 110. Preliminary indications, however, indicate a sharp reduction to 106 for 1979. The average index for the last 4 years of the 1970s was 108.2 compared with 101.2 for the same period a decade earlier. The annual growth in per capita food production for the period 1966–1969 to 1976–1979 was approximately 0.7%. This may seem low, but it was higher than the growth rate for the 1960s.

Viewed in terms of the performance of agriculture, the growth of food production during the 1970s in the low-income countries reflects a remarkable performance. For the decade, food production grew at 3.2% annually, compared to 2.0% for the high-income countries. The modest rise in the per capita food production figure was due to the rapid growth in population.

Imports and Food Supply

The consumption of food in a given year is generally not the same as the amount of food produced. The supply actually consumed consists of food produced, changes in stocks, and net trade. We have inadequate data on changes in stocks for the low-income countries. If we are interested, however, in average food consumption for a number of years, changes in stocks have only a limited effect. The major

---

[3]D. Gale Johnson, *World Food Problems and Prospects* (Washington, D.C.: American Enterprise Institute, 1975), p. 81.

source of a difference between food production and food consumption is net trade.

As a group, the low-income countries are net importers of grain. During the 1970s their grain imports increased by 25 million tons to 48 million tons net in 1979–1980. The increase in grain imports would provide about 40 calories per day for more than 2 billion people. On the basis of an average daily per capita intake of 2000 calories, the increase in grain imports added 2% to the available calories. This is not to imply that the increase in grain imports made a major contribution to the improvement of food supplies in the low-income countries but rather to make it clear that the increase in per capita food supplies was equal to or greater than the increase in per capita food production during the 1970s.

Increased imports of food are often assumed to be a necessity caused by failure of agricultural production to increase at an appropriate pace. An FAO study, for example, recently noted that the developing countries increased their grain imports by more than 50% between 1975 and 1979, and stated that this increase portends both increasing dependence upon high-income countries (especially the United States) and increasing difficulties in paying for a rising level of food imports.[4] But for many developing countries, increasing food imports may be an efficient use of their resources and a response to rising real incomes—not a signal of imminent or eventual disaster. Associated with the notion that significant food imports are evidence of agricultural failure is the view that most, if not all, developing countries should be self-sufficient in food.[5]

The fact that the vast majority of developing countries are net exporters of agricultural products is often lost sight of in the discussion of food self-sufficiency. In 1977 the developing market economies had an excess of $17 billion of agricultural exports over agricultural imports; in terms of percentage, the excess of exports over imports was almost 60%. If the oil exporters are excluded, the value of agricultural exports was nearly double the value of agricultural imports in 1977 for the developing market economies.[6] The best course for some nations may be to produce crops for export and to import a significant fraction of their food.

It is interesting to note that although concern has been expressed about the

---

[4]In a discussion of recent trends in world trade in agricultural products in the United Nations report, *Agriculture: Toward 2000*, the following was stated: "every developing region . . . shared in both the downward share of world agricultural exports and the rising share of world agricultural imports. . . . A major feature of this deterioration—from the point of view of the developing countries—of trade in agricultural products was the stubborn upward trend in their cereals imports" (p. 12). It was noted that the degree of cereal self-sufficiency declined from 96% in 1963 to 92% in 1975.

[5]*Agriculture: Toward 2000* is somewhat ambivalent about the merits of self-sufficiency in food and export expansion. For example, "indeed, the pursuit of the objective of greater self-sufficiency in food is not necessarily inconsistent with a drive toward commodity development aimed at enhancing export earnings. Import substitution for food saves foreign exchange and production for foreign exchange earns foreign exchange. With limited land resources and with the need for foreign exchange earnings—for promoting industrialization and other development efforts—the most profitable use of agricultural resources would depend upon the relative gains from import substitution and export promotion. The individual countries would need to select the right mix of foodstuff production and export crop production, taking into account the relative costs and returns" (p. 189).

[6]*FAO Commodity Review and Outlook: 1977–79* (Rome: FAO, 1979), p. 11.

increase in grain and other food imports by the developing countries, little attention has been given to the even larger increase in the value of agricultural exports by the same group of countries. Although food imports of the non-oil-producing developing countries increased at an annual rate of $1.4 billion between 1970 and 1977, the value of their agricultural exports increased by $2.9 billion per year.[6]

Grain Prices

Another measure of the supplies of food available to the low-income countries is the price of grain in international markets. If demand had been growing more rapidly than supply, as many predicted would occur during the latter half of the 1970s, the real or deflated prices of grain would have increased. But the United States export prices of wheat and corn, in 1967 dollars per ton for the period from 1910 to date, reveal a long-term downward trend for the real prices of both products. In fact, prices during the late 1970s have been below those that prevailed from 1930–1934, during the Great Depression, and significantly below the prices of the late 1930s. Prices in recent years are also lower than during the late 1950s and very near to the low prices of the late 1960s.

These price data indicate that for the grains the supply to the international market has increased somewhat more than demand during the last seven decades. In fact, compared with the late 1920s, it is an understatement to say that supply has increased at a ''somewhat'' faster rate than demand. The real prices of both wheat and corn have fallen by approximately one-third in a half century. During this time output has grown substantially as, of course, has demand. It may be noted that what were considered to be the very high grain prices in 1974 were less than one-tenth higher than average prices for 1925–1929 and below the prices that prevailed after World War II. Within 3 years after 1974, the real export price for wheat fell by almost half, and the corn price fell by one-third. Clearly the world market for grains was not under strong demand pressure during the late 1970s. The prices prevailed even though the total world trade in grains doubled during the 1970s as did the volume of grain imports by the low-income market economies.

MALNUTRITION—HOW MUCH?

I have argued that the availability of food in the low-income countries improved during the 1970s, as it had during the previous two decades. I have confidence that the 1980s will see further improvement. However, the extent of malnutrition or hunger that exists in the world has not been considered. Unfortunately our knowledge of the number of percentage of people inadequately fed, either in the past or today, is limited.

Estimates for recent years of the number of people who are malnourished vary enormously. The Presidential Commission on World Hunger, in its preliminary report issued in December 1979, presented no new estimates of the extent of hunger and malnutrition. It relied upon previous estimates made by FAO and the World Bank, yet one finds in the opening paragraph of the preface the following:

Widespread hunger is a cruel fact of our time. In 1974, after poor harvests and oil price increases disrupted the international food system, the World Food Conference called on all governments to accept the goal that in ten years' time no child would go to bed hungry, no family would fear for its next day's bread, and no human being's future and capacities would be stunted by malnutrition. *Today, however, the world is even farther from that goal than it was then.* While the good harvests of recent years have prevented widespread famine, the next world food crisis will find the world not much better prepared than it was in 1974. This need not be the case [Emphasis added].[7]

It is true that in the resolutions of the World Food Conference there was a call for the elimination of hunger within a decade. The elimination of hunger, as defined in the quotation, is an impossibility; it is impossible for the world to ensure that there will always be enough food for everyone all of the time. Nonetheless, it is a worthy goal to move toward a reduction of hunger and malnutrition. The sentence in the preceding quotation shown in italics is an astounding statement to have been produced by a commission appointed by the President of the United States. It is stated as a fact that the world is farther from the goal of reducing hunger and malnutrition than it was in 1974. Not the slightest bit of evidence is presented to back up the statement. It is not even clear what the sentence actually means. Is it that half of the 10 years has passed and there has been little improvement? Or is it that conditions are now actually worse, with more children going to bed hungry in 1979 than in 1974 and with more families fearing for their next day's bread? Whatever may be intended, most readers will interpret the sentence to say that in 1979 the food situation was even more serious for the world's poor people than it was in 1974 with its poor harvests.

It is not my intention to engage in a battle of numbers or to claim that the world's poorer poeple do not face serious problems in obtaining adequate amounts of nutritious food.[8] Instead my objective is to try to measure recent progress or change in per capita food availability and to assess the prospects for improvements in the years ahead. Nor, in emphasizing food production and food prices and costs, am I denying that the primary reason for inadequate nutrition is poverty. In the lower-income countries of the world, limited availability of food for purchase is not the reason poor people have inadequate diets. The reason for inadequate diets is insufficient income to buy enough food. But I hasten to add that the majority, perhaps as many as $\frac{3}{4}$, of the poor people in the low-income countries live in rural areas. Thus, for many of these people there are intimate relationships among income, food, and agricultural production. Thus, while the primary source of food inadequacy is low income, an important factor in the low incomes for hundreds of millions is the limited productivity of agriculture. In this situation, many of the measures that

[7]Presidential Commission on World Hunger, *Preliminary Report of the Presidential Commission on World Hunger,* Washington, D.C., 1979, preface.

[8]In a section headed "Problems of Nutrition" in *Agriculture: Toward 2000,* the obvious truth is stated: "This is an area of relative ignorance, with limited clinical and anthropometrical data" (p. 147). Yet estimates of the number of malnourished continue to be made.

result in increased productivity in agriculture will also increase incomes and the adequacy of diets.

PRICE INSTABILITY

Recent grain export prices are low by comparison with the past. The data for the 1970s, however, indicate a high degree of price instability for the decade. Although there have been some positive changes affecting world food supply and demand during the 1970s, there has been little change with respect to the potential for price instability for grains in international markets and in countries where prices are permitted to vary with international market prices. Was the much greater grain price instability of the 1970s compared with the 1960s due to greater variability in grain production? The evidence clearly supports the conclusion that the source of the increased price instability was not nature, but man.

Much of the increase in grain prices from 1972 to 1974, and much of the subsequent decline, was due to governmental policies rather than to variations in production.[9] The policies responsible for a major fraction of the upward movement of prices (and the subsequent reductions) were those designed to achieve domestic price stability through varying net international trade. A large fraction of the world's consumption of wheat and other grains occurs in countries that divorce their domestic prices from international prices. In other words, numerous countries solve their own problems of instability by imposing that instability on the rest of the world by varying net trade.

The policies of the European Community, the Soviet Union, the Eastern European countries, China, and Japan did not change during the 1970s. Each still maintains a high level of domestic price stability by imposing its internal instability on the rest of the world. The most notorious example is the Soviet Union, which has highly variable grain production but has attempted to stabilize domestic availability of grain by varying net imports. The Soviet Union follows a policy of stable prices for livestock products; a production shortfall does not result in higher retail prices in the state stores, but rather in longer queues at the retail markets. The policy decision to maintain retail meat prices constant in current rubles puts a high premium on providing the feed supplies required to keep meat production growing at a reasonably constant rate. To meet this objective when grain production declines requires grain imports.

The shortfalls in Soviet grain production are sometimes greater than can be made up by imports. There is some evidence that part of the shortfall not met by imports is met by stock changes. Since the size of grain stocks is regarded as a state secret, changes in grain stocks can only be inferred. For example, the 1975 grain crop was 55 million tons below the 1974 crop (all references to tons are in metric tons); in 1975–1976 Soviet net grain imports were 25 million tons larger than during the prior year; net grain imports in 1979–1980 in the absence of the United States

[9]Johnson, *World Food Problems and Prospects,* op. cit. p. 33–34.

suspension of grain exports would have been approximately 34 million tons as an offset to a production decline of 58 million tons.[10] To some degree the amount of grain imported is influenced by the capacities of the Soviet ports and transport facilities to move the grain away from the ports. It is probable that the intended 1979–1980 level of imports was at or near that capacity, and this may also have been true in 1975–1976.

Since countries that consume well over half of the world's grain stabilize internal grain prices, sharp increases in international market prices such as occurred in 1973 and 1974, cannot be ruled out. In fact, it is probable that a similar pattern of price increases could occur during the 1980s. A rather modest decline in world grain production below trend levels could create the potential for similar price changes. Until or unless domestic price policies are changed in many countries, the countries that permit their domestic prices to vary with international market prices will be subject to significant price instability.

FOOD SECURITY, POVERTY, AND MALNUTRITION

As already noted, the primary reason for inadequate food consumption and malnutrition in the low-income countries is poverty rather than any lack of food availability. Barring war and civil insurrection, food is available almost anywhere in the world today if there is income to purchase it. Such was not always the case. It has only been in the past two centuries that famine was not a potential danger facing the majority of the world's population. Less than a century ago, famine was a threat to life for millions in most of Asia and Russia.

The twentieth century has brought a revolutionary change in world food security. Improvements in communication and transportation have brought all but a tiny minority of the world's population into a world food community. The world's food supply is now available to virtually anyone anywhere in the world who has the money to pay for food, except when governments block such purchases. The purchase price now approaches the lowest at which the primary food products (grains) have been available during the past century. The statement that food is now available to anyone who has the money to pay for it is not a cynical description of the alternatives available to the poor people of the world. It is a statement that realistically applies to a large and increasing fraction of the world's population, including the majority of the poorest people.

Unfortunately, the great deal of attention given to food problems during the mid-1970s has resulted in almost no improvement in the factual base for improving our understanding of malnutrition, its causes, and its extent. True, we know that most malnutrition is associated with low incomes, but we also know that some very poor people are adequately fed while others with equal or higher incomes have less than adequate diets. If we better understood why such differences exist in consump-

[10]U.S. Department of Agriculture, Foreign Agricultural Service, *Foreign Agriculture Circular, Grains*, FG-4-80, January 15, 1980.

tion patterns and what health effects, if any, such differences induce, we would be better able to assist those in the greatest need.

PROSPECTS FOR THE 1980s

Per capita food production in the world and in the developing countries increased during the 1970s. The improvement in the developing countries was modest overall and in some areas, particularly Africa, per capita food production declined. But the increase achieved in per capita food production during the 1970s represented a continuation of past trends.

There is no significant reason to expect that the 1980s will show less improvement in the per capita food production of the low-income countries than each of the last two decades. The potential for greater improvement clearly exists, though a cautious and realistic view is that during the 1980s, as during the previous two decades, the realization will fall short of the potential. However, there are some positive factors that may result in a higher rate of growth of per capita food production and consumption in the low-income countries during the 1980s than during the 1970s.

Three reasons have been emphasized to support a pessimistic view of the outcome of the race between world demand and supply of food: higher energy prices, the near disappearance of uncultivated arable land, and the competition between livestock and people for grain. Of these three issues, only higher energy prices merits discussion. There remains much land that can be brought under cultivation.[11] The presumed competition for grain between livestock and people has always been a false issue. It remains a false issue because the amount of grain produced in the world is as much a function of demand as of supply. If less grain were demanded, less grain would be produced. It is as simple as that. And because it is so simple, this point is frequently misunderstood or neglected.

Energy

Energy prices will continue to increase in real terms, and the real prices of farm inputs using significant amounts of energy will increase with the higher energy prices. However, the experience of the 1970s shows there is no simple, one-to-one relationship between the price of energy and the price of an input, such as fertilizer, that has a high energy component. Whereas the index of fertilizer prices paid by United States farmers has increased less since 1970 than the index of prices for all farm production items, the index of prices of fuels and oil has increased by about 35% more than all production items.[12] The share of fertilizer, oil, and fuel expenditures in total farm production expenses increased between 1970 and 1978, but probably by less than most think. Such expenditures on energy products accounted

[11]*Agriculture: Toward 2000* indicates that arable land in the low-income countries (excluding China) could increase from 730 million ha in 1975 to 830 million ha in 1990 and to 930 million ha by 2000 (p. 30).

[12]U.S. Department of Agriculture, Economics, Statistics, and Cooperatives Service, Crop Reporting Board, *Agricultural Prices,* various issues.

for 9.1% of all production expenditures in 1970 and 11.1% in 1978. Preliminary estimates indicate that approximately 11.7% of all 1979 farm production expenses were devoted to these energy products.[13]

I do not intend to minimize the importance of energy prices in affecting the costs of producing agricultural products in the United States and other high-income countries. Food and other agricultural products would be priced lower today and the output of food would be somewhat greater if energy prices were at their pre-OPEC real levels. But we should not exaggerate the effect of energy prices on agriculture nor should we assume that farmers can make no adjustment to the higher real prices.

One additional point should be made about energy prices. Energy derived from fossil fuels is a much smaller component of farm production costs in low-income countries than in the United States or Western Europe.[14] Consequently, increased energy prices have had less effect on agriculture in the poor countries than in the United States. This difference will persist in the years ahead. And we have seen that the effect of higher energy costs on United States agriculture has been quite small so far. One indication of this is that real grain prices are now approximately the same as they were a decade ago, when energy prices were much lower.

The Green Revolution

For many, a look ahead at what the 1980s holds for food supplies in the low-income countries is influenced by their answer to this question: "What happened to the Green Revolution?" The question often implies that the benefits of research leading to the new grain varieties and the cultivation practices that together were called the *Green Revolution* were less than had been anticipated. One reason the question is asked was the unfortunate designation of the new high-yielding varieties of rice and wheat as miracle varieties. The use of the term *Green Revolution* also held out the hope of major, indeed revolutionary, changes in food supplies. The development of new varieties was a remarkable achievement, but it was unfortunate that they were tagged as revolutionary. One lesson must be learned about research and agriculture—a single revolution is never enough. What is required is a stream of revolutions or changes, each perhaps with a rather modest effect but with significant cumulative influence.

For several reasons the new high-yielding varieties did not have the effects on output expected by their most enthusiastic supporters. First, the new varieties were well-adapted to only part of the areas producing rice and wheat; second, the yield differentials between the new and old varieties were significantly smaller on the farm than under experimental conditions; and, third, farmers had to learn how to use

[13]U.S. Department of Agriculture, Economics, Statistics, and Cooperatives Service, *Farm Income Statistics,* Statistical Bulletin No. 627, October 1979, pp. 42, 46. These data do not include expenditures on electricity. The 1979 estimate is made by the author.

[14]It is estimated that in the low-income countries, agriculture produced approximately 24% of the total output of the economies but used only 3.1% of all fossil energy consumed in 1975 (*Agriculture: Toward 2000,* p. 233). In the high-income countries, agriculture consumes approximately the same amount of fossil energy per unit of output as the economy as a whole.

the new varieties effectively. Specifically in the case of the new varieties, they could be used only under irrigation that permitted effective control of water depths. Many of the irrigation systems in South and Southeast Asia do not provide effective control of water levels. On the other hand, since most wheat irrigation is done with tube wells in South Asia, there has been much wider adoption of the new varieties of wheat than of rice. In India in 1976–1977, 35% of all rice was sown with the new varieties, whereas more than 70% of the wheat area was sown with new varieties. The doubling of wheat yields and the trebling of wheat output in India would have been impossible without the new wheat varieties.

Hybrid Corn

When hybrid corn was first introduced in the 1930s, the general methods of cultivating and producing corn had been unchanged for several decades. Little or no fertilizer was used on corn. In this setting the yield advantage of hybrid corn over the traditional (open pollinated) varieties was approximately 15%. The average corn yield in the United States prior to the introduction of hybrids in years of average weather was 1.5 tons/ha (25 bushels/acre). Thus hybrid corn would have increased average yield by about 0.22 tons/ha (less than 4 bushels/acre). In the Corn Belt, where yields were higher than the national average and hybrids were first introduced, the absolute yield advantage of the hybrids was of the order of 0.3 tons/ha (5 bushels/acre). Corn yields are now 6.2 tons/ha (100 bushels/acre) with average weather. Hybrid corn has been an important contributor to the quadrupling of yield over the past four or five decades. But there were many other changes that made the recent yields possible—fertilizer, herbicides, insecticides, more plants per unit of land. Increasingly, corn hybrids are adapted to the climatic and soil and moisture conditions of quite small areas, and some part of the yield increases in the last decade or two are a result of such increased adaptation of hybrid seeds.

Grain Yield Trends

The 1970s saw repeated references to the possibility, if not the probability, that the growth rate of grain yields was declining in the world. The feeling of unease was buttressed for many by United States grain yields, especially corn, that were below prior peak levels in 1975, 1976, and, to a lesser degree, in 1977. Thus, some concluded that grain yields in the United States were slowing down and perhaps had reached their peak.

However, research undertaken at the University of Illinois has shown that the tapering off of corn yield growth after 1974, at least in Illinois, was due to climatic factors. After account was taken of the climatic effects, there was no evidence of a slowing down of the growth in yields of corn or soybeans. In 1978 and 1979, weather variables influencing corn production were more favorable than in 1975 and 1976, and United States corn yields increased substantially, reaching an average yield of 109 bushels per acre (6.7 ton/ha) in 1979. This was between 9% and 10% in excess of the trend level of corn yields for that year.

Prior to 1975 most developing countries held down the price of at least one important food crop and protected farm input-producing industries, such as fertilizer. Although there remain numerous examples of exploitation of farmers for the presumed benefit of consumers or input-producing sectors, many developing countries now have support and purchase prices for major farm crops that are in excess of world market prices. Agricultural exports are still often burdened by an overvalued currency, as in Argentina and, until very recently, in Brazil. The probable improvement in the structure of incentives for farmers in the low-income countries will have a positive impact on the growth of agricultural output.[15]

Agricultural Research

During the past two decades there has been a major growth in the expenditures for agricultural research on the problems of increasing farm production in the low-income countries. In the 15 years between 1959 and 1974, agricultural research in the major developing regions (Latin America, Africa, and Asia) increased from $228 million to $957 million (in 1971 constant United States dollars). This increase occurred both in the international agricultural research centers and in the research institutions of the low-income countries. As a share of an increasing world expenditure on agricultural research, the expenditures in the three low-income regions increased from 17% in 1959 to 25% in 1974.[16] Since there is a lag of 5–10 years between research investment and actual application on farms, most of the effects of the increased investments made after 1973 have still not been felt.

Irrigation

Earlier it was noted that during the past decade there has been a substantial increase in the irrigated area in low-income countries. Much of the increase in irrigation has occurred in the densely populated regions of the world, principally Asia. Current rates of investment in irrigation in South and Southeast Asia are high by historical standards. Irrigation, whether it comes about through new projects or improvement of existing systems, is capital-intensive. This is an investment area where the availability of foreign capital may be important in improving per capita food availability. A report of the Trilateral Commission indicated that it would require more than $50 billion (in 1975 purchasing power) of investment to provide the irrigation expansion and improvements in South and Southeast Asia required for a doubling of rice production by the early 1990s.[17] Approximately one-third of the required investment could come from sources within the region.

[15]For a discussion of the effects of incentives and of distortions of those incentives upon agricultural development, see Theodore W. Schultz (ed.), *Distortions of Agricultural Incentives* (Bloomington: Indiana University Press, 1978).

[16]Robert Evenson, "The Organization of Research to Improve Crops and Animals in Low-Income Countries," ibid., p. 224. The reader interested in further exploration of the potential contributions of agricultural research to improving food production and nutrition may wish to consult the following: Steering Committee of the National Academy of Sciences, *World Food and Nutrition Study: The Potential Contributions of Research* (Washington, D.C.: National Academy of Sciences, 1977). See also, Sterling Wortman and Ralph W. Cummings, Jr., *To Feed This World: The Challenge and the Strategy* (Baltimore: Johns Hopkins University Press, 1978). At the end of each chapter there is an excellent classified bibliography.

[17]Umberto Colombo, D. Gale Johnson, and Toshio Shishido, *Reducing Malnutrition in Developing Countries: Increasing Rice Production in South and Southeast Asia* (New York: The Trilateral Commission, 1978).

Income Growth

Two other factors will have a positive effect on per capita food consumption by the end of the 1980s. One of these is the continued growth of per capita income in the developing countries. The World Bank projects the annual growth of per capita gross domestic product of the low-income (per capita income of less than $300) developing countries during the 1980s at 2.7%.[18] The middle-income developing economies are projected to have a significantly higher growth rate of 3.4%. The population (as of 1976) of the low-income developing countries was 1193 million and of the middle-income countries, 1037 million. An income growth rate of 2.7% annually means a 30.5% growth in income level in a decade. Such a growth of income would, on the average, result in at least a 15% increase per capita in real food expenditures for low-income persons. If this growth in demand for food is reasonably well distributed among all segments of the population, the growth will go a substantial distance toward reducing both severe and moderate malnutrition in the low-income countries.

Slower Population Growth

The other factor that will have a positive effect on per capita food consumption is the likely decline in the rate of population growth in many low-income countries. The decline in the rate of population growth will not significantly alleviate the world's food deficiencies during the 1980s. A slowing down of population growth has two effects on per capita food supply—a larger fraction of the population is in the working ages during the transition period to a lower rate of population growth, and there are fewer people eating from a given food supply after some period of time. These effects will not be large during most of the 1980s, though they will be of modest significance. The difference in a decade between 2.3% and 2.1% annual growth rates is a little less than 2% for the total population. The two growth rates are those for India for the 1960s and from 1970 to 1977. If there is a further decline in the population growth rate for the 1980s to 1.9%, a further 2% lower total population would result by 1990. These differences appear to be small, but compared with annual per capita increases in food consumption of 0.5% or 0.6%, the effect on per capita food consumption of a 2% difference in population size would increase the growth of consumption by one-third. It is by small and additive measures that the nutrition of the world's poorest people will be improved during the rest of this century.

CONCLUDING COMMENTS

It is common in the discussion of the potential growth of food production to emphasize the restraints imposed by nature—the finite limits of our natural resources and the vagaries of climate. It is easy to paint a gloomy picture of the future of the world, if you accept the view that our supplies of fossil energy will be exhausted in some finite period, that erosion will destroy a large part of the land

---

[18]*World Development Report, 1979* (Washington, D.C.: The World Bank, August 1979), p. 13. The population data and growth estimates exclude China.

used for crops, and that future scientific discoveries increasingly will be less relevant to increasing food production.

But if there is an enemy that will prevent improving the nutrition of the world's
poor people, it is man and not nature. Man, not nature, will be the primary factor in
determining the rate of growth of food production in the rest of this century. Nature
is often niggardly and at times terribly cruel. But we now know enough about what
is required to expand food production not to blame our failures upon nature.

When I say that man, not nature, will impose the greatest barriers to the potential
expansion of food production, I am not referring to the consequences of the acts of
farmers, traders, processors, or suppliers, but to man as he functions in the political
process. If policies are adopted that give appropriate incentives for farmers, provide
them access to supplies at reasonable prices, and permit farmers to sell at the best
possible prices, production growth will increase. And if policies are followed that
encourage research on problems of the agriculture of the low-income countries, all
will gain. The mistakes of the past have been especially costly for the world's poor;
we can only hope that fewer mistakes will be made in the next decade.

UPDATE

THE WORLD FOOD SITUATION: DEVELOPMENTS DURING THE 1970s

AND PROSPECTS FOR THE 1980s   and 1990s

D. Gale Johnson

The original paper was both an analysis of the changes in the world
food situation during the 1970s and an effort to evaluate what might occur
during the 1980s. There has been no new information that indicates a need
to change the description of developments during the 1970s. We now know a
great deal more about China than we did earlier but the general picture of
the food situation at the end of the 1970s remains as stated in the earlier
article. Most of the years of the 1980s have now come and gone. How have
the conclusions concerning the prospects for the 1980s stood the test of
time? On the whole, rather well.

The trends with respect to factors affecting the growth in the supply
of food were much as projected for the 1980s. Fertilizer prices in the
United States, which reflect the prices in international markets, declined

during the 1980s. It was noted that between 1970 and 1980 fertilizer prices paid by U.S. farmers increased just 3 percent more than prices farmers paid for all production items. From 1980 to mid-1987 the deflated price of fertilizer fell by 19 percent. In part due to the slowdown in economic growth during the 1980s, the feed use of grain has not increased as a share of world grain use during the 1980s.

The basic patterns of changes in per capita food production during the 1970s persisted into the 1980s. For developing market economies per capita food production increased by 4 percent between 1980 and 1986, representing a modest improvement. However, the downward trend in Africa continued, though the trend moderated with only a 3 percent decline so far in the 1980s. While there were increases in per capita food production in Asia, both South and East Asia, the long term upward trend in Latin America was halted and per capita food production in the mid-1980s was the same as at the beginning of the decade.

The downward trends in real grain export prices continued and, if anything, accelerated. The 1979 prices (in 1967 $ per ton) were $67 for wheat and $50 for corn. In mid-1987 the wheat price had fallen to $40 and the corn to a little less than $30. It is likely that these prices will increase over the next two or three years but will remain well below the 1979 prices. Thus the basic foods—the cereals—which supply more than half of the calories eaten in the low income developing countries continue to be available at lower and lower real prices.

Unfortunately we know little, if any, more on the basis of direct evidence about the extent of malnutrition in the world than we did at the beginning of the 1980s. What we do know is that life expectancy at birth has continued to increase. For all low income countries (less than $400 per capita in 1985), life expectancy at birth increased from 48 years in 1965 to 60 years in 1985. In India the increase was from 45 to 56 years and in China from 55 to 69. True there have been famines during the 1980s but the most serious ones such as in Ethiopia and Uganda have been due to a combination of bad policies and civil war.

World trade in grain grew rapidly during the 1970s. The trade continued to increase until 1984/85 but then declined sharply (20 percent), recovering somewhat by 1987/88 to 194 million metric tons but still some 15 million tons below the 1980/81 volume. As of mid-1987 world grain stocks as of a percentage of world annual use were at the highest level since 1961.

The most surprising development in the food situation in the developing world that has occurred during the 1980s occurred in China.* During the early 1980s China undertook a radical reform of its agriculture. The communes were abolished and by the mid-1980s almost all of the farm land in China had been assigned to households who had a reasonable degree of freedom to produce what they wanted. Prices paid by the state for farm products increased, starting in 1979, and farmers were permitted to sell their excess output in free markets. For the first time in more than a decade it was legal for farmers to sell their products directly to urban people.

The effect on output was remarkable. Between 1978 and 1984 the production of farm products increased by 52 percent, representing an annual growth rate of 7 percent. Production growth slowed to 3 percent for both 1985 and 1986, still quite respectable. Grain production, according to the official Chinese data that were not available when the article was written, increased from 305 million tons in 1978 to a record of 407 million tons in 1984 declining to 380 million in 1985 with a modest recovery to 393 million tons in 1986. Grain is defined more broadly than in the United States and includes both soybeans and potatoes (converted to a grain equivalent basis). It is important to note that after 20 years of stagnation in per capita grain production, per capita output increased from 319 kilograms in 1978 to 380 kilograms in 1984-85. The improvement in food production was associated with a dramatic increase in the incomes of farm people. After adjusting for inflation, the incomes of farm people approximately doubled between 1978 and 1986. This is an indicator both of the enormous inefficiency of the commune

system and of the ability of the ordinary Chinese farmer to make effective
use of his or her resources, when permitted to do so.

During the early 1980s China became a major grain importer, importing
16 million tons in 1982. However, with the improvement in grain production,
Chinese imports fell sharply and while continuing to import wheat, China
became an important corn exporter with exports reaching 7 million tons in
1985/86 but declining subsequently as feed use increased in response to the
rising demands for livestock products.

India continued to increase its food production during the 1980s
though the upward trend was interrupted by a failure of the monsoons in
1987. India had accumulated large supplies of grain and had enough grain in
storage to offset most of the decline in grain production. The hardship and
hunger that may have occurred in 1987 was due primarily to the loss of income in areas seriously affected by the drought and not by the dearth of
food in India as a whole.

One of the major points of the article was that poverty, not lack of
available food, was the primary source of hunger and malnutrition. The
evidence from the 1980s substantiated this conclusion. Having food available is not enough; people must have the means to purchase it. There remain
a few cases where due to war and civil strife people are prevented access to
food. But here the cure is to settle the conflicts not to increase food
availability by food aid.

The general tone of the article was optimistic in the sense that the
food situation for people in low income countries had improved and would
continue to improve. Except for Africa, the optimism was justified. And in
the case of Africa it was clear a decade ago that with the policies governments were following there would be further deterioration in per capita food
production. It can be noted that several African countries have modified
their policies to provide greater incentives for their farmers and in most
cases positive results have followed.*
*The Chinese data are from Statistical Yearbook of China 1984 and 1986,
English edition. State Statistical Bureau, People's Republic of China.
Printed in Hong Kong

Part IV

Common Markets

Developed Countries

Viner
Lipsey
Robson
Dornbusch

Developing Countries

Mikesell
Prebisch
Okita

THE ECONOMICS OF CUSTOMS UNIONS

CUSTOMS UNION AS AN APPROACH TO FREE TRADE

The literature on customs unions in general, whether written by economists or noneconomists, by free-traders or protectionists, is almost universally favorable to them, and only here and there is a skeptical note to be encountered, usually by an economist with free-trade tendencies. It is a strange phenomenon that unites free-traders and protectionists in the field of commercial policy, and its strangeness suggests that there is something peculiar in the apparent economics of customs unions. The customs union problem is entangled in the whole free-trade–protection issue, and it has never yet been properly disentangled.

• • •

A customs union is more likely to operate in the free-trade direction, whether appraisal is in terms of its consequence for the customs union area alone or for the world as a whole:

1. the larger the economic area of the customs union and therefore the greater the potential scope for internal division of labor;

2. the lower the "average" tariff level on imports from outside the customs union area as compared to what that level would be in the absence of customs union;

3. the greater the correspondence in kind of products of the range of high-cost industries as between the different parts of the customs union that were protected by tariffs in both of the member countries before customs union was established, that is, *less* the degree of complementarity—or the *greater* the degree of rivalry—of the member countries with respect to *protected* industries, prior to customs union;[1]

4. the greater the differences in unit costs for protected industries of the same kind as between the different parts of the customs union, and therefore the greater the economies to be derived from free trade with respect to these industries within the customs union area.

5. the higher the tariff levels in potential export markets outside the customs union area with respect to commodities in whose production the member countries of the customs union would have a comparative advantage under free trade, and therefore the less the injury resulting from reducing the degree of specialization in production as between the customs union area and the outside world;

6. the greater the range of protected industries for which an enlargement of the

---

[1] In the literature on customs union, it is almost invariably taken for granted that rivalry is a disadvantage and complementarity is an advantage in the formation of customs unions. See *infra*, pp. 73 ff., with reference to the Benelux and Franco-Italian projects.

Reprinted from "The Customs Union Issue," (taken from) pp. 41–56, with permission of Carnegie Endowment for International Peace, New York. Copyright 1950.

market would result in unit costs lower than those at which the commodities concerned could be imported from outside the customs union area;

7. the smaller the range of protected industries for which an enlargement of the market would not result in unit costs lower than those at which the commodities concerned could be imported from outside the customs union area but which would nevertheless expand under customs union.

Confident judgment as to what the overall balance between these conflicting considerations would be, it should be obvious, cannot be made for customs unions in general and in the abstract, but must be confined to particular projects and be based on economic survey thorough enough to justify reasonably reliable estimates as to weights to be given in the particular circumstances to the respective elements in the problem. Customs unions are, from the free-trade point of view, neither necessarily good nor necessarily bad; the circumstances discussed in the preceding are the determining factors.

● ● ●

CUSTOMS UNION AND THE "TERMS OF TRADE"

There is a possibility, so far not mentioned, of economic benefit from a tariff to the tariff-levying country, which countries may be able to exploit more effectively combined in customs union than if they operated as separate tariff areas. This benefit to the customs area, however, carries with it a corresponding injury to the outside world. A tariff does not merely divert consumption from imported to domestically produced commodities—this is, from the free-trade point of view, the economic disadvantage of a tariff for the tariff-levying country and one of its disadvantages for the rest of the world—but it also alters in favor of the tariff-levying country the rate at which its exports exchange for the imports that survive the tariff, or its "terms of trade," and within limits— which may be narrow and which can never be determined accurately—an improvement in the national "terms of trade" carries with it an increase in the national total benefit from trade. The greater the economic area of the tariff-levying unit, the greater is likely to be, other things being equal, the improvement in its terms of trade with the outside world resulting from its tariff.[2] A customs union, by increasing the extent of the territory that operates under a single tariff, thus tends to increase the efficacy of the tariff in improving the terms of trade of that area vis-à-vis the rest of the world.

[2]The greater the economic area of the tariff unit, other things equal, the greater is likely to be the elasticity of its "reciprocal demand" for outside products and the less is likely to be the elasticity of the "reciprocal demand" of the outside world for its products, and consequently the greater the possibility of improvement in its terms of trade through unilateral manipulation of its tariff.

THE THEORY OF CUSTOMS UNIONS:
A GENERAL SURVEY [1]

Richard G. Lipsey

THIS paper is devoted mainly to a survey of the development of customs-union theory from Viner to date; since, however, the theory must be meant at least as an aid in interpreting real-world data, some space is devoted to a summary of empirical evidence relating to the gains from European Economic Union. It is necessary first to define customs-union theory. In general, the tariff system of any country may discriminate between commodities and/or between countries. Commodity discrimination occurs when different rates of duty are levied on different commodities, while country discrimination occurs when the same commodity is subject to different rates of duty, the rate varying according to the country of origin. The theory of customs unions may be defined as that branch of tariff theory which deals with the effects of geographically discriminatory changes in trade barriers.

Next we must turn our attention to the scope of the existing theory. The theory has been confined mainly to a study of the effects of customs unions on welfare rather than, for example, on the level of economic activity, the balance of payments or the rate of inflation. These welfare gains and losses, which are the subject of the theory, may arise from a number of different sources: (1) the specialisation of production according to comparative advantage which is the basis of the classical case for the gains from trade; (2) economies of scale; [2] (3) changes in the terms of trade; (4) forced changes in efficiency due to increased foreign competition; and (5) a change in the rate of economic growth. The theory of customs unions has been almost completely confined to an investigation of (1) above, with some slight attention to (2) and (3), (5) not being dealt with at all, while (4) is ruled out of traditional theory by the assumption (often contradicted by the facts) that production is carried out by processes which are technically efficient.

Throughout the development of the theory of customs unions we will find an oscillation between the belief that it is possible to produce a general conclusion of the sort: " Customs unions will always, or nearly always, raise welfare," and the belief that, depending on the particular circumstances present, a customs union may have any imaginable effect on welfare. The

---

[1] An earlier version of this paper was read before the Conference of the Association of University Teachers of Economics at Southampton, January 1959. I am indebted for comments and suggestions to G. C. Archibald, K. Klappholz and Professor L. Robbins.

[2] Points (1) and (2) are clearly related, for the existence of (1) is a *necessary* condition for (2), but they are more conveniently treated as separate points, since (1) is not a *sufficient* condition for the existence of (2).

Reprinted with permission from *The Economic Journal* **52**, 496–513. Copyright 1960.

earliest customs-union theory was largely embodied in the oral tradition, for
it hardly seemed worthwhile to state it explicitly, and was an example of an
attempt to produce the former sort of conclusion.   It may be summarised
quite briefly.   Free trade maximises world welfare;   a customs union
reduces tariffs and is therefore a movement towards free trade;   a customs
union will, therefore, *increase* world welfare even if it does not lead to a
world-welfare *maximum*.

Viner showed this argument to be incorrect.   He introduced the now
familiar concepts of trade creation and trade diversion [1] which are probably
best recalled in terms of an example.   Consider the figures in the following
Table:

TABLE I

*Money Prices (at Existing Exchange Rates) of a Single
Commodity (X) in Three Countries*

Country	A	B	C
Price	35s.	26s.	20s.

A tariff of 100% levied by country A [2] will be sufficient to protect A's
domestic industry producing commodity X.   If A forms a customs union
with either country B or country C she will be better off; if the union is
with B she will get a unit of commodity X at an opportunity cost of 26
shillingsworth of exports instead of at the cost of 35 shillingsworth of other
goods entailed by domestic production.[3]   This is an example of trade
creation.   If A had been levying a somewhat lower tariff, a 50% tariff, for
example, she would already have been buying X from abroad before the
formation of any customs union.   If A is buying a commodity from abroad,
and if her tariff is non-discriminatory, then she will be buying it from the
lowest-cost source—in this case country C.   Now consider a customs union
with country B.   B's X, now exempt from the tariff, sells for 26s., while
C's X, which must still pay the 50% tariff, must be sold for 30s.   A will now
buy X from B at a price, in terms of the value of exports, of 26s., whereas
she was formerly buying it from C at a price of only 20s.   This is a case of
Viner's trade diversion, and since it entails a movement from lower to higher
real cost sources of supply, it represents a movement from a more to a less
efficient allocation of resources.

[1] Jacob Viner, *The Customs Union Issue* (New York: Carnegie Endowment for International
Peace, 1950).   See the whole of Chapter 4, especially pp. 43–4.

[2] In everything that follows the "home country" will be labelled A, the "union partner" B
and the rest of the world C.

[3] This argument presumes that relative prices in each country reflect real rates of transformation.   It follows that the resources used to produce a unit of X in country A could produce any
other good to the value of 35s. and, since a unit of X can be had from B by exporting goods to the
value of only 26s., there will be a surplus of goods valued at 9s. accruing to A from the transfer of
resources out of X when trade is opened with country B.

This analysis is an example of what Mr. Lancaster and I have called
" The General Theory of Second Best ": [1] if it is impossible to satisfy *all* the
optimum conditions (in this case to make all relative prices equal to all rates
of transformation in production), then a change which brings about the
satisfaction of *some* of the optimum conditions (in this case making some
relative prices equal to some rates of transformation in production) may
make things better or worse.[2]

Viner's analysis leads to the following classification of the possibilities
that arise from a customs union between two countries, A and B:

> 1. Neither A nor B may be producing a given commodity. In
> this case they will both be importing this commodity from some third
> country, and the removal of tariffs on trade between A and B can cause
> no change in the pattern of trade in this commodity; both countries
> will continue to import it from the cheapest possible source outside of
> the union.
>
> 2. One of the two countries may be producing the commodity
> inefficiently under tariff protection while the second country is a non-
> producer. If country A is producing commodity X under tariff pro-
> tection this means that her tariff is sufficient to eliminate competition
> from the cheapest possible source. Thus if A's tariff on X is adopted
> by the union the tariff will be high enough to secure B's market for A's
> inefficient industry.
>
> 3. Both countries may be producing the commodity inefficiently
> under tariff protection. In this case the customs union removes tariffs
> between country A and B and ensures that the least inefficient of the
> two will capture the union market.[3]

In case 2 above any change must be a trade-diverting one, while in case 3
any change must be a trade-creating one. If one wishes to predict the
welfare effects of a customs union it is necessary to predict the relative
strengths of the forces causing trade creation and trade diversion.

This analysis leads to the conclusion that customs unions are likely to
cause losses when the countries involved are complementary *in the range of
commodities that are protected by tariffs.* Consider the class of commodities
produced under tariff protection in each of the two countries. If these
classes overlap to a large extent, then the most efficient of the two countries
will capture the union market and there will be a re-allocation of resources
in a more efficient direction. If these two classes do not overlap to any

[1] R. G. Lipsey and K. J. Lancaster, " The General Theory of Second Best," *Review of Economic
Studies,* Vol. XXIV (1), No. 63, 1956–57.

[2] The point may be made slightly more formally as follows: the conditions necessary for the
maximising of *any* function do not, in general, provide conditions sufficient for an increase in the
value of the function when the maximum value is not to be obtained by the change.

[3] One of the two countries might be an efficient producer of this commodity needing no tariff
protection, in which case, *a fortiori,* there is gain.

great extent, then the protected industry in one country is likely to capture the whole of the union market when the union is formed, and there is likely to be a re-allocation of resources in a less-efficient direction. This point of Viner's has often been misunderstood and read to say that, in some general sense, the economies of the two countries should be competitive and not complementary. A precise way of making the point is to say that the customs union is more likely to bring gain, the greater is the degree of overlapping between the class of commodities produced under tariff protection in the two countries.

A subsequent analysis of the conditions affecting the gains from union through trade creation and trade diversion was made by Drs. Makower and Morton.[1] They pointed out that, *given that trade creation was going to occur*, the gains would be larger the more dissimilar were the cost ratios in the two countries. (Clearly if two countries have almost identical cost ratios the gains from trade will be small.) They then defined competitive economies to be ones with similar cost ratios and complementary economies to be ones with dissimilar ratios, and were able to conclude that unions between complementary economies would, if they brought gain at all, bring large gains. The conclusions of Viner and Makower and Morton are in no sense contradictory. Stated in the simplest possible language, Viner showed that gains will arise from unions if both countries are producing the same commodity; Makower and Morton showed that these gains will be larger the larger is the difference between the costs at which the same commodity is produced in the two countries.[2]

We now come to the second major development in customs-union theory —the analysis of the welfare effects of *the substitution between commodities* resulting from the changes in relative prices which necessarily accompany a customs union. Viner's analysis implicitly assumed that commodities are consumed in some fixed proportion which is independent of the structure of relative prices. Having ruled out substitution between commodities, he was left to analyse only bodily shifts of trade from one country to another. The way in which Viner's conclusion that trade diversion necessarily lowers welfare depends on his implicit demand assumption is illustrated in Fig. 1. Consider the case of a small country, A, specialised in the production of a single commodity, Y, and importing one commodity, X, at terms of trade independent of any taxes or tariffs levied in A. The fixed proportion in

[1] H. Makower and G. Morton, "A Contribution Towards a Theory of Customs Unions," ECONOMIC JOURNAL, Vol. LXII, No. 249, March 1953, pp. 33–49.
[2] Care must be taken to distinguish between complementarity and competitiveness in costs and in tastes, both being possible. In the Makower–Morton model these relations exist only on the cost side. An example of the confusion which may arise when this distinction is not made can be seen in F. V. Meyer's article, "Complementarity and the Lowering of Tariffs," *The American Economic Review*, Vol. XLVI, No. 3, June 1956. Meyer's definitions, if they are to mean anything, must refer to the demand side. Hence he is not entitled to contrast his results with those of Makower and Morton, or of Viner, all of whom were concerned with cost complementarity and competitiveness.

which commodities are consumed is shown by the slope of the line OZ, which is the income- and price-consumption line for all (finite) prices and incomes. OA indicates country A's total production of commodity Y, and the slope of the line AC shows the terms of trade offered by country C, the lowest cost producer of X. Under conditions of free trade, country A's equilibrium will be at e, the point of intersection between OZ and AC. A will consume Og of Y, exporting Ag in return for ge of X. Now a tariff which does not affect A's terms of trade and is not high enough to protect a domestic industry producing Y will leave her equilibrium position un-changed at e.[1] The tariff changes relative prices, but consumers' purchases

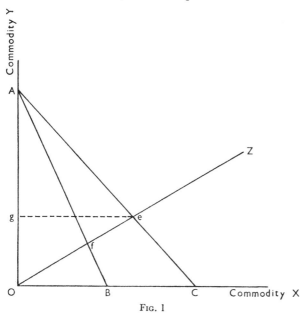

Fig. 1

are completely insensitive to this change and, if foreign trade continues at terms indicated by the slope of the line AC, the community must remain in equilibrium at e. Now consider a case where country A forms a trade-diverting customs union with country B. This means that A must buy her imports of X at a price in terms of Y higher than she was paying before the union was formed. An example of this is shown in Fig. 1 by the line AB. A's equilibrium is now at f, the point of intersection between AB and OZ; less of both commodities are consumed, and A's welfare has unambiguously diminished. We conclude therefore that, under the assumed demand conditions, trade diversion (which necessarily entails a deterioration in A's terms of trade) *necessarily* lowers A's welfare.

[1] It is assumed throughout all the subsequent analysis that the tariff revenue collected by the Government is either returned to individuals by means of lump-sum subsidies or spent by the Government on the same bundle of goods that consumers would have purchased.

Viner's implicit assumption that commodities are consumed in fixed proportions independent of the structure of relative prices is indeed a very special one. A customs union necessarily changes relative prices and, in general, we should expect this to lead to some substitution between commodities, there being a tendency to change the volume of already existing trade with more of the now cheaper goods being bought and less of the now more expensive. This would tend to increase the volume of imports from a country's union partner and to diminish both the volume of imports obtained from the outside world and the consumption of home-produced commodities. The importance of this substitution effect in consumption seems to have been discovered independently by at least three people, Professor Meade,[1] Professor Gehrels [2] and myself.[3]

In order to show the importance of the effects of substitutions in consumption we merely drop the assumption that commodities are consumed in fixed proportions. I shall take Mr. Gehrels' presentation of this analysis because it illustrates a number of important factors. In Fig. 2 OA is again country A's total production of Y, and the slope of the line AC indicates the terms of trade between X and Y when A is trading with country C. The free-trade equilibrium position is again at e, where an indifference curve is tangent to AC. In this case, however, the imposition of a tariff on imports of X, even if it does not shift the source of country A's imports, will cause a reduction in the quantity of these imports and an increase in the consumption of the domestic commodity Y. A tariff which changes the relative price in A's domestic market to, say, that indicated by the slope of the line $A'C'$ will move A's equilibrium position to point h. At this point an indifference curve cuts AC with a slope equal to the line $A'C'$; consumers are thus adjusting their purchases to the market rate of transformation and the tariff has had the effect of reducing imports of X and increasing consumption of the home good Y. In these circumstances it is clearly possible for country A to form a trade-diverting customs union and yet gain an increase in its welfare. To show this, construct a line through A tangent to the indifference curve I'' to cut the X axis at some point B. If A forms a trade-diverting customs union with country B and buys her imports of X from B at terms of trade indicated by the slope of the line AB, her welfare will be unchanged. If, therefore, the terms of trade with B are worse than those given by C but better than those indicated by the slope of the line AB, A's welfare will be increased by the trade-diverting customs union. A's

[1] J. E. Meade, *The Theory of Customs Unions* (Amsterdam: North Holland Publishing Company, 1956).

[2] F. Gehrels, "Customs Unions from a Single Country Viewpoint," *Review of Economic Studies*, Vol. XXIV (1), No. 63, 1956–57.

[3] R. G. Lipsey, "The Theory of Customs Unions: Trade Diversion and Welfare," *Economica*, Vol. XXIV, No. 93, February 1957. My own paper was first written in 1954 as a criticism of the assumption of fixed ratios in consumption made by Dr. Ozga in his thesis (S. A. Ozga, *The Theory of Tariff Systems*, University of London Ph.D. thesis, unpublished).

welfare will be diminished by this trade-diverting union with B only if B's terms of trade are worse than those indicated by the slope of *AB*.

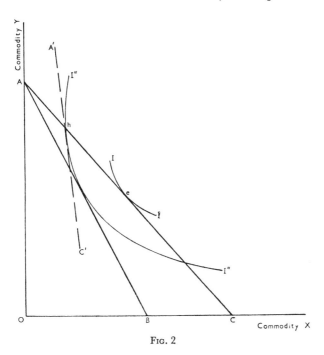

Fig. 2

The common-sense reason for this conclusion may be stated as follows:

" The possibility stems from the fact that whenever imports are subject to a tariff, the position of equilibrium must be one where an indifference curve [surface or hyper-surface as the case may be] cuts (*not* is tangent to) the international price line. From this it follows that there will exist an area where indifference curves higher than the one achieved at equilibrium lie below the international price line. In Fig. 2 this is the area above *I''* but below *AC*. As long as the final equilibrium position lies within this area, trade carried on in the absence of tariffs, at terms of trade worse than those indicated by *AC*, will increase welfare. In a verbal statement this possibility may be explained by referring to the two opposing effects of a trade-diverting customs union. First, A shifts her purchases from a lower to a higher cost source of supply. It now becomes necessary to export a larger quantity of goods in order to obtain any given quantity of imports. Secondly, the divergence between domestic and international prices is eliminated when the union is formed. The removal of the tariff has the effect of allowing . . . consumer[s] in A to adjust . . . purchases to a domestic price ratio which now is equal to the rate at which . . . [Y] can be transformed into . . . [X] by means of international trade. The final welfare effect of the trade-diverting customs union must be the net effect of these two opposing tendencies; the first working to lower welfare and the second to raise it." [1]

On this much there is general agreement. Professor Gehrels, however, concluded that his analysis established a general presumption in favour of gains from union rather than losses. He argued that " to examine customs unions in the light only of *production* effects, as Viner does, will give a biased judgment of their effect on countries joining them," [2] and he went on to say that the analysis given above established a general presumption in favour of gains from union. Now we seemed to be back in the pre-Viner world, where economic analysis established a general case in favour of customs unions. In my article " Mr. Gehrels on Customs Union " [3] I attempted to point out the mistake involved. The key is that Gehrels' model contains only two commodities: one domestic good and one import. There is thus only one optimum condition for consumption: that the relative price between X and Y equals the real rate of transformation (in domestic production or international trade, whichever is relevant) between these two commodities. The general problems raised by customs unions must, however, be analysed in a model containing a minimum of three types of commodities: domestic commodities (A), imports from the union partner (B) and imports from the outside world (C). When this change is made Gehrels' general presumption for gain from union disappears. Table II

TABLE II

Free trade (col. 1)	Uniform *ad valorem* tariff on all imports (col. 2)	Customs union with country B (col. 3)
$\dfrac{P_{Ad}}{P_{Bd}} = \dfrac{P_{Ai}}{P_{Bi}}$	$\dfrac{P_{Ad}}{P_{Bd}} < \dfrac{P_{Ai}}{P_{Bi}}$	$\dfrac{P_{Ad}}{P_{Bd}} = \dfrac{P_{Ai}}{P_{Bi}}$
$\dfrac{P_{Ad}}{P_{Cd}} = \dfrac{P_{Ai}}{P_{Ci}}$	$\dfrac{P_{Ad}}{P_{Cd}} < \dfrac{P_{Ai}}{P_{Ci}}$	$\dfrac{P_{Ad}}{P_{Cd}} < \dfrac{P_{Ai}}{P_{Ci}}$
$\dfrac{P_{Bd}}{P_{Cd}} = \dfrac{P_{Bi}}{P_{Ci}}$	$\dfrac{P_{Bd}}{P_{Cd}} = \dfrac{P_{Bi}}{P_{Ci}}$	$\dfrac{P_{Bd}}{P_{Cd}} < \dfrac{P_{Bi}}{P_{Ci}}$

Subscripts A, B and C refer to countries of origin, d to prices in A's domestic market, and i to prices in the international market.

shows the three optimum conditions that domestic prices and international prices should bear the same relationship to each other for the three groups of commodities, A, B and C.[4] In free trade all three optimum conditions

[1] R. G. Lipsey, " Trade Diversion and Welfare," *op. cit.*, pp. 43–4. The changes made in the quotation are minor ones necessary to make the notation in the example comparable to the one used in the present text.

[2] Gehrels, *op. cit.*, p. 61.

[3] R. G. Lipsey, " Mr. Gehrels on Customs Unions," *Review of Economic Studies*, Vol. XXIV (3), No. 65, 1956–57, pp. 211–14.

[4] If we assume that consumers adjust their purchases to the relative prices ruling in their domestic markets, then the optimum conditions that rates of substitution in consumption should equal rates of transformation in trade can be stated in terms of equality between relative prices ruling in the domestic markets and those ruling in the international market.

will be fulfilled.   If a uniform tariff is placed on both imports, then the relations shown in column 2 will obtain, for the price of goods from both B and C will be higher in A's domestic market than in the international market.   When a customs union is formed, however, the prices of imports from the union partner, B, are reduced so that the first optimum condition is fulfilled, but the tariff remains on imports from abroad (C) so that the third optimum condition is no longer satisfied.   The customs union thus moves country A from one non-optimal position to another, and in general it is impossible to say whether welfare will increase or diminish as a result. We are thus back to a position where the theory tells us that welfare may rise or fall, and a much more detailed study is necessary in order to establish the conditions under which one or the other result might obtain.

The above analysis has lead both Mr. Gehrels and myself [1] to distinguish between *production effects* and *consumption effects* of customs unions.   The reason for attempting this is not hard to find.   Viner's analysis rules out substitution in consumption and looks to shifts in the location of production as the cause of welfare changes in customs unions.   The analysis just completed emphasises the effects of substitution in consumption.   The distinction on this basis, however, is not fully satisfactory, for consumption effects will themselves cause changes in production.   A more satisfactory distinction would seem to be one between *inter-country substitution* and *inter-commodity substitution.* Inter-country substitution would be Viner's trade creation and trade diversion, when one country is substituted for another as the source of supply for some commodity.   Inter-commodity substitution occurs when one commodity is substituted, at least at the margin, for some other commodity as a result of a relative price shift.   This is the type of substitution we have just been analysing.   In general, either of these changes will cause shifts in both consumption and production.

Now we come to Professor Meade's analysis.   His approach is taxonomic in that he attempts to classify a large number of possible cases, showing the factors which would tend to cause welfare to increase when a union is formed and to isolate these from the factors which would tend to cause welfare to diminish.[2]   Fig. 3 (i) shows a demand and a supply curve for any imported commodity.   Meade observes that a tariff, like any tax, shifts the supply curve to the left (to $S'S'$ in Fig. 3) and raises the price of the imported commodity.   At the new equilibrium the demand price differs from the supply price by the amount of the tariff.   If the supply price indicates the utility of the commodity to the suppliers and the demand price its utility to the purchasers, it follows that the utility of the taxed import is higher to purchasers than to suppliers, and the money value of this difference in utility is

---

[1] Gehrels, *op. cit.*, p. 61, and Lipsey, " Trade Diversion and Welfare," *op. cit.*, pp. 40–1.

[2] The point of his taxonomy or of any taxonomy of this sort, it seems to me, must be merely to illustrate how the model works.   Once one has mastered the analysis it is possible to work through any particular case that may arise, and there would seem to be no need to work out all possible cases beforehand.

the value of the tariff. Now assume that the marginal utility of money is the same for buyers and for sellers. It follows that, if one more *unit of expenditure* were devoted to the purchase of this commodity, there would be a net gain to society equal to the proportion of the selling price of the commodity composed of the tariff. In Fig. 3 the rate of tariff is $\frac{cb}{ab}$ %, the supply price is ab and the demand price is ac, so that the money value of the " gain " (" loss ") to society resulting from a marginal increase (decrease) in expenditure on this commodity is bc.

Now assume that the same *ad valorem* rate of tariff is imposed on all imports so that the tariff will be the same proportion of the market price of

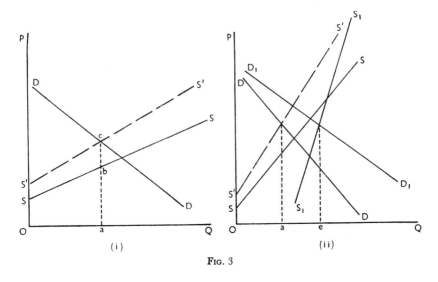

Fig. 3

each import. Then the gain to society from a marginal increase in expenditure (say one more " dollar " is spent) on any import is the same for all imports, and this gain is equal to the loss resulting from a marginal reduction in expenditure (one less " dollar " spent) on any import. Now consider *a marginal reduction* in the tariff on one commodity. This will cause a readjustment of expenditure, in the various possible ways analysed by Meade, so that in general more of some imports and less of others will be purchased. Since, *at the margin*, the gain from devoting one more unit of expenditure to the purchase of any import is equal to the loss from devoting one less unit of expenditure to the purchase of any import, the welfare consequences of this discriminatory tariff reduction may be calculated by comparing the increase in the volume of imports (trade expansion) with the decrease in the volume of other imports (trade contraction). If there is a net increase in the volume of trade the customs union will have raised economic welfare. A study of the welfare consequences of customs unions can, therefore, be devoted to the factors which will increase or decrease the volume of international trade.   If the influences which tend to cause trade expansion are found to predominate it may be predicted that a customs union will raise welfare.   The main body of Meade's analysis is in fact devoted to a study of those factors which would tend to increase, and to those which would tend to decrease, the volume of trade.   Complications can, of course, be introduced, but they do not affect the main drift of the argument.[1]

Meade's analysis, which makes use of demand and supply curves, suffers from one very serious, possibly crippling, limitation.   It will be noted that we were careful to consider only *marginal reductions* in tariffs.   For such changes Meade's analysis is undoubtedly correct.   When, however, there are *large* changes in many tariffs, as there will be with most of the customs unions in which we are likely to be interested, it can no longer be assumed that the demand and supply curves will remain fixed; the *ceteris paribus* assumptions on which they are based will no longer hold, so that both demand and supply curves are likely to shift.   When this happens it is no longer obvious how much welfare weight should be given to any particular change in the volume of trade (even if we are prepared to make all of the other assumptions necessary for the use of this type of classical welfare analysis).   In Fig. 3 (ii), for example, if the demand curve shifts to D_1D_1 and the supply curve to S_1S_1, what are we to say about the welfare gains or losses when trade changes from Oa to Oe?

There is not time to go through a great deal of Professor Meade's or my own analysis which attempts to discover the particular circumstances in which it is likely that a geographically discriminatory reduction in tariffs will raise welfare.   I shall, therefore, take two of the general conclusions that emerge from various analyses and present these in order to illustrate the type of generalisation that it is possible to make in customs-union theory.

The first generalisation is one that emerges from Professor Meade's analysis and from my own.   I choose it, first, because there seems to be general agreement on it and, second, although Professor Meade does not make this point, because it is an absolutely general proposition in the theory of second best; it applies to all sub-optimal positions, and customs-union theory only provides a particular example of its application.   Stated in terms of customs unions, this generalisation runs as follows: when only some

---

[1] For example, the same rate of tariff might not be charged on all imports.   In this case it is only necessary to weight each dollar's increase or decrease in trade by the proportion of this value that is made up by tariff—the greater is the rate of tariff the greater is the gain or loss.   It is also possible, if one wishes to make inter-country comparisons, to weight a dollar's trade in one direction by a different amount than a dollar's trade in some other direction.   These complications, however, do not affect the essence of Meade's analysis, which is to make a *small change* in some tariffs and then to observe that the welfare consequences depend on the net change in the volume of trade and to continue the study in order to discover in what circumstances an increase or a decrease in the net volume of trade is likely.

tariffs are to be changed, welfare is more likely to be raised if these tariffs are merely *reduced* than if they are completely *removed*. Proofs of this theorem can be found in both Meade [1] and Lipsey and Lancaster,[2] and we shall content ourselves here with an intuitive argument for the theorem in its most general context. Assume that there exist many taxes, subsidies, monopolies, etc., which prevent the satisfaction of optimum conditions. Further assume that all but one of these, say one tax, are fixed, and inquire into the second-best level for the tax that is allowed to vary. Finally, assume that there exists a unique second-best level for this tax.[3] Now a change in this one tax will either move the economy towards or away from a second-best optimum position. If it moves the economy away from a second-best position, then, no matter how large is the change in the tax, welfare will be lowered. If it moves the economy in the direction of the second-best optimum it may move it part of the way, all of the way or past it. If the economy is moved sufficiently far past the second-best optimum welfare will be lowered by the change. From this it follows that, if there is a unique second-best level for the tax being varied, a small variation is more likely to raise welfare than is a large variation.[4]

The next generalisation concerns the size of expenditure on the three classes of goods—those purchased domestically, from the union partner, and from the outside world—and is related to the gains from inter-commodity substitution. This generalisation follows from the analysis in my own thesis [5] and does not seem to have been stated in any of the existing customs-union literature. Consider what happens to the optimum conditions, which we discussed earlier, when the customs union is formed (see Table II). On the one hand, the tariff is taken off imports from the country's union partner, and the relative price between these imports and domestic goods is brought into conformity with the real rates of transformation. This, by itself, tends to increase welfare. On the other hand, the relative price between imports from the union partner and imports from the outside world are moved away from equality with real rates of transformation. This by itself tends to reduce welfare. Now consider both of these changes. As far as the prices of the goods from a country's union partner are concerned, they are brought

[1] *Op. cit.*, pp. 50–1.
[2] *Op. cit.*, Section V.
[3] A unique second-best level (*i.e.*, the level which maximises welfare subject to the existence and invariability of all the other taxes, tariffs, etc.) for any one variable factor can be shown to exist in a large number of cases (see, for example, Lipsey and Lancaster, *op. cit.*, Sections V and VI), but cannot be proved to exist in general (*ibid.*, Section VIII).
[4] This may be given a more formal statement. Consider the direction of the change—towards or away from the second-best optimum position—caused by the change in the tax. Moving away from the second-best optimum is a *sufficient*, but not a necessary, condition for a reduction in welfare. Moving towards the second-best optimum is a *necessary*, but not a sufficient, condition for an increase in welfare.
[5] R. G. Lipsey, *The Theory of Customs Unions: A General Equilibrium Analysis*, University of London Ph.D. thesis, unpublished, pp. 97–9, and Mathematical Appendix to Chapter VI. This thesis was subsequently published (1973) by Weidenfeld and Nicholson.

into equality with rates of transformation *vis à vis* domestic goods, but they are moved away from equality with rates of transformation *vis à vis* imports from the outside world. These imports from the union partner are thus involved in both a gain and a loss and their size is *per se* unimportant; what matters is the relation between imports from the outside world and expenditure on domestic commodities: the larger are purchases of domestic commodities and the smaller are purchases from the outside world, the more likely is it that the union will bring gain. Consider a simple example in which a country purchases from its union partner only eggs while it purchases from the outside world only shoes, all other commodities being produced and consumed at home. Now when the union is formed the " correct " price ratio (*i.e.*, the one which conforms with the real rate of transformation) between eggs and shoes will be disturbed, but, on the other hand, eggs will be brought into the " correct " price relationship with all other commodities —bacon, butter, cheese, meat, etc., and in these circumstances a customs union is very likely to bring gain, for the loss in distorting the price ratio between eggs and shoes will be small relative to the gain in establishing the correct price ratio between eggs and all other commodities. Now, however, let us reverse the position of domestic trade and imports from the outside world, making shoes the only commodity produced and consumed at home, eggs still being imported from the union partner, while everything else is now bought from the outside world. In these circumstances the customs union is most likely to bring a loss; the gains in establishing the correct price ratio between eggs and shoes are indeed likely to be very small compared with the losses of distorting the price ratio between eggs and all other commodities. If, to take a third example, eggs are produced at home, shoes imported from the outside world, while everything else is obtained from the union partner, the union may bring neither gain nor loss; for the union disturbs the " correct " ratio between shoes and everything else except eggs, and establishes the " correct " one between eggs and everything else except shoes. This example serves to show that the size of trade with a union partner is not the important variable; it is the relation between imports from the outside world and purchases of domestic goods that matters.

This argument gives rise to two general conclusions, one of them appealing immediately to common sense, one of them slightly surprising. The first is that, *given a country's volume of international trade*, a customs union is more likely to raise welfare the higher is the proportion of trade with the country's union partner and the lower the proportion with the outside world. The second is that a customs union is more likely to raise welfare the lower is the total volume of foreign trade, for the lower is foreign trade, the lower must be purchases from the outside world relative to purchases of domestic commodities. This means that the sort of countries who ought to form customs unions are those doing a high proportion of their foreign trade with their union partner, and making a high proportion of their total expenditure on domestic trade. Countries which are likely to lose from a customs union, on the other hand, are those countries in which a low proportion of total trade is domestic, especially if the customs union does not include a high proportion of their foreign trade.

We may now pass to a very brief consideration of some of the empirical work. Undoubtedly a serious attempt to predict and measure the possible effects of a customs union is a very difficult task. Making all allowances for this, however, a surprisingly large proportion of the voluminous literature on the subject is devoted to guess and suspicion, and a very small proportion to serious attempts to measure. Let us consider what empirical work has been done on the European Common Market and the Free Trade Area, looking first at attempts to measure possible gains from specialisation. The theoretical analysis underlying these measurements is of the sort developed by Professor Meade and outlined previously.

The first study which we will mention is that made by the Dutch economist Verdoorn, subsequently quoted and used by Scitovsky.[1] The analysis assumes an elasticity of substitution between domestic goods and imports of minus one-half, and an elasticity of substitution between different imports of minus two. These estimates are based on some empirical measurements of an aggregate sort and the extremely radical assumption is made that the same elasticities apply to all commodities. The general assumption, then, is that one import is fairly easily substituted for another, while imports and domestic commodities are not particularly good substitutes for each other.[2]

Using this assumption, an estimate was made of the changes in trade when tariffs are reduced between the six Common Market countries, the United Kingdom and Scandinavia. The estimate is that intra-European trade will increase by approximately 17%, and, when this increase is weighted by the proportion of the purchase price of each commodity that is made up of tariff and estimates for the reduction in trade in other directions are also made, the final figure for the gains from trade to the European countries is equal to about one-twentieth of one per cent of their annual incomes. In considering this figure, the crude estimate of elasticities of substitution must cause some concern. The estimate of an increase in European trade of 17% is possibly rather small in the face of the known fact that Benelux trade increased by approximately 50% after the formation of that customs union. A possible check on the accuracy of the Verdoorn method would have been to apply it to the pre-customs union situation in the Benelux countries, to use the method to predict what would happen to

[1] T. de Scitovsky, *Economic Theory and Western European Integration* (Allen and Unwin, 1958), pp. 64–78.

[2] Note also that everything is assumed to be a substitute for everything else; there are no relations of complementarity.

Benelux trade and then to compare the prediction with what we actually know to have happened. Whatever allowances are made, however, Scitovsky's conclusion is not likely to be seriously challenged:

"The most surprising feature of these estimates is their smallness. . . . As estimates of the total increase in intra-European trade contingent upon economic union, Verdoorn's figures are probably underestimates; but if, by way of correction, we should raise them five- or even twenty-five-fold, that would still leave unchanged our basic conclusion that the gain from increased intra-European specialisation is likely to be insignificant." [1]

A second empirical investigation into the possible gains from trade, this time relating only to the United Kingdom, has been made by Professor Johnson.[2] Johnson bases his study on the estimates made by *The Economist* Intelligence Unit of the increases in the value of British trade which would result by 1970, first, if there were only the Common Market and, second, if there were the Common Market and the Free Trade Area. Professor Johnson then asks what will be the size of the possible gains to Britain of participation in the Free Trade Area? His theory is slightly different from that of Professor Meade, but since it arrives at the same answer, namely that the gain is equal to the increased quantity of trade times the proportion of the purchase price made up of tariff, we do not need to consider the details. From these estimates Johnson arrives at the answer that the possible gain to Britain from joining the Free Trade Area would be, *as an absolute maximum*, 1% of the national income of the United Kingdom.

Most people seem to be surprised at the size of these estimates, finding them smaller than expected. This leads us to ask: might there not be some inherent bias in this sort of estimate? and, might not a totally different approach yield quite different answers? One possible approach is to consider the proportion of British factors of production engaged in foreign trade. This can be taken to be roughly the percentage contribution made by trade to the value of the national product, which can be estimated to be roughly the value of total trade as a proportion of G.N.P., first subtracting the import content from the G.N.P. This produces a rough estimate of 18% of Britain's total resources engaged in foreign trade. The next step would be to ask how much increase in efficiency of utilisation for these resources could we expect: (1) as a result of their re-allocation in the direction of their comparative advantage, and (2) as a result of a re-allocation among possible consumers of the commodities produced by these resources. Here is an outline for a possible study, but, in the absence of such a study, what would we guess? Would a 10% increase in efficiency not be a rather conservative

[1] Scitovsky, *op. cit.*, p. 67.
[2] H. G. Johnson, "The Gains from Free Trade with Europe: An Estimate," *Manchester School*, Vol. XXVI, September 1958.

estimate? Such a gain in efficiency would give a net increase in the national income of 1·8%. If the resources had a 20% increase in efficiency, then an increase in the national income of 3·6% would be possible. At this stage these figures can give nothing more than a common-sense check on the more detailed estimates of economists such as Verdoorn and Johnson. Until further detailed work has been done, it must be accepted that the best present estimates give figures of the net gain from trade amounting to something less than 1% of the national income (although we may not, of course, have a very high degree of confidence in these estimates).

When we move on from the possible gains from new trade to the question of the economic benefits arising from other causes, such as economies of scale or enforced efficiency, we leave behind even such halting attempts at measurement as we have just considered. Some economists see considerable economies of scale emerging from European union. Others are sceptical. In what what follows, I will confine my attention mainly to the arguments advanced by Professor H. G. Johnson.[1] His first argument runs as follows:

> " It is extremely difficult to believe that British industry offers substantial potential savings in cost which cannot be exploited in a densely-populated market of 51 million people with a G.N.P. of £18 billion, especially when account is taken of the much larger markets abroad in which British industry, in spite of restrictions of various kinds, has been able to sell its products.[2]

Let us make only two points about Professor Johnson's observation. First, many markets will be very much less than the total population. What, for example, can we say about a product sold mainly to upper middle-class males living more than 20 miles away from an urban centre? Might there not be economies of scale remaining in the production of a commodity for such a market? Secondly, in the absence of some theory that tells us the statement is true for 51 and, say, 31, but not 21, million people, the argument must remain nothing more than an unsupported personal opinion. As another argument, Professor Johnson asks, " Why are these economies of scale, if they do exist, not already being exploited? "[3] It is, of course, well known that unexhausted economies of scale are incompatible with the existence of perfect competition, but it is equally well known that unexhausted economies of scale are compatible with the existence of imperfect competition as long as long-run marginal cost is declining faster than

---

[1] In singling out Professor Johnson, I do not wish to imply that he is alone in practising the sort of economics which I am criticising. On the contrary, he is typical of a very large number of economists who have attempted to obtain quantitative conclusions from qualitative arguments.

[2] H. G. Johnson, " The Criteria of Economic Advantage," *Bulletin of the Oxford University Institute of Statistics*, Vol. 19, February 1957, p. 35. See also "The Economic Gains from Free Trade with Europe," *Three Banks Review*, September 1958, for a similar argument.

[3] Johnson, " Economic Gains," *op. cit.*, p. 10, and " Economic Advantage," *op. cit.*, p 35.

marginal revenue.   Here it is worthwhile making a distinction, mentioned by Scitovsky,[1] between the long-run marginal cost of producing more goods, to which the economist is usually referring when he speaks of scale effects, and the marginal cost of making and selling more goods (which must include selling costs).   This leads to a distinction between increasing sales when the whole market is expanding and increasing sales when the market is static, and thus increasing them at the expense of one's competitors.   The former is undoubtedly very much easier than the latter.   It is quite possible for the marginal costs of *production* to be declining while the marginal costs of *selling* in a static market are rising steeply.   This would mean that production economies would not be exploited by the firms competing in the market, but that if the market were to expand so that *all* firms in a given industry could grow, then these economies would be realised.

Let us also consider an argument put forward in favour of economies of scale.   Writing in 1955, Gehrels and Johnson argue that very large gains from economies of scale can be expected.[2]   In evidence of this they quote the following facts: American productivity (*i.e.*, output per man) is higher than United Kingdom productivity for most commodities; the differential is, however, greatest in those industries which use mass-production methods.   From this they conclude that there are unexploited economies of mass production in the United Kingdom.   Now this may well be so, but, before accepting the conclusion, we should be careful in interpreting this meagre piece of evidence. What else might it mean?   Might it not mean, for example, that the ratios of capital to labour differed in the two countries so that, if we calculate the productivity of a factor by dividing total production by the quantity of one factor employed, we will necessarily find these differences?   Secondly, would we not be very surprised if we did not find such differences in comparative costs between the two countries?   Are we surprised when we find America's comparative advantage centred in the mass-producing industries, and, if this is the case, must we conclude that vast economies of mass production exist for Europe?

Finally, we come to the possible gains through forced efficiency.   Business firms may not be adopting methods known to be technically more efficient than those now in use due to inertia, a dislike of risk-taking, a willingness to be content with moderate profits, or a whole host of other reasons.   If these firms are thrown into competition with a number of firms in other countries who are not adopting this conservative policy, then the efficiency of the use of resources may increase because technically more efficient production methods are forced on the business-man now facing fierce foreign competition.   Here no evidence has as yet been gathered, and, rather than report the opinions of others, I will close by recording the personal guess that this

[1] Scitovsky, *op. cit.*, pp. 42 ff.
[2] Gehrels and Johnson, " The Economic Gains from European Integration," *Journal of Political Economy*, August 1955.

is a very large potential source of gain, that an increase in competition with foreign countries who are prepared to adopt new methods might have a most salutary effect on the efficiency of a very large number of British and European manufacturing concerns.[1]

R. G. LIPSEY

London School of Economics.

[1] Milton Friedman's argument that survival of the fittest proves profit maximisation notwithstanding (see *Essays in Positive Economics*, Chicago: University of Chicago Press, 1953). What seems to me to be a conclusive refutation of the Friedman argument is to be found in G. C. Archibald, " The State of Economic Science," *British Journal of the Philosophy of Science*, June 1959.

THE THEORY OF CUSTOMS UNIONS

Rereading my article nearly thirty years after its publication, I was surprised to see how well it seems to have stood the test of time. In 1958, I rejected offers of publication of my PhD dissertation on customs union's on the grounds that the analysis was not of sufficient quality. When, over a decade later, I found economists still working on questions I had discussed, I authorized its belated publication by Weidenfeld & Nicolson (London, England) in 1972.

I guess the thing I liked most about my thesis was its emphasis on the exchange rate as an equilibrating mechanism. Crude though the "general equilibrium analysis" of Chapter 6 was, it gave a message still not understood in the U.S. Congress, and elsewhere: you cannot judge long-run international competitive positions while ignoring the long-run equilibrium exchange rate.

Rereading my paper, I was interested to be reminded of one proposition which appears to have been ignored. This is that the welfare effects of a customs union are unrelated to the size of the

trade done with one's union partners. This proposition -- argued
intuitively in my paper, and proven formally in my dissertation, --
has been ignored, for example, in the recent discussion on a
Canadian-American Free Trade Area (a CAFTA). Canadian economists
have typically argued that Canada is likely to gain from a CAFTA,
since most of Canadian foreign trade is done with its prospective
partner, the U.S. As the theory shows, however, what matters is the
ratio: <u>trade with non-partners</u> / <u>domestic trade</u>. Fortunately for
Canada, this ratio is small so that economists were correct in
arguing that the trade volumes were such that net gain was more
likely than net loss -- even if they did so for the wrong reasons.

Probably the biggest change since I wrote my essay is in
empirical measures of the gains from trade. The experience of the
EEC taught economists that most of the specialization following on
tariff reductions was intra-industry. Whole industries did not
disappear, instead each country established product niches in each
industry so that the main growth of trade was intra-industry. For
example, fashion goods produced in London, Paris, Milan, Stockholm
and Dusseldorf, pass each after going in opposite directions.
Modern industrial organization theory stresses this phenomenon of
product differentiation and shows that unexploited economies of
scale will be the typical situation in each of the hundreds of
product lines produced by a single industry. Because of these scale
effects the potential gains for tariff reduction are much greater
than was estimated earlier. For example, when such scale effects
were allowed for, estimates of the gains from Canadian-American
trade liberalization, based on levels of tariffs in the early 1970s,
rose from the range 0.5-1.0 percent of Canadian GNP to the range
5-10 percent --an order of magnitude increase!

One point on terminology has become important. The
dominant form of trade liberalizing pact when Viner wrote seemed to
be customs unions. Hence the generic term has become "The Theory of
Customs Unions". But, three types of trade-liberalizing
arrangements are important. A _free trade area_ removes tariffs
between the contracting parties but leaves each country free to set
its own duties against the rest of the world. Thus customs points
are still needed on the borders between member countries in order to
prevent imports coming into the FTA through the lowest tariff
country. So also are rules of origin to prevent trans-shipment,
with only minimal value added, through the lowest tariff partner
into the higher tariff partners. A _customs union_ has a common
tariff against the outside world and so avoids this problem. It
raises another problem, however, in that the politically dominant
partner will tend to set the trade policy with respect to the
outside world. A _common market_ is a customs union plus the free
movements of factors of production.

In the recent Canadian-American negotiations, Canadians who
wished to retain their policy independence towards the outside world
found a customs union unacceptable. For example, Canadians have not
forgotten that they traded with China for a decade during which the
U.S. regarded that country as an "evil empire" to be quaranteened
from world trade. Fortunately, the institution of a free trade area
was available to offer the two countries the benefit of free trade
between themselves, while preserving each member's independence in
setting its commercial policy with respect to the rest of the world.

The Theory of Common Markets

Peter Robson

The microeconomic theory of international economic integration largely consists of the static theory of customs unions and free trade areas, a central assumption of which is that factors of production are immobile both amongst the member countries and vis-à-vis the rest of the world. A common market, by contrast, involves not only the integration of product markets through the trade liberalization that results from customs union, but also the integration of factor markets through the elimination of obstacles to the free movement of factors within the bloc. The concept of a common market is a fairly new one, probably introduced by the Spaak Report of 1956, but in any case the term was in widespread use from the mid-1950s. The Treaty of Rome itself prescribed the establishment of a common market within twelve years, which would entail 'the abolition, as between Member States, of obstacles to freedom of movement for persons, services and capital'.

In a narrow sense the basic concern of a theory of common markets is with the additional benefits that can be derived by going beyond a simple customs union to the establishment of a common market. At the very least such a market would require the removal of legislative restrictions upon the free movement of factors between the member states, but an effective integration of factor markets would in practice also call for the adoption of positive harmonization measures with respect to the regulation of the markets for labour, capital and enterprise.

At a purely static level, the benefits, if any, to be derived from the superimposition of a common market upon a customs union are allocational gains. If, within a customs union, differences subsist in the marginal social productivity of the different factors in the various member states, a reallocation of factors that equalizes their marginal productivities can increase the income and welfare of the group. A migration of factors from countries where such productivities are relatively low, to those where they are higher, will

Reprinted from "The International Economics of Development, Third Edition", pp. 65–88 and 233–259, wiht permission of Routledge Books Inc., Copyright 1987.

213

then be beneficial. This will be accompanied by a tendency for disparities in factor earnings among the different member countries to be reduced.

In orthodox terms the operation of a customs union would itself, through its trade effects, reduce intra-union disparities in factor earnings and marginal productivities. If these effects could be relied upon to equalize intra-union marginal productivities of factors, resources would then be utilized in the most efficient way in the area, and a move from a customs union to a common market would not result in any further increase in allocational efficiency. In terms of that criterion alone therefore, there would be no advantage in establishing a common market.

The conditions required in order that trade alone should equalize marginal productivities are, however, extremely restrictive, and the empirical relevance of the factor-price equalization theorem is generally accepted to be extremely limited. In practice, various reasons such as differences in production functions between member states, or the existence of economies of scale in production, mean that further gains may be anticipated from an advance from a customs union to a common market. These and other sources of gain from factor movement have been analysed in a purely orthodox framework by Meade (1953, pp. 61–73).

In this chapter the principal economic implications of common markets are discussed in a much broader context, although for reasons of simplicity the analysis is conducted entirely in terms of capital flows. The chapter first considers the additional benefits that may be derived by superimposing an integrated factor market upon an existing customs union. It is assumed that the resulting common market chooses an appropriate combined level of capital controls vis-à-vis the outside world so that the possibility of net losses – akin to those that accompany trade diversion – can be disregarded. Secondly it considers the modifications required to the orthodox criteria for evaluating the welfare effects of a customs union in the presence of foreign factors. Thirdly it discusses whether the orthodox analysis of integration calls for qualification where production is carried on by transnational enterprises possessing market power. Fourthly it comments on some dynamic aspects of common markets. It goes on to consider the impact of the European Community on the strategies of transnational enterprises. In conclusion, it briefly considers policy and experience in the EC with respect to the liberalization of the markets for capital, labour and enterprise, and the programme currently under way to 'complete' the common market. The analysis deals mainly with allocational and distributional aspects of the issues. If a complete common market exists, however, and in particular if there is full financial integration (including substantially integrated bond markets), major constraints will be implied for the autonomy of national macroeconomic policies. Likewise, factor mobility will imply major limitations on the effective jurisdictional autonomy of national policies in other areas of policy such as taxation and social security. All of these considerations must be fully taken into account in evaluating both the costs and benefits of the introduction of a common market and the issue of whether a common market can be a stable stage of economic integration.

INTEGRATION AND CAPITAL FLOWS

Formal analysis may usefully commence with an application of orthodox partial equilibrium neoclassical analysis of capital flows to the case of a customs union, utilizing for simplicity a two-country model. It is assumed that two countries, H and P, have established a customs union, but that in the pre-common market phase obstacles to intra-regional factor mobility exist, as a result of which the customs union coexists with divergences in the marginal social productivity of capital. Factor supplies in each country are given. A single aggregate product is produced.

Figure 6.1 depicts production conditions in each country. The lines M_H and M_P relate capital stocks in the two countries to the marginal product of capital, given the amount of the other factor, namely labour. Initially, in the customs union phase, the capital stock is assumed to be OM in country H and OQ in country P. In the pre-common market phase, since capital is assumed to be internationally immobile, all capital stock must be nationally owned. Taxation is ignored. In a competitive model, profits per unit of capital equal its marginal product. Hence total profits in country H are $q + t$. Total output is $p + q + r + s + t$, and labour's share is $p + r + s$. In country P similarly, profits will amount to $x + z$, and the share of labour will amount to y. Despite the existence of the customs union, the rewards of capital are different in the two countries, being higher in P, reflecting partly that country's more favourable productive 'atmosphere'.

Let it now be assumed that the two countries decide to superimpose a common market for capital upon the existing customs union, so that obstacles to capital flows between the two countries are eliminated, although existing restrictions are maintained vis-à-vis

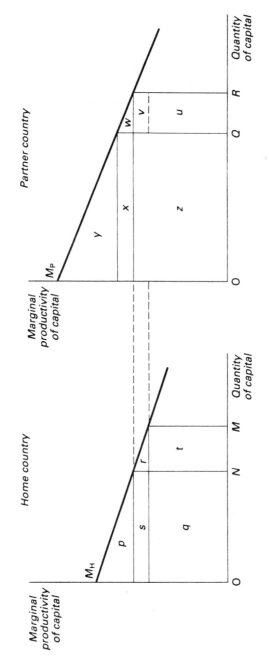

Figure 6.1 The impact of free intra-regional capital flows

the rest of the world. In order to remain initially within the static realm of discourse, it will be assumed that capital continues to be completely immobile vis-à-vis the rest of the world. The total stock of capital of the customs union is thus unaffected by the introduction of the common market for capital.

Following the establishment of the common market, capital will flow from H to P in search of higher rewards and a new equilibrium will be established when the distribution of capital between the two countries is such that its marginal productivity is equal, giving H ON and P OR of the stock.

The outcome is that H's domestically produced product declines to $p + q + s$, but its *national* product, including inward remittances of profit on capital employed in P, namely $v + u$ will increase by $v - r$. In country P *domestic* product increases by $u + v + w$, but *national* product, after allowing for outward profit remittances of $u + v$, increases only by w. In each country the share of labour in national product is altered in favour of owners of capital in country H, and against owners of capital in country P. If intra-market capital flows do not merely entail the application of known and existing technologies in the respective countries (represented by a move along given M_P and M_H curves) but are also accompanied by a significant transfer of new techniques and know-how, as is very often the case, the consequences of intra-group mobility would be more complex and the conclusions of the static neoclassical analysis would need modification. Qualifications on this account (and others) are discussed in MacDougall (1960) and Grubel (1982).

FOREIGN CAPITAL AND THE COSTS AND BENEFITS OF INTEGRATION

Customs unions are rarely, if ever, established in circumstances of complete international immobility of factors. Foreign capital has been an important element in the economies of most of the countries that have sought to establish customs unions and other forms of international integration during the past quarter of a century. How does the presence of foreign capital affect the criteria for evaluating customs unions? At the level of the orthodox neoclassical analysis, the principal qualification is that trade creation and trade diversion then cease to be sufficient indicators of costs and benefits for a member country. Basically this conclusion follows directly from the point just noted, namely that when foreign capital is present the impact of integration on a country's national income is

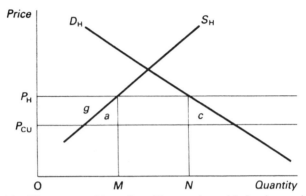

Figure 6.2   The costs and benefits of integration with foreign capital

not identical to its impact on the country's geographical or domestic income.

Whenever foreign direct investment is present in an economy in the shape of foreign enterprises, the effects of integration will be determined partly by its impact on the net economic rents earned by those enterprises from the use of their exclusive assets. These assets include superior technologies, and special administrative and entrepreneurial capacities. These and other factors permit foreign enterprises to produce at lower costs and thus to earn pure or quasi rents even in competitive industries. In a simple partial equilibrium neoclassical analysis, these rents are measured by the producers' surplus. In the presence of foreign rents, a consideration of the gains and losses of integration cannot be limited to the orthodox trade creation and trade diversion effects. *Additional* gains or losses for the host country will arise from changes in the rents earned by foreign companies because these imply a redistribution of income as between the country of origin of the foreign capital and the host country. For instance, in the case of an importable commodity produced by foreign enterprises whose price falls after integration as a result of trade creation, the host country will gain from the reduction in foreign company rents. This additional benefit has been termed by Tironi (1982) the *foreign profit diversion effect*.

Figure 6.2 illustrates the point. S_H and D_H represent the demand and supply curves for an importable produced by country H. Prior to customs union, an amount OM is produced at a price P_H. Assume that if a customs union is formed, the price falls to P_{CU}. If producers are wholly domestic, the gain to country H will be denoted by areas $a + c$, as has been explained in Chapter 2. If, instead, the commodity is produced wholly by foreign enterprise and capital, there will be an additional national gain equal to area g, which represents the reduction in remittable profits, and *mutatis mutandis* for intermediate cases. Area *g* denotes the *foreign profit diversion effect*.

Similarly, if there are foreign enterprises in the home country that enjoy a regional comparative advantage then, in addition to the standard trade and welfare effects, a further effect termed by Tironi *the foreign profit creation effect*, would have to be taken into account in evaluating the costs and benefits of forming a customs union. This foreign profit creation effect is represented by the additional rents or profits that would, as a consequence of the customs union, be obtained by foreign enterprises from their sales in the host country and their exports to the preferential markets of the partner country. For the host country, the counterpart of these additional rents from home sales is a fall in consumers' surplus, which in this case represents a national income loss from its point of view. At the same time, the additional rents earned on sales to the partner country do not – unlike the cases analysed in Chapter 2 – represent a national gain from the host country's standpoint. For the importing partner country on the other hand, the additional rents earned on its imports by the foreign enterprise in the host country are reflected in the trade diversion that it experiences. This loss is already accounted for in the orthodox analysis and no further adjustment on its account is therefore required.

Typically of course, host countries participate through taxes in rents or profits earned by both foreign and domestic enterprises. On one view indeed, this is the principal benefit derived by a host country from foreign inward investment (MacDougall, 1960), because the host country gains from more advanced technologies and skills imported only to the extent that it can use them without fully paying for them in the form of rents and profit remittances. If a country participates in profits through taxation, the benefit from the foreign profit diversion effect would be reduced to $(1 - t)(d)$, where t is the rate of profits tax and d is the profit diversion effect. In the limiting case therefore, where the rate of tax on foreign profits were 100 per cent, the welfare effects of forming a customs union when foreign enterprises are present would be identical to those arising when there are only national enterprises. Similarly, if taxes are paid by a foreign firm that exports to a partner country, then the loss to the host country will be smaller.

TRANSNATIONAL ENTERPRISES AND INTEGRATION

The previous section has explained how the introduction of foreign investment affects the calculation of gain from integration to members of the group, assuming competitive conditions to prevail. In fact, much of contemporary foreign direct investment is undertaken by enterprises that possess a significant degree of market power, and whose operations in many cases are conducted on a multi-country basis. These two characteristics of foreign investment pose a number of important questions for an analysis of integration. The basic question is whether the orthodox analysis linking domestic costs and prices with the direction, composition and extent of intra-group trade and the distribution of its costs and benefits continues to be valid when the operations of such transnational corporations are explicitly taken into account.

This issue is posed in part by the ability of the transnational enterprise (TNE) to bypass the operations of the market, which, in the orthodox model, determines the effects of integration on the efficiency of resource allocation. Within a transnational enterprise the activities of subsidiaries can be regulated as an intra-firm matter in ways that, although they may be optimal from the standpoint of the global interests and objectives of the TNE, are not necessarily so from the standpoint of the individual enterprise considered as a profit-maximizing unit, or from the standpoint of the host country itself. One important aspect of TNE policy from this point of view concerns the prices at which intra-firm transactions take place. These 'transfer prices', which are not market determined, can have an important influence on production, trade flows and the distribution of costs and benefits. At one level, of course, a major source of the TNE's strength is its ability to reduce by 'internalization' the transactions costs that would otherwise be involved in 'arms-length' contractual relationships between independent enterprises. The incentive to engage in 'transfer pricing' will be greater, the greater are the fiscal differences and the impediments to trade and capital movement amongst the countries concerned. The more 'complete' the internal market becomes, the less important this factor is likely to be.

In the simplest of static models with given cost and demand conditions, it can be shown that, if a transnational enterprise is the sole producer of a particular product in an integration group, neither the quantities of goods traded, nor the direction of trade and specialization, need be affected by the phenomenon of transfer prices (Horst, 1973). But when competitors exist, other issues arise. If transfer prices are used for such purposes as to cross-subsidize a subsidiary in order to eliminate local competition, or to maintain a position of market dominance, or to hinder potential competitors from entering, their manipulation must be expected to affect not only trade patterns, but also the character of industrial production, static and dynamic efficiency and the intra-regional distribution of benefits from integration.

The simpler static models that attempt to deal with these issues are certainly open to the objection that they exclude crucial aspects of TNEs' operations. But broader organizational analyses of TNEs sometimes reach similar conclusions. Starting from such approaches, a number of economists (McManus, 1972; Buckley and Casson, 1976; Dunning, 1977) have contended that a transnational's ownership links, which generate economies in transaction costs and benefits from coordination, do not themselves significantly affect the locational distribution of its physical production activities or the scale of its plants – a proposition that Caves (1980, p. 322) has termed the 'separation' theory. These analyses again suggest the conclusion that the international location of production should not, merely as a result of the transnational character of enterprises conducting it, impede the attainment of the pattern indicated by considerations of regional cost minimization.

An important objection to some of these further analyses is that they too disregard the interdependence of enterprises in arriving at their conclusions. Typically, the operations of TNEs take place in an oligopolistic context. In such situations it is well established that patterns of oligopolistic rivalry among TNEs do affect their investment decisions. Knickerbocker (1973), for instance, found that American TNEs had an imitative pattern of behaviour that implies an exaggerated shift of output towards the national markets entered by imitative rivals, and an investment in smaller-scale production facilities, than if no such imitation occurred. In the same way, where TNEs seek to preserve a balance of interest vis-à-vis their rivals, it appears that their investment in production facilities may not serve to minimize costs of production.

In situations of market interdependence and oligopoly it is difficult if not impossible to make *a priori* predictions about the impact of TNEs in the context of integration. It is clearly necessary to be cautious before applying without qualification the resource allocation conclusions of the simple competitive model to sectors in which TNEs dominate. But it should also be borne in mind that often TNEs are in competition with national enterprises, and moreover that, except in a limited range of industries, they may not be dominant (apart from the situation in certain groupings of developing countries). Where that is the case, although the policies of TNEs may influence the outcomes, they need not predominate, and the broad conclusions of the simple models may still hold.

COMMON MARKETS, FACTOR SUPPLIES, DYNAMIC EFFECTS AND CONVERGENCE

Up to this point this chapter has been concerned mainly with the static implications of factor mobility for regional integration.

However, just as the institution of a customs union is likely to affect cost and demand conditions and the supplies of factors and possibly also the rate of growth of the economy partly through dynamic effects, so also may the elimination of restrictions on factor mobility and progress towards a common market. A number of insights into these impacts can be derived from the literature on trade and investment, but strong predictions are few and empirical studies are sparse. In general, the literature suggests that taking these factors into account would merely reinforce the presumed static effects. Starting from different but plausible assumptions however, crucial objections can be made to certain of the qualitative predictions of static neoclassical theory.

In static analysis, the intra-regional movement of factors (here specifically the movement of capital) is seen as an instrument for promoting the convergence of real income. In a growth context also, the intra-regional movement of capital and other factors is orthodoxly viewed as a vehicle for distributing the fruits of technical progress and of productivity growth more evenly throughout a common market. If, however, there is a tendency for those countries whose growth is most vigorous to attract direct investment and other factors from the rest of the economically integrated area, this may produce contrary effects and have adverse consequences for geographical balance. Member states are unlikely to be indifferent to these effects, even if incomes per capita should thereby be rendered more equal, so confronting them with a trade-off between the goals of geographical balance and of income convergence.

Some radical critics of the neoclassical theory argue however, that there is no such trade-off, because the geographical redistribution of factors that is stimulated by the institution of a common market does not contribute to a convergence of incomes, still less to a convergence of growth rates of income. Instead, it is claimed, the impact of economies of scale and of agglomeration effects, together with the progressive adjustments of costs and demands that accompany the interregional migration of factors, will produce self-reinforcing dynamic effects – termed polarization – that accentuate rather than ameliorate regional imbalances of real incomes.

Some empirical support can be found for the existence of such effects, although it is seldom easy to determine to what extent the widening disparities can be attributed to a common market effect rather than to the impact of structural factors that would in any case have produced a similar result even in the absence of a common market – as in the case of Britain's altered position in relation to her partners in the EC. The supposed importance of these dynamic effects constitutes an important part of the general case for instituting a regional policy in a common market.

THE IMPACT OF THE EUROPEAN COMMUNITY ON THE STRATEGY AND PERFORMANCE OF TRANSNATIONAL ENTERPRISES

The establishment of the EC, and its later enlargement, has been accompanied by much debate on how the common market would affect (*ex ante*) and has affected (*ex post*) the strategies and performance of multinational corporations (MNCs), which account for a significant and growing share of the Community's output, employment and trade, and on how, if at all, the EC should attempt to influence their operation. In seeking to understand these issues it is necessary to start from the factors that influence the behaviour of multinational enterprises across national boundaries, that is to say, the theory of international production. The factors to be explained are the ability of firms to compete in foreign markets, and the reasons why they would choose to exploit their advantages by foreign production, rather than by exporting to the market or by selling access to their special advantages by means of licensing, etc. This is typically explained in terms of an interaction between the ownership advantages that a firm possesses in the form of its command of technology, the internalization factor, which, because of market failure, may make it advantageous for the firm to use the advantages itself rather than to sell the right to their use to producers in other countries, and the locational factor, which makes it advantageous to combine its assets with factors that are located in foreign countries rather than to serve the market by exports (Dunning, 1977).

A closely related way of looking at the issues distinguishes simply between factors specific to the firm, industry or product, on the one hand, and environmental factors on the other. In the specific context of integration, relevant environmental factors would include: the impact of the negative integration that is brought about by trade liberalization; the impact of more positive harmonization measures in the shape of EC health and industrial standards, patent and trade mark legislation (particularly relevant to the internalization factor); and, lastly, the legislation of member states and their overt or covert practices with respect to such factors as public procurement, capital flows, ownership and acquisition.

The earliest aspect of the subject to be given attention was the impact of the EC through the size of the market, its rate of growth, and tariff discrimination, on the inflow of foreign direct investment from outside the Community, and more specifically from the US. In the quantitative aggregative studies that have been undertaken a strong relationship has commonly been found between the size of the EEC markets and American foreign direct investment (FDI) in the EC (Balassa, 1977). However, the links between the reported changes in FDI and growth are mixed, or weak. None the less the issue cannot be regarded as wholly settled. In a recent survey, Pelkmans (1984) suggests that an industrial economics approach might be more promising.

Apart from the question of the impact of the EC on inflows of FDI into Europe interest in the impact of the EC on multinational strategy and performance has focused on the two issues mentioned above, namely inter-industry and intra-firm plant specialization, and on the employment impact of intra EC foreign direct investment. Of late these issues have been increasingly viewed in the context of innovation and technological change.

The variety of factors at work with respect to decisions on international production and the interaction that is to be expected between firm-specific and environmental variables suggest that any uniform pattern of behaviour with respect to the impact of the EC factor on the strategies and performance of multinational businesses in Europe is hardly to be looked for. And indeed it is the case that few strong generalizations emerge from the more realistic of the models of international business or market structure and foreign trade. *A priori,* however, it is widely supposed that the integration of national economies might be expected to have two opposing effects on the strategy of multinational enterprises in an economic community:

(1)   The removal of tariffs and barriers to trade and investment may be expected to result in decreased horizontal integration. Firms producing substantially identical products in plants in different countries should be stimulated to remove duplication if costs differ or if economies of scale are significant, and to concentrate their activities – by divestment – on fewer countries and plants;

(2)   The opportunity that integration affords for a better international division of labour might also be expected to stimulate increased vertical integration and perhaps component specialization by MNCs searching for lower costs and scale economies.

One of the earliest systematic studies of these issues was made by

Franko (1976). Using data for the period 1958–71 derived from the Harvard Comparative Multinational Enterprise Project, he analysed the experience of more than eighty of the largest European multinationals – i.e. those with headquarters in the original six member states of the EC. He found little evidence in their conduct of either of the effects distinguished above. On the contrary, despite the fact that tariff barriers in Europe were crumbling during this period, there was a proliferation of international operations in Europe by European multinationals at a rate faster than their rate of growth of foreign production in most other parts of the world. Moreover, particularly high concentrations of foreign subsidiaries in Europe were reported for a number of oligopolistic industries where economies of scale were presumptively very large, such as cans, glass, power turbines, iron and steel, processed foods, industrial chemicals and paints. In the products of these industries, intra-EC trade expansion in the period was relatively low. Only in a very limited number of sectors, such as automobiles, electrical appliances and white goods, were there relatively few acquisitions, even some divestments and an extremely rapid growth of intra-European trade. He concluded that 'reallocation of production did not seem to be a major preoccupation for most Continental firms prior to 1971' and that the behaviour reported is to be explained in terms of efforts by both MNCs and governments to protect existing patterns of activity and investments.

Franko's analysis, which is based on an enumeration of legally incorporated entities, may understate the degree of actual plant closures and product reallocation in the period. Furthermore, his data disregarded the experience of all multinationals with headquarters outside the Six, including the numerically important and, in the case of some industries, dominant US multinationals. Many of these firms – Honeywell, Ford, International Harvester – operate in industries where technology is an important source of competitive strength. In such firms there has been a well-documented tendency, since 1960, for European plants that were previously truncated replicas of their parent companies, each producing similar products for individual national markets without much trade between them, to specialize in particular products and processes for all markets in the region and to trade these products across national boundaries (Dunning, 1983). The formation of Ford (Europe) in 1967, specifically to coordinate and integrate European production, was a major step towards the international rationalization of the motor industry that was undoubtedly stimulated by the progress of the EC.

The numerous studies of the operation of multinational enterprises in Europe that have appeared since the mid-1970s convey a
complex picture with respect to the issues that have been singled out
for discussion here, and one that cannot be briefly presented. But it
is plain that, whatever may have been the case prior to 1970, in the
following years 'European' firms – stimulated no doubt in some
industries by American MNC behaviour and Japanese competition
– have actively sought to rationalize European production, in part
by decreased horizontal integration and increased vertical integration and component specialization, although not always with success. Rationalization has been particularly noticeable in the
European-owned motor industry, in agricultural machinery and in
domestic electrical appliances (refrigerators, freezers, washing
machines and driers). In the bearing industry also, significant
rationalization took place after 1972, stimulated by the enlargement of the EC and the completion of the EC–EFTA free trade
provisions. On the other hand, rationalization has occurred hardly
at all in pharmaceuticals, where its progress has been hindered by
government controls on the registration of new products and controls over prices (Cantwell, 1987). At the same time, it is clear that
frequently European producers based in one country have continued to feel obliged to establish a presence in other countries of
the EC – not merely for the purpose of servicing goods imported
from headquarters, but also to manufacture. The establishment of
such a presence has been attempted in a variety of ways – by
acquisition of interests, by mergers and less commonly by the
construction of new projects. The experience of the UK's multinationals has been well documented by Stopford and Turner
(1985). Their examination of the difficulties encountered by industrial reconstruction initiatives prior to and since 1973 leads them to
the conclusion that entry into the European market cannot be
achieved by acquisition on a major scale. 'The spirit of the Treaty of
Rome does not extend to allowing control of a key national
resource to slip into foreign hands, even when those hands are also
European.'
    One crucial problem in attempting to determine empirically what
has been the impact of the EC on multinational strategy, and
through it on a variety of variables affecting the incomes and
welfare of member states, is to determine, first, what would have
happened in the absence of the identified developments, and secondly what part of them is attributable to the presence of the EC.
This problem is present in all empirical evaluations of the EC and
alternative approaches to its solution are reviewed in Chapter 13.
The former issue has been posed most squarely in those studies that

have attempted to throw light on the effect of intra-EC direct investment and its employment impact. The *anti-monde* issue is usually tackled in the first instance by reference to the putative relevance of three limiting cases suggested by Hufbauer and Adler (1968). They are:

(1) *The classical case.* This postulates that intra-Community direct investment produces a corresponding net addition to capital formation in the host country but an equivalent decline in the source country so that, overall, capital formation remains unchanged. This implies that intra-Community direct investment is a direct substitute for investment at home and that the output of the investment replaces exports from the source country. Investment in other parts of the Community to take advantage of cheap labour could fall into this category.

(2) *The reverse classical case.* In this case the investment is assumed to be a substitute for investment in the host country and to leave investment in the source country unchanged. This corresponds to the case of defensive investment where restrictions prevent imports into the markets of other Community countries or a presence is required to penetrate them. Without the investment, the source country could not penetrate those markets and would lose it to host country producers.

(3) *The anti-classical case.* In this case, foreign investment is not a substitute for capital investment in the source country and does not reduce investment in host country firms.

These categories can be criticized on account of their rigidity and their static nature and because they ignore market servicing strategies, which concern the decisions with respect to which plants should service which markets and through which channels. Empirical studies of such strategies – which should take account of the significant firm-specific and environmental factors to which reference has been made – illustrate the complexity of these decisions (Buckley and Pearce, 1981). Nevertheless, some anti-monde assumption must be made, and the choice will evidently be crucial to the results reported.

A recent case study (Buckley and Artisien, 1987) that investigates the politically charged question of the impact of intra-EC direct investment on employment in the EC illustrates the issue. The study examines nineteen cases of direct investment by enterprises belonging to more advanced members (France, Germany, the UK) in three less developed members (Greece, Portugal and Spain). The study concludes that the effects on the level of income and employment in the host country were almost invariably positive, but those on the source country were often negative. In itself this study throws no light on the EC effect of multinational behaviour on the level and distribution of employment because it cannot be assumed that this development would not have taken place in the absence of the EC. It is, indeed, highly probable that a large part of the multinational integration that has taken place among enterprises in the EC is to be attributed to the globalization of their operations, and can only be fully understood in the light of the pressures and incentives that have given rise to that phenomenon. Nevertheless, the effect of having intra-EC free trade in force or in prospect is to induce direct investments towards a localization that strengthens *inter*-industry specialization inside the common market. The authors' interpretation of the material suggests that this process has been important.

EC Policy towards MNCs

However MNCs are judged (in terms of private or social efficiency criteria) to have responded to the impact of European integration, it is clear that the outcome has been significantly affected by environmental factors, and in particular by the industrial policies of the member states, and more recently by those of the EC. Many of the factors that impede a more effectual rationalization of European industry geared to the common market are to be attributed not so much to shortcomings of multinational strategies as to a failure on the part of the EC to complete the common market. Some institutional aspects of this issue will be considered in the following section. Here we touch briefly on the question of the EC's MNC policy – perhaps attitudes would be a better term – which has undergone substantial evolution in the past decade.

Initially MNCs as such were not a target of the orthodox instruments of EC policy that impinge on business. These policies (and notably competition policy which intervenes when there is a threat to intra-EC trade) were basically free trade in inspiration and EC actions in the field of company legislation and labour affairs were similarly designed to promote market neutrality and to prevent abuses. Inevitably, however, the importance of the MNCs in the European market and the potential impact of their decisions to invest and divest on individual member states of the EC in terms of employment and income have meant that their operations have attracted particular interest in the actual administration of policy.

None the less, it was not until 1973, with the enunciation of the Commission's action programme with respect to multinationals (Commission, 1973b), that the question of an MNC policy *per se* overtly arose. In that action programme the Commission envisaged controls specifically directed at MNCs (echoing earlier measures proposed by UN and OECD – in those cases largely ineffective). But the Commission's approach to multinationals was not entirely negative; steps were also promised to foster the transnational integration of the member countries' industrial structures. These initiatives and the attitudes they reflected nevertheless appear to have been perceived by the MNCs as a threat. The more aggressive competition policy that was pursued during the 1970s, and the Vredeling draft directive of 1980 (*Bulletin of the European Communities*, Supplement 3, 1980; *Bulletin of the European Communities* 10/1980) aimed at facilitating worker participation and consultation in the affairs of industrial groupings, did nothing to allay those fears.

Whether or not it really was the case that the Commission's attitude towards transnationals at that time was adversarial, it is certainly true that the economic crisis experienced by the EC during the mid-1970s subsequently produced a significant shift of attitudes. From that time it had become plain that the European economy was faced with a severely worsening competitive position vis-à-vis the Third World and the US and Japan. It was widely felt that the problem could not be overcome without a more effectual restructuring of European industry. Within the Commission, an acceptance of this view has been reflected, *inter alia*, in the dominance of a more flexible approach to competition policy that seeks to take greater account of the need not to impede European producers in their attempts to regroup and reorganize in the face of competition, and to facilitate changes in other policy fields designed to speed up institutional changes that could foster such needed development. In the process, business enterprise as a whole, but transnationals in particular, have come to be seen as crucial instruments and allies rather than as adversaries in the achievement of the EC's goals or market integration. The promotion by the EC of transfrontier links in certain key sectors regarded as essential to enable the European economy to withstand the competitive challenge from the US and Japan is an important aspect of this development. It is reflected not only in the initiation and conduct of new projects such as ESPRIT, RACE and BRITE, which presuppose such transnational business links, but also in the new approach to the development of industrial standards and to the harmonization of other areas of policy such as patents and trade marks where

progress will in future be predominantly the responsibility of European business – more and more willingly accepted – and of their
organizations. In the process it seems not unlikely that the former
even-handed treatment of foreign and European transnationals
that has hitherto been a particular feature of EC policy may
undergo modification. In any event, the Europeanization of standards and of patent and trade mark legislation cannot fail to have
important implications for the relative strength and conduct of
European and foreign transnationals.

COMPLETING THE
EUROPEAN COMMON MARKET

The European Economic Community is based on the idea of a
common market, and the term itself is used as the colloquial equivalent of the EEC; but in fact there is not yet anything like a full
common market in Western Europe. The pursuit of market integration in Europe may be evaluated in two main ways: first by defining
the measures needed to realize a true common market and comparing them with the prescriptions of the Treaty of Rome; and second
by considering the state of market integration that has been arrived
at by EC decisions and their implementation in member states and
comparing it with the Treaty's prescriptions. From the first point of
view it is indisputable that Treaty prescriptions go a long way in the
direction of the requirements of a full common market, although in
certain respects falling short of an ideal. In this sense a perfect
common market would be a degree of market integration among
member countries in which neither national frontiers, nor residency
nor nationality of economic agents have any differential economic
significance (Pelkmans and Robson, 1987). At the same time, if the
issue is approached from the second point of view, it is equally
indisputable that the actual arrangements of the EC – the *acquis
communautaire*' – with respect to market integration fall far short of
Treaty requirements. This has led to sometimes exaggerated criticisms of the alleged failure of market integration in Europe, cari-
catured by unsympathetic critics as 'the uncommon market'
(Holland, 1980) or centring on criticisms that the EC has become
merely an area of free trade.

Even today's incomplete common market embodies a number of
respectable achievements. What the EC has accomplished in terms
of market integration is both historically unique – given the absence
of coercion that has accompanied it – and economically significant.
Disillusion derives from the even greater aspirations that the EC

proclaims and its failure to live up to them. Of late, an awareness of the costs involved in maintaining an incomplete common market, in terms of the obstacles it imposes to industrial reconstruction and rationalization, has greatly increased. This partly explains why an appreciation of the achievements of the common market has lately been overshadowed by a lamentation over its omissions and failures.

It is in this context that the Commission's White Paper (Commission, 1985) on completing the common market is to be viewed. This paper represents a plan for a large scale assault on the limitations of the common market with the objective of completing it by 1992. Unlike some other EC initiatives, the plan has not been launched in a political vacuum. It has been embraced by the European Council. The aim of completing the common market has moreover been included in the Single European Act (Lodge, 1986) in a formulation that is stronger than the Rome Treaty, which itself contains no reference to eliminating frontiers in the common market. What progress has been made towards the establishment of a common market in Europe? What remains to be done? What are the Commission's proposals?

The European Common Market: Institutional Progress, Gaps and Plans

If purely physical and administrative obstacles are put on one side, together with the fiscal barriers that will be discussed in Chapter 8, the principal remaining obstacles to an undivided internal market in Europe may be divided into (1) those affecting the movement of products, including both goods and services; and (2) those affecting the free movement of factors – labour, capital and enterprise.

FREE MOVEMENT OF PRODUCTS

With respect to the movement of goods, it has already been noted that a variety of non-tariff barriers associated with 'voluntary' industrial standards and governmental health and safety regulations impede the free movement in Europe and the establishment of a single unified market. Hitherto the Community has utilized Article 100 of the Treaty of Rome in its efforts to bring about a harmonization of technical regulations. This article provides for the issue of directives on the basis of unanimity for the harmonization of national legal provisions that directly affect the functioning of the common market. Progress along this line has been painfully slow, in part because of the need to incorporate detailed technical specifications into directives. Henceforward the two-stage procedure that is envisaged in the 'new approach' of the White Paper will consist of laying down, it is hoped in most cases on the basis of qualified majority voting, only those identical requirements or objectives that are seen to be 'essential' in the interests of health, safety and environmental protection. The tasks of actually laying down the technical specifications necessary to meet the requirements as defined in the regulations, will be left to European standards bodies (CEN, CENELEC, etc.). This approach is calculated to make it much more difficult for harmonization to be resisted by vested interests.

A second area of difficulty in relation to the free movement of goods relates to public procurement. In principle, the basic rules of the Treaty apply fully to the supply of goods to public purchasing bodies, as do the rules relating to the freedom to provide services without discrimination. But whereas member states meet 20–40 per cent if not more of the requirements of private consumption by supplies from another member state, the corresponding ratio for public procurement is probably rather less than 1 per cent, if not zero. Since 1971 public works contracts are supposed to be advertised in the *Official Journal* and contracts awarded to the most economic tender. Since 1978 similar provisions have also applied to supply contracts. Reports prepared by the Commission in 1984 (*Bulletin of the European Communities* 12/1984, 6/1985) and endorsed by the European Parliament suggest that neither the letter nor the spirit of the directives is being adhered to. For instance, according to the Commission, less than a quarter of the public expenditure involved in public contracts in fields covered by the existing directives is advertised in the *Official Journal*. Recession is encouraging the use of national suppliers. The Commission's reports do suggest, however, that an important factor hindering effectual Community-wide competition is the lack of harmonization of technical standards. The Commission has proposed a number of measures to open up this important area of the market, including the broadening of the field of application of the relevant directives to cover certain transport services, energy, water and telecommunications, and the establishment of a public procurement unit to monitor action.

Freedom to provide services across the internal frontiers of the Community is also provided for in the Treaty, but progress has been still slower in this area, not only in relation to traditional services such as transport and insurance and banking, but also in relation to services associated with the development of new technologies such as audiovisual services, information and data processing services and certain forms of telecommunications. The importance of making progress in this area is underlined by the growing role of the service sector in the economies of the EC, where it now accounts for a more substantial share of GDP than industry – and by contrast to that sector is generating a growing volume of employment. Any liberalization of the financial service sector in banking and insurance is necessarily closely linked to the free movement of capital, which is discussed below.

FREE MOVEMENT OF LABOUR

Freedom of movement for workers and the abolition of discrimination by nationality is required by the Treaty of Rome and the provisions for it are formally almost complete except for a limited right of public authorities to reserve posts for nationals. The Treaty provisions on labour mobility have been supported by the adoption of social security provisions that entitle migrants who are nationals of member states to the same benefits as those of nationals of the host countries.

Despite substantial differences in levels of wages and social security benefits among the EC countries, intra-Community labour migration, at least of non-professional workers, has to date been modest. Until the 1970s the main internal source of Community migrants was Italy. Migration seems to have been stimulated largely by the lack of employment opportunities rather than by differences in wage rates and earnings. The principal source of migrants has in fact been non-Community states, such as Turkey, Yugoslavia and Portugal, the latter a member since 1986.

In the field of the professions, and the right of establishment for the self-employed, on the other hand, very slow progress has been made towards freedom of movement. The complexities of harmonizing the requirements for professional recognition have proved to be immense. Considerable freedom has nevertheless been secured for those engaged in medicine and nursing. But the right of establishment for architects and pharmacists was not approved until 1985, after respectively seventeen and fourteen years of discussion!

CAPITAL FLOWS: POLICY AND EXPERIENCE IN THE EC

With respect to the integration of capital markets, the Treaty of Rome commits member states progressively to abolish restrictions on intra-EC capital movements to the extent necessary to secure the proper functioning of the Common Market, including the abolition of discriminatory restrictions based on nationality and place of residence. However, under Article 73, if the movement of capital disturbs the capital market of a member state, the Commission may, after consulting the Monetary Committee, authorize a state to take protective measures. The Council itself may revoke or amend such authorization. In addition, under Article 109, which relates to balance of payments policy, a member state is allowed to take certain measures in the event of a crisis, which could include control of capital movements.

Unlike the Treaty provisions relating to free trade in goods and services, the principle of freedom of capital movements does not apply directly. All progress towards liberalization requires the imposition of Community obligations by agreed adoption of directives by the Council. Two such directives were agreed in 1960 and 1962. They resulted in the removal of restrictions on direct investment, portfolio investment in quoted securities, transactions involving real estate, and certain others. These provisions can only be revoked under the emergency provisions of Articles 73 and 109. Liberalization was also agreed in principle for certain other capital flows, but on certain grounds member states were permitted to seek a dispensation from the applications of EC regulations in those fields. The Commission also attempted to liberalize capital flows by means of a third directive that required each member to permit new foreign issues on its security markets up to a certain percentage of all new public issues, but this directive was not adopted.

At Community level, the position that had been reached in 1962 remained formally unchanged until November 1986 when finance ministers agreed to widen the range of capital movements to be freed from exchange controls. This latest directive, which should come into effect in 1987, is the first element of a three-stage liberalization plan. The directive largely reflects the status quo and the separate easing of exchange controls that has already occurred in a number of member states, several of which – West Germany, the UK, Belgium, Luxemburg, the Netherlands and Denmark – have virtually no controls left. Other members however, such as France, Italy and Ireland, have enjoyed dispensations from existing provisions on grounds of balance of payments difficulties. Although they and other members have also eased their controls recently, they fall short of compliance with the latest regulation and will either have to try to liberalize further or seek a dispensation from the new rules.

Apart from the exchange controls that currently remain, many national legal and administrative regulations obstruct the free operation of a Community capital market, as do differences in national systems of direct taxation. Efforts by the Commission to deal with these national regulations have so far made little progress. Similarly, although a proposal for a directive on the harmonization of corporation tax was made some years ago by the Commission, it has yet to be adopted by the Council.

The Community has thus made some progress towards freeing capital flows and integrating its capital markets but a completely free and integrated market certainly does not yet exist.

ENTERPRISE

Apart from the formal removal of restrictions on foreign direct investment, there is also the question of what positive measures are required if cooperation and integration amongst enterprises in the Community are to be effectual – if there is to be a Community-wide integration of enterprise. In this area the absence of a legal framework for cross-border activities by enterprises and for cooperation amongst enterprises from different member states may have hampered cooperation and the development of joint projects. To overcome this the Commission has proposed to establish a new type of association to be known as the European Economic Interest Grouping, which would be governed by uniform Community legislation, with the object of making it easier for enterprises from different Community states to undertake specific activities. A statute for a European company has also been proposed.

Another important area that impinges on transnational integration and the mobility of enterprise is the differences in trade mark and patent legislation from one country to another. This inevitably has a negative impact on intra-Community trade and prevents enterprises from treating the common market as a single environment for their activities. Proposals are under consideration for a Community trade mark and for the harmonization of national trade mark laws. In the field of patents, a Convention on the Community Patent was signed in 1975 but it has not yet entered in force.

This brief review of the stage reached in progressing towards a complete common market highlights the areas in which progress is needed if the internal market of the EC is to be freed of barriers to its full integration. The Commission's White Paper is an action plan of breathtaking ambition for overcoming those barriers. Its implementation is likely to throw into sharp relief the need for the Community to expand the effectiveness of measures and to develop new policies to assist member states to deal with the acute adjustment problems that are likely to be entailed. Indeed, without such measures, the prospect of full implementation is not only likely to be remote; it would also be undesirable.

CONCLUSION

Even if macroeconomic policy issues are disregarded, an assessment of the effects and of the costs and benefits of factor market integration involves many complex issues. Although important efficiency gains may be secured by a move from a customs union to a common market, the need for an effective regional policy will almost certainly become more acute if structural forces contributing to economic divergence and possible losses for certain member states are to be contained. Moreover, if the presence of monopoly is strengthened by a common market through increased opportunities to exploit scale economies, there may be adverse allocational consequences to take into account, in addition to adverse distributional effects. Above all, if integration significantly expands the role of transnational corporations – at least of those based outside the common market and therefore less amenable to its control – the assessment becomes still more complex, for the maintenance of national sovereignty is likely to be an important policy objective for most member states. In terms of political economy considerations, a neoclassical preoccupation with competitive allocational gains that neglects such crucial aspects of the problem as seen by policy makers is of limited value.

RUDIGER DORNBUSCH

Europe 1992: Macroeconomic Implications

Only a few years ago Europe was beset with stagnation and mass unemployment. A Brookings study, concluding that accepting the state of European unemployment was not a solution, recommended a two-pronged attack involving macroeconomic stimulus and microeconomic flexing.[1] Europeans, particularly the Germans, considered the first a typically American naivete. They accepted the second as an inevitable suggestion, about which nothing much could be done.

Under the heading of Europe 1992, the discussion has now moved from Eurosclerosis to the growth potential of the internal market, and Europessimism has yielded to pervasive Europhoria. Together with the sharp fall in oil prices in 1987, the disinflationary effects of dollar depreciation, and expansionary policy measures, Europe 1992 has set the stage for growth. Table 1 shows an outlook for European economic growth that two years ago would have been considered extravagant. Where stagnation had almost seemed inevitable, with discussion of work-sharing a routine response, the prospects have now shifted altogether.

This paper first assesses the macroeconomic implications of the internal market project. That assessment highlights the sources of improved macroeconomic performance, its likely magnitude, and its spillover to the rest of the world. I turn then to three special areas, the prospects for European protectionism, the implications of financial integration, and the fiscal effects of the present exchange rate system.

Reprinted from Brookings Papers on Economic

Activity, Brookings Institution, Washington, D.C.

Copyright 1989.

Table 1. European Growth, Actual, 1961–87, Selected Years, and Projected, 1988–90
Percent per year

Item	1961–73	1974–81	1982–87	1988–90[a]
GDP	4.8	1.9	2.1	3.4
Investment	5.6	5.6	1.7	6.7
Employment	0.3	−0.1	0.2	1.4

Source: Commission of the European Communities (1989b).
a. Forecast, May 1989.

The Aggregate Effects

Europe 1992 is a supply-side revolution designed to generate growth by overcoming the segmented, uncompetitive markets that have survived the lowering of tariff barriers. The removal of physical, fiscal, and regulatory obstacles to competition across borders is at the center of the initiative. European Community estimates of the medium-term (six years) macroeconomic effects anticipate a 4.5 percent higher GDP as a result of these changes.

Four broad categories of policy measures are expected to generate beneficial effects. The first is removal of border controls. The second is EC-wide access to public procurement. The third is full capital mobility both for asset holders and for suppliers of financial services. And the fourth is measures to encourage increased competition and scale economies.

Modeling Productivity Gains

Some of the Europe 1992 benefits can be represented as gains in productivity, or output. These gains can arise in several ways as a result of opening and unifying the European market. Suppose the production function for output is linear homogeneous in capital, labor, and intermediate inputs, X.

$$(1) \qquad Q = F(K, L, X).$$

The value-added function, V, can then be written as

$$(2) \qquad V = \Theta(p)G(K, L),$$

where p measures the real price of intermediate goods.[2] A decline in the real price of intermediate goods because of competition or reduced costs of transborder shipment therefore operates in the way of technical progress by shifting out the aggregate production function.

Productivity gains from the removal of transborder obstacles can also be modeled as arising from an increase in the variety of intermediate products available to firms. A formulation by Paul Romer emphasizes the size of the market in sustaining the profitable production of specialized intermediate goods.[3] Because of the presence of fixed costs, the larger the market the larger the range of specialization that can take place. Let the production function for final goods be

$$Y = L^{1-\alpha} \Sigma x_i^{\alpha},$$

where x denotes the quantity of an intermediate good.[4] Let there be M intermediates and assume that it takes one unit of labor to produce a unit of the intermediate. The labor requirement for intermediates then is $L_I = Mx$ and that leaves $L_F = L - L_I$ of labor for final goods production. The aggregate production function for final goods can be rewritten as

$$Y = (L - L_I)^{1-\alpha} L_I^{\alpha} M^{\alpha}.$$

The Romer formulation points out that in addition to labor input, variety (proxied by M, the number of different inputs) is a determinant of the level of output. Merging two equal-sized economies increases -the aggregate output, not because of scale economies to labor, but because it allows the production of a larger variety of specialized inputs. Scale is essential to exploit this variety bonus because of fixed costs.[5] There is also a gain from the more traditional scale economies that result from declining average variable cost. Raising the scale of operation of individual firms is in this case the source of gain in productivity. Europe-wide operation for firms with scale economies raises their productivity and frees resources as firms merge into more efficient scale.

2. See, for example, Bruno and Sachs (1985).
3. Romer (1989).
4. For simplicity, assume that the quantity of each intermediate good used is the same, so that $x_i = x$. This symmetry result would emerge if the production of each intermediate had the same constant unit labor cost.
5. This analysis applies to intermediate goods, but the same argument can be brought for the benefits of increased variety to consumers.

Measuring Productivity Gains

There are two ways to conceptualize and possibly measure the benefits of Europe 1992. One is to use a general equilibrium model of production to assess the impact of the policy measures on potential output and its growth, assuming that the economy is always at full employment. The other is to evaluate the benefits in terms of a medium-term macroeconomic model where demand factors are critical. An example shows the contrast between these approaches.

Consider the removal of border controls and the associated red tape. The effect is to increase the value of potential real GNP, measured in a welfare perspective. The labor services involved in transborder inspection and red tape, both in the private and the public sector, are part of GNP as officially measured. But the services do not directly contribute to welfare. When they are shifted to alternative uses, aggregate measured GNP does not rise, but welfare associated with the unchanged output increases. In the full-employment model, removal of border formalities appears as a reduction of an implicit tax on traded intermediates or final goods and as an increase in the labor and capital resources available for regular production. In the macroeconomic perspective, by contrast, the possibility of unemployment emerges. The question is by what mechanism former customs officers are absorbed into productive employment.

Both perspectives capture some important issues, but miss others. The full-employment view risks missing cyclical problems of adaptation, and the macroeconomic view is likely to downplay changes in the level and path of potential output. The EC projections rely substantially on macroeconomic channels, feeding Europe 1992 effects into the model as shocks—either reductions in interest cost (fed into the investment equation) or general increases in exogenous productivity growth. The former works through aggregate demand effects on growth; the latter translates into a more favorable growth-inflation trade-off and from there into higher growth.

An aggregate demand and supply model helps show the effects. On the aggregate demand side the chief net effects are two. First, trade diversion toward Europe raises aggregate demand. Because of the removal of intra-European obstacles to trade, European locations are favored, and hence demand for output produced in Europe rises. Second,

Figure 1. The Effect of Europe 1992 on Output and Prices

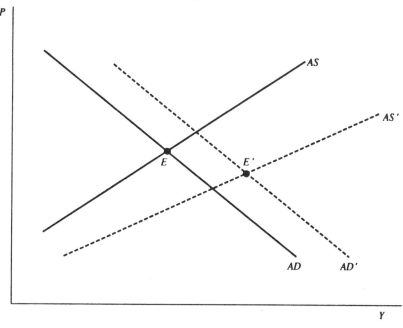

the increased profitability translates into a rise in investment. Financial integration, by reducing credit rationing and lowering financial costs, works in the same direction. Thus, as figure 1 shows, aggregate demand rises from AD to AD', holding constant the structural budget and the nominal quantity of money. On the aggregate supply side, productivity growth shifts the aggregate supply schedule out from AS to AS'. The reduction in trade impediments and increased competition likewise reduce supply prices. The new equilibrium at point E' shows that Europe 1992 leads to higher output and a change in the price level that will depend on the relative strength of demand- and supply-side effects.

Europe 1992 will succeeed to the extent that it raises demand while at the same time creating a favorable inflation-growth trade-off and a favorable external balance. In such a scenario, demand will create growth, and the policy authorities will not feel compelled to stop the growth because of inflation concerns or because of fears that unsustainable external imbalances might develop. Table 2 shows European Community estimates of the direct effects of Europe 1992 policies,

Table 2. Macroeconomic Impact of the Internal Market after Six Years
Percent except as noted

Item	GDP	CPI	Budget (percent of GDP)	External balance (percent of GDP)	Employment (millions)
Removal of border controls	0.4	−1.0	0.2	0.2	0.2
Public procurement	0.5	−1.4	0.3	0.1	0.3
Financial services	1.5	−1.4	1.1	0.3	0.4
Supply effects	2.1	−2.3	0.6	0.4	0.8
Total[a]	4.5	−6.1	2.2	1.0	1.8

Source: Emerson (1988, table 10.2.1).
a. Average estimate.

including any induced macroeconomic effects, but without taking into account changes in macroeconomic policy reactions such as increased public spending.

The first three rows of the table report on the effects of measures that are straightforward, even if the economic measurements of gains may be difficult: removal of border controls, Europe-wide competition in public procurement, and cross-border competition in financial services are all clearly defined. The remaining category of dynamic supply-side effects is less clear. Under this heading comes a large range of deregulation measures that are expected to promote more competitive markets and markets that use scale economies more powerfully, two expectations that could be in conflict. Financial service integration and supply-side policies account for most of the effect on real GNP. All policies tend to reduce inflation relative to the baseline scenario, improve the budget, and improve the external balance.

The stronger the productivity effects—here is where the supply-side effects in table 2 come into play—the more likely that there can be a substantial increase in output without significant inflation. In fact, by predicting a decline in inflation, the EC has explicitly created a scenario with room for further policy initiatives, initiatives that can exploit the decline in inflation and the improvement in the budget arising from stronger growth.

Table 3 sets out EC simulations of expansionary fiscal policies—increased government spending—that reinforce the direct impact of the program, taking advantage of the perceived elimination of inflation,

Table 3. The Role of Macroeconomic Policy
Percent except as noted

Policy	GDP	CPI	Budget (percent of GDP)	External balance (percent of GDP)	Employment (millions)
Unchanged policy	4.5	−6.1	2.2	1.0	1.8
Expansionary policy[a]					
Budget unchanged	7.5	−4.3	0	−0.5	5.7
Current account unchanged	6.5	−4.9	0.7	0	4.4

Source: Emerson (1988, table 10.2.2).
a. Increases in government spending.

budget, and external constraints on expansionary policy. These simulations are made in two ways: assuming that the actual budget deficit is kept unchanged and assuming that the external balance is kept unchanged. The expansionary policies trade off a reduction in the disinflation effects for increased growth—2 percent to 3 percent. On the employment side the impact is massive, presumably because the fiscal support is targeted toward employment with major European infrastructure projects. One more percentage point of real GDP translates into 1.3 million more jobs. Four million jobs would reduce unemployment by about one-third.

Evaluation

The EC simulations show that output rises under both assumptions in the first two years, but that actual employment declines initially except as a result of freeing up public procurement.[6] The initial decline in employment sustains the expansionary impact of the measures because it reduces inflationary pressure and, therefore, for a given growth path of nominal money or nominal income, allows an increase in real growth that ultimately creates employment.

How seriously must these EC estimates be taken? They are the only available estimates, but otherwise there is no reason to attach undue significance to them. The margin of error is large simply because there are no available models with which to evaluate multicountry, multisector

6. See Emerson (1988, tables B.1–B.4).

supply-side economics both in terms of long-run growth and short-run macroeconomics. A more interesting question is whether important policy issues are bypassed or whether the modeling leaves issues unsettled. That seems the case in several respects. There is no clear distinction between the effect of the measures on potential as opposed to actual output. There is no explicit consideration of whether the aggregate demand effects would work fast enough to harvest the gains in potential output. And there is no consideration of whether real wage rigidity could stand in the way of employment gains.

The EC estimates include no measure of the gain in potential output that Europe 1992 could deliver. The only gains that are estimated represent a mix of productivity shocks and macroeconomic adjustment. As a result, one cannot even determine whether the full potential of Europe 1992 is implemented or whether the actual growth gains fall short of potential. And if the latter is the case, it is not apparent what stands in the way. There is clearly an implicit model of inflation constraints on allowable growth that never comes entirely to the forefront.

Regarding short-run dynamics, many of the policy measures initially translate into labor redundancy. At given output levels, labor demand would decline and unemployment would rise. An expansion in employment requires a significant increase in real aggregate demand. The demand expansion relies on increased investment and on the trade diversion effects relative to the rest of the world, and it is implicitly assumed that the decline in employment at the initial level of output does not have important aggregate demand effects. Unemployment compensation, for example, could eliminate aggregate demand effects, but then budget improvement would not be as strong as it is represented in table 2. Thus, if there are substantial immediate productivity benefits, the employment-demand relation needs to be given more emphasis. By contrast, if productivity growth depends substantially on investment, an initial demand-driven phase needs to be implemented that would bring with it more, not less, inflation.

The estimates of the direct effects of the internal market project show a quite significant fiscal improvement. Even if these projections are assumed to be plausible, the question remains whether governments will be willing to use these resources for infrastructure projects or environmental plans or whether they will use them to contain the buildup of public debt. In most European countries debt ratios have not stabilized, and in some they are extremely high. Therefore, it would seem that the assumption of increased government spending or tax reductions may be optimistic.

The assumption of expansionary fiscal policy is also in question because of possible distribution effects. The internal market project in itself assumes fiscal harmonization, particularly in respect to value-added taxes; and that may require new fiscal resources in some countries, including, for example, Italy. More generally, some regions may do very well, both in terms of growth and the budget, and others poorly. The implication, in the absence of a transfer mechanism, is that the complementary fiscal expansion might not take place. Some regions that can afford it may not need it, and others may operate under fiscal constraints that do not permit expansionary measures.

The macroeconomic simulations reveal the implicit constraints and instruments. Monetary policy is not one of the instruments even though the internal market project itself is perceived as a program that leads to disinflation and labor market slack. Macroeconomic stimulus is seen as coming entirely from fiscal expansion, not from a transitory increase in monetary growth. The reason is presumably a super-monetarist view that links inflation directly to money growth, not to employment, unemployment, slack, or shocks.

A more appropriate complementary macroeconomic policy setting would be to use both monetary and fiscal policy. Easier money (used fully to absorb the entire disinflation) could help reduce real interest rates and thereby provide even more scope for fiscal policies to aid expansion.

It is not surprising that the Commission in Brussels did not tread this path. Money growth is made in Germany, where the authorities, quite beside abhorring the notion of European settings for money growth, believe that there is already full employment. Monetary stimulus in response to potential results would be expected simply to cause inflation.

Thus, expansionary macroeconomic policies may be forthcoming if in fact budgets do improve and disinflation is apparent. But European governments will not start a macroeconomic expansion early to absorb any initial adverse employment effects of Europe 1992. That in turn lessens the dynamism of the project and puts policymakers more on the defensive as they contemplate serious productivity measures.

Another problem with the projections concerns employment gains.

The implicit European model emphasizes real wage and labor market rigidities as obstacles to employment. Some of the Europe 1992 measures taken by themselves reduce employment at each level of output, yet the projections call for employment gains between 1.8 million and 5.7 million jobs, depending on macroeconomic policies. Even 1.8 million is an ambitious estimate, since it amounts to a gain of about 1 percent in total employment, and a regression of employment growth on output growth for the period 1961–88 suggests that it takes a 5 percent increase in output growth to raise employment by 1 percent. But that does not allow for the fact that at least part of the output growth in the years ahead is due to an unusual productivity bonus that in itself will reduce employment. Thus, the net employment gains reported in table 2 may well be too generous. That is certainly the case for the simulations that envisage fiscal expansion.

The macroeconomic discussion is also incomplete because it does not make fully explicit the effects on real interest rates and terms of trade and the effects on relations with the outside world. There are two opposing forces at work. European output growth raises demand for goods worldwide and hence leads to a terms of trade improvement for outsiders. But part of the adjustment to Europe 1992 specifically involves trade diversion: a European production location, because of the reduction in intra-European barriers, becomes the preferred option. That will tend to worsen the terms of trade for outsiders.

Figure 2 combines the investment effects discussed above and the impact of Europe 1992 on the trade balance. The vertical axis shows the world real interest rate, r, and the horizontal axis, the terms of trade of outsiders, R. An increase in R is a gain in competitiveness for the rest of the world, RoW. Along RoW there is market clearing in the rest of the world: higher real interest rates reduce demand and require a gain in competitiveness to sustain full employment. Along the schedule EC Europe has goods market equilibrium. Starting at point E, Europe 1992 creates investment effects in Europe. There are also offsetting effects on the trade balance from the gain in potential output and from trade diversion. Supposing that the latter two cancel, thus leaving the schedule RoW unchanged, the net effect is the increase in investment opportunities that shifts EC out and to the right. At the new equilibrium point E' there is a higher world real interest rate and a real appreciation for Europe.

Figure 2. The International Effects of Europe 1992

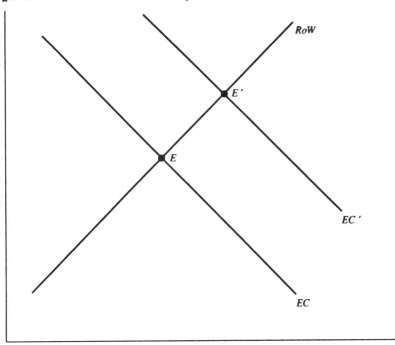

The gain in European terms of trade is required to sustain full employment in the rest of the world as higher real interest rates crowd out demand. But higher real interest rates imply that fiscal balances, because of debt service, might not improve as much as predicted, and that means the scope for extra fiscal expansion would be reduced.

In conclusion, the growth effects of Europe 1992 are open to many questions, and it is tempting to argue that the disinflation-with-growth scenario is primarily a politically convenient portrait. But as everybody can see, Europe's economy is growing. Investment, output growth, and employment growth all are showing a sharp upward movement. One explanation that is not captured in the EC projections is animal spirits— an investment and employment boom brought about by a wave of optimism.

Animal Spirits

The animal spirit effect can be expressed in terms of the new Keynesian economics of investment.[7] The possibility of increased market size offered by Europe 1992 may lead firms to invest to position themselves for the exploitation of oligopolistic rents. The argument can be put in terms of the models of the option value of waiting and the emphasis on the interdependence of profits. Oligopolistic firms that face uncertain returns on quasi-irreversible investments will expand capacity only when the return on such a move is sufficiently front-loaded to overcome the value of waiting. This front-loading emerges in the Europe 1992 context in two ways. First, firms need a market presence to exploit their profit opportunities. A changing market profile requires investments now to preserve or exploit opportunities that otherwise are lost by the entry of other firms. Thus the race to be first triggers a competitive burst of investment. Second, because profits are strategically interdependent, the expectation of a Europe 1992 effect leads to the expectation of an increased profit opportunity for those firms who have the capacity in place. In the language of the new Keynesian economics, Europe 1992 works as a coordination mechanism.

Of course, increased investment profitability must be linked with saving for investment actually to take place. The increase in potential output at a given saving rate would provide resources for investment. If planned investment rises more than the increase in saving, real interest rates will rise and attract saving from the rest of the world. The more Europe 1992 leads to the perception of dynamic gains, the more likely it is to bring with it a high real interest rate environment.

Increased Protection in Europe?

Non-Europeans often wonder whether the European internal market project will lead to a "Fortress Europe." Will Europe, as a result of the competitive tensions that emerge in the completion of the internal

---

7. See Bentolila and Bertola (1987); Pindyck (1986); Dixit (1989); and Murphy, Shleifer, and Vishny (1989).

market, turn more protectionist toward the rest of the world?[8] And, more generally, is Europe 1992 primarily good or bad news for the rest of the world, particularly the United States? Naturally, European policymakers publicly declare that there is no risk of protection. But the possibility already attracts investment by outside producers.

Even without specific protectionist measures, Europe 1992 is expected to have some adverse effects on the rest of the world. The gain in competitiveness of European locations—for example, shipping from France to Germany becomes easier—will bring about trade diversion at the expense of extra-EC suppliers. Detailed estimates of the impact of such measures as removing barriers to trade suggest that imports from outside Europe will decline between 7.9 percent and 10.2 percent.[9] As the scenario reviewed in table 2 shows, the EC external balance is expected to improve by 1 percent of GDP as a result of trade-diverting effects of the internal market. The EC scenarios leave no question that adverse effects on the rest of the world are expected.

Adverse effects can also come from outright protectionist measures—or the threat of such measures. In sectors where scale economies increase market concentration and hence cause plant closings, for example, protection will seem justified: if Europe can achieve operations of minimum efficient scale on her own, import limitation will seem a natural counterpart of the internal opening up. And the political pressure will clearly run in that direction. A second area of vulnerability is public procurement. It is one thing to open up procurement to cross-border competition in Europe; it is quite another to open it to outside suppliers. The question of import content is certain to arise—as it has already for Nissan cars produced in the United Kingdom—and a tendency toward minimum European content is virtually certain. As a third example, multinationals, already anticipating the implicit or explicit adverse effects on outsiders, are preemptively making relocation decisions. Even if no outright protection ever occurs, the risk is enough to create tariff factories precisely in the way they have been created in the United States. The effect of these investments is to move production away from the rest of the world. Once plants are relocated inside Europe, production has been relocated whether there is a tariff or not.

---

8. See Skolnik (1988) for some reactions.
9. See Emerson (1988, tables A.5 and A.6).

That Europe 1992 carries the potential of protection against outsiders is apparent from the scramble of the countries of the European Free Trade Association to position themselves by a direct association. The EFTA countries, for all intents and purposes, are seeking to enlarge Europe 1992 with the concept of a "European Space." With so much emphasis on Europe, one is hard pressed to believe that the rest of the world will not be hurt.

The main reason that protection may ultimately increase stems from Europe 1992's "social dimension," which involves a harmonization of labor market arrangements, from job security and job place safety to wages and social security benefits. The issue is important because labor cost disparities, unadjusted for productivity, are extraordinary. If they are significantly reduced, by increases in labor cost in the low-wage countries, the latter will become uncompetitive relative to outsiders and will be likely to call for protection.

Table 4 shows hourly compensation in various EC countries. From the extent of the divergences, it is clear that a full leveling cannot happen in the near future, but it is equally clear that far more mobility of goods, services, and labor will make some harmonization likely.

How far harmonization will go is unsettled. It is highly unlikely that Spain, Portugal, and Greece will become high-wage countries unable to compete internally or externally. But it is also unlikely that the social dimension will go nowhere: unions are an integral part of the (continental) European political scene, and socially responsible behavior involves recognition of union participation in major political decisions. Unions, therefore, will help shape Europe 1992, and that means a fair part of the social dimension will take place. With some tendency toward harmonization, Spain, Portugal, and Greece will become higher-cost producers and lose some of their competitiveness relative to outside suppliers. Protection will thus arise as a natural complement to European labor market harmonization.

In its 1988–89 annual report, the Commission notes:

Catching-up in economic terms must go hand in hand with catching-up in social terms, while maintaining basic social standards in the more advanced countries. Thus, apart from its regional aspects, the social dimension of the internal market is essential. The lower real wage levels and less onerous social regulations in the less advanced countries are comparative advantages which enable them to make progress in the catching-up process. In addition, minimum health and safety

Table 4. Hourly Compensation in Manufacturing, Seven European Countries, 1988
Index, United States = 100

Country	Compensation
West Germany	130
Italy	93
France	93
United Kingdom	76
Spain	63
Greece	34
Portugal	20

Source: U.S. Bureau of Labor Statistics, unpublished data.

standards at work and the pursuit by Member States, according to Article 118a of the EEC Treaty, of the objective of harmonizing conditions in this area, while maintaining the improvements already made, will contribute to better working and living conditions as well as to avoidance of distortions in competition between the firms of different Member States.[10]

There is clearly a tension between harmonization and competitiveness, leveling and upgrading, that remains unresolved.[11] European protection, if it does occur, is expected to be primarily directed against Asia rather than the United States. That seems commonly accepted even if it is not written on paper.

Financial Integration

The macroeconomic simulations give an unreal impression of what can be said about the effects of Europe 1992. Not only is the social dimension a wide open issue, but the way in which other measures operate is still to be determined. This is especially the case for financial intermediation.

The EC study envisages that cross-border competition in financial services will have a major impact on financial service prices, spreads, and the cost of capital. Compared with the average of the four lowest-price countries, Germany, for example, has at present a very high cost of consumer credit, while Belgium has a low cost. Price divergences at

10. Commission of the European Communities (1988a, pp. 38–39).
11. Giersch (1989) has especially noted the implications of a corporatist strategy where harmonization within leads as a natural counterpart to protection against outsiders.

the retail level would shrink substantially for banking services, insurance, and security transactions. In Spain the decline in financial service prices might be as large as 21 percent, in Germany 10 percent, and in the Netherlands only 4 percent.[12] A complementary, but rarely discussed, aspect of trade in financial services is the impact on credit rationing. The restrictions on capital mobility for asset holders and the inability to compete in services across borders at present leaves the regional and national saving pools substantially unconnected. In the wholesale Eurodollar there is already substantial mobility, as Giavazzi and Giovannini have documented.[13] But in the retail market many forms of credit remain segmented and nontraded. There is local lending of local deposits, and small and medium-sized firms are typically unable to obtain credit except locally. Credit rationing is pervasive, and financial integration, drawing on the U.S. experience with securitization, may be a very radical experiment.[14]

Financial integration is likely to have two effects. One is that while spreads narrow, interest rates that are now repressed may actually rise throughout Europe and especially in high-saving countries like Spain. At the same time, firms and households will find it easier to finance themselves in a more competitive market so that credit rationing will be less pervasive.

In the past, in the presence of budget deficits, credit rationing has crowded out business investment and consumer spending. With the internationalization of markets, this tendency can lessen significantly as firms can tap the European capital market, crossing national borders. The possibility therefore emerges that those countries where credit rationing has kept investment low will now borrow in the European capital market both to finance public sector deficits and to increase investment rates as well. Forecasts for Spain and Italy anticipate such increases in foreign borrowing.[15]

12. See Emerson (1988, p. 105).
13. Giavazzi and Giovannini (1989b).
14. The analogy with the U.S. mortgage market is useful. In the 1960s local savings and loans collected local deposits and made local loans. Today U.S. mortgages are securitized and traded internationally.
15. Commission of the European Communities (1989b).

Fiscal Convergence and Public Debt

Fiscal policies in the EC countries have converged in the 1980s. Differences in inflation have narrowed, and fiscal convergence has meant a shift toward primary budget surpluses everywhere. Table 5 shows the progress in reducing primary deficits and turning them into surpluses.

The internal market project has also strengthened the prospect of increased and perhaps complete monetary integration. The European Monetary System was invented to shield Europe from financial instability exported by the United States in the late 1970s. Initially created as a zone of monetary stability in Europe, it later became a project of disinflation.[16] But although the disinflation effort has been quite successful, a formal system of fully fixed exchange rates has not been established. That creates a delicate situation: interest rates reflect the possibility of further exchange rate alignments even though governments are more or less committed to maintain current exchange rates. For countries with high debt ratios, this represents the worst possible situation because realized real interest rates are high and debts are growing rapidly.

The favored approach at this time, as presented for example in the Delors Report, is to solidify, if not institutionalize, monetary integration. One possibility, favored by Germany, is to broaden rapidly the scope for capital mobility, which would test just how far the partner countries are willing to go in the direction of German monetary policy. With sharply increased capital mobility scheduled to be implemented by 1991, no important departure from German performance can be consistent with the free flow of capital and fixed rates.

The same direction is favored by central banks, in Italy especially, but also in Spain and France, where they traditionally have been appendages (or cash windows) of the national Treasuries. The disinflation experience of the 1980s in which exchange rate stability was central to establishing lower inflation and, possibly, a reputation for anti-inflation commitment, had an extraordinary side effect: it made central banks

16. See Giavazzi and Pagano (1988); Giavazzi and Giovannini (1989a, 1989b); Giavazzi, Micossi, and Miller (1988); de Cecco and Giovannini (1989); Ungerer (1989); Cobham (1989); and Schinasi (1989).

Table 5. Debt and Deficits, European Community, 1981 and 1988
Percent of GDP, general government, except as noted

Country	1981			1988		
		Deficit[a]			Deficit[a]	
	Debt-GDP ratio	Total	Primary	Debt-GDP ratio	Total	Primary
Europe 10	0.41	3.8	1.4	0.59	2.9	−1.8
Belgium	0.76	12.6	4.8	1.27	5.9	−4.5
Denmark	0.39	6.9	1.6	0.63	−1.0	−8.5
Germany	0.33	3.7	1.4	0.45	0.8	−2.0
Greece	0.29	11.0	7.9	0.74	12.8	3.2
France	0.25	1.9	−0.1	0.37	1.7	−1.1
Ireland	0.77	13.4	6.8	1.19	5.1	−4.3
Italy	0.59	11.3	5.2	0.94	9.9	1.0
Luxembourg	0.14	3.6	2.7	0.10	−5.6	−6.7
Netherlands	0.46	5.5	1.0	0.79	4.5	−1.5
Portugal	0.37	9.2	4.1	0.72	6.1	−2.4
Spain	0.18	3.9	3.1	0.48	3.2	−0.3
United Kingdom	0.52	2.6	2.4	0.49	−1.2	−4.7

Source: Commission of the European Community, *European Economy*, various issues.
a. A minus sign denotes a surplus. The primary budget deficit excludes interest payments.

independent. The bureaucratic response, especially in Italy, has been a fervent commitment to more of the same—aggressive deepening of monetary integration. Better to be a branch of the Bundesbank than an agency of the Tesoro.

But even though the experience of the 1980s has progressively hardened nominal exchange rates, there remain doubts about just how fixed the rates are and how permanently inflation differentials have vanished. For example, in 1988 unit labor costs (in dollars) increased by 3.4 percent and 2.9 percent, respectively, in Denmark and Italy, while they rose only 1.9 percent in Germany.

Asset markets clearly have not taken the view that exchange rates are now fixed. The last realignment, in January 1987, was preceded by general realignments in 1986 and 1983. In the fall of 1989 the possibility of another realignment to accommodate the Danish loss of reserves was widely discussed. The fact that inflation differentials have narrowed sharply and no realignment has occurred in two and a half years has not

Table 6. Interest Rates in the EMS, 1989:2
Percent except as noted

Country	Deposit rate	Money market	Government bond	Debt-GDP ratio
Belgium	5.1	6.5	8.4	1.27
Denmark	8.3	8.7	10.6	0.63
France	5.6	8.6	8.8	0.37
Germany	5.2	6.2	7.0	0.45
Ireland	3.9	9.2	9.1	1.19
Italy	7.0	12.5	10.6	0.94
Netherlands	3.5	6.6	7.2	0.79
Spain	9.5	14.8	13.6	0.48

Sources: Figures for Spain from Morgan Guaranty Trust Company (1989); for all other countries, from International Monetary Fund (1989). Debt-GDP ratios from Commission of the European Communities (1988a).

translated into an equalization of long-term interest rates. Yield differentials remain substantial, as table 6 shows.

The long-term interest differentials, assuming they do not primarily reflect taxation, suggest that markets anticipate general depreciation against the deutsche mark, except in the Netherlands. Moreover, the extent of anticipated depreciation is sizeable.

Interestingly, the term structures are quite flat. One cannot therefore take the view that there is a high probability either of a near-term realignment (the case of a negative term structure) or a distant one, reflected in a "peso problem" term premium. In fact, it is not clear what the yield differential relative to Germany suggests, other than that fixed rates are not expected to last forever.[17] And this uncertainty about exchange rates translates into a fiscal problem in countries with high government debt.

The countries with the weakest fiscal position are also the ones with the highest interest rates and the ones most committed to fixed rates. As a result, their budget deficits are large, and their government debt ratios are growing (see table 7). The problem worsens the more a government is actually committed to maintaining exchange rates and the less it is believed: in that case large realized real interest rates add year after year to the debt burdens. In 1985–87, for example, realized short-term interest

17. For a further discussion, see Dornbusch (1989a) and Giavazzi and Giovannini (1989b).

Table 7. The European Problem Debtors, 1989
Percent of GDP except as noted

Item	Belgium	Ireland	Italy
Debt-GDP ratio	1.28	1.18	0.98
Deficit			
Total	5.9	5.1	9.9
Primary	−4.8	−4.6	0.9
Inflation-adjusted	2.3	1.1	4.7

Source: Commission of the European Communities (1988a).

rates averaged 2.1 percent in Germany. By contrast, they averaged 4.3 percent in Italy, 9.4 percent in Denmark, and 6.4 percent in Ireland.[18] Because of these high realized real interest rates, debts kept growing relative to GDP. A related difficulty, also a by-product of the low-inflation policy, was the shift in deficit finance. Before the disinflation and fixed exchange rate commitment, Italy, for example, had financed a significant share of the deficit by money creation. But with fixed exchange rates and low inflation, the scope for inflationary finance was gone, and debt creation was the rule.[19] The growing debt ratios, of course, imply increased tax burdens in the future. Although the form and incidence of these taxes is uncertain, their presence makes high-debt countries poor locations for production.

The debt issue points to the need for major reform in two directions. One is to reduce the exchange risk premiums that now exist in real interest rates, the other is to reduce the budget deficits. The two policies are strictly complementary. Increasing ratios of debt to GDP are clearly not possible for a long time once the 100 percent threshold has been passed. Without a prospect of significantly higher growth or much lower future real interest rates, there is a need for reduced deficits. Without a prospect of deficit reduction and lower real interest rates, asset holders must ultimately expect debt repudiation in some form. That expectation would lead to yet larger risk premiums and even more rapid growth in debt.

Along with increased taxation and a more productive tax structure, a move toward much more rapid and firmly committed monetary policy

18. See OECD (1989).
19. On this point, see Dornbusch (1988) and Giavazzi (1989).

must also take place. To avoid the fiscal costs associated with exchange rate uncertainty, governments in soft-currency countries like Italy can pressure for increasing exchange rate fixity. They can immediately discard the 6 percent margin for exchange rate fluctuations and peg the deutsche mark without any margin. This would signal a much stronger commitment to fixed rates. The strategy is attractive because it is already widely believed in Europe that monetary policy is no longer effective. Monetary policy is made in Frankfurt, and any independence is not only an illusion, but is also expensive in terms of debt service.

Making the EMS fixed exchange rate project more credible may be even more important than the internal market project. The sheer passage of time makes this so, particularly when on strategic occasions a government denies itself the comfort of a devaluation. But the progress is far too slow, given the adverse fiscal results of lingering exchange rate uncertainty.

It is not obvious that a fixed nominal exchange rate offers a solution for all of the EC members at this time. Spain has an inflation rate of 7 percent; Portugal, 13 percent; and Greece, 15 percent. Clearly these countries are far away from German inflation, and any use of fixed nominal exchange rates to control inflation is misguided since it will produce overvaluation and ultimately a currency devaluation crisis. These countries would be better off pursuing a fixed real exchange rate policy, depreciating their currencies at a rate equal to the inflation differential with Germany. They would have inflation, and the fiscal advantage of seigniorage, but they would avoid high real interest rates and instability from real exchange rate variability. The argument against such a proposal is that without a nominal anchor there is no stability of inflation. That is true, but with a nominal anchor real instability may be worse.[20]

International Financial Competition

The formation of a European financial block has a major impact on world financial markets because it creates a viable and even attractive alternative to the U.S. capital market. The issue is not whether there

20. See Dornbusch (1982, 1988) and Canzoneri and Rogers (1989).

will be an ECU market; more likely, the European capital market wil rapidly adapt to the U.S. experience and offer money market account: denominated in deutsche marks and with favorable tax treatment.[2] What will the availability of a convenient market in mark (or equivalent money market instruments do to the dollar? Surely, with such competi· tion the demand for dollar-denominated assets declines relatively. There is no suggestion, even remotely, that the dollar will disappear as an international asset. The fact, though, is that a market of the size of Europe and with the support of German monetary orthodoxy, which now has become the common denominator, does offer a major alternative. Adverse current account effects of Europe 1992 for the United States and financial integration with the creation of a competitive European asset are bound to imply a major dollar depreciation in the 1990s.

21. Earlier this year Germany rolled back an already announced increase in withholding taxes on income from capital in the face of an exodus of tax payers. The lesson would seem to be that there is no obstacle to Germany as a low-tax location for a European money market.

References

Aujean, Michael. 1988. "Evaluation des economies d'echelle pouvant resulter de l'achevement du marche interieur." In Commission of the European Communities, *Research on the "Cost of Non-Europe," Basic Findings,* vol. 2. Luxembourg: Office for Official Publications of the European Communities.

Baldwin, R. 1989. "On the Growth Effects of 1992." *Economic Policy.*

Baltensperger, Ernst, and Jean Dermine. 1989. "European Banking, Prudential and Regulatory Issues." University of Bern.

Bank for International Settlements. 1986. "Recent Innovations in International Banking." Prepared by a Study Group for the Central Banks of the Group of Ten Countries. Brussels.

Belassa, Bela. 1988. "Europe 1992 and Its Possible Implications for Nonmember Countries." Washington: Institute for International Economics.

Bentolila, Samuel, and Giuseppe Bertola. 1987. "Firing Costs and Labor Demand. How Bad Is Eurosclerosis?" Massachusetts Institute of Technology.

Blum, Richard H. 1984. *Offshore Haven Banks, Trusts, and Companies: The Business of Crime in the Euromarket.* New York: Praeger.

Brown, Fred, and John Whalley. 1980. "General Equilibrium Evaluations of Tariff-Cutting Proposals in the Tokyo Round and Comparisons with More Extensive Liberalisation of World Trade." *Economic Journal* 90:838–66.

Bruno, Michael, and Jeffrey D. Sachs. 1985. *Economics of Worldwide Stag-flation*. Cambridge, Mass.: Harvard University Press.

Cabellero, Ricardo J., and Richard Lyons. 1989a. "Increasing Returns and Imperfect Competition in European Industry." Columbia University.

————. 1989b. "The Role of External Economies in U.S. Manufacturing." Discussion paper 431. Columbia University Department of Economics.

Calingaert, Michael. 1988. *The 1992 Challenge from Europe: Development of the European Community's Common Market*. Washington: National Planning Association.

Canzoneri, Matthew B., and Carol Ann Rogers. 1989. "Is the European Community an Optimal Currency Area: Optimal Taxation versus the Cost of Multiple Currencies." Georgetown University.

Cawley, Richard, and Michael Davenport. 1988. "Partial Equilibrium Calculations of the Impact of Internal Market Barriers in the European Community." In Commission of the European Communities, *Research on the "Cost of Non-Europe," Basic Findings*, vol. 2. Luxembourg: Office for Official Publications of the European Communities.

Cecchini, Paolo. 1988. *The European Challenge: 1992: The Benefits of a Single Market*. Aldershot: Wildwood House for the Commission of the European Community.

Central Planning Bureau of the Netherlands. 1989. *Economische Statistische Berichten* 24 (May 31).

Chambost, Edouard. 1983. *Bank Accounts: A World Guide to Confidentiality*. New York: John Wiley & Sons.

Cobham, David. 1989. "Strategies for Monetary Integration Revisited." *Journal of Common Market Studies* 27:203–18.

Cole, Harold L., and Maurice Obstfeld. 1989. "Commodity Trade and International Risk Sharing: How Much Do Financial Markets Matter?" Working Paper 3027. Cambridge, Mass.: National Bureau of Economic Research.

Commission of the European Communities. 1988a. "Annual Economic Report 1988–89: Preparing for 1992." *European Economy* 38 (November).

————. 1985. "Completing the Internal Market: White Paper from the Commission to the European Council." COM (85)310 final. Brussels (June).

————. 1989a. "Documents—Proposals for Council Directives." COM (89) 60 final. Brussels (February 8).

————. 1989b. *Economic Forecasts 1989–1990: Summary*. Brussels.

————. 1989c. "Horizontal Mergers and Competition Policy in the European Community." *European Economy* 40:33.

————. 1989d. "Proposal for a Council Directive on Investment Services in the Securities Field." COM (88) 778-SYN 176. *Official Journal of the European Communities* No. C 43/7 (February 22).

————. 1988b. "Proposal for a Second Council Directive." COM (87) 715 final. Brussels (February).

————. 1989e. *Report on Economic and Monetary Union in the European Community*. Luxemburg.

Council of the European Communities. 1977. "Amending the First Banking Directive." 77/780/EEC. *Official Journal of the European Communities* No. L 332 (December 17).

————. 1988. "Council Directive of 24 June 1988 for the Implementation of Article 67 of the Treaty." 88/361/EEC. *Official Journal of the European Communities* No. L 178.5 (July 8).

Curzon, Gerard. 1989. "Ten Reasons to Fear Fortress Europe." McGill Economics Centre.

Davis, Evan, and others. 1989. "1992: Myths and Realities." London Business School Center for Business Strategy.

de Cecco, Marcello, and Alberto Giovannini, eds. 1989. *A European Central Bank*. Cambridge: Cambridge University Press.

Denison, Edward. 1967. *Why Growth Rates Differ: Postwar Experience in Nine Countries*. Washington: Brookings.

Dixit, Avinash. 1989. "Intersectoral Capital Reallocation under Price Uncertainty." *Journal of International Economics* 26:309–25.

Dornbusch, Rudiger. 1989a. "Credibility, Debt, and Unemployment: Ireland's Failed Stabilization." *Economic Policy* 8:173–209.

————. 1989b. "Europe 1992: Macroeconomic Implications." *BPEA, 2:1989*.

————. 1988. "Money and Finance in European Integration." In *EFTA Money and Finance in European Integration: EFTA Seminar*. Geneva.

————. 1982. "PPP Exchange Rate Rules and Macroeconomic Stability." *Journal of Political Economy* 90:158–62.

Emerson, Michael, and others. 1988. *The Economics of 1992: The EC Commission's Assessment of the Economic Effects of Completing the Internal Market*. Oxford: Oxford University Press.

European Community Office of Press and Public Affairs. 1987. *A Guide to the European Community*. Luxembourg: Office for Official Publications of the European Community.

Eurostat. 1988. *Basic Statistics of the Community: Comparison with Some European Countries, Canada, the U.S.A., Japan, and the U.S.S.R.* Luxembourg: Office for Official Publications of the European Communities.

Giavazzi, Francesco. 1989. "The Exchange Rate Question in Europe." In Commission of the European Communities. *Economic Papers* No. 74.

Giavazzi, Francesco, Stefano Micossi, and Marcus Miller, eds. 1988. *The European Monetary System*. Cambridge: Cambridge University Press.

Giavazzi, Francesco, and Alberto Giovannini. 1989a. "Can the EMS Be Exported? Lessons from 10 Years of Monetary Policy Coordination in Europe." Discussion Paper 285. London: Center for Economic Policy Research.

————. 1989b. *Limiting Exchange Rate Flexibility*. Cambridge, Mass.: MIT Press.

Giavazzi, Francesco, and Marco Pagano. 1988. "The Advantage of Tying One's Hands: EMS Discipline and Central Bank Credibility." *European Economic Review* 32:1055-75.

Giersch, Herbert. 1989. "Europe's Prospects for the 1990s." In Commission of the European Communities. *Economic Papers*. No. 74.

Giovannini, Alberto. 1989. "National Tax Systems vs. the European Capital Market." *Economic Policy* (forthcoming).

Grilli, Vittorio. 1989. "Europe 1992: Issues and Prospects for the Financial Markets." *Economic Policy* (forthcoming).

Grilli, Vittorio, and Rony Hamaui. 1989. "Toward European Financial Integration: Would Temporary Controls Help?" In *L'apertura internazionale dell'economia italiana: Aspetti teorici e la loro rilevanza empirica*, edited by Enrico Colombatto. SIPI.

Grossman, Gene M., and Elhanan Helpman. 1989. "Comparative Advantage and Long Run Growth." Working Paper 2809. Cambridge, Mass.: National Bureau of Economic Research.

Hall, Graham, ed. 1986. *European Industrial Policy*. Dover, N. H.: Croom Helm.

Heig, Rodolfo, and Ranci, Pippo. 1988. "Economies of Scale and Integration of Europe: The Case of Italy." In Commission of the European Communities, *Research on the "Cost of Non-Europe,"* Basic Findings, vol. 2. Luxembourg: Office for Official Publications of the European Communities.

International Monetary Fund. 1988a. *Government Finance Statistics Yearbook*. Washington: IMF.

———. 1989. *International Financial Statistics* 42 (November).

———. 1988b. *International Financial Statistics Yearbook*. Washington: IMF.

Key, Sidney J. 1989. "Financial Integration in the European Community." International Finance Discussion Paper 349. Washington: Board of Governors of the Federal Reserve System (April).

Kiyotaki, Nobuhiro, and Randall Wright. 1989. "On Money as a Medium of Exchange." *Journal of Political Economy* 97:927-54.

Lawrence, Robert Z., and Charles L. Schultze, eds. 1987. *Barriers to European Growth: A Transatlantic View*. Washington: Brookings.

Layard, Richard G. 1986. *How to Beat Unemployment*. Oxford: Oxford University Press.

Lee, Mark Pearson, and Stephan Smith. 1988. *Fiscal Harmonization: An Analysis of the European Commission's Proposals*. London: Institute for Fiscal Studies.

Levich, Richard M. 1989. "The Euromarkets after 1992." New York University.

Ludvigsen Associates, Ltd. 1988. "The EC 92 Automobile Sector." In Commission of the European Communities, *Research on the "Cost of Non-*

Europe," Basic Findings, vol. 1. Luxembourg: Office for Official Publications of the European Communities.

McDonald, Frank, and George Zis. 1989. "The European Monetary System: Towards 1992 and Beyond." *Journal of Common Market Studies* 27:183–202.

Morgan Guaranty Trust Company. 1989. *World Financial Markets* 3 (October).

Mundell, Robert. 1968. *International Economics*. New York: Macmillan.

Murphy, Kevin M, Andrei Shleifer, and Robert W. Vishny. 1989. "Industrialization and the Big Push." *Journal of Political Economy* 97:1003–26.

Organization for Economic Cooperation and Development. 1987a. *Bank Profitability: Financial Statements of Banks, 1980–84*. Paris.

———. 1987b. *Bank Profitability: Financial Statements of Banks, Statistical Supplement, 1981–85*. Paris.

———. 1987c. *Controls and Impediments Affecting Inward Direct Investment in OECD Member Countries*. Paris.

———. 1980. *Controls on International Capital Movements*. Paris.

———. 1987d. *International Investment and Multinational Enterprises*. Paris.

———. 1987e. *International Tax Avoidance and Evasion: Four Relative Studies*. Paris.

———. 1984. *International Trade in Services: Banking*. Paris.

———. 1987f. *International Trade in Services: Securities*. Paris.

———. 1989. *OECD Economic Outlook. Historical Statistics*. Paris.

———. 1981. *Regulation Affecting International Banking Operations of Banks and Nonbanks in Belgium, Luxembourg, France, Germany, the Netherlands, Switzerland, and the United Kingdom*. Paris.

———. 1978. *Regulation Affecting International Banking Operations of Banks and Nonbanks in France, Germany, the Netherlands, Switzerland, and the United Kingdom*. Paris.

Pindyck, Robert S. 1986. "Irreversible Investment, Capacity Choice and the Value of the Firm." Working Paper 1980. Cambridge, Mass.: National Bureau of Economic Research.

Pratten, Cliff. 1988. "A Survey of the Economies of Scale." In Commission of the European Communities, *Research on the Cost of Non-Europe, Basic Findings*, vol. 2. Luxembourg: Office for Official Publications of the European Communities.

Price Waterhouse. 1988. *The Cost of Non-Europe in Financial Services*. In Commission of the European Communities, *Research on the "Cost of Non-Europe," Basic Findings*, vol. 9. Luxembourg: Office for Official Publications of the European Communities.

Romer, Paul M. 1989. "Capital Accumulation in the Theory of Long-Run Growth." In *Modern Business Cycle Theory*, edited by Robert J. Barro. Cambridge, Mass.: Harvard University Press.

———. 1986. "Increasing Returns and Long-Run Growth." *Journal of Political Economy* 94:1002–38.

Rose, Nancy L. 1985. "Union Wage Gains under Regulation: Evidence from the Trucking Industry." Working Paper 1683-85. Sloan School of Management (M.I.T.).

Sarver, Eugene. 1987. *The Eurocurrency Market Handbook: The Global Eurodeposit and Related Markets.* New York: Prentice-Hall.

Schinasi, Garry. 1989. "European Integration, Exchange Rate Management, and Monetary Reform: A Review of the Major Issues." International Finance Discussion Paper 364. Washington: Board of Governors of the Federal Reserve.

Schwalbach, Joachim. 1988. "Economies of Scale and Intra-Community Trade." In Commission of the European Communities, *Research on the "Cost of Non-Europe,"* Basic Findings, vol. 2. Luxembourg: Office for Official Publications of the European Communities.

Skolnik, Amy. 1988. "How Will 1992 Affect the Rest of the World? The Reactions of Some Major Countries and Trade Blocks towards EC Integration." Discussion Paper 24. Bank of Finland.

Smith, Alasdair, and Anthony Venables. 1988. "An Assessment Based on a Formal Model of Imperfect Competition and Economies of Scale." In Commission of the European Communities, *Research on the "Cost of Non-Europe,"* Basic Findings, vol. 2. Luxembourg: Office for Offical Publications of the European Communities.

Swann, Dennis. 1984. *The Economics of the Common Market,* 5th ed. Middlesex, England: Penguin Books Ltd.

Ungerer, Horst. 1989. "The European Monetary System and the International Monetary System." *Journal of Common Market Studies* 27:231–48.

U.S. Council for International Business. 1989. *Statement on the European Single Market.* New York (May).

U.S. Department of Commerce. 1989. *EC 1992: A Commerce Department Analysis of European Community Directives,* vol. 1. Washington (May).

U.S. International Trade Commission. 1989. *The Effects of Greater Economic Integration within the European Community on the United States.* Washington (July).

United Nations. 1988. *1985/86 Statistical Yearbook.* New York: United Nations.

Walter, Ingo. 1985. *Secret Money: The World of International Finance Secrecy.* Lexington, Mass.: Lexington Books.

W. S. Atkins Management Consultants in Association with Eurequip SA—Roland Berger & Partner—Eurequip Italia. 1988. In Commission of the European Communities, *Research on the "Cost of Non-Europe,"* Basic Findings, vol. 1. Luxembourg: Office for Official Publications of the European Communities.

Wolf, Martin. 1989. "The Conflict between Liberalism and Mercantilism: Global Implications on the European Community's Programme to Complete the Internal Market." New York: Lehrman Institute (April).

THE THEORY OF COMMON MARKETS AS APPLIED TO REGIONAL ARRANGEMENTS AMONG DEVELOPING COUNTRIES

BY

R. F. MIKESELL

University of Oregon, Eugene, Oregon

I. INTRODUCTION

By and large the theory of customs unions has been confined to considerations of welfare gains or losses arising from a disturbance of the existing pattern of trade which is assumed to reflect comparative advantages in the commodities traded as determined by existing factor endowments. Some attention has been paid to the realization of gains from the economies of scale and from increased competition. However, the effects of the creation of regional markets on the more fundamental problems of developing countries such as increasing opportunities for profitable foreign and domestic investment, broadening the export base, achieving balance of payments equilibrium, mobilizing unemployed resources and avoiding economic dualism, have been largely neglected. Some of these problems, which are concerned with the dynamics of economic growth, are of interest to under-developed and to industrially advanced countries alike. I doubt, for example, if the most significant gains from the creation of the European Economic Community are to be discovered through a comparison of trade-diverting and trade-creating effects on welfare, even if we could measure them. Rather, the major impact will occur as a consequence of the effects on entrepreneurial decisions arising out of the new market structure and out of the acute awareness of the continual generation of new products, new processes and new methods of distribution on the part of competitors within the broad regional market. In other words, broadening of the area of unfettered activity of competitive enterprise creates opportunities for innovations and forces changes in investment patterns which constitute the dynamic elements of growth. These intangible factors, which are basic to business

Reprinted from "International Trade Theory in a Developing World" (R. Harrod and D. Hague, eds.), pp. 205–229, with permission of Macmillan, London, Copyright 1964.

decisions and expectations, often lie outside the economist's analytical framework.

But the fact that analytical work on common markets has been largely directed to problems of welfare under somewhat static assumptions which permit the employment of the analytical tools at our disposal, does not mean that the conclusions reached have no relevance for economic growth or for developing countries generally. I believe, however, that the theoretical analysis of customs unions or of regional preference arrangements generally should be directed more towards the problem of their impact on the direction of investment in the developing countries for future output rather than limited to an analysis of the welfare implications of shifting existing trade patterns. There are two general reasons for this conclusion, the first of which also has applicability for regional markets among industrially advanced countries. One is that plans for the creation of a customs union or free trade area usually involve relatively long time-periods for fruition so that the initial impact, and perhaps the most important one, is on expectations regarding future market opportunities rather than on existing trade patterns arising directly out of changes in intra-regional trade restrictions. Thus what is most relevant are the effects on investments which will determine trade and production patterns a decade in the future, as compared with what they might have been in the absence of the creation of the regional trading arrangements. The second factor, which is related to the first, is that developing countries are undergoing rapid and far-reaching changes in the structure of their production and trade. Very often there is relatively little trade among the members of regional trading blocs to begin with and virtually no exports of manufactures either between members or to the rest of the world. Hence, while the European Common Market and the European Free Trade Area are striving to achieve an expansion of intra-regional trade within the framework of an existing economic structure, developing countries, such as the members of the Latin American Free Trade Area, are seeking to bring about within the next decade or two a fundamental change in the structure of their production and trade and have sought to fashion a regional trade mechanism which will help to orient their economies in the direction of regional specialization.

Although no two economic regions or groups of countries which regard themselves as a region capable of economic integration are alike, we might begin by setting forth certain characteristics, some if not all of which under-developed regions tend to have in common. These characteristics are frankly based on those of the countries making up the Latin American Free Trade Area or Montevideo Treaty Association. I have chosen this group as a model because it constitutes the most important group of under-developed countries that have formulated, and are actually in initial stages of carrying out, a free trade area plan. The only other group where significant progress has been made is the Central American group, the countries of which are in a much less advanced stage of development and whose domestic markets are smaller. The Central American group also differs from the Montevideo group in that a much larger proportion of the total income of the Central American countries is derived from foreign trade, and for most of them, at least, balance of payments problems have been less acute.

The characteristics of our model group of countries contemplating the formation of a customs union or free trade area are as follows :

(1) Intra-regional trade in primary commodities is not likely to be affected immediately by the regional trading arrangements either because (a) the countries are complementary and do not have significant restrictions if they are not substantial producers of these commodities, or (b) they are competitive and sell the same commodities in world markets. In addition, the agriculture escape clauses in the agreement may take agricultural products out of the regional trading arrangement.

It should also be noted that in Latin America, bilateral agreements and multiple exchange rates which favour exports to convertible currency areas (to say nothing of the U.S. dumping of surplus agricultural commodities) have tended to put trade within the region at a disadvantage compared with trade with the outside. Hence we begin with a system of trade restrictions which discriminates against trade among countries forming the free trade area or customs union.

(2) Trade in industrial products is virtually non-existent. Production for the domestic market is being initiated in more and more commodities and industrialization is moving into intermediate products and investment goods, especially in the more advanced members of the regional group. The expansion of output takes over a larger share of the market from imports in commodity after commodity, mainly as a consequence of trade restrictions, although in many cases domestic costs may be competitive with imports. Frequently former suppliers of imports from abroad with well-established distribution channels will have undertaken domestic production either directly or under licensing arrangements, perhaps including the provision of management and technical services. The same foreign firms may be suppliers of imports or may be producing

locally in other members of the region. Domestically owned firms usually lack marketing outlets in other members of the region even if they were permitted to compete on a cost basis in the markets of their regional partners.

(3) Slowly growing, if not stagnating, export proceeds from primary commodities, together with rapidly expanding import requirements and debt service plus the necessity of finding employment for unemployed workers, have directed national policies towards the promotion of rapid industrialization with special emphasis on the production of substitutes for imported commodities. The policy of directing or influencing production on the basis of achieving direct savings in foreign exchange, rather than on the basis of relative efficiency, usually leads to substantial cost and price disparities for the same products produced within the region and also to overcapacity sometimes for the same commodities in more than one country in the region. For example, there is substantial overcapacity in Argentina, Brazil, Mexico and certain other Latin-American countries for the production of consumers' durable goods such as refrigerators.

(4) Members of the regional trade group include relatively advanced countries with well-developed industrial sectors, such as Argentina, Brazil and Mexico, and less advanced and little-industrialized countries such as Paraguay and Uruguay. This creates the problem of assuring a balanced distribution of the welfare gains from regional trading arrangements or at least of preventing certain countries from gaining at the expense of others.

On the basis of the foregoing characteristics of our model regional trade group encompassing several developing countries, we shall examine the relevance of certain generalizations formulated by recent contributions to the theory of customs unions.

II. THE BALANCE BETWEEN TRADE-DIVERTING AND TRADE-CREATING EFFECTS

We may begin with the well-known argument of Professor Jacob Viner that trade diversion tends to be harmful to welfare while trade creation is beneficial, and the net effects of a customs union on welfare will depend upon the balance of these opposing forces.[1] By and large the traditional primary exports of developing countries to the rest of the world will not be significantly affected by the

[1] Jacob Viner, *The Customs Union Issue*, Carnegie Endowment for International Peace, New York, 1950, Chapter 4.

creation of a regional trading arrangement. Moreover, their total purchases from the rest of the world will continue to depend very largely upon the growth of their primary commodity exports. However, the improved competitive position of their manufactures and semi-manufactures as a consequence of the creation of the competitive regional market may very well enable them to increase their total exports to the rest of the world. Also, if the regional market creates trade in other primary products not previously sold abroad, members may be able to broaden their primary commodity export base with respect to both regional and extra-regional trade. Hence, the long-run impact of a regional trading arrangement is not to decrease trade with the rest of the world but rather to change its pattern and possibly to enlarge it. In this sense, therefore, there is no over-all trade diversion, only trade creation. Thus, the basic questions which we must examine are : (i) whether the new regional pattern of trade with the rest of the world will become more economical as a consequence of the trading arrangements than would have otherwise have been the case ; and (ii) whether the newly created trade is economical or increases economic welfare.

As regards the first question, imports from the rest of the world will be determined by the effects of the regional trading arrangement on the pattern of production and trade within the region. In the absence of intra-regional trade in manufactures, each member will seek to produce as many commodities as possible for sale in the domestic market and import the rest from abroad. In order to save exchange, many commodities that cannot be produced domestically (because of limitations on investment capital and foreign exchange or otherwise) will be subjected to heavy duties or restrictive quotas or prohibitions. The creation of a regional market, however, will enable individual countries to obtain many of these goods from regional markets and to expand their own output for sale to the region. This will not only change the pattern of investment but will increase the total volume of investment. The additional foreign exchange required for the larger imports of capital goods, raw materials and fuel not produced by the regional partners will become available as a consequence of the reduced demand for consumers' goods and other commodities (including some capital goods) from outside the region. Thus, the new pattern of imports from the rest of the world will contribute to the process of greater specialization within the region.

There seems little doubt that a pattern of industrialization based on greater specialization within the region will be more economical than one based on production by each country for its own domestic market. To the extent that greater specialization is permitted in agricultural commodities, there will also be gains from the removal of intra-regional trade barriers. The welfare gains will arise from the availability of a greater variety of goods at lower average cost, but substantial changes in price relationships may occur. Recent discussions of customs union theory which have emphasized *inter-commodity substitution* as against *inter-country substitution* have special relevance for the case of developing countries.[1] While a customs union will not establish the optimum relations between internal prices of domestic and internationally traded goods for maximizing welfare, intra-regional trade and specialization will change relative prices and consumption patterns toward optimum conditions. The increased consumption of commodity x in country A resulting from a lowering of the tariff on commodity x supplied from regional partner B as a consequence of increased investment and production for exploiting the larger regional market, will change consumption patterns in country A in the direction of increased welfare. In turn, investment in country A can be diverted to expanding output of commodity y rather than towards the production of more commodity x in which it is relatively less efficient.

It might be objected that resources will be transferred from production for the world market to production for the regional market and that this would result, in effect, in a reduction in the terms of trade since imports will be acquired from a higher-cost source. However, for reasons noted earlier, this is not likely to take place as a consequence of the creation of the regional market *per se*, although the urge to industrialize as a means of finding employment for labour has undoubtedly shifted capital resources out of primary production for world markets.[2] Of course, as incomes within the regional market grow, Chile and Peru may sell somewhat more copper to Argentina, Brazil and Mexico, and Brazil may sell more coffee to her southern neighbours. These exports will not be displacing the exports of copper and coffee from other areas of the world, and depending upon long-run supply conditions, they may not even be at the expense of exports of Chilean copper or Brazilian coffee to the rest of the world. Certainly it could not be argued that greater production and income promoted by the existence of a regional market, which in turn expands the demand for primary

[1] See R. G. Lipsey, 'The Theory of Customs Unions: a General Survey" *The Economic Journal*, Sept. 1960, p. 504, and J. E. Meade, *The Theory of Customs Unions*, North Holland Publishing Co., Amsterdam, 1955, pp. 34–41.

[2] Whether or not this is desirable for primary-producing countries as a whole depends upon the demand elasticities for primary goods and effects on their terms of trade. However, one can easily cite examples, e.g. Argentina, where this has been disastrous for the particular economy.

products from relatively efficient producers for the world market —
which happen to be members of the regional trading area — are
harmful to economic welfare.

All that we have said on this point with reference to developing
economies reinforces the view of Professor Meade and others that
there is a gain in welfare if there is a net expansion of trade. This
point seems to be particularly evident when we consider that the
alternative to directing investment to the production of those commodities in which countries have a relative competitive advantage
within the regional market, is a haphazard directing of investment
into production for the domestic market of those commodities which
can most readily displace imports from the rest of the world.

III. COMPLEMENTARY VERSUS COMPETITIVE PARTNERS AND THE PATTERN OF EXISTING TRADE

Recent contributions to customs union theory have evolved
certain hypotheses with respect to the potential welfare gains from
discriminatory regional trade arrangements which relate to the
existing patterns of production in the member countries and to the
proportion which trade among regional partners bears to their total
trade. We shall present these generalizations without necessarily
taking a position as to their correctness within the context of the
assumptions under which they are made, and then seek to determine
their relevance for our typical developing regional group.

(a) A regional trading arrangement is more likely to increase
economic welfare if the economies of the members are very competitive but potentially very complementary.[1]

(b) Welfare is likely to be the greater, the higher the proportion
of trade among the partners relative to their total trade.

(c) Welfare is likely to be the greater, the lower the proportion
of the foreign trade of each member to purchases of domestic
commodities.[2]

In our typical case of a regional group encompassing developing
countries, members at the same stage of industrialization tend to be

[1] See Meade, op. cit. p. 107.
[2] See Lipsey, op. cit. pp. 508-9. Professor Meade concludes that 'a customs
union between two countries will be the more likely to raise economic welfare,
if each is the principal supplier to the other of the products which it exports to
the other and if each is the principal market for the other of the products which it
imports from the other'. He also concludes that 'the formation of a customs
union is more likely to raise economic welfare the greater is the proportion of the
world's production, consumption, and trade which is covered by the members of
the union'. See Meade, op. cit. pp. 108-9.

producing many of the same manufactured goods, but there is little
or no trade between them. So far as primary commodities are concerned, they may in some cases be highly competitive in the sense
that both are producing the same commodities for world markets.
For example, both Brazil and Mexico, which are members of the
Montevideo group, produce both coffee and cotton for world markets.
On the other hand, they may be quite complementary with respect
to some primary commodities which each sells in world markets.
The creation of a regional market is not likely to have much effect on
trade in either of these two groups of primary commodities. Where
they are competitive in primary commodities which they do not
export on world markets, but each maintains import restrictions
in order to support domestic output and prices, the elimination
of trade restrictions within the group is likely to bring about a much
more efficient utilization of resources and result in some displacement
of imports from outside the group; the reduced prices and production
costs for total regional output are likely to outweigh any loss from
trade diversion for the region as a whole.

As regards developing countries, it might be said that because
of the emphasis on industrialization, all members are actually or
potentially competitive and certainly all members of a regional
group are potentially complementary. Thus it would not be correct
to say that the outlook for achieving economic welfare gains through
a customs union of Central American states is poor because the
members are at such a low stage of industrialization that they are
actually not competitive at the present time ; nor would it make
much sense to argue that because they all produce coffee and bananas
and hence are actually competitive, this augurs well for a net increase
in welfare from the creation of a customs union. They are not going
to trade in coffee and bananas anyway, except possibly for some
border trade. As industrialization proceeds, they are going to be
more competitive ; but what these countries should strive for is a
pattern of investment which will introduce a substantial degree of
complementarity for the future.

When we come to consider the generalization noted in paragraph (b) above regarding the proportion of intra-regional to total
trade, it might be concluded that there is little prospect for increasing
welfare through a customs union or free trade area for our typical
regional group. This conclusion would be wrong, however, because
the alternative to increased intra-regional trade is not reduced trade
with the outside world but, rather, the production of a larger proportion of each country's requirements within its borders, thus inevitably leading to a less efficient utilization of resources as compared

with regional specialization. Nor can we accept the implication in paragraph (c) above, that because the proportion of foreign trade to domestic expenditures is quite high for many developing countries, their chances for achieving welfare gains from the formation of regional trading groups is severely limited. The reason is that if the countries are going to develop on the basis of a rather slow growth of export proceeds (and perhaps a large part of these going to pay for debt service), the ratio of foreign trade to domestic expenditures will decline rapidly in the future. Welfare gains will be achieved through the creation of regional markets because they will tend to retard the rate of decline in the ratio of foreign trade (including intra-regional trade) to domestic expenditures.

It is for these reasons that I seriously question the applicability of the generalizations of the theory of customs unions which relate to complementarity, competitiveness and trade patterns, to the potential gains from regional trading arrangements for developing countries. It is necessary to look beyond the existing patterns of production and trade to those which are likely to emerge in the absence of the formation of a customs union or a free trade area.

IV. PARTIAL VERSUS COMPLETE REMOVAL OF RESTRICTIONS ON INTRA-REGIONAL TRADE

Contrary to the traditional approach to customs unions and that which is embodied in the General Agreement on Tariffs and Trade,[1] recent theories of customs unions have suggested that a *partial* reduction of duties on imports from regional trading partners is more likely to increase welfare than is a *complete* removal of restrictions on trade within the preference area.[2] The basis for this generalization is that each successive reduction of duties within the preference area will contribute less to the gains from the expansion of trade between the partners, but the loss from trade diversion will continue as the degree of discrimination within the preference trade area continues to increase. This generalization is usually made on the assumption of an all-round reduction of tariffs affecting all commodities.[3]

---

[1] See Article XXIV of the General Agreement on Tariffs and Trade.
[2] See Meade, *op. cit.* pp. 110-11 ; see also Lipsey, *op. cit.* pp. 506-7.
[3] Closely related to this generalization is the one which states that the formation of regional preference arrangements is the more likely to increase welfare, 'the higher are the initial rates of duty on imports into the partner countries'. See Meade, *op. cit.* p. 108.

From the standpoint of the long-run effects on investment decisions within the regional trading bloc, and again considering the fact that individual countries will, over time, seek a maximum displacement of imports with domestic production in the absence of a regional arrangement, I seriously doubt the validity of the above generalization. I do not believe that a preferential trading arrangement can possibly have the same impact on resource distribution as one which looks towards the removal of *all* barriers to trade within a given time-period. Again, we are not concerned simply with the readjustment of existing trade patterns, but rather with alternative principles for the direction of investment which will establish the trade and production patterns a decade or so hence.

In this connection mention might be made of another generalization of Professor Meade's to the effect that 'a customs union is less likely to have adverse secondary repercussions upon economic welfare in a world in which trade barriers take the form of fixed quantitative restrictions rather than of taxes on imports'.[1] The reasoning here, of course, is that the removal of quantitative restrictions on trade among the partners, while maintaining the same quantitative restrictions against imports from the outside world, is likely not to affect the imports within the quotas from the outside world and hence there would be no trade diversion. On the other hand, the use of quantitative restrictions as against tariffs and discriminatory tariff treatment favouring imports from regional partners removes the necessity of competing for markets on a price and quality basis. In short, I would favour the use of tariffs over quantitative restrictions as a means of providing a discriminatory advantage to intra-regional trade.

To a considerable degree import restrictions of developing countries have taken the form of quotas or outright prohibitions on imports. Moreover, as developing countries become relatively self-sufficient in additional commodities in the future, they will, in the absence of a regional trade arrangement, restrict or eliminate foreign competition one way or the other. It might also be said that there has been a tendency to maintain the most restrictive import measures on the very commodities which might have been imported from neighbouring countries, since it is in these commodities — at least in the industrial field — that developing countries tend to be most competitive with their neighbours. Again, so far as the future is concerned, it is not so much a matter of trade diversion as between the outside world and the regional group, but rather whether policies will be adopted which favour regional specialization as against those

[1] *See* Meade, *op. cit.* p. 110.

which favour the maximum degree of self-sufficiency at whatever cost on the basis of domestic markets alone.

V. THE ECONOMIES OF SCALE

While the gains from economies of scale are usually mentioned as a significant argument for the formation of customs unions or free trade areas, there is considerable difference of opinion as to its importance and some are frankly sceptical regarding its significance for Western Europe.[1] First of all, the possibilities of realizing economies of scale differ greatly for different types of commodities for the same market, and for the same commodity for countries of varying market size. For countries like Brazil and Argentina, the domestic market may be large enough to permit realization of economies of scale for a wide range of consumers' goods and even intermediate goods ; this is certainly not true for the countries of Central America, most of which could not support an economically sized soap factory or fertilizer plant on the basis of the domestic market alone. On the other hand, the domestic market even in the largest and most industrially advanced of less-developed countries is not large enough to justify a plant of economical size for a large number of items, such as specialized machinery, transport equipment, certain chemicals, and electronics.

In a recent study on 'Patterns of Industrial Growth',[2] Professor Chenery has shown that as *per capita* income rises from $100 to $600, the percentage of production of investment goods to total manufacturing output approximately triples according to the normal pattern based on a sample of some fifty countries, including both industrialized and under-developed. When allowance is made for variations in the size of the country, deviations from the normal pattern are 'smallest for services, agriculture, and most manufactured consumer goods', while the greatest variation from the normal is found in 'industries producing machinery, transport equipment, and intermediate goods, where economies of scale are important'.[3] Chenery points out that in modern developing countries, the leading sectors of the economies — or those which provide the impetus to growth — are 'likely to be the industries in which import substitution becomes profitable as markets expand and capital and skills

[1] See, for example, H. G. Johnson, 'The Criteria of Economic Advantage', *Bulletin of the Oxford University Institute of Statistics*, Feb. 1957, p. 35 ; see also 'The Economic Gains from Free Trade with Europe', *Three Banks Review*, Sept. 1958.
[2] See Hollis B. Chenery, 'Patterns of Industrial Growth', *American Economic Review*, Sept. 1960, pp. 624-54.   [3] *Ibid.* pp. 650-1.

are acquired'.[1] Hence he concludes that limitations on market size are an important factor in preventing normal growth of developing countries by their being unable to move into the production of investment and intermediate goods where economies of scale are especially important. Thus he lays special emphasis on the creation of regional trading arrangements which will increase market size as a means of promoting development in accordance with the normal pattern of industrial growth.[2]

Any realistic discussion of the advantages to be derived from economies of scale must take into account the nature of the market in which producers are operating. Outside of Communist countries, few manufacturing industries are complete monopolies and in most cases the existence of several producers, some or all of which may already have excess capacity, prevents the realization of potential economies of scale on the basis of the domestic market alone. Imperfect competition, government restraints and private collusion of various kinds prevent individual producers from establishing new low-cost plants which would force competitors out of business by taking over a larger share of the market, or prevent new foreign enterprises from doing so. Hence the impetus for the establishment of new low-cost plants may need to come from the opening up of an external market where conditions of competition, either with firms in the export market or from third countries, may be such as to require lower-cost production achieved through economies of scale. Moreover, if production is in the hands of a foreign firm which has established distribution facilities throughout the regional market, the foreign firm may be able to supply its entire regional market by expanding the output of one country, or the foreign firm may be able to lower costs by producing certain components in individual countries while continuing to assemble the finished product in the plants of several individual countries within the common market. Finally, this same firm may as a consequence of reduced costs of the finished product or, more likely, of components, be able to supply markets outside the regional group, thereby broadening the export base of the regional group.

The contribution of Professor Tibor Scitovsky to the economies of scale which might be realized from economic integration is especially relevant for developing countries.[3] The high degrees of market imperfection, the factor of risk and uncertainty arising from political instability, and the tendency on the part of domestically

[1] See Hollis B. Chenery, 'Patterns of Industrial Growth', *American Economic Review*, Sept. 1960, pp. 624-54.   [2] *Ibid.*
[3] See Tibor Scitovsky, *Economic Theory and Western European Integration*, Stanford University Press, 1958, Chapter 3.

owned firms to favour high margins and low output, greatly limit the willingness of firms to build plants which will be optimal for the level of domestic demand, say, five or ten years hence. Therefore, accretions in demand tend to be supplied by the addition of sub-optimal equipment. On the other hand, an expansion of the market area to other countries in the region may lead some firms to establish plants with equipment permitting substantial economies of scale. Unfortunately, several of the countries in the Montevideo group are already highly competitive in a number of industries, such as durable consumers' goods and steel, in which significant economies of scale could probably be realized. Therefore, reductions in trade barriers affecting these commodities are likely to proceed very slowly if indeed much progress is made at all in the next few years. Greater progress will be made in the reduction of barriers to trade in goods, the domestic production of which is not yet substantial and imports still supply the vast bulk of the region's requirements. However, in the absence of a regional trade arrangement, relatively high-cost plants for the production of these commodities will eventually be established in some of the countries as the process of substitution continues. On the other hand, more economically sized plants might be established if production for a regional market could be assured. The reduction of intra-regional barriers on new goods, such as specialized capital equipment, will be determined on the basis of intra-regional bargaining, since the first interest of each country will be to preserve the potential domestic market for its own production of a given commodity, an interest that it will compromise only if each country is assured the opportunity of exploiting the regional market for other commodities. Tariff negotiations among the members of the Montevideo Free Trade Area are therefore likely to lead to agreements or understandings regarding the establishment of plants, and this will not always mean production in the most efficient country. It can be argued, of course, that this will increase the extent of trade diversion, but it should be kept in mind that trade diversion will take place in any case and that *total* trade with the outside world is not likely to be greatly affected.

VI. THE EFFECTS OF COMPETITION

As we have already noted, any discussion of the gains from the economies of scale cannot be separated from the nature of the markets and the degree of competition within countries and competition between members of the regional group. Most discussions of the benefits of customs unions have tended to emphasize the gains from competition that are likely to result from the more impersonal competitive forces arising from the creation of the regional market, impinging upon the imperfect or oligopolistic structure of domestic markets. This argument undoubtedly has significance for Western Europe and perhaps should apply with even greater force with respect to developing countries which are characterized by mono-polistic elements of all kinds.[1] However, competition is by no means a popular principle in developing countries, and in Latin America regional trading arrangements are viewed more as mechanisms for development planning on a regional basis than as providing the basis for intra-regional competition. In fact, the term competition is not found in the text of the Montevideo Treaty and has been virtually absent from discussions of the gains from regional integra-tion. The emphasis is on the principles of 'reciprocity' and of 'planned complementarity'.[2] Hence, we may find, initially at least, that the intra-regional trade liberalization measures within the Montevideo group will emphasize reductions in barriers on industrial commodities in which members are not currently competitive, while avoiding those in which they are competitive. In other words, the arrangements would seem to favour trade diversion over net trade expansion. However, as we have already indicated, we must look beyond the shorter-run impacts on the existing pattern of trade to the effects on future patterns of production and trade as determined by alternative policies affecting investment and resource allocation. If the Montevideo Treaty programme moves toward its long-term goal of complete free trade — at least in industrial commodities — members must begin undertaking reductions in barriers which will affect the commodities in which they are competitive. This will be easier to do if the reductions take place gradually so that, given the general accretion of demand, serious damage will not be done to existing firms, but, rather, there will be a gradual increase in the proportion of the market represented by intra-regional trade. Such a development cannot help but have an impact on breaking down internal market rigidities. In fact, the major gains in this respect may occur in the countries which become important exporters of certain commodities, since in order to compete abroad, these firms

[1] See Tibor Scitovsky, 'International Trade and Economic Integration as a Means of Overcoming the Disadvantages of a Small Nation', *Economic Con-sequences of the Size of Nations* (Proceedings of a Conference held by the Inter-national Economic Association), Macmillan, London, 1960, pp. 282-90.

[2] See Raymond F. Mikesell, 'The Movement Toward Regional Trading Groups in Latin America', *Latin America Issues : Essays and Comments* (edited by Albert O. Hirschman), Twentieth Century Fund, New York, 1961, pp. 125-51.

will inevitably undertake cost-reducing measures and introduce optimal equipment which will result in lower prices and perhaps the forcing out of marginal firms in the exporting country. The political repercussions of such developments will be less severe than in cases where marginal firms are forced out as a consequence of import competition.

Even the threat of eventual competition from abroad or a stepped-up pace of competitive activity for exporting abroad will shake a number of Latin American industries out of their lethargy and stagnation. They will see that sooner or later they must adopt new methods in both production and distribution. Moreover, the creation of a regional trading area will lead to greater contacts among business men with the consequent increase in the exchange of ideas. Finally, as a spur to a competitive activity within the region, competing foreign firms will enter on the expectation of being able to exploit a larger regional market, either directly with their own subsidiaries or through joint ventures. Such firms are accustomed to competing with one another in markets throughout the world and will spread the arena of their competitive activities to Latin America.

As has already been mentioned, Latin American policy-makers are hoping to work out complementary agreements in certain industries as a basis for trade, rather than simply lowering the barriers and letting competition take its course. In Central America this principle has been formalized in the General Treaty on Central American Integration, which, among other things, provides for joint planning and certification of manufacturing firms in particular industries which would be given free access to the Central American market under conditions which would avoid over-capacity and unrestricted competition. Although formal provisions for the certification of industries are not included under the Montevideo Treaty, the idea of special complementarity agreements is well established.

In a recent article Professor Jan Tinbergen [1] argues for regional planning as opposed to competition in the heavy industry field on grounds that free entry and competition in these industries are not likely to produce optimal development. Tinbergen favours planned production with the aid of economic models by means of which the optimum pattern of heavy industry development, including plant size and location, could be determined for the region as a whole.

---

[1] See Jan Tinbergen, 'Heavy Industry in the Latin American Common Market', *Economic Bulletin for Latin America*, United Nations Economic Commission for Latin America, Santiago, Chile, March 1960, pp. 1-5.

He gives several reasons why free entry and competition would not achieve these conditions, including: (1) the long construction period required for the individual projects, which would reduce the accuracy of decisions arising out of the market mechanism ; (2) the large amount of capital required to establish plants of optimum size which would not be forthcoming except under conditions of planning and assured demand ; and (3) the failure of free enterprise to establish heavy industry in optimum locations.[1]

It is undoubtedly true that regional planning of heavy industry based on Professor Tinbergen's economic models would provide a closer approximation to the optimal size and location of heavy industry than that which would be achieved under the operation of completely unfettered competition. However, freely competitive conditions in this field may be ruled out as unrealistic in any case because of the oligopolistic nature of heavy industry and of the role played by governments as providers of credits or of direct participants in the enterprises. Moreover, I do see a danger in leaving the planning of heavy industry to government negotiators. Agreements in this field are likely to be negotiated by political representatives with a view to achieving a kind of 'balance of industrialization' among the countries within the regional group, rather than on the basis of optimal size and location of plants in accordance with a rational programme. Also, I can think of few processes more stifling to growth than to leave the development of heavy industry to the almost interminable deliberations of government negotiators. This problem might be dealt with by the creation of an independent or supra-governmental authority such as the European Coal and Steel Community, which would have the power to control investments in heavy industry, but such an institution, so far as I am aware, has not been contemplated for the Latin American Free Trade Area. The price of achieving or attempting to achieve optimal solutions may be a considerably slower rate of investment and a prevention of the full operation of the inducement mechanisms. For countries in a hurry to develop, this is far too great a price to pay. However, the formulation of long-range economic programmes prepared by ECLA or other regional groups, which would serve as a guide to domestic and foreign private investors, to governments, and to external lending institutions, together with arrangements for regional consultations on plans for major investment expenditures in the heavy industry field, would be of immense value.

[1] See Jan Tinbergen, 'Heavy Industry in the Latin American Common Market', *Economic Bulletin for Latin America*, United Nations Economic Commission for Latin America, Santiago, Chile, March 1960, pp. 2-4.

VII. UNEQUAL WELFARE EFFECTS AND
ECONOMIC DUALISM

Customs union theory has recognized that some members of a customs union or free trade area may gain in terms of economic welfare while others may lose. For example, if one of the members does not appreciably increase its exports but simply shifts its imports from lower- to higher-cost sources, membership in a preferential trading area may mean little more than a deterioration in its terms of trade. An extreme case would be one in which a country, as a consequence of joining a customs union, would have to raise its import duties on commodities from the outside world in order to provide a market for higher-cost imports from its partners, while at the same time there was no offsetting export gain. Even if it did not raise its duties, and consumers were able to import at somewhat lower prices or at least no higher prices, from partner countries, the government would lose the tariff revenue on imports diverted from external sources and presumably would have to make up the revenue by taxing its citizens in some other way.

Looked at from the standpoint of the longer-run impact on developing countries, a customs union or other regional preference arrangement might have an even more adverse impact upon certain members. Capital, skills and entrepreneurs, both from within the preference region and from abroad, might be drawn to the major industrial centres of the more advanced partners in order to take advantage of external economies in these areas, and to locate their plants closer to the major markets. In his study of the *Strategy of Economic Development* Professor Hirschman warns against what he calls the *polarization* effects which operate in developing countries to create a situation in which progress in certain areas, mainly the rapidly industrializing regions, is accompanied by, and even contributes to, stagnation in other regions.[1] The creation of free trade areas or customs unions which include countries encompassing less advanced regions and partners representing the more industrially advanced regions may well reinforce these polarization effects. While there are some offsetting forces resulting from the increase in demand for primary commodities from the less advanced regions, these may not be strong enough to offset the polarization effects.

The problem of dualism can be handled by a single country or

---

[1] Albert O. Hirschman, *The Strategy of Economic Development*, Yale University Press, New Haven, 1958, Chapter 10.

an economic union with a strong central government and centralized fiscal system. Special encouragements can be given to the location of industries outside the metropolitan centres by means of tax inducements, and by heavy expenditures for transportation, power and other overhead facilities in advance of immediate industrial needs. Loan capital can be distributed in a way which favours the development of the hinterland. However, if economic integration programmes do not include some mechanism by means of which the less advanced countries are given somewhat more favourable treatment in the distribution of capital expenditures for economic overhead projects or possibly special measures for attracting direct private investment, the net results of combining less advanced and more advanced countries in a regional trade arrangement may very well be to increase the degree of dualism with its attendant political and social frictions and frustrations. This problem has been recognized in the EEC by the creation of special financial institutions such as the European Investment Bank and the European Social Fund, but it is likely to be much more serious among the developing countries forming common markets and free trade areas.

Although the Central American integration plan provides for the establishment of a Central American Integration Bank, the Montevideo Treaty has thus far not established financial facilities which would help to balance the advantages as between the less advanced and the more advanced partners. Provision is made in the Montevideo Treaty for the less advanced members to proceed more slowly with import liberalization than the more advanced members, but what is needed is something more positive which will help the less advanced members to broaden their export markets within the region, particularly in industrial commodities, rather than simply retard the impact of regional competition on their own markets. It would seem highly desirable, therefore, that either there be established a special long-term financing institution to operate as a part of the Montevideo Treaty Organization, or the Inter-American Development Bank play a special role in dealing with this problem in close co-operation with the Montevideo Organization.

There is little doubt that the less advanced members of the Latin American Free Trade Area have an actual or potential cost advantage in a number of industrial and agricultural products with respect to other members of the regional group. But for these advantages to be exploited there must be enterprise, capital, better transportation facilities, and perhaps distribution facilities in other members in addition to reduced trade barriers. Disadvantages arising from high transportation costs and location relative to the major markets may well outweigh the cost advantages of producing in the less advanced members.

The fact that the Montevideo Treaty takes the form of a free trade area rather than a customs union undoubtedly reduces the extent of welfare loss on the part of the less advanced members, while at the same time it reduces the possibilities for trade expansion within the area. Countries like Uruguay and Paraguay, which cannot expect to produce their own tractors or capital equipment for a long time to come, tend to have low rates of duty on these commodities so that they can provide little margin of preference for imports of these goods from Brazil and Argentina even though they abolish all of their restrictions on industrial imports from partner countries. On the other hand, such industrial goods as they are likely to be able to export successfully in competition with producers in other members of the regional group are likely to have a high margin of preference. The tendency for countries to have low tariffs or few restrictions (except for balance of payments or revenue purposes) on commodities which they do not produce or expect to produce in the near future themselves, but a high degree of restriction on commodities they are producing for the domestic market, has led many Latin American economists to the position that the Montevideo Treaty Organization must be converted into a customs union if it is to be successful in expanding intra-regional trade. In other words, there is a fear that countries will not be willing to afford to partner members a discriminatory wall of protection on the commodities they are willing to import from them ; while they are not willing to make concessions to their partners on the commodities on which they are maintaining a high level of protection as a means of securing the market for their domestic producers.

This position seems to arise from a view that a Latin American preference area should be mainly trade-diverting and that intra-regional trade is possible only if a high and fairly uniform tariff wall around the entire region is maintained. I think this is a rather static and short-sighted view of the potential benefits from a regional free market. I suspect that the principal incentive to the expansion of investment in one country in order to market a portion of its output in neighbouring countries is the assurance or expectation that it will have free access to those markets with low or non-existent restrictions, rather than the expectation that it will have a substantial margin of preference over exports from third countries. Moreover, I do not believe that it is possible to create a successful regional trading area on a basis of raising prices to consumers in one country in order to provide a market for the goods of partner countries.

Finally, there is reason to believe that given equilibrium rates of exchange and adequate transportation facilities which will permit the realization of locational advantages, costs of production in developing countries will not be significantly higher (in fact, they might well be lower) for the goods which they are exporting within the region than those from industrially advanced countries outside of the preference region.

While admitting that a free trade area can and will provide a considerable degree of regional preference over external goods, the deliberate creation of a common high wall of protection against outside competition for all goods sold within the region does not appear to be either feasible or desirable from the standpoint of the long-run development of the region. In fact, the long-run aim of the region should be a gradual reduction of barriers on imports from outside as well as within the region itself.

VIII. THE PAYMENTS PROBLEM

So much has been written regarding the payments problem in relation to common markets and free trade areas, and the subject has so many ramifications, that an adequate discussion of this problem for developing countries would require a separate paper in itself. Students of customs unions have evolved sharply conflicting positions with respect to the payments problem and the means of dealing with it. Dr. Thomas Balogh and Dr. Raul Prebisch (and his colleagues in the United Nations Economic Commission for Latin America) tend to favour a multilateral compensation system for financing trade among members of a regional preference area which would avoid, or largely avoid, the necessity for settlements in convertible exchange or gold.[1] At the other extreme are those who believe that a successful customs union or free trade area is not possible except under conditions of financing with freely convertible currencies and the maintenance of over-all balance of payments equilibrium by individual members without restrictions. According to this view, the attempt to achieve freedom of payments internally, while at the same time permitting individual countries to maintain balance of payments restrictions on trade and payments with the

[1] See T. Balogh, 'The Dollar Crisis Revisited', *Oxford Review Economic Papers*, Sept. 1954, and 'The Dollar Shortage Once More, a Reply', *Scottish Journal of Political Economy*, June 1955 ; for a discussion of the position of Dr. Prébisch and of the ECLA Secretariat, see *The Latin American Common Market*, United Nations Economic Commission for Latin America, Mexico, July 1959, pp. 17-22 ; see also Victor L. Urquidi, *Trayectoria del Mercado Comun Latinoamericano*, Centro de Estudios Monetarios Latinoamericanos, Mexico City, 1960.

outside world, is unworkable since such an arrangement would lead
to large imbalances within the preferential system. Even a common
policy with regard to trade and payments relations with third
countries is difficult to maintain in the absence of a full economic
union.[1] Professor Meade favours a system of fluctuating exchange
rates as perhaps the best means of maintaining balance of payments
equilibrium and freedom from restrictions, while others, including
myself, believe that the uncertainties resulting from frequent changes
in exchange rates would greatly reduce the benefits from the formation of customs unions.

As regards developing countries which meet the conditions for
our model, those who favour a multilateral compensation system
involving no settlements in external currencies are usually identified
with the position that it is necessary to establish a highly discriminatory system in which each member country's trade is balanced
over time with the group, and no country is permitted to earn convertible exchange by increasing its exports to the group. This view
is based in turn upon the conviction that manufactured exports
from one partner to another simply cannot be competitive with
external goods or, more generally, that there exists within the group
a shortage of convertible currency which would lead members to
avoid using their convertible exchange for purchases within the area.
There is really little basis for this approach, which reflects adherence
to a 'dollar shortage' philosophy long after there is any justification
for it. There is no general shortage of convertible means of payment in the world today. Nearly all Latin American countries have
adopted realistic exchange rates for the bulk of their trade with the
outside world and they urgently need to remove existing price and
cost disparities among themselves artificially created by subsidies,
bilateral trade agreements and import controls of various kinds. If
the problem is one of providing additional liquidity for financing
an expanded volume of trade among themselves by means of convertible currencies rather than bilateral agreements, this can and
should be handled by special assistance from external sources such
as the International Monetary Fund.

Apart from this, the attempt to create a multilateral compensation
scheme among countries whose existing intra-regional trade is
relatively small is fraught with difficulties, since anything approaching a regional balance would be little short of a miracle. If the
desire for a balanced expansion of trade is an important aspect of the

[1] For a discussion of the balance of payments problems of customs unions, see
Scitovsky, *Economic Theory and Western European Integration*, *op. cit.* pp. 95-100 ;
and Meade, *op. cit.* pp. 14-28 and pp. 116-19.

regional trading scheme, it should be achieved by means other than through a payments scheme. In fact, the results of the operation of a payments scheme is only a reflection of the operation of the fundamental trade liberalization programme, and if the payments positions cannot be compensated multilaterally over time, it will be necessary to change the basis of the trade liberalization programme. Hence all that is really needed is some means of keeping track of the intra-regional balances on current account, and an elaborate payments mechanism is unnecessary for this purpose.

A more fundamental question is whether the *trade* arrangements should be such as to achieve an approximate balance of each member with the group. Personally, I do not believe that this should be a fundamental aim since the existence of a surplus or a deficit of an individual member with the group does not measure the welfare gain or loss from membership. As the economies of partners progressively grow, the pattern of their production and trade will change and the determination of the long-run benefits of individual partners from membership in the preference area will require far more subtle means of measurement. For some countries, for example, there may be no loss whatsoever involved in increasing the share of imports from regional sources in their total imports, while at the same time they are enjoying the gains from a broader market for their export. Indeed, they may find their terms of trade improving even though they develop with their regional partners which they must finance with convertible currencies. Likewise, the achievement of a surplus on intra-regional account by one partner country is not a necessary measure of its relative benefits from membership in the regional preference area. Conceivably it could be paying too much in terms of a deterioration in its terms of trade from the intra-regional surplus that it is achieving.

All of this is not to say that there is not a problem in making sure that the benefits and losses from the creation of a regional preference area are equitably shared, but this must be done by means much more fundamental than setting up a multilateral compensation scheme.

IX. THE INDUCEMENT EFFECTS ON INVESTMENT FROM BROADENING THE MARKET AREA

Development literature is full of examples of the impact of market growth upon investment and productivity and on the revitalization of stagnating industries serving a local market. As a rule this has come about through the development of transportation within a country, through improved marketing methods and the expansion of incomes. For modern developing countries the expansion of external demand has not provided the basis for the growth of investment in manufacturing, and for many countries exports of primary commodities have been growing slowly or stagnating and have provided little inducement for increased investment. Also, the surplus of labour in the agricultural regions has provided little inducement for increasing productivity. Inducements to investment based solely on internal developments have certain limitations. First, for a large number of industries, income elasticities may be rather low and production of new goods as substitutes for imports depends upon whether or not the internal market has grown to the point where plants of an economical size can be established. Such substitution can be forced by high or prohibitive import restrictions, but this may mean an uneconomical use of capital through the creation of excess capacity or of very high-cost productive facilities. Once these industries are established, they tend to stagnate for lack of dynamic growth of demand.

A second difficulty with internally induced investment is that it does not provide any additional foreign exchange to meet import costs of investment goods, intermediate goods, raw materials and fuel, unless, of course, the industries are established by foreign capital. But even here, the actual foreign exchange contribution of foreign manufacturing enterprises is likely to be small since they depend for their growth upon reinvested profits and perhaps for a part of the capital for their initial establishment on domestic sources. There is, of course, an offset against these additional foreign exchange expenditures from increased supplies of the import-competing goods, but this does not occur fast enough for the country to maintain a high level of investment with slowly rising or stagnating export receipts. Hence, domestically induced investment is hampered by exchange shortages which result in the imposition of import restrictions and/or exchange depreciation. The import restrictions or steadily depreciating exchange rates in the face of growing domestic demand creates a condition of chronic inflation which brings about a misdirection of investment and a tendency for savings to flow into less productive uses or to find their way to foreign capital markets.

Investment induced by an expansion of external demand for export goods avoids these disadvantages. Export demand does not depend upon slowly growing domestic income and provides the foreign exchange for the increase in investment in productive facilities. The opening-up of markets in neighbouring countries adds a new dimension to market growth.   Demand and supply elasticities will increase substantially, particularly because they tend to be rather low in countries of limited industrial development.   This will increase economic flexibility and open up new opportunities for investment, both foreign and domestic.

The literature dealing with the importance of broadening the export base for regional economic growth is of particular relevance for the creation of regional trading arrangements among developing countries.[1]   Successful regional growth cannot be a 'bootstrap operation', but depends upon the creation of an export base which permits specialization in the production of those goods and services for which the region's resources are best suited and the creation of external economies.   Of course, successful regional centres of economic growth soon develop local industries producing mainly for local consumption, but it is the exports to other regions that provide the external impetus which then has a multiplier effect.   By analogy, the same reasoning can be applied to nations : for maximum growth they need the stimulus of an external demand for their products and the possibility of broadening their export base to include new export industries as the old ones lose their earlier vitality.

X. CONCLUSION

In concluding this paper I would say that the principal way in which customs union theory needs to be modified for application to the problems of developing countries is by taking into account the likely long-term changes in the pattern of production.   This is especially important for those countries where the export industries do not constitute the leading sector, but rather as a consequence of the slow growth of export proceeds there is a strong drive towards substitution.   Growth is inhibited by the fact that (a) substitution cannot take place fast enough to keep import requirements within the limits of exchange availabilities ; and (b) efforts to create new industries on the basis of supplying the domestic market alone result in high-cost production and misdirected resources.   Because countries cannot or do not specialize in their industrial production, they either produce with sub-optimal equipment or create over-capacity, or both.   In addition, they cannot take advantage of the opportunities to specialize in the production of commodities in which they have peculiar advantages resulting from access to raw

[1] See Douglass C. North, 'Location Theory and Regional Economic Growth', *Journal of Political Economy*, June 1955, pp. 243-58.

materials, location, etc. Moreover, the problem is not so much that countries may be producing the wrong things, since in time, and given broad enough markets and access to skills, techniques and know-how from abroad, they might become reasonably productive in any one of a very large range of industrial commodities. Rather, the problem stems from the fact that they are unable to specialize, and in trying to grow on the basis of limited exchange resources, they are seeking to produce too many things, including finished commodities, intermediate goods and, to an increasing extent, capital goods as well.

The creation of regional trading arrangements provides an opportunity for specialization and increased trade, thereby broadening the export base of individual countries and increasing the productivity of the trading region as a whole. It might, of course, be argued that the gains would be greater if each country broadened its export base by expanding its export of both primary commodities and of manufactures to the rest of the world. This is a good doctrine to preach, but it has not happened and it is not likely to happen until developing countries learn to trade and compete with one another on a regional basis. At a later stage, just as the countries of Western Europe soon began to compete actively in a wide range of commodities with the United States once they had learned to compete with one another, so also, I believe, trade and competition in industrial products among developing countries will provide the experience and discipline for them to sell their industrial products on world markets, thereby broadening the export base of the entire region. This process, of course, will be assisted by the operations of international corporations with distribution facilities throughout the world. Moreover, increased investment by foreign enterprise in developing countries will be greatly encouraged if they can produce finished products or components for sale throughout the preference region.

There is, of course, another pattern by which development can and will take place, at least for some countries : that is, for the export sectors to be the leading sectors and industrialization to develop, first for supplying the local market, and later for sale to world markets. Such countries may be able to develop along the same lines as the United States, Canada and Japan and certain Western European countries developed during the nineteenth century. However, I fear that this pattern of development may be the exception to the rule in the twentieth century.

During the late 1950s and early 1960s regional economic integration was regarded as an important or even necessary condition for economic development. Since controls on trade and payments with the industrial world were accepted by most development economists as inevitable or even desirable for developing countries, the road to broader markets for domestically-produced goods other than primary products produced for international markets was to be found in various forms of discrimination for promoting intra-regional trade. As a result of the efforts of Dr. Raul Prebisch and other Latin American leaders, plus substantial encouragement and financial support from the United States government, several institutional arrangements were created, including the Latin American Free Trade Area (LAFTA) (1961), the Central American Integration Program (1962), and later the Andean Common Market (1969). Promotion of these integration efforts constituted a major objective of the Alliance for Progress initiated by President Kennedy in 1961. None of the regional integration efforts accomplished their goals and by the mid-1970s the institutions and their programs were largely dormant. Economic integration initiatives in developing countries outside Latin America were mainly political statements with little economic content.

The reasons for this failure may be found in my essay presented at the September 1961 Conference of the International Economic Association and reprinted in this volume. The most important reason is that the economic integration programs in Latin America were designed to expand intra-regional trade without significantly promoting competition. In fact, competition both within and among the countries of the Latin American region was disparaged and not regarded as necessary or desirable for the success of the integration programs. Government economic controls and planning were believed to be compatible with intra-regional trade, which was to be promoted by government-sponsored complementarity agreements. A second reason for failure was that the arrangements did not permit the realization of the dynamic benefits from intra-regional trade, which arise from the promotion of domestic and foreign investment to exploit a wider market. Foreign investment was explicitly prohibited from enjoying the benefits of the regional market in the

LAFTA treaty, and was subjected to regional control and severe limitation in the Andean Common Market. Foreign investment was rejected in large part because domestic firms did not want competition from more efficient foreign enterprise.

The third reason for failure is to be found in the international payments arrangements. Since nearly all Latin American countries were in overall balance of payments disequilibrium and maintained overvalued exchange rates, countries were reluctant to settle their intra-regional balances with convertible currencies (which could buy lower priced and better quality goods in international markets). Therefore, intra-regional trade was forced into bilateral balance. Prebisch's scheme for multilateral settlements within LAFTA could not deal with the payments problem since it implied that each country must be in overall balance with all of the members of the multilateral payments system. Such a system distorted normal trade patterns and was not workable.

A regional common market can provide substantial benefits by encouraging foreign investment and forcing individual countries to liberalize their economies. This has been the major contribution of the European Economic Community (EEC). Simply expanding intra-regional commerce that is largely trade-diverting cannot enhance economic welfare or development. Over the past decade or so development economists have learned that competition and general trade liberalization are the keys to development progress. Clearly the Latin American model for regional integration did not promote these objectives.

CEPAL REVIEW
April 1981

The Latin American periphery in the global system of capitalism*

Raúl Prebisch**

In a series of articles, appearing above all in this *Review*, the author has gradually been giving form to his mature view of the economic, social and political structure and transformations of Latin America. In this process of further perfecting his ideas by giving them greater depth and coherence, the present article represents a major step, being a concise summary of the main lines of thought which he is developing in three closely interrelated spheres.

To begin with, he returns to his long-standing concern for the relationship between the centres and the periphery, which he analyses in the light of a number of salient features of the contemporary scene. In his opinion, the topic is of the utmost importance, in that the nature of those relations conditions, limits and orients the Latin American countries' forms and possibilities of development. Secondly, he broaches the question of the internal dynamics of peripheral capitalism in order to throw light upon its main components, contradictions and trends. Thus, he asserts that peripheral capitalism is driven by its internal contradictions towards structural crises which it can overcome only by turning to authoritarian political régimes. This thesis has a corollary which is the starting point for his third line of thought: a stable and democratic solution to those structural crises calls for a profound change in the bases of peripheral capitalism, and particularly of its predominant forms of appropriation and use of the surplus. As a contribution to thinking on this controversial topic, he outlines his theory of change, guided by the hope of finding a synthesis of liberal and socialist ideals.

*This article was especially prepared for the Seminar on Latin American Development Policies held between September 1980 and May 1981 by the Development Training Centre (CECADE) of the Ministry of Planning and the Budget of the Mexican Government.

**Director of the *CEPAL Review*.

I

The dynamics of the centres

Peripheral development is an integral part of the world system of capitalism, but the conditions in which it takes place are different from those in the centres, whence the specificity of peripheral capitalism.

Technology plays a fundamental role in this: its development in the centres is accompanied by continuous changes in their social structure, and this is also true of the peripheral countries when the same technology penetrates them much later. The relations between the two correspondingly alter.

In the course of these continuous changes, some highly important constants are to be found. We shall mention the main ones.

While exerting considerable influence on peripheral development, the dynamics of the centres is limited in scope, on account of the centripetal nature of capitalism. Thus it fosters peripheral development only to the extent that concerns the interests of the dominant groups in the centres.

The centripetal nature of capitalism is constantly manifested in the relations between the centres and the periphery. It is in the former that technical progress originates and that the benefits of the concomitant rise in productivity tend to be concentrated. Thanks to the higher demand which accompanies the rise in productivity, industrialization is likewise concentrated there, spurred on by ceaseless technological innovation which diversifies the production of goods and services to an ever greater extent.

Thus, in the spontaneous course of development the periphery tends to be left on the margin of this industrialization process in the historical evolution of capitalism.

Rather than deliberate, this exclusion is the consequence of the play of market laws at the international level.

At a later stage, when becoming industrialized as a result of international crises the periphery again tends to be shut off from the major trade flows in manufactures of the centres. The periphery has had to learn to export, and it is doing so primarily through its own efforts, as the transnationals have contrib-. uted far more to the internationalization of forms of consumption than to the internation- alization of production through trade with the centres.

This largely explains the inherent tenden- cy towards external disequilibrium in past and present peripheral development: an attempt has been made to correct this tendency first through import substitution and subsequently through the export of manufactures.

The centres have by no means encouraged this process through changes in their produc- tion structure; and by failing to open their doors to manufacturing imports from the periphery, they force the latter to continue with import substitution. Substitution is not the result of any doctrinaire preference, but rather some- thing imposed by the centripetal nature of capi- talism. However, it has been taking place with- in narrow national compartments, at the ex- pense of economic efficiency and of vigorous development.

The economic interest of the dominant groups of the centres form a cluster with stra- tegic, ideological and political interests in the centres, giving rise to stubborn forms of de- pendence in centre-periphery relations.

In those relations, the economic interests of the dominant groups of the centres are ar- ticulated with those of the peripheral coun- tries, and in the play of these power relations the technical and economic superiority of the former weighs heavily. The structural changes which accompany the development and spread of technology are highly important. In the periphery, besides their significance for its development these changes eventually give

rise to disruptive pressures when the internal conflictive tendencies characteristic of devel- opment spill over towards the centres, where they arouse an adverse reaction from the power cluster. This is a clear manifestation of the above-mentioned dependence.

The economic interest of the dominant groups continues to prevail in the centres as in the periphery. Its efficiency in the market, at the national and international level, cannot be denied. But the market, despite its enormous economic and political importance, neither is nor can be the supreme regulator of the devel- opment of the periphery and of its relations with the centres.

This is patently clear in the present crisis of those relations. The market has not been able to cope with the ambivalence of technology, which has had an incalculable effect on mate- rial wellbeing, but has also brought irresponsi- ble exploitation of non-renewable natural re- sources and a striking deterioration of the biosphere, not to mention other serious con- sequences.

Nor have the laws of the market remedied the major flaws in centre-periphery relations, nor still less the exclusive and conflictive ten- dencies in peripheral development.

Individual decisions in the market-place must be combined with collective decisions outside it which override the interest of the dominant groups. All this, however, calls for a great vision, a vision of change, both in peri- pheral development and in relations with the centres; a vision based on far-reaching projects combining farsighted economic, social and po- litical considerations.

II

The internal dynamics of peripheral capitalism

The dynamics of the centres does not tend to penetrate deeply the social structure of the pe- riphery; it is essentially limited.

In contrast, the centres propagate and spread in the periphery their technology, forms of consumption and lifestyles, institutions,

ideas and ideologies. Peripheral capitalism increasingly draws its inspiration from the centres and tends to develop in their image and likeness.

This imitative development takes place belatedly in a social structure which differs in major respects from the developed structures of the centres.

The penetration of technology takes place through capital accumulation, in terms both of physical means and of the training of human beings. As the process develops, changes continuously take place in the social structure, which embraces a series of partial structures linked together by close relations of interdependence; the technical, production and employment structures, the power structure and the distribution structure. These changes must be analysed to throw light on the complex internal dynamics of peripheral capitalism.

1. Structural changes, surplus and accumulation

The penetration of technology gradually creates successive layers of rising productivity and efficiency which are superimposed upon less productive and efficient technical layers, while at the base of this technological structure precapitalist or semicapitalist layers usually persist. These changes in the technical structure are accompanied by changes in the employment structure, as labour is continuously shifting from the less to the more productive layers. However, the income structure does not develop in line with the changes in technology and occupation. Thus, the mass of the labour force does not increase its earnings correlatively with the growth of productivity in the play of market forces.

This is explained by the regressive competition of the new manpower in the technical layers of low productivity, or else unemployed, which is seeking to enter productive activity. Only a part of the fruits of technical progress are transferred to a limited fraction of the labour force which, above all through its social power, has been able to acquire the ever greater skills required by technology.

The part of the fruits of higher productivity which is not transferred constitutes the surplus, which is appropriated primarily by the upper social strata, where most physical capital as well as land ownership are concentrated.

The surplus does not tend to disappear through a fall in prices resulting from competition among enterprises —even if this were un-

restricted— but rather is retained and circulates among them. This is a structural and dynamic phenomenom. The growth of production of final goods, thanks to the continuous accumulation of capital, means that there must be a preceding growth of production in process which will later give rise to the final goods. For this purpose, enterprises pay higher incomes, giving rise to the greater demand which absorbs the final supply increased by the growth of productivity, without prices falling.

In fact, the incomes thus paid in the successive stages of the process (including the surplus) through the creation of money are much greater than would be necessary to prevent prices from falling. The reason for this is that only part of those incomes immediately becomes demand for final goods. Another part is diverted towards demand for services, in the market and the State spheres, where it circulates and gradually returns to demand for goods. In addition to the incomes paid to factors of production, enterprises purchase imported goods, and thus the exporting countries recover the incomes they paid in producing them as well as the corresponding surplus. The opposite occurs in the case of exports.

There is no strict correspondence between demand for goods and supply, but the necessary adjustments are made spontaneously or through the precautionary corrective intervention of the monetary authority when the capacity for sharing out the surplus has not yet developed.

The unequal distribution of income in favour of the upper strata encourages them to imitate the forms of consumption of the centres, an imitation which tends to spread to the middle strata. The privileged-consumer society which thus develops represents a considerable waste of capital accumulation potential.

This waste concerns not merely the amount but also the composition of capital. Closely linked with the technology which increases productivity and income, use is made of technology which constantly diversifies production of goods and services. As this change occurs in the production structure, together with other forms of investment, the proportion of non-reproductive capital increases without any growth of productivity or multiplication of employment, to the detriment of the reproductive capital necessary for fostering development.

These trends inherent in the internal logic of capitalism in the centres appear prematurely in the periphery on account of the great inequality in distribution.

In addition to all this, again at the expense of accumulation, there is the exorbitant siphoning-off of income by the centres, especially through the transnationals, as a result of their technical and economic superiority and hegemonic power.

This insufficient, stunted accumulation of reproductive capital, aggravated by the trend towards hypertrophy of the State and the extraordinary growth of the population, is the main reason why the system cannot intensively absorb the lower strata of the social structure and cope with other manifestations of redundancy of labour. This is the system's exclusive tendency.

These lower strata abound in agriculture, and as the demand for agricultural goods scarcely becomes diversified, labour tends to shift towards other activities. However, given the system's inadequate capacity to absorb labour, a serious redundancy arises which explains the relative deterioration of labour income in agriculture.

As long as this insufficient capacity to absorb labour lasts, technical progress in agriculture will not raise those incomes and correct their relative decline. Instead, it tends to harm relative prices when production outstrips demand. This is usually true of agricultural exports in particular, and has the effect of checking their growth to the detriment of development.

2. Changes in the power structure and crisis of the system

As technology penetrates the social structure, changes take place which are reflected in the power structure. The middle strata expand, and as the process of democratization advances their trade-union and political power develops and increasingly forms a counterweight to the economic power of those, especially in the upper strata, in whose hands most of the means of production are concentrated. It is therefore in these strata that the labour force possessing social power is mainly found. These power relations between upper and middle strata exist both in the market and in the State spheres. In this way ever-increasing pressure develops for sharing out the fruits of the growth of productivity.

This twofold pressure is largely manifested through a rise in the remuneration of the labour force, either to increase its share in the fruits of productivity or to offset the unfavourable effects of certain factors, above all the tax burden which it bears directly or indirectly and through which the State copes with the trend towards its own hypertrophy.

Bureaucratic power and military power have their own dynamics in the State apparatus, supported by the political power of the middle strata in particular, as a result of which State activities develop beyond considerations of economic efficiency, both as concerns the amount and diversification of State services and in terms of the spurious absorption of labour.

In this way, through the growth of employment and social services the State seeks to correct the system's insufficient absorption of labour and its distributive unfairness; and this is a major factor in its hypertrophy

To express the foregoing in a nutshell: the distribution of the fruits of the system's rising productivity is fundamentally the result of the changing play of power relations, in addition, of course, to individual differences in ability and dynamism.

As the labour force's sharing capacity increases and it acquires the ability to recoup its tax burden and compensate for the effects of other factors, the rise in remuneration tends to overtake the drop in the costs of enterprises resulting from successive rises in productivity. The excess then tends to be transferred to prices, and this is followed by fresh rises in remuneration in the familiar inflationary spiral.

In these circumstances, for it to be possible to absorb supply, increased by higher costs, it is essential that demand, and the incomes underpinning it, should increase in a correlative manner.

If the monetary authority resists the necessary creation of money in order to avoid or
check the spiral, the growth of demand will be
insufficient to meet the growth of final production, leading to economic recession which will
continue until the authority changes its attitude
and prices can rise in line with the higher costs.
The rise in prices means that the surplus may
once again increase through new rises in productivity, but only temporarily since it is once
again compressed by the subsequent rise in
remuneration. Thus accumulation declines
with adverse consequences for development,
besides the disturbances which accompany the
heightening of the distributive quarrel.

It should be noted, however, that these
phenomena occur when, thanks to the process
of democratization, the labour force's trade-
union and political power becomes ever
greater in both the market and the State
spheres, and the latter's expenditure steadily
expands through its own dynamics.

In these circumstances, the spiral becomes
inherent in peripheral development; and the
conventional rules of the monetary game are
powerless to avert or suppress it.

These rules are highly valid when distributive power (for sharing out and recouping) is
non-existent or very incipient. This is the case
when the democratization process is very weak
or obstructed or manipulated by the dominant
groups: democracy in appearance but not in
substance.

Such, then, is the crisis of the system when
the arbitrary play of power relations becomes
very strong, which is what occurs in the advanced stage of peripheral development. The
crisis of the system may be postponed for some
time, particularly when plentiful resources are
available from the exploitation of non-renewable natural wealth.

The political power of the upper strata,
apparently on the wane with the advance of
democracy, surges up again when the disturbances brought about by the inflationary crisis
give rise to economic disorder and social disin-
tegration. At that point the use of force is introduced, which makes it possible to break the
trade-union and political power of the disadvantaged strata.

If the holders of military power are not
necessarily under the sway of the economic
and political power of the upper strata, one is
tempted to ask why they intervene to serve the
privileged-consumer society. Here undoubtedly a complex set of factors comes into play.
The fundamental explanation, however, is that
since the upper strata hold the dynamic key of
the system, i.e., the capacity for capital accumulation, they must be left to get on with it
from a desire to restore smooth development;
but the social cost is tremendous, not to
mention the political cost.

What in fact happens is that democratic
liberalism breaks down, while the ideas of
economic liberalism flourish: a fake liberalism
which, far from leading to the dissemination of
the benefits of development, flagrantly consol-
idates social inequity.

Democratic liberalism has not yet
managed to become firmly rooted in the Latin
American periphery. We are all too familiar
with its vicissitudes, its promising advances
and painful setbacks. But the past cannot
account for everything: new, complex elements spring up as changes occur in the social
structure. And the significance of the use of
force is not what is was in the past: the creation
of that total split between democratic liberalism and economic liberalism, despite the fact
that both sprang from the same philosophical
source.

3. The great paradox of the surplus

The foregoing considerations lead to very important conclusions, perhaps the most important in our interpretation of peripheral capitalism.

The surplus is subject to two contrary
movements. On the one hand, it grows through
successive increases in productivity. On the
other, it shrinks through the pressure for
sharing which stems from the market and from
the State. The system functions smoothly as
long as the surplus grows continuously as a
result of those two movements.

Consequently, the upper strata, in whose
hands most of the means of production are concentrated, can increase capital accumulation

and at the same time their privileged consumption: they possess the dynamic key of the system.

This essential condition is satisfied so long as the sharing out of the surplus, both in the market and the State spheres through the play of power relations, occurs at the expense of successive rises in productivity. The surplus will continue to expand, although at a dwindling rate. However, the sharing out cannot go beyond the threshold at which the surplus would begin to shrink.

At that limit, however, the surplus will have become proportionately greatest in relation to the total product. Why is it impossible to continue improving the sharing, when there would be plenty of room for doing so by reducing the surplus? This is the weak point of the system of distribution and accumulation, because if the pressure for sharing outstrips the increase in productivity, the rise in the cost of goods will cause enterprises to raise prices.

The total surplus would undoubtedly allow much more sharing out at the expense of size, but there is nothing in the system to make this happen. It is conceivable that enterprises might take part of the surplus and transfer it to the labour force without raising costs; this would be direct participation in the surplus. But the system does not work like that. Any rise in remuneration over the increment in productivity raises costs, with the consequences described above.

Not all the pressure for sharing, however, takes the form of higher remuneration. As was pointed out earlier, in order to share out the surplus the State resorts to taxes falling on the labour force, which the latter seeks to recoup through higher remuneration; but the State also has the possibility of directly taxing the surplus or the incomes of the social groups in the upper strata who have no capacity for recouping such taxes. These taxes are not transferred to costs, but if their amount squeezes the surplus the rate of accumulation and of growth is weakened, thus accentuating the exclusive and conflictive tendencies.

Whatever the angle from which it is approached, there is no solution to the problem within the system, so long as the capacity for redistribution is strengthened in the advanced stage of the democratization process. Either the result is the inflationary spiral, if sharing leads to higher production costs —which, in addition to the upheaval caused by the spiral, undermines the dynamics of the surplus— or else some of the surplus is taken directly, again with adverse consequences for its dynamics, which sooner or later must be resolved using inflationary means.

However much thought one devotes to the question, it appears that the rules of the game of peripheral capitalism do not allow for an attack on its two major flaws: its exclusive tendency, which may only be remedied by a more intense accumulation of capital at the expense of the privileged strata and of the income transferred to the centres; and its conflictive tendency, unrelentingly heightened in the unrestricted play of power relations.

There is a great paradox in all this. When the surplus grows so far as to reach its ceiling and the pressure for sharing continues, the system reacts by seeking to achieve continued growth of the surplus. In order to attain this objective, it resorts to the use of force. However, the use of force is not a solution; the only solution is to change the system.

4. *Crisis of the system and the use of force*

Given the nature of the system, at the advanced stage of peripheral development and of the democratization process it is impossible to avert the tendency towards crisis. In the system's internal logic there is no lasting way of ensuring that the pressure for sharing does not jeopardize the dynamic role of the surplus and lead inevitably to the inflationary spiral.

The attempt to restore the dynamics of the system through the use of force entails the risk of serious disruption, usually involving a combination of theoretical inconsistency and practical incongruity.

If the system is handled skillfully, however, particularly in favourable external conditions, high rates of accumulation and of development may be achieved with striking prosperity for the privileged social strata, but at the cost of severe compression of the income of a considerable part of the labour force.

This solution, however, by no means strikes at the roots of the system's exclusive and conflictive nature. When the democratization process is resumed sooner or later, the pressure for sharing will tend to lead the system into a new political cycle, aggravated by the deformation which has taken place in the production structure to satisfy the exaltation of the privileged-consumer society.

III

Towards a theory of change

1. The two options for a change

The system of accumulation and distribution of the benefits of technical progress is not subject to any regulating principle from the standpoint of the collective interest. If appropriation is arbitrary when market laws prevail, so is redistribution when political and trade-union power becomes a counterweight to those laws.

It is therefore essential for the State to regulate the social use of the surplus, in order to step up the rate of accumulation and progressively correct distributive disparities of a structural nature, which are quite distinct from functional disparities.

At bottom, there are only two ways in which the State can undertake this regulatory activity: by taking into its own hands the ownership and management of the means of production which give rise to the surplus; or by using the surplus in a spirit of collective rationality without concentrating ownership in its own hands.

The political and economic significance of these two options is essentially different. I lean towards the second on account of two fundamental considerations. In the first place, because the major flaws of the system do not lie in private property itself but rather in the private appropriation of the surplus and the harmful consequences of the concentration of the means of production. Secondly, because the first option is incompatible with the paramount concept of democracy and the human rights inherent in it, while in the second that concept becomes fully compatible, both in theory and in practice, with vigorous development and distributive equity.

2. The dissemination of capital and self-management

The transformation of the system necessarily calls for raising the rate of accumulation of reproductive capital, particularly at the expense of the consumption of the upper strata. The social use of the surplus enables this to be done by disseminating ownership of capital among the labour force thanks to the surplus of the large enterprises in whose hands most of the means of production are concentrated.

In the remaining enterprises, greater accumulation would be undertaken by the owners themselves, but as they rose in the capital scale an increasingly proportion would have to go to the labour force in order to avoid concentration.

The change in the social composition of capital thus occurring in the large enterprises would have to be accompanied by gradual participation in capital until reaching self-management. Some principles of this type of management could also be followed in State enterprises, in special conditions which justified doing so.

These guidelines refer to countries which have attained advanced stages in their development; at less advanced stages, the social use of the surplus could take different forms. In any event, in either case it would be necessary to establish suitable incentives so that the transformations could take place without major upheavals.

This latter concern could lead to intermediate solutions, one of which might be to encourage greater accumulation, even in the large enterprises, in the same hands as at present, together with measures for the redistribution of some of the surplus.

3. The market and planning

In the new system all enterprises, whatever their nature, could develop freely in the market, in conformity with some basic, impersonal conditions established by the regulatory action of the State concerning both the social use of the surplus and other responsibilities pertaining to the State.

This regulatory activity has to fulfil objectives which the market itself cannot attain, but which would enable it to achieve great economic, social and ecological efficiency.

The criteria guiding the State's regulatory activity should be established through democratic planning. Planning means collective rationality, and that rationality requires that the surplus should be devoted to accumulation and redistribution, as well as to State expenditure and investment. Accumulation and redistribution are closely linked, since productivity and income should gradually rise as the labour force in the lower strata, as well as the labour employed spuriously by the system, are absorbed more and more productively. This is a dynamic redistribution, accompanied by other direct forms of social advancement responding to pressing needs.

Planning involves technical work of the utmost importance, which cannot be undertaken without a high degree of functional independence; it is, however, a technical and not a technocratic task, as it must be subordinated to democratically-adopted political decisions.

All this requires constitutional changes in the State machinery and new rules of the game ensuring both stability in the social use of the surplus and flexibility in responding to major changes in prevailing circumstances.

4. Synthesis of socialism and liberalism and power structure

The option for change outlined here represents a synthesis of socialism and liberalism. Socialism in that the State democratically regulates accumulation and distribution; liberalism in that it enshrines the essence of economic freedom, closely linked to political freedom in its original philosophical version.

This option calls for very important changes in the structure of political power, as does the option of concentrating ownership and regulatory activity in the hands of the State. In the course of the alterations of the social structure, the power of the upper strata is counterbalanced by the redistributive power of the middle and, possibly, lower strata. The latter, however, eventually shatters itself against the former in the dynamics of the system. Nevertheless, the crisis of the system opens the way for changing it, as it opens the possibility of reducing the power of the upper strata.

These changes in the power structure would perforce be confined to the periphery, as the power relations between the periphery and the centres, under the hegemony of the latter, especially the leading dynamic centre of capitalism, could not be radically changed by the action of the periphery alone. The power of the centres is considerable, and furthermore it lacks a sense of foresight, as is evidenced by its serious disruptions of the biosphere. This crisis may perhaps have the virtue —as has often been true of major crises in the past— of making the centres aware of the need for great foresight in their relations with the periphery and for containing their own power. I am inclined to think that if the main dynamic centre of capitalism had had this awareness, the breakdown of the international monetary system might have been avoided.

The myth of the worldwide expansion of capitalism has been exploded, as has that of the development of the periphery in the image and likeness of the centres. The myth of the regulatory virtue of market laws is also being dispelled.

Major changes are needed; but it is necessary to know why, how and for whom the changes are made. A theory of change is also needed; these pages, called forth by the pressing need for debate and enlightenment, seek to contribute to the formulation of such a theory.

THE EMERGING PROSPECTS FOR DEVELOPMENT AND THE WORLD ECONOMY

Mr. Secretary-General, Your Excellencies, Ladies and Gentlemen,

It is a great honour for me to be able to present my views on development and the world economy from this platform. I still remember vividly the long and trying months from March to June in 1964 when the first session of UNCTAD was held here in Geneva. I was a member of the Japanese Delegation to the Conference. The first Conference had some elements of creative confusion, trying to elaborate a mechanism where Western countries, socialist states and developing countries could jointly endeavour to consider ways to promote trade and development. Since then, I have participated in the activities of UNCTAD in various capacities. In the course of these years of my involvement in UNCTAD as well as in various activities in other places, I had the privilege and the pleasure to work with Dr. Prebisch. The many and varying virtues he had are well known. Among these, his quality which impressed me most was his ability to combine deep ethical commitments and the rigorous scientific analysis of economic issues in considering complicated questions of development. Based on these two major concerns, Dr. Prebisch's approaches to development and the world economy appear to have evolved pragmatically, addressing key issues of the day. I would also like to attempt to present my views in the same spirit. I would, firstly identify briefly key issues which face us now; secondly, present a historical retrospect from the viewpoint of dynamism of the North-South dialogue, and, lastly, offer my thoughts on areas where actions are possible and useful.

I.   Present issues in North-South relations

The global economy is now faced with dangerous possibilities of a recession, after several years of a growth path, however feeble it has occasionally been. The imminence of it originates in adjustment requirements of an enormous proportion. The United States Government is trying to reduce its huge budget deficit and has to find ways to reduce the trade deficit. Indebted developing countries have to reduce their domestic demands and to export as much as possible. While some countries, such as Japan, have decided to expand government spending, the gap in the global context between demand-generating efforts and demand-reduction requirements points to a recession.

I would now like to quote some parts of the Economic Declaration of the recently held Summit at Venice. "We can look back on a number of positive developments since we met a year ago. Growth is continuing into its fifth consecutive year, albeit at lower rates. Average inflation rates have come down. Interest rates have generally declined. Changes have occurred in relationships among leading currencies which over time will contribute to a more sustainable pattern of current account positions and have brought exchange rates within ranges broadly consistent with economic fundamentals. In volume terms the adjustment of trade flows is underway, although in nominal terms imbalances so far remain too large.

How would Dr. Prebisch see the global situation where we are in? He might see some similarities of the problems we are facing with those he encountered in the 1930s as a young economist and a high government official in his country, Argentina. But, I suppose, he might also look at the issues before us in the light of his own experiences of the whole of the past half century. I also would like to present my views on those issues briefly, based on the experiences I have gone through in the past several decades.

A. Diversification of the interests of countries

The first issue which comes to my mind is the diversification of the interests and developmental stages of countries. Of course, the differences of the interests and perceptions among developing countries were already significant in 1964 when the first session took place. However, the degree of these divergences has increased in the past 15 years to such a level that it has become impossible to consider just a set of policies which are equally effective in all developing countries. Beyond some simple typologies of development policies, we now need to consider various elements in elaborationg policies in individual developing countries. Upon my insistence, the Report of the Committee for Development Planning elaborated this point somewhat in 1979. I suggested four categories of developing countries then OPEC and other oil-exporting countries, newly industrialised countries, poorer developing countries, and others. While it is essential for developing countries to maintain political solidarity, it is increasingly important for the world community to recognize different categories of countries which can benefit from and contribute to the world economy in different ways. It seems that there is now clearer recognition of this point. In the course of the intervening eight years, the global economic situation has again changed dramatically. The major impacts of the this alternation on the divergencies of developing countries are two-fold. Firstly, the salience of oil-producing countries in the world economy has diminished considerably. While there may be some possibilities that these countries might again become an important group in the world in the 1990s, they cannot be conceived of as a category of countries in the present world economy. Secondly, some countries in addition to the newly industrialized countries have emerged in the course of the past 10 to 15 years as major forces in the world economy. This emergence is due, to a large extent, to the successful management of their economic policies in their struggles with the turbulence of the world economy. In the present situation, it appears, therefore, that there are three cateogries of countries which need to pursue different policy objectives in the world economy.

The first category of countries can be called <u>major emerging economies</u> which comprise newly industrialized countries and several other countries whose economic performances in the past fifteen years of turbulence have been significantly better than others (such as China, India and Thailand). These countries can benefit more by integrating themselves progressively into the international economic system which is now dominantly market oriented.

The second category of countries consists of <u>poorer developing countries</u> which include not only the least developed countries as recognized by the United Nations but also 20 or 30 other developing countries whose economic performances have been stagnant. The viability of the national entities of these countries is increasingly becoming a global issue. While national efforts to combine attempts at revitalizing national economies and a fresh look at nation-building requirements are essential, it is also important for industrailzied countries to respond more positively to these double efforts of poorer developing countries, as promised at, for example, the Special Session of the United Nations on Africa last year.

All other countries will need to learn from the experiences of themselves and of others, in particular those in the emerging country category during the past two to three decades. Rich experiences of the developing countries themselves will be the biggest source of inspiration for these countries. Some devices to make this mutual learning possible may have to be considered. Industrialized countries will have to listen to the presentation of these countries more attentively once these countries will have learned from the experience of each other.

B. Relative roles of the government and the market in the development process

The second issue is related to the roles to be played by the government and the market in the development process. This question was a highly ideological issue 20 years ago. The discussion of this subject was largely rhetorical. However, it appears that this issue has now acquired a measure of pragmatism and seems amenable to useful discussion. The following three considerations are of particular importance:

In broad terms, it is important to liberalize microeconomic areas, whereas it should be essential to articulate broad guidelines within which macroeconomic policies are to be established.

Another factor is related mainly to developing countries. It appears that stronger government intervention is more effective for those countries which attempt to catch up with more developed countries than for those countries which are already at the forefront of the world economy.

The third dimension is the requirement for planners to read the market signals carefully and to incorporate them in their planning work. This means planning with market forces rather than planning against market forces.

C. Low prices of commodities

The third issue is the question of low prices of commodities. Some observers even suggest de-linkage between economic performances and commodity prices. While prices of commodities are indeed low on practically all fronts, it is particularly important to differentiate between commodities in analysing even the current situation. For

example, in examining agricultural commodities in Africa, it is essential
to differentiate between cash crops and food crops. Considering that
there is a relatively easy changeability between the two, this rather
banal distinction can have important policy implications. For the
purpose of enhancing the capacity of individual countries to maximize
this flexibility, it is important to examine positive contributions that
various technologies can make through such a mechanism as the
Consultative Group on International Agricultural Research. In other
commodity areas as well, differentiation between commodities should be
able to elaborate approaches to break out of the present situation.
Thus, while there is certainly a structural element in the present
situation of low prices of commodities, there are ways to improve the
supply and demand equilibrium.

D. Indebtedness of developing countries

The next issue which characterizes the current sitaution of
development and the world economy is the gravity of the indebtedness
question of developing countries. The interdependent nature of this
issue is now well known. The one trillion dollar debt of developing
countries has a significantly depressive impact on the world economy. In
the face of the slow growth of the world economy, in spite of the efforts
at the Western Economic Summit and other places, the export prospects of
indebted countries are not bright. With regard to the problems which
Latin American indebted countries are facing, we are now forced to learn
three lessons.

The first lesson is that recycling of surplus savings practically
only through commercial banks is a vulnerable endeavour. In the
course of the latter half of the 1970s, there were many proposals
for recycling OPEC money, including some which could have combined
private channels and the official interventions. I, myself,
proposed an idea jointly with Bob Roosa, Armin Gutowski and others
in Foreign Affairs in the January 1975 issue. However, what in
fact happened was the recycling of most of those OPEC surplus
savings through commercial banks, an action which at that time was
praised as being very efficient. This efficiency, however, was
achieved, in some cases, by sacrificing rigorous observance of
bankability tests.

The second lesson is that it requires tremendous efforts on the
part of the Latin American leaders to persuade their people to
reduce their high propensity to consume. This is one of the major
points which Dr. Prebisch stressed just before his passing away.
Unless external financing is invested in activities which are
likely to develop into areas of comparative advantage, the debt
burden originating in that external financing will inevitably
become impossible to bear.

The third lesson is the increased need for improved capacity of the
world community in economic forecasting or prediction of likely
development. This exercise comprises not only pure economic
analysis but also examination of political economy. The second oil
shock of 1979, combined with staunch non-accommodating policies of
the OECD countries, led the world economy into the recession of the
early 1980s which triggered Latin American debt problems. In the

late 1970s, real interest rates reached zero, or even negative, and the dollar exchange rates were very low. Awash with liquidity, international banks resorted to considerable levels of salesmanship, in particular, in Latin American countries. This situation changed dramatically in a few years' time as we all know very well. Living in a world where uncertainty is prevailing, improved capacity for forecasting political economy, though not easy, will contribute significantly to avoiding the repetition of the Latin American type of indebtedness problems.

With regard to the indebtedness problems of sub-Saharan countries, we have learned three lessons in hard ways:

The first lesson is that the official development aid increased significantly in the wake of the famine in these countries in the early 1970s without carefully measuring the impact of the aid. Action was seen to be more important than its effect. The external aid, in the form of lending, led to unbearable debts in recipient countries.

The second lesson is that without appropriate policy mixes in the medium- to long-term context in individual recipient countries, no amount of aid will be able to surmount the problems of hunger, but will lead only to burdens of indebtedness.

The third lesson is that it is essential for donors to respond more positively to the adjustment policy efforts of individual African countries as agreed at last year's Special Session of the United Nations General Assembly on the critical economic situation of Africa.

The focal point for considering the debt of these countries is the Paris Club. There have been improvements in the fucntions of this forum. The recent meeting of the Western Summit agreed on this point as follows:

"For those of the poorest countries that are undertaking adjustment effort, consideration should be given to the possibility of applying lower interest rates to the existing debt and agreement should be reached, especially in the Paris Club, on longer repayment and grace periods to ease the debt-service burden."

To the extent that these various elements which led developing countries into the indebtedness trap exist, some Asian countries are also suffering, though to a lesser extent, from the same problems.

Given these lessons which we have been compelled to learn, it is important to recognize that all the relevant parties, such as the governments of creditor countries and of debtor countries, the IMF, the World Bank and the commercial banks, will have to be involved in attempting to solve the problems of indebtedness.

E.   **Relations between domestic policies and the international**
     environment

The next issue is related to the linkages between domestic policies
and the international environment. One important aspect of this
recurrent issue is the question of broad policy choices betrween
export-oriented growth and import substitution. While there are
different mixes of the two ingredients which should be appropriate for
individual countries, it is, in principle, desirable to increase export
orientation as much as possible. There has been a broad understanding of
this effect in recent years. However, import substitution policies are
gaining ground again in some policy circles. This new trend is
apparently related to protectionist tendencies in the industrailzed
countries. When it is difficult to increase exports due to the
unfavourable international environment, it is natural for some people to
begin to think about going back to import substitution policies. This
resembles ominously the climate of the 1930s when, according to Dr.
Prebisch, Latin American countries had nowhere else to go but to domestic
markets, owing to increasing protectionism in the developed centre
countries. This is a typical case of a vicious cycle. He observed it as
follows:

> "When did import substitution begin in Latin America? During the
> great world depression, when the monetary policy of the United
> States and the enormous rise in customs duties shattered the whole
> system of bilateral trade and payments that had been working very
> well. The slump in our countries' exports was formidable. And
> import substitution was the only way out. I had an active part to
> play at that time, and I do not remember that in the existing
> situation there was anyone crazy enough to say 'The thing is not to
> substitute domestic production for imports but to export
> manufactures'. Export manufactures where? To a world that was out
> of joint and where protectionism was a normal way of safeguarding
> economies? Import substitution was the only solution possible. It
> was not a doctrinaire imposition. It was imposed by force of
> circumstances."

In the face of the slow growth of the world economy, it is, in
general, necessary to attempt to generate domestic demands in developing
countries. As one might say, "growth begins at home". This may, in some
circumstances, include import substitution to some extent. This approach
can be valid in the current circumstances for medium to large developing
economies. With regard to smaller countries, expansion of intra-regional
trade and investment should be able to optimise growth gains in the
generally unfavourable international climate. More broadly, South-South
trade is becoming increasingly important due to slow growth in
industrialized countries. With increasing differentiation among
developing countries, South-South trade, in fact, should become more
productive if trade liberalization among developing countries is
achieved. These efforts should be pursued as an integral part of the
global endeavour to liberalize the trading environment as much as
possible.

The roles of industrial countries and developing countries are becoming only relative in producing a trading climate. In the current situation where there are certain signs of increasing protectionism in some industrial countries, it is for developing countries, in particular those which are more industrialized than others, to attempt to improve the international climate by maximizing openness in the international environment.

F. Weakening multilateralism

The last current issue, as I look at development and the world economy, is the question of weakening multilateralism. Despite the difficulties multilateralism is facing now, the broad trend toward increasing multilateralism is a natural historical tendency. Given increasing economic interdependence, as well as technological developments in, in particular, transport and communications, which make it easier to get together, multilateralism will become an increasingly important element in international life. In considering this issue, it is essential to differentiate between forum organizations and operational bodies at all levels of multilateral endeavours (sub-regional, regional, inter-regional and global). The major objective of forum organizations such as this body, UNCTAD, is to build up elements of legitimacy in the international community. Understandings arrived at in multilateralism are seen to constitute "common goods". To put it differently, the weakening multilateralism in forum organizations means decreasing elements of legitimacy in the world community. Unfortunately, we are witnessing this tendency.

The major objective of operational bodies such as the World Bank is to de-politicise the actions. For instance, aid policies, which tend to become highly political instruments in the bilateral context, can be de-politicised by such bodies as UNDP and the World Bank. Weakening multilateralism in operational bodies tends to generate an increase in politicization of the relevant actions.

Among various issues which the world community faces in the field of development and the world economy, these six are the ones that I see as the present major questions.

II. The dialogue in retrospect

Let us now review the broad context of the North-South dialogue in which these issues have been dealt with. The major objectives of the North-South dialogue being to enhance development of developing countries, and to gradually integrate developing countries into the international economic system. It is important to examine the dynamism of the dialogue in order to look into prospects for development and the world economy.

Among various facets the North-South dialogue has, it is particularly important to consider it as a political movement of the developing countries. Like any other political movements such as labour movements and student movements, the North-South dialogue has three phases: mobilization, peak and decline. The major factors which cause this dynamism are leadership, organization and ideology, while the economic environment in which the dialogue is carried out is not negligible. Reflecting the wax and wane of these factors, two cycles of the North-South dialogue appear to have been completed. The first cycle harvested such fruits as global systems of preferences for trade and the 0.7 per cent of GNP target for ODA. This cycle began with the preparatory meetings in 1963 for the first session of the Conference and ended in the early 1970s. The leadership of this period was marked by the activities of Dr. Prebisch. Organizationally, this body, UNCTAD, was created, and the Group of 77 was formed.

The second cycle began immediately after the end of the first cycle in the early 1970s. Its ideological focal point was the New International Economic Order. The real forces behind the NIEO movement was the oil power of OPEC. In contrast to the emphasis on trade (GSP) and aid (0.7 per cent target) in the first cycle, it was the area of commodities which became the major focal point among various activities which were dealt with in several North-South fora. However, given the broad nature of the NIEO, the focus tended to be lost, and with it, the power of the developing countries. Therefore, while the major fruit of the second cycle was the Common Fund, the forces behind it were not strong enough to implement it. At the same time, the recession of the early 1980s set in. The declining phase of the second cycle has been continuing in the course of the 1980s.

The industrialized countries maintained reactive attitudes throughout these two cycles of the North-South dialogue. They have been institutionalizing themselves, partly owing to the pressures of the developing countries throughout these years. These have taken various forms, including the Western Summit and various new committees at the OECD. The major drawback of institutionalization of the Western countries has been to encourage these countries to consider ways to re-establish some equilibria, mainly among themselves. In a way, pressures of the developing countries in the North-South dialogue have encouraged this tendency. This is not a particularly healthy trend. For example, the balance of trade disequilibria between, on the one hand, the United States, and, on the other hand, Japan and the Federal Republic of Germany could be approached from the viewpoint of global balances including the developing countries. However, this question tends now to be treated as an issue between the United States and the surplus countries in such fora as the Western Summit and the OECD. Instead, recycling of part of the surplus into developing countries would enable them to increase their imports from the United States, thus reducing the trade gap of the United States.

III. **Prospects for development and the world economy and some
       suggestions with regard to the evolving role of UNCTAD**

Enormous amounts of effort, both political and intellectual, have been devoted to maximizing prospects for development and the world economy in recent years. The World Commission on Environment and Development, of which I was a member, chaired by Mrs. Gro Bruntland of Norway, has also attempted to examine these aspects considerably in the past three years. In its report, entitled Our Common Future, we have pointed out as follows:

"Humanity has the ability to make development sustainable - to ensure that it meets the need of the present without compromising the ability of future generations to meet their own needs. The concept of sustainable development does imply limits - not absolute limits but limitations imposed by the present state of technology and social organization on environmental resources and by the ability of the biosphere to absorb the efforts of human activities. But technology and social organization can be both managed and improved to make way for a new era of economic growth. The Commission believes that widespread poverty is no longer inevitable. Poverty is not only an evil in itself, but sustainable development requires meeting the basic needs of all and extending to all the opportunity to fulfill their aspirations for a better life. A world in which poverty is endemic will always be prone to ecological and other catastrophes."

Thus, the issue of sustainable development has to be considered from a global perspective. The major task of enhancing prospects for development and the growth of the world economy, then, is to break out of the North-South bind. Major disequilibria in trade and finance need to be addressed not only between key industrialized countries, but in a broader context where developing countries should be involved. It is important at this juncture to aim for building up policy approaches to address the complicated tasks by producing creative patchworks, rather than to aim for an ambitious comprehensive package. The major elements of these patchworks should be as follows:

A.   **Surplus savings to be transferred to developing countries**

As we observed in a recent report of the WIDER (a recently established institution in Helsinki under the United Nations University), where I serve as Chairman of the Governing Board, 'the complementarity between the urgent resource requirements of developing countries for increased investment and growth, and the availability of capacity in developed countries which may otherwise become idle on an unprecedented scale has never been as striking as it is today'. However, as I pointed out earlier, we have learned from the experiences of the recycling of the oil dollars that channeling surplus savings to developing countries only through private routes tends to invite indebtedness problems. Government actions on the part of surplus countries are required. The Japanese Government has recently announced specific actions for recycling $20 billion or more toward developing countries.

Surplus savings do exist almost always in some economies in the world community. In the 1940s and the 1950s, the surplus savings of the United States were a main feature in the world economy, in the 1970s those in OPEC countries, and in recent years those in Japan and the Federal Republic of Germany. While each surplus economy has its own constraints, it should be useful to consider the policy options available for it to rechannel its surplus savings to developing countries. It would be important to examine this from a global perspective as well and it would be for UNCTAD to play a constructive role in this context.

B. Global indicative guidelines

A related activity that would be useful is to attempt to arrive at some broad indications of development and the world economy for the coming years. Some good works exist already. They have been done by a few international organizations, including UNCTAD, and by some private forecasting groups. Based on these, it would be possible to elaborate broad indicative guidelines for development and the world economy. Strengthening the exercise of the annual Trade and Development Report, UNCTAD could attempt to perform this function. For individual countries, particularly for developing countries, these indicative guidelines will be useful in considering their own policy options.

C. Strengthening governmental capacity in economic policy-making and implementation of policies

To advance this logic a step further, it is essential for individual developing countries to have stronger capacities in making policies and in implementation of the policies. Based on some major studies, there are indications that the strongest correlation exists between development and the quality of government. It appears that various relevant factors such as capital and raw materials are not by themselves the determining forces for development, but that the capacity of government to organize available resources for productive purposes is the most crucial factor which makes a difference in development.

There are two ways to strengthen the government's capacity in this respect. The first approach is a rather traditional one, namely technical assistance. This is, in fact, pursued by various international bodies, bilateral donors and some professional associations. It should be useful to do research on what is being done in this area and to map it out. Perhaps, UNCTAD might consider doing it. Then, it should be possible to identify gaps. Consideration should be given to filling these gaps by multilateral and bilateral agencies.

The second approach is to devise a mechanism through which individual developing countries can learn from the experiences of each other. Perhaps the richest potential resources developing countries have are their own experiences of both successes and failures in the past two to three decades. It is important for the world community to make arrangements for turning these potentials into real resources. One way to do so might be to establish a forum where interested developing countries could learn from the experiences of each other. UNCTAD may be able to undertake such a function.

D. Strengthening commodity markets

There is no magic in attempting to deal with the current situation of commodity markets. As I suggested in a session of the Committee for Development Planning in the late 1970s, it is essential to distinguish four categories of countries in considering commodity issues. They consist of the following: resource rich-rich countries, resource rich-poor countries, resource poor-rich countries, and resource poor-poor countries. The impact of the price behaviour of commodities are different, depending on these categories of countries. The first task of the international community must be to enhance the analytical capacity of the prospects of the commodity markets. Considerable efforts have already been made to comprehend these markets by various bodies, notably by UNCTAD. It should be possible to enhance this capacity of UNCTAD significantly. UNCTAD should continue to play a major role in the commodities field, particularly in analysis of their prospects. A good and reliable analysis in this area is bound to affect both multilateral and bilateral donors and other investors, including developing country governments and private entrepreneurs.

The major new demand generators of commodities should be the emerging countries which I referred to earlier. These are the countries which are rapidly increasing manufacturing capacities, in particular in highly commodity-consuming product lines. Enhanced analytical capacity should be able to make it possible for the international community to have a better grasp of this new trend.

At the same time, high technologies, in particular, new materials and biotechnology might make it possible for commodity-producing countries to control production better than before. This might become a new weapon against the formidable factors of the structural elements.

E. **The debt problem**

The problem of indebtedness of developing countries is deteriorating, slowly, but, unfortunately steadily. In order to tackle this problem, an approach based on inter-linkages among debt, trade, finance and growth has been discussed in various fora in recent years. Indications of recent months point to a need to emphasize growth in this list. Reflecting the concerns over indebtedness questions in the context of inter-linkages among these policy elements, a number of broad agreements have emerged recently. The policy packages addressed to the so-called 'Baker countries' and some sets of understandings with regard to poorer countries, least developed countries and African countries, which have been formulated by UNCTAD and the United Nations General Assembly, have been pursued. These would have been correct approaches. But, in reality, the partial implementation of them on the part of all relevant parties is bringing about the current difficult situation. What we are seeing is a series of sporadic and unilateral decisions on the part of some indebted countries as well as on the part of some banks.

The policy approaches to be taken are, therefore, either to confirm the existing Baker packages and UNCTAD/United Nations 'understandings' more strongly and to try to implement them, or in addition, to attempt something more. My assessment of the situation is tilting toward the latter, namely, to try to do something more.

Broad approaches toward policies on indebtedness in addition to these past commitments are twofold. With regard to bank loans, broadly speaking, additional actions should be based on the indications coming from the secondary markets of these loans. Individual banks are already taking some measures, and they need to be encouraged to elaborate their schemes further which should be aimed at ensuring steady flows of capital into developing countries. As mentioned earlier, a large-scale recycling of savings from surplus countries to developing countries will be required for the fundamental solution of debt problems. Because surplus savings are mostly accumulated in the private sector, government or multilateral financial institutions should provide measures for reducing investment risks by strengthening guarantee, insurance, tax incentives or subsidies.

With regard to indebtedness originating in official development assistance, consideration should be given to strengthening the commitments made in this Organization in 1978 and thereafter. Further actions on the part of donors with regard to the coverage of countries as well as to the terms and amount of the commitments could be sought. They, however, should be accompanied by an improvement of the policies of indebted governments.

These additions will contribute significantly to the improvement of the climate of the international community. Given the uncertainty prevailing over the financial markets, this psychological dimension is of particular importance.

The patchwork of these policy actions will need to be elaborated in various fora, some of which will be existing multilateral institutions, while others will be more flexible arrangements but of a multilateral character. This policy-making process in the area of development and the world economy will gradually build up a sense of legitimacy in the international community, a factor which is sorely needed now. Thus as I see it, we stand now at the starting-point of the third phase of the North-South dialogue. This phase, however, is significantly different from the previous two phases. This time, it is not the Southern countries only which set the tone of the dialogue. It has to be the joint task of both the North and the South. Individual countries will, at the same time, need to break out of the bounds of the North and of the South. They will need to form various patterns of partnership depending on the issues involved while political solidarity of developing countries may need to be maintained. It is going to be a complicated endeavour, requiring enormous capacity for intellectual insight and imagination on the part of the global community. Overviewing the progress on various fronts of discussion and negotiation will be of particular importance. I believe it is the biggest challenge for UNCTAD to perform this task in the third cycle of the North-South dialogue.

Part V

International Cartels, Commodity Agreements, and the Oil Problem

Caves
Behrman
Houthakker

International Cartels and Monopolies in International Trade

RICHARD E. CAVES

The formal niceties of pure competition make it the stock-in-trade market structure in theoretical models of the international economy. Yet imperfect competition calls out for attention as a matter of international economic policy and, therefore, poses issues for theoretical and empirical research that cannot in good conscience be ignored. This chapter addresses two major ways in which imperfect competition impinges on the making of international economic policy. First, governments engage in or promote the formation of international cartels in order to maximize national monopoly gains, or they seek to evade exploitation by such cartels. Second, governments maintain competition in their national markets by means of policies that should recognize the presence or absence of international competition. The two main sections of this paper summarize the theory and empirical evidence relevant to governments' policy choices as exploiters of monopoly power and as enforcers of competition.

I. CREATION AND MAINTENANCE OF INTERNATIONAL CARTELS

By an international cartel, I shall mean an agreement among producers of a given good or service located in different countries and covering the bulk of the market decision variables that must be manipulated or constrained in order to achieve significant joint monopoly profits. Cartels have often been organized among private-sector producers. For this analysis, however, I shall assume that they are either the direct work of national governments or that governments enforce them in the pursuit of national economic objectives. This approach is responsive to the recent role of governments in forming or seeking to form primary-product cartels, and it focuses our attention on the behavioral conditions necessary for forming and maintaining cartels. That is, we can take the key structural conditions

Reprinted from "International Economic Policy: Theory and Evidence" (R. Dornbusch and J.A. Frenkel, eds.), pp. 39–75, with permission of The Johns Hopkins University Press, Baltimore. Copyright 1979.

as given—a certain number of countries possessing bauxite deposits, for example—and concentrate on the game-theoretic depiction of their behavior that is the heart of traditional cartel theory. In the second part of this chapter, where we consider the problems of governments trying to maintain secure, effective, industrial performance, we shall be back in structuralist territory. The exposition of this section uses the microeconomic terminology that is standard for cartel theory. Some remarks about the process of translating the conclusions into the realm of national economies and general equilibrium come at the end.

Under what conditions do potential participants join a cartel? Once the cartel is under way, what are the incentives to defect, and what causes the parties to resist the temptation to cheat? It is useful to begin our answer by drawing upon the Cournot–Nash duopoly theory, in which Cournot's solution to the classic duopoly problem supplies a reference-point outcome for the case in which the parties achieve no cooperation. This solution of course is not in the core, but while we address the possibilities of a collusive bargain between sellers it is hardly unreasonable to put aside the possibility of a subsequent deal with the exploited buyers to supply them at marginal cost.[1]

The familiar "prisoner's dilemma" game explains why the Cournot solution emerges in single-period games. It would also emerge from a model involving trade in n successive periods, if trade in all periods is arranged by means of binding contracts reached on the initial day. More surprising, the Cournot solution also emerges in a market operating for a finite number of trading days, if sales are determined afresh each period and there is an enforcement mechanism that penalizes each period's noncolluders in the next time period. As Shubik (1959) and Telser (1972) have shown, this proposition is easily proved by backward induction. In the last (nth) time period, no punishment is possible for violators of a monopolistic consensus, and so the Cournot solution prevails in the nth period. But given that expected outcome, nothing can deter a party from cheating on that consensus in period $n - 1$, on the assumption that enforcement consists of reverting to the Cournot solution, which will obtain in period n in any case. The proof continues back to the initial period. The empirically interesting point that emerges from this analysis is that avoidance of the prisoner's-dilemma solution requires that the participants not know when the game is going to end. Telser develops this property by assuming that each duopolist supposes in each period that the game will continue for one (or more) additional periods with some exogenously

---

[1] Telser (1972, pp. 138–39) shows that the Cournot solution lies in the core of a reduced market—one in which the buyers extramarginal in the actual Cournot solution are assumed absent from the market.

given probability a. The temptation to cheat on a joint-monopoly consensus depends on the severity of punishment (modeled by Telser as retrogression for k periods to the Cournot outcome), but given that severity it is greater the smaller is a. Telser also points out that, if cheating is expected to be profitable, it will in this model be undertaken immediately; a joint monopoly once attained should be stable indefinitely if k and a values are stationary and high enough to deter cheating.[2]

The creation of cartels

The Shubik–Telser analysis, reported so far, is useful for introducing the central concerns of cartel theory—the essential terms of agreement and the conditions under which an agreement once reached will continue to be honored. Yet there is something peculiar about distinguishing the conditions under which sellers can reach an agreement from those under which they can sustain it. Why not suppose that potential cartel members correctly anticipate the enforcement loopholes of an agreement when it is first drafted? With that rationality assumed, we could predict a cartel would be undertaken if and only if the present value of its joint monopoly profit exceeds the present value of its expected costs of operation and enforcement. Outside interference apart, a potentially profitable cartel then is blocked only by its members' lack of inventiveness with devices that bind their commitment to follow the terms of the agreement. As Schelling (1960, especially chap. 5) points out, the strategies for achieving binding commitment may be rather rich. Nonetheless, the received body of cartel theory puts most of its emphasis on the problems of punishment and defection from incomplete cartel agreements without explaining why—aside from observed fact—this contractual incompleteness should pertain.

It is useful at this point to remind ourselves what is required for a contractually complete cartel. It is not enough to divide markets or agree on a common price. Joint profits from the cartel's activity cannot simply pass to each member as the net revenues resulting from his apportioned sales. Without pooling profits and dividing them according to some pre-agreed formula, the members will find that the allocation of production among themselves must meet an inconsistent set of objectives: it must minimize the aggregate cost of producing the joint-profit-maximizing output, and it must also generate whatever division of profits is consistent with the bargaining power of the parties. Without profit pooling, the feasible locus of efficient profit outcomes will contain many points that fall short of maximum joint profit. Only with profit-pooling or side-payments can the

---

[2] See Telser (1972, pp. 142–45). Recent developments in game theory seem to identify devices capable of sustaining collusive outcomes in noncooperative games that may have some empirical counterparts. They include the use of randomized strategies and the presence of differing subjective priors. Unfortunately, it is beyond the scope of this paper to survey these developments.

parties attain the maximum joint profit and divide the spoils in a way consistent with their bargaining power.[3] Securing a cost-minimizing distribution of outputs that sum to the group's profit-maximizing joint output level poses its own problems for the optimizing cartel. If the participants have different cost curves, the efficient distribution of output requires that all active producing units operate at a common marginal cost and that the output level of the least efficient unit in operation be such that its average cost is at a minimum.[4] Cartel members might obtain this efficient allocation by creating rights to produce given quantities of the profit-maximizing joint output, issuing these to the charter members as part of the basic agreement, and allowing them to be traded among sellers. Fully efficient trade would produce the optimal allocation of output just described.[5] Many decision variables besides the division of output and profits may affect the attainment of maximum joint profits, when output is heterogeneous and the transaction offered to the buyer can vary in a number of dimensions besides price.

When we consider these requirements for agreement, it is evident that contractual costs and uncertainties are an important potential limit on the ability of sellers to reach accord. The heterogeneity of sellers' preferences and of their perceived opportunity sets contributes to these costs. Oligopoly theory in the Fellner–Chamberlin tradition deals with these influences as limitations on how closely the market bargain can approach full joint profit maximization, and the field of industrial organization contains a large literature on the structural conditions and sellers' strategies capable of sustaining a noncompetitive market bargain. However, these valuable insights into the structural conditions for a cartel agreement do not generally take the form of deterministic cartel models, and so I reluctantly put them aside. Consider instead two formal propositions about the terms of cartel agreements.

First, a cartel agreement can potentially be made enforceable without an elaborate mechanism to defuse what would otherwise be a strong temptation to cheat. Osborne (1976) and Spence (forthcoming) show that the adoption by duopolists of reaction functions that commit them to maintaining constant shares of the value of total sales can lead them to a point on the contract curve with respect to their profits. That is, an agreement on market shares has a certain superiority over other forms of agreement on the key market variables.[6] The cartel's charter members can make other choices of terms that ease the enforcement burden. One frequently observed empirically is to divide markets (classes of customers, geographic areas,

---

[3] Telser (1972, chap. 5, esp. pp. 192–94).
[4] Patinkin (1947); Telser (1972, chap. 5).
[5] See Stigler (1952, chap. 14).
[6] Of course, the problem remains of finding a mutually agreeable set of market shares. See Cross (1969, pp. 207–14).

etc.) among the various members. Enforcement costs are then reduced to those of assuring that no one sells to a forbidden customer. There has been some analysis of optimally imperfect terms of agreement for cartels that cannot achieve complete joint maximization. For instance, Comanor and Schankerman (1976) point out that, for industries selling on the basis of bids on individual transactions, identical bids are less costly to enforce than a scheme of rotated bids that requires explicit agreement on market shares, so that we expect (and find) schemes involving the rotation of bids typically to encompass smaller numbers of sellers.

Second, a cartel may have a positive value to its members even if it achieves no long-run departure from a competitive market outcome. Consider the simple story often told in the institutional literature on cartels operated between World Wars I and II: A cartel is formed without the accession of all actual or potential producers of the good in question. The price is raised. The outsiders find price comfortably in excess of their marginal costs and expand output. Newcomers observe the elevated price to exceed their minimum attainable average costs and enter the industry. The cartel members start to lose market share, and the cartel-managed price gives way. The usual account then concludes that the cartel failed, and a soporific moral is drawn about the ultimate triumph of pure competition. The trouble is that the cartel members did expropriate consumers' surplus and cause deadweight losses of welfare while the cartel was in operation. And it could be rational to enter a cartel expected to be temporary (whether due to entry by outsiders or the defection of nominal signatories), even if the profits of the cartel members in the competitive period after the cartel's collapse are expected to be less than the competitive profits they earned before its formation.

The maintenance of cartels

Conventional cartel theory becomes more loquacious on the maintenance of a cartel agreement—the incentive to cheat, the chances that cheating will be detected, and the mechanisms of enforcement against the cheater. As the preceding discussion has suggested, this focus is unsatisfying because the enforcement problem results from the incompleteness of the cartel agreement—itself unexplained theoretically. Therefore, models of cartel enforcement float in an undefined structural context, and they are specific to an arbitrary set of initial conditions. I shall stress this problem of structural context in surveying these models.

The fundamental problem of maintaining cartel arrangements is that in order to obtain monopoly profits they must elevate price above producing members' marginal costs. In the absence of a common sales agency or binding profit-sharing arrangement, each member can potentially increase his own profits in the short run by any maneuver that lets him sell an extra unit for net revenue less than the official cartel price though greater than marginal cost. The factors affecting the net revenue gain expected by the potential cheater can be classified into three groups. First, consider the behavior of short-run marginal costs as the cartel members collectively restrict output and elevate the market price. The more steeply sloped their marginal cost curves in the neighborhood of the precartel output are, the greater becomes the gap between price and marginal cost. A familiar generalization is that a high level of fixed costs as a percentage of total costs should be associated with a steeply sloped marginal-cost curve.[7] Strictly speaking, the observation that fixed costs make up a large proportion of total costs tells us only about the magnitude of *total* variable costs—the integral under the marginal-cost curve up to the precartel output. Nonetheless, there is a probabilistic relation between high fixed costs and a steeply sloped marginal-cost curve, in that the average slope of the marginal-cost curve over its whole range must be steeper.

Another factor affecting the temptation to cheat is the elasticity of the cheater's demand curve, i.e., the responsiveness of the quantity he sells to whatever terms he offers to buyers. That responsiveness depends first on whether his product is a perfect substitute for those supplied by other members of the cartel. If it is differentiated in any way, or if transportation or other transaction costs differ for each buyer, depending on the seller chosen, the elasticity of the demand curve faced by the cheater will be reduced. The elasticity also depends on the method used by the price-cutter to lure extra business—an across-the-board announced price cut or clandestine price reductions to selected buyers. Between these extremes lie price cuts offered to all inquiring buyers but not publically announced and disguised price cuts in the form of quality or service improvements; these disguised improvements in the terms of the transaction can also be offered either selectively or to all buyers. The potential cheater presumably selects the method of defecting from the cartel agreement that has the highest expected present value. This is not necessarily the one corresponding to the most elastic demand curve for the cheater, because the behavior of costs and the likelihood of detection and enforcement also affect the calculation. The average sizes and size distribution of buyers are prominent among the factors determining the response of the quantity that the price-cutter sells to the terms he offers. A seller offering secret price cuts will certainly favor large buyers, if the likelihood that his cheating will become known depends on the number of buyers to whom cuts are offered and not their size. Conversely, the large buyer's threat to take his business elsewhere is more effective in forcing a selective price cut under any circumstances

[7] See Scherer (1970, pp. 192–98).

wherein the seller incurs some fixed contact cost per customer in securing new business.[8]

The third influence on the incentive to cheat is the probability of detection and the costliness of the enforcement that follows. One component is the expected lag between the offering of a reduced price and its detection by cartel members. The model developed by Orr and MacAvoy (1965) assumes that price information is transmitted only with a lag, so that the seller cutting price enjoys some increased profits before discovery, although reduced profits afterward. They show that if enforcement takes the form of matching the cheater's price cut, the potential cheater can calculate the optimal price cut (if any) to offer; and if the lag before detection is long enough, the present value of the profits expected from cheating will exceed those of remaining loyal to the cartel's terms. Besides the lag, the price-cutter's expected return will also depend on the chances of detection (within a given time) and the form of the punishment he expects. These features of cartel behavior demand treatment on their own.

The detection of cheating

The existence of a stochastic lag before cartel members detect cheating and a probability that they will discover it within a given period of time are alternative ways of formulating the same thing. The potential cheater who considers ways of offering price cuts in some sense seeks the one most effective in reaching buyers relative to its speed in reaching cartel-member competitors. Detection depends on the forms in which information passes through the market. If all prices are openly quoted, the same price must presumably be offered to all buyers (unless the structural conditions for price discrimination are present) and will become known to all buyers and sellers at the same time. If price quotations are made to individual buyers, the situation becomes more complicated. A favored buyer has an incentive to conceal his boon from other buyers, because their propensity to demand equally favorable treatment is probably hostile to the preservation of his own favored status. On the other hand, he may have an incentive to tattle about a below-market offer to other sellers in hope of getting a better price still. The seller who expects favored buyers to report the bonanza to other sellers will tend to refrain from cheating; the seller who expects them to switch to his custom and keep quiet will cheat more freely.

[8] Costs of switching to different trading partners, whether incurred by buyer, seller, or both, affect market equilibria in numerous ways that cannot be explored here. For example, the existence of switching costs for the seller are sufficient to guarantee large buyers a lower price, even if there are no scale economies in the transaction itself. If the buyer has no incentive to enter into a long-term supply contract with a particular seller, he can never be deprived of a credible threat to switch suppliers, and thus the seller in each market period rationally offers a discount that depends on the size of these contact costs and the difference between the sizes of the large and the average buyers.

In the face of these diverse possibilities, one model that has attracted much attention is Stigler's (1964) "A Theory of Oligopoly," which is really a theory of the detection of cheating under rather specific conditions. Stigler assumes that each seller recognizes his regular customers and can perceive whether or not he is losing an abnormally large percentage of them in a given time period. Stigler's sellers do not, however, know the prices that other sellers are charging, although these price offers are disseminated by any given seller both to the established customers of other sellers and to buyers new to the market. The Stiglerian seller may hear indirectly about price cutting, with a probability that increases with the number of buyers contacted—hence cheating grows more likely, the fewer buyers per seller. Cartel members' main defense against cheating, however, is to stand guard with probability tables in hand, inferring cheating from any movements of customers in the market that are sufficiently improbable if all sellers are maintaining the agreed price. These movements include the following: the loyal seller can lose too many old customers; the price-cutter can be observed to retain too large a fraction of his own old customers; or the price-cutter can be found attracting too many of the customers new to the market. The latter two tests of violation generally require that the loyal sellers pool their information, and there is always some gain to the loyalists from pooling. It emerges from this model that cheating is more likely to occur the more numerous the sellers, the fewer customers are present per seller, and the more random shifting of buyers among suppliers normally taken place (i.e., shifts not motivated by price cuts). The likelihood of cheating is reduced where large loyal firms are present, because the gains to equal-size firms from pooling information about customer movements are equivalent to the advantages in statistical confidence enjoyed by the large-firm observer of the market.

The process of enforcement

The process of detecting cheating in cartels holds no importance unless there is some mechanism to punish cheaters. And, as Yamey (1973) pointed out, even with a mechanism identified, we still require an explanation why it is in the interest of some cartel members to apply the indicated punishment.

In formal duopoly models it is usually assumed that the punishment for cheating on the cartel consensus is a reversion to the Cournot solution, either permanently or for some predetermined number of time periods. If there are lags in detecting a member's price cut, even a threat of permanent reversion to the Cournot solution will not deter cheating in all cases. To end the cartel, however, is an analytically uninteresting form of punishment, and there are other possibilities to consider:

1. The optimal price response of loyal cartel members is not necessarily to revert to the Cournot solution. In the model of Orr and MacAvoy (1965), where information lags permit price differentials between sellers to persist, matching the cutter's price is neither a sufficient deterrent nor optimal for the cartel. Rather, a reaction-function equilibrium can emerge between the price-cutter and the cartel members, and Orr and MacAvoy show that it is stable under certain conditions. This adaptive behavior between price-cutter and cartel members is reminiscent of a pattern observed empirically in industries with an oligopolistic core or dominant firm but also a fringe of price-taking small firms. The fringe cannot be kept from undercutting the core group's price by some amount. However, some constraints restrict the rate at which fringe firms can expand their joint market share; usually unspecified, these constraints might result either from information lags or adjustment costs in adding capacity for the fringe. The core holds to its collusive price (or perhaps chooses an optimal differential over the fringe) and loses market shares over time.[9] Finally, Salant (1976) develops the properties of an optimal reaction by a natural-resource cartel to the existence of noncooperative fringe producers. The essence of monopolistic exploitation of a natural resource is to charge a higher price initially than would competitive exploiters, but to raise it less rapidly over time and to make the resource last longer. Where a competitive fringe takes the cartel's behavior as parametric, Salant shows that the cartel maximizes its present value by producing nothing, or very little, until the competitive extractor's resources are exhausted, then producing on a schedule that maximizes the present value of the cartel's resource stock. An analysis somewhat similar to Salant's is provided by Hnyilicza and Pindyck (1976), who assume different discount rates for the fringe and core of the resource-extracting producers and thereby provide the basis for a Pareto-optimal extraction schedule that maximizes a weighted average of the welfare functions for the two groups.

2. A punishment more onerous than a return to a noncooperative equilibrium is a threat to ruin a price-cutter, and a formal analysis of games of survival can be employed to identify possible patterns.[10] Telser (1966) develops this analysis in the context of the capital structures of business firms. The firm in an uncertain environment, facing a rising marginal supply price of funds, must keep a portion of its capital in liquid assets for unforeseen contingencies. These liquid funds defend the value of the firm's fixed capital (to be exact, its value in use over its salvage value) by permitting it to operate for a period with its variable but not its fixed costs covered. If this firm is caught cutting prices, the cartel's enforcer may be able to put

---

[9] See Worcester (1957); Stigler (1968, chap. 9).
[10] See Shubik (1959, chap. 10).

prices lower still and force fatal losses on the price-cutter. The cost of predation to the potential monopolistic survivor is at least the liquid assets of the potential victim plus the present value of the profits lost by the enforcer during the period of price warfare. The feasibility of such enforcement is greater, the shorter the victim's liquid reserves and credit lines, and the higher the victim's minimum average variable costs relative to the long-run average costs of the enforcer. If the enforcer's fully allocated costs are actually less than the victim's variable costs, the victim's enterprise in any case has no economic value. Certain structural conditions in the market increase the feasibility of price warfare for eliminating a price-cutter. For instance, the price-cutter may operate in a more limited market segment that the enforcer; or the enforcer may be able to identify the price-cutter's "regular" customers and direct his retaliatory price cuts only at them. These conditions make predation a more feasible enforcement strategy, but they do not necessarily make it optimal; the factors determining the minimum cost of the attack to the enforcer are still the victim's liquid reserves plus foregone profits on some quantity of sales.

3. An enforcement strategy potentially preferable to predatory attacks on a price cutter is to buy him out, or to offer a bribe to induce him to leave the market. There is room for such a deal, as an alternative to a predatory attack, because the price-cutter is better off taking a price (or bribe) slightly greater than his liquid reserves, whereas the potential monopolist is better off paying anything up to these same liquid reserves plus the present value of the monopoly profits he expects to lose during a predatory attack. Telser (1966) shows, however, that the lower limit to the merger price or bribe just stated may be too small. This is because the cost to the potential monopolist of extending an actual price war for another time period always exceeds the cost to the price-cutter (because the former equals the latter plus the present value of the monopolist's foregone profits). Therefore, the price-cutter, as a blockade to monopoly profits, is a valuable market asset, and the price-cutter should be able to secure outside funds to enable him to hold out for at least the value of his total capital, not just the value of his liquid funds. The proposition remains that it is generally more profitable for a cartel to dispose of a single price-cutter through a bribe than through predatory action. However, a vital qualification is that the effects of the two strategies on the profits expected by potential entrants are quite opposite. The supply of potential entrants must be limited for the bribe strategy to be superior.

Although cartel theory identifies these possible enforcement strategies, it is reticent about what structural conditions might mark one seller a price-cutter, another an enforcer of a joint-maximization agreement. Among the few clear factors is relative size. The larger the firm's share of sales under the joint-maximization agreement, the smaller are its potential gains from diverting additional sales by price cutting (because there is less to divert), and the larger are its losses from foregoing monopoly profits.[11] Another discriminant sometimes listed is the relative efficiency of firms; the reasoning holds that for two otherwise identical cartel members, the one with the lower marginal cost curve will experience the greater gap between market price and marginal cost and thus the greater temptation to snatch at extra sales. The trouble with this inference is that the assumed difference in marginal costs at the outputs stipulated in the cartel arrangement indicates that the cartel members are not minimizing their total costs of production, and it also implies that they would not have identical preferences for the common cartel price. The cartel agreement thus is incomplete, to begin with. A few other factors might discriminate between price-cutters and loyalists. Short time horizons or high discount rates dispose participants toward price-cutting; the price-cutter trades short-run profits against long-run sacrifices, whereas the trade for the enforcer is of foregone short-run profits against the preservation of long-run monopoly returns.

In conclusion, these mechanisms for detecting and punishing cheaters are specific to the terms of the cartel agreement within which the behavior takes place. The mechanisms may be interesting if cartel agreements in fact do contain incomplete provisions for policing their terms. However, the reasons why the terms should be incomplete are left unexplained. If punishment A is an insufficient deterrent to cheating, why does the cartel not employ heavier punishment B? The loyalists can afford the punishment costs, because the seller who cheats on an optimal cartel destroys more surplus for the loyalists than he annexes for himself.

Strategic responses to cartels

What of the buyers in a cartelized market? Traditional cartel theory offers them little but the option to bribe the cartel to sell at marginal cost. The possibility of a mutually beneficial arrangement rests on the familiar conclusion that the gain to the cartel (its monopoly profits) is less than the loss to the buyers (monopoly profits plus deadweight loss), except in the case of perfect price discrimination. Recently Nichols and Zeckhauser (1977) have revived Abba Lerner's (1944) proposal of government counterspeculation as an antidote to monopoly. Lerner pointed out that public authority could hold a stock of a monopoly's output, offering to sell unlimited quantities at long-run marginal cost, and thereby force the monopolist to accept marginal-cost pricing. Nichols and Zeckhauser deal with the problem that the government must first acquire a stock of the cartel's output before this strategy can be employed. Working with simulations based on two-period and multiperiod models, they analyze a strategy that basically reduces to the following. With the full knowledge of the cartel, the consuming-country government (or governments) purchases on

[11] This analysis assumes that the cartel members do not pool profits, so that individual members' profits are related to their sales.

the market in the first period and sells its holdings in the second period. This strategy can be mutually beneficial, despite the existence of storage and holding costs for the consumer-nation government, because the cartel gets its profits moved forward in time (from the second period to the first) and the consuming nation averts enough deadweight loss in the second period to offset the holding and storage costs and any increase in the cartel's profit-maximizing price that occurs during the first period. (It is not even necessarily optimal for the cartel to raise the first-period price when it knows stockpiling is taking place.) If several importing countries independently undertake counterspeculation, it will be underprovided, because part of the gain from A's stockpile sales is in surplus for B's consumers.

Because the cartel nations must benefit from the occurrence of stockpiling,[12] the cartel is actually worse off when stockpiling is underprovided and will lower its initial period price somewhat as a partial offset to this underprovision. To that extent, the "weakness" of divided (noncollusive) consuming nations becomes a virtue.

Cartels in the international economy

The preceding analysis has mainly dealt with firms as actors and proceeded in a microeconomic context. However, translating the conclusions to the circumstances of countries cartelizing their exports is generally a straightforward process. The process of monopolizing barter trade for a single country is familiar from the theory of optimal tariffs, and joint monopolization by several countries is merely a matter of calculating the optimal export tax from the joint foreign reciprocal demand curve. The analysis of countries combining to exploit joint monopoly power is closely related to customs-union theory, in which the welfare-maximizing country seeking a customs-union partner is simply a general-equilibrium discriminating monopolist looking for the submarket with the elastic demand curve, and the rest of the world becomes the loser from price discrimination.[13]

A good deal of current writing on international primary-product cartels implicitly employs the analysis of cartel agreements developed above. Without attempting a full survey, some points of contact can be noted.

1. The structural requisites for reaching initial agreement have been discussed in terms reminiscent of Fellner's (1949) analysis of oligopolistic bargains. Because the objectives of national governments are multiple and vaguely defined, a shared set of values (e.g., a common religion) may be more helpful than purely economic facilitating factors, such as a small number of participants. Sharing profits—or even defining them exactly—is

---

[12] They cannot be excluded from benefits because the cartel can always frustrate the stockpiling strategy by charging the no-stockpiling monopoly price each period.
[13] The relation between customs-union theory and price discriminating monopoly is developed by Caves (1974a).

not an easy matter when governments are traders, so the quest for cartels is constrained to agreements in which profits can be acceptably shared as the outcome of the division of output. Potential participants seem conscious that cartel efforts are unproductive where the demand curve and/or the supply of potential entrant producers is elastic.[14]

2. Because of the incompleteness of observed and practicable cartels, policing and enforcement become major problems. When the agreement is simply to raise price, total demand declines, while individual participants are motivated to expand their outputs; the cartel is visible only if dominant members possess extra-economic threat capabilities or are willing themselves to make the necessary output cutbacks. The latter course has apparently been followed by the largest oil-exporting countries. The international aluminum industry employs a consortium arrangement to buy up the otherwise unsold supplies of fringe producers.[15]

3. Another important implication of incomplete agreements is that the distribution of output cannot be rationalized and marginal costs equalized among the producers. This incompleteness either prevents agreement on a joint-maximizing price at the start, or brings about divisive disputes when the price is subsequently adjusted. Producers whose output has been expanded to its long-run equilibrium level, or the extraction of whose stock resource is far advanced, experience a high perceived marginal cost and therefore prefer high prices, even if all sellers are in agreement about the elasticity of demand. One systematic (and rational) divergence does occur, however, in estimates of the demand elasticity facing individual producers. For selling countries in which buyers have already invested in fixed plant to extract the resource, the relevant demand elasticity for price increases is reduced by the sunk character of this plant. For producer countries whose deposits are not yet developed, the operative elasticity of derived demand reflects the buyer's ability to vary the combination (and location) of complementary inputs.[16]

4. International governmental cartels were often formed between World Wars I and II at times when market price had dropped to a very low level, due to declining demand or the intrusion of substitutes. Although this source of cartelization efforts is often attributed to a psychological propensity to "do something" when and only when the existing situation has become unsatisfactory, a more economic rationale can be found in cartel theory. At such times the proportional gap (and probably the absolute

---

[14] See Rowe (1965, part IV), Bergsten (1974), Krasner (1974), and Mikdashi (1974).

[15] See Litvak and Maule (1975), on aluminum, and Blair (1967), on quinine.

[16] See Greene (1977), on the International Bauxite Association. Greene also shows that the presence of concentrated buyers complicates the formation of a sellers' cartel, because a series of arm's-length prices and price differentials between buyers' locations does not exist. The cartel must grope with limited information not only for a price level but also for a price structure.

gap) between Cournot profits and joint-maximum profits increases. It becomes rational for the potential cartel member to incur higher policing costs, higher risks of retaliation, or whatever costs might probabilistically be incurred in pursuit of elevated profits.

5. The debate over importing-country policies toward the Organization of Petroleum Exporting Countries touches upon the policing of cartel arrangements and the detection of cheating. Adelman (1972) has argued that the OPEC countries' use of a "tax" as a nonnegotiable base for pricing oil and the intermediary roles of the international oil companies have reduced the opportunity for the importing countries to exert their bargaining power as large buyers. There is ground for dispute, however, whether that bargaining power is better exercised by conversion of the crude-oil market into one of bilateral monopoly or by a number of large but independent buyers who can exploit the intrinsic difficulties of policing the cartel.[17]

6. Hexner (1945, chap. 4) demonstrates how the risks of failure in a cartel create distrust that further reduces the completeness of the cartel agreement that can be achieved. For instance, optimal allocation of output to a changing group of customers generally requires a collective mechanism to assign customers to suppliers. However, individual suppliers are apt to prefer keeping their old customers in order to build loyalty against the day of the cartel's collapse.

II. POLICY TOWARD COMMERCIAL MONOPOLY

In the balance of this chapter I consider the policy-making country not as a participant in an international cartel or an adversary of other nations forming cartels, but rather as a welfare maximizer dealing with commercial monopoly in national product markets. Market monopoly may pose three issues for the national policy-maker: (1) it may affect the nation's gains from trade and its efficient participation in international trade; (2) trade policy provides an instrument of competition policy by limiting or extinguishing monopoly in national markets; (3) patterns of collusion in noncompetitive markets may affect the short-run dynamics of the economy's response to changes in the international economy.

Monopoly and the gains from trade

A small country participating in international trade by definition faces an externally determined world price ratio. If one of its domestic industries is monopolized, it therefore follows that exposure to trade will eliminate the monopolist's perceived distinction between price and marginal revenue and force him to act as a pure competitor on the world market. This effect, which amplifies the conventional gains from trade, will be

[17] Compare Adelman (1972) and Roberts (1974).

considered in the next section. What must be recognized first, however, is that the standard propositions about gains from trade acquire some important qualifications if monopoly extends beyond a single industry in a small country. Melvin and Warne (1973) analyze the conventional two-by-two general-equilibrium model in which one or both of the two sectors is monopolized in each country. (It turns out not to matter whether monopolistic control affects both industries in each of the two countries, or only one industry—the same one—in each.) Their model employs explicit utility functions which assure that at any relative price ratio demand elasticities for a given good are the same in both countries.[18]

In this model, one trading country must wind up worse off than with purely competitive free trade, and both can wind up worse off. More alarmingly, one country can experience a lower level of welfare with trade carried on by monopolies than it would with monopolized production and no trade at all. The potential loser can be identified—the country having a comparative advantage in the good with the higher elasticity of demand at equilibrium world prices. If only one sector (the same one) is monopolized in each country, the nation with a comparative advantage in the competitively produced good may suffer from the introduction of trade. These conclusions from a two-by-two model do not translate easily into policy conclusions for an n-sector trading nation, but they provide a suitable cautionary note about the effect of monopolies that persist in the presence of international trade.

Some significant findings about monopoly and the gains from trade have been developed in a partial-equilibrium context. Corden (1967) considered the problem of a decreasing-cost industry—a natural monopoly—facing import competition. When should such an industry be established, given that the country can instead acquire its product through international trade? Corden shows that there is a critical import price that makes its establishment just socially desirable; that price lies below the one that would allow the monopoly to cover its average costs and above the one that would prevail in an equilibrium with price equal to its marginal costs. When the world price lies below the monopoly's average-cost price, however, the gain from establishing the natural monopoly is contingent on a lump-sum transfer arrangement that permits (forces) it to price at marginal cost. Corden demonstrates that a tariff can play no useful role in this situation. Raising the landed price of imports by less than the amount needed to establish the industry merely costs consumers' surplus. Raising it to or above the price that permits the monopoly to cover its costs permits it to price at or above average cost and impose a welfare loss.

[18] In this model the introduction of trade does not change the degree of monopoly; the two national producers of any given good behave as if they were jointly monopolizing the world market, with their market shares determined by the general-equilibrium adjustment of trade to tastes and factor endowments.

Corden assumed that his decreasing-cost firm was somehow probihited from expanding to minimum-cost scale and charging forth into export markets. Basevi (1970) and Pursell and Snape (1973) point out that an export market affects the decision to establish a decreasing-cost industry, even if the net world price received by the exporter is below his minimum attainable long-run average cost with all scale economies exhausted. Their case is essentially that of the decreasing-cost producer who can cover his costs only through price discrimination. Domestic demand by itself is not substantial enough to permit the industry to cover its costs at any level of output. And the world-market price, as mentioned, lies below the minimum attainable average cost. Nonetheless, if the activity is carried on by a discriminating monopolist, output may be sufficiently expansible through foreign sales that a higher price in the domestic market will yield enough profits to cover total costs. Thus, there can be cases in which welfare is increased by permitting a decreasing-cost monopolist to discriminate between home and foreign markets, as the price of bringing him into existence. As in Corden's case, a tariff is no help for reaching the optimum, and indeed an import subsidy may be desirable to curb excess monopoly price in the domestic market. Frenkel (1971) points out that discrimination against the domestic market is not always necessary; the cost reduction attainable through selling on price-elastic export markets may make a natural monopoly viable, charging a single price at home and abroad. White (1974) indicates some consequences of monopolized production of exportables for the volume of goods exported. The discriminating monopolist who sells at a competitive world price will supply more exports than would a competitive industry experiencing the same costs, because he elevates the domestic price, reducing demand at home and freeing more goods for the world market. If the monopolist of exportable goods cannot price-discriminate, however, the quantity he exports will be at most equal to what a competitive industry would supply, and he may opt for exporting nothing at all.[19]

In this section we have taken as a given either a monopolized market or decreasing costs as a structural basis for natural monopoly. Empirical research in industrial organization treats markets not as dichotomously monopolistic or competitive, but as capable of showing degrees of "market power," i.e., departing by varying amounts from conditions of pure competition. There is, in fact, a feedback loop running from the structural conditions that create market power to the pattern of a country's foreign trade, because certain fundamental characteristics of technology and demand underlie both comparative advantage and market power. The specific

[19] White also points out that a risk-neutral import-competing monopolist will produce less than a risk-neutral competitive industry facing the same distribution of expected import supply prices.

relation between trade patterns and market structure must, of course, vary from country to country because not all countries can export the same thing, and so the evidence will not be summarized here.[20] Instead we turn to international trade as a limit on market power.

International trade and competition policy

Eliminating a market distortion due to monopoly is an extra dividend that may be associated with the gains from trade. Put the other way around is the old American saying, "the tariff is mother of the Trusts." The two-sector general equilibrium model provides some simple comparative-statics findings about the effect of opening an economy to competitive trade when one industry is initially monopolized. If the monopolized sector is the export industry at externally given world prices, that sector's output will definitely expand, but the pretrade domestic price could either rise or fall. If the monopolized sector turns out to be import-competing, the domestic price will definitely fall, but the pretrade output could either expand or contract. In any of these cases, the world's gains from trade are greater than if the economy had been initially competitive.[21] In each instance, unrestricted international trade is a sufficient remedy for monopolistic distortions of domestic markets, in the sense that the marginal conditions for a competitive welfare optimum will hold after the introduction of trade. Feenstra (1977) points out, however, that international trade is not a complete remedy to monopolistic distortions in this general-equilibrium case, if the monopolist also exercises his monopsony power in national factor markets.[22]

The last few years have brought a burst of statistical research on the effect of international trade on monopoly or—more generally—the extent of market power exercised by oligopolistic industries. These studies examine rates of profit on equity capital or price-cost margins as indicators of the fruits of exercised monopoly power. These dependent variables are related by means of multivariate regression analysis to assorted measures of trade exposure for a sample of manufacturing industries. There is a problem of how to evaluate the extent of import competition facing an industry—

[20] Relevant studies are Pagoulatos and Sorenson (1976b), Caves and Khalilzadeh-Shirazi (1977), and Caves et al. (1977).

[21] See Caves (1974c); also Melvin and Warne (1973).

[22] Feenstra (1977) demonstrates that monopsony in the two-by-two general equilibrium case could be exercised in two ways. The conventional monopsonist recognizes his influence on individual factor markets, depressing the relative price of the factor used intensively in the monopolized industry and forcing the economy onto an inferior transformation curve. The "multiplant monopolist" buys factors of production competitively (say, because branch plant managers fail to recognize their collective influence on the price of each individual factor); however, the monopolist recognizes (as numerous pure competitors in the same industry would not) that expansion of his output along a convex transformation surface drives up his marginal cost. The multiplant monopolist's decisions leave the economy on its competitive transformation curve, though not at the optimal output, either with or without free trade.

specifically, how to proxy the position and elasticity of the excess-supply curve of competing goods importable into the national market. Reliable econometric estimates of import-supply elasticities are not found in droves. Most researchers have settled for using the share that imports comprise of domestic production or domestic disappearance as a proxy for the missing parameters. The proxy could obviously be faulty; e.g., the import-supply curve might be perfectly elastic, and yet domestic supply might fall just slightly short of domestic demand at the world price, making the import share very small. Still, given that the "industries" identified in published statistics and used in these statistical analyses only roughly approximate homogeneous markets, the import-share proxy is probably not a bad indicator of what proportion of the finely defined goods marketed by a group of sellers actually face close competition from foreign suppliers.

In any case, this variable has been found to have a statistically significant negative influence on measures of monopolistic distortion in several studies. Effects of import competition for U.S. manufacturing industries were reported by Esposito and Esposito (1971) and Pagoulatos and Sorenson (1976a). Both studies cover relatively large samples of manufacturing industries and secure statistical results that seem robust to minor changes in statistical specifications.[23]

With such strong results found for the large and relatively closed U.S. economy, one would expect even clearer findings for the smaller industrial nations. The pattern has been a bit murky, however. Khalilzadeh-Shirazi (1974) undertook a similar analysis of U.K. manufacturing industries and secured a regression coefficient for the import-share variable that was correctly signed, but only marginally significant. Hart and Morgan (1977) found no significant relation in their analysis of U.K. data for 1968. A very likely explanation for their negative result is the 1967 devaluation of the pound sterling, which raised the landed price of competing imports and should have given import-competing industries a temporary windfall. Pagoulatos and Sorenson (1976c) studied the determinants of price-cost margins for France, Italy, Germany, the Netherlands, and Belgium–Luxembourg in 1965, reporting a significant negative influence of import competition for all but Italy. Adams's (1976) coefficient for a transnational sample of large companies is negative, but not always significant. For Canada, Schwartzman (1959) employed a different research design that involved comparing the performance of more concentrated Canadian manufacturing industries to their less concentrated U.S. counterparts. He recognized that higher concentration in Canada should lead to higher price-cost margins only when the Canadian industry's trade exposure is

[23] The Espositos report separate regressions for consumer and producer-good industries. When a correction has been made for heteroscedasticity, the import variable appears significant for the consumer goods but not the producer goods.

attenuated. However, the concentration-profit relation that he found for the trade-sheltered industries became even more significant when the import-competing industries were added to the sample. Jones, Laudadio, and Percy (1973) chose to represent import competition by dummy variables designating high (imports over 30 percent of domestic shipments) and medium (imports between 15 and 30 percent) import competition with Canadian manufacturing industries. Their medium-imports dummy proved insignificant, their high-imports dummy *positive* and significant.[24]

Two modifications of these analyses may help to explain their incomplete support for the hypothesis that import competition limits the exploitation of monopoly positions. Most important of these is Bloch's (1974) development of the proposition that import competition should affect industries' profitability only if their seller concentration is indeed high enough that excess profits would be taken in the absence of foreign rivals. Bloch's own statistical work, discussed below, deals with the effect of tariffs rather than import competition. In research in progress on Canadian industrial organization,[25] we find that monopoly profits are significantly related to a variable that is a measure of seller concentration divided by imports as a percentage of domestic-industry shipments. There is not a significant relation to either concentration or the import share when they are included separately in a regression equation. Because the import share is a small fraction with a skewed distribution, the interaction variable tends to "turn on" concentration as an influence on profits only when import competition is low.[26] Another modification recognizes the weakness of the import-share variable as a proxy for the parameters of the excess-supply curve of imports. Turner (1976, chap. 4) utilized the 1967 devaluation of sterling, which provided a substantial disturbance to the import competition faced by U.K. manufacturing industries, as an opportunity to improve this specification. Given that the devaluation should have elevated world prices relative to U.K. domestic prices and costs by about the same proportion in all industries, variations among industries in the change in imports' share of the market in the years immediately following devaluation years should be correlated with the elasticity of the unobserved excess-supply function.

---

[24] For this they offer an unsatisfactory explanation that might apply to a short-run time-series analysis, but not to a cross-sectional analysis in which (one normally assumes) the entities are observed only randomly displaced from their long-run equilibria.

[25] This study, undertaken jointly with M. E. Porter, M. Spence, and J. T. Scott, draws upon a data base constructed with the support of the Royal Commission on Corporate Concentration. Caves et al. (1977) provides a preliminary report on this project that does not include the result mentioned in the text.

[26] Pagoulatos and Sorenson (1976c) also employ an interaction between concentration and import share, but they inappropriately formulate it as a product rather than as a quotient. Naturally, it is not significant.

Turner seeks to explain variations in price-cost margins in 1973 both by imports as a percentage of domestic disappearance in 1973 and by the recent change in a somewhat similar variable, the proportional change in import share. He finds that the change in imports has much more explanatory power.[27] Pagoulatos and Sorenson (1976a) employ a somewhat similar variable, the proportional change in the level of imports 1963–67 as an alternative to the 1973 share of imports for explaining price-cost margins in 1967; the rate of import growth is marginally significant, but appears to have considerably less explanatory power than the level of the import share.

Some evidence from surveys and case studies supports and extends these statistical findings about imports and monopoly in the United States. Sichel (1975) queried large manufacturing firms in the United States as to the identity of their three principal competitors—foreign or domestic. At least one foreign company was listed among the principal rivals of 23 percent of his respondents, although only 5 percent listed a foreign firm as the leading rival. When the respondents were classified to their principal industries, at least one response in 42 of 69 industries designated a foreign company among the chief competitors. Frederiksen (1975) studied several highly concentrated U.S. industries that had experienced increased foreign competition since World War II, finding that foreign rivals had increased price competition in two industries selling undifferentiated products, but that foreign rivalry had been less effective in two differentiated-product industries for which a significant proportion of imports are "captive" purchases by the leading companies in the U.S. industry.

The evidence on import competition, taken together, suggests that imports are a substantial limit on monopolistic distortions. A principal implication of this finding is that tariffs facilitate the collusive behavior of domestic sellers in concentrated industries and can thereby cause welfare losses in such markets that are greater than the familiar deadweight losses expected when a purely competitive industry receives protection. The proposition that tariffs increase the incidence of monopolistic distortion has been tested directly in some statistical studies. Pagoulatos and Sorenson (1976a) report a significant and correctly signed regression coefficient for a variable indicating the proportion of competing imports that are subject to nontariff barriers, but nominal tariff rates are not significant. For Canada, McFetridge (1973) found no influence of effective rates of protection on price-cost margins. Bloch (1974) likewise found that the gross profits of heavily protected Canadian industries, relative to the gross profits of their U.S. counterparts, were no higher than for industries with low tariffs. He did find, however, that selling prices of the heavily protected industries

---

[27] It makes no important difference whether the change is calculated for 1968–73, 1970–73, or 1971–73.

were higher, suggesting that the effect of tariff protection may be on efficiency rather than profitability.[28] We return to this question below. This analysis provides a strong case against tariffs because they can amplify the scope for monopolistic distortion. But the policy implications go beyond a preference for free trade over tariffs. Vicas and Deutsch (1964) point out that the government could force even a monopoly not facing import competition to price at marginal cost by offering a subsidy to imports equal to the difference between the higher world price and the monopolist's marginal cost at the output that equates his marginal cost to price. If his average costs are covered, the monopolist would produce the "competitive" output, and no imports would actually enter.

The theory of the effect of trade exposure on monopoly indicates that the consequences for a small country's domestic monopoly should be the same whether the industry emerges as competing with imports or making net exports. Either way, it faces a parametric price on the world market. In a sample of actual industries, however, two factors could upset the implied prediction of a negative relation between the proportion of an industry's output exported and its rate of profit. For a concentrated and collusive industry, dumping may be possible, so that the presence of international trade is associated with discriminating monopoly. This would imply (if anything) a positive relation between exporting and profitability. Second, under some microeconomic assumptions efficiency rents could accrue to exporting firms, even if they lack shared monopoly power. For instance, if the industry's product is differentiated, the presence of foreign markets should shift the demand curve facing the average seller outward and lift the profit rate above the normal rate of return implied by the Chamberlinean tangency solution. Hence we have no determinate empirical prediction about the effect of export-market participation on profitability.

Actual statistical results have turned out correspondingly diverse. For the United States, Pagoulatos and Sorenson (1976a) report no consistent relation (even as to sign) between profit rates and exports as a percentage of the industry's value of shipments. In their study of five European countries, Pagoulatos and Sorenson (1976c) get negative signs for all five countries, but the coefficients are significant only for France and Italy. Consistent with this, Jenny and Weber (1976) secure a significant negative relation for France, and the result is robust when several alternative measures of profit are empolyed as the dependent variable. Adams's (1976)

---

[28] There are reasons, having to do with sample properties, why the theoretically certain effect of tariffs on an industry's potential market power fails to show up in cross-section studies. As Bloch's (1974) analysis suggests, protecting an industry results in excess profits only if free entry of domestic sellers does not compete away the resulting rents. Nonetheless, governments may choose to ignore this fact and award high tariffs to many sectors that are purely competitive or employ large quantities of low-wage labor. Some of the highest tariffs therefore may generate no monopoly profits.

transnational sample gives an insignificant negative result. The outlier is the United Kingdom, for which Khalilzadeh-Shirazi (1974) found a significant positive relation between exports and price-cost margins. Additional exploration of this result by Caves and Khalilzadeh-Shirazi (1977) suggests the following interpretation: (1) for the United Kingdom, like other countries,[29] there is a strong relation between export participation and the sizes of companies and manufacturing establishments; (2) because U.K. exports run heavily to differentiated goods, efficiency rents associated with larger scale might be captured by the companies rather than dissipated through competitive entry; (3) the positive statistical relation between exports and profits, rationalized in this way, is weaker in the more concentrated industries, consistent with export-market participation having some dampening effect on the exercise of monopoly power. Taken together, the evidence on the exports and profitability of manufacturing industries suggests that extensive participation in foreign markets is (*ceteris paribus*) hostile to effective achievement of monopoly power in the domestic economy, and that it may also bring dividends in the achievement of more efficient scales of production.

A brief account is needed of the relation of the multinational company to monopoly and international trade.[30] Foreign direct investment tends to occur in industries where the average firm is large and sellers are concentrated. Although there are ways in which high concentration can promote foreign investment, and the presence of multinationl companies can increase the degree of monopoly, probably the most important fact is that concentration and foreign investment share a number of common fundamental causes. We can develop, however, some more positive propositions about the behavior of the multinational company that are relevant to international economic policy. It is seldom recognized that the multinational company is a favored entrant to industries with high barriers to entry. Monopoly is a long-run problem only where entry barriers deter the elimination of monopoly profits through entry, and analysis of the differing incidence of multinational companies from industry to industry establishes that the firm-specific assets that induce them to invest abroad tend to be what is needed for scaling the principal sources of barriers to entry (ample supplies of funds, established ability to differentiate their products, and perhaps other forms of technical and marketing skill). Thus the multinational company is a likely potential entrant into national industries that might otherwise be cloistered by even higher entry barriers.[31] When a foreign auto company begins assembly in the U.S. market, or a steel company develops

---

[29] Sue, for example, Scherer et al. (1975, p. 396).

[30] Brief because I have dealt with the subject at length elsewhere; see Caves (1974*b*) and Caves (1974*c*, pp. 17–28).

[31] Gorecki (1976*a*) demonstrates that multinational companies are not halted by the same entry barriers that affect other companies.

an iron ore deposit in a difficult piece of terrain, it may be providing an additional market participant that could come from few other sources. Besides its ability to enter a market, there is also some possibility that the multinational may be an entrant particularly disruptive of an oligopolistic consensus, especially in the early period of its presence. Its alien status may make it initially less sensitive to signals about an oligopolistic consensus emanating from established native firms. And its superior access to information about alternative returns to resources placed elsewhere in the world may make it less risk-averse than firms dependent on a single market.

The analysis so far supports a general policy of openness to market entry by multinational companies. The case is not completely clear-cut, however, for some considerations run the opposite direction. If the multinational company is good at scaling existing industrial barriers to the entry of new firms, it is also good at building up such barriers. The resources required to contrive such barriers (maintaining excess capacity, integrating forward to control distributive outlets, advertising heavily, accelerating the frequency of "model changes," etc.) are often found in the portfolios of multinational companies. It is also true that the multinational possesses the "long purse" that might drive out single-market rivals (see preceding section).[32] Of course, the most direct approach of public policy to such offensive forms of market behavior is to regulate or prohibit the behavior directly rather than blocking the very presence of international ownership links. Conduct designed to reduce the competitiveness of an industry is socially undesirable whatever sort of firm undertakes it.

One policy instrument that appears to have strong leverage on the activity of multinational companies is the tariff, in the case of companies whose foreign subsidiaries normally produce the same line of goods as the parent. A tariff elevates a company's cost of landing its goods within a national market relative to the cost of producing them there through a subsidiary, and hence tends to increase the flow of foreign investment. Many historical accounts affirm this effect of increased tariff rates. The statistical evidence, except for Horst (1972), is less consistent, but a cross-section statistical analysis is ill-suited for testing the hypothesis.[33] If we nonetheless accept the hypothesis, it has interesting implications about monopoly in national markets. Multinational-company entrants are likely to be a significant competitive force in industries that are protected from import competition by tariffs. The same holds for industries subject to

[32] Statistical research on the profitability of U.S. manufacturing industries suggests that profit rates are higher, the larger is the extent of foreign investment by member firms in the industry, after we control for the extent of monopoly or market power. This profit increment could represent the return to intangible assets garnered by working them in foreign markets, or it could measure the effect of additional monopolistic distortion due to international entry-barrier building or similar practices.

[33] Because some industries lack the structural requisites for direct investment to occur, and so no tariff is high enough to induce significant foreign investment.

product differentiation of the Chamberlinean stripe, in which multinational companies flourish on the basis of their success in establishing intangible good-will assets. Conversely, international trade is a more effective curb on monopoly where tariffs are low and where products are homogeneous, so that elaborate marketing organizations are not necessary to sell substantial quantities in a foreign market.

In considering international trade as a restraint on monopoly, economic analysis habitually concentrates on costs of allocative inefficiency—the deadweight loss due to monopoly. However, where competition is imperfect, trade—and trade restrictions—can have important effects on the degree to which costs are minimized. It is a commonplace that the welfare gains from policy changes that reduce unit costs can easily exceed those due to the recapture of deadweight-loss triangles. I shall concentrate on the relation between trade and cost minimization through attaining efficient scales of production.[34]

Trade changes the effective size of the market in which the firm sells. The connections can be illustrated by the firm in the position of the Chamberlinean monopolistic competitor, facing its individual, downward-sloping demand curve though not necessarily taking part in oligopoly. The total size of the market affects the typical firm's scale of production by changing the slope or position of the demand curve that it faces. Access to export markets shifts the curve outward and may also render it more elastic, if the firm's output faces closer substitutes in the international market than in the domestic market. Both changes tend to move the monopolistic competitor's profit-maximizing scale toward that which minimizes long-run average cost. The presence of competing imports has an ambiguous effect, shifting the import-competing seller's demand curve to the left, but also making it flatter, with an indeterminate effect on its profit-maximizing scale of production.[35]

This analysis can also be applied to the organization of Chamberlinean industries marked by either of the following conditions: (1) each "variety" of the product is subject to the same production function, but buyers' preferences are distributed unevenly among the varieties (some are popular, some are not); (2) each of n varieties is preferred by $1/n$ buyers when all varieties sell at the same price, but production functions differ so that some varieties are subject to greater scale economies than others (i.e., must

[34] This is only one channel through which competition and technical efficiency may be interrelated. Others are the outright inefficiency of the enterprise that employs more inputs than necessary to produce a given output and—a special case of this—chronic excess capacity.

[35] In referring to a Chamberlinean industry, I am assuming that entry by new firms propels existing ones *toward* the tangency solution but not invariably *to* it. Oligopoly (mutual dependence recognized) is assumed absent, but the average firm can still command a rent. Enlargement of market size can enlarge the rents of those firms not pressed to the tangency solution.

attain larger volumes to achieve minimum average cost). With free trade, the international distribution of production will be influenced from the cost side by the classic forces of comparative advantage. Given those forces, however, production in the small national market will tend to be confined to popular varieties and those subject to minimal scale economies (in the sense just defined). Large countries will tend to specialize in the unpopular varieties and those subject to extensive scale economies.[36] The effect of tariff protection for any national market—though especially a small one— is to make viable the production of less popular varieties demanded domestically in smaller quantities. Also, domestic production may become viable for varieties subject to more extensive economies of scale. Taking these effects together, it is possible that surrounding a small national market with tariff protection actually reduces the average size of enterprises. And it necessarily follows that tariffs imposed by any country tend to reduce the average scale of production for the world industry as a whole.[37]

A good deal of statistical evidence has accumulated that provides at least indirect support for these propositions about trade, scale, and efficiency. Scherer et al. (1975, pp. 117–20), analyzing the branches of twelve manufacturing industries located in six industrial countries, found that the extent to which plants attain minimum efficient scale in manufacturing industries depends sensitively on the proportion of total shipments that is exported. Eastman and Stykolt (1976, chap. 3) and Gorecki (1976b, chap. 5) report similar results for Canadian manufacturing industries. Owen (1976) found an association for pairs of European countries between the relative sizes of manufacturing plants and the balance of trade. Relatively larger plants (though not larger firms) are associated with larger net exports, although Owen's analysis does not clearly identify the direction of causation between the variables. Other studies have noted a simple correlation between the proportion of output exported and the average sizes of plants and firms,[38] and Pryor (1973, chaps. 5, 6) finds for a large sample of countries that the average sizes of both plants and companies (measured in various ways) are associated with the share of output exported after controlling for the size of the national market. On the import side, we saw that the effect of trade (and its impediment by tariffs) on efficient scale is ambiguous. Scherer's six-country study correspondingly finds that the extent to which an industry's plants achieve efficient scale is negatively but in-

---

[36] The analysis assumes that transportation and transactions costs are greater between than within national economies.

[37] This relation between trade policy and efficient scale depends on the individual firm facing a downward-sloping demand curve, and economists enchanted with the siren song of pure competition may suppose that this is an uncommon market condition. Therefore, I must stress the abundance of evidence supporting the principal corollary of the preceding analysis, namely, that the sizes of plants and firms will be related to the size of the national market in which they are embedded; for example, Pryor (1973, chaps. 5, 6).

[38] Caves and Khalilzadeh-Shirazi (1977); Caves et al. (1977, chap. 7).

significantly related to the extent of import competition. For Canada, however, several studies lean toward the conclusion that tariffs reduce the average plant scale of production or the degree to which efficient scale is attained.[39] Broadly speaking, the evidence confirms that trade restrictions reduce the average scale of production in an industry worldwide, but they may increase it within the markets of some tariff-imposing countries.

Monopoly and short-run adjustments

A final consequence of monopoly in open economies is that it may change the path of short-run adjustment to disturbances from what would prevail in the presence of pure competition. The difference arises not from the behavior of the theoretical pure monopolist but rather mainly from the pricing practices employed in oligopolies with incomplete collusive arrangements. Such industries' prices may be relatively sticky in the short run, because each change in list prices incurs the risk of a breakdown in the oligopolistic consensus. Such pricing behavior can affect both the imports and exports of the country in question.

If an industry's comparative advantage is deteriorating, or if the nation's money price and cost structure is getting too high relative to its fixed exchange rate, the short-run inflexibility of a domestic price can have the effect of inflating the volume of imports. This consequence has been documented for U.S. steel imports by Krause (1962), who found the prices of domestically produced steel products insensitive to changes in import prices and market shares. Rowley (1971, pp. 220–21) describes a period in which the U.K. steel industry showed similar behavior.

Other possibilities pertain to the concentrated exporting industry. Suppose that prices in the domestic market are maintained at a sticky collusive level, while the producers also sell as pure competitors on the world market. First of all, this behavior inflates the average volume of exports above what a competitive industry would sell abroad, as White (1974) pointed out. It can also influence the variability of exports. If the domestic price is inflexible in the face of shifts in the demand curve for the product, the induced fluctuations in the volume of exports will have a greater amplitude than if the domestic price adjusted competitively. Such competitive adjustments in the domestic price would reduce the variability of the quantity sold in the domestic market by a sticky-price oligopoly. Given the position of the sellers' marginal-cost curves, larger fluctuations in the volume of exports are implied by greater fluctuations in the oligopoly's domestic sales.

The presence of product differentiation also affects the adjustment of trade flows. Differentiated goods by definition lack perfect substitutes in

[39] Gorecki (1976b, chap. 5) reports an insignificant negative influence of tariffs. Eastman and Stykolt (1967) and English (1964) stressed the tendency of the tariff to hold an umbrella over firms that were inefficient for whatever reason, and the proclivity of multinational companies to locate inefficiently small-scale production facilities behind a tariff wall.

foreign markets. What adjustments are made to their export prices following a devaluation therefore can depend on pricing practices and market conditions in the domestic market. Turner (1976, chap. 3) found that after the 1967 devaluation U.K. producers of differentiated goods raised their domestic-currency prices of exports significantly less than producers of homogeneous goods.[40] The lower increase by itself does not prove a noncompetitive response, of course, but it does establish a potential influence for collusive practices in the domestic market.

The normative significance of monopoly for short-run adjustments in international trade is not clear and probably varies from one situation to the next. The point is simply that paths of adjustment can be different where elements of monopoly are present.

National and international policy toward monopoly

An "optimum tariff" serves the interest of the single country imposing it, but it imposes a net cost on the rest of the trading world. A similar problem of national versus international welfare arises in the making of national policy toward competition in an open economy. Consider first an industry that is monopolized and sells all of its output abroad. Suppose that some application of antitrust policy by the nation's government can potentially force the industry to sell competitively at a price equal to marginal cost. If, for simplicity, we assume that marginal cost is constant, application of the policy will have two effects. It relieves foreign consumers of a deadweight loss, and it transfers the monopoly profits formerly earned by the monopoly to the consumers' surplus of foreign buyers. The nation enforcing competition is necessarily a net loser, although the world as a whole is better off. If the monopoly has been selling some of its output at home (without import competition) and some abroad, the same antitrust policy now eliminates some deadweight loss at home. Given elasticities of demand in the home and foreign markets, one could evidently identify a share of output exported just small enough that the country would become a net gainer by enforcing competition for its exportable-goods monopolist.[41] The optimal national policy would, of course, be to establish competition in the industry, while applying an optimal export tax.[42] Without that

---

[40] Also see Hague, Oakeshott, and Strain (1974).

[41] This critical export share could be larger if the country attaches some utility to the redistribution of income from domestic profit recipients to domestic final buyers.

[42] That governments are not indifferent to the joys of monopoly profits taken from foreigners hardly needs to be argued in the days of OPEC. Less familiar, however, is the common practice of permitting domestic companies to collude on export sales, even when such behavior is illegal in the domestic market. In the United States the Webb–Pomerene Act is the vehicle for the exercise of joint monopoly in international trade. Part of the Act's rationale was to assist small companies to meet the heavy transaction costs of exporting through joint associations—a sensible policy by itself. However, Larson (1970) has shown that the Act has primarily benefitted already concentrated industries, and that the Webb–Pomerene associations have assisted in monopolizing the domestic as well as foreign markets.

option, however, the government must choose between the potential national gains from cartel participation outlined in the first part of this chapter and the advantages of domestic-market competition attainable partly through appropriate international economic policies.

This problem can be analyzed formally in terms of optimal competition policy for the exporting industry, on the assumption that policy instruments can secure any outcome from pure competition to pure monopoly, but must accept the same degree of monopoly in both domestic and export markets (Auquier and Caves, 1978). The larger the export market relative to the domestic market, the less competition should be enforced to maximize national welfare. The optimal degree of competition is greater, the more elastic is domestic demand and the less elastic is demand in the export market.[43] These partial-equilibrium conclusions can be transplanted to a general-equilibrium setting, using the model of Melvin and Warne (1973). For instance, if the same degree of competition characterizes a given industry in each country (the degrees may differ between industries, though), a nation can lose by entering into international trade either because its exportable good faces an elastic demand (Melvin–Warne's conclusion) or because a high level of competition in its export industry allows that industry to claim little of its potential monopoly profit. If the home country's industries are monopolized, while those abroad are competitive, the home country can lose from entering into international trade.

The general clash between national and international interests considered in this formal analysis has many simple implications for competition policy. A familiar form of international cartel agreement is for sellers in countries A and B to divide up world markets, with C's market assigned to A, and D's market assigned to B. Countries A and B may well be net beneficiaries of the cartel. C and D could potentially bribe them to terminate it, but handing over voluntary tribute to a foreign exploiter is not a policy proposal that commonly wins elections. The divergence of national interests bears not just on policy toward outright monopolies and collusive arrangements but also toward potentially monopolistic practices engaged in by multinational companies. It was pointed out above that the practices generating good-will assets that permit companies profitably to invest abroad also can create or augment contrived barriers to entry into their industry—whether in the multinational's home market or in the market where its subsidiary operates. Once again, prohibiting the practices might not be in the interest of the home-country government.[44]

A different problem of divergent national interests can arise when a multinational company in country A acquires or merges with a national firm in a country B engaged in producing the same line of goods. Suppose

[43] A related analysis demonstrates the use of an optimal export tax or subsidy on the assumption that competition policy is inoperable and the degree of monopoly must be taken as given.

[44] Other examples are discussed in Caves (1975).

that A's producer has not previously been exporting to country B, and that each country's competition authorities regulate mergers only on the basis of the effect on seller concentration in the national market. Concentration conventionally measured is unaffected by the merger in either of the national economies, yet there has been an increase for the two markets taken together. If concentration should be high enough in the international market, this merger could impose real costs on the trading world as a whole. Even if the producer in A has previously been exporting to B, the same misperception could occur if B's competition authorities follow the common practice of watching concentration ratios calculated only over domestic production and not over all sellers present in the domestic market.

Actual antitrust policy in the United States has been fairly sensitive to such spillovers from anticompetitive actions—even in cases where the United States is the beneficiary from monopoly rents. United States companies have been stopped from acquiring foreign companies that are their actual or potential competitors in the U.S. market (and elsewhere). United States and British companies in one instance were prosecuted for agreeing jointly to monopolize the Canadian market.[45] The internationalized competition policy of the European Economic Community has dealt with a number of cases that probably had divergent effects on the national economic welfare of Common Market members (see de Jong, 1975). Despite these favorable patterns, divergent national and international interests in competition create a general problem similar to the problem of tariff reduction addressed by the General Agreement on Tariffs and Trade. A possible (though not necessary) interpretation of that agreement is that countries agree to multinational tariff reduction on the conjecture that the losses they incur from reducing their own tariffs below "optimal" levels will be more than offset by their gains in consumers' surplus (including reduced deadweight losses) from foreign countries' reductions of monopolistic tariffs. One can imagine a similar declaration of faith in the averaging out of gross losses that could occur if all countries agreed that each would apply its competition-policy instruments to whatever monopolistic structures or practices lay within its reach, wherever the resulting social benefits might be felt.

The provisions of competition policy dealing specifically with international trade pose a somewhat different set of issues. All industrial countries allow their domestic sellers greater freedom to collude in the export market than at home, and most of them restrict monopolization of their export trades little or not at all.[46] This policy represents a consistent pursuit of national welfare maximization, in the sense that the prices charged abroad

[45] For details see Brewster (1958).
[46] See Organization for Economic Cooperation and Development (1974) and Gribbin (1976). Jacquemin (1974) suggests that the EEC takes a symmetrically tough line against foreign firms with market power in member-country markets.

by monopolistic exporters could in principle be identical to the "optimum tax" on exports. The only qualm about this policy for a government maximizing its own national welfare lies in the possibility that collusion among exporters may unavoidably spill over and increase distortions in the domestic market. In that case, the country faces the same tradeoff identified above between capturing consumers' surplus abroad and suffering deadweight losses at home. There has been little or no public recognition of the divergence between national and global welfare resulting from these policies, and the policies open to the individual country to combat foreign monopolization of its imports are limited (see the first section of this chapter).

The familiar applications of competition policy to imports are generally concerned not with getting them more cheaply but with restricting the sale of imported goods whose prices are affected by dumping or export subsidies. There is generally little or no foundation for such policies in the maximization of national welfare. The restriction of dumping from a nationalistic point of view makes sense only in the special case of short-run predatory dumping.[47] From an international viewpoint the case is more complicated, because dumping as a form of monopolistic price discrimination is efficient only if total costs can be covered in that way and no other. The case of an export subsidy is somewhat different, assuming that the exporting industry itself is competitive and the subsidy creates rather than removes a market distortion. The importing country maximizes its national welfare by doing nothing and accepting the improvement in its terms of trade. From an international viewpoint, however, all importing countries should impose a counter-vailing duty to offset the distortion induced by the subsidy, and this duty should not be contingent on the occurrence of injury to import-competing domestic producers.

III. CONCLUSIONS

This chapter has surveyed policy toward monopoly in the open economy. The national government may find itself dealing with two classes of issues. First, the nation may possess monopoly power over its export goods, if it colludes successfully with other producing nations. The literature of cartel theory, which concentrates on the conditions for sustainable collusion, supplies a number of useful predictions about the circumstances that render such alliances stable and supply countries with a self-interest in joining them. Some helpful hints are also available for nations whose terms of trade have been worsened by cartels; a version of counterspeculation may retrieve a portion of their losses.

Countries may also find themselves using international economic policy

[47] See Barcelo (1972).

to deal with imperfections in their national markets for goods and services. Where natural monopoly exists due to extensive scale economies, tariffs are no help; however, dumping may sometimes be desirable, and the analysis indicates conditions under which it is desirable to offer lump-sum subsidy to an import-competing monopolist. The power of unrestricted international trade to eliminate market distortions due to monopoly has recently been subject to extensive empirical testing. The general conclusion is that import competition (definitely) and export opportunities (probably) reduce the ability of concentrated industries to exercise their joint monopoly power. Conversely, tariffs augment or preserve this power and may also induce organizational patterns in industries that are inconsistent with cost minimization. The multinational company offers the advantage of being a well-equipped entrant into national product markets surrounded by high entry barriers, but it may also contribute in some ways to long-run anticompetitive conditions.

These two strands of national policy-making can be brought together around the situation of a national authority contemplating its policy toward a monopolized export industry. If the industry sells only in foreign markets, the national (though not global) welfare is served by allowing it to extract the rents available to it. On the other hand, if it sells partly in the domestic market, there is an offsetting deadweight loss to domestic consumers that might be greater than the profits corresponding to surplus captured from foreign buyers. The best nationalistic policy is to make the industry competitive, but levy an optimal tax on exports. If this cannot be done (e.g., because the monopoly power is holistic, due to patents or trademarks, and cannot be preserved one place but not another), a choice must be made by weighing the foreign loss against the domestic gain from enforcing competition. National competition policies implicitly recognize this dilemma by permitting collusion more freely in foreign than domestic markets. United States antitrust policy shows some tendency to recognize international competition and treat it in order to maximize global rather than national welfare.

REFERENCES

Adams, W. J. 1976. "International Differences in Corporate Profitability." *Economica* 43: 367–79.
Adelman, M. A. 1972. *The World Petroleum Market*. Baltimore: The Johns Hopkins University Press for Resources for the Future.
Auquier, A., and Caves, R. E. 1978. "Monopolistic Export Industries and Optimal Competition Policy." Harvard Institute of Economic Research, Discussion Paper No. 607.
Barcelo, J. J. 1970. "Antidumping Laws as Barriers to Trade—the United States and the International Antidumping Code." *Cornell Law Review* 57: 491–560.

Basevi, G. 1970. "Domestic Demand and Ability to Export." *Journal of Political Economy* 78: 330–37.

Bergsten, C. F. 1974. "The Threat Is Real." *Foreign Policy*, no. 14, pp. 84–90.

Blair, J. M. 1967. "Statement," in U.S. Senate, Committee on the Judiciary, Subcommittee on Antitrust and Monopoly, *Prices of Quinine and Quinidine*, Part 2, Hearings pursuant to S. Res. 26, 90th Cong., 1st sess., pp. 180–223. Washington, D.C.: Government Printing Office.

Bloch, H. 1974. "Prices, Costs, and Profits in Canadian Manufacturing: The Influence of Tariffs and Concentration." *Canadian Journal of Economics* 7: 594–610.

Brewster, K. 1958. *Antitrust and American Business Abroad.* New York: McGraw–Hill.

Caves, R. E. 1974a. "The Economics of Reciprocity: Theory and Evidence on Bilateral Trading Arrangements." In *International Trade and Finance: Essays in Honour of Jan Tinbergen*, edited by W. Sellekaerts, pp. 17–54. London: Macmillan & Co.

——. 1974b. "Industrial Organization." In *The Multinational Enterprise and Economic Analysis*, edited by J. H. Dunning, pp. 115–46. London: George Allen & Unwin.

——. 1974c. *International Trade, International Investment, and Imperfect Markets*, Special Papers in International Economics, no. 10. Princeton, N.J.: International Finance Section, Princeton University.

——. 1975. "International Enterprise and National Competition Policy: An Economic Analysis." In *International Conference on International Economy and Competition Policy*, edited by M. Ariga, pp. 183–90. Tokyo.

Caves, R. E., and Khalilzadeh-Shirazi, J. 1977. "International Trade and Industrial Organization: Some Statistical Evidence." In *Welfare Aspects of Industrial Markets: Scale Economies, Competition and Policies of Control*, edited by A. P. Jacquemin and H. W. de Jong, pp. 111–27. Leiden: Martinus Nijhoff.

Caves, R. E., et al. 1977. *Studies in Canadian Industrial Organization.* Ottawa: Information Canada.

Comanor, W. S., and Schankerman, M. A. 1976. "Identical Bids and Cartel Behavior." *Bell Journal of Economics* 7: 281–86.

Corden, W. M. 1967. "Monopoly, Tariffs and Subsidies." *Economica* 34: 50–58.

Cross, J. G. 1969. *The Economics of Bargaining.* New York: Basic Books.

de Jong, H. W. 1975. "EEC Competition Policy towards Restrictive Practices." In *Competition Policy in the UK and EEC*, edited by K. D. George and C. Joll, chap. 2. Cambridge: Cambridge University Press.

Eastman, H. C., and Stykolt, S. 1967. *The Tariff and Competition in Canada.* Toronto: Macmillan & Co.

English, H. E. 1964. *Industrial Structure in Canada's International Competitive Position.* Montreal: Canadian Trade Committee.

Esposito, L., and Esposito, F. F. 1971. "Foreign Competition and Domestic Industry Profitability." *Review of Economics and Statistics* 53: 343–53.

Feenstra, R. C. 1977. "Trade, Competition, and Efficiency: A General Equilibrium Analysis." Senior honors thesis, University of British Columbia.

Fellner, W. 1949. *Competition Among the Few.* New York: Knopf.

Frederiksen, P. G. 1975. "Prospects of Competition from Abroad in Major Manufacturing Oligopolies." *Antitrust Bulletin* 20: 339–76.

Frenkel, J. A. 1971. "On Domestic Demand and Ability to Export." *Journal of Political Economy* 79: 668–72.

Gorecki, P. K. 1976a. "The Determinants of Entry by Domestic and Foreign Enterprises in Canadian Manufacturing Industries: Some Comments and Empirical Results." *Review of Economics and Statistics* 58: 485–88.

———. 1976b. *Economies of Scale and Efficient Plant Size in Canadian Manufacturing Industries*, Research Monograph No. 1, Bureau of Competition Policy. Ottawa: Department of Consumer and Corporate Affairs.

Greene, R. S. 1977. "Cartel Action and Forward Integration by the Bauxite Producing Nations." Senior honors thesis, Harvard College.

Gribbin, J. D. 1976. "Review of OECD, *Export Cartels.*" *Antitrust Bulletin* 21: 341–50.

Hague, D. C., Oakeshott, A., and Strain, A. 1974. *Devaluation and Pricing Decisions*. London: Allen & Unwin.

Hart, P., and Morgan, E. 1977. "Market Structure and Economic Performance in the United Kingdom." *Journal of Industrial Economics* 25: 177–93.

Hexner, E. 1945. *International Cartels*. Chapel Hill, N.C.: University of North Carolina Press.

Hnyilicza, E., and Pindyck, R. S. 1976. "Pricing Policies for a Two-Part Exhaustible Resource Cartel: The Case of OPEC." *European Economic Review* 8: 139–54.

Horst, T. 1972. "The Industrial Composition of U.S. Exports and Subsidiary Sales in the Canadian Market." *American Economic Review* 62: 37–45.

Hu, S. C. 1975. "Uncertainty, Domestic Demand, and Exports." *Canadian Journal of Economics* 8, 258–68.

Jacquemin, A. P. 1974. "Application to Foreign Firms of European Rules on Competition." *Antitrust Bulletin* 19: 157–79.

Jenny, F., and Weber, A. P. 1976. "Profit Rates and Structural Variables in French Manufacturing Industries." *European Economic Review* 7: 187–206.

Jones, J. C. H., Laudadio, L., and Percy, M. 1973. "Market Structure and Profitability in Canadian Manufacturing Industry: Some Cross-Section Results." *Canadian Journal of Economics* 6: 356–68.

Khalilzadeh-Shirazi, J. 1974. "Market Structure and Price-Cost Margins in United Kingdom Manufacturing Industries." *Review of Economics and Statistics* 56: 67–76.

Knickerbocker, F. T. 1973. *Oligopolistic Reaction and Multinational Enterprise*. Boston: Division of Research, Harvard Business School.

Krasner, S. D. 1974. "Oil Is the Exception." *Foreign Policy*, no. 14, pp. 68–83.

Krause, L. B. 1962. "Import Discipline: the Case of the United States Steel Industry," *Journal of Industrial Economics* 11: 33–47.

Larson, D. A. 1970. "An Economic Analysis of the Webb–Pomerene Act." *Journal of Law and Economics* 13: 461–500.

Lerner, A. P. 1944. *The Economics of Control*. New York: Macmillan & Co.

Litvak, L. A., and Maule, C. J. 1975. "Cartel Strategies in the International Aluminum Industry." *Antitrust Bulletin* 20: 641–63.

McFetridge, D. G. 1973. "Market Structure and Price-Cost Margins: An

Analysis of the Canadian Manufacturing Sector." *Canadian Journal of Economics* 6: 344–55.

Melvin, J. R., and Warne, R. D. 1973. "Monopoly and the Theory of International Trade." *Journal of International Economics* 3: 117–34.

Mikdashi, Z. 1974. "Collusion Could Work." *Foreign Policy*, no. 14, pp. 57–67.

Nichols, A. L., and Zeckhauser, R. J. 1977. "Stockpiling Strategies and Cartel Prices." *Bell Journal of Economics* 8: 66–96.

Organization for Economic Cooperation and Development. 1974. *Export Cartels—Report of the Committee of Experts on Restrictive Business Practices.* Paris: OECD.

Orr, D., and MacAvoy, P. W. 1965. "Price Strategies to Promote Cartel Stability." *Economica* 32: 186–97.

Osborne, D. K. 1976. "Cartel Problems." *American Economic Review* 66: 835–44.

Owen, N. 1976. "Scale Economies in the EEC: An Approach Based on Intra-EEC Trade." *European Economic Review* 7: 143–63.

Pagoulatos, E., and Sorenson, R. 1976a. "International Trade, International Investment and Industrial Profitability of U.S. Manufacturing." *Southern Economic Journal* 42: 425–34.

———. 1976b. "Domestic Market Structure and International Trade: An Empirical Analysis." *Quarterly Review of Economics and Business* 16: 45–60.

———. 1976c. "Foreign Trade, Concentration and Profitability in Open Economies." *European Economic Review* 8: 255–67.

Patinkin, D. 1947. "Multi-Plant Firms, Cartels, and Imperfect Competition." *Quarterly Journal of Economics* 61: 173–205.

Pryor, F. L. 1973. *Property and Industrial Organization in Communist and Capitalist Nations.* Bloomington, Ind.: Indiana University Press.

Pursell, G., and Snape, R. H. 1973. "Economies of Scale, Price Discrimination and Exporting." *Journal of International Economics* 3: 85–91.

Roberts, M. J. 1974. "Review of Adelman, *The World Petroleum Market.*" *Journal of Economic Literature* 12: 1363–68.

Rowe, J. W. F. 1965. *Primary Commodities in International Trade.* Cambridge and London: Cambridge University Press.

Rowley, C. K. 1971. *Steel and Public Policy.* London: McGraw–Hill.

Salant, S. W. 1976. "Exhaustible Resources and Industrial Structure: A Nash–Cournot Approach to the World Oil Market." *Journal of Political Economy* 84: 1079–93.

Schelling, T. C. 1960. *The Strategy of Conflict.* Cambridge, Mass.: Harvard University Press.

Scherer, F. M. 1970. *Industrial Market Structure and Economic Performance.* Chicago: Rand McNally.

Scherer, F. M., et al. 1975. *The Economics of Multi-Plant Operation: An International Comparisons Study.* Cambridge: Harvard University Press.

Schwartzman, D. 1959. "The Effect of Monopoly on Price." *Journal of Political Economy* 67: 352–67.

Shubik, M. 1959. *Strategy and Market Structure: Competition, Oligopoly, and the Theory of Games.* New York: John Wiley.

Sichel, W. 1975. "The Foreign Competition Omission in Census Concentration Ratios: An Empirical Evaluation." *Antitrust Bulletin* 20: 89–105.

Spence, M. (forthcoming). "Tacit Coordination and Imperfect Information." *Canadian Journal of Economics.*

Stigler, G. J. 1952. *The Theory of Price,* rev. ed. New York: Macmillan & Co.

————. 1964. "A Theory of Oligopoly." *Journal of Political Economy* 72: 44–61.

————. 1968. *The Organization of Industry.* Homewood, Ill.: Richard D. Irwin.

Telser, L. G. 1966. "Cutthroat Competition and the Long Purse." *Journal of Law and Economics* 9: 259–77.

————. 1972. *Competition, Collusion, and Game Theory.* Chicago: Aldine-Atherton.

Turner, P. P. 1976. "Some Effects of Devaluation: A Study Based on the U.K.'s Trade in Manufactured Goods." Ph.D. dissertation, Harvard University.

Vicas, A. G., and Deutsch, A. 1964. "The Paradox of Employment Creation through Import Subsidies." *Economic Journal* 74: 228–30.

White, L. J. 1974. "Industrial Organization and International Trade: Some Theoretical Considerations." *American Economic Review* 64: 1013–20.

Worcester, D. A., Jr. 1957. "Why 'Dominant Firms' Decline." *Journal of Political Economy* 65: 338–46.

Yamey, B. S. 1973. "Notes on Secret Price-Cutting in Oligopoly." In *Studies in Economics and Economic History: Essays in Honour of Professor H. M. Robertson,* edited by M. Kooy, pp. 280–300. London: Macmillan & Co.

Caves, "International Cartels and Monopolies in International Trade"

This paper was originally written against the background of the 1970s and with reference to the policy problem of international cartels as it then appeared. The question of primary-product cartels receded from the public attention in the 1980s after the Organization of Petroleum Exporting Countries seemed to lose its coherence and other, more tentative, efforts to form primary-product cartels came to naught. However, the reports of OPEC's demise may turn out to be exaggerated. While the history of international trade since World War II is dominated by the proliferation of sources of supply and thus with reduced chances for the successful organization of cartels, our record of successes in forecasting cartel formation (which often seems to depend on random events) is too poor to warrant complacency.

International cartels and monopolies in industrial goods reclaimed some
concern in the 1970s, partly because the success of multilateral
negotiations at lowering conventional tariffs led to renewed interest in
concerted efforts to address other distortions in international trade--
both nontariff barriers (direct and indirect) installed by governments and
those due to positions of market power obtained and held by private
decision-makers. Little or no headway was made at international cooperation
to secure more competitive product markets; as we shall see, nations instead
have slid back into the noncooperative pursuit of market power for national
advantage over their neighbors.

New Thinking About Cartels and Monopolies

The conditions for sustaining a collusive agreement, set forth in the
paper, still hold in essentially the same forms and support the same
substantive conclusions. Nonetheless, the technical sophistication of
theoretical research in this area has advanced considerably in the past
decade. In particular, the theory of multiperiod games has shed
considerable light on the conditions for sustaining cartel arrangements.
One clarification takes a rather negative form: Whereas the theory
of pure competition derives a single, determinate result for each market,
modern game theory stresses the possibility of multiple equilibria. For
example, a given group of international oligopolists might sustain a
moderate level of monopoly rents if they can agree on a moderately severe
punishment of defections from the cartel's arrangements, or higher
monopoly gains if they can agree on dire punishment for cheating.

Another relevant strand is concerned with conditions under which
cartels can be sustained in spite of periodic breakdowns. For example,
Green and Porter (1984) showed that a stable cartel arrangement could be
sustained if participants agree to revert from cooperative outputs to
enlarged, noncooperative outputs for a predetermined period of time when the
market price drops below a threshold level. Market demand is assumed
subject to random influences, so that price could drop below the trigger

value either because somebody cheated on the cartel or because there
occurred a random falloff of demand (which the cartel members by assumption
cannot observe directly). Thus, a cartel could persist, setting a monopoly
output part of the time, breaking down into "cutthroat competition" part of
the time, with the breakdowns sometimes due to cheating by participants,
sometimes due only to "bad" states of demand.

Another line of theoretical research has shown that a cartel can be
stable even if its membership is incomplete (d'Aspremont et al., 1983). The
larger is a firm's market share, the greater is its incentive (cet. par.) to
join and remain loyal to a cartel. Small-share participants, conversely,
have the most to gain from cheating or staying outside. A stable cartel can
persist with all the larger participants taking part and the smaller ones
staying out; the smallest member just barely benefits from staying loyal,
while the largest nonmember on balance benefits from not taking part in the
cartel's output-reducing function. This point is clearly relevant to some
attempted primary-product cartels, although it fails to address the question
of the entry of new producers once price is raised to a monopolized level.

Strategic Behavior in International Industries

A new line of theoretical research on international oligopolies emerged
and flourished in the past decade as an adjunct to concerns over "industrial
policy." Suppose that members of a concentrated world industry produce in a
few countries--at the limit, a duopoly consisting of home and foreign
sellers. The home government, seeking to maximize national welfare, takes a
negative view of output sold in the home market by the foreign duopolist--
because any excess profits flow into the foreign country's national income.
Symmetrically, it applauds sales made abroad at monopoly prices by the home
firm: the profits seized from foreign buyers flow into its national income.
It has long been understood that the home and foreign countries together (if
they make up the whole world) gain from forcing the duopoly to produce a
competitive output. Recent theoretical research, however, has reverted to
the nationalistic question how a country may benefit from intervening in

such a market solely for its national self-interest--and not to bring the
market closer to a competitive equilibrium.

Many theoretical possibilities have surfaced (Krugman, 1986, provided a
nontechnical survey). The government may act on its home duopolist in such
a way that the foreign duopolist reduces its output or raises its price,
thus transferring some of the duopoly rents to the home team. (Whether the
government should use a tax or a subsidy to achieve this outcome turns out,
dismayingly, to depend on hard-to-observe aspects of the way the duopolists
compete.) The government may simply stiffen the backbone of its domestic
duopolist by "sinking" costs on its behalf and providing it with a credible
commitment not to leave the market if pressed by the foreign rival;
subsidizing research and development outlays has been put forth as an
example. The government may use tariffs or quotas to curb sales in the home
market by the foreign seller. Such a strategy might keep monopoly rents
from landing in foreign pockets. Alternatively, the import restrictions
might aid the domestic seller to reduce its costs if they exhibit a
"learning curve" relationship to its cumulative output; then import
restriction serves to promote exports, and the hoary "infant industry"
argument for protection gains a high-tech justification.

While this literature provides an engaging set of theoretical models,
it is difficult to see it as a major practical addition to policy-making.
First, as mentioned, it flies in the face of the global interest of the
trading world in effectively competitive market that has been pursued--
admittedly with rebuffs and backsliding--through the General Agreement on
Tariffs and Trade. Second, the conditions for an unambiguous recommendation
for national policy are typically quite stringent. That is, to play this
game right, the government must know things that governments cannot readily
find out. One need not be an extreme pessimist to fear that these policy
models may be put into service mainly to warrant ad hoc policy interventions
that serve neither national nor global interests.

REFERENCES

d'Aspremont, D., et al., 1983. "On the Stability of Collusive Price Leadership," Canadian Journal of Economics 16:17-25.

Green, E. J., and R. H. Porter, 1984. "Noncooperative Collusion under Imperfect Information," Econometrica 52: 87-100.

Simple Theoretical Analysis of International Commodity Agreements

Jere Behrman

Simple economic theory provides useful guidelines for considering some important issues about which there is some confusion in much of the speculation about commodity market agreements. Therefore it is useful to discuss briefly the following four theoretical questions: What are the implications of price stabilization attempts for producers' revenues? Who benefits from stabilization? What are the normative implications of market solutions to economic problems? Under what conditions is it probable that collusive action by producers alone can raise market prices? Each of the first four sections in this chapter explores one of these questions. The last section gives conclusions.

3.1 IMPLICATIONS OF PRICE STABILIZATION ATTEMPTS FOR VARIABILITY AND LEVEL OF PRODUCERS' REVENUES

Advocates of international commodity agreements recognize that stabilization of export revenues probably is of much more interest to the developing countries than is stabilization of prices. In principle, of course, a buffer stock authority might buy and sell with the intent of stabilizing revenues.[1] Such an operation would be much more difficult than price stabilization,

---

1 It could attempt to act so that the total market demand curve facing producers approached a unit elastic curve with constant revenue implications. Elasticity is defined below as the percentage change in quantity in response to a given percentage change in price. For a unit elastic demand curve this value is unitary or one. Therefore as one moves along the demand curve every change of x percent in price causes a change of x percent in the opposite direction of the quantity demand, so revenue (the product of the two) remains constant.

Reprinted from "Development, the Internationl Economic Order, and Commodity Agreements," pp. 29–46, with permission of Addison-Wesley, Reading, Massachusetts, Copyright 1978.

352

however, for several reasons. Day-to-day operations would be harder because of the greater lags in the availability of quantity than price data. If such an arrangement were successful, strong inducements would exist for supply reductions because the same revenues could be earned with lower sales, which would release factors of production for other uses.[2] The concurrence of importing nations with a revenue-stabilizing scheme, finally, seems unlikely.

For such reasons, advocates of international commodity agreements argue for price stabilization instead of revenue stabilization. But this strategy raises the question: What are the implications of price stabilization attempts for revenues?

A preeminent international economist, Harry G. Johnson [1], states that "elementary economic analysis" suggests that international commodity agreements are dubious on these grounds. His argument is illustrated in Fig. 3.1. The basic average supply and demand curves for a purely competitive international commodity market are given by solid straight lines. The average supply curve (SS) gives the average quantity supplied for each possible price.[3] The average demand curve (DD) gives the average quantity demanded for each possible price. The assumption of pure competition implies that the total market supply is the sum of the quantities supplied at various prices by a large number of individual producers, each of whose production is so small that it cannot perceptibly change the market price by altering its quantity supplied. There is a parallel assumption on the demand side. The solid supply curve is an average curve in the sense that it is halfway between the two equally likely dashed-line actual supply curves, where the different locations reflect differences in some nonprice supply determinant (say, good and bad weather). A parallel situation holds for demand due to two different and equally likely values of some determinant of demand other than price (say, high and low income). P_0 is the average equilibrium price, at which level average quantity demanded just equals average quantity supplied (and both equal Q_0). P_0 also is the price at which the buffer stock is assumed to stabilize prices by purchasing the commodity if otherwise the price would fall, and selling it if otherwise the price would rise.

---

2 Such an outcome probably would not occur if there were a large number of relatively small producers each operating independently, but only if supply were organized in decision units of large enough size so that their individual impact on market prices was noticeable.

3 In Fig. 3.1a, for example, only the demand curve shifts so that the supply curve is traced out. When the demand curve is high the equilibrium price is P_2 and the quantity supplied is Q_2. When the demand curve is low the equilibrium price is P_1 and the quantity supplied is Q_1. The loci of quantities supplied at different prices (such as Q_2 at P_2 and Q_1 at P_1) is the supply curve.

Similar comments apply for the demand curve in Fig. 3.1b.

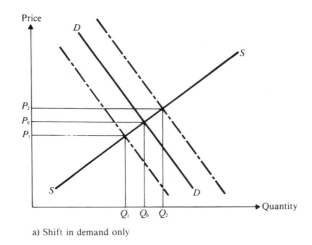

a) Shift in demand only

Fig. 3.1 Impact on revenues of shifts in demand and supply curves with and without price stabilization at P_0 by a buffer stock

Consider first the case of instability due to demand shifts alone (Fig. 3.1a). Without price stabilization, producers' revenues are P_2*Q_2 when the demand curve is shifted up and P_1*Q_1 when the demand curve is shifted down.[4] The average is $(P_1*Q_1 + P_2*Q_2)/2$. With a buffer stock stabilization scheme, the buffer stock sells $Q_2 - Q_0$ units when the demand curve shifts down in order to keep the price at P_0. Whether the demand curve is shifted up or down, producers receive P_0*Q_0 when the buffer stock operates, so this also is the value of their average revenues. Therefore price stabilization clearly implies producers' revenue stabilization in this case. But it also causes a reduction in the average value of producers' revenues since P_0*Q_0 is smaller than $(P_1*Q_1 + P_2*Q_2)/2$, as can be seen by comparing in Fig. 3.1a the size of two rectangles each of which is P_0*Q_0 with the sum of the areas in the rectangles that are P_1*Q_1 and P_2*Q_2. In the case of instability due to demands shifts alone, therefore, price stabilization causes producers' revenue stabilization, but at the cost of a reduction in those revenues.

Consider next the case of instability due to supply shifts alone. Here we must distinguish between various subcases that differ depending upon the supply and demand responsiveness to price changes. To summarize this price responsiveness it is useful to define the concept of elasticity. The price *elasticity of a curve* indicates by what percentage the quantity changes along a curve when the price changes by 1 percent. If the quantity changes by a

---

4 Here and below the standard notation of an ''*'' to mean multiplication is used. P_1*Q_1, for example, should be read as P_1 multiplied by Q_1.

larger percentage than does the price, the absolute value[5] of the price elasticity for that curve is greater than one and the curve is price elastic for that range of price changes (for example, the demand curve and the supply curve in Fig. 3.1b). If the quantity changes by a smaller percentage than does the price, the absolute value of the price elasticity for that curve is less than one and the curve is price inelastic for that range of price changes (for example, the demand curve and the supply curve in Fig. 3.1c). If the quantity does not change at all when the price changes, the price elasticity is zero and the curve is completely price inelastic (for example, the supply curve in Fig. 3.1c).

Now let us consider the case of instability due to supply shifts alone. Johnson considers the most normal subcase to be one with price-elastic supply and demand curves (Fig. 3.1b). Following reasoning parallel to the case of demand shifts alone, we can find the average producers' revenues by considering what they are for both equally likely positions of the supply curve. Without price stabilization, producers' average revenues are $(P_2*Q_2 + P_3*Q_3)/2$. With stabilization they are $P_0*(Q_1 + Q_4)/2$. In this subcase price stabilization increases producers' revenues, as can be seen by comparing the sizes of the relevant rectangles once again.

What about the stability of revenues under price stabilization when supply curves alone shift? In the subcase of price-elastic supply and demand curves, price stabilization increases the instability of revenues.

Of course one also can consider mixed cases in which both demand and supply curves shift. The net result depends on the size of the two shifts and the size of the price elasticities. The tradeoff between level and instability of revenues nevertheless seems to persist in a number of theoretical cases.

Therefore Johnson concludes that price stabilization generally leads to a tradeoff between revenue stabilization and the level of revenues and that advocates of international commodity agreements lump together two different economic problems (instability of demand and instability of supply) that require quite different solutions. He is quite critical of the UNCTAD proposal and of the analysis underlying it.

Is Johnson right? This depends on exactly what are the objectives and what is the empirical reality regarding the relative importance of shifts in supply and demand and regarding the shapes of these curves. We can identify several subcases in which Johnson, not the advocates of international commodity agreements, apparently is wrong:

1. Suppose that, while the developing economies desire higher revenues, *ceteris paribus,*[6] they are *very* risk averse in wanting very much to avoid

---

5 We refer to the absolute value because normally along a demand curve the quantity changes in the opposite direction from the price, while along a supply curve both change in the same direction.

6 *Ceteris paribus* means ''everything else being equal'' or ''everything else held constant.''

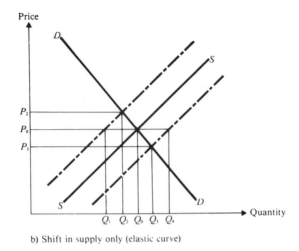

b) Shift in supply only (elastic curve)

Figure 3.1 [continued].

fluctuations in producers' revenues because of the perceived great disruptive effects of such fluctuations on their own economies. Then the proposal makes sense if either demand shifts dominate (Fig. 3.1a) or the curves are sufficiently inelastic (Fig. 3.1c).

2. Suppose that the objectives are weighted in the reverse order: While the developing countries would like revenue stabilization, they really care *much* more about increasing revenues. Then the proposal makes sense if shifts in supply curves are dominant (Figs. 3.1b-c). If the underlying curves are sufficiently price inelastic (Fig. 3.1c), moreover, producers' revenues may be increased at the same time fluctuations in those revenues are reduced.

3. Suppose that the assumptions of linear curves and/or parallel shifts are not valid. Then some of the conclusions of Johnson's "elementary economic analysis" may be changed. For example, consider the case in which the demand curve is very price inelastic above P_0 but very price elastic below this price and the completely price inelastic supply curve shifts (Fig. 3.2). Price stabilization may reduce revenues but increase their stability. This is the opposite outcome from what Johnson considers to be the normal result based on a shift in the supply curve with linear and price elastic curves (Fig. 3.1b).

4. Yet another possibility is that destabilizing speculation causes large price fluctuations that lower the long-run demand curve by inducing substitution of synthetics and other goods for the commodities of concern by risk-

---

7 Note that in the subcase of a supply shift and sufficiently price-inelastic curves, price stabilization leads to revenue stabilization and increased revenues (Fig. 3.1c).

averse manufacturers. Commodity producers, therefore, might rationally prefer price stabilization in order to limit the downward long-run shift in the market demand curve even if the short-term result may be lower immediate revenues or greater instability in revenues.

These possibilities all emphasize that in important respects the manner is an empirical question. Johnson's "elementary economic analysis" is not enough. Without empirical knowledge concerning preferences, long-run movements, the shapes of the curves, risk aversion, the elasticities, and the causes of shifts, whether they are additive or multiplicative, and so on, we cannot state with assurance what is the impact of price stabilization on producers' revenues.

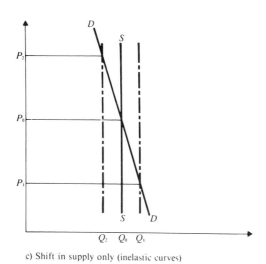

c) Shift in supply only (inelastic curves)

Figure 3.1 [continued].

At this point, it is useful to refer to some available empirical evidence: (1) For many of the relevant commodities, existing estimates indicate that short-run nonprice shifts in the supply curves tend to be larger than those in the demand curves, suggesting that Figs. 3.1b-c generally are more relevant than is Fig. 3.1a. (2) The estimated supply and demand price elasticities indicate for most of the relevant commodities quite low short-run price responsiveness. Therefore, the subcase of low price elasticities with price stabilization leading to larger revenues and less fluctuations in them (Fig. 3.1c) may be "normal," rather than the high price elasticities subcase with a tradeoff between the levels and instability of revenue (Fig. 3.1b) that Johnson emphasizes. (3) For foodgrains, Sarris, Abbott, and Taylor [2]

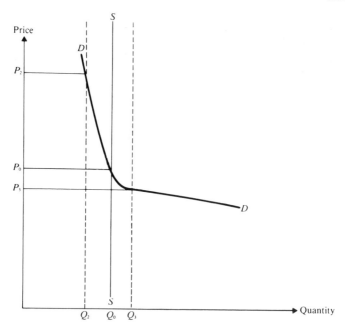

Fig. 3.2 Impact on producers' revenues of shift in inelastic supply curve with non-linear demand curve, with and without price stabilization at P_0 by a buffer stock

maintain that the nonlinear demand curve in Fig. 3.2 better represents reality than does the linear case.

And where does this empirical evidence lead us? For many of the UNCTAD core commodities it suggests that price stabilization may lead to revenue increases *and* greater revenue stability because of the dominance of supply shifts and low price elasticities. This may result in substantial benefits to the developing countries that, as a group, are net exporters of these commodities, independently of whether higher revenues or lower fluctuations in revenues are valued more highly. The possibility of forestalling long-run substitution for their exports by risk-averse users, also mentioned above, may increase the benefits of price stabilization to the developing countries.

For foodgrains, producers' revenues may be lowered, together with fluctuations therein, by price stabilization programs if Sarris, Abbott, and Taylor are right about the shape of the demand curve. However, Third World countries taken as a whole[8] still might benefit because they are net

---

8 A few developing countries (eg. Thailand, Burma, Argentina) are net exporters of foodgrains and thus, would not benefit under these assumptions.

importers of foodgrains. The lower level of producers' revenues in this case means lower consumer expenditures and import bills for them.

Thus, contrary to the assertions made by Johnson, simple economic theory in conjunction with this empirical evidence suggests that the developing countries as a whole well might benefit from effective price stabilization programs for many of the UNCTAD core commodities and for foodgrains. This is but a tentative conclusion, however, because we have not yet incorporated the dynamic adjustments of the interaction between supply and demand into our analysis. We return to such questions in Chapter 5, where we simulate the impact of price stabilization programs with models that incorporate empirical estimates of the relevant elasticities and of the dynamic adjustment paths.

3.2 WHO GAINS FROM PRICE STABILIZATION?

This question is related to the subject of the previous section, but the impact on consumers also needs to be incorporated. We explore it here under simplifying assumptions that ignore risk aversion, the question of distributional effects among consumers or among producers, storage and transaction costs for the buffer stock, and general-equilibrium aspects outside of the market of interest. We measure the benefits (losses) to producers by the additional (lessened) revenues they receive. We measure the benefits (losses) to consumers by the additional (lessened) consumer surplus they receive.

Consumer surplus is measured by the sum, for all units of a commodity, of the difference between what consumers would be willing to pay for each unit and what they have to pay. To illustrate, consider the downward sloping demand curve in Fig. 3.3. To purchase the first unit consumers are willing to pay a price P_3. To purchase the next unit they are willing to pay a price slightly less than P_3. To purchase the Q_2th unit they are willing to pay P_2. If the market price is P_2, then P_2 must be paid for each of the Q_2 units demanded. To measure the consumer surplus given a market price of P_2, we subtract P_2 from what consumers would be willing to pay for each of the Q_2 units actually purchased. But that is just the difference between the demand curve and the horizontal price line at P_2, or the area indicated by the triangle labeled J in Fig. 3.3. Likewise, with a market price of P_0, the consumer surplus would be $J + F + G$.

Now let us return to the question of who gains and who loses from price stabilization. Let us consider the case in Fig. 3.3 in which the completely price inelastic supply curve is equally likely to be at Q_1 or Q_2, so on average it is at Q_0. Assume that the demand curve is fixed, so the only source of instability is the shifting supply curve. P_0 is the average price and the one at which the buffer stock stabilizes the price when it is in operation.

When the supply curve shifts out to Q_1, the buffer stock purchases $Q_1 - Q_0$ units. The change in consumer surplus due to paying P_0 instead of

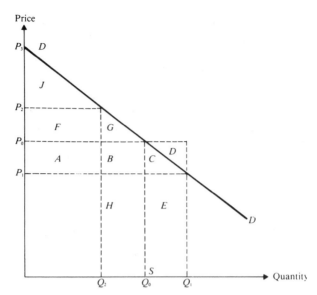

Fig. 3.3 Gains and losses from price stabilization (shifts in inelastic supply curve only)

the price P_1 that would have prevailed without a buffer stock is negative, $-A - B - C$. The producers' revenue gain due to the higher prices is positive, $A + B + C + D$. The cost to the buffer stock of purchasing $Q_1 - Q_0$ units is $-C - D - E$. The total benefit (summing these three components) is $-C - E$.

When the supply curve shifts to Q_2, $Q_0 - Q_2$ units are sold by the buffer stock at price P_0. This precludes the price from rising to P_2, as it otherwise would. The benefit to the consumers is $F + G$ due to the lower price and the larger quantity. The benefit to the producers is $-F$ since they receive a lower price for their Q_2 units than they would without the buffer stock. The financial inflow to the buffer stock is $B + H$. The total benefit is the sum of these three components, $B + G + H$.

If the sequencing over time of the supply shifts is ignored,[9] the total benefits to each of the three groups is the sum of those obtained from buffer stock operation with supply at Q_1 and at Q_2. For consumers the sum is $F + G - A - B - C$. For producers the sum is $A + B + C + D - F$. For the buffer stock the sum is $B + H - C - D - E$. For the total benefit the sum is $B + G + H - C - E$. Under these assumptions the sum for the buffer

9 In Section 5.1 we discuss how events in the distant future might be discounted to make them comparable to current events. In the terminology of that discussion, we here are assuming a zero discount rate.

stock is zero and the overall sum is positive.[10] However, whether or not consumers or producers, respectively, benefit depends on the exact shape of the curves. The issue basically is an empirical one.

The thoughtful reader will realize that Fig. 3.3 represents only one of the alternative cases and subcases considered in the previous section. We could examine each of these and others in which the curves are not linear or the shifts are not parallel. To do so would only reinforce the conclusion that either the producers or the consumers might gain, but the issue is basically empirical. Instead of examining each theoretical possibility, therefore, in Chapters 5 and 6 we focus on the gains that are implied by the empirical estimates of actual supply and demand curves for the commodities of interest.

3.3 NORMATIVE IMPLICATIONS OF MARKET SOLUTIONS[11]

Pure competition is defined to be the situation in which no single participant has the capacity to affect market prices more than infinitesimaly (in other words, no single participant has market power). From the point of view of individual entities in the market place, prices seem to be given (not necessarily fixed over time) parameters independent of their own behavior. Pure competition generally is considered an interesting paradigm for reasons summarized below, but not of very general applicability in the real world. However, most of the initial producers of agricultural commodities that enter into international commodity markets (and agricultural products account for about 85 percent of total nonpetroleum commodity exports from developing countries) and most of the ultimate consumers (generally in processed form of both the agricultural and nonagricultural internationally traded commodities sell and purchase these goods, respectively, under conditions approximating pure competition. At both ends of the marketchain for the relevant international commodities (but not in the middle, where marketing boards, other government agencies, and large companies dominate), therefore, the purely competitive model has substantial applicability.

What are the advantages of pure competition? Some answers are in the area of political economy and thus derivative of particular value systems. Under pure competition the basic economic problems (for example, what is produced, how is it produced, and for whom is it produced) are solved in an

---

10 To see this, note in Fig. 3.3 that $B + H = C + D + E$ (so the sum for the buffer stock is zero) and $B + G + H$ is greater than $C + E$ (so the total benefit is positive).
11 The distinction often is made between positive and normative economics. Positive economic analysis reveals what happens under certain conditions (for example, if the demand curve is downward sloping, the quantity demanded declines as the price increases, everything else held constant). Normative economics pertains to what should occur, and, therefore, incorporates value judgments. Appendix A provides a more detailed analysis of the issues in this section for the interested reader.

impersonal manner, independently of personal ties or characteristics such as race or national origin.[12] The atomistic structure of buyers and sellers required for competition also decentralizes and disperses power. Moreover, if the conditions necessary for pure competition to exist do in fact prevail, freedom of entry into various industries and individual mobility will both be high.

In response to the question about the advantages of pure competition, most economists focus on answers related to economic efficiency. In a world with the correct initial distribution of input ownership for a given social welfare function, with easy entry (for instance, due to a lack of legal restrictions and limited increasing returns to scale relative to the size of industries), with no externalities, with no uncertainty, and with pure competition everywhere else, pure competition in international commodity markets results in maximization of the social welfare function.[13]

This is a strong result. But what does it really mean? Appendix A explores this questions in some depth, and interested readers are encouraged to study it for more details. Here it suffices to expand on the notion of efficiency by distinguishing among efficiency in production, efficiency in exchange, and overall efficiency. Under the assumptions of the previous paragraph, pure competition leads to all three kinds of efficiency, as well as to maximization of social welfare.

Efficiency in production occurs if production of one good cannot be increased without lessening the production of some other good. That is, the economy is on the production frontier of Fig. 1.1 so that no more manufactured products can be made without reducing the output of agricultural products (or vice versa). Under pure competition each firm chooses to sell the number of units of product at which its marginal cost (the cost of producing the last unit) just equals the market price of the product in order to maximize its profits. Also, each firm selects its inputs so that the marginal products (i.e. the additional products obtained from using the last units of inputs) for the last dollars spent on all inputs are identical in order to minimize the costs of producing the profit-maximizing level of output. This means that an individual firm satisfying this condition could not gain by substituting one input for another. It also means that society as a whole could not increase the output of one good without reducing the output of some other good since every firm minimizes its cost by equalizing across inputs the marginal product for the last dollar spent on each input and every firm faces the same input prices. The last unit of each input is everywhere valued the same, so no overall output increase can result from merely shifting inputs around. Such behavior assures efficiency in production.

---

12 Given certain sets of values, this impersonality is a negative dehumanizing feature.

13 The assumptions made here are defined and discussed below.

Efficiency in exchange means that for a given level of production of all goods, no one individual can be made better off merely by exchanging goods with someone else without making at least one other person worse off. Under pure competition all individuals maximize their satisfactions (or utilities) by choosing a combination of goods so that the last bit of satisfaction (that is, marginal utility) obtained from the last dollar spent on the good is the same for all goods. Since every person faces the same product prices, every person values the last unit of one good that they purchase relative to the last unit of another in the same relative way. Therefore everyone could not be made better off merely by switching given levels of goods among individuals. Such behavior assures efficiency in exchange.

Overall efficiency exists when the rate at which the last unit of product of one good can be transformed into another by moving along the production possibility frontier is the same as the rate of which individuals substitute the last unit of one good for the other. The rate at which the last unit of one commodity can be transformed into the other is given by the ratio of the marginal costs of the two commodities, or the slope of the production possibility frontier. Given that purely competitive firms choose an output at which the marginal cost is equal to the product price, this rate of transformation between two goods is equal to the ratio of the product prices. But satisfaction-maximizing consumers also choose combinations of goods so that their ratios of marginal satisfactions (or marginal utilities) are equal to these same ratios of product prices. Marginal consumption decisions among goods are made on the basis of true relative marginal costs of production for society. Therefore, pure competition assures overall efficiency. In such a situation no one can be made better off—by changing inputs among firms, by changing the composition of output among commodities, or by changing the distribution of output among consumers—without making someone else worse off.

Social welfare maximization occurs if there is a social welfare function that depends on the levels of satisfactions of all individuals and if the maximum value of this function is obtained for a given supply of inputs, technology, and preferences of individuals. Given any particular social welfare function, pure competition leads to its maximization if there is overall efficiency *and* if the initial ownership of inputs is exactly right so that the market solutions lead to just the right incomes for that particular social welfare function.[14]

---

14 For example, if the social welfare function weighted everyone's preferences equally, a very unequal distribution of ownership of inputs probably would not lead to maximization of the function. On the other hand, if the socal welfare function put very high weight on the satisfaction of one individual, it probably would not be maximized by an equal distribution of ownership of inputs.

Reservations

The result that pure competition leads to social welfare maximization is a strong result. But the necessary conditions are very strong too, and obviously not even approximately satisfied in the real world. Let us consider them one by one.

First, maximization of a social welfare function depends upon having exactly the right distribution of income and therefore of ownership of inputs. Within a static framework, much of the conflict between the developing and developed nations may arise at this point. Even if all the other conditions given above are satisfied so that economic efficiency is attained, the initial distribution of assets is seen by many to be so inequitable that the world is far away from a welfare maximization. Efficiency concerns may be unimportant in light of this maldistribution.

Second, leaving aside the question of welfare maximization, pure competition leads to overall efficiency if all of the other conditions are satisfied. No shift in resources and so on exists that would improve the welfare of any one individual without reducing the welfare of at least one other individual. Attainment of this state seems desirable, everything else being equal, and its virtues are emphasized (perhaps overemphasized) by many economists. But the existence of pure competition alone is not enough to guarantee even efficiency. To obtain efficiency in the above discussion we had to assume that there are no externalities. That is, we had to assume that the production of one product depends only on the market inputs used directly in the production process for it and that the utility of an individual depends only on the market goods he or she consumes. In the real world, however, externalities abound. Individuals' satisfactions depend not only on their consumption of purchased items, but also on such factors as the consumption of others (for example, "keeping up with the Jones") or non-market products like pollution. Likewise, production of one good may depend not only on the inputs purchased for use in its production process, but also on other nonmarket factors such as pollution. The existence of these nonmarket interdependencies or externalities precludes overall efficiency even if the conditions exist to permit pure competition.

Third, even if all of the conditions for the existence of pure competition are satisfied and there are no externalities, the behavioral assumptions assumed above may not be satisfied. For example, it is assumed that firms maximize profits. But firms may have other objectives or considerations in mind. Possibilities include avoiding risk in an uncertain world or providing perquisites (such as nice offices and company cars) for the managers. If such other considerations are important, behavior of these firms may not be approximated well by profit maximization—and efficient outcomes do not result.

Fourth, the conditions for pure competition to exist often are not satisfied even if profit maximization and the lack of externalities are both assumed. Entry into an industry is not easy in many cases due to legal, natural, and technological monopolies or due to increasing returns to scale that are large relative to the industry. If there are relatively few firms in an industry, they perceive correctly that they have market power in that they can affect their product price by changing their output. Fig. 3.4 illustrates the profit-maximizing behavior of a monopolist in the M industry. Since the demand curve is sloping downward, to sell more the monopolist must lower the price. As a result, the marginal revenue (or additional revenue generated from selling one more unit) is below the demand curve since the price must be lowered on all previous units to sell one more unit. The profit-maximizing level of output is M_1, at which level the marginal revenue equals the marginal cost.[15] At lower outputs the marginal revenue exceeds the marginal cost, so profits can be increased by expanding output and sales (and vice versa at higher levels of output). To sell M_1 units of output, the monopolist must charge the price PM_1, as is indicated by the demand curve. But this profit-maximizing condition for the monopolist implies a price greater than marginal cost. Therefore, if industry A is purely competitive and industry M is a monopoly, the economy no longer satisfies the overall efficiency condition. Instead, people are substituting between A and M at the margin at a different rate than the relative marginal cost of A to M.

Let us pursue one implication of this example further. Ignore the possibilities of externalities for the moment and presume that the only nonpure competition in the system is the existence of monopoly in the production and sale of M. To obtain overall efficiency, the "first best" solution would be to make M act as a pure competitor, perhaps by breaking it up into enough small units so that none has perceptible influence on the market price. But suppose that such an option is not available? What is best to do? Under the assumptions we have made, the "second-best" solution is for A to charge the same ratio of price to marginal cost as does M. Then the overall efficiency condition is satisfied.

This is an illustration of the "theory of second best": If all of the conditions for an optimum cannot be satisfied, efficient outcomes can be ensured by introducing particular new distortions. The problem is that the desirable new distortions depend on the exact nature of the particular situation. The second-best solution indicated in the previous paragraph, for example, works under the particular assumptions indicated, but would not be efficient if one or both industries produced inputs for the other or if total vari-

---

15 The next section discusses the case of limit pricing to preclude entry by firms with market power, in which case the optimal strategy may not be to maximize short-run profits.

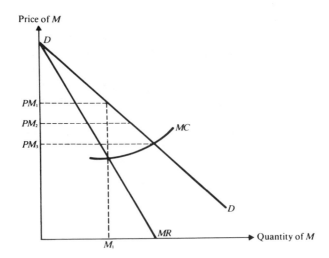

Fig. 3.4 Market behavior of a monopoly

able input supplies were not fixed. Thus, to devise second-best solutions in the real world requires much more knowledge than policy-makers normally have.

What does this discussion of the possibility of nonpurely competitive markets mean in the consideration of international commodity markets? Clearly, substantial market power exists in markets other than the commodity markets in the real world. In principle, if such market power in the rest of the world cannot be eliminated, in the interests of efficiency the theory of the second-best suggests that it *might* be desirable to introduce it into international markets (if it does not already exist), not resist interfering in these markets because of supposed advantages of pure competition!

Realistically, substantial market power already exists in most international commodity markets. In the majority of cases, a relatively few buyers (governments or large firms) account for most of the purchases. In many cases sales are also quite concentrated. If there is no new attempt to regulate these markets, therefore, the alternatives are not an efficient, purely competitive system as many of the critics of the international commodity agreements seem to assume, but systems with considerable existing market imperfections.

Fifth, the whole analysis above is at a point of time without uncertainty. Incorporation of risk aversion and dynamic considerations well might vitiate the claim that pure competition leads to efficient outcomes over time. Schumpeter, for example, placed great emphasis on the importance of market power to lead to new technological developments that are much more important in a dynamic context than is static efficiency (see Behrman [3]). Although such claims are not uncontested, the possibility that they are right raises further doubts about advocating unregulated markets on short-run efficiency grounds above.

Conclusion

Where does this discussion leave us? Unhindered markets may be relatively efficient devices for processing a great deal of information to signal short-ages or surpluses through price or inventory changes. However, one has to be quite careful in regard to their normative implications. They lead to max-imization of a given social welfare function only with the correct distribu-tion of assets and the satisfaction of all of the other conditions discussed above. They lead to economic efficiency only under strong and unrealistic assumptions. The "theory of second best" at worst implies that, in the real world, policies directed at economic efficiency should be abandoned. At best it suggests the advocation of "third-best," very general, policies that have a reasonable probability of leading to greater economic efficiency but that do not guarantee a step in that direction when applied in a specific case. Dynamic considerations may weaken further the argument for unhindered markets leading to overall efficiency.

Economic theory leads us to this highly qualified view of the normative properties of unhindered market solutions. It is a much weaker view than that of many who oppose international commodity agreements on the basis that they would lessen the gains from free market operations. One can un-derstand why economists from developing countries might wonder if the position of the strongest advocates of unhindered free market operations is based on a lack of understanding of underlying economic theory, or a dis-guised defense of vested interests in the status quo.

3.4 CONDITIONS UNDER WHICH COLLUSIVE ACTION BY PRO-DUCERS ALONE CAN RAISE MARKET PRICES

The basic motivation behind the advocacy of international commodity agreements may have little to do with stabilization per se. Instead, the ma-jor concern may be to raise the real resources of the developing countries who export the affected commodities. Under certain conditions discussed in Section 3.1 above (for example, dominant supply shifts), stabilization itself may lead to increased revenues for the exporters. The content of the UNCTAD documents, however, suggests that the concern goes further than this to a desire to raise market prices (or prevent real market prices from falling) to levels above that which otherwise would prevail. If market de-mand curves are price inelastic, successful price raising is rewarded by greater revenues since the quantities demanded do not decline by as large a percentage as prices rise.

This leads us into a much less rigorous area of economic theory: oligopoly formation and behavior. An oligopoly is an industry than has a small number of producers. Each member of an oligopoly can perceive that not only does its own output decision affect the market price, but also the output decisions of all its fellow oligopolists affect the market price. This interdependency creates a rivalry (although not necessarily price competition) among the oligopolists in regard to the division of the existing market. If the oligopolists are able to agree how to divide the market shares, they can maximize their joint profits by acting as a monopolist and selecting that output for which industry marginal cost is equal to marginal revenue (M_1 in Fig. 3.4).

However, this is a very static view. If the oligopolists collude to raise prices, new firms may be induced to enter into the industry or new substitutes may be developed to compete with the product of the industry. This brings us to the possibility of limit pricing to discourage entry. In Fig. 3.4 the collusive short-run static profit-maximizing price is PM_1. Suppose, however, that at any price above PM_2, new entrants are induced. To maximize long-run profits it may be desirable from the point of view of the colluding oligopolists to set the price below the short-run profit maximizing level in order to limit the inducement for new firms to enter. The effective long-run demand curve for the current colluding oligopolists has a horizontal segment at PM_2 until it hits the downward-sloping demand curve DD. The colluders have to decide how to balance off higher short-run and long-run prices and profits. The easier is entry or the possibility of others substituting for the product, the less are the colluding oligopolists able both to gain large current profits and to maintain longer-run market power.

The theory of limit pricing and a number of theories[16] of how oligopolists divide a given market share lead to a checklist of conditions that seem to facilitate oligopolistic coordination of pricing and output decisions: (1) the perception that joint action will lead to greater returns for producers, (2) common output preferences due to similar cost structures and market shares, (3) cheap and rapid communication, (4) high concentration of production in relatively few firms, (5) a small (or no) competitive fringe, (6) repetitive small transactions, (7) homogeneity and simplicity of products, (8) the willingness to utilize inventory and order backlogs as buffers instead of making overly sensitive price adjustments, (9) limited or no substitution for the product, and (10) high barriers to entry (for example, restricted technological knowledge, restricted control over exhaustible resources, legal re-

---

16 See any standard intermediate economic theory or industrial organization textbook. None of these theories is completely persuasive.

strictions on new firms, returns to scale at a high level of production relative to market size).

How do the UNCTAD core commodities stack up against such a checklist? In some respects they do rather well: product homogeneity, frequent transactions, and a common perceived interest—at least currently among the developing country producers. But in other respects they generally fare poorly: low barriers to entry, limited returns to scale, an active competitive fringe, substantial current and potential substitution for the products. And for the commodity that probably is most promising by these criteria—copper—the developing countries account for about only 40 percent of world production. Thus the developing countries indeed may be advocating international commodity agreements that include both producers and consumers because they perceive little likelihood of developing successful producer cartels for the ten core commodities on their own. In an important sense, therefore, the oil cartel of OPEC may seem *not* to be a model that can be imitated by producers of the UNCTAD core commodities.

3.5 CONCLUSIONS

The theoretical considerations of this chapter give important insights into the arguments for and against international commodity agreements. They suggest that the developing-country producers of the ten UNCTAD core commodities may be advocating such agreements because the chances of success of producers' cartels for these commodities are not high. They also indicate that normative arguments against international commodity agreements on the grounds of efficiency or social welfare maximization are *not* well based. Finally, they imply that whether producers or consumers gain from international commodity agreements and whether or not there is a tradeoff between the level and instability of producers' revenues cannot be established on the basis of economic theory. Instead, empirical analysis is required. The rest of this book attempts to provide such analysis.

REFERENCES

1. H. G. Johnson. "Commodities: Less Developed Countries' Demands and Developed Countries Response." Paper presented at MIT Workshop on Specific Proposals and Desirable DC Response to LDC Demands Regarding the New International Economic Order, 17-20 May 1976.
2. A. H. Sarris, P. Abbott, and L. Taylor. *World Grain Reserves*. Washington, D. C.: Overseas Development Council, 1977.
3. J. R. Behrman. "Development Economics." *Modern Economic Thought*. Ed. by S. Weintraub. Philadelphia: University of Pennsylvania Press, 1977.

The Ups and Downs of Oil

Hendrik S. Houthakker

Summary

The sharp fall in oil prices during late 1985 an early 1986 came as a surprise only to those who believed that oil, as a supposedly essential commodity, is somehow exempt from the laws of supply and demand. Actually, fluctuations in oil prices can be explained by market forces, both within and without the industry. In the 1950s and 1960s the world price had a declining trend resulting from massive discoveries in many parts of the world. When demand, stimulated by a worldwide boom, caught up with supply, the trend was reversed. In the early 1970s the inflationary pressures released by the break-down of the Bretton Woods system of fixed exchange rates in due course had their impact on the world oil market. The United States, whose oil reserves had been prematurely exhausted by the import quota system, became dependent on the Persian Gulf countries, already the main suppliers of Europe and Japan.

The leading oil exporters had already organized themselves into a poten-tial cartel, and in late 1973 OPEC seized the opportunity provided by the Arab-Israeli war to impose its price. Acting with due regard to long-run prospects, OPEC was able to maintain its price in real terms until the fall of the shah of Iran. Saudi Arabia, the cartel's leader, could have offset the ensuing loss of production but chose not to do so for apparently political reasons. OPEC abandoned its prudent long-term strategy, focusing instead on short-term profits. High oil prices strengthened production and weakened consumption outside the cartel, thus causing OPEC to lose control of the world market; its market share fell from over 50 percent in 1973 to 30 percent in 1985. In 1986 the world price dropped below $10 per barrel, although it has recovered somewhat since then.

The cartel is now trying to reassert its power to fix the world price and will probably succeed in doing so once the current excess of inventories has been worked off. OPEC, however, is not likely to return to the go-for-broke tactics that led to its recent downfall. The cartel's steady performance of the 1970s offers a better example.

The importing countries now have an opportunity to reconsider their oil policies. The experience of the past thirteen years should have taught them to rely primarily on market forces. Competition, in fact, has become much more effective in the oil market in recent years. The introduction of futures trading in crude and refined products has been an especially valuable development.

In the United States the most urgent task for national security is to establish adequate spare capacity in the domestic industry to reduce our vulnerability to economic and political pressures. In view of our rather limited prospects for new discoveries, this goal is more desirable than keeping up domestic output. A variable tariff, designed to guarantee a minimum price for domestic producers without imposing undue burdens on consumers, appears to hold the most promise. Although a fixed tariff could be used to capture some of OPEC's monopoly profits, it would further worsen the allocation of resources, which has already been seriously impaired by the cartel.

Only a few years ago the words "energy crisis" were heard every day. Most people believed that the days of cheap oil were gone forever, while the president of the United States described the efforts allegedly needed to secure our energy as the "moral equivalent of war." Now the same media that spread this hysteria are full of sad stories about the plight of producers at home and abroad who can no longer sell their oil at the prices to which they had become accustomed. After reaching a high of some $35 per barrel at the beginning of the 1980s, the world price of crude[1] plunged to around $7 in the early summer of 1986; it has recovered to around $16 more recently.[2] In real terms the current price is less than one-half its level of five years earlier, although it is still more than twice what it was fifteen years ago.

How did these drastic changes come about? Was the recent downturn just a fluke, soon to be reversed by the increasing tightness of supplies so widely forecast until recently? Alternatively, was the experience from 1973 to 1981 merely a bubble that was finally deflated by overwhelming market forces? And what, under either explanation, are the consequences for the U.S. and the world economy? To what extent can these consequences be influenced by policy? These are the main questions to be addressed in this essay.

Historical Background

A thumbnail history of the world oil market may be helpful in understanding recent developments. Until the end of World War II a handful of countries accounted for nearly all the world's output. The largest among these was the United States, which remained a net exporter until the 1950s. The quarter of a century after 1945 was a period of massive discoveries in many parts of the world, notably the Arab countries on the Persian Gulf, several countries in Africa, the

North Sea, Alaska, and certain new oil provinces in the Soviet Union.
    As a result, the trend in world oil prices was downward in real
terms, with four important consequences.

• Consumption, which has a low price elasticity in the short run but
a much larger one in the long run, grew rapidly, with considerable
substitution of oil for coal.
• In the late 1950s the United States adopted import quotas to
protect its domestic industry and to reduce its vulnerability to politically inspired interruptions in imports. Combined with the already
existing system of market demand prorationing, the quotas served to
keep the crude price in the United States above its equivalent in the
world market.
• With a view to safeguarding their royalties, a number of third
world oil producers set up the Organization of Petroleum Exporting
Countries (OPEC) in 1960. Together these countries accounted for
more than half of global output by the early 1970s.
• Finally, the major oil companies (particularly the group then
known as the "seven sisters") lost their dominance over the market
outside the United States. The main reasons for this development
were expropriations by host countries, large discoveries by companies
outside the group, and adverse antitrust actions. In the Teheran
agreement of 1971 the majors in effect recognized the power of OPEC
to determine crude prices.

    In early 1973 the United States abandoned the quota system,
which had become an impediment when domestic consumption rose
steadily at the same time that domestic output declined from the peak
of 10 million barrels per day (Mb/d) reached in 1970. One of the
assumptions underlying quotas had been that the permitted imports
would come from nearby sources such as Canada and Venezuela.
When the gap between consumption and domestic output widened
sharply, it became necessary to draw on more distant sources, including the countries in the Persian Gulf. Until then these countries had
sold most of their oil to Europe and Japan. When the United States
also became a buyer, the market power of the Persian Gulf nations
increased considerably.
    The macroeconomic background of the first oil shock is also
important. The 1960s had been a period of unprecedented growth in
the world economy. Since in the long run oil consumption, aside from
the effect of price changes, tends to be proportional to income, this
growth had a powerful effect on the world oil market. By the end of
the decade, inflation, especially in the United States, started to accelerate, and one of its first victims was the Bretton Woods system of

fixed exchange rates. Not only did the dollar, in terms of which world oil prices are expressed, begin to depreciate, but the initial efforts by various countries to keep their currencies from appreciating greatly also increased world liquidity. This (and not, as is often believed, the first oil shock itself) was the origin of the Great Inflation of the 1970s. The inflationary pressures first became manifest in commodities other than oil, such as grains and sugar. The principal reason why these pressures did not show up more quickly in petroleum prices appears to have been the weakness of competition in the oil market, in which there was as yet no futures trading and relatively little spot trading by independent dealers. Nevertheless the inflationary influence was ready to assert itself.

The First Oil Shock and Its Effects

Such was the situation in the early 1970s that made the first oil shock possible. The immediate occasion for that unexpected event was political, namely an embargo proclaimed by the Arab producers against the United States and Holland because of their alleged support for Israel in the 1973 war. The embargo accomplished nothing in the political sphere, but its economic effects were spectacular. The spot market in petroleum came to life, with some cargoes trading as high as $17 per barrel compared with the prevailing "official" price of about $2.50. This appears to have convinced OPEC that a concerted curtailment of oil supplies could be extremely profitable. At the end of 1973 the members agreed not to export crude at less than the equivalent of $10 per barrel. No formal output quotas were set; instead, frequent consultations among the members were to prevent excess supplies from undermining the cartel price (see figure 5–1).

Whatever their feelings about the new price may have been, the major oil companies were no longer in a position to influence it. The consuming countries were equally powerless. Most of them permitted the higher price of crude to be reflected in product prices. The United States, however, maintained price controls, which had the unfortunate effect of delaying and limiting the necessary adjustments in domestic consumption and production. In the years immediately following the first oil shock American petroleum output continued to decline, consumption remained high, and imports soared. Although there was much talk about conservation and alternative energy sources, the price increases that would have led most rapidly to these goals were not permitted.

OPEC, meanwhile, managed to keep the cartel price more or less constant in inflation-adjusted dollars. This apparent stability masked

FIGURE 5–1
WORLD OIL PRODUCTION, 1973–1985

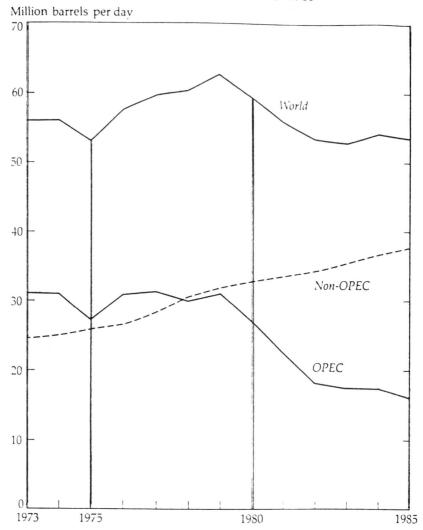

SOURCE: U.S. Energy Information Administration, *International Petroleum Statistics Report*, July 25, 1986.

a growing discord among the members over the appropriate pricing policy. Saudi Arabia with its enormous reserves and small population is naturally concerned about the long-run danger of pricing oil out of the energy markets. It has usually been supported in this postion by its neighbors, Kuwait and the United Arab Emirates. The other members of OPEC have generally taken a much shorter view.

In the middle 1970s the market could probably have borne an even higher price than OPEC had set, but Saudi Arabia prevented this by expanding its output. At one point it temporarily surpassed the United States by producing more than 10 million barrels per day. It had, in effect, become the swing producer within OPEC, adjusting its output to maintain the cartel price. The risk inherent in this role was that it would weaken the commitment of other members to the cartel's goals. These other members came to believe that they could produce as much as they liked since the Saudis would adjust their output as needed. When this risk became a reality in 1977, Saudi Arabia was driven to use the ultimate weapon of any cartel leader: it set its own export price below the cartel price. The resulting two-price pattern lasted only until the second oil shock, which (for reasons discussed below) Saudi Arabia could not or would not prevent.

The value of oil in international trade is by far the largest of any commodity. The sharp and sudden price increase therefore had significant macroeconomic effects, though in retrospect they appear less serious than was thought at the time. The combined current account surplus of the OPEC countries increased from $4 billion in 1973 to $65 billion in 1974, and the current account of the oil-importing nations deteriorated correspondingly.[3] The OPEC surplus resulted from the members' inability to increase their imports in line with their exports at short notice and was therefore essentially transitional. Moreover, this surplus remained in the international banking system, where it was available to finance the oil importers' deficits. The contemporary worries about "recycling the petrodollars" were therefore largely misplaced. As a matter of policy the cartel members did not sell crude on credit, but the net effect was much the same as if they had done so.[4]

Rightly or wrongly, however, many importing countries reacted to their external deficits (and to the continuing inflation) by restrictive domestic policies. It may well be argued that after the strong growth of the preceding period a worldwide slowdown was inevitable, but these policies helped aggravate the slowdown into a severe recession during the middle 1970s. The recession had no permanent effect on inflation, which resumed its acceleration soon afterwards.

As far as the oil market was concerned, the recession was useful in reducing the demand. The supply situation in the non-OPEC world also showed the first signs of improvement. Overriding the objections of environmentalists, the U.S. Congress acted to ensure construction of the Alaska pipeline. Its completion in 1977 helped reverse the downward trend in domestic supply. The first oil from the North Sea was produced in 1975, and that area gradually became a sufficiently large source of crude to turn Britain and Norway into net exporters. The Soviet Union and Mexico also brought their large discoveries into production. In many parts of the world—the OPEC countries were a significant exception—exploration moved into high gear.

The Second Oil Shock

Given enough time the developments just described would conceivably have forced the cartel to lower its price. Before this could happen, however, another political event provided unexpected support to those who believed the price was bound to rise indefinitely.[5] The overthrow of the shah of Iran in 1979 had a drastic effect on the cartel's second largest producer; output was reduced from 5.2 Mb/d in 1978 to 1.7 Mb/d in 1980 and even less in 1981. The religious fundamentalists who assumed power abhorred the modernization plans pursued by the shah and saw no need for the oil revenue with which those plans were to be financed. Saudi Arabia soon abandoned the attempt to make up the resulting shortfall in supply, a major change in policy to be discussed further. All OPEC members ultimately agreed on a new price of about $33 per barrel, in line with the spot market at that time.[6]

Further alarm was caused by the outbreak of war between Iran and Iraq, which had replaced Iran as number two in the OPEC hierarchy. Both countries attacked each other's oilfields and export facilities. Since Iran had already curtailed its production, the effect there was minor, but Iraq's output fell from 2.5 Mb/d in 1979 to 1.0 Mb/d in 1981. Although not participating directly, other countries in the Persian Gulf (including Saudi Arabia) became involved in this war by their support for Iraq, thus creating a potentially explosive situation. It did not take much imagination to paint the world oil outlook in dark colors.

Yet it is clear in retrospect that the market was not as vulnerable as it seemed. To be sure, an extension of the Iran-Iraq hostilities to the Western Gulf would have had dire consequences; the industrial nations might have been forced to safeguard the oilfields in that area by military intervention. Fortunately the war did not spread, perhaps because of a reinforced naval presence by the United States and some of its allies or because Iran had enough trouble dealing with its much smaller neighbor. There was some interference with shipping in the Persian Gulf, but by and large the oil kept flowing. In fact Iran had to increase its oil exports to pay for the war, and Iraq found ways of resuming some of its exports.

Indeed it is indicative of the underlying weakness in the world market that the eruption of the Iran-Iraq war did not lead to a third oil shock. The nominal price remained very high in the early 1980s, but it did not keep up with inflation.[7] In addition there was a partly speculative increase in worldwide inventories, whose liquidation had a dampening effect in subsequent years.

The market's weakness was most evident in the prices of refined products, which are of central importance because crude oil has few uses until it is refined.[8] In the past few years much OPEC crude has been sold on a "netback" basis, according to which the crude price is calculated from the value of the refined products less transportation and refining costs. This practice has tended to make the cartel price for crude less relevant.

OPEC Loses Control

In 1973, the year preceding the first oil shock, OPEC accounted for nearly 56 percent of world crude output.[9] As usual when a cartel is established, its market share dropped, mostly because of a continuing rise in non-OPEC production. The cartel's was still close to one-half when the second oil shock occurred; subsequently it fell steadily to 30 percent in 1985. Moreover, domestic consumption in the member countries has risen, contrary to what happened elsewhere; it doubled between 1975 and 1985. More than 20 percent of OPEC's oil production is now consumed internally, further reducing the cartel's leverage.

In light of these figures it is not surprising that OPEC has lost control over the world market. If a group of suppliers has 56 percent of the market, they can impose a cartel price relatively easily; to do so with less than 30 percent is quite another matter. The question of OPEC policy is so essential to our topic that a brief digression into the relevant microeconomics may be in order.

As pointed out earlier, the demand for oil and other forms of energy is much more price sensitive in the long run than in the short run. The main reason is that oil products can be used only in durable equipment, such as cars and furnaces. The design of the equipment in existence at any time is the main determinant of energy consumption, though use can also be varied to some extent. In an adjustment of energy consumption to a significant change in prices, it is usually optimal to replace the equipment, and that takes time. The short-run effect consists largely of changes in utilization; the long-run effect also reflects changes in equipment.

Much the same is true on the supply side. Oil production from existing fields can be adjusted within limits, but a sustained increase in production calls for exploration and development of new fields, a process that normally extends over several years. In the case of a falling price it may also take a long time before some of the existing wells are abandoned because it no longer pays to maintain them.

The distinction between the short run and the long run is depicted in figure 5-2, where aa' represents the short-run world demand for a commodity and AA' the long-run demand, with aa' steeper than AA'.[10] The suppliers are divided in two parts: a group of producers who have agreed to form a cartel, and all others who will be referred to as the "outside suppliers." The supply curves (bb' for the short run and BB' for the long run) refer only to the outside suppliers; a cartel has no supply curve in the ordinary sense.

The figure represents a competitive equilibrium prior to the actual

FIGURE 5-2
PRICE FIXING BY A CARTEL

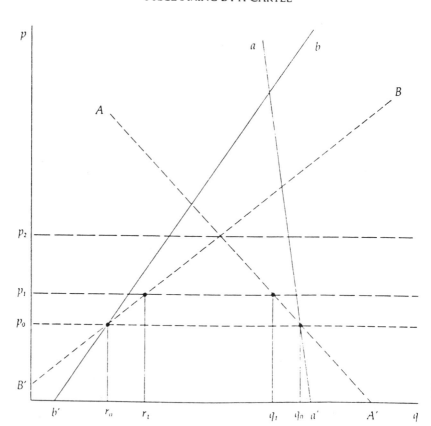

implementation of the cartel. Accordingly, the long-run and the short-run supply curves intersect at the precartel price p_0, as do the two demand curves. The quantity sold is q_0, of which r_0 is accounted for by the outside suppliers and s_0 ($= q_0 - r_0$) by the would-be cartel. To create some resemblance to the oil market at the end of 1973, s_0 is drawn to be larger than r_0.

The question for the cartel is now where to set its price, which in the circumstances will become the market price. Let this price be called p_1, and the corresponding quantities sold q_1 for the total and r_1 and s_1 for the two components. The cartel will presumably set p_1 to maximize its revenue $p_1 s_1$. The location of the maximizing p_1, however, depends on whether the cartel looks at the short run or the long run. It would not be rational to look only at the short run, since this would require frequent reductions of the cartel price as the long run catches up. Cartels generally aim for steady prices in real terms, and OPEC (at least until the second oil shock) was no exception.

Disregarding the cost of production (which is small for most OPEC producers), it may be assumed, therefore, that the cartel will seek to maximize its long-run revenue. In the example this is accomplished by setting p_1 halfway between the horizontal axis (where the price is zero) and p_2, the price at which the entire demand is satisfied by outside suppliers.[11]

There is reason to believe that the leaders of OPEC knew the importance of the long run when they set a price of $10 per barrel at the end of 1973. They could have gone higher, but realized that this would be inconsistent with cartel stability. In fact this price was maintained in real terms until the second oil shock; whether it could have been maintained if the United States had followed less short-sighted energy policies is another matter.

Why then did OPEC change its pricing policy after the revolution in Iran and the start of the war between Iran and Iraq? From a strictly economic point of view the previous strategy with its implicit emphasis on the long run could have been continued because Saudi Arabia and its allies had enough spare capacity to make up for the lower output of the belligerents. The most plausible explanation for the policy change is that the Saudis did not want to antagonize the new regime in Iran, whose influence in other Moslem countries represented a serious threat to the monarchy. In dollar terms Iran received about as much for its sharply reduced production after the second oil shock as it had received before the overthrow of the shah; it would have been a hostile act for the Saudis to upset this agreeable outcome by flooding the market.

Nevertheless OPEC's new policy of charging what the traffic

would bear in the short run carried the seed of its own destruction. The cartel had lost control; it was following the market instead of leading it. Competition finally asserted itself. With its share of the world supply dropping steadily, OPEC was powerless to prevent a gradual decline of the market price that became precipitous in the winter of 1985–1986 and continued into the following summer.

To many observers, and certainly to the public at large, the sharp fall in oil prices was as surprising as the sharp increases of the preceding decade had been. It should be stressed that the recent turbulence in the world oil market cannot be attributed to the much-publicized dissension within OPEC. No doubt the tactics used by Saudi Arabia to get the attention of its fellow members—specifically the increase in its output during the first half of 1986—aggravated the price slump. OPEC's basic problem, however, is not so much internal disagreement as rising outside production and shrinking outside consumption. From reports of recent cartel meetings it appears that most members are well aware of this reality. The price targets that were recently agreed upon are relatively modest. It these targets could be attained, which is by no means certain, the group would in effect be returning to the pricing policy that served it so well from 1974 to 1979.

The cartel has learned two other lessons. One is that the informal supply management of the 1970s, with Saudi Arabia acting as the swing producer, is no longer feasible. Under this mode of operation the kingdom would at times be forced to stop producing altogether, so that it might as well leave OPEC. Although formal production quotas were adopted some years ago, many members chose to ignore them. A binding agreement on more realistic quotas and on stricter enforcement was high on OPEC's agenda; if it had been postponed much longer, the continued existence of the cartel would be in serious doubt.

The other lesson is that OPEC must come to an understanding with at least some of the major outside producers. The admission of additional members would make the setting of output quotas even more difficult, but the group has had some success in getting informal cooperation. Countries such as Mexico, Egypt, and Norway have promised not to undercut OPEC's efforts to reassert its control of the world market. Even the U.S.S.R. has made a token gesture in this direction, but Britain has stuck to its procompetitive policy and the United States has stood aside.[12] In any case a sizable part of the increase in non-OPEC production has come from countries (including the United States) that remain net importers; OPEC can hardly expect to enlist their support.

The Cost and Supply of Oil

To obtain a better perspective on the future of oil prices, let us return for a moment to the theoretical analysis. The two supply curves shown in figure 2 for the outside producers assume competitive behavior on their part, which means that they take the market price as given. The outside supply is therefore determined by the cost of production, which is different in the short run and in the long run.

In the short run (that is, for the already existing oilfields) the marginal cost will typically be close to zero. The oil is normally under pressure and will come to the surface unless it is deliberately shut in. Stripper wells, in which the pressure has declined to the point where the oil must be pumped from the reservoir, are an exception to this statement.[13] A more important exception is provided by fields under secondary recovery, of which there are many in the United States. One analyst puts the average operating cost (which may not be conceptually equal to the short-run marginal cost) for 1984 at $3.87 per barrel in the United States, at $2.12 in the offshore United Kingdom, and at well below $1 in Saudi Arabia.[14]

Even at a very low price the cash flow from the well will be positive, and the operator may well decide to keep it running. Shutting it in may be justified, however, if the operator expects to receive a higher price (properly discounted) in the future. Although the short-run marginal cost is normally zero, this "user cost"[15] is in theory an important determinant of mineral supply. Its practical importance is less clear. In the United States, output in late 1986 was only 1 percent below that of a year earlier, despite a price fall of more than 50 percent. While this small price response is consistent with a short-run marginal cost close to zero, it suggests either that operators paid little attention to user cost—a concept that assumes definite views on future prices—or that they did not expect prices to recover to previous levels.

The effect of a price fall is more pronounced in the longer run because the maintenance and other investments necessary for optimal recovery of the oil in a reservoir will not be justified. When prices are low, therefore, production will decline at a higher rate. The cost of preventing an unduly steep decline of output is part of the long-run marginal cost. Even with optimal maintenance and the adoption of secondary and tertiary recovery, the production from an oilfield will approach zero ultimately, although this may take a very long time.

Exploration serves to replenish and expand the stock of minerals available for extraction. It is often believed that the cost of finding new oilfields is constantly rising, but that is not obvious. The uncertain success of exploration makes it difficult to generalize about the cost of finding oil. Advances in geology and in the technology of extracting oil in difficult environments, such as the deep sea and the Arctic, have played an important role. Some of the largest fields in the world (the Ghawar field in Saudi Arabia is a prime example) were found with minimal effort. On the other side, the vast sums spent on finding oil in the Atlantic off the United States and in the Beaufort Sea have not established any producing fields so far. Moreover, the result of successful exploration cannot be assessed until the necessary development, involving the drilling of additional wells, has been performed. As a rule development is much more expensive than exploration.

The usual measure of success in exploration and development is barrels proved per foot drilled. The cost per foot depends, among other things, on the current activity in exploration and development; drilling rigs, for instance, command much higher rentals when activity is high. Once the cost per foot is known, the cost of finding a barrel of oil in the ground can be found by capitalization as a function of the current interest rate. With this approach the development cost per barrel has been estimated as $9.04 in 1984 in the United States, as $4.43 in the British part of the North Sea, as below $.50 in the Persian Gulf countries, and as $1.81 in Nigeria.[16]

The finiteness of the earth places an upper limit on the global supply of oil, regardless of price. There is little reason to believe, however, that this limit constitutes an effective constraint on exploration in the foreseeable future. In recent decades oil has been found in many areas previously considered nonprospective. In some of these areas the cost of extraction is high, but in others—like southeastern Mexico—it is very low. The principal constraint on exploration since the first oil shock has been OPEC, which has not wanted to undermine its market power by new discoveries in the member countries. Saudi Arabia already has the world's largest proved reserves, but much more could probably be found if the kingdom permitted it. In 1983 Kuwait fortuitously discovered a large oilfield when attempting to augment its domestic gas supply.

Since the United States has been more thoroughly explored than any other country, the prospects are necessarily more limited. At present the largest undeveloped resource is the West Sac deposit in northern Alaska, where oil in place exceeds even Prudhoe Bay. It appears, however, that serious technical problems have to be solved before this deposit can be taken into production, and if it is, additional pipeline capacity may have to be built. At current prices this may not be profitable, but it demonstrates that the United States cannot be written off entirely as a source of future supply. While the level of exploration is very low at present, some recovery is likely when the outlook for prices becomes clearer.

In the unlikely event that conventional crude oil ever runs out, there are still enormous supplies of closely related materials to draw on. These include the Athabasca tar sands in Canada, the Orinoco heavy oils in Venezuela, and the oil shales of the Rocky Mountain area in the United States. Since these are not liquids, they cannot be extracted by drilling wells, but they yield essentially the same refined products as ordinary crude. The Canadian tar sands have been produced for several years; in oil shale a pilot operation in Colorado has been running with government subsidy. Venezuela, a member of OPEC, has been reluctant to open its Pandora's box. Materials of this kind also occur in the Soviet Union and elsewhere.

Most of these oil-bearing solids are high-cost resources and would become reserves only if crude prices rose well above the peak reached a few years ago; some of them are also troublesome from an environmental point of view. Nevertheless their existence in vast quantities, exceeding all known or suspected oil liquids, in effect puts a ceiling on crude prices in the long run. The world price of oil may well reach new highs in the coming decades, but it will not rise without limit.

Competition and Futures Trading

When, for reasons listed earlier, the major companies lost their market power in the 1960s, the alternative entities needed for effective competition were not yet in place. There were only a few independent oil traders and no futures market. After the initial impetus of the 1973 embargo, a competitive spot market in crude and products developed gradually. It is often known as the Rotterdam spot market because of the eminence of that city in transportation and refining; actually it covers much of Europe as well as North America and Southeast Asia, most of the trading being conducted by telex. This market filled the gap created when OPEC assumed control over crude prices without having much involvement in refining and marketing.

The progressive decline of OPEC after the second oil shock made the spot market even more prominent. By the early 1980s oil had become a commodity like copper or soybeans, and like other commodities it provided opportunities for that ultimate embodiment of competition, the futures market. In markets where a few firms are dominant, futures trading is not viable since it requires open entry and public participation. The main economic function of futures trading is in the management of inventories, where it permits price risks to be assumed by those willing to do so in hopes of speculative gain. It thus enables inventory-holding merchants to focus on what they do best, namely merchandizing.

It is no accident that futures trading first emerged in heating oil, a product used mostly for space heating in the northeastern United States. Since in the short run consumption depends primarily on winter temperatures in that area, it is quite risky to hold stocks. The heating oil futures market makes it possible to transfer the risk to those brave enough to take a view on winter weather and other determinants of heating oil prices. After this market proved to be fairly successful, the New York Mercantile Exchange was encouraged to start futures trading in crude oil.

At first crude prices were still under OPEC control and not variable enough to put the new market to the test, but in late 1985 it became clear that the cartel had fumbled and that the price of crude was increasingly governed by market forces. The volume of trading and the open interest[17] expanded rapidly to make crude futures a rival to such long-established markets as those for grains. Initially the futures had for the most part followed the spot market; gradually the price came to be effectively determined by futures trading, as is the case in other commodities. There is also a futures market in gasoline now, and in London futures contracts in gas oil (similar to heating oil) are actively traded.

Entry into a futures market is easy; all one has to do is to find a broker and make a modest security deposit known as margin. Futures trading serves to enlarge the number of individuals whose expectations determine prices. This is socially useful when the price prospects in a market are very uncertain, as is now the case in petroleum. It may seem that outsiders are necessarily less knowledgeable than insiders, but that is only true in the short run. An analysis of pronouncements by oil industry leaders over the past fifteen years would probably show that they were no better at predicting prices two or three years ahead than were people outside the industry. Since spot and futures prices tend to be highly correlated, the expectations expressed in futures prices also affect the spot price. Hedging (that is, arbitrage between the cash and futures markets) helps determine the size of inventories: the higher futures prices are in relation to the spot price, the more profitable it is to hold stocks.

The establishment of futures trading in crude and in products reflected the trend toward competition and has in turn reinforced that trend. This does not mean that the market is now fully competitive. OPEC is still very much alive, and much of the speculation in futures involves guessing what OPEC will do. Moreover, participation in futures trading is still incomplete. As far as is known, OPEC members do not trade in futures, and the major oil companies also appear to be standing aside.[18] Nevertheless the futures markets are now large enough to facilitate the holding of large commercial inventories, and these inventories in turn circumscribe OPEC's power to raise prices.

While futures trading tends to improve the short-run performance of a commodity market, it does not provide much help in long-term investments, such as those necessary to open a new oil-field. This is so because the trading is concentrated in nearby contracts (those calling for delivery within the next few months). In fact, crude futures contracts for delivery more than about nine months ahead are not traded at all. In due course, the crude futures market will possibly expand enough to permit trading in more distant contracts, which would make it more attractive to producers.[19]

In November 1986 the New York Mercantile Exchange started trading in options on crude futures contracts. These differ from the futures themselves in that the owner of an option is not obliged to exercise it, whereas the parties to a futures contract must either take or make delivery of the underlying commodity when the contract expires. The buyer of an option, therefore, has no more at risk than the amount for which the option was originally purchased, while his or her potential profit is theoretically unlimited. The introduction of options is likely to increase public participation, thus making the futures market still more representative of current expectations.

The Outlook

The main conclusion from the preceding analysis is that, barring major political upheavals and ignoring short-term irregularities, the world price of oil is not likely to go much above $20 per barrel in the next few years (through 1990, for example). Indeed, OPEC may need patience in raising the price to its present target of about $18 from the level of around $12 in the fall of 1986. The large inventories still overhanging the market will have to be reduced before a significant price increase can be made to stick.

The underlying price trend during the remainder of this decade, however, is likely to be upward as long as OPEC holds together. Non-OPEC production from existing fields will probably decline, since some of the investments necessary to maintain the present rate of output will not be justified at current prices. Some discoveries already made will not be taken into production, and the slowdown in exploration will reduce the number of new discoveries. These effects will be especially marked in the United States, where oil production may decline by about 25 percent, or more than 2 Mb/d, between 1986 and 1990.

Consumption, in contrast, is likely to turn around in the next few years as the depressing effect of earlier high prices gradually disappears. These past prices still have a depressant effect on demand because of adjustment lags. In the United States, for instance, automobiles have become much more fuel efficient, partly as a result of government regulation. In fact, cars purchased now consume only about half the gasoline per mile as the old cars they replace. Similarly, the substitution of natural gas for oil products in space heating will not soon be reversed. In electricity generation oil is continuing to lose ground to nuclear power, especially outside the United States. Even more important, world GNP is growing at a modest but sustainable rate, and that also stimulates oil demand.

The anticipated changes in production and consumption will lead to an increase in oil imports in the industrial countries and in many developed countries. Toward the end of the decade U.S. oil imports, including refined products, may rise from the current rate of about 6 Mb/d to exceed the peak rate of 10 Mb/d reached briefly in the middle 1970s. Less than half our consumption would then come from domestic sources.

Around 1990, therefore, the world oil market may again be under OPEC control. This does not necessarily imply a third oil shock, since the cartel is now presumably more aware of the dangers of short-run revenue maximization to cartel stability. If so, OPEC is likely to choose a gradual firming of the world price in real terms during the 1990s; if not, the boom-bust cycle of 1979–1986 may be repeated.

Obviously there are major risks in any such forecast. The principal economic uncertainty lies in production; thus some industry sources have predicted a U.S. output as low as 5 Mb/d by 1990. There may also be unpleasant surprises in foreign non-OPEC production; the long-predicted but as yet unrealized decline of North Sea output, for instance, may be steeper than now seems likely. As for consumption, another accident of the Chernobyl type could have a disastrous effect on nuclear power everywhere and force electricity producers to turn to oil. Although it is easier to think of bad news than of good news in this area, the possibility that OPEC will break up cannot be entirely overlooked, and a major discovery in non-OPEC territory is also conceivable.

The principal political uncertainty affecting the world price of crude is the outcome of the war between Iraq and Iran. More than six years after Iraq's initial attack, Iran clearly has the upper hand, especially on the ground. It took Iran several years to translate its numerical superiority into territorial gains, but Iraq is still much stronger in the air. Iraq is supported financially by Saudi Arabia and other Arab nations; it has also been tacitly favored by the West and by the Soviet Union, which facilitates its access to foreign equipment and supplies. Iran has recently managed to improve its external relations somewhat, but it continues to have difficulty in finding supplies.[20] Attempts at a peaceful settlement of the war have come up against Iran's insistence on removing the Iraqi leader, Saddam Hussein. There now appear to be three scenarios:

1. Iran's long-threatened "final offensive" is successful and leads to the installation of a puppet government in Baghdad.

2. Following less catastrophic military reverses, Saddam Hussein is overthrown by an Iraqi group acceptable to Iran; in a negotiated settlement Iraq remains independent.

3. The war continues without either side gaining a decisive advantage; Saddam Hussein remains in power. This scenario includes the possibility that growing popular dissatisfaction in Iran forces the fundamentalist regime to be more receptive to peace initiatives.

As far as oil supply is concerned, the second scenario is the most appealing though not necessarily the most probable. Under that scenario both Iran and Iraq would be able to restore oil exports to more normal levels, and Iraq at least would have strong incentives to do so in order to finance reconstruction from war damage. OPEC, of course, might try to offset the increased output of the former belligerents by reducing output elsewhere, but recent experience suggests that would be very difficult.

The first scenario, by contrast, would have very adverse effects on world oil supplies since Iran would have no interest in restoring, or even maintaining, Iraqi production. Moreover, the prestige of a military victory would raise Iran's standing in the entire Middle East and in OPEC; it might also endanger the pro-Western regimes in several Arab countries, including not only Saudi Arabia and Kuwait but Egypt and Jordan as well. Indeed, the implications of the first scenario are so disturbing that the West will probably do everything, short of military intervention, to prevent it from being realized. Taking all this into account, the first scenario may be judged less likely than the third, at least for the next few years.

The Iraq-Iran conflict is not the only source of political risk. Although the tension between Israel and its Arab neighbors is less acute than ten or fifteen years ago, no comprehensive peace settlement is in sight. The situation in Lebanon remains volatile. Another Arab-Israeli war cannot be ruled out, and the first oil shock has shown how disruptive it could be to the oil market.

To sum up, the supply-demand balance remains relatively favorable to consumers over the next few years; the market will gradually tighten, however, and around 1990 OPEC may again be firmly in the saddle. Although this forecast appears to be close to the consensus, the economic and political uncertainties inherent in it are large. Most of these uncertainties suggest higher prices, except if OPEC disintegrates or a peace settlement between Iraq and Iran is negotiated. It is against this background that policy options will be discussed.

The Role of Government

Government intervention in the oil market has a long history, particularly in the United States. Although its achievements are mixed at best, such intervention will no doubt continue for the following reasons:

1. Oil is one of the very few commodities that truly affects national security. The United States, which depends on imports for a large part of its consumption, is vulnerable to supply interruptions; moreover, the threat of interruption can be used to influence our foreign policy. This argument also applies to other oil-importing countries.

2. Governments are involved in the production process because they own the areas where exploration and extraction take place, and sometimes the deposits themselves. Even without government ownership, licensing is often needed for environmental reasons.

3. When oil transactions are a large factor in the balance of payments, they may be of special concern to macroeconomic policy.

4. Minerals, including oil, require special tax treatment because of depletion, a phenomenon rarely encountered in other goods and services. Exploration, especially when it is unsuccessful, also presents peculiar tax problems.

5. The existence of a foreign cartel casts doubt on the competitive assumptions under which government abstention is optimal.

6. The domestic oil industry may have enough political power to enlist government aid in accomplishing its economic objectives.

Because it is impossible to go into all these considerations here, the focus, rather, will be on the foreign trade regime applied to oil. Before this topic is discussed, the Strategic Petroleum Reserve (SPR) should be briefly mentioned because it bears directly on points 1 and 5 listed above. The SPR continues to be filled at a fairly steady rate to its target level of ninety days' imports; the target is likely to increase in volume over time because imports are likely to rise. The SPR represents a large investment, and a sizable capital loss has already been incurred on the oil that was bought at high prices. Nevertheless, the filling should go on because the long-term world oil outlook is far from reassuring. The oil put into the SPR should come from foreign sources to conserve domestic reserves; use of the SPR as a support program for domestic producers would be contrary to its national security objective.

The Strategic Petroleum Reserve is our first line of defense against attempted blackmail by oil-producing countries, a risk that has not vanished. It would not be realistic to rely entirely on private inventories; as the earlier discussion of futures trading showed, private traders are inevitably more concerned with short-term price fluctuations than with long-term political risks. More thought is needed, however, on the method of making the SPR available in case of an emergency; market forces should be engaged as much as possible.

It is more difficult to be positive about another element of current oil policy, the International Energy Agency (IEA). Its main purpose is to reallocate oil supplies among the member countries in case of a supply interruption. The IEA institutionalizes earlier sharing agreements among the industrial countries that were of some value during the 1973–1974 embargo against the United States and the Netherlands. At that time the spot market was still in its infancy, but at present it would seem that supplies could be at least as efficiently reallocated by the market as by the IEA. In principle, the agency could be useful as a vehicle for a common policy of the oil-importing countries with respect to OPEC; no such policy has emerged, however.[21]

Alternative Trade Policies

Turning now to the foreign trade regime, we will examine four possibilities: import quotas, a fixed tariff, a variable tariff, and free trade.

Import Quotas. Mandatory import quotas were in force from 1959 to 1973. Licenses to import, known as "tickets," were provided without charge to refiners who could use them or sell them. The government did not collect any revenue; yet consumers had to pay much more than the prevailing world price. Apart from its manifest inequity, which could have been corrected by auctioning the tickets instead of giving them away, this system actually worked against the national security interest it was supposed to serve. It stimulated domestic oil extraction to the point where U.S. reserves were being exhausted prematurely; thus it was correctly accused of "draining America first."

Ostensibly justified by national security, the quota system was actually a shortsighted response to the insistence of domestic producers and refiners on protection from low-cost imports. This does not mean that the national security argument itself is invalid; it means, rather, that the argument should not be invoked unless supported by plausible evidence that national security will in fact be enhanced. The effect of the Mandatory Oil Import Program, in the end, was to expose the United States to political pressure and to exploitation by OPEC. The idea of quotas deserves to be buried once and for all.

Fixed Tariff. A fixed tariff (that is, a tariff at a rate that does not change over time) was belatedly adopted by the United States in 1973. It soon became irrelevant to the alleged needs of domestic producers when OPEC solved the problem of low-cost imports with a vengeance. If it had been adopted earlier, a tariff would have had a more positive effect on national security than the quota system actually in force. Since imports would not have been subject to a ceiling, domestic production would not have expanded as much, and the reserves thus kept in the ground would have been available when they were most needed. The adjustments in the world oil market would have been more gradual. Perhaps OPEC would still have had an opportunity to take control of the world price, but the cartel price would probably have been lower.

Since 1973 circumstances have changed so drastically that the case for a fixed tariff (sometimes euphemistically called an "import fee") has to be made on different grounds. It is not enough to point to the difficulties of the domestic industry, manifested by numerous bankruptcies. The industry's problems are attributable to the abnormally high prices of the early 1980s rather than to current prices which, after correcting for inflation, are still twice as high as they were before the first oil shock. The firms that failed had capital losses, not current losses. Acting on the once widespread conviction that oil prices could only go up, they invested and borrowed too much. They, and the banks that financed them, must now pay the normal penalty for their imprudence. It appears that at present prices the bulk of the industry remains profitable in its current operations, though more write-offs of past unsound investments may be expected.

Given the existence of a foreign cartel, the principal argument in favor of a fixed tariff, advanced by Houthakker in 1976 and by Broadman and Hogan ten years later, is that some of the burden could be shifted to OPEC.[22] The federal government would in effect be capturing part of the cartel's monopoly profits. Put briefly, the argument runs as follows. The imposition of a tariff would raise output and lower consumption in this country, thus reducing the demand for imports. Since the United States accounts for a large fraction of OPEC exports, the cartel would find it optimal to set the world price at a lower level than in the absence of a tariff.[23] OPEC would lose revenue because both its price and its exports would be lower. The United States, by contrast, would gain revenue from the tariff on the remaining imports. Thus there would be a transfer from OPEC to the United States.

The net impact of a tariff on American consumers would probably be negative, however. The transfer from OPEC to the United States could be accomplished only if the domestic price (including the tariff) were higher than it would be without a tariff. In other words, the world price would not fall by the full amount of the duty because the United States is not the only oil importer. Although a more detailed quantitative assessment is necessary, it would seem that this adverse effect will not be fully offset by the reduction of nonoil taxes made possible, at least in principle, by the tariff revenue. The main beneficiaries of a U.S. tariff, oddly enough, would be consumers in oil-importing countries that do not impose a tariff: they would gain from the lower world price. If all oil-importing nations imposed the same tariff, OPEC's market power would be effectively destroyed, but that would require an unprecedented degree of international cooperation.[24]

If consumers do not get the benefit of a tariff, who does? Apart from foreign consumers, the benefits would go to the domestic oil industry. The owners of existing wells, in particular, would have a windfall gain; in due course the higher domestic price would enable them to extract more oil from these wells. In addition, some of the benefits would be invested in exploration and other high-cost investments. For essentially geological reasons, the cost of finding and producing oil in the United States has long been rising relative to the rest of the world. The quota system reinforced this tendency; the first and second oil shocks did so more strongly, and a fixed tariff would add further impetus. At some point we must ask ourselves how high the cost of domestic oil should go.

In this connection it is important to realize that the cartel in its heyday created a net loss to the world economy by inducing importing countries, particularly the United States, to substitute their high-cost oil for OPEC's low-cost oil. As far as the efficient allocation of world resources is concerned, a fixed tariff would make a bad situation even worse by encouraging more such substitution. This is the main reason for surmising that American consumers would be net losers under a fixed tariff.

Variable Tariff. Since the effect of a tariff on the domestic price will be very visible, while the net advantage to consumers is uncertain at best, a fixed tariff is likely to be strongly resisted, especially if it is as high as the $10 per barrel proposed by Broadman and Hogan. From this point of view a variable tariff has stronger claims to consideration. With this device the rate of duty is not constant but set daily at the difference (if positive) between a domestic indicator price and the landed price of imports.[25] The effect is to keep the domestic price at or above the indicator price. The domestic market is then effectively insulated from excess supply in the world market. Like a fixed tariff, a variable tariff generates revenue for the government, but at a lower rate; the effect on consumers is correspondingly smaller.

The desirability of a variable tariff hinges on the level of the indicator price. If this price is high relative to the average world price, the duty will usually be positive, and the variable tariff becomes similar to a fixed tariff. Conversely, if the indicator price is low, the duty will be zero most of the time. Although the effect on consumers will then be small, the variable tariff may still be valuable to domestic producers as a "safety net."

Only as a safety net does the variable tariff merit consideration. As long as OPEC is able to set the world price, the domestic industry hardly needs protection. When the cartel loses control, however, the world price may fall precipitously; thus it went briefly below $7 per barrel in 1986. Indeed OPEC might under certain circumstances drive the world price down deliberately to discipline outside suppliers, just as Saudi Arabia did within OPEC on two or three occasions. If very low prices persisted for some time, sizable parts of the American industry might not survive, many wells would be capped, and exploration would come to a virtual halt. Together these developments would make the country more vulnerable to political pressures and to future exploitation by OPEC. It follows that national security considerations may justify a variable levy with a low indicator price.

The purpose of a variable tariff would not be to guarantee comfortable profits to a majority of domestic producers regardless of the world price, as quotas and fixed tariffs tend to do. On the contrary, fluctuating prices can contribute to the health of any industry by weeding out inefficient suppliers when prices are low and attracting new firms when prices are high. Neither would the purpose be to maintain domestic production at a high rate. What matters for national security is not the actual rate of output but the capacity to produce more when needed. Just as the Strategic Petroleum Reserve provides a short-term defense against supply interruptions, spare producing capacity would provide longer-term security. It would constrain OPEC's power to fix prices and the possible desire of some of its members to use oil as a political weapon.

For many years—since about 1970, to be precise—the United States has had little or no spare capacity. Even the Naval Petroleum Reserves, originally intended as spare capacity, are currently being produced flat out, apparently for shortsighted budgetary reasons. The reestablishment of spare capacity, especially in the private sector, deserves high priority in our energy policy. It would require more emphasis on exploration and less on current production; changes in taxation may be needed to provide the necessary incentives. A variable tariff with a low indicator price would give some insurance to the industry against disastrously low prices while permitting adequate variability in prices.

If the concept of a variable tariff is adopted, what would be the optimal indicator price? A precise answer would call for a detailed cost study of the domestic industry and of regional price variations. In the absence of such a study the figure may be tentatively put in the neighborhood of $10 per barrel, with due allowance for grade and location. If a price below that prevailed for some time, a substantial fraction of the nation's wells would probably be abandoned. At the price of around $19 per barrel prevailing in early 1987, the duty would therefore be zero. A similar degree of protection would have to be extended to refined products to prevent circumvention of the duty on crude when it is in force; there is no apparent reason for additional protection of the refining industry.

Free Trade. To those who rightly believe that free trade is the best general prescription for the public interest and for international harmony, any talk of a tariff, whether fixed or variable, is distasteful. The basis for exempting oil from this general rule has already been stated. The mere existence of a foreign cartel is clearly not a sufficient argument against free trade. Such cartels have existed in other commodities, such as coffee and tin, and the United States has at times found it prudent to cooperate with these cartels instead of opposing them with a tariff. This was not just because in these instances there was no significant domestic industry to protect; American consumers, after all, were being harmed.

The critical difference between oil and the cases just mentioned is that in the latter there was no political danger. The politics, if anything, went the other way: the United States saw tolerance of a cartel as a relatively painless way of promoting good relations with the countries involved. Occasional rhetoric aside, OPEC has never shown any serious interest in cooperation with importing countries; from the first oil shock on, it has acted unilaterally. Strictly speaking, even that attitude is not a sufficient reason for departing from free trade, though it comes close. The decisive reason is the demonstrated willingness of leading members to use exports as a means of exercising political pressure. The national security argument is essentially a political argument. It should be added that a variable tariff with a low indicator price would protect our national security with only minimal interference with free trade.

Suppose now that, ignoring these considerations, we maintain an essentially free trade regime in oil. Could any domestic policy measures improve the situation? An increase in the federal excise tax on gasoline and diesel fuel has sometimes been suggested; various European countries took this step when crude prices declined, thus keeping domestic fuel prices more or less unchanged. No doubt a tax increase would have a depressing effect on fuel consumption, especially in the longer run. To that extent it would lessen our dependence on OPEC, though at considerable cost to consumers.

The question is complicated by the Federal Highway Trust Fund, to which revenues from taxes on highway users are dedicated. Many interstate highways need expensive repairs; if current revenues are not enough to finance them, an increase in user taxes would be entirely appropriate. Except as user taxes, however, excise taxes have little merit from an economic point of view. Relatively cheap transportation is an important contributor to the efficiency of the widely dispersed U.S. economy; it should not be lightly interfered with.

Concluding Remarks

The world price of oil has fluctuated more in the past year than at any time since the 1930s. This is not by itself a reason for alarm: such fluctuations are common and salutary in other commodities, and with the advent of competition, oil has become a commodity. Oil, however, differs from most other commodities in at least two respects: it has important national security aspects, and until this year the market was controlled by a cartel. The analysis of this paper suggests that the present respite from high prices is unlikely to last more than a few years.

Although past policies have sometimes been ill conceived, the government does have a role in this area. The Strategic Petroleum Reserve remains necessary as a first line of defense against supply interruption; it should continue to be filled, preferably with foreign oil. Although a fixed tariff could transfer some of OPEC's monopoly profits to the United States, its distributive and allocative effects make

it undesirable. A variable tariff on oil, by contrast, deserves consideration as a safety net preventing permanent damage to the industry
from very low prices. Oil policy should aim at reestablishing spare
capacity in the domestic industry, thus creating a second line of
defense. These measures could make the United States less dependent on whatever OPEC attempts to do in the future.

Notes

1. By "world price" is generally meant the dollar price for Arab Light crude at
Ras Tanura, the principal export terminal of Saudi Arabia. Prices elsewhere are
mostly higher because of transportation differentials.

2. At current freight rates a world price of $16 is equivalent to about $19 for the
standard grade on the New York futures market.

3. According to 1976 estimates of the Bank for International Settlements. It
should be borne in mind that there is a large statistical discrepancy in global
current-account statistics.

4. The main beneficiaries of this indirect form of financing were the banks.
Furthermore, the absence of alternative uses of the OPEC funds was probably the
main reason why real interest rates in the 1970s were close to zero and indeed
frequently negative.

5. This thesis, according to which the high crude prices of the 1970s were
attributable to a scarcity of resources rather than to OPEC, was recently refuted by
M.A. Adelman, "Scarcity and World Oil Prices," *Review of Economics, and Statistics*
68, pp. 387–97.

6. With a weighted basket of major currencies the increase was much less since
the dollar had declined sharply in the late 1970s.

7. At least not in dollars. The dollar strengthened considerably between 1980
and 1985.

8. Verleger and others have argued that crude prices are determined by product prices, although this does not mean that the cartelization of crude was without
effect. P.K. Verleger, "The Determinants of Official OPEC Crude Prices," *Review of
Economics and Statistics* 64, pp. 177–83.

9. The world includes the Communist countries, which should not be left out
in a global analysis. Since 1974 the U.S.S.R. has been the world's largest oil
producer, with substantial exports to both Western and Eastern Europe. More
recently, China has become a net exporter on a modest scale.

10. Straight lines are used for ease of exposition, not because they are realistic.
Certain details aside, the argument carries over to more general functions. Income
effects are ignored, and the cartel's internal demand is deducted from its output.

11. The particular value of one-half is an artifact of the linearity assumption and
has to be modified for differently shaped demand and supply curves.

12. In May 1986 Vice President Bush suddenly went to the Persian Gulf,
apparently to convey the U.S. oil industry's concern over low prices. Whether a
hint of cooperation by the industry was intended is unclear. When he arrived,
Bush learned of strong domestic opposition to any such plan.

13. Absent special tax provisions there would probably be few stripper wells in
operation. The high-cost output from these wells would hardly be missed, except
perhaps by those who like to think of them as the energy counterpart of the family

farm. As is true in agriculture, the importance of very small operations is political rather than economic; they serve as a pretext for policies that benefit the larger producers.

14. M.A. Adelman, "The Competitive Floor to World Oil Prices," MIT Energy Laboratory, Working Paper no. MIT-EL 86-011WP, 1986.

15. Defined as the expected profit forgone by extracting a barrel from the ground now rather than at some future date.

16. See the working paper by Adelman cited in footnote 14.

17. The number of outstanding commitments to buy or sell; this is the most revealing measure of the importance of a futures market.

18. The absence of really large players is fortunate since futures markets are vulnerable to manipulation. A "corner," in particular, is an attempt to drive up the price by accumulating dominant positions in both the cash and the futures markets. Arab traders took part in the 1979–1980 corner in silver.

19. In the most active of all futures markets, the one in Treasury bonds, contracts for delivery more than two years from the present are traded.

20. The recently revealed U.S. approach to Iran appears to have been a temporary aberration.

21. For a detailed discussion of the IEA, see George Horwich and David Leo Weimer, *Oil Price Shocks, Market Response, and Contingency Planning* (Washington, D.C., 1984).

22. Hendrik S. Houthakker, *The World Price of Oil* (Washington, D.C.: American Enterprise Institute, 1976); and Harry G. Broadman and William W. Hogan, "Oil Tariff Policy in an Uncertain Market," Kennedy School of Government, Harvard University, Discussion Paper E-86-11, 1986.

23. In terms of figure 2, *AA'* would shift to the left and *BB'* to the right.

24. For a quantitative analysis of a tariff imposed jointly by the industrial countries, see Hendrik S. Houthakker and Michael Kennedy, "Long-Range Energy Prospects," *Journal of Energy and Economic Development* 4 (1979).

25. Its prototype is the variable levy on imported farm products, a component of the EEC's agricultural policy. In Europe domestic farm prices are generally well above world prices, but that is not essential to the concept. A variable levy should not be confused with an *ad valorem* tariff, in which the rate of duty is fixed as a percentage of the price.

Part VI

Multinational and
International Investments

Caves
Vernon
Hymer

FOREIGN DIRECT INVESTMENT
AND MARKET PERFORMANCE

Richard E. Caves

The other international force affecting the performance of national markets is the multinational corporation. In this section I consider the sorts of markets in which we can expect the multinational firm to appear, and then outline the probable market behavior of these firms in the context of both national and international markets. This analysis leads to predictions of the effects of the multinational firm on market performance.

Causes of Foreign Direct Investment

In recent years, economists' analysis of the causes of foreign direct investment has moved away from macroeconomic explanations (e.g., national gluts or shortages of entrepreneurship) to sector-specific explanations. Rather than losing generality, this shift in focus has allowed us to explain many phenomena—the large interindustry differences in the importance of direct investment and the significant gross exports of equity capital from many industrial countries—that had previously resisted understanding. We can now explain the occurrence of the multinational firm, starting from a coherent model of profit-maximizing behavior and moving to empirical predictions about its incidence, behavior, and welfare significance.[31]

Briefly, the analysis starts from the proposition that the entrepreneurial unit has a natural national identity. Economically, this means that it automatically comes by a large stock of knowledge about the language, laws, and customs of its native land—intangible capital that is productive in guiding the firm toward profit-maximizing decisions. A firm that invests in a foreign market is at an intrinsic disadvantage, because it must consciously recruit this information (or run the risk associated with action under relative ignorance). On this view, the dice are loaded to some degree against the multinational firm, and its emergence thus demands an explanation.

The explanation for much foreign investment—certainly that in manufacturing industries[32]—lies in the fact that the successful firm

---

[31] For a synthesis with references to earlier contributions, see Caves (1971).

[32] The following discussion concentrates exclusively on what I call "horizontal" direct investment—the firm produces abroad the same general line of goods as at home. An important volume of foreign investment instead involves backward vertical integration, to provide the parent with components or raw materials at minimum cost or risk. The explanation of this sort of direct investment is rather

Reprinted from "International Trade, International Investment, and Imperfect Markets—Special Papers in International Economics No. 11, Nov. 1974," pp. 17–29, with permission of Princeton University Press, Princeton, Copyright 1974.

also gains intangible capital in the form of patents, trademarks, or general knowledge about how to produce and distribute its products. Being intangible, these assets can in some measure be moved from one national market to another, gaining rents in new locations without impairing the stock left in service at the home base. And the advantage to the firm investing abroad can offset the disadvantage noted above—the cost of gathering intangible capital for the foreign subsidiary.[33]

A firm that has acquired such intangible capital chooses among several methods of exploiting it in foreign markets. One is simply to export goods that embody the design, formula, trademark, or reputation that the firm has established. Another is to license producers abroad to employ the firm's technology or replicate its product. The third is to establish a producing subsidiary to exploit these assets directly in the foreign market. The choice among these alternatives will depend on many factors. An explanation of foreign direct investment thus must answer not only the question "Why invest abroad at all?" but also "Why investment, rather than exports or licensing?" The answers to the second question will depend on characteristics specific to the firm and its industry—the realm of industrial organization—and on the nation's factor endowment—the realm of international trade.

Take first the market-specific characteristics. Intangible capital is heterogeneous: knowledge about production processes, knowledge about adapting the firm's basic product to local demand conditions, etc. Certain components of intangible capital are much more suited than others to employment via direct investment—notably, knowledge about how to serve a market. When the product must be adapted to local tastes and conditions and when the existence of nearby production facilities is complementary to servicing the product after sale, or even just to forging a reputation for quality, direct investment tends to be the preferred alternative. In terms of the standard concepts of

---

different from that for horizontal investment. In the case of large natural-resource investments in the industrial countries, it turns on the role of capital costs and the avoidance of uncertainty that would otherwise surround bilateral oligopoly bargaining among firms with high fixed costs and long-lived investments. Vertical integration, including that via direct investment, can have its disfunctional consequences in such situations, but market failures of one kind or another are hard to avoid. See Caves (1971, pp. 10-11, 27) and Caves (1974c). The latter paper develops the industrial-organization framework of direct investment in more detail than the present essay.

[33] The analysis of the role of intangible capital leans heavily on Harry G. Johnson, "The Efficiency and Welfare Implications of the International Corporation," in Kindleberger, ed. (1970, Chap. 2).

market structure, a strong affinity exists between direct investment and *product differentiation*.[34]

Conversely, if the knowledge takes the form of specific production techniques that can be written down and transmitted objectively, licensing may be a prime vehicle. Exporting stands as a contender when the intangible advantage can be embodied in the firm's product only at its primary locus of production, or at least when no special need arises for local adaptation.

Another leading market-specific determinant that favors direct investment is size of the parent firm. Direct investment clearly entails a larger and riskier fixed cost than the alternatives, exporting or licensing, because of the substantial and relatively fixed information and search costs that must precede any actual investment abroad. Licensing entails much lower costs of search and real investment, but it is also a more rough-edged method of extracting quasi-rents. Given the presence of lender's risk or outright imperfections of capital markets, direct investment becomes the province of the large firm with substantial internally generated funds to finance the initial fixed charges. On a probabilistic basis, this requirement of large size for the investing firm implies that foreign investment will occur principally in industries where sellers are few in number.[35] Putting all this together, we expect to find direct investment in manufacturing industries marked by differentiation and fewness of sellers, or *differentiated oligopoly*.

The other characteristics determining direct investment lie in the realm of international trade. One characteristic is evidently the position of the parent's industry in the nation's scale of comparative advan-

[34] In connection with Porter's (1973) research, I noted evidence of an important subdivision of differentiated consumer goods according to the relative monopsony power of the distributive channels and scale economies in nationwide sales promotion. It was suggested that trade is apt to be the more effective international market constraint in the case of specialty and shopping goods. Conversely, the multinational firm should be relatively more important where convenience goods are involved. The economies of scale in nationwide sales promotion require a large-scale market entry if the multinational firm is to make any effective use of its intangible assets, and the uncertainties of international trade probably impel the seller toward local production facilities if high-density distribution activities are to be carried out successfully. Statistical research (Caves, 1974b) does not directly confirm this prediction, but it does show that foreign investment in the two sectors responds to various determinants in ways consistent with Porter's model.

[35] The importance of size of firm as a predictor of direct investment is shown by Horst (1972b). Other connections may exist between concentration and foreign investment. A firm with market power must diversify if it wishes to grow faster than its "base" market; otherwise, its growth entails a struggle for market share. The diversification might take the form of expansion into a foreign market, rather than into other domestic markets.

tage. A favorable position encourages exporting, against the alternatives of direct investment and licensing. Because two-way trade can clearly occur in direct investment as well as in a differentiated industry's flow of merchandise, we can say that an industry that is a net importer on trade account is apt (*ceteris paribus*) to be a net exporter on the balace of international indebtedness. An important corollary is that direct investment, unlike other forms of international capital flow, should be sensitive to the exchange rate (as the link between nations' production-cost levels, and apart from any expectations concerning future exchange rates); a country that devalues can hope for improvement in its balance of payments on direct investment as well as on goods and services.

Another trade-related variable that should influence direct investment is tariffs and transport costs. A finding from many of the surveys of foreign subsidiaries is that the initial investment was often made after the parent firm had established an export trade that was threatened by a higher tariff; with a substantial goodwill asset already created in the market, the parent chose to establish local production facilities rather than abandon its goodwill entirely. Transport costs should affect the choice in similar ways. A firm that makes a product that is costly to ship per unit value and that requires only ubiquitous raw materials will be disposed toward establishing multiple plants close to its customers. In this and other respects, the multinational firm may be viewed simply as a multiplant enterprise that happens to sprawl across national boundaries.[36]

One conclusion evident from this analysis of the interindustry distribution of direct investment is that it goes where trade does not. Not only are exporting and direct investment alternative strategies for the individual firm, but direct investment tends also to occur in differentiated products where international trade may be a relatively ineffective constraint on poor market performance. We return to this proposition after examining the probable effects of the multinational firm on market behavior and performance.

Multinational Firms and Market Behavior

Is the multinational firm a constraint on market distortions, in the same sense that a perfectly elastic world supply of cabbage at 10 cents a pound constrains what the domestic cabbage monopoly can charge?

[36] This and the preceding predictions, save for the influence of tariffs, find strong statistical support in Caves (1974b). On the influence of tariffs, see Horst (1972a). The multiplant hypothesis is developed in Eastman and Stykolt (1967, Chap. 4) and McManus (1972).

It may be, for two reasons. First, multinational firms tend to develop in just those industries where barriers to the entry of new firms tend to be high. The formation of a new subsidiary, at least on a "green field" basis without takeover of a going enterprise or establishment, amounts to entry by an established firm in another (geographical) industry; counting as a specially well-endowed potential entrant, the multinational renders the supply of potential entrants larger and in effect makes the barriers to entry lower than they otherwise would be.[37]

Second, multinational firms actually operating in a given national industry may behave differently from domestic firms holding equivalent shares of the market. These possible differences in conduct are vital to the multinational's effects on market performance, and I shall thus consider them in some detail. A national branch of a multinational firm might behave differently from an equal-sized independent company for three reasons:

1. *Motivation.* I accept the conventional view that, as a first approximation, the maximization of profit can safely be assumed to be the prevailing motivation of the firm, multinational or not. Indeed, the available evidence supports the view that the multinational maximizes profits from its activities as a whole, rather than, say, telling each subsidiary to maximize independently and ignoring the profit interdependences among them (Stevens, 1969). But overall maximization by the multinational can lead its subsidiary to behave differently from an independent firm. The rate of earnings retention is a possible example. A subsidiary might pass up an otherwise profitable local use of funds if the expected yield would be higher elsewhere in the global corporation, whereas a local firm would make the local commitment. Another difference arises because the multinational firm almost automatically spreads its risks, and could therefore behave quite differently in an uncertain situation from an independent having the same risk/return preference function (Shearer, 1964; Dunning and Steuer, 1969; Schwartzman, 1970, p. 205). It is hard to generalize, though, about the consequences of such differences in opportunity costs and allocative choices.

2. *Cognition and information.* Its corporate family relations give the multinational unit access to more information about markets located in other countries—or (what is equivalent in effect) information to which it can attach a higher degree of certainty. This information need not be unavailable or even more costly to the national firm. The point is that at any given time the multinational has this stock in hand; its

---

[37] The reasons why the multinational firm has a potential advantage against each of the conventional barriers to entry are set forth in Caves (1974c).

national rival may or may not. The national firm therefore is probably
more dependent on its home base in the national market, and this difference could color the multinational's view of actions that might increase its market share (and its own profits) at the expense of its rivals'
shares (and total profits). With better information about extranational
alternative uses of its resources and less dependence on the local scene
for organizational survival, it has less to lose from rivalrous market
actions. It could be more disposed than a national enterprise toward
strategies yielding a larger profit but with a larger variance. The multinational unit could also collaborate less closely with its local rivals,
especially in its early years, for the simple reason than its ear is less
attuned to the "focal points" of tacit collusion among its unfamiliar
new neighbors. The young subsidiary, even if formed by the acquisition of a going national firm, stands outside the network of tacit understandings and rules of the game developed by the previous market
occupants, and is more apt to rock the boat. As the subsidiary ages
and loses its parvenu status, however, it tends to play by the rules of
the local game; also, it may tread softly at any time because of its
political vulnerability.[38]

3. *Opportunity set.* Each player in a complex oligopoly game is apt
to hold a somewhat different set of assets and to seek to slant the
game along lines that will make his own asset bundle most productive
of profits. The asset bundle of the multinational unit can differ from
its national rival's in various ways. Its skill in differentiating its product, arguably a precondition for direct investment, inclines it to prefer
nonprice forms of rivalry. Holding other traits of market structure
constant, the presence of subsidiaries thus disposes an industry toward
venting its competitive animal spirits through nonprice rather than
price competition. Another asset that the subsidiary holds is the option
to call on the financial assets of its corporate siblings—the "long purse"
that makes it relatively secure from the predatory conduct of its rivals
and a possible predator itself (Telser, 1966).

What do these behavioral differences mean for the performance of
markets populated by multinational firms? The conclusions evidently
will be ambiguous. Let us see where they fall. Because of the multinational's advantages over new firms, it provides a clear increase in the
supply of potential entrants to the industries in which it operates and
should thus constrain the departure of industry profits from normality
—lowering the "limit price," to use the concepts of industrial organiza-

[38] The range of behavior patterns suggested in this paragraph seems to match
those reported in surveys of subsidiaries' behavior (see Brash, 1966, pp. 182-192;
Stonehill, 1965, pp. 98-99).

tion.[39] Furthermore, the cognitive and information resources of the multinational may dispose it to exhibit less collusive and restrictive conduct in the national market than would a similar domestic firm. There is thus some chance that multinational firms reduce allocative distortions in a certain range of industries. This effect is subject to some offsets, however. The multinational's predisposition toward product rivalry and advertising may cause it to devote excessive resources to these activities. Differentiated varieties of a good originating abroad do offer users genuine welfare-increasing expansions of the choices available to them. But the commitment of resources to sales promotion may count at least in part as a minus, especially when we consider that such nonprice competition feeds back to augment barriers to the entry of new firms and thus raises the long-run potential for market distortions.[40]

The presence of multinational firms may also change an industry's probable quality of performance in two other dimensions—technical efficiency and progressiveness. The multinational probably tends to be a technically efficient firm itself—if only on the assumption that the market tends to deny inefficient firms the chance to go multinational. Furthermore, it enjoys an option for avoiding diseconomies of small scale that may not be open to its domestic rivals: producing components subject to extensive economies of scale at a single world location. However, operating in industries subject to product differentiation, the profit-maximizing multinational need not always build efficient-scale facilities. Where a nation's market for manufactures is relatively small and heavily protected by tariffs (e.g., Canada), multinationals may crowd in with inefficiently small facilities; each firm profits from a small group of loyal customers and none is induced to lower its price-cost margin and expand its scale of operations (English, 1964).

Any favorable rating of the multinational on technical progressiveness probably turns on its role as a conduit for transferring new productive knowledge from one country to another. Does it raise the speed (or lower the cost) of technology transfers, considering the al-

[39] A weak negative relation has been found, among Canadian manufacturing industries, between the profit rate of domestic firms and the share of sales accounted for by foreign subsidiaries. The effect is partly explained, though, by variations in the relative size of the domestic firms; i.e., where their profits are relatively low, it is also because their size is relatively small (see Caves, 1974a).

[40] Another adverse structural feedback could result from the multinational's "long purse." The size of American multinationals serves as reason—or excuse—for horizontal mergers, often government-encouraged, among relatively large European firms. Whether or not the multinational is by nature a predatory species, the fact of this reaction is itself important.

ternative channels through which they can take place? Both the analytical issues and the empirical evidence are complex. My tentative impression from both survey and statistical evidence is that the multinational firm, in some countries and industries, probably does speed the transfer of technology (see Brash, 1966, Chap. 8).[41]

Multinational Firms and International Industries

In considering the effects of international trade on competition, I argued that its salutary influence is limited by any oligopolistic interdependence that spreads across national boundaries. The national boundary, however, was found to be a fairly effective insulator against international collusion. But the multinational firm may promote international collusion. It extends the tendrils of ownership from one national market to another. Clearly, corporate siblings are not likely to compete with each other. Furthermore, the multinational could serve as a vehicle for extending oligopoly behavior across national boundaries.

Consider an international industry populated by a number of national and multinational firms, the multinationals based in diverse parent countries. What patterns of oligopolistic interdependence might arise within and among the various national markets? There are two limiting cases:

1. Multinational status (parent or subsidiary) makes no difference in the patterns of conduct adopted by firms in a national market. In this case, the member units of a multinational firm serve as independent profit centers with full autonomy over national price and product decisions. Any cross-national links in market conduct would be due to factors other than ownership status.

2. Multinational enterprises recognize their interdependence comprehensively wherever concentration is high enough and their perceptions sharp enough to permit it. That is to say, firm A sets its actions in market X taking account of B's expected reactions not only in X but also in any other market Y where they both operate. A expects B to react wherever B's interests are best served by so doing.

Between these extremes of cross-national independence and full cross-national interdependence, a variety of patterns could permit dependence across some boundaries but also maintain cordons along others. National origin might tell; firms domiciled in country X might recognize their interdependence in the X market and in host countries $Y, Z, \ldots$, but firms domiciled in X and Y might not perceive their in-

[41] For statistical evidence of the effects of subsidiaries on productivity in competing home-owned firms in Australia, see Caves (1974a).

terdependence comprehensively. Interdependence might be recognized among units (parents or subsidiaries) producing in the largest single national market (as a "home base") and also with parallel operations in other national markets. Interdependence might run outward from a national market where law and custom smile most kindly on overt collusion.

If we try coupling these patterns of possible interdependence with the possible behavior patterns of multinational units outlined above, the taxonomy quickly overtaxes patience. Let us concentrate on one facet of behavior, the decision to establish a subsidiary in a national market. Whatever the international interdependence among firms, the formation of a new subsidiary is clearly a rivalrous or independent move. Even if the parent was previously exporting to the market, local production facilities make it a more effective rival and a greater threat to other sellers. International collusive arrangements of the "sphere of influence" sort should entail nonaggression pacts between firms to keep subsidiaries out of each other's territory. On the other hand, an obvious form of retaliation when A founds a subsidiary in B's home base is for B to invest in A's. Firms domiciled in the same national market might well tend to follow the leader in starting subsidiaries. Assume that A and B both are domiciled in X and have been exporting to Y. When A starts a subsidiary in Y, not only are B's exports to that market threatened, but also it is possible that A's experience with the subsidiary will yield feedback that makes A a more formidable competitor back in X.[42]

Indeed, the empirical evidence does document a good deal of this parallel and reactive behavior in founding subsidiaries. The entry of foreign firms into the U.S. market has sometimes followed on the establishment of U.S. subsidiaries abroad—and the foreign parents' discovery that they could compete with the U.S. giants (Daniels, 1971, p. 47). American industries have shown a strong tendency to parallel behavior in starting subsidiaries in foreign countries. Knickerbocker (1973), studying the dates when subsidiaries were established by U.S. manufacturing companies during the years 1948-1967, found that they were bunched in individual countries more than one would expect on a chance basis (note that scale economies should cut against the simultaneous start-up of new facilities). Furthermore, the tendency to tight parallel action was stronger for firms not highly diversified in the U.S. market and thus exposed to greater risks if rivals should successfully steal a march via foreign investment.

[42] Evidence suggests that this feedback in fact occurs in a majority of cases (see Reddaway *et al.*, 1968, pp. 322-324).

The industry studies are even more reticent on the role of foreign investment than they are on the role of international trade. There is some indication that, while multinational firms have been effective in promoting product rivalry and innovation, they have also bestirred defensive mergers among national firms.[43] Whether these mergers weigh more heavily as a step toward increased technical efficiency or as a sinister move toward a higher level of oligopolistic collusion is, alas, unknown.

IV. SUMMARY: INTERNATIONAL FORCES AND MARKET PERFORMANCE

I have suggested that competitive forces in the international economy complement one another in limiting the distortions that can occur in national markets. Whatever an industry's structural traits, we can pick out some international force as the most likely potential constraint on departures from a reasonable competitive outcome. (One of Panglossier disposition than mine might say that some international force will always ensure competitive performance.) This knowledge of the most probable source of market discipline is valuable for purposes of both research and policy.

Consider how the pieces fit together. Under certain assumptions, the effects of foreign trade via import competition and export opportunities are symmetrical in limiting departures from competitive outcomes. If they are, an industry will tend to face one constraint or another—depending on its comparative-advantage position. This proposition is sharply limited, however, because the disciplining force of export opportunities can easily evaporate when tariffs are present and dumping possible.

The disciplining force of trade flows is probably less when product differentiation is present, but in just those circumstances the multinational firm becomes a more prominent actor. Furthermore, because the firm itself makes a choice between direct investment and export, we conclude that the industry with a comparative disadvantage will face less threat from the entry of multinational firms but more from imports, and vice versa for the industry with a comparative advantage. Both natural and artificial trade impediments blunt the disciplining force of trade, but they may encourage that of foreign investment. Industries producing nontraded goods and services, sheltered from direct

[43] Information on the automobile industry is at least suggestive (see Silberston, 1958, p. 33; Ensor, 1971; Sundelson, "U.S. Automotive Investments Abroad," in Kindleberger, ed., 1970, Chap. 10).

foreign competition, thus are also potential prey to foreign subsidiaries. An important qualification to this universal harmony is that the multinational firm is a mixed blessing as a market force. It is well equipped for scaling barriers to entry and may be less disposed toward oligopoly consensus in a national market than a domestic firm; also, it may speed the transfer of technology and attain (and encourage in its rivals) higher levels of technical efficiency. But it can slant market behavior to an undesirable degree toward advertising and product competition, and it may promote increased concentration and collusion running across national boundaries.

Let me close with some suggestions for economic research and policy. Empirical research on international market forces has at last become active in the field of industrial organization, as the statistical inputs have become available—and not just for the United States. We have some relatively strong conclusions about the role of trade. But even with the copious survey evidence on the multinational firm, it has not been examined very closely as a market force. This is despite the experiments that Nature and statesmen have obligingly performed in recent years—greatly increasing the multilateral penetration of foreign investment, removing tariff barriers within the European Economic Community, etc. The opportunities for research seem great, and the appropriate direction clear. In the international-trade camp, the research performance has been far less satisfactory. Lulled by the mathematical convenience of purely competitive conditions, theoretical research has paid little attention to the causes or consequences of imperfect competition, save for the obligatory bow to optimal tariffs and taxes on capital. And empirical research—lavished on a few safe topics such as the Leontief Paradox and financial capital flows—has elsewhere either been nonexistent or followed its nose with but slender guidance from economic theory. One hopes for both a redirection of research and a more fruitful interchange between theory and empirical investigation.

It is clear that many issues of antitrust and commercial policy turn closely on the results of testing the hypotheses discussed above. Paradoxically, the relation between these branches of policy, once a staple of American political economy ("the tariff is the mother of trusts"), has nearly disappeared from sight. One finds, instead, such spectacles as the U.S. government, bent on restricting certain imports at minimum annoyance to foreign nations, encouraging the cartelization of foreign exporters to reduce competition in U.S. markets! If we can avert our gaze from such squalor, more subtle issues remain to be dealt with. International market links—trade and the multinational firm—logically preclude our dealing with issues of competition on the basis of one-national-market-at-a-time. Policies toward competition, trade, and foreign investment in one country spill over and affect market performance in its trading partners. Issues of policy assignment and interdependence, familiar in international macroeconomics, are clearly present at a microeconomic level as well. One hopes that the further development of theory and empirical research in this area will lead to their due recognition.

REFERENCES

Adams, William James, "Corporate Power and Profitability in the North Atlantic Community," unpublished Ph.D. dissertation, Harvard University, 1973.

Adler, Michael, "Specialization in the European Coal and Steel Community," *Journal of Common Market Studies*, 8 (March 1970), pp. 175-191.

Bain, Joe S., *Industrial Organization*, 2d ed., New York, Wiley, 1968.

Balassa, Bela "Tariff Reduction and Trade in Manufactures among the Industrial Countries," *American Economic Review*, 56 (June 1966), pp. 466-473.

Barker, H. P., "Home and Export Trade," *Economic Journal*, 61 (June 1951), pp. 276-278.

Basevi, Giorgio, "Domestic Demand and Ability to Export," *Journal of Political Economy*, 78 (March/April 1970), pp. 330-337.

Brash, Donald T., *American Investment in Australian Industry*, Cambridge, Mass., Harvard University Press, 1966.

Bright, A. A., Jr., *The Electric-Lamp Industry: Technological Change and Economic Development from 1800 to 1947*, New York, Macmillan, 1949.

Burenstam Linder, S., *An Essay on Trade and Transformation*, Stockholm, Almqvist & Wiksell, 1961.

Caves, Richard E., "International Corporations: The Industrial Economics of Foreign Investment," *Economica*, 38 (February 1971), pp. 1-27.

———, "Multinational Firms, Competition, and Productivity in Host-Country Industries," *Economica*, 41 (May 1974a), pp. 176-193.

———, "Causes of Direct Investment: Foreign Firms' Shares in Canadian and United Kingdom Manufacturing Industries," *Review of Economics and Statistics*, 56 (August 1974b), pp. 279-293.

———, "Industrial Organization," in John H. Dunning, ed., *The Multinational Enterprise and Economic Analysis*, London, George Allen & Unwin, 1974c, pp. 115-146.

Caves, Richard E., and Ronald W. Jones, *World Trade and Payments*, Boston, Little, Brown, 1973.

Caves, "Foreign Direct Investment and Market Performance"

UPDATE

The multinational enterprise has gone through a curious cycle of normative evaluation over the past 15-20 years. At the outset, it was widely attacked as a perpetrator of monopoly, a depressant of the demand for labor (and enemy of trade unions), and a "tax cheat" who shuffled assets and accounts internationally in order to maneuver its profits away from the tax collector. For whatever reason, these charges came to be heard less and less frequently, until a discussion of multinationals and market performance today stirs little excitement. Do we owe this change to swings of fashion, or did policies toward multinationals in fact accomplish their perceived goal of reform? Some of each, I think. While most countries perceived the performance of their economies to deteriorate over the decade from the early 1970s, multinational firms obviously had little to do with the main sources of difficulty. Furthermore, the countries with the strongest perceived interests in taxing or restricting the multinationals simply did so-- consider the success with which raw-material exporting countries have learned to tax away any natural-resource rents that might otherwise fall into multinationals' hands. As a result, broadly speaking, the shares of multinational firms in economic activity peaked in most countries and lines of activity and receded in some. (An excellent survey of policy issues from a United States perspective was provided by Bergsten, Horst, and Moran [1978]; Caves [1982] surveyed recent economic analysis of the multinational.)

The microeconomic view of the multinational firm set forth in this paper has retained its acceptance and continues to dominate research and thinking on the multinational company. Indeed, the main development on the conceptual front has been some incorporation of the intangible-assets and

transaction-cost approach to the multinational firm into general-equilibrium
models of international trade and production (such as Helpman, 1984). The
most dramatic results from extending the analysis of multinational firms in
general equilibrium has come in the realm of normative analysis and policy-
making. Multinational firms that have invested in a country exert claims on
the income stream imputed to capital. Suppose that the country then applies
some policy such as an "optimal tariff" on imports that are capital-
intensive (i.e. the country is capital-scarce in its international
specialization). Whereas the tariff's effect of redistributing income from
labor to capital would ordinarily not be considered to impair the usefulness
of the optimal tariff, it can actually be welfare-reducing when the transfer
flows partly to foreign capitalists (Bhagwati and Brecher, 1980). Clearly,
this example points to a substantial class of policies that have incidental
effects on income distribution.

The positive analysis of foreign investment and market competition has
made steady if incremental progress. Just as the slow growth of the United
States has lowered its profile among the industrial countries, so have U.S.-
based multinationals become less evidently dominant in international
markets. Indeed, investment in the United States by foreign multinationals
has expanded rapidly, resting on the same behavioral forces that earlier
were found to propel U.S. investment abroad (Caves, 1986). Foreign
investment emanating from Japan has grown greatly in importance; it also
seems driven by the same forces as other foreign investment, although it has
underlined the importance of foreign investment as an avenue for acquiring
as well as using technology (Tsurumi, 1976).

REFERENCES

Bhagwati, J. N., and R. A. Brecher, 1980. "National Welfare in an Open

Economy in the Presence of Foreign-owned Factors of Production,"
Journal of International Economics 10:103-15.

Caves, R. E. (1982). Multinational Enterprise and Economic Analysis.
Cambridge: Cambridge University Press.

Caves, R. E., and S. K. Mehra (1986). "Entry of Foreign Multinationals into
U.S. Manufacturing Industries," Competition in Global Industries, ed.
Michael E. Porter. Boston: Harvard Business School Press, pp. 449-81.

Helpman, E., 1984. "A Simple Theory of International Trade with Multinational
Corporations," Journal of Political Economy 92:451-71.

Tsurumi, Y., 1976. The Japanese Are Coming: A Multinational Spread of
Japanese Firms. Cambridge: Ballinger.

INTERNATIONAL INVESTMENT AND
INTERNATIONAL TRADE
IN THE
PRODUCT CYCLE *

RAYMOND VERNON

Anyone who has sought to understand the shifts in international trade and international investment over the past twenty years has chafed from time to time under an acute sense of the inadequacy of the available analytical tools. While the comparative cost concept and other basic concepts have rarely failed to provide some help, they have usually carried the analyst only a very little way toward adequate understanding. For the most part, it has been necessary to formulate new concepts in order to explore issues such as the strengths and limitations of import substitution in the development process, the implications of common market arrangements for trade and investment, the underlying reasons for the Leontief paradox, and other critical issues of the day.

As theorists have groped for some more efficient tools, there has been a flowering in international trade and capital theory. But the very proliferation of theory has increased the urgency of the search for unifying concepts. It is doubtful that we shall find many propositions that can match the simplicity, power, and universality of application of the theory of comparative advantage and the international equilibrating mechanism; but unless the search for better tools goes on, the usefulness of economic theory for the solution of problems in international trade and capital movements will probably decline.

The present paper deals with one promising line of generalization and synthesis which seems to me to have been somewhat neglected by the main stream of trade theory. It puts less emphasis upon comparative cost doctrine and more upon the timing of innovation, the effects of scale economies, and the roles of ignorance and uncertainty in influencing trade patterns. It is an approach

* The preparation of this article was financed in part by a grant from the Ford Foundation to the Harvard Business School to support a study of the implications of United States foreign direct investment. This paper is a by-product of the hypothesis-building stage of the study.

with respectable sponsorship, deriving bits and pieces of its inspiration from the writings of such persons as Williams, Kindleberger, MacDougall, Hoffmeyer, and Burenstam-Linder.[1]

Emphases of this sort seem first to have appeared when economists were searching for an explanation of what looked like a persistent, structural shortage of dollars in the world. When the shortage proved ephemeral in the late 1950's, many of the ideas which the shortage had stimulated were tossed overboard as prima facie wrong.[2] Nevertheless, one cannot be exposed to the main currents of international trade for very long without feeling that any theory which neglected the roles of innovation, scale, ignorance and uncertainty would be incomplete.

LOCATION OF NEW PRODUCTS

We begin with the assumption that the enterprises in any one of the advanced countries of the world are not distinguishably different from those in any other advanced country, in terms of their access to scientific knowledge and their capacity to comprehend scientific principles.[3] All of them, we may safely assume, can secure access to the knowledge that exists in the physical, chemical and biological sciences. These sciences at times may be difficult, but they are rarely occult.

It is a mistake to assume, however, that equal access to scientific principles in all the advanced countries means equal probability of the application of these principles in the generation of new products. There is ordinarily a large gap between the knowledge of a scientific principle and the embodiment of the principle in

---

1. J. H. Williams, "The Theory of International Trade Reconsidered," reprinted as Chap. 2 in his *Postwar Monetary Plans and Other Essays* (Oxford: Basil Blackwell, 1947); C. P. Kindleberger, *The Dollar Shortage* (New York: Wiley, 1950); Erik Hoffmeyer, *Dollar Shortage* (Amsterdam: North-Holland, 1958); Sir Donald MacDougall, *The World Dollar Problem* (London: Macmillan, 1957); Staffan Burenstam-Linder, *An Essay on Trade and Transformation* (Uppsala: Almqvist & Wicksells, 1961).

2. The best summary of the state of trade theory that has come to my attention in recent years is J. Bhagwati, "The Pure Theory of International Trade," *Economic Journal*, LXXIV (Mar. 1964), 1–84. Bhagwati refers obliquely to some of the theories which concern us here; but they receive much less attention than I think they deserve.

3. Some of the account that follows will be found in greatly truncated form in my "The Trade Expansion Act in Perspective," in *Emerging Concepts in Marketing*, Proceedings of the American Marketing Association, December 1962, pp. 384–89. The elaboration here owes a good deal to the perceptive work of Se'ev Hirsch, summarized in his unpublished doctoral thesis, "Location of Industry and International Competitiveness," Harvard Business School, 1965.

a marketable product. An entrepreneur usually has to intervene to accept the risks involved in testing whether the gap can be bridged.

If all entrepreneurs, wherever located, could be presumed to be equally conscious of and equally responsive to all entrepreneurial opportunities, wherever they arose, the classical view of the dominant role of price in resource allocation might be highly relevant. There is good reason to believe, however, that the entrepreneur's consciousness of and responsiveness to opportunity are a function of ease of communication; and further, that ease of communication is a function of geographical proximity.[4] Accordingly, we abandon the powerful simplifying notion that knowledge is a universal free good, and introduce it as an independent variable in the decision to trade or to invest.

The fact that the search for knowledge is an inseparable part of the decision-making process and that relative ease of access to knowledge can profoundly affect the outcome are now reasonably well established through empirical research.[5] One implication of that fact is that producers in any market are more likely to be aware of the possibility of introducing new products in that market than producers located elsewhere would be.

The United States market offers certain unique kinds of opportunities to those who are in a position to be aware of them.

First, the United States market consists of consumers with an average income which is higher (except for a few anomalies like Kuwait) than that in any other national market — twice as high as that of Western Europe, for instance. Wherever there was a chance to offer a new product responsive to wants at high levels of income, this chance would presumably first be apparent to someone in a position to observe the United States market.

Second, the United States market is characterized by high unit labor costs and relatively unrationed capital compared with practically all other markets. This is a fact which conditions the demand for both consumer goods and industrial products. In the case of consumer goods, for instance, the high cost of laundresses contributes to the origins of the drip-dry shirt and the home washing machine. In the case of industrial goods, high labor cost leads to the early

4. Note C. P. Kindleberger's reference to the "horizon" of the decision-maker, and the view that he can only be rational within that horizon; see his *Foreign Trade and The National Economy* (New Haven: Yale University Press, 1962), p. 15 *passim*.

5. See, for instance, Richard M. Cyert and James G. March, *A Behavioral Theory of the Firm* (Englewood Cliffs, N.J.: Prentice-Hall, 1963), esp. Chap. 6; and Yair Aharoni, *The Foreign Investment Decision Process*, to be published by the Division of Research of the Harvard Business School, 1966.

development and use of the conveyor belt, the fork-lift truck and the automatic control system. It seems to follow that wherever there was a chance successfully to sell a new product responsive to the need to conserve labor, this chance would be apparent first to those in a position to observe the United States market.

Assume, then, that entrepreneurs in the United States are first aware of opportunities to satisfy new wants associated with high income levels or high unit labor costs. Assume further that the evidence of an unfilled need and the hope of some kind of monopoly windfall for the early starter both are sufficiently strong to justify the initial investment that is usually involved in converting an abstract idea into a marketable product. Here we have a reason for expecting a consistently higher rate of expenditure on product development to be undertaken by United States producers than by producers in other countries, at least in lines which promise to substitute capital for labor or which promise to satisfy high-income wants. Therefore, if United States firms spend more than their foreign counterparts on new product development (often misleadingly labeled "research"), this may be due not to some obscure sociological drive for innovation but to more effective communication between the potential market and the potential supplier of the market. This sort of explanation is consistent with the pioneer appearance in the United States (conflicting claims of the Soviet Union notwithstanding) of the sewing machine, the typewriter, the tractor, etc.

At this point in the exposition, it is important once more to emphasize that the discussion so far relates only to innovation in certain kinds of products, namely to those associated with high income and those which substitute capital for labor. Our hypothesis says nothing about industrial innovation in general; this is a larger subject than we have tackled here. There are very few countries that have failed to introduce at least a few products; and there are some, such as Germany and Japan, which have been responsible for a considerable number of such introductions. Germany's outstanding successes in the development and use of plastics may have been due, for instance, to a traditional concern with her lack of a raw materials base, and a recognition that a market might exist in Germany for synthetic substitutes.[6]

6. See two excellent studies: C. Freeman, "The Plastics Industry: A Comparative Study of Research and Innovation," in *National Institute Economic Review*, No. 26 (Nov. 1963), p. 22 *et seq.*; G. C. Hufbauer, *Synthetic Materials and the Theory of International Trade* (London: Gerald Duckworth, 1965). A number of links in the Hufbauer arguments are remarkably similar to

Our hypothesis asserts that United States producers are likely to be the first to spy an opportunity for high-income or labor-saving new products.[7] But it goes on to assert that the first producing facilities for such products will be located in the United States. This is not a self-evident proposition. Under the calculus of least cost, production need not automatically take place at a location close to the market, unless the product can be produced and delivered from that location at lowest cost. Besides, now that most major United States companies control facilities situated in one or more locations outside of the United States, the possibility of considering a non-United States location is even more plausible than it might once have been.

Of course, if prospective producers were to make their locational choices on the basis of least-cost considerations, the United States would not always be ruled out. The costs of international transport and United States import duties, for instance, might be so high as to argue for such a location. My guess is, however, that the early producers of a new product intended for the United States market are attracted to a United States location by forces which are far stronger than relative factor-cost and transport considerations. For the reasoning on this point, one has to take a long detour away from comparative cost analysis into areas which fall under the rubrics of communication and external economies.

By now, a considerable amount of empirical work has been done on the factors affecting the location of industry.[8] Many of these studies try to explain observed locational patterns in conventional cost-minimizing terms, by implicit or explicit reference to labor cost and transportation cost. But some explicitly introduce problems of communication and external economies as powerful locational forces. These factors were given special emphasis in the analyses which were a part of the New York Metropolitan Region Study of the 1950's. At the risk of oversimplifying, I shall try to summarize what these studies suggested.[9]

some in this paper; but he was not aware of my writings nor I of his until after both had been completed.

7. There is a kind of first-cousin relationship between this simple notion and the "entrained want" concept defined by H. G. Barnett in *Innovation: The Basis of Cultural Change* (New York: McGraw-Hill, 1953) p. 148. Albert O. Hirschman, *The Strategy of Economic Development* (New Haven: Yale University Press, 1958), p. 68, also finds the concept helpful in his effort to explain certain aspects of economic development.

8. For a summary of such work, together with a useful bibliography, see John Meyer, "Regional Economics: A Survey," in the *American Economic Review*, LIII (Mar. 1963), 19–54.

9. The points that follow are dealt with at length in the following publications: Raymond Vernon, *Metropolis, 1985* (Cambridge: Harvard Uni-

In the early stages of introduction of a new product, producers were usually confronted with a number of critical, albeit transitory, conditions. For one thing, the product itself may be quite unstandardized for a time; its inputs, its processing, and its final specifications may cover a wide range. Contrast the great variety of automobiles produced and marketed before 1910 with the thoroughly standardized product of the 1930's, or the variegated radio designs of the 1920's with the uniform models of the 1930's. The unstandardized nature of the design at this early stage carries with it a number of locational implications.

First, producers at this stage are particularly concerned with the degree of freedom they have in changing their inputs. Of course, the cost of the inputs is also relevant. But as long as the nature of these inputs cannot be fixed in advance with assurance, the calculation of cost must take into account the general need for flexibility in any locational choice.[1]

Second, the price elasticity of demand for the output of individual firms is comparatively low. This follows from the high degree of production differentiation, or the existence of monopoly in the early stages.[2] One result is, of course, that small cost differences count less in the calculations of the entrepreneur than they are likely to count later on.

Third, the need for swift and effective communication on the part of the producer with customers, suppliers, and even competitors is especially high at this stage. This is a corollary of the fact that a considerable amount of uncertainty remains regarding the ultimate dimensions of the market, the efforts of rivals to preempt that market, the specifications of the inputs needed for production, and the specifications of the products likely to be most successful in the effort.

All of these considerations tend to argue for a location in which communication between the market and the executives directly concerned with the new product is swift and easy, and in which a wide

versity Press, 1960), pp. 38–85; Max Hall (ed.), *Made in New York* (Cambridge: Harvard University Press, 1959), pp. 3–18, 19 *passim*; Robert M. Lichtenberg, *One-Tenth of a Nation* (Cambridge: Harvard University Press, 1960), pp. 31–70.

1. This is, of course, a familiar point elaborated in George F. Stigler, "Production and Distribution in the Short Run," *Journal of Political Economy*, XLVII (June 1939), 305, *et seq.*

2. Hufbauer, *op. cit.*, suggests that the low price elasticity of demand in the first stage may be due simply to the fact that the first market may be a "captive market" unresponsive to price changes; but that later, in order to expand the use of the new product, other markets may be brought in which are more price responsive.

variety of potential types of input that might be needed by the production unit are easily come by. In brief, the producer who sees a market for some new product in the United States may be led to select a United States location for production on the basis of national locational considerations which extend well beyond simple factor cost analysis plus transport considerations.

THE MATURING PRODUCT [3]

As the demand for a product expands, a certain degree of standardization usually takes place. This is not to say that efforts at product differentiation come to an end. On the contrary; such efforts may even intensify, as competitors try to avoid the full brunt of price competition. Moreover, variety may appear as a result of specialization. Radios, for instance, ultimately acquired such specialized forms as clock radios, automobile radios, portable radios, and so on. Nevertheless, though the subcategories may multiply and the efforts at product differentiation increase, a growing acceptance of certain general standards seems to be typical.

Once again, the change has locational implications. First of all, the need for flexibility declines. A commitment to some set of product standards opens up technical possibilities for achieving economies of scale through mass output, and encourages long-term commitments to some given process and some fixed set of facilities. Second, concern about production cost begins to take the place of concern about product characteristics. Even if increased price competition is not yet present, the reduction of the uncertainties surrounding the operation enhances the usefulness of cost projections and increases the attention devoted to cost.

The empirical studies to which I referred earlier suggest that, at this stage in an industry's development, there is likely to be considerable shift in the location of production facilities at least as far as internal United States locations are concerned. The empirical materials on international locational shifts simply have not yet been analyzed sufficiently to tell us very much. A little speculation, however, indicates some hypotheses worth testing.

Picture an industry engaged in the manufacture of the high-income or labor-saving products that are the focus of our discussion. Assume that the industry has begun to settle down in the United States to some degree of large-scale production. Although the first

3. Both Hirsch, *op. cit.*, and Freeman, *op. cit.*, make use of a three-stage product classification of the sort used here.

mass market may be located in the United States, some demand for the product begins almost at once to appear elsewhere. For instance, although heavy fork-lift trucks in general may have a comparatively small market in Spain because of the relative cheapness of unskilled labor in that country, some limited demand for the product will appear there almost as soon as the existence of the product is known.

If the product has a high income elasticity of demand or if it is a satisfactory substitute for high-cost labor, the demand in time will begin to grow quite rapidly in relatively advanced countries such as those of Western Europe. Once the market expands in such an advanced country, entrepreneurs will begin to ask themselves whether the time has come to take the risk of setting up a local producing facility.[4]

How long does it take to reach this stage? An adequate answer must surely be a complex one. Producers located in the United States, weighing the wisdom of setting up a new production facility in the importing country, will feel obliged to balance a number of complex considerations. As long as the marginal production cost plus the transport cost of the goods exported from the United States is lower than the average cost of prospective production in the market of import, United States producers will presumably prefer to avoid an investment. But that calculation depends on the producer's ability to project the cost of production in a market in which factor costs and the appropriate technology differ from those at home.

Now and again, the locational force which determined some particular overseas investment is so simple and so powerful that one has little difficulty in identifying it. Otis Elevator's early proliferation of production facilities abroad was quite patently a function of the high cost of shipping assembled elevator cabins to distant locations and the limited scale advantages involved in manufacturing elevator cabins at a single location.[5] Singer's decision to invest in Scotland as early as 1867 was also based on considerations of a sort sympathetic with our hypothesis.[6] It is not unlikely that the

---

4. M. V. Posner, "International Trade and Technical Change," *Oxford Economic Papers*, Vol. 13 (Oct. 1961), p. 323, *et seq.* presents a stimulating model purporting to explain such familiar trade phenomena as the exchange of machine tools between the United Kingdom and Germany. In the process he offers some particularly helpful notions concerning the size of the "imitation lag" in the responses of competing nations.

5. Dudley M. Phelps, *Migration of Industry to South America* (New York: McGraw-Hill, 1963), p. 4.

6. John H. Dunning, *American Investment in British Manufacturing Industry* (London: George Allen & Unwin, 1958), p. 18. The Dunning book

overseas demand for its highly standardized product was already sufficiently large at that time to exhaust the obvious scale advantages of manufacturing in a single location, especially if that location was one of high labor cost.

In an area as complex and "imperfect" as international trade and investment, however, one ought not anticipate that any hypothesis will have more than a limited explanatory power. United States airplane manufacturers surely respond to many "noneconomic" locational forces, such as the desire to play safe in problems of military security. Producers in the United States who have a protected patent position overseas presumably take that fact into account in deciding whether or when to produce abroad. And other producers often are motivated by considerations too complex to reconstruct readily, such as the fortuitous timing of a threat of new competition in the country of import, the level of tariff protection anticipated for the future, the political situation in the country of prospective investment and so on.

We arrive, then, at the stage at which United States producers have come around to the establishment of production units in the advanced countries. Now a new group of forces are set in train. In an idealized form, Figure I suggests what may be anticipated next.

As far as individual United States producers are concerned, the local markets thenceforth will be filled from local production units set up abroad. Once these facilities are in operation, however, more ambitious possibilities for their use may be suggested. When comparing a United States producing facility and a facility in another advanced country, the obvious production-cost differences between the rival producing areas are usually differences due to scale and differences due to labor costs. If the producer is an international firm with producing locations in several countries, its costs of financing capital at the different locations may not be sufficiently different to matter very much. If economies of scale are being fully exploited, the principal differences between any two locations are likely to be labor costs.[7] Accordingly, it may prove wise for the international firm to begin servicing third-country markets from the new location. And if labor cost differences are large enough to offset transport

is filled with observations that lend casual support to the main hypotheses of this paper.

7. Note the interesting finding of Mordecai Kreinin in his "The Leontief Scarce-Factor Paradox," *The American Economic Review*, LV (Mar. 1965), 131–39. Kreinin finds that the higher cost of labor in the United States is not explained by a higher rate of labor productivity in this country.

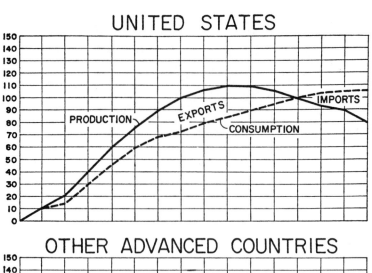

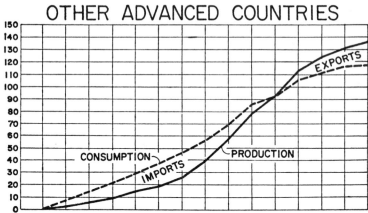

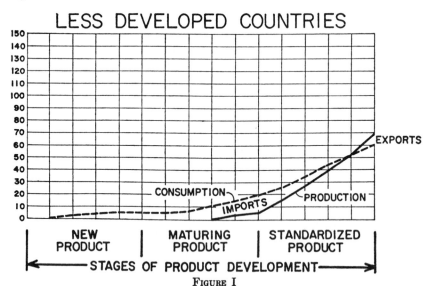

FIGURE I

costs, then exports back to the United States may become a possibility as well.

Any hypotheses based on the assumption that the United States entrepreneur will react rationally when offered the possibility of a lower-cost location abroad is, of course, somewhat suspect. The decision-making sequence that is used in connection with international investments, according to various empirical studies, is not a model of the rational process.[8] But there is one theme that emerges again and again in such studies. Any threat to the established position of an enterprise is a powerful galvanizing force to action; in fact, if I interpret the empirical work correctly, threat in general is a more reliable stimulus to action than opportunity is likely to be.

In the international investment field, threats appear in various forms once a large-scale export business in manufactured products has developed. Local entrepreneurs located in the countries which are the targets of these exports grow restive at the opportunities they are missing. Local governments concerned with generating employment or promoting growth or balancing their trade accounts begin thinking of ways and means to replace the imports. An international investment by the exporter, therefore, becomes a prudent means of forestalling the loss of a market. In this case, the yield on the investment is seen largely as the avoidance of a loss of income to the system.

The notion that a threat to the status quo is a powerful galvanizing force for international investment also seems to explain what happens after the initial investment. Once such an investment is made by a United States producer, other major producers in the United States sometimes see it as a threat to the status quo. They see themselves as losing position relative to the investing company, with vague intimations of further losses to come. Their "share of the market" is imperiled, viewing "share of the market" in global terms. At the same time, their ability to estimate the production-cost structure of their competitors, operating far away in an unfamiliar foreign area, is impaired; this is a particularly unsettling state because it conjures up the possibility of a return flow of products to the United States and a new source of price competition, based on cost differences of unknown magnitude. The uncertainty can be reduced by emulating the pathfinding investor and by investing in the same area; this may not be an optimizing investment

8. Aharoni, *op. cit.*, provides an excellent summary and exhaustive bibliography of the evidence on this point.

pattern and it may be costly, but it is least disturbing to the status quo.

Pieces of this hypothetical pattern are subject to empirical tests of a sort. So far, at any rate, the empirical tests have been reassuring. The office machinery industry, for instance, has seen repeatedly the phenomenon of the introduction of a new product in the United States, followed by United States exports,[9] followed still later by United States imports. (We have still to test whether the timing of the commencement of overseas production by United States subsidiaries fits into the expected pattern.) In the electrical and electronic products industry, those elements in the pattern which can be measured show up nicely.[1] A broader effort is now under way to test the United States trade patterns of a group of products with high income elasticities; and, here too, the preliminary results are encouraging.[2] On a much more general basis, it is reassuring for our hypotheses to observe that the foreign manufacturing subsidiaries of United States firms have been increasing their exports to third countries.

It will have occurred to the reader by now that the pattern envisaged here also may shed some light on the Leontief paradox.[3] Leontief, it will be recalled, seemed to confound comparative cost theory by establishing the fact that the ratio of capital to labor in United States exports was lower, not higher, than the like ratio in the United States production which had been displaced by competitive imports. The hypothesis suggested in this paper would have the United States exporting high-income and labor-saving products in the early stages of their existence, and importing them later on.[4] In the early stages, the value-added contribution of industries engaged in producing these items probably contains an

9. Reported in U.S. Senate, Interstate and Foreign Commerce Committee, *Hearings on Foreign Commerce*, 1960, pp. 130–39.

1. See Hirsch, *op. cit.*

2. These are to appear in a forthcoming doctoral thesis at the Harvard Business School by Louis T. Wells, tentatively entitled" International Trade and Business Policy."

3. See Wassily Leontief, "Domestic Production and Foreign Trade: The American Capital Position Re-examined," *Proceedings of the American Philosophical Society*, Vol. 97 (Sept. 1953), and "Factor Proportions and the Structure of American Trade: Further Theoretical and Empirical Analysis," *Review of Economics and Statistics*, XXXVIII (Nov. 1956).

4. Of course, if there were some systematic trend in the inputs of new products — for example, if the new products which appeared in the 1960's were more capital-intensive than the new products which appeared in the 1950's — then the tendencies suggested by our hypotheses might be swamped by such a trend. As long as we do not posit offsetting systematic patterns of this sort, however, the Leontief findings and the hypotheses offered here seem consistent.

unusually high proportion of labor cost. This is not so much because the labor is particularly skilled, as is so often suggested. More likely, it is due to a quite different phenomenon. At this stage, the standardization of the manufacturing process has not gotten very far; that is to come later, when the volume of output is high enough and the degree of uncertainty low enough to justify investment in relatively inflexible, capital-intensive facilities. As a result, the production process relies relatively heavily on labor inputs at a time when the United States commands an export position; and the process relies more heavily on capital at a time when imports become important.

This, of course, is an hypothesis which has not yet been subjected to any really rigorous test. But it does open up a line of inquiry into the structure of United States trade which is well worth pursuing.

THE STANDARDIZED PRODUCT

Figure I, the reader will have observed, carries a panel which suggests that, at an advanced stage in the standardization of some products, the less-developed countries may offer competitive advantages as a production location.

This is a bold projection, which seems on first blush to be wholly at variance with the Heckscher-Ohlin theorem. According to that theorem, one presumably ought to anticipate that the exports of the less-developed countries would tend to be relatively labor-intensive products.

One of the difficulties with the theorem, however, is that it leaves marketing considerations out of account. One reason for the omission is evident. As long as knowledge is regarded as a free good, instantaneously available, and as long as individual producers are regarded as atomistic contributors to the total supply, marketing problems cannot be expected to find much of a place in economic theory. In projecting the patterns of export from less-developed areas, however, we cannot afford to disregard the fact that information comes at a cost; and that entrepreneurs are not readily disposed to pay the price of investigating overseas markets of unknown dimensions and unknown promise. Neither are they eager to venture into situations which they know will demand a constant flow of reliable marketing information from remote sources.

If we can assume that highly standardized products tend to have a well-articulated, easily accessible international market and to sell largely on the basis of price (an assumption inherent in the definition), then it follows that such products will not pose the problem of market information quite so acutely for the less-developed countries. This establishes a necessary if not a sufficient condition for investment in such industries.

Of course, foreign investors seeking an optimum location for a captive facility may not have to concern themselves too much with questions of market information; presumably, they are thoroughly familiar with the marketing end of the business and are looking for a low-cost captive source of supply. In that case, the low cost of labor may be the initial attraction drawing the investor to less-developed areas. But other limitations in such areas, according to our hypothesis, will bias such captive operations toward the production of standardized items. The reasons in this case turn on the part played in the production process by external economies. Manufacturing processes which receive significant inputs from the local economy, such as skilled labor, repairmen, reliable power, spare parts, industrial materials processed according to exacting specification, and so on, are less appropriate to the less-developed areas than those that do not have such requirements. Unhappily, most industrial processes require one or another ingredient of this difficult sort. My guess is, however, that the industries which produce a standardized product are in the best position to avoid the problem, by producing on a vertically-integrated self-sustaining basis.

In speculating about future industrial exports from the less-developed areas, therefore, we are led to think of products with a fairly clear-cut set of economic characteristics.[5] Their production function is such as to require significant inputs of labor; otherwise there is no reason to expect a lower production cost in less-developed countries. At the same time, they are products with a high price elasticity of demand for the output of individual firms; otherwise, there is no strong incentive to take the risks of pioneering with production in a new area. In addition, products whose production process did not rely heavily upon external economies would be more obvious candidates than those which required a more elaborate industrial environment. The implications of remoteness also would be critical; products which could be precisely described by standardized specifications and which could be produced for inventory without fear of obsolescence would be more relevant than those

5. The concepts sketched out here are presented in more detail in my "Problems and Prospects in the Export of Manufactured Products from the Less-developed Countries," U.N. Conference on Trade and Development, Dec. 16, 1963 (mimeo.).

which had less precise specifications and which could not easily be ordered from remote locations. Moreover, high-value items capable of absorbing significant freight costs would be more likely to appear than bulky items low in value by weight. Standardized textile products are, of course, the illustration par excellence of the sort of product that meets the criteria. But other products come to mind such as crude steel, simple fertilizers, newsprint, and so on.

Speculation of this sort draws some support from various interregional experiences in industrial location. In the United States, for example, the "export" industries which moved to the low-wage south in search of lower costs tended to be industries which had no great need for a sophisticated industrial environment and which produced fairly standardized products. In the textile industry, it was the grey goods, cotton sheetings and men's shirt plants that went south; producers of high-style dresses or other unstandardized items were far more reluctant to move. In the electronics industry, it was the mass producers of tubes, resistors and other standardized high-volume components that showed the greatest disposition to move south; custom-built and research-oriented production remained closer to markets and to the main industrial complexes. A similar pattern could be discerned in printing and in chemicals production.[6]

In other countries, a like pattern is suggested by the impressionistic evidence. The underdeveloped south of Italy and the laggard north of Britain and Ireland both seem to be attracting industry with standardized output and self-sufficient process.[7]

Once we begin to look for relevant evidence of such investment patterns in the less-developed countries proper, however, only the barest shreds of corroboratory information can be found. One would have difficulty in thinking of many cases in which manufacturers of standardized products in the more advanced countries had made significant investments in the less-developed countries with a view of exporting such products from those countries. To be sure, other

6. This conclusion derives largely from the industry studies conducted in connection with the New York Metropolitan Region study. There have been some excellent more general analyses of shifts in industrial location among the regions of the United States. See e.g., Victor R. Fuchs, *Changes in the Location of Manufacturing in the United States Since 1929* (New Haven: Yale University Press, 1962). Unfortunately, however, none has been designed, so far as I know, to test hypotheses relating locational shifts to product characteristics such as price elasticity of demand and degree of standardization.

7. This statement, too, is based on only impressionistic materials. Among the more suggestive, illustrative of the best of the available evidence, see J. N. Toothill, *Inquiry into the Scottish Economy* (Edinburgh: Scottish Council, 1962).

types of foreign investment are not uncommon in the less-developed countries, such as investments in import-replacing industries which were made in the face of a threat of import restriction. But there are only a few export-oriented cases similar to that of Taiwan's foreign-owned electronics plants and Argentina's new producing facility, set up to manufacture and export standard sorting equipment for computers.

If we look to foreign trade patterns, rather than foreign investment patterns, to learn something about the competitive advantage of the less-developed countries, the possibility that they are an attractive locus for the output of standardized products gains slightly more support. The Taiwanese and Japanese trade performances are perhaps the most telling ones in support of the projected pattern; both countries have managed to develop significant overseas markets for standardized manufactured products. According to one major study of the subject (a study stimulated by the Leontief paradox), Japanese exports are more capital-intensive than is the Japanese production which is displaced by imports; [8] this is what one might expect if the hypothetical patterns suggested by Figure I were operational. Apart from these cases, however, all that one sees are a few provocative successes such as some sporadic sales of newsprint from Pakistan, the successful export of sewing machines from India, and so on. Even in these cases, one cannot be sure that they are consistent with the hypothesis unless he has done a good deal more empirical investigation.

The reason why so few revelant cases come to mind may be that the process has not yet advanced far enough. Or it may be that such factors as extensive export constraints and overvalued exchange rates are combining to prevent the investment and exports that otherwise would occur.

If there is one respect in which this discussion may deviate from classical expectations, it is in the view that the overall scarcity of capital in the less-developed countries will not prevent investment in facilities for the production of standardized products.

There are two reasons why capital costs may not prove a barrier to such investment.

First, according to our hypotheses, the investment will occur in industries which require some significant labor inputs in the production process; but they will be concentrated in that subsector of the

---

8. M. Tatemoto and S. Ichimura, "Factor Proportions and Foreign Trade: the Case of Japan," *Review of Economics and Statistics*, XLI (Nov. 1959), 442–46.

industry which produces highly standardized products capable of self-contained production establishments. The net of these specifications is indeterminate so far as capital-intensiveness is concerned. A standardized textile item may be more or less capital-intensive than a plant for unstandardized petro-chemicals.

Besides, even if the capital requirements for a particular plant are heavy, the cost of the capital need not prove a bar. The assumption that capital costs come high in the less-developed countries requires a number of fundamental qualifications. The reality, to the extent that it is known, is more complex.

One reason for this complexity is the role played by the international investor. Producers of chemical fertilizers, when considering whether to invest in a given country, may be less concerned with the going rate for capital in that country than with their opportunity costs as they see such costs. For such investors the alternatives to be weighed are not the full range of possibilities calling for capital but only a very restricted range of alternatives, such as the possibilities offered by chemical fertilizer investment elsewhere. The relevant capital cost for a chemical fertilizer plant, therefore, may be fairly low if the investor is an international entrepreneur.

Moreover, the assumption that finance capital is scarce and that interest rates are high in a less-developed country may prove inapplicable to the class of investors who concern us here.[9] The capital markets of the less-developed countries typically consist of a series of water-tight, insulated, submarkets in which wholly different rates prevail and between which arbitrage opportunities are limited. In some countries, the going figures may vary from 5 to 40 per cent, on grounds which seem to have little relation to issuer risk or term of loan. (In some economies, where inflation is endemic, interest rates which in effect represent a negative real cost are not uncommon.)

These internal differences in interest rates may be due to a number of factors: the fact that funds generated inside the firm usually are exposed to a different yield test than external borrowings; the fact that government loans are often floated by mandatory levies on banks and other intermediaries; and the fact that funds borrowed by governments from international sources are often re-

9. See George Rosen, *Industrial Change in India* (Glencoe, Ill.: Free Press, 1958). Rosen finds that in the period studied from 1937 to 1953, "there was no serious shortage of capital for the largest firms in India." Gustav F. Papanek makes a similar finding for Pakistan for the period from 1950 to 1964 in a book about to be published.

loaned in domestic markets at rates which are linked closely to the international borrowing rate, however irrelevant that may be. Moreover, one has to reckon with the fact that public international lenders tend to lend at near-uniform rates, irrespective of the identity of the borrower and the going interest rate in his country. Access to capital on the part of underdeveloped countries, therefore, becomes a direct function of the country's capacity to propose plausible projects to public international lenders. If a project can plausibly be shown to "pay its own way" in balance-of-payment and output terms at "reasonable" interest rates, the largest single obstacle to obtaining capital at such rates has usually been overcome.

Accordingly, one may say that from the entrepreneur's viewpoint certain systematic and predictable "imperfections" of the capital markets may reduce or eliminate the capital-shortage handicap which is characteristic of the less-developed countries; and, further, that as a result of the reduction or elimination such countries may find themselves in a position to compete effectively in the export of certain standardized capital-intensive goods. This is not the statement of another paradox; it is not the same as to say that the capital-poor countries will develop capital-intensive economies. All we are concerned with here is a modest fraction of the industry of such countries, which in turn is a minor fraction of their total economic activity. It may be that the anomalies such industries represent are systematic enough to be included in our normal expectations regarding conditions in the less-developed countries.

* * * * *

Like the other observations which have preceded, these views about the likely patterns of exports by the less-developed countries are attempts to relax some of the constraints imposed by purer and simpler models. Here and there, the hypotheses take on plausibility because they jibe with the record of past events. But, for the most part, they are still speculative in nature, having been subjected to tests of a very low order of rigorousness. What is needed, obviously, is continued probing to determine whether the "imperfections" stressed so strongly in these pages deserve to be elevated out of the footnotes into the main text of economic theory.

Raymond Vernon

When the editors of the Quarterly Journal of Economics decided to publish my article on the product cycle in 1966, my reaction was not one of unalloyed joy. I was already aware of the fact that the paper had some of the qualities that usually go with articles that are remembered. It had a relatively simple central theme that seemed to cast light on an important phenomenon of the moment, the dominance of the U.S. economy in technology-intensive exports. But the very attractiveness of the product cycle hypothesis was bothersome, because of the risk that some readers might try to apply it more widely than its author intended. Some of the causal sequences described in the hypothesis rested on certain external conditions that prevailed in the 1950s and 1960s, notably, the relatively high income levels and high labor costs of the U.S. economy; and it was clear to me even then that these conditions might be ephemeral.

To reduce the risk that the paper might be received as an enunciation of a grand theory, therefore, I was at some pains to refer to my ideas on the role of the product cycle as an hypothesis, one that purported to explain some selected features of U.S. trade and investment patterns in a particular period.

In 1971, when I published Sovereignty at Bay,[1] my unease had grown to such an extent that I felt the need to include a section entitled, "Toward Another Model." That section included five or six pages of speculation on the significance of the new trade and investment patterns that might emerge as the income and labor costs of the United States converged toward those of Europe and Japan.

By 1979, I felt that my ideas regarding "another model" had matured
sufficiently to justify an article on the subject, an article I entitled
"The Product Cycle Hypothesis in a New International Environment." [2]
Predictably, the article evoked much less interest than the original
product cycle article; the picture it portrayed was much muddier and much
less compact, a reflection of the complexity of the transition in U.S.
economic relations with the rest of the world. Moreover, by that time,
international economists were energetically at work trying to deal more
formally with the effects of scale economies, technological leadership, and
oligopoly, attempting to incorporate these elements in traditional models
based on comparative advantage and resource abundance.

Some portions of the 1966 article, to be sure, have proved quite
durable and useful. Oddly, these portions have included some of the most
speculative ideas in the article, namely, the likely patterns of exports
emanating from the developing countries. Soon after the publication of the
article in 1966, a number of developing countries pushed their way into the
export markets for standardized, capital-intensive products such as steel
and base chemicals. That development was quite consistent with the product
cycle hypothesis, having been adumbrated in the 1966 article. On the other
hand, there was nothing in the body of conventional international economic
theory that would satisfactorily explain those developments.

The contribution of the product hypothesis so far has been to provide
a plausible set of generalizations that have proved to have some predictive
value. But the generalizations have been partial and dynamic in character,

detached from the basic model that is at the core of international economic theory. Some progress has been made in relating its usable ideas to that basic model. But a great deal remains to be done.

FOOTNOTES

1. Raymond Vernon: <u>Sovereignty at Bay</u>. Basic Books, New York, 1971 [in Moffit under AD 2795 V48]

2. _____: "The Product Life Cycle Hypothesis in a New International Environment". Oxford Bulletin of Economics & Statistics; Nov. '79; 79,41 (4)

THE MULTINATIONAL CORPORATION AND

THE LAW OF UNEVEN DEVELOPMENT

by Stephen Hymer

"The settlers' town is a strongly-built town, all made of stone and steel.
It is a brightly-lit town; the streets are covered with asphalt, and the gar-
bage-cans swallow all the leavings, unseen, unknown and hardly thought
about. The settler's feet are never visible, except perhaps in the sea; but
there you're never close enough to see them. His feet are protected by strong
shoes although the streets of his town are clean and even, with no holes
or stones. The settler's town is a well-fed town, an easy-going town, its belly
is always full of good things. The settler's town is a town of white people,
of foreigners.

The town belonging to the colonized people, or at least the native town,
the Negro village, the medina, the reservation, is a place of ill fame peopled
by men of evil repute. They are born there, it matters little where or how;
they die there, it matters not where nor how. It is a world without spacious-
ness; men live there on top of each other, and their huts are built one on
top of the other. The native town is a hungry town, starved of bread, of
meat, of shoes, of coal, of light. The native town is a crouching village, a
town on its knees, a town wallowing in the mire. It is a town of niggers and
dirty Arabs. The look that the native turns on the settler's town is a look of
lust, a look of envy . . ." Fanon, *The Wretched of the Earth.*

We have been asked to look into the future towards the year 2000.
This essay attempts to do so in terms of two laws of economic development: the Law of Increasing Firm Size and the Law of Uneven Development.[1]

Since the beginning of the Industrial Revolution, there has been a
tendency for the representative firm to increase in size from the *workshop* to the *factory* to the *national corporation* to the *multi-divisional
corporation* and now to the *multinational corporation.* This growth has
been qualitative as well as quantitative. With each step, business enter-

Reprinted from "Economics and the World Order: From the 1970s to
the 1990s" (J.N. Bhagwati, ed.), pp. 113–140, with permission of
The Free Press, New York, Copyright 1972.

prises acquired a more complex administrative structure to coordinate its activities and a larger brain to plan for its survival and growth. The first part of this essay traces the evolution of the corporation stressing the development of a hierarchical system of authority and control.

The remainder of the essay is concerned with extrapolating the trends in business enterprise (the microcosm) and relating them to the evolution of the international economy (the macrocosm). Until recently, most multinational corporations have come from the United States, where private business enterprise has reached its largest size and most highly developed forms. Now European corporations, as a by-product of increased size, and as a reaction to the American invasion of Europe, are also shifting attention from national to global production and beginning to "see the world as their oyster."[2] *If* present trends continue, multinationalization is likely to increase greatly in the next decade as giants from both sides of the Atlantic (though still mainly from the U.S.) strive to penetrate each other's markets and to establish bases in underdeveloped countries, where there are few indigenous concentrations of capital sufficiently large to operate on a world scale. This rivalry may be intense at first but will probably abate through time and turn into collusion as firms approach some kind of oligopolistic equilibrium. A new structure of international industrial organization and a new international division of labor will have been born.[3]

What will be the effect of this latest stage in the evolution of business enterprise on the Law of Uneven Development, *i.e.,* the tendency of the system to produce poverty as well as wealth, underdevelopment as well as development? The second part of this essay suggests that a regime of North Atlantic Multinational Corporations would tend to produce a hierarchical division of labor between geographical regions corresponding to the vertical division of labor within the firm. It would tend to centralize high-level decision-making occupations in a few key cities in the advanced countries, surrounded by a number of regional sub-capitals, and confine the rest of the world to lower levels of activity and income, *i.e.,* to the status of towns and villages in a new Imperial system. Income, status, authority, and consumption patterns would radiate out from these centers along a declining curve, and the existing pattern of inequality and dependency would be perpetuated. The pattern would be complex, just as the structure of the corporation is complex, but the basic relationship between different countries would be one of superior and subordinate, head office and branch plant.

How far will this tendency of corporations to create a world in their own image proceed? The situation is a dynamic one, moving dialectically. Right now, we seem to be in the midst of a major revolution in international relationships as modern science establishes the technological basis for a major advance in the conquest of the material world and the beginnings of truly cosmopolitan production.[4] Multinational corporations are in the vanguard of this revolution, because of their great financial and administrative strength and their close contact with the new technology. Governments (outside the military) are far behind, because of their narrower horizons and perspectives, as are labor organizations and most non-business institutions and associations. (As John Powers, President of Charles Pfizer Corporation, has put it, "Practise is ahead of theory and policy.") Therefore, in the first round, multinational corporations are likely to have a certain degree of success in organizing markets, decision making, and the spread of information in their own interest. However, their very success will create tensions and conflicts which will lead to further development. Part III discusses some of the contradictions that are likely to emerge as the multinational corporate system overextends itself. These contradictions provide certain openings for action. Whether or not they can or will be used in the next round to move towards superior forms of international organization requires an analysis of a wide range of political factors outside the scope of this essay.

Part I. THE EVOLUTION OF THE MULTINATIONAL CORPORATION

The Marshallian Firm and the Market Economy

What is the nature of the "beast?" It is called many names: Direct Investment, International Business, the International Firm, the International Corporate Group, the Multinational Firm, the Multinational Enterprise, the Multinational Corporation, the Multinational Family Group, World Wide Enterprise, La Grande Entreprise Plurinationale, La Grande Unité Interterritoriale, La Grande Entreprise Multinationale, La Grande Unité Pluriterritoriale; or, as the French Foreign Minister called them, "The U.S. corporate monsters." (Michel Debré quoted in *Fortune*, August 1965, p. 126.)

Giant organizations are nothing new in international trade. They were a characteristic form of the mercantilist period when large joint-stock companies, e.g., The Hudson's Bay Co., The Royal African Co., The East India Co., to name the major English merchant firms, organized long-distance trade with America, Africa and Asia. But neither these firms, nor the large mining and plantation enterprises in the production sector, were the forerunners of the multinational corporation. They were like dinosaurs, large in bulk, but small in brain, feeding on the lush vegetation of the new worlds (the planters and miners in America were literally *Tyrannosaurus rex*).

The activities of these international merchants, planters and miners laid the groundwork for the Industrial Revolution by concentrating capital in the metropolitan centre, but the driving force came from the small-scale capitalist enterprises in manufacturing, operating at first in the interstices of the feudalist economic structure, but gradually emerging into the open and finally gaining predominance. It is in the small workshops, órganized by the newly emerging capitalist class, that the forerunners of the modern corporation are to be found.

The strength of this new form of business enterprise lay in its power and ability to reap the benefits of cooperation and division of labor. Without the capitalist, economic activity was individualistic, small-scale, scattered and unproductive. But a man with capital, *i.e.*, with sufficient funds to buy raw materials and advance wages, could gather a number of people into a single shop and obtain as his reward the increased productivity that resulted from social production. The reinvestment of these profits led to a steady increase in the size of capitals, making further division of labor possible and creating an opportunity for using machinery in production. A phenomenal increase in productivity and production resulted from this process, and entirely new dimensions of human existence were opened. The growth of capital revolutionized the entire world and, figuratively speaking, even battered down the Great Wall of China.

The hallmarks of the new system were *the market* and *the factory,* representing the two different methods of coordinating the division of labor. In the factory entrepreneurs consciously plan and organize cooperation, and the relationships are hierarchical and authoritarian; in the market coordination is achieved through a decentralized, unconscious, competitive process.[5]

To understand the significance of this distinction, the new system should be compared to the structure it replaced. In the pre-capitalist system of production, the division of labor was hierarchically structured at the *macro* level, *i.e.* for society as a whole, but unconsciously structured at the *micro* level *i.e.,* the actual process of production. Society as a whole was partitioned into various castes, classes, and guilds, on a rigid and authoritarian basis so that political and social stability could be maintained and adequate numbers assured for each industry and occupation. Within each sphere of production, however, individuals by and large were independent and their activities only loosely coordinated, if at all. In essence, a guild was composed of a large number of similar individuals, each performing the same task in roughly the same way with little cooperation or division of labor. This type of organization could produce high standards of quality and workmanship but was limited quantitatively to low levels of output per head.

The capitalist system of production turned this structure on its head. The macro system became unconsciously structured, while the micro system became hierarchically structured. The market emerged as a self-regulating coordinator of business units as restrictions on capital markets and labor mobility were removed. (Of course the State remained above the market as a conscious coordinator to maintain the system and ensure the growth of capital.) At the micro level, that is the level of production, labor was gathered under the authority of the entrepreneur capitalist.

Marshall, like Marx, stressed that the internal division of labor within the factory, between those who planned and those who worked (between "undertakers" and laborers), was the "chief fact in the form of modern civilization, the 'kernel' of the modern economic problem."[6] Marx, however, stressed the authoritarian and unequal nature of this relationship based on the coercive power of property and its anti-social characteristics. He focused on the irony that concentration of wealth in the hands of a few and its ruthless use were necessary historically to demonstrate the value of cooperation and the social nature of production.[7]

Marshall, in trying to answer Marx, argued for the voluntary cooperative nature of the relationship between capital and labor. In his view, the *market* reconciled individual freedom and collective production. He argued that those on top achieved their position because of their superior organizational ability, and that their relation to the workers below them was essentially harmonious and not exploitative. "Undertakers" were not captains of industry because they had capital; they could obtain capital because they had the ability to be captains of industry. They retained their authority by merit, not by coercion; for according to Marshall, natural selection, operating through the market, constantly destroyed inferior organizers and gave everyone who had the ability— including workers—a chance to rise to managerial positions. Capitalists earned more than workers because they contributed more, while the system as a whole provided all its members, and especially the workers, with improved standards of living and an ever-expanding field of choice of consumption.[8]

The Corporate Economy

The evolution of business enterprise from the small workshop (Adam Smith's pin factory) to the Marshallian family firm represented only the first step in the development of business organization. As total capital accumulated, the size of the individual concentrations composing it increased continuously, and the vertical division of labor grew accordingly.

It is best to study the evolution of the corporate form in the United States environment, where it has reached its highest stage.[9] In the 1870s, the United States industrial structure consisted largely of Marshallian type, single-function firms, scattered over the country. Business firms were typically tightly controlled by a single entrepreneur or small family group who, as it were, saw everything, knew everything and decided everything. By the early twentieth century, the rapid growth of the economy and the great merger movement had consolidated many small enterprises into large national corporations engaged in many functions over many regions. To meet this new strategy of continent-wide, vertically integrated production and marketing, a new administrative structure evolved. The family firm, tightly controlled by a few men in close touch with all its aspects, gave way to the administrative pyramid of the corporation. Capital acquired new powers and new horizons. The domain of conscious coordination widened and that of market-directed division of labor contracted.

According to Chandler the railroad, which played so important a role in creating the national market, also offered a model for new forms of business organization. The need to administer geographically dispersed operations led railway companies to create an administrative structure which distinguished field offices from head offices. The field offices managed local operations; the head office supervised the field offices. According to Chandler and Redlich, this distinction is important because "it implies that the executive responsible for a firm's affairs had, for the first time, to supervise the work of other executives."[10]

This first step towards increased vertical division of labor within the management function was quickly copied by the recently-formed national corporations which faced the same problems of coordinating widely scattered plants. Business developed an organ system of administration, and the modern corporation was born. The functions of business administration were sub-divided into *departments* (organs)—finance, personnel, purchasing, engineering, and sales—to deal with capital, labor, purchasing, manufacturing, etc. This horizontal division of labor opened up new possibilities for rationalizing production and for incorporating the advances of physical and social sciences into economic activity on a systematic basis. At the same time a "brain and nervous" system, *i.e.,* a vertical system of control, had to be devised to connect and coordinate departments. This was a major advance in decision-making capabilities. It meant that a special group, the Head Office, was created whose particular function was to coordinate, appraise, and plan for the survival and growth of the organism as a whole. The organization became conscious of itself as organization and gained a certain measure of control over its own evolution and development.

The corporation soon underwent further evolution. To understand this next step we must briefly discuss the development of the United States market. At the risk of great oversimplification, we might say that by the first decade of the twentieth century, the problem of production had essentially been solved. By the end of the nineteenth century, scientists and engineers had developed most of the inventions needed for mass producing at a low cost nearly all the main items of basic consumption. In the language of systems analysis, the problem became one of putting together the available components in an organized fashion. The national corporation provided *one* organizational solution, and by the 1920s it had demonstrated its great power to increase material production.

The question was which direction growth would take. One possibility was to expand mass production systems very widely and to make basic consumer goods available on a broad basis throughout the world. The other possibility was to concentrate on continuous innovation for a small number of people and on the introduction of new consumption goods even before the old ones had been fully spread. The latter course was in fact chosen, and we now have the paradox that 500 million people can receive a live TV broadcast from the moon while there is still a shortage of telephones in many advanced countries, to say nothing of the fact that so many people suffer from inadequate food and lack of simple medical help.

This path was associated with a choice of capital-deepening instead of capital-widening in the productive sector of the economy. As capital accumulated, business had to choose the degree to which it would expand labor proportionately to the growth of capital or, conversely, the degree to which they would substitute capital for labor. At one extreme business could have kept the capital-labor ratio constant and accumulated labor at the same rate they accumulated capital. This horizontal accumulation would soon have exhausted the labor force of any particular country and then either capital would have had to migrate to foreign countries or labor would have had to move into the industrial centers. Under this system, earnings per employed worker would have remained steady and the composition of output would have tended to remain constant as similar basic goods were produced on a wider and wider basis.

However, this path was not chosen, and instead capital per worker was raised, the rate of expansion of the industrial labor force was slowed down, and a dualism was created between a small, high wage, high productivity sector in advanced countries, and a large, low wage, low productivity sector in the less advanced.[11]

The uneven growth of per capita income implied unbalanced growth and the need on the part of business to adapt to a constantly changing composition of output. Firms in the producers' goods sectors had continuously to innovate labor-saving machinery because the capital output ratio was increasing steadily. In the consumption goods sector, firms had continuously to introduce new products since, according to Engel's Law, people do not generally consume proportionately more of the same things as they get richer, but rather reallocate their consumption away from old goods and towards new goods. This non-proportional growth of demand implied that goods would tend to go through a life-cycle, growing rapidly when they were first introduced and more slowly later. If a particular firm were tied to only one product, its growth rate would follow this same life-cycle pattern and would eventually slow down and perhaps even come to a halt. If the corporation was to grow steadily at a rapid rate, it had continuously to introduce new products.

Thus, product development and marketing replaced production as a dominant problem of business enterprise. To meet the challenge of a constantly changing market, business enterprise evolved the multidivisional structure. The new form was originated by General Motors and DuPont shortly after World War I, followed by a few others during the 1920s and 1930s, and was widely adopted by most of the giant U.S. corporations in the great boom following World War II. As with the previous stages, evolution involved a process of both differentiation and integration. Corporations were decentralized into several *divisions,* each concerned with one product line and organized with its own head office. At a higher level, a *general office* was created to coordinate the division and to plan for the enterprise as a whole.

The new corporate form has great flexibility. Because of its decentralized structure, a multidivisional corporation can enter a new market by adding a new division, while leaving the old divisions undisturbed. (And to a lesser extent it can leave the market by dropping a division without disturbing the rest of its structure.) It can also create competing product-lines in the same industry, thus increasing its market share while maintaining the illusion of competition. Most important of all, because it has a cortex specializing in strategy, it can plan on a much wider scale than before and allocate capital with more precision.

The modern corporation is a far cry from the small workshop or even from the Marshallian firm. The Marshallian capitalist ruled his factory from an office on the second floor. At the turn of the century, the president of a large national corporation was lodged in a higher building, perhaps on the seventh floor, with greater perspective and power. In today's giant corporation, managers rule from the top of skyscrapers; on a clear day, they can almost see the world.

U.S. corporations began to move to foreign countries almost as soon as they had completed their continent-wide integration. For one thing, their new administrative structure and great financial strength gave them the power to go abroad. In becoming national firms, U.S. corporations learned how to become international. Also, their large size and oligopolistic position gave them an incentive. Direct investment became a new weapon in their arsenal of oligopolistic rivalry. Instead of joining a cartel (prohibited under U.S. law), they invested in foreign customers, suppliers, and competitors. For example, some firms found they were oligopolistic buyers of raw materials produced in foreign countries and feared a monopolization of the sources of supply. By investing directly in foreign producing enterprises, they could gain the security implicit in control over their raw material requirements. Other firms invested abroad to control marketing outlets and thus maximize quasi-rents on their technological discoveries and differentiated products. Some went abroad simply to forestall competition.[12]

The first wave of U.S. direct foreign capital investment occurred around the turn of the century followed by a second wave during the 1920s. The outward migration slowed down during the depression but resumed after World War II and soon accelerated rapidly. Between 1950 and 1969, direct foreign investment by U.S. firms expanded at a rate of about 10 percent per annum. At this rate it would double in less than ten years, and even at a much slower rate of growth, foreign operations will reach enormous proportions over the next 30 years.[13]

Several important factors account for this rush of foreign investment in the 1950s and the 1960s. First, the large size of the U.S. corporations and their new multidivisional structure gave them wider horizons and a global outlook. Secondly, technological developments in communications created a new awareness of the global challenge and threatened established institutions by opening up new sources of competition. For reasons noted above, business enterprises were among the first to recognize the potentialities and dangers of the new environment and to take active steps to cope with it.

A third factor in the outward migration of U.S. capital was the rapid growth of Europe and Japan. This, combined with the slow growth of the United States economy in the 1950s, altered world market shares as firms confined to the U.S. market found themselves falling behind in the competitive race and losing ground to European and Japanese firms, which were growing rapidly because of the expansion of their markets. Thus, in the late 1950s, United States corporations faced a serious "non-American" challenge. Their answer was an outward thrust to establish sales production and bases in foreign territories. This strategy was possible in Europe, since government there provided an open door for United States investment, but was blocked in Japan, where the government adopted a highly restrictive policy. To a large extent, United States business was thus able to redress the imbalances caused by the Common Market, but Japan remained a source of tension to oligopoly equilibrium.

What about the future? The present trend indicates further multinationalization of all giant firms, European as well as American. In the first place, European firms, partly as a reaction to the United States penetration of their markets, and partly as a natural result of their own growth, have begun to invest abroad on an expanded scale and will probably continue to do so in the future, and even enter into the United States market. This process is already well underway and may be expected to accelerate as time goes on. The reaction of United States business will most likely be to meet foreign investment at home with more foreign investment abroad. They, too, will scramble for market positions in underdeveloped countries and attempt to get an even larger share of the European market, as a reaction to European investment in the United States. Since they are large and powerful, they will on balance succeed in maintaining their relative standing in the world as a whole—as their losses in some markets are offset by gains in others.

A period of rivalry will prevail until a new equilibrium between giant U.S. firms and giant European and Japanese firms is reached, based on a strategy of multinational operations and cross-penetration.[14] We turn now to the implications of this pattern of industrial organization for international trade and the law of uneven development.

Part II. UNEVEN DEVELOPMENT

Suppose giant multinational corporations (say 300 from the U.S. and 200 from Europe and Japan) succeed in establishing themselves as the dominant form of international enterprise and come to control a significant share of industry (especially modern industry) in each country. The world economy will resemble more and more the United States economy, where each of the large corporations tends to spread over the entire continent and to penetrate almost every nook and cranny. What would be the effect of a world industrial organization of this type on international specialization, exchange and income distribution? The purpose of this section is to analyze the spatial dimension of the corporate hierarchy.

A useful starting point is Chandler and Redlich's[15] scheme for analyzing the evolution of corporate structure. They distinguish "three levels of business administration, three horizons, three levels of task, and three levels of decision making . . . and three levels of policies." Level III, the lowest level, is concerned with managing the day-to-day operations of the enterprise, that is with keeping it going within the established framework. Level II, which first made its appearance with the separation of head office from field office, is responsible for coordinating the managers at Level III. The functions of Level I—top management— are goal-determination and planning. This level sets the framework in which the lower levels operate. In the Marshallian firm, all three levels are embodied in the single entrepreneur or undertaker. In the national corporation a partial differentiation is made in which the top two levels are separated from the bottom one. In the multidivisional corporation, the differentiation is far more complete. Level I is completely split off from Level II and concentrated in a general office whose specific function is to plan strategy rather than tactics.

The development of business enterprise can therefore be viewed as a process of centralizing and perfecting the process of capital accumulation. The Marshallian entrepreneur was a jack-of-all-trades. In the modern multidivisional corporation, a powerful general office consciously plans and organizes the growth of corporate capital. It is here that the key men who actually allocate the corporation's available resources (rather than act within the means allocated to them, as is true for the managers at lower levels) are located. Their power comes from their ultimate control over *men* and *money* and although one should not overestimate the ability to control a far-flung empire, neither should one underestimate it.

> The senior men could take action because they controlled the selection of executive personnel and because, through budgeting, they allocated the funds to the operating divisions. In the way they allocated their resources—capital and personnel—and in the promotion, transferral and retirement of operating executives, they determined the framework in which the operating units worked and thus put into effect their concept of the long term goals and objectives of the enterprise . . . Ultimate authority in business enterprise, as we see it, rests with those who hold the purse strings, and in modern large-scale enterprises, those persons hold the purse strings who perform the functions of goal setting and planning.[16]

What is the relationship between the structure of the microcosm and the structure of the macrocosm? The application of location theory to the Chandler-Redlich scheme suggests a *correspondence principle* relating centralization of control within the corporation to centralization of control within the international economy.

Location theory suggests that Level III activities would spread themselves over the globe according to the pull of manpower, markets, and raw materials. The multinational corporation, because of its power to command capital and technology and its ability to rationalize their use on a global scale, will probably spread production more evenly over the world's surface than is now the case. Thus, in the first instance, it may well be a force for diffusing industrialization to the less developed countries and creating new centers of production. (We postpone for a moment a discussion of the fact that location depends upon transportation, which in turn depends upon the government, which in turn is influenced by the structure of business enterprise.)

Level II activities, because of their need for white-collar workers, communications systems, and information, tend to concentrate in large cities. Since their demands are similar, corporations from different industries tend to place their coordinating offices in the same city, and Level II activities are consequently far more geographically concentrated than Level III activities.

Level I activities, the general offices, tend to be even more concentrated than Level II activities, for they must be located close to the capital market, the media, and the government. Nearly every major corporation in the United States, for example, must have its general office (or a large proportion of its high-level personnel) in or near the city of New York because of the need for face-to-face contact at higher levels of decision making.

Applying this scheme to the world economy, one would expect to find the highest offices of the multinational corporations concentrated in the world's major cities—New York, London, Paris, Bonn, Tokyo. These, along with Moscow and perhaps Peking, will be the major centers of high-level strategic planning. Lesser cities throughout the world will deal with the day-to-day operations of specific local problems. These in turn will be arranged in a hierarchical fashion: the larger and more important ones will contain regional corporate headquarters, while the smaller ones will be confined to lower level activities. Since business is usually the core of the city, geographical specialization will come to reflect the hierarchy of corporate decision making, and the occupational distribution of labor in a city or region will depend upon its function in the international economic system. The "best" and most highly paid administrators, doctors, lawyers, scientists, educators, government officials, actors, servants and hairdressers, will tend to concentrate in or near the major centers.

The structure of income and consumption will tend to parallel the structure of status and authority. The citizens of capital cities will have the best jobs—allocating men and money at the highest level and plan-

ning growth and development—and will receive the highest rates of remuneration. (Executives' salaries tend to be a function of the wage bill
of people under them. The larger empire of the multinational corporation, the greater the earnings of top executives, to a large extent independent of their performance.[17] Thus, growth in the hinterland subsidiaries implies growth in the income of capital cities, but not *vice
versa*.)

The citizens of capital cities will also be the first to innovate new
products in the cycle which is known in the marketing literature as
trickle-down or two-stage marketing. A new product is usually first introduced to a select group of people who have "discretionary" income and
are willing to experiment in their consumption patterns.[18] Once it is
accepted by this group, it spreads, or trickles down to other groups via
the demonstration effect. In this process, the rich and the powerful get
more votes than everyone else; first, because they have more money to
spend, second, because they have more ability to experiment, and third,
because they have high status and are likely to be copied. This special
group may have something approaching a choice in consumption patterns; the rest have only the choice between conforming or being isolated.

The trickle-down system also has the advantage—from the center's
point of view—of reinforcing patterns of authority and control. According to Fallers,[19] it helps keep workers on the treadmill by creating an
illusion of upward mobility even though relative status remains unchanged. In each period subordinates achieve (in part) the consumption
standards of their superiors in a previous period and are thus torn in
two directions: if they look backward and compare their standards of
living through time, things seem to be getting better; if they look upward they see that their relative position has not changed. They receive
a consolation prize, as it were, which may serve to keep them going by
softening the reality that in a competitive system, few succeed and many
fail. It is little wonder, then, that those at the top stress growth rather
than equality as the welfare criterion for human relations.

In the international economy trickle-down marketing takes the form
of an international demonstration effect spreading outward from the
metropolis to the hinterland.[20] Multinational corporations help speed
up this process, often the key motive for direct investment, through their
control of marketing channels and communications media.

The development of a new product is a fixed cost; once the expenditure needed for invention or innovation has been made, it is forever a by-
gone. The actual cost of production is thus typically well below selling
price and the limit on output is not rising costs but falling demand due
to saturated markets. The marginal profit on new foreign markets is

thus high, and corporations have a strong interest in maintaining a system which spreads their products widely. Thus, the interest of multinational corporations in underdeveloped countries is larger than the size of the market would suggest.

It must be stressed that the dependency relationship between major and minor cities should not be attributed to technology. The new technology, because it increases interaction, implies greater interdependence but not necessarily a hierarchical structure. Communications linkages could be arranged in the form of a grid in which each point was directly connected to many other points, permitting lateral as well as vertical communication. This system would be polycentric since messages from one point to another would go directly rather than through the center; each point would become a center on its own; and the distinction between center and periphery would disappear.

Such a grid is made *more* feasible by aeronautical and electronic revolutions which greatly reduce costs of communications. It is not technology which creates inequality; rather, it is *organization* that imposes a ritual judicial asymmetry on the use of intrinsically symmetrical means of communications and arbitrarily creates unequal capacities to initiate and terminate exchange, to store and retrieve information, and to determine the extent of the exchange and terms of the discussion. Just as colonial powers in the past linked each point in the hinterland to the metropolis and inhibited lateral communications, preventing the growth of independent centers of decision making and creativity, multinational corporations (backed by state powers) centralize control by imposing a hierarchical system.

This suggests the possibility of an alternative system of organization in the form of national planning. Multinational corporations are private institutions which organize one or a few industries across many countries. Their polar opposite (the antimultinational corporation, perhaps) is a public institution which organizes many industries across one region. This would permit the centralization of capital, *i.e.*, the coordination of many enterprises by one decision-making center, but would substitute regionalization for internationalization. The span of control would be confined to the boundaries of a single polity and society and not spread over many countries. The advantage of the multinational corporation is its global perspective. The advantage of national planning is its ability to remove the wastes of oligopolistic anarchy, *i.e.*, meaningless product differentiation and an imbalance between different industries within a geographical area. It concentrates *all* levels of decision-making in one locale and thus provides each region with a full complement of skills and occupations. This opens up new horizons for local development by making possible the social and political control of economic decision-making. Multinational corporations, in contrast, weaken political control because they span many countries and can escape national regulation.

A few examples might help to illustrate how multinational corporations reduce options for development. Consider an underdeveloped country wishing to invest heavily in education in order to increase its stock of human capital and raise standards of living. In a market system it would be able to find gainful employment for its citizens within its *national boundaries* by specializing in education-intensive activities and selling its surplus production to foreigners. In the multinational corporate system, however, the demand for high-level education in low-ranking areas is limited, and a country does not become a world center simply by having a better educational system. An outward shift in the supply of educated people in a country, therefore, will not create its own demand but will create an excess supply and lead to emigration. Even then, the employment opportunities for citizens of low-ranking countries are restricted by discriminatory practices in the center. It is well-known that ethnic homogeneity increases as one goes up the corporate hierarchy; the lower levels contain a wide variety of nationalities, the higher levels become successively purer and purer. In part this stems from the skill differences of different nationalities, but more important is the fact that the higher up one goes in the decision-making process, the more important mutual understanding and ease of communications become; a common background becomes all-important.

A similar type of specialization by nationality can be expected within the multinational corporation hierarchy. Multinational corporations are torn in two directions. On the one hand, they must adapt to local circumstances in each country. This calls for decentralized decision making. On the other hand, they must coordinate their activities in various parts of the world and stimulate the flow of ideas from one part of their empire to another. This calls for centralized control. They must, therefore, develop an organizational structure to balance the need for coordination with the need for adaptation to a patch-work quilt of languages, laws and customs. One solution to this problem is a division of labor based on nationality. Day-to-day management in each country is left to the nationals of that country who, because they are intimately familiar with local conditions and practices, are able to deal with local problems and local government. These nationals remain rooted in one spot, while above them is a layer of people who move around from country to country, as bees among flowers, transmitting information from one subsidiary to another and from the lower levels to the general office at the apex of the corporate structure. In the nature of things, these people (reticulators) for the most part will be citizens of the country of the parent corporation (and will be drawn from a small, culturally homo-geneous group within the advanced world), since they will need to have the confidence of their superiors and be able to move easily in the higher management circles. Latin Americans, Asians and Africans will at best be able to aspire to a management position in the intermediate coordinating centers at the continental level. Very few will be able to get much higher than this, for the closer one gets to the top, the more important is "a common cultural heritage."

Another way in which the multinational corporations inhibit eco-nomic development in the hinterland is through their effect on tax capacity. An important government instrument for promoting growth is expenditure on infrastructure and support services. By providing trans-portation and communications, education and health, a government can create a productive labor force and increase the growth potential of its economy. The extent to which it can afford to finance these inter-mediate outlays depends upon its tax revenue.

However, a government's ability to tax multinational corporations is limited by the ability of these corporations to manipulate transfer prices and to move their productive facilities to another country. This means that they will only be attracted to countries where superior infrastructure offsets higher taxes. The government of an underdeveloped country will find it difficult to extract a surplus (revenue from the multinational corporations, less cost of services provided to them) from multinational corporations to use for long-run development programs and for stimu-lating growth in other industries. In contrast, governments of the ad-vanced countries, where the home office and financial center of the multinational corporation are located, can tax the profits of the corpora-tion as a whole, as well as the high incomes of its management. Govern-ment in the metropolis can, therefore, capture some of the surplus gene-rated by the multinational corporations and use it to further improve their infrastructure and growth.

In other words, the relationship between multinational corporations and underdeveloped countries will be somewhat like the relationship between the national corporations in the United States and state and municipal governments. These lower-level governments tend always to be short of funds compared to the federal government which can tax a corporation as a whole. Their competition to attract corporate invest-ment eats up their surplus, and they find it difficult to finance extensive investments in human and physical capital even where such investment would be productive. This has a crucial effect on the pattern of govern-ment expenditure. For example, suppose taxes were first paid to state government and then passed on to the federal government. What chance is there that these lower level legislatures would approve the phenomenal expenditures on space research that now go on? A similar discrepancy can be expected in the international economy with overspending and waste by metropolitan governments and a shortage of public funds in the less advanced countries.

The tendency of the multinational corporations to erode the power of the nation state works in a variety of ways, in addition to its effect on taxation powers. In general, most governmental policy instruments (monetary policy, fiscal policy, wage policy, etc.) diminish in effectiveness the more open the economy and the greater the extent of foreign investments. This tendency applies to political instruments as well as economic, for the multinational corporation is a medium by which laws, politics, foreign policy and culture of one country intrude into another. This acts to reduce the sovereignty of all nation states, but again the relationship is asymmetrical, for the flow tends to be from the parent to the subsidiary, not *vice versa*. The United States can apply its antitrust laws to foreign subsidiaries or stop them from "trading with the enemy" even though such trade is not against the laws of the country in which the branch plant is located. However, it would be illegal for an underdeveloped country which disagreed with American foreign policy to hold a U.S. firm hostage for acts of the parent. This is because legal rights are defined in terms of property-ownership, and the various subsidiaries of a multinational corporation are not "partners in a multinational endeavor" but the property of the general office.

In conclusion, it seems that a regime of multinational corporations would offer underdeveloped countries neither national independence nor equality. It would tend instead to inhibit the attainment of these goals. It would turn the underdeveloped countries into branch-plant countries, not only with reference to their economic functions but throughout the whole gamut of social, political and cultural roles. The subsidiaries of multinational corporations are typically amongst the largest corporations in the country of operations, and their top executives play an influential role in the political, social and cultural life of the host country. Yet these people, whatever their title, occupy at best a medium position in the corporate structure and are restricted in authority and horizons to a lower level of decision making. The governments with whom they deal tend to take on the same middle management outlook, since this is the only range of information and ideas to which they are exposed.[21] In this sense, one can hardly expect such a country to bring forth the creative imagination needed to apply science and technology to the problems of degrading poverty. Even so great a champion of liberalism as Marshall recognized the crucial relationship between occupation and development.

For the business by which a person earns his livelihood generally fills his thoughts during the far greater part of those hours in which his mind is at its best; during them his character is being formed by the way in which he uses his facilities in his work, by the thoughts and feelings which it suggests, and by his relationship to his associates in work, his employers to his employees.[22]

Part III. THE POLITICAL ECONOMY OF THE MULTINATIONAL CORPORATION

The viability of the multinational corporate system depends upon the degree to which people will tolerate the unevenness it creates. It is well to remember that the "New Imperialism" which began after 1870 in a spirit of Capitalism Triumphant, soon became seriously troubled and after 1914 was characterized by war, depression, breakdown of the international economic system, and war again, rather than Free Trade, Pax Britannica and Material Improvement.

A major, if not the major, reason was Great Britain's inability to cope with the byproducts of its own rapid accumulation of capital; *i.e.*, a class conscious labor force at home; a middle class in the hinterland; and rival centers of capital on the Continent and in America. Britain's policy tended to be atavistic and defensive rather than progressive, more concerned with warding off new threats than creating new areas of expansion. Ironically, Edwardian England revived the paraphernalia of the landed aristocracy it had just destroyed. Instead of embarking on a "big push" to develop the vast hinterland of the Empire, colonial administrators often adopted policies to slow down rates of growth and arrest the development of either a native capitalist class or a native proletariat which could overthrow them.

As time went on, the center had to devote an increasing share of government activity to military and other unproductive expenditures; they had to rely on alliances with an inefficient class of landlords, officials and soldiers in the hinterland to maintain stability at the cost of development. A great part of the surplus extracted from the population was thus wasted locally.

The new Mercantilism (as the Multinational Corporate System of special alliances and privileges, aid and tariff concessions is sometimes called) faces similar problems of internal and external division. The center is troubled: excluded groups revolt and even some of the affluent are dissatisfied with their roles. (The much talked about "generation gap" may indicate the failure of the system to reproduce itself.) Nationalistic rivalry between major capitalist countries (especially the challenge of Japan and Germany) remains an important divisive factor, while the economic challenge from the socialist bloc may prove to be of the utmost significance in the next thirty years. Russia has its own form of large-scale economic organizations, also in command of modern technology, and its own conception of how the world should develop. So does China to an increasing degree.[23] Finally, there is the threat presented by the middle classes and the excluded groups of the underdeveloped countries.

The national middle classes in the underdeveloped countries came to power when the center weakened but could not, through their policy of import substitution manufacturing, establish a viable basis for sustained growth. They now face a foreign exchange crisis and an unemployment (or population) crisis—the first indicating their inability to function in the international economy, and the second indicating their alienation from the people they are supposed to lead. In the immediate future, these national middle classes will gain a new lease on life as they take advantage of the spaces created by the rivalry between American and non-American oligopolists striving to establish global market positions. The native capitalists will again become the champions of national independence as they bargain with multinational corporations. But the conflict at this level is more apparent than real, for in the end the fervent nationalism of the middle class asks only for promotion within the corporate structure and not for a break with that structure. In the last analysis their power derives from the metropolis and they cannot easily afford to challenge the international system. They do not command the loyalty of their own population and cannot really compete with the large, powerful, aggregate capitals from the center. They are prisoners of the taste patterns and consumption standards set at the center, and depend on outsiders for technical advice, capital, and when necessary, for military support of their position.

The main threat comes from the excluded groups. It is not unusual in underdeveloped countries for the top 5 percent to obtain between 30 and 40 percent of the total national income, and for the top one-third to obtain anywhere from 60 to 70 percent.[24] At most, one-third of the population can be said to benefit in some sense from the dualistic growth that characterizes development in the hinterland. The remaining two-thirds, who together get only one-third of the income, are outsiders, not because they do not contribute to the economy, but because they do not share in the benefits. They provide a source of cheap labor which helps keep exports to the developed world at a low price and which has financed the urban-biased growth of recent years. Because their wages are low, they spend a moderate amount of time in menial services and are sometimes referred to as underemployed as if to imply they were not needed. In fact, it is difficult to see how the system in most under-developed countries could survive without cheap labor, since removing it (*e.g.*, diverting it to public works projects as is done in socialist countries) would raise consumption costs to capitalists and professional elites. Economic development under the Multinational Corporation does not offer much promise for this large segment of society and their antagonism continuously threatens the system.

The survival of the multinational corporate system depends on how fast it can grow and how much trickles down. Plans now being formulated in government offices, corporate headquarters and international organizations, sometimes suggest that a growth rate of about 6 percent per year in national income (3 percent per capita) is needed. (Such a target is, of course, far below what would be possible if a serious effort were made to solve basic problems of health, education and clothing.) To what extent is it possible?

The multinational corporation must solve four critical problems for the underdeveloped countries, if it is to foster the continued growth and surviv̇al of a "modern" sector. First, it must break the foreign-exchange constraint and provide the underdeveloped countries with imported goods for capital formation and modernization. Second, it must finance an expanded program of government expenditure to train labor and provide support services for urbanization and industrialization. Third, it must solve the urban food problem created by growth. Finally, it must keep the excluded two-thirds of the population under control.

The solution now being suggested for the first is to restructure the world economy allowing the periphery to export certain manufactured goods to the center. Part of this program involves regional common markets to rationalize the existing structure of industry. These plans typically do not involve the rationalization and restructuring of the entire economy of the underdeveloped countries but mainly serve the small manufacturing sector which caters to higher income groups and which, therefore, faces a very limited market in any particular country. The solution suggested for the second problem is an expanded aid program and a reformed government bureaucracy (perhaps along the lines of the Alliance for Progress). The solution for the third is agri-business and the green revolution, a program with only limited benefits to the rural poor. Finally, the solution offered for the fourth problem is population control, either through family planning or counterinsurgency.

It is doubtful whether the center has sufficient political stability to finance and organize the program outlined above. It is not clear, for example, that the West has the technology to rationalize manufacturing abroad or modernize agriculture, or the willingness to open up marketing channels for the underdeveloped world. Nor is it evident that the center has the political power to embark on a large aid program or to readjust its own structure of production and allow for the importation of manufactured goods from the periphery. It is difficult to imagine labor accepting such a re-allocation (a new repeal of the Corn Laws as it were[25]), and it is equally hard to see how the advanced countries could create a system of planning to make these extra hardships unnecessary.

The present crisis may well be more profound than most of us imagine, and the West may find it impossible to restructure the international economy on a workable basis. One could easily argue that the age of the Multinational Corporation is at its end rather than at its beginning. For all we know, books on the global partnership may be the epitaph of the American attempt to take over the old international economy, and not the herald of a new era of international cooperation.

CONCLUSION:

The multinational corporation, because of its great power to plan economic activity, represents an important step forward over previous methods of organizing international exchange. It demonstrates the social nature of production on a global scale. As it eliminates the anarchy of international markets and brings about a more extensive and productive international division of labor, it releases great sources of latent energy.

However, as it crosses international boundaries, it pulls and tears at the social and political fabric and erodes the cohesiveness of national states.[26] Whether one likes this or not, it is probably a tendency that cannot be stopped.

Through its propensity to nestle everywhere, settle everywhere, and establish connections everywhere, the multinational corporation destroys the possibility of national seclusion and self-sufficiency and creates a universal interdependence. But the multinational corporation is still a private institution with a partial outlook and represents only an imperfect solution to the problem of international cooperation. It creates hierarchy rather than equality, and it spreads its benefits unequally.

In proportion to its success, it creates tensions and difficulties. It will lead other institutions, particularly labor organizations and government, to take an international outlook and thus unwittingly create an environment less favorable to its own survival. It will demonstrate the possibilities of material progress at a faster rate than it can realize them, and will create a worldwide demand for change that it cannot satisfy.

The next round may be marked by great crises due to the conflict between national planning by governments and international planning by corporations. For example, if each country loses its power over fiscal and monetary policy due to the growth of multinational corporations (as some observers believe Canada has), how will aggregate demand be stabilized? Will it be possible to construct super-states? Or does multinationalism do away with Keynesian problems? Similarly, will it be possible to fulfill a host of other government functions at the supranational level in the near future? During the past twenty five years many political problems were put aside as the West recovered from the depression and the war. By the late sixties the bloom of this long upswing had begun to fade. In the seventies, power conflicts are likely to come to the fore.

Whether underdeveloped countries will use the opportunities arising from this crisis to build viable local decision-making institutions is difficult to predict. The national middle class failed when it had the opportunity and instead merely reproduced internally the economic dualism of the international economy as it squeezed agriculture to finance urban industry. What is needed is a complete change of direction. The starting point must be the needs of the bottom two-thirds, and not the demands of the top third. The primary goal of such a strategy would be to provide minimum standards of health, education, food and clothing to the entire population, removing the more obvious forms of human suffering. This requires a system which can mobilize the entire population and which can search the local environment for information, resources and needs. It must be able to absorb modern technology, but it cannot be mesmerized by the form it takes in the advanced countries; it must go to the roots. This is not the path the upper one-third chooses when it has control.

The wealth of a nation, wrote Adam Smith two hundred years ago, is determined by "first, the skill, dexterity and judgement with which labor is generally applied; and, secondly by the proportion between the number of those who are employed in useful labor, and that of those who are not so employed."[27] Capitalist enterprise has come a long way from his day, but it has never been able to bring more than a small fraction of the world's population into useful or highly productive employment. The latest stage reveals once more the power of social cooperation and division of labor which so fascinated Adam Smith in his description of pin manufacturing. It also shows the shortcomings of concentrating this power in private hands.

EPILOGUE

Many readers of this essay in draft form have asked: Is there an alternative? Can anything be done? The problem simply stated is to go beyond the multinational corporation. Scholarship can perhaps make the task easier by showing how the forms of international social production devised by capital as it expanded to global proportions can be used to build a better society benefiting all men. I have tried to open up one avenue for explanation by suggesting a system of regional planning as a positive negation of the multinational corporation. Much more work is needed to construct alternative methods of organizing the international economy. Fortunately businessmen in attacking the problem of applying technology on a world level have developed many of the tools and conditions needed for a socialist solution, if we can but stand them on their head. But one must keep in mind that the problem is not one of ideas alone.

A major question is how far those in power will allow the necessary metamorphosis to happen, and how far they will try to resist it by violent means. I do not believe the present structure of uneven development can long be maintained in the light of the increased potential for world development demonstrated by corporate capital itself. But power at the center is great, and the choice of weapons belongs in the first instance to those who have them.

Theodor Mommsen summed up his history of the Roman Republic with patient sadness.

> It was indeed an old world, and even the richly gifted patriotism of Caesar could not make it young again. The dawn does not return till after the night has run its course.[28]

I myself do not view the present with such pessimism. History moves more quickly now, the forces for positive change are much stronger, and the center seems to be losing its will and self confidence. It is becoming increasingly evident to all that in contrast to corporate capitalism we must be somewhat less "efficient" within the microcosm of the enterprise and far more "efficient" in the macrocosm of world society. The dysutopia of the multinational corporate system shows us both what is to be avoided and what is possible.

NOTES

1. See Marx, *Capital*, Vol. 1, Chapter XXV, "On the General Law of Capitalist Accumulation," Chapter XII, "Co-operation" and Chapter XIV, part 4, "Division of Labour in Manufacturing and Division of Labour in Society," and Vol. 3, Chapter XXIII.

2. Phrase used by Anthony M. Salomon in *International Aspects of Antitrust*, Part I. Hearings before the Sub-Committee on Antitrust and Monopoly of the Senate Committee on the Judiciary. April 1966, p. 49.

3. These trends are discussed in Stephen Hymer and Robert Rowthorn, "Multinational Corporations and International Oligopoly: the Non-American Challenge" in C. P. Kindleberger, ed., *The International Corporation* (Cambridge, M.I.T. Press, 1970).

4. Substituting the word *multinational corporation* for *bourgeois* in the following quote from *The Communist Manifesto* provides a more dynamic picture of the multinational corporation than any of its present day supporters have dared to put forth.

The need of a constantly expanding market for its products chases the multinational corporation over the whole surface of the globe. It must nestle everywhere, settle everywhere, establish connections everywhere. The bourgeoisie has through its exploitation of the world-market given a cosmopolitan character to production and consumption in every country. To the great chagrin of Reactionists, it has drawn from under the feet of industry the national ground on which it stood. All old-established national industries have been destroyed or are daily being destroyed. They are dislodged by new industries, whose introduction becomes a life and death question for all civilized nations, by industries that no longer work up indigenous raw material, but raw material drawn from the remotest zones; industries whose products are consumed, not only at home, but in every quarter of the globe. In place of the old wants, satisfied by the production of the country, we find new wants, requiring for their satisfaction the products of distant lands and climes. In place of the old local and national seclusion and self-sufficiency, we have intercourse in every direction, universal interdependence of nations. And as in material, so also in intellectual production. The intellectual creations of individual nations become common property. National one-sidedness and narrow-mindedness become more and more impossible, and from the numerous national and local literatures there arises a world literature.

The multinational corporation, by the rapid improvement of all instruments of production, by the immensely facilitated means of communication, draws all, even the most barbarian, nations into civilization. The cheap prices of its commodities are the heavy artillery with which it batters down all Chinese walls, with which it forces the barbarians' intensely obstinate hatred of foreigners to capitulate. It compels all nations, on pain of extinction, to adopt the bourgeois mode of production, it compels them to introduce what it calls civilization into their midst, i.e., to become bourgeois themselves. In a word, it creates a world after its own image.

The multinational corporation has subjected the country to the rule of the towns. It has created enormous cities, has greatly increased the urban population as compared with the rural, and has thus rescued a considerable part of the population from the idiocy of rural life. Just as it has made the country dependent on the towns, so it has made barbarian and semi-barbarian countries dependent on the civilized ones, nations of peasants on nations of bourgeois, the East on the West.

The multinational corporation keeps more and more doing away with the scattered state of the population, of the means of production, and of property. It has agglomerated population, centralized means of production, and has concentrated property in a few hands. The necessary consequence of this was political centralization. Independent, or but loosely connected provinces, with separate interests, laws, systems of taxation, and governments, became lumped together in one nation, with one government, one code of laws, one national class-interest, one frontier, and one customs tariff.

5. See R. H. Coase for an analysis of the boundary between the firm and the market: "outside the firm, price movements direct production which is coordinated through a series of exchange transactions on the market. Within the firm these market transactions are eliminated and in place of the complicated market structure with exchange transactions, is substituted the entrepreneur co-ordinator who directs production." R. H. Coase, "The Nature of the Firm," reprinted in G. J. Stigler and K. E. Boulding *Readings in Price Theory* (Homewood, Richard D. Irwin, Inc., 1952).

6. "Even in the very backward countries we find highly specialized trades; but we do not find the work within each trade so divided up that the planning and arrangement of the business, its management and its risks, are borne by one set of people, while the manual work required for it is done by higher labour. This form of division of labour is at once characteristic of the modern world generally and of the English race in particular. It may be swept away by the further growth of that free enterprise which has called it into existence. But for the present it expands out for good and for evil as the chief fact in the form of modern civilization, the 'kernel' of the modern economic problem." Marshall, *Principles of Economics*, 8th edition, pp. 74-75. Note that Marshall preferred to call businessmen Undertakers rather than Capitalists (p. 74).

7. "Division of labour within the workshop implies the undisputed authority of the capitalist over men that are but parts of a mechanism that belongs to him . . . The same bourgeois mind which praises division of labour in the workshop, lifelong annexation of the labourer to a partial operation, and his complete subjection to capital, as being an organisation of labour that increases its productiveness —that same bourgeois mind denounces with equal vigour every conscious attempt to socially control and regulate the process of production, as an inroad upon such sacred things as the rights of property, freedom and unrestricted play for the bent of the individual capitalist. It is very characteristic that the enthusiastic apologists of the factory system have nothing more damning to urge against a general organization of the labour of society, than that it would turn all society into one immense factory." K. Marx, *Capital*, Volume I (Moscow, Foreign Language Publishing House, 1961), p. 356.

8. The following analysis by E. S. Mason of current attempts to justify hierarchy and inequality by emphasizing the skill and knowledge of managers and the technostructure is interesting and of great significance on this connection:

"As everyone now recognizes, classical economics provided not only a system of analysis, or analytical 'model,' intended to be useful to the explanation of economic behaviour but also a defense—and a carefully reasoned defense—of the proposition that the economic behaviour promoted and constrained by the institutions of a free-enterprise system is, in the main, in the public interest.

It cannot be too strongly emphasized that the growth of the nineteenth-century capitalism depended largely on the general acceptance of a reasoned justification of the system on moral as well as on political and economic grounds.

It seems doubtful whether, to date, the managerial literature has provided an equally satisfying apologetic for big business.

The attack on the capitalist apologetic of the nineteenth century has been successful, but a satisfactory contemporary apologetic is still to be created. I suspect that, when and if an effective new ideology is devised, economics will be found to have little to contribute. Economists are still so mesmerized with the fact of choice and so little with its explanations, and the concept of the market is still so central to their thought, that they would appear to be professionally debarred from their important task. I suspect that to the formulation of an up-to-date twentieth-century apologetic the psychologists, and possibly, the political scientists will be the main contributors. It is high time they were called to their job."

Edward S. Mason, "The Apologetics of Managerialism," *The Journal of Business of the University of Chicago,* January 1958, Vol. XXXI, No. 1, pp. 1-11.

9. This analysis of the modern corporation is almost entirely based on the work of Alfred D. Chandler, *Strategy and Structure* (New York, Doubleday & Co., Inc., 1961) and Chester Barnard, *The Functions of Executives* (Cambridge, Harvard University Press, 1938).

10. Alfred D. Chandler and Fritz Redlich, "Recent Developments in American Business Administration and Their Conceptualization," *Business History Review,* Spring 1961, pp. 103-128.

11. Neoclassical models suggest that this choice was due to the exogenously determined nature of technological change. A Marxist economic model would argue that it was due in part to the increased tensions in the labor market accompanying the accumulation of capital and the growth of large firms. This is discussed further in S. Hymer and S. Resnick, "International Trade and Uneven Development," in J. N. Bhagwati, R. W. Jones, R. A. Mundell, Jaroslave Vanek, eds., *Kindleberger Festschrift* (Cambridge, M.I.T. Press, 1970).

12. The reasons for foreign investment discussed here are examined in more detail in S. Hymer, "La Grande Corporation Multinationale," *Revue Economique,* Vol. XIX, No. 6, Novembre 1968, pp. 949-973, and in Hymer and Rowthorn, *op. cit.*

13. At present, U.S. corporations have about 60 billion dollars invested in foreign branch plants and subsidiaries. The total assets of these foreign operations are much larger than the capital invested and probably equal 100 billion dollars at book value. (American corporations, on the average, were able to borrow 40 percent of their subsidiaries' capital requirements locally in the country of operation.) The total assets of 500 large U.S. firms are about 300-350 billion dollars, while the total assets of the 200 largest non-U.S. firms are slightly less than 200 billion dollars. See U.S. Department of Commerce, *Survey of Current Business,* September 1969 and *Fortune* list of the 500 largest U.S. corporations and 200 largest non-American.

14. At present unequal growth of different parts of the world economy upsets the oligopolistic equilibrium because the leading firms have different geographical distributions of production and sales. Thus, if Europe grows faster than the United States, European firms tend to grow faster than American firms, unless American firms engage in heavy foreign investment. Similarly, if the United States grows faster than Europe, U.S. firms will grow faster than European firms because Europeans have a lesser stake in the American market. When firms are distributed evenly in all markets, they share equally in the good and bad fortunes of the various submarkets, and oligopolistic equilibrium is not upset by the unequal growth of different countries.

15. Chandler and Redlich, *op. cit.*

16. Chandler and Redlich, *op. cit.*, p. 120.

17. See H. A. Simon, "The Compensation of Executives," *Sociometry*, March 1957.

18. Sean Gervasi, "Publicité et Croissance Economique," *Economie et Humanisme*, (Novembre/Decembre, 1964).

19. Lloyd A. Fallers, "A Note on the Trickle Effect," in Perry Bliss, ed., *Marketing and the Behavioural Sciences*, (Boston, Allyn and Bacon, 1963), pp. 208-216.

20. See Raymond Vernon, "International Investment and International Trade in the Product Cycle," *Quarterly Journal of Economics*, LXXX, May 1966.

21. An interesting illustration of the asymmetry in horizons and prospectives of the big company and the small country is found in these quotations from *Fortune*. Which countries of the world are making a comparable analysis of the Multinational Corporation?

A Ford economist regularly scans the international financial statistics to determine which countries have the highest rates of inflation; these are obviously prime candidates for devaluation. He then examines patterns of trade. If a country is running more of an inflation than its chief trading partners and competitors and its reserves are limited, it is more than a candidate; it is a shoo-in. His most difficult problem is to determine exactly when the devaluation will take place. Economics determines whether and how much, but politicians control the timing. So the analyst maintains a complete library of information on leading national officials. He tries to get "into the skin of the man" who is going to make the decision. The economist's forecasts have been correct in sixty-nine of the last seventy-five crisis situations.

DuPont is one company that is making a stab in the direction of formally measuring environmental incertainty, basically as a tool for capital budgeting decisions. The project is still in the research stage, but essentially the idea is to try to derive estimates of the potential of a foreign market, which is, of course, affected by economic conditions. The state of the economy in turn is partly a function of the fiscal and monetary policies the foreign government adopts. Policy decisions depend on real economic forces, on the attitudes of various interest groups in the country, and on the degree to which the government listens to these groups.

In the fiscal and monetary part of their broad economic model, the DuPont researchers have identified fifteen to twenty interest groups per country, from small land-owners to private bankers. Each interest group has a "latent influence," which depends on its size and educational level and the group's power to make its feelings felt. This influence, subjectively measured, is multiplied by an estimate of "group cohesiveness": i.e., how likely the group is to mobilize its full resources on any particular issue. The product is a measure of "potential influence." This in turn must be multiplied by a factor representing the government's receptivity to each influence group.

Sanford Rose, "The Rewarding Strategies of Multinationalism," *Fortune*, September 15, 1968, p. 105.

22. This quote is taken from the first page of Marshall's *Principles of Economics.* In the rest of the book, he attempted to show that the economic system of laissez-faire capitalism had an overall positive effect in forming character. As we noted above, his argument rested upon the existence of competitive markets (and the absence of coercion). Because multinational corporations substitute for the international market they call into question the liberal ideology which rationalized it. (See footnote 9 above, quoting E. S. Mason).

23. A. A. Berle, Jr., has put the problem most succinctly:
The Industrial Revolution, as it spread over twentieth-century life, required collective organization of men and things . . . As the twentieth century moves into the afternoon, two systems—and (thus far) two only—have emerged as vehicles of modern industrial economics. One is the socialist commissariat; its highest organization at present is in the Soviet Union, the other is the modern corporation, most highly developed in the United States.
Foreword to *The Corporation in Modern Society,* E. S. Mason, ed. (New York, Atheneum, 1967), p. IX.

24. S. Kuznets, *Modern Economic Growth* (New Haven, Yale University Press, 1966), pp. 423-24.

25. See K. Polanyi, *The Great Transformation* (New York, Farrar and Rinehart, Inc. 1944), on the consequences after 1870 of the repeal of the Corn Laws in England.

26. See Kari Levitt, *Silent Surrender: The Multinational Corporation in Canada* (Toronto, Macmillan Company of Canada, 1970) and Norman Girvan and Owen Jefferson "Corporate vs. Caribbean Integration" *New World Quarterly,* Vol. IV, No. 2.

27. See A. Smith, *The Wealth of Nations* (New York, The Modern Library, 1937), p. 1 vii.

28. See Theodor Mommsen, *The History of Rome* (New York, Meridian Books, Inc., 1958), p. 587.

Part VII

Commercial Policies

Developing Market Economies

Belassa
Myint

From Centrally Planned to Market Regulated Economies

Wolf

Developed Market Economies, the New GATT, and Foreign Aid

Patterson and Patterson
Chenery and Strout

The Choice of a Development Strategy: Lessons and Prospects

Bela Belassa

Inward- vs. Outward-Oriented Development Strategies

The evidence is quite conclusive: countries applying outward-oriented development strategies performed better in terms of exports, economic growth, and employment than countries with continued inward orientation, which encountered increasing economic difficulties. At the same time, policy reforms aimed at greater outward orientation brought considerable improvement to the economic performance of countries that had earlier applied inward-oriented policies.

It has been suggested, however, that import substitution was a necessary precondition for the development of manufactured exports in present-day developing countries. In attempting to provide an answer to this question, a distinction needs to be made between first-stage and second-stage import substitution.

I have noted that, except in Britain and Hong Kong, the exportation of nondurable consumer goods and their inputs was preceded by an import-substitution phase. At the same time, there were differences among the countries concerned as regards the length of this phase and the level of protection applied. First-stage import substitution was of relatively short duration in the present-day industrial countries and in the three Far Eastern developing countries that subsequently adopted an outward-oriented strategy; it was longer in most other developing countries, and these countries also generally had higher levels of protection.

Nor did all nondurable consumer goods and their inputs go through an import-substitution phase before the Far Eastern countries began to export them. Synthetic textiles in Korea, plastic shoes in Taiwan, and fashion clothing in Singapore all began to be produced largely for export markets. Plywood and wigs, which were Korea's leading exports in the late sixties and early seventies, did not go through an import-substitution phase either.

Wigs provide a particularly interesting example, because they reflect the responses of entrepreneurs to incentives. Korea originally exported human hair to the industrial countries, especially the United States. Recognizing that human hair was made into wigs by a labor-intensive process, entrepreneurs began to exploit what appeared to be a profitable opportunity to export wigs, given the favorable treatment of exports in Korea and the limitations imposed by the United States on wigs originating from Hong Kong. The supply of human

Reprinted from "The Process of Industrial Development and Alternative Development Strategies—Essays in International Finance No. 141, December 1980," pp. 18–27, with permission of Princeton University Press, Princeton, Copyright 1981.

hair soon proved to be insufficient, however, and firms turned to exporting wigs made of synthetic hair. Wigs made with synthetic hair were for a time Korea's second-largest single export commodity, after plywood.

The example indicates that entrepreneurs will export the commodities that correspond to the country's comparative advantage if the system of incentives does not discriminate against exports. It also points to the need to leave the choice of exports to private initiative. It is highly unlikely that government planners would have chosen wigs as a potential major export or that they would have effected a switch from human to synthetic hair in making them. Even if a product group such as toys were identified by government planners, the choice of which toys to produce would have to be made by the entrepreneur, who has to take the risks and reap the rewards of his actions. At the same time, providing similar incentives to all export commodities other than those facing market limitations abroad and avoiding a bias against exports will ensure that private profitability corresponds to social profitability. This was, by and large, the case in countries pursuing an outward strategy.

These considerations may explain why Singapore and Taiwan did not need a planning or targeting system for exports. Export targets were in effect in Korea, but the fulfillment of these targets was not a precondition of the application of the free-trade regime to exports or of the provision of export incentives. While successful exporters were said to enjoy advantageous treatment in tax cases and export targets may have exerted pressure on some firms, these factors merely served to enhance the effects of export incentives without introducing discrimination among export products. At any rate, most firms continually exceeded their targets. A case in point is the increase in Korean exports by two-thirds between the second quarter of 1975 and the second quarter of 1976, exceeding the targets by a very large margin.

The reliance on private initiative in countries that adopted an outward-oriented development strategy can be explained by the need of exporters for flexibility to respond to changing world market conditions. Furthermore, government cannot take responsibility for successes and failures in exporting that will affect the profitability of firms. For these reasons Hungary, among socialist countries, gave firms the freedom to determine the product composition of their exports after the 1968 economic reform and especially after 1977.

In the Latin-American countries that reformed their incentive systems in the period preceding the 1973 oil crisis, the expansion of manufactured exports was not based on export targets either. The question remains, however, whether the development of exports in these countries was helped by the fact that they had undertaken second-stage import substitution.

This question can be answered in the negative as far as nondurable consumer goods and their inputs are concerned. Had appropriate incentives been provided, these commodities could have been exported as soon as first-stage import substitution was completed, as was the case in the Far Eastern countries. In fact, to the extent that the products in question had to use some domestic inputs produced at higher than world market costs, exporters were at a disadvantage in foreign markets. It can also be assumed that the inability to exploit fully economies of scale and the lack of sufficient specialization in the production of parts, components, and accessories in the confines of the protected domestic markets retarded the development of exports of intermediate products and producer and consumer durables.

More generally, as a Hungarian economist has pointed out, there is the danger that second-stage import substitution will lead to the establishment of an industrial structure that is "prematurely old," in the sense that it is based on small-scale production with inadequate specialization and outdated machinery. Should this be the case, any subsequent move toward outward orientation will encounter difficulties. Such difficulties were apparent in the case of Hungary and may also explain why, although exports grew rapidly from a low base, their share in manufacturing output remained small in the Latin-American countries that moved toward outward orientation from the second stage of import substitution.

In contrast, in the period following the oil crisis the Far Eastern countries increasingly upgraded their exports of nondurable consumer goods and began exporting machinery, electronics, and transport equipment. For several of these products, including shipbuilding in Korea, photographic equipment in Singapore, and other electronic products in Taiwan, exporting was not preceded by an import-substitution phase. There are even examples, such as color television sets in Korea, where the entire production was destined for foreign markets.

Intermediate goods, machinery, and automobiles require special attention, given the importance of economies of scale on the plant level for the first; the need for product (horizontal) specialization for the second; and the desirability of vertical specialization in the form of the production of parts, components, and accessories on an efficient scale for the third. In all these cases, production in protected domestic markets will involve high costs in most developing countries, and the establishment of small-scale and insufficiently specialized firms will make the transition to exportation difficult. This contrasts with the case of nondurable consumer goods and their inputs, where efficient production does not require large plants or horizontal and vertical specialization.

It follows that, rather than enter into second-stage import substitution as a prelude to subsequent exports, it is preferable to undertake the manufacture of intermediate goods and producer and consumer durables for domestic and foreign markets simultaneously. This will permit the exploitation of economies of scale and ensure efficient import substitution in some products, while others continue to be imported. At the same time, it will require the provision of equal incentives to exports and to import substitution instead of import protection that discriminates against exports.

Vulnerability and Policy Responses to External Shocks

Outward orientation involves increasing the share of exports in GNP, and the high share of exports in the national economies of countries undertaking such a strategy has been said to increase their vulnerability to foreign events. The experience of the post-1973 period casts some light on the validity of this claim.

Available evidence indicates that the Far Eastern countries applying an outward-oriented strategy weathered the effects of the quadrupling of oil prices in 1973-74 and the world recession of 1974-75 better than countries with continued inward orientation. This may be explained by differences in the "compressibility" of imports and in the flexibility of the national economies of countries applying different strategies. Outward orientation is associated with high export *and* import shares that permit reductions in nonessential imports without serious adverse effects on the functioning of the economy. By contrast, continued inward orientation involves limiting imports to an unavoidable minimum, so that any further reduction will impose a considerable cost in terms of growth. Furthermore, the greater flexibility of the national economies of countries pursuing an outward-oriented strategy, under which firms learn to live with foreign competition, makes it possible to change the product composition of exports in response to changes in world market conditions, whereas inward orientation entails establishing a more rigid economic structure.

I come next to policy responses to external shocks. In the Far Eastern countries there were pressures for a shift toward inward orientation in the immediate aftermath of the oil crisis and the world recession. These countries nevertheless continued their outward-oriented development strategy, which made it possible for them to maintain high rates of growth of exports and GNP. Taking the 1973-79 period as a whole, per capita GNP rose at average annual rates of 8.3 per cent in Korea, 6.1 per cent in Singapore, and 5.5 per cent in Taiwan. Growth rates declined, however, after 1978 in Korea as its currency became increasingly overvalued and some large capital-intensive investments were undertaken.

Brazil attempted to maintain past rates of economic growth by relying on foreign borrowing and increased import protection. The high capital intensity of import-substitution projects, however, raised capital-output ratios and led to a decline in the rate of economic growth. Per capita incomes rose 5.2 per cent a year in 1966-73, 4.5 per cent in 1973-76, and 2.4 per cent in 1976-79. At the same time, the servicing of foreign loans imposed an increasing burden on Brazil's balance of payments.

Policy changes in the opposite direction were made in Chile and Uruguay, which had applied an inward-oriented strategy until the 1973 oil crisis. These countries responded to the deterioration of their terms of trade and the slowdown in the growth of foreign demand for their export products by reforming the system of incentives. The reforms involved eliminating quantitative restrictions, reducing the bias against exports, liberalizing financial markets, and adopting positive real interest rates.

In Uruguay, which had had a stagnant economy in the previous decade, the reforms led to rapid increases in exports and GNP; per capita GNP rose 3.1 per cent a year between 1973 and 1976 and 4.3 per cent a year between 1976 and 1979. The growth of exports and GNP accelerated in Chile after a period of dislocation caused by the application of a severe deflationary policy that was aggravated by rapid reductions in tariffs.

Argentina and Colombia rely on domestically produced oil and hence were unaffected by the quadrupling of petroleum prices. Colombia also enjoyed higher coffee prices, which more than offset the shortfall in exports due to the slowdown in the growth of foreign demand. But it reduced incentives to nontraditional exports, with attendant losses in export market shares, and it was not able to translate increases in foreign-exchange earnings from traditional exports into higher GNP growth rates. The distortions caused by rapid inflation were largely responsible for low GNP growth rates in Argentina.

Mexico lost export market shares in both traditional and non-traditional exports following the adoption of domestic expansionary policies, financed in large part by the inflow of foreign capital. And while the discovery of large oil deposits benefited Mexico's balance of payments, it increased the overvaluation of the currency, thus discriminating against agricultural and manufacturing activities. Finally, no substantive policy changes occurred in India, which continued to lose export market shares.

Policy Prescriptions and Prospects for the Future

The experience of developing countries in the postwar period leads to certain policy prescriptions. First, while infant-industry considerations call for the preferential treatment of manufacturing activities, such treatment should be applied on a moderate scale, both to avoid the establishment and maintenance of inefficient industries and to ensure the continued expansion of primary production for domestic and foreign markets.

Second, equal treatment should be given to exports and to import substitution in the manufacturing sector, in order to ensure resource allocation according to comparative advantage and the exploitation of economies of scale. This is of particular importance in the case of intermediate goods and producer and consumer durables, where the advantages of large plant size and horizontal and vertical specialization are considerable and where import substitution in the framework of small domestic markets makes the subsequent development of exports difficult. The provision of equal incentives will contribute to efficient exportation and import substitution through specialization in particular products and in their parts, components, and accessories.

Third, infant-industry considerations apart, variations in incentive rates within the manufacturing sector should be kept to a minimum. This amounts to the application of the "market principle" in allowing firms to decide on the activities to be undertaken. In particular, firms should be free to choose their export composition in response to changing world market conditions.

Fourth, in order to minimize uncertainty for the firm, the system of incentives should be stable and automatic. Uncertainty will also be reduced if the reform of the system of incentives necessary to apply the principles just described is carried out according to a timetable made public in advance.

It has been objected that the application of these principles—characteristic of an outward-oriented development strategy—would encounter market limitations, aggravated by protectionist policies, in the industrial countries. To address this issue, one needs to examine recent and prospective trends in trade in manufactured goods between the industrial and the developing countries.

Notwithstanding protectionist pressures in the industrial countries, their imports of manufactured goods from the developing countries rose at a rapid rate during the period following the oil crisis, averaging 10.2 per cent a year in volume terms between 1973 and 1978. Moreover, the "apparent" income elasticity of demand for these imports, calculated as the ratio of the growth rate of imports to that of gross domestic product, increased from 3.6 in 1963-73 to 4.1 in 1973-78.

Given the increased volume of manufactured imports from the developing countries, the apparent income elasticity of demand for manufactured goods originating in these countries can be expected to decline in the future. Assuming an elasticity of 3.2 and a GDP growth rate of 3.9 per cent in the industrial countries, I have projected their imports of manufactured goods from the developing countries to rise at an average annual rate of 12.5 per cent between 1978 and 1990. This projection assumes unchanged policies in the industrial countries, including the maintenance of the Multifiber Arrangement.

If this import growth rate were realized, the share of the developing countries in the consumption of manufactured goods in the industrial countries would rise from 1.5 per cent in 1978 to 4.0 per cent in 1990, with an incremental share of 8.9 per cent. The incremental share would be the highest in clothing, 28.1 per cent; it would be 7.2 per cent in textiles and 6.6 per cent in other consumer goods. Nonetheless, the production of textiles and clothing would rise at an average annual rate of 2 per cent in the industrial countries. And these countries would have a rising export surplus in trade in manufactured goods with the developing countries, which would contribute to the growth of their manufacturing sector.

At the same time, in accordance with the "stages" approach to comparative advantage, changes would occur in the product composition of the manufactured exports of the developing countries as they proceeded to higher stages of industrial development. This process is exemplified by Japan, which shifted from unskilled-labor-intensive to skill-intensive to physical-capital-intensive exports and is increasingly expanding its technology-intensive exports.

Shifts in export composition are now occurring in the newly industrializing developing countries, including the Far Eastern and Latin-American countries that carried out policy reforms after the mid-sixties. The Far Eastern countries that have a relatively high educational level may increasingly take the place of Japan in exporting skill-intensive products, while Latin-American countries may expand their exports of relatively capital-intensive products. Countries at lower stages of industrial development, in turn, may take the place of the newly industrializing countries in exporting products that require chiefly unskilled labor.

To the extent that the exports of newly industrializing countries replace Japanese exports, and their exports are in turn replaced by the exports of countries at lower stages of industrial development, the threat to the domestic manufacturing industries of the industrial countries is reduced. Nor does the upgrading and diversification of manufactured exports by the newly industrializing countries represent a serious threat, inasmuch as the exports of individual commodities would account for a relatively small proportion of the consumption and production of these commodities in the industrial countries. This conclusion also applies to the international division of the production process, exemplified by the development of Ford's "world car," which will entail manufacturing in nineteen countries.

It follows that it is in the interest of the newly industrializing developing countries to upgrade and diversify their exports in line with their changing comparative advantage. This is also in the interest of countries at lower stages of industrial development, as they can replace exports of unskilled-labor-intensive commodities from the newly industrializing countries to industrial-country markets.

There are also considerable opportunities for the expansion of trade in manufactured goods among the developing countries themselves. With increased oil earnings, the largely open markets of the OPEC countries will experience rapid growth. Furthermore, the newly industrializing countries can trade skill-intensive and physical-capital-intensive goods among themselves and exchange these commodities for the unskilled-labor-intensive products of countries at lower stages of industrial development.

The expansion of this trade requires the pursuit of outward-oriented strategies by the newly industrializing countries, so as to provide appropriate incentives to exports and to allow imports from other developing countries. The pursuit of such a strategy would also contribute to efficient import substitution by ensuring low-cost manufacture through international specialization and the international division of the production process. Similar conclusions apply to countries at lower stages of industrial development.

Finally, lowering protection in the industrial countries would lead to increases in their imports of manufactured goods from the developing countries over and above projected levels. This would also be in the interest of the industrial countries, properly conceived. They would benefit from shifts to high-technology products within the manufactured sector as higher export earnings permitted the developing countries to increase their imports of these products.

Trade liberalization in the industrial countries could proceed over a ten-year horizon without involving excessively large adjustment costs. One could accept, for example, a decline in the production of textiles and clothing over time that would involve not replacing the normal attrition of workers and depreciated equipment in branches that utilized largely unskilled labor. In turn, new entrants into the industrial labor force would increasingly enter technologically advanced industries where productivity levels are substantially higher.

Apart from expanding the volume of trade, then, the pursuit of appropriate policies by developed and developing countries would permit shifts in the pattern of international specialization in response to the changing structure of comparative advantage in countries at different levels of industrial development. As a result, the efficiency of resource allocation would improve and rates of economic growth would accelerate, with benefits to all concerned.

THE "CLASSICAL THEORY" OF INTERNATIONAL TRADE AND THE UNDERDEVELOPED COUNTRIES[1]

Hal Myint

THERE has recently been a considerable amount of controversy concerning the applicability of the " classical theory " of international trade to the underdeveloped countries.[2] The twists in this controversy may be set out as follows. The critics start with the intention of showing that the " nineteenth-century pattern " of international trade, whereby the underdeveloped countries export raw materials and import manufactured goods, has been unfavourable to the economic development of these countries. But instead of trying to show this directly, they concentrate their attacks on the " classical theory," which they believe to be responsible for the unfavourable pattern of trade. The orthodox economists then come to the defence of the classical theory by reiterating the principle of comparative costs which they claim to be applicable both to the developed and the underdeveloped countries. After this, the controversy shifts from the primary question whether or not the nineteenth-century pattern of international trade, as a historical reality, has been unfavourable to the underdeveloped countries to the different question whether or not the theoretical model assumed in the comparative-costs analysis is applicable to these countries. Both sides then tend to conduct their argument as though the two questions were the same and to identify the " classical theory " with the comparative-costs theory.

It will be argued in this paper that this has led to the neglect of those other elements in the classical theory of international trade which are much nearer to the realities and ideologies of the nineteenth-century expansion of international trade to the underdeveloped countries. In Sections I and II we shall outline these elements and show that they are traceable to Adam Smith and to some extent to J. S. Mill. In Section III we shall show how one of Adam Smith's lines of approach can be fruitfully developed to throw a more illuminating light on the past and present patterns of the international trade of the underdeveloped countries than the conventional theory. In Section IV we shall touch upon some policy implications of our analysis and show certain weaknesses in the position both of the orthodox economists

---

[1] This paper has benefited from comments by Sir Donald MacDougall, Professor H. G. Johnson, R. M. Sundrum and G. M. Meier.

[2] Of the very extensive literature on the subject, we may refer to two notable recent works, the first stating the orthodox position and the second the position of the critics: J. Viner, *International Trade and Economic Development*, and G. Myrdal, *An International Economy*.

Reprinted with permission from *The Economic Journal* **68**, 317–337, Copyright 1958.

in relation to the ideological than to the actual economic forces which characterised the nineteenth-century expansion of international trade to the underdeveloped countries. It is true, as we shall see later,[1] that both the total value and the physical output of the exports of these countries expanded rapidly. In many cases the rate of increase in export production was well above any possible rate of increase in population, resulting in a considerable rise in output per head. But it is still true to say that this was achieved not quite in the way envisaged by Smith, viz., a better division of labour and specialisation leading on to innovations and cumulative improvements in skills and productivity per man-hour. Rather, the increase in output per head seems to have been due: (i) to once-for-all increases in productivity accompanying the transfer of labour from the subsistence economy to the mines and plantations, and (ii) what is more important, as we shall see later, to an increase in working hours and in the proportion of gainfully employed labour relatively to the semi-idle labour of the subsistence economy.

The transfer of labour from the subsistence economy to the mines and plantations with their much higher capital–output ratio and skilled management undoubtedly resulted in a considerable increase in productivity. But this was mostly of a once-for-all character for a number of reasons. To begin with, the indigenous labour emerging from the subsistence economy was raw and technically backward. Moreover, it was subject to high rates of turnover, and therefore not amenable to attempts to raise productivity. Unfortunately, this initial experience gave rise to or hardened the convention of " cheap labour," which regarded indigenous labour merely as an undifferentiated mass of low-grade man-power to be used with a minimum of capital outlay.[2] Thus when the local labour supply was exhausted the typical reaction was not to try to economise labour by installing more machinery and by reorganising methods of production but to seek farther afield for additional supplies of cheap labour. This is why the nineteenth-century process of international trade in the underdeveloped countries was characterised by large-scale movements of cheap labour from India and China.[3] This tendency was reinforced by the way in which the world-market demand for raw materials expanded in a series of waves. During the booms output had to be expanded as quickly as possible along existing lines, and there was no time to introduce new techniques or reorganise production; during the slumps it was difficult to raise capital for such purposes.

[1] See footnotes on pp. 324 and 327 below. See also Sir Donald MacDougall's *The World Dollar Problem*, pp. 134–43. Sir Donald's argument that the productivity of labour in the underdeveloped countries has been rising faster than is generally assumed is mainly based on figures for productivity *per capita*. These figures are not inconsistent with our argument that on the whole the expansion of the export production has been achieved on more or less constant techniques and skills of indigenous labour, by increasing working hours and the proportion of gainfully employed labour rather than by a continuous rise in productivity per man-hour.

[2] Cf. S. H. Frankel, *Capital Investment in Africa*, pp. 142–6, and W. M. Macmillan, *Europe and West Africa*, pp. 48–50.

[3] Cf. Knowles, *op. cit.*, pp. viii and 182–201.

This failure to achieve Adam Smith's ideal of specialisation leading on to continuous improvements in skills can also be observed in the peasant export sectors. Where the export crop happened to be a traditional crop (*e.g.*, rice in South-East Asia), the expansion in export production was achieved simply by bringing more land under cultivation with the same methods of cultivation used in the subsistence economy. Even where new export crops were introduced, the essence of their success as peasant export crops was that they could be produced by fairly simple methods involving no radical departure from the traditional techniques of production employed in subsistence agriculture.[1]

Thus instead of a process of economic growth based on continuous improvements in skills, more productive recombinations of factors and increasing returns, the nineteenth-century expansion of international trade in the underdeveloped countries seems to approximate to a simpler process based on constant returns and fairly rigid combinations of factors. Such a process of expansion could continue smoothly only if it could feed on *additional* supplies of factors in the required proportions.

II

Let us now turn to Smith's " vent for surplus " theory of international trade. It may be contrasted with the comparative-costs theory in two ways.

(*a*) The comparative-costs theory assumes that the resources of a country are given and fully employed before it enters into international trade. The function of trade is then to reallocate its given resources more efficiently between domestic and export production in the light of the new set of relative prices now open to the country. With given techniques and full employment, export production can be increased only at the cost of reducing the domestic production. In contrast, the " vent for surplus " theory assumes that a previously isolated country about to enter into international trade possesses a surplus productive capacity [2] of some sort or another. The function of trade here is not so much to reallocate the given resources as to provide the new effective demand for the output of the surplus resources which would have remained unused in the absence of trade. It follows that export production can be increased without necessarily reducing domestic production.

---

[1] Thus A. McPhee wrote about the palm-oil and ground-nut exports of West Africa: " They made little demand on the energy and thought of the natives and they effected no revolution in the society of West Africa. That was why they were so readily grafted on the old economy and grew as they did " (*The Economic Revolution in West Africa*, pp. 39–40). Some writers argue that there was a studied neglect of technical improvements in the peasant sector to facilitate the supply of cheap labour to other sectors. Cf., for example, W. A. Lewis, " Economic Development with Unlimited Supplies of Labour," *Manchester School*, May 1954, pp. 149–50. For a description of imperfect specialisation in economic activity in West Africa see P. T. Bauer and B. S. Yamey, " Economic Progress and Occupational Distribution," Economic Journal, December 1951, p. 743.

[2] A surplus over domestic requirements and *not* a surplus of exports over imports.

(*b*) The concept of a surplus productive capacity above the requirements of domestic consumption implies an inelastic domestic demand for the exportable commodity and/or a considerable degree of internal immobility and specificness of resources. In contrast, the comparative-costs theory assumes either a perfect or, at least, a much greater degree of internal mobility of factors and/or a greater degree of flexibility or elasticity both on the side of production and of consumption. Thus the resources not required for export production will not remain as a surplus productive capacity, but will be reabsorbed into domestic production, although this might take some time and entail a loss to the country.

These two points bring out clearly a peculiarity of the " vent-for-surplus " theory which may be used either as a free-trade argument or as an anti-trade argument, depending on the point of view adopted. (*a*) From the point of view of a previously isolated country, about to enter into trade, a surplus productive capacity suitable for the export market appears as a virtually " costless " means of acquiring imports and expanding domestic economic activity. This was how Adam Smith used it as a free-trade argument. (*b*) From the point of view of an established trading country faced with a fluctuating world market, a sizeable surplus productive capacity which cannot be easily switched from export to domestic production makes it " vulnerable " to external economic disturbances. This is in fact how the present-day writers on the underdeveloped countries use the same situation depicted by Smith's theory as a criticism of the nineteenth-century pattern of international trade. This concept of vulnerability may be distinguished from that which we have come across in discussing the " productivity " theory of trade. There, a country is considered " vulnerable " because it has adapted and reshaped its productive structure to meet the requirements of the export market through a genuine process of " specialisation." Here, the country is considered " vulnerable " simply because it happens to possess a sizeable surplus productive capacity which (even without any improvements and extensions) it cannot use for domestic production. This distinction may be blurred in border-line cases, particularly in underdeveloped countries with a large mining sector. But we hope to show that, on the whole, while the " vulnerability " of the advanced countries, such as those in Western Europe which have succeeded in building up large export trades to maintain their large populations, is of the first kind, the " vulnerability " of most of the underdeveloped countries is of the second kind.

Let us now consider the " vent-for-surplus " approach purely as a theoretical tool. There is a considerable amount of prejudice among economists against the " vent-for-surplus " theory, partly because of its technical crudeness and partly because of its mercantilist associations. This may be traced to J. S. Mill, who regarded Smith's " vent-for-surplus " doctrine as " a surviving relic of the Mercantile Theory " (*Principles*, p. 579).

The crux of the matter here is the question: why should a country isolated from international trade have a surplus productive capacity? The answer which suggests itself is that, given its random combination of natural resources, techniques of production, tastes and population, such an isolated country is bound to suffer from a certain imbalance or disproportion between its productive and consumption capacities. Thus, take the case of a country which starts with a sparse population in relation to its natural resources. This was broadly true not only of Western countries during their mercantilist period but also of the underdeveloped countries of South-East Asia, Latin America and Africa when they were opened up to international trade in the nineteenth century. Given this situation, the conventional international-trade theory (in its Ohlin version) would say that this initial disproportion between land and labour would have been equilibrated away by appropriate price adjustments: i.e., rents would be low and relatively land-using commodities would have low prices, whereas wages would be high and relatively labour-using commodities would have high prices. In equilibrium there would be no surplus productive capacity (although there might be surplus land by itself) because the scarce factor, labour, would have been fully employed. Thus when this country enters into international trade it can produce the exports only by drawing labour away from domestic production. Now this result is obtained only by introducing a highly developed price mechanism and economic organisation into a country which is supposed to have had no previous economic contacts with the outside world. This procedure may be instructive while dealing with the isolated economy as a theoretical model. But it is misleading when we are dealing with genuinely isolated economies in their proper historical setting; it is misleading, in particular, when we are dealing with the underdeveloped countries, many of which were subsistence economies when they were opened to international trade. In fact, it was the growth of international trade itself which introduced or extended the money economy in these countries. Given the genuine historical setting of an isolated economy, might not its initial disproportion between its resources, techniques, tastes and population show itself in the form of surplus productive capacity?

Adam Smith himself thought that the pre-existence of a surplus productive capacity in an isolated economy was such a matter of common observation that he assumed it implicitly without elaborating upon it. But he did give some hints suggesting how the " narrowness of the home market," which causes the surplus capacity, is bound up with the underdeveloped economic organisation of an isolated country, particularly the lack of a good internal transport system and of suitable investment opportunities.[1] Further his concept of surplus productive capacity is not merely a matter of surplus land by itself but surplus land combined with surplus labour; and the

---

[1] *Op. cit.*, Vol. I, pp. 21 and 383. This is similar to what Mrs. J. Robinson has described as " primitive stagnation." Cf. *The Accumulation of Capital*, pp. 256–8.

surplus labour is then linked up with his concept of "unproductive" labour. To avoid confusion, this latter should not be identified with the modern concept of "disguised unemployment" caused by an acute shortage of land in overpopulated countries. Although Smith described some cases of genuine "disguised unemployment" in the modern sense, particularly with reference to China, "unproductive" labour in his sense can arise even in thinly populated countries, provided their internal economic organisation is sufficiently underdeveloped. In fact, it is especially in relation to those underdeveloped countries which started off with sparse populations in relation to their natural resources that we shall find Smith's "vent-for-surplus" approach very illuminating.

III

Let us now try to relate the "vent-for-surplus" theory to the nineteenth-century process of expansion of international trade to the underdeveloped countries. Even from the somewhat meagre historical information about these countries, two broad features stand out very clearly. First the underdeveloped countries of South-East Asia, Latin America and Africa, which were to develop into important export economies, started off with sparse populations relatively to their natural resources. If North America and Australia could then be described as "empty," these countries were at least "semi-empty." Secondly, once the opening-up process had got into its stride, the export production of these countries expanded very rapidly, along a typical growth curve,[1] rising very sharply to begin with and tapering off afterwards. By the Great Depression of the 1930s, the expansion process seems to have come to a stop in many countries; in others, which had a later start, the expansion process may still be continuing after the Second World War.

There are three reasons why the "vent-for-surplus" theory offers a more effective approach than the conventional theory to this type of expansion of international trade in the underdeveloped countries.

(i) The characteristically high rates of expansion which can be observed in the export production of many underdeveloped countries cannot really be explained in terms of the comparative-costs theory based on the assumption of given resources and given techniques. Nor can we attribute any significant part of the expansion to revolutionary changes in techniques and increases in productivity. As we have seen in Section I, peasant export

---

[1] For instance, the annual value of Burma's exports, taking years of high and low prices, increased at a constant proportional rate of 5% per annum on the average between 1870 and 1900. Similar rates of expansion can be observed for Siam and Indonesia (Cf. J. S. Furnivall, *Colonial Policy and Practice*, Appendix I; J. H. Boeke, *The Structure of Netherlands Indian Economy*, p. 184; and J. C. Ingram, *Economic Change in Thailand since 1850*, Appendix C). African export economies started their expansion phase after 1900, and the official trade returns for the Gold Coast, Nigeria and Uganda show similar rates of increase after that date, although the expansion process was arrested by the depression of the 1930s.

production expanded by extension of cultivation using traditional methods of production, while mining and plantation sectors expanded on the basis of increasing supplies of cheap labour with a minimum of capital outlay. Thus the contributions of Western enterprise to the expansion process are mainly to be found in two spheres: the improvements of transport and communications [1] and the discoveries of new mineral resources. Both are methods of increasing the total volume of resources rather than methods of making the given volume of resources more productive. All these factors suggest an expansion process which kept itself going by drawing an increasing volume of hitherto unused or surplus resources into export production.

(ii) International trade between the tropical underdeveloped countries and the advanced countries of the temperate zone has grown out of sharp differences in geography and climate resulting in absolute differences of costs. In this context, the older comparative-costs theory, which is usually formulated in terms of qualitative differences [2] in the resources of the trading countries, tends to stress the obvious geographical differences to the neglect of the more interesting quantitative differences in the factor endowments of countries possessing approximately the same type of climate and geography. Thus while it is true enough to say that Burma is an exporter of rice because of her climate and geography, the more interesting question is why Burma should develop into a major rice exporter while the neighbouring South India, with approximately the same type of climate and geography, should develop into a net importer of rice. Here the " vent-for-surplus " approach which directs our attention to population density as a major determinant of export capacity has an advantage over the conventional theory.[3]

(iii) Granted the importance of quantitative differences in factor endowments, there still remains the question why Smith's cruder " vent-for-surplus " approach should be preferable to the modern Ohlin variant of the comparative-costs theory. The main reason is that, according to the Ohlin theory, a country about to enter into international trade is supposed already to possess a highly developed and flexible economic system which can adjust its methods of production and factor combinations to cope with a wide range of possible variations in relative factor supplies (see Section II above). But in fact the economic framework of the underdeveloped countries is a

[1] This is what Professor L. C. A. Knowles described as the " Unlocking of the Tropics " (*op. cit.*, pp. 138–52).
[2] Cf. J. Viner, *International Trade and Economic Development*, pp. 14–16.
[3] Those who are used to handling the problem in terms of qualitative differences in factors and differential rent may ask: why not treat the surplus productive capacity as an extreme instance of " differential rent " where the transfer cost of the factors from the domestic to export production is zero? But this does not accurately portray the situation here. The transfer cost of the factors is zero, not because land which is used for the export crop is not at all usable for domestic subsistence production but because with the sparse population in the early phase there is no demand for the surplus food which could have been produced on the land used for the export crop. As we shall see, at a later stage when population pressure begins to grow, as in Java, land which has been used for export is encroached upon by subsistence production.

much cruder apparatus which can make only rough-and-ready adjustments. In particular, with their meagre technical and capital resources, the under-developed countries operate under conditions nearer to those of fixed technical coefficients than of variable technical coefficients. Nor can they make important adjustments through changes in the outputs of different commodities requiring different proportions of factors because of the inelastic demand both for their domestic production, mainly consisting of basic foodstuff, and for their exportable commodities, mainly consisting of industrial raw materials. Here again the cruder " vent-for-surplus " approach turns out to be more suitable.

Our argument that, in general, the " vent-for-surplus " theory provides a more effective approach than the comparative-costs theory to the international trade of the underdeveloped countries does not mean that the " vent-for-surplus " theory will provide an exact fit to all the particular patterns of development in different types of export economies. No simple theoretical approach can be expected to do this. Thus if we interpret the concept of the surplus productive capacity strictly as pre-existing surplus productive capacity arising out of the original endowments of the factors, it needs to be qualified, especially in relation to the mining and plantation sectors of the underdeveloped countries. Here the surplus productive capacity which may have existed to some extent before the country was opened to international trade is usually greatly increased by the discovery of new mineral resources and by a considerable inflow of foreign capital and immigrant labour. While immigrant labour is the surplus population of other under-developed countries, notably India and China, the term " surplus " in the strict sense cannot be applied to foreign capital. But, of course, the existence of suitable surplus natural resources in an underdeveloped country is a pre-condition of attracting foreign investment into it. Two points may be noted here. First, the complication of foreign investment is not as damaging to the surplus-productive-capacity approach as it appears at first sight, because the inflow of foreign investment into the tropical and semi-tropical underdeveloped countries has been relatively small both in the nineteenth century and the inter-war period.[1] Second, the nineteenth-century phenomenon of international mobility of capital and labour has been largely neglected by the comparative-costs theory, which is based on the assumption of perfect mobility of factors within a country and their imperfect mobility between different countries. The surplus-productive-capacity approach at least serves to remind us that the output of mining and plantation sectors can expand without necessarily contracting domestic subsistence output.

The use of the surplus-productive-capacity approach may prove in particular to be extremely treacherous in relation to certain parts of Africa,

[1] Cf. R. Nurkse, " International Investment To-day in the Light of Nineteenth Century Experience," ECONOMIC JOURNAL, December 1954, pp. 744–58, and the United Nations Report on *International Capital Movements during the Inter-war Period.*

where mines, plantations and other European enterprises have taken away from the tribal economies the so-called " surplus " land and labour, which, on a closer analysis, prove to be no surplus at all.   Here the extraction of these so-called " surplus " resources, by various forcible methods in which normal economic incentives play only a part, entails not merely a reduction in the subsistence output but also much heavier social costs in the form of the disruption of the tribal societies.[1]

When we turn to the peasant export sectors, however, the application of the " vent-for-surplus " theory is fairly straightforward.   Here, unlike the mining and plantation sectors, there has not been a significant inflow of foreign investment and immigrant labour.   The main function of the foreign export–import firms has been to act as middlemen between the world market and the peasants, and perhaps also to stimulate the peasants' wants for the new imported consumers' goods.   As we have seen, peasant export production expanded by using methods of production more or less on the same technical level as those employed in the traditional subsistence culture. Thus the main effect of the innovations, such as improvements in transport and communications [2] and the introduction of the new crops, was to bring a greater area of surplus land under cultivation rather than to raise the physical productivity per unit of land and labour.   Yet peasant export production usually managed to expand as rapidly as that of the other sectors while remaining self-sufficient with respect to basic food crops.   Here, then, we have a fairly close approximation to the concept of a pre-existing surplus productive capacity which can be tapped by the world-market demand with a minimum addition of external resources.

Even here, of course, there is room for differences in interpretation.   For instance, there is evidence to suggest that, in the early decades of expansion, the rates of increase in peasant export production in South-East Asian and West African countries were well above the possible rates of growth in their working population.[3]   Given the conditions of constant techniques, no significant inflow of immigrant foreign labour and continuing self-sufficiency with respect to the basic food crops, we are left with the question how these peasant economies managed to obtain the extra labour required to

[1] Cf. The United Nations Report on the *Enlargement of the Exchange Economy in Tropical Africa*, pp. 37 and 49–51.

[2] It may be noted that the expansion of some peasant export crops, notably rice in South-East Asia, depended to a much greater extent on pre-existing indigenous transport facilities, such as river boats and bullock carts, than is generally realised.

[3] For instance, cocoa output of the Gold Coast expanded over forty times during the twenty-five year period 1905–30.   Even higher rates of expansion in cocoa production can be observed in Nigeria combined with a considerable expansion in the output of other export crops.   Both have managed to remain self-sufficient with regard to basic food crops (cf. West African Institute of Economic Research, *Annual Conference*, Economic Section, Achimota, 1953, especially the chart between pp. 96 and 98; *The Native Economies of Nigeria*, ed. M. Perham, Vol. I, Part II).   In Lower Burma, for the thirty-year period 1870–1900, the area under rice cultivation increased by more than three times, while the population, including immigrants from Upper Burma, doubled. (Cf. also, Furnivall, *op. cit.*, pp. 84–5.)

expand their export production so rapidly. A part of this labour may have been released by the decline in cottage industries and by the introduction of modern labour-saving forms of transport in place of porterage, but the gap in the explanation cannot be satisfactorily filled until we postulate that even those peasant economies which started off with abundant land relatively to their population must have had initially a considerable amount of under-employed or surplus labour. This surplus labour existed, not because of a shortage of co-operating factors, but because in the subsistence economies, with poor transport and little specialisation in production, each self-sufficient economic unit could not find any market outlet to dispose of its potential surplus output, and had therefore no incentive to produce more than its own requirements. Here, then, we have the archetypal form of Smith's " unproductive " labour locked up in a semi-idle state in the underdeveloped economy of a country isolated from outside economic contacts. In most peasant economies this surplus labour was mobilised, however, not by the spread of the money-wage system of employment, but by peasant economic units with their complement of " family " labour moving *en bloc* into the money economy and export production.

The need to postulate a surplus productive capacity to explain the rapid expansion in peasant export production is further strengthened when we reflect on the implications of the fact that this expansion process is inextricably bound up with the introduction of the money economy into the subsistence sectors. To the peasant on the threshold of international trade, the question whether or not to take up export production was not merely a question of growing a different type of crop but a far-reaching decision to step into the new and unfamiliar ways of the money economy.

Thus let us consider a community of self-sufficient peasants who, with their existing techniques, have just sufficient land and labour to produce their minimum subsistence requirements, so that any export production can be achieved only by reducing the subsistence output below the minimum level. Now, according to the conventional economic theory, there is no reason why these peasants should not turn to export production if they have a differential advantage there, so that they could more than make up for their food deficit by purchases out of their cash income from the export crop. But, in practice, the peasants in this situation are unlikely to turn to export production so readily. Nor is this " conservatism " entirely irrational, for by taking up export production on such a slender margin of reserves, the peasants would be facing the risk of a possible food shortage for the sake of some gain in the form of imported consumers' goods which are " luxuries " to them. Moreover, this gain might be wiped off by unfavourable changes in the prices of both the export crop they would sell and the food-stuffs they would have to buy and by the market imperfections, which would be considerable at this early stage. Thus, where the margin of resources is very small above that required for the minimum subsistence output, we should expect the spread of export production to be inhibited or very slow, even if there were some genuine possibilities of gains on the comparative costs principle.[1]

In contrast, the transition from subsistence agriculture to export production is made much easier when we assume that our peasants start with some surplus resources which enable them to produce the export crop *in addition* to their subsistence production. Here the surplus resources perform two functions: first they enable the peasants to hedge their position completely and secure their subsistence minimum before entering into the risks of trading; and secondly, they enable them to look upon the imported goods they obtain from trade in the nature of a clear net gain obtainable merely for the effort of the extra labour in growing the export crop. Both of these considerations are important in giving the peasants just that extra push to facilitate their first plunge into the money economy.

Starting from this first group of peasants, we may picture the growth of export production and the money economy taking place in two ways. Firstly, the money economy may grow extensively, with improvements in transport and communications and law and order, bringing in more and more groups of peasants with their complements of family labour into export production on the same " part-time " basis as the first group of peasants. Secondly, the money economy may grow intensively by turning the first group of peasants from " part-time " into " whole-time " producers of the export crop.[2] In the first case, surplus resources are necessary as a lubricant to push more peasants into export production at each round of the widening circle of the money economy. Even in the second case, surplus resources are necessary if the whole-time export producers buy their food requirements locally from other peasants, who must then have surplus resources to produce the food crops above their own requirements. Logically, there is no reason why the first group of peasants who are now whole-time producers of the

---

[1] Of course, this argument can be countered by assuming the differences in comparative costs to be very wide. But, so long as export production requires withdrawing some resources from subsistence production, some risks are unavoidable. Further, remembering that the middlemen also require high profit margins at this stage, the gains large enough to overcome the obstacles are likely to arise out of surplus resources rather than from the differential advantages of the given fully employed resources. The risk of crop-failure is, of course, present both in subsistence and export production.

[2] In either case the expansion process may be looked upon as proceeding under conditions approximating to constant techniques and fixed combinations between land and labour once equilibrium is reached. The distinctive feature of peasant export economies is their failure to develop new and larger-scale or extensive methods of farming. It is true that in subsistence agriculture " fixed factors," such as a plough and a pair of bullocks, were frequently used below capacity, and one important effect of cash production was to increase the size of the holding to the full capacity of these " fixed factors." But this may be properly looked upon as equilibrium adjustments to make full use of surplus capacity rather than as the adoption of new and more land-using methods of production. Increasing the size of holding to make a more effective use of a pair of bullocks is different from the introduction of a tractor! Our assumption of constant techniques does not preclude the development of large-scale ownership of land as distinct from large-scale farming.

export crop should buy their food requirements locally instead of importing them. But, as it happens, few peasant export economies have specialised in export production to such an extent as to import their basic food requirements.

The average economist's reaction to our picture of discrete blocks of surplus productive capacity being drawn into a widening circle of money economy and international trade is to say that while this " crude " analysis may be good enough for the transition phase, the conventional analysis in terms of differential advantages and continuous marginal productivity curves must come into its own once the transition phase is over. Here it is necessary to distinguish between the expansion phase and the transition phase. It is true that in most peasant export economies the expansion process is tapering off or has come to a stop, as most of the surplus land suitable for the export crop has been brought under cultivation. This, of course, brings back the problem of allocating a fixed amount of resources, as we shall see in the next section when we consider issues of economic policy. But even so, the surplus-productive-capacity approach is not entirely superseded so long as the transition from a subsistence to a fully developed money economy remains incomplete. In most underdeveloped countries of Asia and Africa [1] this transition seems not likely to be over until they cease to be underdeveloped.

The continuing relevance of the surplus-productive-capacity approach may be most clearly seen in the typical case of a peasant export economy which with its natural resources and methods of production has reached the limit of expansion in production while its population continues to grow rapidly. According to the surplus-productive-capacity approach, we should expect the export capacity of such a country to fall roughly in proportion as the domestic requirement of resources to feed a larger population increases. This common-sense result may, however, be contrasted with that obtainable from the conventional theory as formulated by Ohlin. First, it appears that the Ohlin theory puts to the forefront of the picture the *type* of export, *i.e.*, whether it is more labour-using or land-using as distinct from the total export capacity measured by the ratio of total exports to the total national output of the trading country. Secondly, in the Ohlin theory there is no reason why a thickly populated country should not also possess a high ratio of (labour-intensive) exports to its total output.

The ideal pattern of trade suggested by the Ohlin theory has a real counterpart in the thickly populated advanced countries of Europe, which for that very reason are obliged to build up a large export trade in manufactures or even in agriculture as in the case of Holland. But when we turn to the thickly populated underdeveloped countries, however, the ideal

[1] Cf. the United Nations Report cited above on the *Enlargement of the Exchange Economy*. Even in the most developed peasant export economies the money economy has not spread to the same extent in the market for factors of production as in the market for products.

and the actual patterns of international trade diverge widely from each other. Indeed, we may say that these countries remain underdeveloped precisely because they have not succeeded in building up a labour-intensive export trade to cope with their growing population. The ratio of their export to total production could, of course, be maintained at the same level and the pressure of population met in some other way. But given the existing conditions, even this neutral pattern may not be possible in many underdeveloped countries. Thus, in Indonesia there is some evidence to suggest that the volume of agricultural exports from the thickly populated Java and Madura is declining absolutely and also relatively to those of the Outer Islands, which are still sparsely populated.[1] Of course, there are other causes of this decline, but population pressure reducing the surplus productive capacity of Java seems to be a fundamental economic factor; and the decline spreads from peasant to plantation exports as more of the plantation lands, which were under sugar and rubber, are encroached upon by the peasants for subsistence production.[2] In general, given the social and economic conditions prevailing in many underdeveloped countries, it seems fair to conclude that the trend in their export trade is likely to be nearer to that suggested by the surplus-productive-capacity approach than to that suggested by the theory of comparative costs.[3]

IV

This paper is mainly concerned with interpretation and analysis, but we may round off our argument by touching briefly upon some of its policy implications.

(i) We have seen that the effect of population pressure on many under-developed countries, given their existing social and economic organisation, is likely to reduce their export capacity by diverting natural resources from export to subsistence production. If we assume that these natural resources have a genuine differential advantage in export production, then population pressure inflicts a double loss: first, through simple diminishing returns, and secondly, by diverting resources from more to less productive use.

---

[1] Cf. J. H. Boeke, *Ontwikkelingsgang en toekomst van bevolkings-en ondernemingslandbouw in Neder-landsch-Indie* (Leiden, 1948), p. 91. I owe this reference to an unpublished thesis by Mr. M. Kidron.

[2] The same tendency to transfer land from plantation to subsistence agriculture may be observed in Fiji with the growing population pressure created by the Indian immigrant labour originally introduced to work in the sugar plantations. The outline is blurred here by the decline in the sugar industry. The reason why this tendency does not seem to operate in the West Indies is complex. But it may be partly attributable to the tourist industry, which helps to pay for the food imports of some of the islands.

[3] The surplus-productive-capacity approach also partly helps to explain why underdeveloped countries, such as India, which started off with a thick population tend to retain large and persistent pockets of subsistence sectors in spite of their longer contacts with the world economy, while the subsistence sectors in thinly populated countries, such as those in West Africa, tend to disappear at a faster rate in spite of their much later start in international trade.

Thus, if Java has a genuine differential advantage in growing rubber and sugar, she would obtain a greater amount of rice by maintaining her plantation estates instead of allowing them to be encroached upon by peasants for subsistence rice cultivation. The orthodox liberal economists, confronted with this situation, would, of course, strongly urge the removal of artificial obstacles to a more systematic development of the money economy and the price system. Now there are still many underdeveloped countries which are suffering acutely from the economic rigidities arising out of their traditional social structure and/or from discriminatory policies based on differences in race, religion and class. Here the removal of barriers, for instance, to the horizontal and vertical mobility of labour, freedom to own land and to enter any occupation, etc., may well prove to be a great liberating force.[1] But our analysis has suggested that it is much easier to promote the growth of the money economy in the early stage when a country is newly opened up to international trade and still has plenty of surplus land and labour rather than at a later stage, when there are no more surplus resources, particularly land, to feed the growth of the money economy. Thus in a country like Java there is a considerable amount of artificial restriction, customary or newly introduced, which the liberal economists can criticise, e.g., restriction on land ownership. But given the combination of population pressure, large pockets of subsistence economy and traditional methods of production which can no longer be made more labour-intensive, it seems very doubtful whether the mere removal of artificial restrictions can do much by itself without a more vigorous policy of state interference. The truth of the matter is that in the underdeveloped countries where, for various reasons described above, the exchange economy is still an extremely crude and imperfect apparatus which can make only rough-and-ready responses to economic differentials, it may require a considerable amount of state interference to move toward the comparative-costs equilibrium. Thus given that Java has genuine differential advantages in the production of rubber and sugar, a more optimal reallocation of her resources may require, for instance, the removal of her surplus population either to the thinly populated Outer Islands or to industries within Java and a vigorous export-drive policy supplemented by bulk purchase and subsidies on the imported rice. Here we come to a fundamental dilemma which is particularly acute for the orthodox liberal economists. On a closer examination it turns out that their free-trade argument, although ostensibly based on the comparative-costs principle, is buttressed by certain broad classical presumptions against protection and state interference:[2] e.g., the difficulty of selecting the right

---

[1] This is why the case for the "liberal" solution is strong in places such as East and Central Africa, where due both to the general backwardness of the indigenous population and the presence of a white settler population, both types of rigidity prevail (cf. *The Royal Commission Report on East Africa*).
[2] Cf. J. Viner, *International Trade and Economic Development*, pp. 41-2. See also Sidgwick, *Principles of Political Economy*, Book III, Chapter V.

industry to protect, the virtual impossibility of withdrawing protection once given, the tendency of controls to spread promiscuously throughout the economic system strangling growth, and so on. These presumptions gain an added strength from the well-known administrative inefficiency and sometimes corruption of the governments of some underdeveloped countries. Thus even if we believe in the " nineteenth-century pattern " of international trade based on natural advantages, how can we be sure that the state is competent enough to select the right commodities for its export-drive policy when it is considered incompetent to select the right industry for protection?

(ii) We have seen that the rapid expansion in the export production of the underdeveloped countries in the nineteenth century cannot be satisfactorily explained without postulating that these countries started off with a considerable amount of surplus productive capacity consisting both of unused natural resources and under-employed labour. This gives us a common-sense argument for free trade which is especially relevant for the underdeveloped countries in the nineteenth century: the surplus productive capacity provided these countries with a virtually " costless " means of acquiring imports which did not require a withdrawal of resources from domestic production but merely a fuller employment for their semi-idle labour. Of course, one may point to the real cost incurred by the indigenous peoples in the form of extra effort and sacrifice of the traditional leisurely life [1] and also to the various social costs not normally considered in the comparative-costs theory, such as being sometimes subject to the pressure of taxation and even compulsory labour and frequently of having to accommodate a considerable inflow of immigrant labour creating difficult social and political problems later on. One may also point to a different type of cost which arises with the wasteful exploitation of natural resources.[2] But for the most part it is still true to say that the indigenous peoples of the underdeveloped countries took to export production on a voluntary basis and enjoyed a clear gain by being able to satisfy their developing wants for the new imported commodities. Thus our special argument for free trade in this particular context still remains largely intact. The orthodox economists, by rigidly insisting on applying the comparative-costs theory to the underdeveloped countries in the nineteenth century, have therefore missed this simpler and more powerful argument.

[1] It may be formally possible to subsume the surplus-productive-capacity approach under the opportunity-cost theory, by treating leisure instead of foregone output as the main element of cost. But this would obscure the important fact that the underdeveloped countries have been able to expand their production very rapidly, not merely because the indigenous peoples were willing to sacrifice leisure but also because there were also surplus natural resources to work upon.

[2] The social cost of soil erosion can be very great, but this may be caused not merely by an expansion of export production but also by bad methods of cultivation and population pressure. The problem of adequately compensating the underdeveloped countries for the exploitation of their non-replaceable mineral resources belongs to the problem of the distribution of gains from trade. Here we are merely concerned with establishing that the indigenous peoples do obtain some gains from trade.

(iii) We have seen in Section I that the deep-rooted hostility of the critics towards the " classical theory " and the nineteenth-century pattern of international trade may be partly traced back to the time when Western colonial powers attempted to introduce export-drive policies in the tropical underdeveloped countries; and tried to justify these policies by invoking the " classical theory " of free trade and the Adam Smithian doctrine of international trade as a dynamic force generating a great upward surge in the general level of productivity of the trading countries. To the critics, this appears as a thinly disguised rationalisation of the advanced countries' desire for the markets for their manufactured products and for raw materials. Thus it has become a standard argument with the critics to say that the nineteenth-century process of international trade has introduced a large " export bias " into the economic structure of the underdeveloped countries which has increased their " vulnerability " to international economic fluctuations.

In Section II we have seen that once we leave the ideal world of the comparative costs theory in which the resources not required for the export market can be re-absorbed into domestic production, every country with a substantial export trade may be considered " vulnerable." Thus a country may be said to be vulnerable because it has built up a large ratio of export to its total production simply by making use of its pre-existing surplus productive capacity. *A fortiori*, it is vulnerable when it has genuinely improved upon its original surplus productive capacity. How does the idea of " export bias " fit into our picture?

The term " export bias " presumably means that the resources of the underdeveloped countries which could have been used for domestic production have been effectively diverted into export production by deliberate policy. The implication of our surplus-productive-capacity approach is to discount this notion of " export bias." In the peasant export sectors, at the early stage with sparse populations and plenty of surplus land, the real choice was not so much between using the resources for export production or for domestic production as between giving employment to the surplus resources in export production or leaving them idle. In the later stage, when the population pressure begins to increase as in the case of Java, we have seen that the bias is likely to develop against, rather than in favour of, the export sector. Even when we turn to the mining and plantation sectors, it is difficult to establish a significant " export bias " in the strict sense. Here the crucial question is: how far would it have been possible to divert the foreign capital and technical resources which have gone into these sectors into the domestic sector? The answer is clear. For a variety of reasons, notably the smallness of domestic markets, few governments of the underdeveloped countries, whether colonial or independent, have so far succeeded in attracting a significant amount of foreign investment away from the extractive export industries to the domestic industries. In criticising the colonial governments it should be remembered that the only choice open to them was whether to attract a greater or a smaller amount of foreign investment within the export sector and not whether to attract investment for the domestic or the export sector.

This is not to deny that the colonial governments had a strong motive for promoting export production. Apart from the interests of the mother country, the individual colonial governments themselves had a vested interest in the expansion of foreign trade because they derived the bulk of their revenues from it.[1] In their search for revenue they have pursued various policies designed to attract foreign investment to the mining and plantation sectors, such as granting favourable concessions and leases, favourable tariff rates for rail transport, taxation policy designed to facilitate the supply of labour, provision of various technical services, etc.[2] But on the whole it is still true to say that the most important contribution of the colonial governments towards the expansion of the colonial exports is to be found, not in these export-drive policies, but in their basic services, such as the establishment of law and order and the introduction of modern transport, which enabled the pre-existing surplus productive capacity of the colonies to be tapped by the world market demand. If we wish to criticise the export-drive policies of the colonial governments it would be more appropriate to do so, not on the ground of " export bias " but on the ground that they may have diverted too great a share of the gains from international trade and of the public services of the colonies to the foreign-owned mines and plantations at the expense of indigenous labour and peasant export producers.

It may be argued that we have given too strict an interpretation of the " export-bias " doctrine which is merely meant to convey the general proposition that, whatever the exact cause, the nineteenth-century process of international trade has landed many underdeveloped countries with a large ratio of raw materials exports to their total national products, making it desirable to reduce their " vulnerability " to international economic fluctuations. But the trouble is that the " export bias " doctrine tends to suggest that the raw-materials export production of the underdeveloped countries has been artificially over-expanded, not merely in relation to their domestic sector, but absolutely. Given the strong feelings of economic nationalism and anti-colonialism in the underdeveloped countries, this can be a very mischievous doctrine strengthening the widespread belief that to go on producing raw materials for the export market is tantamount to preserving the " colonial " pattern of trade. Thus already many underdeveloped countries are giving too little encouragement to their peasant

---

[1] This is true for the governments of most underdeveloped countries, whether colonial or independent, past or present.

[2] For a discussion of the question of the possible export bias through the operation of the 100% sterling exchange system of the colonies, see A. D. Hazlewood, " Economics of Colonial Monetary Arrangements," *Social and Economic Studies*, Jamaica, December 1954.

export sectors by diverting too much of their capital and technical resources to industrial-development projects, and are also crippling their mining and plantation export sectors by actual or threatened nationalisation and various restrictions and regulations. The effect is to reduce their foreign-exchange earnings so urgently needed for their economic development. Of course, no competent critic of the nineteenth-century pattern of international trade would ever suggest the drastic step of reducing exports absolutely; some would even concede the need for vigorous export drive policies.[1] But having built up a pervasive feeling of hostility and suspicion against the " nineteenth-century " or the " colonial " pattern of international trade, they are not in a position to ram home the obvious truths: (a) that, even on an optimistic estimate of the possibilities of international aid, the underdeveloped countries will have to pay for the larger part of the cost of their economic plans aiming either at a greater national self-sufficiency or at the export of manufactured goods; (b) that the necessary foreign exchange for these development plans can be earned by the underdeveloped countries at the present moment only by the export of raw materials (though not necessarily the same commodities for which they were supposed to have a differential advantage in the nineteenth century); and (c) that therefore to pursue their development plans successfully it is vitally important for them to carry out the " export-drive " policies, which in their technical properties may not be very different from those of the colonial governments in the past.[2] In trying to carry out their development plans on the foreign-exchange earnings from raw-materials export they would, of course, still be " vulnerable "; but this should be considered separately as a problem in short-term economic stability [3] and not as a criticism of the nineteenth-century pattern of international trade in relation to the long-term development of the underdeveloped countries. From a long-term point of view, even countries which have successfully industrialised themselves and are therefore able to maintain their population at a higher standard of living by building up a large export trade in manufactures, such as Japan or the

---

[1] Cf., for example, Gunnar Myrdal, *An International Economy*, p. 274.

[2] Colonial governments have frequently defended their export-drive policies as the means of taxing foreign trade to finance services needed for internal development. But because they were colonial governments, their motives were suspect. At first sight we might imagine that the new independent governments of the underdeveloped countries would be free from this disability. But unfortunately, given the atmosphere of intense nationalism and anti-colonialism, this is not true. In some cases the hands of the newly independent governments seem to be tied even more tightly, and economic policies admitted to be desirable are turned down as " politically impossible." Here those economists who regard themselves as the critics of the classical theory and the nineteenth-century pattern of international trade have a special responsibility. Instead of dealing tenderly with the " understandable " emotional reactions which they have partly helped to create, they ought to be emphatic in pointing out the conflicts between rational considerations and " understandable " mental attitudes. The underdeveloped countries are too poor to enjoy the luxury of harbouring their emotional resentments.

[3] Cf. the United Nations Report on *Measures for International Economic Stability* and Myrdal's comments on it, *op. cit.*, pp. 238–53.

thickly populated countries of Western Europe, will continue to be " vulnerable." [1]

H. MYINT

Oxford.

[1] It is particularly in relation to the thickly populated advanced countries of Western Europe which have specialised and adapted their economic structure to the requirements of the export market that Professor J. H. Williams found Adam Smith's " vent-for-surplus " approach illuminating. We have, in this paper, interpreted the " surplus " more strictly in its pre-existing form without the improvements and augmentation in productive capacity due to genuine " specialisation." (Cf. J. H. Williams, " International Trade Theory and Policy—Some Current Issues," *American Economic Review, Papers and Proceedings,* 1951, pp. 426–7.)

Foreign Trade in Planned Economies

by

Thomas A. Wolf*

* European Department, International Monetary Fund. This chapter
is based on the author's more comprehensive monograph, Foreign Trade in
the Centrally Planned Economy, volume 27 in the series Fundamentals of
Pure and Applied Economics, ed. by Jacques Lesourne and Hugo Sonnenschein
(London: Harwood Academic Press, 1988). The views reflected herein do not
necessarily reflect those of the institution with which the author is
affiliated.

This chapter considers a stylized version of the foreign trade system to be found in the Soviet Union and, since the early postwar period, in the planned economies of Eastern Europe. These centrally planned economies (CPEs) not only constitute a distinctive economic system, but also embody a specific and fairly common set of basic policies that has been deeply influenced by the particular historical circumstances in which the CPEs were established. The first section discusses the main institutional and policy determinants of foreign trade behavior in the CPEs. Foreign trade decision making and the role of the exchange rate are considered in greater detail in section 2, and this is followed by a discussion of the CPE trade offer curve in the third section. The fourth section considers several issues that are relatively unique to trade among planned economies, while the fifth section explains the role of foreign trade in macroeconomic adjustment in CPEs. The final section of the chapter considers the impact that the recent pressures for economic reform have exerted on the foreign trade systems of these economies.

1.   Institutions and policies of the CPEs

In the CPE the overwhelming bulk of the means of production is owned by the state. Central authorities formulate detailed plans for the inputs and outputs of state-owned enterprises, but these plans are the outcome of extensive hierarchical bargaining. Information flows, as well, take place in an essentially bureaucratic rather than market setting. Enterprise management is judged on the basis of plan fulfillment, rather than profit maximization. Producer prices are generally set by the central authorities, and held fixed for long periods. The labor market is relatively free, but the enterprise wage fund is closely

regulated from the center. The state banking system is a monolith in

which the commercial banks passively supply the credit required by

enterprises in their fulfillment of their physical plans, and in which

the money supplies of households and socialized enterprises are effec-

tively dichotomized. These systemic features are combined in the CPE

with a strategy of rapid industrialization based principally on the

rapid mobilization of capital and labor, the latter drawn mainly from

agriculture which becomes the neglected sector. The intended legitimacy

of the economic leadership is based on the pillars of retail price

stability, minimal wage differentiation, full employment and, indeed, a

degree of individual job security not found in market economies. 1/

Foreign trade is almost exclusively carried out by state-owned

foreign trade organizations (FTOs) that are subordinate to the Ministry

of Foreign Trade (MFT). The industrial branch ministries may have some

influence on the FTOs, but generally the industrial enterprises under

their control have little direct contact with enterprises abroad.

Normally the FTOs do not compete with one another, and each FTO thus has

an effective monopoly over the foreign trade in a particular set of pro-

ducts. The annual and five-year plans for foreign trade are worked out by

the MFT on the basis of information provided by the FTOs and in close

cooperation with the Central Planning Commission in its drawing up of

the aggregate national economic plan. The foreign trade plan is thus an

integral part of the overall national plan and it specifies in

---

1/ For comprehensive descriptions of the establishment and operation
of the prototype CPE, see Campbell (1974) and Nove (1977).

considerable detail the commodity and geographical composition of
foreign trade that is to be carried out by the FTOs. Most imports and
exports are incorporated in the so-called material balances elaborated
by the planners, which may cover hundreds or even thousands of products
that are considered crucial to fulfillment of the basic indicators in
the national economic plan. 2/

Institutional determinants of foreign trade behavior

This institutional set-up has a number of implications for the
foreign trade behavior of CPEs. The institutional monopoly of foreign
trade under the MFT effectively insulates domestic production and trade
enterprises from foreign markets. This means in turn that domestic producers of tradables are insulated from world market standards for technology, product quality, marketing and distribution, and this isolation
is reflected quite naturally in the difficulty that CPEs have in exporting finished and even many semifinished manufactures on competitive
international markets. The essentially vertical, hierarchic relationships governing economic behavior, including the concentration of enterprise transactions with other firms belonging to the same ministry,
tends to limit the degree of specialization within industry. This
restricts, in turn, the extent to which FTOs have been able to base
their export strategies on specialization and is a further reason for
their lack of competitiveness in world markets for manufactures. This
problem is compounded by the importance placed, in practice, on the

---

2/   In-depth descriptions of the organization of the foreign trade
sector and the planning of foreign trade in the CPEs appear in Pryor
(1963) and Gardner (1983).

fulfillment of physical plans of enterprises in the CPE. Quality of
output tends to suffer as a result, and this is manifested in particular
in the inability to export high quality manufactured products. 3/

In addition to generating a system that is institutionally incap-
able of competing effectively in world markets for manufactures, the
central planners may be expected to be somewhat "trade averse" (Brown,
(1968)). Even if they were able to calculate precisely the economy's
comparative advantages (section 2 discusses why this is unlikely), they
might be unwillng to expand foreign trade to the extent suggested by the
familiar Pareto-optimal conditions given the risks to plan fulfillment
that a high degree of dependence on uncertain world markets might
involve. A CPE would therefore tend to have a less specialized structure of production and trade and a lower level of foreign trade relative
to its national income, than an otherwise comparable market economy. It
is difficult to say, however, to what extent a general policy of import
substitution is the result of this systemic trade aversion or other
factors that may argue for a policy of relative self-sufficiency. 4/

The fixing of prices at the producer level for very long periods
greatly facilitates for the planners their job of aggregating across
thousands of products and evaluating the performance of enterprises.
This practice, however, has the effect of completing the isolation
of domestic enterprises from world market forces. Partial insulation of

---

3/ On these and other institutional constraints on the competitiveness of CPEs in world markets and determinants of their foreign trade
behavior, see Holzman (1966, 1979).
4/ On these issues see Pryor (1963), Kaser (1967), Wiles (1968) and
Winiecki (1986).

even the FTOs is intended by the planners, through the so-called system

of price equalization. Abstracting from commissions and operating

costs, the FTOs as a group earn a profit (T) in foreign trade equal to:

$$(1) \quad T = Q_m(P_m - P_m^\star e') + Q_x(P_x^\star e' - P_x),$$

where Q_m and Q_x are (composite) import and export volumes respectively,

P_m is the average price at which FTOs resell imports to domestic trading

enterprises, P_x is the average price at which the FTOs purchase exports

from domestic producers, $P_m^\star$ and $P_x^\star$ are the foreign currency prices of

the composite import and export respectively, and e' is the valuta

exchange rate, expressed in units of the nominal valuta currency per

unit of foreign currency. This profit is only a nominal profit from the

standpoint of the FTOs, because under the price equalization system it

is exactly taxed away (subsidized, if negative) by the financial

authorities. (Pryor (1963) and Wolf (1980a)).

Although not permitted to retain their profits, FTOs in some cases

have been evaluated, and their employees rewarded, on the basis of their

nominal profit, T. The FTOs typically have only very limited autonomy,

however, thus their ability to arrange the level and composition of

their trade in order to maximize this profit is severely circumscribed.

In large part this restricted autonomy is due to the necessity to main-

tain the material balances already worked out for the national economy.

In general, the FTOs are therefore less likely to be sensitive to

changes in foreign currency prices than their foreign trade partners;

and domestic enterprises, as the result of the price equalization

process, are in general indifferent as to whether their output is directed towards the domestic or external market. Finally, while the

FTOs as a group may be considered to have an institutional monopoly over

foreign trade, they may or may not have external market power; if they

do, there should be no presumption that they will exercise it

analogously to a monopolist in a market economy (see section 3). 5/

   The circumscribed autonomy of the FTOs and the insulation of domes-

tic enterprises from external markets is reinforced by a policy of

de jure resident inconvertibility of the CPE's currency. Export earn-

ings of the FTOs in foreign currency will be paid over directly to the

Foreign Trade Bank or the Ministry of Finance, which will credit the

FTOs with so-called valuta earnings ($P_x'Q_x = P_x^*e'Q_x$ in equation (1))

which, net of the value of valuta imports ($P_m'Q_m = P_m^*e'Q_m$), will be

periodically taxed away as noted earlier. Only in particular cases, as

in the event of authorized trips abroad, will conversion of the domestic

currency (which is not the same as the nominal valuta currency) into

foreign exchange be permitted.

   Because intermediate and final investment goods are centrally

allocated in the CPE, and all foreign trade is stipulated in the plans

of the FTOs, there is little scope for unplanned trade. A foreign com-

pany exporting to the CPE would therefore have little incentive to

accept, if offered, the CPE's currency because it would not, in general,

be readily convertible into goods, or at least not into goods already

prescribed for other uses by the plan. The CPE's currency therefore

---

5/ A more detailed discussion of the issue of FTO behavior under
different conditions may be found in Wolf (1988) and the references
therein.

lacks "commodity convertibility" regardless of whether the currency is
convertible in a legal sense (Holzman (1966)). In general,
foreign enterprises will not want to hold the CPE's currency, except to
cover local costs of doing business. In trade with market economies,
most transactions not involving some type of barter operation will be
settled in the convertible currencies of the market economies. Trade
with other CPEs has since 1964 been largely settled in terms of the
common clearing unit of the Council for Mutual Economic Assistance
(CMEA), the transferable ruble (TR). 6/

   Policy determinants of foreign trade behavior

   In addition to the rigidity of prices at the producer level, a
reflection mainly of the dictates of central planning, a basic policy
commitment was made in the CPEs to price stability at the retail level.
The concern was mainly to avoid open inflation and the uncertainties of
price fluctuations, and to make at least the basic necessities such as
staple food items, clothing and housing affordable to all members of
society. The retail price structure was therefore constructed essentially independently of the producers' price structure and that faced by
wholesalers, with this independence achieved through a system of differentiated turnover taxes. All levels of prices were consequently
established independently of world market prices, as well as being set
without regard to underlying marginal costs of production or the
requirements of market equilibrium.

   6/ The members of the CMEA, an economic grouping of CPEs, are
Bulgaria, Cuba, Czechoslovakia, the German Democratic Republic, Hungary,
Mongolia, Poland, Romania, the Soviet Union and Viet Nam.

As a result, the domestic price structure cannot be taken as an accurate measure of comparative advantage or as an indicator of the prices at which trade should be carried out with other CPEs. Furthermore, the structure and level of official prices in the CPE, being rigid in the short and medium run, cannot serve as a transmission belt for economic disturbances or as a signaling device for adjustment to these disturbances.

Because consumption goods sold at distorted prices are not in general centrally allocated to individual consumers (except when formal rationing is in effect), such products could be bought up by foreigners seeking to engage in international commodity arbitrage. So as to avoid such practices, which could even lead to a net loss for the national economy, the authorities may well impose a ceiling on the amount of domestic currency that foreigners can purchase, i.e., nonresident convertibility will be limited (Holzman, 1966).

A second major policy objective in CPEs, in addition to price stability, has been the strategy of rapid industrialization. This has been accompanied by an underpricing of capital, due to a zero or only a nominal interest charge on its use. Although it is debatable to what extent the unrealistically low cost of capital has affected the structure of production, the CPEs do tend to have a commodity structure of both exports and imports that is relatively capital intensive, both in trade with other planned economies and with the market economies.

Another policy feature of CPEs is the tendency toward excess demand for resources at the enterprise level. This may either be because of conscious overfull employment planning on the part of the planners in

the classical CPE (Holzman, 1953, 1966) 7/ or the implicit output
maximizing behavior of enterprises that perceive that this is what is
most valued by superior organs in the planning hierarchy (Kornai, 1980).
In this environment the planners (in the first case) and enterprises
will see exports as draining the economy of scarce resources; FTOs are
therefore unlikely to be able to launch sustained export drives or
aggressively to hold onto market positions already achieved (Winiecki,
1986). With a domestic sellers' market, enterprises will also give less
attention to quality, packaging and reliability of deliveries, which
will further limit the ability of the economy's FTOs to compete abroad,
particularly in export markets for manufactures. At the same time, however, excess demand on producers' good markets will lead to bottlenecks
in domestic production, further constraining exports as well as raising
the effective demand for imports above that embodied in the plan (Brown,
1968).

Yet another policy orientation is the stress on full employment and
individual job security. This will lead policy makers to try to minimize the transmission of economic disturbances from abroad. While the
system of price equalization fulfills this function on the price side,
this objective is also achieved by limiting the economy's involvement in
foreign trade in general. The result is a policy of import substitution
which reinforces the trade aversion factor mentioned earlier.

7/ This phenomenon, which is not a necessary result of central planning, could come about if the planners perceive that output, especially
in key sectors, will be maximized by setting overly-ambitious plans.

A final feature of planned economies that influences their foreign
trade but may be the result of both system and policy factors is "storming", or the all-out mobilization of resources by enterprises toward the
end of the planning period in order to fulfill or overfulfill output or
export plan targets. Storming can have negative effects on a country's
export performance as a result of the lowering of average product
quality, reduced reliability with respect to delivery times, and terms
of trade deterioration as abnormally large quantities are unloaded on
world markets in a relatively short period of time.

2. The efficiency of foreign trade and the exchange rate 8/

In the CPE, the system of price equalization insulates both the
level and the structure of domestic prices from those prevailing on
world markets. This is reflected in the following equation:

$$(2) \quad P_i = P_i^* e'(1 + \alpha_i),$$

where P_i is the domestic currency price at which the ith product is
transferred between a FTO and domestic industrial or wholesale trade
enterprise, P_i^* is the foreign currency price of this product, e' as
before is the valuta (or external) exchange rate, and α_i denotes the
ex post implicit variable commodity-specific trade tax rate on this
product. This implicit tax rate will vary inversely with fluctuations
in the foreign currency price received or paid by the FTO for this good.
This is because both the domestic price for the ith product and the
valuta exchange rate are typically held fixed for long periods by the

_____

8/ This discussion draws directly from Wolf (1985b).

authorities. The quantity $(1 + \alpha_i)$ could be thought of as an <u>implicit</u> <u>internal</u> exchange rate for the ith good, because it is equal to the ratio of its domestic price (P_i) to its valuta, or external price $(P_i' = P_i^* e')$.

Once the system of price equalization was established the planners came to realize that they were not in a position to plan foreign trade on efficiency grounds. This is because the valuta exchange rate was in general selected independently of the level and structure of domestic relative prices, and these prices in any event did not in general reflect the true pattern of relative scarcities at home (Boltho (1971) and Hewett (1974)). By the late 1950s, economists in some CPEs were developing various indices of "foreign trade effectiveness" so as to assist in more rational foreign trade planning. The basic index can be characterized as an <u>official internal</u> exchange rate (e''). This rate, expressed as the number of units of domestic currency per unit of the nominal, or valuta currency, might be established for aggregate trade with a particular currency region, or differentiated according to industrial branch or commodity group. It would be roughly equal to the average <u>implicit</u> internal exchange rate for that reference group.

Using this official internal exchange rate, a so-called <u>calculative</u> price (P_i'') could be established:

(3) $P_i'' = P_i^* e' e''(1 + t_i),$

where all variables are as defined earlier and t_i would be the actual explicit trade tax (subsidy) rate for the ith product. If the calculative price for this product were greater (smaller) than its domestic

currency price, this might suggest that this product would be a profitable export (import), at least relative to the other products in its
reference group. Because the level and structure of domestic prices are
dissociated from world markets, such an approach was recognized as not
really answering the question of which products, and in what quantity,
should be exported or imported.

Such limitations of the more primitive foreign trade effectiveness
indices led to attempts to estimate the shadow exchange rate using
large-scale linear programming models (Trzeciakowski (1962, 1978)).
Their objective was to minimize costs or maximize consumption, subject
to linear constraints regarding production possibilities and the balance
of trade. Fixed coefficient production functions and constant costs
were assumed, for both domestic- and foreign-produced goods. The optimization process yielded real trade requirements as well as a domestic
shadow price for each commodity.

Derivation of the shadow exchange rate using this approach is
illustrated in Figure 1. Importables are arrayed in descending order
according to the ratio of their estimated domestic shadow price (Z_{mi}) to
their valuta price (P'_{mi}). Exportables are arranged in ascending order
according to the ratio of their real domestic cost of production (Z_{xi})
to their valuta price (P'_{xi}). The cumulative valuta values of these
imports ($V'_{mi} = P^*_{mi} e' Q_{mi}$) and exports ($V'_{xi} = P^*_{xi} e' Q_{xi}$) are measured along
the horizontal axis. Marginal costs are assumed to be constant for each
product; the valuta expenditure (V'_{mi} ()) and revenue ($V'_x()$) curves in

the figure are therefore approximations to bar graphs composed of individual products (for example, importables a, b, and c and exportables d and f).

FIGURE 1
DETERMINING THE OPTIMAL EXCHANGE RATE
UNDER CENTRAL PLANNING

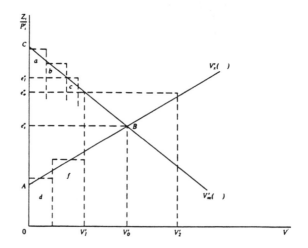

As long as an import involves a real saving of resources or a use value to the economy greater than the real value of the domestic resources used to produce the exports earning the foreign exchange for their purchase, it should take place. Trade should therefore be expanded as long as $(Z_{mi}/P'_{mi}) > (Z_{xi}/P'_{xi})$, where the ith products are the marginal importable and exportable respectively. The intersection of the $V'_x()$ and $V'_m()$ schedules therefore yields the shadow internal exchange rate, e''_s, at which the average domestic relative shadow price of the marginal export and import is equal to their relative price abroad. When trade is balanced at V'_o, the net welfare gain to the

economy is measured by triangle ABC. A different pattern of trade,

whether or not balanced, would yield a smaller sum of producer and

consumer surpluses in foreign trade.

Figure 1 resembles the foreign exchange market diagram frequently

drawn for the market economy, but it should be interpreted quite dif-

ferently. The downward sloping demand curve for foreign exchange in the

market economy denotes the aggregate demand of economic agents for

foreign exchange at different exchange rates that are, from their stand-

point, exogenous. The $V'_m()$ schedule in Figure 1, by contrast, would

measure the planners' demand for valuta at different shadow exchange

rates in the event that they were willing to plan trade on the basis of

a shadow exchange rate approach. The planners themselves, however, will

determine the applicable shadow exchange rate, depending on their trade

balance target. Moreover, since the whole exercise reflects the

planners' own preferences with regard to the structure of production and

consumption, the shapes and positions of the $V'_x()$ and $V'_m()$ schedules

are also determined indirectly by the planners.

Another difference between Figure 1 and the foreign exchange market

diagram for the market economy is that the schedules in the latter

reflect the summation of interdependent foreign exchange demand curves

for different products. For example, a depreciation in the exchange rate

in a market economy would generally lead to a reduction in the demand

for imports of all products, but by amounts that vary directly with

their different price elasticities of import demand. In the CPE, on the

other hand, an increase in the shadow internal exchange rate from e''_o

to, say, e''_1, would lead the planners to eliminate entirely imports of product c, but goods a and b would continue to be imported in the same quantities. This is because in this shadow price approach one is assuming constant costs of production and constant use values.

Finally, although the "optimal" trade pattern in figure 1 involves balanced trade at shadow exchange rate e''_s, this rate should not be confused with the notion of an "equilibrium" exchange rate in a market economy. For example, if the planners liberalized the domestic allocation of resources and abolished all controls on international transactions, only coincidentally would the resulting market-clearing exchange rate be equal to e''_s in the figure.

3. The trade offer curve of a CPE

The discussion of the institutional determinants of CPE foreign trade in section 1 suggested that FTOs have little autonomy with regard to the overall volume and the commodity and geographical composition of their trade. The offer curve of a CPE is therefore likely to be determined by the center, rather than by the combined activities of mutually independent and autonomous enterprises as in the market economy.

The elasticity of the trade offer curve may be expressed as:

(4) $\varepsilon = \beta + m - 1$,

where ε is the elasticity of supply of the exportable X with respect to a change in its price in foreign currency relative to that of the importable M: $(\varepsilon = \hat{X}/\hat{q}$, where q is the terms of trade, and a caret denotes the percentage change in a variable); β is the net substitution effect in domestic supply and demand: $(\beta = (S\eta_s - D\eta_d)M^{-1}$, where S and D represent domestic output and consumption respectively of the importable, and η_s and η_d are the elasticities of supply and of compensated demand for the importable, respectively, with respect to the relative price), and m is the marginal propensity to consume the importable out of income. 9/

For the stylized market economy, X and M are usually assumed to be normal goods (i.e., $0 < m < 1.00$) and substitution is assumed in both domestic production and consumption ($\eta_s > 0$ and $\eta_d < 0$; therefore $\beta > 0$). As long as the substitution effects are large enough, ($\beta + m$) will exceed unity and the market economy's offer curve will have the familiar positive slope.

In the classical CPE, by contrast, foreign trade is determined by the central planners, who might well be insensitive, in their short- and medium-run decisions on domestic resource allocation, to changes in the external terms of trade. On the production side, their plan for output, as between the exportable and importable, might well be insensitive to changes in world market conditions. In the short-run, therefore, the effective production possibilities curve reduces to a point. On the expenditure side, the planners might realistically be viewed as allocating goods to consumers on the basis of predetermined proportions embodied in the plan, not according to the criteria of equalizing consumers' rates of commodity substitution with the domestic relative price (which in any event will not in general be systematically related to the terms of trade prevailing on the world market). In effect, the planners have what approximates a family of fixed-coefficient preference func-

9/ This expression is derived by totally differentiating the export normalized trade balance constraint ($X = q^{-1}M(1-k)^{-1}$, where k is a constant and is equal to zero when balanced trade is assumed) with respect to q, and manipulating and simplifying the resulting expression.

512   THOMAS A. WOLF

tions. Should the economy's real income change as the result of an
unexpected change in output or a movement in the external terms of
trade, the planners may be imagined as reallocating the two composite
tradables domestically in a way that reflects their marginal propensities to have society consume these goods. In terms of equation (4), β
will equal zero and, as long as the planners view the composite tradables as normal goods (0 < m < 1.00), the elasticity of the trade offer
curve (ε) will be negative, or backward-bending. 10/

In analyzing the behavioral implications of this backward bending
offer curve it is useful to consider separately the CPE's trade with
market economies, as a group, and other planned economies. The CPE's
offer curve is illustrated in Figure 2 as OC_s, which alternatively
intersects the composite market economy's offer curve OC_r^1 or OC_r^2. The
backward bending offer curve of the CPE implies that as its terms of
trade with market economies improve (deteriorate), the planners will
reduce (increase) their export offer. The planners' preoccupation with
the terms of trade in their foreign trade behavior is only apparently
inconsistent with their presumed insensitivity to the terms of trade in
the domestic allocation of resources. The former simply reflects their
assumed need to satisfy some trade balance constraint (see footnote 9),
while the latter dictates the shape and size of their trade offer curve.

10/ A model of such a price-insensitive Soviet-type economy is elaborated and estimated in Wolf (1982). From equation (4) it is also evident, however, that relaxation of the assumption of zero terms of trade
sensitivity in either production and/or consumption could result in a
positively-sloped offer curve. Earlier work suggesting a backward-
bending offer curve for CPEs included Brown (1968) and Holzman (1968).

FIGURE 2
TRADE BETWEEN THE PRICE-INSENSITIVE CPE
AND MARKET ECONOMIES

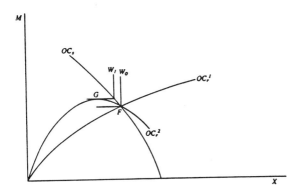

If the market economy offer curve is elastic (i.e., OC_r^1) at its intersection with the CPE offer curve, the planners maximize their welfare by trading at F. In this case, and unlike planners in some hypothetical price-sensitive CPE or policy makers in a market economy pursuing an "optimum tariff" policy,, the planners will be indifferent as to whether the FTOs as a group have external market power. Their offer will be at F regardless of whether OC_r through F is as shown or is a straight line (in which case the CPE is a "small" country). If the offer curve of the market economy is inelastic at F (i.e., OC_r^2) , how-ever, the planners will maximize their welfare by moving off of OC_s and reducing their export offer to G, thereby behaving as revenue maximizers in foreign trade. In effect, if the planners face an elastic market economy offer curve, they will have a well-defined offer curve (OC_s), regardless of whether the CPE has market power. For this reason, the CPE will be more vulnerable to the possible use of market power by the market economy than would another market economy or a hypothetical price-sensitive CPE.

The price-insensitive CPE will confront a somewhat different situation in its trade with other price-sensitive planned economies, as illustrated in Figure 3. Here the planners face a backward-bending offer curve (OC_0) similar to their own. Trade would take place at E if the planners in each CPE ignored their own market power in bilateral trade. If they choose to use this power, however, the result becomes indeterminate, as in most cases of bilateral monopoly (Wolf (1988)).

Figure 3 Trade Between Price-Insensitive
Planned Economies

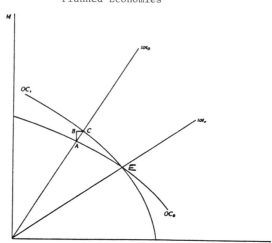

4.   Foreign trade among planned economies

Price negotiations between any two CPEs are complicated by the recognition on the part of the planners that the domestic price structure in neither economy will in general reflect the pattern of relative scarcities existing domestically or within the CMEA as a whole. To rely on bilateral bargaining over prices, without reference to some regional standard, would produce a degree of complexity and price discrimination

that could hamper the development of trade and economic integration more

generally among these economies. 11/ Fairly soon after the formation of

the CMEA in 1949 its members adopted the principles of uniform pricing

in intra-CMEA trade and basing these prices at least indirectly on world

market prices. Successive price-setting schemes have been adopted for

adjusting documented world market prices, and final "contract" prices

are bilaterally negotiated on the basis of commonly agreed principles

embedded in these schemes. Because the final prices are still

bilaterally negotiated, however, de facto price discrimination can and

does occur in intra-CMEA trade. 12/

Because the degree of strict documentation of world prices is more

difficult for manufactures than for fuels, raw materials and inter-

mediates, and because the degree of "adjustment" applied to these prices

varies across products, the structure of relative prices in trade among

CPEs has tended to differ from that found on world markets; in particu-

lar, the relative price for manufactures in the CMEA trade has consis-

tently tended to exceed their relative price on world markets (Hewett

(1974) and Marrese and Vanous (1988)). This has created significant

potential for arbitrage, although the relative rigidity of the foreign

---

11/ Ellis (1945) early recognized the considerable potential for
price discrimination in trade among planned economies. The complex
issues involved in measuring and interpreting price discrimination in
intra-CMEA trade were highlighted by Holzman (1962, 1965) and have been
revived in response to the controversial work of Marrese and Vanous
(1983a).
12/ On the evolution of intra-CMEA pricing rules and practices, see
Hewett (1974), Marrese and Vanous (1983a) and van Brabant (1985).

trade apparatus in CPEs and the writing-in of limitations on re-exports in bilateral trade agreements has constrained the extent of arbitrage in practice (Marrese and Vanous (1983b)).

The possibility also exists that a CPE, even if trading broadly in line with its comparative advantage, and avoiding being discriminated against in intra-CMEA trade, could incur a net welfare loss, in a narrow efficiency sense, from trade with other planned economies. One type of loss, in an opportunity cost sense, might arise from trading with other planned economies at terms of trade inferior to those available to the CPE on the world market (Marrese and Vanous (1983a)). Another type of loss would arise from trading with other planned economies at a terms of trade so different from the CPE's actual marginal rate of transformation that it could end up inside its production possibilities function and worse off than in autarky (Hewett (1977)). Both of these possibilities and the empirical evidence for them, however, are controversial.

Trade between planned economies is likely for several reasons to be subject to severe pressures toward bilateralism. The logic of central planning itself will lead to an institutional framework that accommodates these pressures. The planners, taking into account the material balances embodied in the plan and the terms of trade, would presumably find that it eased their job if they could negotiate the volume and prices of both exports and imports as a package in their dealings with other countries. In trade with the market economies, the planners will be confronted with the reality that most trade of this type is negotiated by profit-oriented and autonomous enterprises. When negotiating with CPEs, however, the planners will be faced with a mirror image of themselves and their own institutional preferences. Trade negotiations carried out at

the highest levels on both sides will therefore be possible, and will be

reflected in annual and longer-term bilateral agreements (for illustra-

tive details, see Hewett (1977)).

As noted earlier, trade with market economies will be settled

largely in convertible currencies and, given the fungibility of these

currencies, there is little reason (except possibly as a negotiating

ploy in order to expand access for its products to a market economy) for

the CPE to press for bilateral balance with individual trade partners.

Bilateralism pressures will arise in trade with other CPEs, however,

because the lack of commodity convertibility of their currencies will

lead each CPE to want to avoid accumulating financial claims on the

other in the latter's currency. Each CPE will want to minimize its

bilateral surplus with the other, and even to maximize its bilateral

deficit provided it can avoid settling the deficit in convertible cur-

rencies. Trade among the CPEs is therefore settled on the basis of

bilateral clearing agreements or, since 1964 in the CMEA, on the basis

of a clearing currency, the TR. Even this common currency, however,

will remain inconvertible as long as the underlying determinant of the

de facto inconvertibility of the national currencies, namely commodity

inconvertibility, persists (Holzman (1978)).

Another form of bilateralism, called "structural bilateralism",

arises from the price-setting mechanism of the CMEA described earlier.

In general the prevailing structure of prices in intra-CMEA trade will

not clear all bilateral markets in the region. This gives rise to the

phenomenon of trade in "hard" and "soft" goods depicted in Figure 3.

The figure shows for simplicity the trade between one CPE and all other
CMEA members as a group. 13/ At the prevailing terms of trade, tot_0,
which is the result of application of the common CMEA price rules and
bilateral bargaining, product M is in excess demand (= BA) and X is in
excess supply (= BC).

If the relative price of X on the world market is equal to or
greater than tot_0, the CPE with offer curve OC_s would find it profitable
to switch its excess supply of X to the world market in exchange for M,
thereby eliminating the imbalances within the CMEA. If the relative
price of X on the world market is less than tot_0, the other CPE, with
offer curve OC_0, would be induced to shift some of its export offer of M
to the world market, while CPE with offer curve OC_s might try to arbitrage, by re-exporting to the world market M purchased (relatively
cheaply) within the CMEA and re-exporting to the other CPE some of its
imports of X from the world market. These actions would tend to exacerbate the imbalances within the CMEA (Wolf (1988)).

It is this second case that has tended to characterize intra-CMEA
trade (i.e., excess supply of manufactures, which command within the
CMEA a relative price higher than that prevailing on the world market),
and the M and X goods have come to be dubbed "hard" and "soft" goods
respectively in CMEA parlance. This situation has led to the phenomenon
of "structural bilateralism" by which a CPE will be willing to export
so-called hard goods to another CPE only to the extent that it can

---

13/ It will be recalled that the situation is much more complex than
indicated in the figure, because in general the structure of relative
prices will not be identical across all bilateral trading relationships.

obtain equally hard goods in return (van Brabant (1973)). 14/ In return
for deliveries of hard goods with a value above reciprocal supplies of
such products, a CPE may demand valuation at world market prices and
settlement in convertible currencies.

Finally, the logic of central planning, with its emphasis on certainty of supplies, would suggest that planners would want to trade
more, ceteris paribus, with other planned economies than with market
economies. This preference, however, might be somewhat offset in practice by the pressures for imports from market economies resulting from
domestic excess demand pressures. While there is evidence that the
degree of mutual trade within the CMEA is greater than in customs unions
composed of market economies, it is extremely difficult to sort out the
effects of different possible determinants, including political considerations. 15/ The issue of attempts to achieve economic integration
within the CMEA lies outside the scope of this chapter. It can be noted,
however, that the various institutional factors that restrict the efficiency and degree of specialization in a CPE's trade more generally may
act to inhibit as well economic integration with other planned economies
(Marer and Montias (1980)).

14/ "Structural bilateralism" has not, however, characterized Soviet
trade with individual East European countries. See Marrese and Vanous
(1983a).
15/ See Hewett (1976 and 1980). On the notion of CMEA as a "customs
union", see Holzman (1985).

5. Internal and External Balance in Planned Economies

The fundamental identities relating the output and expenditure

sides of national income are of course the same for a CPE as for a mar-

ket economy. 16/ The familiar monetary definition of the balance of

payments also applies:

$$(5) \quad B_T' = (\Delta M - \Delta D) = \Delta NFA,$$

where B_T' is the valuta trade balance (= $P_x'Q_x - P_m'Q_m$; see equation (1)

and section 2), ΔM denotes the change in the nominal money supply, ΔD

represents the change in net domestic credit extended by the CPE's

monolithic banking system, and ΔNFA is the change in net foreign assets

expressed in terms of domestic currency. (It is assumed for simplicity that the
only international capital flows are associated with real trade flows.)
Analysis of the stylized market economy usually involves assuming

that holders of money are able to adjust rapidly to temporary disequi-

libria in the money market. In that case the change in the money supply

in equation (5) is assumed to be equal to the change in the combined

flow demand for money of households and enterprises. In the CPE, how-

ever, domestic prices are typically rigid in the short run and enter-

prises cannot be presumed to respond to an emergent excess demand for

goods, particularly in the consumption goods market, with an increase in

supply. This means that it would not be realistic to assume that money

---

16/ In the planned economies, however, national income has historically been measured and interpreted in terms of the Material Product
System, in which the value of services not used in the production of
material product, or NMP, has been ignored. This is in contrast to the
System of National Accounts approach, with its more comprehensive
measure of national product, GDP. See Marer (1985).

holders, particularly households, are always in flow equilibrium.

Changes in the money supply held by households (ΔM_h) will in general be equal to:

$$(6) \quad \Delta M_h = \Delta M_h^* + C^d - C,$$

where ΔM_h^* is the flow household demand for money, C^d denotes the aggregate demand for consumption goods, and C represents actual consumption spending. Excess household liquidity occurs when $(C^d - C) > 0$, and could reflect either excess demand for consumption goods in the aggregate (a controversial assumption), 17/ or microlevel imbalances, in which case the accumulation of excess liquidity would be exactly offset by an increase in unplanned or undesired enterprise inventories of consumption goods (Wolf 1985a).

Substitution of equation (6) into (5) yields, for the CPE:

$$(7) \quad B_T' = (\Delta M_h^* + C^d - C) - \Delta D',$$

where $\Delta D'$ is the change in net domestic credit extended to government and enterprises together plus the change in gross credit extended to households. A change in net domestic credit may affect the trade balance and/or the flow demand for money (i.e., influence desired

---

17/ See Portes (1984) on the controversy over the issue of chronic excess demand for consumption goods in planned economies. To the extent that households respond to excess demand for consumption goods offered by the socialized sector by bidding up prices in the second economy, "forced substitution" of goods in abundant supply for those for which there are shortages, and/or reducing their effective supply of labor, they may achieve a "constrained equilibrium" and, technically speaking may no longer have excess liquidity. See Wolf (1985a) and the references therein.

velocity), as in the market economy, but also, in the CPE, it may
influence the degree of imbalance in the market for consumption goods.
Consequently, the relationship between monetary policy and the trade
balance may be even less straight-forward than in the market economy
(Wolf (1985a)).

The reaction of a CPE to an exogenous adverse disturbance in
foreign trade would tend to differ from that of a market economy. In
the latter, with international commodity arbitrage, a deterioration in
the terms of trade, for example, would cause an immediate decline in
real incomes of economic agents and a shift in domestic relative prices
in favor of production of the importable and consumption of the exportable. With a fixed exchange rate, the terms of trade deterioration
would lead to a temporary worsening of the trade balance and, if monetary policy were not accommodative, a decline in the real money supply.
Together with the loss in real income, this would lead to a lower level
of real expenditure and eventual elimination of the trade deficit. If
instead the market economy had a flexible exchange rate, the terms of
trade deterioration would lead to an incipient deterioraton in the trade
balance, which in turn would cause the currency to depreciate. This
would lead to an increase in the domestic price level and a decline in
the real wage and real money balances, which in turn would induce a
reduction in real domestic expenditure. Along with the substitution
effects in production and expenditure caused by the shift in the terms
of trade, the fall in real spending would eliminate the excess demand

for foreign exchange. Under either exchange rate regime the decline in
expenditure and reallocation of resources may involve a temporary fall
in employment.

Although the authorities in the CPE may utilize the price equalization system to insulate the level and structure of domestic prices from
a shift in the external terms of trade, the operation of this system
alone will not, as is frequently believed, necessarily totally insulate
the domestic economy from such a disturbance. To show this,
equation (1) may be rewritten as:

$$(8) \quad T = B_T' - B_T,$$

where as before T is the net profit earned by FTOs in the aggregate on
price differences in foreign trade (equal to net price equalization
taxes) and B_T' and B_T are the trade balances expressed in valuta and in
domestic prices respectively. Combining expressions (8) and (5) gives:

$$(9) \quad \Delta M = (B_T' + \Delta D) = (B_T + T + \Delta D).$$

In accordance with the earlier depiction of the CPE's offer curve,
it could be reasonably assumed that the authorities would not permit an
adverse shift in the terms of trade to affect in the short run either
the structure or level of output or the level of employment. The
extreme cases of short-run adjustment to the disturbance may be illustrated using equation (9). In both cases it is assumed, for simplicity,
that trade is initially balanced both in valuta and domestic currency
prices; in other words, T is initially equal to zero.

If the authorities are willing and able to permit a decline in the
economy's net foreign assets equivalent to the deterioration in the
valuta trade balance caused directly by the disturbance, they could
leave real trade flows unchanged which, given fixed domestic prices,
would leave the domestic trade balance (B_T) equal to zero. Net foreign
trade profits would fall by the amount of deterioration in the valuta
trade balance ($B_T' = T < 0$) and the resultant fall in net price equalization taxes received by the budget would mean an equal increase in net
credit to government (ΔD) . The domestic money supply would remain
unchanged and the domestic economy would be completely unaffected by
this external disturbance in the short run, although at the expense of a
decline in the economy's international reserves. In this case the trade
offer curve in Figure 2 would be perfectly vertical.

At the other extreme, the authorities might feel compelled to manipulate trade flows so as to maintain the initial balance in valuta trade
and the level of international reserves. In this case the domestic
money supply would increase by the amount by which the trade balance in
domestic prices improves ($\Delta M = B_T > 0$), as the result of the decline in
domestic absorption occasioned by some combination of an increase in
export volumes and decline in import volumes. At the same time the fall
in net price equalization taxes (see equation (8)) would be exactly
offset by increased net credit to the budget ($\Delta T = (-\Delta D)$; Wolf
(1980a)). In this case the trade offer curve would be backward bending.

Although the expenditure-reducing and trade balance outcomes in
this second case are similar to those expected in the market economy,
these outcomes in the CPE are not the result of economic agents

responding to domestic price signals. Instead, in the CPE most or all short-run adjustments are quantity adjustments. Given the relatively rigid prices, market imbalances will typically develop in the course of adjustment, rather than being alleviated, particularly but not exclusively in the household sector. Whereas the adverse external disturbance may have a deflationary effect and an adverse impact on output and employment in the market economy, particularly in the event of downwardly sticky money wages and a fixed exchange rate, the impact in the CPE, if real trade flows are manipulated to maintain external balance, is much more likely to be inflationary in the sense that the buildup in liquidity combined with rigid prices will lead to repressed inflation (Holzman (1968), Wiles (1968) and Wolf (1985a)). Such pressures may be exacerbated by multiplier effects because of the heavy concentration of CPE imports in intermediate products and capital goods critical to fulfillment of the national economic plan (Holzman (1974) and Brada (1982)). Diversion of resources away from consumption may also characterize the planners' response to an adverse domestic supply disturbance or to excess demand generated by so-called investment cycles. Given the high likelihood of disequilibrium in one or more markets in such cases, macro-modeling of planned economies has become increasingly characterized by explicitly disequilibrium approaches. 18/

Given the lack of autonomy of the FTOs and, in part due to confiscatory fiscal policies, their possible lack of profit "interestedness", together with domestic prices that are invariant to changes in the

---

18/ See Portes (1979) for an elaborate model of internal-external balance in the CPE, in an explicitly disequilibrium framework.

valuta exchange rate, this exchange rate is likely to have essentially
an accounting, rather than an economic function in the CPE. The
authorities are therefore unlikely to attempt to use the valuta exchange
rate as an instrument of economic policy (Wolf (1980a, 1988)). 19/

6.   Economic reform and foreign trade

The state monopoly over foreign trade has generally performed well
in insulating the CPE somewhat from external disturbances and ensuring
the import of various products considered essential to plan fulfillment.
At the same time, however, the institutions and policy priorities of
CPEs have tended to result in a foreign trade system and policies that
have severely hampered the efficiency of their foreign trade and kept it
from playing a dynamic role in the development of these economies.

As economic development has proceeded in the CPEs, the scope has
progressively diminished for high rates of economic growth based on an
extensive development strategy based on the rapid accumulation of production factors. The extensive planning and administrative apparatus
has also proved to be less and less able to cope with the direction of
an ever more complex economy. Over the past quarter century attention
in these economies has increasingly been directed toward the necessity

---

19/ The existence of the valuta exchange rate, the price equalization
system, a distorted domestic price structure and price distortions in
intra-CMEA foreign trade create significant problems for the measurement, on a basis comparable to that for market economies, of national
income, the structure and level of foreign trade and the degree of
openness of planned economies. These problems are discussed in Wolf
(1988).

of shifting to a more _intensive_ development strategy, one emphasizing
the need to raise the quality and efficiency of both inputs and outputs,
rather than mainly their accumulation.

An intriguing hypothesis is that those planned economies that are
relatively poorly endowed in natural resources, and therefore for which
the potential for export of conventional "hard" goods is smaller, will
be under particular pressure to reform. In effect, the relative lack of
hard goods accelerates the time when a fundamental shift to a more
intensive development strategy is required, in order to maintain rapid
economic growth and become competitive in trade with market economies
and maintain the ability to import hard goods from other CPEs (Brown and
Marer (1973)).

Whatever the factors pointing to the need for a shift in development strategy, it has been recognized in most CPEs that this change
requires the reform of economic institutions as well as changes in
policy. The basic choice for reformers has been between a reform that
is confined to attempts to improve the efficiency of central planning
and its implementation, and a reform that seeks to give enterprises a
considerable degree of autonomy and to increase significantly the role
of the market in the allocation of resources.

These two approaches to reform have fundamentally different implications for the organization and carrying out of foreign trade. In the
less ambitious reform model, which is frequently characterized as
improving or "perfecting" the system of planning and management, the
authorities will seek to provide the mechanisms for better coordination
between domestic enterprises or combines and the FTOs, perhaps subordi-

nating the latter to some degree to the former. Greater emphasis will
be placed on "realized sales" or possibly value added or profit of producing enterprises as a basis for central evaluation, instead of the
traditional dominant criterion of gross output. The intent may be to
allow prices to play an enhanced role in resource allocation, but these
prices will still be set centrally and not necessarily in light of the
foreign currency prices prevailing on the world market. The foreign
trade system will also continue to be characterized by a valuta exchange
rate and a system of official internal exchange rates. 20/

The second, more market-oriented reform strategy leads to what may
be called a "modified planned economy" (MPE). 21/ In the MPE, detailed,
mandatory central plans governing the inputs and outputs of enterprises
will be abolished, and plan fulfillment is replaced by enterprise profit
or value added as the basis for evaluating the enterprise's performance
and the remuneration of its employees. Enterprises will be encouraged
to shift their efforts from vertical, bureaucratic bargaining toward
"horizontal" dealings with other enterprises, even outside of their own
industrial ministries. So as to promote this use of the "market,"
greater price flexibility will be permitted for a broad range of producer and nonstaple consumer goods. Enterprises will be given more
autonomy with respect to wages, with indirect wage regulation systems,
using various parameters or a system of taxation of "excessive" wages,

---

20/ Gardner (1983) summarizes developments of this type in the Soviet
Union through the early 1980s.
21/ This stylized model was first developed in Wolf (1978); Marer
(1986) provides a more detailed description of the prototypical MPE,
Hungary.

replacing the direct assignment of the wage bill from the center. In
the MPE less reliance is to be placed on budgetary subsidies for investment and more importance given to bank credits, allocated in part on the
basis of interest rates, and the self-financing of enterprises.

In the foreign trade area more direct, export-oriented linkages
will be encouraged between domestic producers and foreign markets, with
many enterprises now being granted direct foreign trading rights or the
ability to contract with FTOs on a strictly commission basis. Establishment of these more direct connections with foreign markets have been
portrayed as somewhat analogous to the organizational evolution, within
large corporations in market economies, from a separate international
division, with responsibility for all of a company's foreign trade, to
world product divisions that produce and directly market abroad a distinct category of products, thereby establishing a more intimate knowledge of changing world market requirements than their predecessor
international division (Brada and Jackson (1978)).

Linkages will also be established for certain groups of tradables
between domestic and foreign currency prices, and the scope of the
system of price equalization will be considerably reduced. A so-called
foreign trade multiplier or commercial exchange rate will be initiated
by in effect folding together the existing valuta exchange rate (e') and
the average official internal exchange rate (e"; see equation (3)). In
the MPE, therefore, the so-called calculative price for the ith product
(P_i'' in equation (3)) becomes a regulated "transaction" price which in
principle will be the price that the exporting enterprise, whether a FTO
or a producer with direct exporting rights, will actually receive per

unit of export (after the obligatory sale of its foreign exchange earnings at the commercial exchange rate), and these proceeds will in principle be directly convertible into goods on the domestic market. This transaction price paid or received in foreign trade is also intended to influence, directly or indirectly, the price at which a given tradable is sold domestically (Wolf (1985b) and Marer 1986)).

The modified planned economy is more difficult to "stylize" than either the CPE or the market economy. The MPE operates partially on market principles and partly through informal mechanisms that de-facto may perpetuate many of the patterns of hierarchical bargaining and bureaucratic intervention in enterprise affairs that characterize the CPE (Bauer (1983) and Kornai (1986)). Although enterprises in principle are meant to behave analogously to the profit-maximizing firm in the market economy, in practice they may give greater attention to bargaining with the authorities over prices, subsidies, tax reliefs and other preferences than to efforts to increase or maximize pre-tax profits through raising efficiency or developing new export markets. Those enterprises that do earn exceptionally high profits may find that these profits are subject to arbitrary confiscation in order to provide the budget the revenues to subsidize loss-making enterprises (Kornai (1986) and Tardos (1988)). The authorities, for their part, may feel compelled to intervene in the pricing, production and export decisions of enterprises in order to satisfy various social objectives, to forestall the bankruptcy of unprofitable firms, or to ensure that a particular investment project is undertaken to satisfy local political authorities. While in theory foreign trade decision-making in the MPE may be the province of profit-oriented enterprises, possessing both the authority

and responsibility to respond mainly to market forces, in reality these

firms will be heavily influenced by various institutions, relationships

and policies built up over a number of years in the CPE from which the

modified planned economy has evolved.

Continued pervasive bureaucratic intervention and the "soft budget

constraint" (Kornai (1979)) of these enterprises, together with the

immobility, relative to the market economy, of both labor and capital

(the latter due in part to the lack of an efficient capital market), are

likely to cause the so-called trade elasticities of export supply and

import demand at the enterprise level to be lower in the MPE than in an

otherwise comparable market economy. Despite these similarities with

the CPE, however, and the blunted pre-tax (pre-subsidy) profit motive of

enterprises in the MPE, these firms may well be more sensitive to rela-

tive prices than their CPE counterparts. Consequently, the aggregate

offer curve of the MPE may well have the positive slope usually assumed

for the market economy (i.e., (β + m > 1.00) , rather than the backward

bending offer curve of the price-insensitive CPE. As noted, however,

this offer curve will probably be more steeply sloped than that of the

market economy. The continuing commitment of the MPE to undertake, say,

one half of its trade with other planned economies also may constrain

its own reform efforts in foreign trade, particularly if most of these

economies remain closer to the classical CPE mold. 22/

22/ Other possible complications resulting from a MPE engaging a
major share of its trade with CPEs are discussed in Wolf (1988).

The modified planned economy, as noted, is difficult to stylize,
and thus formal modeling of issues of internal-external balance in the
MPE is not easy. The dilemma for the modeler is that while the institutional reality of this type of economy may be too complex to model
effectively, to abstract from most of these institutional complexities
would simply result in a model that would resemble a market economy with
various important price distortions. This latter approach to MPEs may,
however, generate some useful analytical insights.

For example, consider an MPE in which the domestic price of the
importable remains administratively fixed, but in which the domestic
price of the exportable is linked to its foreign currency price by the
commercial exchange rate or foreign trade multiplier discussed earlier.
In effect, the importable is still subject to full price equalization
but the exportable is not. Assume that the economy is subjected to a
particular external economic disturbance, such as inflation on world
markets that raises the foreign currency price of the MPE's importable
more rapidly than the price of its exportable. In the case at hand, under
certain conditions, this deterioration in the external terms of trade would
actually be accompanied by an improvement in the internal terms of trade
because the domestic price of the importable is administratively fixed, while
the domestic price of the exportable would rise proportionately to its foreign
currency price. To the extent that enterprises in the MPE were price-
sensitive, and the economy could afford a decline in its net foreign assets,
domestic resources would be reallocated into production of the exportable
and imports would increase. The resulting deterioration in the trade balance

denominated in foreign currency prices would be even larger than that

incurred by a CPE in which the authorities, faced with a similar disturbance,

attempt to completely insulate the domestic economy from the disturbance (see

section 5). In a more complex model, with an imported intermediate good,

the same type of disturbance could result (in the MPE) in positive relative

effective protection of its export, despite the deterioration in its external

terms of trade. 23/

    This case of a "perverse" reaction to an exogenous disturbance

highlights a serious issue for the authorities in a planned economy with

a partially decentralized system. The problem is that many prices

remain distorted in the MPE, but enterprises may now have both the

autonomy and the motivation to utilize this modified system to their

own, but not necessarily to the economy's, advantage. In the stylized

market economy there is a tendency for micro- and macro-interests to

coincide; this outcome cannot necessarily be expected in the MPE, how-

ever, unless the authorities are able to eliminate price distortions.

The authorities will generally be aware of this problem, although per-

haps only after experiences similar to that outlined above. This aware-

ness may well prompt them to tighten formal and informal controls over

enterprise activities, which in effect will move the system back in the

direction of the CPE.

    The foregoing example of a "perverse" response depends, of course,

on enterprises being sensitive to changes in relative prices. As noted,

---

23/ Wolf (1980b) develops detailed models that allow of such effects,
and shows their relevance to the actual experience of one and possibly
two MPEs in the aftermath of the first oil price shock in the mid-1970s.

there are a number of reasons to suppose that this sensitivity may be
effectively blunted in an MPE. Either way, the effectiveness of the
exchange rate as an instrument for macroeconomic stabilization in MPEs

is thrown into question. If enterprises are indeed relatively price
sensitive, a devaluation of the commercial rate could well have perverse
effects along the general lines discussed earlier (Wolf (1978)). On the
other hand, relatively low price sensitivity would tend to mean little
trade balance response, one way or another, to devaluation. Several
arguments have been developed for the notion that devaluation in the MPE
is likely to have mainly, or only, an inflationary effect, but not all
these arguments stand up to scrutiny. 24/ Perhaps the most persuasive
arguments regarding the relative ineffectiveness of devaluation in the
MPE (vis-à-vis the market economy) are those which note that enterprises
may not in general be subjected to financial discipline, profitable
enterprises may expect confiscation of "excessive" profits, exporting
firms may be subject to informal pressures to supply domestic markets at
artificially low prices, and enterprises may find significant constraints on labor and capital mobility in the short and medium run. All
these limiting factors, which incidentally could potentially be relaxed
by the authorities, may lower the effective supply elasticities of MPE
enterprises.

24/ For a summary critique of these arguments, see Wolf (1988) and
the references therein.

References

Bauer, T. (1983), "The Hungarian Alternative to Soviet Type Planning," Journal of Comparative Economies, 7, pp. 304-316.

Boltho, A. (1971), Foreign Trade Criteria in Socialist Economies. London: Cambridge University Press.

Brada, J.C. (1982), "Real and Monetary Approaches to Foreign Trade Adjustment Mechanisms in Centrally Planned Economies," European Economic Review, 19, pp. 229-244.

_____, and M.R. Jackson (1978), "The Organization of Foreign Trade Under Capitalism and Socialism," Journal of Comparative Economics, 2, p. 293-320.

Brown, A.A. (1968), "Towards a Theory of Centrally Planned Foreign Trade," in A.A. Brown and E. Neuberger (eds.) International Trade and Central Planning, pp. 57-93. Berkeley: University of California Press.

_____, and P. Marer (1973), "Foreign Trade in the East European Reforms," in M. Bornstein (ed.) Plan and Market, pp. 153-205. New Haven: Yale University Press.

Campbell, R.W. (1974), The Soviet-Type Economies. Boston: Houghton Mifflin.

Ellis, H.S. (1945), "Bilateralism and the Future of International
    Trade," Essays in International Finance, No. 5.

Gardner, H.S. (1983), Soviet Foreign Trade: The Decision Process.
    Boston: Kluwer-Nijhoff.

Hewett, E.A. (1974), Foreign Trade Prices in the Council for Mutual
    Economic Assistance. London: Cambridge University Press.

_____ (1976), "A Gravity Model of CMEA Trade," in J.C. Brada (ed.).
    Quantitative and Analytical Studies in East-West Economic
    Relations, pp. 1-15. Bloomington, Ind.: IDRC, Indiana University.

_____ (1977). "Prices and Resource Allocation in Intra-CMEA Trade," in
    A. Abouchar (ed.), The Socialist Price Mechanism, pp. 95-128.
    Durham, N.C.: Duke University Press.

_____ (1980), "Foreign Trade Outcomes in Eastern and Western Economies,"
    in P. Marer and J.M. Montias (eds.). East European Integration and
    East-West Trade, pp. 41-69. Bloomington, Ind.: Indiana University
    Press.

Holzman, F.D. (1953), "The Profit-Output Relationship of a Soviet
    Firm: Comment," Canadian Journal of Economics and Political
    Science, 19, pp. 523-531.

_____ (1962), "Soviet Foreign Trade Pricing and the Question of Discrimination: A 'Customs Union' Approach," Review of Economics and Statistics, 54, 134-147.

_____ (1965), "More on Soviet Bloc Discrimination," Soviet Studies, 17, pp. 44-65.

_____ (1966), "Foreign Trade Behavior of Centrally Planned Economies," in H. Rosovsky (ed.), Industrialization in Two Systems: Essays in Honor of Alexander Gerschenkron, pp. 237-263. New York: Wiley.

_____ (1968), "Soviet Central Planning and Its Impact on Foreign Trade Behavior and Adjustment Mechanisms," in A.A. Brown and E. Neuberger (eds.), International Trade and Central Planning, pp. 280-305. Berkeley: University of California Press.

_____ (1974), "Import Bottlenecks and the Foreign Trade Multiplier," in F.D. Holzman (ed.), Foreign Trade Under Central Planning, pp. 126-155. Cambridge, Mass.: Harvard University Press.

_____ (1978), "CMEA's Hard Currency Deficits and Convertibility," in N.G.M. Watts (ed.), Economic Relations Between East and West, pp. 144-163. New York: St. Martin's Press.

_____ (1979), "Some Theories of the Hard Currency Shortages of Centrally Planned Economies," in Joint Economic Committee, U.S. Congress Soviet Economy in a Time of Change, Vol. 2. Washington, D.C.: U.S. Government Printing Office.

_____ (1985), "Comecon: A 'Trade Destroying' Customs Union?," Journal of Comparative Economics, 9, pp. 410–423.

Kaser, M. (1967), Comecon. London: Oxford University Press.

Kornai, J. (1979), "Resource-Constrained Versus Demand-Constrained Systems," Econometrica, 47, pp. 801–819.

_____ (1980), Economics of Shortage, 2 vols. Amsterdam: North-Holland.

_____ (1982), "Adjustment to Price and Quantity Signals in the Socialist Economy," Economie Appliquée, 35, pp. 503–524.

_____ (1986), "The Hungarian Reform Process: Visions, Hopes and Reality," Journal of Economic Literature, 24, pp. 1687–1737.

Marer, P. (1985), Dollar GNPs of the U.S.S.R. and Eastern Europe. Baltimore: Johns Hopkins University Press.

----- (1986), "Economic Reform in Hungary: From Central Planning to Regulated Market", in Joint Economic Committee, U.S. Congress, East European Economies: Slow Growth in the 1980s, vol. 3, pp. 223-297. Washington, D.C.: U.S. Government Printing Office.

_____, and J. M. Montias (1980), "Theory and Measurement of East European Integration," in P. Marer and J.M. Montias (eds.), East European Integration and East-West Trade, pp. 3-38. Bloomington, Ind.: Indiana University Press.

Marrese, M. and J. Vanous (1983a), Soviet Subsidization of Trade with Eastern Europe. Berkeley:

_____ (1983b), "Unconventional Gains from Trade," Journal of Comparative Economics, 7, pp. 382-399.

_____ (1988), "The Content and Controversy of Soviet Trade Relations with Eastern Europe, 1970-84," in J.C. Brada, E.A. Hewett and T.A. Wolf (eds.), Economic Adjustment and Reform in Eastern Europe and the Soviet Union: Essays in Honor of Franklyn D. Holzman, pp. 185-220. Durham, N.C.: Duke University Press.

Nove, A. (1977), The Soviet Economic System. London: Allen and Unwin.

Portes, R. (1979), "Internal and External Balance in a Centrally Planned Economy," Journal of Comparative Economics, 3, pp. 325-345.

____ (1984), "The Theory and Measurement of Macroeconomic Disequilibrium in Centrally Planned Economies," presented at the Conference on the Soviet Union and Eastern Europe in the World Economy, Washington, D.C., October 1984.

Pryor, F.L. (1963), The Communist Foreign Trade System. Cambridge, Mass.: MIT Press.

Tardos, M. (1988), "How to Create Markets in Eastern Europe: The Hungarian Case," in J.C. Brada, E.A. Hewett and T.A. Wolf (eds.), Economic Adjustment and Reform in Eastern Europe and the Soviet Union: Essays in Honor of Franklyn D. Holzman, pp. 259-284. Durham, N.C.: Duke University Press.

Trzeciakowski, W. (1962), "Model optymalizacjii biezacej handlu zagranicznego i jego zastosowanie," Przeglad Statystyczny, 2.

____ (1978), Indirect Management in a Centrally Planned Economy. Amsterdam: North Holland.

van Brabant, J.M.P. (1973), Bilateralism and Structural Bilateralism in Intra-CMEA Trade. Rotterdam: Rotterdam University Press.

(1982), "Optimal Foreign Trade for the Price-Insensitive Soviet-Type Economy," Journal of Comparative Economics, 6, pp. 37-54.

(1985a), "Economic Stabilization in Planned Economies: Toward an Analytical Framework," Staff Papers, International Monetary Fund, 32, pp. 78-131.

(1985b), "Exchange Rate Systems and Adjustment in Planned Economies," Staff Papers, International Monetary Fund, 32, pp. 211-247.

(1988) Foreign Trade in the Centrally Planned Economy. London: Harwood Academic Publishers.

van Brabant, J. M. P. (1977) The Relationship Between Domestic and Foreign Trade Prices in Centrally Planned Economies: The Case of Hungary. Osteuropa Wirtschaft, 22, 235-258.
van Brabant, J. M. P. (1985) Exchange Rates in Eastern Europe: Types, Derivation and Application. World Bank Staff Working Paper No. 778. Washington, D.C.: World Bank.
van Brabant, J. M. P. (1985) The Relationship Between World and Socialist Trade Prices—Some Empirical Evidence. Journal of Comparative Economics, 9, 233-251.
Wilczynski, J. (1969) The Economics and Politics of East-West Trade. New York: Praeger.
Wiles, P. J. D. (1968) Communist International Economics. New York: Praeger.
Winiecki, J. (1986) Central Planning and Export Orientation. Eastern European Economics, 24, 67-89.
Wolf, T. A. (1978) The Theory of International Trade with an International Cartel or a Centrally Planned Economy: Comment. Southern Economic Journal, 44, 987-991.
Wolf, T. A. (1978) Exchange Rate Adjustments in Small Market and Centrally Planned Economies. Journal of Comparative Economics, 2, 226-245.
Wolf, T. A. (1980) On the Adjustment of Centrally Planned Economies to External Economic Disturbances. In East European Integration and East-West Trade, edited by P. Marer and J. M. Montias, pp. 86-111. Bloomington, Ind.: Indiana University Press.
Wolf, T. A. (1980) External Inflation, the Balance of Trade, and Resource Allocation in Small Centrally Planned Economies. In The Impact of International Economic Disturbances on the Soviet Union and Eastern Europe, edited by E. Neuberger and L. D. Tyson. pp. 63-87. New York: Pergamon.
Wolf, T. A. (1980) Devaluation in 'Large' Modified Centrally Planned Economies. Journal of Comparative Economics, 4, 415-419.

UPDATE by Thomas A. Wolfe "Foreign Trade in Planned Economies"

7. The Transition to the Market Economy

Recent years have witnessed the overthrow of existing regimes in
many planned economies and an acceleration of--indeed, in some cases a
qualitatively new commitment toward--market-oriented reforms. While in
some cases the target system still remains vaguely defined, in others
the goal of a market economy has been more clearly elaborated. The
issue has generally become how to make the transition to a market
economy as quickly but as painlessly as possible.

While the precise path and pace of the transition will understandably differ for each of these economies, certain common developments can be expected. There will be substantial further price
liberalization, significant steps towards the development of integrated
capital and labor markets, expanded enterprise autonomy and competition
(accompanied by hardened budget constraints), and increasing
privatization of economic activity. Reforms in these areas will
fundamentally affect these economies' foreign trade; at the same time,
the pace and extent of reform of the domestic economy, including the
scope for expanded competition and price liberalization, will depend as
well on the speed and degree of transformation of the foreign trade and
exchange systems. A significant development in this connection is the
demise of the traditional CMEA trading mechanism (Section 1). Beginning
in 1991, trade among CMEA members is to be conducted in principle at

world market prices and settled in convertible currencies, although
there may be various transitional arrangements. 1/

   With price liberalization and the pursuit of sufficiently tight
macroeconomic policies, including a realistic exchange rate, economies
embarked on the transition will ultimately be in a position to establish
the convertibility of their currencies. This in turn will effectively
broaden the autonomy of firms to choose freely--subject to their budget
constraints--the resources they need to maximize profits. In this way,
the reforming economies may come to the point at which they are trading
with the rest of the world on the basis of their true competitive
advantage.

   The achievement of convertibility at a realistic exchange rate is
no simple matter, however, for many planned economies, due to their
history of domestic price distortions, in some cases chronic excess
liquidity, and the use of exchange rates as mere accounting units. In
some reforming economies, foreign exchange auctions have been
established, with the supply of foreign currency coming from both the
authorities and exporting enterprises that may be permitted to retain a
portion of their foreign exchange earnings. These auctions, if
broadened quickly, can serve as a transitional mechanism for providing
valuable information to the authorities regarding the possible exchange
rate at which the different foreign exchange markets may at one point be
unified.

1/ For some of the implications, see Kenen (1990).

As long as various domestic prices continue to be administered, the
question will still persist as to the extent to which the potential
price effects of exchange rate changes designed to improve the balance
of trade should be "passed through" to the domestic price level. To the
extent that administrative passthrough does not take place, the
devaluation could be expected to have an _expenditure switching_ effect,
as the higher transaction prices received by exporters induce them to
shift production away from the home market towards exports. This
reaction on the part of exporters would tend, however, to lead to excess
demand pressures on the domestic market which in turn could provoke the
type of ad hoc intervention in foreign trade--in the form of export
controls--that characterizes the MPE. Full passthrough of exchange rate
changes, on the other hand, may reduce the expenditure switching effect
but will--under suitably tight financial policies--lead to an
expenditure reducing effect and generally raise the efficiency of the
exchange rate as a policy instrument and ensure balance on domestic
markets. 1/

Even if the prices of all essential tradables are liberalized, the
effective elasticity of the domestic price level with respect to a
change in the exchange rate--what could be called the passthrough
elasticity--may be lower than that expected in the traditional market
economy. This is so because while markets increasingly come to dominate
the process of resource allocation, the transitional economy is likely
to have a predominantly state-owned enterprise sector, the inherited

---

1/ For a more detailed discussion, see Wolf (1990a).

production structure will be only gradually modified, capital and labor mobility may still be relatively low, and financial discipline may be less than complete. As a result, the effective weight of the tradable sector and the combined elasticity of substitution between tradables and nontradables is likely to be less than in the traditional market economy and this may weaken the passthrough effect and thus the effectiveness of exchange rate policy. 1/

Nonetheless, as market-oriented reforms proceed, issues such as the relative size of the passthrough elasticity will tend to fade away and questions of the relationship between exchange rate policy--for example, the relative fixity of the rate and the basis on which it is managed-- and domestic inflation and stabilization in general will increasingly come to be discussed, using the same basic conceptual frameworks as are already used to analyze issues of macroeconomic stabilization in market economies.

Bibliography

Kenen, P. "Transitional Arrangements for Trade and Payments Among the CMEA Countries," International Monetary Fund, Working Paper WP/90/79.

Wolf, T.A. "Market-Oriented Reform of Foreign Trade in Planned Economies," in O. Bogomolov (ed.) Market forces in Planned Economies (London: Macmillan 1990a).

_____, "The Exchange Rate and The Price Level in Socialist Economies," International Monetary Fund, Working Paper WP/90/50, 1990b.

1/ This topic is developed in greater detail in Wolf (1990b).

A NEW AGENDA FOR THE GATT
by
Gardner Patterson and Eliza Patterson

IN ANTICIPATION of the new round of multilateral trade negotiations, within the framework of the General Agreement on Tariffs and Trade (GATT), four important non-governmental reports on the matters to be discussed have been produced recently:

The first, *Trade Policies for a Better Future*, was prepared for the Director-General of the GATT by a group of 'wisemen' under the chairmanship of Fritz Leutwiler, then Chairman of the Swiss National Bank (hereinafter referred to as the Leutwiler report). [1]

The second, *Trading for Growth*, was prepared by Gary Hufbauer and Jeffrey Schott at the Institute for International Economics in Washington (hereinafter referred to as the Hufbauer-Schott study). [2]

The third, *Trade Talks*, was prepared by Michael Aho and Jonathan Aronson at the Council on Foreign Relations in New York (hereinafter referred to as the Aho-Aronson study). [3]

The fourth, *Trade Route to Sustained Economic Growth*, was prepared by a study group of the Trade Policy Research Centre, London, under the chairmanship of Amnuay Viravan, Chairman of the Executive Board of the Bangkok Bank (hereinafter referred to as the Viravan report). [4]

Each of the works warrants serious consideration by those interested in the functioning of the international trading system. [5]

Although these studies differ considerably in their approach, emphasis and coverage, as well as in their specific findings and recommendations, the writers of this article draw from them four conclusions. We agree with them all. (i) The international trading system is in deep trouble. It cannot simply go on as it stands. But abandoning it in favour of additional sectoral, bilateral and regional arrangements would not serve the world well. (ii) Negotiations in the new GATT round are going to be the most difficult yet. (iii) The GATT system should be expanded to cover several new areas and further liberalisation is called for in various old ones. (iv) A most important task facing the negotiators will be to restore respect for, and to strengthen, reform or bring up to date, many of the present norms, rules and procedures of the GATT. Dealing effectively with the systemic problems is absolutely crucial. In the absence of success here, any agreements on further trade liberalisation will have little value.

GARDNER PATTERSON was Deputy Director-General of the General Agreement on Tariffs and Trade (GATT), Geneva, in 1966-67 and 1969-80, having been Professor of Economics at Princeton University (1949-69); and he is the author of *Discrimination in International Trade* (1966). ELIZA PATTERSON is a lawyer specializing in international trade.

Reprinted with permission from *The World Economy*, a quarterly journal of the Trade Policy Centre, London, Vol. 9, No. 2 (June 1986), pp. 153–169.

THE GATT SYSTEM: SHOULD IT HAVE A FUTURE?

On the first of the conclusions, the Hufbauer-Schott study notes that the GATT system is more frequently cited for its shortcomings than for its accomplishments, while the Aho-Aronson study states that it is in 'disarray'. The Viravan report characterises the GATT (as an agreement on basic norms and principles) as 'moribund'; and the Leutwiler report finds that the system is 'suffering serious and continuing erosion'. The GATT system is, indeed, widely perceived to be outmoded. Given all the changes in the world economy and, too, the redistribution of economic power since it was drafted, the GATT's rules are often seen as irrelevant and, even when not, they are more honoured in the breach than in the observance. There is a strong feeling that, without the new negotiations, the system would probably collapse.

In view of the difficulties, sketched below, of conducting a new GATT round at this time, it has to be asked — and fortunately is in these studies — whether greater progress could not be made in smaller negotiations, seeking bilateral agreements, sectoral pacts or limited free trade areas — a trend already under way.

These approaches are examined in some detail in the Aho-Aronson[6] and Hufbauer-Schott[7] studies. They marshall all the respectable arguments. Not all trade problems are multilateral. Those unwilling to negotiate further trade liberalisation should not prevent those who are willing from proceeding. Smaller negotiations can be less subject to paralysing ideological disputes. Limited agreements among 'like-minded' countries serve as building blocks for wider agreements later. And limited agreements could have a useful 'demonstration effect' — serving as an example of the benefits of trade liberalisation to participants and of the costs to non-participants.

But proceeding in this *ad hoc* way is fraught with risks. Powerful vested interests are created by the preferential treatment normally involved in schemes with limited participation and those interests can make any subsequent expansion of membership exceedingly difficult to achieve. Experience before World War II showed that bilateral or plurilateral arrangements do not provide stability and growth; they simply nourish cartels. The regional free trade areas of the post-war period, the Leutwiler report asserts, have 'set a dangerous precedent for further special deals, fragmentation of the trading system and damage to the trade interests of non-participants'.[8] A fragmented trading system, as history has also shown, all too easily leads to bitter political problems between countries. More fundamentally, and easily overlooked in the heat of debate, limited approaches to trade liberalisation restrict the benefits which are the *raison d'être* for international trade, namely more efficient production making for increased output and wider consumer choice.

Given the apparent attractiveness for many of bilateral, regional and *à la carte* approaches, the authors of these studies have performed an important service in spelling out both the case for, and the probable costs of, moving further in these directions. In that event, the Viravan report suggests that 'the best that could be hoped for is a more or less comprehensive network of continually renegotiated international cartel arrangements, [while] the worst would be . . . a return to the chaos of the 1930s',[9] which seems to us to be overstating the case. We heartily agree, though, with the conclusion of the Hufbauer-Schott study that 'a genuine multilateral round offers the best approach for improving the world trading system and improving the welfare of all GATT members'.[10]

CONSTRAINTS ON THE NEGOTIATIONS

Turning to the second of the above conclusions, the new GATT round will be the most difficult one to date, not only because of the complexity, diversity and intractability of the substantive issues, to which we turn shortly, but also because of what Dr Aho and Dr Aronson call 'constraints'. They devote nearly a third of their analysis to the latter problem. And the Viravan report focusses on the deep-seated nature of the difficulties which governments face in trying to get the adjustment process of the market working, a prerequisite for a well-functioning and efficient international trading system. The others give it less space, but all, explicitly or implicitly, recognise and stress the difficulties for negotiations resulting from the expansion of government intervention in the market process, the accumulated effects of failures to adjust to foreign competition, the emergence of 'excess capacity' in basic industries and low rates of growth, high levels of unemployment and widespread protectionist sentiment in many of the major economies.

Laying all this out has been a good thing. The difficulties and constraints are real. They will affect both the negotiating process and the outcome. Any failure by the interested public, especially in national parliaments and the media, to acknowledge that they must be addressed will only lead to disenchantment. Bringing out in the open the difficulties and constraints before the new GATT round actually began should also have the salutary effect of setting reasonable expectations and discouraging all but the most committed, courageous and hardy people from participating. Those who do participate would be well advised to read these publications.

PROCEDURAL PROBLEMS

The way a negotiation is organised has an important bearing on the results. In thinking about the new GATT round there are four 'procedural' problems of special significance.

First, an issue that must be resolved before the negotiations begin is the status of participating countries' obligations during the negotiations. Experience has shown that in preparing for negotiations aimed at reducing barriers to trade, governments are tempted to create new barriers as a means of enhancing their bargaining positions. By creating ill-will and setting back the starting point, such actions make it less likely that substantial liberalisation will result from the negotiations. We agree with the Hufbauer-Schott and Aho-Aronson studies that the proper answer to these tendencies is a commitment by participants to a standstill on trade restrictions at the start of a new round, an undertaking not to introduce new ones, an undertaking which should continue throughout the negotiations. In past negotiations, there has been an implicit understanding that there would be a standstill and, by and large, it was honoured. We think a *formal* undertaking, as these two studies propose, is only worthwhile if the debate on its precise wording and on the procedures for monitoring and enforcement does not threaten to become a major negotiation in itself, such that it seriously delays the negotiations proper.

Secondly, is it to be, as in the past, a negotiation in which nothing is final until all is final and there is more or less simultaneous negotiation on all issues? Or is it to be more in the nature of a 'rolling' negotiation with intermediate deadlines and perhaps a seriatim treatment of particular issues? The great advantage of the more or less simultaneous negotiation on all issues and a final deadline is that it permits the maximum number of trade-offs and so the greatest final results. But it can, of course, fail. Experience shows, however, that the risk of that happening is not great. Too much, politically and economically, is at stake to permit a negotiation to fail after years of effort have been devoted to the task. The Hufbauer-Schott study argues for a rolling agenda, punctuated from time to time by subject or country agreements. The Aho-Aronson study also makes a strong case for intermediate deadlines, but with simultaneous negotiation on all issues, some more active than others at any given time. Our guess is that this would not yield substantial results, unless intermediate agreements on balanced packages of issues were subject to change, in the light of subsequent negotiations. Would it then differ significantly from the traditional approach?

A third major procedural problem is how to organise the negotiations on agriculture. The issue here is whether farm products should be dealt with in the same negotiating groups that deal with manufactured goods (the subsidies group, for example, would consider the problem of subsidies to the production and/or export of *all* products) or whether all aspects of trade in farm products should be dealt with in a separate group dealing only with agricultural matters. Although the former procedure is more conducive to liberalisation, we expect the weight of tradition and the European Community's intransigence will result, after much bitter debate, in the latter. It is greatly to be regretted that none of the studies deals with this problem. Participants in the new GATT round would benefit from a careful and detailed analysis by non-participants of the costs and benefits of the two approaches.

A fourth big procedural problem is also ignored by the studies. Who gets into the room? The success of the new GATT round will depend on the extent to which the interests of the others, especially the developing countries, are considered *before* the three giants — the European Community, Japan and the United States — strike their deals and create a 'take it or leave it' situation. Experience has shown that the giants often can quite easily accommodate many of the needs of others *provided* this is arranged before they reach their final agreements. After that, any changes are strongly resisted, lest they upset the delicate balance achieved. There is no obvious or simple solution to this problem. The major trading powers do have to reach agreement among themselves or nothing happens. Negotiating difficulties increase rapidly as the number sitting around the table increases. And not all participants in the round have a stake in matters of concern to the 'big three'. Experience in the Tokyo and Kennedy rounds suggests that these difficulties can be significantly reduced (i) if the giants do their negotiations in Geneva rather than in Brussels, Washington or Tokyo, (ii) if the GATT Secretariat is permitted to play an active and confidential role as a go-between in passing information on positions of interests back and forth and (iii) if the others, whenever they have important interests in common, join together and have a single spokesperson, thus becoming a 'big' party to the discussions. Moreover, if the smaller countries are to be more effective, they must define those issues of particular importance to them and concentrate on those issues.[11]

THE LIBERALISATION AGENDA

Although the distinction is often blurred in practice and conceptually, it is useful for analytical purposes to divide a negotiation into liberalisation measures (achieving improved market access), on the one hand, and improving the framework of norms, rules and procedures, on the other. It is our thesis that the latter will be critically important in the new GATT round because, without reforms, any progress in liberalising trade will not long endure. At the same time, the purpose of norms, rules and procedures is to ensure that the benefits of trade liberalisation are realised. They are not an end in themselves. Moreover, it is unlikely that the authority, effort and time needed to reach agreement on the reform of norms, rules and procedures will be forthcoming unless countries can also anticipate the benefits of lowered barriers to trade.

All the major issues that were the subject of the Tokyo Round negotiations should be on the agenda again. Conventional wisdom has it that tariffs are no longer an important barrier to trade; and this seems to have led governments of some major countries to conclude that this is one item that can be put aside, given the danger of overloading the agenda. This would be a great mistake. As the Hufbauer-Schott study points out,[12] and as those who followed the Tokyo Round know, there is still need for work here. In the developed countries, high tariffs remain on many items, even though the average tariff is now in the 5 per cent range for most of those countries. These higher tariffs are frequently on goods of high labour content coming from the developing countries. Tariff escalation (increasing the tariff at each successive stage of processing) is also a major impediment to developing-country exports. Moreover, even the low tariffs in the developed countries on a wide range of imports from all sources have a treasured protective effect. How else can the vigour with which further cuts were resisted in the last round be explained? And surely the time has now come for a major effort to reduce the often exorbitant tariffs with which most of the developing countries have burdened themselves.

Given the disappointments and frustrations in previous efforts to liberalise trade in agricultural products, it would be tempting to conclude that the new GATT round should not be burdened with this task. But to exclude farm products would be another great mistake, bleak as the prospects may be for what the Leutwiler report calls increasing the 'scope for the interplay of market forces in agricultural trade'. Trade in farm products is too important to ignore. There is wide agreement that successful negotiations to reform and rationalise agricultural trade policies are not possible until the costs of the current farm-support policies which create the international problems become politically unacceptable.[13] There is increasing evidence that this is beginning to happen in the United States and the European Community. Moreover, agricultural policy is in transition all around the world and this, too, argues for another attempt in the GATT to liberalise agricultural trade. It is too much to hope for acceptance in the new round of the attractive solution proposed in the Hufbauer-Schott study: international agreement that each country place a 'cap' (degressive over time) on the amount of its farm output benefiting from existing government programmes and a commitment to the principle that additional output only be produced and marketed at world prices, without deficiency payments. But given the public recognition of the costs of current farm-support policies, some progress should be possible in reducing the present levels of subsidy competition and, also, in liberalising some import restrictions.

All these studies correctly conclude that a review of the Code on Subsidies and Countervailing Duties, negotiated in the Tokyo Round deliberations, must have a prominent place on the agenda of the new GATT round. As is often stated, subsidies are at the heart of the 'fairness' issue, especially in agricultural products and, more recently, in high-technology ones. The Code has not worked well. Among the aspects calling for improvement are placing agricultural export subsidies and export credits under essentially the same disciplines as other export subsidies. Involved here, with respect to agriculture, would be the hard work of making more precise such concepts in the existing norms and rules as 'fair and equitable market share', 'primary product', 'subsidy', 'representative period' *et cetera*. The Code's treatment of domestic subsidies was a step forward — a small step — but the range of permitted domestic subsidies is uncertain. Removing the ambiguities here and dealing with the problem of natural-resource pricing policies will not be easy, but it should be tried. The Tokyo Round negotiators were not able to reach any agreement on controlling competition from subsidised exports in third-country markets and this thorny problem needs to be broached again.

The other codes negotiated in the Tokyo Round talks also need to be reviewed, but the problems with them are far less serious than in the subsidy area. Indeed, the committees overseeing the Agreement on Government Procurement and the Agreement on Trade in Civil Aircraft have already improved and extended the coverage of those codes. The problems encountered with the agreements on Customs Valuation, Technical Barriers to Trade and Import Licensing Procedures are not of major proportions, but there is room for reducing restrictions in each of these areas and the opportunity should not be missed.

With few exceptions, trade in textiles and clothing between developed countries is restricted only by tariffs. By contrast, most trade between developed and developing countries is not only subject to these tariffs but also restricted by a complex network of bilaterally negotiated quotas under the Multi-fibre Arrangement (MFA). Although the MFA was negotiated and is implemented under the aegis of the GATT, its principles and practices are in violation of GATT rules on quantitative restrictions and non-discrimination.

Negotiations for the renewal of the third MFA were completed in July 1986, prior to the inauguration of the new GATT round. Many observers believe that apart from some reduction in tariffs on textiles and clothing, this action will effectively remove this sector from the new round. Fortunately, "textiles and clothing" has at least formally been placed on this agenda.

Although there has been a large expansion in international trade in textiles under the MFA regime, it certainly is far less than it would have been in its absence and the costs to consumers have been substantial.[14]

Nevertheless, any attempts to dismantle the MFA in short order are doomed to failure and could jeopardise success in other areas of trade policy. That is why the Hufbauer-Schott proposal that one accept the fact of a renewal now, but place the matter of *eventual* retirement of the MFA on the agenda of the new round, is so attractive. Their imaginative proposal calls for each major importing country to establish a system of global quotas on major imports of textiles and clothing. At the outset, global quotas of individual importing countries would be expanded by 6 per cent, while the *national* quota of each exporting country would be cut by 10 per cent. The resultant unallocated quota rights would then be auctioned off by the importing country to the highest bidder. Over time, the national quotas would be reduced to nearly zero, while the global quotas would be expanded to a point where they no longer restricted trade. The proceeds from the quota auction could be allocated to adjustment programmes for the domestic textile and clothing industry.[15] This is a promising idea for liberalising trade in textiles and for assisting in the adjustment of the protected industry. While the details of such a scheme would clearly be a matter for domestic policy, and would vary from country to country, the commitment to phase out the MFA would be an international one. The possibilities set out in this proposal could make it easier for countries to make that commitment.

In recent GATT discussions, no issue has generated so much interest and dissent as whether the new GATT round should attempt to consider ways and means of liberalising trade in services, an area not now subject to GATT disciplines. The developed countries have become increasingly insistent that services have a prominent place on the agenda, in spite of a lack of precision in their official proposals about what to include and what the objectives should be. A number of developing countries have been adamantly opposed, fearing that the effect would be to prevent the growth and development of their own 'infant' service industries, also fearing that less attention would be given to the more important task of reducing barriers in developed countries to their exports of goods.

All the studies serving as the focus of this article agree that services now represent such a large and growing part of the world economy and are so burdened with, or threatened by, restrictions that the time has come to attempt to reach agreement on international rules on rights and obligations, whose purpose would be to facilitate and expand trade in services. As the Leutwiler report notes, the alternative would be discriminatory rules on a bilateral or regional basis which; given the growing importance of trade in services and the fact that it is increasingly commingled with trade in goods, could well bring the GATT system down.

The studies do not provide much guidance on the critical questions of which services should be considered and whether the approach should be to extend the GATT to trade in services or to work out in the GATT forum, or elsewhere, a separate self-contained agreement. None of the studies emphasises sufficiently the necessity, before negotiations begin, for a broad agreement among the service industries in each country, and among governments, on the content and coverage of the negotiations. [16] Such an agreement or consensus does not yet seem to exist. The Aho-Aronson and Hufbauer-Schott studies set out some thoughtful proposals on the modalities and general objectives. [17] They argue for an attempt to negotiate first an 'umbrella' code of fundamental principles for national policies on services, including transparency (making publicly available information on all barriers to trade in services), non-discrimination and rights of establishment. They would leave for a second stage, or perhaps parallel negotiations, specific rights and obligations with respect to specific service industries. We have seen no other proposals that are more convincing, but this is virgin territory and much will have to be learned as the negotiations proceed.

Finally, given the growing importance to many countries of trade in patented and trade-marked products and given, too, the widespread practice of counterfeiting and infringing copyrights and patent rights, seriously inhibiting exports, the time has come to put these issues on the GATT agenda. In light of the seemingly inadequate preparatory work and political sensitivity of the subject, we think that it would overload the agenda, though, to include investment issues as such.

NORMS, RULES AND PROCEDURES: THE GATT ITSELF

The closer and longer one examines the international trading system and the problems of making significant progress on the various items on the GATT agenda, the more evident it becomes that the major task of the new GATT round — if the multilateral trading system is to survive — is nothing less than a comprehensive review, article by article, of the General Agreement and the practices and procedures that have developed since 1948. The purpose of this would be to make such changes as nearly four decades of experience and a greatly altered world economy seem to dictate and to reaffirm and strengthen those norms, rules and procedures found to be furthering trade liberalisation and preserving its results. The need to restore the systemic elements of the GATT system (we would add and emphasise 'revise and bring up to date') is the central theme of the Viravan report. The other studies also propose a good many 'institutional' reforms, but they do not give them the comprehensiveness and pride of place we think they warrant.

A full-dress review [18] of the General Agreement in the context of the new GATT round would no doubt result in some provisions and procedures being amended, some abandoned and some left intact. Such an examination would go far towards restoring respect for, and confidence in, the GATT system. Renewed respect for and confidence in the *system* seems to us to be an essential requirement for making trade liberalisation effective and for restoring one of the GATT's key functions, namely protecting governments against themselves. [19] We hasten to add that it does not seem feasible, or necessary, formally to redraft the various GATT articles. The appropriate method of updating would be that used in the Tokyo Round negotiations. The Tokyo Round codes effectively amended certain articles for those who signed them. And the Agreements Relating to the Framework for the Conduct of International Trade, which were 'adopted' by consensus by the Contracting Parties on 25 November 1979, *effectively* amended such important articles as I, XII, XVIII, XXII and XXIII.

Which of the GATT articles most need a searching review? The first is Article I, often referred to as the cornerstone of the GATT system, which requires all signatory countries to accord most-favoured-nation (MFN) treatment unconditionally to all other signatory countries except in certain circumstances laid down elsewhere in the General Agreement. Most observers believe that unconditional MFN treatment has served the world well, both economically and politically. But it has been badly mangled in recent years — most notably in the various so-called orderly marketing arrangements (OMAs), voluntary export-restraint agreements (VERs), the MFA, the Generalised System of Preferences (GSP) and in some free trade areas and customs unions. The major villains, as the Viravan report points out, have been the three giants: the European Community and the United States for their willingness to discriminate and Japan for her willingness to accept discrimination.

We agree in part that the solution which should be sought in the new GATT round should be to change the practices, not the rules. But as efforts are made to expand the GATT's coverage — whether by adding new items, such as services, or extending, amending or elaborating existing rights and obligations, such as those covered by the Tokyo Round codes — the problem of the 'foot dragger' and the 'free rider' seems serious enough that, unless the unconditional MFN rule is modified, either nothing will happen or, more likely, 'like-minded' countries will strike their deals outside the GATT framework. The answer, therefore, would seem to lie in what could be called 'participatory MFN'; that is to say, MFN treatment in all *new* undertakings (additional tariff cuts excepted) would be accorded only to those who adhere to them. To preserve and expand the multilateral aspects of the system, it would be essential for two conditions to be met. First, any new agreement or arrangement, any extension or elaboration, must not come into effect until countries accounting for a substantial amount — at least half, say — of the activity covered have signed. Second, all new accords must be open to all countries and the rights and obligations of a new member should be the same as for the founding members and not 'conditional' on a new negotiation. [20]

The GATT articles and procedures on anti-dumping and countervailing duties and on subsidies (Articles VI and XVI) are prime candidates for review and possible modification. This should be part of an examination and strengthening of the Subsidies and Anti-dumping Codes. Similarly, Articles VII, VIII, IX and X should be re-examined in the light of past experience and as part of a review of the agreements on Customs Valuation, Import Licensing Procedures and Technical Barriers to Trade.

Far more difficult, and important, will be improving the adequacy of Article XIX, the GATT's main escape clause, which provides for the introduction of emergency protection against a sudden surge of imports of a particular product. Efforts to improve the operation of this central feature of the GATT system foundered in the Tokyo Round negotiations on the issue of condoning 'selectivity' in the application of emergency protection. At that time the selectivity being discussed was directed against Japan and certain newly industrialising countries. There was, and still is, widespread agreement on several broad principles that should govern the use of any safeguard measures. These are transparency, degressivity (steady and progressing relaxation of import restrictions imposed for safeguard reasons), time limits et cetera. But, as all the studies find, the issues that must now be resolved in this area go far deeper and wider than those in the previous discussion. What is involved here is the extremely difficult matter of adjustment and those inherently discriminatory bilateral and sectoral arrangements (often relying on VERs, OMAs and similar 'understandings') which in recent years have been used to avoid adjustment and have undermined and threatened the GATT system. Here, then, is an international problem of truly major dimensions with which Article XIX of the GATT does not adequately deal and, until it does, the GATT system will be found inadequate.

We agree with the conclusions in the four studies (some more explicit and detailed than others) that what is necessary if a multilateral liberal trading system is to survive is a renewed and firm commitment (i) to honour GATT Articles XI and XIII (these articles provided for the general elimination of quantitative restrictions and for the non-discriminatory administration of any that remain) and, except as therein provided, to replace quantitative restrictions *in all forms* by non-discriminatory tariffs or, in some cases, auctioned global quotas and (ii) to accompany safeguard measures with adjustment measures designed to remove the need for continued protection. It should be noted that often the second commitment would require only that governments not impede or obstruct market forces.

Even with such an heroic commitment, there would remain the problem of unwinding the existing maze of bilateral and sectoral arrangements. Some of them may disappear as adjustments are made and markets widen. This may be possible, for example, in the case of the restraints on Japanese exports of automobiles to the United States. But for reasons noted in the studies, left alone such arrangements have a very strong tendency to become entrenched because exporters, importers, domestic producers and government officials have a stake in their continuation. The consumer is without allies. As we have seen, the authors of the Hufbauer-Schott and Aho-Aronson studies believe that one way — and we have seen no other convincing ideas — would be to change the method of protection in the existing schemes to auctionable global quotas (or the conversion of the existing quotas to tariffs) and use the proceeds of such auctions or tariffs to finance adjustment programmes in the domestic industry. It must be accepted, as the Hufbauer-Schott study states, that individual governments cannot be expected to refrain from protecting, or to remove protection from, industries where there is worldwide 'excess capacity' unless other countries with the same problem also undertake internationally-monitored obligations to run down their industry. Specific issues regarding the financing of adjustment are not, of course, a matter to be negotiated internationally, but a commitment to do *something* to facilitate adjustment is. The role of the GATT is to provide rules and procedures for discussing and negotiating these obligations to adjust.

International trade generates disputes as well as promoting economic welfare. The procedures which have developed under the consultation and dispute-settlement articles of the GATT (Articles XXII and XXIII) have been criticised for being slow, sometimes resulting in fuzzy findings and recommendations, and for being weak on enforcement. A close examination of the record shows that the system has worked much better than is commonly perceived, that the United States and the European Community are responsible for most of its failures and that the reforms agreed in the Tokyo Round negotiations and in subsequent meetings of the Contracting Parties have noticeably improved the system. But there is no question that *perceived* inadequacies are important and that the system does need further strengthening. The proposals in the Leutwiler report strike us as the right ones, as far as they go. (i) A permanent roster of non-governmental experts should be built up to serve on GATT panels. (ii) The panels should be required to indicate clearly the rationale for their findings. (ii) Tighter time limits should be set. And (iv) *third parties* should be encouraged and facilitated to use their rights to complain.[21] Provisions for mediation by the Director-General of the GATT at an early stage in disputes would also be an improvement and so might procedures for binding arbitration. More controversial, but worth considering in the context of a general review of the GATT, would be to instruct the GATT Secretariat to notify the Council of actions that they believe have seriously violated the GATT. The Secretariat does report semi-annually on various restrictive and protectionist actions by member countries, but it specifically states that citing an action should not be taken to imply any judgment on its legal status under the General Agreement.

Some of the deficiencies in the operation of the GATT system stem from ambiguities or gaps in the provisions of various GATT articles and associated codes — ambiguities and gaps often reflecting the inability to reach agreement in earlier negotiations. This leads to the sensible proposal in the Hufbauer-Schott study that when a case turns on a disputed interpretation of the GATT, as opposed to questions of fact or law, the panel should make recommendations for the revision or interpretation of the relevant provision. Because any such revision or interpretation could easily alter the previously negotiated balance of concessions, the issue should be sent to the appropriate committee or special working party for negotiation.[22]

A revision of the dispute-settlement procedures must also tackle the most difficult matter of all, that of compliance or implementation. The suggestion in the Leutwiler report that the GATT Council should be required to fix specific dates for carrying out recommendations and conduct regular reviews of how this is being done is modest, but it is probably as much as can be expected. Making public the degree of compliance might bring the recalcitrant around.

No one disputes the close interrelationships between trade, money and international debts. Closer collaboration among those responsible for monetary policy and those responsible for trade policy, at both national and international levels, is essential. But in spite of the support now, as well as during the preparations for the Tokyo Round, for parallel negotiations, the proposals for collaboration have not gone beyond bland generalities. This complex matter is seen as important, but it is not examined in detail in the four studies and one could not reasonably have expected the GATT negotiating mandate to say much beyond the general statement of the need to do something. It is important, however, that the new GATT round be so set up that it could accommodate major monetary reforms negotiated elsewhere. This is yet another reason to include a review of the *entire* General Agreement in the negotiating mandate. An examination of Article XV,[23] which provides for cooperation between the International Monetary Fund (IMF) and the GATT, could provide the up-to-date political authority for the trade negotiators to participate in appropriate ways in any parallel negotiations that may be undertaken. Experience in previous negotiations has demonstrated the importance of including in the negotiating mandate all those things one may want to discuss. If they are not provided for, they may well require a ministerial meeting to get them on the table, a difficult procedural matter that could fail.

The GATT discussions on the formation of free trade areas and customs unions have been long and often bitter. Rarely if ever has there been full agreement that a proposed arrangement meets the requirements of Article XXIV of the GATT. Fortunately, the Leutwiler report addresses this problem. It states that many of the agreements fall short of meeting the requirements of Article XXIV and that the 'exceptions and ambiguities . . . have seriously weakened the trade rules' and set a 'dangerous precedent for further special deals, fragmentation of the trading system and damage to the trade interests of non-participants'.[24] The report concludes that the time has come to re-examine and re-define the GATT rules so as to avoid ambiguity and ensure more strict application of the rules in the future. It is difficult to imagine the European Community and the United States, among others, agreeing to such an item being placed on the agenda by itself; but it is also difficult to think that they would insist on its exclusion from a review of the General Agreement as a whole.

There is one important gap in the four studies, namely improving the rules and procedures for trade between market-oriented and non-market economies. By common consent, the arrangements that have been made for GATT membership by Poland, Hungary and Romania are not satisfactory. The problem is now of considerable importance not least because of the stated intention of the People's Republic of China to resume its affiliation with the GATT. There is no GATT article dealing specifically with this problem. Article XVII, on state trading enterprises, was designed to cover particular state enterprises in an otherwise market-oriented economy. But the experiences, under their special protocols of accession, of the GATT members which are non-market economies have created useful precedents for interpreting rules and procedures. This experience shows that if the non-market economies are to be satisfactorily incorporated into the GATT system, major changes are needed in the so-called entrance fee or market-access provisions, the application to non-market economies of anti-dumping and countervailing duties, the requirements for transparency in the activities of the non-market economy, discriminatory quantitative restrictions, the periodic review and consultation procedures and 'graduation'. None of these reforms will be easy to negotiate, but with the People's Republic of China clearly moving towards GATT membership, they have a place on the agenda of the new GATT round.[25]

The new GATT round will be permeated by 'North-South' issues and, in particular, by the questions of 'special and preferential' treatment, on the one hand, and, with the emergence in recent years of several developing countries–the NICs–as strong international competitors in a wide range of sophisticated manufactured goods, on the other. It would be unwise and fruitless to make either a specific item on the agenda, but a review of the whole General Agreement, including Part IV, could be the basis for making some progress in the important task of differentiating the rights and obligations of the newly industrialising countries (NICs) from those of other developing countries. But we think this differentiation–or 'graduation' (an unfortunate term)–is more likely to be accomplished by the specific concessions demanded and exchanged in the negotiations on specific substantive matters, namely tariffs, subsidies, quantitative restrictions, customs administration *et cetera*, than in a negotiation focussed on North-South issues.

The Leutwiler report and the Hufbauer-Schott study have performed a useful service in concluding that the special and preferential treatment which the developing countries have worked so hard to obtain has been of 'very limited value'. Preferential treatment has served to distract attention from action on more important issues, such as the reduction of tariff escalation in the developed world, and from action by developing countries in reducing their own barriers to trade in exchange for improvements in their access to developed-country markets. In this connection, it should be mentioned that observers of previous GATT rounds have often noted that the developed countries were willing to make additional concessions if the developing countries were prepared to reciprocate in kind. But developed countries found it politically very difficult to justify unilateral actions to their home constituencies.

There is not much new on the North-South issue in the studies. Nor do we have any fresh insights or solutions. What does need emphasising, however, is that the risks are higher than ever before. An unwillingness by the larger and more advanced of the developing countries to participate actively in the new GATT round is likely to lead quite quickly to negotiations only among some of the developed countries, with a disastrous effect on the GATT system and, as all the studies agree, on the long-term interests of the developing world.

In previous rounds the role of the GATT Secretariat has not been a matter of much concern. The GATT Secretariat has a deservedly high reputation as a small highly competent, professional and discreet group which takes seriously its obligations as guardian of the General Agreement and whose loyalty is to the GATT and not to the countries whose passports they carry. The criticisms have been limited largely to what has been seen as a failure to take more initiatives and to provide more leadership, although specific attempts to do so have usually been followed by strong criticism from those who did not find a particular initiative in their interest.

In the new GATT round it seems likely, and altogether desirable, that there will be an effort to increase significantly the GATT Secretariat's responsibilities. There seems to be a growing feeling in the international trading community that, if the GATT system is to function adequately, there must be more and better information on, and justification of, the policies and actions of member countries. That is to say, a vastly improved system of monitoring and surveillance is needed. This led the authors of the Leutwiler report to recommend that the GATT Secretariat be given a central role in the task of surveillance. This would involve preparing reports on trade policy developments to serve as a basis for periodic reviews of individual member countries, initiating studies of national trade policies and calling for clarification of particular policy measures and actions and arranging for discussion of them. These recommendations, which were supported by the other studies, seem to have struck a responsive chord among many GATT member countries. If they survive the negotiations, a truly major reform will have been introduced into the GATT system and a significant deterrent will have been created to the spread of the bilateral, plurilateral and sectoral arrangements that have been so corrosive to the GATT system, all measures that the Secretariat could be expected to denounce.

But one should not underestimate the probable opposition once governments examine the implications of the proposal. It is one thing to have periodic examinations of national economic policies in the Organisation for Economic Cooperation and Development where there are no international legal obligations and rights. It is quite another to have an examination and assessment of a country's trade policies in the GATT where such an exercise would be against the background of formal legal undertakings. It is this difference that may help to explain why, for example, talks on steel in recent years have been held in Paris and not in Geneva. Given that most observers see the fundamental weakness of the GATT system being non-observance of the rules, this proposal may be the litmus test of whether the member countries are serious about refining and strengthening the GATT system.

CONCLUDING REMARKS

The Aho-Aronson study and, to a somewhat lesser extent, the Hufbauer-Schott study set out elements of what the authors consider to be an economically sound and achievable package of results. We lack both the courage and information to assess them. Nonetheless, we applaud their efforts because what they do show is that it is clearly possible for each *country* to gain. A multilateral trade negotiation is not a zero-sum game. The 'losers', as the Hufbauer-Schott study states, 'are not countries, but industries that have already lost their ability to compete'.[26] Belief in the various parliaments and in the executive branches of government that this is so is a prerequisite for the successful conclusion of the new GATT round.

---

1. *Trade Policies for a Better Future: Proposals for Action*, Report of an Independent Group under the Chairmanship of Fritz Leutwiler (Geneva: GATT Secretariat, 1985), hereinafter referred to as the Leutwiler Report.

The members of the independent group were: Fritz Leutwiler, Chairman of Brown Boveri, Baden, Switzerland, and formerly Chairman of the Swiss National Bank and President of the Bank for International Settlements; Bill Bradley, Senator from New Jersey in the Congress of the United States; Pehr Gyllenhammar, Chairman and Chief Executive, AB Volvo, Göteborg, Sweden; Guy Ladreit de Lacharrière, Vice President of the International Court of Justice in the Hague and a former Legal Adviser to the Ministry of Foreign Affairs in the Government of France; I.G. Patel, Director of the London School of Economics and Political Science and a former Governor of the Reserve Bank of India; Mario Henrique Simonsen, Director of the Postgraduate School of Economics, Getulio Vargas Foundation, Rio de Janeiro, and a former Minister of Finance and Minister of Planning in the Government of Brazil; and Sumitro Djojohadikusumo, Professor of Economics at the University of Indonesia, Jakarta, and a former Minister of Trade and Industry, Minister of Finance and Minister of Trade in the Government of Indonesia.

2. Gary Clyde Hufbauer and Jeffrey J. Schott, *Trading for Growth*, Policy Analyses in International Economics No. 11 (Washington: Institute for International Economics, 1985).

3. C. Michael Aho and Jonathan David Aronson, *Trade Talks: America Better Listen!* (New York: Council on Foreign Relations, 1985).

4. Amnuay Viravan *et al.*, *Trade Route to Sustained Economic Growth* (London: Macmillan, for the United Nations, forthcoming), hereinafter cited as the Viravan Report, which we read in its mimeograph form. The report is based on a draft discussed at an Asian-Pacific trade conference held in Tokyo on 15-17 March 1985 to mark the fortieth anniversary of the United Nations.

The members of the study group were: Amnuay Viravan, Chairman of the Executive Board, Bangkok Bank, Bangkok; José Concepcion, President of the RFM Corporation, Manila; Hugh Corbet, Director of the Trade Policy Research Centre, London; Victor Fung Kwok-King, Managing Director of Li & Fung, Hong Kong; Keith Hay, Professor of International Economics, Carleton University, Ottawa; Jean-Pierre Lehmann, Research Fellow at the Euro-Asia Centre, Institut Européen d'Administration des Affaires, Fontainebleau; Mohammed Ramli Kushairi, Chairman of South Malaysian Industries, Kuala Lumpur; Brian Scott, Deputy Chairman, ACI International, Melbourne; Hadi Soesastro, Director of Studies, Centre for Strategic and International Studies, Jakarta; Augustine Tan, Member of Parliament, Singapore; Martin Wolf, Director of Studies at the Trade Policy Research Centre, London; Bunroku Yoshino, Chairman of the Institute for International Economic Studies, Tokyo; and Soogil Young, Senior Fellow at the Korea Development Institute, Seoul.

5. This is not a review article. It is, rather, an essay on the possible content and structure of the new GATT round, using the four studies as the focus of the discussion.

6. Aho and Aronson, *op. cit.*, ch. 7.

7. Hufbauer and Schott, *op. cit.*, pp. 91 *et seq.*

8. Leutwiler Report, *op. cit.*, p. 41.

9. Viravan Report, *op. cit.*, ch. 6.

10. Hufbauer and Schott, *op. cit.*, p. 94.

11. These matters are discussed in more detail in Gardner Patterson, 'The GATT and Negotiating International Trade Rules', in A.K. Hendrikson (ed.), *Negotiating World Order: the Artisanship and Architecture of Global Diplomacy* (Boston:Scholarly Resources, 1986).

12. Hufbauer and Schott, *op. cit.*, pp. 76 *et seq.*

13. See Aho and Aronson, *op. cit.*, pp. 39 *et seq* and 140 *et seq.*, and Hufbauer and Schott, *op. cit.*, pp. 47 *et seq.*

14. See Viravan Report, *op. cit.*, ch. 5, and the references cited there.

15. Hufbauer and Schott, *op. cit.*, pp. 39 *et seq.*

16. We are indebted to Rodney de C. Grey for pointing out the importance of this.

17. Aho and Aronson, *op. cit.*, pp. 42-44, and Hufbauer and Schott, *op. cit.*, pp. 66-73.

18. The negotiations on services will, of necessity, require close study of the relevance of many GATT articles for services, but this is not the same thing as a review and examination of the same articles for trade in goods.

19. This last point is made by Aho and Aronson, *op. cit.*, p. 149, and the Viravan Report, *op. cit.*, ch. 2. For an elaboration of this aspect, see Frieder Roessler, 'The Scope, Limits and Functions of the GATT Legal System', *The World Economy*, September 1985, based on a paper prepared for the Leutwiler Report.

20. In Hufbauer and Schott, *op. cit.*, p. 19, a similar case is made for what the authors call 'conditional MFN', but they do not include our first requirement, which we think is necessary to prevent bilateral deals so narrowly constructed that no one else could or would want to join.

21. Leutwiler Report, *op. cit.*, pp. 46-47.

22. Hufbauer and Schott, *op. cit.*, p. 80.

23. Article XV of the GATT states: 'The Contracting Parties shall seek cooperation with the International Monetary Fund to the end that the Contracting Parties and the Fund may pursue a coordinated policy with regard to exchange questions within the jurisdiction of the Fund and questions of . . . trade measures within the jurisdiction of the Contracting Parties.'

24. Leutwiler Report, *op. cit.*, p. 41.

25. The problems and possible solutions are spelled out in Eliza Patterson, 'Improving GATT Rules on Trade between Market and Non-market Economies', *Journal of World Trade Law*, Geneva, March/April 1986.

26. Hufbauer and Schott, *op. cit.*, p. 85.

A NEW AGENDA FOR THE GATT

In late September 1986, at Punta del Este Uruguay,

ministers of the GATT member countries agreed on a

"Ministerial Declaration" launching new Multilateral

Trade Negotiations, quickly labeled the Uruguay Round.

It had taken four years of difficult preparatory

negotiations to obtain this mandate and the document

established an agenda and process intended - in ways not

yet known - to result in a greatly altered international

trading system.

   The overall objective of the new round is to "bring

about further liberalization and expansion of world trade

to the benefit of all countries "[1]. Of course, this

hides differences in specific objectives and most

informed observers believe that the problems are so

difficult that the stated goal of concluding the

negotiations within four years will probably have to be

---

[1]
The text of the "Ministerial Declaration" may be found
in General Agreement on Tariffs and Trade, Geneva, FOCUS,
No. 4, Oct. 1986. Excerpts were reproduced in The New
York Times, Sept 21, 1986. P. A 18.

extended.

The principal, although by no means the only, source of discord that made reaching agreement on the mandate so difficult was the question of the inclusion of services. For reasons noted in our earlier paper, several developing countries, led by Brazil and India, strongly opposed their inclusion, while for the United States and several others this was a _sine qua non_ . The procedural compromise reached at Punta del Este was to formally divide the negotiations into two parts, one on "negotiation on trade in goods " and one on "negotiations on trade in services." The two sets of negotiations would, however, be treated as a single undertaking. The Chairman of the former group is the Director General of the GATT, the Chairman of the latter is the Columbian ambassador to the GATT.

The mandate on trade in goods sets out an agenda and negotiating objectives for the following fourteen subjects: Tariffs, Non-Tariff Barriers, Natural Resource- Based Products, Textiles/Clothing, Tropical Products, Agriculture, GATT Articles, MTN Agreements and Arrangements, Dispute Settlement, Intellectual Property, Subsidies and Countervailing Measures, Trade- Related Investment Measures, Safeguards, and Functioning of the

GATT System. For each a brief and very generally worded
negotiating objective was agreed upon, typically it is to
"reduce barriers" or "eliminate restrictions" or"achieve
the further liberalization of trade" or "improve and
strengthen rules and procedures" or "elaborate provisions
to avoid adverse effects on trade" etc. The problem of
the negotiations is to give these aims specific content.

Not surprisingly, in view of the background, the agreed
agenda and negotiating objectives for services was much
briefer, citing no specific service sectors. It stated:
"Negotiations in this area shall aim to establish a
multilateral framework of principles and rules for trade
in services, including elaboration of possible disciplines
for individual sectors, with a view to expansion of such
trade under conditions of transparency and progressive
liberalization and as a means of promoting economic growth
of all trading partners and the development of developing
countries, Such framework shall respect the policy
objectives of national laws and regulations applying to
services and shall take into account the work of relevant
international organizations."

Finally, the mandate contained a commitment by each
nation, for the duration of the negotiations, to a
"standstill"(not to take any trade restricting or

distorting measures inconsistent with the GATT or any
trade measure designed to improve its negotiating
position) and to a "rollback" (trade restrictions
inconsistent with the GATT shall be phased out or brought
into conformity not later than the formal completion of
the negotiations.).

In the year-and-a-half following the Punta del Este
meeting formal negotiating groups were established for
each of the fifteen agenda items and each group held three
or four meetings on what is regarded as the "initial
phase"- essentially collecting facts, a first examination
of issues to be covered, submission of preliminary
proposals or concepts etc.[2]   Space here permits only the
briefest sketch of the more important developments in
those groups where significant policy issues were
discussed.   This is not to deny, however, that such work,
in these and other groups, as collecting and agreeing on
the facts, discussing possible approaches to the
negotiations in a particular sector, or agreeing on the
specific products to be covered are a necessary and

---

[2]
The primary source material for the balance of this
epilogue is General Agreement on Tariffs and Trade,
Geneva, Document series NUR, issues 001-011. We have also
benefitted from non-attibutable discussions with various
officials participating in the negotiations.

important component of a successful negotiation.

The work of the Group on Agriculture was dominated by the tabling in July 1987 of a proposal by the United States calling for a very extensive reform of trade in farm goods. It calls for a ten year phase-out of agricultural subsidies; the phase-out of import barriers over the same period; and a series of actions on health and sanitary regulations aimed at reducing their trade restrictive effects. This proposal calls for massive changes in many countries' domestic farm programs. Although most of the participants will delay taking a formal position until they have studied the implications for them and the system, it is already clear that there will be a good bit of opposition to something this drastic ("unrealistic","visionary", some said). In the initial view of some it would threaten their food security needs. Others said it failed to take account of the wide disparaties in average farm size; others asserted it ignored the geographic and climatic disadvantages of some; and several believed it would threaten to undercut various social objectives of their farm support programs. It was also criticized because it made no provision for special treatment for developing countries.

Late in 1987 initial major proposals were also tabled

by the European Communities and the "Cairnes Group"
(thirteen major agricultural producers). The Communities'
proposal stressed the need for action that would achieve a
better balance between demand and supply in the farm
sector and called for a phased reduction in the negative
effects of agricultural support policies.

The fundamental aim of the Cairnes Group proposal was
to achieve fully liberalized trade in agriculture via the
gradual removal of most market access retraints and
phasing down of farm support measures.

Although there are fundamental differences in these
proposals, they have the great merit of forcing
negotiations on the central issue: domestic farm policies
that have operated in the past virtually to remove trade
in most farm goods from the GATT system.

In the Functioning of the GATT System Group,
attention was focused in the initial meetings on how to
strengthen the effectiveness of surveillance: Regular
reviews of the trade policies of specific countries? A
larger role for the Secretariat? A standing surveillance
body? Some opposition quickly developed to the idea of
individual countries being subject to detailed examination
and review. The Group also began its examination of how
to achieve greater coordination in monetary and trade

policies and how to strenghthen the relationship between the GATT, the IMF and the World Bank. Preliminary discussions also took place on how to increase the involvement of Ministers-as distinct from career civil servants-in GATT affairs to the end of better dealing with major policy issues before a crisis develops.

The Group on Dispute Settlement began discussion on various ways of speeding up the process, on the possibilities and modalities of binding arbitration and improved mediation practices, and on mechanisms for insuring better and quicker implementation of panel reports.

The initial attention of the Group on GATT Articles was on reviewing the current provisions on state trading enterprises, customs unions and free trade areas, the procedure for granting waivers, the modification of tariff schedules, and the use of quantitative restraints to safeguard the balance of payments. It should be noted that this group is required to review any GATT article that any contracting party requests. It is to be expected, therefore, that before the end of the Uruguay Round many, if not most, of the present GATT provisions will have been examined in the context of contemporary conditions- an exercise we stressed in our original piece was of great importance.

In our view it also bodes well for the system that in the Safeguards Group several governments stated that this matter was central to the Uruguay Round as a whole. It is important and significant that from the very first meeting some delegations insisted on the need to examine the proliferation and status of the so called "grey area measures": orderly marketing arrangements, voluntary export restraints etc. and a proposal has been tabled to make their elimination an objective of any new safeguard rules. Proposals have also been tabled dealing with rules to limit the duration of safeguard measures, requiring degressivity in their application, giving priority to domestic adjustment assistance for domestic producers as a way of dealing with problems requiring safeguard actions, creation of a special body to deal with safeguard-related disputes, and according priority to compensation rather than retaliation for a country adversely affected by safeguard measures. There has of course been much debate on whether safeguard measures can be applied selectively.

On the delicate issue of Trade-Related Investment Measures, the first year was spent reviewing some seventeen GATT Articles identified as related to the trade-restricive and trade distorting effect of investment measures. Widely divergent views emerged as to the adequacy of these Articles.

Although all the concerns noted above that led to the reluctance of many developing countries to include services in the agenda were still present, the Negotiating Group on Services held several meetings during 1987 and some of the previously reluctant developing countries appear to have concluded that active participation in the negotiations was in their interests. Because trade in services is an unplowed field in the GATT most of the initial discussion was exploratory. Thus, the problem of obtaining adequate information on production and trade in services occupied much of the Group's attention.

As noted earlier, the Ministerial Declaration endorsed the notion that the negotiations should aim to establish a "multilateral framework", (some spoke of an "umbrella") as well as "possible disciplines" for individual service sectors. During 1987 the substantive discussions on this were limited to the significance and relevance of some of the concepts which might be incorporated in the umbrella: non-discrimination, transparancy (rules for notifying procedures , requirements, practices etc. affecting trade), national treatment, right of establishment, and mutual advantage. Not surprising, it was too early to have discussed in any systematic way such difficult problems as the relationship of any agreement on services to the GATT itself, whether the framework should be designed so as to encourage the maximum number of signers at the cost of the rigor of obligations and coverage, what precisely should be the relationship of individual sector agreements to the umbrella, and what was the minimum number of sectors to be covered and which service sectors should be in the minimum list.

One must conclude that the Uruguay Round agenda is remarkably comprehensive and that if the stated objectives are met in as large a measure as were the objectives in previous GATT rounds, there will be a new and greatly improved international trading system. Although the problems and constraints on these negotiations are awesome and success in substantially meeting the objectives is by no means assured, hope can be taken from the pace of the work during the first year and from the fact that, by and large, the tough problems have been put on the table and not swept under the rug.

INTERNATIONAL ASSISTANCE POLICIES

H. B. Chenery and A. M. Strout

Our analysis has shown the conditions under which external assistance may make possible a substantial acceleration in the process of economic development. It has focused on the interrelations among external resource requirements and the development policies of recipient countries. Analysis of these interrelations leads to several principles of general applicability to international assistance policy.

The central questions for assistance policy are the measurement of the effectiveness of external assistance, the policies that recipient countries should follow to make best use of external resources, and the basis for allocating assistance among countries. This chapter summarizes the main implications of our analysis for each of these questions and adds some qualitative elements which have been omitted from the formal analysis.

THE EFFECTIVENESS OF ASSISTANCE

In the short run the effectiveness of external resources depends on their use to relieve shortages of skills, saving, and imported entities. The productivity of additional amounts of assistance over longer periods can be measured by the increase in output resulting in the fuller use of domestic resources which they make possible.

Over longer periods, the use that is made of the initial increase in output becomes more important. Even if the short-run productive aid is high, the economy may continue to be dependent on outside assistance indefinitely unless the additional output is allocated so as to increase saving and reduce the trade gap. Over the whole period of transition to self-sustaining growth, the use that is made of the successive increments in GNP is likely to be more important than the efficiency with which external assistance was utilized in the first instance. To emphasize this point, let us assume that the productivity investment in the first 5 years of the upper-limit development sequence outlined above for Pakistan had been one-third lower, requiring a correspondingly larger amount of investment and external aid to achieve the same increase in GNP. The effect would be to increase the total aid required over the 17-year period to achieve self-sufficiency by some 45%. This, however, is less than the effect on aid requirements of a reduction in the marginal saving rate from .24 to .22% if critical elements in the development sequence are getting the increase in the rate of growth, channeling the increments in income into increased saving, and allocating investment so as to avoid balance of payments bottlenecks. These long-run aspects are likely to be considerably more important than the efficiency with which external capital used in the short run.[1]

[1]This conclusion is demonstrated in the evaluation of the effectiveness of aid to Greece in Organization for Economic Cooperation and Development, *Development Assistance Efforts and Policies:* 1965 Review, Report of the Chairman of the Development Assistance Committee, Paris, 1965.

Reprinted with permission from *The American Economic Review*
56(4), 723–729, Copyright 1966.

The long-run effectiveness of assistance is also likely to be increased by supporting as high a growth rate as the economy can achieve without a substantial deterioration in the efficiency of use of capital. There are also several factors omitted from the formal models that argue for more rapid growth:

1. the fact that a smaller portion of the increase in GNP is offset by population growth;

2. the gain in political stability and governmental effectiveness that is likely to result;

3. the greater likelihood of being able to raise marginal saving rates and export growth when GNP is growing more rapidly;[2]

4. the greater likelihood of attracting foreign private investment to finance the needs for external capital.

While the last three factors cannot be measured with any accuracy, they appear to have been important in most countries that are successfully completing the transition, such as Israel, Greece, Taiwan, Mexico, Peru, and the Philippines. These examples support the theoretical conclusion that the achievement of a high rate of growth, even if it has to be initially supported by large amounts of external capital, is likely to be the most important element in the long-term effectiveness of assistance. The substantial increases in internal saving ratios that have been achieved in a decade of strong growth—from 7% to 12% in the Philippines, 11% to 16% in Taiwan, 6% to 14% in Greece, and 9% to 12% in Israel—demonstrate the speed with which aid-sustained growth can be transformed into self-sustained growth once rapid development has taken hold.

POLICIES FOR RECIPIENT COUNTRIES

While the receipt of external assistance may greatly reduce the time required for a country to achieve a satisfactory rate of growth, dependence on substantial amounts of external resources creates some special policy problems. One lesson from the preceding analysis is that the focus of policy should vary according to the principal limitations to growth. Just as optimal countercyclical policy implies different responses in different phases of the business cycle, optimal growth policy requires different ''self-help'' measures in different phases of the transition.

In Phase I, where the growth rate is below a reasonable target rate, the focus of policy should be on increasing output, implying an increase in the quality and quantity of both physical capital and human resource inputs. Our statistical comparisons suggest that a rate of growth of investment of 10–12% is a reasonable target for countries whose initial investment level is substantially below the required level. Phase I can be completed by most countries in a decade if this increase in investment is accompanied by sufficient improvement in skills and organization to

---

[2]The advantages of more rapid growth with constant per capita marginal savings rates are demonstrated by J.C.H. Fei and D.S. Paauw, ''Foreign Assistance and Self-Help: Reappraisal of Development Finance,'' *Rev. Econ. Stat.*, Aug. 1965, 67, 251–67.

make effective use of the additional capital that becomes available. Although it is probably more important in this phase to focus on securing increases in production and income, a start must also be made on raising taxes and saving if international financing is to be justified by performance.

As Phase I is completed, the rate of increase in investment can be allowed to fall toward a feasible target rate of GNP growth, which is unlikely to be more than 6–7%. The focus of development should then be increasingly on (1) bringing about the changes in productive structure needed to prevent further increases in the balance of payments deficit, and (2) channeling an adequate fraction of increased income into saving. Although theoretical discussion has tended to stress the second requirement, the first appears to have been more difficult in practice for many countries. Since substantial import substitution is required just to prevent the ratio of imports to GNP from rising, export growth at least equal to the target growth of GNP is seen to be necessary in order to reduce external aid.

As the focus of development policy changes, the instruments of policy must change accordingly. Somewhat paradoxically, successful performance in Phase I, which would justify a substantial and rising flow of foreign assistance, may make success in Phase III more difficult. If investment and other allocation decisions are based on the exchange rate that is appropriate for a substantial flow of aid, they are not likely to induce sufficient import substitution or increased exports to make possible a future reduction in the capital inflow. Planning should be based on the higher equilibrium exchange rate that would be appropriate for a declining flow of aid in order for the necessary changes in the production structure to be brought about in time.

It is the need for rapid structural change that sets the lower limit for the time required to complete the transition to self-sustaining growth. Although there is the possibility of completing this transition in less than 20 years starting from typical Asian or African conditions, it is very unlikely that any such country can meet all the requirements of skill formation, institutional building, investment allocation, etc. in less than one generation.

POLICIES FOR DONOR COUNTRIES

Donors are concerned with criteria for the allocation of aid among recipients, and the means for controlling its use. Allocation policies are complicated by the mixture of objectives that motivate international assistance, the most important of which are (1) the economic and social development of the recipient, (2) the maintenance of political stability in countries having special ties to the donor, and (3) export promotion. This mixture of motives has led to a complex system of aid administration in all countries.

The predominant basis for development loans is the individual investment project, for which external financing is provided to procure capital goods from the donor country. Loans not limited to equipment for specific projects are provided to a few selected countries against the balance-of-payments needs of development programs.[3] Substantial but declining amounts of grants are also furnished for budgetary support of ex-colonies and other dependent areas.

Our analysis suggests some directions in which improvements can be sought in the present methods of supporting economic development, which is the objective on which all parties agree. We first consider methods of transferring resources to individual countries and then allocation of assistance among countries.

The Transfer of Assistance

Any system for transferring resources must include: (1) a basis for determining the amount of the transfer, (2) specification of the form of resources to be furnished, and (3) a basis for controlling their use. On all these counts the project system has the virtue of simplicity. It also provides for detailed evaluation of the investments that are directly financed from external aid—which may be 10% or so of total investment—and for increasing their productivity through technical review.

While the project system has much to commend it when the main focus is on increasing the country's ability to invest, it becomes increasingly inappropriate as the development process gets under way. As the rate of growth increases, we have shown that the effectiveness of aid depends more on the use that is made of the additional output than on the efficiency with which a limited fraction of investment is carried out. Furthermore, an attempt to finance the amount of external resources needed during the peak period of an optimal growth path—which may imply aid equal to 30–40% of total investment—by the project mechanism alone may greatly lower the efficiency of use of total resources. Limiting the form of assistance to the machinery and equipment needed by substantial investment projects is likely either to lower the rate of growth or to distort the pattern of investment.

In these circumstances, assistance would be more effective if the range of commodities supplied could be broadened to permit the recipient's pattern of investment and production to evolve in accordance with the principle of comparative advantage.[4] While domestic supply can—and indeed must—lag behind demand in some sectors to accommodate the needed resource transfer, the country should also be preparing to balance its international accounts by the end of a specified transitional period.

Since donors fear that uncontrolled imports may be wasted in increased consumption without the restraints imposed by the project mechanism, an alternative means of control is needed. Part of the solution lies in relating the amount of aid supplied to the recipient's effectiveness in increasing the rate of domestic saving, so that the added aid necessarily increase saving and investment as income grows. As development planning and statistics on overall performance improve, this kind of

---

[3]In the terminology of AID, the latter are called program loans. About half of United States development lending is on a program basis in contrast to a much smaller proportion for other Organization for Economic Cooperation and Development (OECD) Development Assistance Committee members, or the World Bank.

[4]This observation applies to aid in the form of agricultural commodities as well as to aid in the form of machinery or any other specified goods.

"program approach" is becoming increasingly feasible, both from the point of view of determining the amounts of assistance needed and assessing the results.[5]

The strongest argument for the program approach arises for countries in Phase III where the balance of payments is the main factor limiting growth and where there is typically excess capacity in a number of production sectors. In this situation, the highest priority use of imports is for raw materials and spare parts to make more effective use of existing capacity; project priorities should give primary weight to import substitutes and increased exports. In this situation donor controls should be primarily concerned with the efficient use of total foreign exchange resources, which can only be assessed adequately in the framework of a development program.

Allocation of Assistance

If the objectives of the donor countries could be expressed as some function of the growth of each recipient, it would be possible to allocate aid primarily on the basis of expected development performance. The varying political objectives of the donors complicate the problem because each would give somewhat different weights to a unit of increase in income as among recipients. Even with this limitation, however, there may be considerable scope for reallocating a given amount of aid or for selective increases in individual country totals in accordance with criteria of self-help.

The predominant project approach now in use favors countries whose project preparation is relatively efficient. Other qualities that are equally important to successful development—tax collection, private thriftiness, small-scale investment activity, export promotion—are ignored in focusing on this one among many aspects of better resource use.[6]

Where fairly reliable statistics are available, an alternative procedure would be to establish minimum overall performance standards for each country and to share the aid burden among interested donors through a consortium or other coordinating mechanism. For example, a country starting in Phase I might have as its principal performance criteria: (1) growth of investment at 10% per year at a minimum standard of productivity, and (2) the maintenance of a marginal saving rate of .20 (or alternatively a specified marginal tax rate). There would be little possibility to waste aid on these terms, since the required increase in savings would finance a large proportion of total investment. Appropriate overall standards for saving rates and balance-of-payments policies for countries in Phase II and Phase III could also be established without great difficulty. A country maintaining high standards—say a marginal savings rate of .25 and a marginal capital-output ratio of less than 3.3—could safely be allotted whatever amount of aid it requested in the knowledge that the larger the amount of aid utilized, the higher would be its growth rate, and the more rapid its approach to self-sufficiency.

---

[5]The United States government has been using the program approach in India, Pakistan, Turkey, Tunisia, Chile, Colombia, and Brazil.

[6]It is perhaps more than coincidence that most of the striking successes in development through aid—Greece, Israel, Taiwan, etc.—were financed largely on a nonproject basis.

UPDATE

There have been two assessments of the projections in this chapter since its original publication. Morawetz (1977) compares the actual growth of forty-five of the fifty countries to that predicted for the period 1962 to 1975. He finds that twenty countries exceeded the plan projections by more than 0.5 percent, thirteen equalled the projected rates, and twelve fell below them. Morawetz concludes that the actual outcome was about half way between the medium and upper limit projections when equal weight is given to each observation.

Chenery and Carter (1973, 1976) evaluate the overall performance of the two-gap model and analyze the relations among trade, capital flows, and growth. They consider only the first projection period (1962–70) and limit the sample of countries to thirty-seven that are representative of the performance of the international system.[65] For this period the average growth of the sample countries was 5.3 percent, approximately the same as that projected. The analysis focuses on the modifications needed in the two-gap model to improve its usefulness and on the sources of variation in country performance. This postscript summarizes some of the conclusions that emerge from the Chenery-Carter assessment.

Analytical framework

Most discussion of the framework of two-gap analysis has focused on its relevance to developing countries and only indirectly on its usefulness to the suppliers of capital. The main criticisms of this approach fall under two headings: (a) a neoclassical critique, which denies the validity of the trade limit concept, and (b) skepticism that an increase in external resources is likely to lead to higher investment rather than a rise in consumption.

The neoclassical case is effectively presented by Bruton (1969), who argues that the trade limit is unlikely to occur in a well-managed economy and, furthermore, that basing aid policy on this hypothesis provides the wrong incentives to developing countries. There is no issue between us on the first question: model 2 of the present chapter —as well as the studies of Israel and Pakistan in chapters 8 and 9—all demonstrate that a trade gap in excess of the savings gap will not appear if resources are optimally allocated over time. But this norma-tive argument does not reduce the probability that a dominant

---

65. For this purpose, ten of the fourteen countries with populations below 5 million are omitted as are three abnormal cases (Algeria, Vietnam, and Rhodesia).

trade limit will actually occur with some frequency as a result of either ineffective national policies or unanticipated changes in external markets.[66]

The extent to which countries typically use external resources to increase investment or consumption is also an empirical question. Econometric studies by a number of authors have shown the need to modify the savings function used in this chapter (equation 10.5), to allow for this choice.[67] The more general hypothesis is that inflows of external resources have several origins and will normally lead to increases in both investment and consumption. Since saving is conventionally measured as the difference between investment and the capital inflow (equation 10.2), an increase in consumption with given GNP must be reflected in a fall in saving.[68]

This hypothesis can be incorporated by adding a term to the savings function (10.5):

$$S_t \leqq \bar{S}_t = S_o + \alpha' (V_t - V_o) - \alpha'' F_t,$$

where α'' is the proportion of the capital inflow that is used for consumption. The original form thus becomes the extreme case in which all of the external flow is invested and $\alpha'' = 0$.

Since $\bar{S}_t$ is defined as the savings that would result from given government policies in periods when this constraint is binding, the parameters in the savings function can only be properly estimated from a sample of observations for which this assumption is valid. Of the authors who have analyzed this relation, only Weisskopf (1972) obtained a separate estimate of α'' (0.23) for a group of countries for which this assumption could be made. A number of other studies that did not attempt to make such a separation produced estimates of α'' in the range of 0.45 to 0.55 for the negative effect of

---

66. Bruton's other main objection to the two-gap approach is that a shift to less import-intensive forms of investment can eliminate the "gap between the gaps." As was pointed out in my reply (1969b), however, using all the potential saving for less productive investment is not equivalent to getting rid of the trade limit nor does it reduce the desirability of external borrowing.

67. See, for example, Strout (1969), Chenery and Eckstein (1970), Griffin and Enos (1970), Landau (1971), Singh (1972), Papanek (1972), and Weisskopf (1972). A survey of these and other studies of the relations between capital inflow and savings is given by Mikesell and Zinser (1973).

68. This relation is discussed at length by Papanek (1972).

capital inflow on measured savings.[69] These results are consistent with the two-gap hypothesis, which implies that actual savings will be less than potential savings when either the ability to invest [equation (10.4)], or the trade limit is binding.

In analyzing the role of capital inflows in development policy from the viewpoint of either the borrower or the lender, α'' should be treated as a policy variable. An effective development policy is one that channels a high proportion of external resources into investment when savings constitute the binding constraint. The projections in this chapter used the optimistic assumption that $\alpha'' = 0$. Actual experience will be compared to the projections made on this basis in the following subsection.[70]

Overall results

An overview of the structural characteristics of the Chenery-Strout projections is given in table 10-12, which compares average values of the basic parameters projected for 1962–70 under the intermediate (plan) assumptions to the observed values as well as to the historical values for 1957–62. Of the internal parameters, the incremental capital-output ratio (ICOR) fell somewhat more than was anticipated, while the mean marginal savings rate (0.18) was between the ex ante and ex post rates projected (0.196 and 0.140). For the external parameters, the average growth of exports and the marginal propensity to import turned out to be slightly higher than projected. The variance around these means was generally underestimated, however—as it is in most projections—as shown by a comparison of the upper and lower quartile values for each distribution.

These unweighted averages can be quite misleading in assessing the overall performance of the international system because they ignore both the size of countries and their initial levels of income. To remedy these defects, table 10-13 compares the aggregate results for three groups of countries in terms of GNP growth and the sources of foreign exchange.

---

69. See Strout (1969) and Chenery and Carter (1976, page 308). A comparison of time-series and cross-country estimates is given in Chenery and Syrquin (1975). Differing interpretations of the evidence for individual countries are given by Griffin and Enos (1970) and Papanek (1972).

70. Since the effects of the past capital inflow are incorporated in statistical estimates of α', it is only changes in the relative importance of F that will affect predicted savings.

Table 10-12. *Summary of Structural Parameters and Growth Rates* (37-country sample)

	Upper quartile	Median	Mean	Lower quartile
Historical estimates (1957–62)[a]				
ICOR	4.310	3.270	3.600	2.830
Marginal savings ratio	0.205	0.150	0.162	0.115
Marginal import ratio	0.250	0.205	0.202	0.135
Rate of growth of exports (percentage)	7.120	4.450	5.125	3.425
Rate of growth of GDP (percentage)	5.050	4.400	4.381	4.000
Chenery-Strout "plan" estimates (1962–70)[b]				
ICOR	3.770	3.270	3.340	2.720
Marginal savings rate (ex post)	0.235	0.200	0.140	0.150
Marginal savings rate (ex ante)	0.235	0.200	0.196	0.150
Marginal import rate (ex post)	0.331	0.200	0.251	0.260
Marginal import rate (ex ante)	0.236	0.190	0.204	0.164
Rate of growth of exports (percentage)	7.120	4.450	5.080	3.160
Rate of growth of imports (percentage)	6.470	4.770	5.270	3.720
Rate of growth of GDP (percentage)	6.000	5.300	5.290	4.750
Actual values (1960–70)[b]				
ICOR	3.800	3.000	3.250	2.450
Marginal savings rate	0.245	0.212	0.180	0.100
Marginal import rate	0.332	0.228	0.214	0.078
Rate of growth of exports (percentage)	8.090	5.370	5.140	2.640
Rate of growth of imports (percentage)	8.910	6.030	5.820	3.100
Rate of growth of GDP (percentage)	6.450	5.100	5.360	3.900

a. Computed from table 10-7.
b. Chenery and Carter (1976, table 3), based on intermediate (plan) assumptions in table 10-7.

The middle-income countries (group A) were relatively successful in expanding their exports and thereby reduced their need for external capital compared to what had been projected. As a result, the inflow of capital was less than half the anticipated requirement, while the growth of GNP fell only slightly short of that projected.

India has been treated as a separate category because of its size and the significant differences in its experience from that of other poor countries. For the poor countries in group B, the capital supplied was 83 percent of what was projected, while GNP growth was 10 percent higher. For India, however, the capital supplied was only 55 percent of that calculated to be necessary to support GNP growth of 5.3 percent, and actual growth of GNP was only 3.2 percent. As indicated below,

Table 10-13. *Aggregate Growth, 1960–70*
(billions of 1970 U.S. dollars)

	Population (millions)	Total GNP 1960	Total GNP 1970 Projected	Total GNP 1970 Actual	GNP growth (percentage) Projected	GNP growth (percentage) Actual	Capital inflow Projected	Capital inflow Actual
Group A Sixteen countries with per capita income more than $190	321	74	135	129	6.1	5.7	30	13
Group B Twenty countries with per capita income less than $190	606	43	69	72	4.8	5.3	24	20
Group C India	538	35	59	50	5.3	3.5	12	6
Total	1,465	153	263	251	5.6	5.1	66	40

Source: Chenery and Carter (1973, p. 463). Country detail is given in table 10-14.

this is the principal case in which slow growth can be attributed to a substantial extent to the limited supply of external capital.

The transition

The growth sequence implied by the Chenery-Strout projections has three main features: (a) acceleration of growth to an acceptable level (assumed to be at least 5.5 percent); (b) use of external capital to supplement both savings and exports; and (c) eventual reduction in dependence on external capital to sustain satisfactory growth. Although it is not possible to verify the functioning of this mechanism by conventional econometric tests because of the interaction of the several limiting factors, table 10-14 presents some elements of country performance that facilitate less formal judgments.

In the 1962–70 period, twenty-five out of the thirty-seven countries in the sample accelerated their growth, and almost all of these sustained satisfactory rates through 1975. The rate of success was much greater among the middle-income countries, three-quarters of which achieved growth in excess of 5.5 percent through 1975. By contrast less than half of the poor countries managed to do so. This difference was somewhat more pronounced than had been anticipated.[71]

Two systematic differences in the external factors contributed to these results. Although primary exports grew about as expected (3 percent for 1962–70), manufactured exports grew much more rapidly (15 percent compared to the 6 percent projected). More middle-income countries were able to benefit from the favorable development of manufactured exports, but these exports also provided the basis for spectacular growth in Taiwan and Korea.

The statistical relations between real growth of GNP and real growth of exports and imports for the present sample are given by the following regression equations (t ratios in parentheses):

$$G_y = 3.9 + 0.24\,G_e \qquad \bar{R}^2 = 0.58 \qquad \text{and}$$
$$ (11.7)\ (6.9)$$
$$G_y = 3.3 + 0.29\,G_m \qquad \bar{R}^2 = 0.63,$$
$$ (9.4)\ (8.0)$$

71. In the plan projections, eleven of the sixteen middle-income countries and nine of the twenty-one poor countries were expected to achieve at least 5.5 percent growth through 1975. The actual results were twelve middle-income and eight poor countries (including two beneficiaries of the rise in oil prices).

Table 10-14. Comparison of External Aspects of Growth Projections

	Per capita GNP (1960) (1)	Popula- tion (millions) (1970) (2)	Growth of GNP				Financing of imports (1960) (Share)		
			Histori- cal (1957– 62) (3)	Actual (1960– 70) (4)	Actual (1962– 75) (5)	Plan rate (1962– 75) (6)	Primary exports (7)	Other exports (8)	Capital inflow (F) (9)
A. Middle-income countries 1960 GNP per capita above $190									
1. Israel	843	3	9.0	7.9	8.3	9.0	0.13	0.40	0.47
2. Venezuela	752	10	4.5	5.8	5.7	6.0	1.61	0.00	-0.61
3. Argentina	681	23	3.1	4.0	4.5	4.3	0.81	0.09	0.10
4. Greece	417	9	6.0	7.3	7.2	6.5	0.34	0.05	0.61
5. Jamaica	388	2	4.0	5.1	5.7	4.5	0.87	0.12	0.01
6. Chile	371	10	3.5	3.9	3.0	5.0	0.74	0.08	0.18
7. Mexico	352	51	5.0	7.2	6.6	6.0	0.77	0.13	0.10
8. Costa Rica	340	2	5.5	6.5	6.3	6.0	0.78	0.04	0.18
9. Guatemala	253	5	4.0	5.1	5.9	5.0	0.81	0.06	0.13
10. Peru	247	14	5.5	4.5	4.7	5.5	0.80	0.33	-0.13
11. Colombia	221	22	5.0	4.9	5.8	6.1	0.99	0.01	0.00
12. Turkey	217	35	5.3	6.4	6.6	6.0	0.49	0.06	0.45
13. El Salvador	210	4	5.0	5.4	4.9	6.0	0.74	0.08	0.18
14. Malaysia	208	11	4.0	6.2	6.5	5.0	1.22	0.08	-0.30
15. Brazil	193	93	5.5	5.3	7.8	5.5	0.73	0.09	0.18
16. Iran	192	29	4.4	8.3	10.8	5.5	1.21	0.07	-0.28
Subtotal		321							

B. Low-income countries 1960 GNP per capita below $190

17. Ecuador	182	6	4.2	5.1	6.4	5.0	1.00	0.02	-0.02
18. Morocco	167	15	2.8	3.9	4.5	4.0	0.82	0.22	-0.04
19. Jordan	160	2	5.6	6.4	2.9	5.6	0.25	0.02	0.73
20. Ghana	158	9	4.5	2.2	2.4	5.5	0.77	0.06	0.17
21. Tunisia	156	5	4.1	3.5	6.8	5.0	0.51	0.26	0.23
22. Philippines	149	37	5.0	5.9	5.6	5.5	1.03	0.05	-0.08
23. Taiwan	147	14	6.0	10.0	9.4	7.0	0.52	0.08	0.40
24. Sri Lanka	131	13	4.2	3.9	4.2	5.0	0.90	0.01	0.09
25. Egypt	129	33	4.5	4.2	3.7	5.5	0.92	0.09	-0.01
26. Thailand	111	36	5.0	8.0	7.7	6.0	0.72	0.20	0.08
27. Korea, Republic of	104	32	4.3	9.4	10.1	5.0	0.22	0.04	0.74
28. Kenya	101	11	1.7	6.7	6.7	3.5	0.96	0.18	-0.14
29. Indonesia	89	116	1.0	3.0	5.3	3.0	1.05	0.01	-0.06
30. Uganda	89	10	1.7	5.1	3.9	4.0	1.10	0.08	-0.10
31. Sudan	88	16	5.1	3.9	5.8	5.5	1.04	0.00	-0.04
32. Pakistan	71	130	4.5	5.1	—	5.3	0.45	0.26	0.29
33. Nigeria	70	55	4.0	3.0	6.4	4.5	0.71	0.01	0.27
34. Tanzania	65	13	4.2	6.1	5.2	5.0	1.01	0.07	-0.08
35. Burma	56	28	3.2	2.7	2.9	4.0	0.91	0.04	0.05
36. Ethiopia	45	25	4.5	5.0	4.2	4.5	0.85	0.03	0.12
Subtotal		606							
C. India	83	538	4.3	3.5	3.4	5.3	0.35	0.28	0.37
Total		1,465							

(table continues on the following page)

582

Table 10-14 (continued)

	Total exports (predicted) (10)	Total exports (actual) (11)	Growth of Primary exports (12)	Growth of Manufactured exports (13)	Imports (14)	Cumulative capital inflow Projected (1962–70) (15)	Cumulative capital inflow Actual (1962–70) (16)
A. *Middle-income countries* 1960 GNP per capita above $190							
1. Israel	14.7	15.4	15.3	17.8	12.5	3,657	4,488
2. Venezuela	2.8	4.3	4.7	72.6	8.6	-6,111	-3,007
3. Argentina	3.7	2.6	1.1	10.1	0.3	4,565	-1,197
4. Greece	7.1	8.6	3.6	22.8	6.9	2,635	5,218
5. Jamaica	4.5	5.4	5.1	6.1	6.6	197	225
6. Chile	2.5	6.2	6.7	-0.3	2.5	2,884	-113
7. Mexico	7.0	4.7	3.6	12.2	5.5	670	424
8. Costa Rica	4.6	9.7	-4.3	26.7	11.4	362	343
9. Guatemala	4.5	10.4	7.0	28.0	9.2	836	185
10. Peru	6.9	2.2	2.3	3.1	1.6	1,015	-167
11. Colombia	3.6	3.8	1.8	28.8	3.9	4,409	411
12. Turkey	4.0	7.7	13.0	13.3	6.3	3,587	1,820
13. El Salvador	4.9	7.5	3.8	22.5	7.9	185	157
14. Malaysia	2.8	5.4	4.1	13.7	5.7	-112	-921
15. Brazil	3.7	6.2	7.6	14.4	3.8	4,936	-114
16. Iran	7.1	10.7	10.8	6.3	13.3	-14	-3,070
Subtotal						29,939	13,270[a]

B. *Low-income countries*

1960 GNP per capita below $190

	(1)	(2)	(3)	(4)	(5)	(6)	(7)
17. Ecuador	4.5	2.0	1.0	-1.4	4.8	393	166
18. Morocco	2.7	2.7	2.1	2.3	2.8	1,422	265
19. Jordan	7.5	8.3	8.4	19.3	7.5	1,041	1,076
20. Ghana	2.1	-1.3	-4.4	15.7	-4.2	1,311	234
21. Tunisia	4.5	5.5	6.3	3.0	3.4	1,062	1,553
22. Philippines	4.1	9.2	6.8	18.3	9.9	1,041	774
23. Taiwan	7.1	20.7	2.9	46.6	15.5	1,435	411
24. Sri Lanka	2.3	-0.7	1.0	4.8	0.7	531	394
25. Egypt	1.8	0.2	-2.9	12.6	1.9	3,539	1,697
26. Thailand	6.1	7.9	9.1	0.4	9.9	192	1,024
27. Korea, Republic of	7.6	27.1	11.2	53.3	17.8	2,769	4,026
28. Kenya	4.5	2.4	2.6	2.9	6.7	110	75
29. Indonesia	1.4	5.0	-3.2	43.5	10.1	2,508	3,431
30. Uganda	3.6	4.5	4.6	6.3	6.0	362	209
31. Sudan	8.0	2.6	3.5	-4.6	3.4	255	245
32. Pakistan	4.9	2.7	-3.6	13.9	5.2	3,998	3,478
33. Nigeria	7.1	7.6	6.1	15.9	3.6	2,210	854
34. Tanzania	4.4	5.6	3.4	4.1	6.4	402	-51
35. Burma	10.2	-11.7	-12.2	-3.0	-7.6	-116	89
36. Ethiopia	7.1	5.6	5.7	-6.9	6.5	218	208
Subtotal						24,799	20,207ᵃ
C. *India*	2.7	2.0	0.2	3.9	-0.4	11,457	6,313
Total						66,195ᵃ	39,791ᵇ

Source: Chenery and Carter (1976, tables 4, 5, and 8). Column (5) from Morawetz (1977) and World Bank data tapes.

Note: Totals may not add due to rounding.

a. Median projections of Chenery and Strout.

b. Excluding outflows.

where G_y, G_e, and G_m are the growth rates of GNP, exports, and imports. Table 10-14 suggests that a shortfall from projected exports was a significant factor in the slow growth of Peru, Ghana, Sri Lanka, Sudan, and Burma. Conversely, accelerated export growth contributed to high GNP growth in Greece, Malaysia, Iran, Taiwan, Korea, and Indonesia. The causal nature of the export relation is supported by Michaely (1977).

The second main difference arises from the conditions under which external capital has been supplied. The volume of capital available on concessional terms has been considerably less than anticipated, and India has been the country primarily affected. Of the shortfall in total capital flows to the poor countries—$10 billion over the 1962–70 period—more than half was in the projected flow to India.

In summary, although overall progress toward achieving self-sustaining growth has been as substantial as that projected for 1962–75, such growth has proven considerably harder for the poor countries.[72] The rapid expansion of trade has been of more benefit to the middle-income countries that were able to develop manufactured exports, and to the exporters of oil and a few other minerals, but less favorable to the bulk of the poorer countries.[73] It should also be recognized that the growth potential of poor countries is somewhat lower so long as most of their production comes from agriculture, where possibilities for expansion are rarely as great as 5 percent.

The importance of the trade limit to growth appeared to have diminished in the export boom of the early 1970s, but this situation was reversed after 1974 as a result of the rise in the price of petroleum and the slowdown in world growth. Since then the trade limit has again become widespread and exerts a major influence on development policy. To sustain growth, many developing countries have had to change the structure of their external trade and also to increase their external borrowing to levels exceeding those of the 1960s.

The international system of allocating both concessional and nonconcessional capital has favored the middle-income countries through-

---

72. Chenery and Carter (1976) discuss some of the more notable examples of retarded growth. For example, the failure to diversify out of stagnant primary exports was a major factor in countries such as Ghana and Sri Lanka.

73. In a number of cases it was the failure of developing countries to take advantage of export markets, because of policies that discriminated against exports, that was primarily responsible for this result.

out this period. Edelman and Chenery (1977) show that only half of
the total commitments of concessional loans and grants were made to
poor countries during the 1967–74 period, and that countries with
per capita incomes under $200 (in 1970 dollars) received only half as
much on a per capita basis as did those in the income bracket of
$200 to $500.[74] Although donor countries have stated their intentions
to favor the poorer countries, progress in this direction has been slow.
The distribution of private capital is considerably more skewed, since
it is based on export performance and other determinants of credit-
worthiness.

This combination of internal and external factors has produced the
major weakness in the postwar pattern of development: the failure of
the poor to share equitably in the benefits of rapid world growth. The
dimensions of this problem and the extent to which it can be reduced
by alternative policy measures constitute the subject matter of the
following chapter.

74. These figures are based on the grant equivalent of loans to allow for differences in terms. Omission of India—which receives only half the poor country
average—reduces but does not eliminate this discrepancy.

Part VIII

The New International Economics

Krugman
Baldwin
Fishlow

IMPERFECT COMPETITION, INCREASING RETURNS, AND
DIFFERENTIATED PRODUCTS IN INTERNATIONAL TRADE

PAUL KRUGMAN

ABSTRACT

This paper reviews recent work on the relationship between industrial organization and international trade. Five strands in the theoretical literature are discussed. First is the role of economies of scale
as a cause of intra-industry trade, modelled using monopolistic competition. Second is the effect of tariffs and quotas on domestic market
power. Third is the analysis of dumping as international price discrimination. Fourth is the potential strategy role of government policy as an
aid to domestic firms in oligopolistic competition. Finally, the paper
discusses recent work that may provide a new argument for protectionism.
A concluding section discusses recent efforts at quantification of new
trade theory.

This paper is part of the National Bureau of Economic
Research program in International Studies.

In retrospect,it seems obvious that the theory of international trade should draw heavily on models of industrial organization. Most of world trade is in the products of industries that we have no hesitation in classifying as oligopolies when we see them in their domestic aspect. Yet until quite recently only a handful of papers had attempted to apply models of imperfect competition to international trade issues. Indeed, in 1974 Richard Caves still felt that a lecture on the relationship between trade and industrial organization needed to begin with an apology for the novelty of the idea.

Only in the last decade have we seen the emergence of a sizeable literature that links trade theory and industrial organization. This new literature has two main strands. One is fundamentally concerned with modelling the role of economies of scale as a cause of trade. To introduce economies of scale into the model requires that the impact of increasing returns on market structure be somehow taken into account, but in this literature the main concern is usually to get the issue of market structure out of the way as simply as possible - which turns out to be most easily done by assuming that markets are characterized by Chamberlinian monopolistic competition. The first section of this paper summarizes the main insights from this approach.

Since this paper is aimed primarily at an audience of I-O researchers rather than trade theorists, however, most of it will be devoted to the second strand in recent literature, which views imperfect competition as the core of the story rather than an unavoidable nuisance issue raised by the attempt to discuss increasing

returns. Here there are four main themes, each represented by a

section of the paper. First is the relation between trade policy and

the market power of domestic firms. Second is the role of price

discrimination and "dumping" in international markets. Third is the

possibility that government action can serve a "strategic" role in

giving domestic firms an advantage in oligopolistic competition.

Fourth, there is the question of whether industrial organization gives

us new arguments in favor of protectionism. A final section of the

paper will review some recent attempts at quantifying these

theoretical models.

      Generality in models of imperfect competition is never easy to

come by, and usually turns out to be illusory in any case. In this

survey I will not even make the attempt. Whatever is necessary for

easy exposition will be assumed: specific functional forms, constant

marginal cost, specific parameters where that helps. And at least one

part of the tradition of international trade theory will be retained:

much of the exposition will be diagrammatic rather than algebraic.

THE MONOPOLISTIC COMPETITION TRADE MODEL

Origins of the model

The monopolistic competition model of trade began with an empirical observation: neither the pattern of trade nor its results seem to accord very well with what traditional trade models would lead us to expect. The most influential of trade models is the Heckscher-Ohlin-Samuelson model, which tells us that trade reflects an interaction between the characteristics of countries and the characteristics of the production technology of different goods. Specifically, countries will export goods whose production is intensive in the factors with which they are abundantly endowed - e.g., countries with a high capital-labor ratio will export capital-intensive goods. This model leads us to expect three things. First, trade should typically be between complementary countries   capital-abundant countries should trade with labor-abundant. Second, the composition of trade should reflect the sources of comparative advantage. Third, since trade is in effect an indirect way for countries to trade factors of production, it should have strong effects on income distribution - when a country trades capital-intensive exports for labor-intensive imports, its workers should end up worse off.

What empirical workers noticed in the 1960s was that trends in world trade did not seem to accord with these expectations. The largest and rapidly growing part of world trade was trade among the industrial countries, which seemed fairly similar in their factor endowments and were clearly becoming more similar over time. The trade between industrial countries was largely composed of two way exchanges of fairly similar goods - so called "intra-industry" trade. Finally, in several important episodes of rapid growth in trade - notably formation of the European Economic Community and the Canadian-US auto pact - the distributional effects turned out to be much less noticeable than had been feared.

From the mid-60s on, a number of researchers proposed a simple explanation of these observations. Trade among the industrial countries, they argued, was due not to comparative advantage but to economies of scale. Because of the scale economies, there was an essentially arbitrary specialization by similar countries in the production of different goods, often of goods produced with the same factor intensities. This explained both why similar countries traded with each other and why they exchanged similar products. At the same time, trade based on increasing returns rather than indirect exchange of factors need not have large income distribution effects. Thus introducing economies of scale as a determinant of trade seemed to resolve the puzzles uncovered by empirical work.

The problem, of course, was that at the time there was no good way to introduce economies of scale into a general equilibrium trade model. Without being embedded in a formal model, the theory of intra-industry trade could not become part of mainstream international economies. The crucial theoretical development thus came in the late 1970s, when new models of monopolistic competition were seen to allow a remarkably simple and elegant theory of trade in the presence of

increasing returns. This marriage of indusrial organization and trade

was first proposed independently in papers by Dixit and Norman (1980),

Krugman (1979), and Lancaster (1980). It was further extended by

Helpman (1981), Krugman (1980, 1981), Ethier (1982), and others. Now

that a number of years have gone into distilling the essentials of

this approach, it is possible to describe in very compact form a basic

monopolistic competition model of trade.

The basic model

    Consider first a single economy without any foreign trade. We

will suppose that this economy has two factors of production, capital

and labor. These factors are employed in two sectors, Manufactures

and Food.

    Food we will take to be a homogeneous product, with a constant

returns technology and thus a perfectly competitive market structure.

Manufactures, however, we assume to consist of many differentiated

products, subject to product-specific economies of scale. There is

assumed to be a suitable choice of units such that all of the

potential products can be made to look symmetric, with identical cost

and demand functions. Further, the set of potential products is

assumed to be sufficiently large, and the individual products

sufficiently small, that there exists a free-entry noncooperative

equilibrium with zero profits.

Much effect has gone into the precise formulation of product
differentiation. Some authors, including Dixit and Norman (1980),
Krugman (1979, 1980, 1981), and Ethier (1982) follow the Spence (1976)
and Dixit-Stiglitz (1977) assumption that all products are demanded by
each individual, and thus build product differentiation into the
utility function. Others including Lancaster (1980) and Helpman
(1981), follow Lancaster's approach in which the demand for variety
arises from diversity of tastes. It turns out that for the purposes
of describing trade it does not matter at all which approach we take.
All we need is the result that equilibrium in the Manufactures sector
involves the production of a large number of differentiated products,
and that all profits are competed away.

Figure 1 represents the endowment of the economy as the sides of
a box. With full employment this endowment will be exhausted by the
resources used in the two sectors. We let OQ be the resources used in
Manfuactures, and O* be the resources used in Food. Thus
Manufactures is assumed to be capital-intensive.

Next we want to introduce international trade. As Dixit and
Norman (1980) have shown, this is most simply done not by adding a
second economy, but instead by breaking our first economy up. Let us
imagine that the resources of our original economy are now split
between two countries, Home and Foreign. If we measure Home's
endowment using O as origin and Foreign's with O* as origin, we can
represent the division of the world's resources by a single point such

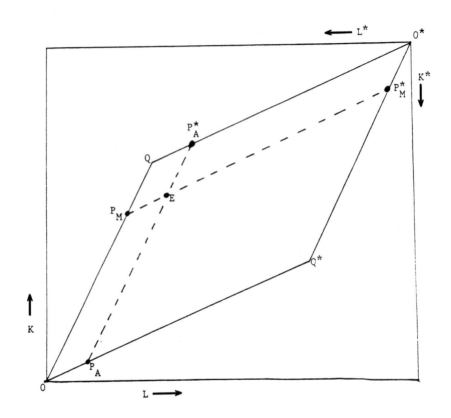

<u>Figure 1</u>

as E. By putting E above the diagonal we have assumed that Home is
capital-abundant, Foreign labor-abundant.

What can we now say about the world's production? The answer is
that as long as the resources are not divided too unequally
specifically, as long as E lies inside the parallelogram OQO^*Q^*
aggregate world production will not change. We can determine the
allocation of that production between the countries by completing
parallelograms. Thus Home will devote resources OP_M to Manufactures,
OP_A to Food; Foreign will devote $O^*P_M^*$ and $O^*P_A^*$ to Manufactures and
Food respectively.

Now it is immediately apparent that a redistribution of resources
from one country to another will have a strongly biased effect on the
distribution of world production. Suppose, for example, that Home
were to have more capital and Foreign less. Then it is clear that
Home would produce more Manufactures and <u>less</u> Food - a familiar result
for trade theorists. It follows, given identical demand patterns,
that capital-abundant Home will be a net exporter of Manufactures and
a net importer of Food. Thus at the level of <u>interindustry</u> trade
flows conventional comparative advantage continues to apply.

Where economies of scale and monopolistic competition enter the
story is in <u>intra</u>-industry specialization. When production of
Manufactures is split between Home and Foreign, economies of scale
will imply that output of each individual differentiated product is
concentrated in one country or the other. Which country produces

which products is indeterminate, but the important point is that within the Manufactures sector each country will be producing a different set of goods. Since each country is assumed to have diverse demand, the result will be that even a country that is a <u>net</u> exporter of Manufactures will still demand some imports of the manufactures produced abroad.

The pattern of trade will be such that these will be two-way "intraindustry" trade within the manufacturing sector, as well as conventional interindustry trade. The former will in effect reflect scale economies and product differentiation, while the latter reflects comparative advantage. We can notice two points about this pattern of trade. First, even if the countries had identical resource mixes (i.e., if point E in Figure 1 were on the diagonal) there will still be trade in Manufactures, because of intra-industry specialization. Second, the more similar the countries are in their factor endowments, the more they will engage in intra- as opposed to inter- industry trade.

Extensions of the model

A number of authors have applied the monopolistic competition approach to models that attempt to capture more complex insights than the one we have just described. Many of these extensions are treated in Helpman and Krugman (1985); here I describe a few of the extensions briefly.

Intermediate goods: Ethier (1982) has emphasized that much intraindustry trade is in reality in intermediate goods. Models that reflect this are Ethier (1982), Helpman (1984) and Helpman and Krugman (1985, ch. 11). As it turns out, this extension makes little difference.

Nontraded goods: Helpman and Razin (1984) and Helpman and Krugman (1985, ch. 10) introduce nontraded goods into the model. Again, this doesn't make much difference. The major new implication is that differences in the size of national markets can give rise to new incentives for factor mobility.

Market size effects: Krugman (1980), Helpman and Krugman (1985), and Venables (1985b) develop models in which transport costs make the size of the domestic market an important determinant of trade. Specifically, other things equal countries tend to export the products of industries for which they have large domestic markets.

Multinational firms: Helpman (1985) and Helpman and Krugman (1985) develop models in which it is assumed that economies of scope and/or vertical integration lead to the emergence of multi-activity firms. Within the monopolistic competition framework it is then possible to let comparative advantage determine the location of activities, allowing models that describe both trade and the extent of multinational enterprise. Horstmann and Markusen (1984) have further extended the analysis with a model that describes the dynamics by which firms may move from an initial strategy of exporting to a later stage of direct foreign investment.

Alternative market structures: Helpman and Krugman contains some efforts to extend the insights of the monopolistic competition model beyond the highly special Chamberlinian large-group market structure. The insights survive essentially intact when the structure is instead assumed to be one of "contestable markets" in the manner of Baumol, Panzar, and Willig (1982). (Helpman and Krugman Ch. 4). A much more qualified set of results occurs when the structure is instead assumed to be one of small-group oligopoly. (Chs. 5 and 7).

Evaluation

The monopolistic competition model has had a major impact on research into international trade. By showing that increasing returns and imperfect competition can make a fundamental difference to the way we think about trade, this approach was crucial in making work that applies industrial organization concepts to trade respectable. In effect, the monopolistic competition model was the thin end of the I-O /trade wedge.

From the point of view of I-O theorists, however, the monopolistic competition trade model may be the least interesting part of the new trade theory. In essence, theorists in this area have viewed imperfect competition as a nuisance variable in a story that is fundamentally about increasing returns. Thus the theory has little to teach us about industrial organization itself. By contrast, the other

strand of the new trade theory is interested in increasing returns
primarily as a cause of imperfect competition, and it is this
imperfect competition that is the main story. Thus it is this second
strand which will occupy the rest of this survey.

PROTECTION AND DOMESTIC MARKET POWER

    Many economists have noted that international trade reduces the
market power of domestic firms, and argued that conversely protection
increases domestic market power. The interest of trade theorists has
been centered on two extensions of this argument. First is the
proposition that the effects of protection depend on the form it takes
—specifically, that quantitative restrictions such as import quotas
create more domestic market power than tariffs. This proposition was
first demonstrated by Bhagwati (1967) in a model in which a domestic
monopolist faces competitive foreign suppliers; only with recent work
by Krishna (1984) has the analysis been extended to the case where
both domestic and foreign firms are large agents. More recently
still, Rotemberg and Saloner (1986) have argued that when collusive
behavior is backed by the threat of a breakdown of that collusion,
import quotas may actually perversely increase competition.
    The second proposition is that protection, by initially
generating monopoly rents, generates excessive entry and thus leads to

inefficiently small scale production. This proposition, originally

proposed by Eastman and Stykolt (1960), is backed by substantial

evidence, and has been modelled by Dixit and Norman (1980).

Bhagwati's model

Consider an industry in which one firm has a monopoly on domestic

production, but is subject to competition from price-taking foreign

suppliers. Why the domestic market structure should differ from that

in the rest of the world is left unexplained; presumably there are

unspecified economies of scale that are large relative to the domestic

market but not relative to the world market. Although economies of

scale may explain the existence of the monopoly, however, the marginal

cost curve is assumed to slope upward. Foreign supply is assumed for

simplicity to be perfectly elastic (this differs slightly from

Bhagwati, who allowed for upward-sloping foreign supply; nothing

crucial hinges on the difference. Also, Corden (1967) analyzed the

case when domestic marginal cost is downward sloping. In this case any

tariff sufficient to establish the domestic firm also eliminates

imports).

Figure 2 can be used to analyze the effects of tariffs in this

model. In the figure, D is the domestic demand curve facing the

monopolist, MC the monopolist's marginal cost curve. P_w is the world

price, i.e., the price at which imports are supplied to the domestic

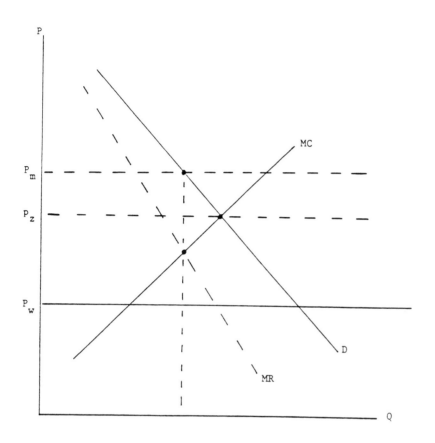

Figure 2

market. P_z is the price that would obtain if all domestic demand were supplied by the monopolist but the monopolist were to behave as a price taker. P_m is the price the monopolist would charge if there were no import competition.

Consider first the case of free trade. The domestic firm cannot raise the price above P_w, so the profit-maximizing strategy is to set marginal cost equal to P_w, producing Q_0. In this case the monopolist has no monopoly power.

Now suppose the government imposes a tariff. The effect is to raise the price at which imports will come into the market. As long as the tariff-inclusive import price lies between P_w and P_z, however, it remains true that the domestic firm acts like a price-taker, setting output where price equals marginal cost.

In a competitive industry, a tariff that raised the import price to P_z would be prohibitive, and any increase in the tariff beyond that level would have no effect — there would be "water in the tariff." Here the monopoly position of the domestic firm matters. A tariff that raises the price above P_z allows the firm to raise its own price to the same level, something that will be profitable as long as the tariff price is below P_m. That is, even when no imports actually occur, the threat of imports keeps the monopolist from exercising its monopoly power fully, and raising an already prohibitive tariff therefore leads to domestic price increases. It also follows that such tariff increases actually reduce domestic output.

features of the model. One is the asymmetry between domestic and foreign firms; we would like foreigners also to be modelled as imperfectly competitive. The other is the lack of any model of the process of entry that leads to imperfect competition. Both features have been the subject of recent research, the first most notably by Krishna (1984), the second by Dixit and Norman (1980).

Krishna's model

To get away from an arbitrary asymmetry between a domestic monopolist and price-taking foreign firms, it seems natural to examine a duopoly. We can let there be a single domestic firm that supplies the market with local production, and a single foreign firm that exports to the market. Collusion is of course possible, but as a modelling device we would prefer to assume noncooperative behavior. (For some possible implications of collusion, however, see below).

In modelling noncooperative oligopolies, the choice of strategy variables is crucial. The two main alternatives are of course the Cournot approach, in which firms take each others' outputs as given, and the Bertrand approach, in which prices are taken as given. In analyzing the effects of protection, both approaches turn out to be problematic. The Cournot assumption fails to capture Bhagwati's insight regarding the difference between quotas and tariffs; the Bertrand assumption fails to yield a pure strategy equilibrium.

Now consider the effects of an import quota. In perfectly competitive models a quota is equivalent in its effects to a tariff that limits imports to the same level. Once we have domestic market power, however, an important difference emerges. A monopolist protected by a tariff cannot raise its price above the tariff - inclusive import price without losing the domestic market to imports. By contrast, a firm sheltered by quantitative restrictions need not fear increased imports, and is free to exercise its market power. The result is that an import quota will lead to a higher domestic price and lower domestic output than an "equivalent" tariff, defined as a tariff that leads to the same level of imports.

Figure 4 illustrates the non-equivalence of tariffs and quotas. As before, D is the domestic demand curve, MC marginal cost, P_w the world price. We compare a tariff t that reduces imports to $\bar{I}$, and an import quota that restricts imports to the same level.

With a tariff, the domestic firm simply sets marginal cost equal to P_w+t. With the equivalent quota, however, the firm now face the demand curve D^1, derived by subtracting $\bar{I}$ from the domestic demand curve D. Corresponding to D^1 is a marginal revenue curve MR^1. The profit-maximizing price with the quota is therefore P_Q; the quota leads to a higher price and lower output than the tariff.

Bhagwati's model produces a clear and compelling result. Better still, it yields a clear policy message: if you must protect, use a tariff rather than a quota. There are, however, two troubling

The problem with the Cournot approach may be simply stated.
Bhagwati's model argued that a quota creates more market power than a
tariff because the domestic firm knows that an increase in its price
will lead to an increase in imports. In the Cournot approach,
however, the domestic firm is assumed to take the level of imports as
given in any case; so a quota and a tariff that leads to the same
level of imports once again have equivalent effects on the domestic
firm's behavior.

If Bhagwati's argument for a lack of equivalence between tariffs
and quotas is right, however — and most international economists feel
that it is — then this approach is missing an important insight. The
alternative is a Bertrand approach. What Krishna shows is that this
leads to unexpected complexities.

Krishna considers a market in which a domestic and foreign firm
produce imperfect substitutes (an assumption that is necessary if
Bertrand competition is not to collapse to marginal cost pricing). In
the absence of quantitative trade restrictions, that is, either under
free trade or with a tariff, Bertrand competition can be treated in a
straightforward fashion. Each firm determines a profit-maximizing
price given the other firm's price; given reasonable restrictions, we
can draw two upward-sloping reaction functions whose intersection
determines equilibrium.

But suppose that an import quota is imposed. This creates an
immediate conceptual problem, which in turn leads to a problem in the
understanding of equilibrium.

The conceptual problem is how to handle the possibility of excess demand. Suppose that at the prices set by the domestic and foreign firms, domestic consumers demand more foreign goods than the import quota allows. What happens? Krishna assumes, plausibly, that an unspecified group of middlemen collects the difference between the price charged by the foreign firm and the market-clearing consumer price. That is, incipient excess demand is reflected in an increased "dealer markup" rather than in rationing.

This now raises the next question, which is how to interpret Bertrand competition in this case. Which price does the domestic firm take as given, the foreign factory price or the dealer price? Here Krishna assumes, again sensibly, that the domestic firm takes the foreign factory price rather than the dealer price as given. This means that the domestic firm recognizes its ability to affect the consumer price of foreign substitutes when the import quota is binding.

But this seemingly innocuous assumption turns out to imply a basic discontinuity in the domestic firm's response function. The domestic firm in effect has two discrete pricing options: an "aggressive" option of charging a low price that limits imports to less than the quota, or a "timid" option of retreating behind the quota and charging a high price. A small rise in the foreign firm's price can shift the domestic firm's optimal response from "timid" to "aggressive."

Figure 3 illustrates the point. It shows the demand curve and the associated marginal revenue curve facing the domestic firm for a given foreign firm factory price. The price $\bar{p}$ is the price at which the quota becomes binding. That is, at domestic firm price above $\bar{p}$ there is an incipient excess demand for imports, which is reflected in dealer markups that the domestic firm knows it can affect. By contrast, at prices below $\bar{p}$ the dealer price of imports is taken as given. That is, at prices below $\bar{p}$ the domestic firm takes the prices of the imported substitute as given, while at prices above $\bar{p}$ it believes that increases in its own price will increase the prices of the substitutes as well. The result is a discontinuity in the slope of the perceived demand curve, which is steeper just above $\bar{p}$ than it is just below; and hence a discontinuity in the level of the marginal revenue curve, which jumps up at the quantity corresponding to $\bar{p}$.

What is clear from the figure is that there are two locally profit-maximizing domestic prices: the "timid" maximum p_T, and the "aggressive" maximum p_A. Which maximum is global depends on the price charged by the foreign firm. The profitability of the timid option is unaffected by what the foreign firm does, but the higher the foreign price, the more profitable the aggressive option.

The result is that at low levels of the foreign price p^*, the domestic firm retreats behind the quota and therefore chooses a price locally independent of

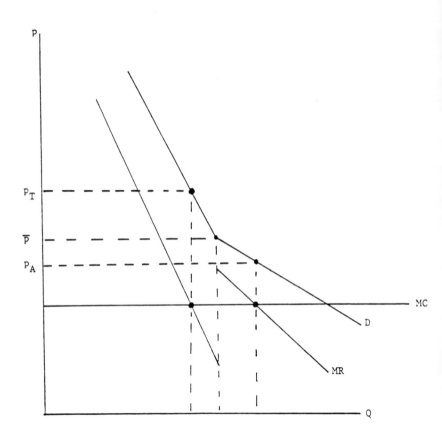

<u>Figure</u> 3

p^*. At a sufficiently high p^*, however, the domestic firm abruptly sallies out from behind the quota with a cut in its price.

The foreign best response function has no such discontinuity. However, if the quota matters at all, no pure strategy equilibrium exists.

A mixed strategy equilibrium does exist. If the foreign firm charges p_E^*, the home firm is indifferent between p_T and p_A; by randomizing its choice of p_A and p_T with the right probabilities, the home firm can induce its competitor to choose p_E^*.

In this mixed strategy equilibrium, we notice that the foreign firm, despite its monopoly power, does not always raise its price enough to capture all of the quota rents, a result in contrast to conventional wisdom. We can also note that with some probability the quota will fail to be binding, in the sense that imports are strictly less than the quota -- yet both domestic and foreign prices are unambiguously higher even in this case than under free trade.

A point stressed by Krishna is that in this duopoly case a quota can easily raise the profits of <u>both</u> firms. Consider for example a quota that only restricts imports not to exceed their free trade level. Clearly if the domestic firm charges p_T, it is because this is more profitable than the free trade price, while the foreign firm will sell the same output as under free trade, yet at a higher price. On the other hand, if the domestic firm charges p_A, this "aggressive" price is still above the free trade price, so the foreign firm must be earning higher profits. (The domestic firm of course earns the same in both states). So profitability of both firms increases unambiguously.

Protection vs. collusion

Almost all theoretical work on industrial organization/trade issues assumes that firms act noncooperatively. In industrial organization theory itself, however, there has recently been a drift toward taking the possibility of collusive behavior more seriously. Key to this drift has been the recognition that collusive behavior may be individually rational in an indefinitely repeated game, where each player believes that his failure to play cooperatively today will lead to noncooperative behavior by others tomorrow. The influential experimental work of Axelrod (1983) suggests that reasonable strategies by individuals will indeed lead to cooperative outcomes in a variety of circumstances.

Recently Davidson (1984) and Rotemberg and Saloner (1986) have proposed analyses of the effects of protection on collusion that seem to stand Bhagwati on his head. They argue that precisely because protection tends to raise profitability in the absence of collusion, it reduces the penalty for cheating on a collusive agreement. By thus reducing the prospects for collusion, the protection actually increases competition.

The case is clearest for an import quota, analyzed by Rotemberg and Saloner. To understand their argument, consider Krishna's model again, but now suppose that the two firms attempt to agree on prices higher than the noncooperative level. Suppose also that the only enforcement mechanism for their agreement is the belief of each firm that if it cheats this period, the other firm will thenceforth play noncooperatively. Then collusion will succeed only if the extra profits gained by cheating now are more than offset by the present discounted value of the profits that will subsequently be lost by the collapse of collusion. A viable price-fixing agreement must therefore set prices low enough to make cheating unappealing.

But as we saw in our discussion of Krishna's model, a quota can actually raise the profitability of both firms in noncooperative equilibrium. This paradoxically makes collusion more difficult to sustain, by reducing the penalty for cheating. If the firms manage to collude nonetheless, they may be forced to agree on lower prices in order to make their collusion sustainable. So in this case an import quota actually leads to more competition and lower prices than free trade!

Davidson considers the case of a tariff, which raises the noncooperative profits of the domestic firm but lowers that of the foreign competitor. If the result is to encourage the domestic firm to cheat, the tariff will likewise increase competition.

It remains to be seen whether this argument will shake the
orthodox presumption that protection is bad for competition. The
modelling of collusive behavior is still in its infancy. To me, at
least, the approach taken in this new line of work seems an odd mix of
ad-hoc assumptions about retaliation with hyper-rational calculations
by firms about the consequences of such retaliation. Yet the argument
is profoundly unsetttling, which means that it must be valuable
(though not that it must be right!).

Protection and excessive entry

In the 1950s, during the honeymoon period of import-substituting
industrialization strategies, it was often argued that economies of
scale in production provided an argument for protection -- a view with
a lineage going back to Frank Graham. At first, the point seems
obvious: protection raises the sales of domestic firms, and thus
allows them to slide down their average cost curves. In an influential
paper, however, Eastman and Stykolt (1960) argued that often the
reverse is true. In their view, bolstered by an appeal to Canadian
experience, protection typically leads to a smaller scale of
production and thus reduced efficiency.

The Eastman-Stykolt view was not couched in terms of an explicit
model. Basically, however, they considered the typical case to be that
where the number of firms permitted by economies of scale is more than

one but small enough to allow effective collusion. Such a collusive industry will seek to raise its price to monopoly levels unless constrained by foreign competition. A tariff or quota will thus lead initially to higher prices and profits. The long run result, however, will be entry of new firms into the industry. If integer constraints do not bind too much, this entry will eliminate profits by driving scale down and average cost up. Thus the effect of protection is to create a proliferation of inefficiently small producers. Such proliferation is indeed one of the favorite horror stories of critics of protection in less-developed countries, with the history of the Latin American auto industry the classic case.

This original version of the inefficient entry problem depended on the assumption of collusion among domestic producers. The problem could however arise even with noncooperative behavior, as is clear from a model offered by Dixit and Norman (1980). They show that in a Cournot market with free entry, expanding the size of the market leads to a less than proportional increase in the number of firms, and to a fall in average cost. Since international trade in effect links together national markets into a larger world market, it would presumably have the same result. Protection, on the other hand, fragments the world market and hence leads to a proliferation of firms and a rise in costs.

We will return to the inefficient entry problem below. It plays a key role in the debate over "strategic" trade policy, and is also central to some attempts to quantify the effects of trade policy.

Evaluation

The basic Bhagwati model of protection and market power is admirably clear and simple, and has been in circulation for long enough to have percolated into practical policy analysis. Market power analysis along Bhagwati's lines has become part of the book of analytical recipes used by the International Trade Commission (Rousslang and Suomela 1985). Market power considerations have now and then helped dictate the form taken by protection; for example, the trigger price mechanism on steel during the Carter administration was deliberately designed to minimize the effect of protection on the monopoly power of both domestic and foreign firms. And perceptions of the impact of trade policy on market power seem to be playing a role in antitrust decisions: in the steel industry, for example, it appears that the Justice Department appreciates that foreign competition is less effective a discipline than import penetration would suggest thanks to import quotas and voluntary export restraints.

More sophisticated models have yet to find application. It is at this point hard to see how Krishna's model might be made operational, let alone the inverted logic of the collusion models. The one exception is the excess entry story, which as we will see is the central element in Harris and Cox's (198?) effort to quantify the effect of protection on Canada's economy.

PRICE DISCRIMINATION AND DUMPING

The phenomenon of "dumping" - selling exports at less than the domestic price - has long been a major concern of trade legislation. It is also self-evidently an imperfect competition issue. It is therefore not surprising that the new literature on trade and I-O sheds some further light on dumping as a particular case of price discrimination. More surprising, perhaps, is the fact that the new literature on dumping actually identifies a new explanation of international trade, distinct from both comparative advantage and economies of scale.

Much as in the case of protection and market power, the initial insight here comes from an asymmetric model in which a domestic monopolist confronts price-taking foreign firms. This insight becomes both enlarged and transformed when rival oligopolists are introduced. Finally, the welfare effects of trade based on dumping are of some interest.

An asymmetric model

An extremely simple model of dumping is presented by Caves and Jones (1985) and illustrated in Figure 4 . As in the case of

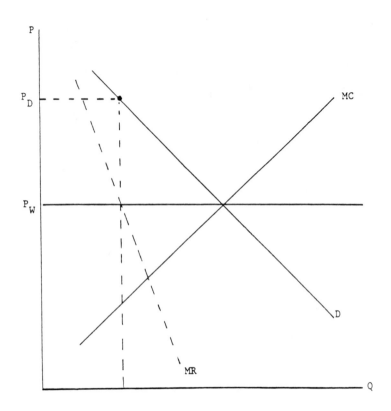

Figure 4

protection and market power, a single domestic monopolist is assumed

to face a given world price p_w. We now, however, reverse the

assumptions about the possibilities for trade. Before, we let the

firm face import competition while disregarding the possibility of

exports. Now we assume that the domestic market is somehow closed to

imports, while allowing the domestic firm to export.

In the figure I have drawn a particular case, where with a price-

taking domestic firm there would be neither imports nor exports. If

the domestic firm acts as a monopolist, however, it will want to set

marginal revenue equal to marginal cost in both the domestic and the

foreign markets. Marginal revenue on the foreign market is however

just p_w, so the profit-maximizing solution is the one illustrated.

The firm sets a domestic price above p_w, yet it exports, "dumping" on

the world market where additional sales do not depress the price

received on inframarginal units.

Three points should be noted about this example. The first is

that while for simplicity it has been assumed that p_w is given, this

is not essential. What is important is that the firm perceives itself

as facing a higher elasticity of demand on exports than on domestic

sales. That is, dumping is simply international price discrimination.

Second, the figure illustrates a case in which a price-taking

domestic firm would not export - in the usual sense of the term, the

domestic industry has neither a comparative advantage nor a

comparative disadvantage. Yet the firm does in fact export. Clearly we could have an industry which has at least some comparative

disadvantage, and yet dumps in the export market. In other words,

dumping can make trade run "uphill" against conventional determinants

of its direction.

Third, the difference between the domestic and foreign markets

remains unexplained. Why should the domestic firm be a price-setter

at home, a price-taker abroad (or more generally, face more elastic

demand for exports)? We would like to have a model in which this

asymmetry is derived, rather than built in by assumption. In the new

I-O trade literature, such models have finally emerged.

Brander's model

A duopoly model of dumping was developed by Brander (1981) and

elaborated on by Brander and Krugman (1983). This model goes to the

opposite extreme from the asymmetrical model we just described, by

postulating instead a perfectly symmetrical situation. We assume that

some good is consumed in two countries, each of which has the same

demand; and we assume that there is a single firm in each country, and

that the two firms have identical costs. There is some positive cost

of transporting the good internationally, so that in a perfect

competition setting there would be no trade.

If the transport costs are not too large, however, and if the

firms behave in a Cournot fashion, trade will nevertheless result. To see why, consider what would happen in the

absence of trade. We see each firm acting as a monopolist, and thus

each country having a price that exceeds marginal costs. The firms do

not expand their output, however, because this would depress the price

on inframarginal units.

But suppose that the markup over marginal cost exceeds the

transport cost between the markets. In this case each firm will have

an incentive to absorb the transport cost so as to export to the

other's home market. The reason is that an extra unit sold abroad,

even though it yields a price net of transportation less than a unit

sold domestically, does not depress the price of inframarginal sales

(it depresses the price the other firm receives instead). So as long

as price less transportation exceeds marginal cost, it is worth

exporting.

The result is a mutual interpenetration of markets, described by

Brander and Krugman as "reciprocal dumping." With Cournot behavior,

equilibrium will take the following form: each firm will have a

larger share of its home market than the foreign market, and will thus

perceive itself as facing a higher elasticity of demand abroad than at

home. The difference in perceived elasticity of demand will be just

enough to induce firms to absorb transport costs. The result will

therefore be a determinate volume of "cross-hauling": two-way trade

in the same product. In the symmetric example considered, this

pointless trade will be balanced.

From a trade theorist's point of view, this result is startling:
here we have international trade occurring despite a complete absence
of comparative advantage and without even any direct role for
economies of scale (although an indirect role can be introduced if we
suppose that increasing returns is the explanation of oligopoly).
From an industrial organization point of view, the result may not seem
quite so outlandish, since it bears a family resemblance to the theory
of basing-point pricing (Smithies 1942). Nonetheless, the trade-
theorist's approach offers the new possibility of an explicit welfare
analysis.

Reciprocal dumping and welfare

Reciprocal dumping is a totally pointless form of trade since the
same good is shipped in both directions, and real resources are wasted
in its transportation. Nonetheless, the trade is not necessarily
harmful. International competition reduces the monopoly distortion in
each market, and the pro-competitive effect can outweigh the resource
waste.

The welfare effects of reciprocal dumping are illustrated in
Figure 5. Since the countries are assumed to be symmetric, looking at
only one market will do. We note two effects. First, some of the
exports that are dumped in each country are a net addition to
consumption. In the figure this is represented as an increase of

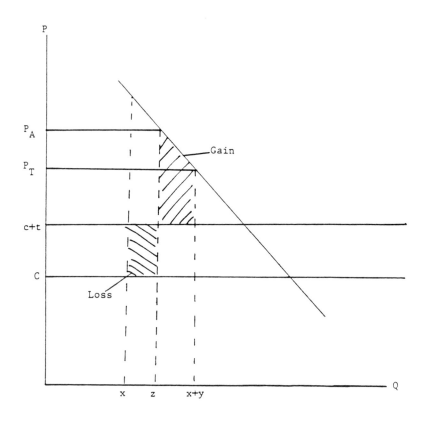

<u>Figure</u> 5

total deliveries from an initial level z to the level x+y. Since the
initial price P_A exceeds marginal cost c plus transportation cost t,
this represents a net gain, and can be equated with the pro-
competitive effect. On the other side, some of the imports displace
domestic production for the domestic market. This is represented as a
fall of deliveries from the domestic firm to its own market from z to
x, with the quantity y both imported and exported. Since this involves
a waste of resources on transportation, this constitutes a loss. From
the diagram it seems impossible to tell whether the net effect is a
gain or a loss.

We know, however, that in one case at least there must be a gain.
If transport costs are zero, cross-hauling may be pointless but it is
also costless,and the pro-competitive effect yields gains. Presumably
this remains true for transport costs sufficiently low.

This suggests that we examine how welfare changes as we vary
transport costs. Consider the effects of a small reduction in
transport costs, illustrated in Figure 6 . There will be three
effects. First, there will be a direct reduction in the cost of
transporting the initial level of shipments — a clear gain. Second,
there will be an increase in consumption, which will be a gain to the
extent that the initial price exceeds marginal cost plus
transportation cost. Third, there will be a displacement of local
production by imports, which will be a loss by the change times the
initial transport cost.

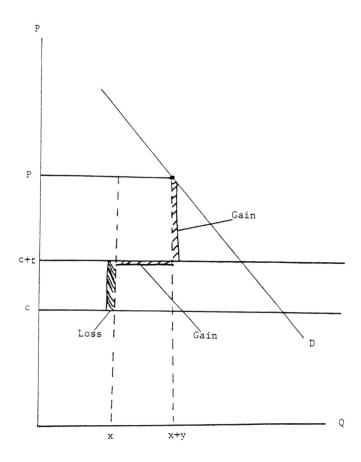

<u>Figure</u>   6

Can we sign the total effect? We can do so in two cases. First, suppose that transport costs are near zero. Then the last effect is negligible, and a reduction in transport is clearly beneficial.

More interestingly, suppose that initially transport costs are almost large enough to prohibit trade. Recalling our discussion above, this will be a situation where price is only slightly above marginal cost plus transport, and where the volume of trade is very small. This means that when transport costs are near the prohibitive level, the two sources of gain from a small decline in these costs become negligible, and a decline in transport costs thus reduces welfare.

Putting these results together, what we see is the following relationship. If transport costs are high, but not high enough to prevent trade, trade based solely on dumping leads to losses. If they are low, trade is beneficial.

Evaluation

The new literature on dumping has so far been resolutely non-policy and non-empirical. Still, nothing that suggests a previously unsuspected explanation of international trade can be dismissed as without importance. Furthermore, the modelling techniques developed in the dumping literature are beginning to find at least some application. As we will see, attempts to calibrate models to actual

data have so far relied on assumptions that bear a clear family
resemblance to those introduced by Brander and Brander and Krugman.

STRATEGIC TRADE POLICY

One of the most controversial ideas of the new I-O/trade
literature has been the suggestion that government intervention can
raise national welfare by shifting oligopoly rents from foreign to
domestic firms. The starting point of this debate was several papers
by Brander and Spencer (1983,1985), who showed that in principle
government policies such as export subsidies can serve the same
purpose as, for example, investment in excess capacity in the I-O
literature on entry deterrence. That is, government policies can serve
the "strategic" purpose of altering the subsequent incentives of
firms, acting as a deterrent to foreign competitors. The "strategic"
analysis seems to offer a possible rationale for trade policies, such
as export subsidies, that have been almost universally condemned by
international economists in the past.

The Brander-Spencer analysis, coming at a time of heated debate
over US international competitiveness, appears dangerously topical,
and other economists have been quick to challenge the robustness of
their results. The critiques are themselves of considerable analytic
interest. In this survey I consider four important lines of research

suggested by the critique of Brander-Spencer strategic trade policy.
First is the dependence of trade policy recommendations on the nature
of competition between firms, analyzed by Eaton and Grossman (1984).
Second is the general equilibrium issue raised by the fact that
industries must compete for resources within a country, analyzed by
Dixit and Grossman (1984). Third is the question of entry, studied by
Horstmann and Markusen (1986) and Dixit (1986). Finally is the
question of who is behaving strategically with respect to whom,
analyzed by Dixit and Kyle (1985).

The Brander-Spencer analysis

As is often the case in the IO/trade literature, the initial
insight in strategic trade policy was obtained by subtraction rather
than addition: by simplifying a trade issue to a form where a familiar
model of imperfect competition can be easily applied.

Consider an industry in which there are only two firms, each in
one country. The clever simplification that Spencer and Brander
suggest is to assume that neither country has any domestic demand for
the industry's products. Instead, both countries export to a third
market. Also, distortions other than the presence of monopoly power in
this industry are ruled out -- i.e., the marginal cost of each firm is
also the social cost of the resources it uses. The result is that for

each country national welfare can be identified with the profits
earned by its firm.

   Since the firms are themselves attempting to maximize profits,
one might imagine that there is no case for government intervention.
However, this is not necessarily the case. To see why, we assume for
now that the two firms compete in Cournot fashion, and illustrate
their competition with Figure 7 .

   Each firm's reaction function will, for reasonable restrictions
on cost and demand, slope down, and the Home firm's reaction function
will be steeper than its competitor's. Point N is the Nash
equilibrium. Drawn through point N is one of the Home firm's iso-
profit curves. Given that the reaction function is constructed by
maximizing Home's profits at each level of Foreign output, the iso-
profit curve is flat at point N.

   Now it is apparent that the Home firm could do better than at
point N if it could only somehow commit itself to produce more than
its Cournot output. Indeed, if the Home firm could pre-commit itself
to any level of output, while knowing that the Foreign firm would
revise its own plans optimally, the outcome could be driven to the
Stackleberg point S. The problem is that there is no good reason to
assign the leadership role to either firm. If no way to establish a
commitment exists, the Nash outcome is what will emerge.

   What Spencer and Brander pointed out was that a government policy
could serve the purpose of making a commitment credible. Suppose that

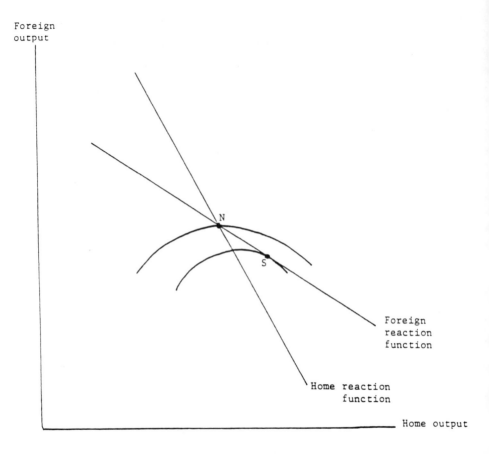

Figure 7

the Home government establishes an export subsidy for this industry. This subsidy will shift the Home reaction function to the right, and thus the outcome will shift southeast along the Foreign reaction function. Because the subsidy has the deterrent effect of reducing Foreign exports, the profits of the Home firm will rise by _more_ than the amount of the subsidy. Thus Home national income will rise. The optimal export subsidy is of course one that shifts the reaction function out just enough to achieve the Stackleberg point S.

It is possible to elaborate considerably on this basic model. Most notably, we can imagine a multi-stage competitive process, in which firms themselves attempt to establish commitments through investment in capital or R&D. In these models, considered in Brander and Spencer (1983), optimal policies typically involve subsidies to investment as well as exports. The basic point remains the same, however. Government policy "works" in these models for the same reason that investing in excess capacity works in entry deterrence models, because it alters the subsequent game in a way that benefits the domestic firm.

The nature of competition

Eaton and Grossman (1984) have argued forcefully that the argument for strategic trade policy is of limited use, because the particular policy recommendation depends critically on details of the

model. In particular, they show that the Brander-Spencer case for
export subsidies depends on the assumption of Cournot competition.
With other assumptions, the result may go away or even be reversed.

To see this, suppose instead that we have Bertrand competition,
with firms taking each others' prices as given. (As in our discussion
of import quotas above, we must assume the the two firms are producing
differentiated products if the model is not to collapse to perfect
competition). Then the reaction function diagram must be drawn in
price space.

Figure 8 shows the essentials. Each firm's best responses
describe a reaction function that is upward-sloping. With reasonable
restrictions, Home's curve is steeper than Foreign's. The Nash
equilibrium is at N, and the Home iso-profit curve passing through N
is flat at that point.

The crucial point is that now Home can increase its profits only
by moving northeast along the Foreign reaction function. That is, it
must persuade Foreign to charge a _higher_ price than at the Nash
equilibrium. To do this, it must commit to a higher price than will ex
post be optimal. To achieve this, what the government must do is
impose, not an export subsidy, but an export _tax_!

So what Eaton and Grossman show is that replacing the Cournot
with a Bertrand assumption reverses the policy recommendation. Given
the shakiness of any characterization of oligopoly behavior, this is
not reassuring.

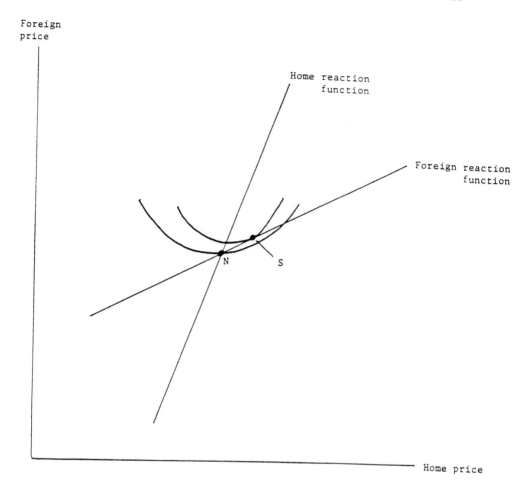

Figure 8

Eaton and Grossman go further by embedding both Cournot and Bertrand in a general conjectural variations formulation. The result is of course that anything can happen. One case that these authors emphasize is that of "rational" conjectures, where the conjectures actually match the slope of the reaction functions (a case that I do not find particularly interesting, given the problems of the conjectural variation approach in general). In this case, not too surprisingly, free trade turns out to be the optimal policy.

Competition for resources

Dixit and Grossman (1984) offer a further critique of the case for strategic trade policy based on the partial equilibrium character of the models. Their point may be made as follows: an export subsidy works in the Brander - Spencer model essentially by lowering the marginal cost faced by the domestic exporter. Foreign firms, seeing this reduced marginal cost, are deterred from exporting as much as they otherwise would have, and this is what leads to a shifting of profits. But in general equilibrium, an export industry can expand only by bidding resources away from other domestic industries. An export subsidy, while it lowers marginal cost in the targeted industry, will therefore raise marginal cost in other sectors. Thus in industries that are not targeted the effect will be the reverse of deterrence.

Dixit and Grossman construct a particular tractable example where
a group of industries must compete for a single common factor,
"scientists". An export subsidy to one of these sectors necessarily
forces a contraction in all the others. As we might expect, such a
subsidy raises national income only if the deterrent effect on foreign
competition is higher in the subsidized sector than in the sectors
that are crowded out. As the authors show, to evaluate the
desirability of a subsidy now requires detailed knowledge not only of
the industry in question but of all the industries with which it
competes for resources. Their conclusion is that the likelihood that
sufficient information will be available is small.

Entry

The strategic trade policy argument hinges on the presence of
supernormal profits over which countries can compete. Yet one might
expect that the possibility of entry will limit and perhaps eliminate
these profits. If so, then even in oligopolistic industries the bone
of contention may be too small to matter.

Horstmann and Markusen (1986) have analyzed the Brander-Spencer
argument when there is free entry by firms. The number of firms in
equilibrium is limited by fixed costs, but they abstract from the
integer problem. The result of allowing entry is to restore the
orthodox argument against export subsidy, in a strong form: _all_ of a

subsidy is absorbed either by reduced scale or worsened terms of trade, and thus constitutes a loss from the point of view of the subsidizing country.

Dixit (1986) is concerned with a more dynamic version of the same problem. He notes that in industries characterized by technological uncertainty, there will be winners and losers. The winners -- who will actually make up the industry -- will appear to earn supernormal profits, but this will not really indicate the presence of excess returns. Ex ante, an investment, say in R&D, may be either a winner or a loser, so that the costs of those who did not make it should also be counted. Dixit develops a technology race model of international competition in a single industry, and shows that in such an industry high profits among the winners of the race do not offer the possibility of successful strategic trade policy.

A larger game?

The Brander-Spencer analysis assumes that the government in effect can commit itself to a trade policy before firms make their decisions. They also leave aside the possible reactions of foreign governments. Yet a realistic analysis would surely recognize that firms also make strategic moves designed to affect government decisions, and that governments must contend with the possibility of foreign reactions. Many of the ramifications of these larger games have been explored by Dixit and Kyle (1985).

To see what difference this extension makes, consider two cases
First, suppose that there is a firm that faces the following
situation: it can commit itself to produce by making an irreversible
investment. Once this cost is sunk, it will be socially optimal to
provide the Brander-Spencer export subsidy, and with this subsidy the
firm will find that its entry was justified. From a social point of
view, however, it would have been preferable for the firm not to have
entered at all.

In this case, what is clear is that if the firm can move first,
the government will find itself obliged to provide the subsidy. Yet it
would have been better off if it could have committed itself not to
provide the subsidy, and thus deterred the undesirable entry. The
possibility of an export subsidy, though it raises welfare <u>given</u>
entry, in the end is counterproductive. The government would have been
better off if it had never heard of Brander and Spencer, or had a
constitutional prohibition against listening to them.

Alternatively, consider the case of two countries, both able to
pursue Brander-Spencer policies. It is certainly possible that both
countries may be worse off as the result of a subsidy war, yet they
will find themselves trapped in a prisoner's dilemma.

The point of the extended game analysis, then, is that even
though interventionist policies may be shown to be locally desirable,
it may still be in the country's interest that the use of such
policies be ruled out.

Evaluation

Strategic trade policy is without doubt a clever insight. From the beginning, however, it has been clear that the attention received by that insight has been driven by forces beyond the idea's intellectual importance. The simple fact is that there is a huge external market for challenges to the orthodoxy of free trade. Any intellectually respectable case for interventionist trade policies, however honestly proposed -- and the honesty of Brander and Spencer is not in question -- will quickly find support for the wrong reasons. At the same time, the profession of international economics has a well developed immune system designed precisely to cope with these outside pressures. This immune system takes the form of an immediate intensely critical scrutiny of any idea that seems to favor protectionism. So Brander-Spencer attracted both more attention and more critical review than would normally have been the case.

That said, does the marriage of trade and I-O offer an important new case for protectionism? To answer this we must go beyond the Brander-Spencer analysis of export competition to consider a wider range of models.

A NEW CASE FOR PROTECTION?

To the extent that the I-O/trade linkage offers any new comfort to protectionists, it takes the form of four not wholly distinct arguments. First is the possibility that trade policy can be used to extract rent from foreign monopolists. Second is the potential for shifting rent from foreign to domestic firms. Third is the possible use of protectionist policies as a way to get firms further down their average cost curves. Last is the use of protection to promote additional entry, where this is desirable.

Extracting rent from foreigners

The possibility of using a tariff to extract gains from a foreign monopolist has been emphasized in two papers by Brander and Spencer (1981,1984). In its simplest version, their analysis considers a foreign monopolist selling to the domestic market without any domestic competition. They point out that under a variety of circumstances a tariff will be partly absorbed by the foreign firm rather than passed on to domestic consumers. For example, suppose that demand is linear and that a specific tariff is imposed: then only half of the tariff will be passed on in prices, with the rest coming out of the firm's markup.

This observation suggests a terms-of-trade justification for tariffs similar to the traditional optimum tariff argument. The difference is that there is no requirement that the tariff-imposing

country be large relative to world markets. As long as the foreign
seller is charging a price above marginal cost, and as long as it is
able to discriminate between the domestic market and other markets, it
will be possible for a tariff to lower prices.

In one extension of their analysis, Brander and Spencer go on to
consider the case where the foreign firm is attempting to deter entry
by a potential domestic competitor. They follow an early Dixit model
in which the incumbent firm does this by setting a limit output high
enough that if it were to be maintained post-entry this entry would be
unprofitable (this was before Dixit acquired enlightenment and became
perfect). The result in this case is that any tariff low enough that
the limit pricing strategy is maintained will be wholly absorbed by
the foreign firm.

Rent-shifting

Clearly a tariff can give domestic firms a strategic advantage in
the domestic market, in the same way that export subsidies can give
them an advantage in foreign markets. Welfare assessment of strategic
tariff policy is however complicated by the need to worry about
domestic consumers. What Brander and Spencer (1984) point out,
however, is that rent shifting will generally reinforce rent
extraction. That is, if in the absence of domestic competitors a
tariff would be partly absorbed by foreign firms, the presence of
domestic competitors will reinforce the case for a tariff.

Reducing marginal cost

In Krugman (1984a) it is pointed out that protection of the domestic market can serve as a form of export promotion. The model is a variant of Brander and Krugman (1983), where two firms interpenetrate each others' home markets through reciprocal dumping. Instead of constant marginal cost, however, each firm has downward-sloping marginal cost. Suppose now that one firm receives protection in its home market. The immediate result will be that it sells more and the other firm less. This will reduce the home firm's marginal cost, while raising its competitor's cost; this will in turn have the indirect effect of increasing the Home firm's sales in the unprotected foreign market. In the end, "import protection is export promotion": protection of the home market actually leads to a rise in exports. The same results obtain when the economies of scale are dynamic rather than static, arising for example from R&D or a learning curve.

Is this policy desirable from the point of view of the protecting country? We can surmise that it might be, because it is in effect a strategic export policy of the kind with which we are now familiar. A numerical example in Krugman (1984b) shows at least that such a policy could be worth carrying out -- if there is no retaliation.

Promoting entry

Venables (1985a) considers another variant of the Brander-Krugman model in which marginal cost is constant, but there are fixed costs. This time, however, he allows free entry and waives integer constraints on the number of firms. He now asks what the effects of a small tariff imposed by one country would be.

It is immediately apparent that such a tariff would raise the profitability of domestic firms and lower the profitability of foreign, leading to entry on one side and exit on the other. This makes the home market more competitive, and the foreign market less competitive. What Venables is able to show, surprisingly, is that for a small tariff this indirect effect on competition has a stronger effect on prices than the direct effect of the tariff itself. The price of the protected good will <u>fall</u> in the country that imposes the tariff, while rising in the rest of the world!.

To understand this result, first note the first-order condition for a firm's deliveries to each market:

$$p + x(dp/dx) = c,$$

where x is the firm's deliveries to the market and c is marginal cost. In a Cournot model dp/dx as perceived by the firm will be the slope of the market demand curve, and thus will itself be a function of the market price p. Thus x will be a function of p, as will the revenues earned by the firm in that market.

Since everything is a function of p, we can write the zero-profit condition that must hold with free entry as a function of p and of p* the price in the foreign market. In Figure 9   the schedule HH represents the combinations of p and p* consistent with zero profits for a representative firm producing in Home, FF the zero-profit locus for a firm producing in Foreign. In the presence of transport costs it will ordinarily be true that HH is steeper than FF, i.e., Home firms are relatively more affected by the Home price than Foreign firms. A free entry equilibrium will occur when both zero-profit conditions are satisfied.

Now suppose that a tariff is imposed by Home. The zero-profit locus for Home firms will not be affected, but Foreign firms will face increased costs on shipment to Home. They will have to receive a higher price in at least one market to make up for this, so FF shifts out. We now see Venables' result: the price in Home must actually fall, while that in Foreign rises.

The welfare calculation is now straightforward. Profits are not an issue, because of free entry. Consumers are better off in the protecting country. And there is additional government revenue as well.

Evaluation

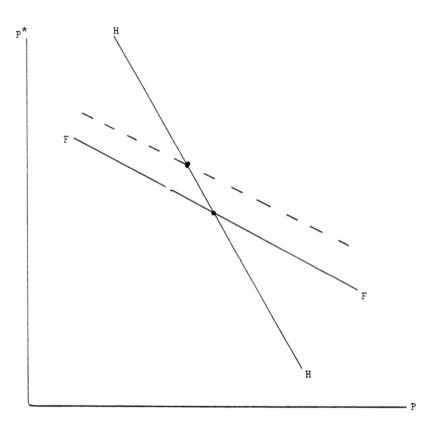

<u>Figure</u> 9

The new literature on I-O and trade certainly calls into question the traditional presumption that free trade is optimal. Whether it is a practical guide to productive protectionism is another matter. The models described here are all quite special cases; small variations in assumptions can no doubt reverse the conclusions, as was the case in the Brander-Spencer model of export competition.

It may be questioned whether our understanding of how imperfectly competitive industries actually behave will ever be good enough for us to make policy prescriptions with confidence. What is certain is that purely theoretical analyses will not be enough. Until very recently, there was essentially no quantification of the new ideas in trade theory. In the last two years, however, there have been a handful of preliminary attempts to put numbers into the models. I conclude the paper with a discussion of these efforts.

QUANTIFICATION

Efforts to quantify the new theoretical models have been of three kinds. First have been econometric studies of some of the aggregate predictions of the intra-industry trade model described in the first section of this paper. Second, and most recent, have been efforts to "calibrate" theoretical models to fit the facts of particular industries. Finally, and most ambitiously, Harris and Cox have

attempted to introduce industrial organization considerations into a
general equilibrium model of the Canadian economy.

Testing the intraindustry trade model

The empirical analysis of intra-industry trade, in such studies
as that by Grubel and Lloyd (1975), long predates the monopolistic
competition theory described in this survey. Without a theoretical
base, however, discussion of intraindustry trade often seemed
confused. Only once formal models became available was it possible for
empirical workers to concentrate on propositions derived from these
models.

Two studies focus on the most direct proposition, that the
proportion of intra-industry as opposed to inter-industry trade should
be positively correlated with the degree of similarity between
countries' capital-labor ratios. Loertscher and Wolter (1980) use
differences in per capita income as a proxy for differences in
resource endowments, and confirm the correlation using a cross section
for a single year. Helpman (1984) uses a more extended data set to
confirm the proposition over a number of years; he also shows that as
the industrial countries became more similar over time the relative
importance of intra-industry trade grew, just as the model would
suggest.

Havrylyshyn and Civan (1984) study a proposition that is less clearly implied by the model, but in the same spirit: namely, that intraindustry trade is likely to be more prevalent in the trade between advanced countries than in trade among LDCs, on the presumption that advanced countries produce more differentiated products. They find that this is, indeed, the case.

These regression studies suffer from a common problem of lack of congruence between the data and the concepts in the theoretical model. In the theory, an "industry" is a group of products produced with similar factor intensities, so that trade within an industry cannot be explained by conventional comparative advantage. Whether this concept of an industry has anything to do with a three-digit Standard International Trade Classification category -- the unit to which the analysis is in each case applied -- is anybody's guess. What is clear is that the data does not provide a very good correspondence to the theoretical concept.

Calibrated models

The newest development in the I-O/trade field is the attempt to quantify models by calibrating them to data from actual industries. This style of analysis seems likely to grow, and needs a name; for now we may call these studies Industrial Policy Exercises Calibrated to Actual Cases (IPECACs).

The pioneering work here is Dixit's (1985) model of the auto industry. The US auto market is represented as a noncooperative oligopoly, with foreign autos differentiated from domestic. Demand functions are derived from other published studies; constant terms and cost parameters are derived from actual industry data. In order to make the model fit, Dixit is also obliged to adopt a conjectural variations approach, with the conjectures derived in the process of calibrating the model.

Once the model is calibrated, it is possible to perform policy experiments on it. In particular, Dixit calculates the optimal trade policy when a tariff is the only available instrument, and the optimal trade-cum-industrial policy when a production subsidy is also available. He finds that a modest tariff is in fact justified, for the reaons we described above. The gains from this optimal tariff are however fairly small. When a production subsidy is allowed, the additional role for a tariff is greatly reduced, with the gains from adding tariffs as an instrument extremely small.

A model similar in spirit but quite different in detail is Baldwin and Krugman (1986), which studies the competition in 16K Random Access Memories. The model is a variant of Krugman (1984a), with strong learning-by-doing providing the increasing returns. As in the Dixit analysis, the model's parameters are partly drawn from other published studies, partly estimated by calibrating the model to actual data. Also as in Dixit's study, it proves necessary to adopt a

conjectural variations approach in order to match the observed
industry structure.

In the Baldwin-Krugman analysis, the policy experiment is a
historical counterfactual. How would the competition in 16K RAMs have
been different if the Japanese market, which appears to have been de
facto closed to imports, had been open? The model yields a striking
result: instead of being substantial net exporters, the Japanese firms
would not even have been able to compete in their own home market.
Thus import protection was export promotion with a vengeance.

The welfare implications of this counterfactual can also be
computed. According to the model, Japanese market closure, although it
succesfully promoted exports, did not benefit Japan. Because Japanese
firms appear to have had inherently higher costs than their US rivals,
market closure was a costly policy that hurt both the US and Japan.

At the time of writing, the only other IPECAC is a study by
Venables and Smith (1986). They apply methods that combine those of
the Dixit and Baldwin-Krugman papers, as well as an interesting
formulation of multimodel competition, to study the UK refrigerator
and footwear industries. The results are also reminiscent to some
degree of both other studies: modest tariffs are welfare-improving,
and protection has strong export-promoting effects.

The calibrated trade models are all at this point rather awkward
constructs. They rely on ad-hoc assumptions to close gaps in the data,
and they rely to an uncomfortable degree on conjectural variations --

an approach that each of the papers denounces even as it is adopted.
To some extent the results of this literature so far might best be
regarded as numerical examples informed by the data rather than as
studies that are seriously meant to capture the behavior of particular
industries. Nonetheless, the confrontation with data does lend a new
sense of realism and empirical discipline to the I-O/trade literature.

General equilibrium

The most ambitious attempt to apply industrial organization to
trade policy analysis is the attempt by Harris and Cox to develop a
general equilibrium model of Canada with increasing returns and
imperfect competition built in. This effort, reported in Harris (1984)
and Harris and Cox (1984), stands somewhat apart from much of the
other literature reviewed here. Although some elements of the
monopolistic competition model are present, the key to the results is
the adoption of the Eastman-Stykolt pricing assumption, that firms are
able to collude well enough to raise the domestic price to the foreign
price plus tariff.

Given this assumption, it is naturally true that Canadian import-
competing industries are found to have excessive entry and
inefficiently small scale. The authors also offer a fairly complex
analysis of pricing and entry in export markets, which leads them to
believe that inefficient scale in Canadian export industries results

from US protection. Combining these effects, the authors find that the costs to Canada from its partial isolation from the US market are several times higher than those estimated using conventional computable general equilibrium models. Thus the Harris-Cox analysis makes a strong case for free trade between the US and Canada.

The Harris-Cox study has not yet been followed by a body of work that would enable us to evaluate the robustness of its conclusion. It is unclear, in particular, how much the assumption of collusion-cum-free entry is driving the results; would a noncooperative market structure still imply comparably large costs from protection? It is a fairly safe bet, however, that over the next few years workers in this area will attempt to fill in the space between Harris-Cox and the calibrated models, building more or less general equilibrium models that also have some detailing of the process of competition in individual industries.

Evaluation

The attempts at quantification described here are obviously primitive and preliminary. However, the same could be said of attempts to apply industrial organization theory to purely domestic issues. The problem is that the sophistication of our models in general seems to have outrun our ability to match them up with data or evidence. The first efforts in this direction in international IO are therefore

welcome. One might hope that this effort will be aided by an
interchange with conventional IO research that poses similar issues,
such as the analysis of the effects of mergers.

CONCLUDING COMMENTS

The rapid growth in the application of industrial organization
concepts to international trade seems to be remaking trade theory in
IO's image. Traditional trade theory was, by the late 1970s, a
powerful monolithic structure in which all issues were analyzed using
variants of a single model. The new literature has successfully broken
the grip of that single approach. Increasingly international
economics, like industrial organization, is becoming a field where
many models are taught and research is an eclectic mix of approaches.

This transformation of the subject has been extremely valuable in
several ways. First of all, the fundamental insight is right --
markets are often not perfectly competitive, and returns to scale are
often not constant. Beyond this, the new approaches have brought
excitement and creativity to an area that had begun to lose some of
its intellectual drive.

At this point, however, the central problem of international
trade is how to go beyond the proliferation of models to some kind of
new synthesis. Probably trade theory will never be as unified as it

was a decade ago, but it would be desirable to see empirical work
begin to narrow the range of things that we regard as plausible
outcomes.

References

Axelrod,R. (1983) The evolution of cooperation, New York: Basic Books.

Baldwin, R. and Krugman, P.R. (1986) "Market access and international competition: a simulation atudy of 16K random access memories", mimeo.

Baumol, W.J., J.C. Panzar, and R.D. Willig (1982) Contestable markets and the theory of industry structure, New York: Harcourt Brace Jovanovich.

Bhagwati, J. (1965) "On the equivalence of tariffs and quotas", in Trade, growth, and the balance of payments (ed. R.E. Baldwin) Amsterdam: North-Holland.

Brander, J.A. (1981) "Intra-industry trade in identical commodities", Journal of International Economics 11, 1-14.

Brander, J.A. and P.R. Krugman (1983) "A `reciprocal dumping' model of international trade", Journal of International Economics 15,313-321.

Brander, J.A. and B.J. Spencer (1981) "Tariffs and the extraction of foreign monopoly rents under potential entry", Canadian Journal of Economics 14, 371-389.

Brander, J.A. and B.J. Spencer (1983) "International R&D rivalry and industrial strategy", Review of Economic Studies 50, 707-722.

Brander, J.A. and B.J. Spencer (1984) "Tariff protection and imperfect competition", in H. Kierzkowski (ed) op.cit.

Brander, J.A. and B.J. Spencer (1985) "Export subsidies and international market share rivalry", Journal of International Economics 18, 83-100.

Caves, R.E. and R.W. Jones (1985) World trade and payments, Boston: Little Brown.

Corden, W.M. (1967) "Monopoly, tariffs, and subsidies", Economica 34, 59-68.

Davidson, C. (1984) "Cartel stability and trade policy", Journal of International Economics 17, 219-237.

Dixit, A.K. (1984) "International trade policy for oligopolistic industries", Economic Journal Supplement, 1-16.

Dixit, A.K. (1985) "Optimal trade and industrial policy for the U.S. automobile industry", mimeo.

Dixit, A.K. and G.M. Grossman (1984) "Targeted export promotion with
several oligopolistic industries", Discussion Paper in Economics no.
71, Woodrow Wison School, Princeton University.

Dixit, A.K. and A.S. Kyle (1985) "The use of protection and subsidies
for entry promotion and deterrence", Amercian Economic Review 75, 139-
152.

Dixit, A.K. and V. Norman (1980) Theory of International Trade,
Cambridge.

Dixit, A.K. and J.E. Stiglitz (1977) " Monopolistic competition and
optimum product diversity", American Economic Review 67, 297-308.

Eastman, H. and S. Stykolt (1960) "A model for the study of protected
oligopolies", Economic Journal 70, 336-347.

Eaton, J. and G.M. Grossman (1983) "Optimal trade and industrial
policy under oligopoly", Woodrow Wilson School Discussion paper no.
59.

Ethier, W. (1982) "National and international returns to scale in the
modern theory of international trade", American Economic Review 72,
389-405.

Grubel, H.G. and P.J. Lloyd (1975) Intra-industry trade, Wiley, New York.

Harris, R. (1984) "Applied general equilibrium analysis of small open economies with scale economies and imperfect competition", American Economic Review 74, 1016-1033.

Harris, R. and D. Cox (1984) Trade, industrial policy and Canadian Manufacturing, University of Toronto Press.

Havrylyshyn, O. and E. Civan (1984) "Intra-industry trade and the state of development" in P.K.M. Tharakan (ed) The economics of intra-industry trade Amsterdam: North-Holland.

Helpman, E. (1981) "International trade in the presence of product differentiation, economies of scale, and monopolistic competition: a Chamberlinian-Heckscher-Ohlin approach" Journal of International Economics 11, 305-340.

Helpman, E. (1984) "A simple theory of international trade with multinational corporations", Journal of Political Economy 92, 451-472.

Helpman, E. (1985) "Imperfect competition and international trade: evidence from fourteen industrial countries", mimeo.

Helpman, E. and P. Krugman (1985) Market structure and foreign trade: increasing returns, imperfect competition, and the international economy, MIT Press, Cambridge.

Helpman, E. and A. Razin (1984) "Increasing resturns, monopolistic competition, and factor movements: a welfare analysis" in H. Kierzkowski (ed) op.cit.

Horstmann, I. and J.R. Markusen (1984) "Strategic investment and the development of multinationals"

Horstmann, I. and J.R. Markusen (1986) "Up your average cost curve: inefficient entry and the new protectionism", Journal of International Economics, forthcoming.

Kierzkowski, H. (ed) (1984) Monopolistic competition and international trade, Oxford.

Krishna, K. (1984) "Trade restrictions as facilitating practices", Woodrow Wilson School Discussion Paper in Economics no. 55.

Krugman, P.R. (1979) "Increasing returns, monopolistic competition, and international trade" Journal of International Economics 9, 469-479.

Krugman, P.R. (1980) "Scale economies, product differentiation, and the pattern of trade", American Economic Review 70, 950-959.

Krugman, P.R. (1981) "Intraindustry specialization and the gains from trade", Journal of Political Economy 89, 959-973.

Krugman, P.R. (1984a) "Import protection as export promotion: international competition in the presence of oligopolies and economies of scale" in H. Kierzkowski (ed) op.cit..

Krugman, P.R. (1984b) "The US response to foreign industrial targeting", Brookings Papers on Economic Activity, 1984:1, 77-131.

Krugman, P. R., ed., 1986. Strategic Trade Policy and the New International Economics. Cambridge: MIT Press.

Lancaster, K. (1980) "Intra-industry trade under perfect monopolistic competition", Journal of International Economics 10, 151-175.

Loertscher, R. and F. Wolter (1980) "Determinants of intra-industry trade: among countries and across industries", Weltwirtschaftliches Archiv 8, 280-293.

Rotemberg, J.J. and G. Saloner (1986) "Quotas and the stability of implicit collusion", mimeo, MIT.

Rousslang, D.J. and J.W. Suomela (1985) "Calculating the consumer and net welfare costs of import relief", US International Trade Commission Staff Research Study no. 15.

Spence, A.M. (1976) "Product selection, fixed costs, and monopolistic competition", Review of Economic Studies 43, 217-235.

Venables, A.J. (1985a) "Trade and trade policy with imperfect competition: the case of identical products and free entry", Journal of International Economics 19, 1-19.

Venables, A.J. (1985b) "Trade and trade policy with differentiated products: a Chamberlinian-Ricardian model", mimeo, Sussex.

Venables, A.J. and A. Smith (1986) "Trade and industrial policy under imperfect competition", presented at Economic Policy, Paris, April.

The New Protectionism:
A Response to Shifts
in National Economic Power

ROBERT E. BALDWIN

Introduction

The international trading economy is in the anomalous condition of diminishing tariff protection but increasing the use of nontariff trade-distorting measures. The former trend is the result of the staged tariff cuts agreed on in the GATT-sponsored Tokyo Round of multilateral negotiations concluded in 1979. The latter trend, however, is taking place largely outside the framework of GATT and threatens to undermine the liberal international trading regime established after World War II.

This paper relates the new nontariff protectionism to significant structural changes in world industrial production that have brought about a decline in the dominant economic position of the United States, a concomitant rise to international economic prominence of the European Economic Community and Japan, and the emergence of a group of newly industrializing developing countries (NICs). The first two sections describe the rise of the United States to a dominant position in international economic affairs in the immediate postwar period and indicate the types of "hegemonic" actions taken by this country. "Shifts in International Economic Power" explains how changes in trade, finance, and energy have led to modifications in national trade policy behavior, particularly on the part of the United States. We then speculate about the nature of the international regime that is evolving under the present pattern of economic power among nations. The paper's final section is a summary and conclusion.

From The New Protectionist Threat to World Welfare,
Dominick Salvatore (ed.), New York: North Holland,
1987, pp. 95-112.

The Rise in U.S. Hegemony

The role of the United States in the evolution of the modern trading system has been central. Although this country became an important trader on the world scene after World War I, it gave little indication at the time of a willingness to assume a major international leadership role. The American share of the exports of the industrial countries rose from 22.1 percent in 1913 to 27.8 percent by 1928 (Baldwin, 1958), but during this period the United States chose political and economic isolation by rejecting membership in the League of Nations and by erecting in 1930 the highest set of tariff barriers in its peacetime history. The failure of the London Economic Conference of 1933 due to the inward-looking economic position of the United States marks the low point of U.S. internationalism in the interwar period.

A major policy reorientation toward participation in international affairs began to occur in the United States during the late 1930s and especially in World War II. More and more political leaders and the electorate generally began to accept the view of key policy officials in the Roosevelt administration that continued international isolationism would bring not only renewed economic stagnation and unemployment to the American economy but also the likely prospect of disastrous new worldwide military conflicts. Consequently, active participation in the United Nations was accepted by the American public, as were the proposals to establish international economic agencies to provide for an orderly balance-of-payments adjustment mechanism for individual nations and to promote reconstruction and development. International trade had long been a much more politicized subject, however, and all that was salvaged (and then only by executive action) from the proposal for a comprehensive international trade organization was the General Agreement on Tariffs and Trade (GATT).

The economic proposals initiated by the United States were not, it should be emphasized, aimed at giving this country a hegemonic role. They, instead, envisioned the United States as one of a small group of nations which would cooperate to provide the leadership necessary to avoid the disastrous nationalistic policies of the 1930s. The envisioned leadership group included the United Kingdom, France, China, and it was hoped, the Soviet Union.

Hegemony was thrust upon the United States by a set of unexpected circumstances. First, the failure of the United Kingdom to return to anything like its prewar position as a world economic power was unforeseen. U.S. officials thought, for example, that the U.S. loan of $3.75 billion to the United Kingdom in 1946 would enable that country to restore sterling convertibility and to return to its earlier prominent international role. But the funds were quickly exhausted and it was necessary to restore exchange control. The 1949 devaluation of the pound was equally disappointing in its failure to revitalize the country. Economic reconstruction in Europe also proved much more costly than envisioned. The resources of the International Bank for Reconstruction and Development proved much too small to handle this task and massive foreign aid by the United States became necessary. The U.S. economy also grew vigorously after the war rather than, as many expected, returning to stagnant conditions.

The failure of either China or the USSR to participate in the market-oriented international economy placed an added leadership burden on the United States. But perhaps the most important factor leading to U.S. hegemony was the effort by the Soviet Union to expand its political influence into Western Europe and elsewhere. American officials believed they had little choice from a national viewpoint but to assume an active political, economic, and military leadership role to counter this expansionist policy, an action that most noncommunist countries welcomed.

Hegemonic Behavior

The significant expansion of productive facilities in the United States during the war coupled with the widespread destruction of industrial capacity in Germany and Japan gave American producers an enormous advantage in meeting the worldwide pent-up demands of the 1940s and 1950s. The U.S. share of industrial country exports rose from 25.6 percent in 1938 to 35.2 percent in 1952 (Baldwin, 1958). (The combined share of Germany and Japan fell from 24.0 percent to 11.4 percent between these years.) Even in a traditional net import category like textiles, the United States maintained a net export position until 1958.

Static trade theory suggests that a hegemonic power will take advantage of its monopolistic position by imposing trade restrictions to raise domestic welfare through an improvement in its terms of trade. However, like the United Kingdom when it was a hegemonic nation in the nineteenth century, the United States reacted by promoting trade liberalization rather than trade restrictionism. A restrictionist reaction might have been possible for a highly controlled, planned economy that could redistribute income fairly readily and did not need to rely on the trade sector as a major source of employment generation or growth, but the growth goals of free-market firms together with the nature of the political decision-making process rule out such a response in modern industrial democracies.

Industrial organization theory emphasizes that firms in oligo-

polistically organized industries take a long-run view of profitability
and strive to increase their market share. By doing so, they try both
to prevent new competitors from entering the market and possibly
causing losses to existing firms and old competitors from increasing
their shares to the point where others might suffer progressive and
irreversible market losses. U.S. firms organized in this manner
seized the postwar competitive opportunities associated with American dominance to expand overseas market shares both through increased exports and direct foreign investment. The desire of U.S.
political leaders to strengthen noncommunist nations by opening up
American markets and providing foreign aid complemented these
goals of U.S. business, and business leaders actively supported the
government's foreign policy aims. Even most producers in more
competitively organized and less high-technology sectors such as
agriculture, textiles, and miscellaneous manufactures favored an
outward-oriented hegemonic policy at this time, since they too were
able to export abroad and were not faced with any significant import
competition.

The United States behaved in a hegemonic manner on many
occasions in the 1950s and early 1960s. As Keohane (1984, chapter
8) emphasizes, in doing so, it did not coerce other states into accepting policies of little benefit to them. Instead, the United States usually proposed joint policy efforts in areas of mutual economic interest and provided strong incentives for hegemonic cooperation. In the
trade field, for example, U.S. officials regularly pressed for trade-
liberalizing multilateral negotiations and six such negotiations were
initiated between 1947 and 1962. But the United States traded short-
term concessions for possible long-run gains, since the concessions
by most other countries were not very meaningful in trade terms due
to the exchange controls they maintained until the late 1950s. The
U.S. goal was to penetrate successfully the markets of Europe and
Japan as their controls were eased and finally eliminated.

One instance where the United States did put considerable
pressure on its trading partners to accept the American viewpoint
was in the Kennedy Round of multilateral trade negotiations. At the
initial ministerial meeting in 1963, U.S. trade officials—with President Kennedy's approval—threatened to call off the negotiations
unless the European Community accepted the American proposal
for a substantial, across-the-board tariff-cutting rule. Members of the
Community had regained much of their economic vitality and the
United States wanted economic payment for its earlier nonrecipro-
cated concessions and its willingness to support a customs-union
arrangement that discriminated against the United States.

In the financial area the $3.75 billion loan to the United King-
dom in 1946, the large grants of foreign aid after 1948 under the

Marshall Plan, and the provision of funds to help establish the European Payments Union in 1948 are examples of hegemonic leadership by the United States. American leaders envisioned the postwar international monetary regime to be one with fixed and convertible exchange rates in which orderly adjustments of balance-of-payments problems would take place. When the International Monetary Fund (IMF) proved inadequate to cope with the magnitude of postwar payments problems, the United States provided financial aid until the affected countries were strong enough economically for the IMF to assume its intended role. A U.S. hegemonic role was also exercised in the energy field, as American companies,.with the assistance of the U.S. government, gained control over Arab oil during the 1940s and 1950s.

Shifts in International Economic Power

TRADE COMPETITIVENESS

The hegemonic actions of the United States, aimed at maintaining the liberal international economic framework established largely through its efforts and at turning back the expansion of the Soviet Union, succeeded very well. By 1960 the export market shares of France, Germany, Italy, and Japan had either exceeded or come close to their prewar levels. Among the industrial countries only the United Kingdom failed to regain its prewar position by this time. The restoration of peacetime productive capabilities in these countries meant that the exceptionally high market shares of the United States in the early postwar years declined correspondingly. The 35.2 percent U.S. export share of 1952 had dropped to 29.9 percent by 1960, a figure that was, however, still higher than its 1938 share of 25.6 percent (Baldwin, 1962).

For manufactured products alone, the picture is much the same. The U.S. world export share decreased from 29.4 percent in 1953 to 18.7 percent in 1959, while the shares of Western Europe and Japan rose from 49.0 percent to 53.7 percent and from 2.8 percent to 4.2 percent, respectively (Branson, 1980). The export market share of Western Europe remained unchanged in the 1960s, but the Japanese share continued to rise and reached 10.0 percent in 1971. At the same time the U.S. share of world exports of manufactures fell to 13.4 percent by 1971.

While aid from the U.S. government played an important part in restoring the trade competitiveness of the European countries and Japan, the governments of these nations themselves were the prime driving force for revitalization. The French government, for example, formulated an industrial modernization plan after the war and two-thirds of all new investment between 1947 and 1950 was financed from public funds. Similarly, the British government under the Labour Party created an Economic Planning Board and exercised close control over the direction of postwar investment, while even the relatively free-market-oriented German government channeled capital into key industries in the 1950s. Government investment aid to the steel, shipbuilding, and aircraft industries and the use of preferential government policies to promote the computer sector are other examples of the use of trade-oriented industrial policies in Europe during this period.

Japan is perhaps the best-known example of the use of government policies to improve international competitiveness. During the 1950s and 1960s the Japanese government guided the country's industrial expansion by providing tax incentives and investment funds to favored industries. Funding for research and development in high-technology areas also became an important part of the government's trade policy in the 1970s. Governments of newly industrializing developing countries use industry-specific investment and production subsidies to an even greater extent than any of the developed nations in their import-substitution and export-promotion activities.

Not only had the prewar export position of the United States been restored by the late 1960s, but the period of an absence of significant import pressures in major industries with political clout had also come to an end. Stiff competition from the Japanese in the cotton textiles industry was evident by the late 1950s, and the United States initiated the formation of a trade-restricting international cotton textile agreement in 1962. A broad group of other industries also began to face significant import competition in the late 1960s. The products affected included footwear, radios and television sets, motor vehicles and trucks, tires and inner tubes, semiconductors, hand tools, earthenware table and kitchen articles, jewelry, and some steel items.

Trade-pattern changes in the 1970s and early 1980s were dominated by the price-increasing actions of the Organization of Petroleum Exporting Countries (OPEC). This group's share of world exports rose from 18.2 percent in 1970 to 27.3 percent in 1980 (Economic Report of the President, 1985). By 1984 OPEC's share, however, had fallen to 23.5 percent as the power of the cartel declined. During this period the U.S. export share fell from 13.7 percent to 10.9 percent, while that of the European Community dropped from 36.1 percent to 30.7 percent. Japan, however, managed to increase its share from 6.1 percent to 8.4 percent. The latter figures reflect Japan's continued strong performance in manufacturing. That country's share of industrial countries' manufacturing exports rose from 9.9 percent in 1971 to 15.3 percent in early 1984 (U.S. Department of Commerce, 1985).

The 1970s and early 1980s were a time of relative stability in the U.S. manufacturing export share, with this figure rising slightly—from 19.6 percent in 1971 to 20.1 percent in 1984. In contrast, the European Community's manufacturing export share declined from 59.9 percent in 1971 to 54.6 percent in 1984. Another major development of this period was the increase in the manufacturing export share of the developing countries from 7.1 percent in 1971 to 11.0 percent in 1980.

An important feature of the shifts in trading patterns of industrial countries in the 1970s and 1980s has been that not only have labor-intensive sectors like textiles, apparel, and footwear continued to face severe import competition but that large-scale oligopolistically organized industries such as steel, automobiles, and shipbuilding have had to contend with such competition. Machine tools and consumer electronic goods have also come under increasing import pressure.

The decline in the dominance of the United States in trade policy matters became apparent in the Tokyo Round of multilateral trade negotiations as well as when the United States proposed a new negotiating round in 1982. As it had in the Kennedy Round, the United States proposed an across-the-board linear tariff-cutting rule at the outset of the Tokyo Round, whereas the European Community again proposed a formula that cut high tariff rates by a greater percentage than low duties. This time the United States did not prevail. The other industrial nations treated both the United States and the Community as major trading blocs whose negotiating objectives must be satisfied. The result was a compromise duty-cutting rule that met the U.S. desire for a deep average cut and at the same time produced the significant degree of tariff harmonization sought by the European Community. At the 1982 GATT ministerial meeting the United States again called for a new multilateral exercise that included as major agenda items negotiations aimed at reducing export subsidies in agriculture and barriers to trade in services. The Community and the developing countries both rejected the U.S. proposals, and it has become clear that the United States can no longer determine the pace at which such negotiations will be held.

INTERNATIONAL FINANCIAL AND OTHER ECONOMIC CHANGES

As a decline in the dominant trade-competitiveness position of the United States became increasingly evident in the 1960s, both the United States and many other countries became dissatisfied with the

U.S. role in international monetary affairs. Since the supply of gold in the world increases only slowly, the demand for additional international liquidity that accompanied the rapid growth in world trade had to be met by greater holdings of dollars, the other official form of international reserves. However, as these holdings grew, a number of countries became concerned about the freedom from monetary and fiscal discipline that such an arrangement gave the United States and they resented the seigniorage privileges it granted. The United States also became increasingly dissatisfied with its inability to change the exchange rate of the dollar as a balance-of-payments adjustment means. Another indication of the decline in U.S. hegemony was the creation in 1969 of a new form of international liquidity in the International Monetary Fund (IMF): Special Drawing Rights (SDRs), designed to reduce the dependence of the international economy on the dollar.

The shift to a flexible exchange-rate system in 1971, however, was the clearest manifestation of the decline in U.S. dominance in the monetary field. Although the results of this action have not given countries the expected degree of freedom from U.S. financial influence, the role of the dollar as a reserve and vehicle currency has declined. Another institutional change directed at reducing the monetary influence of the United States was the formation of the European Monetary System in 1979.

The difficulties faced by the industrial nations in the energy field as a consequence of the success of OPEC have already been mentioned, but the importance of this shift in economic power is hard to exaggerate. This development was an especially devastating blow to the international economic prestige of the United States.

Trade Policy Responses to the Redistribution of National Economic Power

The nonhegemonic members of the international trading regime (i.e., countries other than the United States) responded to the inevitable industry disruption caused by the shifts in comparative cost patterns in a manner consistent with their earlier reconstruction and development policies. With the greater postwar emphasis on the role of the state in maintaining full employment and providing basic social welfare needs, these governments intervened to prevent increased imports and export market losses from causing what they considered to be undue injury to domestic industries. Assistance to industries such as steel and shipbuilding injured by foreign competition in third markets took the form of subsidies. These included loans at below-market rates, accelerated depreciation allowances and other special tax benefits, purchases of equity capital, wage subsidies, and the payment of worker social benefits. Not only had such activities been an integral part of the reconstruction and development efforts of the 1940s and 1950s, but the provisions of the GATT dealing with subsidies other than direct export subsidies also did not rule out such measures.

Because of the difficulties of modifying the tariff-reducing commitments made in the various earlier multilateral trade negotiations, import-protecting measures generally did not take the form of higher tariffs. By requiring compensating duty cuts in other products or the acceptance of retaliatory increases in foreign tariffs, increases in tariffs could have led to bitter disputes and the unraveling of the results of the previous negotiations. Therefore, to avoid such a possibility, governments negotiated discriminatory quantitative agreements outside of the GATT framework with suppliers who were the main source of the market disruption. For example, quantitative import restrictions were introduced by France, Italy, the United Kingdom, and West Germany on Japanese automobiles as well as on radios, television sets, and communications equipment from Japan, South Korea, and Taiwan (Balassa and Balassa, 1984). Flatware, motorcycles, and videotape recorders from Japan and the NICs of Asia were also covered by such import restrictions of various European countries. In the agricultural area, which had been excluded from most of the rules of the GATT, governments did not hesitate to tighten quantitative import restrictions (or restrictions like those under the European Community's Common Agricultural Policy that have the same effect) or provide export subsidies to handle surpluses produced by high domestic price-support programs.

In the United States the disrupting effects of the postwar industry shifts in competitiveness throughout the world produced basic policy disputes that continue today. Except for the politically powerful oil and textile industries, up until the latter part of the 1960s import-injured industries were forced to follow the administrative track provided for import relief under the escape-clause provision of the GATT. Moreover, many of the industry determinations by the International Trade Commission were rejected at the presidential level on foreign policy grounds—namely, the need for the hegemonic power to maintain an open trade policy. Industry subsidies provided by foreign governments, though subject to U.S. countervailing duty laws, were also largely ignored by the executive branch for the same reason.

The official position of the United States began to change under the strong import pressures of the late 1960s. As their constituents described the competitive problems they were facing, fewer members of Congress accepted the standard argument that a liberal U.S. trade policy was essential to strengthen the free world against communism. The intensity of congressional views on trade issues is indicated by the rejection by that body of President Lyndon Johnson's 1968 request for new trade authority and by the near-approval in 1970 of protectionist legislation. The growing unwillingness of U.S. allies to accept the unquestioned leadership of the United States in international political, military, and economic affairs also caused officials in the executive branch to question the traditional American position on trade policies.

The view that gradually gained the support of the major public and private interests concerned with trade matters was that much of the increased competitive pressure on the United States was due to unfair foreign policies such as government subsidization, dumping by private and public firms, preferential government purchasing procedures, and discriminatory foreign administrative rules and practices relating to importation. This argument had appeal for several reasons. No new legislation was required to provide import relief; a stricter enforcement of long-existing domestic legislation seemed to be all that was necessary. After a material injury clause was introduced into the U.S. countervailing duty law in 1979, these laws also were consistent with the provisions of the GATT dealing with unfair trade practices. Consequently, a stricter enforcement of U.S. unfair trade laws was unlikely to lead to bitter trade disputes with other countries. By placing the blame for their decline in competitiveness on unfair foreign actions, U.S. managers and workers could avoid the implication that this decline might be due to a lack of efficiency on their part. Finally, government officials could maintain that the United States was still supporting the rules of the liberal international regime that the country had done so much to fashion.

The emphasis on the greater need for fair trade is evident in the 1974 legislation authorizing U.S. participation in the Tokyo Round of multilateral negotiations. In reshaping the proposal of the president, the Congress stressed that the president should seek "to harmonize, reduce, or eliminate" nontariff trade barriers and tighten GATT rules with respect to fair trading practices. Officials in the executive branch supported these directives not only on their merits but because they deflected attention from more patently protectionist policies as well.

The new codes that were approved in the Tokyo Round by no means fully satisfied those who stressed the need for fairer trade, but their provisions and the attention that the subject received established the framework for many U.S. trade policy actions that have followed the conclusion of these negotiations. There has been a marked increase recently in the number of antidumping and countervailing duty cases, determinations in such cases rising between 1981 and 1983 from 21 to 50 in the United States and from 31 to 58 in the European Community (Moore, 1985). Another indication of the greater use of these statutes to gain import protection is the increased number of ITC injury findings in antidumping cases, from 8 in the 1961–1964 period to 32 between 1980 and 1983. The most important protectionist action taken by the United States since the late 1960s—the gradual tightening of controls over steel imports— has also been justified mainly on the grounds of unfair trade practices by foreign producers. For example, the trigger price mechanism (TPM) introduced by President Carter in 1978 that in effect established minimum import prices for steel was designed to offset foreign dumping. When a series of voluntary export-restraint agreements with leading steel-exporting nations was concluded in late 1984, a spokesperson for the U.S. Trade Representative stated: "We are responding to unfair trade in the U.S.; defending yourself against unfair trade is not, in our opinion, protectionism" (*New York Times*, December 19, 1984).

The unfair trade argument has been used in support of most other trade-restricting or trade-promoting actions taken by the United States in recent years. The textile and apparel sectors have been described by government officials as "beleaguered" by disruptive import surges, thus justifying more restrictive import controls. Similarly, when temporary orderly marketing agreements (OMAs) were negotiated in the 1970s with selected East and Southeast Asian countries, the implication conveyed was that these were responses to unfair export activities of these nations. Even the Japanese voluntary export restraints on automobiles were sometimes justified by American industry and government officials on the grounds that industry's competitive problem was in part due to the unfair targeting practices of the Japanese government. On the export-promoting side, it is routinely claimed that subsidized export credits through the Export-Import Bank and special tax privileges to exporters establishing Foreign Sales Corporations are necessary to counter unfair foreign practices in these areas. In short, fair trade arguments using such phrases as the need for "a level playing field" or "to make foreign markets as open as U.S. markets" have become the basic justification for the greater use of trade-distorting measures by the United States.

The Future of the International Trading Regime

The United States fared well economically in its hegemonic role: American exporters and investors established substantial foreign market positions from which they are still benefiting greatly. The open trade policy that U.S. officials were able to maintain for so long also promoted growth and resource-use efficiency and thus extended the period of U.S. economic dominance. But the postwar recovery of Europe and Japan and the emergence of the NICs brought an inevitable relative decline in U.S. economic and political power. The comparative economic position of Western Europe also receded from its postwar recovery level as Japan and the NICs grew more rapidly. The outcome has been an increase in industrial-country protection that takes the form of nontariff trade-distorting measures.

No country or country group is likely to assume a dominant role in the world economy during the rest of the century. Japan seems to be the most likely candidate for this leadership role with its highly competitive industrial sector, but it appears to be too small economically to be a hegemonic power. Moreover, like the United States in the 1920s, Japan is still quite isolationist. Government officials and businesspeople are conditioned by the disastrous outcome of the country's expansionist efforts in the 1930s and 1940s and by its past history of inwardness. Furthermore, when a potential hegemonic nation first demonstrates its competitive strengths over a wide range of products, certain traditional sectors (such as agriculture) that are faced with difficult adjustment problems tend to be able to prevent the national commitment to trade openness required by a dominant economic power. This occurred in the early stages of both the British and the American rise to economic dominance and is now keeping Japan from making a commitment to openness commensurate with its competitive abilities. In addition, Japanese consumers have not yet developed the taste for product variety needed to make Japan an important market for foreign manufactured goods. The European Community possesses the size and resources to be the dominant economic power, but the very diverse economic nature of its members and the severe structural adjustment problems faced by almost all of them preclude a hegemonic role for this economic bloc.

The United States remains the country most able to identify its trading interests with the collective interests of all. However, a number of the industries that were the most competitive internationally during the rise of U.S. hegemony have become victims of their success. The relatively high profits these oligopolistically organized industries were able to maintain provided the investment funds needed to take advantage of the expanding market opportunities at home and abroad. But their economic structures were also favorable to the development of powerful labor unions that wished to share these profits through higher wages. The outcome was wage increases in these industries that far exceeded wage increases in manufacturing in general. Consequently, as other countries developed their productive capabilities, these American industries found themselves penalized by above-average labor costs and an institutional framework that made it very difficult to adjust to the new realities of international competition. Management in some of these industries also failed to keep up with the most advanced practices. Another very important feature of these industries is their ability to obtain protection by exerting political pressure at the congressional and presidential levels, if they fail to gain it through administrative routes involving the import-injury, antidumping, and countervailing duty laws.

As a consequence of these developments, protectionism has gradually spread in the United States as such industries as steel and automobiles have come under severe international competitive pressures. European governments are faced with even stronger protectionist pressures for similar reasons and have also moved toward more restrictive import policies. As Mancur Olson (1983) has argued, organized common interest groups such as these industries tend to delay innovations and the reallocation of resources needed for rapid growth.

There seems to be no reason why the recent trend in nontariff protectionism at the industry-specific level will not continue in the United States and Europe and become more important in Japan. But one should not conclude from this that the present international trading regime will turn into one where protectionism is rampant. There are—and will continue to be—dynamic, export-oriented industries in the older industrial countries that will seek access to foreign markets and see the relation between this goal and open markets in their own country. Moreover, such industries will have considerable political influence, as U.S. high-technology and export-oriented service industries have demonstrated. These sectors will continue to provide the United States, Western Europe, and Japan with the economic power that makes international openness a desirable trade policy objective. Consequently, none of these trading blocs is likely to adopt a policy of general protection.

But will not creeping protection at the industry level eventually bring a de facto state of general protection? This is, of course, a real possibility. However, this conclusion need not follow because protection usually does not stop the decrease in employment in declining industries. Even politically powerful industries usually have only enough political clout to slow down the absolute fall in employment. Furthermore, while employment tends to increase due to the fall in imports from the countries against which the controls are directed, offsetting forces are also set in motion. These include a decrease in expenditures on the product as its domestic price tends to rise; a shift in expenditures to noncontrolled varieties of the product, to either less or more processed forms of the good, and to substitute products; a redirection of exports by foreign suppliers to more expensive forms of the item; and, if the import controls are country-specific, an increase in exports by noncontrolled suppliers. The larger industry profits associated with the increased protection are also likely to be used to introduce labor-saving equipment at a more rapid pace than previously.

The continued decline in employment after increased protection is well-documented from histories of protection in particular industries (e.g., United States International Trade Commission, 1982). In the European Community and the United States even such politically powerful industries as textiles and apparel and steel have been unable to prevent employment from falling despite increased import protection.

There are many factors that determine an industry's effectiveness in protection-seeking. Its size in employment terms is one important factor. With declining employment an industry is likely to face diminution of its political power because of a fall in its voting strength and an attendant decrease in its ability to raise funds for lobbying purposes. The decline in the political power of the U.S. agricultural sector as the farm population has declined is an example that supports this hypothesis. It seems likely, therefore, that highly protected industries such as textiles and apparel will gradually lose their ability to maintain a high degree of import protection. Consequently, in older industrial nations the spread of protection to sectors in which newly industrializing countries gradually acquire international competitiveness may be offset by a decrease in protection in currently protected sectors. Counterprotectionist pressures also build up as industry-specific protection spreads. The stagnating effect of this policy becomes more obvious, as do the budgetary and economic efficiency costs. A state of affairs may thus be reached in which protectionism will not increase on balance in the current group of industrial countries or only at a very slow rate. Meanwhile, export-oriented high technology and service sectors will encourage continued international cooperation to maintain an open trading regime.

Even if this sanguine scenario takes place, the international trading regime is likely to operate quite differently than it did in the years of U.S. dominance. Industrial countries will seek short-run economic reciprocity in their dealings with each other. In particular, the United States will no longer be willing to trade access to the American market for acquiescence to U.S. international political goals and the prospect of long-term penetration of foreign economic markets. The developing countries and nations with special political relationships with particular major trading powers will probably continue to be waived from the full-reciprocity requirement but their trade benefits from this waiver will be closely controlled. Greater emphasis will be placed on bilateral negotiations in reducing nontariff trade distortions, though these negotiations may still take place at general meetings of GATT members. The articles and codes of the GATT will provide the broad framework for such negotiations, but the variety and discriminatory nature of nontariff measures make true multilateral negotiations too cumbersome. Bilateral negotiations will also be used to a greater extent in handling trade disputes. The GATT dispute-resolution mechanism will be utilized by smaller countries in their dealings with the larger trading nations and by the larger nations to call attention to actions by one of their members that are outside of generally accepted standards of good behavior. These means of settling disputes do not differ essentially from the practices followed throughout the history of the GATT.

Greater discrimination in the application of trade restrictions and in the granting of trade benefits is another feature of the emerging international trading regime. The safeguard provisions of the GATT, for example, will probably be modified to permit the selective imposition of quantitative import controls on a temporary basis. It will be justified, at least implicitly, on the grounds that injury-causing import surges from particular suppliers represent a form of unfair competition and thus can be countered with discriminatory restrictions under GATT rules. Greater state assistance for the development and maintenance of high technology and basic industries will be another characteristic of the international trading order likely to evolve during the rest of the century. The governments of industrial countries as well as developing nations will continue to insist on the use of subsidies to develop a certain minimum set of high-technology industries and to maintain a number of basic industries domestically on the grounds that these are needed for a country to become or remain a significant economic power.

The international trading regime described above is not one to gain favor with economists. It will not yield the degree of static economic efficiency or economic growth that economists believe is achievable in an open, nondiscriminatory trading order. But this is an essay on the most likely nature of the future international trading order and not on the regime economists would most like to see evolve. Free trade is not a politically stable policy in an economic world of continuing significant structural shifts involving severe adjustment problems for some politically important sectors and the demands of infant industries for special treatment. But neither is general import protection a politically stable state of affairs in modern industrial democracies with dynamic export sectors. Politically stable conditions in this type of world economy involve openness in some industries and protection in others with the set of industries in each category changing over time. The particular mix of openness and import protection can vary significantly, depending on such

factors as the country distribution of national economic power and
the pace of structural change. The present situation in which there
are three major industrial trading powers plus a rapid rate of new
technology development and international transfer of old technology suggests that the currently evolving trading regime will be characterized by a greater degree of government control and private cartelization than has existed throughout most of the postwar period.

Summary and Conclusion

The new protectionism threatening the international trading regime
is related to significant structural changes in world production that
have brought about a decline in the dominant economic position of
the United States, a concomitant rise of the European Community
and Japan to international economic prominence, and the emergence
of a highly competitive group of newly industrializing countries.

The trading regime expected to develop after World War II
involved a shared responsibility on the part of the major economic
powers for maintaining open and stable trading conditions. However, the unexpected magnitude of the immediate postwar economic
and political problems thrust the United States into a hegemonic
role. U.S. economic dominance manifested itself in the trade, finance, and energy fields and enabled American producers to establish strong export and investment positions abroad. Yet, by facilitating the reconstruction and development of Western Europe and
Japan as well as the industrialization of certain developing countries, U.S. hegemonic activities led eventually to a marked decline in
the American share of world exports and a significant rise of import
competition in both labor-intensive sectors and certain oligopolistically organized industries. These developments also significantly
diminished the leadership authority of the United States.

Most industrial countries responded to the inevitable market
disruptions associated with these shifts in comparative advantage by
providing extensive government assistance to injured industries in
the form of subsidies and higher import barriers. Such behavior was
consistent with the extensive role the governments of these countries played in promoting reconstruction and development. For the
hegemonic power, the United States, the policy adjustment has been
more difficult. However, government and business leaders have
gradually adopted the view that unfair foreign trading practices are
the main cause of the country's competitive problems. By focusing
on more vigorous enforcement of U.S. statutes and GATT rules on
fair trade they are able to press for import protection and still maintain their support for the type of open trading regime the United
States did so much to establish after World War II. Attention has also

been diverted from the role that high labor costs and inefficient managerial practices in certain industries play in explaining these problems.

No other trading bloc seems able or prepared to become a hegemonic power. However, free trade is not a politically stable policy in a dynamic economic world in the absence of such leadership. Without the foreign policy concerns of the dominant power, domestic sectors injured by import competition and the loss of export markets are able to secure protection or other forms of government assistance through the political processes of industrial democracies. Nevertheless, these industries are unlikely to be able to prevent market forces from halting the decline in employment in the industries and thus an erosion of their political influence. General protectionism is also not a politically stable policy in a rapidly changing economic environment. Politically important export industries that are able to compete successfully abroad will press for the opening of foreign markets and realize the need to open domestic markets to achieve this result.

While it is possible that particular protectionism will continue to spread and bring about an essentially closed international trading order, a more sanguine outcome, involving the support of the three major trading powers (the United States, the European Community, and Japan) seems possible. This is the emergence of a regime characterized by more trade-distorting government interventions than at the height of American hegemonic influence and by the existence of a significant group of government-assisted industries. However, while new industries will be added to this group, assistance will be withdrawn from others as they lose political influence so that, on balance, the list does not increase over time or does so only very slowly. Such a regime will not yield the growth and efficiency benefits of an open trading system, but at least it will not lead to the disastrous economic and political consequences brought about by the type of trading order prevailing in the 1930s.

References

Baldwin, R. E. (1958) The Commodity Composition of Trade: Selected Industrial Countries, 1900–1954. The Review of Economics and Statistics 40: 50–68.

Balassa, B. and Balassa, C. (1984) Industrial Protection in the Developed Countries, The World Economy 7: 179–196.

——— (1962) Implications of Structural Changes in Commodity Trade. In Factors Affecting the United States Balance of Payments, Part 1. Washington, D.C.: Joint Economic Committee. 87th Congress, 2nd Session.

Branson, W. (1980) Trends in U.S. International Trade and Investment Since World War II. In *The American Economy in Transition* (M. Feldstein, ed.). Chicago: University of Chicago Press.

Economic Report of the President (1985) Washington, D.C.: U.S. Government Printing Office.

Keohane, R. O. (1984) *After Hegemony: Cooperation and Discord in the World Political Economy.* Princeton, N.J.: Princeton University Press.

Moore, M. (1985) Import Relief from Fair and Unfair Trade in the United States and the European Community. Madison, Wis.: Department of Economics, University of Wisconsin.

Olson, M. (1983) The Political Economy of Comparative Growth Rates. In *The Political Economy of Comparative Growth Rates* (D. C. Mueller, ed.). New Haven: Yale University Press.

United States Department of Commerce (1985) *United States Trade: Performance in 1984 and Outlook.* Washington, D.C.: U.S. Department of Commerce, International Trade Administration.

United States International Trade Commission (1982) *The Effectiveness of Escape Clause Relief in Promoting Adjustment to Import Competition,* USITC Publication 1229. Washington, D.C.: United States International Trade Commission.

Alternative Approaches and Solutions to the Debt of Developing Countries

Albert Fishlow

1 INTRODUCTION

It is more than five years since that fateful Friday the Thirteenth of August when the Mexican Minister of Finance visited Washington to announce that his country could no longer continue to meet its debt service obligations. Other countries soon followed. Since 1982 that rescheduling experience has been repeated for more than 30 countries involving close to $200 billion of debt (IMF, 1986, p. 123). There have also been a variety of other actions to shore up a vulnerable international financial system and to promote debtor adjustment.

The gravity and seeming novelty of the debt problem – the defaults of the 1930s had long since been forgotten, not to mention earlier history – has also given rise to a burgeoning economics literature. It has been characterised by three main thrusts. One is the application of the modern techniques of game theory and the economics of information to issues of sovereign indebtedness.[1] A second focus is more applied, and related to the adjustment/stabilisation experiences of debtor countries.[2] The third line of interest has been in historical precedents and parallels, the better from which to draw lessons about the present.[3]

In this paper I propose to draw upon these three subject areas with the ultimate intent of addressing the appropriate form of potential solutions to the continuing debt problem. My interest here, like that of most of the literature, is with the debts to commercial creditors rather than to official agencies. It thus excludes the largest part of the African problem, about which there is growing consensus for the need of some debt relief and additional net resource flows.

The paper has three parts. One compares the present lending facilities available to developing countries to the characteristics of historical

From Silvio Borner, ed., International Finance and Trade in a Polycentric World, IEA Conference, Volume No. 92, Macmillan, 1988.

capital markets. Return to 'normal' conditions prior to 1982 has been an integral part of the dominant debt strategy; but the striking feature of the rapid increase in indebtedness in the 1970s and early 1980s is its abnormality. The second section considers some implications of the new 'willingness to pay' models of debtor behaviour. A critical difference from an ability to pay approach is the relative neglect of the productive structure and the role of adjustment in debtor countries. The third part takes up the relative merits of debt increasing versus debt relief measures in reducing resource outflows from developing country debtors.

2 HISTORICAL COMPARISONS

The post-1973 expansion in lending to developing countries represented a quantum change in reliance upon debt finance and net capital inflow in the period after the Second World War. From a level of about 2 per cent of GNP in 1960–73, current account financing increased to some 3 per cent in the next several years. Bank loans, excluding export credits, amounted to 50 per cent of the flows by the end of the period compared to 15 per cent at the beginning. Developing country debt, excluding capital exporters, increased from less than $150 billion in 1973 to more than $1.1 trillion at the end of 1986. The ratio of debt to exports rose from little more than 1 to 1.8; as a ratio to income, it again almost doubled from 0.22 to 0.43.[4]

The closest analogue to this recent surge is the burst of foreign lending in the decade before 1914. In absolute terms, net annual foreign investment averaged about $9 billion (in 1984 dollars) between 1900 and 1913.[5] While evidently smaller than recent capital flows that reached and even exceeded $100 billion a year, it was likely that historical investment reached a greater percentage of contemporary incomes. For the principal peripheral countries like Argentina, Canada and Australia, inflows financed more than 5 per cent of GNP.

Modern circumstances differ in three important respects. One is the much greater rise in real debt, at an annual rate of some 12 per cent from 1973 to 1982, compared to 4 per cent in the earlier period.[6] The earlier experience was part of an established process of foreign investment that went back to the 1820s, and the cycle, while pronounced, was not so profound an acceleration. Secondly, as a consequence, ratios of debt to exports and income have shown a tendency to rise more rapidly in recent experience than historically.

Thirdly, the share of industrialised country income allocated to foreign investment was substantially higher earlier than in the more recent period. While flows from industrialised countries averaged only about 1 per cent in the 1970s, Britain was allocating some 5 to 10 per cent of income to overseas investment and France and Germany, 2 to 3 per cent each. That is, there was a large and continuing source of capital supply, not least because the accumulated stock of foreign investment was capable of generating large return incomes that were reapplied abroad. Such service receipts exceeded new applications, even in the period 1900–1913. For borrowers as a whole, resource transfers were negative. Previous recipients of funds were financing investment in new borrowers.

Capital flows in the pre-1914 decades can usefully be categorised into two types. One was development finance provided principally by Britain to the relatively resource-rich and underpopulated countries of the periphery. Such investment, making up something more than half of foreign assets in 1914, helped to forge a global economy extending from the core of Western European industrialisers to latecomers in Eastern Europe, to raw material suppliers on the periphery. At the heart of this expanding trade was a flow of finance that underwrote a significant part of the real investment required for the expansion of primary production.

Another stream of investment was Europe-oriented, accounting for some quarter of all assets. Russia was by far the largest debtor, with additional flows to Scandinavian and Eastern European countries. France and West Germany were the principal sources. In this kind of investment, as well as the holdings in China, Turkey, Egypt, and some of the African colonies, political considerations and not economic return alone played a part.

Developmental investment yielded attractive private returns relative to domestic applications. Edelstein's calculations of realised earnings to securities issued in London show a cyclically adjusted margin varying between 3.9 and 1.6 per cent, depending upon the country and type of investment (Edelstein, 1976). Lindert and Morton's recent recalculation of internal rates of return by country show only Mexico as a prominant exception to a positive premium ranging for developmental borrowers from 1 to 1.5 per cent for the period 1850–1914 (Lindert and Morton, 1987, Table 3). The London capital market successfully mediated between the private financial gains of investors and the social returns attendant upon peripheral infrastructure investment.

Moreover, it did so with virtually no official intervention or restriction. Gunboats were a rarity, and interruptions in payments were generally temporary rather than permanent defaults. Borrowers had clear incentives to pay based upon the benefits of continuing access to the market rather than sanctions or penalties that might be imposed if they failed to do so. Repayment was interrupted largely because of cyclical circumstance: investment was bunched and preceded the lagged response of production and exports needed to service it. New loans in the interim covered the old. When capital flows slowed down, there was a temporary balance of payments problem that was capable of eventual endogenous resolution. In the transition, there would be a difficult time, involving some postponement of service and sometimes more outright assistance. But it was clearly seen as a liquidity problem because of low debt-service ratios and an expected future stream of increased export revenues.

Revenue borrowers, the second category, did not yield as high *ex post* returns and posed larger enforcement problems. Foreign investment afforded little or no increase in local productive capacity; proceeds were used to finance public consumption. Borrowers eventually found themselves in a debt trap paying higher rates for shorter-term finance, until such flows ceased too, and provoked default. Then relief became necessary.

Turkey in the nineteenth century is a classic case. Its loan yielded a negative return to creditors as a result of debt write-downs. Such generous treatment was provided only in exchange for outright political intervention and a large voice in the collection of public revenues and public administration. The Russian experience is more mixed. Some of the foreign investment found its way to productive application, although much supported public consumption. Default came with the Revolution and inflicted large losses on hapless, predominantly French, private investors.[7]

Lending in the 1920s was more akin to the revenue model than the developmental one. Proportionally more loans were directed to European countries in that decade, some with the laudable purpose and high returns of reconstruction finance, but many not. Applications in peripheral countries were not nearly as directed to production of tradables as they had been earlier, and much borrowing was done by state and local government authorities. There was therefore much less of a self-liquidating quality to capital flows after the First World War. That was less apparent at the time for two reasons. Wartime inflation had reduced the previous debt burden, and facilitated continuing service during the 1920s. By the time the pinch might have been felt, the decline of international economic activity during the Great Depression was so severe and prolonged that payment was out of the question. Widespread default ensued without penalty and attention to particular cases.

This brief historical summary helps to highlight several points about the lending in the 1970s and early 1980s.

First, capital flows were largely a product of the international balance of payments liability produced by the oil price increase, rather than a continuing increase of private finance emanating from the industrialised countries in search of application in developing country assets. Holders of deposits in the Euro-currency market, initially the oil surplus countries, subsidised borrowers by making possible low, and even negative, real rates of return, that made debt such an attractive option. Commercial banks held the loans themselves; there was no ultimate lender.

Secondly, the form of the lending instruments placed the risk of changing economic conditions predominantly upon the borrower; short maturities and variable interest rates adjusted every six months required continuing gross flows and imposed a vulnerability to fluctuations in financial markets. Inflation was not only neutralised as a source of potential debt relief, but its inclusion in nominal interest rates served to speed up real amortisation.

Thirdly, the subsequent increase in export capacity was less automatic than with earlier developmental lending; indeed, large capital flight from Argentina, Mexico and Venezuela meant that there was a smaller stock of productive assets in the countries than the amount of public liabilities. Even when that was not the case, the asymmetry between the financial and trade opening in the Latin American borrowers raised doubts about the capacity to mobilise foreign exchange to service the debt. Finally, countries were not prepared for extended export surpluses over a period of years, should lending be slow. There had been no such cycles in the period after the Second World War, and expectations of continuous growth had become the rule.

Fourthly, bank lenders, directly threatened by the crisis, rather than intermediaries, could not readily absorb the losses implied by revaluation of borrowers' prospects as the external situation deteriorated. Their high ratios of developing country debt to capital implied potential insolvency. Maintaining the integrity of the financial system has been a much more prominent objective than in earlier overlending episodes. Consequently, arrangements between debtors and creditors have required the continuity of debt service rather than substantially easing accommodation to new and unanticipated external conditions.

These fundamental differences add up to a very different perspective on the present debt problem than in the pre-1914 period. The discipline, and advantage, of restoration of normal market conditions is not the same, because there is little likelihood that lending of the same form could, or should, take place. The one basic similarity, the role of reduced capital supply in provoking the onset of the crisis, cannot be extrapolated to imply that resumption of flows will eventually occur as they did in the past. And even that inference ignores the typical long cycle lag of two decades that occurred.

Rather, the task of present policy is not to await a typical historical transition to renewed flows based upon growing exports, but to dampen the echo effect of the excessive capital inflows of the 1970s. Future financial flows will be smaller rather than larger if one judges not only from revealed bank lending, but also the increased emphasis upon security. If those future flows are to yield productive effect, new debt cannot simply be taken up, and much more than taken up, in paying interest on the old flows. Otherwise debtors will be condemned to premature, continuing resource outflows in contradiction to continuing capital needs to underwrite economic growth.

3 DEBTOR COUNTRY ADJUSTMENT

That brings us to the heart of the matter, the tradeoff between debt service and economic performance of the debtor countries. Interestingly, that issue is given secondary focus in the new willingness-to-pay models of international debt. Their primary concern, rather, is with the enforceability of sovereign debt where assets are not subject to seizure and where penalties inflict damage but yield little or no benefit to creditors. As such the theory emphasises the moral hazard of debtors and the vulnerability of creditors; the susceptibility to less than full repayment provides a rationale for rising supply curves of credit, risk premia and credit limits.

These models, even when extended to debt renegotiation to avert potential default, give virtually no attention to the productive structure of the debtors and its influence on the outcome. In an adverse state of nature, the only defence of debtors is a threat of default that will provide some relief if to the creditors' advantage. Because debtors are inherently unwilling to pay, and only do so because of penalties that would leave them still worse off, there is no scope for reduced debt service to underwrite improved economic performance and larger future payments to creditors. That contradiction is emphasised by Lindert and Morton, (1987, p. 30, italics theirs) 'Is there no case in which creditors in the aggregate can gain by lending more in a debt crisis? No, not with *sovereign* debt'. And Kohler criticises, from the same perspective: 'Rather than seeking no minimize the number of debtors that request reschedulings, most researchers seem preoccupied with finding improvements in the debt renegotiation process (Kohler, 1986, p. 743)'.

Another conclusion may be that one is overemphasising the special quality of non-enforceability of sovereign debt as a vehicle for understanding the present problem. An ability-to-pay approach, by contrast, places emphasis on constraints to meeting commitments that are accepted as binding. Such a view implicitly rejects continuous recalculation of the utility of default in favour of a rule of thumb of contractual fulfilment. Sovereign governments could choose such a course for two principal reasons. One is reputation. It figures not merely in continuing access to the capital market, but in the whole range of related international transactions, political as well as economic. Note in this respect that the larger debtor countries are themselves sometimes creditors. In the second instance, renunciation of property rights has serious domestic consequences. If external obligations are not paid, it signals a willingness to alter internal rules as well. Both of these effects can be taken as sufficiently compelling to rule out default except if unanticipated deterioration of external circumstances intervenes, and only after attempts to conform. Countries first choose to alter their policies in an effort to pay, and default only reluctantly.

No rigorous econometric evidence has been adduced to establish the superiority of either of these approaches. At best, weak implications are tested. The empirical evidence clearly establishes, however, a vulnerability to default as a consequence of deterioration of debt-export ratios. The ubiquity of the recent rise in this indicator, and the continuation of debt service despite significant reduction in growth, should at least give pause to the uncritical acceptance of a willingness to pay perspective.[8]

Casual support for an alternative ability to pay view can be adduced from the close association of extended default with revolutionary governmental change. Then the continuity of internal rules, and even one's international situation, is of second order. Other interruptions in payment tend to be shorter term and related to a changed economic environment, and in particular, changes in the supply and terms of foreign capital and deterioration in possibilities for external trade. Moreover, the fact that countries have frequently bought up their debt at discounted market prices reflects an expectation about self-fulfilment that markets undervalue during difficult periods.

An ability to pay framework is not without its own problems. Analogies with private corporate insolvency are inappropriate. External debts would exceed national wealth only under exceptional circumstances. That is an objective basis for Walter Wriston's dictum about countries, unlike firms, never going bankrupt. Even a more restrictive version requiring a positive present value of the balance of payments does not go very far. Countries have a capacity to reallocate resources to exports and import substitutes over the medium term. Then, of course, there is no well defined maximum that countries can pay.

It is better to frame the matter explicitly in terms of the tradeoff between current resource transfer and the present value of expected future repayments. As resource transfer increases, as it has, from a positive inflow to a large negative value, economic performance, and with it the base for subsequent debt service fulfilment, is affected. Countries may remain technically solvent, but not forever. Even creditors, and secondary markets, come to recognise that contractual debt service fulfilment is impossible unless something is done.

The central difference from a willingness to pay approach is an explicit identification of why resource transfer impedes economic performance. Constraints to full repayment can emerge in any of the three interrelated processes of transferring the needed debt service: external, consumption-investment and public-private.

The one that has been given most prominence is the balance of payments. The classic transfer problem was first elaborated in the context of the German reparations question. Then the concern was that increased export volume to satisfy payments would be offset by deteriorating terms of trade. It reappears in a modern guise as a result of mounting debt service payments. For Latin America, the largest debtor region, terms of trade declines have more than cancelled an improved post-1979 export volume performance relative to the previous decade. More generally, world trade growth, with the exception of 1984, has been extremely sluggish in this same period. Debtor countries face the need, not merely of reallocating production between export and consumption, but of restructuring production to a more diversified and competitive set of products whose market is expanding. Real exchange depreciation to reduce real wages is a short-term expedient; productivity increases are required in the medium term to assure competitiveness.

An optimistic assessment of the debt problem derives from a view that such a transformation is not only feasible, but relatively easy. Then cumulative export growth with continuous compounding works its magic by significantly reducing debt-export ratios. Resumption of voluntary lending then quickly follows. Such a view has consistently tended to overestimate performance of the world economy, and to underestimate the difficulties faced by debtors in penetrating world markets. Export surpluses have been achieved, but through continuing compression of imports rather than sustained export growth. This outcome has occurred despite much improved exchange rate policies.

Improved external accounts have thus come at the expense of internal equilibrium rather than as a consequence of sound adjustment. The more basic point is that the balance of payments is not the only determinant of debt service capability. Exporting one's way out of the problem is not assured. The resultant resource transfer also has implications for the level of feasible domestive investment. If reduced domestic consumption does not finance the bulk of the transfer, increases in debt service must come at the expense of the level of investment. Capital formation has to be crowded out to permit part of domestic saving to be used for debt service. When consumption is interest-inelastic, as it seems to be, and not fully compressible, real interest rates must be high to achieve the needed low investment rate equilibrium. The rationing of imports, by depriving countries of complementary inputs necessary to permit domestic investment, also contributes. In such circumstances, potential saving will not be fully realised *ex post*. This is the second type of transfer.

Again, for the Latin American debtors, the decline in investment is a dominant reality. Investment ratios since 1982 have averaged 4 to 5 percentage points below earlier levels, approximately equal to the levels of current outward resource transfer. At their present level of 18–19 per cent, capital formation is inadequate to sustain rates of growth of 5–6 per cent a year required to absorb increases in the labour force.

A third transfer set in motion by external debt service is an internal financial flow between surplus and deficit sectors. Real resources to purchase foreign exchange must be chanelled to those servicing the debt. In the majority of cases, the public sector is the principal, if not exclusive, debtor; indeed, one direct consequence of the post-1982 debt crisis was coercive pressure from external creditors for public assumption of private liabilities.

The public sector can acquire such resources by taxes, increases in internal debt or expansion of the money supply. There are limits to any of them, and therefore limits to their sum. Constraints exist on how much can be extracted by taxes, not only by reason of political resistance but also by virtue of incentive consequences. Excessive reliance on internal debt provokes high interest rates by attracting funds from other applications. Reliance on money issue confronts a limit on the inflation tax, and thus beyond a certain point becomes frustrated by accelerating inflation. The mix of policies is further subject to a potential instability problem: at real interest rates well above the growth of governmental revenues, the public debt becomes a destabilising element in its impact on public sector expenditures. Devaluation, while improving the trade balance, can thus stimulate deficits and inflation validating monetary expansion.[9]

Such constraints to efficient transfer, and decisions about appropriate policies, are the essence of determining the ability to pay. Default enters only at a last stage, after other efforts have failed. How debt service influences economic performance is the key question. Paying more today may even imply less sustainable debt service in the future. A low investment, low growth equilibrium will be consistent with this year's export surplus but not with sustained expansion of exports in the future.

Within a willingness to pay context, this relationship between present and future debt service is largely irrelevant. What happens tomorrow is independent of the payment today; economic structure is rudimentary. Creditors, moreover, would never make the mistake of seeking to extract too much. They are maximisers. Yet, the reluctance to offer more generous concessions earlier may be a source of larger losses to lenders today.

Renegotiation of debt service can be better for both lenders and borrowers when 'excess' current payments are being made. 'Involuntary lending' is perfectly rational in the ability to pay framework. It requires co-ordinated action to assure that the interests of individual creditors are subordinated to aggregate gain, and hence to avoid the free rider problem. It also requires some assessment of the debtor country situation to determine the correct form and amount of relief. Precisely because negotiations have proceeded without adequate sense of the consequences of resource transfer on performance, and have been dominated by immediate considerations of weak bank balance sheets, such flows have been inadequate. Effects on world trade growth and feedbacks upon the industrialised countries have been largely ignored.

In the last analysis, the moral hazard issues of willingness to pay are better treated by focusing upon appropriate adjustment policies that would diminish transfer constraints rather than by augmenting penalties and lender toughness. Better internal policies can make greater debt service feasible in the same way that improved external conditions do. The task is how to design proper incentives to implement them so that the burdens of adjustment are more equitably shared.

4 INCREASED CAPITAL FLOWS VERSUS DEBT RELIEF

The analytic debate between willingness and ability to pay takes second place in the policy arena to discussions about the form and extent that intervention should take. From the beginning, there has been a strong presumption in the creditor countries that debtors faced an adverse situation, not only as a result of external shocks, but also of poor policy, and that domestic adjustment could and should be the major form of compensation. Additional lending was as small, delayed and fraught with large conditionality upon domestic policies. There was also an emphasis upon meeting interest obligations in order to avoid the possibility of bank failure. Hence the far-reaching decline in imports of debtor countries in 1982–83. Slower growth was the principal instrument assuring balance of payments equilibrium.

Faith in an OECD-led solution to the debt problem through buoyant exports and return to normal capital flows has progressively faded, however, since the end of 1984, when *World Financial Markets* (1984, p. 1) spoke of 'lasting resolution of the LDC debt problem'. That year, when US import volume increased at an extraordinary rate of 24 per cent, was the exception, not the norm. Continuing poor performance and imbalance among the industrialised countries has slowed world trade growth. At the same time, developing country export prices have shown their largest decline in the post-war period, unmitigated by dollar devaluation as had been predicted.

Under the impulse of inadequate debtor country performance, policy has become more active and explicit in its recognition of the need to mobilise resources collectively. The *quid pro quo* is the conditionality upon debtor country policies to use new resources effectively. This combination is at the core of the first Baker Plan announced at the Fund-Bank meeting in Seoul in 1985, and it is extended by the second one unveiled at the Washington meeting in 1987.

The Baker approach is squarely in the camp of using limited additions of further debt to provide the resources with which to service existing debt while leaving a margin for larger imports and hence economic expansion. Its most recent version, provoked by the failure of commercial bank lending to respond to the first initiative, adds two new features. First, the call for a large increase in the capital of the World Bank recognises the primary role of official finance in providing new resources compared to original expectations of a major role for commercial bank new credits. Secondly, support for an interest rate facility at the IMF to reduce country exposure to rising interest rates recognises the undesirable vulnerability to debtors to such exogenous financial market effects.

The key to the viability of increasing debt as a solution to the debt problem depends critically on the interrelationship between the rate of growth of exports and the interest rate. Debt dynamics dictates that an interest rate in excess of the export growth rate, as has been true for Latin America since 1982, can be made compatible with a stable debt-export ratio only by the device of continuing export surpluses. There is no long-run equilibrium permissive of net resource inflows consistent with this disparity. The fall in nominal interest rates since their peak in the early 1980s conceals their continuing high real level in comparison with historical levels as well as export growth potential. An interest rate facility that caps potential increases is therefore indispensable to the success of the strategy. But it will be effective provided only that the initial level of the rate is itself compatible.

The provision of adequate net flows is an equally central part of the equation in reducing current levels of outward resource transfer. A larger role for the World Bank is welcome, but by itself inadequate to provide the levels needed by debtor countries, both to service past debt and to resume adequate levels of economic growth. Original Baker plan estimates fell short by $10–15 billion a year of requirements for the principal debtors.[10] In the new version, such quantitative estimates are missing altogether. In their place is an appeal to commercial banks to offer a menu of options.

Commercial bank decisions thus remain vital. They are central to the outcome because of the size of the bank debt overhang in the principal debtors. They must either lend, reliably, or find ways to offer relief to curtail debt service. Bank thinking has slowly moved toward the latter alternative. The dramatic decision by Citibank in May 1987 to increase loan loss provisions, followed by other major banks, represents a new phase in dealing with the problem. Private lenders have taken the initiative in recognising that full debt service will not be sustained. Until the losses on profit and loss statements are converted to balance sheet write-downs, however, there is no change in the debtor country position.

The next logical step has now occurred with the Treasury-Morgan

Guaranty plan to exchange new bonds for current Mexican loans valued at a significant discount. Market judgements have jumped ahead of policy. If the debt as constituted cannot be paid, there is some smaller debt that can be. Discounts may now in fact be too great, having fallen rapidly throughout 1987, by their failure to record the benefits that can be anticipated from a reduction in debt service. Markets have led, but not necessarily perfectly.

This opportunity offers considerable advantages compared with the debt-equity option that had previously figured so prominently. In essence an exchange represents two interlinked transactions. Debt is initially acquired with hard currency from an intermediary and later sold, at a more favourable exchange rate, for domestic currency. The principal limitations are correspondingly twofold. Foreign exchange additionality is restricted by diversion to the subsidised rate, and the issuance of currency must correspond to a real resource transfer to redeem the external debt before its maturity. If the public sector already cannot satisfy its needs, and if domestic saving cannot be increased, the needed internal transfer will be frustrated and inflation will result. Since the benefit in reduced annual debt service is relatively small because of the need to redeem principal, the arrangement is not very useful in relaxing the foreign exchange constraint. If only current interest flows were redeemed in this fashion, the advantages for debtor countries would be greater. Then debt for equity swaps become akin to automatic interest capitalisation with a conversion option to domestic currency.

Real debt relief reduces rather than simply postpones debt service. When the debt is too large relative to domestic ability to pay, it is the only solution. Banks now have begun to despair of the false optimism that has characterised treatment of the problem up to now. A solution to the debt problem via increases in debt required a much bolder willingness to lend, both on their part as well as from official sources. 'Involuntary lending' could secure co-ordination only for limited sums that were inadequate to finance the needed adjustment. In preference to any change, banks now prefer explicitly to accept lower payments and revalue their assets. That reality was in fact registered earlier in market valuation of bank equity, and was one of the considerations contributing to the new willingness to move on.[11] But smaller outflows will now leave countries with resources to be applied internally and will yield gains in lesser involuntary lending in the future and more secure prospects for remaining loans.

The potential losses to banks from their misassessment of debtor country prospects are offset by two sources. One is the revenue from continuous payment of a risk premium by debtor countries; the other is tax reductions corresponding to realised write-downs (and even loan loss reserves in many countries other than the United States). A crude calculation can provide some orders of magnitude, at least for the first of these factors. The present value of a constant premium of 1 per cent paid by Latin American countries since 1973 comes to approximately $14 billion in 1986 dollars; that equates to a write-down of about 13 per cent that countries have already purchased. Adding in tax benefits at a rate of 30 per cent would mean that a write-down of 25 per cent of the Latin American debt would leave banks only 10 per cent poorer relative to never having lent to these countries at all.[12] So it is not a fatal blow, the more so since banks have restored their capital base in recent years. None the less, the timing of allocating the losses can make a difference to their financial strength.

The Mexican exchange plan, while a significant step in the direction of debt relief, suffers from four limitations. For one it is not readily generalisable because of its basis in the purchase of United States coupon bonds with Mexican reserves; not all debtors are blessed with similar resources. Secondly, because the arrangement is bilateral, it fails to tap the available resources of the major surplus countries, Japan and Germany, whose support could and should be mobilised. Thirdly, because principal alone is guaranteed, the substitute Mexican bonds will likely trade at a substantial discount since country risk for continuous service of interest will remain. That diminishes the attractiveness of the exchange and limits the effective relief that will be provided. Fourthly, the relief is detached from a comprehensive strategy of domestic adjustment and future financial requirements; the latter are left to the still non-existent market.

One can do better. An opportunity for more efficient mediation exists that can provide greater relief for equivalent bank loss. Instead of selling debts to intermediaries at an excess discount for cash in the secondary market, or exchanging their loans for still uncertain bonds *à la* the Mexican plan, banks could receive a more secure asset in exchange. This arrangement would leave them in a preferred position, while allowing debtor countries the full advantage of the discount. Sale in the secondary market does not translate into equivalence relief, because the discount is shared under debt-equity arrangements, and exchange of a somewhat less risky security means a continuing high yield, i.e., less reduction in debt service.

Figure 1.1 illustrates this point. Banks are indifferent between holding more secure and lower yielding assets and less secure and higher yielding

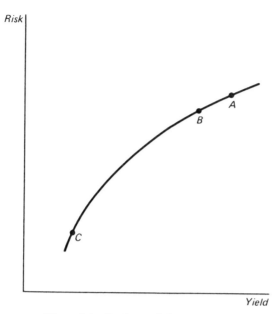

Figure 1.1   Bank portfolio preferences

ones. Their current situation is at point *A*; developing country loans now yield upwards of 15 per cent. An exchange to guaranteed principal alone would move down along the indifference curve only slightly, to point *B*, say. Debt service could not be much reduced, at least on a voluntary basis. Sale for cash provides a certain alternative, but countries do not have the cash; the intermediary that does, thereby, receives much of the gain rather than the country.

Such a situation provides an obvious opportunity for the World Bank, whose initial rationale was precisely the capacity to raise resources more cheaply from capital markets than could individual countries. An exchange of World Bank bonds for developing country loans would mean a move to point *C*, where countries' payments to cover them would be significantly lower, while leaving banks indifferent. Not all debt would have to be transferred, allowing capital gains on the part retained if relief produces sounder development prospects as it should. Nor should the market price necessarily rule in determining the extent of debt relief; that creates obvious moral hazards, giving countries incentives not to pay in order to drive down the value of the debt. The price could be tuned to an analytic assessment of what countries could afford to pay, and banks could register the losses on their balance sheets gradually over time.

Relief organised under World Bank auspices could attract the participation of all of the industrialised countries in creating a fund to guarantee the special issue of bonds exchanged. Only a small proportion of cash would have to be paid in, thereby leveraging direct appropriations considerably. With backing of $10 billion in contributions, $100 billion of bonds could be issued; at prices of 50 per cent, the face value of the debt purchased would amount to $200 billion.

The World Bank is in a unique position as well to support the continuing adjustment efforts countries will have to make, and to co-ordinate the continuing flows of capital that will be required. Debtors will not only have to reduce their current levels of resource transfer, but also return to a situation of net receipts in order to attain needed levels of investment and growth. Present conditionality is flawed by its short-term focus and its preoccupation with return to full service. Adjustment organised under an umbrella of debt relief need not be so obtrusive or uniform. Like historical precedent, there is some price to be paid to creditors for relief in order to guarantee better future performance. Unlike the past, it should not be interventionist and unilateral.

5 CONCLUSION

The contemporary debt problem has been a fertile source of inspiration for economic analysis and review of historical experience. We clearly understand many of the issues of sovereign debt better than we had earlier. It is time for that comprehension to spill over into more appropriate and enduring solutions that recognise the special character of present capital markets and of developing countries. In the end, the developing country debt problem is a development, and not a finance, problem.

Notes

1. See Eaton *et al.* (1986, pp. 481–513) for a useful survey and references.
2. Smith and Cuddington (1985, part IV) is a useful starting point. Other analyses can be found in the WIDER project directed by Lance Taylor and the NBER project directed by Jeffrey Sachs.
3. See Fishlow (1985); Lindert and Morton (1985); and Eichengreen (1987).
4. These data derive from World Bank (1985) and IMF (1987).

5. I draw here and elsewhere on Table 1.1 and other data presented in Fishlow (1985).
6. The deflation of the stock rather than flows is inadequate, not to mention problems of exchange rate revaluation and choice of an appropriate deflator. None the less, the comparative orders of magnitude between present and past should be robust to modifications.
7. For more elaboration of the distinction between development and revenue defaults and discussion of individual cases, see Fishlow (1985, pp. 402 ff). Lindert and Morton (1987) provide evidence of negative returns.
8. The most extensive empirical analysis in McFadden *et al.* (1985). It does not relate its findings to alternative behavioural hypotheses of developing countries. Kaletsky (1985) argues that penalties are small. In conjunction with the large resource outflows, that would suggest the willingness to pay approach is deficient. One cannot simply tautologically infer that penalties must be large by the absence of default.
9. For discussion of the instability question, see Morley and Fishlow (1987).
10. For a quantitative analysis of the adequacy of capital flows under the Baker Plan, and capital requirements more generally, see Fishlow (1987).
11. For evidence on revaluation of bank stocks see Kyle and Sachs (1984), and Ozler (1986).
12. I have converted the risk premium to a post-tax basis for the purpose of the comparison. Needless to iterate, the computation is intended only to provide some quantitive sense of the losses involved rather than a precise estimate.

References

Eaton, J., Gersovitz, M. and Stiglitz, J. (1986) 'The Pure Theory of Country Risk', *European Economic Review*, vol. 30.

Edelstein, M. (1976) 'Realized Rates of Return on UK Home and Overseas Portfolio Investment in the Age of High Imperialism', *Explorations in Economic History*, vol. 13.

Eichengreen, B. (1987) 'Till Debt do us Part', July, Paper for NBER Conference on Developing Country Debt, September (New York: NBER).

Fishlow, A. (1985) 'Lessons from the Past: Capital Markets during the Nineteenth Century and the Interwar Period', *International Organisation*, Summer, pp. 383–439.

Fishlow, A. (1987) 'Financial Requirements for Developing Countries in the Next Decade', *Journal of Development Planning*, no. 17.

IMF (1986) *International Capital Markets*, December (Washington: IMF).

IMF (1987) *World Economic Outlook 1987* (Washington: IMF).

Kaletsky, A. (1985) *The Costs of Default* (New York: Twentieth Century Fund).

Kohler, D. (1986) 'To Pay or not to Pay; A Model of International Defaults', *Journal of Policy Analysis and Management*, vol. 5.

Kyle, S. and Sachs, J. (1984) 'Developing Country Debt and the Market Value of Large Commercial Banks (New York: NBER) Working Paper no. 1470, September.

Lindert, P. and Morton, P. (1987) 'How Sovereign Debt has worked',

U. C. Davis Research in Applied Macroeconomics and Macro Policy Paper no. 45.

McFadden, D. *et al.* (1985) 'Is there Life after Debt?' in Smith, G. and Cuddington, J. (1985) *International Debt and the Developing Countries* (Washington: World Bank).

Morley, S. and Fishlow, A. (1987) 'Deficits, Debt and Destabilisation', *Journal of Development Economics*, vol. 27.

Ozler, S. (1986) 'The Motives for International Bank Debt Rescheduling 1978–83: Theory and Evidence, UCLA Department of Economics Working Paper no. 401.

Smith, G. and Cuddington, J. (1985) *International Debt and the Developing Countries* (Washington: World Bank).

World Bank (1985) *World Development Report* (Washington: World Bank and Oxford University Press).

World Financial Markets (1984) October–November, p. 1.

Reactions of Debtor Countries

From the first Mexican negotiations in 1982, debtor governments have sought to emphasize two externalities inherent in the debt problem. One is the mutual disadvantage of their adjustment via recession and decline in imports, which only reduces markets for exports and slows industrial country growth. The force of this argument was particularly addressed to the United States inasmuch as the principal Latin American debtors were more closely tied to American producers. The other is the political content of the outcome; for many countries, recent transitions to civilian government were in the balance. Neither was properly reckoned in the negotiations with private banks, whose concerns for the future would be exclusively filtered through their own profit maximizing objective.

Despite efforts to elevate the problem to a government to government level, there was only partial and temporary success in the elaboration, but non-implementation, of the Baker Plan. Latin American countries have organized themselves into the Cartagena Group, and most recently at the end of 1988, into a new Rio Group. The declarations of the debtors have chronicled the evolution of the problem: from a concern with adequate liquidity to demands for coordinated efforts to reduce the debt overhang. Despite the implicit threat of a more coordinated response of debtors -formation of a debtors' cartel- cooperation has been rhetorical rather than practical. Brazil stood alone in declaring its unsuccessful moratorium, and other countries in their turn have apparently been rebuffed when they were considering non-compliance.

Successful joint debtor action does not appear to be realistic. In contrast to the bank steering committees, which have been organized under the auspices of the IMF and enforced by the industrial country central banks, there is no comparable natural enforcement mechanism among the debtors. One needs such a device because lenders can make it worthwhile for individual debtors to defect.

This does not make debtor pressure irrelevant. More favorable individual treatment has shown a tendency to become generalized during the sequence of negotiations. Spreads **have** diminished, fees and commisssions have been discarded and **grace** and maturity periods extended. The threat of concerted **action,** even if not a formal cartel, thus has had palpable impact.

The changing political mood in the debtor countries promises to have an even greater effect. National elections in Mexico and local polls in Brazil have evoked strong popular support for more nationalist and independent stands on the debt issue. So do prospective results in Argentina and Peru. The message is clear and undiluted: there is need to resume domestic growth rather than give priority to making space in the external accounts for debt **service.** **Private** creditors ignore this trend at their peril, **for** it diminishes even further the probability of full repayment. Market prices for debt reflect pessimism: even for Brazil, with a record trade surplus and a just concluded resched-uling, prices have fallen.

6. Conclusion

The contemporary debt problem has been a fertile source of

inspiration for economic analysis and review of historical experience. We clearly understand many of the issues of sovereign debt better than we had earlier.

The issue now is whether that comprehension will spill over into more appropriate and enduring solutions that recognize the special character of present capital markets and of developing countries. There has been movement. Debt relief is no longer a taboo discussion. Some banks have even written their portfolios down voluntarily and have argued in favor of an international facility to purchase loans at a discount. The Japanese government has shown increasing interest in a similar approach. The key actor, and question mark, remains the United States.

Coincidence of new Mexican and United States administrations will go far to define an answer. Just as the debt problem initially took on its form in fashioning a response to the Mexican situation, the current Mexican crisis promises to move the discussion to a new stage. There is in place a Mexican government committed to liberalization and a role for market forces; but after unprecedented declines in real wages and reduced economic activity, that government must show immediate results. It can only do so if there is a new priority for domestic performance. External transfers, not economic growth, must become the residual.

That principle is consistent with the initial vision of the Baker Plan. Now as Secretary of State in the Bush Administration rather than of Treasury, Mr. Baker may take the additional step of enforcing implementation. The responsibilities of designing

foreign policy afford a different perspective. Reliance upon the
private market has not been enough.   Banks did not come forward
to lend in the anticipated quantities, themselves inadequate, and
subsequent secondary market transactions in debt have not provided significant alleviation.

     The pieces in the puzzle are now all there.   The essential
step is to recognize that the developing country debt problem is
a development, and not a finance, problem.

Part IX

International Payments

Meade
Johnson
Cooper
Dornbusch
Frankel
Giovannini
Rogoff
Artus and Crockett
International Monetary Fund

THE MEANING OF "INTERNAL BALANCE"*

JAMES MEADE

I

It is a special privilege for me on this occasion to have my name associated with that of Professor Bertil Ohlin. By the younger generation of economists we are no doubt both regarded as what in my country and now in his own are now termed senior citizens; but I am just that much younger than Professor Ohlin to have regarded him as one of the already established figures when I was first trying to understand international economics. His great work (Ohlin, 1933) on *International and Inter-regional Trade* opened up new insights into the complex of relationships between factor supplies, costs of movement of products and factors, price relationships, and the actual international trade in products, migration of persons, and flows of capital. Of the two volumes which I later wrote on International Economic Policy – namely, *The Balance of Payments* and *Trade and Welfare* – (Meade, 1951, 1955) – it is in the latter that the influence of this work by Professor Ohlin is most clearly marked.

Professor Ohlin also made an important contribution to what now might be called the macro-economic aspects of a country's balance of payments. In 1929 in the ECONOMIC JOURNAL he engaged in a famous controversy with Keynes on the problem of transferring payments from one country to another across the foreign exchanges. In this he laid stress upon the income–expenditure effects of the reduced spending power in the paying country and of the increased spending power in the recipient country. In doing so he made use of the usual distinction between a country's imports and exports; but in addition he emphasised the importance of the less usual distinction between a country's domestic non-tradeable goods and services and its tradeable, exportable and importable, goods. I made some use of this latter distinction in my *Balance of Payments*; but looking back I regret that I did not let it play a much more central role in that book.

II

Indeed I realise now, looking back with the advantage of hindsight, that my two books were deficient in many respects. From this rich field of deficiencies I have selected one as the subject for today's lecture, because it raises an issue which in my opinion is at the present time perhaps the most pressing of all for the maintenance of a decent international economic order.

The basic analysis in *The Balance of Payments* was conducted in terms of static

Reprinted with permission from *The Economic Journal* **88**, 423–435,
Copyright by The Nobel Foundation, 1977.

equilibrium models rather than in terms of dynamic growing or disequilibrium models. The use of this method of comparative statics was a result of Keynes's work.

Keynes (1936) in *The General Theory* applied Marshall's short-period analysis to the whole macro-economic system instead of to one single firm or industry. In this model additions to capital stocks are taking place; but we deal with a period of time over which the addition to the stock bears a negligible ratio to the total existing stock. Variable factors, and in particular labour, are applied to this stock with a rising marginal cost until marginal cost is equal to selling price – an assumption which can be modified to accommodate micro-economic theories about determinants of output and prices in conditions of imperfect competition. The rest of the Keynesian analysis with its consumption function, liquidity preference, and investment function can be used to determine the short-period, static, stable equilibrium levels of total national income, output, employment, interest, and so on, in terms of such parameters as the money wage rate, the supply of money, entrepreneurs' expectations, rates of tax, levels of government expenditure, and the foreign demand for the country's exports. The model can then be used to show how changes in these parameters would affect the short-period equilibrium levels of the various macro-economic variables. Keynes was not, I think, interested in the process of change from one short-period equilibrium to another, though he was very interested in the way in which expectations in a milieu of uncertainty would affect the short-period equilibrium, in particular through their effect upon investment. If my interpretation is correct, he judged intuitively that the short-period mechanisms of adjustment were in fact such that at any one time the macro-elements of the system would not be far different from their short-period equilibrium values; and he may well have been correct in this judgement in the 1930s.

The Balance of Payments was essentially based on macro-economic models of this kind. What I tried to elaborate was the international interplay between a number of national economies of this Keynesian type. For this purpose I discussed the different combinations of policy variables which would serve to reconcile what I called "external balance" with what I called "internal balance". By "external balance" was meant a balance in the country's international payments; and although this idea presents, and indeed at the time was realised to present, considerable conceptual difficulties, nevertheless I still instinctively feel that it is not a foolish one. But can the same be said of the idea of "internal balance"? Does it mean full employment or does it mean price stability?

I don't believe that I was quite so stupid as not to realise that full employment and price stability are two quite different things. But one treated them under the same single umbrella of "internal balance" because of a belief or an assumption that if one maintained a level of effective demand which preserved full employment one would also find that the money price level was reasonably stable. The reason for making this tacit or open assumption was, of course, due to a tacit or open assumption that the money wage rate was normally either constant or at least very sluggish in its movements. In this case with the Keynesian model the absolute level of money prices would be rather higher or lower according as the level of effective demand moved the economy to a higher or lower point on the upward-sloping short-period marginal cost curve. But there would be no reason to expect a rapidly rising or falling general level of money prices in any given short-period equilibrium position.

This may have been a very sensible assumption to make in the 1930s. It is more doubtful whether it was a sensible assumption to make in the immediate post-war years when *The Balance of Payments* was being written. In any case if I were now rewriting that book I would do the underlying analysis not in terms of the reconciliation of the two objectives of external balance and internal balance, but in terms of the reconciliation of the three objectives of equilibrium in the balance of payments, full employment, and price stability.

Why did I not proceed in this way in the first place?

I was certainly aware of the danger that trade union and other wage-fixing institutions might not permit the maintenance of full employment without a money cost-price inflation. But I suppose that writing immediately after the war I adopted the basic model which was so useful before the war and simply hoped that somehow or another it would be possible to avoid full employment leading to a wage-price inflation. Having done so I found that there remained quite enough important international relationships to examine even on that simplifying assumption. That is not perhaps a very strong defence of my position, but I suspect that it is the truth of the matter.

I am well aware that I could now adopt a more sophisticated line of defence of my past behaviour. It is quite possible to define as the natural level of employment, that level which – given the existing relevant institutions affecting wage-fixing arrangements – would lead to a demand for real wage rates rising at a rate equal to the rate of increase of labour productivity. One has only to add to this the assumption that one starts from a position in which there is no general expectation of future inflation or deflation of money prices to reach the position in which the maintenance of this natural level of employment is compatible with price stability. If this natural level of employment is treated as "full employment" one has succeeded in defining a situation of "internal balance" in which "full employment" and "price stability" can be simultaneously achieved.

One could then go on to discuss the many institutions which affect this so-called full employment level. Decent support of the living standards of those who are out of work may mean that unemployed persons are legitimately rather more choosey about the first alternative job which is offered to them, quite apart from the existence of a limited number of confirmed "sturdy beggars" who prefer living on social benefits to an honest day's work. The obligation to make compulsory severance or redundancy payments when employees are dismissed may make some employers less willing to expand their labour force in conditions in which future developments are uncertain. Monopolistic trade union action may put an extra upward pressure on money wage demands which means that unemployment must be maintained at a higher level in order to exert an equivalent countervailing downward pressure. Some statutory wage-fixing bodies in particular occupations may exert a similar influence.

It is not very helpful to squabble about definitions. There is, however, a very real difference of substance between those who do, and those who do not, consider these labour market institutions to cause very real difficulties. Is it necessary to achieve some radical reform of these institutions in order to make reasonable price stability compatible with reasonably low levels of unemployment? Or is it a fact that, if affairs could for a time be so conducted as to remove the expectation of any marked future inflation of the money cost of living, we would find that even with present institutions the natural level of unemployment would not be at all excessive? I myself would expect that in many countries including the United Kingdom the recasting of labour market institutions would still be found to be of crucial importance.

As far as the less important question of definition is concerned, I prefer to think of "full employment" and "price stability" as being two separate and often conflicting objectives of macro-economic policies. Anyone who has this preference can, of course, be legitimately challenged to define what is meant by full employment. Perhaps I would be driven to the extreme of defining full employment as that level of employment at which the supply-demand conditions would not lead to attempts to push up the real wage rate more rapidly than the rate of increase in labour productivity if there were perfect competition in the labour market – no monopsonistic employers, no monopolistic trade unions, no social benefits to the unemployed, no obligations on employers to make compulsory severance or redundancy payments to dismissed workers, and so on – though I am not at all sure whether this extreme form of definition has much meaning. However, in so far as full employment could be defined somewhere along these lines, one would end up with price stability and full employment as separate macro-economic objectives in any real world situation with labour market institutions as one of the instruments of policy. This is the way in which I like to think of macro-economic problems.

If one adopted this approach, how should *The Balance of Payments* be recast? In the basic model we would have the three targets of external balance, full employment, and price stability. If one continued to think in terms of matching to each "target" a relevant policy "weapon", one could divide the weapons into three main armouries: the first containing the weapons which directly affect the level of money demands (e.g. monetary and budgetary policies); the second containing the weapons which directly affect the fixing of money wage rates; and the third containing the weapons which directly affect the foreign exchanges, such as the fixing of rates of exchange, measures of exchange control, and commerical policy measures designed directly to affect the total value of imports and exports.

My subsequent education in the rudiments of the theory of the control of dynamic systems suggested to me that this was not the best way to have proceeded. One should not pair each particular weapon off with a particular target as its partner, using weapon A to hit target A, weapon B to hit target B, and so on. Rather one should seek to discover what pattern of combination of simultaneous use of all available weapons would produce the most preferred pattern of combination of simultaneous hits on all the desirable targets. With this way of looking at things no particular weapon is concentrated on any particular target; it is the joint effect of all the weapons on all the targets which is relevant.

There is no doubt that this is the way in which a control engineer will look at the problem and that in a technical sense it is the correct way to find the most preferred pattern of hits on a number of targets simultaneously. For a considerable period between the writing of *The Balance of Payments* and the present time I was fully enamoured of this method.

I am now, however, in the process of having second thoughts and of asking myself whether the idea of trying to hit each particular target by use of a particular weapon or clearly defined single armoury of weapons is really to be ruled out. This onset of second childhood is due to a consideration of the political conditions in which economic policies must be operated. It is most desirable in a modern democratic community that the ordinary man or woman in the streets should as far as possible realise what is going on, with responsibilities for success or failure in the different fields of endeavour being dispersed but clearly defined and allocated. To treat the whole of macro-economic control as a single subject for the mysterious art of the control engineer is likely to appear at the best magical and at the worst totally arbitrary and unacceptable to the ordinary citizen. To put each clearly defined weapon or armoury of weapons in the charge of one particular authority or set of decision makers with the responsibility of hitting as nearly as possible one well defined target is a much more intelligible arrangement.

Of course there are obvious disadvantages in any such proposal. Thus the best way for authority A to use weapon A to achieve objective A will undoubtedly be affected by what authorities B and C are doing with weapons B and C. It depends upon the structure of relationships within the economic system how far these repercussions are of major importance. Perhaps a mysterious dynamic model operated inconspicuously in some back room by control experts for silent information of the authorities concerned might be useful; and in any case in the real world it would be desirable for the different authorities at least to communicate their plans to each other so that, by what one hopes would be a convergent process of mutual accommodation, some account could be taken of their interaction. But in the modern community there is, I think, merit in arrangements in which each authority or set of decision makers has a clear ultimate responsibility for success or failure in the attainment of a clearly defined objective.

III

There are six ways in which each of three weapons can be separately aimed at each of three targets. Some of these patterns make more sense than others. In this lecture I can do no more than give a brief account of that particular pattern which, as it seems to me at present, would make the best sense if one takes into account both economic effectiveness and also comprehensibility of responsibilities in a free democratic society.

With this pattern:

(1) the instruments of demand management, fiscal and monetary, would be

used so to control total money expenditures as to prevent excessive inflations or deflations of total money incomes;

(2) wage-fixing institutions would be modelled so as to restrain upward movements of money wage rates in those particular sectors where there were no shortages of manpower and to allow upward movements where these were needed to attract or retain labour to meet actual or expected manpower shortages. This should result in the preservation of full employment with some moderate average rise in money wage rates in conditions in which demand management policies were ensuring a steadily growing money demand for labour as a whole; and

(3) foreign exchange policies would be used to keep the balance of payments in equilibrium.

This pattern implies the use of the weapons of demand management to restrain *monetary* inflation and of wage-fixing to influence the *real* level of employment and output. Many of my friends and colleagues who share my admiration for Keynes will at this point part company from me. "Surely", they will say, "you have got it the wrong way round. Did not Keynes suggest that the control of demand should be used to influence the total amount of real output and employment which it was profitable to maintain, while the money wage rate was left simply to determine the absolute level of money prices and costs at which this level of real activity would take place?" I agree that this is in fact the way in which Keynes looked at things in the late 1930s when it could be assumed that the money wage rate was in any case constant or rather sluggish in its movements. What he would be saying today is anybody's guess; and I do not propose to take part in that guessing game except to say that he would be appalled at the current rates of price inflation. It is a complete misrepresentation of the views of a great and wise man to suggest that in present conditions he would have been concerned only with the maintenance of full employment, and not at all with the avoidance of money price and wage inflation.

Whatever Keynes's policy recommendations would be in present circumstances, I would maintain that the way in which I have distributed the weapons among the targets is in no way incompatible with Keynes's analysis. In the 1930s Keynes argued, rightly or wrongly, that cutting money wage rates would have little effect in expanding employment because its main effect would be simply to reduce the absolute level of the relevant money prices, money costs, money incomes, and money expenditures, leaving the levels of real output and employment much unchanged. It is a totally different matter, wholly consistent with that Keynesian analysis, to suggest that the money wage rate might be used to influence the level of employment in conditions in which the money demand was being successfully managed in such a way as to prevent changes in wage rates from causing any offsetting rise or fall in total money incomes and expenditures. If one is going to aim particular weapons at particular targets in the interests of democratic understanding and responsibility, it is, in my opinion, most appropriate that the Central Bank which creates money and the Treasury which pours it out should be responsible for preventing monetary inflations and deflations, while those who fix the wage rates in various sectors of the economy should take responsibility for the effect of their action on the resulting levels of employment.

Earlier I spoke of "price stability" as being one of the components of "internal balance". Yet in the outline which I have just given of a possible distribution of responsibilities no one is directly responsible for price stability. To make price stability itself the objective of demand management would be very dangerous. If there were an upward pressure on prices because the prices of imports had risen or indirect taxes had been raised, the maintenance of price stability would require an offsetting absolute reduction in domestic money wage costs; and who knows what levels of depression and unemployment it might be necessary consciously to engineer in order to achieve such a result? This particular danger might be avoided by choice of a price index for stabilisation which excluded both indirect taxes and the price of imports; but even so, the stabilisation of such a price index would be very dangerous. If any remodelled wage-fixing arrangements were not working perfectly – and it would be foolhardy to assume a perfect performance – a very moderate excessive upward pressure on money wage rates and so on costs might cause a very great reduction in output and employment if there were no rise in selling prices so that the whole of the impact of the increased money costs was taken on profit margins. If, however, it was total money incomes which were stabilised, a much more moderate decline in employment combined with a moderate rise in prices would serve to maintain the uninflated total of money incomes.

The effectiveness of the pattern of responsibilities which I have outlined rests upon the assumption that there is a reasonably high elasticity of demand for labour in terms of the real wage rate, since success is to be achieved by setting a money wage rate relatively to money demand prices which gives a full employment demand for labour by employers. I have no doubt myself that in the longer-run the elasticity of demand is great enough. But what of the short-run? What if in every industry there is a stock of fixed capital in a form which sets an absolute limit to the amount of labour which can be usefully employed, while, for some reason or another of past history there is more labour seeking work than can be usefully employed? There will be unemployment in every industry; and any resulting reduction in money wage rates combined with the maintenance of total money incomes would merely redistribute income from wages to profits.

I have explained the danger in its most exaggerated form; but it would remain a real one even in a much moderated form. There should, of course, never be any question of the wholesale immediate slashing of wage rates in every sector in which there was any unemployment. Any such arrangement would, for the reasons which I have outlined, be economically most undesirable even if it were politically possible. What one has in mind is simply that in a milieu in which total money incomes are steadily rising at a moderate rate, money wage rates should be rising rather more rapidly in some sectors and less rapidly or not at all in other sectors according to the supplies of available labour and the prospects of future demands for labour in those sectors. There would be no requirement that any money wage rates must be actually reduced.

Putting more emphasis on supply-demand conditions in the settlement of particular wage claims could only work if there were general acceptance of the idea by the ordinary citizen; and such acceptance would depend *inter alia* upon a marked change of emphasis about policies for influencing the redistribution of the national income. I have for long believed that it is only if, somehow or another, the ordinary citizen can be persuaded to put less emphasis on wage bargaining and more emphasis on fiscal policies of taxation and social security for influencing the personal distribution of income and wealth that we have any hope of building the sort of free, efficient, and humanely just society in which I would like to live. But that raises a host of issues which I cannot discuss today.

There is, however, one feature of this connection between the supply–demand criterion for fixing wage rates and the attitude of the wage earner to his real standard of living on which I do wish to comment. Suppose, for example because of a rise in the world price of oil or of other imported foodstuffs or raw materials, that the international terms of trade turn against an industrialised country. This is equivalent to a reduction in the productivity of labour and of other factors employed in the country in question. If money wage rates are pushed up as the prices of imported goods go up in order to preserve the real purchasing power of wage incomes, money wage costs are raised for the domestic producer without any automatic rise in the selling price of the domestic components of their outputs. Profit margins are squeezed. The demand for labour will fall unless and until profit margins are restored by a corresponding rise in the selling prices of domestic products. But such a rise would in turn cause a further rise in the cost of living, followed perhaps by a further offsetting rise in money wage rates, with a further round of pressure on profit margins. In fact workers are attempting to establish a real wage rate which, because of the adverse effect of the terms of international trade, is no longer compatible with full employment. The resulting rounds of pressure on profit margins, rises in domestic selling prices, further rises in money wage rates, further pressure on profit margins, and so on, may result in stagflation – a level of employment below full employment with a continuing inflation of money prices.

This story may in fact help to explain what has happened recently in some industrialised countries, but my purpose in telling it is merely to give a vivid illustration of the fact that an effective combination of full employment with the avoidance of inflation necessarily requires that wage-fixing should take as its main criterion the supply–demand conditions in the labour market without undue insistence on the attainment and defence of any particular real wage income. The latter must be the combined result of domestic productivity, the terms of international trade, and tax and other measures taken to affect the distribution of income between net-of-tax spendable wages and other net-of-tax incomes.

IV

So much for the specification of targets and for the distribution of weapons among targets, we must now ask "What about the detailed specification of the weapons themselves?"

If the velocity of circulation of money were constant, a steady rate of growth in the total money demand for goods and services could be achieved by a steady rate of growth in the supply of money, and this in turn could be the task of an independent Central Bank with the express responsibility for ensuring a steady rate of growth of the money supply of, say, 5 % per annum. It is a most attractive and straightforward solution; but, alas, I am still not persuaded to be an out-and-out monetarist of this kind. It is difficult to define precisely what is to be treated as money in a modern economy. At the borderline of the definition substitutes for money can and do readily increase and decrease in amount and within the borders of the definition velocities of circulation can and do change substantially. Can we not use monetary policy more directly for the attainment of the objective of a steady rate of growth of, say, 5 % per annum in total money incomes, and supplement this monetary policy with some form of fiscal regulator in order to achieve a more prompt and effective response? For this purpose one would, of course, be well advised to call in aid the skills of the control engineer, in order to cope with the dynamic problems of keeping the total national money income on its target path. Am I to be regarded as a member of the lunatic fringe or as an unconscious ally of authoritarian tyranny if I express this remaining degree of belief in the possibilities of rational social engineering?

I find very attractive the idea that this monetary control should be the responsibility of some body which was not directly dependent upon the government for its day-to-day decisions but which was charged by its constitution independently to achieve this stable but moderate growth of money incomes. But there is real difficulty in endowing any such independent body with powers to use fiscal policy as well as monetary policy to achieve its objective.

Let me take an example. Suppose that overseas producers of oil raise abruptly the price charged to an importing country; and, to isolate the point which I want to make, suppose further that the oil producers invest in the importing country any excess funds which they receive from the sale of an unchanged supply of oil, so that there is no immediate need to cut imports or to expand exports in order to protect the foreign exchanges. The abrupt price change will, however, tend to cause a deflation of money incomes in the importing country whose citizens will, out of any given income, spend less on home produced goods in order to spend more on imported oil, the receipts from which are saved by the oil producers. With the scheme of responsibilities which I have outlined it is now the duty of the demand managers to reflate the demand for goods and services in the importing country in order to prevent a fall in money incomes in that country.

There are at least two alternative strategies for such reflation.

In the first place, the taxation of the citizens of the importing country might be reduced so that, while they have to spend more on imported oil, they have just so much more spendable income to maintain their demands for their own products. In this case the government directly or indirectly borrows funds saved by the oil producers to finance the larger budget deficit due to the reduced tax payments by the domestic consumers. No one's standard of living is immediately affected.

If this solution is adopted, the importing country faces an ever-growing debt to the foreign oil producers with no corresponding growth of domestic or foreign capital to set against it. If this is considered undesirable, the private citizens must not be relieved of tax; their current consumption standards must be allowed to fall as a result of the rise in the price of oil; and the reflation of domestic income must be brought about by measures which stimulate expenditure on extra real capital development at home, the finance of which will mop up the savings of the oil producers. Such action will depend upon monetary policies rather than, or at least as well as, upon fiscal action.

I have told this particular story simply to make the point that the choice between fiscal action and monetary action must often depend upon basic policy issues which should certainly be the responsibility of the government rather than of any independent monetary authority. Perhaps the best compromise is an independent monetary authority charged so to manage the money supply and the market rate of interest as to maintain the growth of total money income on its 5% per annum target path, after taking into account whatever fiscal policies the government may adopt. One would hope, of course, that there would be a suitable discussion of their plans and policies between the government and the monetary authority; but the latter would be given an ultimately independent duty and independent choice of monetary policy for keeping total money incomes on their target path.

The difficulties involved in the specification of the weapons of demand management are real enough; but they fade into insignificance when they are compared with the problems of remodelling wage-fixing arrangements in such a way as to ensure a greater emphasis on supply–demand conditions in each sector of the labour market.

I can think of five broad lines of approach.

First, one can conceive of wage fixing in each sector of the labour market by the edict of some government authority. An efficient use of this method would be extremely difficult in a modern economy with its innumerable different forms and skills of labour in so many different and diverse regions, occupations, and industries. It would, I think, in any case ultimately involve a degree of governmental authoritarian control which I personally would find very distasteful.

Secondly, there is the corporate state solution in which a monopoly of employer monopolies agrees with a monopoly of labour monopolies on a central bargain for the distribution between wages and profits in the various sectors of the economy of the total national money income which the demand managers are going to provide. I suspect that, in the United Kingdom at any rate, any such bargain would be very difficult to attain without leaving some important, but relatively powerless, sectors out in the cold of unemployment or of very low wages. In any case I ought to reveal my prejudice against being ruled by a monopoly of uncontrolled private monopolists.

Thirdly, the restoration of competitive conditions in the labour market would in theory do the trick, since the competitive search for jobs would restrain the wage rate in any sector in which there was unemployed labour and the competitive search for hands by competitive employers would raise the wage rate in any sector in which manpower was scarce. There is little doubt in my own mind that in some cases trade unions have attained an excessively privileged position and that some reduction of their monopoly powers might help towards a solution.

But I do not believe that any full solution is to be found along this competitive road. On the employers' side it may be impossible to ensure effective competition where economies of large scale severely restrict the number of employers. On the employees' side the whole of history suggests the powerful psychological need for workers with common concerns to get together in the formation of associations to represent their common interests. Moreover, reliance on individual competition might well involve the reduction, if not elimination, of support for workers who were unemployed and of compulsory severance or redundancy payments to workers whose jobs disappeared. But what one wants to find is some effective, but compassionate and humane, method which applies supply–demand criteria for the fixing of wage rates for those in employment without inflicting needless hardship and anxiety on those particular individuals who are inevitably adversely affected by economic change.

Fourthly, there are those who see the solution in the labour-managed economy in which workers hire capital rather than capital hiring workers. In such circumstances there would be no wage rate to fix. Workers would share among themselves whatever income they could earn in their concerns after payment of whatever fixed interest or rent was necessary to hire their instruments of production. These ideas are very attractive; but, alas, there is, I think, good reason to believe that satisfactory outcome on these lines is possible only in those sectors of the economy where small scale enterprises are appropriate and where conditions make it fairly easy to set up new competing co-operative concerns.

Finally, there remains the possibility of the replacement in wage bargaining of the untamed use of monopolistic power through the threat of strikes, lock-outs, and similar industrial action by the acceptance of arbitral awards made by trusted and impartial outside tribunals – awards which would, however, have to be heavily weighted by considerations of the supply–demand conditions of each particular case, if they were to achieve what I have suggested should be the basic objective of wage-fixing arrangements.

This is the civilised approach; but I am under no illusion that it is an easy one. It relies upon a widespread acceptance of the idea that some such approach is necessary for everyone's ultimate welfare and, in particular, as I have already indicated, upon the belief that there are alternative fiscal and similar policies to ensure social justice in the ultimate distribution of income and wealth. But even if in the course of time such a general acceptance could be achieved, some form of sanction for its application in some particular cases would almost certainly be needed. The punishment of individuals as criminals for taking monopolistic action to disturb a wage award does not hold out much hope of success, but is it pure dreaming to conceive ultimately of a state of affairs in which (1) in the case of any dispute about wages either party to the dispute or the government itself could apply for an award of the kind which I have indicated and (2) in which certain financial privileges and legal immunities otherwise enjoyed by the parties to a trade dispute would not be available in the case of industrial action taken in defiance of such an award?

Perhaps this is merely an optimist's utopian fantasy; but I can think of nothing better.

V

So much for the attainment of price stability and full employment through the instrumentalities of demand management and wage-fixing, we must now ask "What about the attainment of external balance through foreign exchange policies?"

In my view the appropriate division of powers and obligations between national governments and international institutions is that the national governments should be responsible for national monetary, fiscal, and wage policies which combine full employment with price stability and that external balance should be maintained by foreign exchange policies under the supervision of international institutions.

Variations in the rate of exchange between the national currencies combined with freedom of trade and payments should in my view be the normal instrument of such foreign exchange policies, but this is not to say that there will never be occasion for the use of other instruments of foreign exchange policy. Special control arrangements may be appropriate where the removal of an international imbalance requires wholesale industrial development or structural change, or where abrupt changes in the international flow of capital funds require special offsetting measures, or where differences in national tax regimes would distort international transactions in the absence of offsetting measures. But where such exceptions to the free movement of goods and funds arise, these should be under the rules and supervision of appropriate international institutions.

After the war we managed to lay the foundations of an international system of this kind with the pivotal institutions of the International Monetary Fund, the International Bank for Reconstruction and Development, and the General Agreement on Tariffs and Trade, a system which for a quarter of a century resulted in a most remarkable expansion of international trade. In my opinion there was one important original flaw in this system, namely the insistence on the International Monetary Fund's very sticky adjustable peg mechanism for the correction of inappropriate exchange rates. But even this flaw has now gone as the International Monetary Fund seeks to find the most appropriate rules for running a system of international flexible exchange rates.

Yet we seem now to be faced with the possibility of a gigantic tragedy, with this initial success being fated unnecessarily to end in calamity. Why is this so? In my view the answer is obvious; it is simply because so many of the national governments of the developed industrialised countries have failed to find appropriate national institutional ways of combining full employment with price stability.

If they could do so, not only would the domestic tragic waste and social discontent of heavy unemployment in such countries be removed, but the international scene would be transformed. The pressure for the use by developed countries of massive import restrictions rather than of gradual and moderate changes in exchange rates to look after their balances of payments would, I suspect, be very greatly reduced. It is the spectacle of imports competing with the products of domestic industries in which there is already serious unemployment which is the greatest threat to the freedom of imports into the developed countries. With full employment and price stability at home the balance of payments could with much more confidence be left to the mechanism of flexible foreign exchange rates. The developed countries would then have less difficulty in giving financial aid to the third world; and, what in my opinion is even more important, they could much more readily accept the inflow from the third world of their labour-intensive products.

In this lecture I have marked an occasion which is concerned with international economics with a lecture on internal balance. But I suggest that in present conditions this is not anomalous. I do not, I think, exaggerate wildly when I conclude by saying that one – though, of course, only one – of the really important factors on which the health of the world now depends is the recasting of wage-fixing arrangements in a limited number of developed countries.

Little Shelford, Cambridge

Date of receipt of final typescript: February 1978

REFERENCES

Keynes, J. M. (1936). *The General Theory of Employment, Interest and Money*. London: Macmillan.
Meade, J. E. (1951). *The Theory of International Economic Policy*. Vol. I. *The Balance of Payments*. London: Oxford University Press for the Royal Institute of International Affairs.
—— (1955). *The Theory of International Economic Policy*. Vol. II. *Trade and Welfare*. London: Oxford University Press for the Royal Institute of International Affairs.
Ohlin, B. (1933). *International and Interregional Trade*. Harvard University Press.

MONEY, BALANCE OF PAYMENTS THEORY, AND THE INTERNATIONAL MONETARY PROBLEM

Harry G. Johnson

This Essay is adapted with small modifications from the David Horowitz Lectures that I delivered in Israel in 1975. I was honored by and grateful for the invitation to give them. My only previous visit to Israel had been ten years earlier, for a Rehovoth Conference graced by an address by Governor Horowitz himself. At that time, he was extremely active in two major world economic-policy debates—the reform of the international monetary system, which already appeared as a necessary task but one that could be tackled with due deliberation by economic statesmen of good will, and the problem of devising new ways to transfer resources for development to the less developed countries, a problem to which world attention had been dramatically called by the First United Nations Conference on Trade and Development in Geneva in 1964. Governor Horowitz, in common with many other international monetary experts, sought to solve the two problems simultaneously by linking reserve creation in some way to development assistance. That general class of proposals, I must admit, did not appeal to me then and has never appealed to me any more strongly since. After years of learning to appreciate the necessity and the difficulty of distinguishing between monetary and real phenomena, I find intellectually obscurantist any analysis or proposition that unwittingly or willfully confuses the creation of money with the liberation of real resources, however noble the intention. The world inflation of recent years bears ample evidence to the dangers of the politically popular belief that desirable real results can be achieved by manipulations of monetary magnitudes and maneuvers with monetary mystique. Nevertheless, I admired the combination of ingenuity and economic statesmanship that distinguished the contributions of Governor Horowitz to the debate—a combination that is in some ways reminiscent of John Maynard Keynes at his best as a policy advisor.

There is a second reason why I was glad to return to Israel: so many Israeli economists have contributed to the development of the two main fields of economic theory I am interested in, monetary theory and international economic theory. In particular, at the time of my previous visit the second edition of Don Patinkin's *Money, Interest and Prices* (1965) was just about to appear—in fact, he showed me an advance copy. His book had only begun to establish the classic position in monetary theory that it has since come to enjoy, and neither of us, I am sure, had any thought that it would become a major source of ideas and techniques for the analysis of a problem it did not deal with

Reprinted from "Money, Balance of Payments Theory, and the International Monetary Problem—Essays in International Finance No. 124, Nov. 1977," pp. 1–26, with permission of Princeton University Press, Princeton, Copyright 1977.

at all, the theory of the balance of payments and the international monetary system. In brief, as I shall show later, Patinkin's work on the integration of money and value theory through the real balance effect, and on the interaction of stock and flow adjustments on the establishment and the stability requirements of full economic equilibrium, provided the key to understanding classical income-expenditure, monetary balance-of-payments theory. That key was necessary for an effective return from the post-Keynesian tradition to the classical tradition of analysis of international disequilibrium problems as monetary phenomena.

My two Horowitz Lectures were entitled "Money and the Balance of Payments" and "The International Monetary Problem." That my selection of topics may seem on the one hand an arbitrary linking of two largely unrelated subjects, and on the other hand a choice catering to the widely different interests of two eminent Israeli economists, Governor Horowitz and Don Patinkin, is admitted. But in my own mind the two topics are firmly interwoven: both areas of economic concern illustrate the difficulties that professional economists and policy-makers get into when they forget the fundamental truism that a monetary economy is different from a barter economy because it is monetary, and the corollary that in some broad sense the demand for and supply of money are relevant to what happens to monetary magnitudes in such an economy. One cannot hope to reason effectively about a monetary economy in the terms appropriate to the barter economy of value theory.

Both topic areas exemplify the pitfalls of attempting to analyze a monetary world with the tools of "real" theory. I include under this term theories like sophisticated Keynesianism that attempt to create a simulacrum of a monetary economy by treating money and monetary policy as a determinant of a real quantity or real price in the shape of a real quantity of money or "liquidity" or a rate of interest. Notable examples are the "Yale School's" "portfolio balance" approach and the alternative liquidity approach presented in recent writings of J. R. Hicks. My own experience as both a pure theorist and a minor participant in over fifteen years of discussion of the international monetary system and its possible reform has led me increasingly to ask myself, as a social scientist: Why do policy-makers and their professional economic advisors, who should know better, consistently retreat into "real" analyses of and solutions for monetary problems? I can offer only a brief sketch of an answer here: The "real" world is familiar, and identical with the "monetary" world as long as the price level is reasonably stable; everyone lives his normal life in a partial-equilibrium context in which money price changes are also real price changes. The "money" world of monetary macro-equilibrium and disequilibrium is by contrast unfamiliar and strange. Few people indeed possess either a systemic concept of the economy as a whole, as distinct from their own small corner of it, or the imagination to recognize what seem like "real" changes with "real" causes as being in reality monetary changes with monetary causes. Hence they do "what comes (intellectually) naturally," treating unemployment as due to business pessimism, automation, inadequate training of the labor force, and so on, and inflation as due to the monopoly power and greediness of big business or big labor, or to excessive and wasteful public spending on warfare or welfare, according to political taste.

Money and the Balance of Payments

The new, so-called "monetary approach" to the theory of the balance of payments has been developing and gaining popularity in recent years as an alternative to the "elasticity approach," the "absorption approach," and various other Keynesian approaches which may be termed "the foreign-income multiplier approach" and "the Meade-Tinbergen-Keynesian economic-policy approach." (The meaning of these approaches will be explained more fully later.)

At the outset, it is important to note that the monetary approach is new only in the context of balance-of-payments theory as it has developed since the 1930s, when the collapse of the liberal international economic order based on the gold-standard system was accompanied by the Keynesian revolution in economic theory. The monetary approach actually represents a return to the classical tradition of international monetary theory established by the work of David Hume, summarized in the classical price-specie flow mechanism of adjustment to international monetary disequilibria, and foreshadowed in the work of Isaac Gervaise (1720). This tradition has dominated international economics for most of the two centuries during which economics has existed as a scientific system of thought. It is important to emphasize this point, because the development of the monetary approach to the balance of payments has been confused in many so-called minds with something called "monetarism," which is one side of an argument about domestic macroeconomic policy management that has been conducted mainly in the United States, though with a subsequent and derivative manifestation in the United Kingdom. The argument is between those who place their faith in fiscal policy, following the Hansenian American version of the Keynesian revolution, and those who emphasize the necessity of proper monetary policy for the stabilization of the economy, led but by no means dragooned by Milton Friedman.

The issue has been further confused by the fact that Robert Mundell and I, as the two most visible exponents of the new approach, were associated with the University of Chicago during the crucial period when the approach was developed and hence are easily identified by the unthinking as lesser lights in the contemporary "Chicago School" led by Milton Friedman. Yet we are Canadians by birth and citizenship, did our graduate work at M.I.T. and Harvard respectively, and were strongly influenced in our early professional years by the balance-of-payments theorizing of James Meade of the London School of Economics. Mundell worked out his central ideas at the Johns Hopkins Bologna Center and the International Monetary Fund before he joined the Chicago department. Most of my own work on the subject was done during my periods at the London School of Economics, in response to international monetary developments as seen from—more accurately, not understood by—the United Kingdom. Unfortunately, however, the description of scientific activity as a debate between risible and reasonable schools of thought and the assignment of skeptics about prevailing orthodoxy to a ludicrous school through guilt by association, however tenuous geographically and intellectually, has become a hallmark of post-Keynesian discussion of monetary economics. The ability to do so with fluency and plausibility has been assumed by many to be more than adequate to justify the earning of a Ph.D. at public expense.

In order to explain the nature of the new approach, I find it convenient to begin with a brief history of the development of balance-of-payments theory, an *excursus* that will allow me to make some incidental digressions on the inherent difficulty of monetary theory and the shackles imposed on free theoretical inquiry in economics by the limitations of the tools—particularly the mathematical tools—of theoretical analysis.

Hume's price-specie flow analysis was developed as an answer to the mercantilist contention that the path to augmentation of national wealth and power lay in the development and maintenance of a balance-of-payments surplus through measures to increase exports and decrease imports ("a policy of import substitution," in the modern phrase) so as to produce a continuing inflow of precious metals ("treasure") into the country. Hume's analysis demonstrated that such a policy would inevitably be self-defeating, since the accumulation of money stocks would satiate the demand for them and any excess stocks would "leak out" through a balance-of-payments deficit. (Remember that, in an open system, actual stocks of real balances are adjusted to desired levels not by price inflation or deflation, as in a Patinkinian closed economy, but by outflow or inflow of nominal money through the balance of payments.)[1] In illustrating this proposition, Hume showed that the expansion of issue of paper-currency substitutes for precious metals would lead merely to an outflow of precious metals. The parallel in the contemporary monetary approach is the proposition that excessive expansion of "domestic credit" by a country's banking system will lead to a balance-of-payments deficit under fixed exchange rates and a loss of international reserves. A corollary of Hume's analysis is the assertion that there is a "natural distribution" of the world money or reserve stock among the member countries of the world system toward which the actual distribution will gravitate. (Note the parallel with the Archibald and Lipsey [1958] critique of Patinkin's first-edition analysis of the effects of a disproportionately distributed increase in nominal money.)

Hume's analysis was related to the economic world of his time, but such is the propensity of economists to live with archaic old facts rather than open their eyes to new facts that the work of Hume and his immediate successors left a permanent mark on balance-of-payments theory. The most important and pervasive point of influence was his concentration on the trade account—exports and imports of goods—as the locus of adjustment to international monetary disturbances. This concentration has remained a valid point of complaint by practical men against academic balance-of-payments theory, especially as it has been carried over to, and accentuated in, the post-Keynesian "elasticities," multiplier, and policy approaches to the balance of payments. A second influence, which—apart from some work by Ohlin in the 1920s (see, e.g., Ohlin, 1929)—has only in the last four years begun to be questioned, was the assumption incorporated in the phrase "price-specie flow mechanism" that the domestic price level of a country possessing excess money stocks must rise relative to other countries' price levels before trade flows are affected and a balance-of-payments deficit emerges. This view assumes limited holdings of commodity stocks and long lags in transportation and in the dissemination of information about markets, assumptions appropriate to Hume's time but a decreasingly realistic approximation for contemporary integrated world markets. Furthermore, Hume's

[1] This proposition cleared monetary phenomena from policy discussion and permitted the advocacy of free trade as the way to maximize output from national resources.

account predated the development of large-scale commercial banking subject to control by a central bank. By this century, however, the theory had been extended by the addition of the standard textbook analysis of the role of bank-rate adjustments in stimulating short-term capital movements as substitutes for actual specie movements.

The classical Humean tradition of international monetary analysis, like so much else of value in the classical and neoclassical traditions of monetary theory, was swept aside and, at least transiently, completely suppressed in the wake of the Great Depression and the Keynesian revolution. I attribute the fragility of that tradition, and its vulnerability to attack by what purported to be "common sense," to the inherent difficulty of monetary theory. "Real" theory began with the notion that value is created by the expenditure of human effort over time, a notion that raises no real questions of understanding or ethical justification. But it ran into problems once it became necessary to explain the productive role of material capital and the existence of a return on it, problems that still and needlessly confuse, or are confused by, the present-day Cambridge successors of the English classical tradition. But real capital at least requires sacrifice to accumulate, and it contributes in tangible form to total output. Money, on the other hand, is a stock that ultimately requires confidence, not tangible effort, to create, appears to have no inherent usefulness in its medium-of-exchange function, and yields no explicit return identifiable with an easily measurable contribution to production. Hence it requires a great deal of sophistication to treat money as a stock requiring application of stock-flow adjustment mechanisms. It is not surprising that even great monetary theorists like Wicksell and Keynes have found it more congenial to treat monetary adjustments proximately in terms of income-expenditure flow relationships motivated by the fixing of a disequilibrium relative price (the interest rate) through monetary policy, while politicians and the public prefer to attribute balance-of-payments deficits to prices being too high, businessmen and workers too lazy, or governments too spendthrift with the taxpayers' money.

Be that as it may, the classical approach to international monetary equilibrium and disequilibrium and balance-of-payments problems was swept away in the 1930s in favor of a succession of alternative approaches that attempted to treat balance-of-payments equilibria and disequilibria as flow equilibria. The implicit or explicit assumption on which these approaches were based was that flow trade deficits or surpluses (or, in some cases, surpluses or deficits on the balance of trade and services) entailed corresponding outward or inward flows of international reserves. This brief description, incidentally, encapsulates the two main objections to these approaches made on behalf of the monetary approach. The first, which is one of those blindingly obvious elementary tautological points that economists are carefully trained to disregard in the process of formal model building, is that (in a fixed-exchange-rate system) an excess demand for money can be supplied *either* by the acquisition of international money through a balance-of-payments surplus *or* through the creation of money against domestic credit by the domestic monetary authority. This point has pervasive implications for international economic policy; they can be summarized in the proposition that no policy for improving the balance of payments can be successful unless supported by an appropriate restriction of domestic credit. The second objection, which requires sophisticated understanding of the basics of stock-flow relationships and adjustments subsumed in Patinkin's "real balance effect," is that a balance-of-payments deficit or surplus represents a transient stock-adjustment process evoked by an initial inequality of desired and actual money stocks. It cannot be treated as a continuing flow equilibrium. It is worth noting in passing that Keynes never made that mistake—he dealt entirely with a closed economy and a full stock and flow equilibrium in the goods, money, and bonds market. It was entirely a creation of others, who committed the error of analyzing a disaggregated monetary economy as if overall stock-flow equilibrium was enough and continuing net cash flows between its national parts would leave other flow equilibria unchanged.

The first popular successor to the traditional framework of analysis, one that still prevails in official and public policy discussions, was the so-called "elasticities approach," attributable to a classic essay by Joan Robinson (1950), though traceable to early work by the eccentric Bickerdike. That approach was pre-Keynesian, in the direct tradition of Marshallian partial-equilibrium analysis, which ignored repercussions of changes in production and expenditure in one sector on the equilibrium of the rest of the economy. Specifically, the approach regarded exports and imports as separate small sectors whose equilibria were determined by sector demand-and-supply functions in terms of domestic money prices (proxying for relative prices of traded goods in terms of domestic nontraded goods in general) as affected by the exchange rate applicable to conversion of domestic into foreign prices and vice versa.

The elasticities approach had the advantage of apparently shedding light, mistakenly it now appears, on two questions of contemporary concern apart from the effect of exchange-rate changes on the balance of payments itself: the effect on domestic employment, where improvement in the balance of payments *in domestic currency* (as distinct from foreign) increases demand for domestic output and the amount of employment, and the effect on the terms of trade, assumed to constitute an index of economic welfare. (In the latter connection, Robinson and others attempted to establish a presumption where none can exist, to the effect that the terms of trade will tend to move against the devaluing country.)

The approach had three major drawbacks, however. First, it expressed the criteria for a devaluation to improve the trade balance in terms of separate elasticities for exports and for imports, in an unfamiliar formula making improvement depend in the simplest case on whether the demand elasticities summed to more or less than unity. This formulation concealed the point that the question was one of market stability and concentrated attention on empirical guesswork as to what the magnitudes of the elasticities were likely to be in particular cases. Second, the analysis involved both the minor inelegance of ignoring cross-elasticity relations among exports and imports and the major theoretical error of ignoring the multiplier implications of the increase in demand for domestic output that was the counterpart of an improvement in the balance of payments. (This was *not*, it should be recognized, an error committed by Robinson, who clearly stated the multiplier implications, but an important error in popular interpretation of her analysis.) In consequence of this error, less skilled theorists took the elasticities formulation as the total of the analysis. In the early postwar controversy over elasticity pessimism versus elasticity optimism, they ignored the question of availability of unemployed domestic resources to supply the devaluation-induced increase in demand and attempted to cram this consideration into the determination of the likely magnitudes of the elasticities themselves. Finally, as already mentioned, the model identified an excess flow demand for money with an excess flow demand for international reserves, thereby treating balance-of-payments disequilibria as continuing flow phenomena and ignoring the importance of domestic monetary policy in determining the effect of the presumed cash-flow demand on the flow of international reserves.

In the 1930s, the international-economics application of Keynesian theory proper was primarily concerned with the international extension of the multiplier concept. Initially, there was a controversy over whether the trade balance or total exports should be used as the multiplicand, and whether the marginal propensity to save or the sum of the marginal propensities to save and to import should be used as the multiplier. The controversy about the multiplicand was soon resolved, correctly, in favor of total exports. Later work by Metzler (1942) and Machlup (1943) was concerned with the question of whether quantity adjustments through the multiplier could fully replace the classical relative-price adjustments, the answer being in the negative so long as both countries in the world system had positive marginal propensities to save internationally.

A fully consistent multiplier analysis of the effects of devaluation, however, had to wait until the postwar period. The analysis was simplified by assuming perfectly elastic supplies of exports and imports and no nontraded goods, so that devaluation involved essentially a change in the real relative price of the two goods. This relative price change triggered multiplier expansion and contraction of income depending on whether the demand elasticities summed to more or less than unity *and* whether or not both marginal propensities to save internationally were positive. The two requirements appeared multiplicatively in the overall formula for the effects of a devaluation, and the concept of the marginal propensity to save disguised the fact that what was really represented was a bastard stock-flow concept of a marginal propensity to accumulate international reserves. It was thus easy to interpret the concept as making the effect of a devaluation depend essentially on the standard stability criterion that the sum of the price elasticities of import demand be greater than unity, the result of the devaluation, if successful, being a continuing inflow of international reserves (domestic credit policy being ignored).

Meanwhile, the fact that the immediate postwar situation was one of inflationary pressure rather than mass unemployment led most policy economists to attempt to torture the elasticities approach into conformity with inflationary conditions. Alexander (1952) responded by producing the rival "absorption approach" to devaluation. Alexander's essential contribution was to observe that, for a devaluation undertaken *by itself* under full-employment conditions, the resulting extra inflationary pressure would make the elasticities of export and import demand and supply irrelevant and the effect of the devaluation in reducing the deficit depend on the consequences of the inflation itself in reducing aggregate domestic demand for output. These consequences were of two kinds: Keynesian effects, of theoretically doubtful reliability, working via various kinds of income redistribution, and the monetary-theoretic effect of inflation in reducing real balances.

The absorption analysis, while important in shifting attention from microeconomic elasticities to the macroeconomic balance of aggregate demand and supply, was itself defective in two important respects and is best regarded as constituting a halfway house to a correct analysis. The first important defect lay in taking devaluation *by itself* as a policy for analysis, under circumstances in which a combination of devaluation *and* deflationary macroeconomic policy is clearly required. The second defect was that the absorption approach still concentrates on expenditure flows, not recognizing that a continuing deficit will eventually correct itself without devaluation by reducing the economy's real balances, unless real balances are continually renewed by domestic credit expansion to offset the effects of reserve losses. In such a case, devaluation will not improve the balance of payments by deflating real balances.

The fourth, and most theoretically satisfactory, stage of post-Keynesian development of Keynesian balance-of-payments theory came almost simultaneously with the publication in 1951 of James Meade's *The Theory of International Economic Policy*, Volume I, *The Balance of Payments*. Meade shifted the whole theory from the "positive" analysis of the effects of individual policies on the balance of payments to the "normative" analysis of the combination of policies the authorities must follow if they wish to implement policy objectives with respect to both domestic employment and the balance of payments ("internal balance" and "external balance," in Meade's terminology). (Tinbergen's [1952] contribution, incidentally, was to show that the government must have as many independent policy instruments as it has objectives.)

Basically, Meade's analysis showed that the authorities must have fiscal or monetary policy to control aggregate domestic expenditure, and devaluation or controls over international trade and payments to control the allocation of domestic and foreign expenditure between domestic and foreign output. Note that, insofar as the authorities maintained exact balance-of-payments equilibrium, actual and desired money holdings would balance and there would be no inconsistency with monetary-theoretic requirements. Inconsistency could arise only from the implication that if government policy erred, the result would be a continuing flow-equilibrium deficit or surplus whose elimination would require a change in governmental economic policy.

The final stage of development of Keynesian balance-of-payments theory came with the apparent foreclosure of the possibility of using exchange-rate change or trade and payments controls as policies for affecting the allocation of domestic and foreign demand between domestic and foreign output. Mundell (1962) pointed out that the need for as many policy instruments as policy objectives could be met by recognizing that fiscal and monetary expansion have effects in the same direction on the current account but in opposite directions on the capital account of the balance of payments. This policy model—the so-called "theory of fiscal-monetary policy mix" (Mundell, 1962)—also involved no monetary-theoretic inconsistency in cases of preservation of balance-of-payments equilibrium. It was correctly criticized, however, for treating as continuing flow phenomena what are properly regarded as securities-portfolio stock adjustments in response to changes in international interest-rate differentials, and for neglecting the consequences of such portfolio adjustments on the services-account component of the current account. (Moreover, as a practical policy suggestion for the United States, it turned out to be a resounding failure to the extent that it was tried.)

The alternative "monetary approach" to the balance of payments starts from the proposition that balance-of-payments disequilibrium involves an inflow or outflow of international money and hence must be treated as a monetary phenomenon requiring the application of the tools and concepts of monetary theory (Frenkel and Johnson, eds., 1976). This approach, as mentioned earlier, involves two major changes in theoretical orientation and formulation. The first is the simple tautological point that domestic money can *either* be created or destroyed by domestic monetary policy operating on the volume of domestic credit extended by the banking system *or* be imported or exported by running a surplus or deficit on accounts of the balance of payments other than the money account. (The phrasing here is carefully chosen, for a reason that will appear shortly.) This change implies, most fundamentally, that balance-of-payments theory, analysis, and policy prescription must necessarily include exact specification of domestic monetary policy. The second and more subtle change is that international money flows are a consequence of stock disequilibria—differences between desired and actual stocks of international money—and as such are inherently transitory and self-correcting. This is, of course, nothing more than a contemporary restatement of the Humean price-specie flow mechanism, but one refined by modern understanding of the nature of money as a stock yielding either utility to consumers or productive services to producers and by recognition of the possibility that adjustment of desired to actual stocks of international money may occur through either the trade account (surpluses or deficits on exports relative to imports of goods and services) or the capital account (international capital flows of various descriptions) or both. In other words, the monetary approach frees balance-of-payments theory from its traditional concentration on balance-of-payments adjustment through changes in the trade balance (the modern equivalent of which is concern with the "basic balance" or combined balance on goods, services, and long-term capital accounts, the last account being assumed for some reason to be more predictable and amenable to economic explanation and policy influence than movements in the money and short-term capital accounts).

The monetary approach also has the attraction of clarifying the role of movements in the terms of trade—the prices of imports relative to the prices of exports—in the process of international adjustment. Prevailing theory has strongly implied that the purpose of devaluation is precisely to produce an adverse movement in the terms of trade (thereby making the devaluing government appear to be deliberately choosing to impose a national loss) and has further tended to suggest that the reduction of material welfare consequent on devaluation can be avoided by alternative interventionist balance-of-payments policies. By contrast, the monetary approach indicates that terms-of-trade changes, which in principle may go in either direction, are either a transient feature of a monetary stock-adjustment process or a necessary concomitant of movement from an unsustainable deficit situation (in which a country is "living beyond its income" with the help of distress monetary transfers from the rest of the world) to a sustainable position of balance-of-payments equilibrium.

Recognition of this point has led monetary balance-of-payments theorists to transfer their analytical interest away from models stressing imperfect substitution between foreign and domestic tradeable goods and the role of elasticities of demand for such goods in producing terms-of-trade changes that may go either way. They are concerned instead with models stressing the distinction between traded international and nontraded domestic goods, whose relative prices must change in a particular way as domestic expenditure varies relative to income in the process of international monetary stock adjustment. (For an early example of such a model, see Salter, 1959.) This clarification of the role of elasticities and relative price changes in the process of international adjustment is worth emphasizing. The concentration of analysis by monetary balance-of-payment theorists on the so-called "small country" assumption—that the country under analysis is so small that all goods prices and interest rates can be treated as internationally fixed—has often been mistakenly interpreted to mean that the monetary approach is confined to the analysis of such trivial cases. In fact, the procedure has been prompted by the opposite purpose of clearing secondary and essentially trivial analytical complications out of the way of understanding the essentials.

Insofar as theoretical development in international economics is promoted by the observed failure of existing theories to fit the facts of experience rather than by the refinement of professional standards of theoretical elegance and the instinct of scientific workmanship, the development of the monetary approach to balance-of-payments theory can be attributed to two recent historical events. The first is the failure of the prevalent elasticity approach to account for a mounting accumulation of awkward failures of prescription and prediction with respect to devaluations and revaluations and other balance-of-payments policies, most notably the initial failure of the British devaluation of 1967 and its short-lived success after the British authorities turned temporarily to tight control of domestic credit expansion. The other is the failure of Keynesian theory to explain and account for the world inflation that has been going on since 1965 or so, a phenomenon that is easily explainable on classical Humean lines by the generation of an excessive rate of growth of the world money supply initiated by U.S. monetary policy.

Correspondingly, the ultimate test of the monetary approach is its superiority in empirical explanation of balance-of-payments phenomena. Work on the empirical testing of the theory has been proceeding apace behind the scenes, though constantly impeded by the unfortunate institutional fact of life that the reputations of young economists can be made much more quickly and definitively by elegant and comprehensive mathematical theorizing than by the empirical testing of hypotheses. The main positive findings so far (see Frenkel and Johnson, eds., 1976) have provided underpinning for the proposition that balance-of-payments improvement is inversely connected with domestic credit expansion. The most robust specific proposition is that, contrary to Keynesian predictions, the fastest-growing countries will have the strongest (the surplus) balance-of-payments positions, because their demand for money will tend to grow faster than the supply of domestic credit. Empirical testing has, however, run into two major difficulties: First, there is a dangerous temptation to test and confirm the monetary approach spuriously, by verifying statistically the tautology that an increase in domestic money must be provided either by domestic credit creation or by reserve acquisition. Second, in devising a proper test of the theory, which involves testing the existence and stability of the domestic demand for money, one runs into all the problems previously encountered in domestically oriented research on the quantity theory of money, most noticeably the interdependence of demand and supply of money, lags in the adjustment of actual to desired quantities on both sides, and the division of the effects of monetary changes between price changes and output changes.

In this section, I have dealt with the application of monetary theory to the theory of the balance of payments, criticizing the successive stages of development of balance-of-payments theory since the early 1930s for their attempt to analyze the monetary phenomena of balance-of-payments surpluses and deficits with theoretical constructs designed to deal with a "real" or "barter" system. I outlined a new "monetary" approach to these problems—actually a restatement of the main tradition of international monetary theory going back to David Hume's formulation of the price-specie flow mechanism but improved by the incorporation of modern concepts of stock-flow adjustments in monetary equilibration processes. The fundamentals of the monetary approach involve two central points: the tautology that changes in the domestic money supply may be brought about either through changes in the volume of domestic credit or through international exchanges of international reserve money for goods or securities, and the proposition that a balance-of-payments deficit or surplus is a monetary phenomenon representing a process of adjustment of actual to desired stocks of money and cannot therefore be appropriately treated as a continuing flow phenomenon representable as the residual of inflows and outflows of expenditure on goods (and possibly securities) governed by incomes and relative prices (and possibly relative interest rates).

The International Monetary Problem

I turn now from pure theory to the application of the monetary approach to a practical problem in international economic policy, the international monetary problem. The problem, in simple terms, is that the international monetary system of fixed but "flexible" exchange rates, created at Bretton Woods after the international monetary collapse of the 1930s and centered on the International Monetary Fund, itself collapsed in February-March 1973 into a regime of "dirty" or "managed" floating exchange rates. At the time, the official international monetary experts were still arguing in a rather leisurely fashion about the precise institutional changes required and negotiable to strengthen the International Monetary Fund system against certain weaknesses that had become increasingly evident from the early 1960s on.

What have we learned from the experience of collapse and its aftermath, and where do we go from here? I find it useful, in examining these questions, to concentrate on the international monetary system as a monetary *system*, that is, a system governing monetary relationships among the constituent national members of the international economy, and to visualize in a very long historical perspective the problems of an international monetary system based on the concept of fixed rates of exchange among national currencies. That means starting, though very briefly, with the traditional nineteenth-century gold standard—even though to speak of such a "traditional" system is in part mythological, since one of the safety valves of the nineteenth-century system was that, for most of the period, nations had a choice between the gold and the silver standards. They opted gradually for the gold standard at their own convenience, the United States coming firmly onto gold only in 1900. (By the same token, immediately after World War I, the international experts of the League of Nations saw as one of the chief problems of reestablishing the gold standard in a world of many more independent nations the danger of a shortage of gold relative to the demand for it, and set themselves to propagandizing, largely unsuccessfully, for the adoption of the gold-reserve standard.)

The gold standard, in common with any other fixed-exchange-rate system based either on a produced commodity or on an international credit instrument bearing a zero or uncommercially low rate of return, is subject to two major and interacting difficulties. The first is to provide for a rate of growth of the international-reserve-base money of the system approximately equal or closely related to the growth of demand for international reserves at stable prices. With a stable reserve growth at such a rate, broadly full-employment growth of the world economy can occur at a stable, or only mildly rising or falling, world price level. Without it, the fixed-rate system provides, for its member countries, not monetary stability but the obligation to experience roughly the same degree of price inflation or deflation as all the other members experience. The second difficulty arises from the fact that money derives its function not from its inherent value or characteristics but from confidence in its usability in exchange. Consequently, so long as the base money involves a functionally unnecessary investment of real resources or commitment to hold liquid assets in a zero or low-yielding form, there will be natural economic pressures to find higher-yielding substitutes for the holding of actual base money. This can be done with apparent safety so long as confidence is maintained in the ultimate convertibility of base-money substitutes into base money itself. The result of the process, however, is on the one hand greatly to complicate the problem of determining the rate of expansion of world base money appropriate to the maintenance of reasonable price stability, and on the other hand to make the system vulnerable to waves of excessive confidence and loss of confidence in the convertibility of base-money substitutes into base money itself.

These two difficulties, it may be noticed in passing, are precisely analogous to the problems encountered in the historical evolution of national central banking. Those problems resulted in the conception of the central bank as having two not entirely consistent or easily combinable functions, that of controlling the growth of the money supply in the interests of monetary stability, and that of serving as lender of last resort to the commercial banking system in times of liquidity crisis. The solution in principle to the inconsistency was that in a liquidity crisis the central bank should lend *without stint* but lend *at a penalty rate*, in Bagehot's famous phrase, so that excess money created in a crisis would be returned to the central bank as soon as possible and not remain to overhang the market.

The nineteenth-century gold standard solved these problems surprisingly well, thereby maintaining an international monetary climate conducive to liberal policies of international trade and investment and peaceful world economic growth. But the gold-reserve standard reestablished after World War I very quickly fell victim to a collapse of confidence in national currency substitutes for nonexistent gold. The loss of confidence was triggered by the failure of the U.S. Federal Reserve System to prevent a collapse of the American money supply and was complicated by intra-European national rivalries and American isolationism, which prevented the salvaging of the system by international monetary cooperation. The international monetary system could have been rescued in three relatively painless alternative ways: coordinated national policies of domestic monetary expansion; international agreement to raise the national-currency prices of gold; and the invention by international agreement of a new international credit-reserve asset to replace gold. Failing the requisite willingness to solve the problem in one of these ways by international cooperation and invention, the only remaining alternative was the painful and socially disastrous one of lowering the national-money and gold prices of commodities through savage deflation and its accompanying mass unemployment. (In fact, the 1930s ended with exchange rates among national currencies more or less what they had been at the beginning, but with the national-currency prices some 75 per cent higher and national unemployment levels far higher on the average than the pre–World War I norm.)

The fundamental source of the international monetary collapse was only imperfectly understood at the time. In accordance with what I said in the preceding section about the strong temptations for both "practical" men and professional economists to retreat into the finding of "real" explanations and the proposal of "real" remedies for monetary problems, the monetary causation was increasingly dismissed or disregarded in favor of real explanations and remedies. Thus, the results of a failure of governmental monetary management were transmuted into evidence of the instability of capitalism and its alleged inherent tendencies to depression, and the failure to resort to expansionary monetary policy as evidence that monetary policy was powerless to make capitalism behave properly. The apotheosis of these ideas found expression in the American Hansenian version of Keynesianism, with its faith in the reality of "secular stagnation" and its emphasis on fiscal policy as the only effective tool available for macroeconomic management.

In the narrower context of international monetary organization, the experience gave rise to a number of ideas that constituted the ethos of opinion about the problems that were intended to be solved by the Bretton Woods system. Chief among these were the following: belief in the inherent "deflationary bias" of the gold standard, against which national full-employment policies had to be protected by the freedom to devalue in cases of "fundamental disequilibrium"; fear of a chronic shortage of international liquidity, to be made good by international provision of credit substitutes for gold—a fear that dominated International Monetary Fund thinking well into the 1970s, in spite of accelerating world inflation, and is still evident in the Fund's concern with providing additional short-term credit for consumer-country victims of the oil-price escalation; belief in the need to exercise surveillance to prevent "competitive devaluation," together with "elasticity pessimism," both derived from misinterpretation of a situation in which general devaluation was required to raise the price of gold as one in which devaluation was required to correct individual deviant behavior in an international monetary system in overall equilibrium; and belief that the chief threat to the stability of the system was another great depression in the United States economy.

The related set of preconceptions and problem orientations naturally meant that official opinion was unprepared when the chief problem of the system eventually turned out to be world inflation rather than world depression. The 1930s problem was turned on its head: excessive liquidity, excessive willingness to accept U.S. dollars as credit substitutes for gold or Special Drawing Rights, "unfair" competition meaning reluctance to revalue rather than eagerness to devalue, and a chronic U.S. deficit as the engine of world inflation.

For a while, however, the Bretton Woods system worked well in providing a monetary framework for sustained economic growth and a trend toward a more liberal international trade and payments system. One must be careful, however, not to exaggerate how well it worked, and for how long. The European currencies became convertible only at the end of 1958, and tensions over the U.S. dollar glut and the adjustment of exchange rates began very soon thereafter. The system was buoyed up for a long time after the war's end by the belief that the United States had a disproportionate share of the world's gold and should, if anything, encourage a balance-of-payments deficit to relieve the postwar "dollar shortage" and redistribute the gold. Nevertheless, in the mid-1960s the view was gradually accepted that the reserve-currency position of the United States posed a special problem, and that the solution was gradual replacement of the dollar as international money by the creation and steady augmentation of new genuinely international credit-reserve assets in the form of Special Drawing Rights.

What forestalled this expected leisurely and deliberate progress toward a new fixed-exchange-rate system based on international credit reserves was the decision of President Johnson in 1965 to escalate the war in Vietnam *without* introducing the substantial increase in taxes required to finance that escalation. The result was necessarily inflation, which was compounded by later inflationary mistakes of American monetary policy. Owing to the fixed-exchange-rate system and the dominance of the United States as reserve-currency country and leading trading and investing country, the inflation permeated the world economy.

The period of inflation with fixed exchange rates raises two major problems for analysis. The first problem is why the major countries, primarily the European countries, were unable to cope with the American inflation. The international monetary system did, after all, permit exchange-rate changes in both directions, and it would have been possible in principle to confine most or all of the inflationary pressure to the United States by a series of revaluations of other countries' currencies against the dollar. This procedure would have been more disturbing than the adoption of floating rates against the dollar, since it would have amounted to a speeded-up version of the crawling peg. Nevertheless, there had been enough discussion of the need for smaller and more frequent changes in the adjustable pegs after the

1967 devaluation of sterling to permit not-too-startling innovations. The main reasons why European countries did not cope were two: (1) They had got used to the idea of the dollar as a currency with a fairly stable real purchasing power, in relation to which they could adjust their currency values to take account of more or less inflationary domestic price trends than those of their major trading partners. American inflation deprived the system of this cornerstone of stability and made it necessary for the European countries to learn to cooperate in concerted revaluations against the dollar and American inflation. This they were unwilling and unable to do. (2) The franc-mark realignment of 1969 dashed the hopes of the Common Market establishment that the Common Agricultural Policy of the EEC would make it impossible ever again to change the exchange rates of member countries against each other. The establishment reacted by pressing for the creation of a common European currency directly, rather than implicitly as an uncovenanted implication of the Common Agricultural Policy.

As a start, the "snake in the tunnel" concept narrowed the fluctuations of European currency rates in relation to each other, by comparison with fluctuations against the dollar. Given enough cooperation, the snake might eventually have produced a situation in which the European currencies could be revalued in common against the dollar, thus turning American inflation back onto the United States. But its main actual result was to freeze the exchange values of the European currencies and prevent individual action against world inflation. In the end, it was the United States, worried by its mounting balance-of-payments deficit and especially the adverse trend of its merchandise-trade balance, and not the Common Market countries that forced a revaluation of other currencies in terms of the dollar (or, if one prefers, a devaluation of the dollar) in 1971. The Smithsonian Agreement to this effect lasted barely long enough to let President Nixon win reelection. Thereafter, in 1973, an American decision to devalue by another 10 per cent precipitated the collapse of the fixed-exchange-rate system into a regime of "dirty floating."

The second problem concerning this period is why governments, and official and academic economists, were so determined to deny the existence of a world inflation sparked by U.S. inflation and communicated by the fixed-rate system. The requisite analysis was certainly obvious enough, in conformity with time-tested theory, and not entirely unknown from previous history, especially the well-known case of the effects of Spain's imports of precious metals from conquered Latin America. Yet all the official economists in Europe known to me rushed to present alleged statistical disproof of the contention that I and various European colleagues advanced that the fundamental problem was a world inflation.

The reasons appear, at this juncture, to lie in two basic defects of Keynesian monetary theory (or, perhaps better, vulgar post-Keynesian macroeconomic policy theory), which those convinced of the rectitude of their position regard as a source of invincible strength against alternative "classical" monetary analysis. First, the *General Theory* provides no theory whatsoever about what determines money wages and changes in them. Consequently, when it comes to this question anything goes, and what goes best for the policy-maker accustomed to keep his brains sharp by reading the headlines and occasionally an editorial in his morning newspaper is a mishmash of *ad hoc* sociological analysis of union behavior, ending in the conclusion that what is required is an incomes policy. Second, Keynesian theory, like income-expediture theories in general, insists that monetary influences must affect aggregate output and prices through certain channels defined by the theory itself; if the influence cannot be seen moving in the specified channels, it does not exist. Thus, for a closed economy or one treated as closed, Keynesian theory asserts that monetary policy operates by influencing direct fixed investment. This remains an article of faith even though econometrics has been remarkably unsuccessful in finding such an influence and there is a growing body of evidence that monetary-policy changes have a fairly reliable influence on consumption expenditure (in typical "Keynesian," not sharply inflationary, circumstances). For an open economy, Keynesian theory similarly insists that world inflation must be communicated either through an inflow of reserves or through a sharp increase in the export surplus. Yet elementary monetary theory indicates that the money supply may increase either through reserve inflow or through domestic credit expansion designed to avert unwanted reserve inflow and that, through arbitrage, the prices of exports of closely substitutable goods will tend to stay in alignment in the various supplier countries rather than be forced up by a prior increase in demand.

There is a third and related problem: Why did the very official sources that denied the reality of world inflation during the closing stages of the fixed-exchange-rate system (when it was a necessary implication of the fixed-rate system) turn around within a few months of the switch to a floating-rate system (which made participation of foreign inflation in principle unnecessary) to the position that there was indeed a world inflation whose manifestation in domestic inflation they were powerless to influence? It strains credulity—though not all the way to the breaking point—to hypothesize that it is a professional obligation of official economists to assert the exact opposite of prevailing economic truth in order to give maximum scope for ingenious policy recommendations. But another hypothesis seems plausible. Having tried unsuccessfully to hold back the tide of world inflation by sweeping vainly at it with the domestic brooms of fiscal, monetary, and incomes policy, only to see inflation become an endemic problem arrestable solely by thoroughgoing deflation and unemployment, governments and their economists found it easiest to blame the problem they had created for themselves on a foreign cause they could not be expected to overcome.

Leaving that issue aside, the floating-rate system, "dirty" or "managed" as it has been, especially in its early stages, has in my judgment worked very well. Contrary to the dire predictions of the adherents, defenders, and beneficiaries of fixed rates, and in accordance with the theoretical expectations of exponents of floating rates, the floating-rate system has not led to the fragmentation of the world economy and the cessation of growth of international trade and investment. Early fears of such fragmentation, and particularly of the proliferation of controls over international capital movements, were connected with the initial European effort to maintain a common float against the dollar and the belief of the French, since abandoned by them along with the common float, that this required a system of fixed rates for current-account transactions and a floating rate for capital-account transactions. Well before the oil crisis, the efficacy of the floating-rate system had removed any urgency about fundamental international monetary reform, and the onslaught of the oil crisis produced the spectacle—unfortunately temporary—of former fixed-rate diehards congratulating the world on its wisdom in having opted for a floating-rate system.

Since those halcyon days of winter 1973-74, however, the fixed-rate adherents and the commercial-banking and financial community have once again begun to find grave fault with the floating-rate system. They are not as yet anywhere near the point of recommending a return to fixed rates but only of recommending international cooperation and coordination in smoothing exchange-rate movements. Their criticisms are of two kinds, narrowly technical and broadly policy-evaluative.

The technical criticisms concern chiefly the magnitude of the exchange-rate movements that have occurred, which are judged to have been excessive and erratic in relation to the adjustment necessary, and the failure of forward markets to develop for more than a few currencies, which greatly hampers the safe conduct of international financial business.

With respect to the first criticism, I must confess that I have always been astounded by the confidence with which "practical" men pass judgments about how much movement of a market price is sufficient to restore equilibrium. If the market consistently overshot, one would expect vast profits to be made by currency speculation. But a number of bankers who have tried it have had their fingers badly and most embarrassingly burnt. This is perfectly predictable from the results of economic research on forward exchange markets, using techniques taken over from analysis of the behavior of stock-market prices. These results show that, despite the frequent appearance of apparent purposive patterns, changes in the movement of foreign-exchange rates in a free market are a "random walk." One must also note that foreign-exchange markets, like stock markets, capitalize expected future price movements into current prices, so that prices may be expected to move more sharply in response to new information than consideration of current demands and supplies alone would lead one to expect. (To put this point another way, "practical" men are as guilty as the balance-of-payments theorists they criticize of assuming that international adjustment occurs only through the current account.) In addition, one suspects that there is an important degree of optical illusion in bankers' discussions of the magnitudes of exchange-rate changes. Financial attention tends to concentrate on the rates between currencies that are important in international finance, but these are not necessarily the exchange-rate relationships relevant to international trade and direct investment. Thus, for the United States the rates of the Canadian dollar and Japanese yen are far more important than the rate of the Swiss franc, and the Canadian dollar has remained within a few cents of parity with the American dollar since 1970, while the yen rate has been fairly stable since 1973.

The second technical criticism, concerning the failure of forward facilities to develop on the expected scale, also raises some questions about what one can reasonably expect. To be brief and colloquial, it would obviously be pleasant for me if someone were to operate an all-night bar on the corner of my street, so that I could get a drink if ever I needed one, but I cannot reasonably expect anyone to open such a bar solely on the expectation of having me for a customer. Forward facilities in foreign exchange will develop only if there is enough volume of business to yield a reasonably predictable profit. It would not surprise me, given all the other risks to which private trade and investment are subject in the inflationary and oil-uncertain mid-1970s, if the establishment of futures markets in a broad range of currencies commanded a very low priority.

The policy-evaluative criticism of the floating-rate system is that the world has had more inflation, not less, since floating rates became the system of international monetary relationships. But floating-rate exponents have never argued that floating rates will guarantee more price stability than fixed rates. The original argument, which goes back to the 1930s depression, was that only with floating rates could a country pursue an independent employment and price-stabilization policy. Actually, in that period countries did not in fact employ floating rates at all boldly for that purpose. Recently, the argument for floating rates has been modified, quite logically, into the proposition that only with floating rates can a country pursue an independent price-stabilization policy *if it so desires*. Whether it chooses to do so or, on the contrary, chooses to permit more inflation than would have been consistent with fixed rates is a matter for its own political choice.

Given the head of steam that inflation was permitted to develop under the fixed-rate system, and particularly the unusual degree of synchronization of the up-phases of national business cycles and the consequent pressure of world demand on food prices in 1972-73, it is not surprising that countries should have opted to let inflation rip. There is, in fact, a dangerous parallelism of irrational interpretation building up in this connection: just as the defenders of fixed rates used to attribute the depression and the constriction of world trade of the 1930s to the 1930s floating-rate regime—which relieved the worst of the horror—instead of blaming the predecessor fixed-rate regime that produced them, so those currently hankering after a return to fixed rates are building toward laying the blame for world inflation on the 1970s floating-rate regime, rather than on the predecessor fixed-rate regime that made floating rates necessary.

In any case, it is far too early to conclude that the floating-rate regime is more inflationary than the predecessor fixed-rate regime. The present world recession may succeed in breaking inflationary expectations and restoring rough price stability if contractionary monetary policies are not reversed too sharply and expansively. And the U.S. determination to fight inflation probably owes something to the effects of devaluation and downward flotation of the dollar in bottling up American inflation within the U.S. economy.

Time alone will tell. Meanwhile, it is certain that the world will not return to the fixed-rate system for a long time ahead, if ever. This raises some interesting problems for national economies and their policy-makers as to the best way of living with the floating-rate regime.

My own country, Canada, has chosen in my view the worst possible strategy—to stay virtually pegged to the American dollar while letting the energy-resources boom give the economy a still more inflationary impetus than pegging to the U.S. dollar and the U.S. inflation alone would have done.

In an earlier run of the Horowitz Lectures, my Chicago colleague Milton Friedman surprised some of his audience and, later, of his readers by recommending that Israel should abolish its central bank and instead peg irrevocably to the U.S. dollar. I agree entirely with Friedman's argument that a small country anxious to promote economic development should eliminate the temptations to inflation inherent in central banking by joining irrevocably to a larger currency area, but I do not find it self-evident that the U.S. dollar is the proper currency to peg to. For a country significantly involved in trade with a number of countries, pegging to the currency of the most rapidly inflating country or to the currency depreciating most rapidly in terms of other major currencies (which may not be the same thing) automatically guarantees the most rapid possible rate of domestic inflation. The only relevant argument for doing so—and it is a nonargument—is that a country heavily dependent on another for imported capital and unilateral transfers should peg to the currency of the investing country in order to encourage investor confidence and maintain the domestic-currency value of foreign gifts. The second objective makes no economic sense whatever—the real value of foreign gifts is what they can buy abroad—and the first makes no sense when the relevant risk is created by the irresponsibility of the investing country's financial management and not by that of the recipient country. To be concrete, if Israel as a small country finds it preferable to peg the Israeli pound to a larger foreign country's currency rather than to float independently, the question of whether to peg, say, to the German mark rather than the U.S. dollar should at least be looked at seriously.

I have said that, in my judgment, the regime of floating exchange rates is going to be with us for a long time. This raises the obvious question of whether eventually the world monetary system will return to a regime of fixed rates—or, more likely, "flexible" or "adjustably pegged" rates. My own hunch is that it will. One reason is historical: Britain after the Napoleonic War, the European countries after each of the two world wars, the United States after its period of floating (1860-79), not to speak of lesser countries practicing currency flotation for shorter or longer periods, all returned sooner or later to fixed exchange rates. As an incidental point, worth meditating on and relevant in the event of another major war, note that, in contrast to a more distant past, the advent of World War II led countries to peg the exchange rates of previously floating currencies, presumably to fix the unit of calculation for the external transactions of the controlled war economy. The other reason for my expectation is theoretical. The case for floating exchange rates is always carefully framed to distinguish between exchange rates that are free to move in response to market forces and exchange rates that oscillate significantly over time. The point is that, under stable economic conditions and with stable national economic policies, rates free to move will actually change little and slowly over time. Such a situation of relative stability must come about, if only transiently, at some point in the future. With rates stable, it will seem a trivial step, well worth the additional benefits, to move from *de facto* to *de jure* fixity of exchange rates.

That possibility makes it more, not less, necessary to keep fresh the memory of the intensive debates that were proceeding up until early 1974, after the outbreak of the oil crisis, about the main lines that a reform of the international monetary system (conceived as a fixed-rate system) should take. There are, specifically, three problems that are likely to be more difficult to get to grips with in the light of floating-rate and oil-crisis experience than they already were in the last phase of the International Monetary Fund system: the conditions under which exchange-rate changes in both directions should be sanctioned and indeed internationally required (recall what I said earlier about the financial community's feeling that exchange-rate trends in the past two years have been uncomfortably severe and erratic); the future of the dollar as a nationally created and controlled international reserve currency substitutable for and against Special Drawing Rights under ill-defined and amorphous conditions; and the possible world central-banking role of the International Monetary Fund. The prime function of a world central bank should be to provide stable growth of the international money base of the world financial system. But the International Monetary Fund has two serious distractions from this primary objective. Because of its historical origins in 1930s depression thinking, it is psychologically dominated by the presumption that the main danger to be guarded against is a shortage of international liquidity. And owing to its character, being at least partially a democratically responsible world institution and obliged to develop and maintain popular support among the numerical majority of its constituents, it tends to concern itself with the lender-of-last-resort function of the ultimate source of international credit, to the neglect of the money-supply-control function and of Bagehot's dictum that lending of last resort should be conducted *at a penalty rate*. It must obviously be demoralizing for a central-banking institution to be empowered, by virtue of low conventional lending rates in a period of rapid inflation, to lend at last resort at a negative real cost of borrowing to the borrower and to be under political pressure to ration credit on the basis of the borrower's need for real resources.

References

Alexander, Sidney S., "Effects of a Devaluation on a Trade Balance," *IMF Staff Papers*, 2 (April 1952); reprinted as Chap. 22 in R. E. Caves and H. G. Johnson, eds., *Readings in International Economics*, Homewood, Ill., Irwin, 1969.

Archibald, G. C., and R. G. Lipsey, "Monetary and Value Theory: A Critique of Lange and Patinkin," *Review of Economic Studies*, 26 (October 1958), pp. 1-22.

Frenkel, Jacob A., and Harry G. Johnson, eds., *The Monetary Approach to the Balance of Payments*, London, Allen & Unwin, and Toronto, University of Toronto Press, 1976.

Gervaise, Isaac, *The System or Theory of the Trade of the World*, 1720; reprinted in Economic Tracts series, Baltimore, The Johns Hopkins Press, 1956.

Hume, David, *Political Discourses*, 1752; reprinted in E. Rotwein, ed., *David Hume: Writings on Economics*, London, Nelson, 1955.

Machlup, Fritz, *International Trade and the National Income Multiplier*, New York, Blakiston, 1943; reprinted, New York, Augustus M. Kelley, 1965.

Meade, James E., *The Theory of International Economic Policy*, Vol. I, *The Balance of Payments*, Oxford, Oxford University Press, 1951.

Metzler, L. A., "Underemployment Equilibrium in International Trade," *Econometrica*, 10 (April 1942), pp. 97-112.

Mundell, Robert A., "The Appropriate Use of Monetary and Fiscal Policy for External and Internal Stability," *IMF Staff Papers*, 9 (March 1962), pp. 70-79.

Ohlin, Bertil, "The Reparation Problem: A Discussion," *Economic Journal*, 39 (June 1929), pp. 172-178.

Patinkin, Don, *Money, Interest, and Prices*, 2nd ed., New York, Harper & Row, 1965.

Robinson, Joan, "The Foreign Exchanges," Chap. 4 in H. Ellis and L. A. Metzler, eds., *Readings in the Theory of International Trade*, London, Allen & Unwin, 1950.

Salter, W. E., "Internal and External Balance: The Role of Price and Expenditure Effects," *Economic Record*, 35 (August 1959), pp. 226-238.

Tinbergen, J., *On the Theory of Economic Policy*, Contributions to Economic Analysis series, Amsterdam, North-Holland, 1952.

CURRENCY DEVALUATION
IN DEVELOPING COUNTRIES

Richard N. Cooper

Currency devaluation is one of the most dramatic—even traumatic—measures of economic policy that a government may undertake. It almost always generates cries of outrage and calls for the responsible officials to resign. For these reasons alone, governments are reluctant to devalue their currencies. Yet under the present rules of the international monetary system, laid down in the Articles of Agreement of the International Monetary Fund, devaluation is encouraged whenever a country's international payments position is in "fundamental disequilibrium," whether that disequilibrium is brought about by factors outside the country or by indigenous developments. Because of the associated trauma, which arises because so many economic adjustments to a discrete change in the exchange rate are crowded into a relatively short period, currency devaluation has come to be regarded as a measure of last resort, with countless partial substitutes adopted before devaluation is finally undertaken. Despite this procrastination, over 200 devaluations in fact occurred between the inauguration of the IMF in 1947 and the end of 1970; to be sure, some were small and many took place in the years of postwar readjustment, especially 1949. In addition, there were five upvaluations, or revaluations, of currencies. Two more occurred in May 1971.

By convention, changes in the value of a currency are measured against the American dollar, so a devaluation means a reduction in the dollar price of a unit of foreign currency or, what is the same thing, an increase in the number of units of the foreign currency that can be purchased for a dollar. (The numerical measure of the extent of devaluation will always be higher with the latter measure than with the former; for example, the 1967 devaluation of the British pound from $2.80 to $2.40 was 14.3 per cent and 16.7 per cent on the two measures, respectively.) By law, changes in currency parities are against gold, but since the official dollar price of gold has been unchanged since 1934, these changes in practice come to the same thing. Except when many currencies are devalued at the same time—as they were in September 1949 and to a much less extent in November 1967 (when over a dozen countries devalued with the pound) and August 1969 (when fourteen French African countries devalued their currencies along with the French franc)—a currency devaluation against the dollar is also against

Reprinted from "Currency Devaluation in Developing Countries—Essays in International Finance No. 86, June 1971," pp. 3–31, with permission of Princeton University Press, Princeton, Copyright 1971.

the rest of the global payments system, that is, against all other currencies.

Only a baker's dozen of countries did not devalue their currencies at least once during the period 1947-70 (Japan, Switzerland, and the United States among developed countries, and ten less developed countries, mostly in Central America). Largely because they are so numerous, but partly also because they devalue on average somewhat more often than the developed countries do, less developed countries account for most currency devaluations. Yet the standard analysis of currency devaluation, which has advanced substantially during this period and is still being transformed and further refined, fails to take into account many of the features that are typical of developing countries today, and which influence substantially the impact of currency devaluation on their economies and on their payments positions.

This essay attempts to do three things. First, it sketches very briefly the analysis of currency devaluation as it stands at present. Second, it suggests how this analysis has to be modified to take into account the diverse purposes to which the foreign-exchange system is put in many less developed countries, and the extent to which these diverse purposes influence the nature of devaluation and its effects on the economy. Third, it draws on recent experience with about three dozen devaluations to see to what extent the anxieties of government officials, bankers, and traders, and even some economists, about devaluation and its effects are justified, and interprets some of this experience in light of the earlier theoretical discussion.

I. A SUMMARY OF THE THEORY OF DEVALUATION

In analyzing devaluation, the exact nature of the initial disequilibrium is important, and much analysis misleads by its focus on economies that are assumed to be in equilibrium at the moment of devaluation. To set the stage precisely, suppose we have a country which for reasons past has money costs that are too high to permit it to balance its international payments at a level of domestic economic activity that is both desired and sustainable, and as a result it must finance a continuing payment deficit out of its reserves, a process that obviously cannot continue indefinitely. Thus by assumption we are not dealing with a case in which domestic demand is pressing against productive capacity to an extent that is regarded as undesirable ("inflationary"), although under the circumstances domestic expenditure does exceed domestic output, a necessity to maintain full employment. Correction of the payments imbalance by reducing aggregate demand (the rate of money spending) would lead to unwanted unemployment because of the rigidity of fac-

tor incomes in money terms, especially wages. Perhaps ultimately the
pressure on costs and prices of a depression in activity would restore an
equilibrium level of costs and prices that would lead to payments balance at full employment, but the transitional depression might have to
be long and painful. The recommended alternative is devaluation of the
currency, which at the stroke of a pen lowers the country's costs and
prices when measured in *foreign* currency. Analysis of the effects of devaluation on the country's economy and of the mechanism whereby it
eliminates the payments deficit has proceeded under three quite different and apparently contrasting approaches: the elasticities approach, the
absorption approach, and the monetary approach.

Three Approaches to Analysis

The *elasticities approach* focuses on the substitution among commodities, both in consumption and in production, induced by the relative
price changes wrought by the devaluation. For an open economy such
as the one we are considering here, the principal relative-price change
is between goods, whether imported or exported, whose price is strongly
influenced by conditions in the world market, and those home goods
and services that are not readily traded. For a small country, we
can assume that the prices in domestic currency of foreign-trade goods—
exports, imports, and goods in close competition with imports—will
rise by the amount of devaluation (the larger of the two percentages
mentioned above is the relevant one here). This rise will divert purchases out of existing income to nontraded goods and services, thereby
reducing domestic demand for imports and for export goods, releasing
the latter for sale abroad. When the country is large enough to influence world prices, domestic prices may rise by less than the amount
of the devaluation, since prices in foreign currency will fall somewhat
in response to the reduction in our country's demand for imports or
to the increase in its supply of exports. There is some presumption that
most countries will have a greater influence on their export prices than
on the prices at which they import, so the rise in local prices of exports
will be less, and the terms of trade will deteriorate.

The shift in relative prices operates both on consumption and on production. Consumption will be diverted to lower-priced nontraded goods
and services, releasing some existing output for export and cutting demand for imports. At the same time, increased profitability in the foreign-trade sector, arising from the fact that prices in domestic currency
have risen more than domestic costs, will stimulate new production of
export and import-competing goods, and will draw resources into these
industries. If excess capacity happens to exist in these industries, the

resources drawn in will be variable ones—labor and materials. Otherwise new investment will be required; in agriculture, land may have to be recropped or herds rebuilt.

The elasticities approach gives rise to the celebrated Marshall-Lerner condition for an improvement in the trade balance following a devaluation: that the elasticity of demand for imports plus the foreign elasticity of demand for the country's exports must exceed unity, which is to say that the change in the quantity of imports and exports demanded together must be sufficiently great to offset the loss in foreign earnings consequent upon lowering the price of exports in foreign currency. This condition assumes initially balanced trade, finished goods, and elastic supply of exports both at home and abroad, but may be modified to allow for initial trade imbalance, for less than perfectly elastic supplies of export, and for intermediate products.

The *absorption approach* shifts attention from individual sectors to the overall economy. Its basic proposition is that any improvement in the balance on goods and services must, in logic, require some increase in the gap between total output and total domestic expenditure. It starts from the identity $E + X = Y + M$, where E is total domestic expenditure on goods and services and X is total foreign expenditure on our country's goods and services (exports), the sum of the two representing total "absorption" of the goods and services available to the country, which derive from its own aggregate output, Y, and imports from the rest of the world, M. Rearranging the terms yields $X - M = Y - E$, which shows that any trade surplus reflects an excess of output over domestic expenditure, and vice versa for a trade deficit. It follows that to reduce a deficit requires a corresponding reduction in the gap between output and expenditure. Excess capacity and unemployment will permit an increase in output; otherwise expenditure must be reduced. Without such a reduction, there can be no improvement in the balance, regardless of the elasticities. This analysis points to the policy prescription that devaluation must be accompanied by deflationary monetary and fiscal policy to "make room" for improvement in the balance, a prescription to which we shall return below.

The *monetary approach* to devaluation focuses on the demand for money balances and the fact that an excess demand for goods, services, and securities, resulting in a payments deficit, reflects an excess supply of money. It draws attention to the analytical parallel between a devaluation and a reduction in the supply of money that affects all holders in equal proportion. Devaluation is equivalent to a decline in the money supply and in the value of other financial assets denominated in local currency, when measured in *foreign* currency. Put another way, the real value of the money supply will be reduced by devaluation, because the local prices of traded goods and services, and, secondarily, those of nontraded goods and services to which demand is diverted, will rise. The public will accordingly reduce its spending in order to restore the real value of its holdings of money and other financial assets, which reduction in expenditure will produce the required improvement in the balance of payments. For a country in initial deficit, the right devaluation will achieve just the right reduction in the real value of the money supply, and the deficit will cease. To restore lost reserves the country must devalue by more than that amount, in order to achieve a surplus. But once the public has reattained its desired financial holdings, expenditure will rise again and the new surplus will be eliminated. On this view, a devaluation beyond the equilibrium point has only a once-for-all effect. A key implication of this approach is that if the monetary authorities expand domestic credit following devaluation to satisfy the new demand for money, the effects of the devaluation on international payments will be undermined. (The money supply may of course increase in response to the inflow of reserves; indeed, if it does not, the surplus will continue until some other country takes steps to curtail it.)

These three approaches are complementary rather than competitive—they represent different ways of looking at the same phenomenon, and each has its strengths and weaknesses. The first has its roots in Marshallian, partial-equilibrium analysis, and is most suitable when the foreign-trade sector—like Marshall's strawberry market—is small relative to the total economy, or when there are ample unemployed resources—and even in the latter case it offers only a part of the story. The absorption approach is "Keynesian" in its focus on total output and expenditure, not differentiating among sectors and neglecting monetary effects. But it draws attention to the impact of changes in exchange rates on overall income and expenditure, which the elasticities approach fails to do. The third approach is the international counterpart of the recently revived monetary school of thought propagated by the Chicago-London School of Economics, but its intellectual roots go back to David Hume, where stock adjustments in the real value of money balances were all-important.

It is tempting to think of these three approaches in temporal sequence, with the first stage of the elasticity approach representing the short run, the absorption (income-expenditure) approach applying to the medium run, and the monetary approach applying to the long run, on the grounds that asset portfolios take a long time to adjust following a major dislocation. But this would oversimplify the matter. All factors are present to some degree even immediately following devaluation.

In the first instance relative prices normally do change, however, as assumed by the elasticities approach, and this in turn will alter the patterns of consumption and, in the right circumstances, of production, encouraging the necessary increase in net exports.

With initial excess capacity, these alterations will generate additional income, which by leading to additional expenditure will in turn damp down the improvement in the trade balance; without it, the switch in demand toward home goods will tend to bid up their prices. But unless the monetary authorities expand domestic credit the rise in prices will not be sufficient to eliminate the change in relative prices initially brought about by the devaluation, and some improvement in the trade balance will remain.

All this is consistent with the monetary approach. The initial disequilibrium reflects not only an excess supply of money but also a misalignment of relative prices between home and tradable goods, since the fixed-exchange-rate link with the world market diverts the impact of those excess holdings of money into demand for imports rather than higher prices in the foreign-trade sector. The appropriate devaluation simply corrects this disequilibrium set of relative prices and at the same time lowers the real value of money holdings and, hence, expenditures. It therefore has a durable effect. This contrasts with the case where the starting point is one of monetary equilibrium, as is usually assumed in the theoretical analysis despite the fact that devaluation seems superfluous in such circumstances, in that devaluation from equilibrium can have only a transitory effect, giving rise to the wholly misleading impression that devaluation cannot really "work."

Whether the second stage of the elasticities approach—the new investment in the foreign-trade sector—comes into play depends in large part on whether the structure of potential output was seriously affected during the disequilibrium period before devaluation. If the disequilibrium persisted for some time, or if investors were prompt to respond to profitable opportunities and failed to anticipate the eventual need for devaluation, then there would be excess capacity in the home-goods sector and deficient capacity in the foreign-trade sector from the viewpoint of long-run equilibrium, and the second stage would come into play. Otherwise, there would be sufficient capacity in the foreign-trade sector (not fully utilized before devaluation) and no change in the structure of potential output would be necessary.

The impact of growing cost-price disequilibrium on production in the export industries, and its subsequent reversal after devaluation, can be illustrated graphically by Finland's experience. Here a "zero line" marks the boundary north of which it is unprofitable to cut and transport timber for export. As cost inflation proceeded in the 1950s, this zero line gradually moved southward, to the point in 1957 that it was only about 200 miles from the south coast. Following the 1957 devaluation, the line shifted markedly northward again.

Distributional Effects

There is a distributional counterpart to these allocational changes which should be explicitly acknowledged, since distributional considerations are so important in less developed countries. A devaluation will raise the "rents" on all factors working in the foreign-trade sector, particularly, in the first instance, entrepreneurial returns in industries engaged in export and in competition with imports. At the same time, the real income of other groups (including the government) will decline because of the rise in prices of these goods. If the higher profits are expected to continue, managers in these industries will expand output and in so doing will bid up the prices of other factors of production used extensively in the foreign-trade sector, leaving a distributional effect in the end that may favor, say, labor, even though it favored certain profits initially. Since we started with a disequilibrium pattern of expenditure and a disequilibrium distribution of income (for a given tax regime), both produced by the misalignment of prices between traded and nontraded goods, the new position brought about by appropriate devaluation will persist unless it is disturbed by other factors.

But both the speed with which the initial distributional effect is transformed to the ultimate effect and the chance that the ultimate effect will not be disturbed will vary greatly. It is here that "money illusion" enters the picture, provided that term is interpreted broadly to cover cases where the decline in real income from a rise in prices is perceived (so there is no "illusion" in a literal sense) and accepted, even when a reduction in money wages would not be accepted. There are many reasons for such illusion to be present, not the least of which is the importance of contracts in business transactions. In the long run contracts can be renegotiated, but in the short run there are important costs to breaking and renegotiating them. Even when "contracts" are broken in any case, as when workers leave jobs in the home-goods sector to take up jobs in the foreign-trade sector, they may be willing to move at real wages lower than their pre-devaluation wages in the expectation of greater job security if they do so. Thus, while money illusion is not normally necessary for devaluation to be successful in improving the trade balance, the more widespread it is, and the longer it lasts, the greater will be the gain to reserves in the period following a devaluation of a given amount.

In another respect, however, money illusion is even more important. Some factors of production profited (at the expense of others, and of the national reserves) before the devaluation, when the domestic costs of foreign-trade goods were too high. This state of affairs was not sustainable in the long run, but those factors that did profit may be most reluctant to accept the reduction in real rewards that is in fact necessary, given the regime of taxes and other policies that affect the distribution of income. If through "bargaining power" (strong unions, administered prices) they succeed in raising their money incomes enough to restore their pre-devaluation level of real income, then the initial disequilibrium will also have been restored. The authorities will be forced to devalue again in the hope that it will work (or can be made to work) the second time. Or they may in the end have to reduce domestic demand, thereby creating unemployment and damaging all groups (although not equally) as the only way to resolve the incompatible objectives of payments equilibrium and level of real income (at full employment) acceptable to those who benefit from the disequilibrium. Money illusion will help to resolve the difficulty by permitting the groups in question to accept lower real incomes while still keeping up appearances with high and even somewhat enlarged money incomes.

II. MODIFICATION IN THE ANALYSIS FOR DEVALUATION IN MOST DEVELOPING COUNTRIES

The foreign-exchange system of a country can be used to pursue many objectives other than clearance of the foreign-exchange market, and, faced with inadequate instruments of policy to achieve the many objectives expected of them, the governments of many less developed countries have called upon it to do so. These functions range from fostering industrialization, improving the terms of trade, and raising revenue to redistributing income among broad classes and even doling out favors to political supporters. A practice used frequently to accomplish all three of the first objectives, and also to redistribute income, is to give primary export products a rate of conversion into local currency lower than the rate that importers must pay to purchase foreign exchange (and that exporters of nontraditional products receive). Import-substituting investment is stimulated by the unfavorable rate on imports, foreign export prices are higher than they otherwise would be in the rare event that the country can influence world prices for its products, and the government gains revenue from the often substantial difference between the buying and selling prices of foreign exchange. Similarly, imported consumer goods are often charged a rate much higher than imported investment goods, in an effort to stimulate invest-

ment in manufacturing (and with the undesirable side-effect of encouraging modes of production that use relatively more capital and
relatively more imported ingredients or components). Finally, and not
least, the exchange system can be used to redistribute income between
broad classes, as for example in Argentina when the exchange rate applied to traditional exports, meat and wheat, was deliberately kept low
for a number of years with a view to keeping down the cost of living
for urban workers.

All of these functions involve multiple exchange rates of some kind,
either explicit or implicit, that is, charging different exchange rates according to the commodity or service, the origin or destination, or the
persons involved in the transaction. As such, they inevitably invite
arbitrage and require policing—but so of course do taxes, which they
often replace in function.

Moreover, politicians have learned that an objective achieved indirectly is frequently socially acceptable when direct action would not
be. This is not always because of an imperfect understanding of the
indirect means in contrast to the direct means, although that plays an
important role. It is much easier for an interest group to mobilize successfully against an export tax than it is to mobilize against an over-valued
currency supplemented by high import tariffs and possibly accompanied
by some export subsidies, even though the two systems might have precisely the same economic effects. As Fritz Machlup has said (in connection with Special Drawing Rights): "We have often seen how disagreements among scholars were resolved when ambiguous language was replaced by clear formulations not permitting different interpretations.
The opposite is true in politics. Disagreements on political matters,
national or international, can be resolved only if excessively clear language is avoided, so that each negotiating party can put its own interpretation on the provisions proposed and may claim victory in having
its own point of view prevail in the final agreement." Machlup was
speaking of language, but the same is true of action; a roundabout way
of accomplishing a controversial objective will often succeed where
direct action would fail, because it obscures, perhaps even from the policy-
makers themselves, who is really benefitting and who is being hurt.

The difficulty is that the pursuit of these diverse objectives too often
leads to neglect of the function of the exchange rate in allocating the
supply of foreign exchange. When balance-of-payments pressures develop (sometimes as a result of inflationary policies, which in the short
run are often also a successfully ambiguous way to reconcile conflicting
social objectives), officials then engage in a series of patchwork efforts
and marginal adjustments to make the problem go away (raising tariffs

here, prohibiting payments there), which may disturb the original objectives as well as coping only inadequately with the payments difficulty. When devaluation finally occurs, in consequence, the occasion is also taken (sometimes under pressures from the IMF or from foreign-aid donors) to sweep away many of the ad hoc measures that have been instituted to avoid the necessity for devaluation.

This fact makes currency devaluation in many developing countries (and some developed ones) a good deal more complex than a simple adjustment of the exchange rate, and the analysis must be modified to take these other adjustments into account. Broadly speaking, one can distinguish four types of devaluation "packages": (1) straight devaluation (involving a discrete change in the principal exchange rate, as opposed to a freely depreciating rate or an administered "slide" in the rate, such as was adopted by Brazil, Chile, and Colombia in the late sixties, whereby the rate was depreciated by a small amount every two to eight weeks); (2) devaluation with a *stabilization* program of contractionary monetary and fiscal policy aimed at reducing the level of aggregate demand, or at least the rate of increase of demand; (3) devaluation accompanied by *liberalization*, whereby imports and other international payments that were previously prohibited or subject to quota are allowed to take place under much less restraint than before the devaluation; and (4) devaluation accompanied by partial or full *unification* of exchange rates, whereby a pre-existing diversity of exchange rates is collapsed into a single, unified rate, or at most two rates, the lower one applying to traditional exports of primary products and in effect amounting to a tax on these exports.

It is obvious that these categories are not mutually exclusive. Devaluation may involve simultaneously a stabilization program, liberalization, and exchange-rate unification, and in fact at least some elements of all are often present in devaluation in developing countries. For example, of 24 devaluations studied in some detail (and which will provide the basis for evidence cited below), ten involved a fairly substantial degree of trade liberalization, ten (partially overlapping) involved a major consolidation of rates, and virtually all were accompanied by at least token measures of stabilization. (It might be mentioned in passing that in most developing countries the distinction between monetary and fiscal policy does not have the same meaning it has in more advanced countries. Since capital markets are little developed and access to foreign capital markets is limited, budget deficits, after allowing for foreign assistance, must be financed by the banking system, which results directly or indirectly in monetary expansion. Thus, the usual focus on eliminating government deficits is merely an indirect way to limit the rate of monetary expansion, provided, of course, that bank credit to the private sector is also kept under control.)

These various simultaneous adjustments must be taken into account in analyzing the economic effects of devaluation. In particular, it is necessary to distinguish between devaluation from a position of open payments deficit, such as we considered in the preceding section, and devaluation from a position in which a latent deficit is suppressed by import controls and related measures, which are removed upon devaluation. An additional complication is that less developed countries are more likely at the time of devaluation to be generating new money demand at a rate greater than can be accommodated by total domestic output plus foreign assistance and other long-term capital inflows from abroad; in short, they are pursuing inflationary policies, as opposed merely to having costs that have gotten out of line in the course of *past* inflation.

In fact, most devaluing countries have some combination of an open payments deficit and a suppressed one. But for clarity of exposition, and to bring out the contrast with the analysis above most clearly, we will consider devaluation from a position in which the payments deficit is fully suppressed by other measures, and where the devaluation is accompanied by liberalization and/or unification of the exchange system involving the removal of special taxes, subsidies, and prohibitions that have been installed earlier. In addition, we will suppose that the country is not pursuing inflationary policies at the time of devaluation.

Elasticity Pessimism

The first point to note is that the elasticity of demand for imports is likely to be low when imports are concentrated on raw materials, semi-fabricated products, and capital goods, a structure prevalent in less developed countries. With import substitution in an advanced stage, all the easy substitutions having already been made in the pursuit of industrialization; imports depend largely on output rather than income and are not very sensitive to relative price changes. There is more room for substituting home production for imports of foodstuffs, although it will usually take a season or longer to bring this about. Moreover, import liberalization and exchange-rate unification will actually result in a *reduction* of the prices of those imports most tightly restrained before the devaluation, so consumption of them will be encouraged.

There is greater diversity of experience with regard to exports. Some countries—producers of oil, copper, and cocoa, for instance—have virtually no domestic consumption of the export goods. In others, exports include the major wage good—beef in Argentina and fish in Iceland, for instance. In the former countries, increasing exports require enlarged output and development of new export products, and neither of these courses may be easy in the short run, although tree crops can sometimes be more intensively harvested. In the latter countries, there is more room for immediate increases in exports permitted by reductions in domestic consumption of the export products, but this gain is brought about only by courting a wage-price spiral, on which more will be said below. In developed countries, by contrast, there are many domestically consumed goods that are actual or potential exports, and hence there is more room for short-term increases in export supply by diverting output from the home to the foreign market.

When it comes to incentives to enlarge output and expand capacity, the principal reallocation here is between import-competing goods and exports, rather than between home goods and all foreign-trade goods, as in the case of open economies. This is because by assumption imports have already been stringently limited by high tariffs, disadvantageous exchange rates, and quantitative restrictions, all of which create a strong price incentive for domestic production. Some exports may also have been subsidized and, where this is so, devaluation accompanied by removal of the subsidy may leave no new incentive to increase production for export. But, generally speaking, exports are heavily penalized under the regimes we are considering, and devaluation has the effect of reducing the premium for producing import-competing goods for the home market and increasing the premium for production for export, with the principal shift in incentives coming between these two sectors rather than with respect to the home-goods sector (although of course there will also be some incentive to shift resources into that sector from the import-competing sector and out of it to the export sector).

New investment in the capacity to export will require that investors expect the improvement in their position to last, that the devaluation and associated policies will establish a new regime that will not simply slide back into the old configuration of policies. Establishing these expectations is one of the most difficult tasks of those carrying out the reform. The same problem exists in principle in devaluation from open deficit too, but developing countries that have not relied on restriction of imports for payments reasons stand a better chance of success, because investors will expect any emerging disequilibrium to be corrected rather than suppressed by controls.

Furthermore, the required investment may differ in character from that in developed countries. Where manufactures can be competitively exported under the new regime, conversion from domestic manufacturing may be relatively easy; but opening up export markets for manufactured goods for the first time is a drawn-out process, requiring the establishment of new marketing channels. The shift from domestic to export crops in agriculture—or the opening of new lands—is generally easier; but for livestock and for tree crops the required gestation period may be several years.

For all of these reasons, some pessimism with regard to price elasticities would be quite justified for many developing countries, at least in the short run, but as we will see below it does not usually go far enough to prevent devaluation from improving the trade balance.

Effects on Aggregate Demand

The absorption approach suggests that a devaluation that merely substitutes for other measures, leading to no net improvement in the balance on goods and services, requires no cut in aggregate expenditure or increase in total output. But it is still worth asking what pressure devaluation in these circumstances might put on aggregate expenditure and output, since this will give some guide to the possible need for compensatory macroeconomic policy. To provide a framework for discussion, rewrite the basic equation noted above as $Y = E + D$, where $D = X - M$, the balance on goods and services measured in domestic currency. In order to discover the impact effect on output, Y, we must ask what will be the effects of devaluation on its two components, the level of domestic expenditure and the external balance measured in domestic currency. The impact on output will in turn affect incomes, expenditure, imports, and output again in a multiplier process. But the impact effect will tell us the impetus to this multiplier process, and in particular whether it is expansionary or deflationary.

To take the external balance first, for the reasons given above this might actually worsen in the period immediately following devaluation, when measured in foreign currency, and this by itself would have a deflationary impact upon the economy. The worsening would occur if import liberalization takes effect immediately, giving rise to an increase in imports, while the stimulus to exports occurs only with a lag. In time, of course, the stimulus to exports will also stimulate the domestic economy; but the immediate impact would be a deflationary one. Furthermore, any discrepancy between the local-currency value of a dollar's worth of imports and a dollar's worth of exports, for example due to tariffs, means that even a parallel expansion of imports and exports will be deflationary, provided the government does not spend the additional revenue at once.

Thirdly, devaluation is deflationary to the extent that remaining quotas are replaced in their import-restricting effects by the depreciated exchange rate. Scarcity rents that went to privileged importers before the devaluation would now accrue to the central bank as it sells foreign exchange. In effect, price rationing will have replaced quantitative rationing, with no ultimate effect on the *final* market price, but with a higher domestic-currency price to the importer or firm enjoying the license. (If the licenses are auctioned, of course, these scarcity rents accrue to the government even before devaluation; but auctioning of licenses is in fact rare.)

Finally, the inelasticity of demand for imports suggests that a sharp rise in their local-currency price will lead to an increase in *expenditure* upon them, even if the quantity and foreign-exchange value of imports fall. In this respect devaluation is like an efficient revenue-oriented excise tax, increasing the price far more than it reduces the quantity purchased. Since imports will substantially exceed exports, thanks to inflows of foreign grants and capital, exports will have to expand a great deal before the increased local-currency income from their sale exceeds the increased local-currency expenditure on imports.

For all these mutually reinforcing reasons, the initial impact of devaluation on the domestic economy of a developing country is likely to be deflationary in that it will reduce purchasing power available for expenditure on domestic output. This may be so, paradoxically, even when the trade balance improves in terms of foreign currency. Thus in 14 of 24 devaluations examined, the balance measured in domestic currency worsened following devaluation—without including increased tariff revenues on imports—and in seven of these this worsening occurred despite an improvement in the balance when measured in foreign currency.

The external sector, however, is only one component of demand. It is necessary also to ask how devaluation may affect the level of total domestic expenditure, E. Refined analysis is required to discuss the possible effects satisfactorily, but here it will be sufficient to identify six effects that are likely to be important in developing countries.

(1) There is first the *speculative effect*, which is also important in devaluations from open deficits. If devaluation has been anticipated and is expected to lead to a general increase in prices there will be anticipatory buying before the devaluation and the post-devaluation period will therefore commence with larger-than-usual holdings of goods. Total expenditure by the public may therefore drop in the period immediately following devaluation, until these inventories are worked off. (This effect would also lead to a rise in imports before and a drop after the devaluation, insofar as this is permitted by the system of licensing or other controls.) While the speculative effect will normally lead to a drop in expenditure, however, it may lead to an increase if the price

increases following devaluation are expected to lead to general inflation, or if another devaluation is in prospect, as it did immediately following Britain's devaluation in 1967.

(2) Devaluation will generally lead to a redistribution of income, and this *distributive effect*, while present for any devaluation, is likely to be especially important in developing countries with heavy reliance on primary products for export. Unless checked by special export taxes, a devaluation will lead to a sharp increase in rewards to those in the export industry, who are often landowners. Whether large or small, landowners are likely to have different saving and consumption patterns from urban dwellers, generally saving more out of marginal changes in income, at least in the short run. Thus, a redistribution of real income from workers to businessmen and from urban to rural dwellers is likely, in the first instance, to lead to a drop in total expenditure out of a given aggregate income, and this drop will be deflationary. But of course the redistributional effect could also go the other way, if as a result of devaluation the real income of those with a low marginal propensity to save is increased at the expense of others. The redistributional effect will also affect the level of imports out of a given total income, since consumption pattern of those who gain may differ from that of losers. But this effect is likely to be less marked than the total expenditure effect, partly because much of the import bill of developing countries represents inputs into domestically produced goods and services, so they are somewhat more widely diffused throughout the economy than would be the case for direct imports of manufactured consumer goods. Diaz-Alejandro has documented well the dominating importance of the redistributive effect following the Argentine devaluation of 1959, where the shift of income to the landowners led to a sharp drop in domestic spending and therefore to a secondary drop in imports.

(3) A devaluation will lead to a rise in the domestic costs of servicing *external debt* denominated in foreign currency. Where the liabilities are those of businessmen who do not benefit much from the devaluation, it may lead to bankruptcy and an attendant decline in business activity, even when businesses are otherwise sound. This factor allegedly figured in the decline in investment following the Argentine devaluation of 1962. Even where the debt is held officially, the problem of raising the local-currency counterpart of external servicing charges often poses a serious problem, and sometimes represents a serious inhibition to devaluation.

Indeed (to digress for a moment), these "accounting" relationships, usually ignored by economists, often preoccupy officials and bankers.

Local development banks that have borrowed abroad (for instance, from the World Bank or IDA) in foreign currencies and re-lent to local business in domestic currency have accepted an exchange risk that has occasionally provided the major barrier to devaluation: to allow its development bank to fail might psychologically undermine the government's development plans. But if the bank is to be saved, who is to absorb the devaluation loss, and how? (The obvious retrospective answer is that local borrowers should be charged interest rates sufficiently above what the development bank pays on its foreign debt to cover the exchange risk—with the added advantage that such rates will more closely approximate the true cost of capital in the developing country. But development banks have often failed to do this. Or, if they have done it, they have failed to set aside a sufficiently large reserve out of the difference in rates.) A similar problem arises for net *creditors* when the value of their foreign claims is reduced in terms of local currency by devaluation abroad or revaluation of the home currency. Thus, Hong Kong inadvisedly devalued its currency following the 1967 devaluation of sterling, apparently because the commercial banks in Hong Kong held large sterling assets against their local-currency deposits, and the banking system would have been threatened if the relationship between sterling and Hong Kong dollars had not been preserved. But the government thought better of this decision and revalued again four days later, in the meantime having worked out a way to indemnify the banks out of official reserves. By the same token, the German Bundesbank showed substantial paper losses (in marks) on its assets held in gold and dollars following the revaluations of 1961 and 1969. The 1961 revaluation was delayed until the German government would agree to indemnify the bank for its "losses" (which were entirely paper losses, arising from double-entry bookkeeping conventions) out of the budget over a period of seven years. Where private parties have incurred foreign debt, of course, the loss is real to the firm or bank, and that may have undesirable consequences for the economy as a whole. But a thorough discussion of this important issue is beyond the scope of the present essay.

(4) When the balance of goods and services has turned adverse in terms of domestic currency—as we have seen above may frequently be expected—then in the absence of countervailing monetary action a domestic *credit squeeze* may result, since importers and others will be paying more into the central bank for foreign exchange than exporters are receiving. This in turn may lead to a reduction in domestic expenditure.

(5) On the other hand, the improved earning opportunities in the export industries may (if they are expected to last) induce both *domestic*

and foreign investment in the country. Foreign investors bring their funds with them, as it were, and increase local credit by converting foreign exchange into domestic currency at the central bank. Domestic investors must either activate idle balances or find banks willing and able to lend, in the second instance leading to domestic credit expansion. Of course, the incentives to invest in import-competing industries will be reduced by the devaluation (in sharp contrast to the case of devaluation from a position of open deficit, where they will be stimulated by devaluation); but the stimulus to investment may on balance be positive, partly because there are limits to the rate at which disinvestment can take place. For reasons given earlier, however, the extent of new investment will depend on expectations about the durability of the new regime, and investors may wait awhile to see how things are going.

(6) In the monetary approach to devaluation from an open deficit, attention was drawn to the reduction in the real value of money holdings and reliance was placed on a desire to reconstitute these holdings to reduce expenditure. In the case of devaluation from a suppressed deficit, however, this *money-demand* effect is more complicated, and may not be present at all. If devaluation simply displaces other instruments of policy, with no effect on domestic prices, the real value of money balances will not be altered. If, as is more typically the case, devaluation displaces some other limits on imports but raises the local prices of exports, the effect on the real value of money holdings will depend upon the importance of export products in local expenditure. When export products are extensively purchased by residents, the monetary effect will tend to reduce domestic spending. Import liberalization, on the other hand, cuts the other way insofar as import prices actually fall. Moreover, in the long run another factor comes into play: to the extent that devaluation displaces measures that led to a less efficient use of resources, the devaluation package will lead (after the necessary reallocation of resources has taken place) to an increase in real income, and this in turn will require a supporting increase in money holdings. Unless it is supplied by the monetary authorities, this demand will depress expenditure relative to potential income.

The upshot of these various considerations is that devaluation in developing countries is likely to be deflationary in the first instance, and thus may "make room" for any improvement in the balance on goods and services, without active reinforcement from monetary and fiscal policy. Indeed, for reasons given below, it may sometimes be desirable to accompany devaluation with modestly *expansionary* policies. Frequently, however, the devaluation will take place against a background of excessively expansionary policies. In this case the devaluation-induced deflation will be helpful in bringing the economy under control, but these effects must be taken into account if the government is to avoid overshooting the target with deliberately contractionary measures.

In short, unless the devaluation is very successful in stimulating exports or in stimulating investment, the absorption approach to devaluation is of less relevance to devaluation in developing countries except in manifestly inflationary situations—the real problem will often be getting adequate capacity in the export sector, not in releasing resources overall.

Before turning to the actual experience of devaluations in developing countries, it should be noted that a devaluation will have powerful short-run distributive effects (alluded to above in the discussion of the impact of devaluation on expenditure). When tariffs are reduced (unless they are offset by a reduction in subsidies), the government loses revenue; when quotas are eliminated, quota-holders lose the quasi-rents they enjoyed by getting a scarce resource (the right to import) at a price below its social value. When prices rise, all those on fixed money incomes suffer. Petty officials responsible for licensing or tariff collection may also lose the "fees" they can collect by virtue of their position of control. The gainers are those in the actual and potential export industries and, where a quota system is replaced by a dual exchange-rate system (the lower rate usually applying to traditional exports), the government. These prospective gains and losses influence sectional attitudes toward devaluation and their willingness to help make it succeed.

III. SOME EVIDENCE ON THE IMPACT OF DEVALUATION

Having set out how the conventional analysis of devaluation may have to be adapted to devaluations in developing countries, we turn now to the actual experience of these countries with devaluation. As noted in the introduction, currency devaluations have occurred with some frequency in the last 25 years, averaging nearly ten a year, despite widespread reluctance to engage in them. Many of these were small, or were by countries with inadequate statistics, or were by developed countries, or were part of a larger movement of exchange rates of one block of countries as against another—the last kind of devaluation raising rather different issues for analysis than have been considered above. The evidence drawn on here derives from a study of 24 devaluations occurring over the period 1953-66 and including most of the major devaluations by developing countries in the early 1960s (a more complete description and analysis of these cases is found in Chapter 13 of G. Ranis, ed., *Government and Economic Development*, Yale University Press, 1971), supplemented by some experience drawn from about a dozen devaluations in the late 1960s.

There are many questions that one can ask about the consequences of devaluation and its associated package of policies, which may have profound effects upon the allocation of resources, growth, and the distribution of income in developing economies. We are not concerned with these ultimate effects—although empirical work on them is all too rare—but, rather, with the immediate, impact effects of devaluation. These start the transition to the longer-term effects, if they are given a chance to work themselves out. The reason for focussing on impact effects is that they often determine whether the longer-term effects will be given a chance to work themselves out. Officials have notoriously short planning horizons, and their anxieties about the impact effects of devaluation often lead to a postponement of devaluation and the substitution in its place of numerous ad hoc measures, imposing substantial costs by impeding the efficient operation of the economy.

The reluctance of officials arises in large measure from the considerations adduced in the introduction: devaluation will disturb an implicit social contract among different segments of society—or at least will jar some groups out of their acquiescence in the existing state of affairs, with its numerous implicit compromises—and officials are understandably anxious about rocking an overloaded and delicately balanced boat. But sooner or later the decision may be forced upon them, when for external or internal reasons the external disequilibrium deepens and a suppressed deficit becomes an open deficit which can be corrected only by disturbing the social equilibrium anyway.

More specific anxieties are also expressed about the consequences of devaluation, however, and they can be grouped under four headings: (1) Devaluation, it is feared, will not achieve the desired improvement in the balance of payments, because neither imports nor exports are sufficiently sensitive to relative price changes within the acceptable range of such changes—in a phrase, elasticity pessimism. (2) Devaluation will worsen the terms of trade of the country and thus will impose real costs on it. (3) By raising domestic prices, devaluation will set in motion a wage-price spiral that will rapidly undercut the improved competitiveness that the devaluation is designed to achieve. (4) Whatever its economic effects, it is thought that devaluation will be politically disastrous for those officials responsible for it.

Let us see to what extent these fears are justified by experience, adopting the short-run (one year, say) perspective of the official.

Impact on Trade and Payments

In nearly three-fourths of the three dozen devaluations examined the balance on goods and services, measured in foreign currency (as is appropriate for balance-of-payments analysis, although a number of countries record their payments positions in domestic currency), improved in the year following devaluation. In 90 per cent of the cases either this or the overall monetary balance (often both) improved in the year following devaluation. Of the four countries that showed a worsening on both counts, two involved important import liberalization resulting in a rise in imports, and one (Israel) was engaged in sporadic warfare and was running down reserves to build up its defense position.

Of course, these actual improvements could have taken place for reasons quite independent of the devaluation, for example an increase in world demand for the country's products or a drop in domestic expenditure due to a crop failure. Adjustment of the trade data to allow for movements in world demand and for changes in the level of domestic activity reveals a slight increase in the number of countries improving their trade balance following devaluation.

These improvements occurred despite good reasons for being an elasticity pessimist about developing countries, for the reasons given above. No doubt some part of the improvement both in trade and in overall payments can be explained by the speculative considerations already mentioned—a reversal of flows after the devaluation occurred. But not all of it can be explained in this way, for the second year following devaluation usually showed a preservation of, and sometimes a substantial increase in, the gains. The fact that supply elasticities are low in the short run helps in theory to assure that there is little or no loss in export receipts such as would arise if supply could be increased rapidly at unchanged *domestic* prices. A steadiness in export earnings, combined with some reduction in imports, will assure some improvement in the trade balance, but only a modest one. In only five of the cases examined did the improvement in the trade balance exceed the initial trade deficit, thereby swinging the country into trade surplus—a fact that should not be surprising for countries that normally import capital from the rest of the world.

Interestingly enough, most of the countries that liberalized imports experienced a *reduction* in the volume of imports in the year following devaluation—partly because of a decline in activity and a switching away from imports to domestic sources of supply, but even more because import liberalization was often delayed from three to nine months following the devaluation, apparently reflecting a wait-and-see attitude on the part of the authorities toward the devaluation. In delaying, however, they increased the risk of a wage-price spiral.

Impact on the Terms of Trade

Many countries do not have even reasonably comprehensive data on the prices they pay for imports and receive for their exports, hence on their terms of trade. Among those that do, somewhat under one-half showed a deterioration in the terms of trade following devaluation. But some of these deteriorations were independent of the devaluation, and in any case all were small relative to the size of the devaluation—one or two per cent, compared with nominal devaluations ranging from ten to nearly 70 per cent.

The negligible deterioration observed in the terms of trade may of course have been due to preventive measures taken by the devaluing countries. Most of them imposed special taxes (or a disadvantageous exchange rate, lower than the new principal rate) on certain exports of primary products. But usually these taxes were imposed for distributive or revenue reasons, not to prevent a deterioration in the terms of trade through a fall in foreign-currency prices of exports. A standard pattern, for example, is to impose a tax roughly equivalent to the amount of devaluation on exports out of the current harvest, on the ground that the quantity of such exports can be increased only marginally (unless domestic consumption is substantial) and there is no reason to pass windfall gains on to the farmers. The new exchange rate is applied to subsequent harvests. In other instances the tax has been imposed to prevent an immediate rise in the domestic price of an export product important in local consumption, such as olive oil in Greece. In both cases it is a rise in domestic prices, not a fall in foreign ones, that the authorities are guarding against. Where only one or two foreign marketing organizations dominate a country's export sales, however, these buyers may retain their pre-devaluation buying price for domestic produce, which of course implies a decline in the price in terms of foreign currency. Thus, existing institutional arrangements may permit foreign buyers, in the short run, to improve their terms of trade at the expense of the devaluing country, and a tax will help to prevent this. In the long run, competition from potential foreign buyers will also prevent it, but by that time domestic supplies may also have increased. Finally, there are some commodities—such as hazel nuts in Turkey, jute in Pakistan, cocoa in Ghana—where one country does have a dominant position in the world market, and in these cases too the imposition of an export tax or its equivalent will prevent a deterioration in the terms of trade.

But preoccupation with the terms-of-trade effects of devaluation in fact reflects a misunderstanding of the purposes of devaluation, or at best confuses devaluation theory with optimal-tariff theory. A country that dominates world markets in one or more of its export products can increase its welfare by imposing a tax on those exports up to the point at which the additional gains from further increases in the foreign-currency price (arising from the willingness of foreign buyers to pay part of the tax) just compensate for the additional welfare losses arising from the tax-induced reduction in trade. If the devaluing country has already imposed such optimizing export tariffs—import tariffs alone will not do here, because in equilibrium they also discourage manufactured exports, on which the optimal export tax is surely zero for developing countries—then devaluation will not require their alteration unless the causes of the payments imbalance also happen to have altered the optimum export tax. A pre-devaluation rise in domestic costs and prices, leading indeed to the need for devaluation, will have improved the country's terms of trade *beyond* the optimal point. The objective should be to maximize net returns on exporting, not merely to prevent a deterioration in the terms of trade, and in these circumstances some lowering of export prices in terms of foreign currency will be desirable to stimulate foreign purchases.

As a slight digression, it might be mentioned that at least one country, Jamaica, devalued because of a deterioration in its terms of trade caused by devaluation of *another* currency, the pound sterling. Britain buys Jamaica's sugar and bananas at prices fixed in sterling well above world-market prices. At the same time, Jamaica's imports are much more diversified as to source. When sterling was devalued in November 1967, the real value of Jamaica's export earnings therefore dropped and, more than that, the receipts of Jamaica's major export plantations would have dropped in terms of Jamaican dollars, while their expenditures (including wage bill) would not have dropped by nearly as much. To prevent bankruptcy and large-scale unemployment in these important agricultural industries, Jamaica therefore devalued its currency to maintain its parity with the pound. Similar considerations (as well as balance-sheet ones) may have led the French African countries to devalue their currencies with the French franc in 1969.

Impact on Wages and Prices

Assessing the impact of devaluation on domestic prices and wages is exceptionally difficult, and only partly because price and wage data are sparse and of dubious quality for most developing countries. It is difficult also because exogenous events, expectational patterns based on the same history that led to the devaluation, and policies associated with but sometimes also at variance with the devaluation all may have important influences on both wages and prices.

It is useful first of all to distinguish between demand-induced and cost-induced increases in prices and wages. By conventional analysis, both should be present following a successful devaluation, for the improved trade balance will increase the claims on domestic output, and the devaluation will lead directly to an increase in the local prices of imports and other foreign-trade goods. We have seen, however, that devaluation may lead to a decline rather than an increase in demand for domestic output, and this alone would tend to depress prices. The extent to which devaluing countries have taken the advice normally tendered to pursue deflationary monetary and fiscal policies will reinforce these devaluation-induced pressures. There is of course no contradiction between deflationary pressures and observed price increases; the devaluation here is very much like an excise tax, which reduces demand by withdrawing purchasing power from circulation, but also raises local prices. Where the devaluation merely substitutes for other measures to restrict imports, such as quotas or special tariffs, there need, of course, be no rise in these prices following devaluation, for under competitive conditions the local market prices will have already risen to reflect scarcity values.

In fact, some depression in economic activity is frequently found following devaluation in developing countries, sometimes lasting only a few months, not infrequently lasting more than a year. While it is impossible to disentangle the deflationary effects of devaluation from those of autonomous policy measures designed to facilitate success of the devaluation, there is much circumstantial evidence to suggest that the extent of depression is a surprise to the authorities in the devaluing countries, that they have not adequately taken into account the depressing effects of the devaluation itself, or that they have exaggerated its expansionary impetus. In too many cases, of course, the need to devalue arises from pre-devaluation inflation that has not been brought fully under control even after devaluation, and these cases reinforce the views of those who insist on strongly deflationary measures to accompany devaluation; in those cases further deflation is necessary to make the devaluation work. But in other cases further deflation is not necessary, and on the contrary may aggravate the difficulties of the authorities in keeping the situation under control just as exports are expanding most rapidly. We return to this possibility below.

Despite the theoretical argument that under some circumstances domestic prices need not rise following devaluation, in fact they invariably do. This is partly because there is normally some effective devaluation for imports and export products, even when export subsidies are removed and imports are liberalized, and partly because the instinctive reaction of importers is to pass along to their customers any increase in costs that they have incurred. If they are already charging what the market will bear, however, these higher prices are not sustainable in a given monetary environment, and in the course of time competition among importers will result in a subsequent drop in prices—not to below the pre-devaluation level, but toward it, to an extent governed by the degree to which devaluation substitutes for import quotas as a restraint on imports. Such a pattern can be observed for about half of the few countries for which adequate monthly data on local prices of imports are available: prices rise sharply following devaluation, reach a peak three or four months later, and then gradually drop back, sometimes substantially. In an inflationary monetary environment, of course, one does not observe a post-devaluation decline in prices, but the rate of increase is reduced temporarily.

Higher prices will raise costs directly (especially since many imports are intermediate products and capital goods) and they will also stimulate demands for higher money incomes by local factors of production, especially wage and salary employees. But the cycle of wage and price increases should be self-limiting, unless *all* parties (including the government) attempt to maintain their real incomes in the face of rising import prices, or unless the devaluation stimulates price increases that are quite unrelated to increases in costs. In addition, for either case the monetary authorities must support the increase in money incomes with domestic credit expansion if domestic prices and incomes are to rise by the full amount of the devaluation without generating unemployment.

As we saw in the first section, an open deficit will reflect both a level of expenditure and a distribution of income that is not sustainable at the existing level of output and with the existing structure of taxation and expenditures insofar as they affect distribution. Devaluation requires that some real incomes go down and that total expenditures go down, even though aggregate income need not drop. If, however, those who benefitted from the initial disequilibrium insist on retaining the same level of real income, and if they have the market power through administered prices or through wage bargaining to stake out that claim in monetary terms, then the devaluation cannot succeed without general deflation leading to unemployment—unless, of course, there is some unutilized capacity and the tax system can be so altered as to assure that enough of the increased output will go to the powerful factors in the post-devaluation period. Even this will not work if these factors insist on maintaining their pre-devaluation *share* of income.

Second, the devaluation may stimulate price increases that were overdue in any case, but for reasons of law, custom, fear of public opprobrium, or simply inertia were not made earlier—the liquidation of unliquidated monopoly gains, to use Galbraith's term. This problem arises especially with public utilities subjected to an inflationary environment in the past. Being highly visible to the public, electric companies and bus companies do not readily raise their rates, and they are frequently under substantial government pressure not to do so. A currency devaluation, being little understood by the public, presents a natural occasion to raise such prices and lay responsibility on the devaluation. Several devaluations have led to rioting in the streets—as well as to larger wage claims—when an economically unrelated but psychologically related increase in urban bus fares occurred shortly afterward.

In either case the monetary authorities are confronted with a dilemma; it is here that management of a devaluation is trickiest. Economists have been too little interested in these matters of management, even though they affect the final result (that is, the path is important for determining the equilibrium, or indeed whether equilibrium is achieved). For, if the authorities do not allow some monetary expansion, unemployment and underutilization will result; and if they do allow it, the effects of the devaluation will be weakened and perhaps undermined. That various groups attempt to maintain their pre-devaluation incomes poses a more acute problem in the case of devaluation from open deficit than devaluation from suppressed deficit, since in the latter case much of the adjustment toward equilibrium income distribution will already have been made, except insofar as some firms and individuals are profiting from quantitative restrictions. Since developing countries generally do rely on quantitative restrictions before devaluation, and since they also generally have some open deficit in spite of their ad hoc adjustments, the problem remains a practical one.

In the event, price-wage spiraling does not generally get out of control, at least within the year or so following devaluation. Twelve months after devaluation, wholesale prices of imported goods will generally have risen, but by less than the devaluation (after having fallen from a peak reached three or four months after devaluation, as noted earlier), general wholesale prices will have risen less than this, consumer prices will have risen by about the same as wholesale prices, and, except where devaluations are small, manufacturing wages will have risen by less than consumer prices, showing a decline in real wages following the devaluation. Thus nonwage incomes of employed factors— mostly profits and rents—show an increase in real terms a year later, and it is this increase that provides the incentive for the necessary reallocation of resources, which reallocation may ultimately restore and even raise real wages, depending on the relative factor intensities in the export industries as opposed to the protected industries.

Thus, to sum up briefly the experience following devaluations in less developed countries, it seems that official anxieties concerning the economic effects are exaggerated. The firmest generalization that can be made is that country experiences are highly diverse, which of course may be unsettling to cautious officials. But, for a hypothetical "representative" country, devaluation seems to improve both the trade balance and the payments position within the first year; it does not seem to lead to deterioration in the terms of trade of any consequence; it does lead to price increases, but not by amounts great enough to undermine the devaluation; price increases of imports are substantially less than the devaluation, suggesting that importer margins have been reduced; real wages fall; and there is a slump in economic activity following the devaluation.

The Political Impact

The fourth apprehension concerns the political fate of those responsible for the decision to devalue, and here experience is not nearly so encouraging. A naive test is whether the government fell within a year of the devaluation. In nearly 30 per cent of the cases examined it did. Some of these changes in government were clearly unrelated to the devaluation—Costa Rica and Colombia each happened to have elections within the year, for example, and both countries have quite regularly voted out the incumbent government in recent history, devaluation or not. But in other cases the devaluation and associated policies for managing the economy were the main issue on which the government fell. And there were near misses in both Israel (1962) and India (1966), where the ruling government came under severe criticism for its decision to devalue, but survived the crisis for more than a year.

A check was provided by examining a random control group of similar countries that did not devalue; governments changed within the year in only 14 per cent of the control sample. Thus it appears that devaluation—or the policies that led to the need for devaluation or the policies that followed it—roughly doubles the chance that a ruling group will be removed from power. But the test will have to be refined considerably before it can be regarded as anything more than suggestive, in particular by selecting a control group from countries that seem to be in some balance-of-payments difficulty, either of an open or a suppressed type, rather than just from all developing countries.

Ministers of finance fared much worse. Nearly 60 per cent of them lost their jobs in the year following devaluation—half of them of course when their governments fell—compared with a turnover in a control group of only 18 per cent. So the chances of ouster for the official immediately responsible seems to increase by a factor of three as a result of devaluation. Again the test should be refined. And, in any case, losing one's job as finance minister does not necessarily end a political career; James Callaghan of Britain felt obliged to resign after devaluing sterling, but was immediately promoted to Home Secretary.

IV. CONCLUSIONS

Managing a devaluation through the transition phase to final success requires both judgment and delicacy in handling. Consider first the problem of aggregate demand. As we noted, this frequently falls following a devaluation, and unless the economy was badly overheated beforehand it may lead to a drop in profits and employment. If the slump is sufficiently severe and prolonged, it will evoke calls for expansionary action by the government, for few governments these days can escape responsibility for developments in their economies. If the government then yields to these pressures, the expansionary policies may come when devaluation-induced export expansion is also taking hold with a lag, and thereby increase demand pressures on the economy at just the wrong time. The better course of action, on these grounds, would be to mitigate the slump—that is, to take some modest *expansionary* action with or immediately following the devaluation, contrary to the usual advice—and then to draw back with monetary and fiscal policy when new export demand is becoming important. Properly timed, this would reduce the social and economic costs of the slump and would prevent belated expansionary action, in response to political pressure, from undermining the effects of the devaluations on the trade balance.

On the other hand, we have also seen that there is often a sharp increase in prices in the period immediately following devaluation, as importers attempt to pass on to their customers all or most of the increased cost of foreign goods. To the extent that these price increases, some of which are not otherwise sustainable, get built into wages and other local costs, they will undermine the devaluation. Timing here becomes crucial. The authorities should do what they can to reduce the temporary increase in prices (lest it become permanent), to make sure that it comes quickly and is brief, and to delay any wage settlements or administered price increases until after the peak of import prices has been reached and they are falling.

The size of the temporary increase in prices can be influenced by the speed and extent of import liberalization, and this argues for liberalizing imports at once with devaluation (or even before, if that can be done without signalling the intention to devalue), instead of waiting several months as most countries have done. With respect to the promptness with which prices of imported goods begin to fall after their initial rise, the slump in total demand reinforces the desired outcome, and this factor cuts against the suggestion above that the slump should be mitigated. The timing of prospective wage settlements should if possible be taken into account in choosing the time to devalue, the aim being to allow a considerable lapse of time between devaluation and major wage settlements. Necessary increases in administered prices, such as those of public utilities or of industries in the public sector, should also be delayed until the temporary rise is past and some prices are falling. Finally, the seasonality of food prices should be taken into account; devaluations immediately after a good harvest are more likely to achieve prolonged success than are devaluations after a poor harvest or before the new harvest is in, when food stocks are low and food prices are rising. Bad harvests, in particular, have greatly weakened the impact of several devaluations, notably those of India in 1966 and Colombia in 1962.

New investment in the export sector will take place only if investors believe that the change in relative prices achieved through devaluation is a reasonably durable one. Thus, in terms of the timing of export response, *expectations* about the capacity and the will of the authorities to keep the economy under control are as important as their actual success in doing so. Here history lives in the present. A country with a poor record of monetary and fiscal management, and with a history of inflation, is likely to have greater difficulty in bringing about the required reallocation of resources than one with more favorable experience in these respects. A slump, deep if not prolonged, may (regrettably) be necessary in such a country in order to establish a new pattern of expectations.

Thus there is a dilemma with respect to macroeconomic management in the period immediately following a devaluation, and in the end the authorities must inevitably tailor their policies to the particular requirements of the country, to some extent even playing by ear. Short-term economic management of this type remains very much an art.

At the same time, the apparent political consequences of devaluation —an increased probability that governments will lose their positions and ministers their jobs—is unsettling. For it means that there may be a sharp conflict between the personal interests of those in authority and the interests of the country, a conflict that has to be resolved by those same persons, and which too often may be resolved at the expense of the country. This conflict perhaps plays an even greater role than the "social contract" considerations outlined earlier in leading to procrastination over devaluation and an attempt to substitute ad hoc restrictions and subventions.

It would thus be desirable to depoliticize the whole question of devaluation, by making it less traumatic both for the officials and for the public. This suggests another reason, in addition to more strictly economic ones, for moving toward greater flexibility of exchange rates along the lines of the gliding parity, as Brazil and Colombia have done. Gradual changes in exchange rates would not only eliminate the political jolt and major economic dislocations following a large discrete devaluation, with its sharp alteration of relative prices and hence of factor incomes, but would also avoid the major misallocation of resources that takes place as a disequilibrium builds up under a fixed exchange rate. Taking exchange-rate changes in small, frequent steps would also help to resolve the dilemma posed above: a slump would not be necessary to redirect resources into export industries.

CONTEMPORARY EXCHANGE RATE ECONOMICS

Rudiger Dornbusch

In the past fifteen years key exchange rates have moved in larger and more persistent ways than advocates of flexible rates in the late 1960s would have left anyone free to imagine. Certainly there was no expectation of constancy for nominal exchange rates. But real exchange rate movements of 30 or 40% were certainly not suggested as a realistic possibility. Moreover, where these large movements did occur, they did not obviously appear to be connected with fundamentals, and hence seemed difficult to explain in terms of the exchange rate theories at hand. The persistence of rate movements was as surprising as the rapid unwinding of apparent misalignments when they did ultimately happen. Research on exchange rate economics has grown tired searching for risk premia determinants or for new macroeconomic models. With a shift of interest toward the microeconomic effects of exchange rate movements, research is now turning in a fresh direction. It is therefore a good time to take stock of what is known of exchange rate economics, what has been learnt since the early 1970s and where more research needs to be done.

The past fifteen years provide a natural dividing line between the Keynesian and monetary approaches of the 1960s, and the more recent analysis that takes into account exchange rate expectations and portfolio issues. These took off in the early 1970s as well as the brand-new approaches that concentrate on (partial equilibrium) microeconomics. To review these ideas the paper starts with a brief look at the US experience with flexible exchange rates. From there we proceed to use the Mundell–Fleming model as a comprehensive framework of analysis. The following section draws attention to persistent effects of policy disturbances. The next three topics deal with the link between exchange rates and prices, the political economy of exchange rate movements and the question of policies toward excess capital mobility.

I. THE US EXPERIENCE WITH FLOATING RATES

The most striking result of the flexible rate experience is the recognition that the 'law of one price' is a poor description of the facts. Fig. 1 shows the real exchange rate of the US dollar over the past ten years. In the transition from fixed rates to floating in the early 1970s (not shown), the dollar depreciated by nearly 40%. An index of competitiveness in manufacturing (using the IMF series shown in Fig. 1) stood at 153 in 1968–70 and fell to 112 by 1973–5 which is also about the average for the period 1975–86 . Over the next ten years (1970-80) the

* This paper was originally presented at a meeting on exchange rates of the Royal Economic Society. I am indebted to Charles Goodhart, Stanley Fischer, Simon Johnson and the conference participants for their helpful comments and suggestions. Financial support was provided by a grant from the National Science Foundation.

Reprinted with permission and adapted with minor expansion from Exchange rate economics. 1986. *Economic Journal* 97, 1–18 (March 1987).

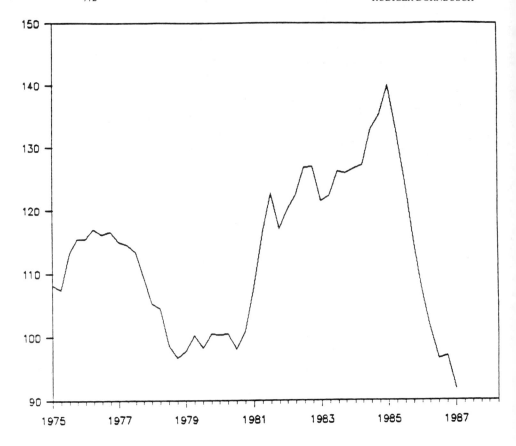

Fig. 1.   U.S. Real Exchange Rate (Index 1980-100.

dollar depreciated sharply until 1980. Then appreciation ensued, raising the dollar well above the level of the 1970s. Since 1985 the follar has been on a slide, taking it back by late 1986 to the average of the 1970s.

The recognition that real exchange rate changes have taken place on a massive scale, and that they have major and potentially persistent macroeconomic effects, points to several important directions for research:

(1) Why do exchange rates move so much and so persistently?

(2) Does the fact that real exchange rates remain misaligned so persistently imply that they must therefore ultimately overshoot to remedy the accumulated consequences of over- or undervaluation?

(3) Does a review of available theories and evidence suggest that exchange rate movements are based on irrational speculation rather than fundamentals?

(4) What are linkages between movements in the exchange rate and changes in relative prices?

(5) Do the large and persistent movements lead to the inevitable conclusion that exchange rate management offers a chance for better macroeconomic performance? If so, what is the externality, and thus what is the appropriate policy instrument, exchange rate-oriented monetary policy or a reduced scope for capital movements?

We are certainly not at a point to answer these questions in a satisfactory manner. But it is worthwhile seeing where the literature has gone and what suggestions are available. We start by asking whether the standard models of exchange rate determination can give a satisfactory account of rate movements in the past decade.

Why Do Exchange Rates Move?

There are two standard models of exchange rate determination. One focuses on an expectations-augmented, open economy IS–LM model in the tradition of Meade, Fleming, and Mundall. The other highlights the role of portfolio diversification and relative asset supplies. In choosing between these models an important question is to decide how relevant portfolio diversification effects are as part of an explanation for exchange rate movements. In other words, are monetary and fiscal policy most of the story, or do relative supplies of debts and other claims also play an important role?

The Extended Mundell–Fleming Models

The textbook model today is an open economy IS–LM model with perfect capital mobility, sluggish price adjustment, rapid asset market or interest rate adjustment, and rational expectations in asset markets.

A streamlined version is written in log-linear form and takes output as given. Complications stemming from output adjustments can easily be introduced but do not actually change the basic dynamics. In the same way we do not explicitly focus on wage–price interaction:[1]

$$m - p = hi, \qquad (1)$$

$$i = i^* + \dot{e}, \qquad (2)$$

$$\dot{p} = \eta[\xi(e-p) + g + \delta(i - \dot{p})]. \qquad (3)$$

Here m and p are the nominal money stock and prices, i and e are the nominal interest rate and the exchange rate respectively, and g is a variable representing fiscal policy. All variables other than interest rates are in logs.

Equation (1) represents monetary equilibrium or the LM schedule. Equation (2) states that with an adjustment for anticipated depreciation, assets are perfect substitutes. Perfect foresight is imposed by equating actual and anticipated depreciation. Equation (3) specifies that price adjustment is linked to the excess demand for goods which in turn depends on the real exchange rate, fiscal policy and the real interest rate.

This model exhibits the familiar overshooting property: a one-time monetary expansion leads to an immediate depreciation of the exchange rate. The exchange rate overshoots its new long run level – which is proportional to the increase in money. In the transition period following the initial overshooting the exchange rate appreciates while prices are rising. The process continues until the initial real equilibrium is re-established.

The overshootiong model can also be stated in terms of relationships between the real interest differential, the current actual real exchange rate and the longrun equilibrium exchange rate. Suppose that the real exchange rate adjusts gradually to its longrun level $\bar{q}$:

$$(4) \qquad \dot{q} = \Omega(\bar{q} - q)$$

The coefficient Ω measures the speed of adjustment of the real exchange rate and hence depends, under rational expectations, on all the structural parameters. From (2), using the definition of the real exchange rate and the real interest rates, we can write the rate of change of the real exchange rate as:

$$(5) \qquad \dot{q} = r - r^*$$

Combining (4) and (5) yields the key relation:

$$(6) \qquad q = \bar{q} - \beta(r - r^*) \quad ; \quad \beta = 1/\Omega$$

The model thus predicts that, when real interest rates are high relative to the rest of the world, the real exchange rate is high and depreciating.

---

[1] See Dornbusch (1976, 1983). Some of the extensions are considered in Dornbusch (1986).

Wilson (1979) has shown that this model also lends itself to the investigation of currently anticipated future disturbances or of transitory disturbances. This exercise highlights the flexibility of asset prices which move ahead of the realisation of disturbances. Exchange rates move immediately, driven entirely by anticipations, and bring about alternations of prices and interest rates before any monetary or fiscal changes are acually implemented.

The strong feature of the model is the contrast between instantly flexible assets prices which are set in a forward-looking manner, and the sluggish adjustment of prices. The linkage of the domestic asset market to foreign rates of interest produces exchange rate dynamics which yield the required rate of return on home assets. Any 'news' will make the exchange rate jump instantly to that level such where the expected capital gains or losses precisely offset the nominal interest differential. In this sense, the structure is extraordinarily rigid, just as was the original Mundell–Fleming model.

Of course, there is room for some flexibility: output adjustment can be brought into the model, import prices can appear in the real money balances' deflator, or a J-curve can be introduced to allow a more gradual response of demand to the real exchange rate. But these are niceties that do not add much to the basic flavour of the results.

Fiscal Policy

A major insight comes from a different application: fiscal policy. A fiscal expansion in this model brings about currency appreciation. Fiscal expansion creates an excess demand for goods, leading to an expansion in output or prices and hence, with a given nominal money stock, to upward pressure on the interest rate. Incipient capital inflows bring about an exchange rate appreciation and full crowding out. This is, of course, exactly the property captured by the Mundell–Fleming model. Fiscal policy works in the way they described even when price adjustments and expectations are introduced.

An interesting extension is to consider a transitory fiscal expansion. This corresponds, for example, to the US experience of the 1980s. Suppose that fiscal policy follows an adjustment process such as:

An Alternative Money Supply Process

A once and for all change in the money stock, with sticky prices in goods markets, perfect foresight in asset markets, leads to an overshooting of exchange rates. Lyons (1987) has rightly pointed out that the "once and for all" model is not very interesting as a policy experiment. In a much richer model of a stochastic money supply process and rational expectations he shows that innovations in money growth, because they are extrapolated into cumulative increases in money, lead to sizeable shortrun movements in exchange rates in response to even small changes in money.

This is a promising direction for modelling exchange rate responses, putting the emphasis on the extrapolation of current events. A simple example can explain what is involved. Suppose that innovations in money are serially correlated and suppose that inflation only adjusts gradually. A positive innovation in money is extrapolated into a cumulative accumulation of money relative to the trend growth. This implies that in the longrun the exchange rate will have moved to a "higher path" as will the price level. Because inflation is not fully flexible in the shortrun, the real money stock is seen as growing and hence nominal interest rates will be declining for sometime before inflation builds up to erode the growth in nominal balances. Ultimately the system returns to the initial rate of inflation, money growth and depreciation.

Figure 2 shows the exchange rate path in response to this experiment. Initially, up to time T₀ the economy moves along the solid line. At T₀ the innovation occurs and is extrapolated. The public recognizes that asymptotically the economy will converge to the "higher" exchange rate path reflecting the cumulative increase in money relative to trend shown by the dashed line. But there will be an immediate depreciation of the exchange rate from A to A'. The overshooting reflects the fact that forward looking asset holders anticipate the cumulative depreciation and will only hold domestic assets, in the face of reduced interest rates, if the exchange rate is appreciating. Along the new exchange rate path the rate of appreciation, following the initial jump, will accelerate for some time as nominal interest rates initially decline. The basic point of the Lyons analysis is that the forward looking expectations about the evolution of money, extrapolating the serial correlation of disturbances, must find their way immediately into the spot exchange rate. The analysis has obvious extensions to fiscal policy and other determinants of the exchange rate.

An interesting extension is to consider a transitory fiscal expansion. This corresponds, for example, to the US experience of the 1980s. Suppose that fiscal policy follows an adjustment process such as:

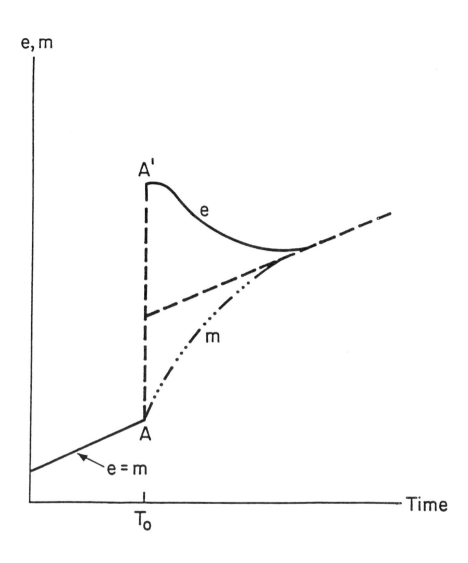

Fig. 2.   Exchange rate path in response to inflation, money growth, and deprivation.

$$\dot{g} = -\beta(g - \bar{g}) \qquad\qquad [7]$$

where $\bar{g}$ is the long-run level of government spending. According to 7 a fiscal expansion is being phased out over time at the rate β.

Now suppose that at time T_0 a fiscal expansion to level g_0 takes place and that from there on fiscal policy will follow the rule of 7 . It is possible to solve for the path of the real exchange rate to establish the following results: There will be an immediate real appreciation. Then, under the impact of excess demand, prices will keep rising so that further real appreciation occurs. Over time, the exchange rate overvaluation builds up even as the fiscal policy is being wound down. A recession develops which now forces deflation and hence, gradually, a return to the initial level of the real exchange rate.

If a future transitory fiscal expansion is anticipated or is gradually phased in, the adjustment process is somewhat more complicated. The adjustment path is shown in Fig 3. Upon the news of the fiscal programme there will be an initial

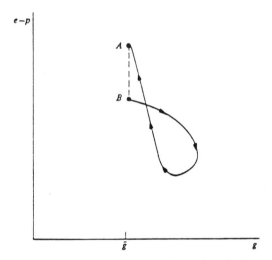

Fig. 3. The real exchange rate effect of a transitory fiscal expansion.

nominal and real appreciation shown as a jump from A to B. Then the overvaluation exerts a deflationary pressure. As prices decline and real balances rise, the nominal interest rate falls. To match the lower interest rate the exchange rate will be appreciating. That process continues until the fiscal expansion actually gets underway, and leads to excess demand and inflation. Only when real balances and hence interest rates have been pushed up beyond their initial level, does the corrective depreciation start. The depreciation then continues, along with the phasing out of the fiscal expansion, until the initial equilibrium is restored.

Fiscal policy thus appears in addition to monetary policy as an important driving force for the exchange rate. Sustained shifts in government spending or taxes will bring persistent movements of the real exchange rate. Feldstein

(1986) Hutchinson and Throop (1985) have documented that shifts in the full employment budget, along with real interest rates, can in fact explain the large shifts in real exchange rates that have occurred. Interestingly the empirical tests hold up not only for the very recent experience in the United States. They work equally well when applied to multilateral exchange rates for the entire floating rate period.

Fiscal policy, including the expectations of correction associated with Gramm–Rudman, provides one interpretation of the dollar movements in the 1980s. The alternative is to argue the case of at least partial irrationality as has been done by Frankel (1985a), Frankel and Froot (1986) and Krugman (1986).

II. PERSISTENCE EFFECTS

Three features of the extended Mundell–Fleming model account for its strong and unambiguous predictions. First, there is the absence of any effects, dynamic or otherwise, associated with the current account. Second, that home and foreign assets are perfect substitutes. Third, that there are only two classes of assets, money and bonds, and no real assets. We consider now what alternative models might look like and what they imply for exchange rate economics.

Current Account Effects

A period of fiscal expansion leading to appreciation will also involve cumulative current account imbalances. The case of the United States stands out, as now more than 2% of GNP is borrowed from the rest of the world in financing the persistent deficit, adding in each year to come to a seemingly ever growing external indebtedness. Sometime in 1985 the United States passed from net creditor to net debtor status.

The accumulated net external indebtedness will, of course, show up in the current account in the form of reduced income from net foreign assets. The reduction in net external assets means that, following a period of deficits, the current account cannot be balanced simply by returning to the initial real exchange rate. Now there will be a deficit stemming from the increased debt service. Therefore, to restore current account balance, an overdepreciation is required.

The current account can be represented in the following manner. Let d be the net external assets and i^* the rate of return on net foreign assets. The term $\dot{d}$ denotes the current account surplus or accumulation of net foreign assets:

$$\dot{d} = f(e-p,g) + i^*d. \tag{8}$$

The real exchange rate that yields current account balance will therefore depend on the rate of return on assets and on the cumulated history of fiscal policy and other shocks to the current account. A transitory fiscal binge requires a subsequent permanent real depreciation to yield the improvement in the non-interest current account that is necessary to service the debt.

Such a permanent response to transitory deficits is clearly not part of the standard model. The question is whether it represents a realistic, quantitatively important effect. This is the case addressed in trade theory under the heading of the 'transfer problem'. It depends in large part on the impact on demand for domestic goods of an international redistribution of wealth and spending, and on the production response to changes in relative prices.

The discussion of the transfer problem is not complete without a consideration of how the budget will be balanced. The fiscal expansion gives rise to a budget deficit which is financed by issuing debt. The debt in turn will have to be serviced at some point by increased taxes. The question then is whether the taxation yields an equal current account improvement at constant relative prices. If so, then there is no need for terms of trade adjustments. At the going levels of output, disposable income and absorption by domestic residents decline but part of reduced spending falls on domestic goods rather than imports. To achieve the transfer *at full employment* ordinarily requires a real depreciation. The real depreciation will shift demand toward domestic goods.

This discussion of fiscal policy effects on real exchange rates clearly provides scope for an application of the Barro–Ricardo equivalence ideas to the open economy. A particularly complete rendition is offered in Frenkel and Razin (1986).

Portfolio Effects

A separate persistence effect can arise via the impact of a fiscal and current account imbalance on the relative supply of assets. Suppose that, contrary to (2), assets are not perfect substitutes, so that there is a risk premium,[1]

$$i = i^* + \dot{e} + \alpha(b - b^* - e), \tag{2a}$$

where b and b^* are the supplies of domestic and foreign debt in national currencies.[1]

If current account imbalances are financed by an increase in the relative supply of domestic debt, then the cumulative imbalance would require an increase in the relative yield on domestic securities or a change in the relatively valuation via exchange rate changes. A depreciation would be a means of correcting an increase in the relative supply of domestic securities by reducing their value in foreign currency, thus restoring portfolio balance at an unchanged yield differential. Other things equal we would therefore expect a period of debt accumulation to have a permanent effect on exchange rates, so as to bring interest differentials in line with the changed relative supply of assets.

[1] The formula for the risk premium here omits wealth terms. It also focusses on debt rather than all nominal outside assets. For a more complete treatment see Dornbusch (1982).

The responsiveness of exchange rates to relative asset supplies has been addressed in a number of important papers by Frankel.[2] He concludes that relative asset supplies in fact do not provide a satisfactory account of relative yields, at least in the context of a capital asset pricing model. The impact of relative asset supplies is practically negligible. That is an uncomfortable conclusion for a whole strand of research which places major emphasis on the imperfect substitutability of assets as a major feature of open economy macroeconomics.

Work by Sachs and Wyplosz (1984), Dornbusch and Fischer (1980) and Giovannini (1983) raises the following problem: if as a result of debt accumulation, via the transfer problem or via risk premia, an ultimate depreciation is required, why should we expect an initial appreciation? Is it not likely that for certain parameters and paths of subsequent budget correction there should be an immediate path of sustained real depreciation. It turns out that all the parameters in the model – trade elasticities, wealth elasticities, risk premium responses, etc. – matter for this question. Even in very highly simplified models no firm conclusions emerge about the path of the exchange rate.

Real Assets

The standard model remains over-simplified even when long-term issues of current account balancing and a risk premium are taken into account. The simplification lies in the omission of real capital from portfolios, and in disregarding the effect over time of investment on the capital stock and thus the supply side of the economy.

Concurrently with the imbalance in the current account and the resulting shift in net foreign assets, capital accumulation takes place. Portfolio adjustments in response to the changing relative asset supplies bring about changes in the value of real assets and in relative yields. The flow of investment and the changes in the value of real capital potentially dominate the effects of current account imbalances. A good week on the stock market produces a change in wealth that is several times the magnitude of an entire year's deficit in the current account. While it is true that the current account is important because persistent imbalances cumulate, exactly the same argument must be made for investment.

Work by Gavin (1986) shows that the inclusion of the stock market in the standard model offers important additional channels for exchange rate dynamics. Unfortunately, the inclusion of the stock market removes at the same time the simplicity of the standard model. Now virtually anything is possible. And that result is arrived at by looking only at the portfolio implications of a money-debt-capital model and the ensuing yield and wealth effects, without even taking into account the accumulation of physical capital. Among the sources of ambiguity are two different effects: an expansion in demand will bring about both an increase in output and an increase in interest rates. The net effect on the valuation of the stock market is therefore uncertain. Thus wealth may rise or fall, and this is important in judging the induced effects on

[1] In a model with a risk premium there is a serious difficulty in linking goods and assets markets. There is certainly no excuse for using the interest rate on bonds in home currency as *the* domestic interest rate used as a determinant of domestic spending. The *ad hoc* model becomes a liability. The correct treatment, drawing on an optimisation model would use the marginal cost of capital which is based on the marginal financing pattern which in turn is derived by solving the firm's and household's complete intertemporal optimisation problem.

[2] See especially Frankel (1985*b*, 1986) and Frankel and Froot (1986).

money demand and spending. The second important consideration is the relative substitutability of money and debt, and debt and capital. This is relevant for the extent of yield changes and hence for the direction and magnitude of exchange rate changes.

The money-debt-capital model is also important in highlighting that current accounts are not necessarily financed by sales of domestic bonds or foreign bonds. There need not be any link between cumulative current account imbalances and yield differentials between home and foreign nominal bonds. There would be a significant distinction, for example, between fiscal deficits and investment deficits. The difference is also relevant from the point of view of the transfer problem. Deficits that arise as a result of increased investment have different implications from deficits that have their source in fiscal imbalances.

Hysteresis Effects

A final channel for persistence effects is introduced by an industrial organisation approach to the consequences of extended rate misalignments. When an industry is exposed to foreign competition and entry by a persistent overvaluation, it may close down and perhaps even re-open in the low wage country. Firms already producing in the low wage country may make the necessary investment to enter the market where home firms are handicapped by overvalued labour. A period of overvaluation or undervaluation thus changes the industrial landscape in a relatively permanent fashion. These considerations are at the centre of a new literature that seeks to interpret the US experience following the five year overvaluation.[1] The upshot of the literature is, of course, that overvaluation leads ultimately to the need for overdepreciation to remedy the accumulation of adverse trade effects.

Overvaluation, for example due to monetary contraction or fiscal expansion for example, brings in foreign firms and displaces domestic firms. When the overvaluation is ultimately undone the foreign firms are still there and the domestic firms may exist no longer. Worse yet, they now may even be producing abroad. A period of sustained undervaluation is required to bring forth the required investment. The possibility of entry and the choice of labour market from which to supply a particular market, thus opens an important dynamic theory of adjustment to the exchange rate. Expectations about the persistence of changes in relative labour costs become important for the determination of relative prices. Now pricing between firms not only involves current strategic interaction, which we consider below, but also the impact of pricing strategies on entry, location and investment.

There is some offset to these considerations from the side of factor prices. To the extent that an industry has a captive factor supply we would expect that wages come down with the exchange rate, thus maintaining a firm in existence. Conversely, in expanding countries, wages might rise and thus offset some of the gain in profitability arising from depreciation.

---

[1] See especially Baldwin (1986), Krugman (1985) and Baldwin and Krugman (1986).

III. EXCHANGE RATES AND PRICING

The monetary approach to the balance of payments used purchasing power parity (PPP) as an essential ingredient in explanations of exchange rate determination. Today, PPP is certainly no longer a corner-stone for modelling. Attention has shifted to modelling changes in equilibrium relative prices. The simple Keynesian model assumes that wages and prices in the national currencies are given, so that exchange rate movements change relative prices one-for-one. A newer approach recognises the sluggishness of wages, but builds on that a theory of equilibrium price determination along industrial organisation lines.[1]

Relative Prices

An interesting setting for exchange rate-wage-price relationships is a world of imperfect competition. Here firms are price setters. They may or may not interact strategically, but they certainly face the problem of how their pricing decision should react to a change in the exchange rate. Consider the simple case of an oligopoly.[2]

The typical setting would be the following. We look at the home market where n home firms and n^* foreign firms compete. The profits of the typical home and foreign firms, with constant unit labour costs in their respective currencies given by w and w^*, are:

$$\pi = (p_i - w)\, D_i(p_i, p_j),$$

$$D_j(p_i, p_j).$$

These profits are maximised subject to the strategic assumptions about the determinants of the demand facing each firm and the responses of other firms in the market. It is clear that there is no general solution to the problem. The impact of an exchange rate change on equilibrium prices will depend on a number of factors. Specifically, these include:

(1) whether goods are perfect substitutes or differentiated products,
(2) the market organisation – oligopoly, imperfect competition, etc.,
(3) the relative number of domestic and foreign firms, and
(4) the functional form of the market demand curve.

Even though there is no presumption about the effects of exchange rates on the changes in equilibrium prices, it is immediately clear that there is an important link between open economy macroeconomics and industrial organisation. There is no presumption that an exchange rate movement affects all markets equally. Some markets may involve a homogeneous good and, for example, a duopoly. Other markets may involve differentiated products and Chamberlinian competition. Yet other markets may be close to perfect competition. But whichever is the case, once the exchange rate changes, given wages, there will be an adjustment in the equilibrium price.

Of course, this pricing issue, depending on market organisation, may be repeated at different levels from import to retail. The same pricing issue arises on the export side.

---

[1] See Dornbusch (1987), Krugman (1986), Feinberg (1986), Mann (1986) and Flood (1986).
[2] This analysis draws on Dixit (1986) and Seade (1983).

Figure 4 shows as an example the dollar transaction prices for imports and exports of scientific and optical instruments. Up to 1985 import prices decline and then, accompanying the depreciation, they rise in dollar terms. Export prices rise throughout as if they were based on domestic costs alone.

FIGURE 4

IMPORT AND EXPORT PRICES
(INDEX 1979·4 = 100)

For the case of differentiated products, an appreciation tends to bring about a rise in the relative price of domestic goods. Imported variants decline in price both absolutely and relatively. For homogeneous products the industry price declines, with the decline being larger the less monopolised the market and the larger the relative number of foreign firms.

An interesting, and perhaps surprising, result appears here: currency appreciation, in certain cases, may lead to a more than proportionate decline in market price. This result occurs because the favourable cost-shock for foreign firms makes expansion overly profitable and overcomes the tendency to preserve profits by restricting output. But these results are very specific to market structure and functional form. In public finance, as Seade (1983) has shown, a similar result occurs: a tax on an oligopolistic industry may raise profits.

To show how specific the results are to the details of the market, consider a simple duopoly market with a domestic and a foreign firm. Let the inverse market demand function be:

$$P = P(Q); \quad P'(Q) < 0, \quad Q \equiv q + q^*, \qquad (11)$$

where Q denotes total quantity demanded and q and q^* are the supplies by the home and foreign firm. Let the elasticity of the slope of the inverse demand function be denoted by σ:

$$\sigma = -(P''/P')\,Q, \qquad (12)$$

which may be zero, as in the linear case, positive or negative.

Suppose that each of the two firms assumes that the other maintains a given level of output. The equilibrium then is the Cournot–Nash solution for industry output and price. The elasticities of output, and of the industry price in response to an exchange rate change, are:

$$\hat{Q} = [(ew^*/P)\,(P/P'Q)/(3-\sigma)]\,\hat{e}; \quad \hat{P} = [(ew^*/P)/(3-\sigma)]\,\hat{e},$$

where a circumflex denotes a percentage change.

Consider now three cases. First, with a linear market demand function the term $\sigma = 0$. Accordingly, the pass-through of depreciation to the prices is one third of marginal cost–price ratio for the foreign country. Because we are in a situation of oligopoly the marginal cost–price ratio is less than unity. The elasticity of industry price with respect to the exchange rate is thus definitely a fraction and much less than a half.

Next we look at a constant semi-elasticity demand curve, $Q = A\exp(-\alpha P)$. For this case the elasticity $\sigma = 1$, and the price elasticity is already increased to a half of the marginal cost–price ratio. Going further to a constant elasticity demand curve $Q = AP^{-a}$ yields a value of $\sigma = 1 + 1/a$. Let $a = 1$ so that spending on the good is constant. In that case the elasticity of price is equal to the marginal cost–price ratio.

The examples show that the impact of exchange rate movements on prices is far from straightforward. Market structure, conjectural variations and functional form all come into play. Even though this application of industrial organisation ideas to the effects of exchange rate movements does not emerge with firm results, it is quite apparent that it offers a major avenue for theoretical research and for applied studies. Exchange rate changes affect home and foreign firms differentially, to an extent which varies between industries. Focusing on the adjustment to major exchange rate movements may therefore help identify market structures and thus enrich industrial organisation research.

Commodity Prices

One of the more interesting price effects of real exchange rate movements between major industrial countries occurs in the area of commodities. It is readily established that a real dollar exchange rate depreciation (in terms of value added deflators for manufactured goods) will lead to a rise in the dollar price of commodities, and a rise in their real price to US users. Conversely, abroad the real price declines as does the absolute price in foreign currencies.

This result can be seen by looking at the commodity market equilibrium condition where J is the excess demand for any particular commodity, say cotton:

$$J(p/P, p^*/P^*, \ldots) = 0, \qquad [13]$$

where p and p^* are the national currency commodity prices and P and P^* are the deflators. Excess demand is a declining function of the real prices in the two regions. In Fig. 5 the market equilibrium schedule is shown as downward sloping. Points above and to the right correspond to an excess supply. Let $\phi = P/eP^*$ be the real exchange in terms of manufacturing deflators rate, and which is shown as the ray OR through the origin. Using the law of one price for commodities, $p = ep^*$, and the definition of the real exchange rate in 13 we obtain:

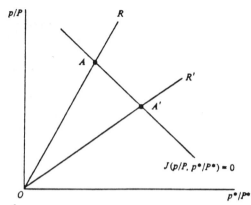

Fig. 5 Real exchange rate movements and the real prices of commodities.

$$J(p/P, \phi, \dots) = 0, \tag{14}$$

or $$p/P = h(\phi, \dots), \quad h' < 0. \tag{14a}$$

A real appreciation of the dollar corresponds to a rise in ϕ rotating downward the OR ray. The model predicts a decline in real commodity prices in the United States as a result of dollar appreciation. Equation (14a) shows that a real appreciation of the dollar will lead to a decline in the real price of commodities to US users, and a real price increase abroad. Given the US deflator, P, the nominal commodity price quoted in dollars will decline. In this perspective the large dollar appreciation of 1980–5 helps explain the sharp decline of dollar commodity prices in world trade. In fact though, the dollar appreciation and world cyclical movements are not enough to explain fully the decline in these prices.

Exchange Rates and Inflation

The impact of exchange rates on inflation is well-established for any Banana Republic and, indeed, for any industrial country. The experience of the 1980s makes it clear that it even applies to the United States. There are several channels through which exchange rates affect inflation. The least controversial effect of exchange rates on inflation concerns the prices of homogeneous commodities traded in world markets.

Changes in commodity prices influence directly the rate of inflation for food and hence influence wages. They also affect industrial materials costs in manufacturing. But exchange rates influence inflation also via several other channels. Their influence is important because they are rapid and quite pervasive.

One channel working in addition to commodity prices involves the prices of traded goods and the prices of those goods directly competing with traded goods. The industrial organisation analysis considered above applies to determine the magnitude and speed of response for prices. The less monopolistic a market, and the lower entry costs, the more pervasive the price effects.

There are also inflation effects via wages. These can arise because wages respond to the competitive pressure of an appreciation or depreciation in affected industries. They also come about as wages respond to changes in the cost of living.

Adding together these various channels yields a pervasive pattern of cost and price effects that are directly or indirectly associated with exchange rate movements. It is interesting to note that in the United States the magnitude of these effects is still under discussion. Estimates of the impact of a 10% dollar appreciation on the price level, range between one and two percentage points. The reason it is so difficult to establish the size of the impact is apparent. There have been only three recent episodes involving a major change in inflation. Each coincided with an oil price change, a large change in unemployment, and a major change in the dollar. As a result, it is nearly impossible to extract a precise estimate for the size of each of these three elements in the inflation process.[1]

IV. THE POLITICAL ECONOMY OF OVERVALUATION

The literature on political business cyles has drawn attention to the systematic pursuit of macroeconomic goals on a timetable dictated by political elections. The exchange rate fits very well into that scheme. It does so via its effects on output and inflation, but also as a highly visible indicator of confidence in policy.

The political business cycle implication of exchange rate movements is strongly enhanced by the relative timing of output and inflation results. A real appreciation quickly raises real wages in terms of tradeables and quickly reduces inflation. The impact on activity is much more gradual. The implication of these timing relationships is that a policy of real appreciation, conducted at the right time, can make an administration look particularly successful at controlling inflation, while at the same time delivering increases in real disposable income.

Diaz Alejandro (1966) was the first to draw attention to the fact that devaluation in the short-term may reduce activity, in addition to having inflationary effects. Only in the long-term do output and employment expand. The reason is that in the short-run a devaluation cuts real wages in terms of tradeables thereby reducing purchasing power and the demand for home goods. These income effects dominate in the short-run. The neoclassical substitution effects take time to build up. The short-time effects are sufficiently powerful to be highly relevant for political decision-making.

The reverse side of this coin is overvaluation. In the short term it involves less inflation and an increase in real income and hence it wins popularity contests. Only over time, as substitution effects become important and output declines due to the loss of competitiveness, do the costs emerge. No wonder that overvaluation is a very popular policy. It created broad short-term political support in Chile for Pinochet, in Argentina for the policies of Martinez de Hoz,

---

[1] See Dornbusch and Fischer 1984., Sachs 1985 and Woo 1984 on the exchange rate effects on US inflation.

for the Thatcher government in the United Kingdom, and in the United States for Reaganomics.

Whether the policy mix was deliberate or not, there is little doubt that for a while the real appreciation was celebrated as a mark of achievement rather than being seen as a highly destructive misalignment. Only as the deindustrialisation effects became visible, and politically alarming did the policymakers back track and start viewing overvaluation with concern. In the meantime it had bought a strong disinflation.

In the US case the oil price decline of 1986 came just in time to offset the cut in real income and the inflationary impact implied by dollar depreciation. The timing of appreciation and depreciation thus looked like a masterpiece of political economy. The only cloud remains the very serious blow to industry, the effects of which do appear to persist even after an already significant depreciation. Of course, in addition, there is the cost of servicing the accumulated debt.

These episodes of overvaluation raise the interesting issue of why an electorate would favour exchange rate misalignment. Given the welfare costs associated with uneven tax structures over time, and the costs resulting from de- and reindustrialisation, one would expect voters to favour steady policies rather than large fluctuations in the real exchange rate and the standard of living. Yet the evidence runs counter to this observation, overvaluation often one of the best tricks in the bag.

There is an international dimension to the issue of inflation stabilisation via overvaluation. Under flexible exchange rates a tightening of monetary policy exerts immediate disinflationary effects via currency appreciation. When used by a large country, such a policy amounts to exporting inflation. Investigation of policy coordination and of the gamethoretic implications of these effects has been an important part of international economics research.[1]

A recent study by Edison and Tryon (1986) makes an important point in this connection. The authors find that in simulations with the Federal Reserve MCM model an asymmetry is apparent. For the United States – the large country – foreign repercussions and the particulars of foreign policy responses are relatively unimportant in their impact on inflation and growth. For foreign countries, by contrast, the details of US policy have a major impact. This asymmetry should be expected to influence the nature of Europe's policy responses to US actions.

V. EXCESS CAPITAL MOBILITY AND POLICY RESPONSES

In this concluding section we consider policy issues that follow from the fact that macroeconomic disturbances exert significant *excess* effects on real exchange rates, trade flows, and on the standard of living. There are broadly two approaches: one is to accept the fact of international capital mobility and use monetary policy coordination to avoid exchange rate effects of disturbances.

---

[1] See Cooper (1969), Hamada (1985), Buiter and Marston (1985) and Oudiz and Sachs (1984).

The other is to interfere with capital flows in order to pursue macroeconomic objectives more freely.

Target Zones and Exchange Rate Oriented Monetary Policy

A strong case for some form of managed exchange rates is returning in the aftermath of the extreme exchange rate fluctuations. In particular, among those arguing for more fixed exchange rates are Williamson (1983) and McKinnon (1984).

The McKinnon position for a fixed exchange rate has at its centre the assumption that international portfolio shifts are behind exchange rate movements. In an initial version of this argument shifts between M1 in one country and another were the source of disturbance. Monetary authorities, being committed to *national* monetary targets, would not accommodate these money demand shifts, and exchange rate volatility was seen as the inevitable consequence. More recent versions of the hypothesis recognise that international portfolio shifts are more likely to take the form of shifts in the demand for interest bearing assets denominated in different currencies. But the recommendation remains to fix exchange rates, using exchange rate-oriented monetary policy to hold rates and accommodate money demand shifts. In other words *unsterilised* intervention is to be used.

This policy recommendation prescribes exactly the wrong kind of intervention. To offset the exchange rate impact of shifts in the demand for bond, the currency denomination of the world bond portfolio should be allowed to change. That means *sterilised* intervention is the correct answer. In response to exchange rate appreciation the authorities should intervene, leaving money supplies unchanged but increasing the supply of home bonds and reducing the supply of foreign currency bonds. That, of course, is sterilised intervention. The case for sterilised intervention is well-established, and has been a basic principle of asset market management ever since Poole's authoritative analysis of the choice between interest rate and monetary targets. The remaining problem, of course, is to determine whether it is portfolio shifts or shifts in fundamentals that are moving rates.

The case for fixing exchange rates whatever the source of disturbance is advanced by those favouring target zones. Their position is that exchange rates do not necessarily reflect fundamentals but rather irrationality, band wagons, and eccentricity. The large movements in exchange rates interfere with macroeconomic stability, but they can and should be avoided by a firm commitment to exchange rate targets. On the surface it is difficult to see any difficulty with this prescription, but on further inspection two serious difficulties emerge. First, it is certainly not an established fact that exchange rates move irrationally and without links to fundamentals. Or, if they do move in this way, it is not clear that they do so more than stock prices or long-term bond prices. Why single out one price for fixing if it may mean that the other prices have to move even further away from their fundamental equilibrium levels?

The second objection concerns a lack of instruments. Governments are unlikely to agree on coordinating their fiscal policies. But if real exchange rates are to remain fixed in the face of uncoordinated fiscal policy changes, then monetary accommodation is required. In the context of the dollar appreciation of 1980–5, for example, that would have meant a more aggressively expansionary monetary policy in the United States and hence no disinflation. It is questionable whether the objective of fixed rates is sufficiently important to warrant bad monetary policy[1].

Policies Toward Excess Capital Mobility

But there is an alternative, extreme answer to international exchange rate instability which is more attractive. The stickiness of wages relative to exchange rates creates a macroeconomic externality which possibly justifies closing or restricting some markets. Tobin (1982) has made the case for throwing more sand into the international financial system, so as to reduce the overwhelming influence of capital flows over productive activity and trade. The proposal, known as the 'Tobin tax', involves a uniform tax on all foreign exchange transactions, to be levied in all countries of the world. The consequence of the tax is to make short-term hot money roundtrips unprofitable. Under this system capital flows would therefore be more nearly geared to considerations of the long-term profitability of investment rather than the overnight speculation which now dominates.

It might be argued that it is too late for stopping the flow of international capital, that throwing sand in the wheels is no longer sufficient. But why stop there and not use rocks? An operational way of doing this is to combine the stability of inflation and real activity that comes from fixed rates with a dual exchange rate system for capital account transactions. If capital markets are irrational and primarily speculative it might be as well to detach them altogether from an influence on real activity. Rather than use scarce macro-policy tools to adapt the real sector to the idiosyncracy of financial markets, a separate exchange rate would detach the capital account and deprive it from distorting influences on trade and inflation[2].

---

[1] For a further discussion see Fischer (1986).
[2] For a discussion of a dual rate system and extensive references to the literature see Dornbusch (1986c).

REFERENCES

Baldwin, R. (1986). 'Hysteresis in trade.' Unpublished manuscript, Massachusetts Institute of Technology, April.

—— and Krugman, P. (1986). 'Persistent trade effects of large exchange rate shocks.' Unpublished manuscript, Massachusetts Institute of Technology, July.

Buiter, W. and Marston, R. (eds.) (1985). *International Economic Policy Coordination.* Cambridge University Press.

Cooper, R. (1969). 'Macroeconomic policy adjustment in interdependent economies.' *Quarterly Journal of Economics,* February.

Diaz-Alejandro, C. (1966). *Exchange Rate Devaluation in a Semi-Industrialized Country: The Experience of Argentina 1955–1961.* MIT Press.

Dixit, A. (1986). 'Comparative statics for oligopoly.' *International Economic Review,* vol. 27, pp. 107–22.

Dornbusch, R. (1976). 'Expectations and exchange rate dynamics.' *Journal of Political Economy,* December.

—— (1982). 'Exchange risk and the macroeconomics of exchange rate determination.' In *International Financial Management* (ed. R. Hawkins *et al.*). Greenwich, Conn.: JAI Press.

—— (1983). 'Flexible exchange rates and interdependence.' *IMF Staff Papers,* March, reprinted in *Dollars, Debts and Deficits.* Cambridge: Mass.: MIT Press, 1986.

—— (1986a). 'Inflation, exchange rates and stabilization.' *Princeton Essays in International Finance,* no. 165, October.

—— (1987). 'Exchange rates and prices.' *American Economic Review.*

—— (1986b). 'Flexible exchange rates and excess capital mobility.' *Brookings Papers on Economic Activity,* no. 1.

—— (1986d). 'Special exchange rates for capital account transactions.' *The World Bank Economic Review,* vol. 1, no. 1.

—— (1986c) 'The open economy implications of monetary and fiscal policy.' in *The Business Cycle* (ed. R. Gordon). University of Chicago Press.

—— (1987). 'Purchasing power parity.' NBER Working Paper No. 1591. In *The New Palgrave's Dictionary of Economics,* Macmillan. (In the Press.)

—— and Fischer, S. (1980). 'Exchange rates and the current account.' *American Economic Review,* December.

Edison, H. and Tryon, R. (1986). 'An empirical analysis of policy coordination in the United States, Japan and Europe.' Board of Governors of the Federal Reserve, International Finance Discussion Papers, no. 286, July.

Feinberg, R. M. (1986). 'The interaction of foreign exchange and market power effects on German domestic prices.' *Journal of Industrial Economics,* no. 1, September.

Feldstein, M. (1986). 'The budget deficit and the dollar.' *NBER Macroeconomics Annual.*

Fischer, S. (1986). 'Symposium on exchange rates, trade and capital flows: comments. *Brookings Papers on Economic Activity,* no. 1.

Flood, E. (1986). 'An empirical analysis of the effects of exchange rate changes on goods prices.' Unpublished manuscript. Stanford University.

Frankel, J. (1982). 'In search of the exchange risk premium: a six-currency test assuming mean-variance optimization.' *Journal of International Money and Finance,* no. 1.

—— (1985a). 'The dazzling dollar.' *Brookings Papers on Economic Activity,* no. 1.

—— (1985b). 'Portfolio crowding-out empirically estimated.' *Quarterly Journal of Economics,* Supplement.

—— (1986c). 'The implications of mean-variance optimization for four questions in international finance.' *Journal of International Money and Finance.* Supplement. March.

—— and Froot, K. (1986). 'The dollar as an irrational speculative bubble.' *The Marcus Wallenberg Papers on International Finance,* no. 1.

Frenkel, J. and Razin, A. (1986). 'The international transmission and effects of fiscal policy.' *American Economic Review,* May.

Gavin, M. (1986). 'The stock market and exchange rate dynamics.' International Finance Discussion Papers, Board of Governors of the Federal Reserve. no. 278.

Giovannini, Alberto (1983). *Three Essays on Exchange Rates.* Unpublished MIT dissertation.

—— (1985). 'Exchange rates and traded goods prices.' Unpublished manuscript. Columbia University.

Hamada, K. (1985). *The Political Economy of International Monetary Interdependence,* MIT Press.

Hutchinson, M. and Throop, A. (1985). 'The U.S. budget deficit and the real value of the dollar.' Federal Reserve Bank of San Francisco. *Economic Review,* no. 4, Autumn.

Krugman, P. (1985). 'Is the strong dollar sustainable?' In *The U.S. Dollar Recent Developments.* Federal Reserve Bank of Kansas.

—— (1986). 'Pricing to market when the exchange rate changes.' *NBER Working Paper Series,* no. 1926, May.

Lyons,R. (1987) "Exchange Rates and Money Supply Expectations"
Unpublished manuscript, Massachusetts Institute of Technology.

Mann, C. (1986). 'Prices, profit, margins and exchange rates.' *Federal Reserve Bulletin*, June.

McKinnon, R. (1984). *An International Standard for Monetary Stabilization*, Institute for International Economics.

Oudiz, G. and Sachs, J. (1984). 'Macroeconomic policy coordination among the industrial economies.' *Brookings Papers on Economic Activity*, no. 1.

Sachs, J. (1985). 'The dollar and the policy mix: 1985.' *Brookings Papers on Economic Activity*, no. 1.

—— and Wyplosz, C. (1984). 'Real exchange rate effects of fiscal policy.' *NBER Working Paper*, no. 1255.

Seade, J. (1983). 'Prices, profits and taxes in oligopoly.' Working Paper, University of Warwick.

Tobin, J. (1982). 'A proposal for international monetary reform.' In *Essays in Economics: Theory and Policy*. Cambridge, Mass.: MIT Press.

Williamson, J. (1983). *The Exchange Rate System*. Institute for International Economics.

Wilson, C. (1979). 'Exchange rate dynamics and anticipated disturbances.' *Journal of Political Economy*, December.

Woo, W. T. (1984). 'Exchange rates and prices of nonfood, nonfuel products.' *Brookings Papers on Economic Activity*, no. 2.

MONETARY AND PORTFOLIO-BALANCE MODELS OF

EXCHANGE RATE DETERMINATION

JEFFREY A. FRANKEL

Abstract

"Monetary and Portfolio-Balance Models of Exchange Rate Determination" was a survey of empirical models of the 1970s, published in Economic Interdependence and Flexible Exchange Rates, edited by J. Bhandari (M.I.T. Press: Cambridge), in 1983. It is here supplemented with a brief epilogue to update the literature to 1987, including some skeptical observations on recent claims that "random walk" results constitute evidence in favor of an "equilibrium" model of the exchange rate.

Monetary and Portfolio-Balance Models of Exchange Rate Determination

Jeffrey A. Frankel

The Asset-Market View of Exchange Rates

The theoretical literature on the "asset-market" view of exchange rates has been expanding voluminously in recent years. The popularity of this view may be attributed to the compelling realism in today's world of both its distinguishing theoretical assumption and its distinguishing empirical implication. The theoretical assumption that all asset-market models share is the absence of substantial transactions costs, capital controls, or other impediments to the flow of capital between countries, an assumption which will here be referred to as perfect capital mobility. Thus the exchange rate must adjust instantly to equilibrate the international demand for stocks of national assets—as opposed to adjusting to equilibrate the international demand for flows of national goods as in the more traditional view. The empirical implication is that floating exchange rates will exhibit high variability, variability that exceeds what one might regard as that of their underlying determinants.

But beyond this common point, the asset-market models diverge down a bewildering complexity of routes. Synthesis models and comprehensive surveys are notably lacking. Furthermore, the specific empirical implications of the various theories conflict with observed events, as well as with each other. Econometric attempts to relate the theory to recent data have

An earlier version of this chapter was presented at the World Congress of the Econometric Society, Aix-en-Provence, France, 29 August 1980, and also appeared as NBER Summer Institute Paper 80-7.

This material is based upon work supported by the National Science Foundation under Grant No. SES-8007162, and further supported by a research grant from the Institute of Business and Economic Research at the University of California, Berkeley. I would like to thank Brian Newton, Charles Engel, Eric Fisher, and Allen Berger for research assistance, and to thank Peter Kenen and Hali Edison for very useful comments and suggestions.

foundered on the dollar depreciation, which, in 1977 and 1978, was too highly correlated with the US current account deficit to be explained readily by the asset-market approach, and which rather seemed to fit the more traditional approach.

This chapter proposes a taxonomy of asset-market models of floating exchange rates, as illustrated in figure 3.1. The most important dichotomy is according to whether or not domestic and foreign bonds are assumed to be perfect substitutes in asset-holders' portfolios. It is important to note the distinction between capital mobility, as the term is used here, and substitutability.[1] Perfect capital mobility between countries means that actual portfolio composition adjusts instantaneously to desired portfolio composition. Assuming no risk of default or future capital controls, perfect capital mobility implies, for example, covered interest parity: The interest rate on a domestic bond is equal to the interest rate on a similar foreign bond plus the forward premium on foreign exchange.[2] Perfect substitutability between domestic and foreign bonds is the much stronger assumption that asset holders are indifferent as to the composition of their bond portfolios as long as the expected rate of return on the two countries' bonds is the same when expressed in any common numeraire. It would imply, for example, uncovered interest parity: The interest rate on a domestic bond is equal to the interest rate on a foreign bond plus the *expected* rate of appreciation of foreign currency.[3]

In one class of asset-market models, domestic and foreign bonds are imperfect substitutes. This is the "portfolio-balance approach" to exchange rates, in which asset holders wish to allocate their portfolios in shares that are well-defined functions of expected rates of return.[4]

In the other class of asset-market models, domestic and foreign bonds are perfect substitutes: Portfolio shares are infinitely sensitive to expected rates of return. Thus uncovered interest parity must hold. But given that it does hold, bond supplies then become irrelevant. The responsibility for determining the exchange rate is shifted onto the money markets. Such models belong to the "monetary approach" to exchange rates,[5] which focuses on the demand for and supply of money.

3.2 The Monetary Approach

3.2.1 The Flexible-Price ("Monetarist") Monetary Model

We have defined the monetary approach by the assumption that not only are there no barriers (such as transaction costs or capital controls) segmenting international capital markets, but domestic and foreign bonds

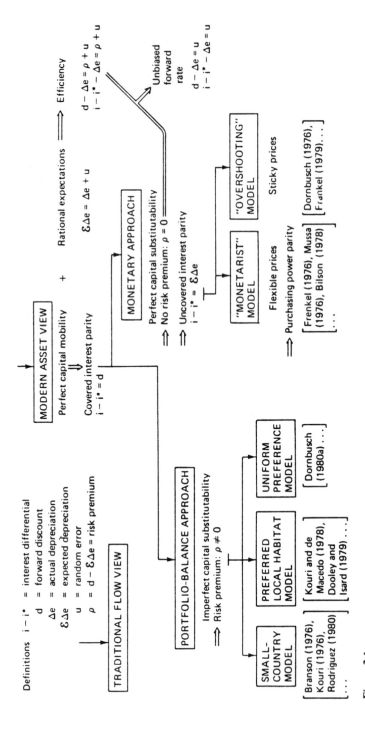

Figure 3.1
Exchange rate models and assumptions.

are also perfect substitutes in investor demand functions. In essence, there is only one bond in the world.

As the starting point within the monetary approach we begin with the model that also makes the analogous assumption for goods markets: Not only are there no barriers (such as transportation costs or trade controls) segmenting international goods markets, but domestic and foreign goods are also perfect substitutes in consumer demand functions. In essence, there is only one good in the world.

This assumption, of course, implies purchasing power parity: The domestic price level is equal to the foreign price level times the exchange rate. Large short-run failures of purchasing power parity have been observed empirically.[6] But the assumption can be useful in certain contexts, for example, hyperinflation. And, in any case, the model that assumes one world good as well as one world bond is a powerfully simple prototype that will serve as a point of departure for more sophisticated models.

If perfect price flexibility is considered the crucial characteristic of monetarism, then the best name for the variety of monetary model that assumes purchasing power parity is the "monetarist model."[7] It has been developed by Frenkel [1976, 1977, 1980], Mussa [1976], Girton and Roper [1977], Hodrick [1978], and Bilson [1980a, b].

The fundamental equation in the monetary approach is a conventional money demand function:

$$m = p + \phi y - \lambda i, \tag{1}$$

where

$m \equiv$ log of the domestic money supply,
$p \equiv$ log of the domestic price level,
$y \equiv$ log of domestic real income,
$i \equiv$ the domestic short-term interest rate,
$\phi \equiv$ the money demand elasticity with respect to income,
$\lambda \equiv$ the money demand semielasticity with respect to the interest rate.

We assume a similar money demand function for the foreign country:

$$m^* = p^* + \phi y^* - \lambda i^*$$

where asterisks denote foreign variables and the parameters are assumed the same in both countries. Taking the difference of the two equations gives us a relative money demand function:

$$(m - m^*) = (p - p^*) + \phi(y - y^*) - \lambda(i - i^*). \tag{2}$$

The one-bond assumption gives us uncovered interest parity:

$$i - i^* = \mathscr{E}(\Delta e) \tag{3}$$

where $\mathscr{E}(\Delta e) \equiv$ the expected depreciation of domestic currency. We combine (2) and (3) and solve for the relative price level:

$$(p - p^*) = (m - m^*) - \phi(y - y^*) + \lambda\mathscr{E}(\Delta e). \tag{4}$$

The one-good assumption gives us purchasing power parity:

$$e = p - p^*, \tag{5}$$

where $e \equiv$ log of the spot exchange rate, defined as the price of foreign currency in terms of domestic. A consequence is that expected depreciation is equal to the expected inflation differential:

$$\mathscr{E}(\Delta e) = \mathscr{E}(\Delta p) - \mathscr{E}(\Delta p^*). \tag{6}$$

We combine (5), (4), and (6) to obtain the monetarist equation of exchange rate determination:

$$e = (m - m^*) - \phi(y - y^*) + \lambda(\mathscr{E}\,\Delta p - \mathscr{E}\,\Delta p^*). \tag{7}$$

Equation (7) says that the exchange rate, as the relative price of currency, is determined by the supply and demand for money. An increase in the supply of domestic money causes a proportionate depreciation. An increase in domestic income, or a decrease in the expected inflation rate, raises the demand for domestic money and thus causes an appreciation. The equation has been widely estimated econometrically.

Assume that expectations are rational and the system is stable. Assume further that income growth is exogenous (for simplicity equal to zero, so $y - y^* = \bar{y} - \bar{y}^*$), as it usually is in monetarist models. Then the expected inflation rate is equal to the rationally expected monetary growth rate. A benchmark specification of the money supply process is that monetary growth follows a random walk. Then the rationally expected future relative monetary growth rate, and thus the last term in equation (7), is simply the current relative monetary growth rate, which we will represent by $\Pi - \Pi^*$:

$$e = (m - m^*) - \phi(\bar{y} - \bar{y}^*) + \lambda(\Pi - \Pi^*). \tag{8}$$

As an alternative to the benchmark specification, a very restrictive special case occurs when we specify the *level* of the money supply, rather than the change in the money supply, to be a random walk. Then the expected relative rate of monetary growth, $\Pi - \Pi^*$, is zero. The level of the exchange rate is perfectly correlated with the level of the relative money supply. But in today's world the existence of secular inflation and its effect on money demand cannot be ignored.[8]

On the other hand, one could generalize beyond the benchmark case of a random-walk specification for money growth. More sophisticated specifications of the money supply process have appeared in monetarist exchange rate models by Mussa [1976], who distinguishes between transitory and permanent monetary disturbances, and Barro [1978], who distinguishes between anticipated and unanticipated disturbances.

3.2.2 The Sticky-Price ("Overshooting") Monetary Model

As mentioned, purchasing power parity may be a good approximation in the long run, but large deviations appear in the short run empirically. The existence of contracts, imperfect information, and inertia in consumer habits means that prices do not change instantaneously but adjust gradually over time.

We now retain the monetary approach's one-bond representation of financial markets but relax the monetarist model's one-good representation of trade. This gives us a class of models in which changes in the nominal money supply are also changes in the real money supply because prices are sticky, and thus have real effects, especially on the exchange rate.

The sticky-price class of monetary models begins with the well-known analysis of perfect capital mobility by Mundell [1963]. Mundell abstracts from expectations, so that uncovered interest parity (3) becomes a simple equality between the domestic and foreign interest rates. In a money demand equation like (1), the combination of a fixed price level and an interest rate tied to the world rate means that a monetary expansion causes a large instant depreciation in the currency: Export demand has to be stimulated sufficiently for the increased income to raise money demand to the level of the new higher money supply *without* lowering the domestic interest rate below the foreign one.

A number of authors have introduced a nonzero expected rate of depreciation into the Mundell model.[9] They argue that as long as the expected future spot rate is less than unit-elastic with respect to the current spot rate, a monetary expansion will not cause as large an increase in the exchange rate and income as in the Mundell model. This is because it is possible for the domestic interest rate to fall below the foreign one without inducing an infinite capital outflow.

At first Argy and Porter [1972] and Dornbusch [1976a] specified

expectations adaptively. But then Dornbusch [1976b] offered a model
in which expectations are specified rationally. In this model purchasing
power parity does hold in the long run, so that a given increase in the
money supply raises the exchange rate proportionately as in the monetarist model, but *only* in the long run. In the short run, because prices are
sticky, a monetary expansion has the liquidity effects of the Mundell
model. The interest rate falls, generating an incipient capital outflow,
which causes the currency to depreciate instantaneously *more* than it will
in the long run; it depreciates just enough so that the rationally expected
rate of future *appreciation* precisely cancels out the interest differential.
The phenomenon just described is known as "overshooting" of the spot
rate. In its honor, this paper will use the name "overshooting model" for
the sticky-price monetary approach to distinguish it from the monetarist
(flexible-price monetary approach) model.[10]

The overshooting model retains the money demand function (1) and
uncovered interest parity condition (3) essential to the monetary approach. It replaces the instantaneous purchasing power parity condition
(5) with a long-run version:

$$\bar{e} = \bar{p} - \bar{p}^*, \tag{9}$$

where bars over variables signify a relation that holds in the long run.
Thus the monetarist exchange rate equation (7) is replaced by a long-run
version:

$$\bar{e} = (\bar{m} - \bar{m}^*) - \phi(\bar{y} - \bar{y}^*) + \lambda(\overline{\mathscr{E}(\Delta p)} - \overline{\mathscr{E}(\Delta p^*)}). \tag{10}$$

Precisely as we did in the monetarist model, we assume that expectations are rational and the system is stable; for simplicity, income growth
is exogenous (or random with mean zero); and as a benchmark specification, monetary growth follows a random walk. It then follows that the
relative money supply, and in the long run the relative price level and
exchange rate, are all rationally expected to follow paths along which
they increase at the current rate of relative monetary growth $\Pi - \Pi^*$.
Equation (10) becomes

$$\bar{e} = (m - m^*) - \phi(y - y^*) + \lambda(\Pi - \Pi^*). \tag{11}$$

It remains only to specify expectations. In the short run, when the
exchange rate deviates from its equilibrium path, it is expected to close
that gap with a speed of adjustment θ. In the long run, when the exchange
rate lies on its equilibrium path, it is expected to increase at $\Pi - \Pi^*$:[11]

$$\mathscr{E}(\Delta e) = -\theta(e - \bar{e}) + \Pi - \Pi^*. \tag{12}$$

We combine (12) with the uncovered interest parity condition (3),

$$i - i^* = \delta(\Delta e) \tag{3}$$

to obtain

$$e - \bar{e} = -(1/\theta)[(i - \Pi) - (i^* - \Pi^*)]. \tag{13}$$

The gap between the exchange rate and its equilibrium value is proportional to the real interest differential. Intuitively, when a tight domestic monetary policy causes the nominal interest differential to rise above its equilibrium level, an incipient capital inflow causes the value of the currency to rise proportionately above *its* equilibrium level.

Now we combine (11), representing the long-run monetary equilibrium path, with (13), representing the short-run overshooting effect, to obtain a general monetary equation of exchange rate determination:

$$e = (m - m^*) - \phi(y - y^*) + \lambda(\Pi - \Pi^*)$$

$$- (1/\theta)[(i - \Pi) - (i^* - \Pi^*)]. \tag{14}$$

As the basis for econometric estimation, equation (14) is identical to the monetarist equation (8) but for the addition of a fourth explanatory variable, the real interest differential. This variable should show up in a regression with a zero coefficient if the monetarist model is correct; the economic interpretation would be that the speed of adjustment θ is infinite.

As we did in the last section, we can depart from the benchmark specification of the money supply process by considering the simple special case when the *level* of the money supply, rather then the *change* in the money supply, is a random walk. Then the expected long-run inflation differential $\Pi - \Pi^*$ is zero. This is precisely the context in which this model was originally developed by Dornbusch. Equation (14) becomes

$$e = (m - m^*) - \phi(y - y^*) - (1/\theta)(i - i^*). \tag{15}$$

The Dornbusch equation (15), like the monetarist equation (8), can be viewed as a nested model which can be tested econometrically by estimating equation (14).

Again as in the last section, one could also depart from the benchmark specification by considering a more general money supply process. More sophisticated specifications of the money supply process have appeared in Dornbusch-type models by Rogoff [1979], who distinguishes between transitory and permanent monetary disturbances, and Wilson [1979] and Gray and Turnovsky [1979], who distinguish between anticipated and unanticipated monetary disturbances.

3.2.3 Empirical Application of the Monetary Approach

Five years or so after exchange rates began to float in 1973, a number of empirical studies of the period appeared.[12] These studies tended generally to support the implications of the monetary approach against those of the traditional flow approach: a coefficient on the relative money supply which is positive or—more precisely—unity, and a coefficient on relative income which is negative and interpretable as the income elasticity of money demand. However, the empirical basis for a choice between the flexible-price and sticky-price variants of the monetary approach was less clear-cut. When the United Kingdom was one of the two countries whose exchange rate was studied, Bilson [1978a] and Hodrick [1978] found the interest differential to show the significant positive coefficient that is implied by the flexible-price model represented by equation (8). But Hodrick [1978] found the German interest rate to show the significant negative effect on the mark/dollar rate that is implied by the sticky-price model represented by equation (15). Estimation of equation (14)— Frankel [1979b]—supported the general monetary model for the mark/dollar rate from July 1974 to February 1978. The coefficient on the short-term interest differential was significantly less than zero, as in the sticky-price model, while the coefficient on the expected long-run inflation differential was significantly greater than zero, as in the flexible-price model.

In 1978 the dollar depreciated sharply. The depreciation prompted increasing political criticism of the noninterventionist policies of the US government and did not come to an end until the November package of increased monetary restraint and direct intervention to support the dollar. Much of the criticism, such as that appearing in repeated *Wall Street Journal* editorials, subscribed to the monetary model. In this view the declining price of dollars was simply due to the rapid increase in the supply of dollars "spewing forth from Federal Reserve printing presses." The behavior of the Bundesbank and the performance of the mark were pointed to as paragons of monetary restraint and its rewards. Unfortunately for this theory, German monetary growth in 1978 was, and has been for some years, actually *higher* than US monetary growth. The reason for the surprisingly high rate of monetary growth in Germany, ironically, was the strength in the value of the mark against the dollar. The Bundesbank resisted this appreciation by buying dollars, without sterilizing the reserve inflow, and thus caused the German money supply to swell.

Empirical studies that tried to update the monetary equation to include the events of 1978 and 1979 were quite unsuccessful from the viewpoint of all versions of the model.[13] The only coefficient to appear statistically significant was that on the expected inflation differential. The coefficient on the relative money supply actually appeared with the incorrect sign, attesting to the mystery of a mark that went up in price even as it was increasing in relative supply.[14]

In 1980 the traditional Keynesian correlation between the interest rate and the value of the dollar strongly reemerged. Both exhibited two sharp peaks centered on April and December. Table 3.1 reports an update of the monetary equation through December 1980. When we correct for serial correlation, the coefficient on the interest differential rejoins the coefficients on the expected inflation rates in appearing statistically significant. This new evidence would tend again to support the general sticky-price form of the monetary model, equation (14). However, the insignificant (or in one case significant but of the wrong sign) coefficient on the money supplies and relative income continue to cast doubt on the monetary model in all forms.

If the money supplies are endogenous, because of either the existence of central bank reaction functions or disturbances in money demand, then the estimates reported in the first row of table 3.1 are not consistent. One remedy is to impose the constraint of a unit coefficient on the relative money supply, in effect moving the endogenous variable to the left-hand side of the regression equation. The results of such regressions (not reported here) are no better than the unconstrained regression.

3.3 The Portfolio-Balance Approach

3.3.1 The Effect of the Current Account
The other popular explanation for the decline of the dollar in 1978, besides US monetary growth, was the large US current account deficit. The old-fashioned view that the level of the exchange rate must clear the current account had been refuted by theorists who pointed to the existence of high capital mobility and by practitioners who pointed to the fact that until the end of 1977 the dollar's trade-weighted value was quite high despite a record current account deficit. But more recently, the correlation between current account deficits and exchange rates has been undeniably strong, not only in 1978 when the dollar depreciated and the currencies

Table 3.1

Estimation of monetary exchange rate equation (14): dependent variable — log of mark/dollar rate[a]

Sample	Technique	c	gml − usmlb	gy	usy	gi − usi	gΠ	usΠ	R^2	D.W.	ρ̂
7401–8012	OLSQ	3.229 (0.570)	−0.835[b] (0.158)	−0.885[c] (0.255)	0.289 (0.195)	−0.190 (0.300)	4.717[c] (0.813)	−3.932[c] (0.301)	0.93	0.92	
	CORC	3.283 (1.018)	−0.770[b] (0.268)	−0.382 (0.271)	−0.199 (0.240)	−0.698[c] (0.328)	3.485[c] (1.187)	−3.444[c] (0.539)	0.95		0.67
7402–8011	FAIR	2.453 (1.217)	−0.503 (0.335)	−0.167 (0.319)	−0.222 (0.294)	−1.465[c] (0.516)	7.244[c] (2.081)	−4.877[c] (0.755)	0.94		0.66

a. Definitions: gml − usmlb ≡ log of relative money supply, Germany/U.S. (M1B); gy, usy ≡ log of real income levels (proxied by industrial production), Germany and United States, respectively; gi − usi ≡ nominal interest differential (short-term money market rates, per annum basis); gΠ, usΠ ≡ expected inflation rates (proxied by average CPI inflation over preceding twelve months): OLSQ, ordinary least squares; CORC, iterated Cochrane-Orcutt: FAIR, Fair's method of correcting for possible endogeneity of gi − usi, gΠ, and usΠ (instrumental variables are the German and US ratios of outstanding government bonds to monetary base, and the German and US long-term government bond interest rates) in the presence of serial correlation (current and lagged values of all endogenous and included exogenous variables are added to the list of instruments). (Standard errors are in parentheses.)

b. Significant at the 95% level and of the incorrect sign.

c. Significant at the 95% level and of the correct sign.

of the surplus countries, Germany and Japan, appreciated, but also in 1979 and 1980 when the pattern was reversed.

There are three main lines according to which current account developments can be argued to affect the exchange rate, without reverting to the traditional flow theory of foreign exchange. The first begins by observing that current account developments have been largely dominated by oil. One could argue within the monetary approach that, because the United States produces oil while Germany and Japan produce none, or else because world oil trade is actually transacted in dollars, the sharp increase in world oil prices that took place in 1979 raised the demand for the dollar at the expense of the mark and yen, much as did the increase that took place in late 1973. On the other hand, financial commentators have often argued more loosely that oil price increases actually *hurt* the dollar because the United States had not yet decontrolled domestic oil prices or else because US political prestige is at stake in the Middle East.[15]

The second line of argument begins by observing that the release by the government of unexpected figures on the trade balance or current account appears to have large immediate "announcement effects" on the exchange rate. In some versions the current account figures reveal new information about shifts in the long-run terms of trade. But the important point is that only the unexpected component of the current account has a large effect, the expected component having already been taken into account by the foreign exchange market.[16]

The third line of argument begins by observing that the counterpart of a current account surplus is a transfer of wealth from foreign residents to domestic residents. The increase in domestic wealth can, in turn, appreciate the currency through any of three channels. First, it can raise domestic expenditure as in the well-established Modigliani consumption function, and thus raise domestic income and the transactions demand for domestic money. Second, it can raise the demand for domestic money directly if wealth enters the money demand function and domestic money is not held by foreigners. Third, if domestic bonds and foreign bonds are imperfect substitutes and domestic residents have a greater tendency to hold wealth in the form of domestic bonds than do foreign residents, the increase in domestic wealth will raise the demand for domestic bonds. Each of these effects might claim a role in a comprehensive model, but we will focus on the last of the three and refer to it as the "portfolio-balance" effect, giving us the second major branch in figure 3.1.[17]

3.3.2 The Portfolio-Balance Equation

We retain our assumption that there are no barriers segmenting international capital markets, but we relax the assumption that domestic and foreign bonds are perfect substitutes. Thus investors allocate their bond portfolios between the two countries in proportions that are functions of the expected rates of return.

There are many reasons why two assets can be imperfect substitutes: liquidity, tax treatment, default risk, political risk, and exchange risk. However, at the level of aggregation relevant for most macroeconomic models (see note 2), and under our assumption of perfect international bond markets, the last of these is the most important. We assume that there is only one respect in which domestic and foreign bonds differ: their currency of denomination. Investors, in order to diversify the risk that comes from exchange rate variability, balance their bond portfolios between domestic and foreign bonds in proportions that depend on the expected relative rate of return (or risk premium):

$$B_j/EF_j = \beta_j(i - i^* - \mathscr{E}\,\Delta e). \tag{16}$$

Here B_j is the stock of domestic-denominated bonds held by investor j; F_j, the stock of foreign-denominated bonds held; and E, the exchange rate. β_j is a positive-valued function; for concreteness let it be $\exp[\alpha_j + \beta_j (i - i^* - \mathscr{E}\,\Delta e)]$.[18] An increase in the interest differential or a fall in the expected rate of depreciation induces investors to shift their portfolios out of foreign bonds and into domestic bonds. (Note that B_j and F_j can be negative, which will be the case if agent j is a debtor.)

We assume at first that all active participants in the market have the same portfolio preferences, as represented by the function β. This assumption allows us to add up individual asset demand functions into the aggregate asset demand equation (17):

$$\frac{B}{EF} = \beta(i - i^* - \mathscr{E}\,\Delta e), \tag{17}$$

where

$$B \equiv \sum_{j=1} B_j \quad \text{and} \quad F \equiv \sum_{j=1} F_j.$$

B and F are the *net* supplies of bonds (domestically denominated and foreign denominated, respectively) in the market. If one market participant is in debt to another, the asset and liability will cancel out. All that matters are the supplies of *outside* assets in the market.

A relation like (17) between asset supplies and expected rates of return is not by itself a theory of exchange rate determination, as Dooley and Isard [1979] have pointed out. Even if the interest rates are omitted or taken as exogenous, expectations must be specified. For example, if either the expected rate of depreciation $\mathcal{E} \Delta e$ or the expected future exchange rate $\mathcal{E} e_{+1}$ is determined, then the exchange rate is uniquely determined.[19] But specifying that expectations are formed *rationally* is not sufficient to determine the exchange rate uniquely; as in so many rational expectations problems, the assumption of stability is also required. The simplest possible portfolio-balance model would specify static expectations: $\mathcal{E} \Delta e = 0$. Then the exchange rate is simply determined by relative bond supplies and the interest differential:

$$e = -\alpha + \beta(i - i^*) + b - f, \tag{18}$$

where $b \equiv \log B$ and $f \equiv \log F$. Equation (18) is estimated below.[20]

So far we have not been very precise about the definitions of B and F. If the market consists of the whole world, and residents of all countries have the same portfolio preferences, then "the supplies of outside assets in the market" include only government-issued liabilities held by the private sector.[21] In (17) B must be interpreted as net domestically denominated government indebtedness and F as net foreign-denominated government indebtedness. B and F will be the same as domestic and foreign government debt, respectively, under the assumption that governments issue debt denominated exclusively in their own currencies.[22]

The proposition that residents of all countries have the same portfolio preferences implies that the indebtedness of residents of one country to residents of the other has no effect. This proposition holds in several recent finance papers—Grauer, Litzenberger, and Stehle [1976]; Frankel [1979a]; Fama and Farber [1979]; and Dornbusch [1980a]—and is represented by the "uniform preference" branch of portfolio-balance models in figure 3.1. These papers derive the asset demand functions as the outcome of maximization of expected utility by risk-averse agents. The proposition that all agents have the same portfolio preference follows from the assumption that they all consume the same good, or basket of goods.[23]

This interpretation of equation (17) contrasts with macroeconomic models of portfolio balance that take asset-demand functions as given. The majority of these models, though they maintain our assumption that no barriers discourage residents of any country from participating in the world market, make the assumption that domestic residents are the only ones who *wish* to hold domestically denominated assets.[24] The domestic country is assumed to be too small for its assets to be of interest to foreign residents.

One motivation for this assumption is to simplify the accounting—it allows the identification of a capital inflow or outflow with an increase or decrease in the supply of foreign assets in the home market by assuming away the problem of currency of denomination of the capital flow. The second motivation for the assumption is that, under floating exchange rates, it leads to the result that a current account deficit causes a depreciation of the home currency, since the counterpart to the current account deficit is a capital inflow: The reduction in the supply of foreign-denominated assets in the market leads to a rise in their price in terms of domestic currency.

Thus as an alternative to (17), we aggregate (16) over all domestic residents only:

$$\frac{B_H}{EF_H} = \beta_H(i - i^* - \mathscr{E} \Delta e), \tag{19}$$

where B_H is defined as the sum of all domestic bonds held by home residents (identical to B, under the small-country assumption), F_H is defined as the sum of all foreign bonds held by home residents (equal to the accumulation of past current account surpluses under the small-country assumption), and β_H is the asset-demand function shared by all home residents. Assuming static expectations, the exchange rate equation is

$$e = -\alpha_H - \dot{\beta}_H(i - i^*) + b - f_H, \tag{20}$$

where $b \equiv \log B$ and $F_H \equiv \log F_H$.

The small-country assumption—the assumption that foreign residents do not hold domestic bonds—is particularly unrealistic if the domestic country is the United States. One alternative is to assume that the *foreign* country is the small country—that domestic residents do not hold foreign bonds. Then (20) is replaced by

$$e = -\alpha_F - \beta_F(i - i^*) + b_F - f, \tag{21}$$

where b_F is defined as the log of domestic bonds held by foreign residents (equal to the accumulation of past foreign current account surpluses under the small-country assumption).[25] Equations (20) and (21) are estimated below.

A realistic portfolio-balance model for large countries must recognize that residents of both countries hold assets issued by both countries. But the (cumulated) current account will still have the expected effect on the exchange rate, provided domestic residents wish to hold a greater proportion of their wealth as domestic assets and foreign residents wish to hold a greater proportion as foreign assets. (Such models are classified under the name "preferred local habitat" in figure 3.1.[26]) This is because the current account will redistribute world wealth in such a way as to raise net world demand for the surplus country's assets, thus raising the price of its currency. We would have to specify a separate asset-demand function for foreign residents:

$$\frac{B_F}{EF_F} = \beta_F(i - i^* - \mathcal{E}\,\Delta e), \tag{22}$$

where $\beta_H \geq \beta_F$ for all values. Equations (19) for the home country and (22) for the foreign country could each be solved independently for the exchange rate and regressed in logarithic form, were data on B_H, B_F, F_H, and F_F available. Unfortunately, data on the four-way breakdown—who owns how much of which asset—are difficult to obtain. Only the two-way breakdowns can be attempted: between domestically and foreign-denominated bonds ($B \equiv B_H + B_F$ versus $F \equiv F_H + F_F$) and between domestically and foreign-held wealth ($W_H \equiv B_H + EF_H$ versus $W_F \equiv B_F + EF_F$).

The nonlinear nature of (19) and (22) prevents solving for the exchange rate as a function of B, F, W_H, and W_F. However, the signs to be expected in such a relation are clear. An increase in the supply of foreign bonds F lowers their relative price E. An increase in the supply of domestic bonds B raises E. An increase in foreign wealth W_F raises the overall world demand for foreign assets and thus raises their relative price E. Finally, an increase in home wealth W_H raises the overall world demand for domestic assets and thus lowers E.

Table 3.2 presents regressions of the dollar/mark exchange rate against the interest differential and bond supplies, which are tests of the portfolio-balance approach under static expectations. Calculation of the net supplies of domestically and foreign-denominated assets requires correcting outstanding treasury debt for exchange intervention by central banks—as mentioned in note 22.[27] In addition, each country's monetary base is subtracted from the supply of its assets to arrive at the supply of its interest-paying bonds. Kouri [1978] argues that all nominally fixed assets should be included in the portfolio, whether interestpaying or not. Proponents of the currency-substitution model argue in effect that *only*

Table 3.2

Estimation of portfolio-balance equations—log of dollar/mark rate, January 1974–October 1978[a]

Asset preferences	Technique	c	usi − gi	usb	gb	usf	gf	R^2	D.W.	$\hat{\rho}$
1. Uniform worldwide	OLS	−0.485 (0.215)	−0.472 (0.579)	−0.798[b] (0.122)	+0.916[b] (0.116)			0.78	0.46	
	CORC	+0.733 (0.971)	−0.387 (0.461)	−0.343[b] (0.173)	+0.431[b] (0.089)			0.94		0.97
2. US bonds held only by US residents	OLS	−6.391 (0.831)	0.240 (0.643)	−0.393[b] (0.098)		+1.255[b] (0.217)		0.71	0.29	
	CORC	−10.312 (3.202)	−0.248 (0.525)	−0.117 (0.171)		+1.639[b] (0.524)		0.92		0.95
3. German bonds held only by German residents	OLS	−1.530 (0.223)	1.920[b] (0.598)		+0.224[b] (0.062)		−0.096 (0.105)	0.61	0.23	
	CORC	+0.632 (1.041)	−0.311 (0.426)		+0.154 (0.106)		−0.521[b] (0.162)	0.94		0.96
4. General case	OLS	−5.648 (0.881)	−1.595[c] (0.491)	−0.607[b] (0.105)	+0.893[b] (0.102)	+1.330[b] (0.226)	−0.295[b] (0.096)	0.87	0.61	
	CORC	−5.620 (2.497)	−0.699 (0.431)	−0.188 (0.106)	+0.271 (0.147)	+1.174[b] (0.423)	−0.463[b] (0.149)	0.95		0.94

a. Definitions: usi − gi ≡ interest differential (short-term money market rates, per annum basis); usb ≡ log of net supply of dollar bonds to the private sector, calculated as US Treasury debt + cumulative Federal Reserve sales of dollar assets in foreign exchange intervention (inferred from Fed international reserves without valuation changes) − dollar assets held by other central banks − US monetary base; gb ≡ log of net supply of mark bonds to the private sector, calculated as German Treasury debt + cumulative Bundesbank sales of mark assets in foreign exchange intervention (inferred from Bundesbank international reserves without valuation changes) − mark assets held by other central banks − German monetary base; usf ≡ log of net supply of foreign bonds to the US private sector, under the (unrealistic) assumption that dollar assets are held only by US residents and that all capital flows are denominated in marks, calculated as the cumulation of (expressed in marks) the US current account − Federal Reserve purchases of foreign assets in foreign exchange intervention + sales by other central banks of foreign assets for dollars; gf ≡ log of net supply of foreign bonds to the German private sector, under the (unrealistic) assumption that mark assets are held only by German residents and that all capital flows are denominated in dollars, calculated as the cumulation of (expressed in dollars) the German current account − Bundesbank purchases of foreign assets in foreign exchange intervention + sales by other central banks of foreign assets for marks. (Standard errors in parentheses.)

b. Significant at the 95 percent level and of the incorrect sign.

c. Significant at the 95 percent level and of the correct sign.

moneys should be included in the portfolio.[28] But regressions based on these alternatives were no more successful than those, based on supplies of bonds alone, reported in table 3.2.

Row 1 is an estimation of equation (18): the portfolio-balance model when residents of all countries have uniform asset preferences, so that the worldwide distribution of wealth via current accounts is irrelevant and government bond supplies are all that matter. Row 2 is an estimation of equation (20), the "domestic small-country" model, in which the relevant stock variables are the supply of domestic government bonds and the supply of foreign bonds to domestic residents, with the United States defined as the domestic country. Row 3 is an estimation of equation (21), the "foreign small-country" model, in which the relevant stock variables are the supply of foreign government bonds and the supply of domestic bonds to foreign residents, with Germany defined as the foreign country. Row 4 uses all four stock variables: the supplies of both domestic and foreign bonds and the cumulated current accounts of both countries.[29] This regression includes each of the first three as special cases.[30]

The results are very poor for the portfolio-balance models. The coefficients on all four stock variables are always of the incorrect sign and usually appear significantly so.

3.4 A Synthesis of the Monetary and Portfolio-Balance Equations

In section 3.2.1 we presented the simple monetarist model of exchange rates which assumes one world bond (i.e., perfect capital substitutability, implying uncovered interest parity) and one world good (i.e., perfect price flexibility, implying purchasing power parity). The result was the monetarist equation in which the exchange rate is determined by the relative money supply, relative income, and the expected inflation differential:

$$e = (m - m^*) - \phi(y - y^*) + \lambda(\Pi - \Pi^*). \tag{8}$$

In section 3.2.2 we relaxed the price flexibility assumption. In empirical terms, we simply added the real interest differential to the other three explanatory variables:

$$e = (m - m^*) - \phi(y - y^*) + \lambda(\Pi - \Pi^*)$$
$$-(1/\theta)[(i - \Pi) - (i^* - \Pi^*)]. \tag{14}$$

In this section we extend the synthesis process by relaxing the perfect substitutability assumption.[31] We integrate the monetary models, as represented by equation (14), with the portfolio-balance models, as represented by equation (17):

$$B/EF = \beta(i - i^* - \mathscr{E}\,\Delta e).\tag{17}$$

In logarithmic form (17) becomes

$$b - e - f = \alpha + \beta(i - i^* - \mathscr{E}\,\Delta e).\tag{23}$$

We repeat the expectation equation (12):

$$\mathscr{E}(\Delta e) = -\theta(e - \bar{e}) + \Pi - \Pi^*.\tag{12}$$

By adding and subtracting the nomial interest differential, we see that (12) implies that the exchange rate deviates from its long-run value by an amount proportional to the real interest differential and the risk premium:

$$e - \bar{e} = -(1/\theta)[(i - \Pi) - (i^* - \Pi^*)] + (1/\theta)[i - i^* - \mathscr{E}\,\Delta e].\tag{24}$$

We substitute in equation (11) for the equilibrium exchange rate:

$$e = (m - m^*) - \phi(y - y^*) + \lambda(\Pi - \Pi^*)$$
$$-(1/\theta)[(i - \Pi) - (i^* - \Pi^*)] + (1/\theta)[i - i^* - \mathscr{E}\,\Delta e].\tag{25}$$

In the monetarist model, purchasing power parity (6) ensured that the real interest differential was zero and uncovered interest parity (3) ensured that the risk premium was zero, so that equation (25) reduced to (8). The sticky-price monetary model relaxed the first condition but maintained the second, so that (25) reduced only to (14).

The synthesis of the monetary and portfolio-balance equations is accomplished simply by relaxing the second condition. We replace uncovered interest parity (3) with the imperfect substitutability condition (23). Now the exchange rate deviates from its equilibrium value not only because sticky goods prices create a real interest differential, but also because imperfect bond substitutability creates a risk premium. We substitute (23) into (25), getting bond supplies into the exchange rate equation in place of the unobservable risk premium:

$$e = (m - m^*) - \phi(y - y^*) + \lambda(\Pi - \Pi^*)$$
$$-(1/\theta)[(i - \Pi) - (i^* - \Pi^*)] + [1/(\theta\beta)][b - e - f - \alpha].\tag{26}$$

Finally, we solve for e:

Table 3.3
Implied regression coefficients of competing exchange rate equations[a]

e against	$(m - m^*)$	$(y - y^*)$	$(i - i^*)$	$(\Pi - \Pi^*)$	$(b - f)$
Traditional flow view		+	−		
Modern asset view					
Monetary approach					
Monetarist equation (8)	+	−	+	+	
Overshooting equation (15)	+	−	−		
Real interest differential equation (14)	+	−	−	+	
Portfolio-balance approach (18)			−		+
Synthesis asset equation (27)	+	−	−	+	+

a. Definitions: $e \equiv$ log of exchange rate: $m - m^* \equiv$ log of relative money supply: $y - y^*$ $\equiv$ log of relative income: $i - i^* \equiv$ nominal interest differential: $\Pi - \Pi^* \equiv$ expected inflation differential: $b - f \equiv$ log of relative bond supply.

$$e = \frac{\alpha}{\theta\beta + 1} + \frac{\theta\beta}{\theta\beta + 1}(m - m^*) - \frac{\theta\beta\phi}{\theta\beta + 1}(y - y^*)$$

$$+ \frac{\beta(\theta\lambda + 1)}{\theta\beta + 1}(\Pi - \Pi^*) - \frac{\beta}{\theta\beta + 1}(i - i^*) + \frac{1}{\theta\beta + 1}(b - f). \quad (27)$$

In empirical terms we have simply added the relative bond supply to the monetary equation (14) as a fifth explanatory variable.

Equation (27) is intended to synthesize many varieties of asset-market model, monetary as well as portfolio balance. Since it contains the individual competing models as special cases, it provides a framework for evaluating them empirically. Table 3.3 summarizes the coefficient signs implied by the various models in a regression of equation (27). The implications of the various models are so conflicting that one would think that regression could hardly help but reject some models in favor of others.

Table 3.4 reports the regression of equation (27). The results are similar to those in tables 3.1 and 3.2. The coefficients of the variables from the monetary equation—the relative money supply, relative income, interest differential, and inflation differential—are usually correct in sign. However, when we correct for serial correlation, most of them lose their significance. The coefficient of the relative bond supply, in the uniform-preference and German small-country version, appears significant but of the *reverse* sign from that hypothesized in the portfolio-balance model.

An examination of the data on dollar and mark bond supplies readily reveals the problem with tables 3.2 and 3.4. During a period when the dollar/mark rate rose on average, the dollar bond supply (like the dollar

Table 3.4
Estimation of synthesis exchange rate Equation (27)—log of dollar/mark rate, January 1974–October 1978[a]

Technique	c	usmlb – gml	usy – gy	usi – gi	usΠ – gΠ	usb – gb	usb – usf	gb – gf	R^2	D.W.	$\hat{\rho}$
1. OLS	0.086	-0.751[b]	0.357	-1.588[c]	2.657[c]	-0.578[b]			0.86	0.56	
	(0.131)	(0.136)	(0.190)	(0.550)	(0.530)	(0.121)					
CORC	-0.260	-0.011	-0.133	-0.396	0.852	-0.398[b]			0.94		0.97
	(0.230)	(0.358)	(0.224)	(0.502)	(0.766)	(0.091)					
2. OLS	-0.520	-0.388	-0.281	0.706	5.559[c]		0.419[c]		0.83	0.84	
	(0.090)	(0.226)	(0.229)	(0.595)	(0.597)		(0.115)				
CORC	-0.674	0.190	-0.355	0.156	0.773		-0.184		0.92		0.98
	(0.256)	(0.416)	(0.255)	(0.570)	(0.928)		(0.194)				
3. OLS	-0.772	-0.687	-0.220	-0.491	4.480[c]			0.284[b]	0.89	0.76	
	(0.086)	(0.116)	(0.167)	(0.420)	(0.371)			(0.041)			
CORC	-1.103	0.050	-0.056	-0.358	1.851[c]			0.313[b]	0.95		0.92
	(0.186)	(0.314)	(0.208)	(0.465)	(0.691)			(0.052)			

a. Definitions: see tables 3.1 and 3.2. (Standard errors are in parentheses.)
b. Significant at the 95 percent level and of the incorrect sign.
c. Significant at the 95 percent level and of the correct sign.

money supply) did *not* increase as fast as its mark counterpart. The problem can be traced to foreign exchange intervention: Foreign central banks rapidly increased their holdings of dollar assets in order to keep their own currencies from appreciating against the dollar. As Hooper and Morton [1982] point out, one cannot use a current account deficit within the portfolio-balance model to explain a currency depreciation if the deficit is more than offset by exchange intervention on the part of foreign central banks.

To the extent that this intervention was sterilized, its failure to maintain the value of the dollar is evidence against the portfolio-balance approach and in favor of the monetary approach.[32] As noted in section 3.2.3, the purchases of dollars by foreign central banks *were* allowed to increase their money supplies. However, the relative German monetary base did not increase anywhere nearly as quickly as the relative German net bond supply. While 1978 remains a mystery for both models, the updated results in table 3.1 appear promising enough, at least in comparison to the disaster of table 3.2 and 3.4, tentatively to justify a return of attention to the monetary approach.

Notes

1. This distinction between capital mobility and substitutability is made precise by Dornbusch and Krugman [1976]. Earlier references to it appear in Girton and Henderson [1976], Girton and Roper [1976], and Dornbusch [1977]. The distinction is far from universally accepted (for example, Mundell [1963] implicitly took perfect mobility to require perfect substitutability), but is useful.

2. Empirical tests have shown covered interest parity to hold to a high degree of approximation, at least in the Eurocurrency market. See, for example, Frenkel and Levich [1977]. Covered interest parity holds less well if the interest rates used refer to treasury bills, commercial paper, or other financial securities that differ from the forward contract with respect to tax treatment, default risk, or other factors. However, at the level of aggregation relevant for most macroeconomic models we speak only of "the" interest rate, abstracting from distinctions such as that between the 30-day Eurodollar interest rate and the 30-day treasury bill rate. This paper presumes that level of aggregation and presumes covered interest parity.

3. It is difficult to test uncovered interest parity empirically because expectations are not observable. Uncovered interest parity (and, by implication, perfect substitutability) can be tested *jointly* with market efficiency by examining the ex post excess return on domestic currency. The excess return is defined as the interest differential in excess of ex post depreciation, or alternatively (given covered interest parity) as the forward discount in excess of ex post depreciation. Under the joint null hypothesis, the ex post excess return should be random; the forward rate should be an unbiased predictor of the future spot rate (see figure 3.1).

Most such tests take the perfect substitutability component of the joint hypothesis as given and interpret the results as evidence on efficiency. See for example Cornell [1977], Cornell and Dietrich [1979], Frankel [1980], and Frenkel [1977]; the literature is surveyed by Levich [1979] and Kohlhagen [1978]. But a few such tests take the market efficiency component of the joint hypothesis as given and interpret the results as evidence on substitutability. See Stockman [1978], Cumby and Obstfeld [1979], and Frankel [1982b].

4. Some of the many examples are Allen and Kenen [1980]; Black [1973]; Branson [1976]; Branson, Halttunen, and Masson [1977]; Calvo and Rodriguez [1977]; Dooley and Isard [1979]; Dornbusch [1980a]; Flood [1979]; Girton and Henderson [1977]; Girton and Roper [1976]; Kouri [1976a, 1978]; Kouri and deMacedo [1978]; McKinnon [1976]; Porter [1979]; Tobin and deMacedo [1980]; and Rodriguez [1980]. The antecedents are the portfolio-balance approach under fixed exchange rates, as represented by Branson [1968], and the portfolio-balance model in a closed economy, as represented by Tobin [1969].

5. Examples are Frenkel [1976, 1977, 1980], Mussa [1976], Dornbusch [1976a,b], Girton and Roper [1977], Bilson [1978a,b], Hodrick [1978], and Frankel [1979b].

6. Officer [1976] surveys the literature on purchasing power parity. Some recent empirical studies are Isard [1977], Genberg [1978], and Krugman [1978].

7. This distinction between the monetary approach to exchange rates and the more restrictive monetarist model follows the distinction made by Whitman [1975] in the theory of fixed exchange rates between the monetary approach to the balance of payments and the more restrictive "global monetarist" model. (In the past— Frankel [1979b]—I have used the term "Chicago model" for what I am here calling the monetarist model.)

8. Little, if any, published monetarist work asserts this restrictive special case, the monetarists having long ago relaxed the quantity theory of money to study the effect of expected inflation on money demand.

A recent paper by Caves and Feige [1980] that purports to test "the monetary approach to exchange-rate determination" uses as its criterion the unusual proposition that the exchange rate is entirely explainable by the past history of the money supplies. Even the most extreme monetarist proponent of the monetary approach recognizes the importance of fluctuations in real income.

In a further confusion, Caves and Feige claim that proponents of the monetary approach "have failed to recognize that one of the consequences of an efficient foreign exchange market is to eliminate the possibility of directly observing a systematic relationship [between] exchange rates and past supplies of national monies. If the foreign exchange market is efficient, all monetary effects on exchange rates will be contemporaneous" [1980, p. 121]. But as is well known, market efficiency requires not that changes in the spot rate be independent of past variables such as money supplies, but that changes in the spot rate *in excess of the interest differential* (or forward discount) be independent of past variables. In any monetary model except the restrictive special case described above, the past history of the money supply may contain information on changes in the spot rate without violating efficiency. In the benchmark monetarist model, for example, the interest differential and the rationally expected change in the spot rate are each equal to the relative rate of expected monetary growth; actual changes in the spot rate will be independent of past money supply *changes*, not *levels*. In the Dornbusch overshooting model, changes in the spot rate are not independent of either past money supply changes *or* levels.

9. See Mundell [1964], Argy and Porter [1972], Niehans [1975], and Dornbusch [1976a,b].

10. The version that follows is based on Dornbusch [1976b] as generalized in Frankel [1979b] to include the case of secular inflation. (In that paper I used the term "Keynesian model" for what I am here calling the overshooting model. We should also note that overshooting is possible in other models, as shown by Flood [1979].) Investigations of the overshooting properties of the Dornbusch model include Mathieson [1977] and Bhandari [1981].

11. In the appendix to Frankel [1979b], it is proved that the form of exchange rate expectations specified in (12) is rational, assuming an additional equation in which the price level adjusts in the short run in response to excess goods demand (itself a function of relative prices, and possibly income and the real interest rate) and increases in the long run at the secular inflation rate (Π).

12. For example, Bilson [1978a,b], Hodrick [1978], Dornbusch [1978], Kohlhagen [1979], Frankel [1979b], and Driskill [1981].

13. For example, Dornbusch [1980], and an earlier version of the present paper.

14. The unexplained fall in demand for dollars relative to marks may be associated with the observed unexplained downward shift in the US money demand function known as "the mystery of the missing money."

15. Krugman [1980] identifies OPEC's asset-holding and importing preferences between the United States and Europe as the key determinants of the effect of oil price increases on the value of the dollar. Obstfeld [1980b] is typical of a number of papers that emphasize oil's role as an intermediate input and are primarily relevant for small countries.

16. For example, Hooper and Morton [1982], Isard [1980] and Dornbusch [1980b].

17. The expenditure channel is represented by Dornbusch and Fischer [1980]. Wealth enters the money demand function in Dornbusch [1976c] and Frankel [1982a]. Both effects are present in Turnovsky and Kingston [1979]. The strategy of attempting to "put the current account back" into the asset-market models through the portfolio-balance effect is made explicit by Kouri [1976a], Kouri and deMacedo [1978], Hooper and Morton [1982], Porter [1979], Dooley and Isard [1979], and Rodriguez [1980]. Dornbusch [1980b] mentions all three wealth effects (pp. 154–57, 164, and 164–68, respectively), but emphasizes the imperfect substitutability effect as "more persuasive."

18. If portfolio-balance behavior is the outcome of the maximization of expected utility by risk-averse investors, then we are implicitly assuming in (16) that the variances of currency values, and covariances with other forms of real wealth, are stationary over time. Only the expected rate of return is assumed to vary.

19. If the expected future exchange rate is $\overline{\mathscr{E}e_{+1}}$, then the solution for the current exchange rate, in log form, is

$$e = -\frac{\alpha}{1 + \beta} + \frac{1}{1 + \beta}(b - f) + \frac{\beta}{1 + \beta}(\overline{\mathscr{E}e_{+1}} - (i - i^*)).$$

20. Kouri [1976a] considers the alternatives of static and rational (or perfect foresight) expectations.

21. If government-issued assets are not considered net wealth by the private sector because they imply off-setting liabilities in the form of future taxation, the Ricardian principle, then the possibility arises that the net supply of outside assets to the world market is zero. If there are no outside assets (including real assets) then exchange risk is completely diversifiable. Under these very special circumstances, investors will consider domestic and foreign bonds perfect substitutes in market equilibrium because they can always cover any exchange risk on the forward market *without* paying any risk premium; the perfect substitutability assumption holds despite risk aversion. (The argument is made in Frankel [1979a]. For an empirical test of perfect substitutability based on equation (17) see Frankel [1982b].)

22. Of course many small countries do sometimes issue debt denomination in foreign currencies, and even the United States began to do so with its Carter notes. (The Roosa bonds of the 1960s do not count because they were held by foreign governments rather than citizens.) In empirical work, any such debt must be counted according to its currency of denomination. A bigger problem is central bank behavior. Purchases of domestically denominated assets in foreign exchange intervention (by foreign as well as domestic central banks) must be subtracted from treasury debt to arrive at the proper measure of the net supply of domestically denominated assets to the private market.

23. At the opposite extreme, Solnik [1974] derives asset-demand functions as the outcome of maximization by agents who consume only goods produced in their own countries.

24. Branson [1976], Kouri [1976a], Flood [1979], Branson, Halttunen, and Masson [1977], Porter [1979], Dornbusch and Fischer [1980], and Rodriguez [1980], among others, assume that domestic assets are not held by foreigners.

25. Shafer [1979] assumes that the foreign country is the small country, that is, the foreign accumulated current account surplus is the supply of domestically denominated bonds.

26. A small but growing number of models allow the foreign preference for holding domestic assets to be less than the domestic preference and yet greater than zero. In the category of finance models that derive asset-demand functions from expected-utility maximization are Kouri [1976b] and Kouri and deMacedo [1978] and the appendix to Dornbusch [1980a]. The necessary assumption at first appears to be only that the foreign preference for consuming domestic goods is less than the domestic preference and yet greater than zero. However, Krugman [1981] shows in a continuous-time stochastic model that it is also necessary that the coefficient of relative risk-aversion be greater than one.

In the category of macroeconomic models of portfolio balance which take asset-demand functions as given are Dooley and Isard [1979] and parts IV and V of Allen and Kenen [1980]. Henderson and Rogoff [1981] use such a model to investigate the possibility that negative holdings of foreign assets cause dynamic instability (a possibility that in a small-country context concerns Branson, Halttunen, and Masson [1977] and Obstfeld [1980a] among others).

27. These calculations become especially difficult after October 1978 because of the issuing of Carter notes by the Treasury, the holding of foreign exchange reserves valued at current exchange rates by the Federal Reserve, and the turning over of reserves to the European Monetary System by the Bundesbank. For this reason the data sample used in tables 3.2 and 3.4 ends in October 1978. Data sources were the *Federal Reserve Bulletin* and the *Bundesbank Monthly Report Statistical Supplements*. Data and details of the calculations are available on request.

28. The term "currency substitution" was originated by Girton and Roper [1981] to describe the allocation of market portfolios between domestic and foreign money. Other examples are Barro [1978] and Calvo and Rodriguez [1977]. In many of the theoretical models, only the use of the words "money" or "currency" distinguishes them from the other portfolio-balance models, which use the words "bonds" or "assets." But one might argue, following note 21, that, to the extent that government debt implies future tax liabilities to pay it off, high-powered money is the only true outside asset, and thus the only asset able to create nondiversifiable exchange risk for the private market.

Presumably if only money is included in the asset measures, the interest rates do not belong in the equation. Some currency substitution models, such as Miles [1978], use interest rates as the opportunity cost of money, thus hypothesizing a *positive* coefficient in the exchange rate equation. It is difficult to distinguish such an equation from the reduced form of the monetarist model (7), in which national moneys are held only in their own countries but bonds and goods are perfect substitutes across countries.

Branson, Halttunen, and Masson [1977, 1979] include bonds in their theoretical model, in addition to money, and use them to solve out the endogenous interest rate. However, they restrict the empirical estimation to money supplies under the rationale that the effect of an increase in the supply of domestic bonds on the exchange rate is ambiguous: The resulting increase in the interest rate has the opposite effect from the increase in total domestic assets. Porter [1979] does the same. Dooley and Isard [1979] restrict their asset measures to bonds throughout, which strategy table 3.2 follows.

29. Of course, if the world really consisted of only two countries, one country's current account would be the negative of the other and row 4 would be subject to perfect multicollinearity. However, there are many wealth holders not residing in either Germany or the United States.

30. Branson, Halttunen, and Masson [1977, 1979] regress the exchange rate against all four stock variables although their theoretical discussion is based on the small-country model. Such an equation cannot be rationalized by the assumption that both the United States and Germany are small countries, aside from the unrealism of such an assumption, unless the current account and intervention figures that enter into usf and gf are cumulated in terms of some third currency such as the

SDR. This method of calculation produces results no better than those in table 3.2.

One possible rationale for such an equation is that it is a log-linear approximation to the two-country relation described after equation (22).

31. Hooper and Morton [1982] and Isard [1980] integrate the risk premium into the monetary equation in a very similar fashion. For a more theoretical synthesis of the portfolio-balance model and the sticky-price monetary model, see Henderson [1980].

32. In the monetary approach, foreign exchange intervention affects the exchange rate *only* to the extent that it is nonsterilized, that is, allowed by the central banks to affect the money supplies. Girton and Henderson [1977], p. 169, and Obstfeld [1980a, pp. 142–43], illustrate this point in portfolio-balance models as the special case in which domestic and foreign bonds are perfect substitutes.

References

Allen, Polly, and Kenen, Peter (1980). *Asset Markets, Exchange Rates, and Economic Integration.* New York: Cambridge University Press.

Argy, Victor, and Porter, Michael (1972). "Forward Exchange Market and the Effects of Domestic and External Disturbances under Alternative Exchange Rate Systems." *IMF Staff Papers:* 503–28.

Barro, Robert (1978). "A Stochastic Equilibrium Model of an Open Economy under Flexible Exchange Rates." *Quarterly Journal of Economics.* February: 149–64.

Bhandari, Jagdeep (1981). "A Simple Transnational Model of Large Open Economics." *Southern Economic Journal.* April.

Bilson, John (1978a). "The Monetary Approach to the Exchange Rate: Some Evidence." *IMF Staff Papers* 25. March: 48–75.

Bilson, John (1978b). "Rational Expectations and the Exchange Rate." In *The Economics of Exchange Rates.* Edited by J. Frenkel and H. G. Johnson. Reading, MA: Addison-Wesley.

Black, Stanley (1973). "International Money Markets and Flexible Exchange Rates." *Princeton Studies in International Finance* no. 32. March.

Branson, William (1968). *Financial Capital Flows in the U.S. Balance of Payments.* Amsterdam: North-Holland.

Branson, William (1976). "Asset Markets and Relative Prices in Exchange Rate Determination." IIES Seminar Paper no. 66, Stockholm. December.

Branson, William, Halttunen, Hannu, and Masson, Paul (1977). "Exchange Rates in the Short Run: The Dollar-Deutschemark Rate." *European Economic Review* 10, no. 3: 303–24.

Branson, William, Halttunen, Hannu, and Masson, Paul (1979). "Exchange Rates in the Short Run: Some Further Results." *European Economic Review* 12, no. 4. October: 395–402.

Calvo, Guillermo, and Rodriguez, Carlos (1977). "A Model of Exchange Rate

Determination under Currency Substitution and Rational Expectations." *Journal of Political Economy* 85, no. 3. June: 617–26.

Caves, Douglas, and Feige, Edgar (1980). "Efficient Foreign Exchange Markets and the Monetary Approach to Exchange-Rate Determination." *American Economic Review* 70, no. 1. March: 120–34.

Cornell, Bradford (1977). "Spot Rates, Forward Rates and Exchange Market Efficiency." *Journal of Financial Economics* 5. Reprinted in *International Financial Management*. Edited by D. Lessard. Boston: Warren, Gorham and Lamont. 1979.

Cornell, Bradford, and Dietrich, J. K. (1979). "The Efficiency of the Market for Foreign Exchange under Floating Exchange Rates." *Review of Economic Statistics* 60, no. 1. February.

Cumby, Robert, and Obstfeld, Maurice (1981). "A Note on Exchange-Rate Expectations and Nominal Interest Differentials: A Test of the Fisher Hypothesis." *Journal of Finance* 36. June.

Dooley, Michael, and Isard, Peter (1979). "The Portfolio-Balance Model of Exchange Rates " International Finance Discussion Paper no. 141, Federal Reserve Board. May.

Dornbusch, Rudiger (1976a). "The Theory of Flexible Exchange Rate Regimes and Macroeconomic Policy." *Scandinavian Journal of Economics* 78, no. 2. May: 255–79. Reprinted in J. Frenkel and H. Johnson, eds., *The Economics of Exchange Rates*. Reading, MA: Addison-Wesley. 1978.

Dornbusch, Rudiger (1976b). "Expectations and Exchange Rate Dynamics." *Journal Political Economy* 84, no. 6. December: 1161–76.

Dornbusch, Rudiger (1976c). "Capital Mobility, Flexible Exchange Rates and Macroeconomic Equilibrium." In *Recent Developments in International Monetary Economics*. Edited by E. Claasen and P. Salin. Amsterdam: North Holland.

Dornbusch, Rudiger (1977). "Capital Mobility and Portfolio Balance." In *The Political Economy of Monetary Reform*. Edited by R. Aliber. London: Macmillan & Co.

Dornbusch, Rudiger (1978). "Monetary Policy Under Exchange Rate Flexibility." In *Managed Exchange Rate Flexibility*, Federal Reserve Bank of Boston Conference Series. Reprinted in D. Lessard, ed., *International Financial Management*. Boston: Warren, Gorham and Lamont. 1979.

Dornbusch, Rudiger (1980a). "Exchange Risk and the Macroeconomics of Exchange Rate Determination." MIT. April. [Published in 1982 in *The Internationalization of Financial Markets and National Economic Policy*. Edited by R. Hawkins, R. Levich, and C. Wihlborg. Greenwich, CT: JAI Press.]

Dornbusch, Rudiger (1980b). "Exchange Rate Economics: Where Do We Stand?" *Brookings Papers on Economic Activity* 1: 143–94. Adapted for this volume, chapter 2.

Dornbusch, Rudiger, and Fischer, Stanley (1980). "Exchange Rates and the Current Account." *American Economic Review* 70, no. 5. December: 960–71.

Dornbusch, Rudiger, and Krugman, Paul (1976). "Flexible Exchange Rates in the Short Run." *Brookings Papers on Economic Activity* 3:537-75.

Driskill, Robert (1981). "Exchange Rate Dynamics: An Empirical Investigation." *Journal of Political Economy* 89, no. 2. April:357-71.

Fama, Eugene, and Farber, Andre (1979). "Money, Bonds and Foreign Exchange." *American Economic Review* 69, no. 4. September: 639-49.

Flood, Robert (1979). "An Example of Exchange Rate Overshooting." *Southern Economic Journal* 46:68-78.

Frankel, Jeffrey (1979a). "The Diversifiability of Exchange Risk." *Journal of International Economics* 9. August:379-93.

Frankel, Jeffrey (1979b). "On the Mark: A Theory of Floating Exchange Rates Based on Real Interest Differentials." *American Economic Review* 69, no. 4. September:610-22.

Frankel, Jeffrey (1980). "Tests of Rational Expectations in the Forward Exchange Market." *Southern Economic Journal* 46, no. 4. April:1083-1101.

Frankel, Jeffrey (1982a). "The Mystery of the Multiplying Marks: A Modification of the Monetary Model." *Review of Economics and Statistics*. August.

Frankel, Jeffrey (1982b). "A Test of Perfect Substitutability in the Foreign Exchange Market." *Southern Economic Journal*. October.

Frenkel, Jacob (1976). "A Monetary Approach to the Exchange Rate: Doctrinal Aspects and Empirical Evidence." *Scandinavian Journal of Economics* 78, no. 2. May: 200-224. Reprinted in J. Frenkel and H. Johnson, eds., *The Economics of Exchange Rates*. Reading, MA: Addison-Wesley. 1978.

Frenkel, Jacob (1977). "The Forward Exchange Rate, Expectations, and the Demand for Money: The German Hyperinflation." *American Economic Review* 67, no. 4:653-70.

Frenkel, Jacob (1980). "Exchange Rates, Prices and Money: Lessons from the 1920s." *American Economic Review* 70, no. 2. May:235-42.

Frenkel, Jacob, and Levich, Richard (1977). "Transactions Costs and Interest Arbitrage: Tranquil versus Turbulent Periods." *Journal of Political Economy* 85, no. 6:1207-24. Reprinted in D. Lessard, ed., *International Financial Management*. Boston: Warren, Gorham and Lamont. 1979.

Genberg, Hans (1978). "Purchasing Power Parity under Fixed and Flexible Exchange Rates." *Journal of International Economics* 8. May:247-76.

Girton, Lance, and Henderson, Dale (1976). "Financial Capital Movements and Central Bank Behavior in a Two Country, Short-Run Portfolio Balance Model." *Journal of Monetary Economics* 2:33-61.

Girton, Lance, and Henderson, Dale (1977). "Central Bank Operations in Foreign and Domestic Assets under Fixed and Flexible Exchange Rates." In *The Effects of Exchange Rate Adjustments*. Edited by P. Clark, D. Logue, and R. Sweeney. Washington: US Government Printing Office, pp. 151-79.

Girton, Lance, and Roper, Don. 1977. "A Monetary Model of Exchange Market

Pressure Applied to the Postwar Canadian Experience." *American Economic Review* 67, no. 4. September:537–48.

Girton, Lance, and Roper, Don (1981). "Theory and Implications of Currency Substitution." *Journal of Money, Credit and Banking*. 13, no 1. February: 12–30.

Grauer, F. L. A., Litzenberger, R. H., and Stehle, R. E. (1976). "Sharing Rules and Equilibrium in an International Capital Market under Uncertainty." *Journal of Financial Economics* 3, no. 3.

Gray, M., and Turnovsky, S. (1979). "The Stability of Exchange Rates Dynamics under Perfect Myopic Foresight." *International Economic Review* 20, October: 643–60.

Henderson, Dale (1980). "The Dynamic Effects of Exchange Market Intervention: Two Extreme Views and a Synthesis." In H. Frisch and G. Schwödiauer, eds., *The Economics of Flexible Exchange Rates*, Supplement to *Kredit und Kapitol* (Heft 6). Berlin: Duncker and Humblot, pp. 156–209.

Henderson, Dale, and Rogoff, Kenneth (1981). "Net Foreign Asset Positions and Stability in a World Portfolio Balance Model." Federal Reserve Board International Finance Discussion Paper no. 178.

Hodrick, Robert (1978). "An Empirical Analysis of the Monetary Approach to the Determination of the Exchange Rate." In *The Economics of Exchange Rates*. Edited by J. Frenkel and H. Johnson. Reading, MA: Addison-Wesley, pp. 97–116.

Hooper, Peter, and Morton, John (1982). "Fluctuations in the Dollar: A Model of Nominal and Real Exchange Rate Determination." *Journal of International Money and Finance* 1, 1. April.

Isard, Peter (1977). "How Far Can We Push the 'Law of one Price'?" *American Economic Review* 67. December: 942–48.

Isard, Peter (1980). "Factors Determining Exchange Rates: The Roles of Relative Price Levels, Balances of Payments, Interest Rates and Risk." Federal Reserve Board International Finance Discussion Paper no. 171. December.

Kohlhagen, Steven (1978). *The Behavior of Foreign Exchange Markets – A Critical Survey of the Literature*. N.Y.U. Monograph Series in Finance and Economics.

Kohlhagen, Steven (1979). "On the Identification of Destabilizing Speculation." *Journal of International Economics*, 9:321–40.

Kouri, Pentti (1976a). "The Exchange Rate and the Balance of Payments in the Short Run and in the Long Run: A Monetary Approach." *Scandinavian Journal of Economics* 78, no. 2. May:280–304.

Kouri, Pentti (1976b). "The Determinants of the Forward Premium." Seminar Paper 62, University of Stockholm. August.

Kouri, Pentti (1978). "Balance of Payments and the Foreign Exchange Market: A Dynamic Partial Equilibrium Model." Cowles Foundation Discussion Paper no. 510, Yale University. November. Also appearing in this volume, chapter 4.

Kouri, Pentti, and de Macedo, Jorge (1978). "Exchange Rates and the International Adjustment Process." *Brookings Papers on Economic Activity* 1:11–50.

Krugman, Paul (1978). "Purchasing Power Parity and Exchange Rates: Another Look at the Evidence." *Journal of International Economics* 8, no. 3. August: 347-407.

Krugman, Paul (1980). "Oil and the Dollar." MIT, June. Also appearing in this volume, chapter 6.

Krugman, Paul (1981). "Consumption Preferences, Asset Demands, and Distribution Effects in International Financial Markets." NBER Working Paper no. 651. March.

Levich, Richard (1979). "On the Efficiency of Markets for Foreign Exchange." In *International Economic Policy*. Edited by R. Dornbusch and J. Frenkel. Baltimore: Johns Hopkins University Press, pp. 246-66.

Mathieson, Donald (1977). "The Impact of Monetary and Fiscal Policy under Flexible Exchange Rates and Alternative Expectations Structures." *IMF Staff Papers*. November: 535-68.

McKinnon, Ronald (1976). "Floating Exchange Rates, 1973-74: The Emperor's New Clothes." In *Institutional Arrangements and the Inflation Problem*. Edited by K. Brunner and A. Meltzer. Carnegie-Rochester Conference Series on Public Policy, vol. 3. New York: American-Elsevier.

Miles, Marc (1978). "Currency Substitution, Flexible Exchange Rates and Monetary Independence." *American Economic Review* 68, no. 3. June: 428-36.

Mundell, Robert (1963). "Capital Mobility and Stabilization Policy under Fixed and Flexible Exchange Rates." *Canadian Journal of Economics and Political Science* 29, no. 4. November: 475-485. Adapted in R. Mundell, *International Economics*. New York: Macmillan. 1968.

Mundell, Robert (1964). "The Exchange Rate Margins and Economic Policy." In *Money in the International Order*. Edited by J. C. Murphy. Dallas.

Mussa, Michael (1976). "The Exchange Rate, the Balance of Payments, and Monetary and Fiscal Policy under a Regime of Controlled Floating." *Scandinavian Journal of Economics* 2. May: 229-48. Reprinted in J. Frenkel and H. Johnson, eds., *The Economics of Exchange Rates*. Reading, MA: Addison-Wesley. 1978.

Niehans, Jurg (1975). "Some Doubts about the Efficacy of Monetary Policy under Flexible Exchange Rates." *Journal of International Economics* 5. August: 275-81.

Obstfeld, Maurice (1980a). "Portfolio Balance, Monetary Policy, and the Dollar-Deutsche Mark Exchange Rate." Columbia U. Discussion Paper 62. March.

Obstfeld, Maurice (1980b). "Intermediate Imports, the Terms of Trade, and the Dynamics of the Exchange Rate and Current Account." *Journal of International Economics* 10(4): 461-80.

Officer, Lawrence (1976). "The Purchasing Power Parity Theory of Exchange Rates: A Review Article." *IMF Staff Papers* 23. March.

Porter, Michael (1979). "Exchange Rates, Current Accounts, and Economic Activity." Federal Reserve Board. June.

Rodriguez, Carlos (1980). "The Role of Trade Flows in Exchange Rate Determination: A Rational Expectations Approach." *Journal of Political Economy*. 88, no. 6. December: 1148–58.

Rogoff, Kenneth (1979). "Anticipated and Transitory Shocks in a Model of Exchange Rate Dynamics." Chapter 2 of Ph.D. dissertation, MIT.

Shafer, Jeffrey (1979). "Flexible Exchange Rates, Capital Flows and Current Account Adjustment." Federal Reserve Board. October.

Solnik, Bruno (1974). "An Equilibrium Model of the International Capital Market." *Journal of Economic Theory* 8, no. 4: 500–24.

Stockman, Alan (1978). "Risk, Information, and Forward Exchange Rates." In *The Economics of Exchange Rates*. Edited by J. Frenkel and H. Johnson. Reading, MA: Addison-Wesley, pp. 193–212.

Tobin, James (1969). "A General-Equilibrium Approach to Monetary Theory." *JMCB* 1. February: 15–29.

Tobin, James, and deMacedo, Jorge Braga (1980). "The Short-Run Macro-economics of Floating Exchange Rates: An Exposition." In *Flexible Exchange Rates and the Balance of Payments: Essays in Memory of Egon Sohmen*. Edited by J. Chipman and C. P. Kindleberger. New York: North-Holland.

Turnovsky, S., and C. Kingston (1979). "Government Policies and Secular Inflation Under Flexible Exchange Rates." *Southern Economic Journal* 47: 389–412.

Whitman, Marina V. N. (1975). "Global Monetarism and the Monetary Approach to the Balance of Payments." *Brookings Papers on Economic Activity* 3: 491–536.

Wilson, Charles (1979). "Anticipated Shocks and Exchange Rate Dynamics." *Journal of Political Economy* 87, no. 3. June: 639–47.

UPDATE

Much has happened in the few years since the exchange rate models of the 1970s were developed and tested.

The early 1980s saw a wave of pessimism among international economists as to the empirical performance of the existing models, or indeed as to the possibility of ever constructing a model that would perform well. Haache and Townend (1981), Dornbusch (1983), Frankel (1984), and Backus (1984) were typical of the mounting pile of studies showing poor results by standard statistical criteria (incorrectly signed coefficients, insignificant magnitudes, low R^2, etc.). Recent surveys of the empirical models include Levich (1985) and Isard (1986).

Rendering the devastation seemingly complete was a series of papers by Meese and Rogoff (1983a,b; 1986). Meese and Rogoff (1983a) showed that the popular models of Frenkel (1976), Bilson (1978), Dornbusch (1976), Frankel (1979), and Hooper and Morton (1982), were of no use whatsoever in predicting exchange rates outside the sample in which the models had been estimated, that in every case a simple random walk predicted better than the structural models. In one sense, this finding should not have been at all surprising. A typical in-sample regression shows unsensible coefficient estimates (for example, near-zero or negative coefficients on the money supply variables, as in Table 3.1 above, attributable to simultaneity bias). Thus it should not have been surprising that the estimated equations made bad predictions out-of-sample.

But Meese and Rogoff (1983b) then tried an alternative to estimating the equations in-sample. They tried out an entire grid of possible combinations of parameter values, for example, a range of possible values of the semi-elasticity of money demand from -3 to -10. This way, any failure to predict could not be blamed on bad estimates arising from small samples or from simultaneity bias. The results were again discouraging. While many plausible combinations of parameter estimates did give predictions that beat a random walk, many other combinations did not, and the predictive performance was in no case very impressive compared to the total variation in exchange rates. What made these findings particularly humiliating is that the authors had from the beginning given the structural models the benefit of the doubt by using ex post realized values of the explanatory variables (money supply, income, interest rates, etc.), rather than making the models forecast them ex ante before forecasting the exchange rate.

Some economists tried to convert the inability of the structural models to predict from a liability into an asset. Their argument, in its least sophisticated form, was essentially a misunderstanding of the point by Dornbusch (1980) and Frenkel (1981) regarding the importance of "news" in determining exchange rates. The argument was that under the assumptions of high capital mobility and rational expectations, which almost all of the standard theoretical models share, new information regarding the money supply or other macroeconomic variables should have a big effect on the contemporaneous exchange rate, and this effect should not have been predictable before the information is known.   While this statement is true so far as it goes, it does not follow that the poor empirical performance of structural models is anything other than a major strike against the standard theory.

There are two respects in which the empirical results are disturbing from the viewpoint of standard theory.   First, the proportion of exchange rate changes that we are able to predict over the short term seems to be, not just low, but close to zero. According to rational expectations theory we <u>should</u> be able to predict that proportion of exchange rate changes that is correctly predicted by participants in the foreign exchange market.   For example, a country that has a record of high money growth and inflation should have a currency that can be predicted to depreciate, at a rate that is appropriately reflected in the expectations of market participants, in the forward discount, and in the interest rate.   Yet the Meese-Rogoff papers found that a random walk beats, not only all the structural models, but also the forward exchange rate, as   well as standard time-series techniques (ARIMA and VAR).[1]   The finding that the forward exchange rate is of zero benefit in predicting which way the spot rate will move is confirmed in the very large literature testing unbiasedness in the forward exchange market.   These studies typically regress the <u>ex post</u> change in the spot rate against the forward discount at the beginning of the period.   Rather than getting a coefficient of 1.0 as would be implied by the hypothesis of unbiasedness, they usually get a coefficient much closer to zero, confirming the random walk.   (For surveys of this literature, see Levich (1985), Boothe and Longworth (1986), or Hodrick (1987).)   A new measure of the expectations of market participants, survey data, shows results similar to those for the forward rate.   Expectations as reflected in the surveys are worse predictors than the contemporaneous spot rate;   investors could improve their forecasts by putting more weight on the contemporaneous spot rate, perhaps even 100 per cent weight   (Frankel and Froot, 1987; and Froot and Frankel, 1987.)   The "random walk" results seem remarkably robust.

The second respect in which existing empirical results are disturbing is that, even if we accept that we are able to predict only a very small part -- or no part-- of exchange rate changes <u>ex ante</u>, for example because the predictable component is statistically dwarfed by the "news," we would still hope to be able to explain a large part of exchange rate changes <u>ex post</u>, after we are able to observe the realized values of the macroeconomic variables.   This we seem unable to do, at least on a monthly basis (without in-sample overfitting).

---

[1] It should be noted that Meese and Rogoff's "random walk" finding was that the simple spot exchange rate was a better predictor than the simple forward rate (or the simple forecasts of structural or ARIMA models).   This is not quite the same thing as saying that these other predictors are of no help at all in predicting changes in the exchange rate.   Meese and Rogoff did not test whether there might exist some <u>convex combination</u> of the forward rate (or model forecasts) and the spot rate that would out-predict the simple spot rate.   This is what the large literature on bias in the forward discount tests for, and the answer is generally "no."   But Somanath (1986) uses updated data sets (to December 1983) to test versions of the monetary models combined with the lagged spot rate, and claims forecasting performance superior to the simple lagged spot rate.   Meese and Rogoff (1986) report some ability of the model based on real interest differentials to predict the direction of change in the 1980s.

The response of international finance economists to their inability to predict or explain exchange rate movements has been to redefine the problem. Many were predisposed in any case to move away from the money-demand or portfolio-balance functions that were assumed in the models above, considering them too <u>ad hoc</u>, and instead to derive investor behavior more rigorously from principles of optimization. This is the way the theory has proceeded in the 1980s. A demand for money is created, within the optimization framework, either by assuming that money enters the utility function directly, or by assuming a "cash-in-advance" constraint for transactions. (Examples include Stockman (1980), Lucas (1982) and Svensson (1985). For a survey, see the last section of Obstfeld and Stockman (1985).)

Whatever their motivation, these models have the distinct advantage, from the viewpoint of their evolutionary survival, that they are generally too abstract to be subjected to genuine empirical testing at all. In fact, proponents of these models, in the economists' public relations coup of the decade, have managed to claim as econometric verification their <u>inability</u> to explain changes in the exchange rate. Examples typical of modern macroeconometric logic are Roll (1979) and Stockman (1987), who argue that the very slow tendency of the exchange rate to return to purchasing power parity supports the optimizing ("equilibrium") models against the overshooting ("disequilibrium") models. It is ironic that the earlier incarnation of equilibrium models, those called "flexible-price monetary" above, claimed support from the alleged empirical observation that the speed of adjustment to purchasing power parity was near-infinite, while the current generation of equilibrium models claims support from the alleged empirical observation that the speed of adjustment to purchasing power parity is near-zero. (Meanwhile, proponents of overshooting have consistently claimed a slow, but positive, rate of adjustment.)

The argument goes essentially as follows. According to the optimization models, exchange rate changes are due to shifts in technology and tastes that, though known to all agents in the economy, are not known to the economist. In fact, the economist doesn't even care to commit himself on questions such as whether the trend in domestic productivity is greater or less than in foreign productivity. Thus, as far as he or she is concerned, the exchange rate could as easily move up as down: the theory--which is admitted to be in its infancy--as yet contains no information that could be used to explain specific changes in the real exchange rate. He then goes to "test" his theory "empirically" by seeing whether he can statistically reject the hypothesis that the real exchange rate follows a random walk. Rather than being humbled or embarrassed about his statistical failure to explain any movement in the macroeconomic variable that he is investigating, he proudly proclaims it as confirming his theory,[2] on the grounds that the theory too did not explain any movement in the variable!

------

[2] This disturbing trend in modern macroeconometrics is an extreme case of the old problem that a statistical failure to reject a null hypothesis does not entitle one to claim an interesting finding. The failure to reject may simply be due to low power in the test, especially if the null hypothesis is a weak one. Traditionally in econometrics, the goal is supposed to be to <u>succeed</u> in statistically rejecting one economically interesting hypothesis in favor of another, i.e., to get results that are "statistically significant at the 95 per cent level," rather than the reverse. What makes the trend away from this principle so remarkable is that the popular null

If the goal is considered to be to explain exchange rate changes rather than not to explain them, then the empirical developments of the 1980s, ironically, are in many respects more supportive of some of the structural models of the 1970s than were the empirical developments of the 1970s. In particular, the broad outlines of the 1981-85 appreciation of the dollar--roughly 50 per cent in either nominal or real terms--and its 1985-87 reversal, are consistent with the theory of exchange rates based on differentials in real interest rates (what is above called the "sticky-price monetary model"). Long-term real interest differentials now seem to explain the real exchange rate better than the short-term real interest differentials that were used in earlier specifications (e.g., Frankel, 1979), and there are good theoretical reasons for preferring them as well.[3]   By a variety of alternative measures, the long-term real interest differential between the United States and its major trading partners rose by about 5 points between 1980 and late 1984.[4]   Thus a ready account is provided by the overshooting theory: the increase in U.S. real interest rates--due, presumably, to a shift in the mix between monetary and fiscal policy--attracted capital into the country, causing the dollar to appreciate, until it had become sufficiently "overvalued" that expectations of future depreciation back toward equilibrium were sufficient in investors' minds to offset the interest differential.   After 1984, the real interest differential declined, and the dollar followed.

A theory that only claims to explain exchange rate movements on the basis of 2 or 3 observations per decade is not very testable when only 15 years of data are available.   A lot more work would be needed before we could claim to have explained exchange rates well.   A number of recent studies on monthly or quarterly data have claimed a degree of success with long-term real interest differentials: Shafer and Loopesko (1983), Hooper (1984), Sachs (1985), Hutchison and Throop (1985), Golub et al (1985), and Feldstein (1986). Given how often in the past a model that appeared to work well for one sample period is observed to go awry subsequently, it would be foolhardy to claim too much from these or any other regression studies.   But neither is it necessary for economists to abjure any ability to explain exchange rate movements at all.

---

hypothesis of a random walk is so weak that a failure to reject it is nothing other than a failure to explain any movement in the variable of interest.   It is true that a problem with the classical econometric criteria is that the author has an incentive to shift through many regressions, and the journal editor has an incentive to sift through many submitted articles, to come up with "good" results.   But it is no solution to this problem to redefine the inability to explain something as a "good" result.

[3] The ten-year real interest differential, corrected for any risk premium, tells us how far the market expects the dollar to depreciate per year in real terms over the next ten years.   The expected real exchange rate in ten years, unlike in 3 months, can in turn be interpreted as the long-run equilibrium. See, for example, Isard (1983).

[4] Frankel (1985).

FURTHER REFERENCES

Backus, David. 1984. "Empirical models of the exchange rate: Separating the wheat from the chaff." Canadian Journal of Economics, 17 824-826.

Boothe, Paul, and Longworth, David. 1986. "Foreign exchange market efficiency tests: Implications of recent findings." Journal of International Money and Finance 5: 135-152.

Dornbusch, Rudiger. 1980. "Exchange Rate Economics: Where Do We Stand?," Brookings Papers on Economic Activity. (Reprinted, this volume.)

Feldstein, Martin. 1986. "The budget deficit and the dollar." NBER Macroeconomic Annual 1986 (September).

Frankel, Jeffrey. 1984. "Tests of Monetary and Portfolio-Balance Models of Exchange Rate Determination." In J. Bilson and R. Marston, eds., Exchange Rate Theory and Practice. (Chicago: University of Chicago Press).

——————————————————. 1985. "Six possible meanings of 'overvaluation': The 1981-85 dollar." Essays in International Finance No. 159 (December), Princeton University.

Frankel, Jeffrey, and Froot, Kenneth. 1987. "Using survey data to test standard propositions regarding exchange rate expectations." American Economic Review, 77, 1 (March): 133-153.

Froot, Kenneth, and Frankel, Jeffrey. 1987. "Findings of forward discount bias interpreted in light of exchange rate survey data." M.I.T. and U.C. Berkeley (June).

Golub, Steven, et al. "Exchange rates and real long-term interest-rate differentials: Evidence for eighteen OECD countries." Economics and Statistics Department Working Papers, Organisation for Economic Cooperation and Development, 1985.

Haache, Graham, and Townend, John. 1981. "Exchange rates and monetary policy: Modelling sterling's effective exchange rate, 1972-1980." In W. A. Eltis and P. J. N. Sinclair, eds., The Money Supply and the Exchange Rate. (Oxford: Clarendon Press).

Hodrick, Robert. 1987. "The empirical evidence on the efficiency of forward and futures foreign exchange markets." Northwestern University. Forthcoming in Fundamentals of Pure and Applied Economics. Chur, Switzerland: Harwood Academic Publishers.

Hooper, Peter. 1984. "International repercussions of the U.S. budget deficit." International Finance Discussion Paper No. 246, Federal Reserve Board, Washington, D.C. (September).

Hutchison, Michael and Throop, Adrian. 1985. "U.S. budget deficits and the real value of the dollar." Economic Review 4, Federal Reserve Bank of San Francisco (Fall): 26-43.

Isard, Peter. 1983. "An accounting framework and some issues for modeling how exchange rates respond to the news." In Exchange Rates and International Macroeconomics, Jacob Frenkel (ed.). Chicago: University of Chicago Press.

_____. 1986. "The empirical modeling of exchange rates: An assessment of alternative approaches". International Monetary Fund. Forthcoming in Empirical Macroeconomics for Interdependent Economies, edited by R. Bryant, D. Henderson, G. Holtham, P. Hooper and S. Symansky. Washington, D.C.: Brookings Institution.

Levich, Richard. 1985. "Empirical studies of exchange rates: Price behavior, rate determination, and market efficiency." In R. Jones, and P. Kenen, eds., Handbook of International Economics. Amsterdam: North Holland.

Lucas, Robert. 1982. "Interest rates and currency prices in a two-country world." Journal of Monetary Economics 10 (November): 335-360.

Meese, Richard, and Rogoff, Kenneth. 1983a. "Empirical exchange rate models of the seventies: Do they fit out of sample?" Journal of International Economics 14 (February): 3-24.

_____. 1983b. "The out-of-sample failure of empirical exchange rate models: Sampling error or misspecification?" In Exchange Rates and International Macroeconomics, edited by Jacob Frenkel. Chicago: University of Chicago Press.

_____. 1986. "Was it real? The exchange rate - interest differential relationship; 1973-1984." U.C. Berkeley.

Obstfeld, Maurice, and Stockman, Alan. 1985. "Exchange rate dynamics." In the Handbook of International Economics, edited by R. Jones and P.Kenen. Amsterdam: Elsevier Science Publishers.

Roll, Richard. 1979. "Violations of Purchasing Power Parity and their Implications for Efficient International Commodity Markets." International Finance and Trade, vol. 1, edited by M. Sarnat and G. Szego, Cambridge, MA: Ballinger.

Sachs, Jeffrey. 1985. "The Dollar and the Policy Mix: 1985." Brookings Papers on Economic Activity 1.

Shafer, Jeffrey and Loopesko, Bonnie. 1983. "Floating exchange rates after ten years." Brookings Papers on Economic Activity 1:1-70.

Somanath, V.S. 1986. "Efficient exchange rate forecasts: Lagged models better than the random walk." Journal of International Money and Finance 5, 2 (June): 195-220.

Stockman, Alan. 1980. "A theory of exchange rate determination." Journal of Political Economy 88: 673-698.

_____. 1987. "The equilibrium approach to exchange rates." Economic Review, Federal Reserve Bank of Richmond (March/April): 12-30.

Svensson, Lars. 1985. "Currency prices, terms of trade and interest rates: A general equilibrium asset-pricing cash-in-advance approach." <u>Journal of International Economics</u> 18: 17-41.

THE EUROPEAN MONETARY SYSTEM

by

Alberto Giovannini[*]

[*] Written for <u>International Economic Policies and their Theoretical Foundations,</u> edited by J.M. Letiche. Parts of this paper summarize the results of my research project on the EMS carried out with Francesco Giavazzi, which appear in Giavazzi and Giovannini [1988, 1989]. I thank Reiko Nakamura for research assistance, and the CEPR for financial support.

1. Introduction

The European Monetary System (EMS) is of great interest to both academic economists and policymakers. To academic economists it offers an experiment of fixed exchange rates within a relatively large area, during a period of substantial fluctuations of the dollar exchange rate. The experience of the EMS provides an opportunity to identify the costs and benefits of a common currency area within Europe, to verify whether exchange rate regimes appear to have an effect on the macroeconomic performance of the member countries, to evaluate the interactions of exchange rate policies and inflation among European countries. To policymakers, the EMS represents the most important experiment at limiting exchange rate flexibility among industrialized countries since the collapse of the Bretton Woods regime. Dissatisfaction with the performance of floating exchange rates has prompted several proposals of reform of the international monetary system, including a return to the gold standard. All proposals of reform of the world monetary system suggest a return, in one form or another, to fixed exchange rates. They point to the EMS as a successful experiment, which could be copied outside of Europe.

The purpose of this paper is to summarize the evidence on the working of the EMS which is of interest to academic economists, and to suggest what the experience in Europe teaches to those who would like to reform the world monetary system. The balance of the paper is divided in 5 sections. Section 2 briefly summarizes the rules of the EMS exchange rate arrangement, and compares them with the rules governing previous fixed exchange rates regimes. Section 3 reviews the evidence on the "real" effects of the EMS, in particular on the behavior of real exchange rates of European countries. Section 4 discusses whether the EMS has played an important role in the disinflation after the

second oil shock. Section 5 examines whether capital controls have been

instrumental in tying the system together. Section 6 contains a number of

concluding observations, which directly address the title of the paper: can the

institutions induce monetary policy cooperation?

2. The Rules Governing the EMS

The EMS consists of an agreement among the central banks of the European

Community to manage intra-Community exchange rates and to finance exchange

market interventions.[1] Thus the exchange rate mechanism of the EMS is only one

aspect of the system. Moreover, while only a subset of the EEC countries[2]

participate in the exchange rate mechanism, all of them belong to the EMS. For

example, the European Currency Unit (ECU), created with the EMS, is a monetary

unit based on a basket of all EEC currencies (including sterling and the drachma

which are not part of the EMS exchange rate mechanism.)[3] Therefore the EMS is

reminiscent of Bretton Woods, not only because the exchange rate regime

incorporated in the two systems is similar--essentially both can be described as

---

[1] For a description of the rules of the EMS see European Economy, no. 12, July
1982, EEC, Monetary Committee [1986], Ungerer et al. [1983, 1986]. For an
"outsider's" view of the EMS, see Cohen [1981].

[2] Germany, France, Italy, Belgium, Luxemburg, Denmark the Netherlands and
Ireland.

[3] As of January 1989, the currencies of the two new members of the EEC, Spain
and Portugal, will also be included in the ECU basket, independent of whether
these two countries decide to join the exchange rate mechanism of the EMS.

"adjustable pegs"--but also because both systems embody provisions and
institutions for granting monetary support to member countries.

The first step taken by the European Council of Ministers in designing the
EMS was the creation of a new monetary unit, the ECU.   The ECU is a composite
unit of account, made up of a basket of specified amounts of each Community
currency. Since the number of units of each currency in the ECU is fixed, the
weights of the various currencies change over time, as intra-European exchange
rates fluctuate.[4]   This is particularly true of the weights of currencies like
the pound, that belong to the ECU but not to the exchange rate mechanism of the
EMS. Exchange rate fluctuations thus could move the composition of the ECU far
away from the initial set of weights which were based on the economic size of
the various countries. To correct this, the units of each currency that make up
one ECU are reviewed every five years, or on request, whenever the weight of any
currency has changed by more than 25%.

The ECU serves four functions in the EMS. It is a reserve asset, and a
settlement instrument for transactions among the Community's central banks. In
addition, it provides a numeraire for the exchange rate mechanism, the basis of
the "indicator of divergence" and the unit of account for the intervention
operations in the EMS.

EMS intervention rules work as follows: each Community currency has an ECU
central rate, expressed as the price of one ECU in terms of that currency. ECU

---

[4] ECU weights are computed in the following way: let z_i be the units of
currency i in one ECU. The weight of currency i in the ECU basket is given by
$w_i = z_i S_i$, where S_i stands for the price of 1 ECU in terms of currency i.

central rates are fixed and are revised only when there is a realignment. The
ratio of any two ECU central rates is the bilateral central rate of any pair of
currencies which together form the parity grid of the system. By joining the
exchange rate mechanism of the EMS, a central bank agrees to keep its market
exchange rate vis-a-vis any other currency participating in the mechanism
within preassigned margins from the bilateral central parity. The parity grid
thus is the core of the exchange rate mechanism of the EMS: in this mechanism,
the ECU is no more than a numeraire. The bilateral margins are set at 2.25
percent on each side of the central parity, so that the width of the fluctuation
band for any bilateral rate is 4.5 percent. The lira is allowed to fluctuate in
a larger band, 12 percent wide; the pound and the drachma belong to the ECU
basket, and thus have an ECU central rate but do not observe the exchange rate
margins.

  While a parity grid is in force, each central bank fulfills its obligation
not to go beyond the margins by intervening in the foreign exchange market.
Intervention is compulsory only when two currencies reach their bilateral
margin, that is when the bilateral exchange rate diverges by +/- 2.25 percent
from the central parity. This is called marginal intervention. Marginal
intervention must be carried out by both central banks involved, in the currency
at the opposite bilateral limit. Financing for marginal intervention is
unbounded: while there are obviously no limits to the purchase of the weaker
currency by the central bank that issues the stronger currency, there are also
no limits to the sales of the strong currency by the "relatively weaker" central
bank.

  The swap arrangements triggered when two currencies reach the bilateral fluctuations margins are labelled Very Short Term Financing Facility, and represents one of the balance-of-payments financing facilities available to member countries. The other facilities are the Short Term Monetary Support and the Medium Term Financial Assistance. The Short Term Monetary Support is designed to provide short term financing for balance of payments needs due to transitory difficulties, while the Medium Term Financial Assistance-- administered by the EEC Council of Ministers--is designed to provide longer term financing.

The EMS agreements also allow central banks to intervene in buying and selling each other's currencies intra-marginally, that is before the outer limits of the bilateral band have been reached. In this case, however, intervention is subject to the approval of the central bank whose currency is being bought or sold. There are no provisions for the automatic financing of intra-marginal intervention. Intervention in non-Community currencies--usually in dollars--is always permitted, and not subject to mutual authorization.

In addition to the rules for marginal intervention, there is within the EMS (Monetary Committee [1986], p.48, article 3) an indicator which signals the divergence of each currency from its ECU-central rate. When this divergence indicator crosses a threshold, a country is expected to act through "diversified intervention, measures of domestic monetary policy, changes in central parities, or other measures of economic policy." None of these actions is compulsory however, in contrast to the obligation to intervene arising when a currency reaches a bilateral margin.

The considerable number of technical innovations in the EMS relative to, for example, the IMF Articles of Agreement, might lead one to conclude that the EMS is not quite a fixed exchange rates regime, and might suggest that the way in which the EMS has worked has fundamentally been different from the way in which other fixed exchange rates regimes have operated. In fact, both these observations are probably wrong. First, all

fixed exchange rates regimes are characterized by bilateral fluctuations bands.[5] Indeed, the original IMF Articles of Agreement implied bilateral fluctuation bands between European currencies that were only 0.5 percent narrower than those prevailing in the EMS--except, of course, for the lira. Similarly, the costs of transporting gold from one country to another determined bilateral fluctuation bands for exchange rates during the International Gold Standard. Second, the role of the ECU in the EMS is very similar to the role of the SDR in the IMF system: the ECU has not--contrary to the expectations of its creators--become the "currency of the EMS". And third, the special provisions that allocate symmetrically the burden of foreign exchange market intervention when exchange rates reach bilateral fluctuation margins cannot bind countries' monetary policies: (a) foreign exchange market intervention can be sterilized, and, as it happened, a large fraction of total foreign exchange market intervention in the first ten years of the EMS occurred well within bilateral fluctuation bands; furthermore it was carried out by countries other than West Germany,[6] and (b) the non-binding nature of the mechanism of the indicator of divergence, as well as its imperfect

---

[5] For a discussion stressing the similarities of fixed-exchange-rates regimes, see Giovannini [1988a].

[6] See Giavazzi and Giovannini [1987].

functioning,[7] led countries to abandon it soon after the start of the EMS.

As a result, during its first ten years the EMS worked as in "imperfect Deutsche mark area," with West Germany setting its own monetary policy targets independently of the other EMS countries, and the other countries accommodating West Germany's policies. The adjective "imperfect" is used since countries like France and Italy were able to avoid a full convergence of their monetary policies to West GErmany's by systematically resorting to capital controls--discussed below in section 5.

The functioning of the EMS strikingly resembles other fixed exchange-rate regimes, like the Bretton Woods system, and the international gold standard. All three regimes are characterized by a "center country" running monetary policy often in disregard of its balance-of-payments constraint--"center countries" being Britain in the international gold standard, and the United States in the Bretton Woods regime. Moreover, in all three cases, the countries at the periphery resorted to capital controls to limit their dependence on the center country's monetary policy.[8]

---

[7] See Spaventa [1982] for an illustration of the properties of the indicator of divergence. Spaventa observes that the indicator crosses the threshold less frequently for those currencies with a smaller weight in the ECU, and therefore it is not really a means of achieving symmetry in the system.

[8] For evidence on the central role of West Germany in the EMS, see Giavazzi and Giovannini [1987] where it is shown that, in an asymmetric system, the center country's interest rates are unaffected by international portfolio shocks, and that this pattern is strongly confirmed by the behavior of West Germany rates, relative, for example, to Italian and French rates. See also Giovannini [1988a] for a discussion of the "center country" hypothesis.

3. Economic Effects of the EMS: Exchange Rates

The main features of the exchange rate mechanism of the EMS are the
bilateral fluctuation bands and the possibility of realignments. Indeed, from
March 1979 to December 1987 there were 10 realignments of bilateral central
rates: only in 1980 and 1984 did bilateral central rates remain unaffected.
Since bilateral fluctuations bands of 4.5% (12% for Italy) are relatively wide,
this experience raises the question of whether the exchange rate mechanisms put
in place by the EMS affect nominal exchange rate fluctuations at all, or whether
they are simply a "veil" over a system of effectively fluctuating exchange
rates. Are the EMS realignments simply accomodating the unstoppable market
forces, without even delaying inevitable exchange rate changes caused by
divergent monetary policies?

Several authors have offered empirical evidence to bear on this question.
Rogoff [1985] studied the variance of the forward rate prediction error for
France and Italy vis-a-vis Germany, and compares it with the variance of the
forward rate prediction error for the dollar/DM, pound/DM and yen/DM exchange
rates.[9] He showed that changes in both the franc and the lira exchange rates

_____

[9] He also computes the root mean square error of forecasts obtained from an
unrestricted vector autoregression, over a 1-month and a 12-month horizon.

relative to the Deutsche mark were significantly more predictable after the
beginning of the EMS than during the earlier period from February 1974 to February
1979. Artis and Taylor [1987] showed that changes in nominal bilateral exchange
rates of European currencies vis-a-vis the DM displayed a smaller variance after
March 1979. Similarly, Giavazzi and Giovannini [1989] found that the EMS had
decreased the volatility of bilateral Deutsche mark rates significantly, at least
in the case of the Guilder, the French franc, and the lira.

Did the observed stabilization of nominal exchange rates end up stabilizing
real exchange rates--a measure of countries' competitiveness? Figures 1 and 2
plot changes in real exchange rates of the Deutsche mark relative to the dollar
and the Italian lira, respectively, from 1960 to the present. This long interval
allows us to compare the behavior of real rates over different regimes, including
the Bretton Woods period and the snake. The real exchange rates are the (log of)
nominal exchange rates adjused by relative wholesale prices, and are computed by
using monthly data. Two facts emerge from these figures. First, the behavior of
real exchange rates was almost identical to the behavior of nominal rates: I
interpret this phenomenon as a strong indication of the presence of price
stickiness.[10] Second, the dollar/lira rate did not display any significant
change in volatility after 1979, while the volatility of the lira/DM rate seems to
have decreased somewhat. The dramatic increase in the volatility of the dollar/DM
rate after the collapse of the Bretton Woods system is especially noteworthy.

The next question of interest regards the behavior of effective exchange

---

[10]See Flood [1981], Dornbusch and Giovannini [1988], and Giovannini [1987,
1988b] for a discussion of the empirical evidence on prices and exchange
rates and price stickiness.

rates. The EMS appears to have stabilized bilateral real exchange rates in Europe, but it is not clear whether the stabilization of European rates did bring about a stabilization of the overall competitiveness of the member countries. The changes in the volatility of West GErmany's real effective exchange rate are reported in the Appendix, Table 1. The Table shows the simplest possible measure of the variability of the real effective excange rate: its standard deviation. The data are monthly, from 1960 to 1985. The volatility of the effective real rate increases dramatically after the end of Bretton Woods, but stabilizes in the EMS. The second column in the Table suggests why this might have happened. It reports the correlation between an index of the real effective exchange rate of the Deutsche mark vis-a-vis its EMS partners and the index of "global" competitiveness. In the 1960s and '70s the correlation between the two indices is very high, indicating that the French franc, the lira and the other EMS currencies did not follow the Deutsche mark--particularly at the time of its large appreciation vis-a-vis the dollar after the collapse of Bretton Woods. This phenomenon was reversed after 1979: the correlation between the global and the intra-EMS indices becomes negative, indicating that the EMS had limited the effects of the fluctuations of the dollar/DM rate on Germany's competitiveness. Similar computations for the other EMS countries show that the phenomenon documented in Table 1 is specific to Germany. Belgium for example offers the mirror immage of the German experience: the correlation between the global and the intra-EMS indices increases after 1979. Given that Belgium is one of Germany's major trading partners, this has stabilized Germany's real exchange rate. The cost for Belgium has been an increase in the volatility of its real effective exchange rate.

4. Economic Effects of the EMS: Inflation Rates

One of the most dramatic changes in the economies of the EMS member
countries since 1979 has been the decrease in the rate of inflation. Table 2
compares inflation rates of various European countries prior to the start (1978)
of the EMS with 1987. The Table suggests both a significant convergence of European
inflation rates towards the West German levels, and a general decrease of
inflation, which is not limited to the countries belonging to the EMS. Since
the conclusion of section 2 is that West Germany's monetary policy has been at
the center of the EMS, and since West German authorities built a wide reputation
as "inflation fighters" in the second postwar period, the natural question
raised by this experience is whether the structure and working of the EMS, and
in particular the central role played by the German monetary authorities, have
played any role in the disinflation experience of countries as different as
Denmark, France and Italy. In this section I review the argument according to
which pegging the exchange rate can help a country in the disinflation effort,
and compare the evidence for a number of EMS countries with that of a country outside
the EMS, namely the United Kingdom. The theoretical model points to the problem of the
credibility of the exchange rate target, and the costs of the exchange rate
union for the center country--West Germany. In the empirical section I report
estimates of the size, timing, and effects of shifts in expectations after 1979.

4.1 Breaking the Inflation Inertia: The Role of Expectations

One fundamental feature of the inflationary process in modern industrial economies appears to be its persistence, a phenomenon that has been linked to the mechanics of wage and price setting. Firms and unions--for a number of reasons that I do not need to explore here[11]--find it more convenient to set prices and wages much less frequently than the rate of arrival of economic news. Therefore wages and prices are crucially affected by workers' and firms' expectations. Workers and firms are concerned, for example, to preserve the purchasing power of their income, and incorporate in their output prices their forecasts of the future evolution of the general price level. Indirectly, wage and price setters concerned about the evolution of the general price level need to forecast the stance of monetary policy.

The special nature of wage and price setting therefore creates a problem of coordination between the central bank and the public. The central bank might want to use monetary policy to steer the economy towards a higher output path, but the public, anticipating future expansionary policies, can neutralize them fully by incorporating in their current pricing decisions the expectation of future monetary expansion and higher inflation. This process, by itself, generates inflation and tends to force the monetary authority to accomodate the higher rate of growth of prices, in order to avoid a severe recession. Hence in equilibrium there is higher inflation, and less output growth, than initially desired by both the public and monetary authorities. This is the inflationary

---

[11] See, for example, Blanchard [1988] and Rotemberg [1988] for excellent surveys.

bias of monetary policy in the presence of price and wage inertia, first described and analyzed by Barro and Gordon [1983].

The coordination problem of   monetary policy and sluggish prices and wages is also at the core of the issue of disinflation. Bringing inflation down requires a change in inflationary expectations on the part of price setters. How can the monetary authorities "convince" price setters that an announced contraction will be lasting and credible? The reputation that a central bank needs to bring down inflation can be obtained in two ways. The first, and more painful method for society as a whole, is by showing that, even in the worst of a depression, the announced monetary targets are not reneged upon. The initial monetary contraction after the announcement of a disinflation plan generates a recession, since it is imposed in a economy where inflation and money growth expectations are high. The recession would tend to be longer and harsher, the slower is the response of the private sector's expectations to the monetary contraction, because the very fact that the monetary authority sticks to the announced contractionary path comes to private agents as a surprise.

Alternatively, the monetary authority could avoid going through this prolonged "initiation" period by seeking a way to influence expectations with some institutional reform. The institutional reform of interest for us is a change in the exchange rate regime. How can the transition from flexible to fixed exchange rates bring about an improvement in the output-inflation tradeoff, and facilitate the disinflation effort? The model by Canzoneri and Henderson can be profitably used to illustrate these effects.

They consider a model with two symmetric countries.   See Appendix I for mathematical details. Supply of output is a negative function of real wages, while demand is allocated between the outputs of the two countries by the real exchange rate. The demand for money (the only asset)[12] is a positive function of income. The central banks attempt to minimize a quadratic-loss function, where deviations from an employment target, and the price level, are the arguments. The employment target levels exceed the natural rate. These employment target levels represent the central banks' attitudes toward expansionary policies.[13] The exchange rate enters the authorities' objective function because a real appreciation lowers the domestic CPI.

---

[12] If we allowed additional assets in the model, it would become necessary to assume capital controls.

[13] These attitudes might be motivated by the presence of distortions in the economy, which move equilibrium output inside the production possibility frontier.

The model is closed with equations specifying how wages are set. Unions
are assumed to set them before the realizations of exogenous shocks, trying to
minimize the fluctuations of employment around equilibrium. Under perfect
foresight, this implies that employment levels are the same in both countries.[14]
Employment is determined by the demand for labor. However, the optimal level of
wages is not independent of the exchange rate regime. To identify the possible
advantages of exchange rate pegging, I compare the flexible exchange rates
regime with fixed exchange rates, assuming that each central bank sets monetary
policy taking as given: 1) price expectations in the domestic labor market, thus
giving rise to a time-consistent equilibrium; and 2) the partner country's
money supply, thus giving rise to a Nash equilibrium in the international
interaction.

In the flexible exchange rate regime, each central bank sets its own money
supply taking the partner's as given. The exchange rate is endogenous. It is
straightforward to show that minimization of the unions' loss function implies
the following wage-setting rule: log wages equal log money, taken to power of
the log exchange rate.

---

[14]Prices, on the other hand, are perfectly flexible in this model.

Assuming perfect foresight, one obtains the Nash equilibrium: the log price level (CPI) equals the log money supply, which in turn equals a function of target employment. Equilibrium inflation is a function of central banks' incentives to "fool" the public with surprise monetary expansions, and of the incentives to export inflation to the rest of the world via a real exchange rate appreciation.

International interactions affect equilibrium inflation to the extent that changes in the real exchange rate affect consumer prices in the two countries. The presence of international interactions actually lowers inflation in a Nash equilibrium.

The lesson from the analysis of flexible rates is that the strategic interaction among countries gives rise to a contractionary bias; this partly offsets the "domestic" inflationary bias associated with the central banks' incentive to affect real wages when nominal wages are pre-set. As Rogoff [1985b] pointed out, this is an example of a second-best situation, where adding one inefficiency improves welfare.

What is the outcome of fixed rates in the two-country model shown here? Assume that the foreign country sets monetary policy, and the partner country accommodates any change in foreign money by changing domestic money accordingly. Ignoring real shocks, the equilibrium employment levels and CPIs will be the same across the two countries. The CPI will be a function of the central bank's weight on employment deviations, and the target employment level.

Comparison of the flexible versus fixed rates equilibrium CPIs clearly points to the conditions for fixed exchange rates to be an attractive option for a central bank facing a credibility problem. Under flexible rates, the equilibrium price level in the domestic country is a function of the central bank's expansionary proclivities. Under fixed exchange rates, the domestic central bank loses all power to affect the domestic price level, which is simply equal to the price level prevailing in the foreign country. If the foreign central bank does not suffer from a credibility problem, fixed rates remove the domestic inefficiency. The domestic central bank acquires the reputation of the foreign central bank and price expectations are automatically stabilized. The more similar the foreign and the domestic country, the less attractive a system of fixed exchange rates. Pegging to a country whose central bank faces a credibility problem similar to the one faced at home clearly does not help. For pegging to be an attractive option, the "credibility gap" must be sufficiently large: fixed exchange rates remove all strategic interactions and, as we have seen, strategic interactions dampen the domestic inflationary bias.

Fixed exchange rates are superior to flexible rates if the "credibility-gap" is large relative to the incentive to affect the exchange rate under flexible rates.

In practice, the EMS has not completely eliminated inflation differentials. Countries with higher inflation rates have resorted to periodic exchange-rate realignments to recover the losses in competitiveness caused by persisting inflation differentials and fixed exchange rates. The disruptions caused by speculators' expectations of these exchange-rate realignments have been limited-- as I stressed above--through the systematic use of capital controls. Even when the exchange rates are periodically realigned, though, pegging to a low inflation country can improve the output-inflation tradeoff. This happens because the terms-of-trade fluctuations that occur during the intervals when exchange rates are not changed provide a strong-enough deterrent to central banks not to deviate from the center-country monetary policies as much as they would under a pure floating rate regime. With periodic realignments, however, the center country's output-inflation tradeoff is affected. During the intervals when exchange rates are kept fixed, the center country's terms of trade worsen, because the partner's inflation rate is higher than its own. As a consequence, the center-country's output-inflation tradeoff also worsens: the inflation-buster exports reputation and imports inflation. This result occurs also in the static model described above. The value of the loss function in the center country is higher ("welfare" is lower) under fixed exchange rates than under flexible rates. under flexible rates.

Hence, the model of imported credibility cannot explain the incentive of the center-country to belong to a fixed-exchange-rates regime. The evidence on Germany's terms-of-trade presented in section 3, however, seems to justify Germany's incentive to promote the EMS. The system has protected Germany from the effects of dollar fluctuations. In the early 1970s, at the time of the first dollar collapse, Germany appreciated both vis-a-vis the dollar and vis-a-vis its European partners: the result was a large swing in the country terms-of-trade. After the dollar fall of 1985 the EMS currencies followed the DM much closer and attenuated the impact on Germany's terms-of-trade. The comparison between the two periods clearly shows the extent to which the EMS has stabilized Germany's overall competitiveness. From November 1969 to March 1973 the Deutsche mark appreciated 25 percent vis-a-vis the dollar; this was accompanied by an 18.6 percent worsening of Germany's overall competitiveness. From January 1985 to December 1987 the DM appreciation was similar--27 percent--but this time it was accompanied by a loss of competitiveness only half as large--9 percent.

Finally, the argument that pegging to West Germany has helped high inflation countries in the disinflation efforts of the 1980s rests crucially on

the assumption that exchange-rate targets are more credible than monetary
targets. Once again, nothing in the model discussed above implies that
exchange-rate targets are more credible than, say, money or interest rate
targets. Giavazzi and Giovannini [1989] offer a number of informal arguments in
support of the view that exchange-rate targets might be more credible than
money targets. The empirical evidence discussed in the next section, where the
effects of the EMS on inflation expectations and the short-run output-inflation
tradeoff among member countries are measured directly, allows us to determine
whether or not exchange-rate targets in the EMS have been credible.

4.2 Measuring the Shifts in Expectations

     This section reviews empirical evidence on the shift in inflationary
expectations in European countries after the start of the EMS. These shifts are
estimated as follows. Private agents (firms and unions) set prices and wages by
forming expectations on future macroeconomic variables, like the overall rate of
inflation. These expectations are necessarily a function of agents' available
information, reflected in current and past realization of all relevant
macroeconomic variables. If a monetary reform like the EMS is put in place,
private agents who believe that the reform will actually change monetary
policies in the way described above, have to reevaluate the methods they use to
extrapolate from past macroeconomic variables their expectations about future
inflation and economic activity. Hence the shift in expectations, and its

effect on the inflationary process, will be reflected in a shift of statistical

equations relating wages and prices to available information.

This section reviews the evidence on the process of disinflation in

Denmark, France, Germany, Ireland, Italy, and, for comparison, the United

Kingdom, by comparing how the relation between price and wage inflation and

output has shifted after the start of the EMS. Estimates of the shifts in

expectations are drawn from a (quarterly) system of three equations specifying

the dynamics of CPI inflation, wage inflation, and output growth, measured by using

industrial production indices. Each equation includes on the right hand side a

time trend, seasonal dummy variables, 4 lags of wage inflation, CPI inflation

and industrial production growth, and dummy variables representing country-

specific events that the model cannot explain.[15] It also includes 4 lags of M1

growth rates, as well as changes in the relative price of imported intermediate

and final goods. This last set of variables are assumed to be determined

outside of the system: while innovations in wage and price inflation are

plausibly correlated with money growth and changes in relative prices of

intermediate and final goods, these variables are assumed to affect inflation

and output growth only with a one-quarter lag.[16]

---

[15] The dummies are the following. For all countries, from 1971:3 to the end of
the sample, fall of the fixed-rates regime. For Italy, 69:2-70:1 Autunno
Caldo, 73:3-74:1 price freeze. For France, 63:4-64:4, 69:1-70:4, 74:1-74:4,
77:1-77:4, 82:3-83:4, wage and price controls; 68:2-68:3 "May 1968". For the
UK, 67:4 sterling devaluation, 73:4-74:4 wage controls.

[16] The estimates are obtained assuming that superneutrality holds, i.e. the sum
of the coefficients of nominal variables is equal to 1 in the equations
explaining wage and price inflation, and is zero in the equation explaining
output growth. These constraints were not rejected in the largest majority
of cases.

The first question is whether the parameters in these statistical equations significantly shift after 1979. A test of stability of the parameter estimates--performed for eqch equation and each country using as a cutting point the first quarter of 1979[17]--indicates the presence of a structural shift only in the case of France: in no other country are the shifts of wage-price dynamics after 1979

statistically significant. While this evidence is against the hypothesis that the EMS has been associated with a shift in expectations, the negative result is very likely to be caused by the low power of the parameter stability tests.

The next question regards the timing and the direction of the shifts in the inflation processes. The parameter estimates obtained over the 1960-79 sample, and the actual realizations of the forcing variables (money growth and relative prices of intermediate and final goods) are used to compute dynamic simulations of wage and price inflation and output growth. Table 3 reports the timing and the direction of estimated shifts in inflation and output dynamics obtained from the simulations. The Table shows, for each country, the date when the simulated paths of inflation and output growth start diverging in a persistent way from the actual paths, and the sign of the divergence. The words "higher" and "lower" reported in parenthesis under each date indicate that the actual realizations of the variables were respectively higher and lower than their simulated values.

The Table suggests a number of impressive regularities. First, for all countries except West Germany, and possibly Denmark, actual and simulated

---

[17] Giavazzi and Giovannini [1989] report a more detailed analysis of the model, and all the statistical results.

inflation and output paths start diverging later than the beginning of the EMS.
Second, simulations for output growth tend to be less clearcut than simulations
for inflation. And third, the direction of the divergences are opposite for
Germany and the other countries in the Table. In Germany actual inflation after
1979 is higher than its simulated value, and output growth is lower. The
opposite results of Germany and the other countries are consistent with the
model of imported reputation. The delayed shifts in the output-inflation
tradeoffs for most countries, which occur well after the start of the EMS, and
the very similar pattern followed by UK inflation and output, raise the question
of the nature of the shift in expectation, and the role played by the reform of
the exchange-rate regime.

     Finally, it is interesting to analyze the magnitudes of the shifts in the
output-inflation tradeoffs. Table 4 reports changes in inflation and cumulative
output growth that occurred in European countries since 1979, and compares them
with simulations of the same magnitudes obtained from the model described above.
Contrast, for example, the experiences of Germany, Ireland and Italy. According
to the simulations, every percentage point of inflation reduction since 1979
would have afforded Germany 10.7 percent growth: by contrast, the output growth
for every point of inflation reduction was only 4.10. In the case of Ireland
and Italy, the simulations predict that every point of inflation reduction could
have afforded those countries 4.10 and 0.67 percent growth, respectively. But
in reality, real growth for every point of inflation reduction was higher in
both cases: 6.94 percent in Ireland and 2.18 percent in Italy. Similarly, the
simulations predicted a fall in output by 1.34 percent for every percent point
reduction of inflation in Denmark, whereas in fact output has increased by 10.6

percent for every percent point reduction of inflation. These comparisons
vividly illustrate the estimated effects of shifts in expectations, and their
uneven distribution among Germany and the European partners.

It is however puzzling that price and wage expectations seem to have
adjusted with a lag. One possible interpretation of this puzzle is that the
effects of the EMS on expectations were not as direct as predicted by the Barro-
Gordon model. The experience in France, Italy and Ireland, and the estimates of
the timing of the shifts in expectations, suggest that the shifts in
expectations were prompted by shifts in domestic policies.

- In Italy the shift in expectations seems to have occurred in the first
quarter of 1985, in the aftermath of a government decree which had set a ceiling
on wage indexation. That decree had been challenged by the unions, and was
eventually ratified by a national referendum. in June 1984.

- In Ireland there was a major turnaround in economic policies in the Summer
of 1982, marked by an announcement of tighter guidelines for monetary policy, a
decision   not to devalue the central parity of the punt in the February and
June 1982 EMS realignments, and to freeze pay increases in the public sector.[18]

- In France, the turnaround in macroeconomic policies occurs in March 1983,
after the expansionary experiment of the first Mitterrand government had produced
a large current account deficit (3.5 percent of GDP) and a speculative attack on
the franc. The government accompanied the EMS exchange realignment with a
freeze in budgetary expenses, an increase in income taxes, and a dramatic

---

[18] Dornbusch [1988].

tightening of credit.[19]

What was the linkage between these policies and the EMS constraint? In the case of Ireland and France the linkage is apparent. In particular, French authorities justified the unpopular policies as a necessary step to insure EMS membership, and linked   membership in the EMS to   participation in the EEC.[20] In the case of Italy, although there is no explicit reference to the EMS in the government pronouncements after the decree on wage indexation, one cannot exclude that the external constraint might have motivated that unpopular policy. In conclusion, EMS membership might have helped countries other than West Germany in their disinflation efforts only to the extent that they provided a justification for unpopular policies vis-a-vis the domestic public, which could have helped to strengthen the credibility of the exchange-rate targets. Thus the unpopular policies were justified by French government officials who argued that EMS membership is an integral part of EEC membership.

---

[19] Sachs and Wyplosz [1986].

[20] Sachs and Wyplosz [1986].

5. The Role of Capital Controls

Like other fixed exchange rate regimes, the EMS is characterized by
widespread use of capital controls by its member countries. While there is no
agreed-upon justification for the imposition of capital controls,[21] the concern
of policymakers with fluctuations of domestic interest rates is the often-cited
reason for their imposition. The main thrust of interest-rate-stability
argument is that, with perfect capital mobility, the discrete exchange rate
realignments occurring in an adjustable peg regime can cause extremely high
interest rate differentials. Large discrete devaluations are not unusual in
adjustable peg regimes. The experience of the Bretton Woods years has shown
several instances where currencies were devalued by more than 5 percent; several
of the EMS realignments resulted in non-negligible jumps in the level of the
exchange rate.[22]

Whenever large exchange rate changes are expected, equilibrium interest rate
differentials widen sharply. To illustrate this fact, assume that uncovered
interest rate parity between domestic and foreign assets holds, so that the
(continuously compounded) interest rate on domestic assets equals the
(continuously compounded) interest rate on foreign assets, plus the expected
rate of change of the price of foreign currency in terms of domestic currency.
Suppose a 5 percent devaluation of the domestic currency is expected to occur in
the next month, but no changes in the exchange rate are expected to take place

---

[21] That justification would have to rely on second-best arguments.

[22] Williamson [1985] stresses the potential disruptive effects of large parity
realignments in the EMS.

afterwards. The expected devaluation twists the term structure of interest rate differentials: the differential between domestic and foreign rates on comparable 1-year instruments in equilibrium is equal to 5 percent; but it increases to 10, 20, and 60 percent, on assets of 6, 3, and 1-month maturity, respectively. In proximity of a devaluation, equilibrium interest rates on overnight assets can easily exceed 100 percent! In general, fluctuations in expected exchange rate devaluations increase the volatility of short-term nominal interest rates to levels that are considered unacceptable by most central banks. While there is no widely agreed-upon welfare justification for the desirability of targeting nominal interest rates, many economists argue that nominal interest rate targeting seems a reasonable description of central banks' activities.[23]

Controls on international capital flows can protect domestic interest rates from the fluctuations associated with expectations of discrete exchange rate realignments. They do so by prohibiting domestic and foreign residents from borrowing at the domestic interest rate in order to lend abroad, in the expectation of the capital gains accruing after the exchange rate realignment.[24]

To what extent have the capital controls been effective in severing the link

---

[23] See Barro [1988] for a recent appraisal of that argument.

[24] However, when a devaluation is expected, accepting the fluctuations of domestic interest rates required to prevent the reallocation of international financial portfolios does not avoid a speculative attack on the reserves of the central bank. A large enough increase in domestic interest rates can compensate portfolio-holders for the capital loss expected on the day of the devaluation, but does not help holders of domestic high powered money. The reluctance of central banks to suffer large swings in their foreign exchange reserves is an additional motive for prohibiting the purchase of foreign exchange by domestic residents.

between the domestic and the international financial market, and thus at
insulating domestic interest rates in the wake of parity realignments? In the
EMS, it is interesting to compare the experience of France and Italy, with that
of the Netherlands, an EMS member where, as in Germany, there are almost no
impediments to international capital flows.

The degree of insulation of the domestic financial market from the
international market can be estimated by looking at the onshore-offshore
differential: that is at the differential between the return on a deposit issued
in the domestic money market and the return on a deposit of the same maturity
issued in the Euromarket and also denominated in domestic currency. Onshore-
offshore differentials signal the presence of unexploited profit opportunities
that can be attributed only to the active enforcement of exchange controls. In
the case of the lira, however, the market for Eurolire deposits is extremely
thin; often no price is quoted. As an alternative to the onshore-offshore
differential, one can use the deviations from the condition of covered arbitrage
between the return on a deposit issued in Milan and denominated in lira and the
covered return on a Eurodollar deposit of the same maturity.[25]

Two arbitrage operations between the domestic money market and the
Euromarket are possible: either borrowing on the domestic market to buy a
Eurodeposit, or borrowing on the Euromarket to invest at home.
In the absence of exchange controls, prices would move so as to eliminate
profit opportunities. If controls are effective at preventing capital outflows,
it would be profitable to borrow at home and buy a Eurodeposit. If controls
are effective at preventing capital inflows, it would be profitable to borrow
on the Euromarket and invest domestically. Table 5 in the Appendix reports
statistics on such profit opportunities for the period October 1980 to December
1987.[26] The Table shows that

---

[25] Under the assumption that covered interest rate parity holds on the
Euromarket, the two differentials are identical.

unexploited profit opportunities were extremely frequent in the cases of France and Italy, especially during the "crisis" months from October 1982 to March 1983. By contrast, the differential between domestic and offshore interest rates for the Netherlands was always within the band defined by transaction costs, Hence capital controls used by France and Italy were effective at partially isolating domestic interest rates from international disturbances.

The use of capital controls, however, could also be at the root of the asymmetric behavior of European exchange rates vis-a-vis the dollar. There appears to be a tendency for currencies like the French franc and the lira to drift away from the DM, in relation to dollar fluctuations. It is often noted that when the dollar is "strong" in foreign exchange markets, the Deutsche mark tends to be "weak" vis-a-vis other European currencies.[27] This observation typically is made in relation to day-to-day exchange rate movements that occur within the bilateral target zones.

Differences in the degree of financial integration are often offered as an explanation of the observed correlations. Capital controls result in increased transaction costs in the exchange of assets denominated in the currencies subject to capital controls. These costs represent the obstacles imposed by controls on free exchange of a country's financial assets for the purpose of international portfolio diversification.[28] The first important effect of these costs is the

[26]Covered interest rate differential for a group of 24 countries--including the three European countries we study here--are analyzed in Frankel and MacArthur [1988].

[27]See, among others, Masera [1981], Thygesen [1981], Baer [1982], Kaufman [1985], Russo [1984], Giavazzi and Giovannini [1985], Frankel [1985a, 1985b], Dennis and Nellis [1984], Padoa Schioppa [1985].

[28]Giavazzi and Giovannini [1986] formally describe a model of international portfolio diversification with capital controls.

limitation of the number of agents who actively trade for portfolio purposes in currencies subject to capital controls. The second effect is to make a country's financial assets less substitutable for assets denominated in other currencies. Finally, transaction costs make price responses to exogenous shocks asymmetric between assets that are costly to trade and assets that are not.

Consider an exogenous and identical increase in expected returns on Deutsche mark and French franc assets. The incipient portfolio shift into marks and francs has different effects on exchange rates if transactions costs differ. If they were higher for French francs, we would observe the effective dollar exchange rate depreciate, and the mark appreciate in terms of francs.

Thus, it appears that capital controls have given rise to two offsetting effects. One one hand, they have allowed the EMS to hold together without full monetary convergence among member countries. On the other hand, by making assets denominated in currencies whose countries impose capital controls less attractive to international investors, they have induced asymmetric reaction of European currencies' prices to common international shocks.

6. Concluding Observations

This paper has offered a review of the main institutional features of the EMS, and of its economic effects. A number of noticeable points have emerged: (a) The institutional innovations that were hailed as the important technical novelty of the EMS--the indicator of divergence and the European Currency Unit-- have played no effective role. Indeed the EMS has worked like the other two major experiments with fixed exchange rates, with a "center" country setting monetary policy targets for the whole system. This has occurred because the institutions of the EMS have not been sufficient to induce a balanced sharing of the burden of international adjustment: no EMS rule imposes constraints on monetary policies of the member countries, and countries are free to sterilize foreign exchange operations undertaken under the EMS obligations.

(b) The lack of coordination among monetary policies has worked to the member countries' advantage: countries like France and Italy were able to import the Bundesbank's reputation as an inflation fighter, and justify unpopular domestic policies that convinced the public of their anti-inflationary stance, and facilitated the disinflation process. West Germany, by contrast, appears to have been able to limit the volatility of its own effective terms of trade, especially in comparison with the early 1970's, when its major European partners were accomodating US policies.

(c) Capital controls have been instrumental to the survival of the EMS, as in the previous fixed-exchange-rates experiences. They have allowed countries to achieve a gradual convergence of inflation rates, characterized by periodic exchange-rate realignments. The wide fluctuations of interest rates around exchange rate realignments have not been transmitted to domestic interest rates.

  Hence the experience of the EMS suggests, once again, that fixed exchange rate systems, or the variations on the theme appearing in the current proposals of the reform of the world monetary system, are not enough to induce monetary policy cooperation, or a symmetric sharing of the burden of international adjustment. In the absence of the conditions that make asymmetric structures like those of the EMS and Bretton Woods system viable, fixed exchange rate systems would most likely be unsustainable.

References

Artis, M.J. and M.P. Taylor "Exchange Rates, Interest Rates, Capital Controls
    the EMS: Assessing the Track Record." University of
    Manchester. Mimeo, 1987.

Baer, G.U. "Some Reflections on a Co-ordinated Dollar Policy
    The Pivotal Role of Germany in the EMS." Aussenwirtschaft 37 (1982)

Barro, R. "Interest Rate Smoothing." Harvard University. Mimeo, 1988.

Barro, R.J., and D. Gordon, "A Positive Theory of Monetary Policy in
    a Natural Rate Model," Journal of Political Economy 91, 1983,
    pp. 589-610.

Blanchard, O.J., "Why Money Affects Output" manuscript, MIT 1988.

Cohen, B.J. "The European Monetary System: An Outsider's View." Essays in
    International Finance No. 142, International Finance Section,
    Princeton University, 1982.

Dennis, G., and Nellis, J. "The Ems and UK Membership: Five Years On."
    Lloyds Bank Review (1984).

Dornbusch, R., "Ireland's Failed Stabilization," manuscript, MIT
    September 1988.

Dornbusch, R. and Giovannini, A. "Monetary Policy in the Open Economy." MIT.
    Mimeo, 1988.

European Community, Monetary Committee Compendium of Community Monetary Texts.
    Brussels, 1986.

Flood, R.P. "Explanations of Exchange-Rate Volatility and Other Empirical
    Regularities in Some Popular Models of the Foreign Exchange Market."
    Carnegie-Rochester Conference Series on Public Policy 15 (1981):219-250.

Frankel, J. "Comments on Williamson and Giavazzi and Giovannini,"
    in A.Giovannini and R.Dornbusch (eds) Europe and the Dollar.
    Torino: Istituto Bancario San Paolo di Torino, 1985a.

Frankel, J. "The Implications of Mean-Variance Optimization For
    Four Questions in International Finance." University of California,
    Berkeley. Mimeo, 1985b.

Frankel, J.A., and A.T. MacArthur "Political vs. Currency Premia in
    International Real Interest Differentials: A Study of Forward Rates for
    24 Countries." NBER Working Paper No. 2309, 1987.

Giavazzi,F., and Giovannini, A. "Asymmetries in Europe, the Dollar
    and the European Monetary System," in
    A. Giovannini and R. Dornbusch (eds.) Europe and the Dollar. Torino:
    Istituto Bancario San Paolo di Torino, 1985.

Giavazzi,F., and Giovannini, A. "The EMS and the Dollar," Economic Policy 2,
    April 1986, pp. 456-484.

Giavazzi, F., and Giovannini, A. "Models of the EMS: Is Europe a Greater
    Deutsche-Mark Area?" in R. Bryant and R. Portes (eds.)
    Global Macroeconomics: Policy Conflicts and Cooperation. London:
    McMillan 1987a.

Giavazzi, F., and Giovannini, A. "Can the EMS Be Exported? Lessons from
    Ten Years of Monetary Policy Coordination in Europe," mimeo,
    Columbia University, 1988.

Giavazzi, F. and A. Giovannini, Limiting Exchange-Rate Flexibility:
    The European Monetary System, Cambridge, MA: MIT Press, 1989.

Giovannini, A., "How Do Fixed-Exchange-Rates Regimes Work: The
    Evidence from the Gold Standard, Bretton Woods and the EMS,"
    mimeo, Columbia Business School, October 1988 (a).

Giovannini, A. "The Macroeconomics of Exchange-Rate and Price-Level
    Interactions: Empirical Evidence for West Germany." NBER Working Paper
    No. 2544, 1988 (b).

Giovannini, A. "Prices and Exchange Rates: What Theory Needs to Explain."
    Paper prepared for the 1987 ASSA Meetings, Chicago, December 1987.

Kaufman, H.M. "The Deutsche Mark Between the Dollar and the
    European Monetary System." Kredit und Kapital (1985)

Masera, R.S. "The First Two Years of the Ems: The Exchange Rate
    Experience." Banca Nazionale del Lavoro Quarterly Review 138 (1981):
    271-296.

Padoa Schioppa, T. "Policy Cooperation and the EMS Experience,"
    in W.H. Buiter and R.C. Marstons (eds.) International Economic Policy
    Coordination. Cambridge (UK): Cambridge University Press, 1985.

Rogoff, K. "Can Exchange Rate Predictability be Achieved Without Monetary
    Convergence?" European Economic Review 28 (1985a):93-115.

Rogoff, K. "Can International Monetary Policy Cooperation Be
    Counterproductive?" Journal of International Economics 18 (1985b):
    199-217.

Rotemberg, J.J., "The New Keynesian Microfoundations" NBER
    Macroeconomics Annual, 1988.

Russo, M. "Cooperazione Monetaria Europea: Cinque Anni di
    Esperienza dello SME" EEC Commission. Mimeo, 1985.

Sachs, J., and Wyplosz, C. "The Economic Consequences of President
    Mitterand." Economic Policy 2 (1986):261-313.

Spaventa, L. " Algebraic Properties and Economic Improperties of the
    'Indicator of Divergence' in the European Monetary System," in R. Cooper
    et al. (eds.) The International Monetary System under Flexible
    Exchange Rates - Essays in Honor of Robert Triffin. Cambridge (Mass.):
    Ballinger, 1982.

Thygesen, N. "Are Monetary Policies and Performances Converging?"
    Banca Nazionale del Lavoro Quarterly Review 138 (1981):297-326.

Ungerer, H., Evans, O. and Young, P. "The European Monetary System: Recent
    Developments." Occasional Paper No. 48.
    Washington, D.C.: International Monetary Fund, 1986.

Ungerer, H., Evans, O. and Young, P. "The European Monetary System: The
    Experience." Occasional Paper No. 19.
    Washington, D.C.: International Monetary Fund, 1983.

Williamson, J. The Exchange Rate System. Washington, D.C.: Institute for
    International Economics, 1985.

APPENDIX 1

This Appendix describes the model developed by Canzoneri and Henderson, and applied in section 4.1 of the text.

$$y = -(w-p)/(1-\alpha)/\alpha \tag{1}$$

$$y^* = -(w^*-p^*)/(1-\alpha)/\alpha \tag{1'}$$

$$y-y^* = \delta(e+p^*-p) \tag{2}$$

$$m-p = y \tag{3}$$

$$m^*-p^* = y^* \tag{3'}$$

$$\Omega = -\sigma(n-k)^2 - (q)^2 \tag{4}$$

$$\Omega^* = -\sigma(n^*-k^*)^2 - (q)^2 \tag{4'}$$

$$q = p + \beta(e+p^*-p) \tag{5}$$

$$q^* = p^* + \beta(p-e-p^*) \tag{5*}$$

The model considers two symmetric countries. All variables are in logs and expressed as deviations from their means. The supply functions (equations (1) and (1')) relate output to real product wages. The level of the real exchange rate determines how demand gets allocated between the outputs of the countries (equation (2)). Domestic and foreign money are the only assets, and they are not traded. [1] Money demand (equations (3) and (3')) is an increasing function of the level of income. The central banks' objectives are described by equations (4) and (4'): they are quadratic in the deviations of employment from a target and in the level of the consumer price index, defined in equations (5) and (5'). The target employment levels (k and k*) exceed the natural rate, which in the model equals zero.

Using the assumptions set forth in the text, one finds in a flexible exchange rate regime that the wage-setting rule is:

$$w = (m)^e \tag{6}$$
$$w^* = (m^*)^e \tag{6'}$$

Substituting these expressions into equations (1) and (1'), assuming perfect foresight, one obtains the Nash equilibrium:

$$n = n^* = 0 \tag{7}$$

$$q = m = \frac{\sigma}{\epsilon+\alpha} k \tag{8}$$

$$q^* = m^* = \frac{\sigma}{\epsilon+\alpha} k^* \tag{8'}$$

[1] If we allowed additional assets in the model, it would become necessary to assume capital controls.

Where $\epsilon = (1-\alpha)\beta/\delta$. Hence equilibrium inflation is a function of σ and ϵ. The larger σ, and k (k*) are, the greater the inflation bias. ϵ, a function of the real exchange rate's weight in the CPI, lowers this inflationary bias.

Fixed exchange rates imply:

$$n = n* = 0 \tag{9}$$

$$q = q* = \frac{\sigma}{\alpha} k* \tag{10}$$

Fixed exchange rates will be superior, on anti-inflation grounds, if the "credibility gap" is sufficiently large:

$$\frac{k-k*}{k*} > \frac{\epsilon}{\alpha} \tag{11}$$

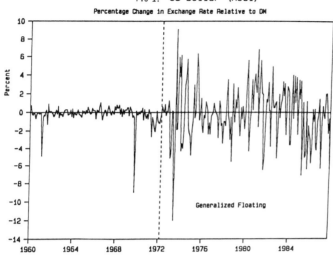

FIG 1: US Dollar (Real)

Percentage Change in Exchange Rate Relative to DM

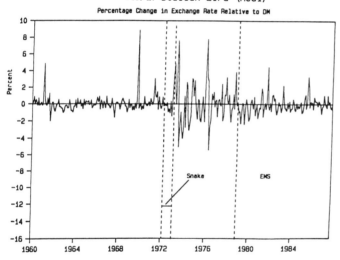

FIG. 2: Italian Lira (Real)

Percentage Change in Exchange Rate Relative to DM

Table 1

Germany's Terms-of-Trade

	Standard Error of the Real Effective Exchange Rate (global index)	Correlation between the Global and the Intra-EEC Indices of Competitiveness
1960:1-1971:8	.041	.824
1960:1-1979:1	.127	.911
1960:1-1985:12	.124	.620
1979:2-1985:12	.114	-.033

Sources: IMF, IFS. Real exchange rates are constructed using wholesale prices. Effective exchange-rate weights are the IMF-MERM weights for 1977, normalized to account for Germany's competitiveness vis-a-vis its eight major trading partners--in the case of the global index--and its four major EMS parners--in the case of the intra-EMS index. Weights are as follows. Global index: Belgium, 0.0588; France, 0.2016; Italy, 0.151; Japan, 0.152; Netherlands, 0.074; Switzerland, 0.043; United Kingdom, 0.058; United States, 0.262. Intra-EMS index: Belgium, 0.121; France, 0.416; Italy, 0.311; Netherlands, 0.152.

Table 2

The European disinflation
(GDP deflator: annual growth, percent)

	1978	1987
Belgium	4.3%	2.1%
Denmark	9.9	4.6
France	9.5	3.3
Germany	4.3	2.1
Ireland	10.5	2.9
Italy	13.9	5.5
Netherlands	5.4	-1.0
United Kingdom	11.3	4.0

Source: European Economy.

Table 3

The timing and direction of the shift in expectations:

	Denmark	France	Germany	Ireland	Italy	U.Kingdom
Price Inflation (direction)	80:1 (lower)	83:2 (lower)	79:2 (higher)	82:3 (lower)	85:1 (lower*)	81:3 (lower)
Wage Inflation (direction)	80:2 (lower)	83:2 (lower)	79:2 (higher)	80:2 (lower)	85:1 (lower*)	81:1 (lower)
Output Growth (direction)	80:3 (higher)	none	79:2 (lower)	none	none	none

Note: The words "higher" and "lower" indicate that the actual realization of
the variables are respectively higher and lower than their simulated values.
The word "none" indicates that no systematic divergence between actual and
simulated values can be detected. In the case of Italy, the divergence between
actual and simulated variables occurs close to the end of the simulation period.

Table 4

The shift in the output-inflation tradeoff

	Denmark	France	Germany	Ireland	Italy	U.Kingdom
End of the Simulations	84:4	85:4	86:4	88:1	86:4	87:1
Change in Inflation	-1.83	-4.86	-3.37	-9.72	-8.38	-6.23
Predicted Change in Inflation	-2.57	6.78	-5.51	-8.57	-12.87	6.63
Cumulative Change in Output	19.43	5.06	13.82	39.84	18.30	12.10
Predicted Cumulative Change in Output	-3.45	26.18	58.95	59.60	8.25	9.98

Table 5

Onshore-Offshore Differentials
(November 1980-December 1987)

Sample No. of observations Direction	1980:11-1987:12 (372)			1982:10-1983:3 (27)			1983:4-1985:11 (138)		
	Out	In	Neither	Out	In	Neither	Out	In	Neither
France									
Number of weeks	309	8	55	27	-	-	115	-	23
Frequency (%)	83	2	15	100	-		83	-	17
Mean rate of return (%)	2.2	0.3		7.2	-		1	-	
Italy									
Number of weeks	112	75	185	25	1	1	1	58	79
Frequency (%)	30	20	50	92	4	4	1	42	57
Mean rate of return (%)	2.7	0.6		3.2	-		0.1	0.6	
Netherlands									
Number of weeks	2	1	369	0	0	27	1	0	137
Frequency (%)	.005	.003	99.9	-	-	100	-	-	100
Mean rate of return (%)	.03	-		-	-		-	-	

Direction indicates the direction in which unexploited arbitrage profits are observed. The mean rate of return represents the instantaneous profit that could have been earned on each riskless and costless arbitrage operation, if there had been no exchange controls. Out refers to observations for which π_1 is positive; in to observations for which π_2 is positive, and neither refers to observations for which $\pi_1 \leq 0$, and $\pi_2 \leq 0$. π_1 and π_2 are defined in equations (16) and (17) in the text. In the case of France and of the Netherlands the data refer to the differentials between onshore and offshore rates, that is to eq. (16) and (17). In the case of Italy they refer to the covered interest rate differentials described in equations (16') and (17)

CAN INTERNATIONAL MONETARY POLICY COOPERATION BE COUNTERPRODUCTIVE?

Kenneth ROGOFF*

Board of Governors of the Federal Reserve System, Washington, DC 20551, USA

Received April 1984, revised version received August 1984

This paper demonstrates that increased international monetary cooperation may actually be counterproductive. The potential problem is that cooperation between central banks *may* exacerbate the credibility problem of central banks vis-à-vis the private sector. Coordinated monetary expansion yields a better output/inflation trade-off than unilateral expansion because it does not induce exchange rate depreciation. Wage setters realize that the incentives to inflate are greater in a cooperative regime, and thus time-consistent nominal wage rates are higher. Cooperation does improve responses to disturbances. Thus, a cooperative regime which contains institutional constraints on systematic inflation is definitely superior.

1. Introduction

Schemes to increase coordination among central banks of employment and inflation-rate stabilization policies have received a great deal of attention.[1] Unfortunately, most analyses focus entirely on how central banks might cooperate to offset unanticipated disturbances, and devote little or no consideration to the problem of systematically maintaining low rates of inflation. The present paper is an effort to provide a simple macroeconomic framework in which to examine both issues. Within the context of a two-country model of a managed floating exchange rate system, we simultaneously analyze the strategic interactions of sovereign monetary authorities across countries, and the strategic interactions of private agents and the monetary authorities within a given country.

The main result of this paper is that, contrary to the usual conclusion (and presumption) of earlier analyses, increased monetary policy cooperation

---

*An earlier version of this paper was written while the author was on leave at the Research Department of the International Monetary Fund. The views expressed in this paper are the author's own, and should not be interpreted as the official views of either institution. The author has benefited from discussions with Matthew Canzoneri and Dale Henderson.

[1]Cooper (1969) and Hamada (1976) were the first to analyze the strategic interactions of two (or more) governments in conducting monetary stabilization policy. More recently, Jones (1982, 1983) as well as Canzoneri and Gray (1985) have examined some game-theoretic aspects of monetary policy under fixed and flexible exchange rates. The above analyses do not incorporate rational expectations. Other recent multi-country analyses of monetary policy include Carlozzi and Taylor (1984), Henderson (1984), Macedo (1983), McKinnon (1982), Miller and Salmon (1983), and Sachs (1983).

between two governments does not automatically increase welfare in either country.[2] In fact, welfare in one or both countries may be higher when central banks conduct their monetary policies independently. The potential danger with inter-central bank cooperation is that it can exacerbate the credibility problem of central banks vis-à-vis the private sector. One reason for such a credibility problem is that the central bank may be tempted to try to exploit the existence of nominal wage contracts to systematically raise employment.[3] Of course, in a time-consistent equilibrium, wage inflation will be high enough so that the central bank's efforts will be futile. International monetary cooperation may raise the rate of wage inflation because wage setters recognize that a noncooperative regime contains a built-in check on each central bank's incentives to inflate. The reason is that when a central bank expands its money supply unilaterally, it causes its country's real exchange rate to depreciate thereby reducing the employment gains and increasing the CPI inflation costs. Cooperation may remove this disincentive to inflate, and thus raise time-consistent nominal wage growth. A cooperative regime does produce better responses to supply shocks or relative shifts in aggregate demand; that is to say, it reduces the variance of the social welfare function around its mean market-determined value. But monetary policy cooperation is unambiguously beneficial only in institutional frameworks which eliminate or ameliorate the central banks' credibility problem vis-à-vis the private sector.

Except for the fact that it incorporates rational expectations (cum wage contracting), the stochastic, two-good, two-country model we employ is quite similar to ones which have been used to characterize the benefits of inter-governmental cooperation. Nominal wage contracts, negotiated a period in advance and only partially indexed to the current price level, provide the fulcrum for monetary policy (though the basic point of the analysis extends to alternative non-neutralities). The details of the underlying macro model are relegated to appendix A, since they are not needed to express the main ideas. Section 2 describes the home and foreign welfare functions, which depend on own employment and CPI inflation. Section 3 details the objectives of wage setters, as well as the nature of a time-consistent equilibrium. Section 4 describes the cross-effects of home and foreign monetary policy; the real exchange rate plays a key role here. The main

[2]An important exception is Vaubel (1983), who has independently suggested that currency competition under floating rates may lead to lower inflation. We will not ask here how a cooperative regime might be implemented. Hamada (1976) stresses that the problem may best be thought of as one in which the central banks cooperate to construct a regime with the best possible (self-enforcing) noncooperative equilibrium.

[3]The analysis of the strategic interactions of private agents and the monetary authorities within a given country is based on Phelps (1967), Kydland and Prescott (1977), Barro and Gordon (1983a) and Rogoff (1985). It is important to recognize that the bank's actions should be interpreted as maximizing social welfare given the institutional framework within which it operates. See sections 3 and 8 below.

result is illustrated in section 5. Section 6 formally derives the stochastic equilibrium path of the world economy when central banks conduct stabilization unilaterally, and are unable to guarantee to wage setters that they will not try systematically to raise employment. Section 7 contrasts the results of section 6 with social welfare under a regime in which central banks again lack credibility with wage setters, but are able to cooperate with each other in conducting stabilization policy. Section 8 stresses that an optimal cooperative regime — one which contains institutional constraints on systematic inflation — is definitely superior to any noncooperative regime.

2. Domestic and foreign social objective functions

Each central bank attempts to minimize a social loss function which depends on deviations of own-country employment and inflation from their optimal (socially-desired) values:[4]

$$\Lambda_t = (n_t - \tilde{n})^2 + \chi(\pi_{It} - \tilde{\pi}_I)^2, \tag{1a}$$

$$\Lambda_t^* = (n_t^* - \tilde{n}^*)^2 + \chi(\pi_{It}^* - \tilde{\pi}_I^*)^2, \tag{1b}$$

where Λ (Λ^*) is the home (foreign) social loss function. Star superscripts denote foreign country variables, t subscripts denote time, and lower case letters represent logarithms. (Henceforth, we will discuss only domestic variables and equations in circumstances where discussion of their foreign counterparts is superfluous.) Employment is given by n, and π_I is the rate of consumer price level inflation, e.g. $\pi_{It} = (p_I)_t - (p_I)_{t-1}$, where the index p_I [defined in eq. (16) of appendix A] includes both the home- and foreign-produced good. The socially-preferred values of n and π_I are denoted by $\tilde{n}$ and $\tilde{\pi}_I$. χ is the relative weight which society places on inflation stabilization versus employment stabilization.[5] As with all of the parameters of the model of appendix A, χ is the same for both countries; also, $\tilde{\pi}_I = \tilde{\pi}_I^*$, and $\tilde{n} = \tilde{n}^*$. This symmetry greatly simplifies the algebra, but is not essential to the analysis. The objective functions (1) are static, but because wage contracts

---

[4]A similar specification of the social loss function is used by Barro and Gordon (1983a), and by Kydland and Prescott (1977).

[5]In most rational expectations macroeconomic models, inflation rate shocks enter the social loss function only indirectly through their effects on employment. It is indeed difficult to strongly justify including the level of inflation as a separate term in Λ. To close the model, however, it is only necessary that the weight on inflation be nonzero. (It is also necessary that Λ be strictly convex in π_I.) Some costs of perfectly anticipated inflation include the administrative costs of posting new prices, the costs of adjusting the tax system to be fully neutral with respect to inflation, and the costs incurred because high rates of inflation force private agents to economize on their holdings of noninterest-bearing money. The optimal rate of inflation may nevertheless be nonzero; it may be optimal to make some use of the seignorage tax when other methods of taxation are also distortionary. See Phelps (1973).

are for one period, the results below would be unchanged even with multiperiod objective functions.[6]

3. The conflict between wage setters and the central banks

The tension between wage setters and the central bank within each country derives from the assumption that $\tilde{n}$, society's target employment rate, is greater than $\bar{n}$, wage setters' target employment rate. Possible factors which might cause equilibrium employment $\bar{n}$ to be too low include income taxation, unemployment insurance and monopolistic unions; see Barro and Gordon (1983a). Income taxation, for example, drives a wedge between private and social marginal product. While an individual would not want to be alone in being fooled by the central bank into working an extra hour (since he would only receive an infinitesimal share of the benefits from his extra taxes), he might be better off if everyone were to work an extra hour (since he would share in the benefits from everyone's taxes).

Of course, the monetary authorities cannot systematically raise the level of employment. In equilibrium, base nominal wage rates are set at a sufficiently high level so that, in the absence of disturbances, the central bank will not *choose* to inflate the money supply beyond the point consistent with wage setters' desired real wage. At this sufficiently high level of inflation the central bank finds that the marginal utility gain from inflating (further) to raise employment above wage setters' desired level is fully offset by the marginal disutility from the added inflation.[7] Note that each individual group of wage setters is indeed concerned with the inflation rate, just as society is. But because the impact of an individual firm's contract on aggregate inflation is small, they have little incentive to temper their nominal wage increases. Thus, the equilibrium is Nash.

Obviously, if the labor market distortion can be removed at low cost, then there is no problem. A second-best equilibrium could be attained if the central bank is able credibly to promise not to systematically inflate. The problem is how to design a system to enforce such a promise without constraining the ability of the central bank to offset unanticipated shocks. For example, if it were possible to anticipate every type of disturbance, one

[6]Even with one-period contracts, it would be necessary to explicitly allow for multi-period objective functions in order to analyze reputational equilibria; see Barro and Gordon (1983b) or Canzoneri (1985). Sachs (1983) examines monetary policy cooperation in an interesting dynamic setting, and Miller and Salmon (1983) examine dynamic games in a very general dynamic open-economy model. The main point of the present paper can be expressed in a model with more dynamic elements.

[7]Phelps (1967) and Kydland and Prescott (1977) demonstrate why a time-consistent macro-economic equilibrium might be characterized by stagflation. While we focus here on labor market distortions, there are other factors which may cause the time-consistent rate of inflation to be too high. Examples include seignorage and the existence of nominal government debt; see Barro and Gordon (1983a).

could write a law specifying an optimal contingent path of the money supply. We shall return to this issue in section 8.

4. The macro model and the linkages between the two central bank objective functions

Aside from the credibility problems which the monetary authorities face vis-à-vis the private sector, there is also scope for strategic interactions between the two central banks. Although it is possible to develop alternative linkages, the analysis here focuses on those which arise in the rational expectations Mundell–Fleming model of appendix A. In that model, each country produces a different good; the two goods enter with equal weights into the CPI in both countries. The demand for each country's good depends on its relative price, the real interest rate, and income at home and abroad. Only home (foreign) residents hold the home (foreign) money; the demand for real balances is a function of real income and the nominal interest rate. Residents of both countries hold both home and foreign bonds, which are perfect substitutes.

One can see that the real exchange rate is the key link between the two central bank objective functions by substituting eqs. (16), (17) and (18) of appendix A into eqs. (1):

$$\Lambda_t = [z_t/\alpha + \gamma(p_t - \bar{w}_t) - \tau q_t - (\tilde{n} - \bar{n})]^2$$

$$+ \chi[p_t - p_{t-1} + 0.5(q_t - q_{t-1}) - \tilde{\pi}_I]^2, \tag{2a}$$

$$\Lambda_t^* = [z_t/\alpha + \gamma(p_t^* - \bar{w}_t^*) + \tau q_t - (\tilde{n}^* - \bar{n}^*)]^2$$

$$+ \chi[p_t^* - p_{t-1}^* - 0.5(q_t - q_{t-1}) - \tilde{\pi}_I^*]^2, \tag{2b}$$

where p is the home-currency price of the home good, p^* is the foreign-currency price of the foreign good, and q is the real exchange rate: $q \equiv e + p^* - p$ (e is the home-currency price of foreign currency). $\bar{w}$ ($\bar{w}^*$) is the home (foreign) base nominal wage rate, and z is a supply shock common to both countries.

The first term in Λ represents squared deviations of home employment from its socially-desired value. It depends on the productivity disturbance z, the unanticipated movement in the real wage $\bar{w} - p$, and the difference between society's and wage setters' target levels of employment, $\tilde{n} - \bar{n}$. The real exchange rate q also enters because wages are indexed to the CPI, which includes the foreign good. A similar term in q would arise if, as in the model of Daniel (1981), the foreign good entered as an intermediate good into the domestic production function. The second term in the social objective function is the squared difference between the actual rate of CPI inflation and society's target rate. Again, the real exchange rate enters.

5. Cooperation can be counterproductive

We have discussed (a) why the central banks cannot systematically alter the mean level of employment in a time-consistent equilibrium, and (b) how the real exchange rate links the objective functions of the two central banks. These are the two key elements of our main result: a cooperative regime may be characterized by systematically higher inflation rates than a noncooperative regime.

This result, which will be proven formally below, can be seen most simply by assuming that there are no disturbances and that the cooperative regime attains the symmetric point on the central banks' contract curve. (Due to the symmetry of the model, this point is achieved if the two central banks credibly agree to fix their exchange rate.) Note that each central bank has two objectives but only one instrument at its disposal: the money supply.[8] Once base wage rates are set, any unilateral effort by either central bank to inflate will cause its country's real exchange rate to depreciate (except in the case of complete wage indexation).[9] By inspection of eqs. (2), we see that this concomitant depreciation puts a check on each central bank's incentive to expand their money supply. A real depreciation directly raises CPI inflation, and tends to lower employment if (a) wages are indexed to the CPI, or if (b) the foreign good enters as an intermediate good in the home production function. Wage setters recognize the tempering influence of the real exchange rate when setting their base nominal wage rates.

This tempering influence is not present in the cooperative regime, since each central bank can count on the other to match any money supply increase. Cooperation thus forces wage setters to set a higher rate of nominal wage growth in order to ensure that the central banks will ratify their target real wage. Since monetary policy does not end up having any systematic effect on employment in either regime, the only thing accomplished by central bank to central bank cooperation is to raise inflation. Of course, as we shall see below, one can construct counterexamples to this counterexample: cooperation can also be productive.

---

[8]See appendix A. We are restricting our attention to contemporaneous money supply feedback rules since, in the setup of the text, 'prospective' (lagged) feedback rules [see Canzoneri, Henderson and Rogoff (1983)] are not time consistent; see Rogoff (1985).

[9]It would, of course, be attractive to extend the present model to allow for an endogenous determination of the coefficient of wage indexation, β. For the full information setup of the text, one can show that individual groups of wage setters would choose $\beta = 0$ if β is bounded between zero and one. Wage setters have no need to worry about aggregate goods market demand and money demand disturbances, because these are fully offset by the central banks. However, wage setters want the central banks to allow some price-level movement in response to productivity shocks in order to stabilize employment around the level which would arise if nominal wages were fully flexible. (See appendix A.) But because the central banks also care about price-level stability, they do not allow sufficient price-level movement to fully stabilize employment. Thus, from the point of view of wage setters at an individual firm, indexation would only serve to further damp desired movements in the real wage.

6. Equilibrium when central banks do not cooperate

Here we will examine the Nash equilibrium which obtains when each central bank perceives that it cannot improve its own objective function through unilateral action. To focus on the game-theoretic aspects of the model, we will assume that central banks and private investors have full current-period information.[10] To further simplify, we will treat the home price of the domestically-produced good as the home central bank's control variable, though implicitly it is actually controlling the home money supply. This simplification can only be rigorously justified because both countries are assumed to experience identical goods market demand and productivity disturbances. (The analysis in appendix B allows for relative shifts in aggregate demand, and explicitly treats the money supplies as the control variables.)

Our solution algorithm is as follows: In the macro model of appendix A we solve for the effects of home and foreign money supply changes, holding base wage rates constant and assuming that CPI inflation rate and exchange rate depreciation expectations are static. In the analysis of the text, we employ the partial derivatives obtained in appendix A to solve for the time-consistent path of wages. We then confirm that static CPI inflation rate and exchange rate depreciation expectations are indeed rational (provided there are no regime changes).

Once base wage rates are set and the current-period disturbances are observed, the Nash first-order conditions for the two noncooperating central banks are[11]

$$(\partial A_t/\partial p_t)^N = 2[\gamma - \tau \Psi][z_t/\alpha + \gamma(p_t - \bar{w}_t) - \tau q_t - (\tilde{n} - \bar{n})]$$

$$+ 2\chi(1 + 0.5\Psi)[p_t - p_{t-1} + 0.5(q_t - q_{t-1}) - \tilde{\pi}_I] = 0, \qquad (3a)$$

$$(\partial A_t^*/\partial p_t^*)^N = 2(\gamma + \tau \Psi^*)[z_t/\alpha + \gamma(p_t^* - \bar{w}_t^*) + \tau q_t - (\tilde{n}^* - \bar{n}^*)]$$

$$+ 2\chi(1 - 0.5\Psi^*)[p_t^* - p_{t-1}^* - 0.5(q_t - q_{t-1}) - \tilde{\pi}_I^*] = 0, \qquad (3b)$$

where N superscripts stand for 'Nash' equilibrium, and $\Psi \equiv (\partial q/\partial dm)/(\partial p/\partial dm) > 0$ [m is the home money supply, $dm \equiv m_t - v_t - E_{t-1}(m_t - v_t)$, v is the home money demand disturbance and E is the expectations operator]. Due to the symmetry of the underlying macroeconomic model of appendix A, $\Psi^* \equiv (\partial q/\partial dm^*)/(\partial p^*/\partial dm^*) = -\Psi$. One can also show that $(\gamma - \tau \Psi) > 0$, i.e. an unanticipated increase in the home money supply raises home employment.

---

[10]The results here extend readily to the case of incomplete contemporaneous information [see Rogoff (1985)]. The operative assumption here is that all agents have the same information set.

[11]The second-order conditions for a local minimum are met; because of the quadratic forms of (1), the minimum is global.

Wage setters are assumed to correctly anticipate whether a cooperative or Nash regime will be in place in the ensuing period. By examining the first-order conditions (3), wage setters can choose base wage rates so that the expected real wage equals their target real wage. The underlying macro model is constructed so that wage setters' target (logarithm of the) real wage is zero, and so that $E_{t-1}(q_t)=0$. Taking $t-1$ expectations across (3), and setting expected real wages and the expected real exchange rate equal to zero yields:[12]

$$(\bar{w}_t)^N = E_{t-1}(p_t)^N = p_{t-1} + 0.5q_{t-1} + \bar{\pi}_I^N = (\bar{w}_t^*)^N, \tag{4}$$

where $\bar{\pi}_I^N \equiv \bar{\pi}_I + (\gamma - \tau \Psi)(\tilde{n} - \bar{n})/\chi(1 + 0.5\Psi)$.

By choosing base wage rates according to eqs. (4), wage setters assure themselves that the noncooperating central banks will, in the absence of disturbances, produce price levels consistent with wage setters' target real wage. Inspection of eqs. (4) reveals that nominal wage growth depends positively on $\tilde{n} - \bar{n}$, the difference between the central bank's and wage setters' target employment rate; wage growth is a decreasing function of the weight society places on stabilizing inflation versus stabilizing employment. Using the fact that $E_{t-1}(q_t)=0$, it is easy to deduce from (4) that the expected rate of change of the CPI, $E_t(p_{t+1} + 0.5q_{t+1}) - (p_t + 0.5q_t)$, is constant and equal to $\bar{\pi}_I^N$. Thus, as assumed in appendix A, rational CPI inflation rate expectations are indeed static.

Using eqs. (3) and (4), one can analyze the responses of the noncooperative system to unanticipated disturbances. Because the two countries are structurally identical, and because they experience identical goods market demand and aggregate supply (but not money demand) shocks, the real exchange rate q always turns out to be zero in Nash equilibrium, regardless of the realization of the disturbances.[13] Assuming that $q=0$ is indeed always a Nash equilibrium, one can solve (3) for p_t and p_{t-1}^* holding $q=0$. Then take $t-1$ expectations and subtract to form:

$$(p_t)^N - E_{t-1}(p_t)^N \equiv (dp_t)^N = -z_t/\alpha[\gamma + \chi(1 + 0.5\Psi)/(\gamma - \tau \Psi)] = (dp_t^*)^N. \tag{5}$$

Feasibility and uniqueness of the $q=0$ Nash equilibrium may be confirmed by using eqs. (26) of appendix A (together with their foreign counterparts) to substitute into eqs. (3) for q, p and p^* in terms of m, m^*, $\bar{w}$, $\bar{w}^*$, $\bar{\pi}$, $\bar{\pi}^*$ and the disturbances (setting $x=0$).

To compare social welfare under the Nash regime with social welfare under a cooperative regime, it will be necessary to compute $E_{t-1}(\Lambda_t)^N$. Using

---

[12]Here is the first of many times where we make use of the fact that certainty equivalence obtains because the objective functions are quadratic; see Sargent (1979).

[13]With relative shifts in demand between home and foreign goods, as in appendix B, the real exchange rate does fluctuate in both the Nash and the cooperative regimes.

the fact that $q^N = 0$, it is possible to decompose the social loss function into three components:

$$E_{t-1}(\Lambda_t)^N = (\tilde{n} - \bar{n})^2 + \chi \Pi^N + \Gamma^N, \tag{6}$$

where

$$\Pi^N \equiv [(\bar{\pi}_I)^N - \tilde{\pi}_I]^2, \Gamma^N \equiv E_{t-1}\{[z_t/\alpha + \gamma(dp_t)^N]^2 + \chi[(dp_t)^N]^2\}.$$

The first element of $E_{t-1}(\Lambda_t)^N$ is nonstochastic; because monetary policy cannot systematically raise the employment rate, $\tilde{n} - \bar{n}$ can be reduced only by directly addressing the underlying cause of the real distortion. (This issue is beyond the scope of the present paper.) The second term, $\chi \Pi^N$, measures the extent to which the expected CPI inflation rate exceeds society's target rate. This second term is also independent of current-period disturbances but, as discussed in section 5, it is a function of the policy regime. The final term, Γ^N, measures the extent to which the central bank succeeds in stabilizing (a weighted average of) the employment rate and the CPI inflation rate around their expected *market-determined* values. Note that although the central banks actually attempt to stabilize inflation and employment around their socially-preferred values, in a time-consistent equilibrium the central banks appear to respond to disturbances as if they were trying to stabilize inflation and employment around their mean market-determined values. (This result is due to the quadratic form of the objective functions.) To evaluate Γ^N, substitute in for $(dp_t)^N$ using eq. (5):

$$\Gamma^N = (\sigma_z^2/\alpha^2)[(\chi')^2 + \gamma^2 \chi]/(\gamma^2 + \chi')^2 = (\Gamma^*)^N, \tag{7}$$

where σ_z^2 is the variance of the zero mean supply shock, $E_{t-1}(z_t^2)$, and $\chi' \equiv \gamma \chi (1 + 0.5\Psi)/(\gamma - \tau\Psi)$.

Note that money demand shocks do not appear in eq. (7) since, to the extent the shocks are known (here information is perfect), they can be completely neutralized through temporary money supply infusions. Complete offset of money demand disturbances is optimal since they present no trade-off between price-level stability and employment stability. Thus, the home central bank will react to home money demand disturbances in the same fashion whether or not it takes the utility function of the foreign central bank into account.[14]

Goods market demand shocks do not disturb the Nash equilibrium only because we have made the simplifying assumption that both countries

---

[14]Henderson (1984) derives a similar result. If the central banks place weight on achieving their money supply targets, as in Canzoneri and Gray (1985), then the cooperative and noncooperative response to money demand shocks will no longer be equivalent.

experience the same goods market demand disturbance. (This assumption is relaxed in appendix B.) Provided that both countries alter their money supplies equally to offset the mutual disturbance, there will be no effect on home and foreign prices and employment. The level of world real interest rates will move to offset the disturbance, but the real exchange rate will remain fixed. The resulting equilibrium is Nash because neither side has any incentive to unilaterally alter its money supply.

On the other hand, aggregate supply disturbances do affect the price levels which arise in Nash equilibrium in spite of our simplifying assumption that the home and foreign supply shocks are perfectly correlated. Because an aggregate supply shock alters the full-information real wage, it creates a trade-off between price level stability and employment stability. In the next section we demonstrate that, ignoring systematic effects on the inflation rate, the cooperative response to supply shocks is superior to the noncooperative response.

7. Equilibrium when central banks cooperate to achieve their stabilization objectives

Examining the first-order conditions for the Nash equilibrium [eqs. (3)], we see that the incentives of the central banks to unilaterally inflate are reduced by their fears of the concomitant effects on the real exchange rate. In this section we will assume that the two central banks engage in a binding cooperative agreement, under which they choose the symmetric point on their contract curve (given the base wage rates they face).[15] Equivalently, they could agree to fix their nominal exchange rate and allow either symmetric country to lead in choosing price levels. We will demonstrate below that such an agreement is mutually beneficial only if the variance of supply shocks is large relative to distortions in the labor markets.

Under the cooperative fixed real exchange rate ($q=0$) regime, the first-order condition for minimization of the home social welfare function is given by:

$$\gamma[z_t/\alpha + \gamma(p_t - \bar{w}_t) - (\tilde{n} - \bar{n})] + \chi(p_t - p_{t-1} - \tilde{\pi}_I) = 0. \tag{8}$$

(The corresponding foreign-country equation is identical.)

In deriving eq. (8), we have made use of the fact that $\partial q/\partial m$ is zero in the cooperative equilibrium, since each central bank can count on the other to

[15]There are other, asymmetric, cooperative schemes which, holding wages constant, lead to Pareto improvements over the Nash equilibrium. Qualitatively, all of these schemes are similar in that they involve higher money growth at home and abroad than in the Nash equilibrium. The symmetric scheme analyzed in the text is a logical one to consider since the two countries are identical in almost every respect. Canzoneri and Gray (1985) have emphasized that fixed exchange rate regimes may be noncooperative in that either country can unilaterally precommit to fix the exchange rate.

match any marginal change in its money supply. Eqs. (9), (10), and (11) are derived using the same algorithm used to derive eqs. (4), (5), and (7) of the previous section; 'C' superscripts stand for 'cooperative regime':

$$(\bar{w}_t)^C = E_{t-1}(p_t)^C = p_{t-1} + (\bar{\pi}_t)^C = (\bar{w}_t^*)^C, \tag{9}$$

$$(p_t)^C - E_{t-1}(p_t)^C \equiv (dp_t)^C = (dp_t^*)^C = -z_t/\alpha(\gamma + \chi/\gamma), \tag{10}$$

$$\Gamma^C = (\sigma_z^2/\alpha^2)[\chi/(\gamma^2 + \chi)] = (\Gamma^*)^C, \tag{11}$$

where $(\bar{\pi}_t)^C \equiv \tilde{\pi}_t + \gamma(\tilde{n} - \bar{n})/\chi$. Comparison of eqs. (9) and (4) reveals that the mean rate of CPI inflation is indeed higher under the cooperative regime than under the noncooperative regime. The intuitive explanation is exactly as discussed in section 5: wage setters anticipate that the two central banks will have stronger incentives to inflate in a regime where each can count on the other's cooperation, so that the benefits of inflation are not reduced by real exchange rate depreciation.

A comparison of eqs. (10) and (5) reveals that $|(dp_t)^C| > |(dp_t)^N|$. In the Nash equilibrium, the central banks allow the supply shock to affect employment more, and inflation less, than in the cooperative equilibrium.[16] It is easy to prove that the cooperative response to disturbances is superior, i.e. $\Gamma^C < \Gamma^N$:

Proof. Note that expressions (11) and (7) can be written in the same general form since $\chi/(\gamma^2 + \chi) = (\chi^2 + \gamma^2\chi)/(\gamma^2 + \chi)^2$. Differentiating the expression $(y^2 + y^2\chi)/(\gamma^2 + y)^2$ with respect to y yields $2\gamma^2(y - \chi)/(\gamma^2 + y)^{-3}$. Note that this derivative is strictly positive for $y > \chi$ (since $\chi > 0$), and note that $\chi' > \chi$. Q.E.D.

It is easy to generalize the foregoing analysis to the case where the two countries are identical except for their labor market distortions. One can then demonstrate that the country with the smaller labor market distortion may prefer the cooperative regime, while the other country would be better off under a noncooperative regime. (If a country had no labor market distortion, it would not have to worry about aggravating its inflation distortion, and thus would always prefer the cooperative regime regardless of the variance of the disturbances.)

While the result that a cooperative regime may produce higher expected inflation rates arises in a sensible way, it is not general. Suppose we alter the

---

[16]Canzoneri and Gray (1985) analyze a one-time supply disturbance and find that the cooperative response to this disturbance may call for either smaller or larger changes in the money supply than in the Nash equilibrium. In their framework, the authorities try to stabilize employment and money growth. The present framework may also yield the result that $|dp_t|^C < |dp_t^N|$ when the central banks adopt the money supply as an intermediate monetary target, along the lines discussed in Rogoff (1985).

central banks' objective functions to depend on employment and money supply growth (instead of employment and inflation); this type of monetary targeting objective function is used by Canzoneri and Gray (1985). When employment/monetary targeting objective functions are combined with the macro model of appendix A, the cooperative regime turns out to have a lower time-consistent inflation rate if, holding base wage rates constant, foreign money supply growth lowers domestic employment.[17] This will be the case provided the expenditure-switching effect of the real foreign currency depreciation (induced by an unanticipated foreign money supply increase) outweighs the expenditure-increasing effect of lower world real interest rates (assuming there is no wage indexation.) If instead the expenditure-increasing effects dominate, then the cooperative regime will be more inflationary. This ambiguity did not arise with the employment-inflation objective functions used in our earlier analysis, since joint money supply growth always produces a better employment/inflation trade-off than unilateral money growth.

8. Institutional designs for superior cooperative regimes

The possibility that the regime we have labeled 'cooperative' might be inferior to the 'non-cooperative' regime does not violate the basic tenets of game theory: the central banks are assumed to cooperate with each other, but not with private sector wage setters. Of course, if the central banks were able credibly to guarantee that they would not systematically try to raise employment, and would only use monetary policy to offset disturbances, then it would be possible to achieve a superior and truly cooperative outcome. (A still better cooperative equilibrium could be obtained if the two countries could eliminate their labor market distortions at low cost.) The present analysis does suggest cases in which government to government cooperation might lead to better institutional reforms. Suppose, for example, each country passed a binding law fixing the future path of its money supply except for prespecified responses to specific disturbances.[18] If the two countries design their monetary constitutions independently, the prespecified response to common supply disturbances might be Nash, whereas if they design their systems jointly, the prespecified response might be closer to the cooperative one.[19] The behavior of governments in other countries will, in general, be a

[17]Oudiz and Sachs (1985) provide an example in which cooperation between central banks eliminates their credibility problems with the private sector.

[18]Buiter (1981) specifies optimal contingent rules. There are, of course, many problems involved in designing an institutional framework in which to implement such rules. Rogoff (1985) and Canzoneri (1985) discuss institutional responses to the central bank's time-consistency problem in a closed economy context.

[19]McKinnon (1982) suggests a cooperative monetary reform. His specific proposal to fix the path of the world money supply would definitely be an improvement over money-supply targeting by individual countries in a world where the main source of disturbances is currency substitution.

consideration in evaluating any institutional response to the time-consistency problem discussed here. Thus, it should be clear that an optimally-designed cooperative regime is superior to any noncooperative scheme.

9. Conclusions

A regime in which governments conduct monetary policy independently may produce lower time-consistent inflation rates than a regime in which central banks cooperate; inter-governmental cooperation can exacerbate the central banks' credibility problems vis-à-vis the private sector. While the conditions under which cooperation leads to systematically higher inflation rates are quite plausible, we have also indicated an example where cooperation ameliorates the central banks' credibility problems. In either event, the cooperative response to unanticipated disturbances is always at least as good as the noncooperative response, in the sense of stabilizing employment and inflation around their mean market-determined values.

While the main result has been expressed in a rational expectations cum wage contracting model, it clearly can arise in models with alternative non-neutralities and different sources of time-consistency problems. Cooperation can be counterproductive, for example, in a flexible-price currency-substitution model, in which each central bank is trying to maximize seignorage. The key point is that it can be misleading to model the strategic interactions of two governments without also modeling the game between the governments and the private sector.

Appendix A: The underlying two-country macroeconomic model

Here we describe the two-country, two-good, rational expectations cum wage contracting model on which the results of the text are explicitly based. Unanticipated monetary policy can have real effects here because nominal wage contracts are negotiated a period in advance; these contracts are only partially indexed to the current-period consumer price level.[20] To facilitate algebraic manipulation, the technological and behavioral parameters in the two countries are constrained to be equal. Indeed, we will refer only to domestic variables and equations where discussion of their foreign counterparts is redundant.

A.1. Aggregate supply

The good produced by home-country firms differs from the good produced by foreign-country firms. But within each country, all firms have identical

---

[20]As Gray (1976) demonstrates, full price-level indexation is suboptimal in the presence of supply (productivity) shocks. Apart from its game-theoretic aspects, the model is quite similar to ones employed by Daniel (1981), Henderson and Waldo (1983), and Canzoneri and Gray (1985).

Cobb–Douglas production functions. Using lower case letters to denote logarithms, the aggregate production function can be written as

$$y = c_0 + \alpha \bar{k} + (1 - \alpha)n + z, \tag{12}$$

where y is output, $\bar{k}$ is the fixed capital stock, n is labor, c_0 is the constant term, and z is a serially uncorrelated aggregate productivity disturbance; $z \sim N(0, \sigma_z^2)$. The foreign country shares the same productivity disturbance, so that $z^* = z$. [Star (*) superscripts denote foreign-country variables.] Time subscripts are omitted where the meaning is obvious; throughout, all parameters are non-negative.

Firms hire labor until the marginal value product of labor equals the nominal wage rate, w:

$$c_0 + \log(1 - \alpha) + \alpha \bar{k} - \alpha n_d + z = w - p, \tag{13}$$

where p is the nominal price of the domestically-produced good, and n_d is aggregate labor demand. The notional labor supply curve is assumed inelastic (the results are not qualitatively affected when labor supply depends positively on the real wage):

$$n_s = \bar{n}. \tag{14}$$

To simplify algebra, $\bar{n}$ is set equal to $\bar{k} + (1/\alpha)[\log(1 - \alpha) + c_0]$, $\bar{n} = \bar{n}^*$ and $\bar{k} = \bar{k}^*$.

CPI-indexed wage contracts for period t are negotiated at the end of period $t - 1$. The base wage rate is $\bar{w}$ and the indexation parameter is β:

$$w = \bar{w} + \beta(p_I - \bar{w}), \quad 0 \leq \beta < 1, \tag{15}$$

$$p_I = 0.5p + 0.5(p^* + e), \tag{16}$$

where e is the (logarithm of the) exchange rate (the domestic currency price of foreign currency). The nature of the employment contract is that laborers agree to supply (ex post) whatever amount of labor is demanded by firms in period t, provided firms pay the negotiated wage. The actual levels of employment in period t are thus found by substituting the wage equation (15) into the labor demand equation (13):

$$n = \bar{n} + \gamma(p - \bar{w}) - \tau q + z/\alpha, \tag{17a}$$

$$n^* = \bar{n} + \gamma(p^* - \bar{w}^*) + \tau q + z/\alpha, \tag{17b}$$

where $\gamma \equiv (1 - \beta)/\alpha$, $\tau \equiv 0.5\beta/\alpha$, and

$$q = e + p^* - p. \tag{18}$$

(Note that q always appears with the opposite sign in the otherwise identical foreign-country equations.) As described in the text, wage setters choose $\bar{w}$ to minimize $E_{t-1}(n_t - \bar{n})^2$; thus $\bar{w} = E_{t-1}[p_t - 0.5\beta q_t/(1 - \beta)]$. The indexation parameter, β, is taken as given; see footnote 9 above.

Eqs. (12) and (17), together with the assumption that $-c_0 = \alpha \bar{k} + (1 - \alpha)\bar{n}$, imply that the aggregate supply equation can be written as

$$y_s = \theta(p - \bar{w}) - \kappa q + z/\alpha, \tag{19}$$

where $\theta \equiv (1 - \alpha)(1 - \beta)/\alpha$ and $\kappa \equiv 0.5(1 - \alpha)\beta/\alpha$.

A.2. Money and bond markets

Only domestic residents hold the domestic money and only foreign residents hold the foreign money. However, residents of both countries hold both domestic- and foreign-currency denominated bonds. The demand for real money balances in each country is a decreasing function of the nominal interest rate and an increasing function of real income:

$$m - p_I = -\lambda r + \phi(p + y - p_I) + v, \tag{20}$$

where m is the logarithm of the nominal money supply and v is the money market disturbance terms; $v \sim N(0, \sigma_v^2)$, and v and v^* are independent.

Domestic- and foreign-currency denominated bonds are perfect substitutes so that uncovered interest parity holds:[21]

$$E_t(e_{t+1}) - e_t = r_t - r_t^*. \tag{21}$$

Private agents are assumed to have full knowledge of the period t disturbances in making their portfolio and investment decisions.

A.3. Goods market demand

Demand for the good produced in each country is a decreasing function of its relative price, an increasing function of real income at home and abroad, and a decreasing function of the real interest rate:

$$y_d = \eta q - \delta(1 - 2\Delta)\{r - E_t[p_{I(t+1)}] + p_{It}\} + \Delta(p + y - p_I)$$
$$+ \Delta(p^* + y^* - p_I^*) + u(1 - 2\Delta) + x, \tag{22}$$

---

[21]There seems little harm in abstracting from the macroeconomic effects of sterilized intervention, since those effects appear to be extremely limited. See, for example, Rogoff (1984).

where $u \sim N(0, \sigma_u^2)$, $x \sim N(0, \sigma_x^2)$ and $\Delta < 0.5$. u is a common goods market demand disturbance and x represents a shift in demand from the foreign good to the home good. (u and δ are multiplied by $1 - 2\Delta$ as a convenient normalization.)

A.4. Solution of the model

To close the model, it is necessary to specify how wage setters and investors form expectations of future prices. The solution algorithm employed here involves first assuming and then proving that rational expectations are equivalent to static expectations for the rate of change of the exchange rate and for the home and foreign CPI inflation rates. [Note that eqs. (16) and (21) imply that $E_t(e_{t+1}) - e_t = \bar{\pi}_I - \bar{\pi}_I^*$.] By imposing the 'static expectations are rational' assumption, we can solve the model of eqs. (17)–(22) for q, p, p^*, p_I, p_I^*, n, and n^* as functions of $\bar{w}$, $\bar{w}^*$, $\bar{\pi}_I$, $\bar{\pi}_I^*$, z, u, x, v, and v^*. Then, in the text, we use the resulting partial derivatives [see eqs. (26) below] to solve for the time-consistent values of $\bar{w}$, $\bar{w}^*$, $\bar{\pi}_I$, $\bar{\pi}_I^*$, and $E_t(e_{t+1}) - e_t$. (These values depend, of course, on whether the central banks are engaged in a cooperative or noncooperative regime.) The analysis of the text confirms that time-consistent expectations for exchange rate depreciation and CPI inflation rates are indeed static (in the absence of regime shifts).

Taking $t-1$ expectations across eqs. (19) and (22) (together with their foreign counterparts) and recalling that wage setters set $\bar{w} = E_{t-1}[p_t - 0.5\beta q_t/(1-\beta)]$, one can solve for

$$E_{t-1}(q_t) = 0 = \bar{w} - E_{t-1}(p_t), \tag{23}$$

$$E_{t-1}(r - \bar{\pi}_I) = E_{t-1}(y_t) = 0, \tag{24}$$

$$E_{t-1}(m_t) = \bar{w} - \lambda \bar{\pi}_I. \tag{25}$$

Given our expectational assumptions, the solutions for q, p, p_I, and n are (solutions for p^*, p_I^* and n^* are symmetric):

$$q = v[(m - \bar{w} + \lambda\bar{\pi}_I - v) - (m^* - \bar{w}^* + \lambda\bar{\pi}_I^* - v^*) - 2(\phi + 1/\theta)x], \tag{26a}$$

$$p = \bar{w} + (vS + H)(m - \bar{w} + \lambda\bar{\pi}_I - v) - vS(m^* - w^* + \lambda\bar{\pi}_I^* - v^*)$$
$$+ \lambda H u/\delta - H(\phi + \lambda/\delta)z/\alpha + [\lambda H/\delta - 2vS(\phi + 1/\theta)]x, \tag{26b}$$

$$p_I = \bar{w} + (vJ + H)(m - \bar{w} + \lambda\bar{\pi}_I - v) - vJ(m^* - \bar{w}^* + \lambda\bar{\pi}_I^* - v^*)$$
$$+ \lambda H u/\delta - H(\phi + \lambda/\delta)z/\alpha + [H\lambda/\delta - 2vJ(\phi + 1/\theta)]x, \tag{26c}$$

$$n = \bar{n} + (Q + Rv)(m - \bar{w} + \lambda\bar{\pi}_I - v) - Rv(m^* - \bar{w}^* + \lambda\bar{\pi}_I^* - v^*)$$

$$+ Q\lambda u/\delta + Q[-\phi - \lambda/\delta + 1/(1-\beta)]z + [Q\lambda/\delta - 2Rv(\phi + 1/\theta)]x,$$

(26d)

where

$$v \equiv [2(\eta + \kappa)/\theta + 2\phi\eta + (1-\phi)]^{-1} > 0, \ H \equiv (1 + \theta\lambda/\delta + \phi\theta)^{-1} > 0,$$

$$S \equiv H[\kappa\phi - (1-\phi)/2 + \lambda(\kappa + \eta)/\delta] \gtreqless 0,$$

$$J \equiv H\{0.5\phi[(1-\alpha)/\alpha + 1] + \lambda/\delta[0.5(1-\alpha)/\alpha + \eta]\} > 0,$$

$$Q \equiv [\phi(1-\alpha) + \lambda(1+\alpha)/\delta + \alpha/(1-\beta)]^{-1} > 0,$$

$$R \equiv Q\{0.5[\phi - 1/(1-\beta)] + \lambda\eta/\delta\} \gtreqless 0.$$

Using eqs. (26), and imposing the assumption that the income elasticity of money demand $\phi \leqq 1$, one can determine the sign of the following partial derivatives (holding $\bar{w}$, $\bar{w}^*$, $\bar{\pi}_I$, and $\bar{\pi}_I^*$ constant):

$$\partial q/\partial m, \ \partial p/\partial m, \ \partial p_I/\partial m, \ \partial n/\partial m, \ \partial p/\partial u, \ \partial p_I/\partial u, \ \partial n/\partial u > 0;$$

$$\partial n/\partial x \geqq 0;$$

$$\partial p_I/\partial x, \ \partial q/\partial x, \ \partial p_I/\partial m^*, \ \partial p_I/\partial z, \ \partial p/\partial z < 0.$$

The partial derivatives $\partial p/\partial x$, $\partial p/\partial m^*$, $\partial n/\partial m^*$, and $\partial n/\partial z$, may be positive or negative. For example, when there is no wage indexation a foreign money supply shock will raise or lower domestic output and employment, depending on whether the expenditure-switching effect of the real appreciation of the domestic currency outweighs the expenditure-increasing effect of lower world real interest rates.[22] Wage indexation increases the possibility that the foreign money supply shock will raise domestic employment.

In the text, we require knowledge of $\Psi \equiv (\partial q/\partial m)/(\partial p/\partial m)$, holding m^*, $\bar{w}$, $\bar{w}^*$, $\bar{\pi}_I^*$, and $\bar{\pi}_I^*$ constant. One can easily demonstrate, using (26), that $\Psi > 0$.

Appendix B: Relative shifts in demand

Throughout the text, shifts in the demand for each country's good are assumed to be perfectly positively correlated. This assumption is analytically

[22]Daniel (1981) discusses these transmission channels, as do Canzoneri and Gray (1985). If $\beta = 0$, so that there is no wage indexation, and if the income elasticity of money demand, ϕ, equals one, then $\partial p/\partial m^*$, $\partial n/\partial m^* < 0$. If $\beta > 0$, then $\partial n/\partial m^*$ may be positive even if $\phi = 1$.

convenient because it turns out to imply that the real exchange rate q does not move in either the Nash or the symmetric cooperative equilibrium. To solve the model when there are relative shifts in the demand for the two goods (denoted by x), use eqs. (26) to substitute into eqs. (1) for $n - \bar{n}$ and $\bar{\pi}_I$:

$$\Lambda = (a_1 dm + a_2 dm^* + a_3 x + \bar{n} - \tilde{n})^2$$

$$+ \chi(b_1 dm + b_2 dm^* + b_3 x + \bar{w} - p_{t-1} - \tilde{\pi})^2, \tag{27}$$

where $dm \equiv m - \bar{w} + \lambda\bar{\pi} - v$, $dm^* \equiv m^* - \bar{w}^* + \lambda\pi_I^* - v^*$, and the coefficients a_i and b_i are the same as in (26). (As a minor expositional convenience, we are abstracting from the common disturbances u and z. Again, the equation for Λ^* is symmetric, except that x enters with opposite sign.) In the Nash equilibrium, $\partial\Lambda/\partial dm = 0 = \partial\Lambda^*/\partial dm^*$. The procedure for finding $\bar{w}^N$ and $(\bar{w}^*)^N$ is the same as in the text, and the resulting equations are the same as eqs. (4). Together, eqs. (4) and (27) (with its foreign counterpart) imply

$$dm^N = -(a_1 a_3 + \chi b_1 b_3) x / [a_1(a_1 - a_2) + \chi b_1(b_1 - b_2)] = -(dm^*)^N, \tag{28}$$

where from eqs. (26), $a_1(a_1 - a_2) + \chi b_1(b_1 - b_3) > 0$, but $a_1 a_3 + \chi b_1 b_3 \gtrless 0$. A positive x represents a shift in world demand from the foreign good to the home good; home CPI inflation falls and home employment rises. In the Nash equilibrium, the home country may respond to unanticipated relative demand shifts with either positive or negative unanticipated money growth, depending (in part) on χ, the relative weight placed on inflation deviations versus employment deviations.

Provided that the responses to relative demand shifts are symmetric, the cooperative $\bar{w}^C$ and $(\bar{w}^*)^C$ are as in the text [eqs. (9)], and

$$dm^C = -[(a_1 - a_2)a_3 + \chi(b_1 - b_2)b_3]x / [(a_1 - a_2)^2 + \chi(b_1 - b_2)^2]$$

$$= -(dm^*)^C. \tag{29}$$

Since $b_2 < 0$ and $a_2 \gtrless 0$, it is perfectly possible that dm^C and dm^N are actually of opposite signs.

References

Barro, Robert J. and David B. Gordon, 1983a, A positive theory of monetary policy in a natural-rate model, Journal of Political Economy 91, August, 589–610.

Barro, Robert J. and David B. Gordon, 1983b, Rules, discretion and reputation in a model of monetary policy, Journal of Monetary Economics 12, July, 101–121.

Buiter, Willem H., 1981, The superiority of contingent rules over fixed rules in models with rational expectations, Economic Journal 91, September, 647–670.

Canzoneri, Matthew B., 1985, Monetary policy games and the role of private information, American Economic Review, forthcoming.

Canzoneri, Matthew B. and Jo Anna Gray, 1985, Monetary policy games and the consequences of non-cooperative behavior, International Economic Review, forthcoming.

Canzoneri, Matthew B., Dale W. Henderson and Kenneth Rogoff, 1983, The information content of the interest rate and optimal monetary policy, Quarterly Journal of Economics 98, November, 545–566.

Carlozzi, Nicholas and John B. Taylor, 1984, International capital mobility and the coordination of monetary rules, in: J. Bhandari, ed., Exchange rate management under uncertainty (MIT Press, Cambridge).

Cooper, Richard N., 1969, Macroeconomic policy adjustment in interdependent economies, Quarterly Journal of Economics 83, February, 1–24.

Daniel, Betty C., 1981, The international transmission of economic disturbances under flexible exchange rates, International Economic Review 22, October, 491–509.

Gray, Jo Anna, 1976, Wage indexation: A macroeconomic approach, Journal of Monetary Economics 2, April, 221–235.

Hamada, Koichi, 1976, A strategic analysis of monetary interdependence, Journal of Political Economy 84, August, 667–700.

Henderson, Dale W., 1984, Exchange market intervention operations: Their role in financial policy and their effects, in: J.F.O. Bilson and R.C. Marston, eds., Exchange rate theory and practice (University of Chicago Press, Chicago).

Henderson, Dale W. and Douglas Waldo, 1983, Reserve requirements on Euro-currency deposits: Implications for the stabilization of real outputs, in: J.S. Bhandari and B. Putnam, eds., Economic interdependence and flexible exchange rate (MIT Press, Cambridge).

Jones, Michael, 1982, Automatic output stability and the exchange rate arrangement: A multi-country analysis, Review of Economic Studies 89, January, 91–107.

Jones, Michael, 1983, International liquidity: A welfare analysis, Quarterly Journal of Economics 98, February, 1–23.

Kydland, Finn E. and Edward C. Prescott, 1977, Rules rather than indiscretion: The inconsistency of optimal plans, Journal of Political Economy 85, June, 473–492.

Macedo, Jorge Braga de, 1983, Policy interdependence under flexible exchange rates, xeroxed (Princeton University, Princeton).

McKinnon, Ronald I., 1982, Currency substitution and instability in the world dollar standard, American Economic Review 72, June, 320–348.

Miller, Marcus and Mark Salmon, 1983, Dynamic games and the time inconsistency of optimal policy in open economies, xeroxed (University of Warwick, U.K.).

Oudiz, Gilles and Jeffrey Sachs, 1985, International policy coordination in dynamic macro-economic models, in: W.H. Buiter and R.C. Marston, eds., International economic policy coordination (Cambridge University Press).

Phelps, Edmund S., 1967, Phillips curves, expectations of inflation and optimal unemployment over time, Economica 34, August, 254–281.

Phelps, Edmund S., 1973, Inflation in the theory of public finance, Swedish Journal of Economics 75, January/March, 68–82.

Rogoff, Kenneth, 1984, On the effects of sterilized intervention: An analysis of weekly data, Journal of Monetary Economics 13, September, 133–150.

Rogoff, Kenneth, 1985, The optimal degree of commitment to an intermediate monetary target, Quarterly Journal of Economics, forthcoming.

Sachs, Jeffrey, 1983, International policy coordination in a dynamic macroeconomic model, National Bureau of Economic Research Working Paper No. 1166 (Cambridge, MA).

Sargent, Thomas J., 1979, Macroeconomic theory (Academic Press, New York).

Vaubel, Roland, 1983, Coordination or competition among national macroeconomic policies? in: F. Machlup et al., eds., Reflections on a troubled world economy (Macmillan, London).

Floating Exchange Rates
and the Need for Surveillance

Jacques R. Artus and Andrew D. Crockett

Introduction

The move from fixed to more flexible exchange rates among major currencies has been rapid and widespread in recent years, but it has fallen far short of a complete shift to a freely floating exchange-rate regime. Rate-management policies continue to play a major role. Such policies may involve intervention by the central bank in the foreign-exchange market, official or quasi-official borrowing or lending, various forms of controls on foreign transactions and payments, monetary-policy measures, and statements by public officials on the appropriateness of prevailing rates. The major issue at the moment is the extent to which national authorities should use such management policies rather than rely on the free play of market forces for the determination of their exchange rate. This issue is central to the definition of the duties and responsibilities of national authorities and of the International Monetary Fund in a world of floating exchange rates.

Two major questions in the current debate relate to the likely behavior of exchange rates in the absence of rate management and to the role of exchange-rate flexibility in the international adjustment process. An important argument for rate management is that the free play of market forces would lead in the short run to an inappropriate rate, i.e., a rate that has been unduly influenced by temporary factors of a cyclical or speculative nature and therefore diverges significantly from some longer-run equilibrium value corresponding to underlying economic conditions.[1] A second argument for rate management is that exchange-rate flexibility is not a very effective means of reducing or eliminating payments dis-

[1] An implicit assumption here is that market forces cannot produce an inappropriate rate in the longer run. This means that political and economic preferences reflected in permanent measures affecting payments flows (e.g., tariffs, capital controls, and fiscal incentives) are taken as given in the determination of the longer-run equilibrium rate. Also, in what follows, the long-run equilibrium rate should be seen as an analytical concept referring to the rate that would clear the exchange market in the absence of temporary factors and once any adjustment lags have worked themselves out, given foreseeable underlying price and economic conditions. Since such conditions are uncertain and may change rapidly, the long-run equilibrium rate is obviously not a precise value and will change whenever the foreseeable conditions that it reflects are modified.

Reprinted from "Floating Exchange Rates and the Need for Surveillance—Essays in International Finance No. 127, May 1978," pp. 1–38, with permission of Princeton University Press, Princeton, Copyright 1978.

equilibrium and may have harmful consequences for domestic economic objectives, in particular the objective of price stability. Exchange-rate movements, in this argument, lead only to offsetting local-currency price changes and result in a vicious circle of depreciation/inflation or appreciation/deflation.

Even if market forces often led to an inappropriate rate or if exchange-rate flexibility was not very effective in bringing about international adjustment, there still might not be a case for an active policy. Such a policy might be ineffective, the potential for policy errors might be large, the cost of the policy measures might be high, and finally the welfare costs of the inappropriate rate might be low.

These issues have obvious implications for the development of effective international surveillance over countries' exchange-rate policies. If the free play of market forces can be presumed to result in exchange rates that contribute to the smooth working of the international adjustment process, the interest of the international community can concentrate on cases involving deliberate rate management; the concern will be whether policy measures affecting the exchange rate are justifiable in the context of a country's overall economic strategy, and whether such measures place undue burden on other members. If, on the other hand, such a presumption about market-determined rates cannot be made, the international community will have a legitimate interest also in the policies of countries that do not pursue an active exchange-rate policy, and ultimately an assessment of whether an active or inactive policy is justified will have to be made.

This essay begins by discussing a number of important issues related to the short-term variability of exchange rates: the role played by exchange-rate risk and the risk preferences of market participants, the effects of various kinds of monetary measures, the role of exchange-rate expectations, and the costs of short-run exchange-rate variations. We conclude that the free play of market forces may lead to inappropriate rates in periods of unstable underlying economic conditions, and that such rates, if they persist, can impose significant economic costs. Inappropriate rates are less likely to result, however, if the underlying economic conditions are stable and if well-developed capital markets exist without strict capital controls.

We go on to discuss issues related to the role of exchange rates in eliminating payments disequilibria. While recognizing that there is solid empirical evidence for large feedbacks from exchange-rate movements to domestic wages and prices, we conclude that there is most often no realistic alternative to the use of exchange-rate flexibility for the elimination of protracted imbalances. While exchange-rate flexibility is a necessary part of the adjustment process, however, it is not a substitute for domestic stabilization policies.

In the final section of the essay, we consider the implications of these judgments for the desirability of various forms of rate-management policies and for the development of effective international surveillance over countries' exchange-rate policies. We conclude that no simple set of rules can adequately cover the various exchange-market circumstances that are likely to arise. There will be occasions when rate management is desirable to counter short-term disturbances in the exchange markets and promote smooth balance-of-payments adjustment. There are risks, however, that deliberate management of the rate will be used to meet short-term economic goals at the expense of underlying adjustment. Effective surveillance of exchange-rate policies cannot therefore rely on a set of mechanical guidelines but must take account of the special circumstances of each individual case. In building experience with operating the new, more flexible system, the International Monetary Fund can be expected to accumulate a body of "case law" that will enable member countries to form a clearer impression of the kind of behavior most conducive to effective international adjustment.

Issues Related to the Short-Run Variability of Exchange Rates

During the first few years of floating exchange rates among the major industrialized countries, short-run exchange-rate movements have been far greater than the corresponding movements in domestic price levels. This is illustrated in Figure 1 by comparing deviations of exchange rates and local-currency consumer price indices from their corresponding thirteen-month centered moving averages. (In this chart, the U.S. dollar and the U.S. domestic price level are used as reference points.) This experience suggests two questions: (1) What are the reasons for the short-run variability of exchange rates? And (2) are there significant economic costs when exchange rates fluctuate widely over the short run? Answering these questions requires, first, a theoretical digression on the nature of the process of exchange-rate determination. This digression provides the context for a discussion of the effects of exchange-rate risk, monetary-policy measures, and speculative excesses on the short-run variability of the exchange rate. The concluding part of the section assesses the costs of exchange-rate variability.

FIGURE 1

Short-Run Variability in Exchange Rates and Relative Consumer Prices

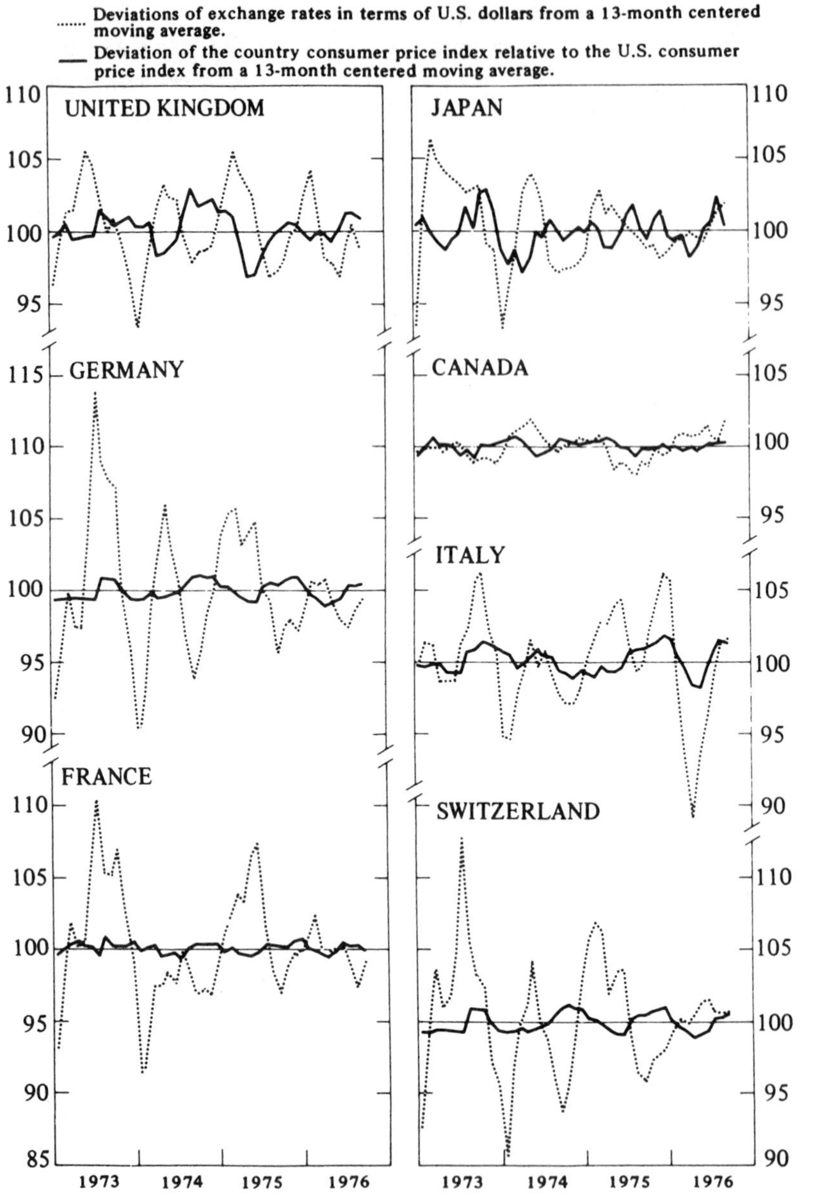

.... Deviations of exchange rates in terms of U.S. dollars from a 13-month centered moving average.
___ Deviation of the country consumer price index relative to the U.S. consumer price index from a 13-month centered moving average.
UNITED KINGDOM
JAPAN
GERMANY
CANADA
ITALY
FRANCE
SWITZERLAND
110
105
100
95
115
90
85
1973
1974
1975
1976

A Simple Analytical Framework

In recent years, a broad measure of support has developed, at least among academic economists, for the asset-market theory of exchange-rate determination. The essence of this approach is to view the exchange rate as an asset price—the relative price at which the stock of money, bonds, and other financial and real assets of a country will be willingly held by domestic and foreign asset holders. The asset-market approach does not, of course, neglect the requirement that exchange rates must balance the current demand for a currency with the current supply (i.e., flow equilibrium), but it highlights the role played in the determination of current (flow) demand and supply by factors affecting the relative desired stocks of domestic and foreign assets.

The asset-market approach has its main relevance for countries with well-developed capital and money markets, where exchange controls are free enough to permit substantial arbitrage between domestic and foreign assets. In countries where the possibility of such arbitrage is limited or nonexistent, the exchange rate is determined by supply and demand in goods markets and by the amount of intervention undertaken by the authorities. For other countries, the asset-market approach has two major advantages. First, it draws attention to the multiplicity of factors affecting the exchange-rate-determination process. Asset holders continuously adjust or attempt to adjust the composition of their portfolios to reflect expected rates of return, adjusted for degrees of risk, on various domestic and foreign assets. Variability in the factors that influence expected rates of return or relative risk will tend to result in variability in exchange rates.

A second advantage of the asset-market approach is that it draws attention to the predominant role of financial factors in the short run. New unexpected financial developments leading to desired portfolio readjustments occur continuously, and they may at times cause sharp exchange-rate changes. In contrast, changes in current-account positions (apart from their effect on expectations) play a more subdued role in the short run, both because prices in goods markets usually change more gradually and because longer lags operate in the adjustment of trade and invisible flows to price changes. Also, expectational factors play a more limited role in determining trade and service flows. Thus, over any short period the potential demand for a currency resulting from changes in desired *stocks* of financial assets will be large relative to the *flow* demand arising from current balance-of-payments transactions and will be more important in determining the short-run equilibrium value of the exchange rate.

Relative prices of goods and of factors of production are dominant factors in exchange-rate determination in the long run, but the usefulness of the asset-market approach is much greater when the focus of the analysis is on the short run. A brief review of this approach will provide an analytical framework for discussing the various issues related to the short-run variability of exchange rates. (A more extensive review of this approach and its implications for the analysis of exchange-rate variability can be found in Schadler, 1977, and Dornbusch and Krugman, 1976.)

The foreign demand (A') for assets denominated in the currency of a given country, net of the demand for foreign assets by the country's residents, can be assumed to be determined by the expected yield on that country's assets relative to the expected yield on assets denominated in other currencies.[2] The expected relative yield reflects the interest-rate differential and the expected exchange-rate change. The elasticity of demand for domestic-currency assets with respect to their expected relative yield will depend on the degree of substitutability between assets denominated in the domestic currency and assets denominated in foreign currencies. Exchange-rate risks and the risk preferences of speculators, which are discussed in more detail below, will be the major determinants of this substitutability.

In terms of flow demand, the change in A' occurring during a given period will be related to changes in the interest-rate differential and in the expected exchange-rate appreciation or depreciation. At the same time, the change in A', which is nothing other than the net balance on private capital flows, will have to be equal *ex post* to the sum of the balance on current transactions, official capital flows, and the net amount of intervention by the monetary authorities in the exchange market.

We have dwelt at some length on the analytical framework of the asset-market approach because it is the key to understanding the potential for exchange markets to produce in the short run exchange rates that are inconsistent with effective adjustment in the longer run. The factors that establish a stock equilibrium in financial markets are not necessarily consistent with those that would produce continuing flow equilibrium in goods markets. In particular, stock equilibrium may be influenced by expectational and risk-aversion factors not relevant to transactions on current account. And because the lags that govern the response of current-account flows to changes in their underlying determinants are generally presumed to be longer than those for the capital account, the exchange rate may move to a level which, while clearing the foreign-

---

[2] Foreign currencies are all grouped together here for purposes of exposition.

exchange market in the short term, is not consistent with continuing equilibrium in the longer term. In such cases, it may be desirable for the authorities to take action which keeps the exchange rate at (or moves it to) a level consistent with longer-term equilibrium. The following sections therefore examine those factors which may give rise to differences between the equilibrium short-term rate that is dominated by asset-market developments and the rate that would result in payments equilibrium over a longer-term time horizon.

Exchange-Rate Risk

The degree of exchange-rate risk and the risk preferences of partici-pants in the foreign-exchange markets influence significantly the behavior of exchange rates in the short term. Financial assets denominated in different currencies and carrying the same yield would be perfect sub-stitutes if speculators were risk neutral.[3] In this case, temporary disturb-ances in the goods markets or temporary changes in "autonomous" capital flows would be rapidly offset by speculative capital flows, with little or no cost in terms of exchange-rate variations.[4] Even substantial capital flows resulting from the speculative activity of a significant number of mis-informed speculators would be offset by the action of the better-informed speculators.

Even if there were variations in the degree of risk attached to par-ticular currencies, say because of changes in the underlying economic and political conditions in the issuing countries, these would not in them-selves be a source of exchange-rate change if speculators were risk neutral. Under such circumstances, it would also be impossible for the authorities to influence their exchange rate by intervening in the foreign-exchange market while offsetting the effect of this policy on the monetary base. Perfect asset substitution implies that excess money creation in one country immediately creates an incentive for capital outflows and pushes the exchange rate down to a point where the higher money stock is willingly held. Thus, the authorities can have a target for the money

[3] Risk neutrality means that speculators would make decisions on whether to acquire or dispose of assets denominated in certain currencies entirely on the basis of the mean values of their expected relative yields (interest plus capital-value change). They would not be influenced by any change in the overall degree of risk (i.e., variance of the expected yield) of their portfolio that such decisions might cause either because of differences in the degrees of risk attached to assets denomi-nated in different currencies or because of diversification considerations.

[4] Examples of changes in "autonomous" capital flows would include, in the present context, bulky overseas direct investments related, say, to the discovery of a new oil field, a large bond issue in the Eurodollar market, or a loan to a foreign government.

supply or for the exchange rate, but not both. Imperfect asset substitution opens the way for exchange-rate variations caused by temporary changes in trade flows or autonomous capital flows, or by the action of misinformed speculators; at the same time, it permits, within limits, an independent monetary policy and provides justification for an active policy of intervention by the central bank in the foreign-exchange market.

Early arguments in favor of a flexible-exchange-rate regime (see, e.g., Friedman, 1953, and Sohmen, 1961) assumed that benign speculators with a firm view of where the equilibrium value of the exchange rate lay and unlimited supplies of funds would ensure the short-run stability of the exchange rate. A few years' experience with floating exchange rates has, however, led to a re-examination of the importance of exchange-rate risk and its effect on the degree of substitution between various currencies.

Essentially, currency risk is related to the perceived likelihood that the exchange rate will vary in an unpredictable way during the period a currency is held. One reason for such uncertainty is to be found in the "thinness" of exchange markets for many currencies, a characteristic that is often the result of exchange restrictions. Even with large markets, currencies of countries with unstable underlying political or economic conditions are likely to be considered particularly risky. Variations in their rate may be dominated by political factors rather than relative prices or other predictable economic variables, and the risk of exchange controls is always present. Since the depth of exchange markets and surrounding economic and political conditions vary among countries, it seems likely that perceived risk will differ considerably between currencies.

As to the risk preferences of banks and other large institutional market participants, there is a growing body of evidence (see, e.g., Mc-Kinnon, forthcoming) which suggests that they are very much risk averters as far as foreign-exchange operations are concerned. Strict legal and regulatory constraints have been imposed on the speculative activity of commercial banks in many countries. In addition to such constraints, difficulties encountered by a number of financial institutions as a result of their foreign-currency dealings have led banks to shy away from taking substantial net open positions in foreign currencies. Oil exporters and multinational corporations tend also to have a "defensive" policy; they are mainly searching for a stable haven for their funds. (Corporations or other transactors with operations in several countries may, of course, have a need to maintain cash balances and other financial assets denominated in various currencies to finance their worldwide operations.

This in itself does not involve risk. The multinational corporation takes risks when it speculates by reallocating its portfolio away from the equilibrium position corresponding to its normal disbursement needs. An "open position" must be understood as a deviation from the portfolio allocation corresponding to normal disbursement needs.)

Perhaps a more important reason why risk aversion can lead to exchange-rate variability is that the willingness of transactors to take additional risks is likely to decrease with their exposure in particular currencies. A small expectation of gain may be sufficient for a multinational corporation to undertake a minor reallocation in its portfolio of liquid assets, but the profit prospects might have to be much greater and more certain to induce it to accept the risk of a large open position. Except in the case where the multinational corporation is betting against a fixed rate that is clearly out of line with underlying factors, it is unlikely that it would be willing to accept a large open position. The degree of currency substitutability may thus be quite low in many cases.

Another aspect of currency substitution is that the smooth working of the adjustment mechanism requires market transactors to take open positions in "weak" currencies. It is countries with weak balances of payments that need to attract a net capital inflow, and the providers of these funds naturally ask themselves what consequences balance-of-payments adjustment will have for the value of their investment. Although an exchange-rate depreciation may appear sufficient to restore external balance, foreign holders may still be reluctant to acquire the currency if they fear that the depreciation might set off a round of domestic inflation or might be perceived as inadequate by other participants in the foreign-exchange market. Further, countries with weak balances of payments also often happen to be countries with unstable underlying economic and political conditions. The cumulative influence of all these factors may lead many transactors to consider investment in assets denominated in certain currencies as "unsuitable" in the same way that they exclude from consideration certain low-quality shares or bonds regardless of yield.

Risk aversion may therefore cause exchange rates to depart from what would be an appropriate level for longer-run equilibrium. This would be particularly likely when there is a large disturbance in trade flows. When such a disturbance occurs (for example, the oil-price increase of late 1973), it is not to be expected that current-account positions will quickly adapt to a balance financed by sustainable capital flows. Additional capital flows are needed during a transitional period while adjustment is taking place. This means that foreign residents must be prepared to take open positions in the currencies of deficit countries. If this is difficult to do

because markets are thin or unattractive or because of the risks involved
in any open position, there is a danger that exchange rates will depreciate
by more than is necessary to secure the needed adjustment in the current
account.

In the case of the oil-price increase of late 1973, countries with large oil
deficits and small financial markets might not have been able to attract
capital on a sufficient scale to maintain an exchange-rate appropriate to
longer-run adjustment. In such a situation, intervention by central banks
financed from reserves or from compensatory official borrowing can have
a key role to play while gradual adjustment takes place in goods markets.
More generally, countries with narrow financial markets may find it
necessary to intervene in the exchange market to offset the effects of
cyclical and other temporary variations in their export receipts and import payments.

Monetary Policies and Exchange Rates

Another way in which exchange rates can be pushed away from their
longer-run equilibrium value is through the response of exchange markets
to unexpected monetary measures, and the resultant shifts in interest
differentials. It is, of course, not surprising that changes in interest differentials should have an influence on exchange rates. What is less well
understood is why relatively small monetary disturbances have in recent
years sometimes been accompanied by disproportionately large exchange-
rate changes. (For an empirical study of the effects of monetary disturbances on the U.S. dollar/deutsche mark rate, see Artus, 1976.) An
explanation that is sometimes advanced to explain these disproportionately large exchange-rate movements is based on the bandwagon hypothesis: the change in the interest-rate differential caused by the
monetary shock leads initially to a small change in the exchange rate;
speculators project further exchange-rate movements in the same direction and act on these projections; their action brings about further
exchange-rate movements. This explanation, as it is usually presented,
implies irrational market behavior. There is, however, an alternative explanation that attributes greater rationality to speculators and is intuitively more appealing. It focuses on the relation between monetary
measures and expected price changes, and it also draws attention to the
effects of monetary measures on nominal interest rates and on portfolio
composition.

For analytical purposes, a discretionary change in monetary policy,
defined as a discretionary change in the money stock, can be viewed as
affecting speculators' expectations in one of three possible ways: it may

be seen as a transitory development, perhaps of a countercyclical nature, that will subsequently be reversed; it may be seen as a one-step change in the money stock that will not be reversed but will not change the future rate of growth of the monetary aggregates; or it may be seen as presaging a more permanent change in monetary growth rates.

If speculators view a change in monetary policy as a temporary measure that will later be reversed, they will have no reason to change their expectations as to the long-run value of the exchange rate. If we ignore for the moment the effect of the policy change on interest differentials, there is no reason to expect such a development to lead to a significant change in the current exchange rate. On the other hand, changes in monetary policies that are viewed by market participants as probably leading to permanent changes in prices can be expected to have a very different effect on the exchange rate. If there is no reason to expect that a 5 per cent increase in the money supply will be reversed at a later stage, market participants will be likely to consider that the long-run equilibrium value of the exchange rate has fallen by about 5 per cent. This fall will reflect the widespread belief that in the long run both the quantity theory of money and the purchasing-power-parity theory hold. Under these circumstances, the spot rate will fall by something close to 5 per cent after the implementation or announcement of the policy change. If the policy change is interpreted by market participants as a sign that the authorities are "giving up" in the fight against inflation and that further accommodating increases in the money supply will take place, the rate may fall by even more.

The cases considered above are illustrative only and are therefore somewhat unrealistic. The argument, however, strongly suggests that it is the effect of monetary-policy measures on expectations that determines the size of the exchange-rate change in the short run. And expectations are more likely to be volatile when domestic underlying economic conditions are unstable, leading to uncertainty about the long-run policy intentions of the authorities. During periods of rapid inflation, monetary-policy changes are likely to be interpreted mainly in relation to the fight against inflation. In such circumstances, policy measures are much less likely to be viewed as purely temporary events without any long-run implications as to prices. In countries with stable conditions, on the other hand, there is less reason to expect countercyclical measures to cause significant exchange-rate movements. Price and exchange-rate expectations would be more stable under such conditions, and in any event monetary-policy changes would probably be smaller.

The effects of movements in the money supply on prices do not come through at once. In the short term, changes in interest rates are more likely to equilibrate the supply and demand for money (although this effect itself depends on how far the inflationary consequences of monetary changes are anticipated). Any change in the interest rate will affect the relative attractiveness of domestic bonds versus foreign bonds; therefore, the spot rate will initially have to move away from the expected longer-run equilibrium level by an amount sufficient to offset the interest-rate differential between domestic and foreign bonds. (For a discussion of this effect, see Dornbusch, 1976.) For example, if the 5 per cent increase in money supply considered above leads to a fall in domestic (real) interest rates in addition to the 5 per cent fall in the longer-run equilibrium value of the spot exchange rate, then the spot rate would fall initially by 5 per cent *plus* an amount that offsets the lower interest rate.[5] The "overshooting" effect is a manifestation of the phenomenon of differences in the speed of adjustment to equilibrium—in this case between the money market and the goods market. The more rapidly domestic prices adjust to the higher money supply and attendant fall in the exchange rate, the more transitory will be the effects of monetary-policy changes on interest rates and the shorter will be the period during which the actual exchange rate differs from its longer-run equilibrium value.

For many years, one of the main attractions of a flexible-exchange-rate system has been assumed to lie in the independence it gives to national monetary authorities. In a formal sense, this occurs because, in the absence of exchange-market intervention, the rate of growth of the monetary aggregates is approximately equal to the domestic credit creation that is directly under the control of the monetary authorities. Hence, the thrust of monetary policy cannot be offset by inflows or outflows of reserves.

The kind of monetary independence allowed for by a flexible-exchange-rate system has, however, been found in recent years to be less beneficial than expected, at least for high-inflation countries, and also possibly to have adverse consequences for the international community at large. Considering first the long-run aspects, it is certainly true that a flexible-exchange-rate system permits a country to "choose" a long-run inflation rate that diverges from the world rate of inflation, since it allows the country to control the rate of growth of its monetary aggregates. If

---

[5] This effect will normally be small. For example, a 1 percentage point fall in the interest-rate differential (at an annual rate) on three-month deposits might cause a fall of about one-fourth of 1 per cent in the exchange rate if the fall in the rate was expected to last three months; the fall of the exchange rate would be about 1 per cent if the fall in the interest rate was expected to last one year, 2 per cent if the fall in the interest rate was expected to last two years, etc.

countries faced a long-run tradeoff between output and inflation and had diverging preferences for inflation rates, the possibility for each country to choose its inflation rate would be an important advantage for all. It is now recognized, however, that in most countries such a tradeoff does not really exist in the long run; any advantage in terms of real output from having a higher-than-average rate of inflation is likely to be short-term in nature. Thus, the only long-run advantage arising from monetary independence may be that countries that are willing and able to maintain lower-than-average rates of inflation do not see their efforts frustrated by inflows of reserves pushing up the money supply.

In the short run, monetary independence may tend to increase the effectiveness of discretionary policy measures, but sometimes to the detriment of other countries. The possibility of using monetary-policy measures to affect real domestic demand is enhanced by the greater degree of control the monetary authorities have over their monetary aggregates. Of course, under a flexible-exchange-rate regime, changes in monetary policy are more quickly translated into price-level effects via the inflationary or deflationary consequences of exchange-rate movements. To the extent that prices adapt more quickly under floating rates to changes in monetary policy, real interest rates are likely to move by less in response to changes in the money supply. Even under a floating-exchange-rate regime, however, price adjustment will not be instantaneous. More important, monetary-policy measures may be quite effective in the short run in achieving real output and price goals in a floating-rate regime because of their effects on the exchange rate. It does seem to be the case that, in the short run, exchange rates are quite sensitive to interest-rate differentials created by differences in monetary policies among countries. It may therefore be tempting for countries to use this mechanism to a greater extent than is warranted in the context of balance-of-payments adjustment needs. A loosening of domestic monetary policy may drive the exchange rate down to levels where trading partners have a legitimate fear that the country concerned is exporting unemployment. Conversely, if a shift in policy toward restraint results in an exaggerated upward movement in the rate, trading partners may be concerned about the inflationary consequences for them.

These fears point to the desirability of pursuing stable monetary policies clearly related to the medium-term needs of the country concerned. They also lend support to the suggestion, adopted by a number of major countries, that market participants should receive guidance (through the establishment of medium-term monetary objectives) on how to adapt their expectations in the light of current developments in the monetary aggregates.

The Danger of Speculative Excesses

So far, we have considered ways in which market participants, acting perfectly rationally given the information available to them and their own preferences regarding risk, can move exchange rates away from their longer-run equilibrium levels. But what of the possibility of irrational speculative behavior, plain and simple?

Attitudes toward speculators have always played a key role in the debate on the merits of flexible-exchange-rate systems. At one extreme, speculators have been viewed as overreacting to most news, and as contributing to a "bandwagon" effect that causes exchange rates to fluctuate widely around their underlying equilibrium value. At the other extreme, speculation has been regarded as a stabilizing force, with speculators instantaneously processing and correctly interpreting all new developments bearing on the appropriate value of the exchange rates. A more balanced view would admit that speculative activity can be either stabilizing or destabilizing, depending on the circumstances. The task then becomes one of identifying the circumstances under which speculation might be destabilizing and considering how such speculation might be offset or its consequences limited.

The possibility of speculative excess in free markets is documented by a wide range of historical experience, from the Dutch tulip-bulb craze and the South Sea Bubble down to the Wall Street boom and bust of 1928-29. Speculative excesses are, however, much less likely to occur in the foreign-exchange market than in markets for individual commodities. A currency is only a right to purchase certain goods at market prices, and the value of a currency in terms of foreign exchange is not likely to become completely divorced from its relative purchasing power. Nevertheless, the degree of constraint imposed by arbitrage opportunities in the goods market should not itself be exaggerated. Large and protracted disturbances from purchasing-power parity can and do occur, as demonstrated by the experience of the French franc in the 1920s (see Rogers, 1929).

Speculative disturbances are more likely to occur as prospective developments in the relative purchasing power of currencies become more uncertain. In such circumstances, the desire of speculators to hold particular currencies will be affected not only by the current purchasing power of those currencies but also by perceptions of how this purchasing power will change in the future. This makes the foreign-exchange market more like a stock market, where price fluctuations are due more to changing expectations of future profitability than to current profits. It follows that the possibility of speculation leading to wide fluctuations in exchange rates is less likely when underlying price developments are reasonably stable than when there is considerable uncertainty in this regard.

The Costs of Exchange-Rate Variability

In assessing the advantages of policies designed to limit movements that might otherwise take place in the exchange rate, attention must be paid to the costs and benefits that are likely to ensue. The case for firm intervention clearly becomes stronger the greater are the potential costs of variability relative to the benefits. The benefits of exchange-rate flexibility have been shown to accrue in the form of a somewhat greater monetary independence and a somewhat greater effectiveness of monetary policies. The costs are reviewed below.

Some of the costs of exchange-rate variability arise because floating exchange rates tend to move, at least in the short run, by amounts different from underlying cost-price relationships. This means that international transactions take place with a somewhat greater risk of exchange-rate changes during the period between contract and settlement of a transaction. Such short-term uncertainty is likely to be a relatively small added cost in international trade, however, since short-term exchange-rate variability is not normally great, and, in any case, hedging mechanisms exist (e.g., through forward markets) that enable traders to protect themselves against such risks at relatively modest cost.

Departures from longer-run equilibrium rates are potentially more serious when they continue for more than a few months. The costs of having a pattern of exchange rates that is not conducive to effective balance-of-payments adjustment are of three types: (1) the static welfare loss from a suboptimal allocation of world resources; (2) the adjustment costs that inevitably ensue when the disequilibrium is eventually eliminated; (3) the political frictions that result when countries' exchange-rate objectives clash.

The static welfare loss from a suboptimal allocation of a given volume of world resources is perhaps the least serious consequence of a pattern of exchange rates that diverges from longer-run equilibrium. So long as exchange-rate fluctuations are no greater than they have been, on average, in recent years, only a small amount of trade is likely to be displaced from "efficient" channels.[6] And the welfare loss of such a misallocation

---

[6] It is assumed that the appropriate equilibrium exchange rate has lain somewhere within the band of fluctuation of the actual rate.

is reduced by the fact that only trade flows that are marginal (in their contribution to welfare) are likely to be affected. Somewhat more significant may be the dynamic consequences of frequent sustained deviations from longer-run equilibrium rates. Such deviations may increase uncertainty and lead to a shift of investment away from the more exposed traded-goods sectors. The consequences may be slower growth of foreign trade, a weaker competitive climate, and decreased incentives for growth of productivity. The influences of uncertainty are very hard to quantify, however.

More serious are the adjustment costs of correcting a disequilibrium. These costs are apt to become greater the longer a disequilibrium has persisted. Effective balance-of-payments adjustment means shifting domestic resources from (or to) producing for domestic consumption into (or out of) exports or import substitution. This normally will involve a change in the relative profitability of industries, with the likely result of redundancies, and even bankruptcies, in certain sectors. Resources cannot be moved costlessly between industries, of course; there is likely to be transitional unemployment of both labor and capital, and perhaps also inflation as the industries that need to expand, relative to the others, bid for the necessary resources.

It is important to note that these adjustment costs fall not only on countries whose exchange rates have gotten out of line with longer-run equilibrium but also on their competitors and trading partners. For example, when the overvalued exchange rate of a country eventually moves to a more appropriate level, this country will inevitably increase its share of world markets at the expense of other producers of similar goods. These other countries then have to adapt, as best they may, to weakness of export demand. In all this, the social and political costs of unemployment and structural change have to be considered along with the direct economic costs in terms of loss of production.

Last, and perhaps most important, are the political consequences of a world in which there is no mechanism for reconciling incompatibilities in exchange-rate policies. These costs are by their nature the least quantifiable. In judging them, it is necessary to balance the potential costs of such conflict (illustrated in extreme form by the events of the 1930s) against the unlikelihood of such a degeneration of international economic relations in a world where cooperation is the order of the day.

In addition to the misallocation and adjustment costs involved in disequilibrium rates, there may be a cost in terms of domestic price stability. This arises from the inflationary and deflationary impulses transmitted through the external sector when the exchange rate moves. In circumstances where inflation is a particular worry and there is thought to be downward price rigidity, an additional problem is a possible ratchet effect on prices. Downward price rigidity may result in prices going up more in response to exchange-rate depreciation than they come down when the exchange rate appreciates. If such an effect exists it would be a powerful argument for stabilizing the exchange rate against disturbances that might turn out to be temporary. The empirical evidence for such a phenomenon is not conclusive, however (see, e.g., Goldstein, 1977). The ratchet effect may be limited to countries where the authorities do not effectively control the money supply, possibly because the economic, social, and political costs entailed in achieving control are believed, either correctly or incorrectly, to be too high. In these countries, an asset-market-related depreciation of the exchange rate may indeed be a source of inflation, and the exchange-rate depreciation may be self-validating.

The Role of Exchange Rates in Eliminating Payments Disequilibria

At the beginning of the generalized-floating period, discussion of the role of the exchange rate in the international adjustment process was overshadowed by concern for the consequences of exchange-rate variability for matters such as inflation and the growth of foreign trade. Indeed, many observers seemed ready to assume that exchange-rate flexibility had solved the external-adjustment problem once and for all. Balance-of-payments developments in various countries put an end to this attitude rather quickly. As Marina v. N. Whitman remarked at the 1975 meeting of the American Economic Association:

> The fundamental question to which we seek an answer from recent experience is, of course, whether greater flexibility of exchange rates is indeed an effective means of reducing or eliminating payments disequilibrium, thus alleviating the burden of adjustment which must otherwise be borne either by internal measures or by direct restrictions on international transactions (Whitman, 1975).

This was the crucial question during the pegged-exchange-rate period, and it remains the crucial question today. Many have come to believe that exchange-rate depreciations lead simply to higher inflation rates without any significant benefit for the current account (see, e.g., Economistes Belges de Langue Française, 1973). Certainly the evidence in Figure 2 indicates that during 1973-76 countries with depreciating currencies have had relatively high inflation rates and rather weak current-balance performances in spite of relatively large depreciations, while countries with appreciating currencies have had relatively low inflation rates and rather

FIGURE 2

Effective Exchange Rate, Relative Prices, and Current Balance

- - - MERM-weighted exchange rate; first half of 1973=100
——— Relative wholesale prices of manufactured goods adjusted for exchange
        rate changes; first half of 1973=100
⊡ Current-account balance (excluding official tranfers) in per cent of GNP (right scale)

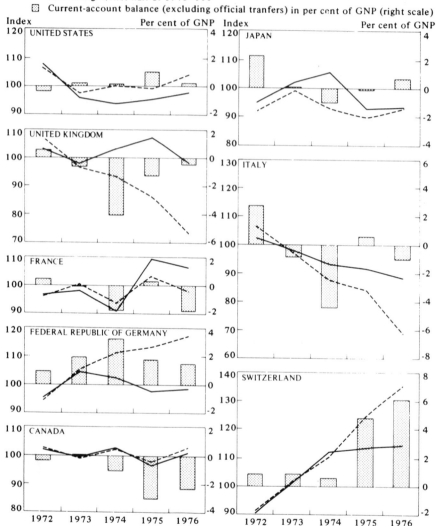

strong current-balance performances in spite of large effective apprecia-
tions. One cannot, of course, conclude from this evidence alone that a
currency depreciation is likely to push a country into a "vicious circle":
Figure 2 does not indicate whether domestic sources of inflation have
been the causal factor for the exchange-rate depreciation, or vice versa.
It does indicate, however, that on the whole the period of flexible exchange rates starting in 1973 has been characterized by a certain divergence between countries with current-account surpluses and countries
with current-account deficits rather than by a move toward a more balanced position, as might have been expected.

This section reviews, first, the "protracted" nature of external imbalances. It goes on to analyze the various forms of the vicious-circle hypothesis, and the effect of exchange-rate flexibility on the behavior of the
authorities and of private economic agents as regards the inflationary
process. The aim is to review the theoretical and empirical underpinnings
of the vicious-circle hypothesis and to make a balanced judgment as to
the appropriate role of the exchange rate in the external-adjustment
process.

The Protracted Nature of External Imbalances

There is considerable empirical evidence that relative-price changes
have a strong effect on the structure of demand and supply in goods
markets and, in particular, on the foreign-trade performance of a
country. However, economists have become more conscious over recent
years of the slowness of the response to relative-price changes, and of the
importance of nonprice factors in the determination of trade performance. Over a given period, relative-price changes may be significant and
in the right direction but they may easily fall short of the changes that are
necessary to offset developments in nonprice factors affecting competitiveness, and this may leave observers with the impression that price
factors are of marginal importance.

Technological innovations and the marketing of new products, the
right product mix at the right time, and a reputation for quality, reliable
delivery schedules, and good after-sales service have been found to explain in large part the trade performances of countries such as the United
States in the 1950s and early 1960s and the Federal Republic of Germany
in the 1960s and 1970s. (The experience of the United States in the 1950s
was reviewed by Kindleberger, 1958, and de Vries, 1956, while Kindleberger, 1976, reviewed the German experience.) Successful trade performance over the years also creates a certain orientation of the economy
toward exports markets. Thus, it is unrealistic to expect a sudden relative-

price change, induced by an inflationary burst or an exchange-rate change, to affect rapidly a pattern of production and demand that reflects such "structural" factors. First, economic agents will have to be sure that the relative-price change is going to last before they undertake the large adjustment costs that are likely to be involved in any reallocation of factors of production or in any change in the allocation of demand among products and supplying countries. Second, even when economic agents are persuaded that the relative-price change is going to last, it may take years, in particular on the supply side, before the effects of the decisions they take are fully felt.

One of the consequences of the slow speed of adjustment in goods markets is the now well-known J-curve effect. In the period immediately following an exchange-rate change, the terms of trade tend to turn against a depreciating country and in favor of an appreciating country, and this may more than offset the volume effect of the exchange-rate change on the balance of trade. Figure 3 shows significant terms-of-trade effects from exchange-rate changes for four countries that have experienced substantial rate changes over the last four years.[7] Combined with the empirical evidence that the volume effects on trade flows of relative price changes take place only with a lag, this suggests that the initial effects of exchange-rate changes on the current account may be perverse. Such perverse effects could result in excessive exchange-rate movements, in particular if developments in the current account affect speculative capital movements in the same direction.

Economic agents are, of course, likely to resist any attempt to eliminate a protracted payments imbalance that has become reflected in the structure of the domestic economy. The longer the imbalance has existed, the more entrenched are the social groups that benefit from it. Resistance to adjustment will first take the form of political pressure against the exchange-rate change. Once the exchange-rate change has occurred, resistance will take the form of an attempt by social groups that benefited from the imbalance to "pass along" the price effects of the exchange-rate change to other social groups. This can be the beginning of a vicious circle of exchange-rate changes and offsetting domestic price movements.

The Vicious-Circle Argument

A better understanding of the vicious-circle argument can be obtained by considering a country which, for whatever reason, needs to reduce

---

[7] To obtain a precise estimate of the J-curve effect, one would need to adjust the prices of the trade flows for factors other than the exchange-rate change. The strong terms-of-trade effects are clearly apparent from the chart, however.

FIGURE 3

EFFECTIVE EXCHANGE RATE AND THE TERMS OF TRADE

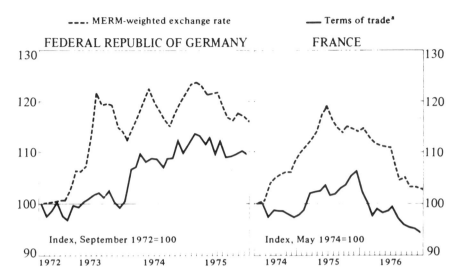

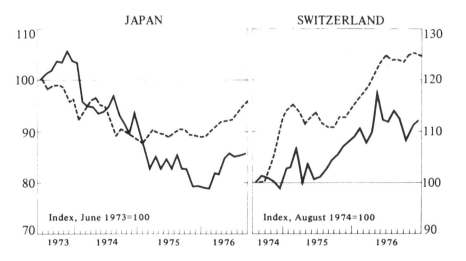

NOTE: This chart considers four particular cases in which a sharp change in the effective exchange rate has occurred.

[a] Export price index divided by import price index, scaled by a trade-weighted average of the terms of trade for the United Kingdom, France, the Federal Republic of Germany, Italy, and Japan.

its current-account deficit. To do so, it will have to reduce its absorption of goods relative to domestic output. It can do this in two ways: (1) it can reduce its domestic demand in terms of domestic currency, or (2) it can let its exchange rate depreciate and its price level increase in terms of domestic currency. If the policy used reduces the real wage rate, the adjustment can take place without a fall in output (an increase in unemployment); if the real wage rate cannot be reduced, the adjustment can be achieved only with a fall in output. Thus the relative effectiveness of the exchange rate as a policy instrument depends in this case on its relative effectiveness in reducing the real wage rate.

The vicious-circle argument, in its extreme form, assumes that a depreciation of the exchange rate is automatically offset by an increase in the money wage rate. Thus, the authorities are left with the choice of letting the money supply rise to accommodate the wage-price increase, in which case they are back to square one, but after experiencing a temporary increase in inflation,[8] or of refusing to accommodate the wage-price increase, in which case they arrive at the same unemployment rate they would have had if they had chosen to reduce nominal domestic demand rather than to let the exchange-rate depreciate. Under the first scenario, the exchange-rate depreciation will lead to further price increases and further depreciations of the rate in an endless succession. Under the second, it has the same consequences as the use of a deflationary policy, but without the added advantage of a temporary fall in the rate of inflation that a deflationary policy is likely to yield.

The issue behind the vicious-circle argument turns on the effectiveness of different policy instruments in bringing about the ultimate reduction in real wages that is essential for adjustment, while minimizing the harmful consequences for such other objectives as the maintenance of reasonable price stability and full employment. Fellner (1975), for example, argues that the exchange rate is more effective in reducing the real wage rate, because the concern of various labor unions with *relative* real wage positions makes it easier for the authorities to cut real wage rates by an increase in consumer prices induced by a change in the exchange rate. Such a change hits every labor group more or less equally and simultaneously, whereas a deflationary policy tends to affect labor contracts

---

[8] The change in the rate of inflation is temporary because the policy change considered here is only a once-and-for-all change in nominal demand (relative to trend). Temporary changes can, of course, lead to permanent changes if, for example, they lead to changes in expectations and accompanying changes in the rate of growth of the money supply.

one at a time when they are renewed. However, in many industrial countries (France, Italy, Belgium, Japan, etc.) most labor contracts are renewed at the same time, and the bargaining process involves a few *national* labor unions. Another argument for using the exchange rate is based on the hypothesis that employees may be influenced by money illusion. This argument has been weakened by the probable erosion of money illusion in periods of high inflation and by the fact that the use of indexation clauses in labor contracts is becoming increasingly widespread (see Braun, 1976).

A strong argument against the vicious-circle view and its policy implication that exchange-rate adjustments should not be relied on is that the alternative policy strategy to reduce real wage rates, a restrictive demand-management policy, seems in many cases even less effective. Is it realistic, for example, to expect countries that in the past have been unable to maintain their inflation rates in line with those of their trading partners to succeed in bringing their inflation rates substantially *below* those of their trading partners so as to gradually restore their competitiveness? Thus, the case for using the exchange rate to bring about a readjustment in real wage rates rests less on its efficiency in doing so than on the evidence that other available instruments are even less efficient. Further, while the effect of an exchange-rate change on real wage rates may not be large, the available empirical evidence shows that it is not insignificant, at least if the proper supporting policies are implemented at the time of the exchange-rate change. The evidence presented in Figure 3 above, for example, of continuing terms-of-trade effects for countries with significant exchange-rate movements is consistent with the hypothesis that exchange-rate changes are not immediately offset by changes in domestic costs. Viewed in this light, the relevant question is how the authorities can increase the effectiveness of an exchange-rate change. Here, deflationary measures, temporary nullification of indexation clauses, etc., have a crucial role to play.

External Constraints on Inflationary Practices

Concern has often been expressed that the wider use of exchange-rate flexibility as a means of achieving balance-of-payments adjustment will weaken the discipline to adopt policies that promote price stability. Under fixed exchange rates, a country that inflates at a rate higher than that of its trading partners will tend to suffer a deterioration in its balance of payments and a loss of international reserves. If the fixed exchange rate is to be maintained, the country will ultimately have to take action to bring its inflation rate into line with that of its trading partners. The usefulness of such a discipline was recognized in the 1970 report of the IMF Executive Directors, which stated:

> ... the need to defend a fixed exchange rate against depreciation may promote willingness to impose unpopular domestic restraints; and where the attempt to defend a parity is ultimately unsuccessful, the psychological shock of a devaluation may promote broad support for the adoption of the necessary associated measures to curtail domestic demand (International Monetary Fund, 1970, p. 32).

A commitment to fixed exchange rates may also act as a limitation on cost-push pressures in the domestic economy. If price setters, either in the labor or goods markets, are aware that the exploitation of market power will lead to a loss of competitiveness and therefore to a reduction in demand, they may be induced to moderate wage or price increases. Such a result is, of course, more likely in economies that are rather open to external competition; in addition, the authorities' commitment to an exchange-rate target must be perceived as strong enough to outweigh countervailing pressures to maintain full employment.

The disciplinary pressures that operate on high-inflation countries under fixed exchange rates have, however, a counterpart in the pressures that operate on countries that have low inflation rates and a tendency toward balance-of-payments surpluses. To the extent that current-account surpluses directly raise the pressure of domestic demand, countries with low rates of price increases will be likely under a system of fixed exchange rates to experience an increase in inflationary pressures.

Which kind of disciplinary pressure will be the stronger depends on a number of factors, including the availability of conditional and unconditional liquidity to finance balance-of-payments deficits. If international liquidity is scarce, or available only on strict conditions, a stronger discipline may be exerted on deficit countries, since the consequences of continued deficits will be perceived as more serious than the consequences of prolonged surpluses. On the other hand, if balance-of-payments finance is readily available deficit countries may be much more willing to accept deficits, and it will be the surplus countries that tend to take prompter action to stem the outflow of the real resources that their surpluses represent.

As Emminger (1973) has pointed out, where finance for payments deficits is relatively freely available, flexible exchange rates may well exercise more effective discipline over inflationary policies. Under fixed exchange rates, a substantial part of the price and output consequences of a high-inflation policy can be exported abroad through a balance-of-pay-

ments deficit. With flexible rates, however, such a policy is more likely to result in a depreciation of the exchange rate and, in turn, an increase in domestic prices in the high-inflation country. Thus, the cost of a high-
inflation policy—declining purchasing power of domestic incomes over
foreign goods—will be more easily and quickly noticed by the public
under flexible rates. Assuming that inflation is unpopular and that governments are responsive to public opinion, the foregoing implies in turn that
inflationary pressures will be restrained more quickly under flexible rates
than under fixed rates when there is the option of financing them by
reserve depletion. Even under flexible rates, however, it is still possible
for high-inflation countries to use exchange-rate policy to avoid, for a
while, the discipline of public opinion. Since governments are always
seeking the least painful way to bring inflation down, there is a danger
that countries with floating rates will try to resist exchange-rate depreciation through intervention and other ways of influencing the exchange
rate.

Crockett and Goldstein (1976) have argued that neither *a priori*
reasoning nor empirical evidence is conclusive in showing that anti-
inflationary discipline is stronger under fixed than under flexible rates.
Rather, inflationary disturbances can disrupt the smoothness with which
the adjustment mechanism works under either exchange-rate regime if
there are not sufficient pressures to adopt timely adjustment measures.
Such a result is likely to occur if balance-of-payments finance is either too
easy or too difficult to obtain. Too easy access to finance is likely to deter
governments from taking effective adjustment action either through domestic policies or through permitting exchange-rate movement. A shortage of liquidity, on the other hand, can prompt overhasty external adjustment, with possible adverse consequences for the stability of domestic
incomes and prices.

Assessing Exchange-Rate Policies

The Case for Intervention

The analysis of the two preceding sections suggests that the case for
intervention (or any other form of active exchange-rate policy) is rather
strong. Asset-market-related disturbances have been shown to be a considerable source of exchange-rate disturbance, at least in certain cases.
They may lead to disorderly conditions in the foreign-exchange market,
wide fluctuations in exchange rates, and even, in certain circumstances,
to an exchange-rate level that interferes with smooth external adjustment

in the longer run. For certain countries, a case can also be made that a freely floating exchange rate is not necessarily conducive to effective external adjustment.

In practice, however, the case for intervention is not so strong. While the free play of market forces may have undesirable effects, in most cases it may be difficult to implement a rate-management policy that would not hinder but help the working of the external adjustment process in the longer run.

The desirability of intervening to prevent disorderly market conditions is widely accepted. It is not always easy, of course, to determine in advance whether a particular disturbance in foreign-exchange markets is a temporary aberration or the beginning of an underlying trend. This would be the case, for example, where a sudden movement in the rate is prompted by political fears. If the political situation that gave rise to the exchange-rate pressures disappears, it would have been appropriate for the authorities concerned to resist the exchange-market consequences. But if the change in political climate is permanent and gives rise to a permanent reappraisal of what constitutes an appropriate exchange rate, a rapid movement in the exchange rate to its new equilibrium might have been more conducive to orderly exchange-market conditions. The important point is that it is exchange-rate movements that are temporary and reversible, not just rapid, that are a cause for concern.

The need to intervene to preserve orderly exchange markets normally arises suddenly, and thus there is no alternative to relying on the judgment of the authorities regarding the suitability of intervention in particular cases. *Ex post*, however, it is relatively easy to reach a judgment on whether such intervention has been warranted. Smoothing intervention will normally cancel out over a short period; if it does not, this can be considered *prima facie* evidence that the authorities have misjudged the nature of exchange-market conditions. Conversely, sharp exchange-rate movements around a stable exchange-rate level (or trend), when unaccompanied by official intervention, would tend to suggest that an opportunity for stabilizing intervention has been missed.

The need for intervention to preserve orderly markets is likely to be less where exchange markets have reasonable depth and breadth. In such cases, individual large transactions can be absorbed without a significant impact on the rate, and a change in sentiment on the part of some speculators is not likely to carry the exchange rate very far before countervailing expectations of other speculators are encountered. It is where exchange markets are narrow (as in the case of many smaller countries or of countries imposing exchange restrictions) or where expectations are particularly volatile (perhaps because of political uncertainties) that the case for smoothing intervention is likely to be strongest.

Much more difficult to appraise is the case for sustained management of the exchange rate, whether by intervention or other means. There are basically two reasons why the authorities may wish to have a rate that is different from the one that would emerge in the absence of intervention.

The first reason is that the short-run market-clearing rate may differ substantially from the longer-run equilibrium rate. A number of causes of such a divergence were examined in the section on short-run variability of exchange rates. Apart from the possibility of irrational market behavior, the most important cause was the risk-averse behavior of private market participants. Faced with the need to assess the longer-term significance of disturbances in countries' balances of payments and monetary policies, private wealth owners seek to maximize the return on their assets and to minimize their risk. In acting to minimize risk, speculators are likely to require an additional incentive to hold open positions in weak currencies. This may mean that speculators will acquire such currencies only when they become "overdepreciated" and there is a significant expectation of capital gain.

The second reason why countries may wish to intervene to influence the exchange rate is that relying on exchange-rate adjustment may complicate the task of using domestic instruments of adjustment to achieve a viable balance of payments. The extreme version of this argument is the vicious-circle hypothesis. Although this hypothesis may not be acceptable in its pure form, there may be truth in the implication that subjecting private and public decision makers to an external constraint (in the form of an exchange-rate target) will make domestic stabilization policies more effective. Since longer-term adjustment requires effective action on domestic demand, it is arguable that the main emphasis of adjustment policies should be domestic. It must be recognized that this argument for intervention implies an acceptance of a "wrong" rate in the short term to improve the prospects of achieving a more durable "right" rate in the longer term. It therefore depends crucially on backing up exchange-rate intervention with a suitable package of measures to restore domestic stability.

Ultimately, the major weakness in the case for intervention is that it is so difficult to recognize cases when intervention is really called for. Further, national authorities are often unwilling to accept significant exchange-rate movements even when they are justified by underlying economic developments. Market forces may not always be "right," but the experience of the past decade indicates clearly that they have been right more often than the authorities. Perhaps the strongest temptation to pursue an inappropriate exchange-rate policy results from viewing as temporary what eventually turns out to be a permanent change in exchange-market conditions. This temptation is likely to be particularly strong when the costs, both political and economic, of adjusting to the change are perceived to be high and when there is a considerable degree of uncertainty concerning future developments affecting the balance of payments. Exchange-rate changes affect the relative profitability of production of traded and nontraded goods. Switching resources between sectors imposes adjustment costs and may also involve transitional unemployment of factors of production. Since there may also be strong economic interests that benefit from the existing structure of production, governments may be unwilling to accept the political consequences of permitting an exchange-rate realignment.

Another temptation, which is particularly prevalent when countries are attempting to bring down excessive rates of price inflation, is to use the exchange rate as part of incomes policy. It is well-known that the rate of increase in prices, particularly consumer prices, is an important element in determining wage settlements. For this reason, governments that attach high priority to reducing the rate of increase in wages are often prepared to accept measures that distort the allocation of resources in order to retard the rise in the consumer price index. This can take place through domestic subsidies, but only at the cost of increasing the budget deficit and complicating the financing of the central government. A simpler mechanism, but one that has much the same result, is to subsidize imports by holding up the exchange rate. The attraction of such a policy is enhanced when the immediate goals of implementing an effective incomes policy bulk larger in the government's overall economic strategy than the more medium-term constraint of attaining external balance.

The costs of maintaining an overvalued rate for incomes-policy purposes should not be underestimated, however. Quite apart from the distorting effect on the allocation of production between traded and nontraded sectors, any beneficial consequences on the rate of price increase in the short term are achieved at the cost of adverse consequences later on, when the rate has to be allowed to move to an equilibrium level. Only if it can be argued convincingly that the consequences of favorable effects on inflation in the short term are likely to be stronger than the consequences of unfavorable effects later will there be a case for using the exchange rate as an anti-inflationary instrument. Even so, care must be taken that any advantages of an active exchange-rate policy for the country adopting it are not purchased at the expense of offsetting disadvantages for trading partners.

Although, in present circumstances, the greater risk seems to be that countries will take action that has the effect of overvaluing their exchange rate, a more long-standing concern has been the use of competitive depreciation to improve domestic employment. The temptation to use exchange policy in this way would presumably become greater if the main objective of economic policy shifted from fighting inflation to promoting employment. Also, growth in output generated by rising exports (as against domestic demand) has the attraction that overall productivity is often thought to be higher in the export sector. Furthermore, in circumstances where finance for balance-of-payments deficits is not readily available, exchange-rate depreciation may appear preferable to domestic measures as a means of promoting employment, since it is less likely to run into an external constraint. The danger of such a policy, of course, is that it promotes domestic employment objectives at the expense of employment in other countries and thus risks retaliation and a chain reaction of beggar-thy-neighbor policies.

The Need for a Case-by-Case Approach to Surveillance

All countries are subject to disturbances in their balance of payments that may be external or internal in origin. The interest of the international community lies in ensuring that the combination of measures chosen by a country is such as to enable timely and effective adjustment to take place, consistent with its other obligations to achieve a satisfactory employment level with reasonable price stability and to avoid actions harmful to other countries.

The need to protect the international community from potentially harmful actions by individual countries is one of the basic *raisons d'être* of the International Monetary Fund. The exchange-rate system of the original Bretton Woods Articles of Agreement sought to achieve this goal through the establishment of par values for currencies that could be changed only with international concurrence. When this system broke down in 1971 and finally collapsed in 1973, alternative means for avoiding harmful and inconsistent exchange-rate policies were sought.

In June 1974, the Fund adopted a set of nonbinding "Guidelines for the Management of Floating Exchange Rates." These guidelines reflected a widespread acceptance that the behavior of governments with respect to exchange rates was a matter for international consultation and surveillance. The main features of the guidelines were to provide encouragement (1) to smooth out very short-term fluctuations in market rates; (2) to offer a measure of resistance to market tendencies in the slightly longer run, and in particular to rapid movements in the rate; and (3) to try to estimate, if possible, a medium-term "norm" for currencies' exchange rates, with a view to resisting movements that appeared to deviate substantially from that norm. In addition, it was recognized that intervention policies should take account of countries' reserve positions and of the effect of intervention on the exchange rate of the currency being used in intervention.

The themes of the guidelines are reflected in a number of academic contributions on the subject. In an earlier essay in this series, Ethier and Bloomfield (1975) suggested the establishment of "reference rates," which would work in much the same way as the "norms" of the guidelines. In other words, countries would not be under any obligation to defend a particular rate, but they would be prevented from intervening against their currency when it was below the reference rate and from intervening in favor of their currency when it was above the reference rate. Tosini (1977) picks up another element of the guidelines in suggesting that countries should always be encouraged to "lean against the wind" so as to moderate exchange-rate movements that would result from market forces. Her rationale for this prescription is that, in practice, rate fluctuations have proved to be excessive and that any action to dampen such swings would tend to lead to a smoother evolution of exchange rates. In a more elaborate analysis of different situations in which rate management might be considered, Mikesell and Goldstein (1975) examine a variety of circumstances in which intervention might be desirable and consider possible rules to protect the interests of the international community. Broadly speaking, their rules relate to permissible changes in official reserves between reporting periods.

The objective of formulating fairly explicit behavior rules for intervention runs into a number of theoretical and practical difficulties, however. Resistance to rapid movements in the exchange rate (or leaning against the wind) is optimal only so long as market forces are moving rates excessively in one direction. There seems to be no valid reason, however, to assume that large and sudden exchange-rate changes are necessarily inappropriate. If, for example, a major policy shift results in a substantial change in the assessment by market participants of the longer-run equilibrium exchange rate for a currency, it may be less disruptive to allow the rate to move quickly to a new value than to slow this movement down through intervention.

The possibility of using changes in official reserves as a standard for permissible intervention is also unlikely to be acceptable in practice. Quite apart from the difficulty of agreeing on country-by-country limits for reserve changes, it is by now widely recognized that official intervention affecting reserve holdings is only one among several ways of managing the exchange rate.

The establishment of an internationally agreed set of "norms" for exchange rates runs into severe practical difficulties, and although such norms were provided for in the IMF's 1974 guidelines, no attempt was made to establish them. Apart from the fact that the move toward greater exchange-rate flexibility has by now gone so far that the establishment of exchange-rate norms can no longer be considered politically feasible, it is obvious that the necessary conditions for the working of such a system, namely relatively stable underlying economic conditions in the major countries and some harmonization of national economic policies, are not satisfied at present.

Partly as a result of the perceived difficulties in applying rules with even the limited degree of precision involved in the 1974 IMF guidelines, the new Articles of Agreement express the obligations of Fund members in the exchange-rate field in more general terms. The relevant provision of the new Article IV is that members shall "avoid manipulating exchange rates or the international monetary system in order to prevent effective balance of payments adjustment or to gain an unfair competitive advantage over other members."

At the time this provision was drafted, late in 1975, it was decided that this general rule would be further codified later on through the adoption of "specific principles" for the guidance of all members in their exchange-rate policies. In fact, however, the decision that was eventually reached by the IMF in April 1977 (and which is reproduced here in an Appendix) was to avoid introducing too much precision in defining members' obligations and to concentrate instead on establishing procedures that would enable continuous and effective surveillance to take place. In other words, the Fund opted for a case-by-case approach to its surveillance responsibilities that would not be based on a specific set of ground rules. However, the procedures that were adopted in 1977 do provide illustrative cases of developments that would be *prima facie* evidence of a need for international consultation and review. For the most part, these developments relate to policies pursued by countries that have the effect of influencing balances of payments and reserve flows. But it is also suggested that the Fund would have an interest in "behavior of the exchange rate that appears to be unrelated to underlying economic and financial conditions . . . ," implying that intervention to counter such exchange-rate developments is to be regarded as desirable.

These new procedures provide the necessary framework for Fund surveillance activities. They take into account that both misguided rate-management policies and the free play of market forces may lead to an "undesirable" exchange rate, but it is clear that misguided rate policies are expected to be the major source of problems.

Another advantage of these procedures is that they make allowance for the divergent interests and preferences of member countries. For a variety of reasons, countries attach different degrees of importance to the objective of exchange-rate stability. In part, these diverging preferences stem from differences among countries in the importance of the exchange rate as a price that influences the level and distribution of national output. For countries where the external sector is relatively small, the impact of external disturbances on the domestic economy is likely to be correspondingly reduced and the main objective will be to ensure that the external-adjustment mechanism does not interfere with the setting of domestic policy instruments. For countries with a larger external sector, however, the exchange rate is likely to be a price that has more pervasive effects on the level and distribution of national output. For this reason, such countries would suffer greater costs if, for whatever reason, market forces tended to move the exchange rate to a level judged incompatible with domestic objectives or inconsistent with medium-term balance-of-payments equilibrium.

The importance of the exchange rate as a disciplinary instrument may also vary between countries. In large, fairly closed economies, external developments will exercise relatively less influence over the setting of domestic policy instruments and over the wage-price formation process. For more open economies (for example those of the smaller snake members) prices and wages are likely to be much more responsive to external developments, so that exchange-rate flexibility will be less effective as an adjustment mechanism relative to domestic measures. Also, the degree to which wages and prices are indexed (formally or informally) will have important implications for the relative efficacy of different adjustment techniques.

Another possible reason for divergences in exchange-market policies is that exchange-market structures may vary between currencies. Not all countries have exchange markets with the depth and breadth of the major industrial countries, where a wide range of traders, arbitrageurs, and speculators participate. In particular, many smaller countries have a restricted market for their currencies, often centralized in the central bank.

Many countries also have capital controls, reducing the scope for arbitrageurs and speculators to smooth disturbances in the supply and demand for foreign exchange arising from current-account transactions. Furthermore, the current account itself may be somewhat unresponsive to exchange-rate variations, particularly where more direct means of controlling imports are employed and where the elasticity of supply of exports is low—as it may be for many primary producing countries.

These differences between countries are important in assessing the need for an active exchange-rate policy in particular cases. While a freely floating exchange rate can ensure a continuous equilibrium between the demand and supply for a country's currency in the foreign-exchange market, other measures may take considerably longer to achieve their intended effect on external payments flows. It has been argued above that exchange-rate flexibility, if unsupported by appropriate measures to influence domestic demand, is likely to be inadequate to achieve durable adjustment. To the extent that these supporting measures affect payments flows with a lag (particularly on current account), there will be a temporary disequilibrium in the balance on current and long-term capital account that has to be covered by short-term financing. If, however, the authorities do not intervene and there is weakness in private speculative demand, the exchange-rate movement needed to induce accommodating flows of private short-term capital may be excessive.

Ultimately, the exchange-rate policy of the authorities should reflect both their assessment of whether there is a large difference between the short-run market clearing rate and the longer-run equilibrium rate for their currency and their views on the appropriate role of the exchange rate in their overall economic strategy. To judge the appropriateness of the authorities' exchange-rate policy, there is no alternative to a full assessment of the implications for the balance of payments of the overall economic strategy adopted by the authorities. This involves an appraisal of the implications for the current account of existing domestic policies and prospective developments in the world economy, combined with an assessment of whether sustainable capital flows are likely to be forthcoming to finance whatever surplus or deficit emerges on current account.

These various points lead us to conclude that the only international monetary system consistent with existing economic and political realities is the present system, where the major countries rely heavily on market forces but intervene whenever these forces tend to push their exchange rates beyond what they assess to be appropriate. This mixed system, however, is bound to lead to frequent conflicts among countries with divergent interests, and surveillance by the International Monetary Fund is needed to avoid harmful and inconsistent exchange-rate policies and to moderate international conflicts. Because of the real divergence in interests among countries and the many uncertainties inherent in the appraisal of exchange-rate policies—in particular, the difficulty of assessing the appropriateness of an exchange rate for the longer term—such surveillance cannot be based on a single objective indicator or even on any precise set of rules. Thus, in arriving at a judgment as to whether a country's exchange-rate policies constitute an unwarranted hindrance to the proper working of the international adjustment process, the Fund must make a comprehensive appraisal of these policies. These points have been taken into account in the new Article IV and in the Fund decision of April 1977. Whether this new system works satisfactorily depends primarily on whether the major countries show sufficient willingness to give it a fair chance.

References

Artus, Jacques R., "Exchange Rate Stability and Managed Floating: The Experience of the Federal Republic of Germany," *IMF Staff Papers*, 23 (July 1976), pp. 312-333.

Braun, Anne W. R., "Indexation of Wages and Salaries in Developed Economies," *IMF Staff Papers*, 23 (March 1976), pp. 226-271.

Crockett, Andrew D., and M. Goldstein, "Inflation under Fixed and Flexible Exchange Rates," *IMF Staff Papers*, 23 (November 1976), pp. 509-544.

De Vries, Tom, "De Theorie van het Comparatieve Voordeel en het Dollartekort," *De Economist*, 104 (January 1956), pp. 1-39.

Dornbusch, Rudiger, "Expectations and Exchange Rate Dynamics," *Journal of Political Economy*, 84 (December 1976), pp. 1161-1176.

Dornbusch, Rudiger, and Paul Krugman, *Flexible Exchange Rates in the Short Run*, Brookings Papers on Economic Activity No. 3, 1976, pp. 537-575.

Economistes Belges de Langue Française, *Economies ouvertes face aux mutations internationales—Rapport du 2e Congrès des Economistes Belges de Langue Française*, Brussels, Centre Interuniversitaire de Formation Permanente, 1977.

Emminger, Otmar, *Inflation and the International Monetary System*, Basle, Per Jacobsson Foundation, June 16, 1973.

Ethier, Wilfred, and Arthur I. Bloomfield, *Managing the Managed Float*, Essays in International Finance No. 112, Princeton, N.J., Princeton University, International Finance Section, 1975.

Fellner, William J., "The Payments Adjustment Process and the Exchange Rate Regime: What Have We Learned?—Comments," *American Economic Review*, 55 (May 1975), pp. 148-151.

Friedman, Milton, "The Case for Flexible Exchange Rates," *Essays in Positive Economics*, Chicago, University of Chicago Press, 1953, pp. 157-201.

Goldstein, M., "Downward Price Inflexibility, Ratchet Effects, and the Inflationary Impact of Import Price Changes: Some Empirical Tests," unpublished, Washington, D.C., International Monetary Fund, DM/77/34, April 1977.

International Monetary Fund, *The Role of Exchange Rates in the Adjustment of International Payments*, Washington, D.C., 1970.

Kindleberger, Charles P., "The Dollar Shortage Revisited," *American Economic Review*, 68 (June 1958), pp. 388-395.

————, "Germany's Persistent Balance-of-Payment Disequilibrium Revisited," *Banca Nazionale del Lavoro Quarterly Review*, 29 (June 1976), pp. 135-164.

McKinnon, Ronald I., "Instability in Floating Foreign Exchange Rates: A Qualified Monetary Interpretation," *Money in International Exchange: The Convertible Currency System*, New York, Oxford University Press, forthcoming.

Mikesell, Raymond F., and Henry N. Goldstein, *Rules for a Floating-Rate Regime*, Essays in International Finance No. 109, Princeton, N.J., Princeton University, International Finance Section, 1975.

Rogers, James H., *The Process of Inflation in France, 1914-1927*, New York, Columbia University Press, 1929.

Schadler, Susan, "Sources of Exchange Rate Variability: Theory and Empirical Evidence," *IMF Staff Papers*, 24 (July 1977), pp. 253-296.

Sohmen, Egon, *Flexible Exchange Rates*, Chicago, University of Chicago Press, 1961.

Tosini, Paula, *Leaning Against the Wind: A Standard for Managed Floating*, Essays in International Finance No. 126, Princeton, N.J., Princeton University, International Finance Section, 1977.

Whitman, Marina v. N., "The Payments Adjustment Process and the Exchange Rate Regime: What Have We Learned?" *American Economic Review*, 65 (May 1975), pp. 133-146.

JACQUES R. ARTUS and ANDREW D. CROCKETT

FLOATING EXCHANGE RATES AND THE NEED FOR SURVEILLANCE

Our 1978 article reached the conclusion that "the only international monetary system consistent with existing economic and political realities is the present system, where the major countries rely heavily on market forces but intervene whenever these forces tend to push their exchange rates beyond what they assess to be appropriate." In our view

this remains a valid conclusion. Nevertheless, the experience of the
intervening ten years has taught several lessons about how the system
reacts to different kinds of disturbance and how it can be managed to
improve its stability.

The most striking development in the field of exchange rates in
the ten years or so following the publication of our article has been
the prolonged rise of the U.S. dollar in 1980-85, and subsequent
more rapid fall. The cumulative real effective appreciation
of the U.S. dollar between late 1980 and its peak in the first quarter
of 1985 was of the order of 70 percent. Two years later, in early
1987, the dollar had returned virtually to its level at the beginning
of the decade.

Swings of this amplitude clearly pose the issue of whether the
system is operating as efficiently as it might. Large and reversible
changes in external competitiveness involve potentially significant
economic costs. While most studies have been unable to detect
significant adverse effects from short-run exchange rate volatility,
longer-run swings are more likely to have harmful consequences. These
consequences stem from the adjustment costs of switching factors of
production back and forth between competing uses; the misallocation
of resources that results when relative prices depart from underlying
equilibrium values; the transitional unemployment that occurs when
competitiveness declines in certain sectors; the added uncertainty
surrounding investment in tradable goods producing sectors; and the
protectionist pressures that build up when particular sectors perceive
they are being disadvantaged by capricious exchange rate movements.

The causes of the rise, and subsequent fall, of the U.S. dollar
are widely agreed to be related to the divergences in fiscal-monetary
mix that occurred among the major countries in the early 1980s.
Monetary restraint was pursued by all the major countries in that
period, and perhaps most strongly by the United States, given the

strength of the inflationary pressures that had to be combated. By
contrast, there was a wide diversity of fiscal stance. In the United
States, the effects of the substantial tax cuts introduced at the
beginning of the Reagan presidency led to a rapid and substantial
widening of the federal fiscal deficit. Meanwhile, in Germany and
Japan, steps were being taken to reduce budget deficits. The result
was that absorption rose relative to output in the United States,
while saving tended to rise in relative terms in the other countries.
The demand for funds to finance the U.S. federal deficit tended to
push up interest rates in the United States, which attracted savings
from abroad. This in turn caused the U.S. dollar to appreciate, and
thus brought about the increase in the trade deficit that made possible
the growth in absorption in the United States.

The appreciation of the dollar would not have been a source of
concern if it was sustainable, that is, if the growing indebtedness
of the United States reflected higher capital formation in that country
and an increase in the underlying growth of output. However, that did
not appear to be the case in practice. By 1985, the U.S. balance of
payments deficit had reached a level at which most market observers
concluded it was unsustainable. Calculations made in early 1985
suggested that if the U.S. dollar remained at its peak level, the net
international indebtedness of the United States would reach $1.3 trillion
within five years, and would continue to rise rapidly thereafter.
(Marris, 1985)

The question therefore arises, what adjustments to the international
monetary system could help correct such problems and avoid their
emergence in future. One approach, that has gained considerable
support, is the use of target or reference zones for exchange rates
(Williamson, 1985). It is argued that if the international community
could agree on such zones, this would provide the discipline countries
need to avoid taking them outside such zones. Of course, further agree-

ments would be still necessary to establish the kinds of policy measures
that should be used to maintain exchange rates within the target ranges.
Those who are more skeptical about target zones generally express
concern that exchange rate objectives, by themselves, are not enough
to bring about a stable functioning of the system. Exchange rate
misalignments are generally traceable to particular domestic policy
divergences, and these divergences need to be corrected in appropriate
ways. If, for example, the appreciation of the U.S. dollar in the
early 1980s is attributed to the fact that fiscal policy was easier,
relative to monetary policy, than in other countries, there are a
number of ways by which this divergence could be corrected: tighter
fiscal policy in the United States; easier monetary policy in the
United States; easier fiscal policy outside the United States; or
tighter monetary policy outside the United States. Certain types
of response might be desirable; others, however, could be highly
undesirable.

Because the choice of policy response depends on circumstances,
the major industrial countries have recently been moving toward a
system of continuous review of economic policy interactions, based
on a system of "indicators." (See Crockett, 1987) The communique of
the June 1987 Venice summit noted the commitment of each of the seven
countries to "develop medium-term objectives and projections for its
economy, and for the Group to develop objectives and projections that
are mutually consistent both individually and collectively." The
Communique also endorsed "the use of performance indicators to review
and assess current economic trends and to determine whether there are
significant deviations from our intended course that require consideration of remedial action."

In summary, there is now a greater awareness than there was ten years or so ago, that exchange rate developments can have significant economic costs. It is generally agreed, therefore, that the system needs more "management" than was earlier envisaged. This management, however, is seen to be primarily in the sphere of coordinating domestic policies so that they are mutually consistent and supportive.

References:

Marris, Stephen, "Deficits and the Dollar," Washington, D.C., Institute for International Economics, 1985.

Williamson, John, "The Exchange Rate System," Washington, D.C., Institute for International Economics, 1985.

Crockett, Andrew, "Indicators of Policies and Economic Performance," in Crockett, Andrew and Morris Goldstein, "Strengthening the International Monetary System," IMF Occasional Paper No. 450, Washington, D.C., 1987.

HOW THE IMF PROVIDES FINANCIAL ASSISTANCE TO MEET MEMBER COUNTRIES' NEEDS

The IMF's financial resources are made available to its members through a variety of facilities and policies, which differ mainly in the type of balance of payments needs they address and in the degree of conditionality attached to them. The IMF derives its finances from

o resources in the General Resources Account, which may be used to provide balance of payments financing to all members, and are derived from members' subscriptions and the IMF's borrowing;

o resources in the Special Disbursement Account, which are used for concessional balance of payments assistance to low-income developing members through the structural adjustment facility (SAF) and the enhanced structural adjustment facility (ESAF), and are derived from the reflow of Trust Fund resources; and

o resources in the ESAF Trust, which are used by the IMF, as trustee, for concessional balance of payments assistance to low-income developing members through the ESAF, and are derived from members' loans and donations.

This article is based on the 1990 Supplement on the Fund,

932

The rules governing access to the IMF's general resources apply uniformly to all members. Access to these resources, which is determined primarily by a member's balance of payments need and the strength of its adjustment policies, is set within well-defined limits in relation to a member's quota, although access can exceed these limits in exceptional circumstances. General resources are used to finance stand-by and extended arrangements as well as special facilities that are open to all members, including the compensatory and contingency financing facility and the buffer stock financing facility. Members may also make use of general resources under temporary policies and facilities that have been financed with borrowed resources. For example, in 1981, as a follow-up to the supplementary financing facility, the IMF established a policy of "enlarged access" to its resources, which allows it to continue to help members whose balance of payments needs are large relative to their quotas by making available resources that it borrows.

The IMF has also generated other resources, in addition to its general resources, to provide low-income developing countries with relatively long-term balance of payments assistance at concessional rates of charge. Concessional assistance is provided through loans under the SAF and the ESAF.

Reserve Tranche. A member has a reserve tranche position in the IMF to the extent that its quota exceeds the IMF's holdings of its currency in the General Resources Account, excluding holdings arising out of purchases under all policies on the use of the IMF's general resources. A member may purchase (draw) up to the full amount of its reserve tranche at any time, subject only to the requirement of balance of payments need. However, the IMF has no power to challenge the member's representation of need for use of the reserve tranche. A reserve tranche purchase does not constitute a use of IMF credit and is not subject to charges or to an expectation or obligation to repurchase (repay).

Credit Tranches. The credit tranche policy is the IMF's basic lending policy on the use of its general resources. Credit is made available in four credit tranches, each equivalent to 25 percent of a country's quota. Larger access can be authorized in exceptional circumstances.

A first credit tranche purchase is defined as one that raises the IMF's holdings of the purchasing member's currency in the credit tranches to no more than 25 percent of quota. Generally, a member requests a use of the IMF's resources in the first credit tranche when confronted with relatively small balance of payments difficulties, and financial assistance is made available if the member demonstrates that it is making reasonable efforts to overcome its difficulties. The member may request use of the first credit tranche as part of a stand-by arrangement.

Subsequent purchases are made in additional tranches, which are collectively known as the "upper credit tranches." A member may use the IMF's resources in the upper credit tranches if it adopts policies that provide appropriate grounds for expecting that the member's payments difficulties will be resolved within a reasonable period. Such use is almost always made under stand-by or extended arrangements. A stand-by or extended arrangement assures the member that it will be able to make purchases from the IMF, up to a specified amount, during a given period, as long as it has observed the performance criteria and other terms specified in the arrangement. Repurchases of drawings under the credit tranches and stand-by arrangements are made in 3 1/4 to 5 years. The period of stand-by arrangements has normally been between 12 and 18 months in recent years, but may extend up to 3 years. Extended arrangements typically run for 3 years, but they may be lengthened to 4 years.

Purchases of the amounts available under a stand-by arrangement in the upper credit tranches or under an extended arrangement are "phased;" in other words, they are made available in installments at specified intervals during the period of the arrangement. The member's right to draw is subject to its observance of the performance criteria and other specified conditions. The performance criteria typically cover credit policy, government or public sector borrowing requirements, and policies on trade and payments restrictions; they also frequently cover the contracting or net use of short-, medium-, and long-term foreign debt, and changes in external reserves.

Performance criteria allow the member and the IMF to assess the member's progress in carrying out policies during the stand-by or extended arrangement, and they signal the need for possible corrective policies. When performance criteria have not been observed, further purchases are permitted only after the IMF and the member reach understandings--following consultations and Executive Board action--for the resumption of purchases.

Extended Fund Facility. Under the extended Fund facility (EFF), which was established in 1974, the Fund may provide assistance to members to meet their balance of payments deficits for longer periods and in amounts larger in relation to quotas than under the credit tranche policies.

A member that requests an extended arrangement is expected to present a program outlining the objectives and policies for the whole period of the extended arrangement, as well as a detailed statement of the policies and measures that it will follow in each 12-month period to meet the objectives of the program. In May 1988, the Board agreed that, in cases where a country has a strong adjustment program, more IMF resources could be made available by increasing actual access within the current limits; and in exceptional circumstances, access might extend beyond the existing quota limits. Also, disbursements and performance criteria can now be phased at semiannual intervals, provided that appropriate monitoring of macroeconomic developments is ensured. In addition, the period of an existing extended arrangement over which purchases can be phased--normally three years--may be lengthened, where appropriate and at the request of the member, to four years.

Purchases under the extended arrangement are made from ordinary resources until the outstanding use of ordinary resources in the upper credit tranches and under the facility equals 140 percent of quota, and from borrowed resources thereafter. Repurchases of drawings of ordinary resources are made 4 1/2 to 10 years after each purchase. Repurchases of purchases financed by borrowed resources under the enlarged access policy are made over a period of 3 1/2 to 7 years.

Enlarged Access Policy. The enlarged access policy enables the IMF to provide additional financing from borrowed resources, in conjunction with its ordinary resources, to members whose payments imbalances are large in relation to their quotas. The enlarged access policy is used when the member needs more financing from the IMF than is available to it in the four credit tranches or under the extended Fund facility, and when its problems require a relatively long period of adjustment and a longer repurchase period. Such purchases are subject to the relevant policies of the IMF, including those on phasing and performance criteria.

The policy on enlarged access and access limits under this policy are reviewed annually by the Executive Board, and, in the latest review in June 1990, the Board decided to leave the limits unchanged. The amount of assistance in individual cases is determined by guidelines that the IMF reviews periodically. The current access limits on stand-by or extended arrangements, individually or combined, are 90 or 110 percent of quota annually; 270 or 330 percent of quota over three years; and a cumulative limit of 400 or 440 percent of quota. The limits, which may be exceeded in exceptional circumstances, exclude drawings under the compensatory and contingency financing and buffer stock financing facilities. For a member that has a stand-by or an extended arrangement involving enlarged access, the amounts available for enlarged access to IMF resources are apportioned between ordinary quota-based resources and resources the IMF has borrowed.

Compensatory and Contingency Financing Helps Members Adjust to External Shocks

Compensatory financing under the compensatory and contingency financing facility (CCFF) helps countries meet shortfalls in their export receipts and/or excesses in the cost of cereal imports. Contingency financing, which was introduced in August 1988, helps countries facing adverse external shocks that are beyond their control to maintain the momentum of adjustment programs, through an appropriate blend of additional financing and adjustment.

The amounts of financing available to a member under the CCFF are up to 40 percent of quota each on account of the export shortfall and the external contingency elements, and up to 17 percent of quota for the cereal element. In addition, members may request an optional tranche of up to 25 percent of quota to supplement any one of these three elements. When a member has a satisfactory balance of payments position--except for the effect of an export shortfall or an excess in cereal import costs--a limit of 83 percent of quota applies for either of these elements. A joint limit of 105 percent of quota applies to the use of any two elements of the CCFF and a joint limit of 122 percent of quota applies to the use of all three.

Purchases under the CCFF are additional those under regular credit tranche policies. This means that a member's use of IMF resources under these special facilities may increase the IMF's holdings of the member's currency beyond the limits set for credit tranche policies.

Export Shortfalls. Shortfalls must be temporary and attributable to circumstances that are largely beyond the member's control. For members whose balance of payments problems go beyond the effects of an export shortfall, the use of the compensatory financing element requires that the member cooperate with the IMF in finding appropriate solutions to its balance of payments difficulties.

The calculated shortfall is the amount by which a country's export earnings in the shortfall year are below the value of their medium-term trend. This trend is defined as the geometric average of export earnings during the 5 years centered on the shortfall year, normally the latest 12-month period for which actual data are available. Projected export earnings for the 2 post-shortfall years may not be more than 20 percent above the level of actual export earnings in the 2 pre-shortfall years. In calculating the shortfall, a member may choose to include travel receipts or workers' remittances.

Excesses in Cereal Import Costs. Compensatory financing can also be provided in connection with a combination of an export shortfall and an excess in cereal import costs. An excess in cereal import costs is calculated as the difference in the cost of such imports in a given 12-month period from the arithmetic average cost for the 5 years centered on that year.

Contingency Financing. At the request of a member, a contingency mechanism is attached to an IMF arrangement, and financing is provided to cover part of the net effect on a member's balance of payments of unfavorable deviations beyond the member's control in key current account variables that are highly volatile and easily identifiable. For example, the variables covered could include key export or import prices and international interest rates. Deviations in the variables covered by a contingency mechanism are measured in relation to baseline projections, which are established at the start of each program or at the time of a review of a multiyear arrangement. The contingency mechanism is triggered once net deviations in the key elements exceed a threshold level and it is clear that movements in current account variables not covered by the mechanism have not offset such deviations. Favorable deviations--such as an unexpected increase in export prices--may trigger the symmetry provision, which may result in an increase in the reserve target under the IMF-supported program, a reduction in the amount available under the IMF arrangement, or an early repurchase of previous contingency purchases.

In addition to the cumulative limit on contingency financing of 40 percent of quota (or 65 percent of quota, including the optional tranche), such financing generally may not exceed 70 percent of access under the associated arrangement (or 70 percent of annual access under a multiyear arrangement). There is also a cumulative sub-limit of 35 percent of quota for contingency financing on account of deviations in international interest rates. Members, when requesting contingency mechanisms, should make every effort to obtain parallel financing from other sources, such as commercial banks, and they are encouraged to use market mechanisms to reduce their exposure to interest rate risks.

Buffer Stock Financing Facility. The buffer stock financing facility (BSFF), was established in 1969 to help finance IMF members' contributions to approved international commodity buffer stock schemes, subject to the existence of balance of payments need. No drawings have been made under this facility for the past six years, and no credits under it are outstanding. Drawings may be made for buffer stock financing up to the equivalent of 45 percent of quota. The member is expected to demonstrate its willingness to cooperate with the IMF to find, where required, appropriate solutions to its balance of payments difficulties. In April 1990, the IMF decided that the BSFF may be used to finance eligible members' contributions to the 1987 International Rubber Agreement.

Concessional Facilities Assist Poorer Countries

The IMF's Executive Board established the structural adjustment facility (SAF) in March 1986 to provide balance of payments assistance on concessional terms to low-income developing countries. The facility is being financed by SDR 2.8 billion of Trust Fund reflows expected to become available during 1985-91. In December 1987, the Executive Board established the enhanced structural adjustment facility (ESAF), which is financed from SAF resources, special loans, and grant contributions.

The SAF provides loans to support the medium-term macroeconomic and structural adjustment programs of low-income developing member countries with protracted balance of payments problems. The objective is to help these countries establish the conditions for sustained growth, strengthen their balance of payments position, and facilitate orderly relations with creditors and a reduction in trade and payments restrictions. Of the 62 countries currently eligible for SAF resources, China and India--the 2 largest--have indicated that they do not intend to make use of the facility, thereby making more resources available to other eligible countries.

The amount potentially available to each eligible member under SAF loans is 70 percent of the member's quota. Disbursements are made in three annual installments equivalent to 20 percent of quota in the first year, 30 percent in the second year, and 20 percent in the third year. SAF loans carry an annual interest rate of 0.5 percent, with repayments to be made semiannually, beginning 5 1/2 years and ending 10 years after the disbursement.

An eligible member seeking to use SAF resources develops, with the assistance of the staffs of the IMF and the World Bank, a policy framework for a three-year adjustment program, which is set out in a policy framework paper (PFP). The PFP describes the authorities' macroeconomic and structural policy objectives and priorities and the measures that they intend to adopt during the three years. It assesses the member's external financing needs and possible sources of finance. The PFP is also intended as a means of catalyzing and coordinating financial assistance in support of the adjustment program. The PFP is reviewed by the Executive Board of the IMF and by Executive Directors of the World Bank in the Committee of the Whole, and is updated annually on a three-year rolling basis.

The first annual loan disbursement under the SAF is made available after the Executive Board approves the three-year SAF arrangement and the first annual arrangement thereunder. In requesting these arrangements, the member is expected to present a program, consistent with the PFP, that describes the specific objectives and policies it will pursue during the three-year program period and the first annual program. The second and third loan installments are made after the IMF approves annual arrangements for those years. Performance during a program year is monitored with reference to benchmarks that reflect the program's key elements. Financial benchmarks that are specified on a quarterly basis usually cover monetary, fiscal, and external debt variables. Structural benchmarks are also usually specified for key structural policies. Although disbursements are not directly related to the observance of benchmarks, deviations would indicate the need for policy adjustments under the subsequent annual program.

The objectives, eligibility, and basic procedural features of the ESAF-- including the role of the PFP--parallel those of the SAF. Differences between the SAF and the ESAF relate largely to the monitoring and the strength of the programs and to the access to, and the funding of, the facilities. The adjustment measures adopted under programs supported by the ESAF are expected to be particularly ambitious, with a view to fostering growth and achieving a substantial strengthening of the balance of payments position during the three-year program. The 62 countries that are eligible for the SAF are also eligible for the ESAF. China has indicated that it does not intend to use ESAF

resources in the present circumstances, and India has indicated that, in the
absence of a fundamental deterioration in its balance of payments position, it
does not expect to borrow from the facility. Eligible members may request
arrangements under either the SAF or the ESAF. Requests for three-year
arrangements under the ESAF must be approved before the end of November 1992.

Total ESAF resources are expected to amount to approximately SDR 6 billion
in special loans and other contributions, in addition to the amounts remaining
undisbursed under SAF arrangements. Access to ESAF resources differs according
to members' balance of payments needs and the strength of their adjustment
efforts. An eligible member country may borrow a maximum of 250 percent of its
quota under a three-year arrangement, although this limit may be exceeded
under exceptional circumstances up to a maximum of 350 percent of quota. ESAF
loans are expected to average about 150 percent of quota.

As with the SAF, ESAF loans are repaid in 10 semiannual installments,
beginning 5 1/2 years and ending 10 years after the date of disbursement. The
interest rate on ESAF loans is currently 0.5 percent a year but will be
reviewed periodically by the Executive Board. Monitoring under ESAF
arrangements is conducted on the basis of quarterly financial benchmarks and
structural benchmarks, as under the SAF. In addition, performance criteria
are established semiannually for financial targets and are set for a few
structural policies. Policies and performance are reviewed at midyear in most
cases. ESAF loans are disbursed semiannually, initially upon approval of an
annual arrangement and subsequently based on the observance of performance
criteria and, in most cases, after the midyear review is completed.

Guidelines Provide for IMF Support Of Debt and Debt-Service Reduction

The Executive Board approved, in May 1989, new guidelines for the IMF's involvement in helping developing member countries that face serious debt problems. Under the guidelines, the IMF may provide resources for debt and debt-service reduction operations. The World Bank has adopted similar guidelines.

The changes are part of the IMF's ongoing efforts to adapt its own policies to assist member countries in coping with their debt problems. They involve its active contribution to designing and implementing a cooperative strategy for dealing with these problems on a case-by-case basis. The ultimate objective of the debt strategy is to ensure satisfactory growth with balance of payments viability and to restore debtor countries' spontaneous access to credit markets. The basic conditions for the success of this strategy continue to be:

o growth-oriented adjustment and structural reform in debtor countries;

o a favorable global economic environment; and

o adequate financial support from official (bilateral and multilateral) and private sources.

The Guidelines. All members are eligible for IMF financial support of debt and debt-service reduction under the new guidelines, provided that the IMF is satisfied that o the member is pursuing an economic adjustment program with strong elements of structural reform, in the context of a stand-by or extended arrangement;

o voluntary, market-based, debt and debt-service reduction will help the country regain access to credit markets and achieve external payments viability with economic growth; and

o financial support for debt and debt-service reduction represents an efficient use of scarce resources.

In assessing the quality of a member's adjustment and structural reform program, the Executive Board will give particular emphasis to policies designed to improve the climate for saving and investment, help reverse capital flight, and attract private capital inflows and direct investment.

Amount of Support. The guidelines provide that the proportion of IMF resources committed under an extended or stand-by arrangement that could be set aside to finance operations involving a reduction in the stock of debt would generally be about 25 percent, although the proportion would be determined on a case-by-case basis. Drawings on set-aside amounts are normally to be phased--in line with the member's performance under the adjustment program--but some front-loading or phasing in accordance with the specific financing needs of the member's debt-reduction plan may be permitted.

Moreover, the IMF is prepared, in certain cases, to provide additional access to its resources, provided that such support would be decisive in promoting further cost-effective debt and debt-service reduction and in catalyzing other financial resources. Such additional access--up to 40 percent of the member's quota--can be used for interest support in connection with debt or debt-service reduction. Actual access is based on the magnitude of the member's balance of payments problems, the strength of its adjustment program, and its efforts to contribute its own resources to support debt and debt-service reduction.

The Executive Board has stressed the importance of close collaboration between the IMF and the World Bank in supporting effective debt and debt-service reduction operations by member countries.

Financing Assurances. The objectives of the IMF's policy on financing assurances are to ensure that:

o adjustment programs are fully financed;

o financing is consistent with a return of the country to a viable balance of payments position and with its ability to repay the IMF;

o the burden of financing is shared equitably; and

o orderly relations between the member country and its creditors are maintained or re-established.

The guidelines of May 1989 also modified the policy on financing assurances in view of changes in the financial environment and the possibility that debtors and creditors may need time to agree on financing packages. Under these guidelines, the IMF may approve an arrangement before the conclusion of a financing package between the member and its commercial bank creditors if prompt IMF support is essential for program implementation, negotiations with banks have begun, and an appropriate financing package is expected to be concluded within a reasonable period of time. When circumstances warrant, the practice of seeking a critical mass, and the possibility of approving an arrangement in principle, will continue to be followed.

To promote orderly financial relations, every effort will be made to avoid arrears, which could not be condoned or anticipated by the IMF in the design of programs. Nevertheless, an accumulation of arrears to banks may have to be tolerated where negotiations continue and the country's financing situation does not allow them to be avoided. The IMF's policy of nontoleration of arrears to official creditors remains unchanged.

Overdue Financial Obligations Affect IMF Operations

Overdue financial obligations to the IMF remained a serious problem in 1989/90. During the financial year, however, a number of countries with overdue obligations continued, or began, to pursue economic policies aimed at restoring growth and external viability as part of their efforts to cooperate with the IMF in addressing the problem of their arrears. Some support groups of creditor and donor countries have been formed to assist countries in clearing arrears to international financial institutions. In late June, Guyana and Honduras cleared their arrears with the IMF; they became the first countries with protracted arrears to do so.

In the few cases in which members have not shown a willingness to cooperate with the IMF in resolving the problem of their overdue obligations, the Executive Board has indicated that it would apply remedial measures according to the guidelines established under the IMF's cooperative strategy. During 1989/90, the Board further defined the procedures, and timetable, for the application of remedial measures and added two new instruments-- communications with IMF Governors and heads of selected international financial institutions and a declaration of noncooperation. Communications have been sent by the Managing Director regarding a member's failure to fulfill its financial obligations to the IMF in four instances, of which three involved ineligible members and one involved a member that was not yet ineligible. The Board issued a declaration of noncooperation in the case of one member (Liberia), which noted, among other points, that if the member did not resume active cooperation with the IMF, the IMF would consider initiating procedures leading to the compulsory withdrawal of the member from the IMF.

In May 1990, the Interim Committee endorsed the concept of a "rights" approach, under which a member with protracted arrears could earn "rights"-- based on sustained performance during the period of a "rights accumulation" program monitored by the IMF--toward future financing once its arrears to the

IMF had been cleared. Such programs would generally span a period of around three years. Under this approach, upon successful completion of a rights accumulation program, clearance of the member's arrears, and approval by the IMF of the successor arrangement, the member would be able to cash in its accumulated rights as the first disbursement under a new successor arrangement.

Future financing could be made available from the IMF's general resources, or for the countries eligible to use the structural adjustment facility (SAF), from the general resources, the SAF, or the enhanced structural adjustment facility (ESAF), or some combination as determined by the Executive Board. The Interim Committee concurred with the proposal that the IMF pledge the use of up to 3 million ounces of gold, if needed, as additional security for use of ESAF resources in connection with financing of accumulated rights.

The Board of Governors of the IMF adopted a Resolution, effective June 28, 1990, approving proposals for a Third Amendment to the IMF's Articles of Agreement. Under the proposed amendment, a member's voting rights and certain related rights may be suspended by the Executive Board, by a 70 percent majority of the total voting power, if the member, having been declared ineligible to use the general resources of the IMF, persists in its failure to fulfill any of the obligations under the Articles. In accordance with the Articles of Agreement, the IMF must now ask all members whether they accept the proposed amendment. In addition, the Executive Board adopted, in June 1990, an extension of IMF mechanisms for the sharing of burdens associated with overdue obligations to cover the risks to the General Resources Account associated with outstanding credit stemming from the encashment of rights.

Table 1

Fund Provides Financial Assistance
To Overcome Balance of Payments Difficulties

Tranche policies

First credit tranche

Member demonstrates reasonable efforts to overcome balance of payments difficulties in program. Performance criteria and purchase installments not used. Repurchases are made in $3^1/_4$–5 years.

Upper credit tranches

Member must have a substantial and viable program to overcome its balance of payments difficulties. Resources normally provided in the form of stand-by arrangements that include performance criteria and purchases in installments. Repurchases are made in $3^1/_4$–5 years.

Extended Fund facility

Medium-term program aims at overcoming structural balance of payments maladjustments. A program is generally for three years, although it may be lengthened to four years, where this would facilitate sustained policy implementation and achievement of balance of payments viability over the medium term. Program states policies and measures for first 12-month period in detail. Resources are provided in the form of extended arrangements that include performance criteria and drawings in installments; repurchases are made in $4^1/_2$–10 years.

Enlarged access policy

Policy used to augment resources available under stand-by and extended arrangements, for programs that need large amounts of Fund support. Applicable policies on conditionality, phasing, and performance criteria are the same as under the credit tranches and the extended Fund facility. Repurchases are made in $3^1/_2$–7 years, and charges are based on the Fund's borrowing costs.

Compensatory and contingency financing facility

The compensatory element provides resources to a member for an export shortfall or excess in cereal import costs that are due to factors largely beyond the member's control. The contingency element helps members with Fund-supported adjustment programs to maintain the momentum of adjustment efforts in the face of a broad range of unanticipated, adverse external shocks. Repurchases are made in $3^1/_4$–5 years.

Buffer stock financing facility

Resources help finance member's contribution to an approved international buffer stock. Repurchases are made in $3^1/_4$–5 years.

Structural adjustment facility

Resources are provided on concessional terms to low-income developing member countries facing protracted balance of payments problems, in support of medium-term macroeconomic and structural adjustment programs. Member develops, and updates, with assistance of the Fund and the World Bank, a medium-term policy framework for a three-year period, which is set out in a policy framework paper (PFP). Detailed annual programs are formulated prior to disbursement of annual loans, and include quarterly benchmarks to assess performance. Repayments are made in $5^1/_2$–10 years.

Enhanced structural adjustment facility

Objectives, eligibility, and basic program features of this facility parallel those of the SAF; differences relate to provisions for access, monitoring, and funding. A policy framework paper and detailed annual program are prepared each year. Arrangements include quarterly benchmarks, semiannual performance criteria, and, in most cases, a midyear review. Adjustment measures are expected to be particularly strong, aiming to foster growth and to achieve a substantial strengthening of the balance of payments position. Loans are disbursed semiannually, and repayments are made in $5^1/_2$–10 years.

Table 2

Potential Cumulative Disbursements Under Arrangements and Facilities

(percent of member quotas)[1]

Under stand-by and extended arrangements[2, 3]

Annual	**90-110**
Three-year	**270-330**
Cumulative	**400-440**

Special facilities[3]

Compensatory and contingency
financing facility (CCFF)

● *Compensatory financing*	**40**
● *Contingency financing[4]*	**40**
● *Optional tranche[5]*	**25**
● *Excess cereal import costs*	**17**
● *Combined[6]*	**122**

Buffer stock financing facility	**45**

Under SAF and ESAF arrangements

Structural adjustment facility[7]

● *First year*	**20**
● *Second year*	**30**
● *Third year*	**20**
● *Cumulative*	**70**

Enhanced structural
adjustment facility[8]

● *Cumulative*	**250**

[1]Under exceptional circumstances, the amounts disbursed may exceed the following limits.

[2]Excludes drawings on available reserve tranches.

[3]These arrangements and facilities are financed directly with Fund resources.

[4]Contingency financing may not exceed 70 percent of access made under the associated arrangement, with a cumulative sublimit of 35 percent of quota on account of deviations in interest rates.

[5]May be applied to supplement the amounts for compensatory financing, contingency financing, or excess in cereal import costs.

[6]Where a member has a satisfactory balance of payments position—except for the effect of an export shortfall or an excess in cereal costs—a limit of 83 percent of quota applies to either the export or cereal element, with a combined limit of 105 percent of quota.

[7]This facility is financed with the SDR 2.7 billion in reflows from the Trust Fund.

[8]This facility is being financed with SAF resources and with special loan and grant contributions.

Table 3

Stand-By, Extended, Structural Adjustment Facility (SAF), and Enhanced Structural Adjustment Facility (ESAF) Arrangements as of June 30

(million SDRs)

Member	Date of Arrangement	Expiration Date	Total Amount	Undrawn Balance
Stand-by arrangements			**2,995.12**	**1,814.75**
Argentina	Nov. 10, 1989	Mar. 31, 1991	920.00	552.00
Chile	Nov. 8, 1989	Nov. 7, 1990	64.00	—
Côte d'Ivoire	Nov. 20, 1989	Apr. 19, 1991	146.50	87.90
Ecuador	Sept. 15, 1989	Feb. 28, 1991	109.90	70.65
Gabon	Sept. 15, 1989	Mar. 14, 1991	43.00	32.50
Haiti	Sept. 18, 1989	Dec. 31, 1990	21.00	6.00
Hungary	Mar. 14, 1990	Mar. 13, 1991	159.21	127.37
Jamaica	Mar. 23, 1990	May 31, 1991	82.00	68.30
Jordan	July 14, 1989	Jan. 13, 1991	60.00	33.20
Pakistan	Dec. 28, 1988	Nov. 30, 1990	273.15	78.67
Papua New Guinea	Apr. 25, 1990	June 24, 1991	26.36	26.36
Poland	Feb. 5, 1990	Mar. 4, 1991	545.00	281.25
Trinidad and Tobago	Apr. 20, 1990	Mar. 31, 1991	85.00	56.25
Yugoslavia	Mar. 16, 1990	Sept. 15, 1991	460.00	394.30
Extended arrangements			**7,765.30**	**5,001.78**
Mexico	May 26, 1989	May 25, 1992	3,263.40	1,491.84
Philippines	May 23, 1989	May 22, 1992	660.60	424.68
Tunisia	July 25, 1988	July 24, 1991	138.20	138.20
Venezuela	June 23, 1989	June 22, 1992	3,703.10	2,947.06
SAF arrangements			**811.02**	**218.62**
Benin	June 16, 1989	June 15, 1992	21.91	15.65
Chad	Oct. 30, 1987	Oct. 29, 1990	21.42	—
Equatorial Guinea	Dec. 7, 1988	Dec. 6, 1991	12.88	9.20
Guinea	July 29, 1987	July 28, 1990	40.53	11.58
Guinea-Bissau	Oct. 14, 1987	Oct. 13, 1990	5.25	1.50
Lao P.D.R.	Sept. 18, 1989	Sept. 17, 1992	20.51	14.65
Lesotho	June 29, 1988	June 28, 1991	10.57	—
Mali	Aug. 5, 1988	Aug. 4, 1991	35.56	10.16
Nepal	Oct. 14, 1987	Oct. 13, 1990	26.11	—
Pakistan	Dec. 28, 1988	Dec. 27, 1991	382.41	109.26
Sao Tome and Principe	June 2, 1989	June 1, 1992	2.80	2.00
Sri Lanka	Mar. 9, 1988	Mar. 8, 1991	156.17	44.62
Tanzania	Oct. 30, 1987	Oct. 29, 1990	74.90	—
ESAF arrangements			**1,455.60**	**662.63**
Bolivia	July 27, 1988	July 26, 1991	136.05	68.02
Gambia, The	Nov. 23, 1988	Nov. 22, 1991	20.52	6.84
Ghana	Nov. 9, 1988	Nov. 8, 1991	368.10	96.00
Kenya	May 15, 1989	May 14, 1992	241.40	120.70
Madagascar	May 15, 1989	May 14, 1992	76.90	38.45
Malawi	July 15, 1988	July 14, 1991	55.80	18.60
Mauritania	May 24, 1989	May 23, 1992	50.85	33.90
Mozambique	June 1, 1990	May 31, 1993	85.40	76.25
Niger	Dec. 12, 1988	Dec. 11, 1991	50.55	33.70
Senegal	Nov. 21, 1988	Nov. 20, 1991	144.67	42.55
Togo	May 31, 1989	May 30, 1992	46.08	23.04
Uganda	Apr. 17, 1989	Apr. 16, 1992	179.28	104.58
TOTAL			**13,027.04**	**7,697.78**

Data: IMF Treasurer's Department

Table IV

Exchange Arrangements of Fund Members 1/
(as of March 30, 1990)

Types of Exchange Arrangements	All Countries	Industrial Countries	Fuel Exporters	Developing Countries			
				Primary Product Exporters	Exporters of Manufactures	Service and Remittance Countries	Other
Pegged to:							
Single currency:							
U.S. dollar	30		3	11		12	4
French franc	14		3	8		1	2
Other	5			2		3	
Currency composite:							
SDR	7		2	4		1	
Other	34	5	2	9	5	10	3
Flexibility limited vis-a-vis a single currency or group of currencies:							
Single currency 2/	4		3				1
Cooperative arrangements 3/	9	9					
More flexible:							
Adjusted according to a set of indicators	4	1		3			
Other managed floating	23	1	3	9	7	2	1
Independently floating	21	6	2	8	1	2	2
TOTAL	151	22	18	54	13	31	13

Data: International Monetary Fund

1/ Data exclude the Democratic Republic of Kampuchea.
2/ U.S. dollar.
3/ Countries participating in the Exchange Rate Mechanism.

Currency		Rate	$ rate
Chile (peso)[8,9,10]		296.98	
China (yuan)[4]	F	4.7221	
Colombia (peso)[8]	F	468.96	
Comoros (franc)	F	50.00	
Congo (franc)	F	50.00	
Costa Rica (colón)[4]	F	86.45	
Côte d'Ivoire (franc)	F	50.00	
Cyprus (pound)	bskt	0.48031	
Denmark (krone)[7]		6.4685	
Djibouti (franc)	$	177.721	
Dominica (EC$)[5]	$	2.70	
Dominican Rep. (peso)	$	6.34	
Ecuador (sucre)[4]	$	710.03	
Egypt (pound)[4]	$	2.633	
El Salvador (colón)[4]	$	7.70	
Equatorial Guinea (franc)	F	50.00	
Ethiopia (birr)	$	2.07	
Fiji (dollar)[4]	bskt	1.54131	
Finland (markka)[11]	bskt	4.002	
France (franc)[7]	F		
Gabon (franc)	F	50.00	
Gambia, The (dalasi)		8.3396	
Germany, Fed. Rep. of (deutsche mark)[7]		1.6944	
Ghana (cedi)[4]		313.0	
Greece (drachma)		163.12	
Grenada (EC$)[5]	$	2.70	
Guatemala (quetzal)[12]			
Guinea (franc)		650.0	
Guinea-Bissau (peso)		2132.11	
Guyana (dollar)	$	33.00	
Haiti (gourde)	$	5.00	
Honduras (lempira)[4]	$		
Hungary (forint)	bskt	65.6438	
Iceland (króna)[13]	bskt	61.06	
India (rupee)[14]	bskt	17.226686	
Mexico (peso)[4]		2718.0	
Morocco (dirham)		8.0581	
Mozambique (metical)	bskt	902.711	
Myanmar (kyat)	SDR	8.50847	6.54080
Nepal (rupee)	bskt	28.9	
Netherlands (guilder)[7]		1.908	
New Zealand (dollar)	$	1.72473	
Nicaragua (new córdoba)[4,12]	$		
Niger (franc)	F	50.00	
Nigeria (naira)[13]		7.9428	
Norway (krone)[13]	bskt	6.559	
Oman (rial Omani)[4]	$	0.3845	
Pakistan (rupee)	bskt	21.5337	
Panama (balboa)	$	1.00	
Papua New Guinea (kina)	bskt		
Paraguay (guaraní)[12]		0.957579	1215.84
Peru (inti)[4]	$	11225.4	
Philippines (peso)		22.75	
Poland (zloty)[4]	bskt	9500.00	
Portugal (escudo)[8]		149.756	
Qatar (riyal)[6]		3.64	
Romania (leu)	bskt	21.28	
Rwanda (franc)	SDR	102.71	78.9573
St. Kitts and Nevis (EC$)[5]	$		
St. Lucia (EC$)[5]	$	2.70	
St. Vincent (EC$)[5]	$	2.70	
Sao Tome and Principe (dobra)[12]			
Saudi Arabia (riyal)[6]		3.745	
Senegal (franc)	F	50.00	
Seychelles (rupee)	SDR	7.2345	
Sierra Leone (leone)[12]	$	5.56145	
Singapore (dollar)		1.8843	
Solomon Islands (dollar)	bskt	2.4876	
Yemen Arab Rep. (rial)	$	12.01	
Yemen, People's Dem. Rep. of (dinar)	$	0.345399	
Yugoslavia (dinar)[17]		11.87	
Zaire (zaire)		515.0	
Zambia (kwacha)[4]	SDR	40.00	21.6488
Zimbabwe (dollar)[4]	bskt	2.3736	

$	U.S. dollar	bskt	Currency basket other than SDR
F	French franc	Re	Indian rupee
R	South African rand	A$	Australian dollar

[1] Rates and arrangements as reported to the Fund and in terms of currency units per unit pegged to; rates determined by baskets of currencies are in currency units per U.S. dollar.

[2] Market rates in currency units per U.S. dollar.

[3] Under this heading are listed those members that describe their exchange rate arrangements as managed floating, floating independently, or as adjusting according to a set of indicators (see footnote 8) and certain other members whose exchange arrangements are not otherwise described in this table. In addition, U.S. dollar quotations are given for the currencies that are pegged to the SDR and for those that participate in the European Monetary System (see footnote 7).

[4] Member maintains exchange arrangements involving more than one exchange market. The arrangement shown is that maintained in the major market. A description of the member's exchange system as of December 31, 1988 is given in the Annual Report on Exchange Arrangements and Exchange Restrictions, 1989.

[5] East Caribbean dollar.

[6] Exchange rates are determined on the basis of a relationship to the SDR, within margins of ±7.25 percent. However, because of the maintenance of a relatively stable relationship with the U.S. dollar, these margins are not always observed.

[7] Belgium, Denmark, France, the Federal Republic of Germany, Ireland, Italy, Luxembourg, the Netherlands, and Spain are participating in the exchange rate and intervention mechanism of the European Monetary System and maintain maximum margins of 2.25 percent (in the case of the Spanish peseta, 6 percent) for exchange rates in transactions in the official markets between their currencies and those of the other countries in this group.

[8] Exchange rates adjusted according to a set of indicators.

[9] Member maintains a system of advance announcements of exchange rates.

[10] The exchange rate is maintained within margins of ±5.0 percent.

[11] The exchange rate is maintained within margins of ±3.0 percent.

[12] Exchange rate data not available.

[13] The exchange rate is maintained within margins of ±2.25 percent.

[14] The exchange rate is maintained within margins of ±5 percent on either side of a weighted composite of the currencies of the main trading partners.

[15] The exchange rate is maintained within margins of ±7.5 percent.

[16] The exchange rate is maintained within margins of ±1.5 percent.

[17] Member maintains a fixed relationship of Din ± = DM1.

Data: IMF Treasurer's and Exchange and Trade Relations Departments

Table 5

Exchange Rates and Exchange Arrangements, March 30, 1990

Member (currency)	Exchange Rate Pegged to[1]	Exchange Rate[1]	Exchange Rate Otherwise Determined[2,3]
Afghanistan (afghani)[4]	$	50.60	
Algeria (dinar)	bskt	7.9674	
Angola (kwanza)	$	29.958	
Antigua and Barbuda (EC$)[5]	$	2.70	
Argentina (austral)			4660.0
Australia (dollar)			1.32591
Austria (schilling)	bskt	11.925	
Bahamas, The (dollar)[4]	$	1.00	
Bahrain (dinar)[6]	bskt	0.376	
Bangladesh (taka)[4]	bskt	33.88	
Barbados (dollar)	$	2.0113	
Belgium (franc)[7]			35.06
Belize (dollar)	$	2.00	
Benin (franc)	F	50.00	
Bhutan (ngultrum)	Re	1.00	
Bolivia (boliviano)			3.085
Botswana (pula)	bskt	1.89798	
Brazil (cruzeiro)[8]			41.933
Burkina Faso (franc)	F	50.00	
Burundi (franc)	SDR	232.14	178.455
Cameroon (franc)	F	50.00	
Canada (dollar)			1.1702
Cape Verde (escudo)	bskt	74.31	
Central African Republic (franc)	F	50.00	
Chad (franc)	F	50.00	
Indonesia (rupiah)			1822.00
Iran, Islamic Rep. of (rial)[4]	SDR	92.30	70.9547
Iraq (dinar)	$	0.310857	
Ireland (pound)[7]			0.633433
Israel (new sheqel)[11]	bskt	1.9940	
Italy (lira)[7]			1249.175
Jamaica (dollar)			6.95
Japan (yen)			157.2
Jordan (dinar)	bskt	1.49031	
Kenya (shilling)	bskt		22.8988
Kiribati (dollar)	A$	1.00	
Korea (won)			700.9
Kuwait (dinar)	bskt	0.29410	
Lao People's Dem. Rep. (kip)			713.50
Lebanon (pound)			571.0
Lesotho (loti)[4]	R	1.00	
Liberia (dollar)[4]	$	1.00	
Libya (dinar)[15]	SDR	0.383929	0.295142
Luxembourg (franc)[7]			35.06
Madagascar (franc)[8]			1538.89
Malawi (kwacha)	bskt	2.9214	
Malaysia (ringgit)[13]	bskt	2.728	
Maldives (rufiyaa)			9.1950
Mali (franc)	F	50.00	
Malta (lira)	bskt	2.993	
Mauritania (ouguiya)			83.87
Mauritius (rupee)	bskt	15.1011	
Somalia (shilling)	bskt	1106.0	
South Africa (rand)[4]			2.65449
Spain (peseta)[7]			108.55
Sri Lanka (rupee)			40.00
Sudan (pound)	$	4.50	
Suriname (guilder)	$	1.785	
Swaziland (lilangeni)	R	1.00	
Sweden (krona)[16]	bskt	6.1255	
Syrian Arab Rep. (pound)[4]	$	11.225	
Tanzania (shilling)	bskt	193.935	
Thailand (baht)	bskt	25.98	
Togo (franc)	F	50.00	
Tonga (pa'anga)	A$	1.00	
Trinidad and Tobago (dollar)	$	4.260625	
Tunisia (dinar)			0.904216
Turkey (lira)			2486.51
Uganda (shilling)	bskt	380.52	
United Arab Emirates (dirham)[6]			3.671
United Kingdom (pound)			0.608717
United States (dollar)			1.00
Uruguay (new peso)			968.0
Vanuatu (vatu)	bskt	120.75	
Venezuela (bolivar)[4]			44.05
Viet Nam (dong)[4]	bskt	4.300	
Western Samoa (tala)	bskt	2.35349	

Table 6

Current and Proposed Fund Quotas
(million SDRs)

Member	Current	Proposed	Member	Current	Proposed	Member	Current	Proposed
Afghanistan	86.7	120.4	Grenada	6.0	8.5	Pakistan	546.3	758.2
Algeria	623.1	914.4	Guatemala	108.0	153.8	Panama	102.2	149.6
Angola	145.0	207.3	Guinea	57.9	78.7	Papua New Guinea	65.9	95.3
Antigua and Barbuda	5.0	8.5	Guinea-Bissau	7.5	10.5	Paraguay	48.4	72.1
Argentina	1,113.0	1,537.1	Guyana	49.2	67.2	Peru	330.9	466.1
Australia	1,619.2	2,333.2	Haiti	44.1	60.7	Philippines	440.4	633.4
Austria	775.6	1,188.3	Honduras	67.8	95.0	Poland	680.0	988.5
Bahamas, The	66.4	94.9	Hungary	530.7	754.8	Portugal	376.6	557.6
Bahrain	48.9	82.8	Iceland	59.6	85.3	Qatar	114.9	190.5
Bangladesh	287.5	392.5	India	2,207.7	3,055.5	Romania	523.4	754.1
Barbados	34.1	48.9	Indonesia	1,009.7	1,497.6	Rwanda	43.8	59.5
Belgium	2,080.4	3,102.3	Iran	660.0	1,078.5	Sao Tome & Principe	4.0	5.5
Belize	9.5	13.5	Iraq	504.0	864.8	Saudi Arabia	3,202.4	5,130.6
Benin	31.3	45.3	Ireland	343.4	525.0	Senegal	85.1	118.9
Bhutan	2.5	4.5	Israel	446.6	666.2	Seychelles	3.0	6.0
Bolivia	90.7	126.2	Italy	2,909.1	4,590.7	Sierra Leone	57.9	77.2
Botswana	22.1	36.6	Jamaica	145.5	200.9	Singapore	92.4	357.6
Brazil	1,461.3	2,170.8	Japan	4,223.3	8,241.5	Solomon Islands	5.0	7.5
Burkina Faso	31.6	44.2	Jordan	73.9	121.7	Somalia	44.2	60.9
Burundi	42.7	57.2	Kampuchea, Democratic	25.0	25.0	South Africa	915.7	1,365.4
Cameroon	92.7	135.1	Kenya	142.0	199.4	Spain	1,286.0	1,935.4
Canada	2,941.0	4,320.3	Kiribati, Republic of	2.5	4.0	Sri Lanka	223.1	303.6
Cape Verde	4.5	7.0	Korea	462.8	799.6	St. Kitts & Nevis	4.5	6.5
Central African Rep.	30.4	41.2	Kuwait	635.3	995.2	St. Lucia	7.5	11.0
Chad	30.6	41.3	Lao People's Dem. Rep.	29.3	39.1	St. Vincent & Grenadines	4.0	6.0
						Sudan	169.7	233.1

Country		
Chile	440.5	621.7
China	2,390.9	3,385.2
Colombia	394.2	561.3
Comoros	4.5	6.5
Congo, People's Rep.	37.3	57.9
Costa Rica	84.1	119.0
Côte d'Ivoire	165.5	238.2
Cyprus	69.7	100.0
Denmark	711.0	1,069.9
Djibouti	8.0	11.5
Dominica	4.0	6.0
Dominican Republic	112.1	158.8
Ecuador	150.7	219.2
Egypt	463.4	678.4
El Salvador	89.0	125.6
Equatorial Guinea	18.4	24.3
Ethiopia	70.6	98.3
Fiji	36.5	51.1
Finland	574.9	861.8
France	4,482.8	7,414.6
Gabon	73.1	110.3
Gambia, The	17.1	22.9
Germany, Fed. Rep. of	5,403.7	8,241.5
Ghana	204.5	274.0
Greece	399.9	587.6

Country		
Lebanon	78.7	146.0
Lesotho	15.1	23.9
Liberia	71.3	96.2
Libya	515.7	817.6
Luxembourg	77.0	135.5
Madagascar	66.4	90.4
Malawi	37.2	50.9
Malaysia	550.6	832.7
Maldives	2.0	5.5
Mali	50.8	68.9
Malta	45.1	67.5
Mauritania	33.9	47.5
Mauritius	53.6	73.3
Mexico	1,165.5	1,753.3
Morocco	306.6	427.7
Mozambique	61.0	84.0
Myanmar	137.0	184.9
Nepal	37.3	52.0
Netherlands	2,264.8	3,444.2
New Zealand	461.6	650.1
Nicaragua	68.2	96.1
Niger	33.7	48.3
Nigeria	849.5	1,281.6
Norway	699.0	1,104.6
Oman	63.1	119.4

Country		
Suriname	49.3	67.6
Swaziland	24.7	36.5
Sweden	1,064.3	1,614.0
Syrian Arab Republic	139.1	209.9
Tanzania	107.0	146.9
Thailand	386.6	573.9
Togo	38.4	54.3
Tonga	3.25	5.0
Trinidad and Tobago	170.1	246.8
Tunisia	138.2	206.0
Turkey	429.1	642.0
Uganda	99.6	133.9
United Arab Emirates	202.6	392.1
United Kingdom	6,194.0	7,414.6
United States	17,918.3	26,526.8
Uruguay	163.8	225.3
Vanuatu	9.0	12.5
Venezuela	1,371.5	1,951.3
Viet Nam	176.8	241.6
Western Samoa	6.0	8.5
Yemen, Republic of	120.5	176.5
Yugoslavia	613.0	918.3
Zaïre	291.0	394.8
Zambia	270.3	363.5
Zimbabwe	191.0	261.3

Data: IMF

Appendix:

IMF Board of Governors Adopts Resolutions

On Quota Increase and Third Amendment

Resolutions proposing increases in members' quotas and the acceptance of a

Third Amendment to the IMF's Articles of Agreement were adopted by the Board

of Governors on June 28, 1990. The proposed increases in quotas--if accepted

by members following their national legislative or other procedures--will

expand the size of the IMF by 50 percent, to approximately SDR 135.2 billion.

When the increases take effect, the Federal Republic of Germany and Japan will

share second place in terms of size of quota after the United States, followed

by France and the United Kingdom, which will also have equal quotas.

No increase in quotas can become effective before the date of the IMF's

determination that, during the period ending December 30, 1991, members having

not less than 85 percent of present quotas have consented to the increases

proposed for them, and, thereafter, that members having not less than 70

percent of present quotas have so consented. In addition, the quota increases

will not be effective until the proposed Third Amendment to the IMF's Articles

of Agreement has taken effect.

The proposed Third Amendment provides that a member's voting rights and

certain related rights may be suspended by the Executive Board, by a 70

percent majority of the total voting power, if the member persistently fails to fulfill any of the obligations under the Articles. The Amendment will take effect when the IMF certifies that three fifths of the members, having 85 percent of the total voting power, have accepted it. The Interim Committee, at its May meeting, urged members to make every effort to ensure that the Resolutions on the quota increase and the Third Amendment are effective before the end of 1991.

Part X

Perspectives and Implications

Klein

SOME ECONOMIC SCENARIOS
FOR THE 1980's

Nobel Memorial Lecture, 8 December, 1980
by

LAWRENCE R. KLEIN

University of Pennsylvania, Philadelphia, Pennsylvania 19104, USA

At the beginning of a decade it is tempting to look ahead for the next ten years. In addition to end-of-decade targets, there is considerable interest, at the present time, in end-of-century targets. Analysis of multi-decade developments depends on an even longer view, and I shall focus my attention on the medium-term outlook for one decade as much as possible.

This analysis will proceed through the medium of two econometric models, one for the United States and one for the World as a whole. I shall refer to available simulations of the Wharton Model of the United States for a single (large) country appraisal. The U.S. weight in the total for all OECD countries is more than one-third of aggregate production. Any sizeable action by the U.S. is, therefore, reflected in the totals.

Other countries are going in their own chosen directions, and it will be useful to try pull them all together in world model simulations from the equation system of project LINK. The LINK system is an amalgamation of econometric models from 17 OECD industrial countries, eight socialist countries, and four regional models of developing countries.[1]

BASE CASE – UNITED STATES

First, let us consider a baseline simulation for the United States. There is general recognition that something large (a "sea change") has come over the leading countries in the OECD area. In the case of the United States, real GNP growth, from the end of World War II until the end of the 1960's, averaged just under 4%. The baseline projection shows a distinct tendency for the economy to hover in the neighborhood of 3% growth. Slower growth, more inflation, high interest costs, an elevated rate of unemployment and balance-of-payments problems are manifest in the long sequence of tables generated by the Wharton Annual Model. Some annual growth rates, recorded at five year intervals, are listed in Table 1.

---

[1] This is the present country/regional make-up of the LINK system. In some versions of system simulations – set up a year or so ago – there are four fewer OECD country models and one fewer centrally planned model.

This is a pattern familiar not only in the United States but in other industrial countries. The changed economic profile between the post World War II recovery/expansion period (1945—1970) and the period since 1970, through the end of the decade, is a result of some profound changes in the underlying economic environment. They are related to such major events as

   (i)   energy supply-demand imbalance and a shift from inexpensive to dear prices;
   (ii) pressure on available food supplies and a shift towards higher food prices;
   (iii) accelerated inflation;
   (iv) declining productivity growth;

Table 1. Five Year Average Annual Percentage Growth Rates

Five Years Ending:	1960	1965	1970	1975	1980[1]	1985[1]	1990[1]
Real GNP	2.4	4.7	3.0	2.3	3.3	3.0	3.0
GNP Deflator	2.4	1.6	4.2	6.8	7.3	8.0	7.6
Nominal GNP	4.9	6.3	7.4	9.2	10.8	11.3	10.8
Real Consumption	2.8	4.3	3.7	3.0	3.6	2.7	3.0
Durables	0.1	6.9	3.9	4.9	3.5	3.1	2.6
Nondurables	2.4	3.2	3.0	1.6	2.8	1.4	2.0
Services	4.1	4.6	4.3	3.6	4.3	3.4	3.8
Total Real Investment	0.2	7.3	0.6	−1.6	5.3	5.9	3.8
Nonresidential	1.5	7.7	2.8	0.6	4.8	3.2	4.5
Residential	−0.1	4.3	−1.3	−0.8	2.2	7.5	2.2
Real Trade Flows							
Imports	5.5	6.2	9.9	0.5	8.8	3.1	3.7
Exports	5.1	6.5	6.4	6.0	7.7	3.9	3.3
Real Government							
Spending	2.8	3.9	3.6	1.0	1.4	1.9	2.2
Federal	0.9	2.1	2.0	−2.7	2.0	3.3	2.0
State and Local	5.1	5.9	5.0	3.6	1.0	0.9	2.3
Employment	1.1	1.6	2.0	1.5	2.7	1.4	1.3
Civilian Labor Force	1.4	1.3	2.1	2.3	2.5	1.3	1.1

[1] Forecast values: Wharton EFA. Real values in prices of 1972

   (v) rapid expansion of the labor force;
   (vi) increasing attention paid to problems of quality of life.

These issues started to appear in the late 1960's, many in the wake of the Vietnam war, and prevailed during the 1970's which proved to be a turbulent decade for the U. S. economy. Averages for the past decade, after smoothing of cyclical movements show changed trends in growth, inflation, unemployment rates, interest rates, internal deficits, and external deficits. It is also a period in which the U. S. economy became highly internationalized; i. e., increasingly subject to pressures of international events, less self-contained, and not at all insulated. The differences between the 1970's and earlier decades are matters of recorded history. The average trends estimated from the decade 1971—1980 govern the projections for the 1980's and 1990's. There is no indication that the trends of the 1970's were aberrations and that we are likely to return to the heady days of earlier postwar decades. The reasons for this changed performance are contained in the six points listed above, but in this essay, I want to look at the problem through the medium of econometric model simulation, rather than point-by-point analysis of the six items.[2]

Table 2. Selected U. S. Economic Indicators Projections to 1990.

WHARTON ANNUAL AND INDUSTRY FORECASTING MODEL
PRE-MEETING CONTROL SOLUTION - OCT 1980

SELECTED INDICATORS

ITEM	1980	1981	1982	1983	1984	1985	1986	1987	1988	1989	1990
GROSS NATIONAL PRODUCT (CUR $)	2559.2	2659.0	3212.8	3552.3	3939.6	4362.5	4859.2	5412.7	5983.2	6614.8	7286.2
% CHANGE	8.01	11.7	12.4	10.6	10.9	10.7	11.4	11.4	10.5	10.6	10.1
GROSS NATIONAL PRODUCT (72 $)	1416.5	1448.8	1511.1	1553.6	1606.9	1645.3	1696.5	1745.2	1795.5	1852.9	1903.2
% CHANGE	-1.01	2.2	4.3	2.8	3.4	2.4	3.1	2.9	2.9	3.2	2.7
GROSS NAT. PROD. DEFL. (1972=100.0)	180.81	197.3	212.6	228.7	245.2	265.1	286.4	310.2	333.2	357.0	382.6
% CHANGE	9.21	9.3	7.7	7.6	7.2	8.1	8.0	8.3	7.4	7.1	7.2
POPULATION (MILLIONS)	222.51	224.57	226.72	228.69	231.08	233.27	235.46	237.63	239.77	241.87	243.93
% CHANGE	0.91	0.9	1.0	1.3	1.0	0.9	0.9	0.9	0.9	0.9	0.8
LABOR FORCE (MILLIONS)	104.53	106.65	108.16	109.41	110.68	112.00	113.42	114.79	116.04	117.16	118.19
% CHANGE	2.01	1.6	1.4	1.2	1.2	1.2	1.3	1.2	1.1	1.0	0.9
PARTICIPATION RATE	63.51	64.1	64.3	64.4	64.5	64.6	64.8	64.9	65.1	65.3	65.4
% CHANGE	-0.21	0.3	0.3	0.1	0.2	0.2	0.3	0.2	0.3	0.3	0.3
EMPLOYMENT (MILLIONS)	97.05	97.93	99.74	101.23	102.80	103.91	105.37	106.84	108.20	109.59	110.91
% CHANGE	0.11	0.9	1.9	1.4	1.6	1.1	1.4	1.4	1.3	1.3	1.2
WAGE RATE PER WEEK, ALL INDUSTRIES	313.61	340.1	384.9	416.2	453.4	496.0	542.5	594.9	650.4	709.8	777.7
% CHANGE	8.41	10.9	10.6	8.7	8.4	9.4	9.3	9.7	9.3	9.1	9.5
PRODUCTIVITY - ALL INDUSTRIES	14.000	14.794	15.143	15.348	15.631	15.835	16.099	16.334	16.595	16.908	17.160
% CHANGE	-1.11	1.3	2.4	1.4	1.8	1.3	1.7	1.5	1.6	1.9	1.5
PRODUCTIVITY - ALL MANUFACTURING	7.927	8.112	8.354	8.563	8.823	9.018	9.287	9.565	9.845	10.158	10.448
% CHANGE	-1.31	2.3	3.0	2.5	3.0	2.2	3.0	3.0	2.9	3.2	2.8
REAL PER CAPITA GNP (THOU 72 $)	6.368	6.451	6.665	6.788	6.954	7.053	7.205	7.344	7.489	7.661	7.802
% CHANGE	-1.91	1.3	3.3	1.8	2.5	1.4	2.2	1.9	2.0	2.3	1.8
REAL PER CAP DISP INC (THOU '72 $)	4.450	4.502	4.603	4.688	4.813	4.870	4.986	5.071	5.171	5.290	5.411
% CHANGE	-1.31	1.2	2.2	1.7	2.6	1.3	2.4	1.7	2.0	2.3	2.3
CORPORATE PROFITS BEFORE TAXES	233.51	236.5	249.1	276.2	321.4	363.2	451.2	530.3	586.9	659.9	724.0
% CHANGE	-2.61	2.6	5.3	10.9	16.3	3.0	2.2	3.0	3.0	2.9	3.2
BOND RATE (%)	12.33	12.28	11.43	10.98	10.73	10.29	10.32	10.66	9.96	9.63	9.54
PRIME COMMERCIAL PAPER RATE (%)	11.23	11.17	9.66	9.61	9.29	9.73	8.87	9.29	8.66	8.23	8.17
MONEY SUPPLY	1424.21	1421.4	1526.9	1539.9	1734.6	1861.8	2190.4	2450.5	2712.0	3020.2	3359.6
% CHANGE	8.51	8.7	8.6	16.0	12.6	13.1	12.0	11.6	10.7	11.4	11.2
UNEMPLOYMENT RATE (%)	7.51	8.17	7.74	7.48	7.12	7.23	7.09	6.92	6.76	6.46	6.17
SAVINGS RATE (%)	4.241	4.79	4.90	5.25	5.58	5.36	5.61	5.44	5.51	5.80	6.04
SURPLUS OR DEFICIT, FEDERAL (CUR $)	-51.11	-58.3	-37.7	-26.0	-13.5	-7.7	-9.8	-0.7	-5.0	3.3	-1.1
SURPLUS OR DEF, STATE & LOC (CUR $)	23.21	31.6	42.6	38.9	39.4	37.9	37.0	36.5	41.3	45.5	44.4
COMPEN. TO EMPLOYEES TO NAT. INCOME	77.01	77.1	77.0	76.6	75.8	75.5	75.0	74.5	74.9	74.8	75.3
PROFITS TO NATIONAL INCOME	11.21	10.3	9.6	9.6	10.1	10.8	11.4	12.0	12.0	12.2	12.2

A trend projection of a large scale econometric model has a special interpretation. In the initial two or three years of such an extrapolation, an attempt is made to introduce as much specific business-cycle content as possible by moving principal policy magnitudes along specified short-run courses that interpret budget commitments, tax statutes, behavior of monetary authorities, and various economic regulations. This portion of the extrapolation may properly be labelled as a multi-dimensional forecast. From that point forward, major inputs are placed on recent medium-term trend paths. A set of exoge-

---

[2] The Wharton Model projections for the United States, reported here, were prepared by Vijaya Duggal, Gene Guill, George Schink, and Yacov Sheinin.

nous inputs are sought, by trial and error, that generate a balanced growth path for the economy. By balanced growth, I refer to several established long run characteristics that are used to constrain the solution. These are:

(a) equality between the real growth rate and real interest rate;
(b) a stable savings ratio;
(c) a stable wage share of GNP;
(d) a stable velocity ratio;
(e) tolerable deficits, internal and external.

It is not easy, but it is generally possible, to find a set of input values which, together with initial conditions, generate a model solution with these properties. There is no guarantee that such a solution, determined from a model of some 1000 or more interrelated equations, is unique, but there is no indication that a very different one exists that also meets these enumerated conditions.

It was evident at the beginning of the 1970's − as early as 1970, in fact − that if we were to try to bring projected solutions of the Wharton Model closer to established long run trends for growth and unemployment that internal pressures would be built up that would unbalance the solution for the economy. Inflation would pick up, the domestic deficit would grow abnormally large, and the net foreign balance would move into serious deficit. It did not seem possible to start from prevailing initial conditions and end up with a solution to the model that moved on a higher growth path, conforming to history and satisfying the constraints imposed on the long run extrapolation. Generally speaking, the model would produce higher rates of inflation and large domestic and foreign deficits. Further development of feedbacks to capital flows and dollar exchange rates were not explicitly developed.

The trial and error simulation procedure gives the following indications:

(i)   the long term growth rate has fallen by about one percentage point;
(ii) the inflation rate has been raised by about five percentage points;
(iii) the current account balance is barely maintained;
(iv) productivity growth is resumed, but at a rate lower by about one percentage point;
(v)   nominal interest rates are generally higher than in the past;
(vi) domestic fiscal balance is eventually attained.

At the very beginning of a new economic situation, determined to a great extent by adverse external circumstances, we should expect to find an immediate decline in the growth rate, but should the production path of the economy be shifted downwards, once and for all by a level amount, and then revert to the former growth rate, or should the growth rate itself, be lowered? Equilibrium growth theory and intuition suggest that after the initial growth decline the economy should return to the old growth rate. The level of production should be shifted downwards, but the rate of expansion should recover to the old position. Large scale econometric models do not seem to produce that result, at least over the period of one decade. There appears to be a downshift of the entire growth rate; thus, the United States are now expected to grow at about 3 % instead of 4 %, and that is a familiar pair of numbers often cited to describe expectations in a number of individual countries of Western Europe. For

Japan, the downshift in long term equlibrium growth is from about 10 percent to 5 %. This is an interesting finding that pervades many econometric modeling exercises for different countries and, as we shall see, for the world, too.

If the economy of the United States is stimulated toward recovery of the higher growth path of the 1950's and 1960's, a gap in trade and payments appears. But if the economy is allowed to proceed along the more moderate path of 3 %, the current account stays close to balance with only slight deterioration in spite of a continuing increase (assumed) in the real price of imported oil. There is some tendency towards energy conservation, but the value of oil imports is expected to grow significantly, year by year. Mainstays of the American current balance are growing agricultural exports and an impressive positive balance for services, or invisible accounts. Among the latter, the most important growth item is investment income. Many U. S. firms unsettled the balance of payments when they invested capital abroad in earlier formative years. But eventually, they made good on their investments, which was always the intention. U. S. based multinational enterprises now enjoy good income from abroad. In many cases, foreign income is much more favourable than domestic income.

Two other developments also contribute to net investment income from invisibles; high interest rates abroad, especially in the Euro-dollar market, enable U. S. corporate treasurers to realize good earnings from short term investments of working capital. High oil prices, which hurt our balance in the visible, merchandise sector, are offset by high earnings of U. S. multinational oil companies.

The U.S. economy is fundamentally beset by "fiscal drag". When the economy is operating in the neighborhood of full employment, present tax and revenue statutes are capable of generating very large receipts, generally large enough to cover all reasonable expenditures, extrapolated along historical growth paths. There will be some fresh tax cuts, and these are, indeed, factored into the baseline projection. But that is not enough to prevent overall expansion, by large sums, of revenues for the account of central government. Although we seldom realize balanced internal budgets, after the year is over, we do project them in baseline simulations. Major disturbances that bring forth new outlays and hold back the expansion of the personal income base cause internal accounts to fall into deficit positions much more frequently than is expected when a decade projection is made.

It is not solely energy considerations, such as the shift to relatively higher energy prices, that have caused the new slower profile of economic expansion in the United States, but energy is a key factor in these aspects of economic change. It is not possible to appreciate fully the new dimensions of the modern economy without devoting a great deal of attention to the role of energy. Accordingly, the Wharton Model, among other econometric interpretations of the United States, has incorporated a great deal of energy detail. It is evident from the accompanying table that progress is expected in energy conservation, a natural component of economic efficiency. Inefficiency in the use of an expensive scarce resource such as energy should eventually result in its more careful use. The baseline projection for the American economy shows a steady downward trend in the energy (BTU) to GNP ratio, from 52.48 (Thou BTU/1972$) in 1980 to 44.57 in 1990. Were it not for energy conservation, in response to a relative price shift, the problem of bringing external trade accounts into current balance would be much more difficult, with added pressure on the dollar and thus on domestic inflation; therefore, energy use in response to the laws of economics forms an important component of this entire look into the future.

It is not only the free working of the market economy that brings about increasing energy efficiency but also legislative mandates on the fuel efficiency of the automobile fleet. The steady improvement of the statistics on average miles-per-gallon is clearly evident in Table 3. By meeting these standards from the side of the fleet supply, consumers and producers are implicitly contributing to the improvement in the energy to GNP ratio. These institutional considerations are part of the exogenous input into the baseline case.

Table 3. Energy and Related U.S. projections to 1990

	1980	1981	1982	1983	1984	1985	1986	1987	1988	1989
Gasoline and oil consumption (bill $72)	24.0	23.3	23.7	23.0	22.3	21.8	21.4	21.1	20.8	20.5
Miles per gallon (new)	17.19	18.84	20.47	22.02	22.78	23.18	23.39	23.59	23.80	24.01
Miles per gallon (all)	13.75	14.23	14.88	15.70	16.64	17.63	18.62	19.60	20.51	21.32
Crude oil imports (m b)	2017	1956	2138	2030	1996	1952	1921	1898	1872	1843
Import price ($/b)	32.25	38.46	44.99	50.39	54.92	59.87	65.25	71.13	77.53	84.51
Energy consumption (quad BTU)	74.35	75.24	77.10	77.57	78.41	78.91	80.11	81.30	82.41	83.73
Energy GNP ratio thous. BTU/1972$)	52.48	51.93	51.02	49.93	48.80	47.96	47.22	46.58	45.90	45.19

The projected decline in energy use per unit of production is not simply a "hope" built into the solution of the Wharton Model; it is, in fact, a continuation of an existing trend that has been apparent but too little appreciated since 1973. The energy-GNP ratio fell from 60.41 to 54.50 over the period 1973−79.

In searching for a set of economic policies that give rise to the balanced solution, termed the baseline case, I have been mindful of contemporary politics. Since the Kennedy-Johnson years, the federal administration in the United States has been conservative, undoubtedly becoming more conservative with the passage of time and with mounting frustration in dealing with inflation. The fiscal and monetary policies of the baseline case are appropriately constrained to be conservative also. They continue basic downward trends in public expenditures as a percent of GNP and keep taxes high enough to generate an eventual domestic budget balance. The growth of money supply is prudent. In the long run there is a tendency for this model to conform to the quantity theory of money, i.e., nominal GNP and money supply expand at the same rate of change.[3] This is shown by a tendency toward steady velocity of

[3] See L.R. Klein, "Money in a General Equilibrium System: Empirical Aspects of the Quantity Theory", *Economie Appliquée*, XXXI (1−2, 1978), 5−14.

circulation. This is a conservative monetary policy, to go hand-in-hand with an assumed conservative fiscal policy.

Table 4. Estimated M4 Velocity in U.S. Baseline Projections

1980	2.28	1984	2.27	1988	2.21
1981	2.34	1985	2.22	1980	2.19
1982	2.42	1986	2.21	1990	2.17
1983	2.31	1987	2.21		

BASE CASE—THE WORLD ECONOMY[4]

In many respects, the economic evolution of the United States over the next decade should indicate a general pattern for most developed industrial economies. To be sure, every country will have its own special situation, but the principal simulation results—moderate growth, less inflation, and overall balance—should prevail for several if not all industrial market economies. Next let us consider the world as a whole, not just the group of industrial countries which comprise the OECD, but the centrally planned and developing countries as well. Interest centers on their interaction and the way the world economy evolves.

During the 1960's economic development was rapid. Among industrialized countries, Japan's growth was unusually high, exceeding 10% annually. The growth rate of all industrialized countries averaged 5.1% over the decade but fell to only 3.2% during the greater part of the 1970's as a result of business cycle swings. The centrally planned economies turned in some individual good performances, but the cultural revolution in China, internal upheavals in Czechoslovakia, and difficulties elsewhere held their growth rate to 4.9%, just under the OECD average. The socialist countries picked up considerably in the 1970's but now face the same problems as the market economies in the period ahead.

For the developing countries, the results are very mixed depending on country classification. According to World Bank estimates, low income countries grew at rates significantly under 4 % in both the 1960's and 1970's. Performance was close to 6 % in the middle income grouping, and even higher for Persian Gulf Oil exporters. These tabulations cut off notably in 1978, just prior to the revolution in Iran, which has disrupted economic activity for some time to come.

[4] Members of the research team of Project LINK contributed markedly to the results reported in this section. They are Victor Filatov, Shahrokh Fardoust, Yuzo Kumasaka, Michael Papaioannou, and Baudouin Velge.

Table 5. Some World Historical Statistics

	GDP Growth		Inflation rate		Export Growth		Import Growth	
	1960−70	1970−78	1960−70	1970−78	1960−70	1970−78	1960−70	1970−78
Low Income Countries	3.9	3.6	3.0	10.6	5.0	−0.8	5.0	3.2
Middle Income Countries	6.0	5.7	3.1	13.1	5.5	5.2	6.8	5.8
Industrial Countries	5.1	3.2	4.2	9.4	8.7	5.7	9.4	5.1
Persian Gulf Oil Exporters	13.0	6.0	1.2	22.2	9.5	−1.2	11.1	21.1
Centrally Planned	4.9	5.6	−	−	−	−	−	−

Source: World Development Report, 1980
              World Bank

Inflation rates were modest prior to the economic dislocations of the past decade, with single-digit rates well under 5 % customary in the non-socialist world. There were some significant exceptions in the developing world. After the large increments in food and fuel prices during the early 1970's, and the absorption of the legacy of Vietnam, prices took off to new heights. The average, 1970−78, was just below 10 % for the industrialized countries, but the situation has worsened considerably in the most recent years. This is one of the bleakest aspects of the future outlook.

There are no satisfactory price reports from the centrally planned economies. Very recently, they have shown a series of once-for-all price changes, but their opening of their borders to trade on a significantly larger scale means that they will have to absorb a large degree of imported inflation. Where appropriate price indexes are available, they indicate price increases comparable to those in the West.

Another dimension in the world economy is the growth and pattern of world trade. The decade of the 1960's was a "golden era" in trade development. Both exports and imports grew faster than did aggregate production. As recession hit the world economy in the 1970's, trade growth also receded, but it remained significantly above the growth in production. On a world scale, the growth in trade volume was about 50 % faster than production growth.

For most of the historical period since the end of World War II, the fixed parity system of the Bretton Woods Agreement took care of adjustments in trade balances, while developing a thriving multilateral system of trade. The build up of large surpluses by countries like Japan and Germany and the relative weakness of the United States, United Kingdom and a few other key countries brought the downfall of this system at the end of the 1960's or beginning of the 1970's. The managed floating system was being given a chance to operate, when the world was shocked by the oil embargo of 1973, followed by high energy pricing by OPEC. Now there are large surpluses and deficits among countries, subject to a great deal of turnover from year to year, as regards who is in surplus and who is in deficit. Overshadowing the short run adjustments among various OECD members is the very large balance of oil exporting nations. After the first buildup of surplus balances by OPEC in 1974−75, the excess funds were recirculated throughout the world economy through inflation, dollar devaluation, and OPEC's high propensity to import.

This situation has been halted, and a large surplus for oil exporting countries is presently matched by a deficit for oil importing countries in both the developed and developing world.

The basic assumption for world model projections into the 1980's is that oil production will be more moderate; price increases will be maintained above western inflation rates; and the surplus of oil exporting countries will be used for the development of the non-oil sectors of their economies or invested throughout the world.

By using the initial conditions of recent world economic history, an assumption about the course of oil prices, and extrapolated trends of major exogenous variables, we can compute a baseline projection of the world economy as a whole. The interrelated system of national and regional econometric models that constitute project LINK is the statistical medium through which this calculated projection is made.[5]

Each component model of the LINK system is put through a trend extrapolation exercise analogous to that described above for the Wharton Model of the United States, the main difference being that the models of project LINK, including the U.S. component, do not have the large detailed input-output and energy sectors that are present in the version of the Wharton Model that is being used for these longer term analyses. In the U.S. case, the projected American economy of the LINK model is monitored by the known results of the annual Wharton Model.

The main advantage of using the integrated LINK system for this medium term projection is to develop the growth patterns of world trade and inflation as part of the outcome of the calculation rather than as assumed inputs. For the individual assessment of growth patterns in each separate country or region, assumed values for world trade and import prices must be established in advance.

The base case projection for the world economy bears some close resemblances to the results discussed already for the U.S. case, since most parts of the world are experiencing the same kinds of economic pressures and converging towards a similar response and outcome.

---

[5] R. J. Ball, ed., *The International Linkage of National Economic Models*, J. Waelbroeck, ed., *The Models of Project LINK*, and J. Sawyer, ed., *Modelling the International Transmission Mechanism*. (Amsterdam: North-Holland Publishing Co., 1973, 1976, 1979). See also B. G. Hickman and L. R. Klein, "A Decade of Research by Project LINK", ITEMS (New York: Social Science Research Council), vol. 33, (December, 1979) 49–56.

Table 6. World Summary Measures of Growth and Inflation 1980−1990 Baseline (annual percentage changes)*

Country Grouping	1980	1981	1982	1983	1984	1985	1986
Gross Domestic Product							
13 LINK OECD							
Countries[1]	1.3	2.3	4.2	3.7	3.4	3.4	3.2
Level[2]	(2613.5)	(2672.5)	(2785.5)	(2889.0)	(2987.9)	(3087.5)	(3184.7)
Developing Countries	5.0	5.6	5.3	5.7	5.4	5.6	5.4
Non-Oil Exporting	5.5	5.6	5.3	5.7	5.4	5.6	5.3
Oil Exporting	2.2	5.3	5.3	5.3	5.3	5.3	6.3
Centrally Planned							
Countries[3]	4.2	3.4	4.3	4.4	4.6	4.4	4.4
World[4]	2.2	3.0	4.3	4.1	3.9	3.9	3.7
Private Consumption Deflator							
13 LINK OECD							
Countries	11.2	8.5	6.4	5.9	5.6	5.4	5.4
(GDP Deflator)	(9.5)	(8.1)	(6.6)	(5.9)	(5.6)	(5.6)	(5.5)
Developing Countries	25.3	29.1	20.7	18.1	16.2	13.0	11.2
Non-Oil Exporting	26.8	31.6	22.7	19.6	17.4	13.8	11.8
Oil Exporting	14.4	11.3	6.3	7.4	8.0	7.5	6.9
World[5]	13.8	12.3	9.1	8.2	7.6	6.8	6.5

* Weighted averages of own country/region growth rates.
[1] 13 LINK OECD countries are Australia, Austria, Belgium, Canada, Finland, France, Federal Republic of Germany, Italy, Japan, Netherlands, Sweden, United Kingdom, and the United States of America.
[2] Billions of 1970 U.S. $ at 1970 exchange rates.
[3] Includes only Eastern Europe CMEA and the U.S.S.R.
[4] World = .6565×OECD+.1494·DEVE+.1851×CMEA.
[5] World = .8145×OECD+.1855 DEVE. Inflation measures for CMEA are not avialable.
Period averages are calculated as the geometric mean of the first through last period growth rates.

On average, the industrialized countries are projected to lose one or two percentage points of growth. During the 1960's they expanded at more than 5%, but a longer stretch of time including the 1950's would reduce that estimate. In the projection, the growth rate is about 3%, the same as in the cyclical decade of the 1970's. GDP growth of the developing countries is reduced in this projection, as is that of the centrally planned economies. All told, when the figures are averaged on a world-wide basis, the resulting figure for growth is between 3.5 and 4.0% for the decade ahead. The corresponding figure was in excess of 5% for the 1960's and somewhat smaller during the 1970's.

Historically, world trade has expanded more rapidly than production, in a ratio of about 1.5. In the projection, however, the ratio falls considerably, so that world trade is expected to grow by little more than 10% above the growth rate of production. This is a new situation, with new large economies entering the world trade system on a large scale − China, the U.S.S.R., and other socialist countries − together with an awareness of an increasing degree of interrelatedness among nations. The United States is noticeably more concerned about its international economic relations, and more involved too. Countering these tendencies are efforts at import substitution, the introduction

1987	1988	1989	1990	1981–1985	1986–1990	1980–1990	1981–1990
2.9	2.9	2.9	2.7	3.4	2.9	3.0	3.2
(3277.2)	(3373.1)	(3471.6)	(3564.4)				
5.3	5.3	5.3	5.3	5.5	5.3	5.4	5.4
5.2	5.2	5.2	5.2	5.6	5.2	5.4	5.4
6.3	6.3	6.3	6.3	5.3	6.3	5.5	5.8
4.6	4.4	4.6	4.6	4.2	4.5	4.3	4.4
3.6	3.5	3.6	3.4	3.8	3.6	3.6	3.7
5.4	5.5	5.4	5.4	6.4	5.4	6.4	5.9
(5.5)	(5.5)	(5.4)	(5.6)	(6.4)	(5.5)	(6.2)	(5.9)
11.1	10.8	10.5	10.3	19.3	11.5	15.9	15.0
11.7	11.4	11.0	10.8	20.9	11.3	17.0	16.0
6.9	6.8	6.8	6.6	8.1	6.8	8.1	7.4
6.5	6.5	6.3	6.3	8.8	6.5	8.2	7.6

of some measures of protectionism, and some attempts by oil exporting nations to restrain the growth of their output.

In this moderate growth, relatively slow trade era, it is expected that eventually anti-inflationary policies will take hold. These are promoted by the conservative economic attitudes of policy makers now prevalent in the United States. The overall inflation rate does not fall back to the very low ranges that prevailed some twenty years ago. In place of the less than 5% rates that we once enjoyed, a reduction to single digit ranges and ultimately to about 5–6% is considered a significant achievement. In the developing world, a reasonable target would be about 15%, on average.

The growth of the OPEC surplus, covered over in these tables as a result of the amalgamation of all developing countries is matched, over the decade, by the deficit of the industrial countries. There is some deficit, as well, among the socialist countries. This projection assumes that these offsetting balances are recycled through the world financial system. The actual process may be quite difficult to accomplish.

Within the OECD area, there is a great deal of shifting between surplus and deficit areas. While the U.S. goes from deficit towards balance by 1990, Japan and Germany initially move into deficit, as do France, Italy, and the United

Table 6. (continued) World trade summary

	1980	1981	% $\triangle$	1982
13 LINK OECD Countries[1]				
Exports[2]	1036.0	1219.3	17.7	1420.8
Imports	1090.0	1275.2	17.0	1439.0
Balance	−54.0	−55.8		−18.2
Developing Countries				
Exports	532.1	631.6	18.7	693.7
Imports	438.5	564.3	28.7	629.2
Balance	93.6	67.4		64.5
Centrally Planned Countries[3]				
Exports	138.4	156.7	13.3	177.2
Imports	146.7	168.2	14.6	186.5
Balance	−8.3	−11.4		−9.3
Rest of the World[4]				
Exports	163.4	203.0	19.8	189.8
Imports	194.7	203.1	4.3	226.8
Balance	−31.3	−0.1		−37.0
World Exports	1869.9	2210.7	18.2	2481.5
World Export Price	3.3	3.8	14.8	4.1
World Exports (Real)*	572.2	589.4	3.0	612.6
World Export Price of Fuel	10.9	13.2	20.8	14.3
World Exports of Fuel (Real)*	40.9	39.6	−3.2	41.3

* Constant dollar measures have base 1970 = 1.0

+ Figures in parentheses are annual average trade balances.

[1] 13 LINK OECD countries are Australia, Austria, Belgium, Canada, Finland, France, Federal Republic of Germany, Italy, Japan, Netherlands, Sweden, United Kingdom and the United States of America.

[2] Measures are for merchandise trade, F.O.B.

[3] Includes only Eastern Europe CMEA and the U.S.S.R.

[4] Period averages are calculated as the compound annual growth rate of the last over first year projection.

Kingdom. The Japanese situation is projected to change drastically and promptly back into surplus by mid-decade, while the German case follows a more moderate path towards balance and reaches a small surplus by 1990.

The analysis of U.S. growth prospects is applicable by analogy to the industrial countries as a whole. Restrictive policies to fight inflation, to pay for expensive oil imports, protect exchange value of the currency, and to recoup productivity losses keep the economy on a moderate path. The slowdown in the industrial world holds back the export potential of developing countries. In order to cope with adverse trade and payments deficits, restrictive policies are followed. In this environment, capital inflows for development are harder to

% △	1983	% △	1984	% △	1985	% △
16.5	1592.3	12.1	1788.9	12.3	2012.7	12.5
12.8	1622.5	12.7	1833.2	13.0	2055.5	12.1
	−30.2		−44.3		−42.7	
9.8	773.5	11.5	859.0	11.1	954.7	11.1
11.5	719.9	14.4	807.2	12.1	912.9	13.1
	53.6		51.8		41.8	
13.0	201.1	13.5	229.7	14.2	261.3	13.8
10.9	207.3	11.2	235.3	13.5	265.9	13.0
	−6.2		−5.6		−4.6	
−6.5	239.7	26.3	286.9	19.7	329.2	14.8
11.7	256.9	13.2	288.9	12.5	323.7	12.0
	−17.2		−2.0		5.5	
12.2	2806.6	13.1	3164.5	12.8	3557.9	12.4
8.0	4.4	7.9	4.7	7.8	5.1	7.5
3.9	641.9	4.8	671.4	4.6	702.3	4.6
8.5	15.8	10.5	17.4	9.9	19.1	9.7
4.3	42.9	3.9	44.5	3.7	46.1	3.5

come by. High debt service burdens, in a number of cases, act as additional constraints. Conservative governments in the OECD area are less disposed than previously to grant concessionary aid.

The centrally planned economies used to consider themselves well insulated against the economic ills of the rest of the world. This is no longer the case.

The centrally planned economies, dissatisfied with the outcome of their own efforts to achieve good economic growth performance, have changed strategy and decided to import high technology from the West, as well as necessary grains to supplement their domestic agricultural supplies. This new approach has opened their economies to Western inflation because imports have been

Table 6. (continued)

	1986	% Δ	1987	% Δ	1988	% Δ
13 LINK OECD Countries						
Exports	2259.8	12.3	2522.4	11.6	2824.7	12.0
Imports	2295.4	11.7	2551.0	11.1	2840.3	11.3
Balance	−35.6		−28.5		−15.6	
Developing						
Exports	1055.8	10.6	1161.0	10.0	1273.5	9.7
Imports	1020.1	11.7	1134.0	11.2	1258.6	11.0
Balance	35.7		27.0		14.8	
Centrally Planned Countries						
Exports	298.2	14.1	333.2	11.7	376.0	12.8
Imports	304.9	14.7	339.5	11.3	383.9	13.1
Balance	−6.7		−6.2		−7.9	
Rest of the World						
Exports	367.8	11.7	408.3	11.0	454.8	11.4
Imports	361.2	11.6	400.7	10.9	446.1	11.3
Balance	6.6		7.7		8.7	
World Exports	3981.6	11.9	4425.1	11.1	4929.0	11.4
World Export Price	5.4	7.1	5.8	7.1	6.2	6.9
World Exports (Real)	733.9	4.5	761.9	3.8	793.7	4.2
World Fuel Price	20.9	9.3	22.9	9.7	25.0	9.2
World Fuel Exports (Real)	47.9	3.9	49.2	2.7	50.7	3.1

reflecting rising world prices. Gold and oil sales at correspondingly rising prices have been used by the Soviet Union to finance part of their import needs, but they are fully enmeshed in world inflation accounting in balancing rising export prices.

The economies of Eastern Europe have had to cope with trade deficits and unusual borrowing in order to pay for imports, over and above their abilities to produce exports for the world markets. As their external accounts have got out of line, they have had to resort to the "stop" phase of familiar "stop-go" policies. In addition, Poland and other Eastern countries have been confronted with domestic labor unrest in an inflationary environment.

The People's Republic of China are resorting to similar trade policies, but mindful of the complications that arise when socialist countries rush headlong into an open economy format, they are taking lessons from the European experience and moderating their original trade and capital import plans. Although the Chinese are approaching this phase of development quite cautiously, they have enough pent-up growth potential at the present time to support a growth rate in excess of the average for centrally planned economies.

1989	% $\triangle$	1990	% $\triangle$	1981–1985 % $\triangle$	1986–1990 % $\triangle$	1980–1990 % $\triangle$	1981–1990 % $\triangle$
3172.8	12.3	3545.1	11.7	13.3	11.9	13.1	12.6
3174.3	11.8	3532.1	11.3	12.7	11.4	12.5	11.9
−1.5		13.0		(−38.2)[+]	(−13.6)[+]	(−28.5)[+]	(−25.9)[+]
1399.8	9.9	1534.0	9.6	10.8	9.8	11.2	10.3
1403.2	11.5	1559.0	11.1	12.7	11.2	13.5	11.9
−3.4		−25.0		(55.8)[+]	(19.8)[+]	(38.3)[+]	(37.8)[+]
424.6	12.9	477.2	12.3	13.6	12.5	13.2	13.1
433.6	12.9	487.2	12.3	12.1	12.4	12.7	12.5
−9.0		−10.0		(−7.4)[+]	(−7.9)[+]	(−7.7)[+]	(−7.7)[+]
512.5	12.7	576.7	12.5	12.8	11.9	13.4	12.3
498.7	11.8	554.7	11.2	12.3	11.3	11.0	11.8
13.9		22.0		(−10.2)[+]	(11.7)[+]	(−2.1)[+]	(0.8)[+]
5509.7	11.8	6133.0	11.3	12.6	11.4	12.6	12.0
6.6	6.8	7.1	7.8	7.6	7.1	8.0	7.2
830.4	4.6	861.9	3.8	4.5	4.1	4.2	4.3
27.3	9.1	29.7	9.0	9.6	9.2	10.6	9.4
52.3	3.2	54.0	3.3	3.8	3.1	2.8	3.5

In the near term, China is growing at 7 percent or more. For the longer term, 6% seems to be attainable, although they could slip backward by another percentage point, or so.

A special group of nations among the developing countries are the OPEC nations or, more broadly, the oil exporting nations. They have little or no balance of payments constraint attached to their development plans for the medium term at least. Although they may be in a position to develop at a more rapid rate, they are reconsidering the experience of the past few years in which rapid exploitation of oil resources did not optimize their purchasing power for capital and other imports and created dangerous or fatal unrest in several countries. Many of these countries were not able to absorb imports efficiently at the more rapid pace. Their overseas investments have been only partially successful. As a consequence of all these problems, oil exporting nations are opting for a more moderate rate of industrialization. Both the oil and non-oil sectors of their economies will be expected to phase down to a slower growth path.

No matter where we look in the assessment of the world economy, there are fundamental reasons for expecting a slower rate of development.

Recognition of lack of abundant energy resources for the world, more particularly crude oil resources, has by itself contributed to the slowing down of the world economy. This can be seen by looking at the results of alternative simulations of the LINK model with different assumptions about energy prices. A standard procedure is to compute a baseline projection, as has already been described here, and then compare this result with an alternative projection where specific changes in external factors have been imposed on the model. In the case being examined here, the change imposed is an increase in the world oil price by 10%; i.e., the exogenous path of world oil prices, set by OPEC, is raised, year by year, to a new path that is uniformly about 10% above the baseline path.

On occasion, we have made simulations in which the oil price was kept fixed at some base year value or in which the *real* price of oil was kept fixed — by allowing the nominal price to move by the same percentage change as an accepted index of inflation, say a general price index in the OECD countries. The LINK system has a basic symmetry property. Results with lower oil prices are opposite in sign, with similar magnitude, to those with an increase in price.

The general findings can best be described by considering main elasticities of the system. These are percentage changes in principal magnitudes associated with a change in oil price, other external inputs remaining unchanged.

In the first place, fuel import demand falls by about 1.1% for a 10% increase in price. The elasticity coefficient is about 0.11. This degree of sensitivity appears in the first year of a projection and persists for a whole decade. After 10 years, if the price is higher by 10%, the trade volume is lower by about 1%.

Higher oil price discourages world economic activity and adds to world inflation. Industrial world GDP falls by about 0.5% when oil prices are initially 10% and then about 6% higher after the first year. This works out to be an elasticity coefficient of 0.06. For this same change in oil price, OECD inflation measured by the GDP implicit deflator is up by about 0.2% and consumer price rises by 0.3% to 0.4%.

When we consider that world energy prices have gone up much more than 10%, after 1973 — they quadrupled and then more than doubled again — we can see that energy issues had much to do with the present state of stagflation. It is not a simple matter of finding a multiple of the 10% change used in the elasticity calculations, because those changes were introduced in an artificial ceteris paribus situation, while many things changed in the actual world environment after oil prices first jumped. In fact, *real* oil prices did not permanently rise after the initial change in 1974–75; they did, however, after the latest change in 1979.

In any event, we can plainly see that world economic activity and world inflation are highly sensitive to world energy prices. The present slowing down of economic growth, accompanied by higher inflation, is due, in part at least, to higher energy prices.

The baseline projections made here for both the United States and the world as a whole are done in a *benign* environment; that is to say, there are no untoward major disturbances contemplated for the 1980's in this case. Since the end of World War II and the immediate readjustment period there have been three completed decades, each with its own disturbing factors that upset an otherwise benign environment. These have been:

1950's   Korean War
          "Cold" War
          Suez Canal Closing
1960's   Vietnam War
1970's   Breakdown of Bretton Woods
          Massive Harvest Failures
          Oil Embargo cum OPEC Cartel Pricing
          Iranian Revolution

These major events had enormous impact on economic performances all over the world. Within each decade there were other disturbances as well, less dramatic, yet economically significant.

In thinking about possible "futures" for the 1980's, it may be convenient to formulate baseline cases without contingency planning for such disturbances because, in many respects, the kinds of formal models that we use decompose, approximately, into a systematic (baseline) component and a disturbance component.

This property is associated with *linearity* in formal model theorizing, and it appears to be a reasonable approximation. Therefore, we proceed by first working out the base case and then superimposing disturbances on it.

Sometime during the 1980's there can very well be—according to many thinkers there *will* be—another significant interruption of delivery of oil supplies and another large harvest failure. During the 1970's there was war in the Middle East but not on the scale and duration of Korea or Vietnam. In a sense, the oil embargo and OPEC pricing listed above are economic surrogates for the Middle East War.

Will the military experience of the 1950's and 1960's be repeated during the 1980's? This is certainly a contingency. There could well be large scale cold or hot war during the coming decade. Also, the international economy has been so upset by events in the food and fuel sectors that we tend to look to those areas for the reappearance of disturbances. It is likely that a large scale economic disruption will occur during the decade, but there will probably be disturbances in surprising new areas. Shortages of basic materials other than food and fuel could develop. There could be a wave of debt defaults running throughout the developing world or among relatively poor countries of the developed world. There could be a massive dislocation in the physical environment, in atmospheric or water pollution, or urban congestion. It is worthwhile exploring in some detail the economic dimensions of a few of these disturbances.

POSSIBLE DISTURBANCES

Cartel Pricing: For the baseline case, we have assumed that, after the immediate effects of the Iranian Revolution have been worked out, crude oil prices would rise, on average, by about 10% annually for the whole decade. This turns out to be about 3% above the inflation rate that is relevant to the oil exporting countries, namely, the export price of OECD countries. In the baseline solution, this key price grows at about 6−7% annually. Between 1980 and the attaining of the trend pattern for the rest of the decade, there is an assumed transitional period before world inflation and the growth rate of oil prices decline; thus, the 1981 real price increases by more than 3%. In addition, a disturbance did appear during 1980, continuing at the end of this year, in the form of war in the Middle East. We are witnessing an unusual event in which two members of an effective cartel are engaged in open warfare. This has significantly reduced oil supplies and provides another reason for marking up the price in the transitional period, at least.

The steady rise of 3% in the real price of oil, together with an approximate solution path for OECD export prices at 7%, amount, in a numerical sense, to the indexation of oil prices. It has often been mentioned that a stated objective of OPEC is to devise an index formula for oil pricing. The simplest of such formulas is implicit in the baseline case. Variations on this case have been worked out with either higher or lower rates of increase of real oil prices. Another route to follow is to have a multivariate indexation formula, in which the oil price is also tied to GDP growth in the developed world, to the exchange value of the dollar, and other relevant indicators.

Indexation formulas give smooth steady paths for the course of oil prices, but at least one unsteady path is worth consideration as a result of a possible disturbance. If forseeable world supplies of oil are balance against estimated world demand, there appears to be a large scale shortfall developing by mid-decade. This deficit could be made up either by having price rise steadily on a faster gradient, by having a one-time large upward step of 50−100%, or by rationing.

The fact that the OPEC Cartel has been as cohesive and long lasting as it has, surprises many economists. At the present time it even appears to be surviving open warfare between two members. We should be prepared, therefore, to experience other surprises of similar proportions. There are, of course, some unique features about OPEC that are not easily duplicated. Cartels in other fields of economic activity may not reach out to such important products from an industrial viewpoint. Cartels in diamonds, mercury, chromite or other industrial products would not have as great an impact on overall world activity. In most food lines, grains for example, large developed countries, which would be more disposed towards maintenance of a multilateral free trade system, are major export suppliers and could, therefore, inhibit or prohibit effective cartel action. Petroleum products are peculiarly concentrated, as far as surplus capacity for export is concerned, in the hands of a fairly cohesive politico-social group, dedicated to pan-Arabism or to aspirations of developing nations. If export capacity of important industrial products were concentrated in the hands of a cohesive group of nations (religious, political, social, geographical) another effective cartel could arise. Such a possible field of action does not presently appear to exist on the world scene.

The world has been economically disturbed by food, as well as by fuel. There is certainly a possibility of unforeseen supply shocks in the provision of food during the 1980's. Harvest failures have been occurring with alarming regularity as ambitious attempts are being made to upgrade diets over a large part of the world. The year 1980 initiates the decade on an insecure footing with some measurable disturbances. The embargo of American grain shipments to the U.S.S.R., as a result of the invasion of Afghanistan has been controversial, not only because of its political impact but also because of doubts about its effectiveness. When all the arguments are sifted, it does appear that the embargo has been effective in delaying the delivery of larger meat supplies to the Soviet population. When it is placed in juxtaposition to the disappointing Soviet harvest of 1980 and the food shortages in Poland, it is evident that there are quite significant stresses on the world economy. To add to the list of food supply setbacks, we can also cite the drought, resulting in a poor crop in feed grains in the United States in 1980. We are starting out the decade with upward pressure on food/agricultural prices. The downward drift in world inflation, which is an important component of the baseline economic scenario for the 1980's is temporarily being thrown off course by rises in food/agricultural prices and in energy prices. If more disturbances like these occur during the course of the decade, we could have significantly worse economic performance than in the base case.

There is an important difference between food and fuel disturbances. The fuel disturbances of the 1970's, stemming from the 1973 Middle East War, were institutionalized and made permanent by the control power of OPEC. Food/agricultural prices, however, fluctuated during the decade, since supply responses to high prices have been relatively quick in agriculture. U.S. grain supplies, in particular, were expanded on a large scale after the massive depletion of stocks by Soviet purchases in 1972/73. The responsiveness of U.S. and other suppliers tends to soften the effect of agricultural disturbances when spread over a two or three year horizon.

The next disturbance to the world economy could well be entirely unforeseen. In searching for new and different areas where contingent planning would be helpful, we may cite the possibility of simultaneous debt default. Many developing countries, some centrally planned economies, and some poorer developed countries are seriously in debt. The degree of seriousness is indicated by debt service ratios showing the extent to which trade gain can cover (or fail to cover) needs for interest payment and debt amortization. There have been several singular cases of a nation's inability to meet current debt service requirements, but they have always been met in recent years without the precipitation of a crisis. Debt rescheduling has been successful for dealing with the specific situations that have arisen—Peru, Zaire, Zambia, Poland, Turkey, to name a few. As long as such cases can be kept isolated from the routine functioning of the world financial system, a major disturbance can be averted. Commercial banks and international institutions have become alerted to the situation as a result of experiences in these singular cases. They have, accordingly, become more prudent in loan activity. This is another reason why moderation in the face of economic activity has become a characteristic of the baseline projection for the decade ahead. Although there is good reason to believe that disturbances in the form of a wave of debt defaults will not occur, such an event is by no means impossible.

AN OPTIMISTIC CASE

While some economists may feel that the base case, itself, is optimistic—at least complacent and trouble free—there are many industrialists, policy makers, financiers, and economists who strive for a better outcome. If there is a single measure, among the many that properly describe the economy, that indicates the unsatisfactory nature of present performance and its extrapolation along the path of the baseline case, it is the poor performance of *productivity*. In Table 2, it can be seen that productivity growth during 1980, in the United States, has been *negative*, while its trend projection, at rates of change that are mainly between 1.0 and 2.0% annually, fall considerably below a previously established long run path. It used to grow at a rate in excess of 3% in the United States. Outside the U.S., across most international lines, it is also true that the productivity improvement factor has fallen, perhaps not as drastically as in the United States, but it is uniformly lower in recent years.

A central focus for policy targets that gives some promise for better economic performance is, therefore, a policy mix that attempts to enhance productivity growth. Since we are not sure of the causes that led to the productivity slowdown it is especially difficult to prescribe policies for productivity improvement. Of the possible sources of productivity decline, it is widely felt that relatively weak capital formation, in the private sector, plays a major role.

Both through general capital expansion, and through modernization, it is expected that higher rates of fixed capital formation will lead to better productivity growth. It is necessary to make firms want to invest and to use the new capital at a high capacity rate.

Capital formation is important but not the whole story, because there is still a long way to go towards revitalizing the economy even after some objectives on capital formation have been reached. In a study for the New York Stock Exchange, last year, the operators of the Wharton Model examined the resulting net gains for the United States as a consequence of raising the investment share of GNP to about 12% from a stagnating level of about 10%.[6]

In a rounded policy package, the raising of the investment and savings rates by 2 percentage points are formidable steps forward, but they apparently do not suffice to restore the rate of growth of productivity to its historical trend of

[6] *Building a Better Future: Economic Choices for the 1980's.* New York Stock Exchange, New York, (December, 1979).

the early 1960's. This drastic upward shift in investment is estimated to add about 0.2 to 0.5 percentage points to the overall rate of productivity expansion. This in turn is associated with an overall improvement of the GNP growth rate by about 0.5 percentage points. These are promising policies but standing by themselves, they are not enough.

It is one thing to assume in a statistical mathematical model solution that the investment ratio is to be higher (by about 2.0 percentage points) and quite another to design policies that will, indeed, raise the share of capital formation in GNP by 2.0 percentage points. The policy discussion in the United States is narrowing to the provision of tax incentives for investment through liberalized depreciation rules and investment tax credits. There is still ample room for improvement of the rate of return on capital through changes in the appropriate tax parameters. Additional policy measures concern tax benefits for R & D outlays, more federal spending for R & D, and more federal spending for basic research. In addition to these standard fiscal measures on the taxing and spending sides of the national budget, there is expectation that productivity growth will be helped by relaxation of restricitve regulations and by the promotion of worker training programs on-the-job. To complement policies designed to raise the investment share of GNP, there should be corresponding policies to raise the savings share. One possible route is to encourage private savings for pension systems, possibly through policies to make retirement pensions portable between jobs. Another way is to exempt some interest on savings accounts from income taxation. The basic issue, however, is to shift the proportions in the make-up of U.S. GNP, namely, to reduce the consumption ratio by 2 percentage points while raising the investment ratio by an equal amount. This is the same thing as saying that the savings ratio should be increased by the same amount as the increase in the investment ratio. In other words, the objective is to shift the U.S. economy from being fundamentally a high consumption to being a high investment economy.

Other countries may view the problem differently, but there should be broad agreement that capital formation has had a relatively poor recovery since the start of the cyclical upswing after 1975. World-wide, the problem is to stimulate investment, but, as in the United States, that will be only a step in the right direction; it will lead to only modest improvement. Clearly, more imaginative policy thinking will have to deal with higher productivity growth.

A feature of the baseline path is the gradual reduction of the average rate of inflation. Many economists would argue that the central economic problem in both the long and short run is to reduce the inflation rate and that many things will "fall-into-place" once inflation has been controlled and gradually reduced.

Many policies can contribute to this worthy end, but a principal line would be to tie changes in the rate of productivity growth to the inflation rate. In the long run, if the rate of inflation is to be lowered, the growth rate of productivity must be significantly increased on a lasting basis.

If the rate of return on capital can be raised, if R & D activity can be made popular again, if economic regulation is liberalized, if worker productivity can be improved through training schemes, and if the rate of inflation can be moderately but steadily decreased, then there is a chance that we can enjoy an investment boom in the 1980's that compares favorably with the great expansionary era of the 1950's and early 1960's.

The appropriate policy measures for raising capital formation and productivity growth are being looked at essentially on individual national bases. But coordinated fiscal and monetary policies offer a new dimension in which to act. If all major countries act synchronously to stimulate capital formation or to ease monetary stringency, there can be added reinforcement effects. International amplification of national fiscal multipliers is estimated to be as large as 1.25 to 1.50. Simultaneous expansions operate through the world trading system because as countries expand, they generally increase import demand. This, in turn, helps partner country export activity and feeds back again on domestic expansion in each individual country. The stronger the response, both nationally and internationally, the less the stimulus has to be in order to arrive at a specified objective. The more we can moderate the use of fiscal/ monetary policy, the better is the prospect for lower inflation. By keeping inflation on a favorable path, we stand to gain much through better trade performance.

The figures in Table 7 give a rough indication of what might be expected if the federal government were to stimulate private fixed investment so that it would grow by an extra 2% annually. The policies are different among countries, but they generally consist of tax changes, support from public capital formation and support from general government spending.

The growth rate of GDP is improved over the course of this scenario by about 0.5 percentage points at the beginning, but gradually the investment stimulus tends to wear off by mid-decade. Similarly, there are gains in reducing inflation, again by 1.0 or 2.0 percentage pints. A major contributing factor to the inflation gains is the improvement in productivity (real output per worker hour). It, too, performs better at the outset than at the end in 1985.

Table 7. Coordinated Investment Stimulus 13 LINK Members in OECD 1979–1985
Differences in Percentage Growth Rates

	1979	1980	1981	1982	1983	1984	1985
GDP	0.3	0.6	0.5	0.2	0.2	0.2	0.1
Inflation							
(consumer prices)	0.0	−0.2	−.1	0.0	0.0	0.0	0.0
Productivity gains	0.3	0.4	0.3	0.0	0.0	−0.3	−0.1

UPDATE

The decade of the 1980s, which is the basic projection horizon for this investigation is now more than one-half complete, and in combining some hindsight with some foresight, I would still stand by the overall growth projections of this essay, both for the United States and for the world economy. This remark is to be interpreted only in an average sense. Each year has not worked out as projected, but the average yearly growth rates for the entire decade look plausible because the early recession, 1980-82, offsets what now appear to be better prospects for the last few years of the decade. Also, the distribution among areas is different from what was expected years ago. In particular, Chinese performance has been extremely strong for a few years, up to the present, and has a good chance of remaining above the world average for the rest of the decade.

In several expositions of the content of this essay, particularly in Europe, the achievement of medium term growth of production near 3 percent for the World and for the OECD countries was viewed as being strongly optimistic, possibly over optimistic, but that view does not at all seem to be unduly optimistic.

The biggest single mistake of the model projections in this essay was the underlying assumption of steadily rising oil prices. Early in the decade, the oil price leveled off and in 1985-86 fell precipitously. Lower oil prices were not entirely ruled out, as evidenced by the passing comment that system sensitivity to a price decline was symmetric with a price rise, but the baseline assumption was one of rising nominal and real oil prices. This contributed to moderation of the global rate of growth, and if falling prices had been assumed, the projections would have been even more optimistic on this account, taken by itself.

But there was one other development, both on the model input and output

sides, namely that the policies in Western Europe and the United States
introduced after 1981 gave rise to widespread recession. The combination of
slow or negative policy-constrained growth early in the decade with faster
growth after mid decade produces an overall result that appears to be
plausible at the present time.

Anti-inflation measures were properly assumed, and the average decline in
the rate of price increase is realistic for the OECD region as a whole, if too
high for the United States alone. It was the severity of the policies and
their monetary-fiscal imbalance that gave rise to very high interest rates,
followed by falling rates that generated a strong cyclical departure from the
trend results of the projection in this essay.

To say that the effects of falling oil prices are symmetric with those of
rising oil prices accounts for the projected gains in world and US economic
performance -- higher growth with lower inflation -- but it carries a risk
that some heavily indebted oil exporting countries may be in such dire straits
that special assistance programs for them upsets the symmetry of the case.

The decade is not over, but clearly the strength and cohesiveness of OPEC
was over in 1980. More optimistic economic outcomes than projected, for the
second half of the decade (not for the first half) have a good chance of
taking place.

ECONOMIC THEORY, ECONOMETRICS, AND MATHEMATICAL ECONOMICS

Series Editor: Karl Shell

CORNELL UNIVERSITY
ITHACA, NEW YORK

Erwin Klein. Mathematical Methods in Theoretical Economics: Topological and Vector Space Foundations of Equilibrium Analysis

Paul Zarembka (Ed.). Frontiers in Econometrics

George Horwich and Paul A. Samuelson (Eds.). Trade, Stability, and Macroeconomics: Essays in Honor of Lloyd A. Metzler

W. T. Ziemba and R. G. Vickson (Eds.). Stochastic Optimization Models in Finance

Steven A. Y. Lin (Ed.). Theory and Measurement of Economic Externalities

Haim Levy and Marshall Sarnat (Eds.). Financial Decision Making under Uncertainty

Yasuo Murata. Mathematics for Stability and Optimization of Economic Systems

Jerry S. Kelly. Arrow Impossibility Theorems

Peter Diamond and Michael Rothschild (Eds.). Uncertainty in Economics: Readings and Exercises

Fritz Machlup. Methodology of Economics and Other Social Sciences

Robert H. Frank and Richard T. Freeman. Distributional Consequences of Direct Foreign Investment

Elhanan Helpman and Assaf Razin. A Theory of International Trade under Uncertainty

Edmund S. Phelps. Studies in Macroeconomic Theory, Volume 1: Employment and Inflation. Volume 2: Redistribution and Growth

Marc Nerlove, David M. Grether, and José L. Carvalho. Analysis of Economic Time Series: A Synthesis

Michael J. Boskin (Ed.). Economics and Human Welfare: Essays in Honor of Tibor Scitovsky

Carlos Daganzo. Multinomial Probit: The Theory and Its Application to Demand Forecasting